Microeconomics

Early Release

Microeconomics

Early Release

B. Douglas Bernheim
Stanford University

Michael D. Whinston
Northwestern University

McGraw-Hill Irwin

Boston Burr Ridge, IL Dubuque, IA New York San Francisco St. Louis
Bangkok Bogotá Caracas Kuala Lumpur Lisbon London Madrid Mexico City
Milan Montreal New Delhi Santiago Seoul Singapore Sydney Taipei Toronto

David Ortega

The McGraw·Hill Companies

McGraw-Hill Irwin

MICROECONOMICS, EARLY RELEASE
Published by McGraw-Hill/Irwin, a business unit of The McGraw-Hill Companies, Inc., 1221 Avenue of the Americas, New York, NY, 10020.

This book is printed on acid-free paper.

1 2 3 4 5 6 7 8 9 0 DOW/DOW 0 9 8 7

ISBN 978-0-07-721199-8
MHID 0-07-721199-5

Editorial director: *Brent Gordon*
Executive editor: *Douglas Reiner*
Developmental editor: *Karen Fisher*
Lead project manager: *Pat Frederickson*
Senior production supervisor: *Debra R. Sylvester*
Lead designer: *Matthew Baldwin*
Senior photo research coordinator: *Jeremy Cheshareck*
Photo researcher: *Jennifer Blankenship*
Cover design: *Artemio Ortiz Jr.*
Interior design: *Artemio Ortiz Jr.*
Typeface: *10.5/12.6 Times New Roman*
Compositor: *Lachina Publishing Services*
Printer: *R. R. Donnelley*

Library of Congress Cataloging-in-Publication Data

Bernheim, B. Douglas.
Microeconomics / by B. Douglas Bernheim, Michael D. Whinston.
p. cm.
ISBN-13: 978-0-07-721199-8 (alk. paper)
ISBN-10: 0-07-721199-5 (alk. paper)
1. Microeconomics. I. Whinston, Michael Dennis. II. Title.
HB172.B485 2008
338.5--dc22
2007030151

www.mhhe.com

About the Authors

B. Douglas Bernheim B. Douglas Bernheim graduated with an A.B. in Economics from Harvard University, Summa Cum Laude and Phi Beta Kappa, in 1979. He entered graduate study at M.I.T. under a National Science Foundation Graduate Fellowship, and completed his Ph.D. three years later. He began his academic career at Stanford University from 1982–1987. He left Stanford in 1988 to assume an endowed chair in the Department of Finance at Northwestern University's J.L. Kellogg Graduate School of Management. In 1990, he moved to Princeton University, where he held an endowed chair in the Department of Economics, and also served as the Co-Director of the Center for Economic Policy Studies. He returned to Stanford in 1994, and is now the Edward Ames Edmonds Professor of Economics.

Professor Bernheim's work has spanned a number of fields, including public economics, political economy, game theory, contract theory, behavioral economics, industrial organization, and financial economics. He is a research associate of the National Bureau of Economic Research, a Senior Fellow of the Stanford Institute for Economic Policy Research (SIEPR), and Co-Director of SIEPR's Tax and Budget Policy Program. He is also a former Director of the Stanford Institute for Theoretical Economics, and Co-Editor of the *American Economic Review*.

Professor Bernheim's teaching has included Principles of Economics, Intermediate Microeconomics, Public Economics, Microeconomic Theory, Industrial Organization, Behavioral Economics, and Insurance and Risk Management.

Michael D. Whinston Michael D. Whinston is the Robert E. and Emily H. King Professor of Business Institutions in the Department of Economics at Northwestern University. He also holds appointments at Northwestern's School of Law and its Kellogg Graduate School of Management. Whinston received his B.S. and M.B.A. from the Wharton School at the University of Pennsylvania and his Ph.D. from MIT. He taught at Harvard from 1984–1997 before moving to Northwestern. His research has covered a variety of topics in microeconomics, including game theory, the design of contracts and organizations, firm behavior in oligopolistic markets, antitrust, and law and economics. He has also conducted empirical research on the airline and pharmaceutical industries, and served as a consultant—for private parties, the government, and the court—in various antitrust cases. Whinston is a co-author of the leading graduate textbook in microeconomics, *Microeconomic Theory* (Oxford University Press, 1995), and is also the author of *Lectures on Antitrust Economics* (MIT Press, 2006). He and Doug Bernheim have collaborated since 1983, and are excited about bringing this collaboration to producing an innovative new microeconomics text for undergraduates.

Letter to Instructors

Dear Instructors,

Our object in writing this book has been to provide students with a treatment of intermediate microeconomics that is clear, accessible, up to date, accurate, useful, and relevant. In this letter, we would like to mention a few features of the book that may enhance its usefulness to you.

Enrichment Material—First, the book contains both core material and optional material. We identify an optional section by placing a star (*) in front of the section heading. Instructors who wish to delve into particular topics more deeply, or to introduce additional topics that enrich and extend the core material, may wish to incorporate one or more of the book's Add-Ons, which can be downloaded at www.mhhe.com/bernheim1e. Each Add-On is listed in the Table of Contents following the chapter with which it is associated, and readers are referred to these Add-Ons within the text ("readers who are interested in learning more about . . ."). As we receive feedback on this book, we may write additional Add-Ons, which will also be available through the same Web site.

Organization—Second, the organization of the book is slightly unconventional. As a discipline, microeconomic theory begins by examining the behavior of individuals in their roles as either consumers or owner-managers of firms. On this foundation, it builds a theory of aggregate economic outcomes, with an emphasis on market equilibria. Logically, it therefore makes sense to study the theory of decision making before diving into an analysis of how markets operate. This book follows the logical structure of the discipline. As a result, basic consumer theory (Chapters 4, 5, and 6) and basic producer theory (Chapters 7, 8, and 9) are followed by a series of chapters on decisions involving time, uncertainty, strategy, and behavioral perspectives on decision making (Chapters 10 through 13). We then cover competitive market equilibrium in Chapters 14 through 16. We do not, however, anticipate that instructors will necessarily teach the material in this order. Many instructors may wish to jump directly from basic producer theory (which concludes in Chapter 9) to competitive equilibrium (which begins in Chapter 14), returning to the special topics on decision making if time allows. The book is written to provide instructors with this flexibility.

Math Flexibility—Third, the book does not require calculus. However, an instructor who wishes to teach a calculus-based course using this book can easily do so. For the most important points, explanations involving calculus appear in footnotes and certain Add-Ons. In addition, the book includes a large number of quantitative Worked-Out Problems and Exercises. Where calculus would ordinarily be required, we simply supply the student with a derivative—for example, a formula for the marginal rate of substitution between goods, or for the marginal product of an input. In the context of consumer theory, the marginal rate of substitution is actually a more natural starting point for analysis than the utility function; after all, the marginal rate of substitution is observable, whereas a utility function is not. For a calculus-based course, an instructor can ask students to verify the derivatives. Supplying the derivatives cleanly separates the calculus portion of problem-solving from the "economic" portion, and prevents the calculus from interfering with the students' understanding of the economics.

Behavioral Economics—Fourth, given the level of interest in and increasing prominence of behavioral economics, the book devotes a separate chapter to this area of inquiry (Chapter 13). The material on behavioral economics is entirely compartmentalized; any instructor who wishes to teach a conventional course on intermediate microeconomics can simply skip the chapter. For those who are interested in introducing behavioral perspectives, we have designed the chapter with a modular structure, so that it can be used in one of two different ways. Most obviously, an instructor can introduce behavioral economics as a stand-alone topic, covering all or part of the chapter. Alternatively, an instructor can integrate behavioral perspectives with traditional perspectives, for example, covering Sections 13.1 and 13.2 after basic consumer theory (Chapters 4 through 6), Section 13.3 after decisions involving time (Chapter 10), Section 13.4 after decisions involving uncertainty (Chapter 11), and Section 13.5 after decisions involving strategy (Chapter 12).

We hope you enjoy using this book, and we look forward to receiving your helpful feedback!

With best wishes,
B. Douglas Bernheim and Michael D. Whinston

Brief Contents

CONTENTS

part I Introduction

part II Economic Decision Making

To Come

IIIB: Imperfectly Competitive Markets

part I

Introduction

Part I The first three chapters of this book lay the groundwork for all the material that follows. In Chapter 1, we'll provide a brief overview of microeconomics, previewing the types of questions it addresses, the tools it employs, the themes it emphasizes, and its uses in personal decision making, business, and public policy. In Chapter 2, we'll review some basic concepts that are typically covered in introductory economics courses, including demand, supply, market equilibrium, and elasticity. In Chapter 3, we'll study some basic principles of good decision making, and develop useful tools for identifying the choice that strikes the best balance between benefits and costs.

chapters

1 Preliminaries

Learning Objectives

After reading this chapter, students should be able to:

- Describe the scope of microeconomics and understand that it concerns the allocation of scarce resources.
- Explain how economists apply the scientific method to common economic questions.
- Identify recurring economic themes within the field.
- Recognize a variety of situations where economic ideas can be applied.
- Explain the goals of microeconomic inquiry.

It is often said that money can't buy happiness. Yet undeniably, people derive both sustenance and pleasure from material goods. Some of those goods, like clean water or a quiet spot on the beach, are found in nature. Others, like automobiles and television sets, are produced from natural resources. All these goods, whether natural or manufactured, have one important characteristic: their supplies are limited, or scarce.

Scarcity forces societies to confront three critical issues. First, each society must decide *what to produce.* All societies convert natural resources, like land, minerals, and labor, into the various things that people want, like food, clothing, and shelter. When we produce more of one good, we use up scarce resources, and this reduces our ability to produce other goods. For example, if a farmer uses an acre of land to produce wheat, he can't use the same acre to grow corn or tomatoes, or to graze livestock. He can't use it as the site for a manufacturing plant or a housing development. Since resources are scarce, every society must develop procedures for determining what is and is not produced.

Second, a society must decide *how to produce goods.* There is usually more than one way to produce a good. For example, if a farmer uses more fertilizer per acre, he can grow the same amount of wheat on less land. This decision frees up scarce land, which then becomes available for other purposes, such as housing or manufacturing. But fertilizer is also scarce. If farmers use more of it to grow wheat, less will remain for other crops. Since different methods of production consume different resources, every society must develop procedures for determining how goods are produced.

Finally, a society must determine *who gets what.* Every society produces goods so that people can eat, wear, use, or otherwise consume them. In some cases, a small number of individuals receive a large share of the goods. In the United States, for example, Bill Gates (cofounder of Microsoft), Larry Ellison (CEO of Oracle), Paul Allen (cofounder of Microsoft), and Warren Buffet (CEO of Berkshire Hathaway) together held more than half a percent of the nation's private wealth in 2006, which entitled them to buy a great deal more than the rest of us. In other cases, goods are distributed more equally. Every society must develop procedures for allocating goods among consumers.

The field of economics examines the ways in which societies address these three issues. In other words, it concerns the allocation of scarce resources. If everyone could have whatever they wanted whenever they wanted it, there would be no need for economics.

In this introductory chapter, we'll cover four main topics concerning microeconomics.

1. *What is microeconomics?* The field of microeconomics concerns decision making by individuals—typically consumers and the managers of firms—and how their decisions determine the allocation of a society's scarce resources. As we'll see, microeconomists address a wide range of issues related to individual and social behavior.
2. *Tools of microeconomics.* Microeconomists try to understand the allocation of scarce resources by applying the scientific method. We'll summarize the main principles of this method and describe its application to economic questions.
3. *Themes of microeconomics.* As you read through this book, you'll notice that some themes come up over and over again. We'll preview the most important ones.
4. *Uses of microeconomics.* Microeconomics can help with the decisions we make in our personal lives and in business. It also provides some useful tools for evaluating the effects and desirability of public policies. We'll briefly describe several problems to which microeconomic principles have been usefully applied.

1.1 WHAT IS MICROECONOMICS?

There are two main branches of economics, microeconomics and macroeconomics. While microeconomics concerns individual decision making and its collective effect on the allocation of a society's scarce resources, macroeconomics concerns aggregate phenomena. Booms and busts (recessions), the pace of economic growth, and the rate of unemployment are all macroeconomic topics. Much of modern macroeconomics involves applications of microeconomics, in the sense that explanations for aggregate outcomes are often rooted in theories of decision making by consumers and firms.

Institutions for Allocating Resources

Microeconomic analysis begins with an understanding of the institutions, including the laws and customs, that define a society's procedures for allocating resources. Those procedures empower various people to make decisions, but they also constrain their choices. For example, in most Western economies, consumers are free to spend their money as they choose, but they can't spend more than they can earn, accumulate, or borrow. Even an absolute dictator is constrained by the scarcity of a country's total resources.

A **capitalist economy** is one in which the means of production are mostly owned and controlled by and for the benefit of private individuals, and the allocation of resources is governed by voluntary trading among businesses and consumers.

A **communist economy** is one in which the state owns and controls the means of production and distribution.

Decentralization versus Centralization In some societies, most economic decisions are decentralized. Capitalism involves a high degree of decentralization. A **capitalist economy** is one in which the means of production are mostly owned and controlled by and for the benefit of private individuals, and the allocation of resources is governed by voluntary trading among businesses and consumers. Typically, this trading is organized into markets, which we discuss below. In capitalist economies, production takes place in thousands of independent firms, which are free to produce whatever their owners and managers choose. Likewise, consumers are free to spend their money as they please.

In some societies, many economic decisions are centralized. Communism involves a high degree of centralization. A **communist economy** is one in which the state owns and controls the means of production and distribution.[1] Government officials decide what to produce, how to produce it, and who gets it. In the old Soviet Union, for example, the managers of manufacturing plants received their production targets and other instructions from government ministries. Government officials also decided who would receive coveted consumer items, such as washing machines and automobiles.

No economy is completely centralized or decentralized. Every society takes a hybrid approach. While there is no foolproof way to measure a society's degree of economic centralization, it is possible to get a general idea by examining statistics on the size of government. Figure 1.1 shows total government spending on goods and services (also

Figure 1.1
Relative Economic Centralization. For each of the 12 countries in this figure, the lengths of the bars show total government spending on goods and services (also known as *government consumption*) and total government expenditure as fractions of gross domestic product (GDP) in 2005.

Source: *OECD in Figures, 2006–2007 Edition,* OECD Publications, 2006.

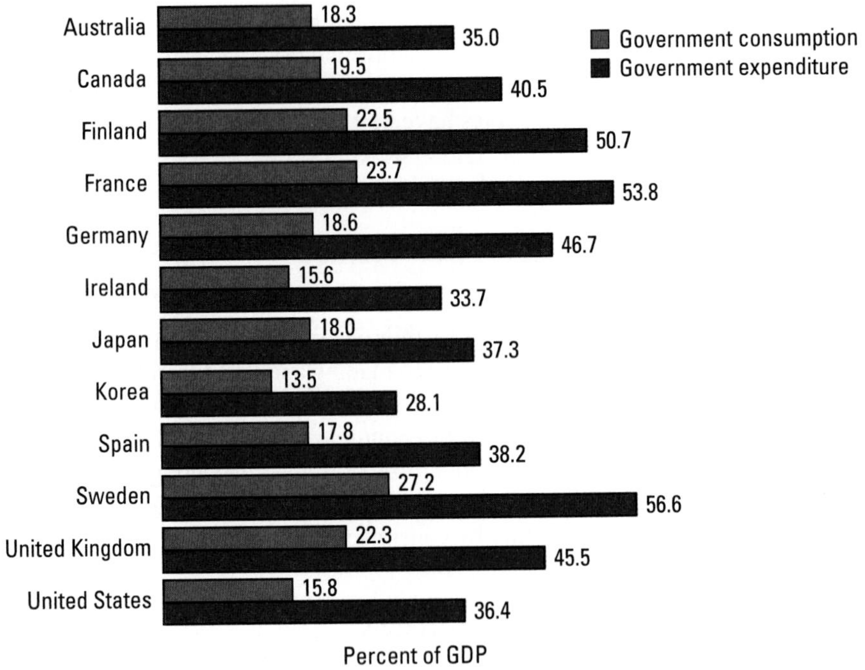

[1]This definition is not intended to encompass the meaning of communism as a political philosophy. The ownership and control of the means of production and distribution are also substantially centralized in socialist economies. As this book is primarily concerned with the operation of capitalist economies, we will not delve into the economic, political, and philosophical distinctions between the various forms of communism and socialism.

Application 1.1

A Pain in the Neck

The United States and other developed nations spend as much as 14 percent of their GDPs on medical care. How is the allocation of resources to medical care determined? In most countries, even those with capitalist economies, decisions that affect medical expenditures are both centralized and decentralized.

Suppose you have severe neck pain and need a strong painkiller. Who picks your medication? To some extent, you are free to purchase the painkiller of your choice. However, your decision is also constrained by government policy. In the United States, the Food and Drug Administration (FDA) regulates pharmaceutical products like painkillers. Before bringing a new drug to market, the manufacturer must first demonstrate to the FDA that it is both effective and reasonably safe. Consumers are not permitted to choose drugs that haven't received FDA approval. For example, when this book was written, doctors were free to prescribe a painkiller called lumiracoxib in Australia, Brazil, Mexico, and the United Kingdom, but not in the United States. Newly approved drugs are usually dispensed only on a prescription basis, according to the judgment of physicians. Prescription painkillers include codeine and morphine. Ultimately, the FDA approves many drugs for over-the-counter (OTC) use. Consumers can purchase and use OTC drugs without a doctor's consent. OTC painkillers include aspirin, acetominophen, ibuprofen, and naproxen.

In short, the choice of a pain killer depends not only on voluntary transactions between consumers and producers, but also on the decisions of health care providers and government regulators. Therefore, the allocation of pain killers is decentralized in some ways, and centralized in others.

known as *government consumption*) and total government expenditure (which includes both consumption and transfer payments like social security and welfare), expressed as percentages of gross domestic product, or GDP (a measure of national economic activity), for 12 countries as of 2005. According to these measures, resource allocation is centralized to a significant degree in all 12 countries. Sweden has the most centralized economy of the twelve; 27.2 percent of GDP goes to government consumption and 56.6 percent to government expenditure. South Korea's economy is the least centralized; there, only 13.5 percent of GDP goes to government consumption and 28.1 percent to government expenditure. The United States lies on the low end of this spectrum, with slightly greater centralization than South Korea and Ireland, and slightly less than Japan, Spain, and Australia.

Sometimes, a country centralizes certain aspects of resource allocation, like spending on national defense, and decentralizes others, like spending on breakfast cereal. (We'll see in Chapter 20 why this can make sense.) However, as Application 1.1 illustrates, there are also situations in which the decisions that affect the allocation of particular goods are both centralized and decentralized.

Markets The most common form of economic decentralization involves markets. **Markets** are economic institutions that provide people with opportunities and procedures for buying and selling goods and services. The procedures are sometimes defined by explicit rules, sometimes by custom. Compare, for example, the strict rules and procedures governing the sale and purchase of corporate stock on the New York Stock Exchange, with the loose customs that prevail in an open bazaar.

Markets are economic institutions that provide people with opportunities and procedures for buying and selling goods and services.

In microeconomic analysis, each market is associated with a single group of closely related products that are offered for sale within particular geographic boundaries. For example, an economist might examine the retail market for ice cream in Boston. Often, it is difficult to say exactly what constitutes an appropriate group of products or geographic boundaries. For example, should we consider a narrower product category, like chocolate ice cream, or a broader one that includes sorbet and frozen yogurt? Similarly, should we consider a smaller geographic area like Beacon Hill, or a larger one like Massachusetts?

Economists think of products as belonging to the same market when they are highly interchangeable. If consumers freely substitute sorbet for ice cream and vice versa, an economist would group those goods into a single market. Likewise, if the consumers who frequent ice cream parlors in Beacon Hill and Back Bay are happy to consider alternatives in the other neighborhood, an economist would group those Boston neighborhoods into a single market. In cases in which any seller can serve any customer regardless of location, the market is worldwide.

A flea market located in San Jose, California

In contrast to economists, most people associate markets with specific physical locations where trading takes place. Picture, for example, a flea market, a farmer's market, or the trading floor of the New York Stock Exchange. To an economist, a flea market doesn't qualify as a market for two reasons. First, a flea market offers a wide variety of goods, from socks to sofas. An economist would distinguish between a sock market and a sofa market. Second, flea market customers can usually buy most of the same goods at other local stores. To an economist, the sock market would include other sources of socks for the flea market's customers, such as local clothing and department stores, and possibly companies that sell socks over the Internet.

In many markets, the sellers are companies and the buyers are individuals. The markets for most consumer products fall into this category. For example, a consumer can buy ice cream from an A&P supermarket and televisions from a Good Guys discount warehouse. But there are also markets in which companies are buyers: A&P buys ice cream from Dreyer's, and Good Guys buys televisions from Sony. And there are markets in which individuals are sellers: employees sell their labor services to A&P and Good Guys. In some markets, buyers and sellers both include mixes of companies and individuals. Think about markets for used cars. You can buy a used car from, or sell one to, either a company or another individual.

A **price** is the rate at which someone can swap money for a good.

In modern markets, trade is usually governed by prices. A **price** is the rate at which someone can swap money for a good. In the markets for many consumer products, each seller establishes a nonnegotiable price at which it is willing to sell the good. For example, an A&P supermarket offers one gallon containers of Dreyer's chocolate ice cream to all customers at a fixed price. In other markets, sellers negotiate different prices with different customers. For instance, while new car dealers set prices for the automobiles in their inventories, most are willing to haggle.

A **property right** is an enforceable claim on a good or resource.

To function, markets require institutions that establish and protect private property rights. A **property right** is an enforceable claim on a good or resource. The notion of property rights is closely related to the idea of ownership. When we say that someone owns an object, we mean that she holds the only enforceable claim on it—in other words, she owns the property rights. If sellers lacked property rights, they would have nothing of value to offer buyers. (That's why you can't sell the Brooklyn Bridge!)

Property rights are **transferrable** if the current owner of a good can reassign those rights to another consenting party.

Trade can occur only if property rights are **transferrable**, in the sense that the current owner of a good can reassign those rights to another consenting party. When you buy a used car, for example, the previous owner transfers the car's title into your name. When property rights aren't transferrable, markets can't operate. For example, though many workers in the United States have rights to pension benefits, those rights aren't legally transferrable, so there's no market for them. You can't buy the rights to someone else's pension benefits.

Nations that allocate scarce resources primarily through markets are said to have **market economies**. Governments can play either large or small roles in market economies. In a **free market system**, the role of government is rather limited. Government enforces and protects property rights but otherwise mostly allows markets to operate as they will, with little regulation or other intervention. Most people equate capitalism with the free market system.

A **market economy** allocates scarce resources primarily through markets. In a **free market system**, the government mostly allows markets to operate as they will, with little regulation or other intervention.

There are, of course, ways to decentralize economic decision making without using markets. For example, many resources, like space on the beach, are allocated on a first-come first-served basis. Others, like seats in an oversubscribed college class, may be allocated by lottery.

One of the main objectives of microeconomics is to determine when each method of allocating scarce resources performs well and when it performs poorly. This knowledge allows us to judge whether specific economic decisions should be centralized or decentralized. In particular, it tells us whether markets are preferable to other economic institutions for allocating specific resources.

Economic Motives

By studying economic institutions, we learn about the constraints people face when they make choices that affect the allocation of resources. To determine which choices they will make, we need to understand their motives.

Microeconomists assume that people are motivated by material self-interest—that is, by the desire for goods and services. Throughout this book (except where we explicitly state otherwise), we'll assume that material self-interest is the *only* motive for behavior. Microeconomic theory can, however, accommodate a broader view of human motivations, including the possibility that someone might care about someone else's well-being.

The procedures used to allocate scarce resources create incentives for people to engage in certain activities and to avoid others. In market economies, people respond to material incentives in a variety of different ways, depending on whether they act as *consumers*, *employees*, or *owners of firms*.

In deciding how to spend their resources, self-interested consumers try to choose the mix of goods and services that provides the highest possible level of personal satisfaction. They respond to incentives created by the prices of those goods and services. Ordinarily, a high price discourages the consumption of a good, while a low price encourages it.

In deciding how to spend their time, self-interested employees try to choose the mix of work and leisure that provides the highest possible level of personal satisfaction. They respond to monetary incentives provided by their employers. For example, if an employer pays a fixed wage for each hour of work, that decision affects the relative attractiveness of work and leisure to the employee.

In directing production, the owners of firms are motivated by material self-interest to choose the mix of inputs and outputs that provides the highest possible level of profit. Because owners can exchange profits for goods and services, higher profits permit greater consumption and greater material satisfaction. Thus, owners respond to incentives created by the prices of inputs and outputs. For inputs, high prices discourage their use. For outputs, high prices encourage their production.

In other institutional settings, the quest for either material self-interest or broader notions of personal satisfaction motivates different types of activities. For example, children respond to incentives to study hard at school; politicians respond to incentives to promote policies that increase the likelihood of their reelection; and military officers respond to incentives to behave in ways that increase the likelihood of their promotion. Microeconomic analysis can help us to understand how people respond to incentives in a wide range of settings, not just in economic markets.

Positive versus Normative Analysis

Positive economic analysis addresses factual questions, also known as **positive questions**, usually concerning choices or market outcomes. It concerns what did, will, or would happen.

One of the main objectives of microeconomists is to address factual questions, also known as **positive questions**, usually concerning choices or market outcomes. This activity is known as **positive economic analysis**.[2] The truth of every possible answer to a positive question is potentially testable—the relevant facts, once known, must either confirm or contradict it.

All positive questions concern what *did* happen, what *will* happen, or what *would* happen. In addressing what *did* happen, economists provide a factual account of the past—for example, how the distribution of wealth among U.S. households changed between 1900 and 2000. In addressing what *will* happen, they forecast the future—for example, how the average interest rate charged on home mortgages will change over the next year. In addressing what *would* happen, they describe the likely consequences of a course of action, based on an understanding of cause and effect.

While historical fact-finding and forecasting are certainly important branches of economics, the cause-and-effect analysis of actions and their consequences is the bread and butter of microeconomics. Here are some examples of questions that address what *would* happen:

- If Dell were to reduce the price of notebook computers by 10 percent, how many more notebooks would the company sell? Would the increase in the sale of notebooks cut into the sales of Dell's desktop computers? If so, by how much?
- If Ford were to launch an advertising campaign to promote its new line of cars, would Toyota respond by advertising more? By lowering prices? By changing how it markets some models?
- If New York were to raise the minimum wage from $6.75 to $7.50, what would be the effect on employment? Would businesses hire fewer workers? Would they relocate to other states?

To answer positive questions accurately, economists must stick to objective facts and avoid value judgments. Sometimes, the facts aren't what we would like them to be. In such cases, positive economic analysis can at times seem callous, insensitive, or politically incorrect.

In 2001, for example, economist Steven Levitt and legal scholar John Donohue teamed up to study the important positive question of whether unwanted children are more likely to commit crimes when they become teenagers and adults.[3] After examining variations in crime statistics across states and across time, they concluded that the legalization of abortion—which presumably reduced the number of unwanted children—led

[2]The word *positive* does *not* mean that the answer admits no doubt. On the contrary, all answers—particularly those involving predictions—involve *some* degree of uncertainty. Rather, in this context, *positive* simply means that the prediction concerns a factual matter.

[3]John Donohue and Steven Levitt, "The Impact of Legalized Abortion on Crime," *Quarterly Journal of Economics* 166, no. 2, May 2001, pp. 379–420.

to lower crime rates among teenagers and young adults roughly 20 years later. The study touched off a firestorm of controversy. The authors received stacks of hate mail; some critics accused them of encouraging genocide. Yet the study drew no implications concerning the desirability of abortion. Its purpose was to investigate the positive, cause-and-effect relationship between neglect and subsequent criminal behavior. Professor Levitt sees a less controversial implication of the study: "We should do the best we can to try to make sure kids who are born are wanted and loved."

The other main objective of microeconomists is to address questions that involve value judgments, also known as **normative questions**, concerning the allocation of resources. This activity is known as **normative economic analysis**. Normative questions concern what ought to happen, rather than what did, will, or would happen. Here are some examples:

Normative economic analysis addresses questions that involve value judgments, also known as **normative questions.** It concerns what ought to happen rather than what did, will, or would happen.

- Is society better off with free trade between countries or with barriers to free trade?
- Which is better, taxing income from labor or income from capital?
- Will a merger between two large firms that produce similar goods benefit society?

Since value judgments are subjective, particular answers to normative questions are neither right nor wrong, and their validity isn't testable. Consider, for example, the following normative statement: "Economic inequality is evil." This statement is a value judgment, and people are free to disagree with each other about it, even when they agree about the objective facts.

If all normative statements are subjective, how can an economist usefully conduct normative analysis? Typically, economists rely on a single overarching value judgment, known as the principle of **individual sovereignty**, which holds that each person knows what's best for him or her. This principle requires us to avoid paternalistic judgments, like the notion that classical music is "better for you" than hip hop. If you choose hip hop, then hip hop must be better for you. Economists apply the same principles to policy questions. If, *with full knowledge of all consequences*, someone would choose trade barriers over free trade, we conclude that he's better off with trade barriers than with free trade. In this way, economists turn normative questions into positive questions. To determine whether a consumer would be better off or worse off with one of two alternatives, they predict which one the consumer would choose, given full and correct information about the effects of each alternative. This type of normative analysis obviously requires accurate positive analysis, both to forecast the consequences of the alternatives and to predict the consumer's choice.

The principle of **individual sovereignty** holds that each person knows what's best for him or her.

Unfortunately, the interests of different people often conflict. A policy that benefits one person may hurt another. This conflict requires us to weigh one person's gain against another's loss. For example, suppose we must choose between two policies, one of which benefits person A at the expense of person B, and the other of which benefits person B at the expense of person A. If person A is poor and person B is wealthy, most people would probably lean toward the first policy. But what if the benefit to A was small, while the cost to B was large? What if the policy involves taking money away from someone who works hard and giving it to someone who makes no effort?

Neither the principle of individual sovereignty, nor any other economic principle, can help us to decide whether the gain to one person outweighs the loss to another, or vice versa. However, if someone supplies a subjective criterion, normative economic analysis can identify the best policy. For example, suppose someone believes that from a social perspective, extra dollars in the hands of person A are worth twice as much as extra dollars in the hands of person B (possibly because person A is poor relative to person B). If positive economic analysis reveals that a policy is likely to raise person A's income by $80 and lower person B's income by $100, then *according to this criterion*, the policy will be beneficial.

The Scope of Microeconomics

Microeconomics isn't just about money. When economists speak of the allocation of resources, they often have in mind a broad definition of resources. Suppose, for example, that you're scheduled to take a test and have only a limited amount of time to study. Since your time is a scarce resource, its allocation between studying, sleep, and recreation is an economic issue.

Virtually every human decision involves the use of some scarce resource. As a result, microeconomists study an extremely broad range of topics, including marriage, crime, addiction, and suicide. In effect, microeconomics has evolved into the study of decision making, the ways in which decisions by many individuals combine to produce social outcomes, and the desirability of those outcomes.

Application 1.2

For Richer or Poorer

Though we make many important decisions over the course of our lives, few affect our happiness as profoundly as the choice of a spouse. Do economists have anything to say about who pairs up with whom?

In the past, the motivation for marriage was often explicitly economic. Betrothals were arranged to advance families' material interests, and marriages were treated as financial transactions. In some cultures, the groom's family made a substantial payment to the bride's family. Called a *bride price*, it was intended as compensation for the costs of the bride's upbringing and the loss of her services to her parents. In other cultures, the bride's family made a substantial payment to the groom's. Such "dowries" were particularly common in societies in which an unmarried adult daughter was considered a burden or an embarrassment to her parents. As in any economic market, the magnitude of the bride price or the dowry reflected the forces of supply and demand (see Chapter 2).

In contemporary western societies, we frown on "gold-diggers" who place financial concerns before romance. According to custom, we choose our spouses based primarily on love. Does that mean that our choice of a spouse is not an economic decision? Not at all. From an unmarried woman's point of view, appropriate mates are scarce—indeed, it's often said that a good man is hard to find. The same principle holds for unmarried men. Potential spouses are a scarce resource, the allocation of which is governed by the customs and institutions associated with dating and marriage.

A skeptic might argue that love is irrational, that it defies logical analysis. But an economist doesn't need to explain why Bob is more attracted to Sally than to Sue, any more than she needs to explain why Bob likes pizza more than popcorn. Rather, an economist tries to explain Bob's *choices*, taking his likes and dislikes, as well as the intensity of those feelings, as givens.

While economists can't predict who will fall in love with whom, they can (and do) investigate the types of traits that men and women value in potential mates. By examining who chooses whom, they can also determine the typical person's willingness to trade off one desirable characteristic, like financial success, for another, like an aspect of physical attractiveness. In one study, economist Raymond Wolff found that where marriage is concerned, income is the most important determinant of a man's desirability to women, while slimness is the most important determinant of a woman's desirability to men.[4] While many people might find these

[4]Raymond Alfred Wolff, "The Relationship between Child Support and Remarriage for Divorced and Separated Women and Men," PhD dissertation, Stanford University, 2000.

conclusions somewhat offensive, it is important to remember that Wolff was describing tendencies, not universal truths, and that he was engaged in *positive* analysis. That is, his objective was to discover the facts, not to make judgments.

Why then does marriage fall within the scope of microeconomics? Economists study how the allocation of scarce resources (including spouses with desirable characteristics) depends on institutions and customs (including those governing who meets whom) given the objectives that motivate choices (including the desire for a wealthy or attractive mate). Equipped with an understanding of the traits that people value in spouses, an economist could, for example, predict how a change in the social customs and institutions that determine who meets whom—resulting perhaps from a technological development like the Internet, which makes it easier to meet potential mates with particular characteristics—will tend to affect the standards applied in evaluating potential mates, the length of time spent searching for mates, and the types of people who ultimately pair up. These effects may lead to further consequences of economic interest. For example, a reduction in the tendency for people to marry spouses with similar social and economic backgrounds will reduce the likelihood that differences in income and wealth will persist across generations.

1.2 TOOLS OF MICROECONOMICS

Economics is a social science—social in the sense that it concerns human behavior, and a science in the sense that, when studying behavior, economists follow the scientific method. In practice, what does that method involve?

"I'm a social scientist, Michael. That means I can't explain electricity or anything like that, but if you ever want to know about people I'm your man."

The Scientific Method

How do scientists uncover the truth about the world? How do they learn about the characteristics, causes, and effects of observed phenomena? Though the details differ from one discipline to another, all scientists follow a common approach known as the **scientific method**, which consists of the following five steps.

Step 1: Initial observation Scientific inquiry starts with the observation of an unexplained phenomenon. Think of Sir Isaac Newton, who wondered why objects (like apples) tend to fall toward the earth rather than away from it. Observation also motivates economic questions. An economist might wonder why water, which is essential to life, costs far less per ounce than diamonds, which are not.

Step 2: Theorizing After observing an unexplained phenomenon, a scientist tries to come up with a possible explanation, known as a **theory**. To account for the behavior of falling objects, Newton proposed the theory of gravity. Likewise, to account for differences between the prices of goods like water and diamonds, economists developed the theory of supply and demand (which we'll review in the next chapter).

Step 3: Identification of additional implications It isn't enough for a theory to explain the observation that motivated its creation. Good theorizing requires the scientist to "stick her neck out." Having formulated a theory, she must look for additional implications that can either be verified or falsified. Virtually every scientific theory implies that there are circumstances under which a phenomenon will reoccur. For example, according to Newton's theory of gravity, apples should *always* fall when separated from their branches.

The **scientific method** is the general procedure used by scientists to learn about the characteristics, causes, and effects of natural phenomena.

A **theory** is a possible explanation for a natural phenomenon.

Sometimes a theory's additional implications are more subtle. Newton's theory implies that in a vacuum, all objects should fall at precisely the same rate, regardless of their weight or size. Similarly, the theory of supply and demand implies that prices should rise following an increase in production costs.

Step 4: Further observation and testing To determine whether a theory is valid, scientists make further observations, gathering data that will allow them to test the theory's additional implications. A physicist might test the theory of gravity by designing an experiment to determine whether different objects do, in fact, fall at the same rate in a vacuum. An economist might gather the data needed to determine whether prices do, in fact, rise following an increase in production costs.

Step 5: Refinement of the theory Sometimes a scientist's further observations are inconsistent with some or all of a theory's additional implications. In some cases, the falsification of the theory is so complete that scientists must go back to the drawing board. In other instances, they can account for the new observations by modifying the theory. In either case, after further theorizing, they return to step 3, identify additional implications of the new or modified theory, and put those to the test.

This process never truly ends. Though a scientist may have enormous confidence in a thoroughly tested theory, she never treats it as absolute truth. Scientists are free to examine and reexamine the validity of any theory, no matter how well-established.

Some theories are more useful than others. A useful theory is both broadly applicable and specific in its implications. The theory of gravity is extremely useful both because it applies to all physical objects and because it has very specific implications about the rate at which any two objects will move toward each other. In contrast, the theory that "anything can happen, anytime, anywhere" may be broadly applicable, but it has no specific implications. Likewise, a theory that explains only why a particular leaf on a particular tree fell at a particular moment may have very specific implications, but isn't useful because it isn't broadly applicable.

Models and Mathematics

A **model** is a simplified representation of a phenomenon.

Scientists usually express their theories through *models*. A **model** is a simplified representation of a phenomenon—a story or analogy that explains how part of the world works. Typically, a model provides an account of cause and effect.

Without realizing it, all of us use simple models in our daily lives. For example, when you get into a car and step on the gas, you expect the car to move forward, because you have in your mind a model of how the car works. If you're not mechanically inclined, your model may be no more complicated than the idea that pressing on the accelerator makes the car move forward. Even so, it's still a model.

Newton's model of gravity starts with a simple principle, that every object pulls every other object toward it. The complete theory adds numerous details. For example, it maintains that the pull between two objects depends on their masses and the distance between them. Since Newton was interested in quantitative questions—for instance, how fast an object moves or how far it travels—the theory involves a great deal of mathematics.

A model needn't be mathematical, however. Take the following statement: "If you study longer for a microeconomics exam, you'll receive a higher grade." This qualitative model is certainly useful, though not as useful as a good quantitative model. For example, if you knew that another hour of studying would improve your numerical score on an exam by 10 percent, you could better assess whether additional studying is worth the time and effort.

Economists usually work with mathematical models. Why? Because most economic choices are quantitative, most of the economic questions raised in business and government call for precise answers. Mathematical models can provide precision; qualitative theories cannot. In addition, mathematical modeling imposes intellectual discipline. It forces us to be specific about our assumptions and prevents us from relying on loose or incomplete reasoning.

In Chapter 2, we'll explore one important economic model in some detail: the model of supply and demand. Economists often use that model qualitatively—for example, to understand whether the price of a good will rise or fall after an increase in production costs. However, by using a mathematical model of supply and demand, they can also say, with some precision, how much the price will rise for a given change in cost.

"Duh!"

Simplifying Assumptions

There's a famous joke about an economist and two scientists stranded on a desert island with a great deal of canned food, but no can opener. The scientists suggest various methods for opening the cans, which the economist dismisses out of hand. When they ask irritably what he would suggest, he smiles and replies, "Assume a can opener."

Though the joke implies otherwise, all scientists—not just economists—make assumptions that are not literally true. By their nature, models are *simplified* representations of the real world. Simplification allows us to wrap our minds around phenomena that might otherwise be too complex to understand.

In formulating a model, scientists often concentrate on the *most important* explanations for a phenomenon. For example, to describe how quickly a paper clip falls from a tabletop to the floor, a scientist might focus exclusively on gravity, using a simple theory that near the earth's surface, objects accelerate downward at the rate of 9.8 meters/sec^2. This model isn't literally correct. Among other things, air resistance affects the rate of descent. Should the scientist factor in air pressure, wind speed, humidity, surface imperfections on the paper clip, and other factors that could in principle affect its speed? The answer depends on her need for precision. In this context, her simple model of acceleration is reasonably accurate and hard to improve on, even though it is literally false.

Economists do much the same thing. Since the social phenomena they study are extremely complex, they must make many simplifying assumptions. Typically, some of those assumptions are easy to criticize. In evaluating economic models, then, we must remember that no model is literally true. The real test of a good model is its usefulness. A model that contributes to our understanding of social phenomenon and does a reasonably good job of predicting outcomes is certainly useful, even if it isn't entirely realistic.

It follows that the same simplifying assumption can be reasonable in one context but unreasonable in another. For example, in studying patterns of household spending on consumption goods like food, clothing, and shelter, it's probably reasonable to assume that people care only about their material self-interest. But in studying charitable contributions, that certainly is *not* a good assumption.

Data Analysis

The scientific method requires us to test our theories by confronting them with data. Sources of economic data fall into three main categories: records, surveys, and experiments.

Records Most companies maintain detailed business records, including financial accounts, personnel records, and client or customer databases. Many companies employ in-house economists to analyze these data, and some companies share their data with independent economists. Other companies compile data for the express purpose of selling it to others. For example, they track the prices of stocks, bonds, and various commodities. Both companies and households are required to supply information to the government, which is, in some cases, available to the public. For example, the U.S. Securities and Exchange Commission requires publicly traded companies to disclose certain financial information. In some cases, economists can also obtain limited access to confidential data, like individual income tax returns and social security records.

Surveys A survey can be used to collect data on virtually anything, including topics for which there are no records, such as the amount of time people devote to work, housekeeping, leisure, and sleep. The U.S. government sponsors many large-scale surveys that collect data on a wide range of topics. The Consumer Expenditure Survey, for instance, tracks people's monthly out-of-pocket spending on housing, clothing, transportation, health care, insurance, and entertainment. Companies, too, sponsor surveys for business purposes and sometimes turn to economists for analyses of the resulting data. In some cases, they provide that data to independent economists, either for a fee or free of charge. In a pinch, an economist can even design and field her own survey.

Experiments Natural scientists routinely test their theories by conducting controlled experiments. Though economics is not primarily an experimental science, over the past two or three decades economic experiments have become increasingly common. To test theories of consumer behavior, economists present experimental subjects with options and then observe their choices. To test market theories, economists set up experimental markets and study their operation.

Through controlled experiments, scientists can determine the causal relationship between circumstances and outcomes. For example, if a medical researcher wants to know whether a new drug will prevent a disease, he randomly assigns subjects to a "treatment group," which will receive the drug, and a "control group," which will receive a placebo (an inactive substance known to have no therapeutic effect). He then attributes any differences in the health outcomes of the two groups to the drug. Experimental economists try to isolate causal relationships in a similar way.

Outside the laboratory, however, there are few controlled experiments. How do economists determine cause and effect using data obtained from the real world? Sometimes, the circumstances of otherwise identical people differ entirely by chance. In those cases, economists can attribute the differences in the average outcomes for different groups of people to the differences in their circumstances, just as in the laboratory. This approach is known as a **natural experiment**.

In a **natural experiment**, the circumstances of otherwise identical people differ entirely by chance. An economist attributes differences in the average outcomes for those people to the differences in their circumstances.

For example, suppose we want to measure the effect of military service on an individual's later earnings as a civilian. The Vietnam draft lottery provides an opportunity for a natural experiment. Since the lottery drawings were entirely random, we can focus on those men who were eligible for the draft and compare the subsequent earnings of those who were drafted and those who were not.[5]

When the circumstances of different people differ entirely by chance, as in a controlled laboratory or natural experiment, we can be reasonably confident that other factors do not explain any observed differences in outcomes. However, in the real world, the circumstances of different people usually do not differ by chance. Those who find themselves in one circumstance are often systematically different from those who find themselves in another. Economists must then control for those differences statistically, rather than experimentally. Suppose, for instance, that we're interested in learning whether men and women prefer to spend their money on different goods. Merely observing differences in their spending patterns won't settle the issue. Why not? Among other reasons, men tend to have higher incomes than women. Before attributing gender differences in spending habits to preferences, then, we need to remove differences that are attributable to income. Statistical methods allow us to adjust data on spending by men and women to reflect a common level of income. The application of statistical methods to empirical questions in economics is known as **econometrics**.

Econometrics is the application of statistical methods to empirical questions in the field of economics.

Why Economists Sometimes Disagree

Though good economists use the scientific method, as in all sciences there is still room for disagreement. In economics, it's important to distinguish between disagreements that concern positive matters and those that concern normative matters.

Disagreements about positive matters usually reflect differences in scientific judgment. Sometimes, two economists look at the same evidence and come to different conclusions. For example, based on the available studies, some economists think that an increase in the minimum wage would significantly reduce employment, and others believe that the effect on employment would be relatively minor. These types of disputes aren't unique to economics. Indeed, most of the leading theories in the natural sciences were at one time controversial.

When two scientists reach different positive conclusions based on the same evidence, it's a safe bet that they've started from different assumptions. For example, what conclusions follow from the observation that college graduates earn more money than high school graduates? If we assume that college attendance is unrelated to ability, then we may conclude that college teaches valuable skills. But if we assume that college teaches nothing of practical value, then we may conclude that college students are more capable to begin with. Fortunately, most assumptions are testable, so we can, at least in principle,

[5] In contrast, a comparison of earnings for people with and without military service would not be as informative, because the decision to enlist is not the result of chance. On the contrary, it is related to personal characteristics (like self-discipline) that can affect job performance.

resolve such disputes by analyzing additional data. In practice, nailing down all the relevant facts can be difficult and time-consuming. As the evidence accumulates, judgments converge, and a scientific consensus emerges.

Through decades of research and stacks of studies, economists have reached a degree of consensus on a number of important issues.[6] However, even when there's widespread agreement about a particular issue, there are usually a few dissenters, who sometimes receive disproportionate attention from the media, particularly when their views are helpful to powerful political interests. While economists do disagree about many things, the extent of this disagreement is therefore often exaggerated.

While the accumulation of scientific evidence can resolve positive disagreements, it can't resolve normative disputes arising from differences in values. For example, it can't tell us whether one person's gain is more or less important than another person's loss. As a result, even when economists reach the same positive conclusions, they may disagree about the desirability of a particular public policy. Two economists may agree that an increase in the minimum wage leads to a moderate reduction in employment, benefitting those who receive higher wages at the expense of those who lose their jobs. Yet they may disagree on whether helping the first group justifies hurting the second. Careful positive inquiry allows us to measure the size of the two effects, but it can't tell us which is more important.

1.3 THEMES OF MICROECONOMICS

Judging by the length and content of this book, microeconomists have a lot to say about a wide range of topics. Still, as you progress through the book, you'll notice that a number of themes come up over and over again. Here we'll preview some of the most important ones.

Decisions: Some Central Themes

The following four themes, which concern decision making, are featured in Chapters 3 through 13.

Theme 1: Trade-offs are unavoidable. Economists like to remind us that there's no such thing as a free lunch. Simply put, scarcity forces us to confront trade-offs. To get something we want, we must usually give up something else.

Every choice involves trade-offs. In selecting one alternative, you forgo others. If you want to get good grades, you have to study, but since your time is scarce, you socialize less. Likewise, when a consumer spends an extra dollar on food, she has one less dollar to spend on other goods like clothes and housing. And when a company decides to shut down, it saves money, but gives up the chance to earn revenue.

Recognizing trade-offs is an essential part of good decision making. When we ignore trade-offs, we risk giving up something we value highly for something that is less important, and we tend to regret our choices. If you pretend that socializing doesn't cut into your study time, you're likely to be disappointed with your grades. Similarly, if a con-

[6]See Richard M. Alston, J.R. Kearl, and Michael B. Vaughn, "Is There Consensus among Economists in the 1990s?" *American Economic Review*, May 1992, pp. 203–209.

sumer ignores trade-offs, he risks spending his money on the wrong things. When a company ignores trade-offs, it risks the loss of profit opportunities.

Theme 2: Good choices are usually made at the margin. While some decisions have an all-or-nothing quality, most are matters of degree. For example, registering for a course in microeconomics is an all-or-nothing choice, but preparing for a test is not—a student can devote as much or as little time to studying as she likes. Likewise, a consumer's decision to purchase 10 gallons of gasoline rather than 11 is a matter of degree, as is a company's decision to produce 20,000 units of a good rather than 21,000.

For decisions involving matters of degree, microeconomic principles teach us to think "at the margin." To determine whether a particular choice is best, we ask whether a small adjustment of the choice—also known as a **marginal change**—will lead to improved results. The typical adjustment has both benefits and costs. If the benefits exceed the costs, then the decision maker will be better off; if the costs exceed the benefits, then he will be worse off. If a marginal change makes the decision maker better off, then the original choice obviously wasn't the best one.

A **marginal change** is a small adjustment of a choice.

Suppose, for example, that a student plans to spend five hours studying for her midterm, which she knows is better than not studying at all. But is it her *best* choice? Thinking at the margin requires her to ask whether she would be better off studying a little bit more—say, an extra 15 minutes—or a little bit less. The answer depends on many factors: how well she knows the material, how much she expects to accomplish in 15 minutes, and the relative importance of other activities.

Thinking at the margin sometimes leads to surprising conclusions. Imagine that you have arranged to stage a play at a 1,000-seat theater at a cost of $15,000. Since the average cost per seat is $15, you might hesitate to sell any tickets for less than $15 a piece. But suppose that just before show time there are still some empty seats, and you believe you can fill some of them by dropping the ticket price to $5. Doing so is clearly worth your while, even though the marginal customer doesn't pay enough to cover the average cost per seat.

The principle of thinking at the margin is so important that we'll devote an entire chapter to it (Chapter 3). In Part II, we'll apply the principle to decisions involving consumption and production.

Theme 3: People respond to incentives. To determine whether an action is desirable, a good decision maker carefully weighs her benefits and costs. Benefits provide incentives to take the action; costs provide disincentives. The action becomes more attractive when benefits rise or costs fall, and less attractive when benefits fall or costs rise. So any development that changes benefits or costs has the potential to alter behavior.

Imagine that it's Friday, and you have a microeconomics exam the next Monday. If a friend decides to throw a party over the weekend, you'll probably spend less time studying than you planned. The prospect of missing the party makes studying more costly, creating a disincentive to hit the books. But what if your professor announces that the exam will count for 40 percent of your final grade instead of 15 percent, as you had expected? In that case, you'll probably study more than you planned. The professor's decision raises the benefits of studying, creating an incentive to hit the books.

Most public policies provide people with incentives to take certain actions and avoid others. Unfortunately, lawmakers often fail to think through all those incentives. As a result, their policies sometimes have unintended and unfortunate consequences.

In 1994, for example, the state of Texas adopted a new system for financing public primary and secondary schools. Among other features, the system provided school districts with extra funds for each child with a qualifying disability. Texas lawmakers were surprised to discover that the fraction of Texas schoolchildren classified as disabled leapt upward by roughly 20 percent between 1992 and 1997, creating an unanticipated strain on the state's financial resources. Little consideration had been given to the possibility that schools might strategically reclassify students with marginal disabilities in order to obtain additional resources. Yet it appears that is precisely what happened. Indeed, many schools hired consultants to help them get the most out of the system.[7]

Theme 4: Prices provide incentives. The costs of buying goods and the benefits of selling them depend on their prices. An increase in the price of a good provides a disincentive to buy, because it raises the costs of buying. It also provides an incentive to sell because it raises the benefits of selling. Conversely, a reduction in the price of a good provides an incentive to buy, because it reduces the costs of buying. It also provides a disincentive to sell, because it reduces the benefits of selling.

Since people respond to incentives, changing prices tend to change people's choices. A price increase tends to reduce the amount people want to buy, and increase the amount they want to sell. A price reduction has the opposite effect. These relationships form the basis for supply and demand curves, which we'll review in the next chapter.

Markets: Some Central Themes

The following four themes, which concern markets, are featured in Part III (Chapters 14 through 21).

Trade occurs whenever two or more people exchange valuable goods or services.

Theme 5: Trade can benefit everyone. Trade occurs whenever two or more people exchange valuable goods or services. Think about what life would be like if you were unable to trade with others. How would you eat? What would you wear? What would you use for shelter? Even if you had the skills needed to survive on your own, your life would be primitive. All of the conveniences and luxuries that we associate with modern life, such as cars, airplanes, cell phones, computers, air conditioning, and television, are available to you only because people trade with each other.

Through trade, someone who owns a good that is of relatively little value to him, but of substantial value to another, can exchange it for something he values more highly. Trade also frees him from the need to produce everything he needs or wants. Instead, he can focus on producing a single good or service that has value to others. By specializing in something that he does well, he can become even more skilled and productive. Talented carpenters can focus on building, talented chefs on cooking, and talented scientists on research. Society ends up with better goods and services, and more of them.

Theme 6: The competitive market price reflects both value to consumers and cost to producers. In a market, every buyer requires a seller, and every seller requires a buyer. The market price adjusts to balance supply and demand, falling when supply exceeds demand and rising when demand exceeds supply. As a result, the market price reflects both demand and supply.

In a competitive market, consumers balance the benefits of a good against the cost of acquiring it (namely, its price). At the margin, those benefits and costs must be equal. Otherwise, the consumer would benefit by consuming a little bit more (if the benefits exceed

[7]According to one study, the financial incentives embedded in the state's new school financing system accounted for 40 percent of the growth in student disability rates. See Julie Berry Cullen, "The Impact of Fiscal Incentives on Student Disability Rates," *Journal of Public Economics* 87, 2003, pp. 1557–1589.

the costs) or a little bit less (if the costs exceed the benefits). Thus, a good's market price is equal to the value consumers place on an extra unit.

Similarly, competitive firms balance the revenue they receive from selling another unit of a good (once again, its price) against the cost of producing it. At the margin, those benefits and costs must be equal. Otherwise, the firm could earn a higher profit by producing more (if the revenue exceeds the cost) or less (if the cost exceeds the revenue). Thus, a good's competitive market price is equal to the cost of producing an extra unit.

Theme 7: Compared to other methods of resource allocation, markets have advantages. The Cold War, which lasted from the end of World War II in 1945 to the fall of the Berlin Wall in 1989, was in large part a struggle between two competing economic systems, capitalism and communism. Ultimately, the communist economies were unable to keep pace with the capitalist economies. Economic pressures caused the collapse of the Soviet Union and forced other communist countries, like the People's Republic of China, to adopt market reforms.

Why do market economies perform so well, even though individuals pursue their own narrow self-interests? How do they manage to achieve such high levels of productivity and growth with so little centralized coordination? The answer to both these questions is that market prices coordinate our activities, providing us with incentives to expend our effort and resources in pursuits that others value.

True, companies usually don't try to advance social goals; instead, they seek profit. But in deciding whether to produce a good, they look to its price, which reflects its value to consumers at the margin. Similarly, most consumers are concerned primarily with their own satisfaction. But in deciding whether to purchase a good, they consider its price, which reflects its cost to firms at the margin. Thus, market prices cause self-interested producers and consumers to consider the costs and benefits that their actions create for other members of society.

For example, suppose new medical research identifies important health benefits from eating grapefruit. In response, a knowledgeable and well-intentioned central planner would presumably shift social resources toward grapefruit production. Yet without any centralized decision making, free markets can and do accomplish exactly the same thing. Learning of the research, consumers demand more grapefruit. With no change in the price of grapefruit, demand will exceed supply, so the price must rise. (We'll explain why in Chapter 2.) The higher price then encourages farmers to produce more grapefruit.

Theme 8: Sometimes, government policy can improve on free-market resource allocations. Though market economies have many advantages, they aren't perfect. There are some legitimate concerns about the way in which markets allocate scarce resources. In many instances, there are potential justifications for government intervention in markets.

In some situations, the market price of a good doesn't accurately reflect its costs and benefits to all consumers and producers, at the margin. When that occurs, markets may fail to allocate resources to their best uses. There are several types of market failure. In some cases, the failure is associated with insufficient competition among producers. If, for example, only one company can provide telephone service, it may set the price of a minute of service well above cost. Consumers react to the high price by using their telephones less often than they would if they had to pay only the true cost. In other cases, markets fail because transactions affect uninvolved third parties. Take gasoline, for example. The market price of gasoline reflects the production costs incurred by gasoline producers. It does not, however, reflect the costs associated with polluting the environment, which fall on the general population. As a result, consumers use more gasoline than they would if its price reflected all the social costs. In still other cases, markets fail because different people have access to different information. For example, potential used car buyers may worry that sellers will try to unload lemons. That fear may prevent a buyer and a seller from consummating a mutually beneficial deal.

When a market fails, government intervention may be beneficial. In the case of the telephone company with no competition, there may be some justification for regulating prices. In the case of gasoline, a tax that reflects the costs of pollution may induce consumers to take those costs into account. In the case of used cars, laws requiring the full and truthful disclosure of a car's history of accidents and repairs may allay the fears of potential buyers. However, it's important to remember that government policy making is imperfect, and that interventions can also fail. Sometimes the cure is worse than the disease. Many forms of government intervention can prevent the economy from performing as well as it might.

Finally, free markets can produce a great deal of inequality across consumers. Some people can afford private jets, while others whose skills are not highly valued, at least at the margin, struggle to make ends meet. Concerns about equity can justify government policies that redistribute resources from the haves to the have-nots.

1.4 USES OF MICROECONOMICS

Why study microeconomics? The simple answer is that microeconomics is extremely useful. It can help us to make important decisions, and it provides tools for understanding and evaluating the effects of public policies.

In terms of decision making, microeconomics offers a wide variety of helpful principles. For example, it stresses the importance of approaching every decision in terms of the trade-offs implied. It also trains us to search for our best choice by thinking at the margin.

In some cases, the principles of economics involve little more than common sense. For example, if your old car requires $3,000 worth of engine work, after which it will be worth only $2,000, it's ready for the junk heap. This conclusion holds even if you've just sunk $1,200 into a complete tune-up and new brakes. Economic principles discourage you from throwing good money after bad.

Other decisions are much more complex, so that common sense takes us only so far. In such cases, the careful application of microeconomic principles guides us toward good choices. Here are two examples:

1. *Business investments.* Suppose a company is considering investing $10 million to build a new manufacturing plant. It expects the plant to generate a net profit of $1.5 million per year for 20 years, at which point it will have a scrap value of $1 million. Is this investment worthwhile? Upon what does the answer depend? Does it matter that the investment doesn't break even until the seventh year? (We explain how to evaluate business investments in Section 10.3.)
2. *Portfolio management.* Most people try to save money for retirement. Should a particular individual accumulate her savings in bank accounts? Should she buy corporate stocks? Corporate bonds? Government bonds? Mutual funds? Upon what does the answer depend? Should she behave differently if she's cautious than if she's

a risk-taker? If so, how? (We discuss some basic principles behind portfolio allocation in Section 11.4 and Add-On 11A.)

Microeconomic tools are also indispensable to the analysis and evaluation of public policy. Those who stand to gain from a public policy often exaggerate its benefits and downplay its costs, while those who stand to lose do the opposite. And as we've seen, sometimes even well-intentioned policymakers overlook important effects of policy changes on incentives. Careful microeconomic analysis can identify beneficial policies and provide reliable, objective measures of the costs and benefits. Here's an example:

Environmental policy. Coal-fired electric plants emit sulfur dioxide (SO_2), which is the main cause of acid rain. Traditionally, the United States government has regulated SO_2 by limiting the emissions of each plant. At the urging of economists, the government adopted a new approach in 1990. The idea is to provide each plant with permits that allow them to emit certain amounts of SO_2 and then allow them to trade those permits. This policy created a market for SO_2 emission permits, thereby ensuring that plants with low abatement costs would trade them to plants with high abatement costs. By harnessing the power of markets, the policy is estimated to have reduced abatement costs by \$225 to \$375 million per year. (We elaborate on this policy in Section 14.5.)

Application 1.3 describes one setting in which microeconomic analysis has had an enormous influence, both on major business decisions and on policy making. Throughout this book, you'll find many other applications to important problems confronting households, companies, and public officials.

Application 1.3

Allocating the Airwaves

Wireless electronics, like cell phones, television, and radio, all make use of "the airwaves"—technically, the electromagnetic spectrum. Doing so requires coordination. If different service providers tried to use the same portion of the spectrum, their signals would overlap, rendering certain frequencies virtually useless. Governments usually solve this problem by assigning different services and service providers to different frequencies within the spectrum.

In the 1980s and early 1990s, advances in communications technologies put pressure on the U.S. government to reevaluate the allocation of the electromagnetic spectrum. In August 1993, President Bill Clinton signed legislation authorizing the Federal Communications Commission (FCC) to assign spectrum licenses through auctions. The legislation required the FCC to develop auction rules and conduct the first spectrum auction within one year.

The FCC found itself in a rather difficult position. While the government had used auctions for a variety of other purposes, spectrum licenses are rather special. Since wireless telecommunications providers require multiple licenses for geographically contiguous areas, the value of any one license to a given company depends critically on the combination of licenses it succeeds in acquiring. The FCC's technical staff understood that traditional auction structures are not well suited to auctioning off multiple licenses with these types of interdependencies.

The most obvious possibility would have been to auction off the licenses one at a time in succession, each to the highest bidder. The main problem with this approach is that the value to a bidder of a license that is auctioned off early depends on the prices it will have to pay for other licenses to be auctioned off later. Bidders in the early auctions must therefore guess the prices that will emerge from the later auctions. When bidders actually participate in a sequence of auctions, they often guess wrong and make poor decisions in the early rounds.[8]

Hoping to discover some new procedure that would allocate spectrum to its most valuable uses while generating substantial revenue for the government, the FCC sought suggestions from interested parties. In response, several economists—most notably Paul Milgrom and Robert Wilson, acting as consultants for what was then Pacific Bell, and Preston McAfee, acting as a consultant for what was then Airtouch—proposed a completely novel auction structure, called the *simultaneous ascending auction.* The rules of the new auction are complex. However, the basic idea is to auction off all licenses at the same time. That way, as the auction proceeds, bidders gradually learn what the prices of *all* licenses will be, and they can make their final decision about each license based on accurate knowledge concerning the prices of other licenses, rather than on guesses. Milgrom, Wilson, and McAfee argued that the new auction structure was therefore more likely to promote good decisions and allocate spectrum to its most valuable uses.

The FCC's staff was understandably reluctant to approve a new auction structure with no track record, particularly since the proposed rules were significantly more complicated than those of any auction with which they were familiar. FCC Chairman Reed Hunt made it clear to the staff that he feared a fiasco, and that the FCC's spectrum auctions were far too important to serve as an economic "beta test site."

Despite these obstacles, the FCC staff eventually became convinced that the basic ideas behind the proposed auction were sound. However, the elegance of the underlying theory was not in itself sufficient to carry the day. The staff insisted on hard evidence. So several economists, including Charles Plott (working for what was then PacTel), turned to experiments. The experimental evidence confirmed that the new auction performed considerably better than traditional alternatives.

The FCC opened its first spectrum auction, based primarily on the economists' proposal, on July 25, 1994. To the surprise of many observers, it ran smoothly and was a great success, generating far more revenue for the U.S. government than anyone had expected, as well as prices that were indicative of more informed decision making on the part of bidders.[9] The FCC was so satisfied with the results that it decided to use the same basic procedures for later spectrum auctions.

As we'll see in later chapters, microeconomic principles have important implications not only for auction design, but for effective bidding strategies. Not surprisingly, when the stakes are high, bidders often turn to economic consultants for advice and guidance.

CHAPTER SUMMARY

1. **What is microeconomics?**
   a. Microeconomics is the study of decision making by individuals, usually consumers or managers of firms. It is also the study of how the separate decisions of many individuals combine to determine the allocation of scarce resources.
   b. Societies differ with respect to their relative centralization or decentralization of economic decision making.
   c. The most common form of economic decentralization involves markets. Economists usually define markets by focusing on one product and place at a time.
   d. Economists often assume that people are motivated by material self-interest. Self-interest leads to different choices in different societies, depending on the procedures used to allocate scarce resources.

[8]For example, virtually identical objects sometimes sell for radically different prices in early rounds versus later rounds.

[9]For example, licenses that were roughly interchangeable sold for similar prices.

e. In a market economy, people make decisions that affect resource allocation in three main ways: as consumers, as employees, and as owners of firms.

f. A positive economic statement concerns factual matters and is testable (the facts either confirm or contradict it). A normative economic statement involves value judgments and is not testable.

g. The scope of microeconomics is extremely broad, encompassing most of human decision making.

2. **Tools of microeconomics**

a. In studying human behavior, economists employ the scientific method.

b. Economists usually express their theories through mathematical models.

c. Models are simplified representations of the real world. As a result, they rely on assumptions that are not literally true.

d. A useful model captures the most important factors that contribute to an economic phenomenon, advances our understanding of it, and leads to reasonably accurate predictions.

e. Sources of economic data fall into three main categories: records, surveys, and experiments.

f. When controlling for multiple factors that contribute to a phenomenon isn't possible through laboratory or natural experiments, economists control for those factors statistically, using econometrics.

g. Economists sometimes disagree about both positive and normative matters. They have achieved a reasonable degree of consensus with respect to a number of positive issues through the accumulation of evidence. However, factual evidence cannot resolve normative disputes.

3. **Themes of microeconomics**

a. Major themes concerning decision making include the following: trade-offs are unavoidable; good choices are usually made at the margin; people respond to incentives; and prices provide incentives.

b. Major themes concerning markets include the following: trade can benefit everyone; the competitive market price reflects both value to consumers and cost to producers; compared to other methods of resource allocation, markets have advantages; and sometimes government policy can improve on free-market resource allocation.

4. **Uses of microeconomics**

a. Microeconomics offers a wide variety of principles that can help us make decisions.

b. Microeconomic tools are indispensable to the analysis and evaluation of public policy.

ADDITIONAL EXERCISES

Exercise 1.1: Name three examples of each of the following (other than those given in the text):

a. Goods that are provided centrally, by the government.

b. Goods that are provided by firms operating in decentralized markets.

c. Goods that are provided *both* centrally by the government and by firms operating in decentralized markets.

d. Goods that are provided through some decentralized procedure other than markets.

Exercise 1.2: Which of the following statements are positive and which are normative? Why?

a. The U.S. government should eliminate the estate tax.

b. The income tax causes people to work less.

c. Public education improves the well-being of the average citizen.

d. Exercise lowers the risk of heart disease.

e. Exercise is good for you.

f. Most people would choose pizza over tacos.

g. Most people are better off with pizza than with tacos.

Exercise 1.3: Every decision involves costs and benefits. As a result, some economists believe that the methods of economic analysis can and should be applied to *all* human decision making. Do you agree or disagree? Are there certain types of decisions that economists shouldn't study? Justify your answer.

Exercise 1.4: Latanya believes that people are irrational; that each person is irrational in his or her own special way; and that the nature of a person's irrationality sometimes changes from one moment to the next. Is her belief a theory? Does it have implications that can be verified or falsified? Is it a useful theory?

Exercise 1.5: Which of the following are models? Explain.

a. Red sky at night, sailors' delight. Red sky at morning, sailors take warning.

b. Let sleeping dogs lie.

c. What goes around comes around.

d. Cleanliness is next to godliness.

e. Absence makes the heart grow fonder.

Exercise 1.6: Economists often assume that most people are motivated only by their own material self-interest. Is this assumption always, usually, sometimes, rarely, or never a good one? Give examples to justify your answer.

Exercise 1.7: Which of the following is a natural experiment? Which is more likely to produce a reliable answer? Explain.

a. Elena wants to determine whether rain causes people to drive less. To do so, she compares the amount of gasoline sold on an average day in March in Seattle, Washington (where it rains a great deal), and in Los Angeles, California (where there is much less rainfall).

b. Annika also wants to determine whether rain causes people to drive less. To do so, she compares the amount of gasoline sold on an average rainy day in March and on an average sunny day in March in San Francisco, California.

Exercise 1.8: Going to college involves trade-offs. What are they? Make your list as complete as possible.

Exercise 1.9: Give some examples of how thinking at the margin is important to making good decisions. Are there times when thinking *only* at the margin can lead to mistakes? Give an example.

Exercise 1.10: Give three examples in which you or someone you know has responded to an economic incentive.

2

SUPPLY AND DEMAND

LEARNING OBJECTIVES

After reading this chapter, students should be able to:

- Explain what supply and demand curves for a good, and supply and demand functions, represent.
- Identify various market forces that shift the supply and demand curves.
- Use the concept of market equilibrium to calculate the equilibrium price and the amount bought and sold.
- Evaluate how changes in demand or supply affect market equilibrium.
- Understand elasticity and the way economists use it to measure the responsiveness of demand or supply.

New Orleans after Katrina

Gas prices after Katrina

When Hurricane Katrina made landfall near New Orleans on August 29, 2005, the results were devastating to residents of the Crescent City and many other communities along the Gulf Coast. Americans were shocked to see a major U.S. city flooded, its residents struggling for survival. Less than a month later, on September 24, Hurricane Rita made landfall near Houston. Together, the two storms disabled a large portion of the coast's oil refineries, representing a significant fraction of the nation's gasoline production capacity. By early October roughly 30 percent of U.S. refining capacity had been shut down by the two storms.

Though less severe than the human suffering caused by the storms, the economic effects of the refinery shutdowns were immediate and dramatic. Within days after Katrina hit, the price of gasoline surged upward. In early October the average price of regular gasoline in the United States rose to $2.92 per gallon—up from $2.51 per gallon only six weeks earlier, even though the price of crude oil (the key input in gasoline) had barely changed.

Why did the price of gasoline rise so dramatically? How much would the price have fallen if half of the sidelined capacity had quickly come back on line? To answer questions such as these, economists often use a model of supply and demand. If you've taken an introductory economics course before, you're no doubt familiar with this model. In that case, this chapter should mostly help to refresh your memory. If, instead, you've never taken an economics course, this chapter will provide an introduction to a simple but important economic model, along with some examples of its usefulness. As you study this book, you'll learn more about the building blocks of supply and demand, as well as about other economic models.

This chapter covers four topics:

1. *Demand.* To analyze a market using a model of supply and demand, we first need to determine the demand for the product. We'll see how demand curves and demand functions summarize this information.
2. *Supply.* The next step is to determine the supply of the product. We'll see how supply curves and supply functions summarize this information.
3. *Market equilibrium.* The price of a product tends to adjust to balance supply and demand. We'll see how to find the equilibrium price and the amount bought and sold. We'll also see how changes in demand or supply can alter those outcomes.
4. *Elasticities of demand and supply.* One factor that affects how changes in demand or supply alter the price and amount bought and sold is the responsiveness of demand and supply to changes in price. We'll see how economists measure that responsiveness, as well as the responsiveness to changes in other economic variables.

2.1 DEMAND

To analyze a market using a model of supply and demand, we first need to determine the demand for the product that is sold in that market. As a general matter, that product could be a manufactured good, a raw material, or a service. We can represent its demand in two ways: graphically, as a demand curve, or mathematically, as a demand function.

Demand Curves

A product's **demand curve** shows how much buyers of the product want to buy at each possible price, holding fixed all other factors that affect demand.

A product's **demand curve** shows how much buyers of the product want to buy at each possible price, holding fixed all other factors that affect demand. Figure 2.1(a) shows a (hypothetical) demand curve for the U.S. corn market. The vertical axis shows the price of a bushel of corn. The horizontal axis shows the annual demand for corn, measured in billions of bushels. For example, when the price of corn is \$3 a bushel, buyers demand 9 billion bushels per year.

The demand for corn comes from a number of sources. Consumers buy corn to include in their meals. Food processors use corn as an ingredient in chowder and soup. Farmers use corn to feed their livestock. A number of companies use corn to make ethanol, which is then mixed into gasoline.

Note that the demand curve in Figure 2.1(a) is downward sloping: the higher the price, the less corn consumers and firms want to buy. For example, if the price is \$2 per bushel, the amount demanded is 11 billion bushels per year, 2 billion bushels more than if the price is \$3 per bushel. Almost all demand curves slope downward. Intuitively, we know that when the price is higher, buying a product is less attractive than when the price is lower. As a result, some potential purchasers will decide to spend their money on other products. In Chapters 5, 6, 8, and 9, we'll discuss this relationship more fully.

Implicitly, a demand curve holds all factors other than the product's price constant. Some other factors that can affect the demand for a product include: population growth,

Figure 2.1

The Demand Curve for Corn. Figure (a) shows the demand curve for corn, which depicts the amount of corn consumers and firms want to buy at each possible price, holding fixed all other factors that affect demand. Figure (b) shows that when the price of potatoes rises, the demand for corn increases at each price, shifting the demand curve to the right.

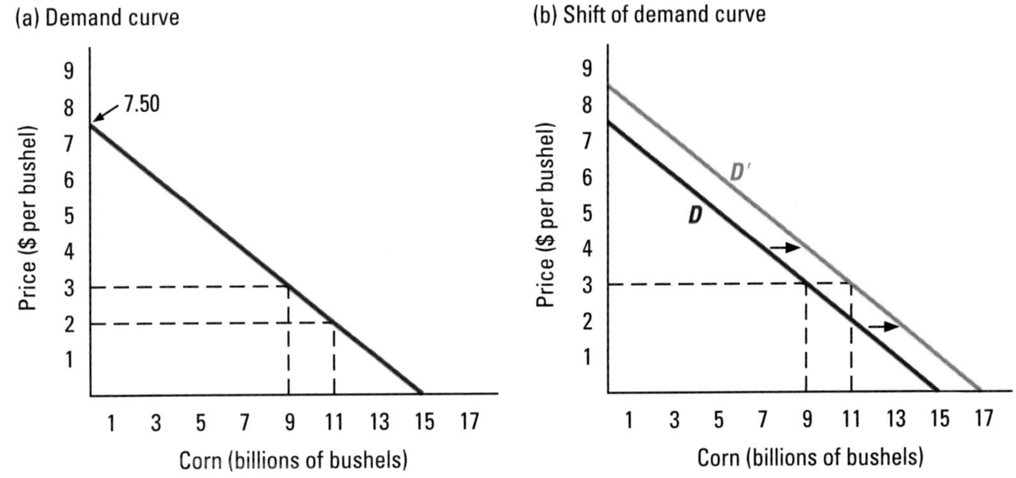

consumer tastes and incomes, the prices of other products, and in some cases, government taxes or regulations. Consider the demand for corn. If a popular diet recommends a low intake of carbohydrates, consumers' desire for corn will decrease, and they will purchase less at any given price. If instead, vegetarianism becomes more popular, consumers' desire for corn will increase, and they will purchase more at any given price. If the price of potatoes—an alternative form of starch—rises, consumers are likely to buy fewer potatoes and more corn at any given price of corn. Potatoes and corn are **substitutes**—all else equal, an increase in the price of one of these products causes buyers to demand more of the other product. If the price of butter—which consumers like to spread on corn—rises, the demand for corn is likely to decrease at any given price of corn because the total cost of a corn-with-butter meal will have increased. Butter and corn are **complements**—all else equal, an increase in the price of one of these products causes buyers to demand less of the other product. Finally, if consumers' incomes rise, they are likely to buy more corn at any given price.

Two products are **substitutes** if, all else equal, an increase in the price of one of the products causes buyers to demand more of the other product.

Two products are **complements** if, all else equal, an increase in the price of one of the products causes consumers to demand less of the other product.

A change in one of these other factors will cause the entire demand curve to *shift*. Figure 2.1(b) shows how the demand curve for corn shifts outward (to the right) when the price of potatoes rises. At each price of corn, buyers demand more corn. For example, the figure shows that the amount of corn demanded at a price of $3 per bushel increases from 9 billion bushels a year to 11 billion bushels a year.

As we have seen, either a change in the price of a product or a change in some other factor can change the amount of the product that buyers demand. However, Figures 2.1(a) and (b) illustrate an important distinction: A change in the price of a product causes a *movement along* its demand curve, whereas a change in some other factor *shifts* the product's demand curve. Accordingly, economists differentiate between a *change in the quantity (or amount) demanded* (which occurs when a change in a product's price produces a movement along its demand curve), and a *change in demand* (which occurs when a change in some other factor shifts a product's demand curve).

> **Movements Along versus Shifts of the Demand Curve** A change in the price of a product causes a *movement along* its demand curve, resulting in a *change in the quantity (or amount) demanded.* A change in some other factor (such as consumer tastes or income, or the prices of other products) causes a *shift* of the entire demand curve, known as a *change in demand.*

Demand Functions

A product's **demand function** describes the amount of the product that is demanded for each possible combination of its price and other factors.

We can represent the demand for a product mathematically as well as graphically. A product's **demand function** is a formula of the form Quantity Demanded = *D*(Price, Other factors). It describes the amount of the product that buyers demand for each possible combination of its price and other factors. For example, if the demand for corn is affected by three factors other than its price—the price of potatoes, the price of butter, and consumers' income—then the demand function for corn might take the form

$$Q^d_{corn} = 5 - 2P_{corn} + 4P_{potatoes} - 0.25P_{butter} + 0.0003M \quad \textbf{(1)}$$

where Q^d_{corn} is the amount of corn demanded per year in billions of bushels; P_{corn} is the price of corn per bushel; $P_{potatoes}$ and P_{butter} are the price of potatoes and butter per pound, respectively; and M is consumers' average annual income. According to this demand function, increases in the prices of corn and butter will decrease the amount that buyers demand (because P_{corn} and P_{butter} are multiplied by negative numbers), while increases in the price of potatoes and consumer income will increase the amount that buyers demand (because $P_{potatoes}$ and M are multiplied by positive numbers).

The demand curve in Figure 2.1(a) shows the relationship between the amount of corn demanded and its price based on the demand function in formula (1) when potatoes cost \$0.50 per pound, butter costs \$4 per pound, and consumers' average annual income is \$30,000. Substituting those values into formula (1), the demand function for corn becomes $Q^d_{corn} = 15 - 2P_{corn}$. According to this formula, for example, if corn were free (that is, if $P_{corn} = 0$), the amount demanded would be 15 billion bushels a year. Graphically, this means that the demand curve in Figure 2.1(a) hits the horizontal axis at 15 billion bushels per year. If the price of corn rose to \$7.50 per bushel (or higher), the amount demanded would fall to zero [since $15 - 2(7.50) = 0$]. At that price, the demand curve in Figure 2.1(a) hits the vertical axis.

The shift in the demand curve shown in Figure 2.1(b) corresponds to a change in the price of potatoes from \$0.50 to \$1 per pound. That \$0.50 increase in the price of potatoes changes the demand function to $Q^d_{corn} = 17 - 2P_{corn}$. (You can check, for example, that when the price of corn is \$3 per bushel, the amount demanded is 9 billion bushels a year if the price of potatoes is \$0.50, versus 11 billion bushels a year if the price of potatoes is \$1.)

Economists determine the demand function for a product by applying statistical techniques to historical data. The appendix to this chapter provides an intuitive and nontechnical summary of these techniques.

WORKED-OUT PROBLEM 2.1

The Problem Suppose that the demand function for corn takes the form in formula (1), that potatoes cost $0.50 per pound, that butter costs $4 per pound, and that consumers' average annual income is $30,000. At what price of corn will consumers demand 8 billion bushels per year? How does your answer change if the price of potatoes rises from $0.50 to $1 per pound?

The Solution We've seen that when potatoes cost $0.50 per pound, butter costs $4 per pound, and the average annual income is $30,000, the demand function for corn is $Q^d_{corn} = 15 - 2P_{corn}$. We want to find the price at which

$$15 - 2P_{corn} = 8$$

Solving this expression for P_{corn}, we find that

$$P_{corn} = 3.50$$

So demand is 8 billion bushels per year when the price of corn is $3.50 a bushel.

If the price of potatoes rises to $1 per pound, the demand function for corn becomes $Q^d_{corn} = 17 - 2P_{corn}$, so we must find the price at which $17 - 2P_{corn} = 8$. The solution is $4.50 per bushel.

IN-TEXT EXERCISE 2.1 **Suppose that the demand function for corn is $Q^d_{corn} = 20 - 4P_{corn} + 8P_{potatoes} - 0.50P_{butter}$. Potatoes cost $0.25 per pound and butter costs $2 per pound. At what price of corn will consumers demand 8 billion bushels a year? How does your answer change if the price of butter rises to $4 per pound?**

2.2 SUPPLY

The second step in analyzing a market using a model of supply and demand is to determine the supply of the product. We can represent supply in two ways: graphically, as a supply curve, or mathematically, as a supply function.

Supply Curves

A product's **supply curve** shows how much sellers of a product want to sell at each possible price, holding fixed all other factors that affect supply. Figure 2.2(a) shows a (hypothetical) supply curve for corn in the United States. The vertical axis shows the price of a bushel of corn; the horizontal axis shows the annual supply of corn, measured in billions of bushels. For example, when the price of corn is $3 per bushel, the amount supplied is 9 billion bushels per year. That supply includes the production of many farmers.

A product's **supply curve** shows how much sellers of the product want to sell at each possible price, holding fixed all other factors that affect supply.

Note that the supply curve in Figure 2.2(a) is upward sloping: the higher the price, the more corn farmers want to sell. For example, when the price is $2 per bushel, the amount supplied is 4 billion bushels per year, 5 billion less than when the price is $3 per bushel. Intuitively, when the price of corn is higher, producing and selling corn is more profitable.

Figure 2.2

The Supply Curve for Corn. Figure (a) shows the supply curve for corn, which depicts the amount of corn farmers want to produce and sell at each possible price, holding fixed all other factors that affect supply. Figure (b) shows that when the prices of diesel fuel and soybeans fall, the supply of corn increases at each price, shifting the supply curve to the right.

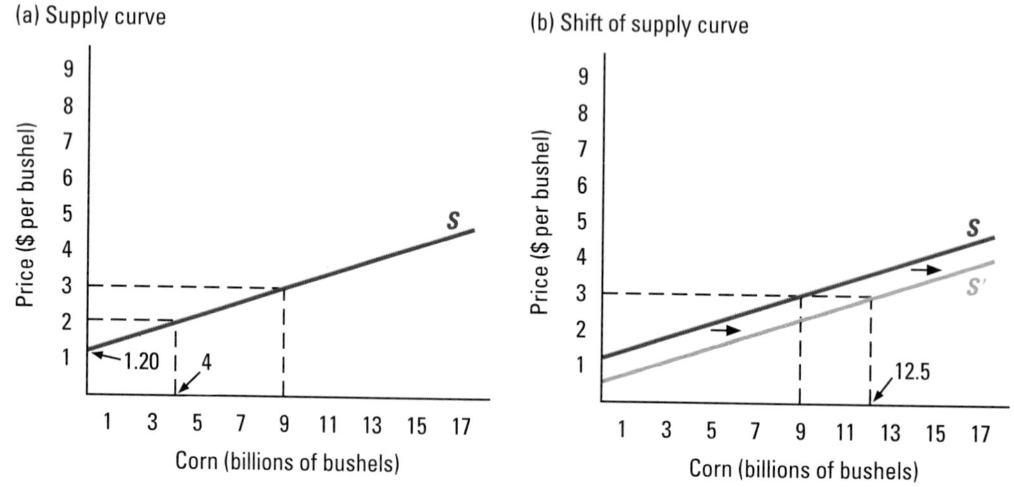

At a higher price, farmers will find it profitable to plant more of their land with corn rather than other crops, such as wheat or soybeans, and fewer farmers will sell their land to real estate developers. In Chapter 9, we'll discuss these trade-offs more fully.

A supply curve holds all factors other than the product's price constant. Many other factors can affect the supply of a product: technology, the prices of inputs, the prices of other possible outputs, and in some cases, government taxes or regulations. Consider the supply of corn. When a new disease-resistant corn hybrid becomes available, farmers can produce more corn using the same quantities of inputs. That lowers the cost of producing corn, making corn more attractive to produce and sell at any given price. Reductions in the price of fertilizer or diesel fuel also lower the cost of production and increase the amount supplied at any given price. On the other hand, increases in the price of other crops that farmers can plant instead of corn, such as soybeans, lower the amount of corn supplied at any given price of corn.

A change in one of these other factors will cause the supply curve for corn to *shift*. Figure 2.2(b) shows how the supply curve for corn shifts outward (to the right) when the prices of diesel fuel and soybeans fall. At each price of corn, the amount supplied increases.

Figures 2.2(a) and (b) illustrate the important distinction between movements along and shifts of supply curves: A change in the price of a product causes a *movement along* its supply curve, whereas a change in some other factor *shifts* the product's supply curve. Accordingly, economists differentiate between a *change in the quantity (or amount) supplied* (which occurs when a change in a product's price produces a movement along its supply curve), and a *change in supply* (which occurs when a change in some other factor shifts a product's supply curve).

Movements Along versus Shifts of the Supply Curve A change in the price of a product causes a *movement along* its supply curve, resulting in a *change in the quantity (or amount) supplied.* A change in *some other factor* (such as technology or input prices) causes a *shift* of the entire supply curve, known as a *change in supply.*

Supply Functions

We can represent the supply of a product mathematically by means of a **supply function**, a formula of the form *Quantity Supplied* = *S*(*Price*, *Other Factors*). It describes the amount of the product supplied for each possible combination of its price and other factors. For example, if the supply of corn is affected by only two factors other than its price—the price of diesel fuel and the price of soybeans—then the supply function for corn might take the form

A product's **supply function** describes the amount of the product that is supplied for each possible combination of its price and other factors.

$$Q^s_{corn} = 9 + 5P_{corn} - 2P_{fuel} - 1.25P_{soybeans} \qquad \textbf{(2)}$$

where Q^s_{corn} is the amount of corn supplied per year in billions of bushels; P_{corn} is the price of corn per bushel; P_{fuel} is the price of diesel fuel per gallon; and $P_{soybeans}$ is the price of soybeans per bushel. According to this supply function, the amount of corn supplied will increase if the price of corn rises, and fall if the prices of fuel and soybeans rise.

The supply curve shown in Figure 2.2(a) shows the relationship between the price of corn and the amount of corn supplied based on the supply function in formula (2) when diesel fuel costs \$2.50 a gallon and soybeans sell for \$8 a bushel. Substituting those values into formula (2), the supply function for corn becomes $Q^s_{corn} = 5P_{corn} - 6$. For example, if the corn price is \$1.20 (or less), the amount supplied falls to zero [since $5(1.20) - 6 = 0$]. At that price, the supply curve in Figure 2.2(a) hits the vertical axis.

The shift in the supply curve shown in Figure 2.2(b) corresponds to a fall in the price of diesel fuel from \$2.50 to \$2 per gallon, combined with a fall in the price of soybeans from \$8 to \$6 per bushel. Those price reductions change the supply function to $Q^s_{corn} = 5P_{corn} - 2.5$ (you should check this). For example, if the price of corn is \$3 per bushel, the amount of corn supplied is 9 billion bushels per year when diesel fuel costs \$2.50 per gallon and soybeans cost \$8 per bushel, versus 12.5 billion bushels per year when diesel fuel costs \$2 per gallon and soybeans cost \$6 per bushel.

As with demand functions, economists determine the supply function for a product by applying statistical techniques to historical data—a topic discussed in the appendix.

2.3 MARKET EQUILIBRIUM

Once we know the demand and supply for a product, the next step is to determine the **equilibrium price**. That is the price at which the amounts supplied and demanded are equal. Graphically, it's the price at which the supply and demand curves intersect. The market "clears" at the equilibrium price, with buyers and sellers making all their desired purchases and sales.

The **equilibrium price** is the price at which the amounts supplied and demanded are equal.

Figure 2.3
Equilibrium in the Corn Market. The price of corn adjusts to equate the amounts supplied and demanded, which occurs when the price of corn is $3 per bushel. At that price there is no excess demand or supply and no pressure for the price to rise or fall. The amount bought and sold at the equilibrium is 9 billion bushels per year.

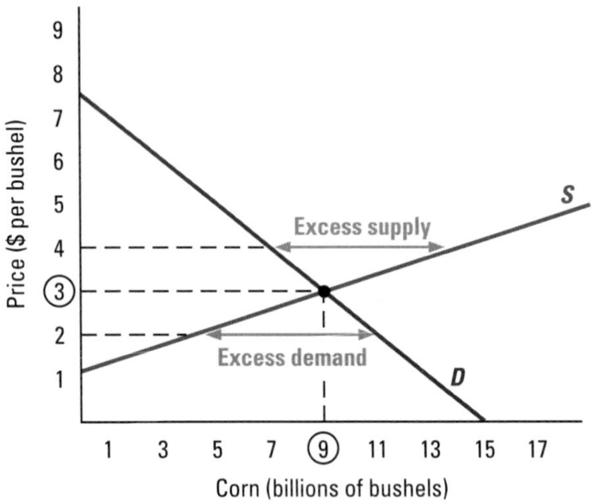

Figure 2.3 shows the equilibrium price of corn. That price, $3 per bushel, is the price at which the demand and supply curves intersect. At that price, the amount that buyers wish to buy, 9 billion bushels, exactly equals the amount that sellers wish to sell.

Market prices tend to adjust so that the amount supplied equals the amount demanded. Suppose, for example, that the price of corn is $2 per bushel. According to Figure 2.3, there is excess demand; the amount demanded exceeds the amount supplied. In that case, some buyers won't be able to purchase as much of the product as they would like at the prevailing price. They'll have an incentive to offer a slightly higher price to acquire their desired amounts. These offers will push the market price upward, reducing buyers' demands and increasing sellers' supply until supply and demand are once more in balance.

Now suppose that the price of corn is $4 per bushel. According to Figure 2.3, there is excess supply: the amount supplied exceeds the amount demanded. In that case, some sellers won't be able to sell as much as they would like at the prevailing price. They'll have an incentive to lower their prices a little to boost sales. These price reductions will push the market price downward, increasing buyers' demands and reducing sellers' supply until supply and demand are once more in balance.

When the price is such that the amounts supplied and demanded are equal, there is neither excess supply nor excess demand. Since everyone can buy or sell as much as they like at the prevailing price, there is no pressure for the market price to rise or fall.

Worked-out problem 2.2 shows how to find the equilibrium price using supply and demand functions and a bit of algebra.

WORKED-OUT PROBLEM 2.2

The Problem Suppose the demand function for corn is $Q^d_{corn} = 15 - 2P_{corn}$ and the supply function is $Q^s_{corn} = 5P_{corn} - 6$. What is the equilibrium price of corn? What are the amounts bought and sold?

The Solution The equilibrium price in the corn market, which equates the amounts supplied and demanded, is the solution to the equation $Q^d_{corn} = Q^s_{corn}$, or equivalently

$$15 - 2P_{corn} = 5P_{corn} - 6$$

The equilibrium price of corn is therefore $P_{corn} = \$3$. We can derive the amount bought and sold from either the demand or supply function, by substituting \$3 for the price: $Q^d_{corn} = 15 - 2(3) = 9$ or $Q^s_{corn} = 5(3) - 6 = 9$.

IN-TEXT EXERCISE 2.2 **Suppose the demand function for corn is $Q^d_{corn} = 20 - 2P_{corn}$ and the supply function is $Q^s_{corn} = 1.6P_{corn} - 7$. What is the equilibrium price of corn? What is the amount of corn bought and sold?**

Application 2.1

Market Equilibrium from Alfred Marshall to Vernon Smith's Laboratory

Economists' use of supply and demand curves to study and predict market equilibrium originated with the publication in 1890 of Alfred Marshall's *Principles of Economics*. Marshall, a professor at Cambridge University in England, was the first to show how the market price is determined as an equilibrium, equating the amount sellers wish to sell with the amount buyers wish to buy. Since then, economists have used Marshall's theoretical framework to analyze a wide variety of markets.

Alfred Marshall (1842–1924)

Marshall's simple framework yielded predictions that matched observed outcomes well. Still, something was missing. Since economists can never *directly* observe a supply or demand curve, how can they be sure that Marshall's theory is right? One sleepless night in 1955, economist Vernon Smith had an idea: perhaps he might see how well supply and demand theory worked by bringing economics into the laboratory.[1]

Smith began to run experiments using students at Purdue University as his subjects. In the early experiments, he tried to create an environment similar to the setting in a stock or commodity market by splitting the students into buyers and sellers. Each buyer received a card listing a value for a unit of the hypothetical product. Each seller received a card listing the cost of producing a unit. The students, who observed only their own cards, were told that they could not buy at a price above their value or sell at a price below their cost. Other than that, they should try to buy or sell at the best price possible. In this way, Smith created an experimental market. Since he created the market conditions, he could

[1] Recall that in the appendix to this chapter we discuss how economists can infer supply and demand curves through their observations of historical market outcomes. However, those methods typically *assume* that markets clear, so that the observed amounts bought and sold reflect buyers' and sellers' desired purchases and sales. This assumption is exactly what Smith wanted to test.

easily compare what actually happened with what supply and demand analysis would predict.

The trading process involved students calling out or accepting offers to buy or sell. For example, a buyer holding a card that said \$2.50 might raise her hand and shout "Buy at \$1." Any seller was then free to accept her offer or shout out a counteroffer to sell (for example, "Sell at \$3.60"). The process continued until no further trades occurred. Then Smith would start the process all over again, to simulate what would happen over time in a market with stable supply and demand conditions.

Vernon Smith (left) accepting the Nobel Prize from the King of Sweden

Figure 2.4 shows the theoretical supply and demand curves from one of Smith's experiments, in which there were 11 buyers and 11 sellers. The highest buyer value was \$3.25; the lowest was \$0.75. The lowest seller cost was \$0.75; the highest, \$3.25. Supply and demand analysis would predict that the equilibrium price in this market should be \$2 and that either five or six units should be traded. In principle, however, many other outcomes were possible. Indeed, if higher-value sellers were to trade with higher-value buyers (for example, the buyer with a value of \$3.25 buying from the seller with a cost of \$3.25), up to 11 voluntary trades could occur in this market.

Smith found that Marshall's theoretical framework worked remarkably well in practice.[2] Since neither buyers nor sellers knew the market conditions, initial trades sometimes took place at prices far from equilibrium. But prices generally converged to the equilibrium level over time, often very rapidly. For example, Smith ran his experiment with the market shown in Figure 2.4 five times for the same group of subjects (who traded in five separate "market periods"). The results are shown on the right-hand side of the figure. In the first period, the average price was \$1.80, but by the third market period and thereafter, it had risen to within a few pennies of the predicted price. The amount bought and sold was always close to the predicted number of trades.

Smith made a number of interesting observations about factors that affect the speed of convergence to market equilibrium. His experiment started an entire new subfield within economics, the experimental study of economic institutions. In 2002 he was awarded the Nobel Prize in Economics for his pioneering work.

Changes in Market Equilibrium

Market conditions often change. Supply can increase or decrease, as can demand. Consider again the corn market. If the price of diesel fuel falls from \$2.50 to \$2 per gallon and the price of soybeans falls from \$8 to \$6 per bushel, the supply curve of corn will shift outward as Figure 2.5 shows. After the supply curve shifts, the market is no longer in equilibrium at the original price of \$3 per bushel. Instead there is excess supply: the buyers still demand 9 billion bushels, but sellers now wish to sell 12.5 billion bushels. Some sellers won't be able to sell their corn at \$3 per bushel and will accept a lower price. As a result, the price will fall to bring supply and demand into balance once more. Figure 2.5 shows that the new price of corn will be \$2.50 per bushel, and that 10 billion bushels of corn will be bought and sold.

Just as in worked-out problem 2.1, we can also find the new price of corn using algebra. When the prices of diesel fuel and soybeans fall, the market supply function becomes $Q^s_{corn} = 5P_{corn} - 2.5$. Since the demand function is unchanged, the new equilibrium price solves the equation

$$15 - 2P_{corn} = 5P_{corn} - 2.5$$

[2] V. L. Smith, "An Experimental Study of Competitive Market Behavior," *Journal of Political Economy* 70, April 1962, pp. 111–137.

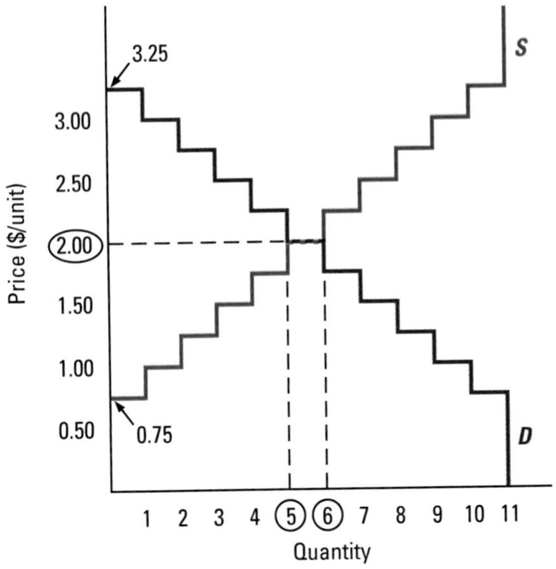

Market Period	Average Price ($)	Quantity Traded
1	1.80	5
2	1.86	5
3	2.02	5
4	2.03	7
5	2.03	6

Figure 2.4
Results of Vernon Smith's Experimental Market. The figure at left shows the supply and demand curves in Smith's experimental market. Supply and demand analysis would predict that five or six units would be traded at a price of $2. The table on the right shows the results in each of five market periods. The number of units traded was always close to the predicted number, and by the third period, the average price was within pennies of the predicted price.

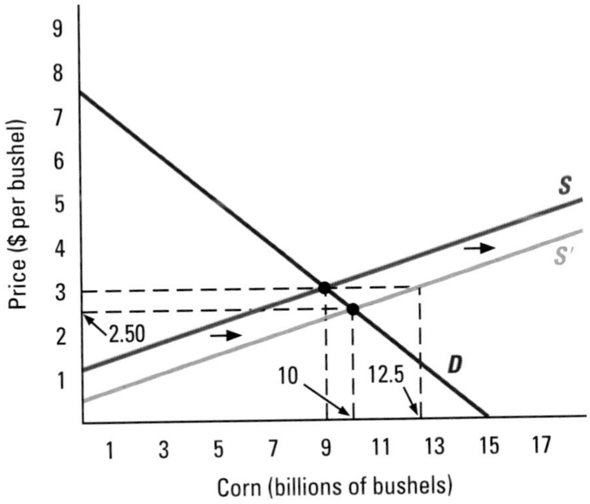

Figure 2.5
A Change in Market Equilibrium. When the price of diesel fuel falls from $2.50 to $2 per gallon and the price of soybeans falls from $8 to $6 per bushel, the supply of corn increases, shifting the supply curve to the right. At the original price of $3 per bushel, there is an excess supply of corn: farmers want to sell 12.5 billion bushels but consumers and firms want to buy only 9 billion bushels. This imbalance puts downward pressure on the market price. The equilibrium price falls to $2.50, and the amount bought and sold increases to 10 billion bushels per year.

The solution is $P_{corn} = \$2.50$. Using the supply and demand functions, we can see that 10 billion bushels of corn will be bought and sold at that price: $Q^d_{corn} = 15 - 2(2.50) = 10$ and $Q^s_{corn} = 5(2.50) - 2.5 = 10$.

Figure 2.6 shows the four possible ways in which either demand or supply curves can shift. Demand can increase or decrease, as in panels (a) and (b) where in each case

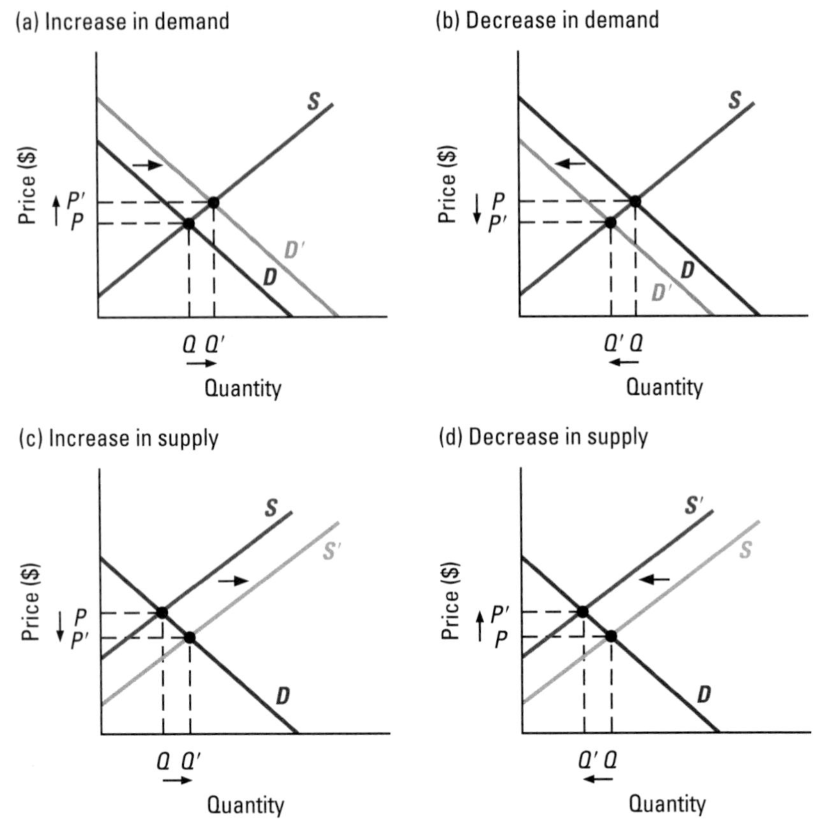

Figure 2.6
The Effects of Shifts in Demand or Supply on Market Equilibrium. The four figures show the effects of various shifts in either demand or supply on price and the amount bought and sold.

the initial demand curve is D and the new curve is D'. Alternatively, supply can increase or decrease, as in panels (c) and (d) where in each case the initial supply curve is S and the new curve is S'. Figure 2.6(a) shows the effects of an increase in demand: the price and the amount bought and sold rise. Figure 2.6(b) shows that when demand instead decreases, shifting to the left, the opposite happens: the price and the amount bought and sold fall. Figure 2.6(c) shows that when supply increases, the price falls but the amount bought and sold rises (just as we saw in Figure 2.5). Figure 2.6(d) shows that when supply decreases, the opposite happens: the price rises and the amount bought and sold falls. Table 2.1 summarizes these conclusions. Applications 2.2 and 2.3 discuss some practical examples of such changes.

Table 2.1
Effects of Changes in Demand or Supply

Source of Change	Effect on Price	Effect on Amount Bought/Sold
Increase in demand	Rises	Rises
Decrease in demand	Falls	Falls
Increase in supply	Falls	Rises
Decrease in supply	Rises	Falls

Application 2.2

A Room with a View (and its Price)

The elegant Bar Harbor Inn overlooks beautiful Frenchman's Bay in Bar Harbor, Maine, just minutes from Acadia National Park. At the height of the summer tourist season, the inn's most expensive rooms cost over $350 per night. Unfortunately, those same tourists have little interest in visiting once the leaves have fallen from the trees. By then, they're thinking of Caribbean beaches or the ski slopes in Colorado and Utah.

The Bar Harbor Inn

As a result, the price of hotel rooms at Bar Harbor's many inns, which together make up the supply in this market, vary greatly by season. As Figure 2.7 shows, the supply curve for hotel rooms in Bar Harbor is the same in November as in July.[3] The quantity $\bar{Q}$ is the total number of rooms. At high prices, innkeepers want to rent all those rooms, but at low prices, they withdraw some rooms from the supply, since the price no longer compensates them for the expense and effort of serving customers. (In the dead of winter, some inn owners close temporarily and take a vacation.) The demand in the two months is very different, however, so that the price in November (P_{Nov}) is much lower than the price in July (P_{July}). In 2005, for example, a tourist paid $369 a night to stay in the Bar Harbor Inn's best room during July, but only $159 a night to stay in the same room during November.

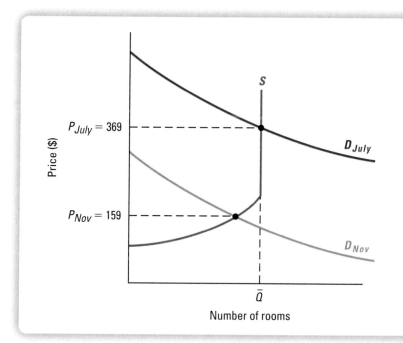

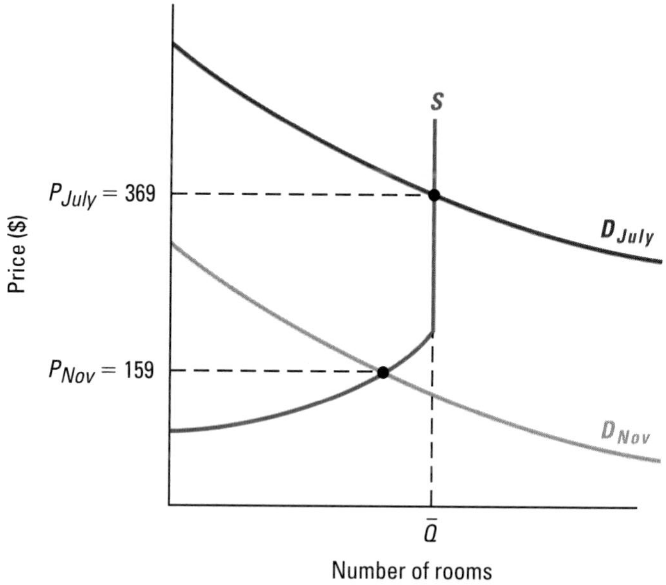

Figure 2.7

Changes in the Market Equilibrium for Hotel Rooms in Bar Harbor. This figure shows the demand curve for Bar Harbor's hotel rooms in July (D_{July}) and November (D_{Nov}). Because of the lower demand in November, the price of a room in November ($159) is much lower than in July ($369).

[3]The supply curve is in reality not exactly the same in all seasons. Utility costs and wage rates, for example, may vary by season, causing the supply curve to shift a bit. We draw it as unchanging here for simplicity. The important point is that the supply curve does not shift very much compared to the shift in the demand curve.

Application 2.3

Hurricanes that Blew a Hole in Consumers' Pockets

In the introduction of the chapter we mentioned that the price of gasoline surged upward after the refinery shutdowns that followed hurricanes Katrina and Rita. Figure 2.8(a) shows why this happened. The refinery shutdowns shifted the U.S. supply curve for gasoline to the left by 30 percent between August and October, from S_{AUG} to S_{OCT}, causing the price to rise sharply, from \$2.51 per gallon to \$2.92 per gallon. That steep price increase caused consumers to reduce their consumption of gasoline, from about 395 million barrels per day in mid-August to about 365 million barrels in early October.[4]

Another example of the effects of hurricanes on market prices occurred the year before in Florida. In August and September of that year, three hurricanes—Charley, Frances, and Jeanne—slammed into Florida's orange groves. Fortunately, the storms didn't inflict much damage on the trees themselves, but they destroyed almost 40 percent of the orange crop. The result can be seen in Figure 2.8(b). The hurricanes shifted the supply curve from $S_{2003\text{–}4}$ in the 2003–2004 growing season to $S_{2004\text{–}5}$ in the 2004–2005 season. Only 150 million (90-pound) boxes of oranges were harvested in 2004–2005, compared to 242 million boxes in 2003–2004. The price that orange growers received for their oranges rose from \$2.35 per box in 2003–2004 to \$3.49 per box in 2004–2005—an increase of nearly 50 percent.[5]

Mike Keefe Hurricane/Oil cartoon, 2005. © Mike Keefe, Denver Post, PoliticalCartoons.com. Used by permission.

Sometimes, changes in market conditions involve shifts in *both* demand and supply. The effects of such changes are a combination of the separate effects of changes in demand and supply. Suppose, for example, that demand and supply both increase. We've just seen that both these changes lead to increases in the amount bought and sold, so we can safely say that the amount bought and sold will increase. But what about the effect on price? The increase in demand alone would make the price rise, but the increase in supply alone would cause the price to fall. Because these effects work in opposite directions, we can't be sure which way the price will change.

Figure 2.9 illustrates this point. In Figure 2.9(a), demand increases a lot but supply increases only a little. These changes move the market equilibrium from point A to B, which brings a higher price. In Figure 2.9(b), demand increases a little but supply increases a lot. These changes move the market equilibrium from point C to E, which brings a lower price. In both cases, the amount bought and sold rises.

In general, when separate shifts in demand and supply each individually move the price in the same direction, the equilibrium price will definitely move in that direction. When separate shifts in supply and demand move the price in opposite directions, the equilibrium price can move in either direction, depending on the relative sizes of the

[4]For information on the gasoline market consult the U.S. Energy Information Administration Web site (www.eia.doe.gov).

[5]For information on oranges and other agricultural products visit the U.S. Department of Agriculture, National Agricultural Statistical Service Web site (www.nass.usda.gov).

Figure 2.8

The Effects of Hurricanes on Market Equilibrium. Figure (a) shows the effects of hurricanes Katrina and Rita on the price and the number of gallons of gasoline bought and sold per day. Figure (b) shows the effects of hurricanes Charley, Frances, and Jeanne on the price and number of boxes of Florida oranges bought and sold. In both cases, the reduction in supply increased the price and decreased the amount bought and sold.

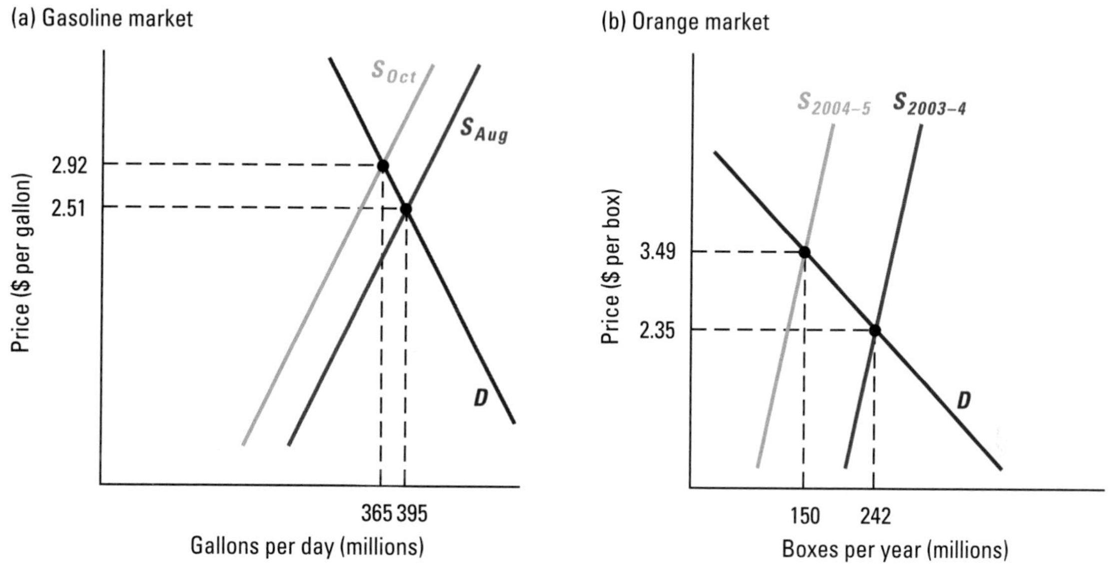

Figure 2.9

The Effects of an Increase in Both Demand and Supply. When both demand and supply increase, the amount bought and sold necessarily increases, but the effect on price is ambiguous. Figure (a) shows that when demand increases a lot but supply increases only a little, the price rises. Figure (b) shows that when supply increases a lot but demand increases only a little, the price falls.

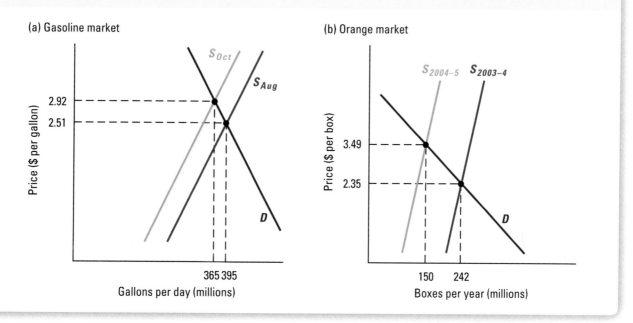

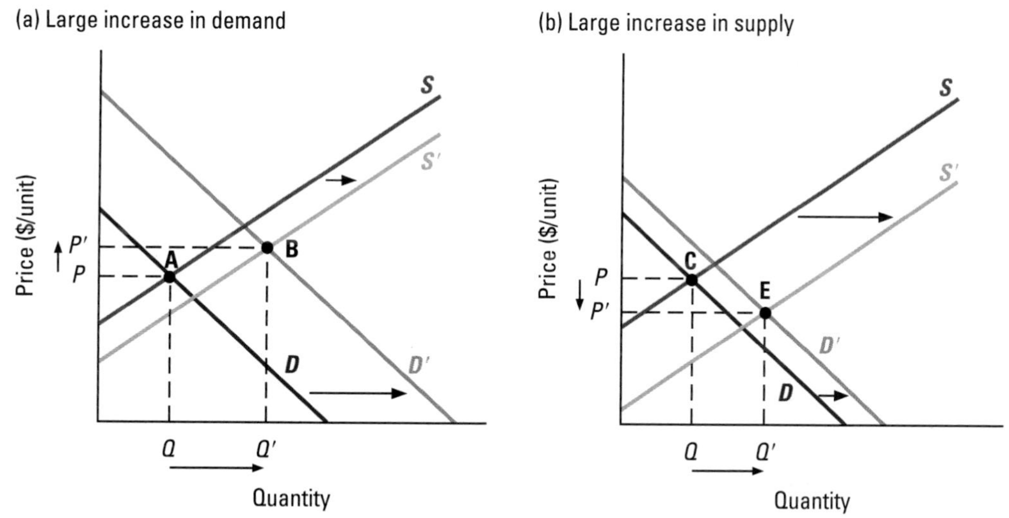

changes. This principle applies as well to effects on the amount bought and sold. Table 2.2 summarizes the effects on price and the amount bought and sold from simultaneous changes in demand and supply. Application 2.4 presents a real-world example of a shift in both demand and supply. (See Add-On 2A for another example.)

Table 2.2
Effects of Simultaneous Changes in Demand and Supply

Source of Change	Effect on Price	Effect on Amount Bought/Sold
Demand increases/supply increases	Ambiguous	Rises
Demand decreases/supply decreases	Ambiguous	Falls
Demand increases/supply decreases	Rises	Ambiguous
Demand decreases/supply increases	Falls	Ambiguous

Application 2.4

Prices of 2004 Boston Red Sox Trading Cards

The 2004 Boston Red Sox were the first Red Sox team to win the World Series since 1918. Even better for Red Sox fans, the team reached the World Series with a historic come-from-behind victory in the American League Championship Series against their archrival, the New York Yankees.

The World Series victory made a lot of Red Sox fans happy. It also increased their desire to own the trading cards of their favorite Red Sox players. Table 2.3 shows the price ranges for several Red Sox players' "rookie cards" in January 2004 and January 2005, before and after the World Series.[6] After the World Series win, those cards' prices were higher than before.

We can understand these changes using supply and demand analysis, as illustrated in Figure 2.10. At any given point in time, the total number of rookie cards for a particular player is fixed. People who don't own the cards can buy them at the market price; people who do own the cards can either sell them or buy more at the market price. At any point in time, these various individuals differ in their willingness to pay to own a particular player's card. Some may be rabid Red Sox fans while others just like collecting; some may feel a strong affinity for the player, while others

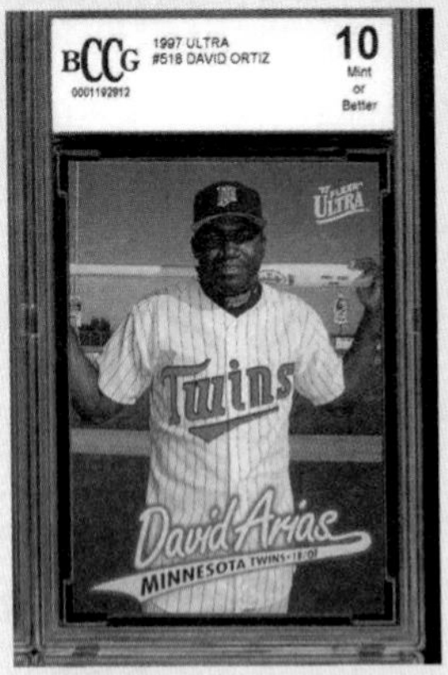

2004 Red Sox Slugger David Ortiz's rookie card

Table 2.3
Prices of Red Sox Players' Rookie Cards Before and After the 2004 World Series

Player	January 2004	January 2005
Bronson Arroyo	$1.25–3.00	$2.00–5.00
Johnny Damon	3.00–8.00	4.00–10.00
David Ortiz	4.00–10.00	6.00–15.00
Manny Ramirez	0.75–2.00	1.00–2.50
Curt Schilling	1.25–3.00	2.00–5.00
Jason Varitek	1.25–3.00	3.00–8.00
Tim Wakefield	1.50–4.00	2.00–5.00

[6] A "rookie card" is a player's first card as a major leaguer, and the most valuable of a player's trading cards. Card-buying guides report a range of prices.

may actively dislike him; and some may be wealthy, while others are strapped for cash.

As a general matter, though, an increase in the price of the card increases the willingness of current owners to sell it and reduces the willingness of others to buy it. The supply curve for a given card, such as for star David Ortiz (the Most Valuable Player in the League Championship Series win against the Yankees), therefore slopes upward, and the demand curve slopes downward, as shown in Figure 2.10. At low enough prices, no current owners want to sell their cards; they think the value of each card exceeds the price they can get for it. As the price increases, more and more owners become willing to sell. At high enough prices, the existing owners will want to sell all of their cards. Since the number of cards is fixed, at that point higher prices cannot bring forth additional supply, so the supply curve becomes perfectly vertical at a quantity equal to the number of existing cards (labeled $\bar{Q}$ in Figure 2.10). The demand curve reflects the behavior of potential purchasers of the cards. As the card's price rises, fewer and fewer of them will think that the card is desirable enough to justify its purchase.

The Series win made owning the cards more desirable both to current owners and to potential buyers. At any given price, buyers became more willing to buy (shifting the demand curve outward from D_{2004} to D_{2005}) and sellers became less willing to sell (shifting the supply curve inward from S_{2004} to S_{2005}). These shifts in both demand and supply raised the equilibrium prices of the cards.[7]

The Size of Changes in Market Equilibrium

Our discussion so far has focused only on the *direction* of changes in the price and the amount bought and sold following shifts in the demand and/or supply curves. We learned, for example, that an increase in demand increases a product's equilibrium price, while an increase in supply lowers it. Often, though, we want to know *how much* the price or amount bought and sold will change. What factors determine the *size* of the price change?

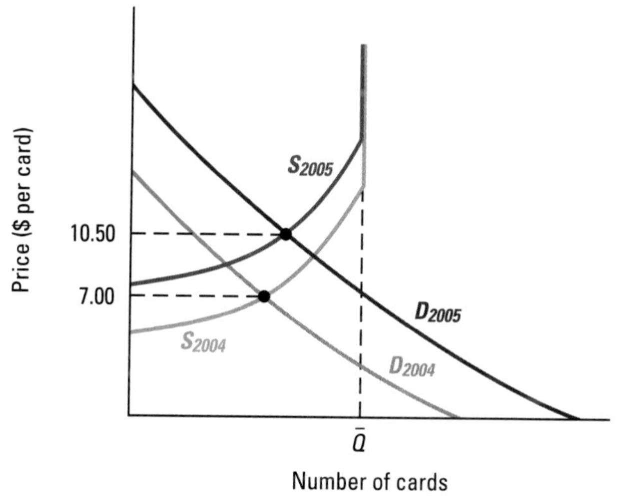

Figure 2.10

Changes in the Market Equilibrium for a David Ortiz Rookie Card. The figure shows the changes in demand and supply for a David Ortiz rookie card from before the Boston Red Sox won the 2004 World Series (curves D_{2004} and S_{2004}) to after (curves D_{2005} and S_{2005}). Winning the World Series increased the quantity demanded and reduced the quantity supplied at any given price. This led the equilibrium price to increase.

[7]In contrast, none of the New York Yankee rookie cards we examined increased in price during the period. It is also interesting to ask why different players' cards sell for different prices. A card's price reflects not only the desirability of owning the card (Is the player a star? Does he have an attractive personality?), but also the number of cards that were originally manufactured, which can vary dramatically between different cards.

Figure 2.11

Changes in Market Equilibrium for Two Extreme Demand Curves. Figure (a) shows that when the demand curve is perfectly horizontal, an increase in supply has no effect on the product's price but increases the amount bought and sold. Figure (b) shows that when the demand curve is perfectly vertical, an increase in supply has no effect on the amount bought and sold but decreases the product's price.

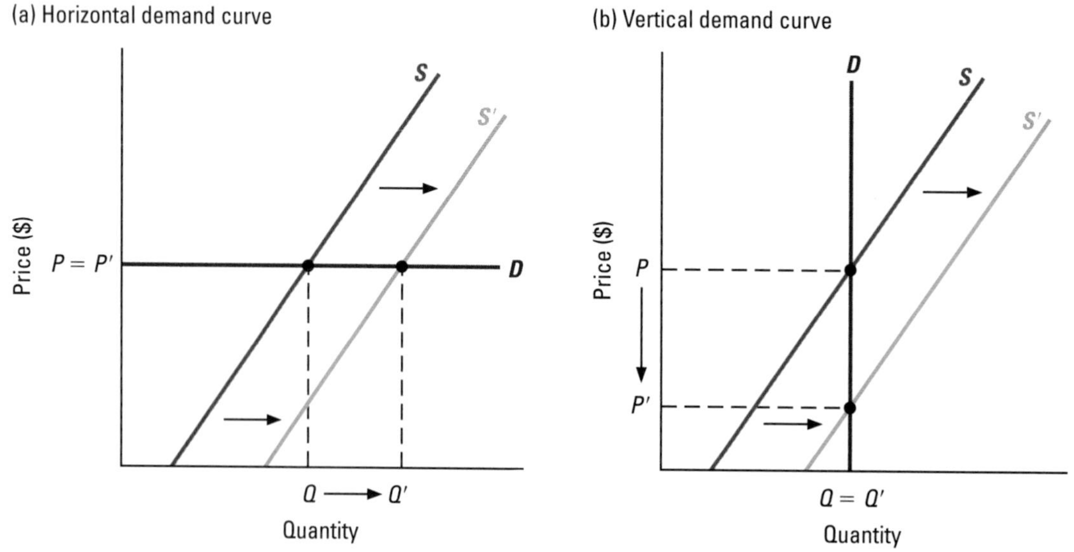

Certainly the size of the change in demand or supply matters. The larger the shift in the demand or supply curve, the larger the effect on price. Perhaps less obviously, the size of the changes in the price and the amount bought and sold also depend on the *steepness* (that is, the slope) of the curve that does *not* shift. Consider an increase in supply. As Figure 2.5 (page 35) showed, when the supply curve shifts outward, the market equilibrium shifts, moving along the fixed demand curve. How much the price and the amount bought and sold will change depends on the steepness of the demand curve. That steepness reflects the responsiveness of buyers' demands to the price. For example, if the demand curve is perfectly horizontal as in Figure 2.11(a), the amount demanded is extremely responsive to price. In that case, when the supply curve shifts outward the amount bought and sold increases from Q to Q', but the price does not change at all. In contrast, if the demand curve is perfectly vertical as in Figure 2.11(b), the amount demanded is completely unresponsive to the price. In that case, when the supply curve shifts outward the price falls from P to P', but the amount bought and sold does not change at all.

Typically, when the supply curve shifts outward, *both* the price and the amount bought and sold will change. However, the steeper the demand curve—that is, the less responsive is the amount demanded to price—the more the price changes and the less the amount bought and sold changes. Figure 2.12 illustrates this point using two demand curves that differ in steepness labeled D_1 and D_2. Suppose that the supply curve is initially the dark red curve labeled S. For both demand curves the initial equilibrium price is P^* and the

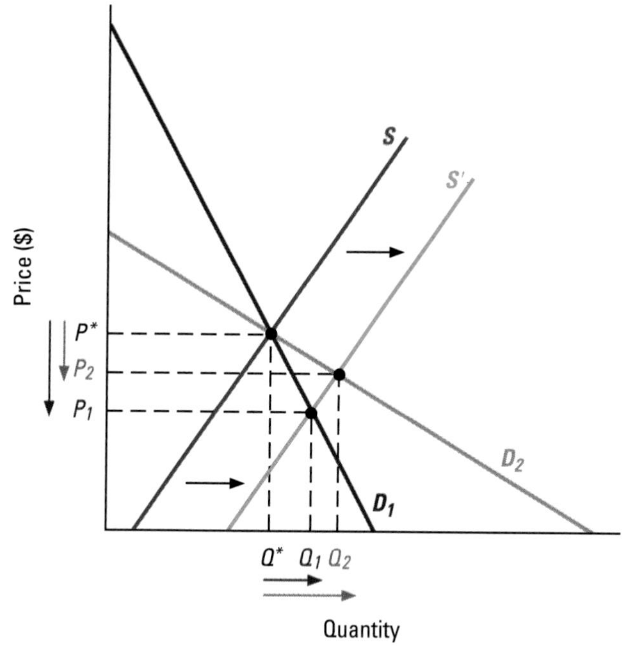

Figure 2.12
Changes in Market Equilibrium for Two Demand Curves. The closer the demand curve is to being vertical, the larger the decrease in the product's price and the smaller the increase in the amount bought and sold when supply increases from S to S'.

amount bought and sold is Q^*. Now suppose the supply curve shifts outward to the light red curve, labeled S'. The steeper demand curve (labeled D_1) results in a *larger* reduction in price than the flatter one (labeled D_2). On the other hand, the steeper demand curve results in a *smaller* increase in the amount bought and sold. (The prices and amounts bought and sold after the change in supply are labeled with the subscripts 1 and 2, corresponding to demand curves D_1 and D_2 respectively.)

A similar point holds for shifts in demand. In that case, the sizes of the price and quantity changes depend on the steepness (that is, the slope) of the supply curve. Figure 2.13(a) shows the extreme case of a perfectly horizontal supply curve, for which the amount supplied is extremely responsive to the price. When the demand curve shifts outward, there is an increase in the amount bought and sold but no change in price. Figure 2.13(b) shows a perfectly vertical supply curve, for which the amount supplied is completely unresponsive to the price. In that case an outward shift in the demand curve increases the price but has no effect on the amount bought and sold. Figure 2.14 shows two intermediate cases. For the dark blue curve labeled D, the two supply curves (labeled S_1 and S_2) result in the same initial equilibrium price P^* and amount bought and sold Q^*. What happens when the demand curve shifts outward to the light blue curve labeled D'? The steeper supply curve, S_1, results in a larger increase in price and a smaller increase in the amount bought and sold than the flatter one, S_2.

In-text exercise 2.3 asks you to confirm that similar effects arise for inward shifts of the demand or supply curves (reductions in demand or supply).

Figure 2.13

Changes in Market Equilibrium for Two Extreme Supply Curves. Figure (a) shows that when the supply curve is perfectly horizontal, an increase in demand has no effect on the product's price but increases the amount bought and sold. Figure (b) shows that when the supply curve is perfectly vertical, an increase in demand has no effect on the amount bought and sold but increases the product's price.

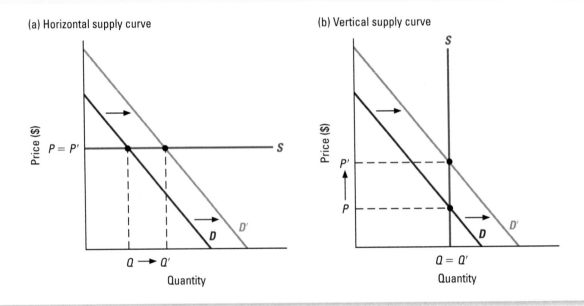

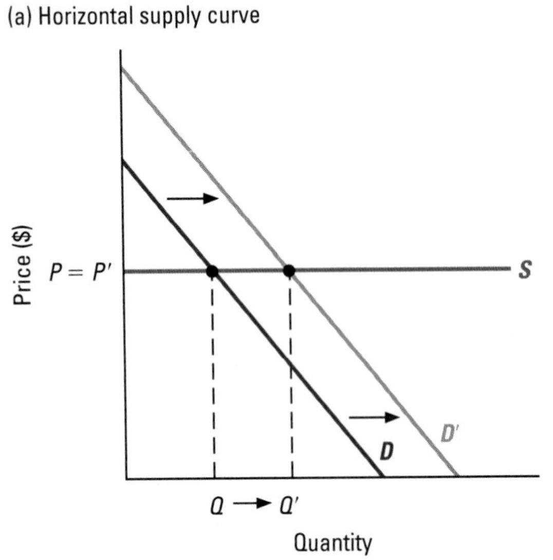

Figure 2.14

Changes in Market Equilibrium for Two Supply Curves. The steeper the supply curve, the larger the increase in the product's price and the smaller the increase in the amount bought and sold when demand increases.

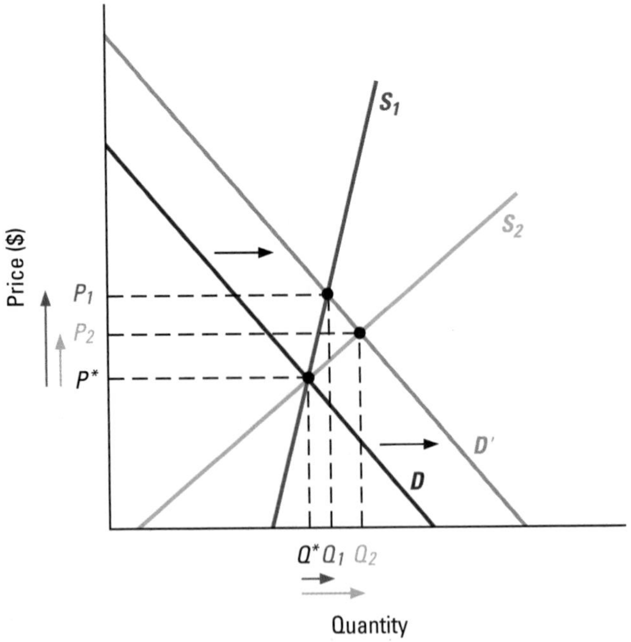

IN-TEXT EXERCISE 2.3 **Draw a picture similar to Figure 2.12 to show that the steeper the demand curve (the less responsive the amount demanded is to price), the larger the change in price and the smaller the change in the amount bought and sold when the supply curve shifts inward. Draw a picture similar to Figure 2.14 to show that the steeper the supply curve (the less responsive the amount supplied is to price), the larger the change in price and the smaller the change in the amount bought and sold when the demand curve shifts inward.**

We can summarize these findings as follows:

Changes in Market Equilibrium and the Price Responsiveness of Demand and Supply

1. When the demand curve shifts: the steeper the supply curve (the less responsive the amount supplied is to price), the larger the price change and the smaller the change in the amount bought and sold.
2. When the supply curve shifts: the steeper the demand curve (the less responsive the amount demanded is to price), the larger the price change and the smaller the change in the amount bought and sold.

Short-Run and Long-Run Changes in Market Equilibrium The responsiveness of a product's demand or supply to its price, and therefore the slopes of supply and demand curves, can depend on the time horizon. For example, once farmers plant their fields, they may be unable to produce much more corn in the short run if the price of corn rises. But in the long run they can plant more of their land with corn and even acquire additional land.

Because the steepness of supply and demand curves can depend on the time horizon, long-run changes in the equilibrium price and the amount bought and sold resulting from a shift in supply or demand can differ from short-run changes. For example, suppose the corn market is in equilibrium at price P^* in Figure 2.14, and the demand curve suddenly shifts from D to D'. The steeper supply curve, S_1, might represent the short-run supply curve, while the flatter one, S_2, might represent the long-run supply curve. If so, then as the figure shows, the price will rise sharply to P_1 in response to the increase in demand, but over time it will fall back toward its original level, eventually reaching P_2 in long-run equilibrium. The amount bought and sold, on the other hand, will increase only to Q_1 at first, but will continue to increase over time, eventually reaching Q_2 in long-run equilibrium.

2.4 ELASTICITIES OF DEMAND AND SUPPLY

In Section 2.3 we saw that changes in market equilibrium depend on the responsiveness of the amounts demanded and supplied to changes in price. How can we measure that responsiveness?

One possibility is to do as we did in Section 2.3, and describe the responsiveness to price changes in terms of the steepness (or slope) of the demand and supply curves. This measure has one problem, though: it depends on the units we are using to measure both the units of the good and its price. For example, if someone says that the demand curve for milk has a slope of -200, what does that mean? It might mean that when the price of milk rises by a penny per quart, 200 fewer quarts are sold. But it might instead mean that when the price of milk rises by a dollar per gallon, 200 fewer gallons are sold. To know which it is, we would have to be careful to specify exactly how we are measuring both the units of the good and the price. Doing so every time we want to measure the responsiveness of demand would be cumbersome and inconvenient.

The **elasticity** of Y with respect to X, denoted E_X^Y, equals the percentage change in Y divided by the percentage change in X, or equivalently, the percentage change in Y for each 1 percent increase in X.

Instead, economists get around this problem by measuring the responsiveness of one variable to changes in another variable using the concept of *elasticity*. Suppose that a change in X causes a change in Y. The **elasticity** of Y with respect to X, denoted E_X^Y, equals the percentage change in Y divided by the percentage change in X:

$$E_X^Y = \frac{\%\text{ change in } Y}{\%\text{ change in } X}$$

For example, if a 2 percent increase in X causes a 4 percent increase in Y, then $E_X^Y = 2$. This value tells us that Y increases by 2 percent for each 1 percent increase in X. If the change in X instead causes Y to *fall*, then the elasticity will be negative. For example, if the 2 percent increase in X causes Y to fall by 4 percent, then $E_X^Y = -2$. This value tells us that Y falls by 2 percent for each 1 percent increase in X. Elasticities are "unit-free measures": for example, if someone tells you the elasticity of demand for a good with respect to some variable X, you can understand what it means without knowing the units in which they were measuring the quantity demanded and the variable X.

Negative elasticity measures sometimes confuse students. An important point to remember is that, for both positive *and* negative elasticities, values that are further from zero indicate greater responsiveness. For example, suppose that initially a 2 percent increase in X causes Y to fall by 4 percent, but due to some new development, Y becomes more responsive to X—a 2 percent increase in X now causes Y to fall by 6 percent. Then the elasticity of Y with respect to X would change from $E_X^Y = -2$ to $E_X^Y = -3$. Because the new elasticity is further from zero, we would say that Y has become *more elastic* with respect to changes in X. We would say the same thing if the elasticity instead changed from $E_X^Y = 2$ to $E_X^Y = 3$.

Let's take a closer look at how economists use elasticity to measure the responsiveness of the amount of a product demanded or supplied to its price.

The (Price) Elasticity of Demand

The **(price) elasticity of demand** at price P, denoted E^d, equals the percentage change in the amount demanded for each 1 percent increase in the price.

First, let's consider the elasticity of demand for a product with respect to its price. Economists use this particular elasticity so often that they usually refer to it simply as the elasticity of demand (omitting the reference to price), writing it as E^d rather than E_P^d. A product's **(price) elasticity of demand** equals the percentage change in the amount demanded divided by the percentage change in the price, or equivalently, the percentage change in the amount demanded for each 1 percent increase in the price.

Since the quantity demanded typically decreases when the price increases, we expect the elasticity of demand to be a negative number. Products tend to have more elastic demands when they have closer substitutes to which consumers can switch in response to a price increase. Demand will also be more elastic when the potential buyers of the product regard it as a discretionary (luxury) purchase, rather than as a necessity. On the other hand, if the potential buyers are all very wealthy and are relatively insensitive to their expenditures, the demand will be less elastic than if the potential buyers are strapped for cash.

In general, the elasticity of demand can differ at different points on the demand curve (we'll see an example of this soon). For example, at high prices consumers may respond differently to a 2 percent price increase than they would at low prices. So, when economists measure the elasticity of demand they usually measure it separately at each possible initial price. To do this, they also focus on the responsiveness of demand to *small* price changes so that they are getting a measure of responsiveness close to the initial price.

Let's be more specific about this. Suppose the price changes from P to P', causing the amount demanded to change from Q to Q'. The change in price is $(P' - P)$. For convenience, we'll call this $\Delta P = (P' - P)$. (Mathematicians use the Greek letter Δ, read as "delta," to represent the *change* in a variable, so ΔP represents a change in price.) The percentage change in price is $100 \times (\Delta P/P)$. [For example, if the initial price P is \$100, and the new price P' is \$101, then $\Delta P = 1$ and the percentage change is $100 \times (1/100) = 1\%$.] The change in the amount demanded is $Q' - Q$; we'll call this $\Delta Q = (Q' - Q)$. The percentage change in Q is $100 \times (\Delta Q/Q)$. So the elasticity of demand at price P is[8]

$$E^d = \frac{\text{\% change in amount demanded}}{\text{\% change in price}} = \frac{100 \times (\Delta Q/Q)}{100 \times (\Delta P/P)} = \frac{(\Delta Q/Q)}{(\Delta P/P)} \quad (3)$$

Application 2.5

Elasticities of Demand for New Cars

The elasticity of demand for a product at a given price depends on how readily consumers will switch to other products if the product's price increases a little. That depends in turn on the prices and characteristics of the other available products. In the new car market, consumers who are considering lower-price cars, such as the Nissan Sentra, can choose from among many fairly similar alternatives. Those consumers also tend to keep a close eye on their budgets. So we'd expect the elasticity of demand for these cars to be high. In contrast, those who are considering certain luxury cars, such as the BMW 7 series, have fewer alternatives and are less concerned about their budgets. Each of those luxury cars also has a much more distinctive cachet that inspires strong loyalty among some buyers. As a result, we'd expect the elasticities for these cars to be relatively low.

The Nissan Sentra

The BMW 750Li

In a study of the demand for cars from 1970 to 1990, economists Steven Berry, James Levinsohn, and Ariel Pakes estimated the elasticities of demand for various models.[9] For low-priced cars like the Nissan Sentra, Mazda 323, and Ford Escort, elasticities of demand were roughly −6. That is, a 1 percent increase in price would cause them to lose about 6 percent of their sales. In contrast, the BMW 735i and Lexus LS400 had demand elasticities of roughly −3. This value implies that they would suffer much smaller percentage reductions in sales in response to a 1 percent increase in price. Between these two extremes were cars like the Honda Accord (with an elasticity of −4.8), the Ford Taurus (with an elasticity of −4.2), and the Lincoln Town car (with an elasticity of −4.3).

[8]You might wonder why we calculate the percentage change in the elasticity formula relative to the initial price and quantity demanded, P and Q, and not the final price and quantity demanded, P' and Q'. The answer is that for small price changes these values will be very close to each other, so it doesn't matter which we use. Sometimes, though not often, economists calculate the elasticity for a *large* price change, using a measure called the *arc elasticity of demand*. This measure replaces P and Q in formula (3) with the average price and average quantity demanded, $\bar{P} = (P + P')/2$ and $\bar{Q} = (Q + Q')/2$. For small price changes, the arc elasticity is approximately equal to the elasticity measure in expression (3) (which is sometimes called the *point elasticity*), because $\bar{P}$ will be close to P, and $\bar{Q}$ will be close to Q.

[9]Steven Berry, James Levinsohn, and Ariel Pakes, "Automobile Prices in Market Equilibrium," *Econometrica* 63, July 1995, pp. 841–90.

Elasticities for Linear Demand Curves Let's examine the elasticity of demand for linear demand curves; that is, demand curves that are straight lines, such as the one shown in Figure 2.1(a) (page 27). Linear demand curves correspond to demand functions of the form $Q^d = A - BP$, where A and B are positive numbers. For example, we've seen that the demand curve in Figure 2.1(a) corresponds to the demand function $Q^d_{corn} = 15 - 2P_{corn}$, so in that case $A = 15$ and $B = 2$.

To calculate the elasticity of demand for a linear demand curve, we rewrite the elasticity formula (3) as follows:[10]

$$E^d = \left(\frac{\Delta Q}{\Delta P}\right)\left(\frac{P}{Q}\right) \quad \textbf{(4)}$$

The first term in parentheses is the change in the amount demanded for each dollar that the price increases (when prices are measured in dollars). For a linear demand curve, that just equals $-B$. [To verify this, observe that for any change in price, ΔP, the change in demand is $\Delta Q = -B(\Delta P)$; dividing both sides by ΔP implies that $(\Delta Q/\Delta P) = -B$.] The second term in parentheses in formula (4) is just the initial price divided by the initial quantity. Thus, the elasticity of demand for a linear demand curve starting at price P and quantity Q is

$$E^d = -B(P/Q) \quad \textbf{(5)}$$

Figure 2.15 reproduces the linear demand curve for corn from Figure 2.1(a), $Q^d_{corn} = 15 - 2P_{corn}$, and indicates the elasticity of demand at three prices along this demand curve: \$6, \$3.75, and \$1.50. For example, when $P = 3.75$, the amount demanded is $Q = 7.5$. Since $B = 2$, that means the elasticity of demand at $P = 3.50$ is $E^d = -2(3.75/7.5) = -1$. Similar calculations imply that when $P = 6$, the elasticity is $E^d = -4$ and that when $P = 1.50$, the elasticity is $E^d = -1/4$.

More generally, formula (5) tells us that, for a linear demand curve, demand is more elastic at higher prices than at lower prices, since then P is larger and Q is smaller. For

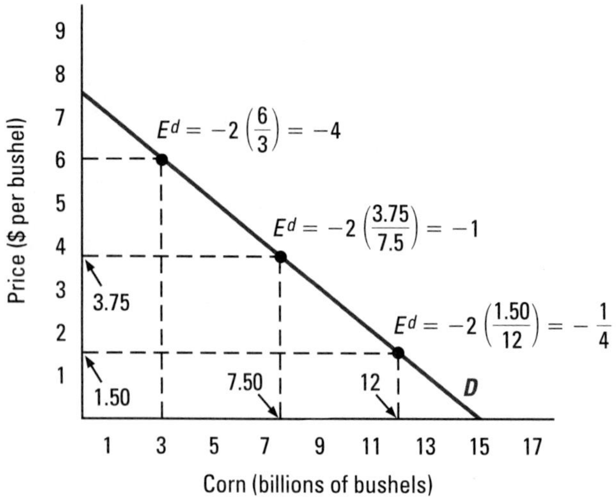

Figure 2.15
Elasticities along a Linear Demand Curve. When the demand curve is linear, the price elasticity of demand, which equals $-B(P/Q)$, is different at different points on the curve. This figure shows elasticities for the demand curve for corn from Figure 2.1(a).

[10] We derive formula (4) by rewriting formula (3) in the following way:

$$E^d = \frac{(\Delta Q/Q)}{(\Delta P/P)} = \left(\frac{\Delta Q}{Q}\right)\left(\frac{P}{\Delta P}\right) = \left(\frac{\Delta Q}{\Delta P}\right)\left(\frac{P}{Q}\right)$$

example, in Figure 2.15, the demand elasticity is less than -1 ($E^d < -1$) at prices above \$3.75, and greater than -1 ($E^d > -1$) at prices below \$3.75.

When the elasticity of demand is less than -1, economists say that demand is **elastic**, which means that the percentage change in the amount demanded is larger (in absolute value) than the percentage change in the price. When the elasticity of demand is greater than -1 (that is, between -1 and 0), economists say that demand is **inelastic**, which means that the percentage change in the amount demanded is smaller (in absolute value) than the percentage change in the price.

Demand is **elastic** when the elasticity of demand is less than -1. It is **inelastic** when the elasticity of demand is greater than -1 (that is, between -1 and 0).

Another useful way to write the elasticity of demand comes from dividing the numerator and denominator of the first term in formula (4) by ΔQ:

$$E^d = \left(\frac{1}{(\Delta P/\Delta Q)}\right)(P/Q) \qquad \textbf{(6)}$$

The denominator of the first term in formula (6), $(\Delta P/\Delta Q)$, is the change in the price divided by the change in quantity. For a linear demand curve, $(\Delta P/\Delta Q)$ is exactly the demand curve's slope (its vertical "rise" divided by its horizontal "run" between any two points on the line), which equals $-(1/B)$.[11] For example, the slope of the demand curve in Figure 2.15, the graph of the demand function $Q^d_{corn} = 15 - 2P_{corn}$ (for which $B = 2$), is $-(1/2)$.

Figure 2.11 (page 42) depicted two extreme cases of demand elasticity. The horizontal demand curve in Figure 2.11(a) has a slope of zero: $(\Delta P/\Delta Q) = 0$. Applying formula (6), we therefore conclude that the elasticity of demand at price P equals minus infinity: $E^d = -\infty$. When a demand curve is horizontal, we say that demand is **perfectly elastic**.

Demand is **perfectly elastic** when the demand curve is horizontal so that the elasticity of demand equals negative infinity.

The vertical demand curve in Figure 2.11(b) is one for which any price change, ΔP, produces no change in the amount demanded, so $(\Delta Q/\Delta P) = 0$. Applying formula (4), we see that the elasticity of demand is zero: $E^d = 0$. When a demand curve is vertical, we say that demand is **perfectly inelastic**.

Demand is **perfectly inelastic** when the demand curve is vertical so that the elasticity of demand is zero.

WORKED-OUT PROBLEM 2.3

The Problem Consider the linear demand curve for gasoline in Figure 2.8(a) (page 39). What is the elasticity of demand at a price of \$2.51 per gallon? What about at \$2.92? Is demand elastic or inelastic?

The Solution First, we need to determine the value of B, which we can compute from the changes in the market equilibrium in Figure 2.8(a) using the formula[12]

$$B = -\frac{\Delta Q}{\Delta P} = -\frac{(365 - 395)}{(2.92 - 2.51)} = 73.17$$

Thus, the elasticity of demand at \$2.51 per gallon is

$$E^d = -B\left(\frac{P}{Q}\right) = -73.17\left(\frac{2.51}{395}\right) = -0.46$$

Similarly, the elasticity of demand at \$2.92 per gallon is -0.59. Demand is inelastic at both prices.

[11] Substituting $-(1/B)$ for $(\Delta P/\Delta Q)$ in formula (6) gives formula (5) again.

[12] Alternatively, we can find the value of both A and B by solving the two equations, $A - B(2.51) = 395$ and $A - B(2.92) = 365$. The solution is $B = 73.17$ and $A = 578.66$.

IN-TEXT EXERCISE 2.4 **Consider the linear demand curve for oranges in Figure 2.8(b). What is the elasticity of demand at a price of \$2.35 per box? At a price of \$3.49?**

Elasticities for Nonlinear Demand Curves Calculating the elasticity of demand at a particular price is a little more complicated for demand curves that are not linear, such as the one in Figure 2.16. To consider this issue, recall the way we expressed the elasticity in formula (6):

$$E^d = \left(\frac{1}{(\Delta P/\Delta Q)}\right)(P/Q)$$

We already saw that for a linear demand curve, $(\Delta P/\Delta Q)$ is exactly the demand curve's slope. What about for a nonlinear demand curve? In that case, for very small price changes starting at the initial price P, $(\Delta P/\Delta Q)$ equals the slope of the black line in Figure 2.16 that is touching the demand curve at the point corresponding to price P, labeled point A.

Figure 2.16 shows why that is so. Consider, for example, a price change from P to P' that is not tiny, that produces a movement along the demand curve from point A to point C, with the amount purchased changing from Q to Q'. The changes in the price and quantity demanded between points A and C, $\Delta P'$ and $\Delta Q'$, are shown along the axes in the figure. The ratio $\Delta P'/\Delta Q'$ equals the slope of the light grey line connecting points A and C, since the line's rise is $\Delta P'$ and its run is $\Delta Q'$. Now consider a smaller price change, from P to P'', that produces a movement along the demand curve from point A to point

Figure 2.16

Slope of the Demand Curve at Price *P*. For the large price change from P to P', the light grey line connecting points C and A has the slope $(\Delta P'/\Delta Q')$. For the smaller price change from P to P'', the medium grey line connecting points B and A has the slope $(\Delta P''/\Delta Q'')$. As the price change grows smaller and smaller, the slope of the lines connecting the new and old demand points comes closer to the slope of the black line that is touching the demand curve at point A, known as the tangent line at point A. Thus, for small price changes, $(\Delta P/\Delta Q)$ comes to equal the slope of that tangent line, which is also called simply the *slope of the demand curve* at point A.

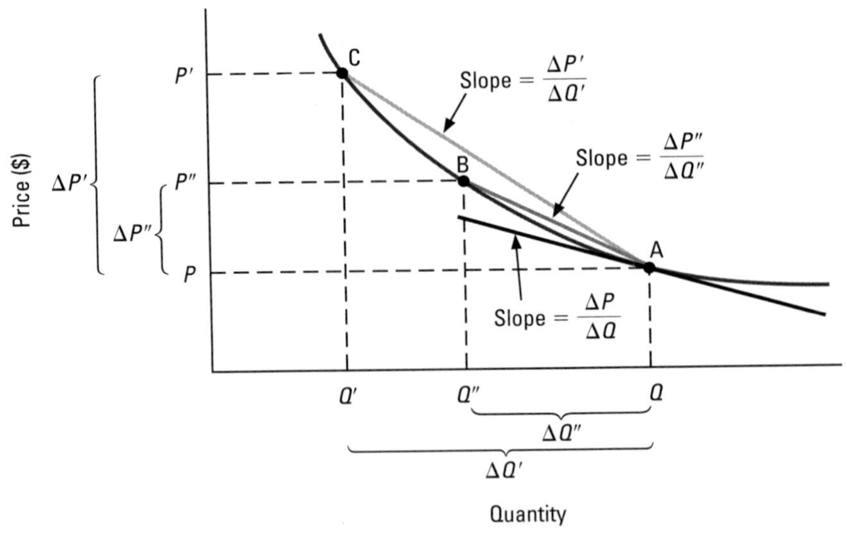

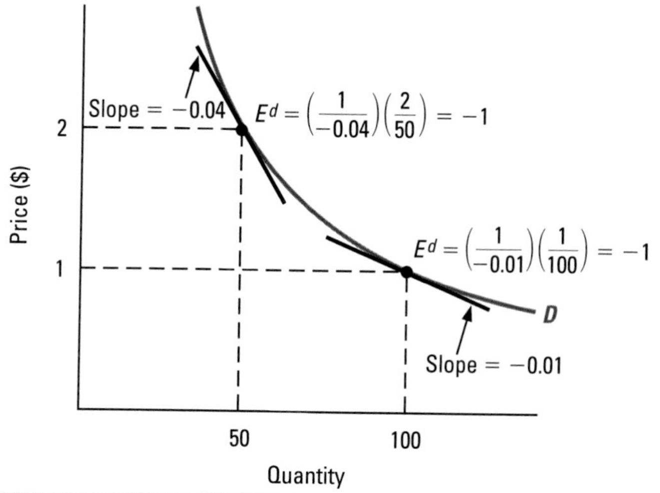

Figure 2.17

A Constant-Elasticity Demand Curve. This figure shows the curve for the demand function $Q^d = 100/P$. At every price P, the elasticity of demand is equal to −1.

B, with the amount purchased changing from Q to Q''. Again, the changes in price and quantity demanded between points A and B, $\Delta P''$ and $\Delta Q''$, are shown along the axes in the figure. The ratio $\Delta P''/\Delta Q''$ equals the slope of the medium-grey line connecting points A and B. This line is steeper than the black line, but less steep than the line connecting points A and C. As the figure suggests, if we were to consider smaller and smaller price changes, the slopes of the corresponding lines would eventually become very close to the slope of the black line that touches the demand curve at point A. That black line is said to be *tangent* to the demand curve at point A.[13]

A common shorthand expression, which we'll often use, says that the slope of the tangent line to a curve at a point is the "slope of the curve" at that point. Using this language, we can restate our conclusion as follows: *for small price changes starting at price P, the ratio* $(\Delta P/\Delta Q)$ *equals the slope of the demand curve at point A.*[14]

Economists sometimes work with demand curves for which the demand elasticity is the same at every price. Those curves, known as **constant elasticity** (or **isoelastic**) **demand curves**, correspond to demand functions of the form $Q^d = A(P^{-B})$, where A and B are positive numbers. For these demand functions, the elasticity of demand is $E^d = -B$.[15] Figure 2.17 shows the demand curve for the constant elasticity demand function $Q^d = 100/P$ [or, equivalently, $Q^d = 100(P^{-1})$], which has an elasticity of $E^d = -1$ at every price P. As shown in the figure, a constant elasticity demand curve gets steeper as the price increases. Why? Looking at formula (6), we see that as P increases (and Q decreases), P/Q increases. For the elasticity to remain constant, the slope of the demand curve, $(\Delta P/\Delta Q)$ must increase too, as shown in the figure.

A **constant elasticity** (or **isoelastic) demand function** has the same elasticity at every price.

[13] In mathematics, a line is said to be tangent to a curve at a point if its slope equals the rise over the run for very small changes along the curve starting at the point.

[14] If you know calculus, you may want to look at Add-On 2B, which discusses elasticities in terms of calculus.

[15] Add-On 2B shows this result using calculus. If you don't know calculus, you can see it another way: Suppose that the price increases from P to αP, where $\alpha > 1$. Then formula (3) tells us that

$$E^d = \frac{\left(\dfrac{A(\alpha P)^{-B} - AP^{-B}}{AP^{-B}}\right)}{\left(\dfrac{\alpha P - P}{P}\right)} = \frac{(\alpha^{-B} - 1)}{(\alpha - 1)}.$$

For very small price changes in which α is very close to 1, this expression equals approximately −B in value. For example, if B equals 5, this expression equals −4.853 when $\alpha = 1.01$; −4.985 when $\alpha = 1.001$; and −4.999 when $\alpha = 1.0001$.

Total Expenditure and the Elasticity of Demand The elasticity of demand for a product tells us how buyers' total expenditure on the product changes when the price increases and we move along the demand curve. That expenditure equals $P \times Q$, the product of the price and the total amount demanded. *Total expenditure will increase with a small increase in price when demand is inelastic and decrease when demand is elastic.* Since sellers' total revenue always equals buyer's total expenditure, the same is true for sellers' revenue.

Why does this relationship hold? Suppose that a 1 percent price increase causes the quantity demanded to fall by 1 percent. With no change in quantity, the 1 percent increase in price would cause total expenditure to rise by 1 percent. With no change in price, the 1 percent drop in quantity would cause total expenditure to fall by 1 percent. So intuitively, the 1 percent increase in price and the 1 percent decline in quantity offset one another, leaving total expenditure unchanged. If a 1 percent price increase causes a less than 1 percent decline in quantity, total expenditure will rise, and if it causes a more than 1 percent decline in quantity, total expenditure will fall. (For a demonstration of this result using algebra, see Add-On 2C.)

Let's look at a couple of examples. First consider constant elasticity demand curves. For the demand function $Q^d = 100/P$ depicted in Figure 2.17, which has an elasticity of -1, total expenditure equals \$100 at every price. This follows from the fact that $P \times (100/P) = 100$. More generally, if $Q^d = A(P^{-B})$ (for which $E^d = -B$), then the total expenditure at price P is $P \times (A \times P^{-B}) = A(P^{1-B})$. Accordingly, a price increase raises total expenditure if $B < 1$ (which implies that E^d is between -1 and 0) and reduces total expenditure if $B > 1$ (which implies that E^d is less than -1).

Now consider linear demand curves. Figure 2.18 graphs the relationship between the total expenditure on corn and its price for the linear demand curve shown in Figure 2.15. The formula for total expenditure is $P_{corn} \times Q_{corn} = P_{corn} \times (15-2P_{corn}) = 15P_{corn} - 2(P_{corn})^2$. Recall that this demand curve is inelastic for prices below \$3.75 per bushel, and elastic for prices above \$3.75 per bushel. As the figure shows, a price increase raises total expenditure when the initial price is below this threshold (so that demand is inelastic) and reduces total expenditure when the initial price is above this threshold (so that demand is elastic).

At what price is total expenditure largest? That must be a price at which the elasticity of demand equals -1. Why? If demand was inelastic (an elasticity between zero and -1), a small increase in price would increase the total expenditure. If it was elastic (an elasticity less than -1), a small decrease in price would raise total expenditure. If expenditure is at its largest possible value, neither a small increase nor a small decrease can increase total expenditure; demand must therefore be neither elastic nor inelastic, so its elasticity must equal -1. In Figure 2.18, for example, the price that maximizes total expenditure is \$3.75 per bushel—the same price for which the elasticity of demand is -1.

To summarize:

Total Expenditure and the Elasticity of Demand A small increase in price causes total expenditure to increase if demand is inelastic and decrease if demand is elastic. Total expenditure is largest at a price for which the elasticity equals -1.

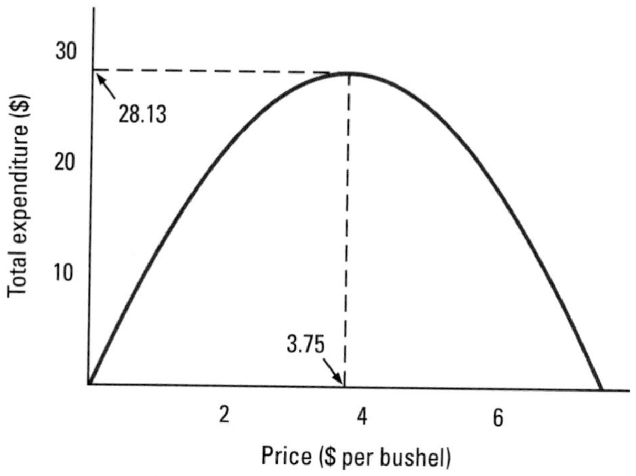

Figure 2.18

The Relationship between Price and Total Expenditure. This figure shows the total expenditure on corn for the demand curve in Figure 2.15. Total expenditure increases when the price rises for prices below \$3.75, where demand is inelastic. It falls when the price rises for prices above \$3.75, where demand is elastic. It is largest when the price is \$3.75, where $E^d = -1$.

WORKED-OUT PROBLEM 2.4

The Problem Consider the linear demand curve for gasoline in Figure 2.8(a) (page 39), which was the subject of worked-out problem 2.3. The demand function for that curve is $Q^d = 578.66 - 73.17\,P$. At what price will total expenditure on gasoline be largest?

The Solution Recall that the elasticity of the linear demand function $Q^d = A - BP$ at price P is $E^d = -B(P/Q)$, where Q is the amount demanded at that price. Substituting for Q, we can rewrite this formula as

$$E^d = -B\left(\frac{P}{A - BP}\right)$$

We know that the largest total expenditure occurs at a price for which the elasticity of demand equals -1. Since $B = 73.17$, that value of P will solve the equation

$$-73.17\left(\frac{P}{578.66 - 73.17P}\right) = -1$$

Multiplying both sides by $578.66 - 73.17P$, we can rewrite this equation as

$$73.17P = 578.66 - 73.17P$$

Solving for P, we find that total expenditure is largest at a price of \$3.95 per gallon.

IN-TEXT EXERCISE 2.5 **The linear demand function for the demand curve shown in Figure 2.8(b) (page 39) is $Q^d = 431.6 - 80.7P$. At what price will the total expenditure on oranges be largest?**

Application 2.6

How Much Were Orange Growers Hurt by Charley, Frances, and Jeanne?

In Application 2.3, we learned that three hurricanes destroyed much of Florida's orange crop in August and September of 2004. Following the storms, President George W. Bush asked Congress to provide emergency aid to the orange growers in the state of Florida. But how severely hurt were the state's orange growers? How much assistance would they have needed to offset their losses?

President George W. Bush and his brother Florida Governor Jeb Bush inspect a hurricane-damaged orange grove

Looking at Figure 2.8(b) (page 39) we see that the number of boxes growers sold fell dramatically, from 242 million in 2003–2004 to 150 million in 2004–2005. But the price of oranges rose from \$2.35 in 2003–2004 to \$3.49 in 2004–2005. Despite the huge reduction in the size of the harvest, the orange growers' total revenue fell by only 8 percent, from \$569 million to \$522 million. Though orange growers were hurt by the storms, the impact was much smaller than the reduction in their harvest might suggest. Over the range of prices charged during 2003 through 2005, the elasticity of demand for oranges averaged out to only a little less than −1—in other words, the demand for oranges was only slightly elastic (recall in-text exercise 2.4).[16] As a result, when the supply curve shifted inward, causing a leftward movement along the demand curve [see Figure 2.8(b)], the impact on Florida orange growers' revenue was small.

The (Price) Elasticity of Supply

The **(price) elasticity of supply** at price *P*, denoted E^s, equals the percentage change in the amount supplied for each 1 percent increase in the price.

Economists also use elasticities to measure the responsiveness of supply to a product's price. The basic ideas are the same as for demand. For example, the **(price) elasticity of supply** at price *P*, denoted E^s, equals the percentage change in the amount supplied for each 1 percent increase in the price,

$$E^s = \frac{\%\text{ change in amount supplied}}{\%\text{ change in price}} = \frac{(\Delta Q/Q)}{(\Delta P/P)} = \left(\frac{\Delta Q}{\Delta P}\right)\left(\frac{P}{Q}\right) \quad \textbf{(7)}$$

where Q is now the amount *supplied* at price P and $\Delta Q/\Delta P$ is the change in the amount supplied for each dollar the price increases (when prices are measured in dollars). Since supply usually increases as the price increases, we expect the elasticity of supply to be a positive number. In parallel with our discussion of demand elasticities, we can also express the elasticity of supply as

$$E^s = \left(\frac{1}{(\Delta P/\Delta Q)}\right)(P/Q) \quad \textbf{(8)}$$

where $\Delta P/\Delta Q$ is the slope of the supply curve.

[16] The arc elasticity for this price change was −1.21.

The horizontal supply curve in Figure 2.13(a) (page 44) has a slope of zero, so applying formula (8) the elasticity of supply at price P is infinite: $E^s = +\infty$. This supply curve is **perfectly elastic**. In contrast, the vertical supply curve in Figure 2.13(b) is one for which any price change, ΔP, produces no change in the amount supplied, so $\Delta Q = 0$. For this supply curve, $(\Delta Q/\Delta P)$ equals 0, so [applying formula (7)] the elasticity of supply is zero: $E^s = 0$. This supply curve is **perfectly inelastic**.

In general, supply curves with an elasticity of supply between 0 and 1 are referred to as **inelastic**; those whose elasticity of supply is greater than 1 are referred to as **elastic.** With an inelastic supply curve, the percentage increase in the amount supplied is less than the percentage increase in price. With an elastic supply curve, the opposite is true.

Supply is **perfectly inelastic** when the supply curve is vertical so that the price elasticity of supply is zero, and **perfectly elastic** when the supply curve is horizontal so that the price elasticity of supply is infinite.

Supply is **elastic** at price P when the elasticity of supply is greater than 1, and **inelastic** when the elasticity of supply is between 0 and 1.

The Size of Changes in Market Demand, Revisited

We've said that elasticities of demand and supply are a more convenient way to measure price responsiveness than is the steepness (or slope) of the demand and supply curves. In Section 2.3 we related the steepness of the demand and supply curves to the size of the change in the market price and the amount bought and sold when, respectively, the supply or demand curve shifts. Let's go back to that discussion to see how it relates to elasticities.

Figure 2.12 (page 43), for example, showed that the price changed more and the amount bought and sold changed less in response to a shift of the supply curve with the steeper demand curve, D_1, than the flatter curve, D_2. How is the steepness of those two demand curves related to their elasticities? When two different demand curves coincide at a particular price, the steeper one is always less elastic at that price. For example, both demand curves in Figure 2.12 run through the initial market equilibrium point, with price P^* and quantity Q^*. Since the slope $(\Delta P/\Delta Q)$ is closer to zero for the flatter curve and the value of P^*/Q^* is the same for both curves at the point of intersection, formula (6) implies that the flatter curve is more elastic at price P^*. Thus, for small shifts in the demand and supply curves, we can restate the conclusion from our discussion in Section 2.3 as follows:

Changes in Market Equilibrium and the Elasticity of Demand and Supply

1. When the demand curve shifts: the less elastic the supply curve at the initial equilibrium price, the larger the price change and the smaller the change in the amount bought and sold.
2. When the supply curve shifts: the less elastic the demand curve at the initial equilibrium price, the larger the price change and the smaller the change in the amount bought and sold.

Other Elasticities

As we explained in Sections 2.1 and 2.2, the demand and supply for a product are affected by factors other than its price. We can use the concept of elasticity to measure the responsiveness of demand and supply to those other factors as well. For example, the elasticity

The income elasticity of demand equals the percentage change in the amount demanded for each 1 percent increase in income.

of demand with respect to income (denoted by M), usually called the **income elasticity of demand**, equals the percentage change in the amount demanded divided by the percentage change in income, or equivalently, the percentage change in the amount demanded for each 1 percent increase in income:

$$E_M^d = \frac{(\Delta Q/Q)}{(\Delta M/M)}$$

When the demand for a product increases when income grows larger, the product is called a **normal good.** If it instead decreases, it is called an **inferior good.**

If an increase in income raises the demand for a product, the income elasticity is positive, and we say that the product is a **normal good**. Sometimes, an increase in income reduces the demand for a product. This usually occurs when the product is of low quality, and higher incomes cause consumers to substitute toward higher quality alternatives. In that case, the income elasticity is negative, and we say that the product is an **inferior good**. We'll discuss these concepts further in Chapter 5.

The **cross-price elasticity of demand** with another product equals the percentage change in the amount demanded of the product for each 1 percent increase in the price of the other product.

Economists also frequently measure the elasticity of demand for a product with respect to the price of another product, known as the first product's **cross-price elasticity** with the second product. Let Q denote the demand for the first product and P_o the price of the second "other" product. Then this elasticity equals the percentage change in the amount demanded of the product divided by the percentage change in the price of the other product, or equivalently, the percentage change in the amount demanded for each 1 percent increase in the price of the other product:

$$E_{P_O}^d = \frac{(\Delta Q/Q)}{(\Delta P_O/P_O)}$$

With products that are substitutes (see Section 2.1), the cross-price elasticity is positive. With products that are complements, it is negative.

In a similar fashion, we can measure the elasticities of supply for a product with respect to other factors, such as the prices of inputs or other outputs.

Application 2.7

Cross-Price Elasticities for the Honda Accord

The similarity of substitute products affects not only a product's elasticity of demand with respect to its own price, but also its cross-price elasticities with other products. Recall from Application 2.5 that the elasticity of demand for a Honda Accord was −4.8: when its price went up by 1 percent, it experienced a 4.8 percent reduction in sales. What happened to the sales of other cars? According to economists Berry, Levinsohn, and Pakes, the Nissan Sentra, Ford Escort, and Ford Taurus—relatively similar cars to the Accord—all had cross-price elasticities with the Accord of about 0.2. That is, each experienced roughly a 0.2 percent increase in sales when the price of a Honda Accord rose 1 percent. In contrast, the much more upscale BMW 735i and Lexus LS400 experienced almost no change in their sales—their cross-price elasticities with the Honda Accord were essentially zero.

The Honda Accord

1. **Demand**

a. The first step in a demand-and-supply analysis of the market for a product is to determine the demand for the product.

b. A product's demand curve shows how much of the product consumers and firms want to buy at each possible price, holding fixed all other factors that affect demand.

c. The demand function for a product is a formula of the form *Quantity Demanded* = *D*(*Price*, *Other Factors*). It gives the total demand for the product at every possible combination of its price and other factors.

d. A change in a product's price leads to a movement along its demand curve. A change in other factors leads to a shift in the entire demand curve.

2. **Supply**

a. The second step in a demand-and-supply analysis of the market for a product is to determine the supply of the product.

b. A product's supply curve shows how many units sellers of the product want to sell at each possible price, holding fixed all other factors that affect supply.

c. The supply function for a product is a formula of the form *Quantity Supplied* = *S*(*Price*, *Other Factors*). It gives the total supply of the product at every possible combination of its price and other factors.

d. A change in a product's price leads to a movement along its supply curve. A change in other factors leads to a shift in the entire supply curve.

3. **Market equilibrium**

a. Once we know the demand and supply in a market, the next step is to determine the equilibrium price—the price at which the demand and supply curves intersect, so that the amounts supplied and demanded are equal. That price can be found graphically or algebraically.

b. Market prices tend to adjust to equate the amounts demanded and supplied. If there is excess demand then some buyers will have an incentive to raise the price they offer in order to acquire their desired quantity. If there is excess supply, then some sellers will have an incentive to lower the price in order to sell their desired quantity. These processes tend to restore the balance between supply and demand.

c. To determine how a change in market conditions, such as a change in the price of an input or a shift in consumer preferences, will change the price and the amount bought and sold, we solve for the market equilibrium before and after the change.

d. Changes that increase demand (shifting the demand curve to the right) raise the price and the amount bought and sold; changes that decrease demand lower them. In contrast, changes that increase supply (shifting the supply curve to the right) raise the amount bought and sold but lower the price; changes that decrease supply have the opposite effect.

e. If both the demand curve and supply curve shift and each would individually increase the price, the overall effect is to increase the price. If the two effects work in opposite directions, the overall effect is ambiguous. The same principle applies to changes in the amount bought and sold.

f. When demand or supply increases, shifting the demand or supply curves, the size of the change in price and the amount bought and sold depends on how much the curve shifts and on the steepness of the nonshifting curve. The steeper the nonshifting curve, the greater the change in the equilibrium price and the smaller the change in the amount bought and sold.

4. **Elasticities of supply and demand**

a. The elasticity of one variable, Y, with respect to another, X, measures how responsive Y is to a change in X. It equals the percentage change in Y divided by the percentage change in X, or equivalently, the percentage change in Y for each 1 percent increase in X.

b. The (price) elasticity of demand at a given price P, denoted E^d, measures the percentage change in the amount demanded for each 1 percent increase in its price, for small price changes. The elasticity of demand is typically a negative number.

c. The elasticity of demand is calculated using the formula $E^d = (P/Q)/(\Delta P/\Delta Q)$. For a linear demand curve of the form $Q^d = A - BP$, $(\Delta P/\Delta Q)$ equals $-(1/B)$, the slope of the demand curve. For a nonlinear demand curve, it equals the slope of the demand curve at the particular price P (which equals the slope of the line that is tangent to the curve at that point).

d. Demand is inelastic at price P when the elasticity of demand is closer to zero than -1 ($E^d > -1$). It is elastic at price P when the elasticity of demand at that price is further from zero than -1 ($E^d < -1$). It is perfectly inelastic when the price elasticity of demand is zero, and perfectly elastic when the price elasticity of demand equals negative infinity.

e. When demand is elastic, a small price increase causes total expenditure to fall. When demand is inelastic, a small price increase causes total expenditure to rise. Total expenditure is largest at a price at which the elasticity of demand equals -1.

f. The price elasticity of supply at a given price P, denoted E^s, measures the percentage change in supply for each 1 percent increase in price.

g. Supply is inelastic when the price elasticity of supply is closer to zero than 1 ($E^s < 1$). It is elastic when the price elasticity of supply is further from zero than 1 ($E^s > 1$). Supply is perfectly inelastic when the elasticity of supply is zero, and perfectly elastic when the elasticity of supply is infinite.

h. For small shifts in the demand curve, the less elastic the supply curve at the equilibrium price, the larger the price change and the smaller the change in the amount bought and sold. For small shifts in the supply curve, the less elastic the demand curve at the initial equilibrium price, the larger the price change and the smaller the change in the amount bought and sold.

i. Economists also study elasticities of a product's demand or supply with respect to other factors, such as income and the prices of other products (for demand), and input prices (for supply).

ADDITIONAL EXERCISES

Exercise 2.1: Consider again the demand function for corn in formula (1). Graph the corresponding demand curve when potatoes and butter cost \$0.75 and \$4 per pound, respectively, and average income is \$40,000 per year. At what price does the amount demanded equal 15 billion bushels a year? Show your answer using algebra.

Exercise 2.2: Consider again the supply function for corn in formula (2). Graph the corresponding supply curve when diesel fuel costs \$2.75 per gallon and the price of soybeans is \$10 per bushel. At what price does the amount supplied equal 21 billion bushels a year? Show your answer using algebra.

Exercise 2.3: What is the equilibrium price for the demand and supply conditions described in exercises 2.1 and 2.2? How much corn is bought and sold? What if the price of diesel fuel increases to \$4.50 per gallon? Show the equilibrium price before and after the change in a graph.

Exercise 2.4: Consider again the demand and supply functions in worked-out problem 2.2 (page 33). Suppose the government needs to buy 3.5 billion bushels of corn for a third-world famine relief program. What effect will the purchase have on the equilibrium price of corn? How will it change the amount of corn that consumers and firms buy?

Exercise 2.5: After terrorists destroyed the World Trade Center and surrounding office buildings on September 11, 2001, some businesspeople worried about the risks of remaining in Manhattan. What effect would you expect their concern to have in the short run (before any of the destroyed office buildings are rebuilt) on the price of office space in Manhattan? What factors does your answer depend on? What about the effect over the long run? Suppose the area around the former World Trade Center is made into a park, so that the destroyed office buildings are never rebuilt. Economically, who would gain and who would lose from such a plan?

Exercise 2.6: If the U.S. government were to ban imports of Canadian beef for reasons unrelated to health concerns, what would be the effect on the price of beef in the United States? How would the typical American's diet change? What about the typical Canadian's? What if the ban suggested to consumers that there might be health risks associated with Canadian beef?

Exercise 2.7: Suppose that the U.S. demand for maple syrup, in thousands of gallons per year, is $Q^d = 6000 - 30P$. What is the elasticity of demand at a price of \$75 per gallon?

Exercise 2.8: Consider again exercise 2.7. At what price is the expenditure on maple syrup by U.S. consumers highest?

Exercise 2.9: Suppose the demand function for jelly beans in Cincinnati is linear. Two years ago, the price of jelly beans was \$1 per pound, and consumers purchased 100,000 pounds of jelly beans. Last year the price was \$2, and consumers purchased 50,000 pounds of jelly beans. No other factors that might affect the demand for jelly beans changed. What was the elasticity of demand at last year's price of \$2? At what price would the total expenditure on jelly beans have been largest?

Exercise 2.10: Consider again the demand and supply functions in in-text exercise 2.2 (page 33). At the equilibrium price, what are the elasticities of demand and supply?

Exercise 2.11: Last September, the price of gasoline in Chattanooga was \$2 a gallon, and consumers bought 1 million gallons. Suppose the elasticity of demand in September at a price of \$2 was -0.5, and that the demand function for gasoline that month was linear. What was that demand function? At what price does consumers' total expenditure on gasoline reach its largest level?

Exercise 2.12: Suppose the annual demand function for the Honda Accord is $Q^d = 430 - 10P_A + 10P_C - 10P_G$, where P_A and P_C are the prices of the Accord and the Toyota Camry respectively (in thousands), and P_G is the price of gasoline (per gallon). What is the elasticity of demand of the Accord with respect to the price of a Camry when both cars sell for \$20,000 and fuel costs \$3 per gallon? What is the elasticity with respect to the price of gasoline?

Exercise 2.13: The demand for a product is $Q^d = A - BP$, where P is its price and A and B are positive numbers. Suppose that when the price is \$1 the amount demanded is 60 and the elasticity of demand is -1. What are the values of A and B?

APPENDIX

ESTIMATING DEMAND AND SUPPLY CURVES

To answer many questions in economics and business, we need to measure the relationships between the amount demanded and/or supplied and various factors, including the product's price. We've already seen that we need to know the demand and supply functions to predict market prices. Later in this book, we'll see that this same knowledge is useful for such diverse purposes as evaluating the effects of a tax and determining a firm's profit-maximizing price. The process of learning about demand and/or supply is known as demand and/or supply function estimation. For the sake of simplicity, and because the issues are very similar, we'll focus here primarily on the estimation of demand functions.

How can we determine the demand function for a product? There are various approaches to this problem. One is to ask buyers about their willingness to buy the product at different prices. Marketing specialists have developed survey methods for this purpose. But while surveys can provide useful information, they suffer from some shortcomings. Consumers may have difficulty providing accurate responses about what they would do in hypothetical situations. And since their well-being doesn't depend on their answers, they may not give these questions much thought.

Given these problems, economists usually take a different approach: they try to learn about demand by studying consumers' *actual behavior.*

The "Ideal Experiment"

Suppose we're interested in studying the weekly demand function for hot dogs in Evanston, Illinois. To start, we'll assume for simplicity that this demand depends only on the price of a hot dog. Suppose the demand function is linear, so that it takes the form $Q^d = A - BP$. We don't know the values of A (the intercept term) and B (which determines how much the amount demanded changes when the price changes).

How can we learn these values? First let's think about an ideal experiment, in which we present consumers with different prices in different weeks and observe their demand. Figure 2.19 shows the amounts demanded at two different prices, $P = \$1$ and $P = \$2$, as black dots. We can find the demand curve, labeled D, by drawing a line through these dots, as in the figure. The value A is the quantity at which this line hits the horizontal axis (corresponding to the amount demanded when hot dogs are free). The demand curve hits the vertical axis at a height equal to A/B. So the value of B equals the horizontal intercept of the demand curve divided by the vertical intercept. [This is also equal to $-$(1/demand curve slope)].

If the demand function isn't linear, we would usually need to observe the demand at more than two prices to trace out the demand curve. And if observable factors other than the price affect demand, such as the season (summer versus nonsummer), we would need to perform a similar experiment in each season.

In reality, if we were to present consumers with a price of \$1 in some weeks and \$2 in other weeks, we would find that the quantities demanded would differ even across weeks in which the price was the same. Variation in other unobserved factors creates this pattern. For example, in some weeks a local university may hold home football games, the youth baseball league may hold a "BaseballFest," or a large church may have a potluck dinner, significantly increasing the demand for hot dogs.

Let's imagine that half the time the demand is high, which we represent by the curve labeled D^H in Figure 2.20, and half the time it is low, which we represent by the demand curve D^L in that figure. In that case, for any given price we face the consumer with (\$1 or \$2), half of the time the amount demanded corresponds to the black dot on D^H, and half of the time to the black dot on D^L. Though we can't determine the demand curve with

Figure 2.19
Identifying the Demand Curve through an "Ideal Experiment." If consumers face different prices in different weeks within each season, their choices will reveal the market demand curve.

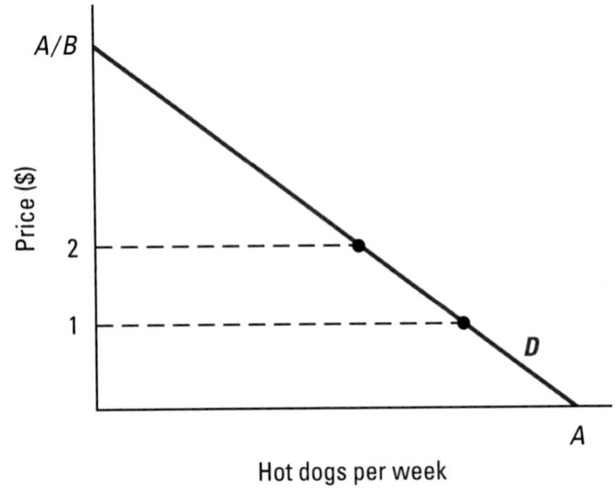

Figure 2.20
Identifying the (Average) Demand Curve, Given Unobservable Factors. When unobservable factors affect demand, the quantity demanded will differ from week to week even when consumers face the same price. In such cases, we can learn how the average demand varies with the price.

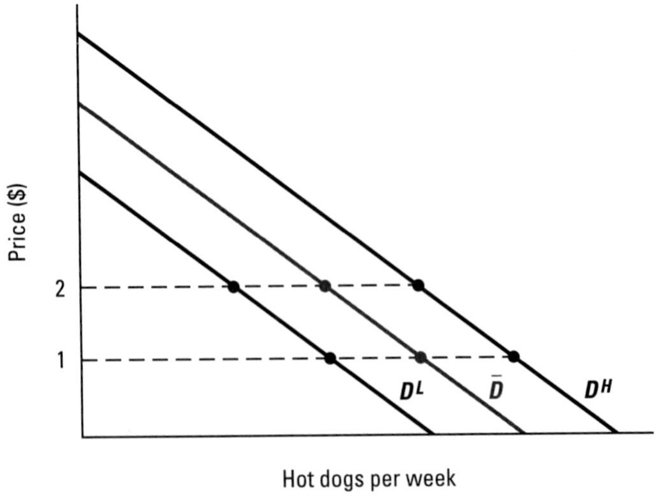

certainty, we *can* learn about the *average* demand curve, which tells us how many hot dogs consumers would demand, on average, at each possible price. To do so, we would calculate the average demand when the price is \$1 and the average demand when the price is \$2, shown as the two blue dots in Figure 2.20. We could then draw a line through those two dots to obtain an estimate of the average demand curve, labeled $\bar{D}$ in the figure.

Economists who specialize in a field called *econometrics* study how best to use such data to derive estimates of average demand. One such method, known as *linear regression*, involves minimizing the sum of the squared distances between the estimated demand curve and the observed demand. In econometrics, the variable whose movements we are trying to explain is called the **dependent variable**. The variables that explain the changes in the dependent variable are called the **explanatory variables**.

In econometrics, the variable whose movements we are trying to explain is called the **dependent variable.** The variables that explain the changes in the dependent variable are called the **explanatory variables.**

Using Actual Market Data

If economists could easily conduct the ideal experiment, our discussion of demand estimation would be complete. Unfortunately, they rarely can perform such experiments. Instead, they must typically use actual market data. To see why doing so creates problems, look at Figure 2.21. The figure shows the same two demand curves as in Figure 2.20, but now also includes a supply curve labeled *S*. When we look at market data, we see the equilibrium prices and amounts demanded. These equilibria correspond to the two black dots, where the demand curves intersect the supply curve.

Like our ideal experimental data, these market data tell us how much consumers purchased at two different prices. Suppose we treat this data the same way as we did in Figure 2.20, drawing a line to connect the two dots. That line, labeled $\hat{D}$, is upward sloping, and doesn't look at all like the actual demand curves. Why isn't our method working? The answer is that we're no longer performing the ideal experiment. In the ideal experiment, the price that consumers faced was unrelated to the unobserved factors that affect demand. In Figure 2.20, for example, we presented consumers with prices of \$1 and \$2 every other week. But when we look at real market data, as in Figure 2.21, *the*

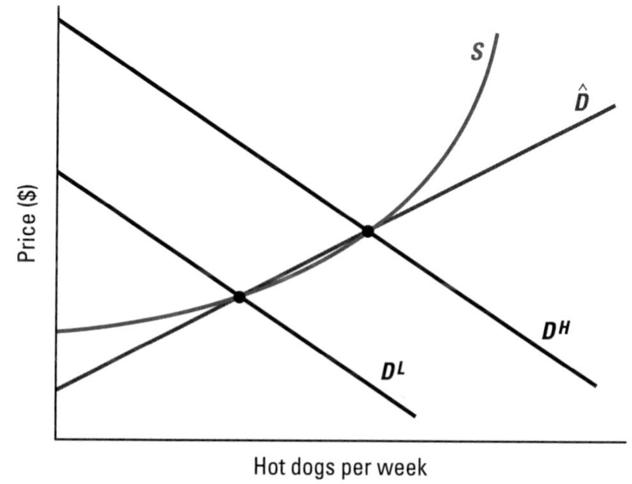

Figure 2.21

The Effect of Unobservable Factors on Demand. This figure shows two different demand curves, a variation in demand that is caused by unobserved factors. Because the equilibrium price is higher when unobserved factors increase demand, demand appears to be higher when the price is higher.

price we observe is affected by the unobserved factors that influence demand. The market price tends to be high precisely when unobserved factors shift the demand curve outward, which in turn increases the amount bought and sold. As a result, we tend to underestimate how much an increase in price reduces demand. In fact, in Figure 2.21, a higher price always goes hand-in-hand with a higher quantity, because both result from an outward shift of the demand curve.

Is there some way to determine the true average demand curve? The answer is "maybe," but it depends on our ability to observe a factor that shifts the *supply* curve while leaving the demand curve unaffected.[17]

Imagine, for instance, that the price of hot dog meat rises, increasing a hot dog vendor's cost by \$1 per hot dog. The cost increase shifts the supply curve for hot dogs to the left (reducing supply). In Figure 2.22, these two supply curves are labeled S (before the increase in the cost of meat) and S' (after the increase). Suppose we compare the prices and quantities demanded when the meat price is high and when it is low. With the higher meat cost, hot dog prices tend to be higher because of the reduced supply. The hot dog prices and quantities we observe correspond to points A and B. When the price of meat is low, the hot dog prices and quantities we observe correspond to points C and D. The blue dots labeled E and F show the *average* price and *average* demand when the cost of meat is high (E) and when it is low (F). If we connect those blue dots by drawing the blue line labeled $\hat{D}$, we see that the line is downward sloping. In fact, it gives us a reliable estimate of the average demand curve.

What's going on here? We would like to perform the ideal experiment in which we face consumers with different prices while holding all other factors that affect demand fixed and estimate the demand curve by plotting the average demand at those prices. We can't do that, because the price consumers actually pay in a market equilibrium depends

Figure 2.22

Using a Supply-Shifter to Identify the (Average) Demand Curve. This figure shows two supply curves, one with a low price of hot dog meat (S) and the other with a high cost of meat (S'). Point E is the average of the market equilibria with a high cost of meat; point F is the average with a low cost of meat. These two points allow us to identify the (average) demand curve, shown in blue.

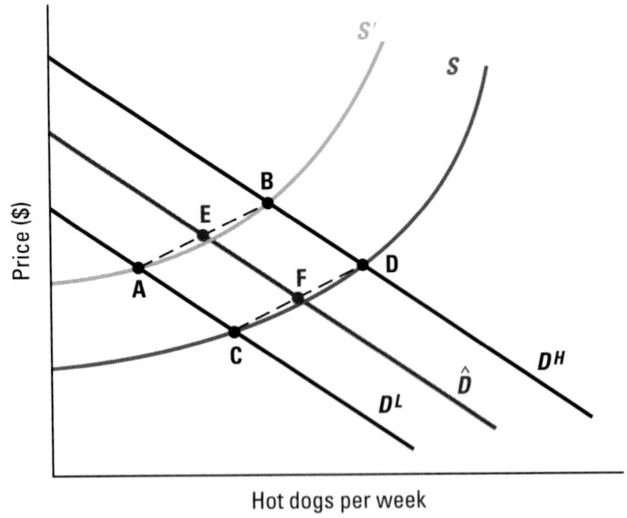

[17]In econometrics, an observed factor that shifts the *other* curve (here the supply curve) rather than the one we are estimating (here the demand curve) is known as an *instrumental variable*.

on unobserved factors that also affect demand. Instead, we perform a different experiment: we compare the average prices and quantities demanded in periods when supply is high to those when supply is low, in this case due to the differences in the price of meat. By computing the average difference in the amount demanded between these two situations, and comparing it to the average difference in the price, we can estimate the average relationship between the price and the quantity demanded. This gives us an estimate of the demand curve.

In fact, we've already put this idea to work in worked-out problem 2.3 (see also in-text exercise 2.4). There we used information about the price and amount of gasoline bought before and after hurricanes Katrina and Rita, which affected the supply of gasoline but left the demand largely unchanged, to learn about the demand curve for gasoline.

The methods for estimating the supply curve parallel those used to estimate demand curves. The main difference is that, when estimating the supply curve, we need to observe factors that shift demand. For example, if we want to estimate the supply curve for hot dogs, we might compare the average prices and amounts sold in summer weeks versus winter weeks. Since the demand is greater in the summer, the price will tend to be higher during summer weeks, and we can use market data to determine how supply responds to that price difference.

3 Balancing Benefits and Costs

Learning Objectives

After reading this chapter, students should be able to:

- Understand the concept of maximizing benefits less costs.
- Describe what it means to think on the margin.
- Explain the concepts of marginal benefit and marginal cost.
- Use marginal analysis to identify best choices.
- Understand why sunk costs can be ignored in making economic decisions.

Last week your 1998 Honda Civic broke down for the second time in a month, jeopardizing your after-school pizza delivery job. You and your "Civ" have been through some good times together, but you've reluctantly concluded that it's time to replace it with another car. Before you sell it, however, you may want to spend some money to fix it up.

Think about the benefits of having a mechanic work on your car: The more problems you fix, the more money you'll get for it. Some things that don't cost that much to fix can greatly increase its resale value. A broken turn signal, streaky windshield wipers, and a cracked windshield strike most car buyers as bad signs. Careful buyers might also discover that your brake pads are worn and your muffler has holes. But fixing your car also has costs. Your mechanic's time isn't cheap, nor are the parts she uses. And while the car is in the repair shop, you won't be able to do your delivery job. Making the right decision involves balancing these benefits and costs.

Many decisions we will study in this book involve such a trade-off. A decision maker is confronted with various options and needs to find the best choice. Doing so means balancing benefits and costs. In this chapter, we'll see how economists think about such problems. We'll use the tools we develop here over and over again throughout the book. The chapter can be studied at the start of a course, or used as a reference while reading later chapters. It covers three topics:

1. *Maximizing benefits less costs.* Economic decisions generate both benefits and costs. We'll discuss how the best choice maximizes benefits less costs.
2. *Thinking on the margin.* Economists often think about a choice in terms of its marginal benefits and marginal costs, which capture its incremental benefits and costs. We'll define these concepts and examine their relationships to best choices.
3. *Sunk costs and decision making.* In some situations, a decision is associated with costs that the decision maker has already incurred or to which she has previously committed. Economists call such costs *sunk costs*. We'll see that a decision maker can always make the right choice simply by ignoring sunk costs.

3.1 MAXIMIZING BENEFITS LESS COSTS

Let's take a closer look at your car repair decision. For the sake of simplicity, we'll assume to start that your mechanic charges for her time in one-hour increments, so that the amount of time you choose must be a whole number, like two hours or four hours, but not two and one-half hours. Also for the sake of simplicity, we'll assume your mechanic has at most six hours of available time.

We'll focus first on the benefits. Table 3.1 shows how much more money you will get for your car for each number of hours your mechanic works on it. Notice that the more repair time, the more your car is worth. For example, your car will be worth $1,150 more if the mechanic works on it for two hours, and $1,975 more if she works on it for four hours.

Now let's think about the costs. First, you'll have to pay for your mechanic's time and the parts she uses. For example, Table 3.2 shows that the cost of two hours of repair work is $355. Second, you won't be able to work at your pizza delivery job while your car is being repaired. For example, Table 3.2 shows that you will earn $25 less if you miss two hours of work, but will earn $75 less if you miss four hours of work. (Your boss will be more annoyed if you miss four hours of work and will reassign you to a delivery route in a less wealthy part of town, where tips are lower.)

Table 3.2 also shows the total cost for each number of repair hours you could choose. Notice that the costs of repairing your car are of two different types. When you hire your

Table 3.1

Benefits of Repairing Your Car

Repair Time (Hours)	Total Benefit
0	$0
1	615
2	1,150
3	1,600
4	1,975
5	2,270
6	2,485

Table 3.2

Costs of Repairing Your Car

Repair Time (Hours)	Cost of Mechanic and Parts	Lost Earnings from Pizza Delivery Job	Total Cost
0	$0	$0	$0
1	140	10	150
2	355	25	380
3	645	45	690
4	1,005	75	1,080
5	1,440	110	1,550
6	1,950	150	2,100

Table 3.3
Total Benefit and Total Cost of Repairing Your Car

	Repair Time (Hours)	Total Benefit	Total Cost	Net Benefit
	0	$0	$0	$0
	1	615	150	465
	2	1,150	380	770
Best choice →	(3)	1,600	690	(910)
	4	1,975	1,080	895
	5	2,270	1,550	720
	6	2,485	2,100	385

An **opportunity cost** is the cost associated with forgoing the opportunity to employ a resource in its best alternative use.

Net benefit equals total benefit less total cost.

mechanic and buy parts, you incur an out-of-pocket cost in the sense that you have to take money out of your pocket (or bank account) to pay her. But when repairing your car forces you to skip your pizza delivery job, the cost is of a different nature. You hand no money to others; instead, you forgo the opportunity to have others hand money to you. That type of cost is known as an opportunity cost. In general, an **opportunity cost** is the cost associated with forgoing the opportunity to employ a resource in its best alternative use.[1] Here, you forgo the opportunity to use your car to deliver pizzas.

To make the right decision, you need to find the number of repair hours that maximizes your **net benefit**—the total benefit you derive less the total cost you incur. Table 3.3 shows the total benefit, total cost, and net benefit for each of your possible choices. The best choice is three hours, which has a net benefit of $910.

Figure 3.1 graphs the total benefits and total costs from Table 3.3. The horizontal axis measures the number of repair hours and the vertical axis measures total benefit and total cost. The figure shows the total benefit for each number of hours in blue and the total cost in red. At the best choice of three hours, the vertical distance between the blue total benefit point and red total cost point is larger than at any other number of hours.

In practice, managers often construct benefit and cost tables using a computer. By entering the various benefits and costs into a spreadsheet program and then using it to calculate the net benefit of each possible choice, they can identify the best choice.

IN-TEXT EXERCISE 3.1 **Suppose your mechanic lowers the amount she charges by $25 an hour. The total benefits are the same as in Table 3.1. What is your best choice?**

Maximizing Net Benefits with Finely Divisible Actions

Many choices involve actions that are finely divisible, that is, that can be adjusted in arbitrarily small increments. Consider again your decision of how much repair time to

[1]As a general matter, the cost you incur in paying your mechanic could also be viewed as an opportunity cost since when you hand over your money you forgo the opportunity to spend that money on something else. However, we will typically reserve the term *opportunity cost* for implicit or hidden costs such as your lost pizza delivery income, and not direct out-of-pocket expenses.

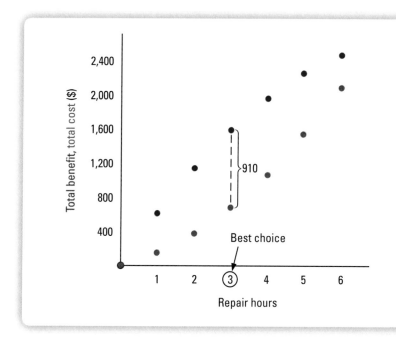

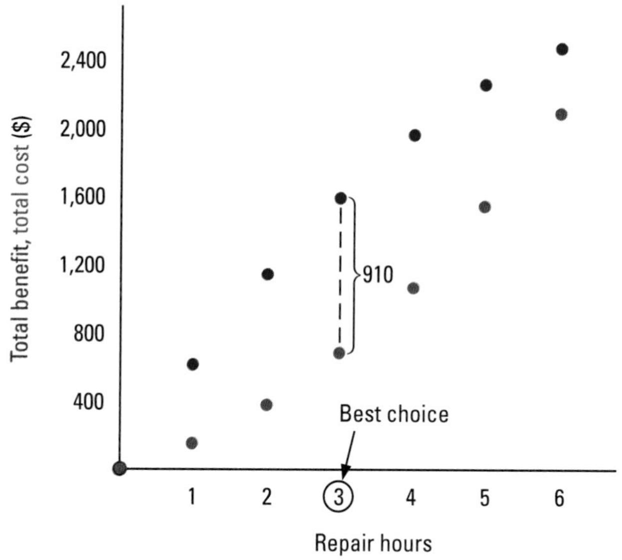

Figure 3.1

Total Benefit and Total Cost of Repairing Your Car. This figure shows the total benefits from Table 3.3 in blue and the total costs in red. The best choice is three hours, which results in a net benefit of $910. That is the number of hours at which the vertical distance between the blue and red dots is greatest.

invest in your Honda Civic. Originally, we assumed that you had to hire your mechanic in one-hour increments. But what if your mechanic charged by the quarter-hour, or even the minute? And what if you were doing the repair work yourself? Then you could even choose the number of seconds.

When a decision maker's choices are finely divisible, we can use total benefit and total cost curves to find the best choice. Figure 3.2(a) shows the total benefit curve for your car repair decision. The horizontal axis measures hours of your mechanic's time. The vertical axis measures in dollars the total benefit you derive (the increase in your car's value). To draw the figure, we assume that the total benefit with H hours of repair work is described by the function $B(H) = 654H - 40H^2$. (The total benefits in Table 3.1 correspond to the values of this function, rounded to the nearest \$5.) Note that the total benefit increases as the amount of repair work rises from zero to six hours.

Figure 3.2(b) shows the total cost curve. Here, we assume that the total cost of H hours of repair work is described by the function $C(H) = 110H + 40H^2$. (The total costs in Table 3.2 correspond to the values of this function, rounded to the nearest \$5.) In this case, the horizontal axis again measures repair hours and the vertical axis measures total cost in dollars. Just like total benefit, total cost increases as the amount of repair work rises from zero to six hours.

Figure 3.2(c) combines these two curves and identifies the best choice. The vertical axis measures total benefit and total cost in dollars. The best choice gives you the largest possible net benefit (total benefit less total cost). Graphically, that point is the number of hours at which the vertical distance between the total benefit and total cost curves is largest. In Figure 3.2(c), your best choice turns out to be 3.4 hours, at which point total benefit is \$1,761.20 and total cost is \$836.40. The difference between total benefit and total cost at 3.4 hours is \$924.80, the largest possible net benefit. With any other choice, the net benefit would be smaller.[2]

[2] This net benefit is larger than the largest net benefit in Table 3.3 and Figure 3.1, where repair hours could only be chosen in increments of an hour. Having more flexibility (the ability to hire your mechanic in finer increments) allows you to do better.

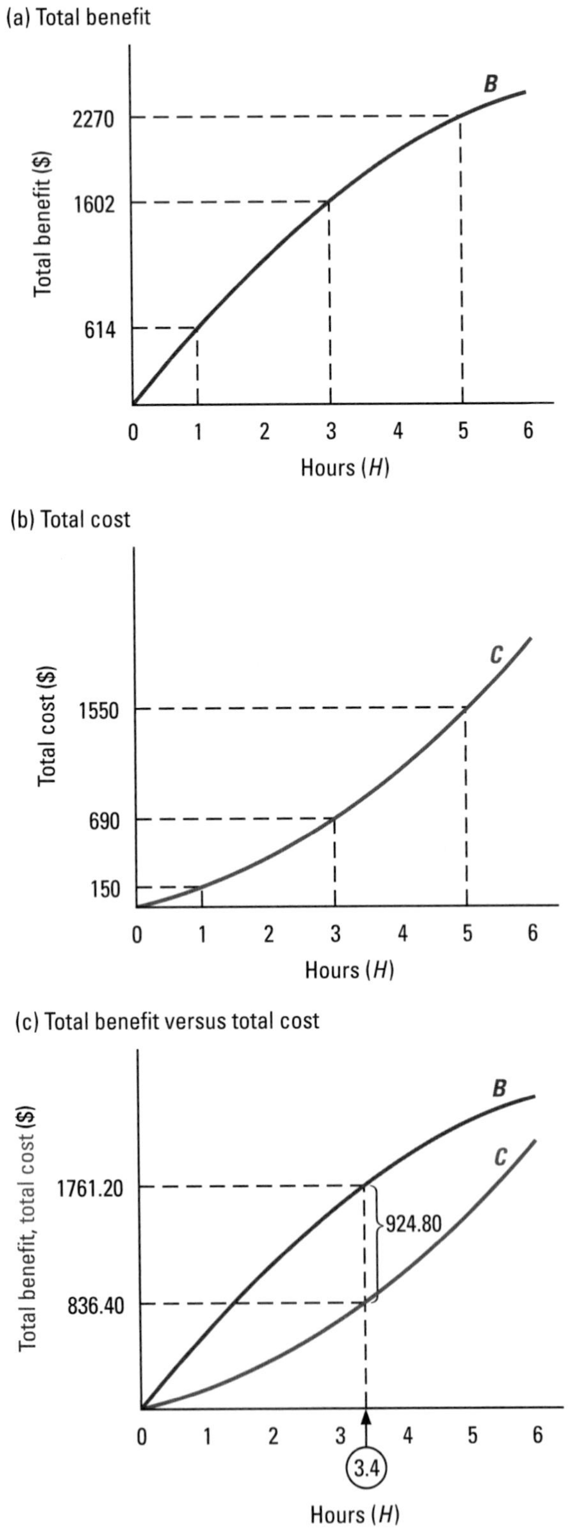

Figure 3.2

Total Benefit and Total Cost Curves When Repair Time Is Finely Divisible. The blue curve in (a) shows the total benefit from repairing your car for each amount of repair work between zero and six hours. It represents the total benefit function $B(H) = 654H - 40H^2$. The red curve in (b) shows the total cost of repairing your car for each amount of repair work between zero and six hours. It represents the total cost function $C(H) = 110H + 40H^2$. The two curves are combined in (c), which shows that the net benefit (which equals the vertical distance between the two curves at any given number of hours) is largest at a choice of 3.4 hours. In this case, total benefit is $1,761.20, total cost is $836.40, and net benefit is $924.80.

Figure 3.3 shows the net benefit, $B - C$, in the form of a curve (the horizontal axis again measures the number of repair hours, while the vertical axis now measures the net benefit, the difference between the total benefit and total cost). The best choice of 3.4 hours leads to the highest point on the curve.

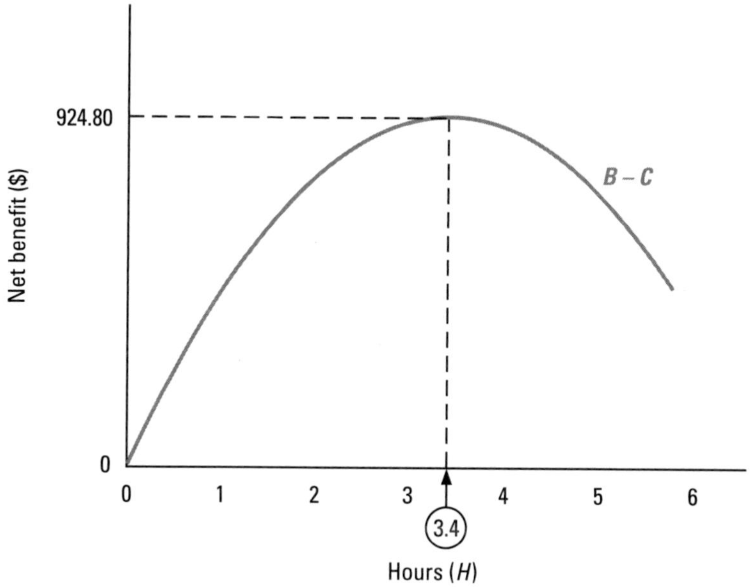

Figure 3.3
Net Benefit When Repair Time Is Finely Divisible. This figure shows the difference between the total benefit and total cost curves in Figure 3.2. Note that the curve is highest at a choice of 3.4 hours, the point here total benefit exceeds total cost by $924.80.

Application 3.1

Benefits and Costs of College Degree

What do Bill Gates and LeBron James have in common, aside from being very, very rich? The answer is that neither got a college degree.

Each year millions of high school students decide to go to college. Is a college degree a good investment for the typical student? The answer involves a comparison of the benefits and costs. While a college education has many benefits (for example, you will become a much more interesting dinner companion), we'll look only at its effects on lifetime earnings.

A recent U.S. Census Bureau report documents the average earnings of high school and college graduates of various ages (see Table 3.4).[3] Clearly college graduates earn quite a bit more than high school graduates. Over a lifetime,

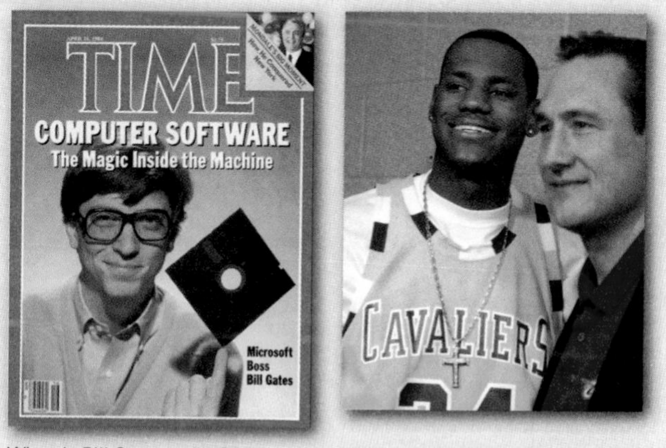

What do Bill Gates and LeBron James have in common?

[3]Jennifer C. Day and Eric C. Cheeseman, "The Big Payoff: Educational Attainment and Synthetic Estimates of Work-Life Earnings," U.S. Bureau of the Census, pp. 23–210 (www.census.gov/prod/2002pubs/p23-210.pdf).

the extra earnings are worth about $615,000 before taxes and about $430,000 after taxes.[4]

But what about the costs of attending college? One obvious cost is tuition, which varies tremendously. Public (state) colleges cost much less than private schools. For example, in 2006, a year at the University of Texas at Austin cost a Texas resident $5,314, while a year at a private college often cost more than $30,000. In fact, over 70 percent of four-year-college students attended colleges where tuition was less than $8,000. In addition, many students paid reduced tuition through their college's financial aid programs. On top of tuition, books cost them roughly $1,000 per year.

But tuition and books are *not* the only costs of going to college. There's also an important opportunity cost: while you're in college you probably can't hold a full-time job. According to Table 3.4, for an average high school graduate of age 25 to 29, this cost is roughly $25,000 per year, which comes to about $17,500 per year after taxes—far exceeding tuition costs for most students. (For college students younger than 25, the lost earnings are probably a little less than this.) On an after-tax basis, this opportunity cost raises the cost of a college education to roughly $100,000, or $200,000 for the most expensive private colleges. (If you can still work at a part-time job, that would reduce the opportunity cost below this amount.)

With a total benefit of over $400,000 and a total cost ranging from $100,000 to $200,000, going to college looks like a good decision![5]

What about Bill Gates and LeBron James? In some cases, the opportunity costs of going to college are so great that getting a degree doesn't make sense, at least not from the perspective of maximizing lifetime earnings. In 1975, Bill Gates dropped out of Harvard to start Microsoft. Had he stayed in school, he would probably have missed the opportunity to found the world's largest, most profitable software producer. More recently, when LeBron James decided to skip college and go directly to the NBA, he signed a three-year $12.96 million contract with the Cleveland Cavaliers, along with a highly lucrative endorsement deal with Nike. For both Bill Gates and LeBron James, the opportunity costs of a college degree were just too high relative to the benefits.[6]

The decision to go to college is a discrete decision, either you go or you don't, at least if you want to get the degree that comes with completing college. But college students make other, finely divisible decisions about their education nearly every day. For example, is it worthwhile studying another 15 minutes for next week's microeconomics test? Doing so has benefits (a better grade, better future job prospects, and greater understanding of the world) but also costs (less time for that pizza delivery job, sleep, or socializing). Making those decisions correctly involves a balancing of benefits and costs.

Table 3.4

Average Annual Earnings of High School and College Graduates

Age	High School Graduates	College Graduates
25–29	$24,997	$38,118
30–34	28,754	47,356
35–39	29,998	53,519
40–44	31,968	56,226
45–49	32,043	57,281
50–54	32,223	61,324
55–59	32,781	60,437
60–64	32,570	53,911

[4] In Chapter 10 we explain how to calculate the value of an income stream that is spread out over time.

[5] These estimates of the effect of a college degree on lifetime earnings have two shortcomings. First, the average income in Table 3.4 for a college graduate is the average for those individuals who have only a college degree, not a more advanced degree. As such, it overlooks the fact that getting a college degree gives you the option to get a more advanced degree that could further increase your lifetime earnings—and therefore it understates the true effect of a college degree on your lifetime earnings. On the other hand, it may also overstate the true increase in earnings that comes with a college degree. If smart people tend to get more education, and employers like to hire smart employees, part of the extra salary that college graduates earn may be due to their intelligence rather than to the extra time they spent in the classroom.

[6] Gates's future earnings from his decision to drop out of college were, however, uncertain. In Chapter 11, we'll discuss how to evaluate uncertain returns.

3.2 THINKING ON THE MARGIN

Another way to approach the maximization of net benefits involves thinking in terms of *marginal effects*. In fact, this is one of the most important ways in which you can learn to "think like an economist." In this section, we'll introduce the basic ideas behind marginal analysis. The chapter's appendix and Add-On 3A provide additional details, focusing in particular on the use of marginal analysis to find best choices, a topic that we discuss at the end of the section.

When economists think about a decision, they focus on its *marginal benefits* and *marginal costs*. Marginal benefits and marginal costs capture the way total benefit and cost *change* as the activity changes just a little bit. Consider again the decision of how much time your mechanic should spend repairing your car. Let H be the number of hours you choose. Marginal benefit and marginal cost measure how much your benefits and costs change due to a small change in repair time—the smallest change that is possible. We'll call the size of this smallest change ΔH. (The Greek symbol Δ, called *delta*, refers to a change in a variable.) In Table 3.1, $\Delta H = 1$, since your mechanic charged for her time in one-hour increments. If instead she were to charge in half-hour increments, then ΔH would equal 0.5. When you are purchasing H hours of repair time, the last ΔH hours you purchase are called the marginal units of repair time. More generally, for any action choice X, the **marginal units** are the last ΔX units, where ΔX is the smallest amount you can add or subtract.

The **marginal units** of action choice X are the last ΔX units, where ΔX is the smallest amount you can add or subtract.

Marginal Cost

Let's look first at your marginal cost, MC. Marginal cost measures the additional cost you incur because of the last ΔH hours of repair time (the marginal units of repair time). Specifically, suppose that $C(H)$ is the total cost of H hours of repair work. [For example, in Table 3.2, the total cost of three hours of repair work is $C(3) = \$690$.] When you are getting H hours of repair work, the extra cost due to the last ΔH hours is $\Delta C = C(H) - C(H - \Delta H)$, which is the amount it costs to get H hours of repair time less the amount it costs to get only $H - \Delta H$ hours.

This is simple enough. The only added complication is that economists measure marginal cost on a *per unit* basis. That is, MC measures the extra cost due to your last ΔH hours of repair time per hour of extra repair time. To obtain this measure, we divide the extra cost by the number of marginal hours, ΔH:

$$MC = \frac{\Delta C}{\Delta H} = \frac{C(H) - C(H - \Delta H)}{\Delta H} \quad (1)$$

This expression tells us how much marginal repair time costs *per hour*. More generally, the **marginal cost of an action** at an activity level of X units is equal to the extra cost incurred due to the marginal units, $C(X) - C(X - \Delta X)$, divided by the number of marginal units, ΔX. That is, $MC = [C(X) - C(X - \Delta X)]/\Delta X$.

The **marginal cost of an action** at an activity level of X units is equal to the extra cost incurred due to the marginal units, $C(X) - C(X - \Delta X)$, divided by the number of marginal units, ΔX.

If measuring the change in cost on a per-unit basis seems confusing, consider a familiar example. Imagine that you're in the supermarket, trying to decide between a one-pound jar of peanut butter that costs \$1 and a one-and-one-half-pound jar that costs \$1.25. Is the larger jar a good deal? That depends on how much the extra peanut butter you get costs per pound. If you choose the larger jar, you're getting an extra one-half pound of

Table 3.5
Total Cost and Marginal Cost of Repairing Your Car

Repair Time (Hours)	Total Cost ($)	Marginal Cost (MC) ($/hour)
0	$0	—
1	150	$150
2	380	230
3	690	310
4	1,080	390
5	1,550	470
6	2,100	550

peanut butter for an extra $0.25. So the extra peanut butter costs only $0.50 per pound ($0.25 divided by one-half pound). When we calculate the marginal cost of repair time using formula (1), we're doing the same thing: we measure the additional cost of the marginal units on a per-unit basis.

Table 3.5 shows the total cost and marginal cost of repair work for each possible number of hours. Since you can vary repair work in one-hour increments ($\Delta H = 1$), formula (1) in this case simplifies to $MC = C(H) - C(H - 1)$. So the entries in the marginal cost column are just the change in cost due to the last hour of time purchased (represented graphically by the dashed arrows). For example, your marginal cost when you choose three hours of repair work ($H = 3$) is $C(3) - C(2) = 690 - 380 = \$310$ per hour.

Marginal Benefit

We can find the marginal benefit of repair work in a similar way. Suppose that $B(H)$ is the total benefit of H hours of repair work. Then when you choose H hours of repair work, the extra benefit from the last ΔH hours is $\Delta B = B(H) - B(H - \Delta H)$. Dividing by ΔH expresses this change on a per-hour basis, which gives the marginal benefit:

$$MB = \frac{\Delta B}{\Delta H} = \frac{B(H) - B(H - \Delta H)}{\Delta H} \qquad \textbf{(2)}$$

The **marginal benefit of an action** at an activity level of X units is equal to the extra benefit produced by the marginal units, $B(X) - B(X - \Delta X)$, divided by the number of marginal units, ΔX.

More generally, the **marginal benefit of an action** at an activity level of X units is equal to the extra benefit produced by the ΔX marginal units, measured on a per-unit basis. That is, $MB = \Delta B/\Delta X = [B(X) - B(X - \Delta X)]/\Delta X$.

Table 3.6 shows the total and marginal benefits for your car repair decision. The marginal benefit corresponds to formula (2) where $\Delta H = 1$, so $MB = B(H) - B(H - 1)$.

IN-TEXT EXERCISE 3.2 **Suppose you can hire your mechanic in quarter-hour increments. For repair work up to two hours, the total benefit (in dollars) is $B(0) = 0$, $B(0.25) = 30$, $B(0.5) = 60$, $B(0.75) = 90$, $B(1) = 120$, $B(1.25) = 140$, $B(1.5) = 160$, $B(1.75) = 180$, $B(2) = 200$. What is the marginal benefit of repair time (measured on a per-hour basis) at each of these possible choices?**

Table 3.6
Total Benefit and Marginal Benefit of Repairing Your Car

Repair Time (Hours)	Total Benefit ($)	Marginal Benefit (MB) ($/hour)
0	$0	—
1	615	$615
2	1,150	535
3	1,600	450
4	1,975	375
5	2,270	295
6	2,485	215

Best Choices and Marginal Analysis

By comparing marginal benefits and marginal costs, we can determine whether an increase or a decrease in the level of an activity raises or lowers the net benefit. For an illustration, look at Table 3.7, which lists together the marginal benefits and marginal costs shown in Tables 3.5 and 3.6. Suppose you are wondering whether one hour of repair work is better than zero. According to the table, the marginal benefit of the first hour is $615, while the marginal cost is $150. Since 615 is larger than 150 (as indicated by the ">" sign in the table), one hour of repair work is better than none—you come out ahead by $465 (that is, $615 – $150). Next, suppose you're thinking about hiring your mechanic for five hours. Is the last hour worthwhile? According to the table, the marginal benefit of the fifth hour is $295, which is less than the marginal cost ($470). So it's better to hire your mechanic for four hours than for five—you lose $175 ($470 – $295) on the fifth hour.

Whenever someone chooses the best level of an activity, a small change in the activity level can't increase the net benefit (if it did, it wouldn't be a best choice!). We call this the

Table 3.7
Marginal Benefit and Marginal Cost of Repairing Your Car

	RepairTime (Hours)	Marginal Benefit (MB) ($/hour)		Marginal Cost (MC) ($/hour)
	0	—		—
	1	$615	>	$150
	2	535	>	230
Best choice →	(3)	450	>	310
	4	375	<	390
	5	295	<	470
	6	215	<	550

No Marginal Improvement Principle. This principle tells us that, at a best choice, the marginal benefit of the *last* unit must be at least as large as the marginal cost, and the marginal benefit of the *next* unit must be no greater than the marginal cost. The reason is simple. If the marginal benefit of the last unit were less than the marginal cost, net benefit would be increased by reducing the activity level by one unit. Similarly, if the marginal benefit of the next unit were greater than the marginal cost, the net benefit would be increased by increasing the activity level by one unit. In either case, the original activity level (before adding or subtracting a unit) wouldn't have been a best choice.

For an illustration, look again at Table 3.7. As you saw in Table 3.3, the best choice is three hours. Notice that the marginal benefit of the third hour exceeds the marginal cost (\$450 versus \$310), and the marginal benefit of the fourth hour is less than the marginal cost (\$375 versus \$390).

In a little while, we'll see that the No Marginal Improvement Principle has many useful implications and can even help us identify best choices. Before illustrating those points, though, we'll first show how to extend its logic to situations in which action choices are finely divisible.

Marginal Benefit and Marginal Cost with Finely Divisible Actions

Now let's examine these same concepts in a setting with finely divisible choices. We'll begin with marginal benefit. Figure 3.4 shows again the total benefit curve from Figure 3.2(a). Suppose we pick any point on the curve, such as the point D associated with H hours (see the figure). The total benefit, $B(H)$, is measured on the vertical axis. When hours are finely divisible, so that the smallest amount of time we can add or subtract is very tiny, what is the marginal benefit of a mechanic hired for H hours?

Figure 3.4

Using the Total Benefit Curve to Find the Marginal Benefit. When actions are finely divisible, the marginal benefit at H hours of repair time is equal to the slope of the line drawn tangent to the total benefit function at point D (shown in this figure as a solid black line) and often called simply the *slope of the total benefit curve* at point D. The light and dark gray lines show why this is so. Their slopes are equal to the marginal benefit for two sizes of the marginal units, $\Delta H'$ and $\Delta H''$, that are not tiny. As the size of the marginal unit grows smaller, the slope comes closer and closer to the slope of the solid black line.

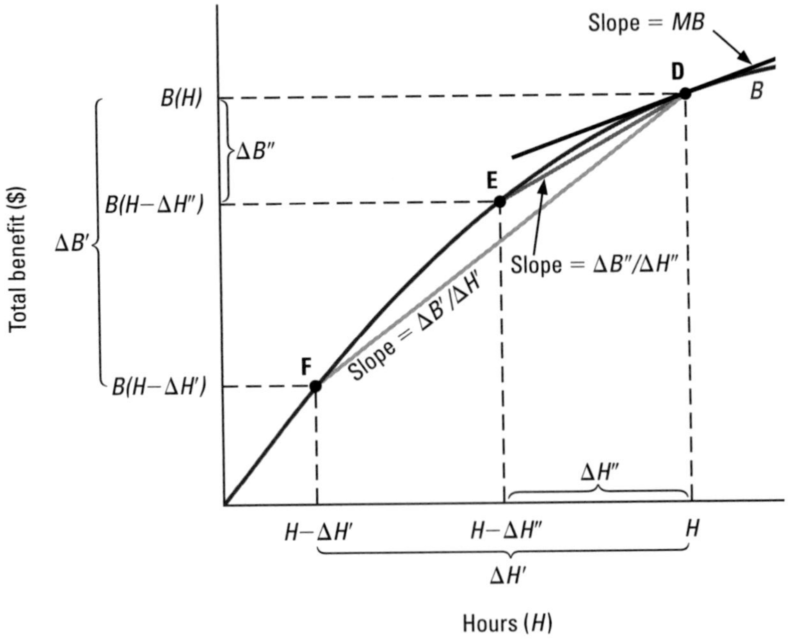

Whatever the size of the smallest possible change in hours, the marginal benefit equals "rise over run" along the total benefit curve. To illustrate, suppose the smallest possible change is $\Delta H'$. Adding the last $\Delta H'$ hours of repair time involves a movement along the total benefit curve from point F to point D in Figure 3.4. This change increases the total benefit by the amount $\Delta B' = B(H) - B(H - \Delta H')$, shown along the vertical axis in the figure. The marginal benefit, $MB = \Delta B'/\Delta H'$, therefore equals the vertical rise divided by the horizontal run along the total benefit curve between points F and D; it is the slope of the straight light gray line connecting these two points. Similarly, if the size of the marginal change is instead the smaller amount $\Delta H''$ (see the figure), the marginal benefit would then be $\Delta B''/\Delta H'' = [B(H) - B(H - \Delta H'')]/\Delta H''$, which equals rise over run along the total benefit curve between points D and E. In other words, the marginal benefit is then the slope of the straight dark gray line connecting points D and E.

In Figure 3.4, we have drawn a straight black line through point D, the slope of which equals rise over run—equivalently, marginal benefit—for very tiny changes in hours, starting from point D. (Notice that the straight gray lines would become closer and closer to the straight black line if we considered smaller and smaller changes in hours.) That black line is said to be *tangent* to the total benefit curve at point D.[7] Accordingly, when goods are finely divisible, the marginal benefit at any given point equals the slope of the straight line that is tangent to the curve at that point. A common shorthand expression, which we'll often use, is to say that the slope of the line that is tangent to a curve at a point is "the slope of the curve" at that point. Using this language, we can restate our conclusion in this simple way: *the marginal benefit with H hours of repair time in Figure 3.4 equals the slope of the total benefit curve at point D.*

Intuitively, the slope of the total benefit curve at D captures the rate at which benefits change with small changes in the amount of repair work starting at H hours. If the curve is steep (a large slope), then benefits increase rapidly when the number of hours increases a little, and the marginal benefit is large; if it is flat (a small slope), then benefits increase slowly when the number of hours increases a little, and the marginal benefit is small. This relationship is summarized as follows:

The Relationship between Marginal Benefit and the Total Benefit Curve
When actions are finely divisible, the marginal benefit when choosing action X is equal to the slope of the total benefit curve at X.

The exact same principle governs the relationship between marginal cost and the total cost curve:

The Relationship between Marginal Cost and the Total Cost Curve
When actions are finely divisible, the marginal cost when choosing action X is equal to the slope of the total cost curve at X.

Marginal Benefit and Marginal Cost Curves By computing the marginal benefit at many different levels of H, we can graph the marginal benefit curve. Figure 3.5(b)

[7]In mathematics, a line is said to be tangent to a curve at a point if its slope equals the rise over the run for very small changes along the curve starting at the point. (If you know calculus, you will recognize the slope of the line tangent to a point on a curve as the derivative of the curve at that point.)

Figure 3.5

The Total and Marginal Benefit Curves When Repair Time Is Finely Divisible. Figure (a) reproduces the total benefit curve in Figure 3.2(a), adding tangents to the total benefit curve at three different numbers of hours ($H = 1$, $H = 3$, $H = 5$). The slope of each tangent equals the marginal benefit at each number of hours. Figure (b) shows the marginal benefit curve: note how the marginal benefit varies with the number of hours. This marginal benefit curve is described by the function $MB(H) = 654 - 80H$.

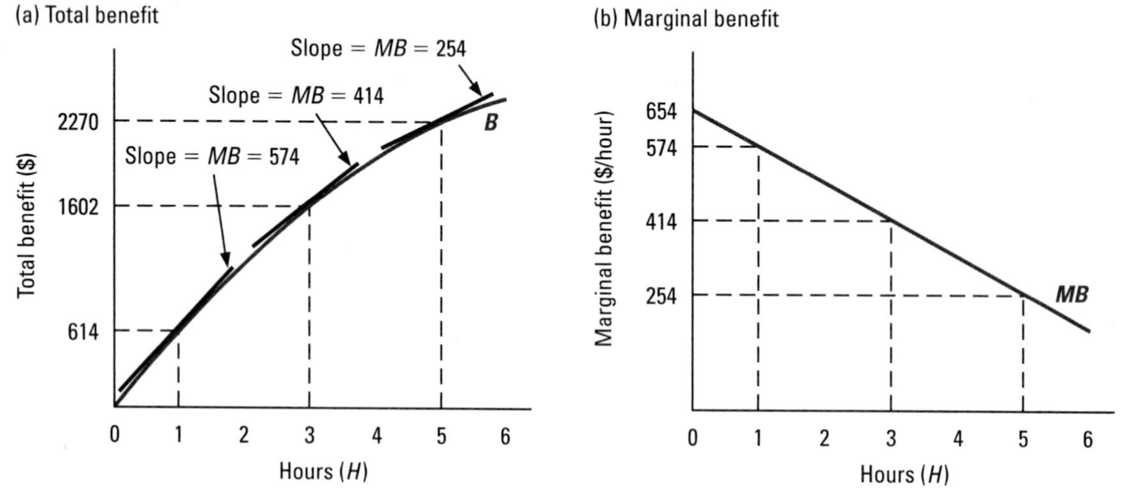

shows the marginal benefit curve for the total benefit curve in Figure 3.4, reproduced in Figure 3.5(a). In Figure 3.5(a), we've drawn straight lines tangent to the total benefit curve at three different numbers of hours: $H = 1$, $H = 3$, and $H = 5$. The slope of each line equals the marginal benefit at each of those levels. Figure 3.5(b) plots the marginal benefit at those levels and others. Note that the marginal benefit curve slopes downward. In other words, marginal benefit shrinks as the amount of repair work increases. This reflects the fact that the tangent lines in Figure 3.5(a) become flatter as we move from left to right along the total benefit curve.

The same idea applies for graphing the marginal cost curve. Figure 3.6(a) reproduces the total cost curve from Figure 3.2(b), with the addition of tangent lines at $H = 1$, $H = 3$, and $H = 5$. The slope of each tangent line tells us the marginal cost at each of those levels. Figure 3.6(b) shows the marginal cost at those levels and others. Note that the marginal cost curve slopes upward. In other words, marginal cost grows larger as the amount of repair work increases. This reflects the fact that the tangent lines in Figure 3.6(a) become steeper as we move from left to right along the total cost curve.

We can describe the particular marginal benefit and cost curves shown in Figures 3.5(b) and 3.6(b) by the functions $MB(H) = 654 - 80H$ and $MC(H) = 110 + 80H$, respectively. How do we know this? Economists usually find formulas for marginal benefits and marginal costs using calculus. The marginal benefit is the derivative of the total benefit function, and the marginal cost is the derivative of the marginal cost function. In this book we do not assume that you know calculus, so whenever you need a marginal benefit or marginal cost function, we will tell you what it is. (If you do know calculus,

Figure 3.6

The Total and Marginal Cost Curves When Repair Time Is Finely Divisible. Figure (a) reproduces the total cost curve in Figure 3.2(b), adding tangents to the total cost curve at three different numbers of hours ($H = 1$, $H = 3$, $H = 5$). The slope of each tangent equals the marginal cost at each number of hours. Figure (b) shows the marginal cost curve: note how the marginal cost varies with the number of hours. This marginal cost curve is described by the function $MC(H) = 110 + 80H$.

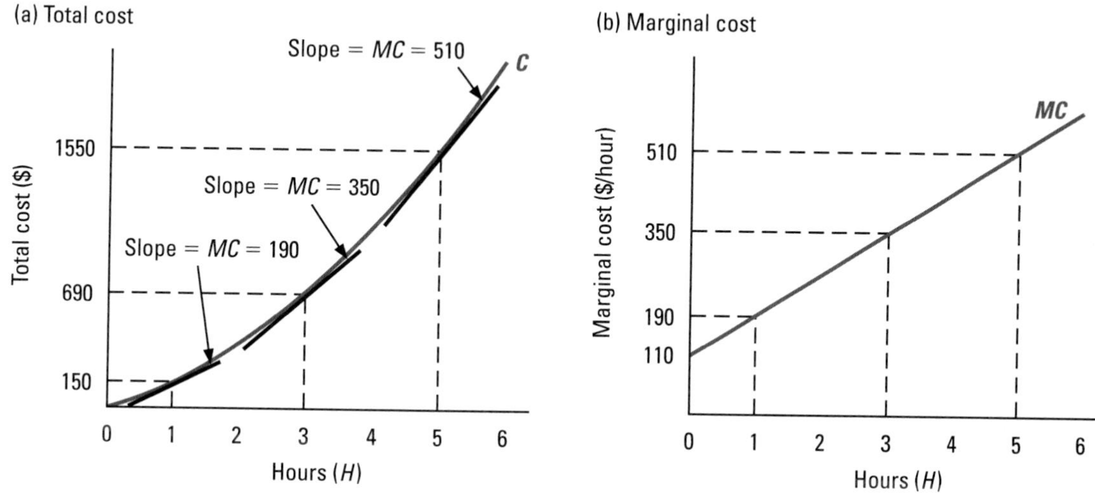

you can use these functions to check your own calculations of the marginal benefit and marginal cost.) You need to understand only (a) what marginal benefit and cost mean and (b) that they are equal to the slopes of the total benefit and cost curves.

Best Choices and Marginal Analysis with Finely Divisible Actions

What can we say about the relationship between marginal benefits and marginal costs at best choices when actions are finely divisible? In that case, we have an even simpler version of the No Marginal Improvement Principle:[8]

The No Marginal Improvement Principle (for Finely Divisible Actions)
If actions are finely divisible, then marginal benefit equals marginal cost ($MB = MC$) at any best choice at which it is possible to both increase and decrease the level of the activity a little bit.

The logic of this principle is again simple. Suppose that action X^* is the best choice. If it is possible to increase the activity level slightly from X^*, then MB must be no greater than MC at X^*. If it were greater (if $MB > MC$), then a small increase in the activity level

[8]If you've had calculus, you will recognize the No Marginal Improvement Principle for Finely Divisible Actions as the first-order condition for a maximum. Specifically, when we are choosing H to maximize the function $B(H) - C(H)$, the first-order condition says that $B'(H) = C'(H)$; that is, marginal benefit must equal marginal cost.

Figure 3.7

Marginal Benefit Equals Marginal Cost at a Best Choice. At the best choice of 3.4 hours, the No Marginal Improvement Principle holds, so $MB = MC$. At any number of hours below 3.4, marginal benefit exceeds marginal cost, so that a small increase in repair time will improve the net benefit (as indicated by the rightward pointing arrow on the horizontal axis). At any number of hours above 3.4, marginal cost exceeds marginal benefit, so that a small decrease in repair time will improve net benefit (as indicated by the leftward pointing arrow on the horizontal axis.)

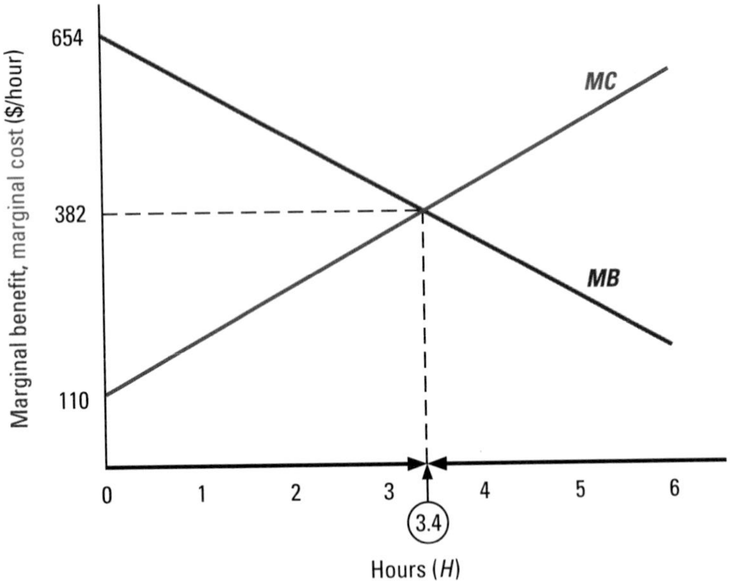

would increase the net benefit. Action X^* would not have been a best choice. Likewise, if it is possible to decrease the activity level slightly from X^*, then MB must be no less than MC at X^*. If it were less (if $MB < MC$), then a small decrease in the activity level would increase the net benefit. Again, action X^* would not have been a best choice. Putting these two facts together, if it is possible to both increase and decrease the activity level from some best choice X^*, we must have $MB = MC$ at X^*.

To illustrate, consider again your car repair problem. Recall that the best choice, as shown in Figure 3.2(c), is to hire your mechanic for 3.4 hours. Figure 3.7 combines the marginal benefit and marginal cost curves from Figures 3.5(b) and 3.6(b). Note that marginal benefit equals marginal cost (visually, the two curves intersect) at $H = 3.4$. When H is less than 3.4, marginal benefit is greater than marginal cost, so an increase in H makes you better off (as indicated by the rightward pointing arrow on the horizontal axis). When H is greater than 3.4, marginal benefit is less than marginal cost, so a decrease in H makes you better off (as indicated by the leftward pointing arrow on the horizontal axis).

Figure 3.8 (like Figure 3.2) shows the total benefit and total cost curves for this decision. Since marginal benefit and marginal cost are equal at the best choice of $H = 3.4$, the slopes of the total benefit and total cost curves at that point must be equal. That is, the tangent lines to the two curves at 3.4 hours must be parallel, as shown in the figure. If that were not the case, then by varying the number of hours in one direction or the other we could increase the distance between the total benefit and total cost curves—and thus the net benefit.

The No Marginal Improvement Principle has numerous important applications in microeconomics. Application 3.2 provides an illustration. You'll see many others throughout this book.

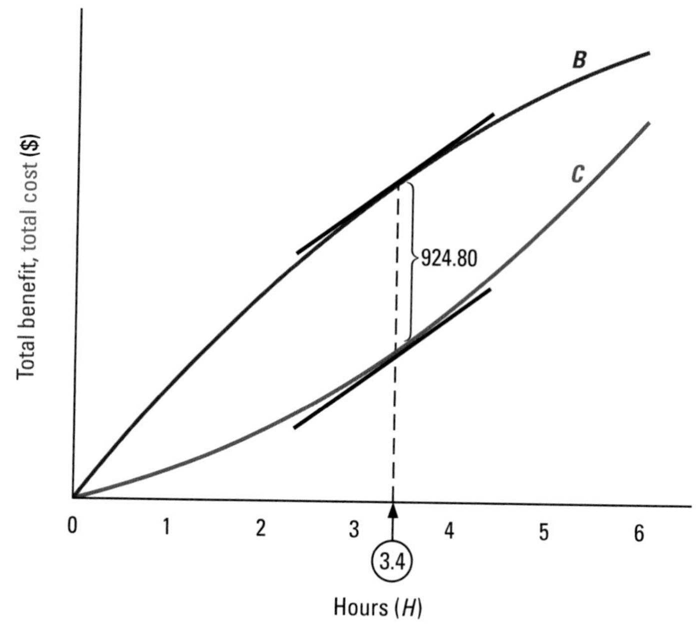

Figure 3.8

Tangents to the Total Benefit and Total Cost Curves at the Best Choice. At the best choice of $H = 3.4$, the tangents to the total benefit and cost curves have the same slope and are therefore parallel. Marginal benefit, therefore, equals marginal cost.

Application 3.2

The Value of a Highway Construction Project

Every day millions of Americans find themselves stuck in traffic. Drivers in many major U.S. cities spend more than 40 hours a year in traffic jams. In the San Bernardino-Riverside area of California, the worst in the country, the figure is closer to *75* hours a year. Similar delays are experienced by drivers in cities such as Toronto, Paris, Mexico City, and Tokyo.

One way that governments try to alleviate traffic jams is by building new highways. These projects can be costly. (At one extreme, the Big Dig in Boston, in which the major highway passing through

A Los Angeles traffic jam

Boston was expanded and put underground and a new harbor tunnel was built, cost more than $14 billion.) Are they worth it? To answer that question, we need to put a dollar value on the time savings from reduced traffic congestion.[9]

If a commuter gains an hour a week because of reduced traffic congestion, what is it worth to him? Does this depend on how he would spend the hour? Would the answer be different depending, for example, on whether he would choose to take an extra hour of leisure or work an extra hour to earn more income?

[9]Time savings is just one component, although usually the most important, of the benefits that arise from these projects. They can also result in improved safety, reduced air pollution, and reduced fuel use.

Fortunately, marginal analysis can help us here. Consider an individual who is allocating his time between two activities, leisure and work, and is free to choose the number of hours he devotes to each (he either has a job with flexible work hours or can choose among jobs with different numbers of hours). The No Marginal Improvement Principle tells us that if he is allocating his time optimally, then his marginal benefit of leisure must equal its marginal cost. The marginal cost of leisure is an opportunity cost—the lost benefit from not being able to spend that hour at work, earning more money. Thus, the No Marginal Improvement Principle tells us that the value of an extra hour spent on leisure must equal the value of an extra hour spent working. In fact, the same logic applies regardless of how many different ways the commuter spends his time: any activity that he can slightly increase or decrease must have a marginal value equal to the value of an extra hour spent working. Thus, the No Marginal Improvement Principle tells us that the value of that extra hour saved in commuting equals the value he would derive by using it to work.

What is that value? If the commuter is not averse to his job, then the value of an extra hour spent working is exactly equal to his hourly wage, *W*. So the value of the hour saved in commuting is exactly his wage rate. What if he instead finds the marginal hour of work unpleasant? Then that hour will be worth less than *W* since the benefit from working an extra hour is the wage rate less the disutility from work.[10] In fact, studies that estimate individuals' values of time typically find values equal to about half of their wage rates, indicating that people are averse to work, at least on the margin.

Measured in this way, the value of time lost due to traffic congestion is enormous. For example, a study by the Texas Transportation Institute estimated that in 2003 the time lost due to traffic congestion in the United States was worth more than $56 billion.

Finding Best Choices Using Marginal Analysis

One of the most useful applications of the No Marginal Improvement Principle is the problem of finding a best choice. When there are just a few possible choices, finding a best choice is a relatively simple matter. We can just compare total benefits and costs directly, as we did in Table 3.3. With more, but still a limited number of, choices, we could instead do this by creating a spreadsheet. However, when choices are finely divisible, it becomes much more difficult and time consuming to precisely identify best choices in this way. It is then often both quicker and more exact to find the best choice by applying the No Marginal Improvement Principle. Here we show how to do this; the appendix to this chapter and Add-On 3A contain further details.

From the No Marginal Improvement Principle we know that, in searching for a best choice, we can limit our attention to activity levels at which either (a) $MB = MC$, or (b) it is impossible to both increase and decrease the activity level. Often, there are only a few activity levels that satisfy these conditions, and we can find the best choice by comparing the net benefit levels for each of them.

As an example, let's return to your car repair problem. Recall that we can describe the marginal benefits and marginal costs shown in Figures 3.5–3.7 by the functions $MB(H) = 654 - 80H$ and $MC(H) = 110 + 80H$. Worked-out problem 3.1 shows how to solve for your best choice using these functions.

[10]Matters are more complicated if the commuter can't adjust the amount of time he spends working. For example, if he must work 40 hours a week, then the marginal benefit from other activities need not equal the value he derives from his last hour of work (that is, the No Marginal Improvement Principle does not apply). In that case, the value of the hour saved in commuting could, in principle, exceed his hourly wage.

WORKED-OUT PROBLEM 3.1

The Problem Suppose that you can hire a mechanic to work on your car for up to six hours. The total cost of repair work is $C(H) = 110H + 40H^2$ and the total benefit is $B(H) = 654H - 40H^2$, where H is the number of hours. The marginal cost is $MC(H) = 110 + 80H$ and the marginal benefit is $MB(H) = 654 - 80H$. What is your best choice?

The Solution Any number of repair hours, H, at which $MB = MC$ solves the equation

$$654 - 80H = 110 + 80H$$

The only solution to this equation is $H = 3.4$. So the best choice is either 3.4 hours, 0 hours (since it is then impossible to reduce hours), or 6 hours (since it is then impossible to increase hours). Your net benefit is \$924.80 for $H = 3.4$, \$0 for $H = 0$, and \$385 for $H = 6$ (where, as in Table 3.3, we have rounded to the nearest \$5 for $H = 6$). So your best choice is to hire your mechanic for 3.4 hours.

IN-TEXT EXERCISE 3.3 **Suppose that you can hire a mechanic to work on your car for up to six hours. The total cost of repair work is $C(H) = 110H + 24H^2$ and the total benefit is $B(H) = 654H - 40H^2$, where H is the number of hours. The marginal cost is $MC(H) = 110 + 48H$ and the marginal benefit is $MB(H) = 654 - 80H$. What is your best choice?**

3.3 SUNK COSTS AND DECISION MAKING

Sometimes a decision is associated with costs that the decision maker has already incurred or to which she has previously committed. At the time she makes her choice, they are unavoidable regardless of what she does. These are called **sunk costs**. For example, suppose that, in addition to the charges discussed earlier, your mechanic collects a \$500 nonrefundable fee when you reserve her time. If you've already paid the \$500 fee, it's a sunk cost. You cannot avoid it even if you subsequently decide not to repair your car. As another example, imagine that you still owe your mechanic \$500 from fixing your transmission three weeks ago. Now you are trying to decide whether to hire her again to work on your car before you sell it. Once again, that \$500 is a sunk cost.

A **sunk cost** is a cost that the decision maker has already incurred, or to which she has previously committed. It is unavoidable.

A sunk cost has *no effect on your best choice*, even though it increases the total costs of repairing your car. Figure 3.9 illustrates this point. It shows the same benefit function as in Figure 3.2(a). In addition, the light red total cost function, labeled C, adds a \$500 sunk cost to the cost function from Figure 3.2(b). (We'll talk about the dark red total cost function labeled C' soon.) The sunk cost shifts the total cost function up by \$500, reducing the distance between the total benefit and total cost curves by \$500 at every number of hours. As the figure shows, the vertical distance between the total benefit function and the light red total cost function is still largest at $H = 3.4$. Including the \$500 sunk cost, the net benefit is \$424.80 (\$500 less than before).

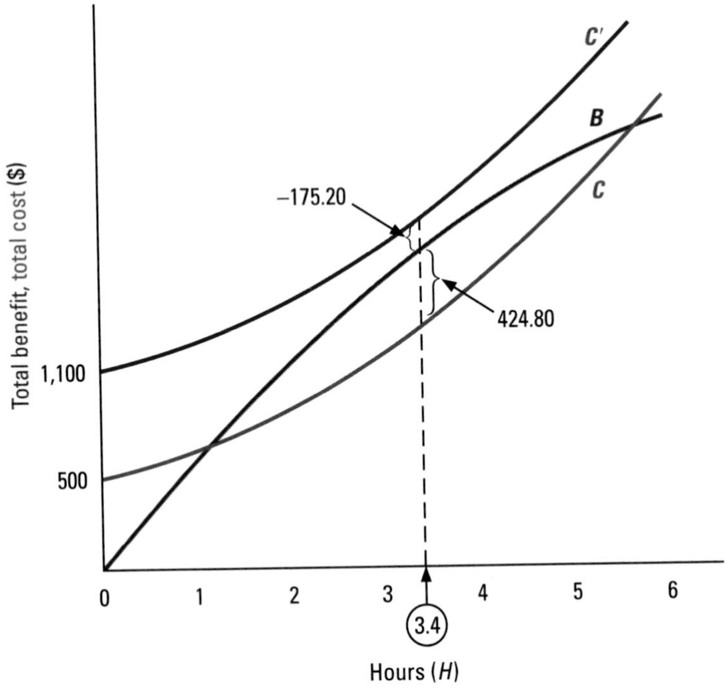

Figure 3.9

Finding a Best Choice with a Sunk Cost. This figure shows a cost-benefit comparison for two possible cost functions with sunk fixed costs. The light red cost curve has a \$500 sunk cost, while the dark red cost curve has an \$1,100 sunk cost. In both cases, the best choice is $H = 3.4$; the level of sunk costs has no effect on the best choice.

This point also follows from thinking on the margin: because you must pay the \$500 sunk cost regardless of the number of hours of repair work you choose, it has no effect on *marginal costs*. The marginal benefit and marginal cost curves are exactly the same as they were in Figure 3.7 without the \$500 sunk cost, so your best choice doesn't change.

In fact, the same conclusion would hold even if the sunk cost was large enough to make your total cost exceed your total benefit. For example, the dark red cost function labeled C′ in Figure 3.9 adds an \$1,100 sunk cost to the cost function from Figure 3.2(b). With the \$1,100 sunk cost, the net benefit from choosing 3.4 hours of repair work is −\$175.20. Nonetheless, this is the best you can do. Given the nonrefundable fee, your net loss is even greater with any other choice.

This observation reflects a general point: *sunk costs never affect a decision maker's best choice*. They are "water under the bridge," as the common saying goes. An implication of this fact is that a decision maker can always make the correct decision by simply ignoring sunk costs—that is, by pretending they are zero.

While sunk costs don't affect a decision maker's best choice, the *sinking* of a cost *can* matter. For example, until you reserve your mechanic's time, you can avoid her nonrefundable fee. In that case, if the fee is large enough, it *can* change your best choice. For instance, if her fixed fee is \$1,100, your best choice if you have not yet made a reservation is to do no repair work. But once you have made a reservation and sunk the \$1,100, your best choice is to employ her for 3.4 hours. (Before you pay the nonrefundable fee, it is known as an *avoidable fixed cost*. For more on avoidable fixed costs, see Add-On 3A.)

Application 3.3

The Chunnel—A Really Sunk Cost

Construction of the Chunnel

In 1802 Albert Mathieu completed plans for connecting England and France via a tunnel under the English Channel. Work on the tunnel began in the early 1880s, only to be abandoned after 11,500 feet because of British fears of an invasion. The project languished until 1984, when Prime Minister Margaret Thatcher of England and President Francois Mitterrand of France revived it.

The ground breaking for the privately financed 31-mile "Chunnel" occurred in 1987. Construction was expected to last six years and to cost roughly £3 billion (British pounds). The project's sponsors anticipated revenue of approximately £4 billion, and a net profit of £1 billion.[11,12]

By 1990, however, prospects did not look so rosy to the Chunnel's investors. Construction was taking longer than anticipated, and costs were escalating. The total estimated cost had risen to £4.5 billion, of which £2.5 billion had already been spent.

Had the project's sponsors foreseen these difficulties in 1987, their best choice would have been not to even start the project. But the £2.5 billion they had already spent by 1990 was a sunk cost, both literally (under the English Channel) and economically. It could not be recovered. Looking forward, investors were clearly better off spending another £2 billion to get the £4 billion in revenue, despite the fact that—including the costs they had already sunk—they would ultimately lose £0.5 billion.

[11]These projected revenues and costs were both uncertain and spread out over time. In Chapters 10 and 11, we will explain how to arrive at total benefit and cost figures in such cases.

[12]See Carmen Li and Bob Wearing, "The Financing and Financial Results of Eurotunnel: Retrospect and Prospect," November 2000, Working Paper No. 00/13, University of Essex.

CHAPTER SUMMARY

1. **Maximizing benefits less costs**

   a. Many economic decisions involve balancing benefits and costs to find a best choice.

   b. A best choice yields the highest net benefit (total benefit less total cost) of all possible alternatives.

2. **Thinking on the margin**

   a. Economists often think about a choice in terms of its marginal benefit and marginal cost, which capture the way benefits and costs change as the decision changes.

   b. The No Marginal Improvement Principle says that if an action is a best choice, then a small (marginal) increase or decrease in the activity level can't increase net benefit.

   c. When actions are finely divisible, the No Marginal Improvement Principle tells us that whenever it is possible to both increase and decrease the activity level a little bit starting at a best choice, marginal benefit equals marginal cost at that choice.

   d. The No Marginal Improvement Principle can be used to help identify best choices.

3. **Sunk costs and decision making**

   a. The size of a sunk cost has no effect on a decision maker's best choice. It is "water under the bridge." A decision maker can always make the correct choice by ignoring sunk costs.

   b. While sunk costs don't matter for a decision maker's best choice, the act of sinking a cost—which turns an avoidable cost into a sunk cost—*can* matter.

ADDITIONAL EXERCISES

Exercise 3.1: Suppose that the cost of hiring your mechanic (including the cost of parts) is \$200 an hour (she charges for her time in one-hour increments). Your benefits and other costs are the same as in Tables 3.1 and 3.2. Construct a table like Table 3.3. What is your best choice?

Exercise 3.2: Suppose that the cost of hiring your mechanic (including the cost of parts) is \$200 an hour up to four hours and \$300 an hour over four hours (she charges for her time in one-hour increments). Your benefits and other costs are the same as in Tables 3.1 and 3.2. Construct a table like Table 3.3. What is your best choice?

Exercise 3.3: What are the benefits you expect to derive and the costs you expect to incur from studying for the final exam in this course?

Exercise 3.4: Economist Milton Friedman is famous for claiming "There is no such thing as a free lunch." What did he mean?

Exercise 3.5: "If the cost of repairing your car goes up you should do less of it." Is this statement correct? If you think the answer is yes, explain why. If you think the answer is no, give an example in which the best choice is higher when cost is higher.

Exercise 3.6: Suppose you can hire your mechanic for up to six hours. The total benefit and total cost functions are $B(H) = 654H - 40H^2$ and $C(H) = 110H + 120H^2$. The corresponding formulas for marginal benefit and marginal cost are $MB(H) = 654 - 80H$ and $MC(H) = 110 + 240H$. What is your best choice?

Exercise 3.7: Suppose you can hire your mechanic for up to six hours. The total benefit and total cost functions are $B(H) = 420H - 40H^2$ and $C(H) = 100H + 120H^2$. The corresponding formulas for marginal benefit and marginal cost are $MB(H) = 420 - 80H$ and $MC(H) = 100 + 240H$. What is your best choice?

Exercise 3.8: Suppose you can hire your mechanic for up to six hours. The total benefit and total cost functions are $B(H) = 400\sqrt{H}$ and $C(H) = 100H$. The corresponding formulas for marginal benefit and marginal cost are $MB = 200/\sqrt{H}$ and $MC(H) = 100$. What is your best choice?

Exercise 3.9: What would be the best choice in worked-out problem 3.1 (page 81) after you have made an appointment that committed you to a \$1,500 nonrefundable fee? What would your net benefit be?

Exercise 3.10: Once the Chunnel investors (in Application 3.3 on page 83) had incurred expenses of £2.5 billion, at what projected total cost would they have decided to abandon the project?

Exercise 3.11: What would be the best choice in worked-out problem 3.2 (in the appendix) if a sunk cost of \$500 were added?

APPENDIX

FINDING A BEST CHOICE USING MARGINAL ANALYSIS

This appendix looks in more detail at how to use marginal analysis to find a best choice when actions are finely divisible.

A TWO-STEP PROCEDURE FOR FINDING A BEST CHOICE

Let's begin by introducing a couple of useful terms. An **interior action**, or **interior choice**, is an action at which it is possible to marginally increase or decrease the activity level. A **boundary action**, or **boundary choice**, is an action at which it is possible to change the activity level in only one direction. (This terminology refers to whether an action is on the inside or the boundary of the set of possible actions.) In your car repair problem, $H = 0$ and $H = 6$ are boundary choices; all repair choices between those two are interior choices.

An **interior action**, or **interior choice**, is an action at which it is possible to marginally increase or decrease the activity level. A **boundary action**, or **boundary choice**, is an action at which it is possible to change the activity level in only one direction.

A simple way to apply the No Marginal Improvement Principle to find a best choice when actions are finely divisible is to use the following two-step procedure, which looks first at interior choices and then at boundary choices:

Two-Step Procedure for Finding a Best Choice when Actions are Finely Divisible:

Step 1: Identify any interior actions that satisfy the No Marginal Improvement Principle. If more than one interior action satisfies $MB = MC$, determine which one is best (which produces the highest net benefit).

Step 2: Compare the net benefits at any boundary actions to the net benefit at the best interior action. The best choice is the action with the highest net benefit.

This two-step procedure is exactly the procedure we followed in Section 3.2 in finding your best choice for repairing your car. For step 1, we found that among the repair choices between zero and six hours, $MB = MC$ only at $H = 3.4$. For step 2, we then found that the net benefit at $H = 3.4$ (\$924.80) was larger than the net benefit at either $H = 0$ (\$0) or $H = 6$ (\$385, rounded to the nearest \$5), the two boundary choices. This meant that $H = 3.4$ was your best choice.

In your car repair problem, there was only one interior action at which $MB = MC$. Sometimes, however, there can be more than one. The two-step procedure described above allows for this possibility. To follow step 1 of the two-step procedure in those cases, we simply need to compare the net benefits of any of those choices to see which is best.

TWO SHORTCUTS

Sometimes there are shortcuts to the two-step procedure that can make finding a best choice easier. Here we describe two of them.

Eliminating Boundary Choices

The No Marginal Improvement Principle can be extended to cover boundary choices. Sometimes this provides a way to eliminate some or all boundary choices as possible best choices without actually calculating their net benefits.

To see how to extend the No Marginal Improvement Principle to boundary choices, recall how we found that $MB = MC$ at an interior best choice. First, we said that if it is possible to marginally increase your activity level at X^*, then MB must be no greater than MC at X^* if X^* is a best choice. If not (if $MB > MC$), then a small increase in the activity level would increase your net benefit. Then we said that if it is possible to marginally decrease your activity level at X^*, then MB must be no less than MC at X^* if X^* is a best choice. If not (if $MB < MC$), then a small decrease in the activity level would increase your net benefit. Together, these two facts implied that $MB = MC$ at an interior best choice, since both a marginal increase and a marginal decrease is possible in that case.

At a boundary choice, though, only one direction of change is possible. The above logic can therefore be applied to boundary choices in the following way:[13]

The No Marginal Improvement Principle for Boundary Choices (with Finely Divisible Actions) If boundary choice X^* is a best choice, then

- If only a marginal increase in the activity level is possible starting from X^*, then $MB \leq MC$ at X^*.
- If only a marginal decrease in the activity level is possible starting from X^*, then $MB \geq MC$ at X^*.

This provides another way to check whether a boundary choice could be best in step 2 of the two-step procedure. In particular, instead of comparing the net benefit of each boundary choice to the net benefit at the best interior choice, you can first eliminate from consideration any boundary choices that do not satisfy the No Marginal Improvement Principle for Boundary Choices. Having done so, you need only compare the net benefit of any remaining boundary choices to the net benefit of the best interior choice.

As an example, in your car repair problem neither $H = 0$ nor $H = 6$ satisfy the No Marginal Improvement Principle for Boundary Choices. At $H = 0$, it is possible to marginally increase the amount of repair work, but MB is bigger than MC, while at $H = 6$ it is possible to marginally decrease the amount of repair work, but MB is less than MC [see Figure 3.7 or note that $MB(0) = 654 > MC(0) = 110$ and that $MB(6) = 174 < MC(6)$

[13]If you are familiar with calculus, you will recognize this requirement as the first-order necessary condition for a maximum at a boundary point. Specifically, when we are choosing H to maximize the net benefit function $N(H) = B(H) - C(H)$ and the maximum occurs at a point where H can only be increased, then $B'(H) - C'(H) \leq 0$ (marginal benefit must not exceed marginal cost at the maximum). If the maximum occurs at a point where H can only be decreased, then $B'(H) - C'(H) \geq 0$ (marginal cost must not exceed marginal benefit at H).

= 590]. Thus, we know that neither $H = 0$ nor $H = 6$ can be a best choice without ever needing to calculate their net benefits and compare them to the net benefits at $H = 3.4$.

Sometimes applying the No Marginal Improvement Principle for both interior and boundary points is enough to conclude that the best choice is actually a boundary choice. Worked-out problem 3.2 provides an example.

WORKED-OUT PROBLEM 3.2

The Problem Suppose the marginal benefit and marginal cost curves for your car repair decision are as shown in Figure 3.10(a). What is your best choice?

The Answer The figure tells us that MC exceeds MB at every value of H. In this case, no value of H greater than zero can be a best choice since none satisfies the No Marginal Improvement Principle. $H = 0$ does satisfy the No Marginal Improvement Principle for Boundary Choices, since only marginal increases in hours are possible at this choice. Thus, $H = 0$ is the best choice.

IN-TEXT EXERCISE 3.4 **Suppose the marginal benefit and cost curves for your car repair decision are as shown in Figure 3.10(b). What is your best choice?**

Just like the No Marginal Improvement Principle discussed in Section 3.2 for interior choices, the No Marginal Improvement Principle for Boundary Choices has applications beyond just finding best choices. We'll see an example when we study so-called corner solutions to a consumer's choice problem in Chapter 5.

When Using the No Marginal Improvement Principle Is Enough

The two-step procedure uses the No Marginal Improvement Property, but also involves calculating and comparing the net benefits of interior and boundary choices. We've just seen, though, that sometimes using the No Marginal Improvement Principle (for both interior and boundary choices) alone is enough to identify the best choice. Is there any easy way to know that this is the case when confronting a particular problem? The following shortcut identifies a condition on marginal benefits and marginal costs that guarantees that using only the No Marginal Improvement Principle (for interior and boundary choices) is enough to find the best choice:

A Shortcut to the Two-Step Procedure for Finding a Best Choice when Actions Are Finely Divisible If MB grows smaller and MC grows larger as the activity level grows larger, then only one action satisfies the No Marginal Improvement Principle and it is the best choice.

This shortcut tells us, for example, that if MB grows smaller and MC grows larger as the activity level grows larger and you find an interior action that equates MB with MC in step 1 of the two-step procedure, you can stop: you have found the best choice.

Figure 3.10
Marginal Benefit and Marginal Cost Curves for Worked-Out Problem 3.2 and In-Text Exercise 3.4.

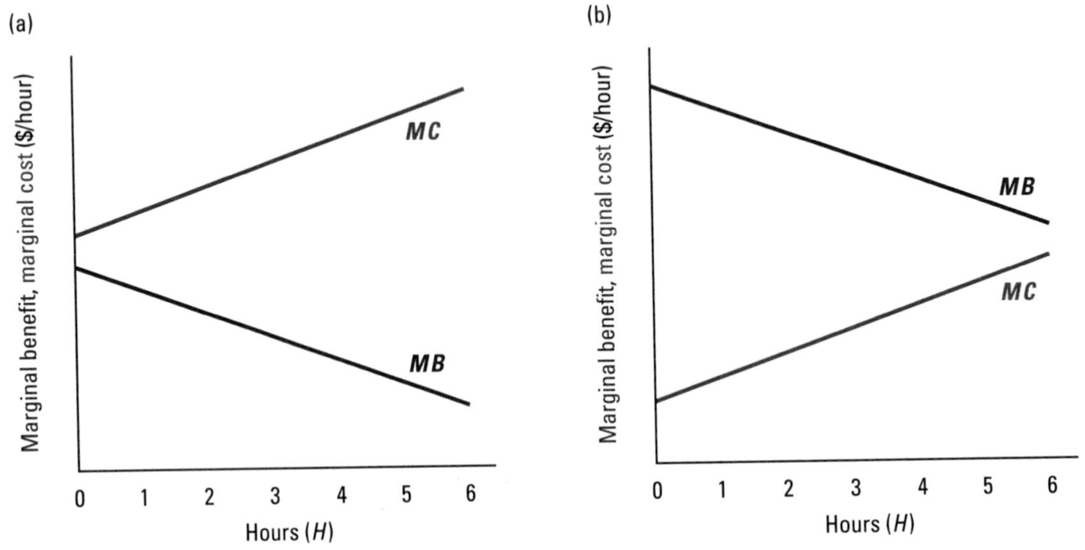

The reason this shortcut works can be seen by looking again at Figures 3.7 and 3.10. In each case, *MB* grows smaller and *MC* grows larger as the activity level grows larger. If there is an interior action at which $MB = MC$, as in Figure 3.7, then (1) no other interior action can have $MB = MC$; (2) at $H = 0$, $MB > MC$; and (3) at $H = 6$, $MB < MC$. As a result, no other choice—either interior or boundary—satisfies the No Marginal Improvement Principle. On the other hand, if there is no interior action at which $MB = MC$, as in Figures 3.10(a) and (b), then one and only one of the two boundary choices satisfies the No Marginal Improvement Principle [$H = 0$ in Figure 3.10(a) and $H = 6$ in Figure 3.10(b)]. That choice must be best.[14]

If you recognize that *MB* grows smaller and *MC* grows larger as the activity level grows larger, this shortcut can make finding a best choice much easier.

---

[14]In fact, the same shortcut works as long as the difference between *MB* and *MC*, $MB - MC$, grows smaller as the activity level grows larger. If you know calculus, you will recognize that this condition means that the net benefit, $N(H) = B(H) - C(H)$, is a strictly concave function. This follows since $N'(H) = MB - MC = B'(H) - C'(H)$, so $MB - MC$ decreases as the activity level grows larger when $N''(H) = B''(H) - C''(H) < 0$, which says that net benefit is a strictly concave function of *H*. So the shortcut amounts to using the *sufficient second-order condition*, which says that if the function being maximized is strictly concave, then any choice that satisfies the first-order condition must maximize the net benefit function.

ECONOMIC DECISION MAKING

part
II

Part II In the next ten chapters, we will study the principles of economic decision making. Part IIA covers decisions by consumers concerning the goods they purchase. Part IIB focuses on firms' decisions about the outputs they produce and the production methods they use. Part IIC examines a number of additional topics including decisions that involve time, uncertainty, and strategic interaction, as well as behavioral theories of economic decision making.

part

IIA

Consumption Decisions

In the next three chapters, we'll investigate the determinants of decisions involving consumption. We'll develop a theory of consumer behavior that helps us to understand and predict choices in a wide range of contexts and provides a solid foundation for evaluating the costs and benefits of public policies. In Chapter 4, we'll introduce some basic principles of decision making and explore the concept of consumer preferences. In Chapter 5, we'll investigate the role of prices and income in constraining consumers' available alternatives, and we'll explain how to identify a consumer's most preferred choice given these and other constraints. In Chapter 6, we'll use our theory of consumer behavior to explore the foundations of demand curve analysis and develop methods of measuring the costs and benefits of public policies.

chapters

PRINCIPLES AND PREFERENCES

4

LEARNING OBJECTIVES

After reading this chapter, students should be able to:

- Explain the Ranking Principle and the Choice Principle.
- Illustrate consumers' preferences for consumption-bundles graphically through indifference curves.
- Understand the properties and functions of indifference curves.
- Determine a consumer's willingness to trade one good for another by examining indifference curves.
- Explain the concept of utility and compare consumption bundles by calculating the numerical values of a given utility function.

If we know the price of a good, we can use its demand curve to determine the amount purchased. But the price isn't always obvious. Take the case of mobile (wireless) telephones. What's the price of service per minute of conversation? If you own a mobile phone, you know this simple question has no simple answer.

In 2006, one wireless company, Cingular, offered more than a dozen different calling plans, each with different prices for different circumstances. In one plan, customers paid a monthly fee of $59.99, received 900 "free" minutes for calls made on weekdays, and paid 40 cents per minute for additional time. In another plan, a monthly fee of $99.99 bought 2,000 free minutes, with additional time charged at 25 cents per minute.

Which price is the relevant one? Free minutes cost nothing—or do they? If a customer incurs a monthly fee of $59.99 and uses exactly 900 "free" minutes, isn't he paying just under 7 cents per minute? And what about additional minutes? Is the price 40 cents, 25 cents, or something else entirely? Even if we knew the demand curve for mobile telephone services, which price would we use to determine the amount purchased? The answers to these questions are far from obvious.

Predicting consumers' choices accurately in such situations is important both to businesses and to policymakers. It requires an understanding of consumer behavior that goes beyond simple demand curves. A general theory of consumer behavior is valuable for at least two other reasons. First, economists are often called on to evaluate the costs and benefits of public policies. For example, the government taxes many goods and services and uses the revenues to finance public activities such as police protection, education, and national defense. Weighing costs and benefits, do the expenditures on any given program benefit taxpayers? A general theory of consumer behavior allows us to determine whether these programs make consumers better or worse off, and by how much.

Second, in analyzing markets, we often make assumptions about the properties of demand. For example, we usually assume that demand curves slope downward. Is that reasonable? Why or why not? Do demand curves typically have any other properties that might be useful in business or policy applications? A general theory of consumer behavior can provide answers to these questions.

This is the first of three chapters on consumer behavior. By the end of Chapter 6, you'll be able to answer each of the questions posed above. In this chapter, we lay the foundations for a theory of consumer behavior by addressing four topics:

1. *Principles of decision making.* We'll introduce and discuss two basic principles of consumer decision making which hold that consumers' choices reflect meaningful preferences.
2. *Consumer preferences.* We'll develop useful ways to describe consumers' preferences graphically and identify some tastes that most consumers share.
3. *Substitution between goods.* All economic decisions involve trade-offs between different objectives. We'll show how to determine a consumer's willingness to trade one good for another by examining his preferences.
4. *Utility.* We'll introduce a concept called *utility*, which economists use to summarize everything we know about a consumer's preferences, including her willingness to substitute one good for another.

4.1 PRINCIPLES OF DECISION MAKING

Three friends order dinner at a restaurant. One picks a salad, another chooses a steak, and the third selects pasta. Why do the three make different choices? They don't pick their meals at random; their decisions reflect their likes and dislikes. Economists refer to likes and dislikes as **preferences**.

Preferences tell us about a consumer's likes and dislikes.

What do we know about consumer preferences? Clearly, different people like (and dislike) different things. Their reasons for preferring one alternative to another may or may not be practical or tangible. Sometimes, those reasons are personal, emotional, and intangible. For example, many people strongly prefer designer jeans to equally functional jeans with unfashionable labels. Even so, each person's preferences, whatever they are, should provide a coherent basis for comparing possible alternatives. This requirement leads to our first main assumption concerning consumer behavior.

The Ranking Principle A consumer can rank, in order of preference (though possibly with ties), all potentially available alternatives.

The Ranking Principle is a simple but important assumption. It tells us that the consumer has a clear idea of what's good (something with a high rank) and what's bad (something with a low rank). It implies that the consumer is never uncertain or befuddled in making comparisons—at least not after some reflection.[1] While the Ranking Principle may not hold in all circumstances, it's a reasonable starting point for thinking about most economic decisions.

Notice that the Ranking Principle allows for ties. This doesn't mean that the consumer is uncertain or befuddled; it simply means that he likes two (or more) alternatives equally. Economists say that the consumer is **indifferent** between such alternatives.

A consumer is **indifferent** between two alternatives if he likes (or dislikes) them equally.

Our second main assumption concerning consumer behavior states that consumers follow their preferences in making decisions:

> **The Choice Principle** Among the available alternatives, the consumer selects the one that he ranks the highest.

Another way to say this is that consumers always try to achieve the highest possible level of well-being.

These two principles are, in a nutshell, the basic building blocks of consumer theory. The rational consumers of economic theory—also known as *homo economicus*—will always follow the Ranking Principle and the Choice Principle. We'll spend the rest of this chapter, as well as Chapters 5 and 6 and portions of several subsequent chapters, exploring the many implications of these principles.

Example 4.1

Dinner Selections and the Ranking Principle

Every Tuesday evening, Ethan has dinner at his favorite restaurant. The chef knows how to cook five dishes: hamburgers, tacos, chili, pasta, and pizza. Because he cannot prepare more than three dishes at once, he always limits the menu to three choices, which he varies from day to day. Ethan is familiar with all five dishes, but he has no way of knowing which three will be available on any given day.

On one particular Tuesday, on the way to the restaurant, Ethan's thoughts turn to his potential dinner selection. After sampling each dish in his imagination, he realizes that he is definitely in the mood for tacos. He would be happy with either pasta or a hamburger (both of which seem equally appealing), and could stomach pizza, but he finds the thought of chili unbearable. With this realization, Ethan has ranked all the alternatives that might be available, thereby satisfying the Ranking Principle. Table 4.1 summarizes Ethan's preference ranking on this Tuesday night.

"The little sad faces next to some items mean they don't taste very good."

[1]The Ranking Principle is equivalent to two assumptions about comparisons between *pairs* of alternatives. The first, *completeness*, holds that, in comparing any two alternatives X and Y, the consumer either prefers X to Y, prefers Y to X, or is indifferent between them. The second, *transitivity*, holds that, if an individual prefers one alternative, X, to a second alternative, Y, which he prefers to a third alternative, Z, then he must also prefer X to Z. If preferences are complete and transitive, then the consumer can rank the alternatives from best to worst, as required by the Ranking Principle. Likewise, if he can rank all the alternatives from best to worst, he can make complete, transitive comparisons between pairs of alternatives.

Table 4.1
Ethan's Preference Ranking

Choice	Rank
Hamburger	2 (tie)
Tacos	1
Chili	5
Pasta	2 (tie)
Pizza	4

Ethan eventually arrives at the restaurant and inspects the menu. On this particular Tuesday, the menu lists chili, pasta, and pizza. Noticing with disappointment that tacos are unavailable, Ethan orders pasta. Based on his preference ranking, this is the best choice he can make given the available alternatives.

Equipped with a knowledge of Ethan's preference ranking, we can accurately predict the choices he would make, no matter what's on the menu. For example, if the menu lists hamburgers, tacos, and pizza, he will select tacos. If it lists hamburgers, chili, and pizza, he will order a hamburger. If it lists hamburgers, pasta, and pizza, he will choose either pasta or a hamburger. (Since he is indifferent between those two options, we cannot be more specific.)

Application 4.1

Preference Rankings, Home Video Rentals, and Netflix

On the way home from dinner, Ethan decides to spend his evening watching a movie. He drives to the nearest Blockbuster and wanders the aisles, scanning row after row of unfamiliar titles. He scratches his head in bewilderment, confounded by the prospect of choosing among so many unknowns. By reading the video jackets, he gleans some superficial information—actors, director, genre, rating, perhaps a brief plot summary, and some carefully selected snippets from reviews. Based on this information, he tries to pick the movie he would enjoy the most. However, he knows from experience that it's very hard to judge a movie by its jacket. Because he lacks all of the information required to evaluate a movie before he sees it, he is often surprised and disappointed. Ideally, Ethan would like to know how he would rank all the movies in the store *had he already seen them.* Then he would be able to make consistently satisfying choices.

Ethan's familiar dilemma creates an opportunity for profit-seeking firms and entrepreneurs to make money by providing him with useful advice. The most common approach employs reviews and ratings. For example, a variety of published movie guides provide summary information and a simple quantitative evaluation—"three stars" or "two thumbs up"—for each title. However, since different people have different tastes, no single rating system can accurately predict everyone's reactions. As all movie lovers know, reviews reflect the tastes, preferences, and moods of the *reviewer* rather than those of the consumer.

Netflix.com, a pioneer in online DVD rental services, solves this problem by offering personalized recommendations. Whenever a subscriber logs into a Netflix account, he or she is invited to rate previously viewed movies, especially recent rentals. Netflix stores this information in an enormous database. A computer program identifies like-minded subscribers based on the similarity of their ratings. For any title that a subscriber has not yet viewed, it consults information supplied by like-minded viewers and predicts the subscriber's rating. Netflix then ranks unwatched movies by these predicted ratings and recommends the most highly ranked selections. In effect, Netflix predicts the subscriber's preference ranking and applies the Choice Principle!

Providing reliable online recommendations is an essential component of the Netflix business model. It is an important aspect of customer service, and it reduces the fees that Netflix pays to movie studios by steering customers toward lesser-known films. Does the approach work? In 2002, Netflix provided more than 18 million personalized recommendations daily. Roughly 70 percent of its rentals were computerized suggestions. Moreover, Netflix viewers enjoyed a much wider range of films than customers of conventional video rental stores.[2] At the typical store, 80 percent of rental activity involved just 200 titles. At Netflix, 80 percent of rental activity involved 2,000 titles. Web site recommendations steered Netflix users to niche films such as *Memento,* which became the seventh-most-rented movie on Netflix (outpacing marquee offerings such as *Harry Potter* and *Moulin Rouge),* despite grossing only $25 million at the box office.

[2]The extent to which Netflix's recommendations account for this pattern is unclear. Netflix may also attract customers with stronger preferences for variety by virtue of its greater selection.

4.2 CONSUMER PREFERENCES

Each of the applications we've considered so far has focused on a single decision in isolation—which meal to order, which movie to rent. In practice, however, our decisions tend to be interrelated in two ways. First, the enjoyment of one activity often depends on other activities. For example, many people enjoy jogging and drinking beer, but usually not at the same time. A decision to jog should not be made independently of a decision to drink beer. Second, when an individual spends money to purchase one good, less money is available for other goods. A decision to consume more of one good is therefore also a decision to consume less of another.

To make sound decisions, consumers need to consider these interrelationships. They must keep an eye on the big picture—a master plan for allocating their limited funds to competing needs and desires over some fixed period, such as an hour, a day, a month, a year, or even a lifetime. By following such a plan, the consumer ends up with a collection of goods, known as a **consumption bundle**, for the period in question.[3]

A **consumption bundle** is the collection of goods that an individual consumes over a given period, such as an hour, a day, a month, a year, or a lifetime.

To illustrate this concept, suppose Ethan cares only for restaurant meals and movie rentals. For a given week, the combination of three restaurant meals and two movie rentals is one possible consumption bundle; the combination of one restaurant meal and eight movie rentals is another. In practice, the consumption bundle for any particular individual includes a very large number of goods.

A consumer's choices should reflect how he feels about various consumption bundles, rather than how he feels about any one good in isolation. Otherwise, he might ignore important interrelationships between decisions. In the rest of this chapter, we'll develop useful ways to describe preferences for alternative bundles, and we'll identify some characteristics of preferences that most consumers share.

How Do People Rank Consumption Bundles?

The Ranking Principle tells us only that consumers can rank consumption bundles. It does not by itself tell us how someone will rank any particular bundle relative to another. Since different consumers have very different tastes, consumer theory allows for a wide variety of rankings.

Despite their differences, consumers do have some things in common. For example, in most contexts, the typical person prefers more to less. Even if people disagree about the relative importance of meals and movies, virtually everyone will agree that three meals and three movies is better than two meals and two movies. We'll state this observation as a third general principle of consumer decision making:[4]

The More-Is-Better Principle When one consumption bundle contains more of every good than a second bundle, a consumer prefers the first bundle to the second. See cartoon on page 97.

[3]Consumption bundles are sometimes called *consumption baskets*, but in this book we'll use the word *bundle*.

[4]This is also known as the Non-Satiation Principle.

No doubt you can think of situations in which someone might have too much of a good thing. Consumer theory can accommodate this relatively rare possibility. But for the typical decision, we can reasonably assume that consumers prefer more to less.

The following example illustrates preferences for consumption bundles.

Example 4.2

Preferences for Meals

Madeline eats all of her meals at a restaurant that serves only soup and bread. The restaurant sells soup by the bowl and bread by the loaf. We'll describe her potential consumption bundles by listing the amounts of soup and bread she eats on a given day.

Table 4.2 shows some of her potential choices. The rows indicate the number of loaves of bread and the columns indicate the number of bowls of soup. Obviously, Madeline's options may include eating more than three loaves of bread or more than three bowls of soup on a given day, but we omit these possibilities to keep the table relatively simple. Each cell in the table corresponds to a single consumption bundle. For example, the arrow identifies the cell corresponding to one bowl of soup and two loaves of bread. Altogether, Table 4.2 has 16 different cells, each associated with a different bundle.

Table 4.2

Madeline's Alternatives and Preference Ranking

(Arrow label: **One bowl of soup, two loaves of bread** → cell with 8)

Bread (loaves) \ Soup (bowls)	0	1	2	3
3	11	7	3	1
2	13	8	4	2
1	15	9	6	5
0	16	14	12	10

According to the Ranking Principle, Madeline can rank all the alternatives potentially available to her. Table 4.2 shows her preference ranking. According to this table, Madeline's top choice (ranked 1 among the 16 bundles) is to eat three loaves of bread and three bowls of soup. Her second best choice (ranked 2) is to eat two loaves of bread and three bowls of soup. Notice that Madeline generally prefers soup to bread. For example, she would rather eat three bowls of soup and two loaves of bread (ranked 2) than two bowls of soup and three loaves of bread (ranked 3). However, since she's hungry, she's happy to trade a bowl of soup for several loaves of bread. For example, she prefers two loaves of bread and no soup (ranked 13) to one bowl of soup and no bread (ranked 14). Her least favorite bundle (ranked 16) is to eat nothing.

The preference ranking shown in Table 4.2 satisfies the More-Is-Better Principle. In any single column (such as the one highlighted in yellow), the numbers at the top are smaller than the numbers at the bottom. This means that, given a fixed amount of soup, Madeline prefers more bread. Similarly, in any row, the numbers at the right-hand side are smaller than the numbers at the left-hand side. This means that, given a fixed amount of bread, Madeline prefers more soup.

WORKED-OUT PROBLEM 4.1

The Problem According to Table 4.2, if Madeline starts with three bowls of soup and no bread, is she willing to trade one bowl of soup for two loaves of bread?

The Solution She ranks the bundle consisting of three bowls and soup and no bread tenth among the listed alternatives. If she trades one bowl of soup for two loaves of bread, she'll have two bowls of soup and two loaves of bread, which she ranks fourth. According to the Choice Principle, she'll choose the second bundle over the first—that is, she'll make the trade.

IN-TEXT EXERCISE 4.1 **According to Table 4.2, which of the following trades is Madeline willing to make? (a) Starting with one bowl of soup and one loaf of bread, swap one bowl of soup for two loaves of bread. (b) Starting with two bowls of soup and no bread, swap two bowls of soup for three loaves of bread. (c) Starting with three bowls of soup and one loaf of bread, swap two bowls of soup for two loaves of bread.**

Consumer Preferences with Finely Divisible Goods

In Example 4.2, each consumption bundle corresponded to a cell in a table. This approach works well when the number of alternatives is small. When the number of alternatives (and cells) is large, such tables are cumbersome, tedious to construct, and difficult to read.

Suppose, for example, that Madeline's favorite restaurant sells soup by the teaspoon and bread by the gram. If we allow for the possibility that she might consume up to 200 teaspoons of soup (a little more than one quart) and 500 grams of bread (a little more than one pound), we have 100,000 (500×200) bundles to consider. To depict all of the alternatives, we would need a table with 100,000 cells!

In analyzing decision-making problems involving goods that either are finely divisible or are consumed in large numbers, economists typically assume that consumers can

Figure 4.1

Identifying Alternatives and Indifference Curves. Starting from bundle A, taking away some soup (moving to bundle C) leaves Madeline no better off. But if we then add enough bread (moving to bundle D), she will be better off than with bundle A. Somewhere on the straight line between C and D, there is a bundle (labeled E) that is exactly as good as A. Similarly, starting from bundle A, adding some soup (moving to bundle F) makes Madeline at least as well off. But if we then take away enough bread (moving to bundle G), she will be worse off than with bundle A. Somewhere on the straight line between F and G, there is a bundle (labeled H) that is exactly as good as A. Bundles E and H lie on the indifference curve running through A.

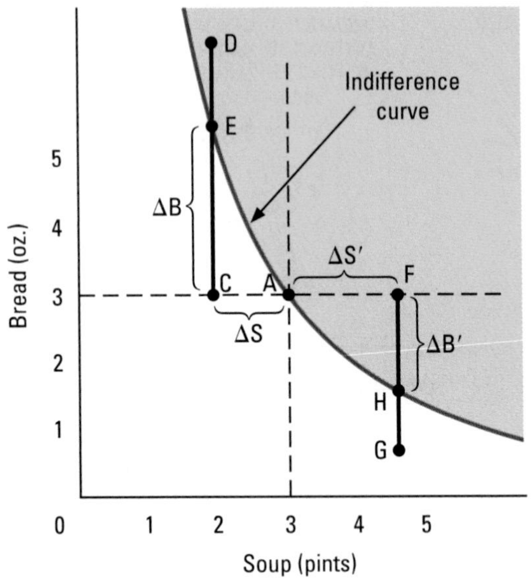

obtain any fraction of a unit, no matter how small. This assumption isn't literally true, but in many situations it's a reasonable approximation. For example, when you prepare your own food, you can vary the amount of soup in a bowl or the size of a loaf of bread.

When goods are available in any fraction of a unit, the number of alternatives is infinite, so we can't show all the consumer's options in a table. Instead, we can represent the alternatives graphically. To illustrate, let's return to Madeline's problem. Here, we'll measure soup in pints and bread in ounces, recognizing that she can obtain any fraction of either. Figure 4.1 shows the set of potential consumption bundles graphically. Each point on the graph corresponds to a possible consumption bundle. For example, point A corresponds to a consumption bundle consisting of three pints of soup and three ounces of bread. Note that the layout of Figure 4.1 resembles Table 4.2 in the sense that the amount of soup is measured on the horizontal axis (columns in Table 4.2), while the amount of bread is measured on the vertical axis (rows in Table 4.2). The main difference is that Figure 4.1 shows the bundles as points rather than as cells.

According to the Ranking Principle, Madeline can rank all the alternatives depicted in Figure 4.1. However, if we tried to write a numerical rank on each point (instead of within each cell, as in Example 4.2), the graph would become completely covered with ink. Clearly, we need to find some other way to represent her preference ranking. We do this by drawing objects called *indifference curves*.

Consumer Indifference Curves

As you learned in Section 4.1, economists say that an individual is indifferent between two alternatives if he or she likes (or dislikes) them equally. In Example 4.1, Ethan is indifferent between eating a hamburger or pasta for dinner (see Table 4.1). This indifference is something of a coincidence; more likely, he would have at least a slight preference for one of those two options. In contrast, when goods are finely divisible, we can start with any alternative and always find others that the consumer likes equally well. An **indifference curve** shows all these alternatives. When we draw an indifference curve, we declare a "tie" between all the points on the curve, much as we declared a tie between pasta and hamburgers in Table 4.1.

Starting with any alternative, an **indifference curve** shows all the other alternatives that a consumer likes equally well.

To illustrate the concept of an indifference curve, let's return to Madeline's problem. Consider the consumption bundle labeled A in Figure 4.1. How do we go about identifying other consumption bundles that are neither more nor less attractive than A? Let's start by taking away ΔS pints of soup, leaving Madeline with bundle C (as shown in the figure). According to the More-Is-Better Principle, she likes bundle A at least as well as bundle C.[5] Suppose that, if we give her enough bread, moving her from bundle C to, say, bundle D, we can more than compensate for the lost soup, and make her better off than with A. Since A is at least as good as C and worse than D, there must be a bundle somewhere on the straight line connecting C and D that is exactly as good as A. In the figure, that bundle is E. By definition, E lies on the indifference curve running through A. To reach bundle E from bundle C, we add ΔB ounces of bread (shown in the figure). So, starting from bundle A, adding ΔB ounces of bread exactly compensates for the loss of ΔS pints of soup.

We can use this procedure to find other points on the same indifference curve. For example, Madeline likes bundle F at least as well as bundle A because it contains the same amount of bread and an additional $\Delta S'$ pints of soup. Suppose that, if we take away enough bread, moving her from bundle F to, say, bundle G, we can make her worse off than with A. Since A is better than G and no better than F, there must be a bundle somewhere on the straight line connecting F and G—call it H—that is exactly as good as A. By definition, H lies on the indifference curve running through A. To reach bundle H from bundle F, we take away $\Delta B'$ ounces of bread. So, starting from bundle A, taking away $\Delta B'$ ounces of bread exactly compensates for $\Delta S'$ extra pints of soup.

Repeating this procedure over and over, we obtain the solid red line in Figure 4.1. Because Madeline is indifferent between bundle A and all other bundles on the red line, such as E and H, the red line is an indifference curve.

Some Properties of Indifference Curves When the More-Is-Better Principle holds, two bundles can't be equally attractive unless, in swapping one for the other, you get more of one good and give up some of another good. If you get more of everything, you're better off, not indifferent. This observation leads to three important conclusions concerning indifference curves.

1. *Indifference curves are thin.* To see why, look at Figure 4.2(a). Since the red curve is thick, we can start at a bundle like A and move to the northeast, reaching a bundle like B, while staying on the curve. Since B contains more soup and more bread than A, the consumer must like B better than A. But this means the thick red curve can't be an indifference curve.
2. *Indifference curves do not slope upward.* To see why, look at Figure 4.2(b). Since part of the red curve slopes upward, we can start at a bundle like C and move to the northeast, reaching a bundle like D, while staying on the curve. Since D contains more soup and more bread than C, the consumer must like D better than C. But this means the red curve can't be an indifference curve.

[5] If she liked bundle C better than bundle A, she would also like C better than some new bundle containing both a tiny bit more soup and a tiny bit more bread than A. The More-Is-Better Principle rules this out, since bundle C contains less soup and less bread than the new bundle.

Figure 4.2

Indifference Curves Ruled Out by the More-Is-Better Principle. Figure (a) shows that indifference curves cannot be thick, since points A and B cannot lie on the same indifference curve. Figure (b) shows that indifference curves cannot have upward sloping segments, since points C and D cannot lie on the same indifference curve.

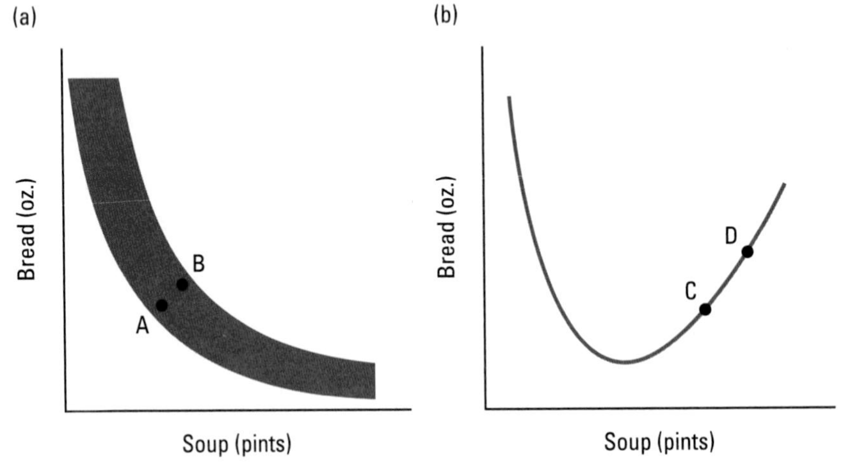

3. *The indifference curve that runs through any consumption bundle—call it A—separates all the better-than-A bundles from the worse-than-A bundles.* Since more is better, the better-than-A bundles lie to the northeast of the indifference curve, while the worse-than-A bundles lie to the southwest. In Figure 4.1, we've shaded the better-than-A bundles light red.

Families of Indifference Curves In Figure 4.1, we constructed an indifference curve by finding all the bundles that were neither more nor less attractive to the consumer than A. As Figure 4.3 shows, we can construct other indifference curves for Madeline starting from other alternatives, such as C, D, E, and F. This figure illustrates what is called a **family of indifference curves**.[6] Two indifference curves belong to the same family if they reflect the preferences of the same individual. Within a family, each indifference curve corresponds to a different level of well-being.

A **family of indifference curves** is a collection of indifference curves that represent the preferences of the same individual.

When the More-Is-Better Principle holds, families of indifference curves have two important properties:

1. *Indifference curves from the same family do not cross.* To see why, look at Figure 4.4, which shows two red curves crossing at bundle A. If the dark red curve is an indifference curve, then the consumer is indifferent between bundles A and B. Since bundle C contains more soup and more bread than bundle B, the consumer prefers C to B, so he also prefers C to A. But that means the light red curve *isn't* one of his indifference curves.

[6]This is sometimes called an *indifference map*, a phrase which emphasizes its similarity to a topographic map. We explain this analogy in Section 4.4.

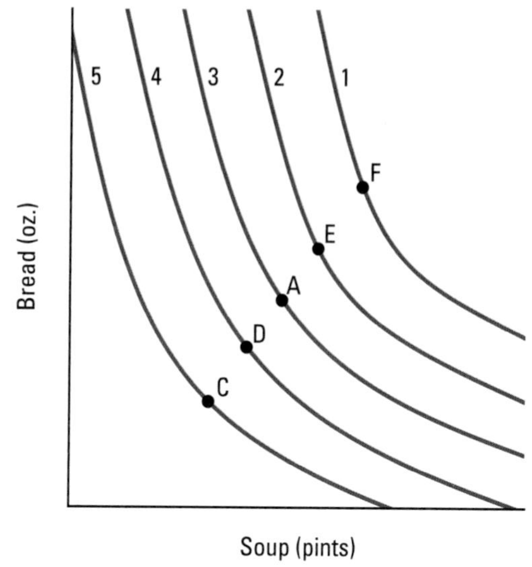

Figure 4.3

A Family of Indifference Curves. This figure illustrates five indifference curves belonging to the same family, all of which represent the preferences of the same consumer. The number next to each curve indicates its rank relative to the other curves. The indifference curve that runs through bundle F recieves a rank of 1 because it is the best from the consumer's perspective. The indifference curve that runs through bundle C recieves a rank of 5 because it is the worst.

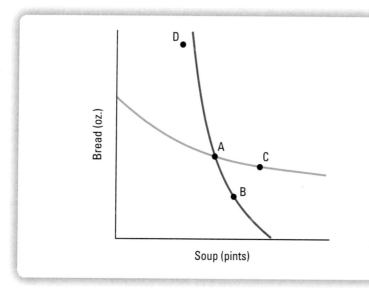

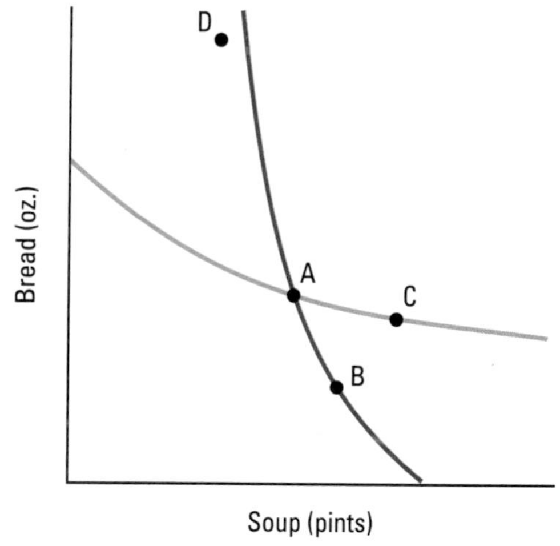

Figure 4.4

Indifference Curves from the Same Family Do Not Cross. If the dark red curve is an indifference curve, then the consumer is indifferent between bundles A and B. Since bundle C contains more soup and more bread than bundle B, the consumer prefers C to B, so he also prefers C to A. But that means the light red curve isn't one of his indifferent curves.

2. *In comparing any two bundles, the consumer prefers the one located on the indifference curve that is furthest from the origin.*[7] This conclusion follows from the fact that, for any bundle A, the better-than-A bundles lie to the northeast of the indifference curve running through A, and the worse-than-A bundles lie to the southwest. For example, Madeline ranks the five indifference curves shown in Figure 4.3 as follows: the curve running through F is first, the curve running through E is second, the curve running through A is third, the curve running through D is fourth, and the curve running through C is last. These ranks appear in the figure.

[7]This observation does *not* imply that the consumer always prefers the bundle that is furthest from the origin. In Figure 4.4, for example, bundle D is further from the origin than bundle A, but a consumer with the dark red indifference curve would prefer bundle A to bundle D.

Let's summarize what we've learned about indifference curves (assuming that the Ranking Principle and the More-Is-Better Principle hold):

Properties of Indifference Curves and Families of Indifference Curves

1. Indifference curves are thin.
2. Indifference curves do not slope upward.
3. The indifference curve that runs through any consumption bundle—call it A—separates all the better-than-A bundles from all the worse-than-A bundles.
4. Indifference curves from the same family never cross.
5. In comparing any two bundles, the consumer prefers the one located on the indifference curve that is furthest from the origin.

Application 4.2

Preferences for Automobile Characteristics

Why does a consumer choose one type of automobile over another? An automobile is a bundle of characteristics and features—style, comfort, power, handling, fuel efficiency, reliability, and so forth. To comprehend the consumer's choice, we must therefore study his preferences for bundles of these characteristics. As with bundles of goods, we can gain an understanding of his preferences by examining indifference curves.

"Nice—but my heart's still set on a helicopter gunship."

In one study, economist Pinelopi Goldberg examined data on purchases of large passenger cars in the United States between 1984 and 1987.[8] Figure 4.5, which is based on her results, shows the preferences of the typical new car buyer for two characteristics, horsepower and fuel economy. Since the curves slope downward, the typical buyer is willing to sacrifice some power and acceleration in return for greater fuel efficiency. For example, consumers are willing to give up roughly 40 horsepower to increase fuel efficiency from 10 to 15 miles per gallon (compare points A and B).

Understanding consumers' willingness to trade horsepower for fuel efficiency is important for both automobile manufacturers and public policymakers. Automobile manufacturers can use information of this type to determine whether a particular design change will improve a car's appeal to consumers. Policymakers can use it to evaluate the likely success of policies that encourage consumers to purchase fuel-efficient automobiles.

[8]Pinelopi Koujianou Goldberg, "Product Differentiation and Oligopoly in International Markets: The Case of the U.S. Automobile Industry," *Econometrica* 63, no. 4, July 1995, pp. 891–951.

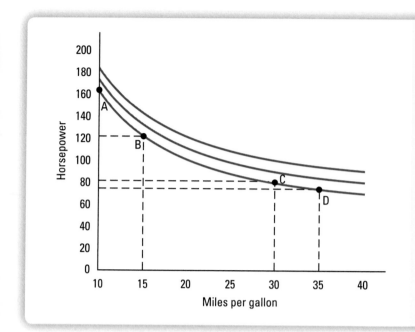

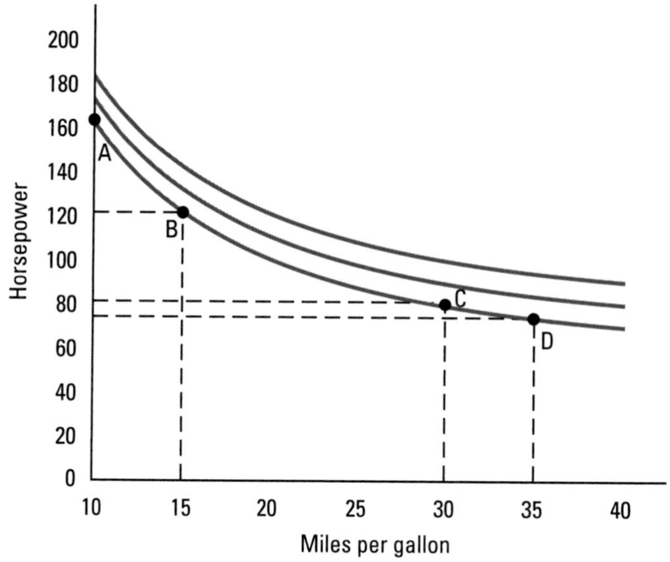

Figure 4.5

Indifference Curves for Horsepower and Fuel Economy. The typical new car buyer's preferences for horsepower and fuel economy correspond to the family of indifference curves shown in this figure. Consumers are willing to give up roughly 40 horsepower to increase fuel efficiency from 10 to 15 miles per gallon (compare points A and B), but they are willing to give up only 6 horsepower to increase fuel efficiency from 30 to 35 miles per gallon (compare points C and D).

Formulas for Indifference Curves So far, we've been studying consumer preferences using graphs. Though the graphical approach helps to build understanding and intuition, it has limitations. First, it isn't quantitative: it doesn't allow us to make precise numerical statements about consumer behavior. Second, graphical illustrations of preferences are always incomplete. A complete family of indifference curves includes curves that run through every single point on the graph. If we tried to draw all of them, the figure would be covered with ink.

To overcome these limitations, economists usually describe consumer preferences using mathematical formulas. As you'll see in Chapter 5, this allows us to treat consumers' decisions as standard mathematical problems.

One way to describe consumer preferences mathematically is to write down the formulas for their indifference curves. For example, the formula for the dark red indifference curve in Figure 4.6 is $B = 10/S$, where B stands for ounces of bread and S for pints of soup. We've graphed this formula by plotting a few points and connecting the dots.[9]

The single formula $B = U/S$ describes an entire family of indifference curves. To obtain a particular indifference curve, we simply plug in a value for the constant U and plot the relationship between B and S. Different values of U will yield different curves. The figure shows curves for the values $U = 10$, $U = 20$, and $U = 30$. Notice that higher values of U lead to indifference curves that are further from the origin. Therefore, the value of U for the indifference curve that runs through any bundle provides an index of the consumer's well-being, or "utility" (hence the letter U), when consuming that bundle. We will elaborate on that interpretation of U in Section 4.4.

[9]You may recall from an algebra course that $B = 10/S$ is the formula for a rectangular hyperbola.

Figure 4.6
Plotting Indifference Curves from a Formula. Using the formula $B = U/S$, we can plot three indifference curves by substituting values of 10, 20, and 30 for the constant U.

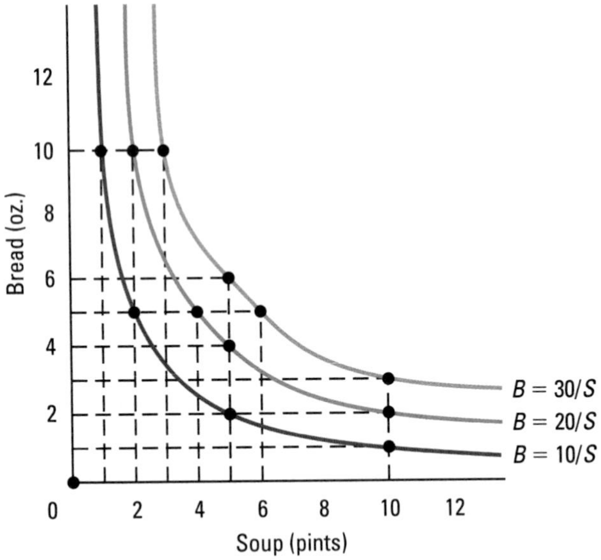

IN-TEXT EXERCISE 4.2 **Judy drinks both Coke and Pepsi. Suppose the formula for her indifference curves is $C = U - 1.2P$, where C stands for liters of Coke and P stands for liters of Pepsi consumed over a month. Draw some of Judy's indifference curves. Which does she prefer, a bundle consisting of one liter of Coke and no Pepsi, or a bundle consisting of one liter of Pepsi and no Coke?**

Goods versus Bads

A **bad** is an object, condition, or activity that makes a consumer worse off.

So far, we have focused on decisions involving things that people desire (goods). But people also often make decisions involving objects, conditions, or activities that make them worse off, and that they wish to avoid (**bads**). Think, for example, about studying for your final exam in this course. Everyone likes to get good grades, and most people like to learn, but few people enjoy studying. (There are, of course, exceptions, such as the odd ones who go on to become professors and write textbooks, but we'll leave them out of this discussion.) Most people are willing to make trade-offs between their grades and their study times. As a consequence, we can summarize their preferences by drawing indifference curves.

Figure 4.7(a) illustrates this trade-off. The vertical axis measures a student's grade on the microeconomics final exam (in percentage points). The horizontal axis measures the number of hours spent studying each evening over some appropriately grueling period, say a full month before the exam. To construct an indifference curve, we first select a starting point. Let's take the professor's ideal: the student spends six hours per evening studying, learns the material perfectly, and receives a perfect score on the final exam.[10] This ideal is

[10]This option, of course, leaves no time to study for other courses, which is reasonable given the importance of microeconomics.

Figure 4.7

Indifference Curves for Studying and Grades. Figure (a) shows an indifference curve for the final exam score, a good, and hours of work per evening, a bad. Figure (b) illustrates the same preferences through an indifference curve for two goods: the final exam score and hours of leisure time per evening.

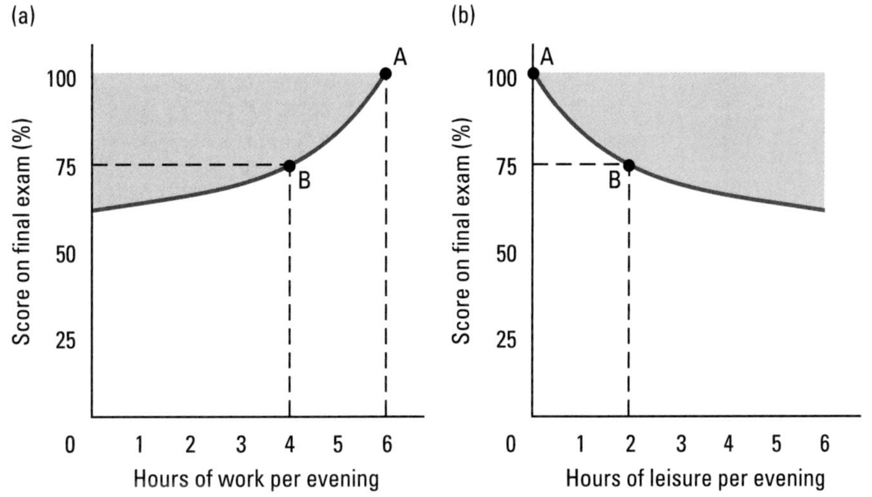

point A in the figure. Oddly, many students feel that academic perfection is not worth the complete absence of a social life. What is the student willing to sacrifice, in terms of exam performance, to get a life? According to the figure, the student is indifferent between point A and point B, which entails studying four hours per night to receive a score of 75 percent. In other words, the student is willing to accept a score that is 25 percentage points lower in return for reducing nightly study time by two hours.

Note that the indifference curve in Figure 4.7(a) slopes upward instead of downward. That is because the More-Is-Better Principle doesn't hold; the student views study time as a bad rather than a good. To compensate him for a lower grade, we have to *reduce* study time. Likewise, since he would like to score higher while studying less, the better-than-A alternatives lie in the red-shaded area to the *northwest* of the indifference curve, instead of to the northeast as in Figure 4.1

Does this mean that we need separate theories for goods and bads? Fortunately, it doesn't. We can always think of a bad as the absence of a good. In our example, studying is a bad because it crowds out leisure time. So let's think about choosing leisure time instead of study time. That way, the student's decision involves two goods, instead of a good and a bad.

Figure 4.7(b) illustrates this idea. Its horizontal axis measures hours of leisure time per evening instead of hours of studying. Six hours of studying corresponds to no hours of leisure, four hours of studying to two hours of leisure, and so forth. Points A and B represent the same outcomes as in Figure 4.7 (a). Note that the indifference curve in Figure 4.7(b) is simply the mirror image of the one in Figure 4.7(a). It slopes downward, and the better-than-A points lie to the northeast. Here, the student's indifference between points

A and B reflects a willingness to give up 25 percentage points on the final exam in return for two hours of leisure time per evening.

This example is important because it suggests a way to address one of the central questions in microeconomics: How do people choose the number of hours they work? Most people regard hours of work as a bad, in the sense that they would rather do something more pleasant. We'll attack this question in Chapter 6 by studying the choice of leisure hours (a good) rather than the choice of work hours (a bad).

4.3 SUBSTITUTION BETWEEN GOODS

All economic decisions involve trade-offs. To determine whether a particular choice benefits or harms a consumer, we need to know the rate at which he is willing to make trade-offs. Indifference curves are important in part because they provide us with that information.

Rates of Substitution

In moving from one bundle to another along an indifference curve, we subtract units of one good and compensate the consumer for the loss by adding units of another good. The slope of the indifference curve is important because it tells us how much of the second good is required to compensate the consumer for giving up some of the first good.

Figure 4.8 illustrates this point using Madeline's preferences. Since bundles A and C lie on the same indifference curve, she is equally happy with either. In moving from bundle A to bundle C, the change in soup, ΔS, is -1 pint, and the change in bread, ΔB, is $+2$ ounces. So starting from bundle A, two additional ounces of bread exactly com-

Figure 4.8

Indifference Curves and Rates of Substitution. In moving from bundle A to bundle C, Madeline loses 1 pint of soup and gains 2 ounces of bread. So the rate at which she is willing to substitute for soup with bread is 2 ounces per pint.

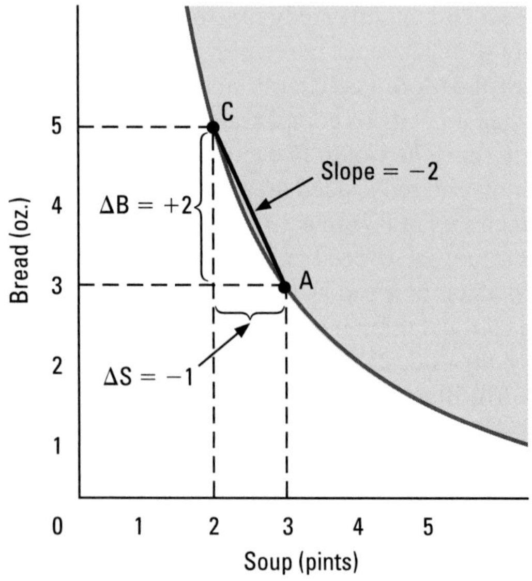

pensate Madeline for the loss of a pint of soup. The rate at which she substitutes for soup with bread in moving from bundle A to bundle C is $-\Delta B/\Delta S = 2$ ounces per pint. The expression $\Delta B/\Delta S$ equals rise over run along the indifference curve between bundles A and C; it is also the slope of the straight line connecting bundles A and C.

In Figure 4.8, the movement from bundle A to bundle C involves relatively large changes in the amounts consumed. Economists usually measure rates of substitution in terms of very small changes in quantities, leading to a concept known as the *marginal rate of substitution*.

Let's refer to the goods in question as X and Y. The **marginal rate of substitution for X with Y**, written MRS_{XY}, is the rate at which a consumer must adjust Y to maintain the same level of well-being when X changes by a tiny amount, from a given starting point. The phrase "for X with Y" means that we measure the rate of substitution *compensating **for** a given change in X **with** an adjustment to Y*. The change in X can be either positive or negative. If it is positive, we must reduce Y to avoid changing the consumer's level of well-being; if it is negative, we must increase Y (as in Figure 4.8). Mathematically, if ΔX is the tiny change in X and ΔY is the adjustment to Y, then $MRS_{XY} = -\Delta Y/\Delta X$. We multiply $\Delta Y/\Delta X$ by negative one because ΔX and ΔY always have opposite signs. Including the negative sign converts the ratio into a positive number, making it easier to interpret (since a larger positive value then indicates that the adjustment to Y must be larger to compensate for a change in X).

The marginal rate of substitution for X with Y, written MRS_{XY}, is the rate at which a consumer must adjust Y to maintain the same level of well-being when X changes by a tiny amount, from a given starting point. Mathematically, if ΔX is the tiny change in X and ΔY is the adjustment to Y, then $MRS_{XY} = -\Delta Y/\Delta X$.

Intuitively, the marginal rate of substitution for X with Y tells us how much Y we need to give a consumer, per unit of X, to compensate for losing a little bit of X. It also tells us how much Y we need to take away from a consumer, per unit of X, to compensate for gaining a little bit of X.

Figure 4.9 illustrates Madeline's marginal rate of substitution for soup with bread, using bundle A as the starting point. Notice that the figure includes a line that lies tangent to her indifference curve at bundle A. (See Section 3.2 for a discussion of tangent lines.)

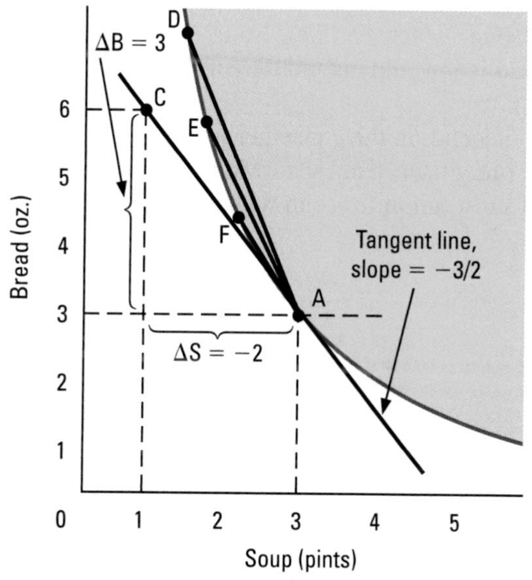

Figure 4.9

Indifference Curves and the Marginal Rate of Substitution. The marginal rate of substitution for soup with bread at bundle A is equal to the slope of the line drawn tangent to the indifference curve running through point A times −1. For smaller and smaller changes in the amounts of soup and bread, the slope of the line between A and the new consumption bundle (first D, then E, then F) grows closer and closer to the slope of the tangent line.

By definition, the slope of the tangent line equals rise over run—that is, $\Delta B/\Delta S$—for very small movements along the indifference curve, starting from bundle A. Therefore, the marginal rate of substitution for soup with bread, MRS_{SB}, at bundle A is simply the slope of this tangent line times negative one.[11] We can measure the slope of the tangent line by selecting a second bundle, like C, and computing $\Delta B/\Delta S$ between the bundles A and C.[12] In this case, since $\Delta B = 3$ ounces and $\Delta S = -2$ pints, we have $\Delta B/\Delta S = -1.5$ ounces per pint. So Madeline's marginal rate of substitution for soup with bread at bundle A is 1.5 ounces per pint.[13]

The value 1.5 ounces per pint signifies that starting at bundle A, Madeline is just willing to give up a small quantity of soup, ΔS pints, in exchange for approximately $\Delta B = 1.5 \times \Delta S$ additional ounces of bread, or to accept ΔS pints of soup in exchange for giving up approximately $\Delta B = 1.5 \times \Delta S$ ounces of bread. The quality of this approximation is better for smaller values of ΔS than for larger values. Figure 4.9 illustrates this point. As we consider smaller and smaller changes in the amounts of soup and bread, the slope of the line between A and the new consumption bundle (first D, then E, then F) grows closer and closer to the slope of the tangent line.

Note that MRS_{XY} is *not* the same as MRS_{YX}. For MRS_{XY}, we compensate for a given change in X with an adjustment to Y, and divide this adjustment by the change in X (that is, we compute $-\Delta Y/\Delta X$). For MRS_{YX}, we compensate for a given change in Y with an adjustment to X and divide this adjustment by the change in Y (that is, we compute $-\Delta X/\Delta Y$).[14]

What Determines Rates of Substitution? Rates of substitution depend on consumers' tastes in predictable and intuitive ways. Figure 4.10 illustrates this point by showing the indifference curves for two consumers. Angie loves soup and likes bread, while Marcus loves bread and likes soup. How do these differences in taste affect their rates of substitution? Starting at bundle A in Figure 4.10, imagine reducing the amount of soup by one pint. Angie needs a large amount of bread, which she likes, to compensate for the lost soup, which she loves. So at A, Angie's marginal rate of substitution for soup with bread is high and her indifference curve, shown in dark red, is relatively steep (it runs through bundle B). In contrast, Marcus needs only a small amount of bread, which he loves, to compensate him for the lost soup, which he likes. So at A, Marcus's marginal rate of substitution for soup with bread is low and his indifference curve, shown in light red, is relatively flat (it runs through C).[15]

Rates of substitution also depend on the consumer's starting point. For example, in Figure 4.11, the slope of the line drawn tangent to Madeline's indifference curve, and therefore her marginal rate of substitution for soup with bread, is different at bundles A, B, and C.

---

[11]Mathematically, the slope of the tangent line is by definition the derivative of the formula for the indifference curve, evaluated at point A.

[12]The location of this second bundle doesn't matter, as long as it's on the tangent line. Because the tangent line is straight, its slope is constant.

[13]Naturally, the value of MRS_{XY} depends on the scale used to measure X and Y. For example, since there are two pints in a quart, substituting for soup with bread at the rate of 1.5 ounces per pint is equivalent to substituting at the rate of 3 ounces per quart.

[14]Though MRS_{XY} and MRS_{YX} measure different things, there is a simple relationship between them. Since $\Delta X/\Delta Y = 1/(\Delta Y/\Delta X)$, it follows that $MRS_{XY} = 1/MRS_{YX}$. So, for example, if the marginal rate of substitution for soup with bread is 1.5 ounces per pint, then the marginal rate of substitution for bread with soup is 0.667 pint per ounce.

[15]Note that the two indifference curves shown in Figure 4.10 cross. Unlike indifference curves that belong to the *same* consumer, indifference curves belonging to *different* consumers with different tastes always cross.

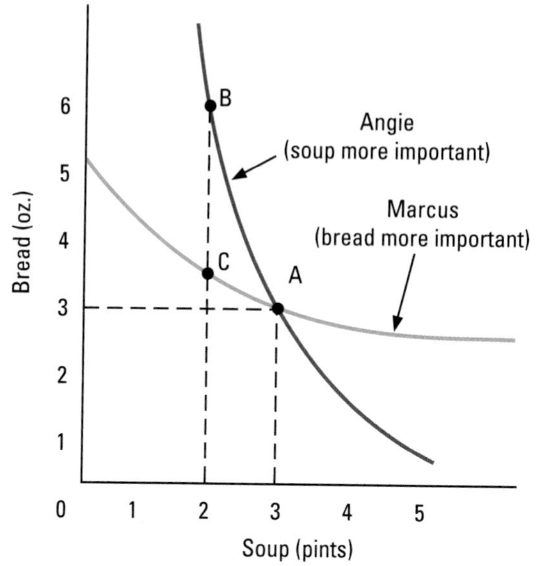

Figure 4.10

Indifference Curves, Marginal Rates of Substitution, and Consumer Tastes. The slope of an indifference curve depends on the consumer's taste. Angie attaches more importance to soup and less to bread than does Marcus. Her MRS for soup with bread is higher than Marcus's, and her indifference curve is steeper.

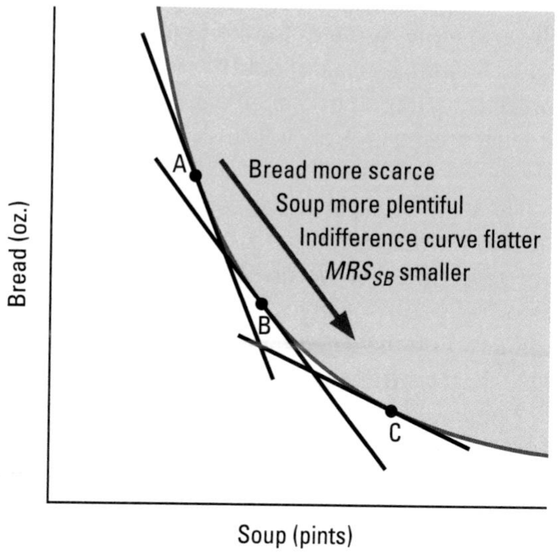

Figure 4.11

The MRS at Different Points on the Same Indifference Curve. The red indifference curve has a declining MRS. Moving in the direction of the blue arrow, bread becomes more scarce and soup becomes more plentiful, so that the MRS for soup with bread falls, and the indifference curve becomes flatter.

Notice that the indifference curve in Figure 4.11 becomes flatter as we move in the direction of the blue arrow, from the northwest (top left) to the southeast (bottom right). This pattern implies that MRS_{SB} declines as we progress toward bundles offering more soup and less bread (for example, from A to B to C). In other words, when soup is more plentiful and bread more scarce, less bread is needed to compensate for the loss of a pint of soup and more soup is needed to compensate for the loss of an ounce of bread.

Why should MRS_{SB} decline when moving from northwest to southeast on an indifference curve? One important reason is that people like variety. To illustrate, suppose we start Madeline off with a great deal of bread but little soup (at a bundle like A in Figure 4.11). As a result, she becomes less enthusiastic about bread and craves soup. This means it would take a great deal of bread to compensate her for the loss of a pint of soup—in other words, her MRS_{SB} is high. Now suppose we start her off with a great deal of soup but little bread (at a bundle like C in Figure 4.11). As a result, she becomes less enthusiastic about soup and craves bread. This means it would take only a small amount of bread to compensate her for the loss of a pint of soup—in other words, her MRS_{SB} is low.

The logic of this discussion applies across a wide range of circumstances. If an indifference curve becomes flatter as we move along the curve from the northwest to the southeast (as in Figure 4.11), we will say that it has a **declining MRS**.[16] When an indifference curve has a declining MRS, the amount of one good, Y, required to compensate a consumer for a given change in another good, X, and hence MRS_{XY}, declines as X becomes more plentiful and Y becomes more scarce.

We will say that an indifference curve has a **declining MRS** if it becomes flatter as we move along the curve from the northwest to the southeast.

Notice that each of the indifference curves in Figure 4.5, which reflects the typical new car buyer's actual preferences for horsepower and fuel efficiency, has a declining MRS. For example, consumers are willing to give up roughly 40 horsepower to increase fuel efficiency from 10 to 15 miles per gallon (compare points A and B), but they are willing to give up only 6 horsepower to increase fuel efficiency from 30 to 35 miles per gallon (compare points C and D).

Formulas for Rates of Substitution As we've seen, one way to describe consumers' preferences mathematically is to write formulas for their indifference curves. Another way is to write formulas for their marginal rates of substitution. An MRS formula tells us the rate at which the consumer is willing to exchange one good for another, given the amounts consumed. For many purposes, that is all we need to know about a consumer's preferences.

To illustrate, suppose the rate at which a particular consumer is willing to substitute for soup with bread is given by the formula $MRS_{SB} = B/S$, where B stands for ounces of bread and S stands for pints of soup. In other words, if the consumer starts out with B ounces of bread and S ounces of soup, tiny changes in the amounts of bread and soup, ΔB and ΔS, will leave him (roughly) on the same indifference curve as long as $\Delta B/\Delta S = -B/S$. When $S = 12$ and $B = 2$, the MRS for soup with bread is 1/6 ounce per pint. In other words, starting with 12 pints of soup and 2 ounces of bread, the consumer must receive $(1/6) \times \Delta S$ ounces of bread to compensate for the loss of ΔS pints of soup (where ΔS is tiny). Likewise, when $S = 5$ and $B = 5$, the MRS for soup with bread is one ounce per pint. In other words, starting with 5 pints of soup and 5 ounces of bread, the consumer must receive ΔS ounces of bread to compensate for the loss of ΔS pints of soup (where again ΔS is tiny).

Checking whether a consumer's indifference curves have declining MRSs using a formula for the MRS is usually easy. For example, when $MRS_{SB} = B/S$, the MRS for soup with bread increases with the amount of bread and decreases with the amount of soup. Every indifference curve must therefore become flatter as we move along the curve from

[16]The notion of a declining MRS is associated with a mathematical concept called *convexity*. Notice that, in Figure 4.11, the set of better-than-A alternatives (shaded light red) is shaped like a convex lens that bulges in the direction of the origin. Economists and mathematicians refer to this type of set as *convex*. The indifference curve illustrated in Figure 4.11 is also called a *convex function*, in the sense that the slope of the line drawn tangent to it increases (becomes less negative) as we move from left to right. These characteristics of preferences are both mathematically equivalent to a declining MRS.

the northwest to the southeast, toward bundles with less bread and more soup. Therefore, those indifference curves have declining MRSs.

For every indifference curve formula, there is an MRS formula that describes the same preferences, and vice versa. In fact, the marginal rate of substitution formula examined here, $MRS_{SB} = B/S$, describes the same preferences as the indifference curve formula discussed in Section 4.2, $B = U/S$. How do we know this? In Section 4.4, we'll see why these two particular formulas correspond to the same preferences. Generally, however, the most direct way to obtain an MRS formula from an indifference curve formula involves calculus.[17] In this book, we do not assume that you know calculus. So whenever you need an MRS formula, we'll give it to you.

Why Are Rates of Substitution Important? We'll emphasize throughout this book that the MRS plays a central role in microeconomic theory. To illustrate its importance, let's consider a basic question that lies at the core of microeconomic theory. Suppose two people meet, and each has something the other wants. Will they voluntarily trade with each other? We can assume they will if doing so is *mutually beneficial*—that is, if they can arrange a swap that benefits both parties. Whether or not the trade is mutually beneficial depends in turn on the parties' rates of substitution. A simple example will illustrate this principle.

Example 4.3

The Lunch Box Problem and Mutual Gains from Trade

Kate and Antonio meet in their school cafeteria and examine the contents of their lunch boxes. Tossing their sandwiches aside, they focus on dessert. Kate discovers a bag of M&Ms, while Antonio finds a box of Milk Duds. Each eyes the other's dessert. Will they exchange some M&Ms for some Milk Duds? The answer depends on their marginal rates of substitution.

Suppose Kate's MRS for Milk Duds with M&Ms is eight M&Ms per Dud, while Antonio's is two M&Ms per Dud. To keep things simple, let's assume that these rates of substitution don't depend on the amounts consumed. In that case, swapping one Milk Dud for, say, five M&Ms makes both of them better off. From Kate's MRS, we know that she is willing to part with up to eight M&Ms for a Milk Dud; since she parts with fewer than eight, she's better off. Likewise, from Antonio's MRS, we know that he requires only two M&Ms to compensate for the loss of a Milk Dud; since he receives more than two, he's also better off. In this example, the same conclusion holds for any trade involving Y Milk Duds and $Y \times Z$ M&Ms, as long as the number Z is between two and eight. (Why?)

Under some circumstances, mutually beneficial trade cannot occur. Suppose, for example, that Kate's MRS for Milk Duds with M&Ms is two M&Ms per Dud, while Antonio's is three. Then Kate is willing to part with no more than two M&Ms for a Milk Dud, while Antonio requires at least three M&Ms to compensate for the loss of a Milk Dud. Meeting both of their requirements is impossible. If Kate and Antonio were to trade, say, 2.5 M&Ms for one Milk Dud, both would be worse off.

"I'd trade, but peanut butter sticks to my tongue stud."

[17] If $B = U/S$, then $dB/dS = -U/S^2 = -B/S$, so $MRS_{SB} = B/S$.

IN-TEXT EXERCISE 4.3 **Suppose you don't know anything specific about Kate and Antonio's preferences. You do know, however, that they were given a chance to swap eight M&Ms for five Milk Duds, and they both voluntarily agreed to this swap. What can you say about Kate's MRS for Milk Duds with M&Ms? About Antonio's? (As in Example 4.3, assume that these rates of substitution don't depend on the amounts consumed.)**

Special Cases: Perfect Substitutes and Complements

Two products are **perfect substitutes** if their functions are identical, so that a consumer is willing to swap one for the other at a fixed rate.

Two products are **perfect complements** if they are valuable only when used together in fixed proportions.

Sometimes consumers use different products to serve essentially the same purpose. When two products' functions are literally identical, so that a consumer is willing to swap one for the other at a fixed rate, we call them **perfect substitutes**. While thinking of products that serve very similar purposes is easy—Coke and Pepsi, Corn Flakes and Special K, Sony PlayStation and Nintendo GameCube—in each case there are some differences. In practice, then, substitutability is a matter of degree. We study the case of *perfect* substitutes because it is one end of the theoretical spectrum.

Sometimes consumers use different products *together* to serve a single purpose. If two goods are valuable only when used together in fixed proportions, we call them **perfect complements**. Again, thinking of examples of products that consumers use together is easy—bicycle tires and frames, left and right shoes, and left and right gloves. However, it is not quite true that these goods are always used in fixed proportions. For example, though most people wear gloves in pairs, some view a single glove as a fashion statement, and others keep unmatched gloves as spares. So in practice, complementarity is also a matter of degree. We study the case of perfect complements because it is the opposite end of the theoretical spectrum.

Graphically, you can identify cases of perfect substitutes and perfect complements by examining families of indifference curves. We'll illustrate this point with a practical application (Application 4.3) and an example.

Application 4.3

Perfect Substitutability Among Pharmaceutical Products

Many examples of near-perfect substitutes can be found in the over-the-counter (OTC) pharmaceutical market, in which products are often differentiated only by dosage. Advil, for example, comes in 200-milligram regular-strength tablets and 400-milligram extra-stength tablets. Obviously, two regular-strength tablets serve exactly the same purpose as one extra-strength tablet. Moreover, as long as a consumer can break a tablet in half, one extra-strength tablet serves exactly the same purpose as two regular-strength tablets. In practice, however, the degree of substitutability may not be perfect; splitting an extra-strength pill in two may be difficult, and some consumers may incorrectly believe that "extra-strength" implies characteristics other than (or in addition to) a higher dosage. Even so, these products are highly substitutable. For illustrative purposes, we'll assume they are perfectly interchangeable.

As a rule, families of indifference curves for perfectly substitutable products are drawn as parallel straight lines. Figure 4.12 shows the indifference curves for regular-strength and extra-strength Advil tablets. Notice that they have a common slope of $-1/2$. Regardless of the starting point, a consumer must receive one extra-strength tablet to compensate for the loss of two regular-strength tablets. Since the consumer cares only about the total number of milligrams of Advil purchased, the marginal rate of substitution for regular tablets with extra-strength tablets is necessarily fixed at one-half extra-strength per regular strength tablet.

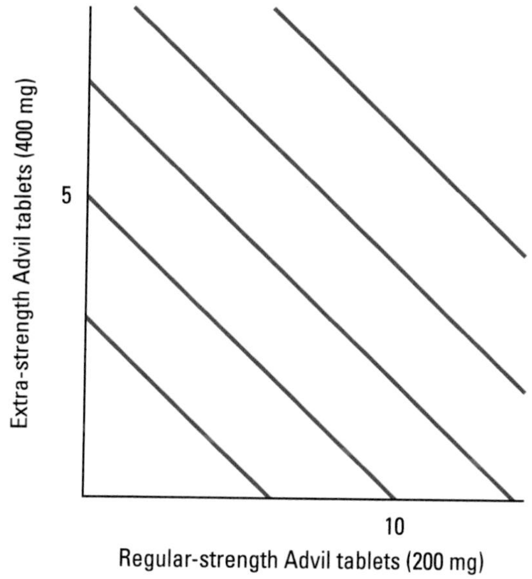

Figure 4.12

Indifference Curves for Perfect Substitutes. The indifference curves for perfect substitutes are straight lines. Because the consumer only cares about the total amount of Advil purchased, two 200-milligram extra-strength tablets are a perfect substitute for one 400-milligram extra-strength tablet.

Example 4.4

Perfect Complementarity between Left and Right Shoes

Figure 4.13 shows a family of indifference curves for left and right shoes, assuming they are perfect complements. For every bundle on the dashed 45-degree line that runs through the origin, the number of left shoes equals the number of right shoes. Consider the point corresponding to five left shoes and five right shoes. What bundles would a consumer find equally attractive? Since extra right shoes are worthless on their own, the consumer would gain nothing from their addition without left shoes. He is therefore indifferent between five left shoes and five right shoes, five left shoes and six right shoes, five left shoes and seven right shoes, and so forth. This conclusion implies that the indifference curve is vertical above the 45-degree line. Similarly, the consumer would gain nothing from the addition of extra left shoes without right shoes. He is therefore indifferent between five left shoes and five right shoes, six left shoes and five right shoes, seven left shoes and five right shoes, and so forth. This conclusion implies that the indifference curve is horizontal below the 45-degree line. Combining these observations, we obtain an L-shaped indifference curve, with a "kink" where it intersects the 45-degree line, as shown in the figure.

Figure 4.13

Indifference Curves for Perfect Complements. Indifference curves for perfect complements are L-shaped. Assuming that a left shoe is of no value without a right shoe and vice versa, a consumer's indifference curves for left and right shoes are vertical above the 45-degree line and horizontal below it, with a kink where they meet.

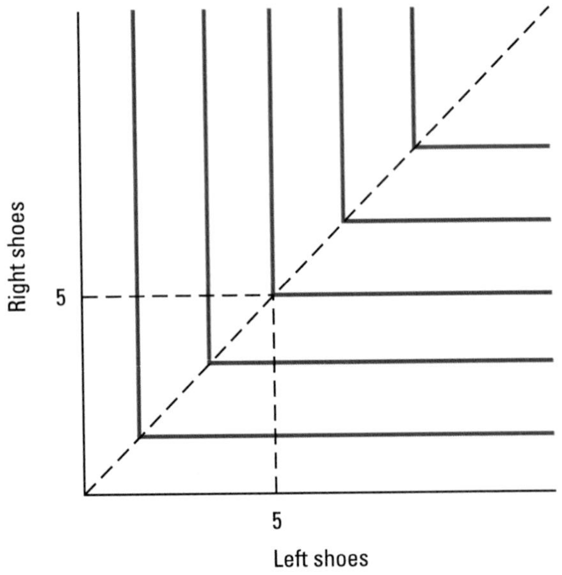

In the real world, product pairs tend to fall somewhere along the spectrum between perfect substitutes and perfect complements. When consumers' indifference curves are reasonably close to straight lines, the degree of substitutability between products is high, and the degree of complementarity is low. When consumers' indifference curves bend sharply, the degree of complementarity between products is high, and the degree of substitutability is low.

4.4 UTILITY

Utility is a numeric value indicating the consumer's relative well-being. Higher utility indicates greater satisfaction than lower utility.

To summarize everything that is known about a consumer's preferences, economists use a concept called **utility**. This is simply a numeric value indicating the consumer's relative well-being—higher utility indicates greater satisfaction than lower utility. The word *utility* reminds us that our objective is to capture the use or benefit that someone receives from the goods he consumes. Every time you rate something from, say, one to ten points, or one to five stars, you're using a utility scale.

To describe a consumer's preferences over consumption bundles, we assign a utility value to each bundle; the better the bundle, the higher the value. To determine which of any two bundles is better, we can simply compare their utility values. The consumer prefers the one with the higher value and is indifferent between bundles whose values are identical.

A **utility function** is a mathematical formula that assigns a utility value to each consumption bundle.

We assign utility values to consumption bundles using mathematical formulas called **utility functions**. For example, the formula $U(S, B) = 2S + 5(S \times B)$ assigns utility values to consumption bundles based on pints of soup, S, and ounces of bread, B. For this function,

$U(12, 3)$, the utility value associated with 12 pints of soup and 3 ounces of bread is 204 $= (2 \times 12) + (5 \times 12 \times 3)$. Likewise, $U(9, 4)$, the utility value associated with 9 pints of soup and 4 ounces of bread is $198 = (2 \times 9) + (5 \times 9 \times 4)$. And $U(17, 2)$, the utility value associated with 17 pints of soup and 2 ounces of bread, is $204 = (2 \times 17) + (5 \times 17 \times 2)$. In this case, the utilities associated with the first and third bundles are the same, and both are higher than the utility associated with the second bundle. Therefore, the consumer is indifferent between the first and third bundles, and prefers both to the second bundle.

WORKED-OUT PROBLEM 4.2

The Problem Mitra enjoys reading books and watching movies. Her utility function is $U(M, B) = M \times B^2$, where M stands for the number of movies and B stands for the number of books enjoyed during a month. How does Mitra rank the following bundles? (1) 4 movies and 5 books, (2) 10 movies and 4 books, (3) 25 movies and 2 books, (4) 40 movies and 1 book, (5) 100 movies and no books.

The Solution Applying Mitra's utility function, we find that (1) $U(4, 5) = 100$, (2) $U(10, 4) = 160$, (3) $U(25, 2) = 100$, (4) $U(40, 1) = 40$, and (5) $U(100, 0) = 0$. Therefore, Mitra ranks the bundles listed in the problem, in order of preference, as follows: first, 10 movies and 4 books; next, either 4 movies and 5 books or 25 movies and 2 books (she is indifferent between those two bundles); next, 40 movies and 1 book; and last, 100 movies and no books.

IN-TEXT EXERCISE 4.4 **Bert enjoys both Coke and Mountain Dew. His preferences correspond to the utility function $U(C, M) = C + 3\sqrt{M}$, where C stands for liters of Coke and M stands for liters of Mountain Dew consumed in a month. How does Bert rank the following alternatives? (1) 5 liters of Coke and 4 liters of Mountain Dew, (2) 20 liters of Coke and no Mountain Dew, (3) 10 liters of Mountain Dew and no Coke, (4) 8 liters of Coke and 7 liters of Mountain Dew, (5) 1 liter of Coke and 6 liters of Mountain Dew.**

From Indifference Curves to Utility Functions and Back

Of course, consumers don't actually have utility functions; they have preferences. A utility function is a formula that an economist develops to summarize consumer preferences. Starting with information about preferences, then, how do we derive an appropriate utility function?

Naturally, a utility function must assign the same value to all the bundles on a single indifference curve. So all we need to do is choose a utility value for each indifference curve, picking higher values for indifference curves that correspond to higher levels of well-being.

When the More-Is-Better Principle holds, we assign higher utility values to indifference curves that are further from the origin. For an illustration, look at Figure 4.14, which shows five indifference curves (labeled I_1 through I_5) for someone who consumes soup and bread. As shown in the figure, we've assigned utility values of 9 to I_1, 12 to I_2, 14 to I_3, 17 to I_4, and 20 to I_5. Between any two bundles, the consumer will always prefer the

Figure 4.14

Representing Preferences with a Utility Function. To create a utility function, we assign the same value to all points on a single indifference curve, using higher values for indifference curves that correspond to higher levels of well-being. Following the More-Is-Better Principle, we assign higher values to indifference curves that are further from the origin.

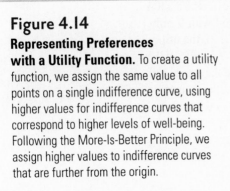

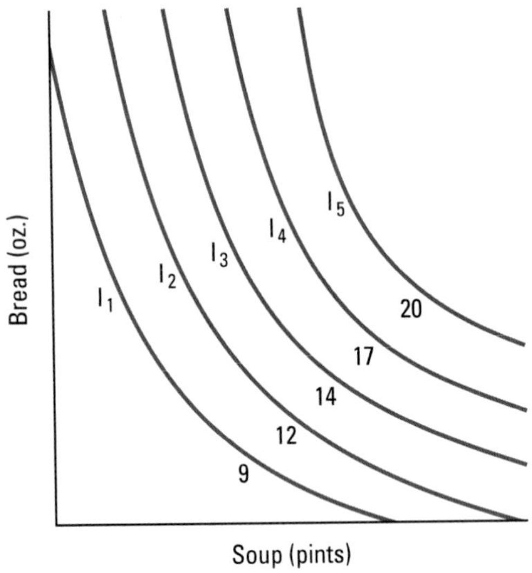

one with the higher utility value, because it lies on a higher indifference curve. The consumer will be indifferent between any two bundles with the same utility value, because they lie on the same indifference curve. Thus, the utility function faithfully represents the consumer's preferences.

We can also start with a utility function and construct the associated indifference curves. To find an indifference curve, all we need to do is fix a level of utility and identify all the bundles that will deliver it. To illustrate, take the utility function $U(S, B) = S \times B$. Choose any utility value, say 10. The consumer will be indifferent between all combinations of soup and bread that satisfy the equation $10 = S \times B$. We can rewrite this equation as $B = 10/S$, a formula that describes a single indifference curve. If we select any other utility value, call it U, the consumer will be indifferent between all combinations of soup and bread that satisfy the formula $U = S \times B$, so the formula $B = U/S$ describes the associated indifference curve. In other words, the utility function $U(S, B) = S \times B$ and the indifference curve formula $B = U/S$ summarize the same preferences. We graphed these indifference curves in Figure 4.6.

Figure 4.15 illustrates another way to think about the relation between utility functions and indifference curves. It is the same as Figure 4.14, except that we've laid the figure on its side and added a third dimension (the vertical axis) measuring Madeline's utility. For any consumption bundle, like A, Madeline's level of utility corresponds to the height of the hill pictured in the figure. The light red curve shows all the points on the hill that are just as high as the point corresponding to bundle A. The dark red line directly below it (at "ground level") shows the combinations of soup and bread that are associated with the points on the light red curve. The dark red curve is the indifference curve passing through bundle A.

If you've gone on a camping trip or taken a geography course, you may have seen contour lines on topographic maps. Each contour line shows all the locations that are at a single elevation. Figure 4.14 is essentially a topographic map for the hill shown in Figure 4.15; each indifference curve in Figure 4.14 is a contour line for a particular elevation.

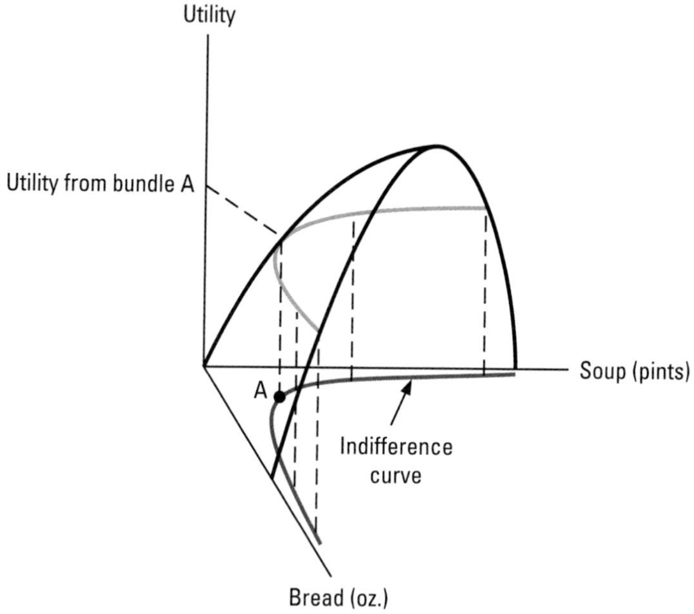

Figure 4.15
Deriving Indifference Curves from a Utility Function. For any consumption bundle, like A, Madeline's utility corresponds to the height of the utility "hill." The indifference curve passing through A consists of all the bundles for which the height of the hill is the same.

Ordinal versus Cardinal Utility

Information about preferences can be either **ordinal** or **cardinal**. Ordinal information allows us to determine only whether one alternative is better or worse than another. Cardinal information tells us something about the *intensity* of those preferences—it answers the question "How much worse?" or "How much better?"

Information about preferences is **ordinal** if it allows us to determine only whether one alternative is better or worse than another. **Cardinal** information tells us something about the *intensity* of those preferences—it answers the question "How much worse?" or "How much better?"

During the 19th century and for much of the 20th century, many prominent scholars, including the influential moral philosopher Jeremy Bentham (1748–1832), thought that utility functions should provide cardinal information about preferences. According to this view, people are "pleasure machines"—they use consumption goods as inputs to produce utility as an output. Bentham and others argued that the aim of public policy should be to maximize the total utility generated through economic activity.

In modern microeconomic theory, utility functions are only intended to summarize ordinal information. If one consumption bundle has a utility value of 10 and a second has a utility value of 5, we know the consumer prefers the first to the second, but it doesn't necessarily make him twice as happy. Today, most economists believe that there's no meaningful way to measure human well-being on an absolute scale, so they reject cardinal interpretations of utility.[18] To understand why this is so, think about your own state of mind. You can probably say whether you're generally happier today than you were yesterday; that's an ordinal statement. But you can't *measure* the difference in your happiness.

From the modern "ordinalist" perspective, the scale used to measure utility is completely arbitrary. Netflix uses a five-star system for rating movies, but it could just as easily have used seven happy faces or ten bowls of popcorn. Likewise, when we measure

[18]Though psychologists have developed reasonably reliable measures of human happiness, these measures also convey ordinal information, rather than meaningful cardinal information. In other words, they can tell us whether someone is happier in one situation than another, but they measure the difference in happiness on an arbitrary scale.

Jeremy Bentham (1748–1832) is regarded as one of the founders of the school of thought on moral philosophy known as "utilitarianism." He continues to be a physical presence at University College London, where, at his request, his skeleton is preserved in a wooden cabinet, dressed in his own clothes and adorned with a wax head. According to one unconfirmed legend, the cabinet is solemnly wheeled into each meeting of the College Council, and the minutes record his presence as "Jeremy Bentham—present but not voting."

the height of the consumer's utility hill (like the one shown in Figure 4.15), we make up the scale and units of measurement. So, for example, in Figure 4.14, we assigned a utility value of 20 to the indifference curve labeled I_5, but we could have just as well used 21, 200, 2,000,000, or any other number greater than the value assigned to I_4.

When we change the scale used to measure utility, the consumer's family of indifference curves, and therefore his preferences, remain unchanged. To illustrate this principle, let's examine the utility function $U(S, B) = 0.5 \times S \times B$, which assigns exactly half as many "utils" (units of utility) to each consumption bundle as the utility function $U(S, B) = S \times B$, considered above. With this new function, the consumer's indifference curve formula is $B = 2U/S$ instead of $B = U/S$. For any given value of U, these two formulas generate different indifference curves. But if we plug any value of U into the formula $B = 2U/S$, and plug a value twice as large into the formula $B = U/S$, we generate the *same* indifference curve. Therefore, the two formulas generate the same family of indifference curves.

Utility Functions and the Marginal Rate of Substitution

Because the marginal rate of substitution tells us the rate at which a consumer is willing to make trade-offs, it's a central concept in microeconomics. In this section, we'll introduce a useful shortcut for deriving an MRS formula, starting from a utility function.

The shortcut involves a new concept, known as **marginal utility**. Marginal utility is defined as the change in the consumer's utility resulting from the addition of a very small amount of some good, divided by the amount added.[19] Mathematically, if ΔX is the tiny change in the amount of a good X and ΔU is the resulting change in the utility value, then the marginal utility of X, written MU_X, is:

Marginal utility is the change in the consumer's utility resulting from the addition of a very small amount of some good, divided by the amount added.

$$MU_X = \frac{\Delta U}{\Delta X}$$

Usually, the calculation of marginal utility requires calculus. However, as illustrated below, there are many special cases for which simple algebra suffices.

The marginal rate of substitution for any good, call it X, with any other good, call it Y, equals the ratio of the marginal utility of X to the marginal utility of Y. In mathematical terms,

$$MRS_{XY} = \frac{MU_X}{MU_Y}$$

Why does this relationship hold? A small change in X, call it ΔX, causes utility to change by approximately $MU_X \Delta X$. Similarly, a small change in Y, call it ΔY, causes utility to change by approximately $MU_Y \Delta Y$. If the combination of these changes leaves us on the same indifference curve, then utility is unaffected, so the changes offset: $MU_X \Delta X = -MU_Y \Delta Y$. Rearranging this formula, we learn that along an indifference curve, $-\Delta Y/\Delta X = MU_X/MU_Y$. Suppose, for example, that an additional unit of X adds 12 utils ($MU_X = 12$) and an additional unit of Y adds 4 utils ($MU_Y = 4$). While utils are meaningless units, a comparison of these numbers nevertheless tells us that the consumer is just willing to exchange one unit of X for three units of Y. Sacrificing one unit of X reduces utility by

[19] If you've taken calculus, you may recognize this as the definition of the derivative of the utility function with respect to the amount of the good in question.

12 utils, but gaining three units of Y increases utility by 12 utils, so the exchange does not alter the consumer's well-being. Therefore, the MRS for X with Y is 3. The preceding formula gives the same answer: $MU_X/MU_Y = 3$.

To illustrate the use of the shortcut, let's again consider the utility function $U(S, B) = S \times B$. For this function, the marginal utility of soup is B (adding ΔS pints of soup increases the utility value by $B \times \Delta S$ units, so $\Delta U/\Delta S = B$), and the marginal utility of bread is S (adding ΔB ounces of bread increases the utility value by $S \times \Delta B$ units, so $\Delta U/\Delta B = S$). Therefore, for this utility function, $MRS_{SB} = B/S$ ounces per pint. As we've explained, the formula $B = U/S$ describes the indifference curves associated with this utility function. Consequently, the formula $MRS_{SB} = B/S$ and the indifference curve formula $B = U/S$ correspond to the same preferences, just as we claimed on page 111.

The concept of marginal utility, though useful, is also the source of much confusion. From our discussion of ordinal and cardinal utility, it should be clear that, by itself, the marginal utility associated with a particular good is completely meaningless. Suppose that Madeline's marginal utility of soup (which we will write as MU_S) is 5. You should be asking yourself, five what? Happy faces? Gold stars? Utils? None of these units has any practical meaning.

If marginal utility is not meaningful by itself, how can the ratio of marginal utilities give us the marginal rate of substitution, which is meaningful? The answer is that when we change the units used to measure utility, we don't change the *ratio* of marginal utilities. To illustrate this point, let's change a utility scale by using the utility function $U(S, B) = 2 \times S \times B$, instead of $U(S, B) = S \times B$, as above. For the new utility function, the marginal utility of soup is $2B$ instead of B (adding ΔS pints of soup increases the utility value by $2 \times B \times \Delta S$ units, so $\Delta U/\Delta S = 2B$), and the marginal utility of bread is $2S$ instead of S (adding ΔB ounces of bread increases the utility value by $2 \times S \times \Delta B$ units, so $\Delta U/\Delta B = 2S$). However, the *ratio* of marginal utilities, and therefore the marginal rate of substitution for soup with bread, remains unchanged: $MRS_{SB} = MU_S/MU_B = B/S$ ounces per pint.

WORKED-OUT PROBLEM 4.3

The Problem Bobby enjoys reading books and watching movies. His utility function is $U(M, B) = M + 2B$. Find a formula for his indifference curves. What do these curves look like? What is Bobby's marginal utility of movies? Of books? What is his MRS for movies with books? From his perspective, are movies and books perfect substitutes, perfect complements, or something else?

The Solution Fixing any utility value U, Bobby will be indifferent between all combinations of books and movies that satisfy the equation $U = M + 2B$. To find the formula for his indifference curves, we just rearrange this: $B = U/2 - M/2$. So each of his indifference curves is a straight line with a slope of $-1/2$ (just like the ones in Figure 4.12). From his utility function, we see that $MU_M = 1$ (adding ΔM movies increases the utility value by ΔM units, so $\Delta U/\Delta M = 1$) and $MU_B = 2$ (adding ΔB books increases the utility value by $2 \times \Delta B$ units, so $\Delta U/\Delta B = 2$). His MRS for movies with books is therefore $MU_M/MU_B = {}^1\!/_2$ book per movie—the same as the slope of his indifference curves, times negative one. From his perspective, movies and books are perfect substitutes.

IN-TEXT EXERCISE 4.5 **Bert's preferences for Coke and Mountain Dew correspond to the utility function given in in-text exercise 4.4 (page 115). Find a formula for his indifference curves. Pick a level of utility, plot a few points on the corresponding indifference curve, and sketch the curve. From Bert's perspective, are Coke and Mountain Dew perfect substitutes, perfect complements, or something else? How would your answer change if his preferences corresponded to the utility function $U(C, M) = C + 3\sqrt{M} + 4$? What about $U(C, M) = (C + 3\sqrt{M})^2$? Or $U(C, M) = 2(C + 3\sqrt{M})$?**

Application 4.4

Ranking College Football Teams

Historically, the identity of the nation's top college football team has been a matter of opinion. The best teams have not always met in season-ending bowl games. Instead, national champions were unofficially crowned according to their standings in nationwide polls of coaches and sports writers. Fifteen times between 1950 and 1979, the college football season ended with more than one team claiming the top spot. Twice, three separate teams finished on top in at least one poll.

Since 1998, the end-of-season bowl match-ups have been governed by a comprehensive agreement known as the Bowl Championship Series (BCS). A central objective of the BCS is to avoid controversy by inviting the two most highly regarded teams to play each other in the national championship game. Selecting those teams, however, can be controversial.[20] There are many possible measures of a team's standing, including various polls and computer rankings. How does the BCS reach a decision? Although BCS officials don't put it this way, their procedure amounts to creating and applying a utility function.

From the perspective of the BCS, each team is a bundle of rankings—one from the USA Today Coaches Poll, one from the Harris Interactive College Football Poll, and six from various computer rankings. Each poll is comparable to a good; a team that has a higher ranking on a particular poll is comparable to a bundle that contains more of that particular good. In selecting teams for the national championship game, the BCS's objective—to minimize controversy by selecting the two most highly regarded teams—is comparable to selecting the best two bundles. When the polls disagree, this objective requires the BCS to make trade-offs. For example, the BCS must decide how much of a lead in the computer rankings is required to compensate for a lower ranking in the Harris Poll. Each year, the BCS uses a formula to assign each team an overall score based on its bundle of rankings. The scores are then used to rank the teams. The formula is in effect a utility function, and the scores are utility values.

For the 2006 season, each team's BCS score was based on (1) the total points it received from voters in the USA Today Coaches Poll, (2) the total points it received from voters in the Harris Interactive College Football Poll, and (3) the total points it received in six computer rankings (throwing out the lowest and highest for each team). In each case, 25 points were assigned for a voter's (or computer's) first-place ranking, 24 points for a second-place ranking, and so forth. The BCS formula averaged these three components after dividing each by the highest possible point score for that component (2,850 for the USA Today Coaches Poll, 1,550 for the Harris Poll, and 100 for the computer rankings).

Knowing this formula, we can identify changes in a team's results that would leave the BCS "indifferent" (that is, the team would end up with the same overall BCS score). As an example, if a team loses 1,000 points in the Harris Poll, its BCS score falls by 1,000/2,850 = 0.351 point. To offset this, its score in the USA Today Coaches Poll would have to be roughly 544 points higher (since 544/1,550 = 0.351). So the BCS's marginal rate of substitution for the Harris Score with the USA Today score is roughly 0.544 USA Today points per Harris point. If we drew a graph with Harris points on the horizontal axis and USA Today points on the vertical axis, each BCS indifference curve would be a straight line with a slope of −0.544.

[20]For example, in 2003, USC was not selected for the BCS championship game, despite finishing the regular season first in both major polls.

CHAPTER SUMMARY

1. **Principles of decision making**

   a. Consumer preferences tell us about people's likes and dislikes.

   b. Consumer theory assumes that consumers' preferences are coherent, in the sense that they respect the Ranking Principle. It also assumes that their decisions reflect preferences, in the sense that they respect the Choice Principle.

2. **Consumer preferences**

   a. Since many consumer decisions are interdependent, decision makers need to compare consumption bundles.

   b. For the typical decision, it's reasonable to assume that consumers prefer more to less. In summarizing the properties of indifference curves below, we make this assumption.

   c. Indifference curves for goods are thin and never slope upward.

   d. The indifference curve that runs through any consumption bundle, call it X, is the boundary that separates all the better-than-X alternatives from all other options. The better-than-X alternatives lie to the northeast of the indifference curve. The worse-than-X alternatives lie to the southwest.

   e. Indifference curves from the same family never cross.

   f. In comparing any two alternatives, the consumer prefers the one located on the indifference curve furthest from the origin.

   g. One way to describe consumers' preferences mathematically is to write formulas for their indifference curves.

   h. For every bad there is an associated good. We can apply consumer theory to bads by thinking about the associated goods.

3. **Substitution between goods**

   a. The marginal rate of substitution varies from one consumer to another according to the relative importance the consumer attaches to the goods in question.

   b. As we move along an indifference curve from the northwest to the southeast, the curve usually becomes flatter. Equivalently, the amount of one good, Y, required to compensate a consumer for a fixed change in another good, X—and hence the MRS for X with Y—declines as X becomes more plentiful and Y becomes more scarce. This feature is known as a declining MRS.

   c. A second way to describe consumers' preferences mathematically is to write formulas for their marginal rates of substitution.

   d. Whether or not two individuals can engage in mutually beneficial trade depends on their marginal rates of substitution.

   e. The indifference curves for perfect substitutes are straight lines.

   f. The indifference curves for perfect complements are L-shaped—vertical above a kink point, and horizontal below it.

4. **Utility**

   a. Economists use the concept of utility to summarize everything that is known about a consumer's preferences.

   b. We can create a utility function from a family of indifference curves by assigning the same utility value to all bundles on an indifference curve, with higher values assigned to indifference curves that correspond to higher levels of well-being. We can construct indifference curves from a utility function by setting the function equal to a constant.

   c. In modern microeconomic theory, utility functions are only intended to summarize ordinal information.

   d. By itself, the marginal utility of a good does not measure anything meaningful. However, the ratio of the marginal utilities for two goods is equal to the marginal rate of substitution between them.

ADDITIONAL EXERCISES

Exercise 4.1: After reading this chapter, a student complains, "What I like and dislike isn't always the same; it depends on my mood." Is this a problem with consumer preference theory? Why or why not?

Exercise 4.2: Suppose there are two types of food, meat and bread. Draw indifference curves for the following consumers.

a. Ed likes variety and prefers to eat meat and bread together.

b. Francis dislikes variety; she likes to eat the same thing all the time.

c. Mia is a vegetarian who doesn't care (one way or the other) about meat.

d. Taka, a sumo wrestler, cares only about the number of calories he consumes; he wants to consume as many calories as possible.

e. Larry loves to eat and enjoys variety, but he also wants to lose weight. He therefore thinks that food is a good at low quantities, and a bad at high quantities.

Exercise 4.3: Gary has two children, Kevin and Dora. Each one consumes "yummies" and nothing else. Gary loves both children equally. For example, he is equally happy when Kevin has two yummies and Dora has three, or when Kevin has three yummies and Dora has two. But he is happier when their consumption is more equal. Draw Gary's indifference curves. What would they look like if he loved one child more than the other?

Exercise 4.4: As in the previous question, suppose that Gary loves Kevin and Dora equally. What is his marginal rate of substitution between Kevin's yummies and Dora's yummies when each has the same number of yummies? Does it become larger or smaller when Kevin has more yummies than Dora? What about when Dora has more yummies than Kevin?

Exercise 4.5: For lunch, Ada prefers to eat soup and bread in fixed proportions. When she eats X pints of soup, she prefers to eat $\sqrt{X}$ ounces of bread. If she has X pints of soup and more than $\sqrt{X}$ ounces of bread, she eats all the soup along with $\sqrt{X}$ ounces of bread, and throws the extra bread away. If she has X pints of soup and fewer than $\sqrt{X}$ ounces of bread (say Y ounces), she eats all the bread along with Y^2 ounces of soup and throws the extra soup away. Draw Ada's indifference curves between soup and bread.

Exercise 4.6: Think of five examples of bads. In each case, what is the associated good? (For example, air pollution is a bad; clean air is the associated good.)

Exercise 4.7: Ryan hates both water pollution and air pollution. He thinks that the harm caused when water pollution increases by a fixed amount rises with the total amount of water pollution, and that the harm caused when air pollution increases by a fixed amount rises with the total amount of air pollution. Sketch Ryan's indifference curves for the amount of water pollution and the amount of air pollution. Indicate how he ranks the curves you've drawn.

Exercise 4.8: Suppose bundles A and B lie on the same indifference curve. Bundle C lies between bundles A and B, on a straight line that connects them. The consumer's preferences satisfy the Declining MRS Principle. Does the consumer prefer C to A and B, or does he prefer A and B to C?

Exercise 4.9: Nora likes to breed rabbits. Clearly, she can't get very far with one rabbit. Thinking about the trade-offs between rabbits and other goods, would you expect the Declining MRS Principle to hold? Can you think of other situations in which it might be violated?

Exercise 4.10: What do you think the indifference curves in Figure 4.5 would look like for the type of person who prefers to purchase a sports car? What about the type of person who prefers to purchase a subcompact?

Exercise 4.11: John's MRS for reading books with watching movies is three movies per book regardless of the amounts consumed. Would he rather read two books and watch no movies, or read no books and watch two movies? What is the formula for his family of indifference curves? What do these curves look like? In this example, are movies and books perfect substitutes, perfect complements, or neither?

Exercise 4.12: Do the following pairs of products serve as complements or substitutes? In each case, is the degree of complementarity or substitutability high or low? Do your answers depend on the contexts in which the goods are used? (1) Bread and butter. (2) Ball point pens and computers. (3) Facsimile service and mail service. (4) Movies and video games. (5) Gasoline and ethanol. (6) Wireless telephone service and standard (wireline) telephone service. (7) Different CDs recorded by the same rock group. (8) Lettuce and ground beef.

Exercise 4.13: Kate has 25 M&Ms and Antonio has 10 Milk Duds. Suppose Kate's MRS for Milk Duds with M&Ms is 4 regardless of what she consumes, and that Antonio's is 3 regardless of what he consumes. Kate and Antonio trade until there is no further opportunity for mutual gain. Can you say anything about what they've traded (how many M&Ms for how many Milk Duds)?

Exercise 4.14: Latanya likes to talk on the telephone. We can represent her preferences with the utility function $U(B, J) = 18B + 20J$, where B and J are minutes of conversation per month with Bill and Jackie, respectively. If Latanya plans to use the phone for one hour to talk with only one person, with whom would she rather speak? Why? What is the formula for her indifference curves? Plot a few of those curves.

Exercise 4.15: Do you think there is a workable way to obtain meaningful *cardinal* information about a consumer's preferences? If so, how might you go about it? If not, why not?

Exercise 4.16: In Exercise 4.14, we discussed Latanya's preferences for telephone conversation. According to our assumption, we can represent her preferences with the utility function $U(B, J) = 18B + 20J$, where B and J are minutes of conversation per month with Bill and Jackie, respectively. What is Latanya's implied marginal utility of speaking with Bill? What is her implied marginal utility of speaking with Jackie? What is her MRS for minutes talking to Bill with minutes talking to Jackie?

Exercise 4.17: Esteban likes both chocolate ice cream and lemon sorbet. His preferences correspond to the utility function $U(C, S) = C^{1/3}S^{2/3}$, where C stands for ounces of chocolate ice cream and S stands for ounces of lemon sorbet. Write a formula for Estaban's family of indifference curves. Plot some of those curves on a graph. Would Esteban rather have four ounces of chocolate ice cream and two ounces of lemon sorbet or two ounces of chocolate ice cream and four ounces of lemon sorbet?

5

Constraints, Choices, and Demand

Learning Objectives

After reading this chapter, students should be able to:

- Demonstrate how price and income affect a consumer's budget line.
- Determine a consumer's best choice based on his preferences and budget line.
- Understand how to find a consumer's best choice by maximizing a utility function.
- Analyze the effects of changes in prices and income on a consumer's demand.
- Explain how economists determine consumers' preferences based on their choices.

Honda Accord (above) and Ferrari Enzo (below)

The Honda Accord has consistently ranked among the best-selling cars in the United States. Yet if you ask your friends to name their favorite automobiles, few would mention the Accord. It lacks the luxury of a Bentley, the engineering of a Mercedes, the sex appeal of a Ferrari, the sophistication of an Aston-Martin, the performance of a Porsche. The Accord simply is a plain-looking car that delivers a safe, comfortable ride with few headaches. The price is reasonable and the maintenance cost is low. The Ferrari Enzo may turn heads, but its $643,330 price tag keeps most buyers out of the showroom.

When the owner of a $23,000 Accord says the Enzo is not affordable, his meaning is obvious. Most people just don't have the cash to buy an Enzo. But when he says he can't afford a $47,000 Mercedes E320, his meaning is probably more subtle. Many Accord owners *could* purchase more expensive cars. They *choose* the Accord because they don't think a flashy car is worth working overtime, skipping vacations, or living in a smaller home.

Consumer choice is all about constraints and trade-offs. The purpose of this chapter is to describe the constraints consumers face and explain how they resolve trade-offs and make decisions. We'll examine six main topics:

1. *Affordable consumption bundles.* A consumer's budget constraint identifies all the consumption bundles he can afford. We'll see how prices and income determine which consumption bundles are affordable.
2. *Consumer choice.* Faced with a budget constraint, the consumer selects the best consumption bundle he can afford. We'll explain how to determine this best choice given his preferences and budget constraint.
3. *Utility maximization.* Many important economic questions are quantitative, which is why economists use mathematics. We'll see that a consumer's best choice corresponds to the solution to a mathematical problem involving the maximization of utility, a concept that we introduced in Section 4.4.
4. *Prices and demand.* When the price of a good changes, each consumer's best affordable consumption bundle may change with it. By studying this relationship, we will develop a better understanding of demand curves.
5. *Income and demand.* When a consumer's income changes, his best affordable consumption bundle changes. Studying this relationship will help us understand how and why demand depends on income.

*6. *How economists determine a consumer's preferences.* Economists can't observe consumers' preferences directly. However, they can observe choices. We'll see how economists learn about consumers' preferences from their choices.

5.1 AFFORDABLE CONSUMPTION BUNDLES

When the owner of a Honda Accord says that a Mercedes E320 isn't worth the sacrifice, he means that by buying an Accord, he can afford a better consumption bundle that contains larger amounts of other desirable items. This example underscores the point that in thinking about what's affordable and what isn't, focusing on consumption bundles rather than individual products is important.

Income, Prices, and the Budget Line

A consumer's **income** consists of the money he receives during some fixed period of time.

A consumer's **income** consists of the money he receives during some fixed period of time such as an hour, a day, a month, or a year. Throughout this chapter and the next, we'll assume that consumers must spend their income during the period in which they receive it—in other words, they can neither save current income nor borrow against future income. (We'll discuss saving and borrowing in Chapter 10.) Therefore, during any time period, a consumer can afford to purchase a particular consumption bundle if its cost doesn't exceed his income for that period:

$$\text{Cost of consumption bundle} \leq \text{Income} \quad (1)$$

A **budget constraint** identifies all of the consumption bundles a consumer can afford over some period of time.

Economists refer to this inequality as the consumer's **budget constraint**.

As an illustration, let's assume that the consumer desires only two goods, soup and bread. In market economies, each good is commonly associated with a price at which consumers can buy as much or as little as they like. We'll use P_S for the price per unit of soup and P_B for the price per unit of bread. We can find the total cost of any good by multiplying its price per unit times the number of units purchased. So if a consumption bundle includes S units of soup and B units of bread, the total cost of soup is $P_S S$, the total cost of bread is $P_B B$, and the total cost of the bundle is $P_S S + P_B B$. The consumer's budget constraint tells us that the bundle is affordable if its total cost does not exceed his income, M:

$$P_S S + P_B B \leq M \tag{2}$$

When each good is available at a fixed price per unit, budget constraints take the form shown in formula (2).

Example 5.1

Budgeting for Meals

In Example 4.2 (page 96), we discussed Madeline's preferences for bundles of soup and bread. Let's assume that the prices are \$2 per bowl for soup and \$2 per loaf for bread, and that Madeline's income is \$6 per day. To determine whether a bundle is affordable, we apply formula (2). The numbers in Table 5.1 indicate the cost of each bundle. For example, a bundle of three bowls of soup and one loaf of bread costs \$8. Madeline can purchase any bundle in Table 5.1 with a cost of \$6 or less. All of her affordable bundles are highlighted in green. Madeline must select one of the green cells.

Table 5.1

Cost and Affordability of Madeline's Consumption Bundles

Soup price = \$2 per bowl, Bread price = \$2 per loaf, Income = \$6 per day

Bread (loaves)				
3	\$6	\$8	\$10	\$12
2	4	6	8	10
1	2	4	6	8
0	0	2	4	6
Soup (bowls)	0	1	2	3

IN-TEXT EXERCISE 5.1 **Suppose the price of soup is \$4 per bowl, the price of bread is \$2 per loaf, and Madeline's income is \$6. Identify Madeline's affordable consumption bundles, as in Example 5.1.**

Example 5.1 describes a situation with lumpy goods. Let's now turn our attention to finely divisible goods. As in Chapter 4, we'll measure the amount of soup, S, in pints and the amount of bread, B, in ounces. The price of soup, P_S, will indicate its cost per pint, and the price of bread, P_B, will indicate its cost per ounce.

Affordable consumption bundles fall into two categories: those that exhaust the consumer's income and those that do not. A bundle exhausts the consumer's income if

Figure 5.1

The Budget Constraint. When soup costs P_S per pint, bread costs P_B per ounce, and income is M, the consumer can purchase any bundle on or below a straight line with the horizontal intercept M/P_S, the vertical intercept M/P_B, and a slope of $-P_S/P_B$.

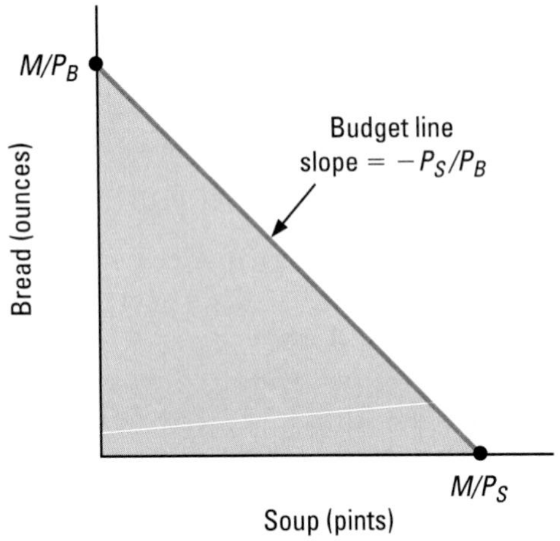

$P_SS + P_BB = M$ (that is, cost equals income). After subtracting P_SS from both sides, and then dividing everything through by P_B, we can rewrite that formula as follows:

$$B = \frac{M}{P_B} - \frac{P_S}{P_B}S \quad \textbf{(3)}$$

A **budget line** shows all of the consumption bundles that just exhaust a consumer's income.

Formula (3) describes a straight line, known as the consumer's **budget line**. By graphing this line, as in Figure 5.1, we can identify all of the consumption bundles that just exhaust the consumer's income.

According to formula (3), the slope of the budget line equals the ratio of the price of soup to the price of bread, times negative one.[1] This price ratio represents the rate at which the consumer can convert pints of soup into ounces of bread by spending money on bread instead of soup. Suppose, for example, that P_S = \$2 per pint and P_B = \$0.50 per ounce. Since \$2 buys either one pint of soup or four ounces of bread, the consumer can convert pints of soup to ounces of bread at the rate of four ounces per pint. In this example, the slope of the budget line, times negative one, is indeed four ounces per pint. (To check this, divide the price of soup, \$2 per pint, by the price of bread, \$0.50 per ounce.)

The budget line intersects the vertical axis at M/P_B ounces, and the horizontal axis at M/P_S pints. For example, suppose that M = \$6, P_S = \$2 per pint, and P_B = \$0.50 per ounce. If the consumer spends all of his money on bread, he can afford 12 ounces (because \$6 ÷ \$0.50 per ounce = 12 ounces). This is the vertical intercept. Likewise, if the consumer spends all of his money on soup, he can afford 3 pints (because \$6 ÷ \$2 per pint = 3 pints). This is the horizontal intercept.

What about consumption bundles that do *not* exhaust the consumer's income? Those satisfy the inequality $P_SS + P_BB < M$, which means they lie in the green-shaded area of Figure 5.1, to the southwest of the budget line. The budget line is the boundary that separates all the affordable consumption bundles from the unaffordable ones. The green shading in Figure 5.1 plays the same role as it does in Table 5.1: it identifies affordable consumption bundles.

[1]Since the slope of a line is rise over run, and since *rise* refers to bread while *run* refers to soup, you might think the slope of the budget line would equal P_B/P_S, rather than P_S/P_B. However, when the price of a good is higher, a smaller change in the amount consumed leads to the same change in expenditure. Therefore, the price of bread is *inversely* related to rise, and the price of soup is *inversely* related to run.

Changes in Income and Prices

Changes in income and prices affect consumption because they move the budget line, altering the set of bundles from which the consumer can choose.

From formula (3), we see that a change in income alters the vertical intercept of the budget line without changing its slope. A reduction in income shifts the budget line inward, shrinking the set of affordable bundles, while an increase in income shifts it outward, expanding the set of affordable bundles. For example, as Figure 5.2 shows, if soup costs \$2 per pint and bread costs \$0.50 per ounce, a reduction in income from \$6 to \$3 shifts the budget line toward the origin, from the line labeled L_1 to the one labeled L_2.[2] All the consumption bundles between L_1 and L_2 become unaffordable. Likewise, an increase in income from \$6 to \$9 shifts the budget line away from the origin, from the line labeled L_1 to the one labeled L_3, making all the bundles between L_1 and L_3 affordable. (Why?) The three budget lines are parallel because their slopes all equal the same price ratio, times negative one.

A change in the price of a good rotates the budget line—outward for a decrease and inward for an increase. The line pivots at the intercept for the good with the unchanged price. To understand why it pivots at that intercept, notice that a change in the price of one good doesn't affect the amount of another good that a consumer can buy if he spends all his income on the good with the unchanged price. For example, as Figure 5.3 shows, if bread costs \$0.50 per ounce and income is \$6, an increase in the price of soup from \$2 per pint to \$6 per pint rotates the budget line toward the origin from the line labeled L_1 to the

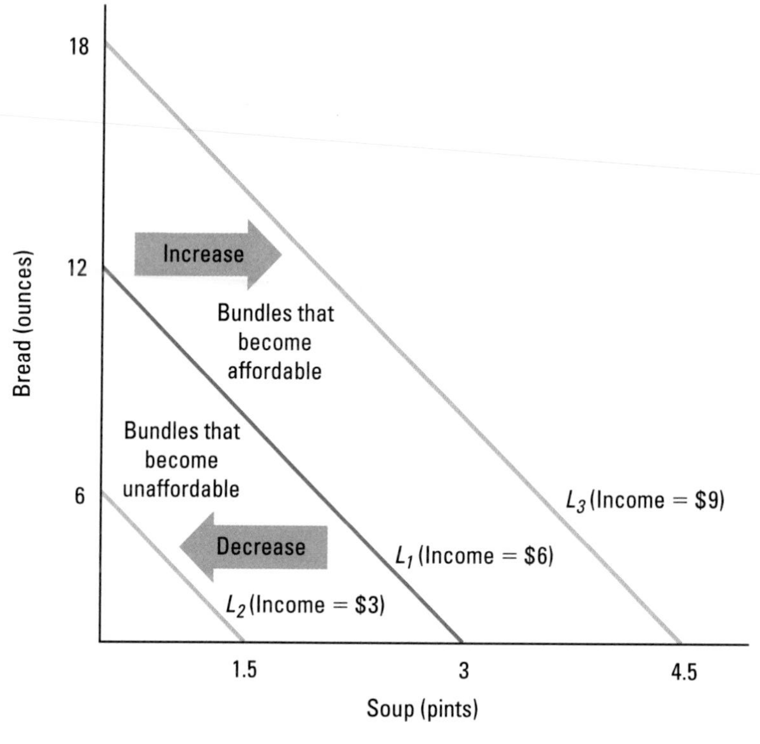

Figure 5.2

Effects of Changes in Income on the Budget Line. Soup costs \$2 per pint and bread costs \$0.50 per ounce. A reduction in income from \$6 to \$3 shifts the budget line toward the origin, making all the bundles between L_1 and L_2 unaffordable. An increase in income from \$6 to \$9 shifts the budget line away from the origin, making all the bundles between L_1 and L_3 affordable.

[2] The ratio M/P_S (and hence the horizontal intercept) falls from 3 pints to 1.5 pints, while the ratio M/P_B (and hence the vertical intercept) falls from 12 ounces to 6 ounces.

Figure 5.3

Effects of a Change in the Price of Soup on the Budget Line. Bread costs $0.50 per ounce and income is $6. An increase in the price of soup from $2 to $6 per ounce rotates the budget line toward the origin (pivoting at the intercept for bread), making bundles between L_1 and L_4 unaffordable. A decrease in the price of soup from $2 to $1 per ounce rotates the budget line away from the origin (pivoting at the intercept for bread), making bundles between L_1 and L_5 affordable.

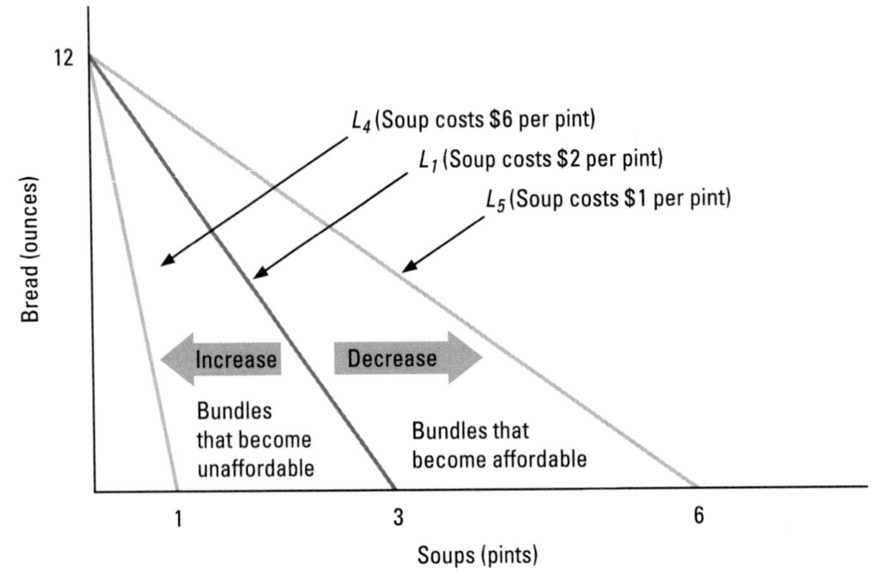

one labeled L_4.[3] All the consumption bundles between L_1 and L_4 become unaffordable. A reduction in the price of soup from $2 per pint to $1 per pint rotates the budget constraint in the opposite direction, from L_1 to L_5, making all the bundles between L_1 and L_5 affordable. (Why?) In each case, the line pivots at the intercept for bread.

Doubling all prices has the same effect on the budget line as cutting income in half—both of these changes eliminate half of the consumer's purchasing power. For example, if the price of soup doubles from $2 to $4 per pint and the price of bread doubles from $0.50 to $1 per ounce while income remains fixed at $6, the budget line shifts from L_1 to L_2 in Figure 5.2.[4] We have already seen that cutting income in half from $6 to $3 with prices fixed has the same effect on the budget line. More generally, multiplying all prices by a single constant has the same effect on the budget line as dividing income by that constant.[5]

[3] The ratio M/P_B (and hence the vertical intercept) is unaffected by the change in the price of soup. The ratio M/P_S (and hence the horizontal intercept) declines from 3 pints to 1 pint. The ratio P_S/P_B (and hence the absolute value of the slope) increases from 4 ounces per pint to 12 ounces per pint.

[4] The ratio M/P_S (and hence the horizontal intercept) falls from 3 pints to 1.5 pints, while the ratio M/P_B (and hence the vertical intercept) falls from 12 ounces to 6 ounces. Since the price ratio, P_S/P_B, doesn't change, the slope of the budget line, -4 ounces per pint, remains the same.

[5] Suppose we multiply all prices by the constant K. The horizontal intercept becomes $M/(KP_S)$, the vertical intercept becomes $M/(KP_B)$. The slope is unchanged: $-(2P_S)/(2P_B) = -P_S/P_B$. Dividing income by K has the same effect.

What if prices and income all change by the same proportion? That scenario would have *no* effect on the budget line, because income changes just enough to compensate for the changing cost of goods. For example, if prices and income all double, the consumer's purchasing power is unchanged.[6]

Let's summarize what we've learned about budget lines:

Properties of Budget Lines

1. The budget line is the boundary that separates all the affordable consumption bundles from all other bundles. Choices that do not exhaust the consumer's income lie to the southwest of the budget line.
2. The slope of the budget line equals the price ratio times negative one, with the price of the good measured on the horizontal axis appearing in the numerator, and the price of the good measured on the vertical axis appearing in the denominator.
3. The budget line intersects the axis that measures the amount of any particular good, *X*, at the quantity M/P_X, which is the amount of *X* the consumer can purchase by spending all income on *X*.
4. A change in income shifts the budget line—outward for an increase and inward for a decrease—without changing its slope.
5. A change in the price of a good rotates the budget line—outward for a decrease and inward for an increase. The line pivots at the intercept for the good with the unchanged price.
6. Multiplying all prices by a single constant has the same effect on the budget line as dividing income by the same constant. Changing prices *and* income by the same proportion has *no* effect on the budget line.

WORKED-OUT PROBLEM 5.1

The Problem For each of the following cases, graph the consumer's budget line. Compute the horizontal intercept, the vertical intercept, and the slope of the budget line. (a) $P_S = \$3$ per pint, $P_B = \$0.60$ per ounce, and $M = \$60$. (b) $P_S = \$1$ per pint, $P_B = \$0.60$ per ounce, and $M = \$60$. (c) $P_S = \$3$ per pint, $P_B = \$0.20$ per ounce, and $M = \$60$. (d) $P_S = \$3$ per pint, $P_B = \$0.60$ per ounce, and $M = \$180$. (e) $P_S = \$9$ per pint, $P_B = \$1.80$ per ounce, and $M = \$180$.

The Solution See Figure 5.4. Notice that the budget constraints in parts (a) and (e) are identical. That's because the prices and income in part (e) are exactly three times as large as in part (a).

[6] The horizontal intercept becomes $(2M)/(2P_S)$, which equals M/P_S (since the twos cancel). Likewise, the vertical intercept becomes $(2M)/(2P_B) = M/P_B$, and the slope becomes $-(2P_S)/(2P_B) = -P_S/P_B$. Since the horizontal intercept, vertical intercept, and slope are unchanged, the budget line doesn't move.

Figure 5.4

Budget Lines for Worked-Out Problem 5.1. This figure shows the budget lines for each combination of prices and income listed in parts (a) through (e) of worked-out problem 5.1, along with their horizontal intercepts, vertical intercepts, and slopes.

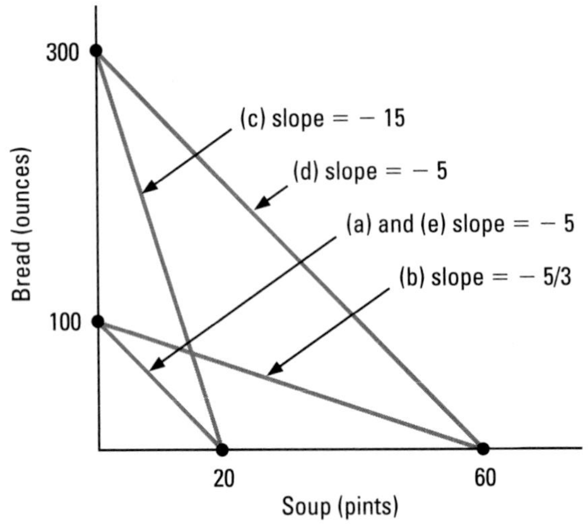

IN-TEXT EXERCISE 5.2 **For each of the following cases, graph the consumer's budget line. Compute the horizontal intercept, the vertical intercept, and the slope of the budget line: (a) P_S = \$2 per pint, P_B = \$0.50 per ounce, and M = \$40. (b) P_S = \$4 per pint, P_B = \$0.50 per ounce, and M = \$40. (c) P_S = \$2 per pint, P_B = \$1 per ounce, and M = \$40. (d) P_S = \$2 per pint, P_B = \$0.50 per ounce, and M = \$80. (e) P_S = \$4 per pint, P_B = \$1 per ounce, and M = \$80.**

Other Limits on Consumption

Sometimes, prices and income aren't the only factors that limit consumption. When the demand for a good exceeds the supply at the prevailing price, governments or suppliers may limit the amount that each consumer can purchase. For example, during the oil crisis of 1973 and 1974, the U.S. government asked gas stations to sell no more than 10 gallons at a time to any customer. In such cases, we say that the good is **rationed.**

When the demand for a good exceeds the supply at the prevailing price, and the government or a supplier limits the amount that each consumer can purchase, we say that the good is **rationed.**

Figure 5.5 illustrates the effect of rationing on the budget line of a consumer who allocates his income, \$200, between food, which costs \$4 per pound, and gasoline, which costs \$2 per gallon. Without rationing, the consumer can choose any bundle on or below the straight line that runs between points A and B (part of which is solid and part of which is dashed). With gasoline rationing (40 gallons per person), he can no longer purchase any bundle containing more than 40 gallons of gasoline. Therefore, his budget line is the solid kinked line through points B, C, and D.

5.2 CONSUMER CHOICE

According to the Choice Principle (Section 4.1), a consumer selects the highest-ranked alternative among the available options. When the number of potential alternatives is small, finding the best one is easy. We'll illustrate by returning to the problem considered in Examples 4.2 and 5.1.

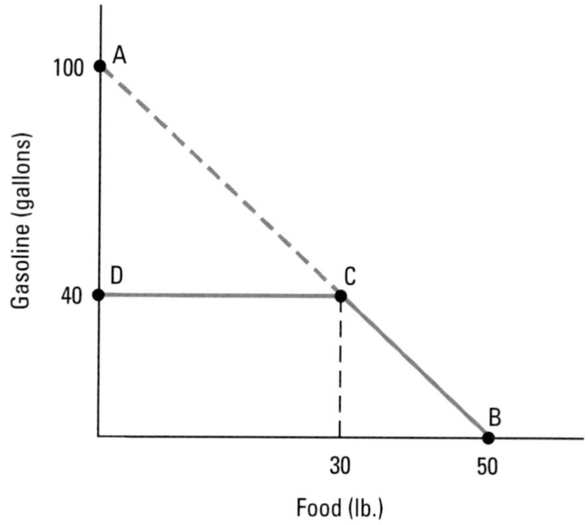

Figure 5.5

A Budget Line with Rationing. A consumer allocates $200 between food, which costs $4 per pound, and gasoline, which costs $2 per gallon. Without rationing, the consumer can choose any bundle on or below the straight line that runs between points A and B. With gasoline rationing (40 gallons per person), the consumer's budget line is the solid kinked line through points B, C, and D.

Example 5.2

Budgeting for Meals, Part 2

As in Example 5.1, let's assume that Madeline's income is $6 per day, soup costs $2 per bowl, and bread costs $2 per loaf. With the preferences shown in Table 4.2 (page 96), what will she choose?

Table 5.2 reproduces Table 4.2 (page 96), which showed Madeline's preference ranking. As in Table 5.1, we've shaded the affordable bundles green. To determine what her decision will be, we can apply the Choice Principle. Since she ranks the bundle consisting of two bowls of soup and one loaf of bread higher (at number 6) than any other green-shaded bundle, this is her best choice.

Since Madeline's cash is limited, the best affordable bundle is not as good as some of the other alternatives listed in Table 5.2 (specifically, those ranked 1 through 5). We use red shading to highlight all of the superior bundles. Notice that the red-shaded portion of the graph does not overlap with the green-shaded portion. Why not? Since Madeline prefers each red-shaded bundle to the best affordable bundle, each must cost more than she can afford.

Table 5.2

Madeline's Best Choice

Soup price = $2 per bowl, Bread price = $2 per loaf, Income = $6 per day

Bread (loaves)				
3	11	7	3	1
2	13	8	4	2
1	15	9	(6)	5
0	16	14	12	10
Soup (bowls)	0	1	2	3

IN-TEXT EXERCISE 5.3 **As in in-text exercise 5.1, suppose that a bowl of soup costs $4 instead of $2, while a loaf of bread still costs $2, and Madeline's income is $6. What will she choose?**

The No-Overlap Rule

When goods are finely divisible, applying the Choice Principle takes a bit more work. However, the basic idea remains the same as in Example 5.2.

Look at Figure 5.6(a), which reproduces the budget line from Figure 5.1. Of all the bundles on or below that line, which one will the consumer pick? According to the More-Is-Better Principle, he'll pick a bundle on the budget line, rather than one below it. Why? A point below the budget line would leave him with unused cash, which he could spend on something he values. For example, in Figure 5.6(a), he would rather pick bundle B than bundle A, because bundle B contains more of everything than bundle A.

The consumer's choice must also lie on the highest indifference curve that touches the budget line. We can easily recognize such bundles by applying the following simple rule:

Figure 5.6

Choosing among Affordable Bundles. In figure (a), the consumer would rather pick bundle B than bundle A because bundle B contains more soup and more bread than bundle A. Bundle C is the best choice because there is no overlap between the red-shaded area above the indifference curve that runs through bundle C, and the green-shaded area below the budget line—in other words, between the bundles that are better than C and the ones that are affordable. In figure (b), bundle D is not the best choice because there is overlap between the area above the indifference curve that runs through D and the area under the budget line—in other words, between the bundles that are better than D and the ones that are affordable. For example, the consumer would rather pick bundle E than bundle D.

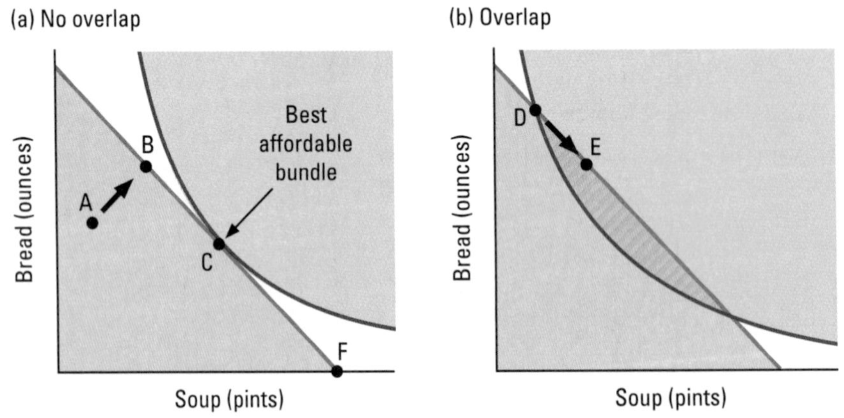

The No-Overlap Rule The area above the indifference curve that runs through the consumer's best bundle does not overlap with the area below the budget line. The area above the indifference curve that runs through any other bundle does overlap with the area below the budget line.

For an illustration, look at Figure 5.6(a). Since the red indifference curve that passes through bundle C does not cross the budget line, the areas above that indifference curve (shaded red) and below the budget line (shaded green) do not overlap. Because none of the better-than-C bundles are affordable, bundle C is the best choice. Notice the similarities between Figure 5.6(a) and Table 5.2. In both cases, the indicated bundle is the best choice because the red and green areas do not overlap (equivalently, no other bundle is both better and affordable).

In contrast, since the red indifference curve that passes through bundle D in Figure 5.6(b) crosses the budget line, the areas above that indifference curve and below the budget line overlap. The overlapping area is striped red and green. Any consumption bundle that lies in the striped area is both affordable (it lies below the budget line) and better than D (it lies above the indifference curve that runs through D). The consumer can therefore do better than D, for example by choosing another bundle, such as E, that lies on the budget line to the southeast of D.

Example 5.3

Purchases of Left and Right Shoes

For an illustration of the no-overlap rule, we'll examine a case involving perfect complements, based on Example 4.4 (page 113). Suppose that Marie has a fixed sum of cash to spend on shoes, and that left and right shoes are sold separately. How many of each will she buy? Figure 5.7 shows her indifference curves for left and right shoes (in red), and her budget line (in green). According to the no-overlap rule, bundle A is Maria's best choice. Since bundle A lies on the 45-degree line, Maria buys the same number of left and right shoes. This conclusion doesn't depend on the slope of the budget line. Even if the prices of left and right shoes differ, Maria will still buy the same number of each. For example, if left shoes cost $10 each, right shoes cost $20 each, and Maria can spend $90 on shoes, she will buy three pairs.

Interior Solutions

An affordable bundle is an **interior choice** if, for each good, there are affordable bundles containing a little bit more of that good and affordable bundles containing a little bit less of it.[7] In Figure 5.6(a), bundles A, B, and C are all interior choices; bundle F is not. When the best affordable choice is an interior choice, we call it an **interior solution.** Bundle C in Figure 5.6(a) is an example.

An affordable bundle is an **interior choice** if, for each good, there are affordable bundles containing a little bit more of that good and affordable bundles containing a little bit less of it. When the best affordable choice is an interior choice, we call it an **interior solution.**

[7] We previously introduced this term in the appendix to Chapter 3.

Figure 5.7

The Best Affordable Bundle with Perfect Complements. According to the no-overlap rule, bundle A is Maria's best choice. Since bundle A lies on the 45-degree line, Maria buys the same number of left and right shoes. This conclusion doesn't depend on the slope of the budget line. Even if the prices of left and right shoes differ, Maria will still buy the same number of each.

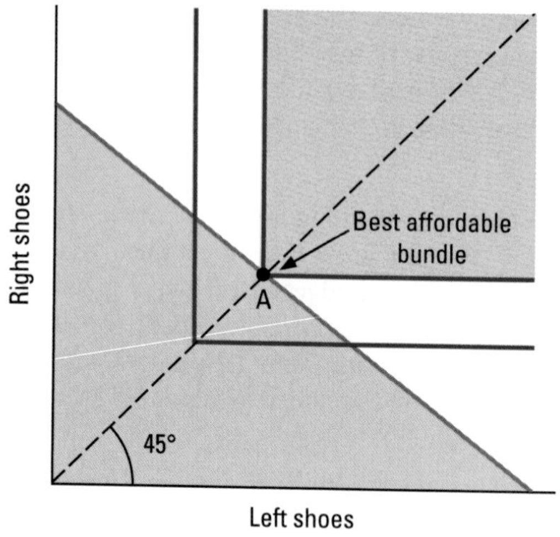

A bundle on the budget line satisfies the **tangency condition** if, at that bundle, the budget line lies tangent to the consumer's indifference curve.

Notice that the consumer's budget line lies tangent to his indifference curve at bundle C. For this reason, we say that bundle C satisfies the **tangency condition**. In fact, interior solutions *always* satisfy the tangency condition.[8] Why? The indifference curve running through any interior choice that does *not* satisfy the tangency condition, like bundle D in Figure 5.6(b), *must* cross the budget line, creating overlap between the areas below the budget line and above the indifference curve. According to the no-overlap rule, such bundles are not best choices.

An Implication of the Tangency Condition At every interior solution, the marginal rate of substitution between two goods equals their price ratio.[9] To understand why, take another look at Figure 5.6(a). Because the interior solution (bundle C) satisfies the tangency condition, the indifference curve and the budget line share the same slope at that bundle. We know that the slope of the indifference curve is the negative of the marginal rate of substitution for soup with bread, MRS_{SB} (Section 4.3). We also know that the slope of the budget line is the negative of the price ratio, P_S/P_B (Section 5.1). Therefore,

$$MRS_{SB} = \frac{P_S}{P_B} \quad (4)$$

We emphasize that formula (4) holds only at interior solutions. It does not hold at other points on the budget line.

Formula (4) has many important implications and applications. For instance, it implies that, as long as consumers can buy and sell all goods at marketwide prices, they will reap all the potential gains from trade. Institutions that promote exchange at marketwide prices, therefore, help the economy to get the most out of its resources. Why? In Example 4.3, "The Lunch Box Problem and Mutual Gains from Trade" (page 111), you learned that two people can benefit from trading with each other when

[8]This statement assumes that the interior solution is not a bundle at which the consumer's indifference curve is kinked. Because the slope of an indifference curve is not well-defined at kink points, such as bundle A in Figure 5.7, it cannot coincide with the slope of any straight line.

[9]This statement also assumes that the interior solution is not a bundle at which the consumer's indifference curve is kinked.

their marginal rates of substitution *differ*. But if everyone buys and sells goods at market-wide prices, each person will choose a bundle that equates his marginal rate of substitution with the same price ratio. Thus, everyone's marginal rate of substitution will be the *same,* which rules out the possibility of further gains from trade. We'll return to this theme in Part III.

Finding Interior Solutions Sometimes, economists need to predict consumers' choices. If the consumers' indifference curves have declining MRSs, this task is particularly easy: we simply find an interior choice that satisfies formula (4) (equivalently, the tangency condition). Any such bundle is an interior solution. To understand why, consider any interior bundle that satisfies the tangency condition, like bundle C in Figure 5.6(a). Because the budget line and the indifference curve that runs through bundle C lie tangent to each other, they don't cross at C. Nor can they cross at any other point. With a declining MRS, the indifference curve becomes steeper to the left of point C and flatter to the right. In either direction, it veers away from and remains above the budget line, as shown. Therefore, the areas below the budget line and above the indifference curve that runs through C cannot overlap. According to the no overlap rule, bundle C is therefore the best choice.

What if the consumer's indifference curves do not have declining MRSs? In those cases, interior choices that satisfy the tangency condition are not necessarily the best affordable choices. For an illustration, we'll examine a case involving cigarette addiction. Suppose that Marlene spends all of her money on food and cigarettes. Figure 5.8 shows her indifference curves. Consider the indifference curve that runs through bundle A. Notice that Marlene's MRS for cigarettes with food *increases* as we move from bundle A to bundle B. Why? As Marlene smokes more cigarettes, she becomes hooked, and her cravings for cigarettes grow more extreme. As a result, the amount of food she is willing to give up to obtain an additional cigarette grows larger. However, if food becomes sufficiently scarce, she grows extremely hungry and is no longer willing to give up as much food to obtain an additional cigarette. That is why her MRS for cigarettes with food declines as we move from bundle B to bundle C. In Figure 5.7, bundles D and E both satisfy the tangency condition. However, according to the no-overlap rule, bundle E is her best choice; bundle D is not.

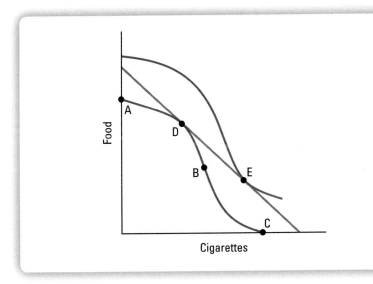

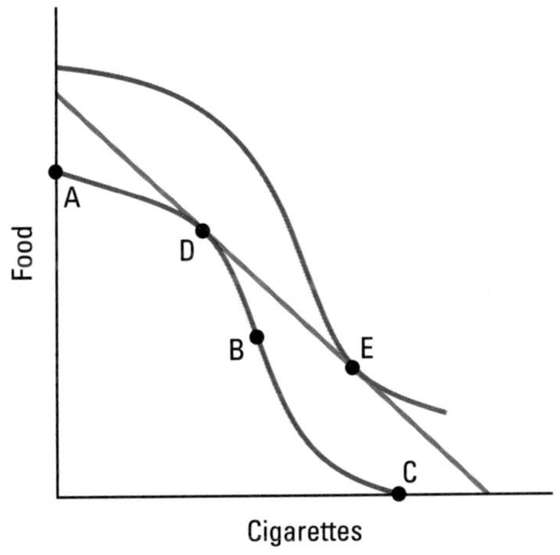

Figure 5.8

A Case in Which Indifference Curves Do Not Have Declining MRSs. Marlene allocates money between cigarettes and food. Because cigarettes are addictive, her indifference curves do not have declining MRSs. She chooses bundle E rather than bundle D, despite the fact that both bundles satisfy the tangency condition.

WORKED-OUT PROBLEM 5.2

The Problem Natasha's income is \$300 per month. She spends all of it on tickets to concerts and films. A concert ticket costs \$15 and a film ticket costs \$10. Her marginal rate of substitution for concerts with films, MRS_{CF}, is F/C, where C stands for the number of concert tickets and F stands for the number of films. (Fractions are allowed—for example, if she buys half of a concert ticket, that means she goes to a concert every other month). How many film tickets will she purchase, and how many concert tickets?

The Solution Notice that MRS_{CF} decreases as C rises and F falls. Therefore, each of Natasha's indifference curves has a declining *MRS*. To find a best choice, we look for a bundle on her budget line that satisfies the tangency condition.

At Natasha's best choice, her marginal rate of substitution between films and concerts equals the price ratio: $MRS_{CF} = P_C/P_F$. Substituting the information contained in the statement of the problem gives us the following: $F/C = 15/10 = 1.5$. In other words, Natasha purchases 1.5 times as many movie tickets as concert tickets.

The formula for Natasha's budget line is $P_C C + P_F F = 300$. Substituting the values of the prices into this formula, we have $15C + 10F = 300$. Using the fact that $F = 1.5C$ gives us $15C + 10(1.5C) = 300$, or $30C = 300$. So $C = 10$, and $F = 15$. Natasha purchases 10 concert tickets and 15 movie tickets.

At a **boundary choice** there are no affordable bundles that contain either a little bit more or a little bit less of some good. When the consumer's best choice is a boundary choice, we call it a **boundary solution.**

IN-TEXT EXERCISE 5.4 **In worked-out problem 5.2, how many of each kind of ticket will Natasha choose if her marginal rate of substitution for concerts with films, MRS_{CF}, is $3F/2C$? If it's $\sqrt{F/C}$?**

Boundary Solutions

In practice, virtually everyone chooses *not* to consume certain goods. Think about your own purchases. There are probably many things that you never consume—possibly octopus, brussels sprouts, or tripe. These types of choices are examples of **boundary choices.**[10] At a boundary choice, there are no affordable bundles that contain either a little bit more or a little bit less of some good. In Figure 5.6(a), bundle F is a boundary choice, because there is no affordable bundle containing a little bit more soup, or a little bit less bread. When the consumer's best choice is a boundary choice, we call it a **boundary solution**.

Boundary solutions often arise when a good provides a consumer with little value per dollar relative to other alternatives. For an illustration, look at Figure 5.9. Notice that the indifference curves (drawn in red) are quite steep. This means that it takes a great deal of bread to compensate the consumer for losing an ounce of soup. According to the no-overlap rule, bundle C is the

"I'll lay it out for you. We're cutting back, and we no longer need a dog."

[10]We introduced this language in the appendix to Chapter 3.

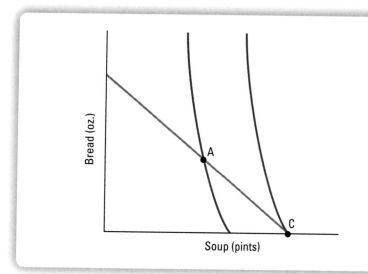

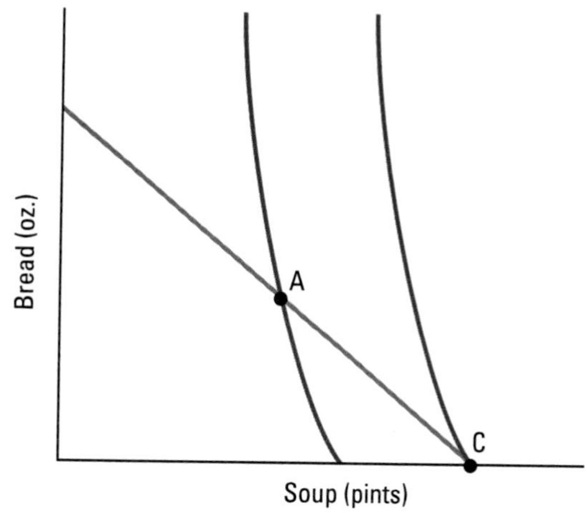

Figure 5.9

A Case in Which the Best Affordable Bundle Is a Boundary Solution. According to the no-overlap rule, bundle C is the consumer's best affordable bundle. The indifference curves through bundles like A are steeper than the budget line, so the consumer is better off purchasing more soup and less bread.

consumer's best choice on the green budget line. Because it contains no bread, it's also a boundary solution. At any bundle that contains some bread (like bundle A), the indifference curve is steeper than the budget line, so the consumer is better off buying more soup and less bread.

Unlike interior solutions, boundary solutions usually do not satisfy formula (4). For instance, at bundle C in Figure 5.9, the consumer's indifference curve is *steeper* than his budget line. As a result, at bundle C, his MRS for soup with bread is *greater* than the price ratio, P_S/P_B. More generally, if bundle C is a boundary solution, then at that bundle,

$$MRS_{SB} \geq \frac{P_S}{P_B} \tag{5}$$

This inequality, which takes the place of formula (4), is intuitive. Starting at bundle C, the consumer has no bread, so his only option is to buy less soup and more bread. He is *willing* to give up one pint of soup for MRS_{SB} ounces of bread, but *able* to buy only P_S/P_B ounces of bread in place of one pint of soup. Since $MRS_{SB} \geq P_S/P_B$, buying more bread and less soup makes him no better off (and indeed makes him worse off if $MRS_{SB} > P_S/P_B$), so he is content to spend all his income on soup.[11]

Let's summarize what we've learned about best choices.

Properties of Best Choices

1. Assuming that more is better, the consumer's best choice lies on the budget line.
2. We can recognize best choices by applying the no-overlap rule.

[11]What if the consumer purchases some soup and some bread, but no octopus? Since this choice is a boundary solution, the marginal rates of substitution for soup with octopus, and for bread with octopus, satisfy inequalities like expression (5). However, the marginal rate of substitution for soup with bread still satisfies formula (4). Why? The choices of those goods are interior: there are affordable bundles containing a little more soup and a little less bread, as well as bundles containing a little less soup and a little more bread.

3. Interior solutions always satisfy the tangency condition. Consequently, if a bundle that includes two goods, *X* and *Y*, is an interior solution, then $MRS_{XY} = P_X/P_Y$ at that bundle.
4. When indifference curves have declining MRSs, any interior choice that satisfies the tangency condition is a best affordable choice.
5. Whenever the consumer purchases good *X* but not good *Y*, then $MRS_{XY} \geq P_X/P_Y$ at the chosen bundle.

Application 5.1

The Food Stamp Program and Food Consumption

The Food Stamp Program subsidizes food purchases by low-income households. The subsidy takes the form of vouchers, or coupons, which the recipient can use in place of cash when purchasing groceries, but for no other purpose. In 2005, food stamp benefits totaled $28.6 billion. During a typical month, 25.7 million people received assistance. The average monthly benefit per person was $93.

Let's examine the effects of food stamps on a consumer's budget line. Suppose he earns $80 and receives another $120 in aid from the government. He spends this money on two goods: food, which costs $4 per pound, and gasoline, which costs $2 per gallon. If he received the $120 aid in cash, he would be able to afford any bundle on or below the straight line that runs between points A and B in Figure 5.10. However, since the aid takes the form of food stamps, he can spend no more than $80 on gasoline, which means he can purchase no more than 40 gallons. Therefore, his budget line is the solid kinked line through points B, C, and D in Figure 5.10. Notice that he would have the same budget line in this example if the government rationed gasoline, limiting his purchases to 40 gallons (see Figure 5.5).

Why does the U.S. government offer food stamps, rather than cash subsidies? The object of the food stamp program is to promote adequate nutrition among the poor. Advocates of the program believe that a dollar spent on food stamps will increase recipients' food consumption more than a dollar spent on cash subsidies. Are they correct?

Figure 5.10 includes indifference curves for two consumers, Barney and Betty, both of whom face the same resource constraint. Barney's indifference curves are shown in dark red. With cash aid, he chooses bundle E (an interior solution), spending less than $120 on food and buying fewer than 30 pounds. With food stamps, he can no longer buy bundle E. Instead, Barney chooses bundle C (a boundary solution), spending exactly $120, his food stamp allotment, on 30 pounds of food. Therefore, providing food stamps rather than cash increases his food consumption. In contrast, with cash aid, Betty chooses bundle F (an interior solution), spending more than $120 on food and buying more than 30 pounds. With food stamps, she also chooses bundle F. Providing food stamps rather than cash has no effect on Betty's choice because the amount she wishes to spend on food exceeds her food stamp allotment.

Our analysis implies that providing assistance through food stamps rather than in cash should increase food purchases by those who would otherwise spend relatively little on food (like Barney). Arguably, this is beneficial because it promotes better nutrition. Notice, however, that bundle C lies on a lower indifference curve than bundle E. Although Barney consumes more food when he receives food stamps, he is worse off than when he receives cash aid.

Does this mean that cash aid is better than food stamps? Not necessarily. Some people fear that the poor will "misuse" cash. This argument assumes that poor people understand their own needs less well than the government. Others are concerned that poor parents may place too little weight on the welfare of their children. Even if these parents view themselves as better off with cash, food stamps can still benefit their children by increasing the availability of nutritious food.

In practice, how does the Food Stamp Program affect expenditures on food? During the late 1980s, the United States government authorized several large-scale experiments with actual food stamp recipients. In each, some households were selected to receive benefits in the form of cash, while others continued to receive food stamp coupons. According to one study by economists Thomas Fraker, Alberto Martini, and James Ohls, food expenditures rose by 18 to 28 cents for each dollar converted from cash assistance to food stamps.[12]

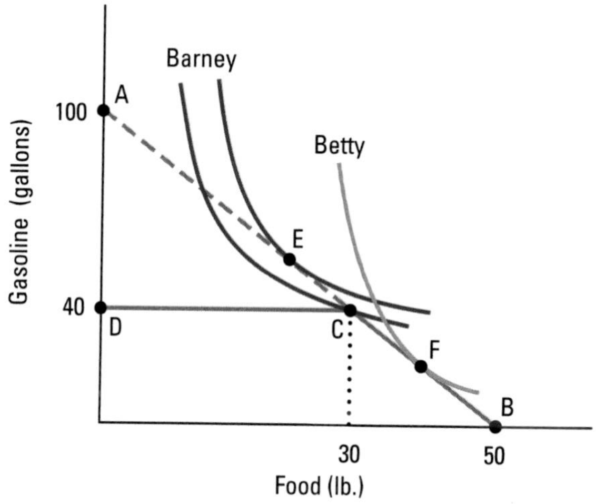

Figure 5.10

The Effect of the Food Stamp Program on Food Consumption. Barney and Betty each earn $80 and receive $120 in aid. Food costs $4 per pound and gasoline costs $2 per gallon. With cash aid, Barney and Betty each choose a bundle on the straight line that runs from bundle A to bundle B. With food stamps, they each choose a bundle on the solid kinked line that runs through bundles B, C, and D. Changing from cash aid to food stamps moves Barney's best choice from bundle E to bundle C, increasing his food consumption. In contrast, Betty chooses point F regardless of whether she receives cash aid or food stamps.

5.3 UTILITY MAXIMIZATION

Many important economic questions are quantitative, which is why economists use mathematics. The notion of utility, introduced in Section 4.4, is valuable because it allows us to analyze consumers' choices using precise mathematics, rather than graphs.

Remember that a utility function assigns a utility value to each consumption bundle. The consumer prefers bundles with higher utility values to bundles with lower utility values. Making the best choice is therefore the same as finding the affordable consumption bundle with the highest utility value. Mathematically, the best bundle maximizes the consumer's utility function while respecting his budget constraint. For example, if he spends his income on soup and bread, we write his problem as follows:

$$\text{Maximize } U(S, B) \text{ subject to } P_S S + P_B B \leq M$$

where $U(S, B)$ is the utility value assigned to a bundle containing S pints of soup and B ounces of bread, P_S is the price of a pint of soup, P_B is the price of an ounce of bread, and M is income.

[12]Thomas M. Fraker, Alberto P. Martini, and James C. Ohls, "The Effect of Food Stamp Cashout on Food Expenditures: An Assessment of the Findings from Four Demonstrations," *Journal of Human Resources* 30, no.4, Autumn 1995, pp. 633–649.

As we illustrate in worked-out problem 5.3, finding the utility-maximizing choice is easy when the number of alternatives is small.

WORKED-OUT PROBLEM 5.3

The Problem As in Examples 5.1 and 5.2, assume that Madeline's income is \$6 per day, soup costs \$2 per bowl, and bread costs \$2 per loaf. Suppose that her preferences correspond to the utility function $U(S, B) = 2S + B + SB$, where S stands for bowls of soup and B stands for loaves of bread. What will Madeline choose? What if her income is \$4 per day instead of \$6 per day?

The Solution Each cell in Table 5.3(a) represents a possible choice. In contrast to Table 5.2, the number in each cell is the utility value for that particular bundle, not Madeline's preference ranking. For example, the utility index associated with three bowls of soup and two loaves of bread is 14, because $(2 \times 3) + 2 + (2 \times 3) = 14$. Since prices and income are the same as in Example 5.2, the affordable bundles (the green-shaded cells) are the same as those shown in Table 5.2. The green-shaded cell with the highest utility index, 7, corresponds to a consumption bundle with two bowls of soup and one loaf of bread. That is Madeline's best choice.

If Madeline can spend only \$4, fewer choices are available to her (see Table 5.3(b)). Two of the available choices share the highest utility index. One offers two bowls of soup and no bread; the other offers one bowl of soup and one loaf of bread. These are Madeline's best choices, and she is indifferent between them.

IN-TEXT EXERCISE 5.5 **Suppose Madeline's preferences correspond to the utility function $U = SB$. Assume that her income is \$8 per day, soup costs \$2 per bowl, and bread costs \$2 per loaf. What will she choose? What if bread costs \$4 per loaf instead of \$2 per loaf? How would your answers change if her preferences corresponded to the utility function $U = 4SB$? To $U = (SB)^2$? What do these comparisons tell you about utility functions?**

Table 5.3
Maximizing Madeline's Utility

Soup price = \$2 per bowl, Bread price = \$2 per loaf, Utility = $2S + 2B + SB$

(a) Income = \$6 per day

Bread (loaves)				
3	3	8	13	18
2	2	6	10	14
1	1	4	(7)	10
0	0	2	4	6
Soup (bowls)	0	1	2	3

(b) Income = \$4 per day

Bread (loaves)				
3	3	8	13	18
2	2	6	10	14
1	1	(4)	7	10
0	0	2	(4)	6
Soup (bowls)	0	1	2	3

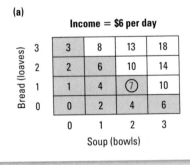

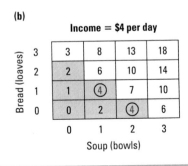

Maximizing Utility with Finely Divisible Goods

In cases with finely divisible goods, we can solve utility maximization problems and thereby identify consumers' best choices using standard mathematical tools, including calculus. That is why the utility maximization framework is so useful. In this book, we do not assume you know calculus. (To learn how to solve utility maximization problems using calculus or numerically, read Add-On 5A.) However, even without calculus, we can still explain the basic principles of utility maximization.

Let's think about decisions involving soup and bread. We know that the consumer's best choice lies on his budget line. To find the bundle on the budget line that delivers the highest level of utility, we'll start at the bundle he obtains by spending all of his income on soup [bundle F in Figure 5.6(a)] and move along the budget line by shifting resources from soup to bread.

In terms of utility, every dollar of income shifted from soup to bread creates both a benefit and a cost. The benefit is the increase in utility resulting from the increase in the amount of bread consumed. The cost is the decrease in utility resulting from the reduction amount of soup consumed. In Section 3.2, we learned that the marginal benefit must equal the marginal cost at any interior choice that maximizes the net benefit. What does that principle imply in this context?

Let's start with the marginal benefit of shifting resources from soup to bread. If the consumer spends one more dollar on bread, he will have $1/P_B$ additional ounces. For example, if bread costs \$0.50 per ounce, then an extra dollar buys 2 ounces. If he adds one ounce of bread, his utility will increase by approximately MU_B, the marginal utility of bread. (We discussed the concept of marginal utility in Section 4.4.) To determine the gain in utility resulting from the additional dollar's worth of bread, we multiply the number of ounces added, $1/P_B$, by the increase in utility per ounce added, MU_B, which gives us MU_B/P_B. This is the marginal benefit of shifting resources to bread.

Now consider the marginal cost of shifting resources from soup to bread. If the consumer spends a dollar less on soup, he will buy $1/P_S$ fewer pints. The loss of one pint causes his utility to fall by approximately MU_S, the marginal utility of soup. So his utility falls by MU_S/P_S with the loss of $1/P_S$ pints. This is the marginal cost of shifting resources to bread.

Setting marginal benefit equal to marginal cost, we have

$$\frac{MU_B}{P_B} = \frac{MU_S}{P_S} \qquad (6)$$

This formula holds at any interior solution. It tells us that the alternative uses of the consumer's resources are equally valuable at the margin.

What about boundary solutions? If the utility maximizing bundle contains no bread, then the marginal benefit of shifting resources from soup to bread must not exceed the marginal cost (see the appendix to Chapter 3). Therefore,

$$\frac{MU_S}{P_S} \geq \frac{MU_B}{P_B} \qquad (7)$$

This formula tells us that, at the boundary solution, the consumer gains at least as much by spending money on soup rather than bread at the margin.

WORKED-OUT PROBLEM 5.4

The Problem As in worked-out problem 5.2, Natasha's income is \$300 per month. She spends all of it on tickets to concerts and films. A concert ticket costs \$15 and a film ticket costs \$10. Her preferences correspond to the utility function $U(C,F) = C \times F$, where C stands for the number of concerts and F stands for the number of films. For that utility function, the marginal benefit of concert tickets is F, the number of film tickets, and the marginal benefit of film tickets is C, the number of concert tickets. (To understand why, refer back to Section 4.4, where we discussed a similar utility function for soup and bread.) As before, fractions are allowed. How many film tickets will she purchase, and how many concert tickets?

The Solution The same logic that led us to formula (6) tells us that $MU_C/P_C = MU_F/P_F$ at an interior optimum. Substituting $MU_C = F$, $MU_F = C$, $P_C = 15$, and $P_F = 10$ into the preceding formula, we discover that $F/15 = C/10$, which implies that $F/C = 1.5$. Reasoning exactly as in the last paragraph of the solution to worked-out problem 5.2, we conclude that $C = 10$, and $F = 15$.

IN-TEXT EXERCISE 5.6 **In worked-out problem 5.4, how many of each kind of ticket will Natasha choose if concert tickets cost \$30 each, and film tickets cost \$15 each?**

Utility Maximization and Best Affordable Bundles

Utility maximization isn't different from the theory of consumer choice described in Section 5.2. It's simply another way to describe the same theory. A consumer's best affordable bundle is also his utility maximizing bundle, and vice versa.

To underscore this point, we'll show that formula (6), which holds for interior choices that maximize utility, is just another way of writing formula (4), the tangency condition for best affordable choices. Let's start by rearranging formula (6) as follows:

$$\frac{P_S}{P_B} = \frac{MU_S}{MU_B}$$

Now recall from Section 4.4 that

$$\frac{MU_S}{MU_B} = MRS_{SB}$$

If we substitute the last formula into the previous one, we obtain formula (4).

Similarly, expression (7), which holds for boundary solutions, is just another way of writing expression (5). To show this, we rearrange expression (7) as follows:

$$\frac{MU_S}{MU_B} \geq \frac{P_S}{P_B}$$

Combining this expression with the previous formula produces expression (5).

5.4 PRICES AND DEMAND

In the last few sections, we developed a theory that explains how consumers allocate their limited resources over available goods. If we know the price of each good together with the consumer's income and preferences, the theory tells us what the consumer will purchase. If a price changes, the theory tells us how the consumer's purchases will change. Put another way, the theory allows us to study the properties of demand curves (which we introduced in Chapter 2).

The Price-Consumption Curve

Oscar spends his income, \$10 per day, on soup and bread. Bread costs \$0.25 per ounce. If his preferences correspond to the red indifference curves shown in Figure 5.11, how will his best choice vary with the price of soup?

If soup costs \$1 per pint, the green line labeled L_1 in Figure 5.11 will be Oscar's budget line, and he will choose bundle A. If soup costs \$2 per pint, the green line labeled L_2 will be his budget line, and he will choose bundle B. If soup costs \$0.50 per pint, the green line labeled L_3 will be his budget line, and he will choose bundle C. Table 5.4 lists his chosen bundle for each of these three soup prices.

If we plotted Oscar's best choices for many other prices in Figure 5.11, the chosen bundles would trace out a curve, drawn as the blue line running through bundles A, B,

Figure 5.11

Effects of a Change in the Price of Soup on Soup and Bread Consumption. The price of bread is \$0.25 per ounce and Oscar's income is \$10. When the price of soup is \$1 per pint, the budget line is L_1 and Oscar chooses bundle A. When the price of soup is \$2 per pint, the budget line is L_2 and he chooses bundle B. When the price of soup is \$0.50 per pint, the budget line is L_3 and he chooses bundle C.

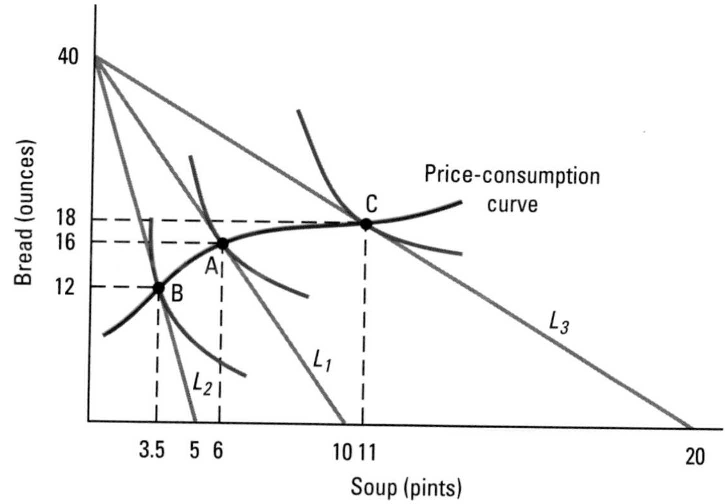

Table 5.4
Best Choices of Soup and Bread at Selected Soup Prices

Assumes the price of bread is $0.25 per ounce and Oscar's income is $10. Based on Figure 5.11.

Price of Soup (per pint)	Best Choice (from Fig. 5.11)	Soup (pints)	Bread (ounces)
$0.50	C	11	18
1.00	A	6	16
2.00	B	3.5	12

The **price-consumption curve** shows how the best affordable consumption bundle changes as the price of a good changes, holding everything else fixed (including the consumer's income and preferences, as well as all other prices).

and C. This is known as the **price-consumption curve**. It shows how the best affordable consumption bundle changes as the price of a good changes, holding everything else fixed (including the consumer's income and preferences, as well as all other prices).

Individual Demand Curves

An **individual demand curve** describes the relationship between the price of a good and the amount a particular consumer purchases, holding everything else fixed (including the consumer's income and preferences, as well as all other prices).

An **individual demand curve** describes the relationship between the price of a good and the amount a particular consumer purchases, holding everything else fixed (including the consumer's income and preferences, as well as all other prices). In the process of finding a consumer's price-consumption curve, we learn everything we need to plot his demand curve.

For an illustration, look at Figure 5.12. The horizontal axis measures pints of soup and the vertical axis measures the price of soup. We've used this graph to plot the data on prices and soup consumption from Table 5.4. The figure shows that Oscar purchases 3.5 pints of soup when the price of soup is $2 per pint (point E), 6 pints when the price is $1

Figure 5.12
An Individual Demand Curve for Soup. According to Table 5.4, Oscar purchases 3.5 pints of soup when soup costs $2 per pint (point E), 6 pints when the price is $1 per pint (point F), and 11 pints when the price is $0.50 per pint (point G). These points lie on Oscar's demand curve for soup, shown here in blue.

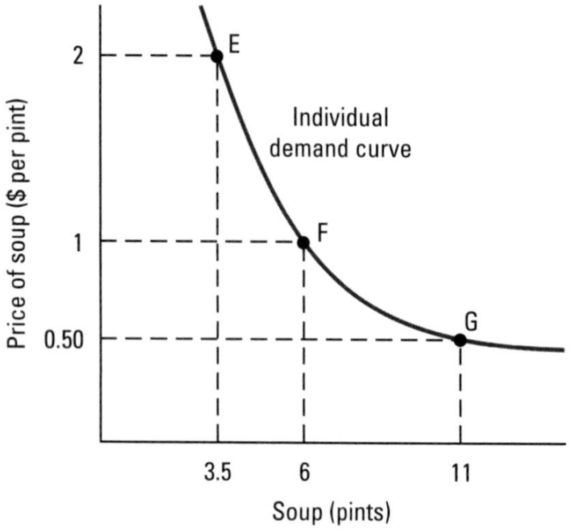

per pint (point F), and 11 pints when the price is $0.50 per pint (point G). If we plotted Oscar's choices for many other soup prices, the chosen bundles would trace out the blue curve running through E, F, and G. This is an individual demand curve for soup. For every soup price, it shows the amount of soup consumed.

Movements along an individual demand curve—for example, from point E to point F in Figure 5.12—show the sensitivity of the amount purchased to the good's price. The price elasticity of demand, which we discussed in Section 2.4, measures this sensitivity; it indicates the percentage change in demand resulting from a 1 percent change in price. When the price elasticity of demand is large in magnitude, a slight increase in price leads to a substantial reduction in the amount purchased, and the demand curve is relatively flat. When this elasticity is small in magnitude, a large increase in price leads to a slight reduction in the amount purchased, and the demand curve is relatively steep. For additional details, review Section 2.4.

Application 5.2

Individual Demand Curves for Groceries

What do individual demand curves actually look like? One study carefully tracked the grocery purchases of 80 British consumers for 16 weeks.[13] Each consumer made multiple shopping trips during that time period. The prices of various products fluctuated from one shopping trip to another, producing variation in the amounts purchased. If we assume that the consumers' demand curves were stable over the 16-week study period, we can plot those curves using the data on prices and the amounts purchased.[14]

Figure 5.13 shows the individual demand curves for five of the 80 consumers and three product categories (biscuits, cheese, and breakfast cereal). Instead of plotting the data points themselves, we have graphed the constant elasticity curves that best fit these points. (For a discussion of how economists estimate demand curves, see the appendix to Chapter 2.) We've used colors to indicate which demand curve belongs to which consumer. For example, the yellow demand curves in Figures 5.13(a), (b), and (c) all belong to the same consumer.

Notice that all of the individual demand curves in Figure 5.13 are downward sloping; these consumers buy less as prices rise. The sensitivity of purchases to prices varies across consumers and across goods. Among these five consumers, the price elasticity of the demand for biscuits ranges from −0.30 (the dark red curve) to −1.02 (the blue curve); the price elasticity of demand for cheese ranges from −0.47 (the yellow curve) to −2.11 (the green curve); and the price elasticity of demand for breakfast cereal ranges from −0.17 (the blue curve) to −0.78 (the green curve, which is almost indistinguishable from the dark red curve). The average demand elasticities for all 80 consumers in the study are −0.54 for biscuits, −1.01 for cheese, and −0.55 for breakfast cereal.

[13]Jorge Oliveira-Castro, Gordon Foxall, and Teresa Schrezenmaier, "Consumer Brand Choice: Individual and Group Analysis of Demand Elasticity," *Journal of the Experimental Analysis of Behavior* 85, no. 2, March 2006, pp. 147–166.

[14]Plots of prices against the amounts purchased will not correspond to demand curves if these curves were not stable during the 16-week study period, and if sellers changed their prices in response to changes in demand. We discussed this type of problem in the appendix to Chapter 2. Simple plots of prices and quantities can also be misleading when prices are correlated with other variables that influence demand. In such cases, economists estimate demand curves using more sophisticated statistical techniques.

Figure 5.13

Individual Demand Curves for Three Product Categories. This figure shows the individual demand curves for five actual consumers and three product categories (biscuits, cheese, and breakfast cereal). The curves are based on prices and the amounts purchased during shopping trips over a 16-week period. Each consumer is associated with the same color in figures (a), (b), and (c).

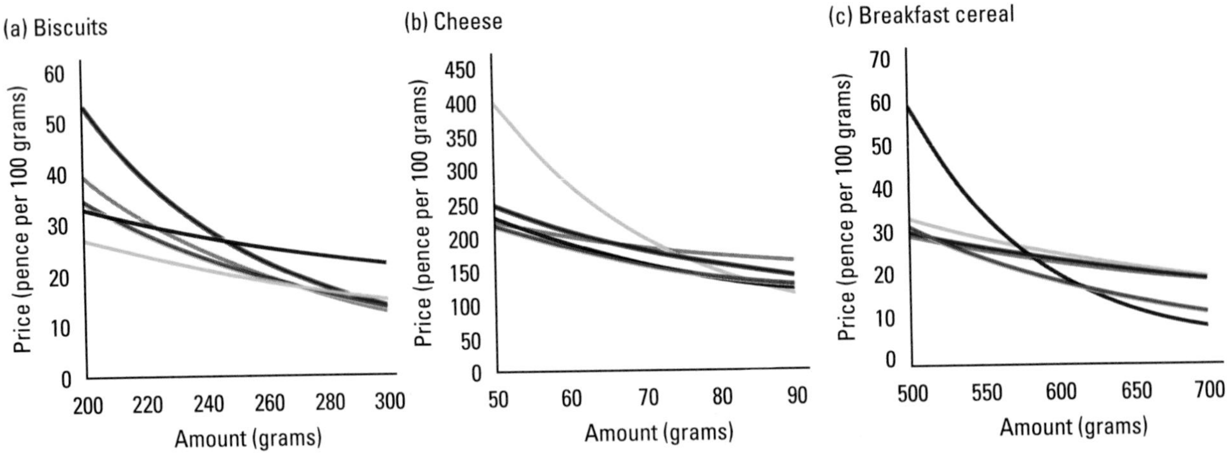

Source: Jorge Oliveira-Castro, Gordon Foxall, and Teresa Schrezenmaier, "Consumer Brand Choice: Individual and Group Analysis of Demand Elasticity," *Journal of the Experimental Analysis of Behavior* 85, no. 2, March 2006, pp. 147–166.

WORKED-OUT PROBLEM 5.5

The Problem As in worked-out problem 5.2, Natasha's marginal rate of substitution for concerts with films, MRS_{CF}, is F/C, where C stands for the number of concert tickets and F stands for the number of films. Natasha's income is \$100 per month, and concert tickets cost \$5 per ticket. Draw her price-consumption curve (allowing the price of film tickets, P_F, to vary) and her demand curve for film tickets. What is her elasticity of demand for film tickets? What fraction of her income does she spend on film tickets, and how does that fraction depend on the price of film tickets?

The Solution Since Natasha's best choice must satisfy the tangency condition, it equates her marginal rate of substitution, F/C, with the price ratio, P_C/P_F, so $F/C = P_C/P_F$. Rearranging this formula, we learn that the tangency condition requires the following relationship between film tickets and concert tickets:

$$F = (P_C/P_F)C$$

Since Natasha's best choice also lies on her budget line, it also satisfies $M = P_C C + P_F F$. To find a bundle that satisfies both the tangency condition formula and the budget line formula, we substitute for F in the budget constraint using the tangency condition formula:

$$M = P_C C + P_F\,(P_C/P_F)C = 2P_C C$$

So $C = M/(2P_C)$. Plugging this into the tangency condition formula gives us $F = M/(2P_F)$. With $M = 100$ and $P_C = 5$, we have $C = 10$ and $F = 50/P_F$. So, for example, when $P_F = 5$, Natasha buys 10 concert tickets and 10 film tickets; when $P_F = 10$, she buys 10 concert tickets and 5 film tickets. We show her price-consumption curve in Figure 5.14(a) and her demand curve for film tickets in Figure 5.14(b). Notice in Figure 5.14(a) that the number of concert tickets does not vary with the price of film tickets. That property is a consequence of Natasha's particular preferences.

Notice that we can rewrite the formula $F = M/(2P_F)$ as $F = (M/2)P_F^{-1}$. From our discussion of demand elasticity in Section 2.4, we recognize this as a constant elasticity demand curve, where the demand elasticity is -1. Multiplying both sides of the demand function by P_F, we see that $FP_F = M/2$, which means that Natasha always spends exactly half her income on film tickets, regardless of the price of film tickets.

IN-TEXT EXERCISE 5.7 **For Alejandro, concert tickets and film tickets are perfect complements—he does not enjoy additional concerts when he has attended more concerts than films, or additional films when he has attended more films than concerts. Assume he can spend \$200 on tickets, and that film tickets cost \$8 per ticket. Draw his price-consumption curve (allowing the price of concert tickets to vary) and his demand curve for concert tickets.**

Figure 5.14

Effects of a Change in the Price of Film Tickets on Natasha's Purchases of Film and Concert Tickets. The solution to worked-out problem 5.5 implies that with an income of \$100 per month, Natasha spends \$50 to buy 10 concert tickets, regardless of the price of film tickets. The price-consumption curve, shown in figure (a), is therefore a flat line. She spends the remaining \$50 on film tickets, so her film ticket purchases fall as the price of a film ticket rises, as shown in figure (b).

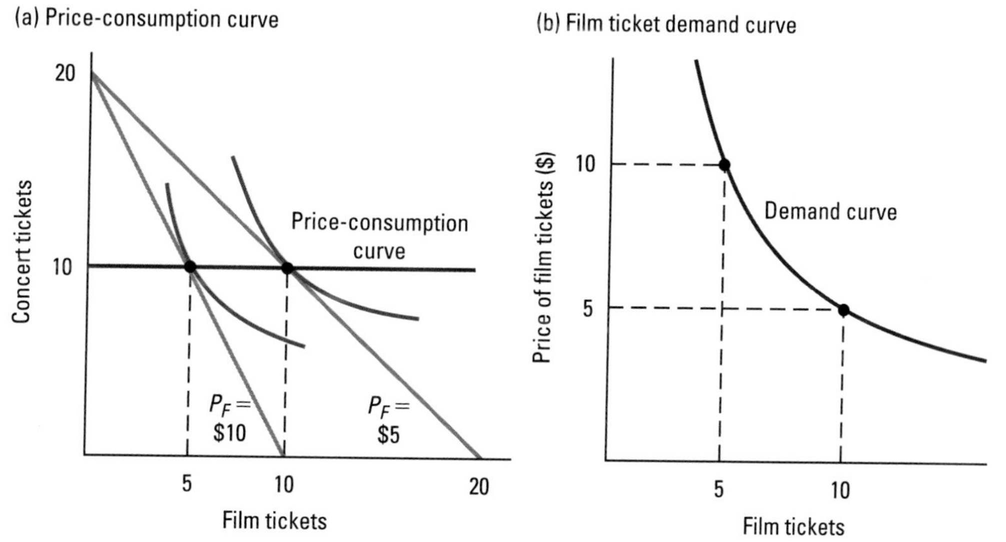

Price Changes and Shifts in Demand

In Section 2.1, we saw that a change in the price of one good can shift the demand curve for a second good. For an illustration of this effect, look back at Table 5.4. To construct this table, we fixed the price of bread at $0.25 per ounce and varied the price of soup. According to the table, when soup costs $0.50 per pint, Oscar buys 18 ounces of bread; this means that his demand curve for bread, labeled D_1 in Figure 5.15, passes through point H. Likewise, when soup costs $1 per pint, he buys 16 ounces of bread, so his demand curve for bread, labeled D_2 in Figure 5.15, passes through point J. Finally, when soup costs $2 per pint, he buys 12 ounces of bread, so his demand curve for bread, labeled D_3 in Figure 5.15, passes through point K. We can trace out the rest of each demand curve by finding his best choice at other bread prices, holding income and the price of soup fixed.

Figure 5.15 shows how changes in the price of soup shift Oscar's demand curve for bread. An *increase* in the price of soup from $1 to $2 per pint shifts the demand curve for bread to the left, and the consumption of bread *falls* at any fixed bread price. A *reduction* in the price of soup from $1 to $0.50 per pint shifts the demand curve for bread to the right; the consumption of bread *rises* at any fixed bread price.

In Section 2.1, we observed that some pairs of goods are complements. When the price of a complement increases, a consumer buys less of the good in question. Since the consumption of complementary goods tends to move together, the price-consumption curve is upward sloping, as in Figure 5.11. For Oscar, soup and bread are complements.

We also observed in Section 2.1 that some pairs of goods are substitutes. When the price of a substitute increases, the consumer buys more of the good in question. Since the consumption of substitutable goods tends to move in opposite directions, the price-consumption curve is downward sloping.

For an illustration, look at Figure 5.16. Daphne purchases butter and margarine. Her preferences correspond to the red indifference curves. Margarine costs 10 cents per ounce and she can spend $10 total over the course of a month. When butter costs 25 cents per ounce, her budget line is L_1, and she chooses bundle A. When butter costs 40 cents per ounce, her budget line is L_2, and she chooses bundle B. When butter costs 10 cents

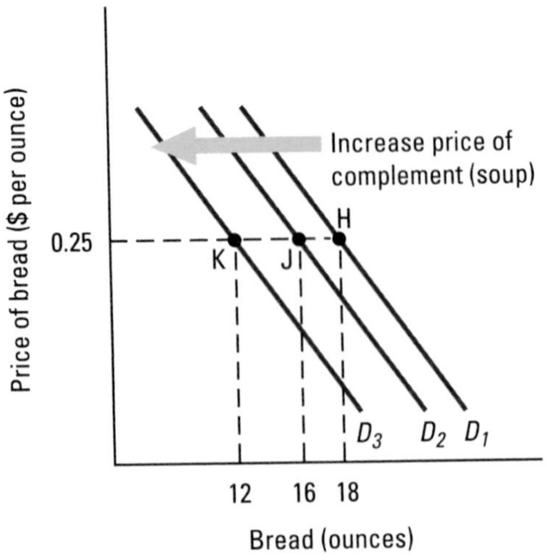

Figure 5.15
Demand for Bread and the Price of Soup. According to Table 5.4, Oscar purchases 18 ounces of bread when the price of soup is $0.50 per pint (point H), 16 ounces of bread when the price of soup is $1 per pint (point J), and 12 ounces of bread when the price of soup is $2 per pint (point K). Each of these points lies on a different demand curve for bread—point H lies on D_1, point J lies on D_2, and point K lies on D_3. In this example, bread and soup are complements: an increase in the price of soup shifts the demand curve for bread to the left.

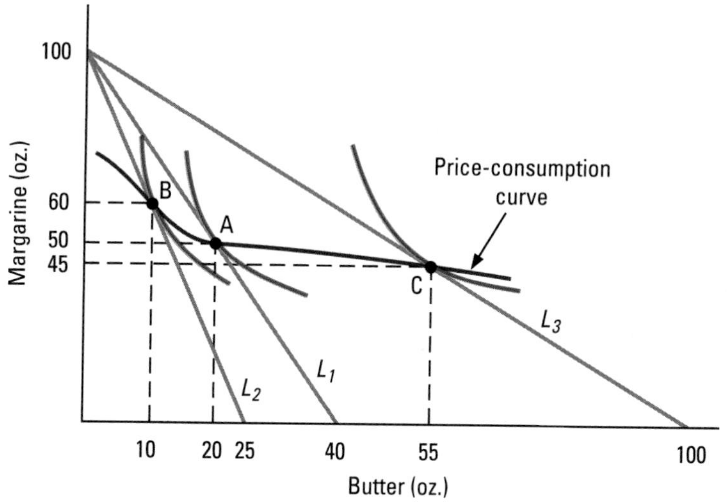

Figure 5.16

Effects of a Change in the Price of Butter on the Consumption of Butter and Margarine. The price of margarine is 10 cents per ounce, and Daphne can spend $10 on butter and margarine. When the price of butter is 25¢ per ounce, her budget line is L_1 and she chooses bundle A. When the price of butter is 40¢ per ounce, her budget line is L_2 and she chooses bundle B. When the price of butter is 10¢ per ounce, her budget line is L_3 and she chooses bundle C. The blue line is her price-consumption curve.

per ounce, her budget line is L_3, and she chooses bundle C. Notice that an increase in the price of butter leads Daphne to purchase more margarine. This means that her margarine demand curve (not shown) shifts to the right. A reduction in the price of butter leads her to purchase less margarine, which shifts her margarine demand curve to the left. For Daphne, butter and margarine are substitutes.

Products tend to be complements when consumers use them together. Think of DVD players and DVDs, bathing suits and sunscreen, or flashlights and batteries. Products tend to be substitutes when consumers use them interchangeably for similar purposes. Think of Corn Flakes and Cheerios, Coke and Pepsi, or voice mail and answering machines. For a practical illustration of substitution between goods, read Add-On 5B.

Unfortunately, it isn't always possible to tell whether goods are complements or substitutes by thinking about whether they are used together or interchangeably. For example, since people use gasoline and automobiles together, these products may seem to be complements. But the truth is not so simple. An increase in the price of gasoline encourages people to buy fuel-efficient cars rather than gas-guzzling sport utility vehicles (SUVs). That means gasoline is a complement to SUVs but may be a substitute for fuel-efficient cars, even though fuel-efficient cars use gas.

5.5 INCOME AND DEMAND

The next time you're in the checkout line at a grocery store, pay attention to the items in other shoppers' carts. If you look closely, you'll see patterns. A well-groomed woman dangles a Lexus key chain while the checker rings up premium cuts of filet mignon and an expensive bottle of French wine. An elderly man who is purchasing basic supplies eyes the register nervously while sorting through his coupons. What do we learn from these observations? Though prices and preferences influence consumers' decisions, they don't explain everything. Income is clearly an important consideration. Were the Lexus driver to lose her high-paying job, she might forgo wine and start clipping coupons. Were the elderly man to win the lottery, he might regularly indulge in premium steaks and fine wine.

An **income effect** is the change in the consumption of a good that results from a change in income.

Economists refer to a change in the consumption of a good that results from a change in income as an **income effect**. For a better understanding of income effects, we turn once more to the theory of consumer behavior.

The Income-Consumption Curve

Let's return to our discussion of Oscar's soup and bread purchases. We'll assume that soup costs $1 per pint and bread costs $0.25 per ounce, and that Oscar's preferences correspond to the red indifference curves in Figure 5.17. How does his choice vary as we change his income? If his income is $10, his budget line is L_1, and he chooses bundle A (just as in Figure 5.11). If his income is $5, his budget line is L_2, and he chooses bundle B. If his income is $15, his budget line is L_3, and he chooses bundle C. Table 5.5 summarizes these choices.

The **income-consumption curve** shows how the best affordable consumption bundle changes as income changes, holding everything else fixed (including prices and the consumer's preferences).

If we plotted Oscar's choices for many other income levels in Figure 5.17, the chosen bundles would trace out a curve, shown as the blue line running through A, B, and C. This is known as the **income-consumption curve**. It shows how the best affordable consumption bundle changes as income changes, holding everything else fixed (including prices and the consumer's preferences).

Normal versus Inferior Goods

If a good is **normal,** an increase in income raises the amount that is consumed.

Economists say that a good is **normal** if an increase in income raises the amount that is consumed. In Figure 5.17, soup and bread are both normal goods. Why? As Oscar's income rises from $5 to $10 to $15, the best choice shifts from bundle B to bundle A to bundle C. The consumption of soup rises with income, as does the consumption of bread—see Table 5.5.

Figure 5.17

Effect of a Change in Income on Soup and Bread Consumption. Soup costs $1 per pint and bread costs $0.25 per ounce. When Oscar's income is $10, his budget line is L_1 and he chooses bundle A. When his income is $5, his budget line is L_2 and he chooses bundle B. When his income is $15, his budget line is L_3 and he chooses bundle C.

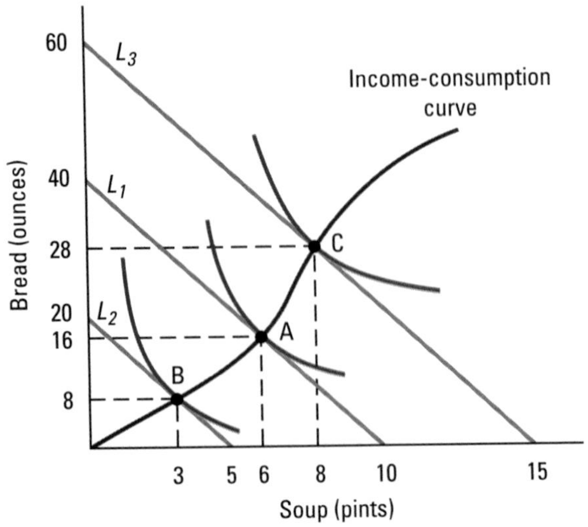

Table 5.5
Best Choices of Soup and Bread with Selected Income Levels

Assumes soup costs \$1 per pint and bread costs \$0.25 per ounce. Based on Figure 5.17.

Income	Best Choice (from Fig. 5.17)	Soup (pints)	Bread (ounces)
\$5	B	3	8
		Normal ↓	Normal ↓
10	A	6	16
		Normal ↓	Normal ↓
15	C	8	28

If a good is **inferior**, an increase in income reduces the amount that is consumed.

Economists say that a good is **inferior** if an increase in income *reduces* the amount that is consumed. This term reflects the fact that the consumption of many goods declines as income rises because people shift toward higher-quality products that fill similar needs. For example, posters are popular among college students who typically have limited funds with which to decorate their rooms and apartments. As incomes rise, most people graduate from posters to prints and reproductions, and finally to original artwork. Few if any posters grace the walls of those who appear on *Lifestyles of the Rich and Famous*.

For a graphical illustration, look at Figure 5.18. The red indifference curves correspond to the preferences of a consumer, Erin, whose diet consists exclusively of beef and potatoes, and who has no other expenses. Erin prefers the taste of meat to potatoes, but her first priority is to avoid hunger. With meat priced at \$3 per pound compared to \$0.50 per pound for potatoes, a dollar spent on meat is much less filling than a dollar spent on potatoes.

When Erin can spend \$18 per month, her budget line is L_1 and bundle A is her best choice. Since she can't afford filling meals, she buys 30 pounds of potatoes and only

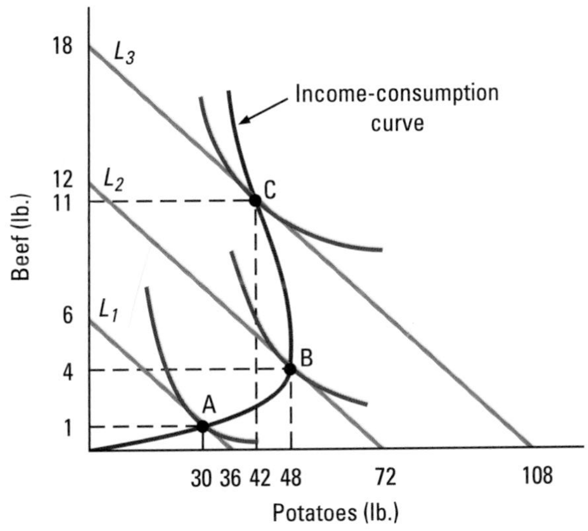

Figure 5.18
Effects of a Change in Income on Potato and Beef Consumption. Beef costs \$3 per pound and potatoes cost \$0.50 per pound. When Erin can spend \$18 in total, her budget line is L_1 and she chooses bundle A. When she can spend \$36 in total, her budget line is L_2 and she chooses bundle B. When she can spend \$54 in total, her budget line is L_3 and she chooses bundle C.

Table 5.6

Best Choices of Potatoes and Beef with Selected Income Levels

Assumes beef costs $3 per lb. and potatoes cost $0.50 per lb. Based on Figure 5.18.

Income	Best Choice (from Fig. 5.26)	Potatoes (lb.)	Beef (lb.)
$18	A	30	1
		Normal ↓	Normal ↓
36	B	48	4
		Inferior ↓	Normal ↓
54	C	42	11

one pound of beef. When her income increases to $36, her budget line is L_2 and her best choice is bundle B. Though she spends much of the extra cash on potatoes, purchasing 48 pounds, she also buys more beef (4 pounds), because her meals are now reasonably filling. When her income increases beyond $36, she tries to make her meals as tasty as possible while making sure that they remain filling. With $54, her budget line is L_3. While she *could* purchase even more potatoes, she wouldn't benefit much from them—they aren't tasty, and she's already full. Instead, she chooses bundle C. Her beef consumption rises to 11 pounds, but her potato consumption *falls* to 42 pounds. Table 5.6 summarizes these choices. Here, beef is a normal good at all levels of income, but potatoes change from normal to inferior as income rises.

In Section 2.4, we studied the income elasticity of demand for a good, which measures the sensitivity of purchases to changes in income. The income elasticity of demand is positive for normal goods because consumption rises with income, and negative for inferior goods because consumption falls with income. For example, according to one study of British households, the income elasticity of demand is 0.20 for butter and −0.37 for margarine.[15] As income rises, these households shift their purchases from margarine, an inferior good, to butter, a normal good.

It's easy to tell whether goods are normal or inferior by examining the income-consumption curve. Figure 5.19 illustrates this point. When the consumer's budget line is L_1, he selects point A. Budget line L_2 corresponds to a higher level of income.

- If the income-consumption curve slopes upward, the best choice on L_2 lies to the northeast of A (for example, the dark blue curve labeled ICC_1 runs through bundle B). That means potatoes and beef are both normal goods.
- If the income-consumption curve bends back toward the vertical axis, the best choice on L_2 lies to the northwest of A (for example, the medium blue curve labeled ICC_2 runs through bundle C). That means potatoes are inferior and beef is normal.
- If the income-consumption curve bends downward toward the horizontal axis, the best choice on L_2 lies to the southeast of A (for example, the light blue curve labeled ICC_3 runs through bundle D). That means potatoes are normal and beef is inferior.

To understand the characteristics of consumer preferences that make a particular good normal or inferior, read Add-On 5C.

[15]Department of Environment, Food, and Rural Affairs, *National Food Survey: 2000*, U.K.

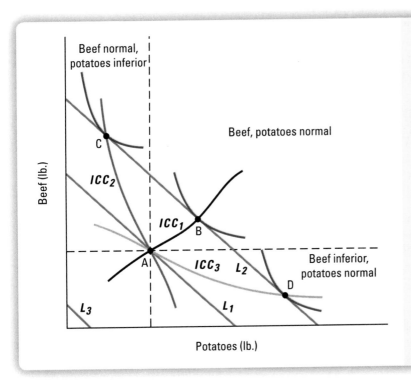

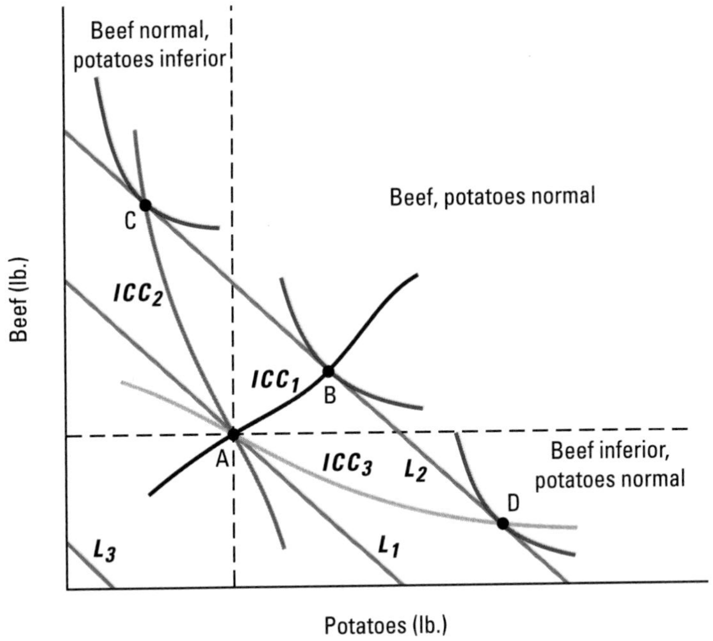

Figure 5.19

Classifying the Effects of a Change in Income on Potato and Beef Consumption. Initially, the consumer's budget line is L_1 and he chooses bundle A. An increase in income shifts his budget line outward to L_2. If he selects a bundle to the northeast of A, such as B, both potatoes and beef are normal goods. If he selects a bundle to the northwest of A, such as C, potatoes are inferior and beef is normal. If he selects a bundle to the southeast of A, such as D, potatoes are normal and beef is inferior.

Can all goods be inferior? No. At least one good must be normal. Look again at Figure 5.19. When the consumer moves from bundle A on the budget line L_1 to a bundle on the new budget line, L_2, the consumption of *something* must rise. If he purchased less of *everything*, the new bundle would have to lie to the southwest of A, which means it would not lie on the new budget line.

Can a good be inferior at all levels of income? No—every good must be normal over some income range. Figure 5.19 again provides the reason. Suppose the consumer's income falls sharply, leaving him on budget line L_3. We know that his best choice must lie somewhere on this new budget line. But *all* the bundles on this line lie to the southwest of A, which means they contain both fewer potatoes and less beef. In general, if income declines sufficiently, the consumption of *every* good must fall.

Let's summarize what we've learned about normal and inferior goods:

Properties of Normal and Inferior Goods

1. The income elasticity of demand is positive for normal goods and negative for inferior goods.
2. We can tell whether goods are normal or inferior by examining the slope of the income-consumption curve.
3. At least one good must be normal.
4. No good can be inferior at all levels of income.

Knowing whether products are normal or inferior is often important in business settings. Companies that sell inferior goods typically target their marketing efforts at lower-income households. But as Application 5.3 illustrates, they can also do quite well during economic downturns and recessions, when household incomes fall.

Application 5.3

Two Buck Chuck

After 10 years of steady growth, U.S. economic activity reached a peak in March 2001 and then slid into a recession. As jobs disappeared and household incomes slipped, many consumers were forced to curtail unnecessary spending. Sales of luxury products, such as high-end wines, were particularly hard hit.

Enter Franzia, best known as the producer of low-end "wine-in-a-box." The company's strategy: capitalize on the recession-driven shift to lower-quality products with an inexpensive but acceptable alternative to mid-range wines. This strategy required careful attention to both packaging and product development.

Reasoning that any acceptable alternative would have to have the look and feel of better products, Franzia's product development team chose expensive-looking wine bottles (rather than boxes or jugs), synthetic corks, and upscale foil capsules. Instead of brewing generic white and red offerings, they made varietals, including a Chardonnay, a Sauvignon Blanc, a Cabernet Sauvignon, and a Merlot. In each case, they created a relatively dry wine to distance the new products from cheap alternatives, which tend to be sweet. Finally, they devised a sophisticated-looking label bearing the name Charles Shaw. There is in fact no Charles Shaw winery, nor even a vintner named Charles Shaw, but the name conveys more refinement than "Franzia."

Franzia introduced the Charles Shaw line in California, selling it for $1.99 a bottle exclusively through Trader Joe's, a well-known discount retailer. Despite a predictably cool reception from skeptical wine experts, who found the quality of the wine little better than other low-end alternatives, "Two Buck Chuck" was an immediate hit with consumers. Stores had trouble keeping the wine in stock. Soon it was outselling famous budget brands, such as Gallo and Mondavi. Franzia expanded distribution into other states, with similar results. By early 2003, Charles Shaw was a national phenomenon, and Franzia was shipping an estimated one million cases a month.

While many factors contributed to the success of Two Buck Chuck, timing was critical. Franzia capitalized on the economic downturn by providing a cleverly designed inferior good (in the sense that economists use the term) just as declining incomes drove consumers away from higher-quality alternatives.

Figure 5.20

Engel Curves for Soup and Potatoes. Figure (a) shows Oscar's Engel curve for soup, based on the information in Table 5.5. Soup is a normal good at all levels of income. Figure (b) shows Erin's Engel curve for potatoes, based on the information in Table 5.6. Potatoes are normal when income is less than $36 and inferior when income is greater than $36.

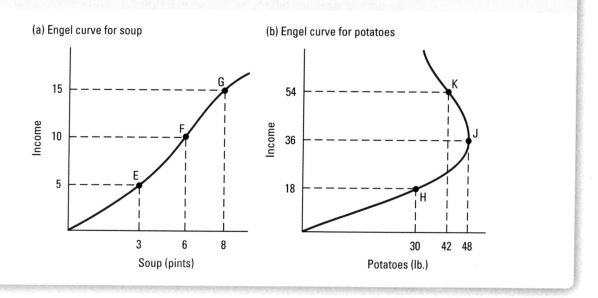

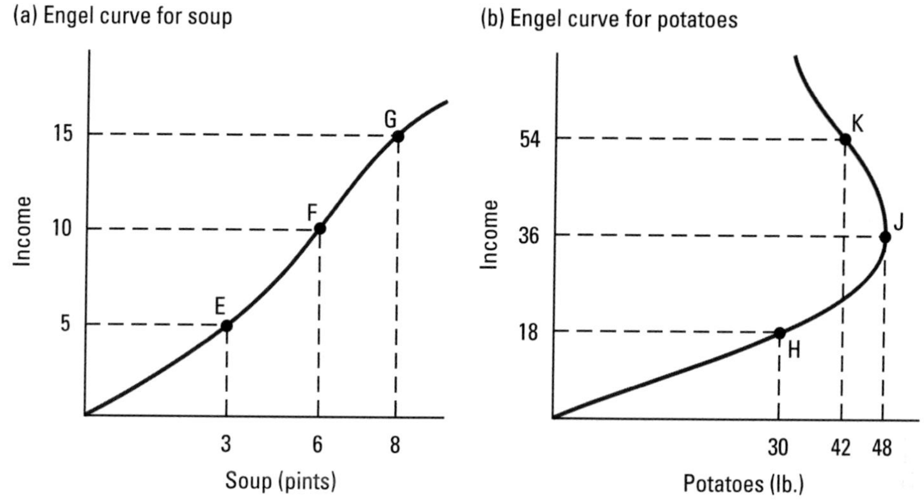

Engel Curves

The **Engel curve** for a good describes the relationship between income and the amount consumed, holding everything else fixed (including prices and the consumer's preferences). To graph an Engel curve, we measure income on the vertical axis and the amount consumed on the horizontal axis. For a normal good, an increase in income raises consumption, so the Engel curve slopes upward. For an inferior good, an increase in income reduces consumption, so the Engel curve slopes downward.

The **Engel curve** for a good describes the relationship between income and the amount consumed, holding everything else fixed (including prices and the consumer's preferences).

Figure 5.20(a) uses the data in Table 5.5 to plot three points (E, F, and G) on Oscar's Engel curve for soup (fixing the price of soup at $1 per pint and the price of bread at $0.25 per ounce). If we plotted Oscar's choices for many other income levels, we would trace out his Engel curve for soup, shown as the blue line that runs through points E, F, and G. In this example, soup is a normal good, so the Engel curve slopes upward.

Figure 5.20(b) uses the data in Table 5.6 to plot three points (H, J, and K) on Erin's Engel curve for potatoes (fixing the price of potatoes at $0.50 per pound and the price of beef at $3 per pound). If we plotted Erin's choices for many other income levels, we would trace out her Engel curve for potatoes, shown as the blue line that runs through H, J, and K. In this example, potatoes are a normal good when income is less than $36, so the lower part of the Engel curve slopes upward. However, since potatoes are an inferior good when income exceeds $36, the upper part of the Engel curve bends backward toward the vertical axis.

WORKED-OUT PROBLEM 5.6

The Problem Keiko spends all her money on two things: airtime for her wireless phone and gasoline for her car. We'll use the symbols W to stand for the number of minutes she spends talking on her wireless phone and G to stand for the number of gallons of gasoline she uses during a week. Her marginal rate of substitution for gasoline with wireless minutes, in minutes per gallon, is given by the formula $MRS_{GB} = 10/\sqrt{G}$. The price of gasoline, P_G, is \$1 per gallon and the price of wireless minutes, P_W, is \$0.50 per minute. Draw Keiko's income-consumption curve and her Engel curves for gasoline and wireless minutes.

The Solution As long as Keiko's best choice includes positive amounts of gasoline and wireless minutes, it equates her marginal rate of substitution, $10/\sqrt{G}$ minutes per gallon, with the price ratio, $P_G/P_W = 1/0.5 = 2$ minutes per gallon. From the resulting formula, $10/\sqrt{G} = 2$, we see that $G = 25$ gallons. Since the price of gasoline is \$1 per gallon, 25 gallons cost \$25. For the moment, we'll suppose that Keiko's income, M, exceeds \$25. If so, she spends \$$(M - 25)$ on wireless minutes. Since a wireless minute costs \$0.50, she buys $W = 2(M - 25)$ minutes. In other words, she spends the first \$25 of her budget on gasoline and the rest on airtime. In Figures 5.21 (a), (b), and (c), choices with income above \$25 account for the blue portions of the income-consumption curve and the Engel curves for gasoline and wireless minutes. Notice that as long as Keiko's income exceeds \$25, her consumption of gasoline does not depend on her income. Gasoline is neither a normal nor an inferior good—for this good in this income range, there are no income effects.

What if Keiko's income is less than \$25? In that case, she spends her entire income on gasoline. Why? Since she purchases fewer than 25 gallons of gasoline, her marginal rate of substitution, $10/\sqrt{G}$ minutes per gallon, is greater than 2, which means it is also greater than the price ratio. At a bundle like X in Figure 5.21(a), her indifference curve is steeper than the budget line, and the indifference curve has a diminishing MRS, so that bundle is a boundary solution. Choices with income below \$25 correspond to the yellow portions of the income-consumption curve and the Engel curves for gasoline and wireless minutes shown in Figures 5.21(a), (b), and (c).

IN-TEXT EXERCISE 5.8 **Alejandro's preferences for concert tickets and film tickets are the same as those described in in-text exercise 5.7 (page 147). Film tickets cost \$8 each and concert tickets cost \$5 each. Draw his income-consumption curve and his Engel curves for film and concert tickets. Are these two goods normal or inferior?**

Changes in Income and Shifts in the Demand Curve

We've seen that a demand curve describes the relationship between the price of a good and the amount purchased, holding everything else fixed, including income. If income changes, the demand curve shifts. When the good in question is normal, an increase in income raises consumption at each price, so the demand curve shifts to the right. A decline in income reduces consumption at each price, so the demand curve shifts to the left. When a good is inferior, these effects are reversed.

Figure 5.21

Keiko's Income-Consumption Curve and Engel Curves. The solution to worked-out problem 5.6 implies that Keiko spends the first $25 of her income on gasoline and the rest on wireless minutes. This choice produces the income-consumption curve shown in figure (a) and the Engel curves shown in figures (b) and (c).

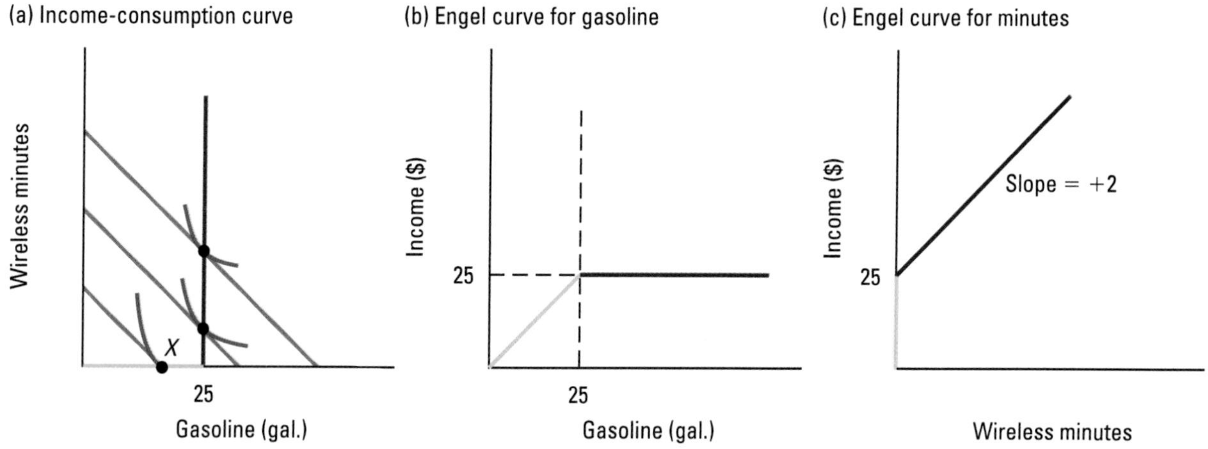

To illustrate, let's revisit Oscar's consumption of soup, a normal good (see Figure 5.17 on page 150, and Table 5.5 on page 151). Suppose that bread costs $0.25 per ounce. With an income of $10, Oscar's demand curve for soup, labeled D_{10} in Figure 5.22, passes through point F. Oscar purchases six pints at a price of $1 per pint. (This demand curve is the same one pictured in Figure 5.12 on page 144.) With an income of $5, Oscar purchases three pints of soup at a price of $1 per pint, so his demand curve for soup, labeled D_5, passes through point H. A *reduction* in income from $10 to $5 therefore shifts his demand curve to the left. With an income of $15, Oscar purchases eight pints of soup at

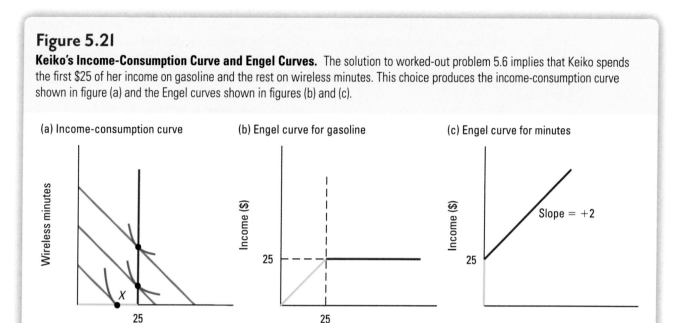

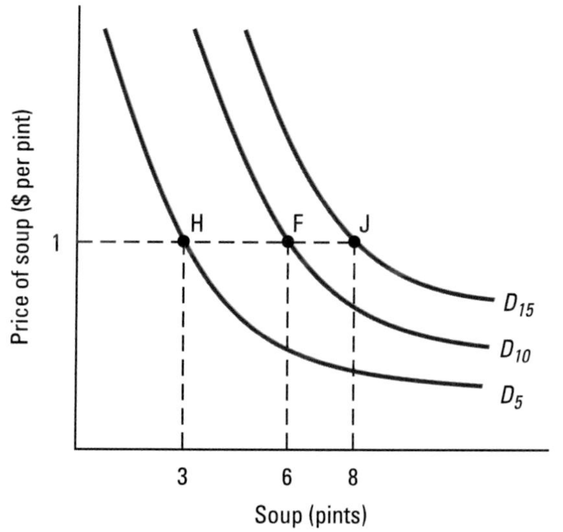

Figure 5.22

Changes in Income Shift the Demand for Soup. According to Table 5.5, which assumes that soup costs $1 per pint and bread costs $0.25 per ounce, Oscar purchases six pints of soup when his income is $10, so his demand curve for soup, D_{10}, passes through point F. He purchases three pints of soup when his income is $5, so his demand curve for soup, D_5, passes through point H. Finally, he purchases eight pints of soup when his budget is $15, so his demand curve for soup, D_{15}, passes through point J. Because soup is a normal good, an increase in Oscar's income shifts the demand curve to the right; a decrease in income shifts it to the left.

a price of \$1 per pint, so his demand curve for soup, labeled D_{15}, passes through point J. An *increase* in income from \$10 to \$15 therefore shifts his demand curve to the right.

To see an example of how a change in income shifts the demand curve for a good that is inferior over some income range, work through the following exercise.

IN-TEXT EXERCISE 5.9 **Using the information in Table 5.6 on page 152, for each level of income plot a point on Erin's demand curve for potatoes and sketch the curve through this point (like Figure 5.22). Does an increase in her income shift her demand curve for potatoes to the left or the right? Does the answer depend on her initial income?**

Application 5.4 illustrates how economists use information about consumer sensitivity to changes in both prices and income to predict choices.

Application 5.4

Forecasting Electricity Demand with Tiered Rates

In the United States, state governments have the authority to regulate the price of electricity. In some cases, the regulated price of extra electricity increases in a series of steps as the consumer's usage rises. This arrangement is known as a *tiered* rate structure. (To learn about consumer choice with other types of volume-sensitive pricing, read Add-On 5D.) The main purpose of tiered rates is to encourage conservation through higher prices, while keeping electricity affordable for the basic needs of low-income households, such as cooking, heating, and refrigeration.

To evaluate a possible change in a tiered rate structure, power companies and regulators need to know how electricity usage will change. Fortunately, forecasting changes in usage patterns requires little more than reliable measures of price and income elasticities.

To keep our analysis simple, let's assume that a consumer, Sean, spends his income on two goods, electricity and food. We'll assume that food costs \$1 per pound, and that Sean's income is \$200. Figure 5.23 shows the affordable consumption bundles associated with two alternative tiered rate structures for electricity. The horizontal axis measures kilowatt hours (kWh) of electricity and the vertical axis measures pounds of food.

Under the first rate structure, electricity costs 10 cents per kWh up to 500 kWh and 20 cents per kWh for each additional kWh. As shown in Figure 5.23, Sean's budget line is kinked; it consists of the solid portions of the lines labeled L_1 and L_2. As long as Sean uses less than 500 kWh, he can choose a bundle on the solid portion of L_1. The slope of that line equals −0.1 pound per kWh (\$0.10 per kWh ÷ \$1 per pound). If he uses more than 500 kWh, electricity becomes more costly, so his budget line becomes steeper; he can choose a bundle on the solid portion of L_2, the slope of which is −0.2 pound per kWh (\$0.20 per kWh ÷ \$1 per pound). Assuming that Sean's preferences correspond to the red indifference curves, his best choice is bundle A.

Under the second rate structure, electricity again costs 10 cents per kWh up to 500 kWh, but only 15 cents for each additional kWh. Sean's budget line consists of the solid segments of the lines labeled L_1 and L_3 (the slope of which is −0.15). His best choice is bundle B.

Let's suppose that the first rate structure is currently in place. Power companies and regulators are studying the consequences of switching to the second rate structure, which means reducing the charge for consumption over 500 kWh from 20 cents to 15 cents per kWh. How might they forecast the resulting change in electricity use?

Notice that Sean would also pick bundle A from the budget line L_2 (the whole thing, not just the solid part). Similarly, he would pick bundle B from the budget line L_3 (again, the whole thing, not just the solid part). So the change in the rate structure has the same effect on his choice as switching from budget line L_2 to budget line L_3.

We can break the switch from budget line L_2 to L_3 into two parts. The first is a reduction in the price of electricity from 20 cents to 15 cents per kWh, which rotates the budget constraint from L_2 to L_4. The second is a reduction in income sufficient to produce a parallel shift of the budget constraint from L_4 to L_3. Knowing the price elasticity of demand, we can forecast the effect of the first part. Knowing the income elasticity of demand, we can forecast the effect of the second part. Putting the two parts together, we can forecast the total impact on electricity usage.

In the spring of 2001, the California Public Utility Commission substantially increased electricity rates for customers with moderate to high usage. Economists Peter Reiss and Matthew White forecasted the effects of the rate change by analyzing data on electricity consumption for 1,307 California households in 1993 and 1997.[16] A central objective of their study was to determine the effects of the change in rate structure on households with different income levels. Did the new rate structure impact primarily wealthy households, or did it also affect the poor? To what extent did it encourage conservation, and by whom? Taking into account the differences in income and price elasticities across consumers with different incomes, Reiss and White forecasted substantial reductions in electricity use (11 percent for high-income households and 9.7 percent for low-income households), as well as substantial increases in average expenditures (28.3 percent for high-income households and 21.6 percent for low-income households). According to these predictions, the burden of the policy fell disproportionately on high-income households (as intended), but the burden on low-income households was still considerable.

Figure 5.23

Effect of a Change in Tiered Rates on Demand for Electricity. Initially, higher rates apply to electricity usage above 500 kWh, and the budget constraint is the solid portions of L_1 and L_2. Sean chooses bundle A. Facing the budget line L_2, he would make the same choice. If the rate for usage over 500 kWh is reduced, the budget constraint becomes the solid portions of L_1 and L_3. Sean chooses bundle B. Facing the budget line L_3, he would make the same choice. The effect of the change in rates is therefore the same as the effect of a shift in the budget line from L_2 to L_4 (a standard price change) plus a shift from L_4 to L_3 (a standard income change). Thus it is possible to forecast the effect of a rate change on electricity consumption using price and income elasticities.

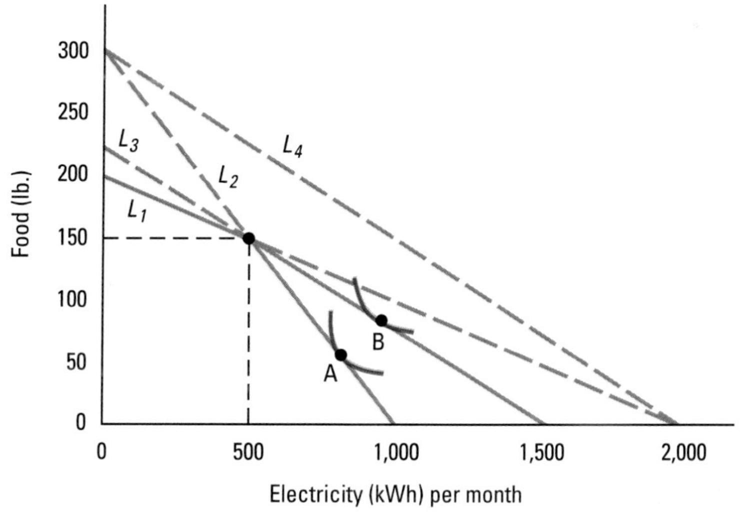

[16]Peter C. Reiss and Matthew W. White, "Household Electricity Demand, Revisited," Working Paper, Stanford University, June 14, 2002.

*5.6 HOW ECONOMISTS DETERMINE A CONSUMER'S PREFERENCES

Our theory of consumer behavior is potentially valuable in a wide range of applications. For example, an economist can use it to advise a government official on the likely effects of a policy proposal, or to forecast the success of a new pricing strategy for a business. To exploit the full power of the theory, however, we need to know a great deal about consumer preferences. How do we obtain this information?

There are two different ways to learn about consumer preferences. First, we can ask about them directly. Marketing organizations often use surveys and questionnaires to acquire information about consumer preferences. This approach has a number of limitations, however. Perhaps most important, questions about preferences are generally hypothetical. Subjects are asked to imagine two or more alternatives and say which they would prefer, but they do not actually make choices. Few people take such hypothetical questions as seriously as they would actual choices. Many also have difficulty forecasting their own behavior, even when they think seriously about it. For example, some people tend to answer questions about hypothetical choices by saying what they think they should do rather than what they actually would do. The answers to hypothetical questions also become less reliable when the comparisons become more complex.

The second approach is to infer a consumer's preferences from his actual choices. In other words, instead of reasoning from preferences to choices as we've done so far in this chapter, we reason backwards from choices to preferences. This method is known as the **revealed preference approach**. Most economists favor this approach because it relies on information about actual behavior rather than hypothetical choices.

The **revealed preference approach** is a method of gathering information about consumers' preferences by observing their actual choices.

The Principle of Revealed Preference

To understand intuitively how the revealed preference approach works, look at Figure 5.24. Imagine that the consumer chooses bundle A on the green budget line. By itself, this

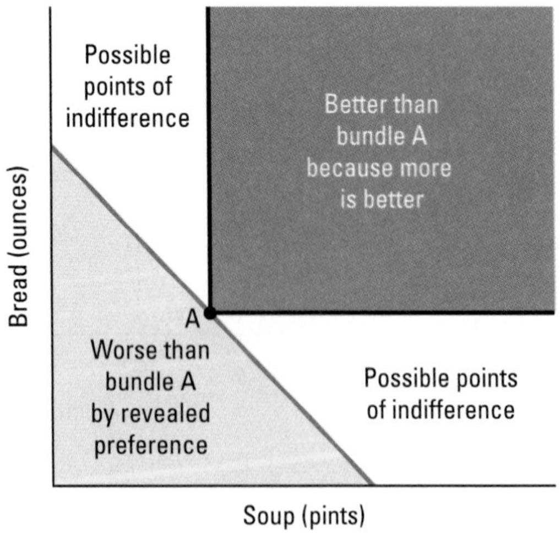

Figure 5.24

Finding the Consumer's Indifference Curve by Process of Elimination: Getting Started. The consumer chooses bundle A on the green budget line. Bundle A is revealed preferred to all the other bundles he could have purchased, which lie in the yellow-shaded area below the budget line. Since bundle A satisfies the no-overlap condition, the indifference curve that runs through bundle A cannot pass through the yellow-shaded area. Neither can it pass through the blue-shaded area, because more is better.

information doesn't pin down the shape of the indifference curve that runs through bundle A, but it does provide us with some useful clues.

First, we can rule out the possibility that the indifference curve running through bundle A crosses into the yellow-shaded area below the budget line. Since bundle A is the best choice on the budget line, this conclusion follows directly from the no-overlap rule. Economists say that bundle A is **revealed preferred** to each of the bundles in the yellow-shaded area. The consumer could have chosen any of the bundles in this area, but instead chose bundle A.

One consumption bundle is **revealed preferred** to another if the consumer chooses it when both are available.

Second, we can rule out the possibility that the indifference curve running through bundle A crosses into the blue-shaded area. Once again, the reason is simple: the bundles in this area contain more soup and more bread than bundle A, and we've assumed that more is better.

From the last two paragraphs, we know that the indifference curve running through bundle A must lie entirely in the two unshaded areas of Figure 5.24 (or along their boundaries). To say more, we must observe the consumer's choices in other settings.

As shown in Figure 5.25(a), we can learn much from the choices the consumer makes when bundle A is not available. We've changed the blue and yellow shading in Figure 5.24

Figure 5.25

Finding the Consumer's Indifference Curve by Process of Elimination: New Choices. In figure (a), bundle A is revealed preferred to bundle B and bundle B is revealed preferred to all the bundles in the yellow-shaded area (like bundle C), so the consumer must prefer bundle A to the bundles in the yellow-shaded area. In figure (b), bundle D is revealed preferred to bundle A, so all bundles that are preferred to bundle D must be preferred to bundle A as well. Since more is better, all of the bundles in the blue-shaded rectangle are preferred to bundle D and, therefore, to bundle A. If the indifference curve has a declining MRS, all of the bundles in the blue-shaded triangle are also preferred to bundle A.

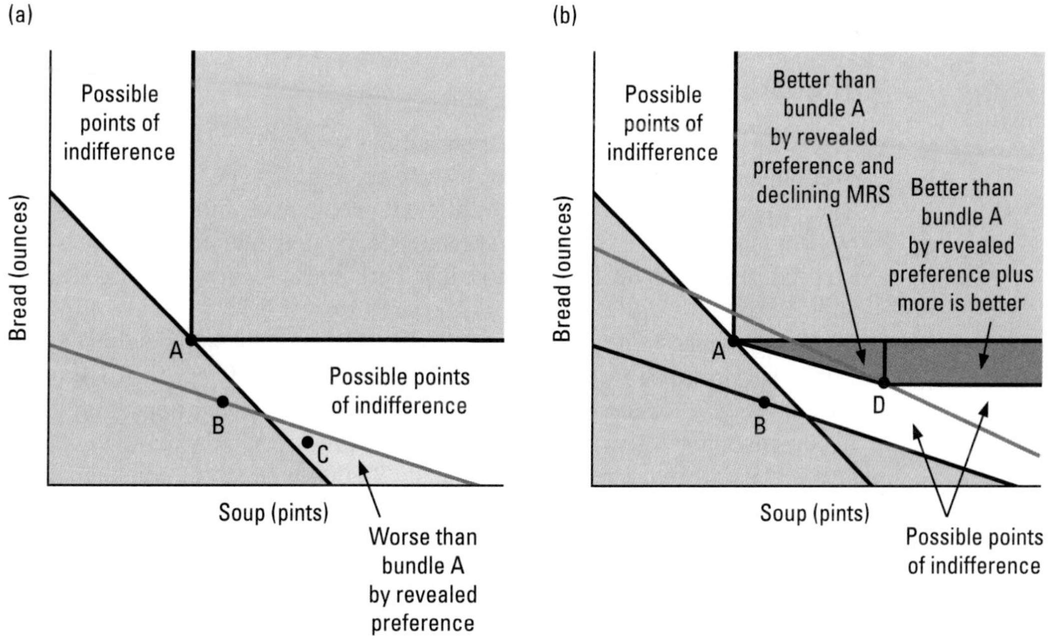

to gray, indicating that we have ruled out those areas. Suppose that when faced with the green budget line in Figure 5.25(a), the consumer chooses bundle B. This choice reveals that he prefers bundle B to all the bundles below the green budget line. Many of those bundles lie in the gray-shaded triangle, but some of them lie in the yellow-shaded triangle—for example, bundle C. The consumer's choices reveal that he prefers bundle A to bundle B, and that he prefers bundle B to bundle C. According to the Ranking Principle, he must therefore prefer bundle A to bundle C. This implies that the indifference curve running through bundle A does not pass through the yellow-shaded triangle.

As shown in Figure 5.25(b), we can also learn much from the choices the consumer makes when bundle A is available. We've changed the yellow shading in Figure 5.25(a) to gray, indicating that we have ruled this area out, along with the other gray-shaded areas. Suppose that when faced with the green budget line in Figure 5.25(b), the consumer chooses bundle D. Since bundle A is available, this choice reveals that the consumer prefers bundle D to bundle A.

We can rule out the possibility that the indifference curve running through bundle A passes through the blue-shaded rectangle to the northeast of bundle D. According to the More-Is-Better Principle, the consumer prefers any bundle in this area to bundle D. According to the Ranking Principle, he must therefore prefer it to bundle A.

As long as we assume that the indifference curve running through bundle A has a declining MRS, we can also rule out the possibility that it crosses into the blue-shaded triangle to the northwest of bundle D. Why? Since the consumer prefers bundle D to bundle A, the indifference curve cannot pass through or above bundle D. To enter the blue-shaded triangle while moving from left to right, it must be flatter than the line connecting bundles A and D. To exit the triangle and pass below bundle D, it must then become steeper than the line connecting bundles A and D. With a declining MRS, that can't happen—moving from left to right, the indifference curve must become flatter, not steeper.

As we observe more consumer choices, we can continue to narrow down the possibilities. With enough observations, we can locate points on the indifference curve with a high degree of precision.

The Use of Statistical Tools

In practice, economists have few opportunities to observe large numbers of choices made by a single individual. Instead, they usually combine data on the choices of many individuals. Doing so can be tricky, since different people have different preferences. However, by using the principle of revealed preference in combination with some statistical tools, we can learn a great deal about consumers' preferences while allowing for the differences among them.

For example, in Application 4.2 (page 102), how did we know that the indifference curves shown in Figure 4.5 correspond to the actual preferences of the typical new car buyer? We derived those curves from the published results of an elaborate statistical study of new car purchases, conducted by economist Pinelopi Goldberg.[17] The data for the study were obtained from interviews of roughly 32,000 households conducted between 1983 and 1987. Those interviews were part of the Consumer Expenditure Survey (CES), which

[17]Pinelopi Koujianou Goldberg, "Product Differentiation and Oligopoly in International Markets: The Case of the U.S. Automobile Industry," *Econometrica* 63 no. 4, July 1995, pp. 891–951.

collects extensive data on consumer spending patterns, including detailed information on automobile purchases.

Though the process Goldberg used to determine consumer preferences is complex, it isn't mysterious. Rather, it's based on the concept of revealed preference. When a household with particular characteristics buys a particular automobile, it reveals that it prefers that alternative to all others. Each new choice reveals a bit more information. An economist usually discovers the nature of consumer preferences through statistical methods that weave together data on many choices by many individuals.

CHAPTER SUMMARY

1. **Affordable consumption bundles**

   a. A budget line consists of all the consumption bundles that just exhaust the consumer's income. It is the boundary that separates all the affordable consumption bundles from all other bundles. Affordable choices that do not exhaust the consumer's income lie to the southwest of the budget line.

   b. The slope of the budget line equals the price ratio times negative one, with the price of the good measured on the horizontal axis appearing in the numerator, and the price of the good measured on the vertical axis appearing in the denominator.

   c. The budget line intersects the axis that measures the amount of any particular good, X, at the quantity M/P_X, which is the amount of X the consumer can purchase by spending all income on X.

   d. A change in income shifts the budget line—outward for an increase and inward for a decrease—without changing its slope.

   e. A change in the price of a good rotates the budget line—outward for a decrease and inward for an increase. The line pivots at the intercept for the good with the unchanged price.

   f. Multiplying all prices by a single constant has the same effect on the budget line as dividing income by the same constant. Changing prices *and* income by the same proportion has *no* effect on the budget line.

2. **Consumer choice**

   a. Assuming that more is better, the consumer's best choice lies on the budget line.

   b. We can recognize best choices by applying the no-overlap rule.

   c. Interior solutions always satisfy the tangency condition. Consequently, if a bundle that includes two goods, X and Y, is an interior solution, then $MRS_{XY} = P_X/P_Y$ at that bundle.

   d. When indifference curves have declining MRSs, any interior choice that satisfies the tangency condition is a best affordable choice.

   e. Whenever the consumer purchases good X but not good Y, then $MRS_{XY} \geq P_X/P_Y$ at the chosen bundle.

3. **Utility maximization**

   a. If a utility function represents a consumer's preference, then the affordable bundle that maximizes the utility function is the consumer's best choice.

   b. At the best choice, a small amount of additional income generates the same increase in the consumer's utility value when spent on any good whose quantity is positive. That is, at the best choice, the ratio of marginal utility to price is the same for all goods. The increase in utility is at least as large as when the additional income is spent on any good whose quantity is zero.

4. **Prices and demand**

   a. The price-consumption curve provides all the information necessary to draw an individual demand curve.

   b. When the price of one good changes, the demand curve for another good may shift. The demand curve shifts to the left when the price of a complement rises and to the right when it decreases. When the price of a substitute changes, these effects are reversed.

5. **Income and demand**

   a. We can determine how the consumption of a good varies with income, and whether it is normal or inferior, by examining the income-consumption curve.

   b. At least one good must be normal.

   c. No good can be inferior at all levels of income.

   d. The income elasticity of demand is positive for normal goods and negative for inferior goods.

   e. When a good is normal, the Engel curve slopes upward; when a good is inferior, it slopes downward.

f. An individual demand curve for a good shifts when income changes. When the good is normal, an increase in income shifts the demand curve to the right, and a decline in income shifts the demand curve to the left. When a good is inferior, these patterns are reversed.

***6. How economists determine a consumer's preferences**

a. If we can observe a sufficient number of consumer choices with sufficient variation in prices and income, we can trace the shape of a consumer's indifference curve. These choices reveal the consumer's preferences.

b. In practice, economists have few opportunities to observe a single consumer make a large number of choices. Instead, they usually combine data on the choices of many individuals, using statistical procedures to allow for differences in individual preferences.

ADDITIONAL EXERCISES

Exercise 5.1: The price of bread is \$0.50 per pound, and the price of butter is \$0.25 per ounce. Channing spends all of her income, buying 12 pounds of bread, 7 ounces of butter, and nothing else. What is her income? Draw her budget constraint and identify her chosen consumption bundle.

Exercise 5.2: The price of bread is \$0.75 per pound, and the price of butter is \$0.20 per ounce. Rupert's income is \$15, with which he buys 6 pounds of bread. How much butter does he buy, assuming that he consumes nothing else? Draw his budget constraint and identify his chosen consumption bundle.

Exercise 5.3: The price of bread is \$0.60 and Aaron's income is \$40. He buys 45 pounds of bread, 26 ounces of butter, and nothing else. What is the price of butter? Draw Aaron's budget constraint and identify his chosen consumption bundle.

Exercise 5.4: As in exercise 4.3, Gary has two children, Kevin and Dora, who consume "yummies" and nothing else. He loves them equally and is happiest when their consumption is equal. Suppose that Kevin starts out with two yummies and Dora with eight yummies, and that Gary can redistribute their yummies. Draw a "budget line" that shows his available choices and indicate his best choice by adding indifference curves. How would your answer differ if Kevin started out with six yummies and Dora with four?

Exercise 5.5: Oscar starts out with budget line L_1, consuming bundle A in Figure 5.17. What point will he choose if the prices of soup and bread double? If they fall by 50 percent? If his income doubles along with prices?

Exercise 5.6: Alan can spend \$10 a week on snacks. He likes ice cream, which costs one \$1 per ounce, and popcorn, which costs 40 cents per ounce. Draw Alan's budget constraint and indifference curves (assuming that each of his indifference curves has a declining MRS) and show his best choice. Now imagine that his older sister Alice hates ice cream but always steals half his popcorn. How does this problem change Alan's budget constraint? On the indifference curves you've drawn, show his new best choice.

Exercise 5.7: Assuming that indifference curves have declining MRSs, could a consumer like the one depicted in Figure 5.6(a) have more than one best choice on the budget line? To answer this question, pick two points on the budget line and try drawing two indifference curves, one through each point, and both tangent to the budget line.

Exercise 5.8: Olivia has received a \$15 gift certificate that is redeemable only for roasted peanuts. Bags of roasted peanuts come in two sizes, regular and jumbo. A regular bag contains 30 peanuts and a jumbo bag contains 50. If a regular bag costs 50 cents and a jumbo bag costs 75 cents, how many of each will Olivia purchase? What if the jumbo bag costs \$1? In each case, draw a budget line that shows her available choices, and indicate her best choice by adding indifference curves. Assume that Olivia cares only about the number of peanuts, and not about the size of the bag.

Exercise 5.9: Natasha's marginal rate of substitution for concerts with films, MRS_{CF}, is F/C, where C stands for the number of concerts and F stands for the number of films. Natasha's income is \$100 per month. Suppose she buys twice as many film tickets as concert tickets. If the price of a film ticket is \$4, what is the price of a concert ticket?

Exercise 5.10: Suppose Table 4.2 describes Madeline's preference ranking. As in Examples 5.1 and 5.2, assume that her income is \$6 per day and bread costs \$2 per loaf. We know from Example 5.2 that when soup costs \$2 per bowl, she eats two bowls of soup and one loaf of bread. From in-text exercise 5.3, you should know how much soup and bread she consumes when soup costs \$4 per bowl. What will she consume if soup costs \$6 per bowl? Each of these choices corresponds to a point on her demand curve for soup. Plot them.

Exercise 5.11: As in worked-out problems 5.2 and 5.5, imagine that Natasha spends all of her monthly income on tickets to concerts and films. Suppose the formula for her marginal rate of substitution is $MRS_{CF} = (3 + F)/(2C)$. (Remember that fractions of tickets are allowed; if she buys half a concert ticket, that means she watches a concert every other month). Suppose Natasha's income is \$300 per month. Concert tickets cost \$5 each. Draw her price-consumption curve (allowing the price of film tickets to vary), and draw her demand curve for film tickets.

Exercise 5.12: Using the information in Table 5.5, plot the Engel curve for bread. Using the information in Table 5.6, plot the Engel curve for beef. Do these curves slope upward or downward? Why?

Exercise 5.13: As in exercise 4.5, Ada prefers to eat soup and bread in fixed proportions. When she eats X pints of soup, she prefers to eat $\sqrt{X}$ ounces of bread. If she has X pints of soup and more than $\sqrt{X}$ ounces of bread, she eats all the soup along with $\sqrt{X}$ ounces of bread, and throws the extra bread away. If she has X pints of soup and fewer than $\sqrt{X}$ ounces of bread (say Y ounces), she eats all the bread along with Y^2 ounces of soup and throws the extra soup away. Assume she spends all her income on soup and bread. Plot her income-consumption curve, her Engel curve for soup, and her Engel curve for bread.

***Exercise 5.14:** Ashley spends all her income on gasoline and food. At first she earns \$100, buys 25 gallons of gasoline at \$2 per gallon, and purchases 10 pounds of food at \$5 per pound. Her income later rises to \$200, but the price of gasoline increases to \$5 per gallon, and the price of food rises to \$7 per pound. Is she better or worse off? Why? Draw Ashley's budget constraint before and after the change in income, and identify her best choice before the change.

***Exercise 5.15:** Make the same assumptions as in exercise 5.14, except that the price of food rises to \$8 instead of \$7. Can you say whether Ashley is better or worse off? What if she purchases 11 pounds of food after the change in prices and income? What if she purchases 15 pounds of food after the change? In each case, draw Ashley's budget constraint before and after the change and identify her best choices.

6

From Demand to Welfare

Learning Objectives

After reading this chapter, students should be able to:

- Distinguish between the two main effects of a price change and understand why demand curves generally slope downward.
- Explain how to use demand curves to measure changes in consumer welfare.
- Explain the purpose of a cost-of-living index and define the Laspeyres index.
- Use cost-of-living indexes to measure changes in consumer welfare and explain why those measures may be biased.
- Understand the trade-off between consumption and leisure and explain how the wage rate affects labor supply.

In 1943, T. J. Watson, Sr., the founder, president, and later chairman of IBM, famously speculated that "there is a world market for maybe five computers." With the benefit of 20-20 hindsight, we know that his forecast was low by a factor of at least several hundred million. But Watson didn't lack vision or imagination—he simply failed to anticipate how inexpensive computers would become. Today, a $1,000 computer that weighs a few pounds and slips into a briefcase performs computations more than a million times as fast as ENIAC, the world's first all-purpose electronic digital computer, built in 1946 at an inflation-adjusted cost of nearly $5 million.

As a result of the dramatic reduction in the price of computing power, consumers are presumably better off today than 10, 20, or 30 years ago—but by how much? We know what we *pay* for our computers, but what are they *worth* to us? In dollar terms, what has the digital revolution contributed to our well-being?

Policymakers have a keen interest in the answers to questions like these. For example, when they use citizens' tax dollars to support the development of new technologies (as they did with digital computing), they are betting that the net social benefits will exceed the costs. Similarly, businesses can sometimes profit from better knowledge of the value that consumers derive from a product or service (see, for example, the discussion of price discrimination in Chapter 18).

In this chapter, we'll continue our exploration of consumer decision making by examining five topics:

1. *Dissecting the effects of a price change.* Price changes affect purchases in two ways. First, consumers shift their purchases toward those goods that have become relatively less expensive. Second, when prices rise, consumer purchasing power falls, because a dollar doesn't go as far as it once did. We'll see that this distinction helps us understand why demand curves usually slope downward.
2. *Measuring changes in consumer welfare using demand curves.* When economists evaluate changes in a consumer's well-being (also known as *consumer welfare*), they use money as a yardstick. We'll examine a common measure of a change in welfare, and we'll explain how to determine its size using demand curves.
3. *Measuring changes in consumer welfare using cost-of-living indexes.* Sometimes, economists are unable to estimate either preferences or demand curves reliably (for example, because there isn't enough data). We'll see that it is still possible to say something about changes in consumer welfare using cost-of-living indexes.
4. *Labor supply and the demand for leisure.* Labor supply is the flip side of the demand for leisure. By dissecting the effects of a change in the wage rate, we'll see why an ordinary consumer's labor supply curve can slope either upward or downward.

*5. *Another type of demand curve.* By dissecting the effects of price changes, we can construct a new type of demand curve—one that holds a consumer's welfare fixed, rather than his income. We'll explain how economists use these demand curves to compute changes in consumer welfare more accurately.

6.1 DISSECTING THE EFFECTS OF A PRICE CHANGE

When the price of a good increases, two things happen:

1. That good becomes more expensive relative to all other goods. Consumers tend to shift their purchases away from the more expensive good and toward other goods.
2. The consumers' purchasing power declines. A dollar doesn't buy as much as it once did. Because consumers can no longer afford the consumption bundles they would have chosen if the price hadn't risen, they are effectively poorer and must adjust their purchases accordingly.

In this section, we'll explain how to divide the effect of a price change into these two components. Why should we bother? Isn't it enough to know the overall effect of a price change? As we'll see, economists have learned quite a bit about consumer demand and welfare from dissecting price changes in this way.

Compensated Price Changes

As the price of a good changes, the consumer's well-being varies. To illustrate this point, let's assume once again that Oscar (whom we introduced in Section 5.4) spends all his income on soup and bread. Oscar can spend \$10 per day, and bread costs \$0.25 per ounce.

Figure 6.1

The Compensated Price Effects of an Increase and a Decrease in the Price of Soup. Initially, Oscar faces budget line L_1 and chooses bundle A. In figure (a), an increase in the price of soup rotates the budget line to L_2, and Oscar chooses bundle B. For a compensated increase in the price of soup, his budget line would shift to L_3, and he would pick bundle C. In figure (b), a reduction in the price of soup rotates the budget line to L_4, and Oscar chooses bundle D. For a compensated decrease in the price of soup, his budget lie would shift to L_5, and he would pick bundle E.

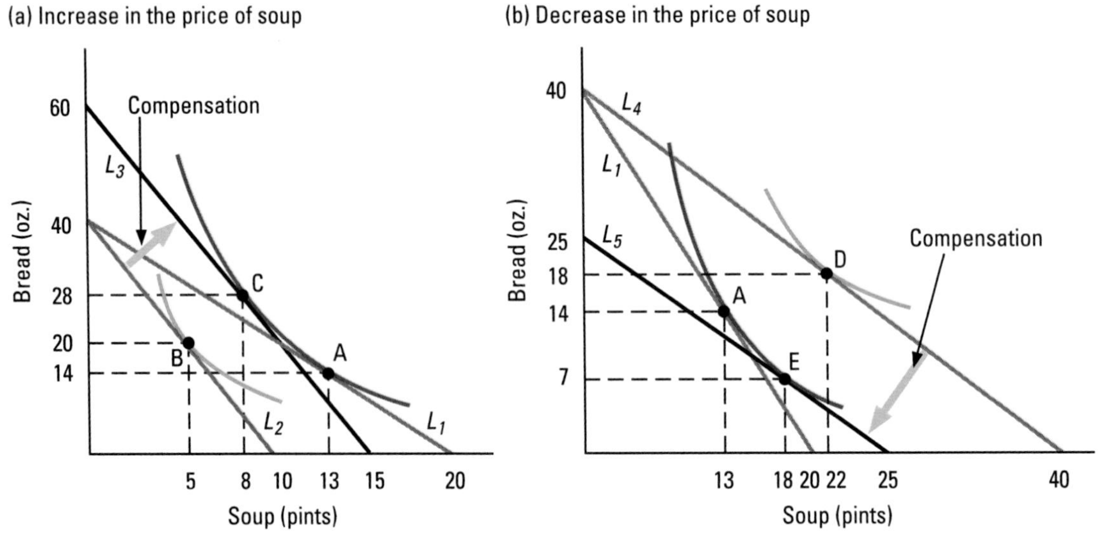

When soup costs $0.50 per pint, Oscar's budget constraint is the line labeled L_1 in Figure 6.1, and he chooses bundle A. When the price of soup rises to $1 per pint, Oscar's purchasing power declines. As shown in Figure 6.1(a), his budget line rotates to L_2 and he chooses bundle B. Notice that bundle B lies on a lower indifference curve than bundle A. The price increase makes him worse off because it reduces his purchasing power.

How much money would we need to give Oscar to compensate him for the higher price of soup? Suppose we give him an extra $5, bringing his income to $15 per day. That level of compensation would allow him to buy any bundle on or below the black budget line (labeled L_3) in Figure 6.1(a). According to the figure, he would choose bundle C. Notice that bundles A and C are on the same indifference curve. The consumer is therefore indifferent between paying $0.50 per pint for soup with an income of $10, and paying $1 per pint for soup with an income of $15. The extra $5 exactly compensates him for the $0.50 increase in the price of soup. The yellow arrow shows the effect of that compensation on his budget line.

An **uncompensated price change** consists of a price change with no change in income. A **compensated price change** consists of a price change and an income change which, together, leave the consumer's well-being unaffected.

The shift from the budget line labeled L_1 to the one labeled L_2 in Figure 6.1(a) illustrates an **uncompensated price change**—it consists of a price change with no change in income. We studied uncompensated price changes in Chapter 5. Usually, we use the phrase *price change* by itself to mean an uncompensated change. The shift from the budget constraint labeled L_1 to the one labeled L_3 in Figure 6.1(a) illustrates a **compensated price change**—it consists of a price change and an income change which, together, leave the consumer's well-being unaffected.

Figure 6.1(b) illustrates the effect of a *reduction* in the price of soup from \$0.50 to \$0.25. The uncompensated price change rotates the consumer's budget line from L_1 to L_4, and his choice shifts from bundle A to bundle D. He is *better off* as a result. To compensate for the price change, we would need to take away income. As indicated by the yellow arrow, taking away \$3.75 shifts his budget line from L_4 to L_5. With L_5, he chooses bundle E, which lies on the same indifference curve as bundle A. He is therefore indifferent between paying \$0.50 per pint for soup with an income of \$10, and paying \$0.25 per pint for soup with an income of \$6.25. In this case, the shift from the budget line labeled L_1 to the one labeled L_5 is the compensated price change.

Substitution and Income Effects

By definition, a compensated price change consists of an uncompensated price change plus compensation. Therefore, the effect of a compensated price change on consumption is the same as the effect of an uncompensated price change, plus the effect of compensation:

Effect of a compensated price change =
Effect of an uncompensated price change + Effect of providing compensation

For example, in Figure 6.1(a), the effect of the uncompensated price change is to shift consumption from bundle A to bundle B, and the effect of the compensation is to shift consumption from bundle B to bundle C. Together, these changes shift consumption from bundle A to bundle C, just like a compensated price change.

We can gain a better understanding of uncompensated price changes by rearranging the preceding formula. Let's add to both sides of the formula the effect on consumption of *removing* the compensation. Since the effect of removing the compensation exactly offsets the effect of providing it, we obtain the following formula:

Effect of an uncompensated price change =
Effect of a compensated price change + Effect of removing compensation **(1)**

For example, in Figure 6.1(a), the effect of the compensated price change is to shift consumption from bundle A to bundle C, and the effect of removing the compensation is to shift consumption from bundle C to bundle B. Together, these changes shift consumption from bundle A to bundle B, just like an uncompensated price change.

Formula (1) tells us that we can break up the effect of an uncompensated price change into two pieces. The first piece—the effect on consumption of a compensated price change—is known as the **substitution effect of a price change**. The name of this effect reminds us that a change in relative prices causes the consumer to substitute one good for another. The substitution effect always involves a movement along an indifference curve to a point where the slope of the indifference curve is the same as the slope of the new budget line. In Figure 6.2, which illustrates the same price changes as Figure 6.1, we indicate the substitution effects with gray arrows. In Figure 6.2(a), the substitution effect of an increase in the soup price from \$0.50 to \$1 per pint shifts the consumer's choice from bundle A on L_1 to bundle C on L_3. In Figure 6.2(b), the substitution effect of a reduction in the soup price from \$0.50 to \$0.25 per pint shifts his choice from bundle A on L_1 to bundle E on L_5.

The effect on consumption of a compensated price change is known as the **substitution effect of a price change.**

The second piece—the effect on consumption of removing the compensation—is known as the **income effect of a price change**. The name of this effect reminds us that a price change affects the consumer's purchasing power. The income effect always involves a parallel shift in the budget constraint, toward the origin for a price increase (since the

The effect on consumption of removing the compensation after creating a compensated price change is known as the **income effect of a price change.**

Figure 6.2

Dissection of the Effects of an Increase and a Decrease in the Price of a Normal Good. In figure (a), an increase in the soup price rotates the budget line from L_1 to L_2. The uncompensated price effect consists of a substitution effect (the movement from bundle A to bundle C) and an income effect (the movement from bundle C to bundle B). In figure (b), a reduction in the soup price rotates the budget line from L_1 to L_4. The uncompensated price effect consists of a substitution effect (the movement from bundle A to bundle E) and an income effect (the movement from bundle E to bundle D). We indicate uncompensated price effects with blue arrows, substitution effects with gray arrows, and income effects with yellow arrows.

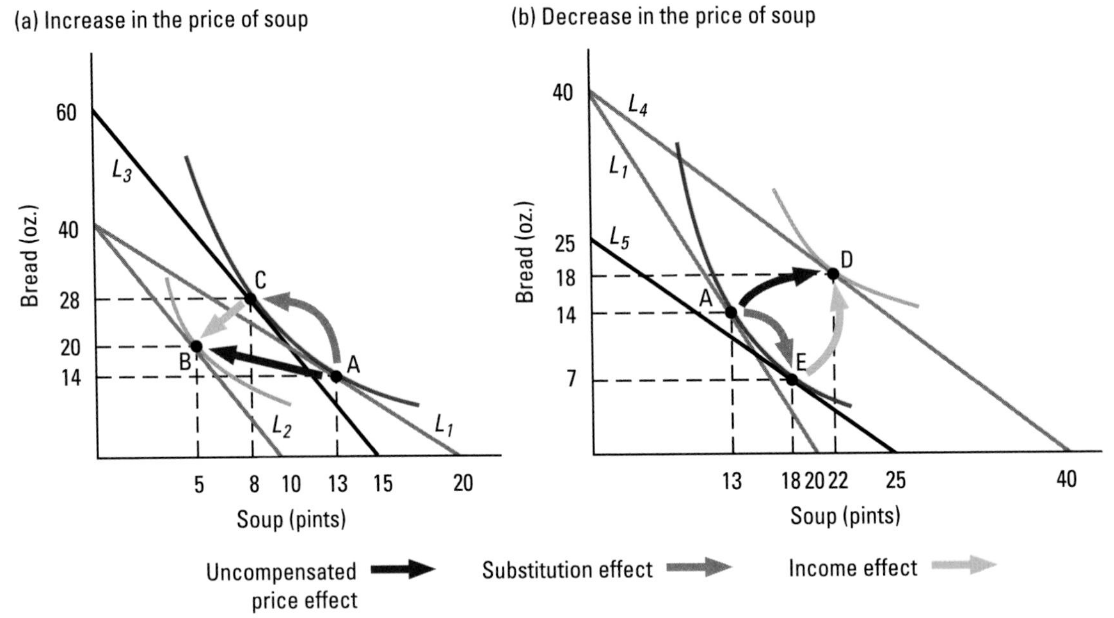

consumer's purchasing power declines) and away from the origin for a price reduction (since his purchasing power rises).[1] In Figure 6.2, we indicate the income effects with yellow arrows. In Figure 6.2(a), the income effect of an increase in the soup price from \$0.50 to \$1 per pint shifts the consumer's choice from bundle C on L_3 to bundle B on L_2. In Figure 6.2(b), the income effect of a reduction in the soup price from \$0.50 to \$0.25 per pint shifts his choice from bundle E on L_5 to bundle D on L_4.

Using these definitions, we can rewrite formula (1) as follows:

$$\text{Effect of an uncompensated price change} = \text{Substitution effect of the price change} + \text{Income effect of the price change} \quad \textbf{(2)}$$

In Figure 6.2, we indicate the effects of the uncompensated price changes with blue arrows. Formula (2) tells us that, together, the gray and yellow arrows start and end at the same bundles as the blue arrows.

In short, an uncompensated price change involves both a change in relative prices (which rotates the budget line) and a change in purchasing power (which causes a parallel

[1] A price increase requires positive compensation, so removing the compensation reduces income, shifting the budget line inward. A price reduction requires negative compensation, so removing the compensation increases income, shifting the budget line outward.

shift of the budget line). The substitution effect isolates the influence of the change in relative prices, while the income effect isolates the influence of the change in purchasing power.

WORKED-OUT PROBLEM 6.1

The Problem As in worked-out problem 5.5 (page 146), Natasha's marginal rate of substitution for concerts with films, MRS_{CF}, is F/C, where C stands for the number of concert tickets and F stands for the number of film tickets. For this problem, you will also need the formula for her indifference curves: $F = U/C$. Natasha can spend \$100 and concert tickets cost \$5 per ticket. Suppose the price of film tickets falls from \$5 to \$1.25 per ticket. What is the uncompensated effect on her purchases of film and concert tickets? What is the compensated effect? How much compensation is involved? Break up the effect of the uncompensated price change into the substitution and income effects.

The Solution From the answer to worked-out problem 5.5, we know that Natasha will choose $F = M/(2P_F)$ and $C = M/(2P_C)$, where M is her income, P_F is the price of a film ticket, and P_C is the price of a concert ticket. So, with $M = \$100$, $P_F = \$5$, and $P_C = \$5$, she chooses $(C, F) = (10, 10)$. If P_F falls to \$1.25, she chooses $(C, F) = (10, 40)$. This uncompensated price reduction raises her film ticket purchases from 10 to 40 and leaves her concert ticket purchases unchanged.

Now let's solve for her choice when the price change is compensated. Since Natasha's best choice must satisfy the tangency condition, it equates her marginal rate of substitution, F/C, with the price ratio, P_C/P_F, so $F/C = P_C/P_F$. With $M = \$100$, $P_C = \$5$, and $P_F = \$1.25$, the tangency condition therefore requires the following relationship between film tickets and concert tickets:

$$F = 4C$$

Natasha's best choice with a compensated price change also lies on the indifference curve that runs through the bundle $(C, F) = (10, 10)$. Since the formula for her indifference curves is $F = U/C$, the value of U for the indifference curve that runs through the bundle $(C, F) = (10, 10)$ must be 100, which means the formula for this indifference curve is

$$F = 100/C$$

A bundle can satisfy both the tangency condition formula and the indifference curve formula at the same time only if $4C = 100/C$. This requires $C^2 = 25$, or $C = 5$. Using either the tangency condition formula or the indifference curve formula, we then see that $F = 20$. So the compensated price effect shifts Natasha from the bundle $(C, F) = (10, 10)$ to the bundle $(C, F) = (5, 20)$.

At the new prices, Natasha requires only \$50 to buy the bundle $(C, F) = (5, 20)$. Since her income is \$100, we would take \$50 away from Natasha to compensate for the price cut.

The substitution effect is the same as the effect of the compensated price change. The income effect is the residual: it shifts Natasha from the bundle $(C, F) = (5, 20)$ to the bundle $(C, F) = (10, 40)$.

IN-TEXT EXERCISE 6.1 **As in worked-out problem 5.6 (page 156), Keiko's marginal rate of substitution for gasoline with wireless minutes, MRS_{GW}, is $10/\sqrt{G}$, where G stands for gallons of gasoline. For this problem, you will also need the formula for her indifference curves: $W = U - 20\sqrt{G}$, where W stands for the number of wireless minutes. Keiko can spend \$40 and wireless minutes cost \$0.50 per minute. Suppose the price of gasoline rises from \$1 to \$2.50 per gallon. What is the effect on her purchases of gasoline and wireless minutes? Break up this effect into the substitution and income effects. How much compensation does the substitution effect involve?**

The Direction of Substitution and Income Effects

A compensated *increase* in the price of a good always causes the consumer to buy *less* of that good—he substitutes *away* from the good as it becomes more expensive. Conversely, a compensated *reduction* in the price of a good always causes the consumer to buy *more* of that good—he substitutes *toward* the good as it becomes less expensive. The substitution effect is therefore negative for a price increase and positive for a price reduction.

Figure 6.3 illustrates this point. In drawing Figure 6.3(a), we have assumed that the consumer's indifference curve has a declining MRS. With the budget line labeled L_1, the

Figure 6.3

The Direction of the Substitution Effect. Figure (a) shows that, with a declining MRS, the point of tangency between an indifference curve and a relatively steep budget line (reflecting a high price of bread) must be to the left of the point of tangency between the same indifference curve and a relatively flat budget line (reflecting a low price of bread). This implies that the substitution effect of an increase in the price of bread reduces bread consumption. Figure (b) makes the same point without assuming a declining MRS. If the consumer is indifferent between his best choice on the budget line L_1 (which reflects a low price of bread) and his best choice on the budget line L_2 (which reflects a high price of bread), then his best point on L_2 must lie to the left of X, and his best choice on L_1 must lie to the right of X.

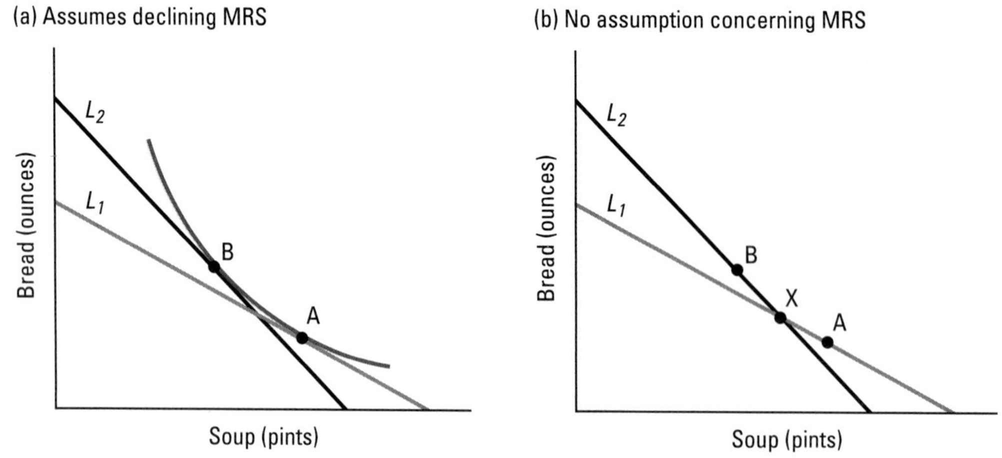

consumer chooses bundle A. After a compensated increase in the price of soup, he faces a steeper budget line (labeled L_2) and chooses another bundle, B, on the indifference curve that runs through A. Since the indifference curve is tangent to a steeper budget line at B than at A, and since it has a declining MRS, B must lie to the northwest of A (as shown), which means it contains less soup.

Figure 6.3(b) makes the same point without assuming that the consumer's indifference curve has a declining MRS. Let's assume that the consumer starts out with the budget line labeled L_1. After a compensated increase in the price of soup, his budget line is L_2. These two lines cross at the bundle labeled X. Because the price change is compensated, the consumer must be indifferent between his best choice on L_1 and his best choice on L_2. Therefore, his best choice on L_1 can't lie below L_2, and his best choice on L_2 can't lie below L_1. This observation implies that his best choice on L_1 must lie to the right of bundle X, like bundle A, and his best choice on L_2 must lie to the left of bundle X, like bundle B. Since the compensated increase in the price of soup moves the customer from the right of X to the left of X, it reduces his soup consumption.

What about income effects? The direction of an income effect depends on whether the good in question is normal or inferior. An increase in the price of a good reduces the consumer's purchasing power, which causes him to buy less if the good is normal and more if it is inferior. Conversely, a reduction in the price of a good increases the consumer's purchasing power, which causes him to buy more if the good is normal and less if it is inferior. If the good is normal, the income effect is therefore negative for a price increase and positive for a price reduction. If the good is inferior, the income effect is positive for a price increase and negative for a price reduction.

For a normal good, the income effect therefore works in the same direction as the substitution effect. Both are negative for a price increase, and both are positive for a price reduction. For a graphical illustration, look again at Figure 6.2. In this figure, soup is a normal good: a shift from L_2 to L_3 in Figure 6.2(a) increases soup consumption, as does a shift from L_5 to L_4 in Figure 6.2(b). In Figure 6.2(a), the substitution and income effects both reduce soup consumption; in Figure 6.2(b), they both increase soup consumption.

For an inferior good, the substitution and income effects work in *opposite* directions. For a price increase, the income effect increases consumption and the substitution effect reduces it. For a price reduction, the directions are reversed.

Figure 6.4 illustrates the opposing substitution and income effects for an inferior good. We'll assume that Erin, whom we introduced in Section 5.5, divides her income between potatoes and beef, and that potatoes are inferior. To start, potatoes cost 50 cents per pound, beef costs $3 per pound, and Erin's income is $36 per month. The budget line is L_1 and Erin picks bundle A. If the price of potatoes falls to 25 cents per pound, the budget line rotates to L_2 and Erin picks bundle B.

Let's break up this change into a substitution effect and an income effect. Bundle C is the point of tangency between the indifference curve that runs through bundle A and a line with the same slope as the new budget constraint. The substitution effect corresponds to the movement from bundle A to bundle C, and the income effect corresponds to the movement from bundle C to bundle B.

The substitution effect in Figure 6.4 involves an increase in the number of potatoes. In other words, when potatoes become less expensive, the consumer substitutes toward potatoes. In this respect, potatoes and soup are similar. However, the income effect in Figure 6.4 involves a *reduction* in the number of potatoes. Why? To compensate for the price

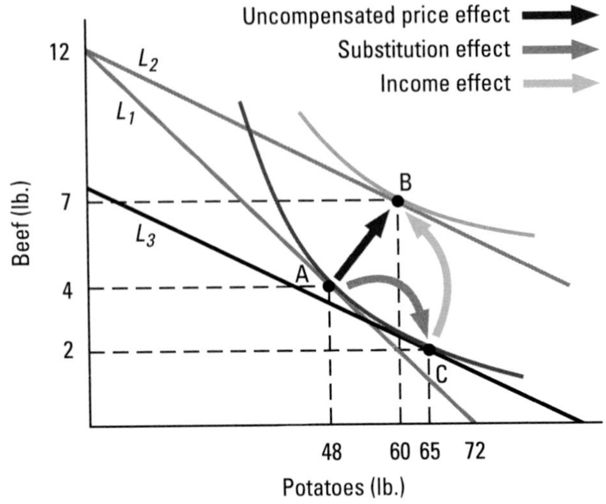

Figure 6.4

Dissection of the Effect of a Reduction in the Price of an Inferior Good. Initially, Erin faces budget line L_1 and chooses bundle A. A reduction in the price of potatoes rotates her budget line to L_2, and she chooses bundle B. This uncompensated price effect, which shifts her choice from bundle A to bundle B (the blue arrow), consists of a substitution effect, which shifts her choice from bundle A to bundle C (the gray arrow), and an income effect, which shifts her choice from bundle C to bundle B (the yellow arrow).

reduction, we have to take away income. When we eliminate this compensation, income rises, shifting the budget line from L_3 to L_2. Since potatoes are inferior, Erin buys fewer potatoes.

Let's summarize our conclusions:

The Direction of Income and Substitution Effects

1. The substitution effect is negative for a price increase and positive for a price reduction.
2. If a good is normal, the income effect reinforces the substitution effect. It is negative for a price increase and positive for a price reduction.
3. If a good is inferior, the income effect opposes the substitution effect. It is positive for a price increase and negative for a price reduction.

Why Do Demand Curves Usually Slope Downward?

The **Law of Demand** states that demand curves usually slope downward.

In Chapter 2, we observed that demand curves usually slope downward. This principle, known as the **Law of Demand**, has very few exceptions (see Application 6.1, below). By dissecting the effects of a price change, we can learn why most but not all goods obey this law.

The substitution effect of a price change is *always* consistent with the Law of Demand. An increase in the price of a good causes the consumer to substitute away from it, reducing demand, and a reduction in the price of a good causes the consumer to substitute toward it, raising demand. If a good violates the Law of Demand, the explanation must therefore involve income effects.

For a normal good, we've seen that the income effect reinforces the substitution effect. As a result, normal goods *always* obey the Law of Demand.

But what about inferior goods? In the previous section, we saw that the income effect for an inferior good *opposes* the substitution effect. Theoretically, if the income effect is large, the substitution effect is small, and the good is inferior, the amount purchased could increase when the price rises, violating the Law of Demand.

Figure 6.5 illustrates this possibility. The figure is identical to Figure 6.4, except that this consumer, Robert, chooses bundle D (instead of bundle B) when the budget line is L_2. The increase in income associated with the outward shift in the budget line from L_3 to L_2 reduces potato consumption by a larger amount than in Figure 6.4 (from 65 to 40 pounds). In other words, potatoes are more inferior in Figure 6.5 than they are in Figure 6.4. In fact, the magnitude of the income effect is larger than the magnitude of the substitution effect, so that the drop in price reduces the consumption of potatoes (from 48 to 40 pounds). As a result, in this example, the demand curve for potatoes slopes upward.

A product is called a **Giffen good** if the amount purchased increases as the price rises. In practice, Giffen goods are extremely hard to find, for two reasons. First, most goods are normal. Second, if spending on a good accounts for a small fraction of a consumer's budget (as it does for most goods), even a large increase in the good's price doesn't have much of an impact on the consumer's overall purchasing power, so the income effect is small. (See the appendix to this chapter for a more detailed explanation of this point).

A product is called a **Giffen good** if the amount purchased increases as the price rises.

Even so, there may be exceptions to the Law of Demand. Application 6.1 discusses two possible cases of Giffen goods.

Figure 6.5

Dissection of the Effect of a Reduction in the Price of a Giffen Good. Initially, Robert faces budget line L_1 and chooses bundle A. A reduction in the price of potatoes rotates his budget line to L_2, and he chooses bundle D. This uncompensated price effect, which shifts Robert's choice from bundle A to bundle D (the blue arrow), consists of a substitution effect, which shifts his choice from bundle A to bundle C (the gray arrow), and an income effect, which shifts his choice from bundle C to bundle D (the yellow arrow).

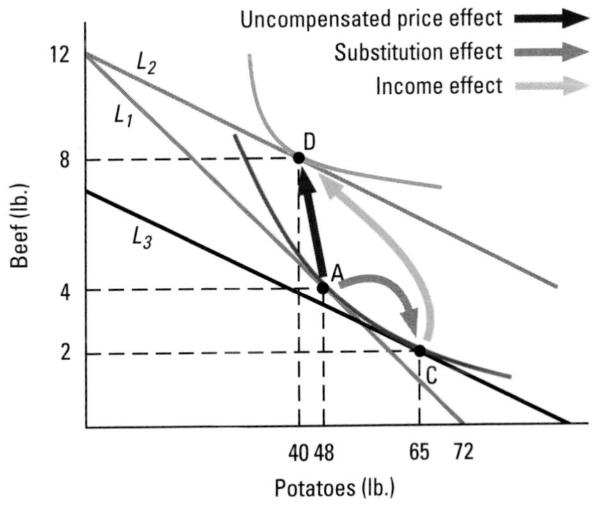

Application 6.1

Irish Potatoes and Japanese Shochu

The potato was introduced in Ireland at the beginning of the 17th century. It caught on rapidly, in large part because it yielded more food per acre than native crops. The resulting abundance of food permitted the Irish population to swell from 3 million in the late 1500s to roughly 8 million by 1840. In the process, Ireland became increasingly dependent on potato production. Of those 8 million inhabitants, roughly 3 million subsisted almost entirely on potatoes.

In 1845, a fungus spread through the Irish potato fields, causing a blight that destroyed most of the crop. The blight struck again in 1846 and 1848. Food became so scarce that the price of potatoes skyrocketed. By the end of the great Irish Potato Famine, nearly a million people had died of starvation and disease, and another million had emigrated to escape those consequences.

From the London Illustrated News, January 30, 1847

Reflecting on his experiences in Ireland as a boy, Sir Robert Giffen later wrote that some Irish families increased their consumption of potatoes during the famine. For families whose diet consisted mainly but not exclusively of potatoes, the price increase took a substantial bite out of their purchasing power. Finding themselves poorer and needing to maintain an adequate caloric intake, they gave up the more expensive foods that had supplemented their diets and turned increasingly to potatoes, their only staple food. Thus the term *Giffen goods.*

Or so the story goes. Some economists have disputed the accuracy of Giffen's recollections, arguing that this alleged violation of the Law of Demand is little more than legend. Surely potato consumption could not have increased for the *average* Irish family, since potatoes were in short supply. Unfortunately, the facts are obscured by the veil of history, so that the truth will never be known with certainty.

More recently, some economists have claimed that shochu, a Japanese alcoholic beverage, may violate the Law of Demand. Like sake, shochu is distilled from rice. In Japan, it is considered the lowest-quality form of rice-based alcoholic beverage, behind second-grade sake, first-grade sake, and special-grade sake. Shochu is consumed disproportionately by lower-income households, whereas special-grade sake is consumed disproportionately by the wealthy.

The consumption of shochu falls sharply with increased income, so it is plainly an inferior good. But is it a Giffen good? As the price of shochu rises, those with lower incomes may feel compelled to give up the better grades of sake so they can afford to maintain their alcohol intake. Such behavior is particularly plausible for those who drink to satisfy an alcohol addiction.

In a recent study, economists Shmuel Baruch and Yakar Kannai examined prices and consumption of shochu and the three grades of sake from January 1987 through March 1989.[2] They used statistical techniques to assess the effect of price on the quantity consumed, accounting for the fact that quantity consumed also affects price, as we saw in the appendix to Chapter 2. The estimated price elasticity of demand for special-grade sake was −6.11. In contrast, the estimated price elasticity of demand for shochu was +8.81. According to these results, the demand curve for special-grade sake slopes downward, but the demand curve for shochu slopes *upward,* violating the Law of Demand!

[2]Shmuel Baruch and Yakar Kannai, "Inferior Goods, Giffen Goods, and Shochu," in Debreu, Neufeind, and Trockel, eds., *Economic Essays, A Festschrift for Werner Hildenbrand,* 2001, pp. 1–9.

6.2 MEASURING CHANGES IN CONSUMER WELFARE USING DEMAND CURVES

Many important questions in microeconomics concern the welfare effects of changes in the prices and quantities of consumer goods. We began this chapter with an example: How much have consumers benefitted from the dramatic drop in the price of computing power over the last few decades? In this section, we'll explain how to measure changes in consumer welfare.

Compensating Variation

When a consumer's economic circumstances change, how can we evaluate his gains and losses in monetary terms? One common measure is called the **compensating variation**. This is the amount of money that exactly compensates the consumer for the change.[3] It is the most he is willing to pay to experience something beneficial, or the least he is willing to receive to experience something harmful. It's an appealing concept because it expresses benefits and costs in a way that is concrete and easy to interpret. If the compensating variation for a road improvement project is −$100, then the consumer is better off with the project as long as his contribution is less than $100. If the compensating variation for a gasoline tax is $50, then he's better off with the tax as long as he receives a rebate for more than $50.

A **compensating variation** is the amount of money that exactly compensates the consumer for a change in circumstances.

A simple example will illustrate the usefulness of this concept. Let's suppose that Carol and Rachel potentially benefit from a $100 project. Can they split the costs in a way that makes both better off? They can if their compensating variations (times negative one) sum to more than $100; otherwise they can't. For example, if Carol's compensating variation is −$80 and Rachel's is −$30, and if we collect $75 from Carol and $25 from Rachel, both are better off because each gives up less than she is willing to pay. Alternatively, if Carol's compensating variation is −$60 and Rachel's is −$30, we can't collect $100 from them without making at least one worse off. If Carol is rich and Rachel is poor, we might be tempted to collect, say, $90 from Carol and $10 from Rachel, leaving Carol worse off and Rachel better off than without the project. However, because Carol's net loss is then $30 while Rachel's net gain is only $20, this is an inefficient way to help Rachel at Carol's expense: both of them would be happier if we skipped the project and simply transferred $25 from Carol to Rachel.

We've actually used the concept of compensating variation earlier in this chapter without naming it. The amount of compensation associated with the income effect of a price change is the compensating variation for the price change: if the consumer receives that amount of compensation following the price change, he will be neither better off nor worse off. For an example, look again at Figure 6.1(a) (page 168). Because $5 fully compensates Oscar for an increase in the price of soup from $0.50 to $1 per pint, the compensating variation for this price increase is $5. Similarly, the compensating variation for the price reduction illustrated in Figure 6.1(b) is −$3.75, and the compensating variation for the price reduction in worked-out problem 6.1 is −$50.

[3]Sometimes, economists also evaluate changes using a concept called the *equivalent variation*. This is the amount of money that produces an equivalent effect on the consumer's well-being; that is, the amount he is just willing to accept *in place of* (rather than in addition to) the change. The equivalent variation for a change from one situation, call it *A*, to another situation, call it *B*, is the same as the compensating variation for the opposite change—that is, from situation *B* to situation *A*.

WORKED-OUT PROBLEM 6.2

The Problem As in in-text exercise 6.1, Keiko's marginal rate of substitution for gasoline with wireless minutes, MRS_{GW}, is $10/\sqrt{G}$, where G stands for gallons of gasoline. The formula for her indifference curves is $W = U - 20\sqrt{G}$, where W stands for the number of wireless minutes. Keiko's income is \$125, gasoline costs \$1 per gallon, and wireless calls cost \$0.50 per minute. How much would we have to pay Keiko to compensate her for the loss of her phone (assuming she can't buy a new one)?

The Solution From our answer to worked-out problem 5.6 (page 156), we know that Keiko buys 25 gallons of gasoline and uses 200 minutes of wireless service. For the indifference curve that runs through this bundle, $U = 300$ (since $200 = 300 - 20\sqrt{25}$). But if Keiko is without her cell phone, $W = 0$. To place her on the same indifference curve as before, we must therefore pick the value of G for which $0 = 300 - 20\sqrt{G}$. But that means $G = 225$. To buy 225 gallons of gasoline, Keiko needs \$225 dollars—an amount that exceeds her budget by \$100. So we have to pay Keiko \$100 to compensate her fully for the loss of her phone. This is her compensating variation.

IN-TEXT EXERCISE 6.2 **Suppose that Keiko's phone malfunctions and will operate for only 100 minutes each week. Otherwise, everything is the same as in worked-out problem 6.2. What is Keiko's compensating variation for the malfunction?**

If we know a consumer's preferences, we can compute the compensating variation for a price change (as in Figure 6.1, and worked-out problems 6.1 and 6.2). However, the task of determining a consumer's preferences can be challenging—recall our discussion of revealed preference in Section 5.6. Fortunately, we can calculate compensating variations directly from demand curves. The rest of this section shows how to do this.

Consumer Surplus

Consumer surplus is the net benefit a consumer receives from participating in the market for some good.

When measuring a consumer's well-being, economists often rely on a concept known as **consumer surplus**. This term refers to the net benefit a consumer receives from participating in the market for some good. Equivalently, it is the amount of money that would fully compensate the consumer (in other words, the compensating variation) for losing access to the market.

To compute the consumer surplus for some particular good, we need to start by measuring the gross benefit of consuming that good. The consumer's demand curve provides us with that information: at any given quantity, its height indicates the consumer's willingness to pay for the marginal unit. This willingness to pay is a measure of the consumer's gross benefit from that unit.

For an illustration, consider the demand curve for computers in Figure 6.6(a). It looks like a staircase instead of a straight line because there's isn't much point in buying a fraction of a computer. For one computer, the height of the demand curve is \$4,000. This

Figure 6.6

Measuring Consumer Surplus Using Standard Demand Curves. The height of the demand curve indicates the consumer's willingness to pay for an additional unit. In part (a), the price of a computer is $1,500 and the consumer buys three computers. For each computer, the net benefit (the area of the green bar) is the difference between the total benefit (the combined areas of the red and green bars) and the price (the area of the red bar). Adding up the areas of the green bars gives us the consumer surplus (total net benefit). Part (b) shows that when a good is finely divisible (like gasoline), consumer surplus is the area under the demand curve and above the horizontal line drawn at the market price.

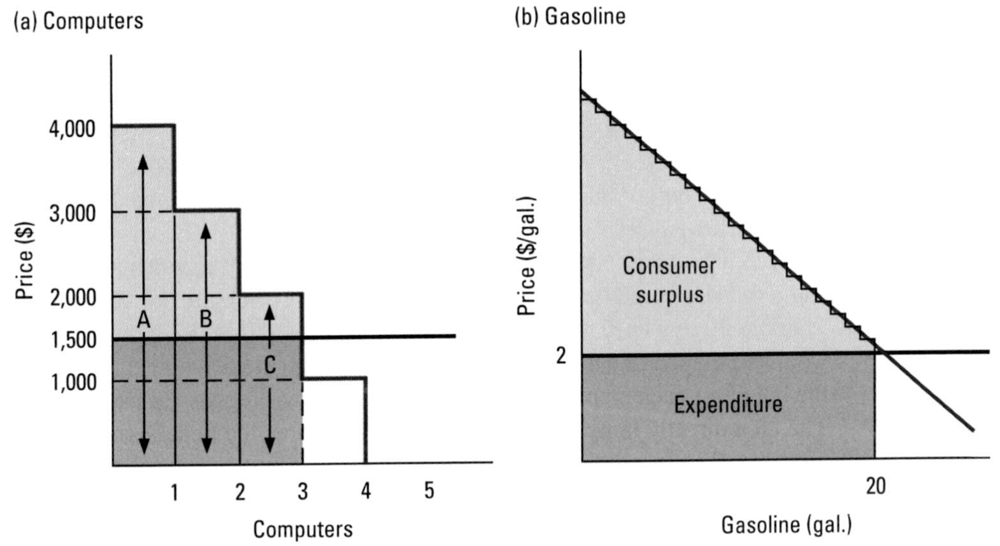

means that the consumer will buy a computer at a price of $4,000 (or any lower price), but will not buy a computer at any higher price. Therefore, his willingness to pay for the first computer is exactly $4,000: since he would buy it at a price of $4,000, his willingness to pay must be at least that high, and it can't be any higher, or he would demand a computer at a higher price. Similarly, for two computers, the height of the demand curve is $3,000. Since he would buy both the first and the second computer at a price of $3,000, his willingness to pay for the second must be at least that high, and it can't be any higher, or he would demand two computers at a higher price. Likewise, according to the figure, his willingness to pay for a third computer is $2,000.

The consumer's net benefit is the difference between his gross benefit and the amount he pays. Let's say computers sell for $1,500 each. According to Figure 6.6(a), the consumer will buy three computers. He is willing to pay $4,000 for the first, so he enjoys a net benefit of $2,500 when he buys it ($4,000 minus $1,500). Similarly, his net benefit from the second computer is $1,500 ($3,000 minus $1,500), and his net benefit from the third computer is $500 ($2,000 minus $1,500). Therefore, his consumer surplus—the total net benefit he receives from participating in the computer market—is $4,500 ($2,500 plus $1,500 plus $500).

Graphically, consumer surplus corresponds to the area below the demand curve and above a horizontal line drawn at the good's price. In Figure 6.6(a), we have shaded that area green. Why does that area represent consumer surplus? The consumer's gross benefit from the first computer equals the height of the bar labeled A ($4,000). The red portion of the bar represents the cost of acquiring this computer ($1,500), so his net benefit equals the green portion of the bar ($2,500). His gross benefit from the second computer equals the height of the bar labeled B ($3,000), and his net benefit equals the green portion of that bar ($1,500); his gross benefit from the third computer equals the height of the bar labeled C ($2,000), and his net benefit equals the green portion of that bar ($500). Therefore, the green-shaded area in the figure represents the consumer's total net benefit, or consumer surplus.

The same principle applies to finely divisible goods. Figure 6.6(b) illustrates this point using gasoline as an example. The weekly demand curve for gasoline is the downward-sloping blue line. At a price of $2 per gallon, the household purchases 20 gallons over the course of a week. As we explain next, consumer surplus once again equals the green-shaded area below the demand curve and above the horizontal line drawn at the price (here, $2 per gallon).

The total gross benefit of 20 gallons of gasoline corresponds to the sum of the green- and red-shaded areas under the demand curve. Why? Imagine for the moment that gasoline is sold only in whole gallons, not in fractions of a gallon. In that case, the demand curve would be shaped like the staircase superimposed on the demand curve. As with computers, the height of each step measures the consumer's willingness to pay for the marginal unit. The area directly beneath the highest step measures the benefit from the first gallon; the area directly beneath the second highest step measures the benefit from the second gallon; and so forth. We can determine the total benefit by adding up these amounts. The result is fairly close to the sum of the green- and red-shaded areas under the demand curve.

Instead of assuming that gasoline is sold only in gallons, we could have chosen a smaller unit—pints, nozzle squeezes, or even drops. As the unit grows smaller, so does each step on the demand curve, so that the staircase becomes harder and harder to distinguish from the blue line. Likewise, the total area under all the steps becomes almost indistinguishable from the total area under the demand curve.

The total expenditure on gasoline corresponds to the area of the red-shaded rectangle. The rectangle's height equals the price ($2 per gallon) and its width equals the quantity (20 gallons). Its area—the height times the width—is therefore the same as the price times the quantity, which produces a total cost, or expenditure, of $40. Since the green- and red-shaded areas represent the total gross benefit, while the red-shaded area represents the total cost, the green-shaded area is the net benefit, or consumer surplus.

The method of computing consumer surplus described above is actually an approximation rather than an exact measure of the compensating variation associated with the loss of access to a market. As we explain in Section 6.5, the quality of the approximation is quite good when the income effects of price changes are small. Consequently, this method is sufficiently accurate for most purposes.

Using Consumer Surplus to Measure Changes in Welfare

Some public policies literally create or destroy markets. Application 6.2 (below) is an example. In these cases, the concept of consumer surplus is clearly applicable: it tells us

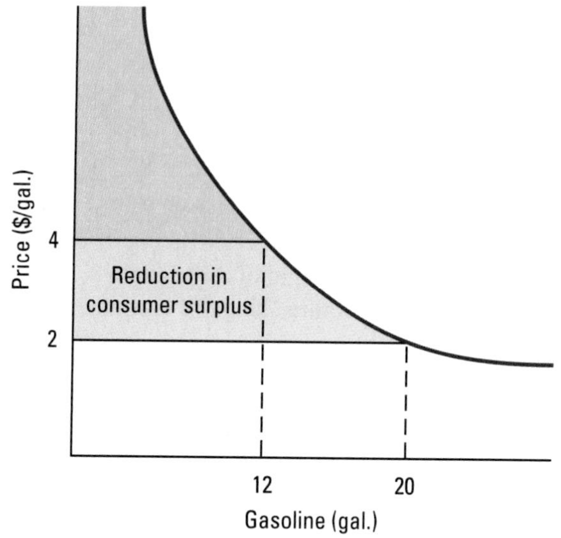

Figure 6.7

Measuring a Change in Consumer Surplus Using a Demand Curve. When the price of gasoline is $2 per gallon, the consumer surplus corresponds to the green- and yellow-shaded areas. When the price of gasoline rises to $4 per gallon, the consumer surplus corresponds to the green-shaded area. The yellow-shaded area is the reduction in consumer surplus that results from the price increase.

how much economic value is created or destroyed. Other public policies alter the prices and amounts of traded goods without affecting a market's existence. For example, gasoline taxes may increase the price of gasoline, but they don't eliminate the gasoline market. In these cases, the concept of consumer surplus is still useful because it allows us to measure the *change* in the net economic benefit that results from the policy. This change in net benefit is simply another way to describe the compensating variation for the policy. For example, if a policy reduces the net benefit that a consumer receives as a participant in a market from $100 to $80, we must provide him with $20 to compensate him fully for the policy's effects.

Figure 6.7 illustrates this point using gasoline as an example. The downward-sloping blue line represents a consumer's demand curve for gasoline. At $2 per gallon, the consumer buys 20 gallons, and his consumer surplus corresponds to the green-shaded area plus the yellow-shaded area. Now imagine the government imposes a large gasoline tax, increasing the price to $4 per gallon. In that case, the consumer buys 12 gallons, and his consumer surplus corresponds to the green-shaded area. The price increase has made the gasoline market less valuable to this consumer. The yellow-shaded area represents his loss; it is also the compensating variation associated with the price change. To determine whether the tax is worthwhile, we can add up the losses for all consumers and compare the total loss to the potential benefits, such as reduced air pollution and revenue for public projects (see Chapter 20).

WORKED-OUT PROBLEM 6.3

The Problem The formula for Abigail's monthly demand curve for minutes of wireless telephone service is $W = 300 - 200P_W$, where W stands for the number of minutes and P_W is the price per minute of service. Suppose that $P_W = \$0.50$ per minute. Using the approach described in this section, calculate Abigail's consumer surplus.

The Solution We have graphed Abigail's demand curve in Figure 6.8. Her consumer surplus is the area of the green triangle. The height of the triangle is 1 and the width is 200, so the area is $1 \times (200/2) = 100$. Therefore, Abigail's consumer surplus is \$100.

IN-TEXT EXERCISE 6.3 **Suppose P_W increases from \$0.50 per minute to \$1 per minute. Calculate the change in Abigail's consumer surplus.**

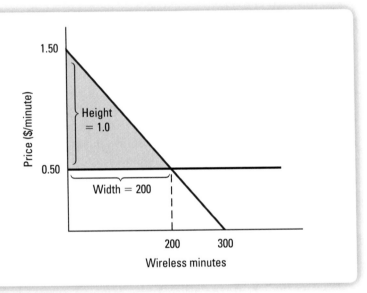

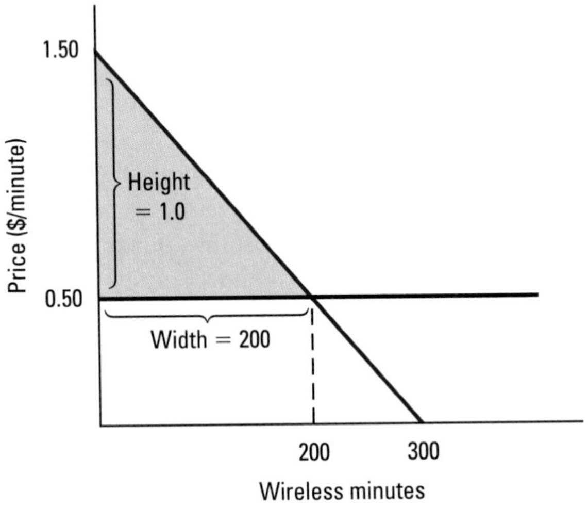

Figure 6.8
Abigail's Consumer Surplus for Wireless Service. The blue line is Abigail's demand curve for wireless telephone service. Her consumer surplus is the green-shaded area below the demand curve and above the horizontal line drawn at the wireless service price, \$0.50 per minute.

Application 6.2

The Introduction of New Telecommunication Services

How much do consumers benefit from the introduction of new goods and services? While many new products are relatively inconsequential, others transform the way we live in a relatively short period of time. Think about handheld wireless telephones. As recently as the early 1980s, they were found only in science fiction novels. Yet in 2004, roughly 50 percent of U.S. citizens owned these devices; in many other countries the percentage was significantly higher. According to one estimate, there were more than 1.3 billion wireless phones in operation worldwide.

It's relatively easy to figure out how much consumers spend on a new product, and it's safe to assume that their benefits exceed their spending. However, the amount of their spending tells us nothing about the good's *net* benefit to them. If we want to know consumers' net gains, the concept to use is consumer surplus.

© The New Yorker Collection 1993 Bernard Schoenbaum from cartoonbank.com. All Rights Reserved.

In one study, economist Jerry Hausman measured the total consumer surplus generated by the introduction of cellular telephones (the first widespread handheld wireless technology).[4] Using data on cellular prices and subscribership in the 30 largest metropolitan areas from 1989 through 1993, Hausman estimated the demand curve for cellular telephone service. He then computed the total consumer surplus from cellular phones by measuring the area between the demand curve and a horizontal line drawn at the market price. On the basis of his calculations, he concluded that in 1994, cellular telephone service generated just under $50 billion of consumer surplus.

Aside from being impressively large, Hausman's estimate of consumer surplus has important implications for public policy. Historically, the telecommunications industry has been heavily regulated. Hausman argued that cellular telephone technology was sufficiently advanced for commercial deployment in the early 1970s—roughly 10 years before its roll-out in the United States. He attributed the 10-year delay to a series of decisions by the Federal Communications Commission (FCC), which oversees the telecommunications industry. In all likelihood, the service would have been more costly and of lower quality in 1975 than it was in 1985. Even so, the delay deprived consumers of the surplus they would have enjoyed had cellular service been available earlier—a loss of more than $100 billion, according to Hausman's estimates.

6.3 MEASURING CHANGES IN CONSUMER WELFARE USING COST-OF-LIVING INDEXES

In this section, we describe an alternative method for measuring changes in consumer well-being, one that requires no information concerning preferences or demand elasticities. Why would we want such a measure? First, it's simple and easy to compute. Second, economists are sometimes unable to estimate either preferences or demand elasticities reliably (for example, because there isn't enough data). This prevents them from measuring changes in consumer well-being using the methods described in Section 6.2. Third, different consumers have different preferences. It's useful to have a measure of the change in well-being—even an approximate one—that applies broadly to a wide range of consumers. The alternative method involves a concept known as a *cost-of-living index*.

What Is a Cost-of-Living Index?

A **cost-of-living index** measures the relative cost of achieving a fixed standard of living in different situations. These indexes are commonly used to measure changes in the cost of living over time. However, they can also be used to measure changes in consumer well-being after the implementation of public policies that alter prices and income.

A **cost-of-living index** measures the relative cost of achieving a fixed standard of living in different situations.

[4]Jerry A. Hausman, "Valuing the Effect of Regulation on New Services in Telecommunications," *Brookings Papers on Economic Activity, Microeconomics*, 1997, pp. 1–38.

The typical cost-of-living index has a base value of one during some specific period. If the value of the index is, say, 1.2 at some later time, then the cost of living has risen by 20 percent. The level of the index in the base period is unimportant. All that matters is the percentage change in the index. To indicate that the cost of living has risen by 20 percent, we could also set the value of the index at two for the base period and at 2.4 for the later period.

Nominal income is the amount of money actually received in a particular period.

Real income is the amount of money received in a particular period adjusted for changes in purchasing power that alter the cost of living over time.

Economists often use price indexes to convert **nominal income** into **real income**. Nominal income is the amount of money that someone actually receives in a particular period. If, for example, your employer pays you $3,000 per month, that is your nominal income. **Real income** is the amount of money received in a particular period adjusted for changes in purchasing power that alter the cost of living over time. To compute real income, we divide nominal income by the cost-of-living index:

$$\text{Real income} = \frac{\text{Nominal income}}{\text{Value of cost-of-living index}}$$

For example, suppose the index is one in the base period and 1.1 at some later time, indicating that the cost of living has risen by 10 percent. If the consumer's nominal income rose from $24,000 to $33,000 over the same period, then his real income increased from $24,000 to only $30,000 (since $30,000 = $33,000/1.1).

Ideally, a cost-of-living index should allow us to quickly evaluate changes in consumer well-being following changes in prices and income. If real income has risen, then nominal income has grown more rapidly than the cost of living, and the consumer should be better off. If real income has fallen, then nominal income has grown more slowly than the cost of living, and the consumer should be worse off. If real income has not changed, then nominal income has kept pace with the cost of living, and the consumer should be equally well off. Moreover, the change in real income should measure the change in the consumer's well-being.

If all prices always changed by the same proportion, constructing a perfect cost-of-living index would be easy; we would simply use the percentage change in prices. So, if prices increased by 20 percent, we would conclude that the cost of living rose by 20 percent. To determine whether the consumer was better or worse off, we would compare that increase to the change in income. If income also increased by 20 percent, then the budget line would be unchanged, and the consumer's well-being would be unaffected, regardless of his preferences. If the consumer's income increased by more than 20 percent, he would be better off because the budget constraint would shift outward; if his income increased by less than 20 percent, he would be worse off because the budget constraint would shift inward—in each case, without rotating.

In actuality, constructing a good cost-of-living index is challenging, because different prices usually change by different proportions. Frequently some prices rise and others fall. As we will see, designing an index that always performs well in practice, let alone one that is perfect, is quite difficult to do.

A Perfect Cost-of-Living Index

If we knew a great deal about a consumer's preferences, then theoretically we could construct a perfect cost-of-living index. Suppose we calculate the compensating variation associated with a change in prices and then divide it by the consumer's initial income. The result (multiplied by 100) would be the *percentage* change in income required to compensate the consumer fully for the price change. The consumer is better off if his income rises by more than this percentage and worse off if it rises by less than this percentage. That is exactly how a perfect cost-of-living index should work.

To illustrate, look back at Figure 6.1(a) (page 168). When the price of soup rises from \$0.50 to \$1 per pint, Oscar's cost of living rises by 50 percent. Why? At the initial price of \$0.50 per pint, and with his initial income of \$10, he chooses bundle A from the budget line labeled L_1. At the new price of \$1 per pint, and with an income of \$15 (including \$5 in compensation), he chooses bundle C from the budget line labeled L_3. Since bundles A and C lie on the same indifference curve, the increase in income from \$10 to \$15 fully compensates him for the rise in price. Notice that the compensating variation for the price change (\$5) is 50 percent of Oscar's initial income. If his actual income increases by exactly 50 percent, he chooses point C and his well-being is unchanged. If his income increases by less than 50 percent, he ends up on a lower indifference curve, and his well-being falls. If his income increases by more than 50 percent, he ends up on a higher indifference curve and his well-being rises.

In practice, there are no perfect measures of changes in the cost of living for two reasons. First, the calculation just illustrated requires detailed and accurate information about consumer preferences. As we've said, that information is often unavailable. Second, preferences vary across the population. The perfect price index for one individual can badly mismeasure the change in cost of living for another individual.

Fixed-Weight Price Indexes

How, then, do we compute cost-of-living indexes in practice? Let's say we want to determine the change in the cost of living in San Francisco between January 2006 and January 2007. The usual approach is to select some consumption bundle and determine its cost in both months using the prices at which the goods were actually available. The percentage change in the cost of the bundle is taken to be the change in the cost of living. So if we choose January 2006 as the base period, and the cost of the fixed bundle rises by 5 percent over the course of 2006, the value of the cost-of-living index is 1 in January 2006 and 1.05 in January 2007. This type of index is known as a **fixed-weight price index**. Fixed-weight indexes are relatively easy to calculate because they require no information about consumer preferences.

A **fixed-weight price index** measures the percentage change in the cost of a fixed consumption bundle.

Of course, the use of a fixed-weight index raises an important question: Which fixed consumption bundle should we use? The choices are almost limitless. Using a bundle that represents the mix of goods that consumers actually purchase certainly makes sense. Even that seemingly innocuous guideline is problematic, however, because the bundles consumers purchase change as prices change.

One common approach is to use a fixed-weight price index based on the consumption bundle actually purchased during the base period. This is known as a **Laspeyres price index**.[5] By comparing the value of a Laspeyres index for different periods, we can determine whether the cost of the base-period consumption bundle has risen or fallen, and by how much. For example, if the base year for a Laspeyres price index is 2003, and the value of the index is 1.2 in 2005 and 1.5 in 2007, then the cost of the bundle consumed in 2003 rose by 20 percent between 2003 and 2005, by 50 percent between 2003 and 2007, and by 25 percent between 2005 and 2007 (since $1.2 \times 1.25 = 1.5$).

A **Laspeyres price index** is a fixed-weight index that is based on the consumption bundle actually purchased in the base period. It tells us whether the cost of the base-period consumption bundle has risen or fallen, and by how much.

[5]Another common choice is a fixed-weight price index based on the consumption bundle actually purchased in the *current* period. This is known as a Paasche price index. The value of a Paasche index tells us whether the cost of the current consumption bundle has risen or fallen since the base period, and by how much. For example, if the base year for a Paasche price index is 2004, and the value of the index is 1.15 in 2007, then the cost of the bundle consumed in 2007 rose by 15 percent between 2004 and 2007.

To illustrate the application of a Laspeyres index, let's return to the problem of computing the change in Oscar's cost of living when the price of soup rises from \$0.50 to \$1 per pint. In the base period, soup costs \$0.50 per pint and bread costs \$0.25 per ounce. According to Figure 6.1(a), Oscar's best choice is bundle A, which contains 13 pints of soup and 14 ounces of bread. We'll construct the index based on this fixed bundle. Initially, the cost of this bundle is \$10. When the price of soup rises to \$1 per pint, the cost of this bundle rises by 65 percent, to \$16.50 (13 pints of soup at \$1 per pint plus 14 ounces of bread at \$0.25 per ounce). The Laspeyres index is therefore 1 in the base period and 1.65 after the price change.

Does the Laspeyres index accurately reflect the true change in the cost of living? The answer is no. For this example, we know from our discussion of the perfect price index that Oscar's income must rise by exactly 50 percent to maintain his level of well-being. The Laspeyres index exaggerates the required increase in income by a substantial amount. If Oscar's income were to increase to \$15 along with the price change, his true standard of living would be unaffected. But according to the Laspeyres index, his real income would be $\$15/1.65 = \$9.09$, a decline of roughly 9 percent compared with the base period!

It is no accident that the Laspeyres index exaggerates the change in the cost of living for this example. A change in the perfect cost-of-living index tells us how much more income is needed to achieve the consumer's original level of well-being. But a change in the Laspeyres index tells us how much more income is needed to achieve the consumer's original level of well-being *by purchasing the consumer's original consumption bundle.* Since the italicized restriction rules out cheaper ways to achieve the original level of well-being, the Laspeyres index overstates the amount of income actually required. When prices are rising, the Laspeyres index exaggerates the increase in the cost of living, an error known as the **substitution bias**. It does so by failing to capture the consumer's tendency to moderate the impact of a price increase by substituting away from goods that have become more expensive.

The **substitution bias** of a Laspeyres price index involves a failure to capture the consumer's tendency to moderate the impact of a price increase by substituting away from goods that have become more expensive. As a result, the index overstates increases in the cost of living.

Figure 6.9 illustrates the substitution bias. We've drawn two budget lines, one for the base period and one for the current period. On each budget line, we've indicated the consumer's best choice. Notice that the consumer has just enough income in the current period to buy the base-period consumption bundle—no more and no less. Therefore, according to the Laspeyres price index, his real income is the same in the base period and

Figure 6.9

A Laspeyres Price Index Overstates Increases in the Cost of Living. If prices have changed between the base period and the current period, and if real income has remained constant according to the index, then the consumer can afford his best choice from the base period. His best choice in the current period is even better. He is therefore better off, even though his real income is supposedly the same.

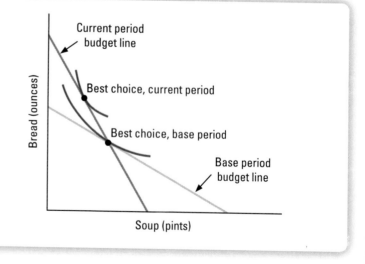

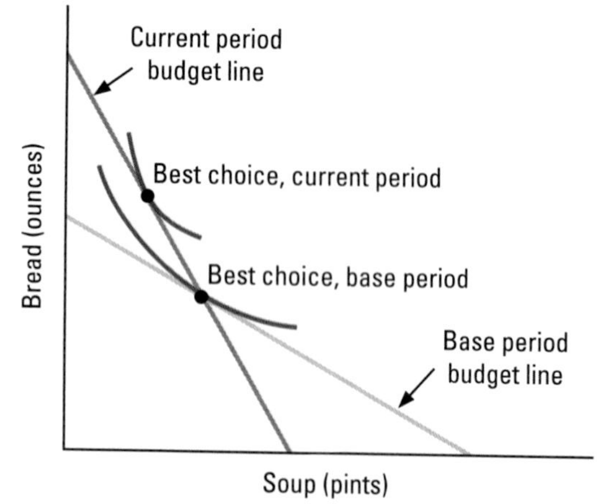

the current period. Yet this conclusion is misleading: the consumer is actually *better off* in the current period than in the base period, which means that the Laspayres index has overstated the increase in the cost of living. How do we know that the consumer is better off in the current period? Because the indifference curve that runs through the base-period best choice is tangent to the base-period budget line, it must cross the current-period budget line, as shown. The best choice in the current period must therefore lie on a higher indifference curve than the base-period best choice.

As Application 6.3 illustrates, such problems are extremely important in practice.

Application 6.3

Bias in the Consumer Price Index

Inflation refers to the change in the cost of living over time. Though measuring the rate of inflation may sound like a tedious bean-counting exercise, it's in fact a controversial subject that stirs impassioned debate, and sometimes even public outcry.

Under current law, Social Security benefits rise automatically with increases in the cost of living, as measured by the U.S. Bureau of Labor Statistics' (BLS) Consumer Price Index (CPI). So do the levels of personal income that define the boundaries between different federal tax brackets. As a result, the federal government could both dramatically reduce retirement benefits and raise taxes over a 20-year period, slicing the national debt by $1 trillion, simply by reducing the *measured* rate of inflation by a mere 0.4 percentage point! Similarly, private-sector contracts between individuals and/or companies often include cost-of-living adjustments that are tied to price indexes such as the CPI. Because of these laws and contractual arrangements, literally trillions of dollars hang in the balance when government statisticians compute the official cost-of-living indexes. No wonder at least one prominent economist received death threats after proposing to change the CPI.

There are several reasons to suspect the CPI exaggerates increases in the true cost of living. First, it's a Laspeyres price index, so it suffers from substitution bias. Second, when the BLS rotates new retail outlets into the sample used to collect data on prices, it attributes all the differences in price between the new outlets and the old ones to the quality of goods sold. Yet the fact that the new outlets have taken business from the old ones strongly suggests that their lower prices reflect better deals, not lower quality.

Third, the CPI understates reductions in the cost of living that result from improvements in the quality of goods purchased. Take personal computers, for example. Each year, these machines become faster and smaller, more reliable and user-friendly. New capabilities and features are constantly being added. Manufacturers come and go; models are retired and new ones introduced. A PC that costs $1,000 today is vastly superior to one that cost the same amount five years ago. Though the BLS tries to adjust for this disparity, one study suggests that it understates the annual decline in quality-adjusted computer prices by four percentage points.[6]

"We project, sir, in '86, a real economic growth of four and five-tenths per cent after adjustment for inflation and ideology."

[6] Aizcorbe, Anna, Carol Corrado, and Mark Doms, "Constructing Price and Quantity Indexes for High Technology Goods," mimeo, Federal Reserve Board, 2000.

These issues received a great deal of attention in 1996, when the Advisory Commission to Study the Consumer Price Index, chaired by economist Michael Boskin, released an influential study containing estimates of the CPI's bias. The "Boskin Commission" concluded that the CPI was overstating the annual increase in the cost of living by roughly 1.1 percentage points (within a plausible range of 0.8 to 1.6 percentage points). This conclusion implied that automatic increases in Social Security benefits had for many years substantially outstripped true increases in the cost of living, adding significantly to the government's budgetary woes.

In recent years, the BLS has made many improvements in the CPI, some in response to the Boskin Commission's report. Even so, significant bias remains. A recent study by two economists with the Federal Reserve System's Board of Governors, David Lebow and Jeremy Rudd, concluded that the CPI continues to overstate the annual increase in the cost of living by 0.87 percentage point (within a plausible range of 0.3 to 1.4 percentage points)*. Lebow and Rudd attribute 0.35 percentage point of that overstatement to substitution bias, 0.05 percentage point to new outlets, 0.37 percentage point to mismeasured quality improvements, and 0.1 percentage point to the use of incorrect weights.

*David E. Lebow and Jeremy B. Rudd, "Measurement Error in the Consumer Price Index: Where Do We Stand?" *Journal of Economic Literature.* March 2003, vol. 41(1), pp. 159–201.

6.4 LABOR SUPPLY AND THE DEMAND FOR LEISURE

Labor supply refers to the sale of a consumer's time and effort to an employer.

So far, we've focused on decisions involving the things consumers buy. But what about the things they *sell*? For example, most adults earn all or part of their incomes by selling their time and effort to employers. This is known as **labor supply**.

Understanding consumer supply—particularly labor supply—is every bit as important as understanding consumer demand. Fortunately, we don't need a separate theory for supply. We mentioned the reason for this in our discussion of goods and bads (Chapter 4, page 104). Let's assume that people regard hours of work as a bad, in the sense that they would rather do something more pleasant.[7] For every bad, there is a corresponding good, defined by the absence of the bad. For labor, the corresponding good is leisure. The price of this good is the wage rate. For example, if a consumer earns $10 per hour, then every hour of leisure costs him $10. To understand the supply of labor, we study the demand for leisure.

Let's consider an example. Javier is taking a year off between high school and college. He doesn't want to work, but he needs money. His wealthy uncle generously gives him an allowance of $210 per week ($30 per day) for living expenses, no strings attached. (Lucky Javier!) The owner of the local 24-hour convenience store has offered him a job that pays $5 per hour and has told Javier that he can work as much or as little as he likes. What should he do?

Javier needs to spend 10 hours per day sleeping, eating, and otherwise taking care of himself. This leaves him with 14 hours per day for work and leisure. Figure 6.10 shows his alternatives. For simplicity, we'll assume that he spends all of his money on food, which costs $1 per ounce. The horizontal axis measures hours of leisure, and the vertical axis measures ounces of food. If Javier chooses not to work, he'll enjoy 14 hours of leisure per day and consume 30 ounces of food. In the figure, this is bundle A. For each hour of leisure he gives up, he'll earn $5, which will allow him to buy another five ounces of food. The slope of his budget line, shown in green, is therefore −5 ounces per hour. For example, if Javier works 14 hours per day, he'll earn $70. Along with his $30-per-day allowance, this income will allow him to buy 100 ounces of food (bundle B in the figure).

[7]Many people derive great satisfaction from their work, or see hard work as virtuous. Consumer theory can also accommodate these possibilities, but we ignore them here for the sake of simplicity.

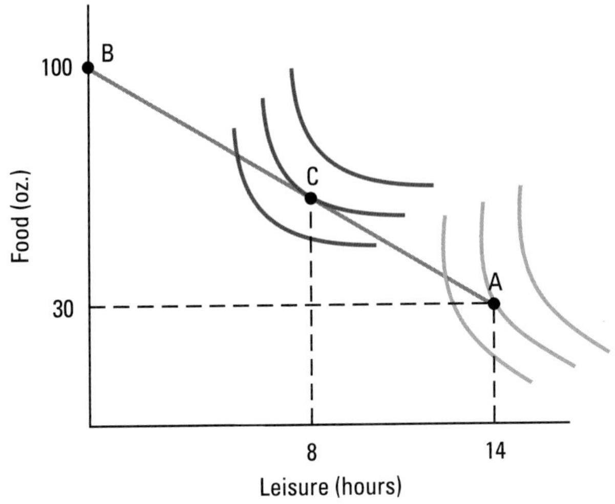

Figure 6.10

A Labor-Leisure Choice. Javier can work for up to 14 hours per day at $5 per hour. He also receives an allowance of $30 per day from a wealthy uncle. He uses his income to buy food, which costs one dollar per ounce. With the dark red indifference curves, he chooses 8 hours of leisure per day, which means he works for 6 hours. With the light red indifference curves, he chooses 14 hours of leisure per day, which means he doesn't work.

The figure shows two families of indifference curves. Compared with the dark red curves, the light red curves attach more importance to leisure and less to food. (Can you explain why?) With the dark red indifference curves, Javier chooses 8 hours of leisure per day, which means he works for 6 hours. With the light red indifference curves, he chooses 14 hours of leisure per day, which means he doesn't work.

In the rest of this section, we study how a change in Javier's wage rate affects his labor supply.

The Effect of Wages on Hours of Work

How does a change in Javier's hourly wage affect his budget line? If he chooses not to work, he'll have $30 to spend on food regardless of his wage. As a result, his budget line always passes through bundle A in Figure 6.10. A change in Javier's wage rotates his budget line, pivoting it around bundle A. With a wage of $3 per hour, he would face the flatter green budget line in Figure 6.11(a). With a wage of $7 per hour, he would face the steeper green budget line. An increase in his hourly wage makes his budget line steeper because it improves the terms at which he can convert his time into food.

Figure 6.11(a) also reproduces the family of dark red indifference curves from Figure 6.10. The points of tangency between the indifference curves and the budget lines form a price-consumption path. Notice that Javier consumes nine hours of leisure with a wage rate of either $3 or $7 (bundles D and E) compared with eight hours of leisure with a wage rate of $5.

We've plotted Javier's leisure demand curve in Figure 6.11(b). Points C, D, and E correspond to the bundles with the same labels in Figure 6.11(a). For low wages, this demand curve slopes downward, but for high wages, it slopes upward—with a higher wage, Javier demands more leisure.

In Section 6.1, we learned that the demand curve for the typical good can slope upward only if the good is inferior, and if the income effect of a price change is sufficiently large. We also pointed out that these conditions are rarely satisfied, which is why Giffen goods are hard to find. In contrast, the demand curve for leisure will slope upward if leisure is a

Figure 6.11

A Leisure Demand Curve and a Labor Supply Curve. Figure (a) shows Javier's choices for three different wage rates: $3, $5, and $7 per hour. Figure (b) uses the information from figure (a) to plot Javier's demand curve for leisure. Since Javier's hours of labor equal his total available hours minus his hours of leisure, his labor supply curve is the mirror image of his leisure demand curve. Javier's labor supply curve is backward-bending.

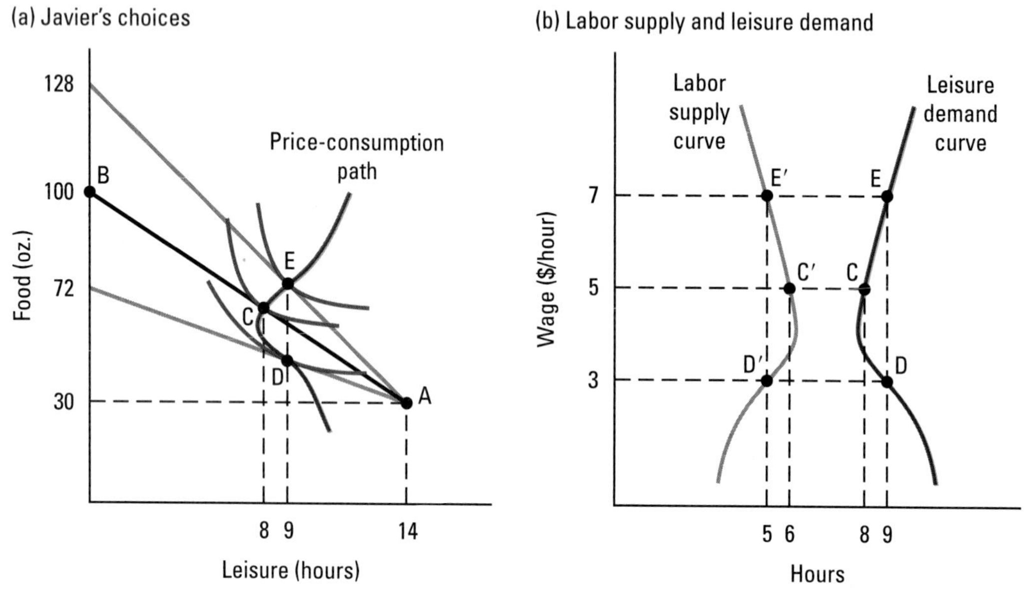

normal good, and if the income effect of a wage change is sufficiently large. Since these conditions are plausible, some consumers may well have upward-sloping leisure demand curves.[8] What accounts for this difference between leisure and typical goods, like soup and potatoes?

For most goods, consumers initially own less than they consume; they buy the difference from producers. In contrast, Javier initially owns more time than he consumes; he sells the difference to his employer. This distinction reverses the direction of the income effect. When the price of soup rises, the typical consumer is *worse* off as a buyer. Assuming soup is a normal good, he therefore demands less soup as a consequence of the income effect. In contrast, when the price of Javier's time rises, he is *better* off as a seller. Therefore, if leisure is a normal good, he demands *more* leisure as a consequence of the income effect. If this effect is sufficiently large, it will more than offset the substitution effect, which involves a shift toward less leisure.

Figure 6.12 illustrates the opposing substitution and income effects for an increase in Javier's wage rate from $5 to $7, assuming that leisure is a normal good. Bundle F is the point of tangency between the indifference curve that runs through bundle C and a line with the same slope as the new budget constraint. The substitution effect corresponds to the movement from bundle C to bundle F. Since leisure becomes more expensive, Javier substitutes away from it, consuming seven hours instead of eight. The income effect cor-

[8] If a consumer's income is derived mostly from employment, then the amount of money required to compensate him fully for a substantial change in his wage rate will be large, in which case the associated income effects may also be large.

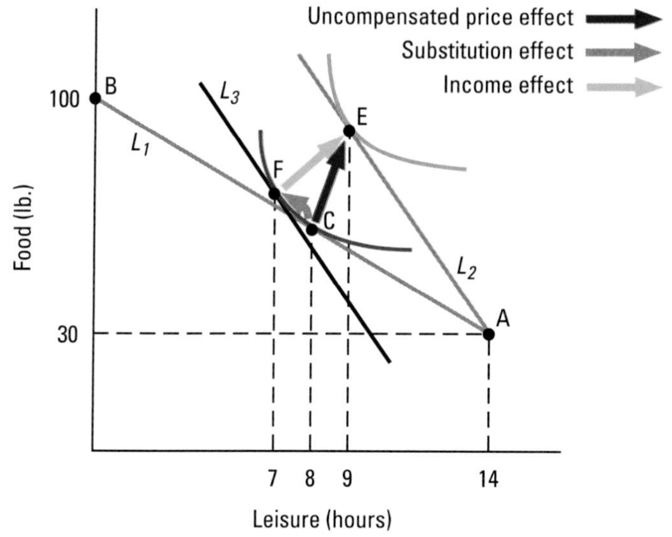

Figure 6.12

Dissection of the Effect of an Increase in a Wage Rate. An uncompensated increase in Javier's wage rotates his budget line upward from L_1 to the L_2, and his choice shifts from bundle C to bundle E (the blue arrow). The movement from bundle C to bundle F is the substitution effect (the gray arrow), and the movement from bundle F to bundle E is the income effect (the yellow arrow). Since Javier consumes less time than he owns, the income and substitution effects work in opposite directions, even though leisure is a normal good. For Javier, the income effect is larger in magnitude than the substitution effect, so an increase in his wage increases his hours of leisure and reduces his hours of labor.

responds to the movement from bundle F to bundle E. Since an increase in Javier's wage raises his purchasing power, and since leisure is a normal good, Javier consumes more of it (nine hours instead of seven). Overall, his leisure time rises.

Using the fact that Javier's hours of labor and leisure must add up to 14, we've also plotted Javier's labor supply curve in Figure 6.11(b). For example, with a wage of \$5, Javier takes eight hours of leisure (point C) and spends six hours working (point C′).

In this example, Javier's labor supply curve is *backward bending*—when the wage is above \$5, an increase in the wage *increases* the amount of leisure he demands, and *reduces* the amount of labor he supplies. There is good evidence that some people actually behave this way. For many prime-age men, labor supply usually does not change much, and may even decline, as the wage rate rises. Our analysis of labor supply decisions attributes this pattern to income effects: since people own more time than they consume, an increase in the wage rate raises their purchasing power, and thereby increases their consumption of normal goods like leisure.

The Effect of Wages on Labor Force Participation

If labor supply curves can bend backward, can a cut in the wage rate cause someone who otherwise would not work to enter the labor market? Can an increase in the wage rate drive someone who otherwise would work out of the labor market?

The answer to both of these questions is no. An increase in the wage rate must increase labor force participation, and a decrease must reduce it. To understand why, look at Figure 6.13. Here we have reproduced Javier's three budget lines from Figure 6.11(a), along with the family of light red indifference curves from Figure 6.10. In the figure, an increase in Javier's wage rate from \$5 to \$7 per hour lures him into the labor market and leads him to choose bundle *G*. However, if the wage rate falls from \$5 to \$3 per hour, his set of affordable bundles shrinks. Since bundle A is his best choice in the larger set of affordable alternatives (with a wage of \$5 per hour), it must also be his best choice in the smaller set (with a wage of \$3 per hour). Therefore, he will definitely remain out of the labor market.

(To check your understanding of this point, use a graph to show why an increase in the wage rate can't drive a worker out of the labor market.)

We can make the same point by dissecting the effects of a wage change. When Javier chooses not to work, the amount of time he owns is the same as the amount of time he consumes. Since he neither sells nor buys his time, a change in the price of his time makes him neither better off nor worse off. That means there's no income effect—only a substitution effect. Since a compensated reduction in the price of leisure cannot produce substitution away from leisure, Javier remains out of the labor force when his wage rate falls.

Figure 6.13

The Effect of the Wage Rate on Labor Force Participation. With the black budget line, Javier chooses not to work. An increase in his wage rotates the budget line upward and leads him to enter the labor force—he chooses bundle G. A reduction in his wage rotates the budget line downward and cannot lead him to enter the labor force.

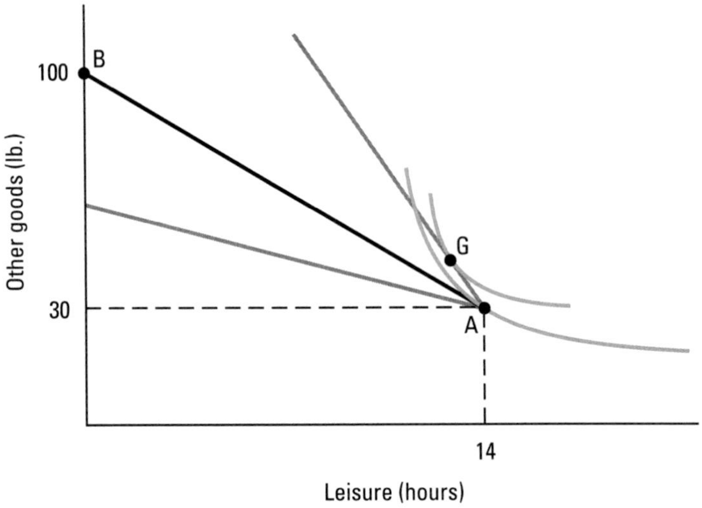

Application 6.4

Women in the Labor Force

At the start of the 20th century, only 5.6 percent of married women in the United States were in the labor force. Women started working in large numbers during World Wars I and II, but this was a temporary measure for most of them. As late as 1950, the labor force participation rate among married women stood at only 23 percent. The second half of the 20th century witnessed much more dramatic changes in female labor force participation. By 1960, 31.7 percent of married women were in the labor force. This figure climbed steadily to 40.2 percent in 1970, 49.9 percent in 1980, 58.4 percent in 1990, and 61.3 percent in 2000. Labor force participation rates for adult men declined somewhat during the same period.

What caused this dramatic change among women? Our analysis of labor supply decisions points to two types of explanations: changing opportunities, including better wages and a wider range of potential careers, and changing preferences.

Let's start with wages. According to the U.S. Census Bureau, in 1967, the typical adult female employee earned only 57.9 percent as much as the typical adult male employee. In 2004, this figure stood at 76.1 percent. In light of the discussion that preceded this application, this sharp increase in wages may well account for a significant fraction of the increase in female labor force participation over this period.

Now let's turn to career choices. Women were once largely confined to traditional "female" occupations, like teaching, nursing, and clerical work. This is no longer the case. Their ability to pursue a wider range of potential careers has two effects. First, it contributes to higher wages. Second, it potentially increases the enjoyment (or at least reduces the displeasure) that women derive from their chosen occupations. This reduces the relative attractiveness of leisure (as well as of unpaid work in the home), flattening the indifference curves in Figure 6.13, and thereby increasing the odds that a woman will choose to join the labor force.

Why did the opportunities for women improve so dramatically? The main causes include changing social norms and customs, measures to discourage discrimination based on gender, and greater educational attainment. Of course, the rising level of educational attainment among women is also a consequence of their expanding opportunities. For example, the number of women pursuing law degrees has grown in part because their career prospects in the field of law have improved.

As a result of changing social norms and customs, women's preferences for paid employment, housework, and leisure have also changed. Today, working women no longer face the social stigma they once did. Many women now grow up with expectations for professional success and measure themselves against these expectations. Those considerations also flatten the indifference curves in Figure 6.13, contributing further to the rise in female labor force participation.

*6.5 ANOTHER TYPE OF DEMAND CURVE

A standard demand curve shows the effect of an uncompensated change in a good's price on the amount consumed. For example, according to the blue demand curve for beef in Figure 6.14(a), an uncompensated increase in the price of beef from \$4 to \$6 per pound reduces beef consumption from 20 to 10 pounds; an uncompensated price cut from \$4 to \$2 per pound increases consumption from 20 to 30 pounds. For this reason, a standard demand curve is sometimes called an **uncompensated demand curve**. It describes the relationship between the price of a good and the amount consumed holding the consumer's income fixed and allowing his well-being to vary. Uncompensated demand curves are also known as **Marshallian demand curves**, in recognition of Alfred Marshall, the 19th-century British economist who originated supply-and-demand analysis, as well as the concept of consumer surplus. When people use the phrase *demand curve*, they generally mean an uncompensated (standard) curve.

An **uncompensated demand curve**, or **Marshallian demand curve**, shows the effect of an uncompensated change in a good's price on the amount consumed. In other words, it describes the relationship between the price and the amount consumed holding the consumer's income fixed and allowing his well-being to vary.

As explained in Section 6.1, we can break up the effect of any uncompensated price change into a substitution effect and an income effect. Fixing a starting price, we can show these effects in the same graph as a standard demand curve. To illustrate, let's assume that the price of beef starts out at \$4 per pound, placing the consumer at point A on the blue demand curve in Figure 6.14(a). Assume that the substitution effect of a price increase from \$4 to \$6 per pound reduces beef consumption from 20 to 15 pounds, while the income effect reduces it from 15 to 10 pounds. Then the substitution effect moves the consumer from point A to point B, and the income effect moves him from point B to point C. Similarly, assume that the substitution effect of a price cut from \$4 to \$2 per pound increases consumption from 20 to 25 pounds, while the income effect raises it from 25 to 30 pounds. Then the substitution effect corresponds to the movement from point A to point D, and the income effect corresponds to the movement from point D to point E.

Now consider the yellow curve that runs through the points A, B, and D. This curve shows *only* the substitution effect of a price change—in other words, the effect of a com-

Figure 6.14

Compensated and Uncompensated Demand Curves. In figure (a), the blue line is the uncompensated demand curve for beef. The yellow line shows the effects of a compensated change in the price of beef starting from $4 per pound; the horizontal distance between the yellow and blue lines is the income effect of the price change. In figure (b), the blue line is the uncompensated demand curve for potatoes. The yellow line shows the effects of a compensated change in the price of potatoes starting from $0.40 per pound; the horizontal distance between the yellow and blue lines is the income effect of the price change. The uncompensated demand curve is flatter than the compensated demand curve in figure (a) and steeper in figure (b) because we have assumed that beef is normal and potatoes are inferior.

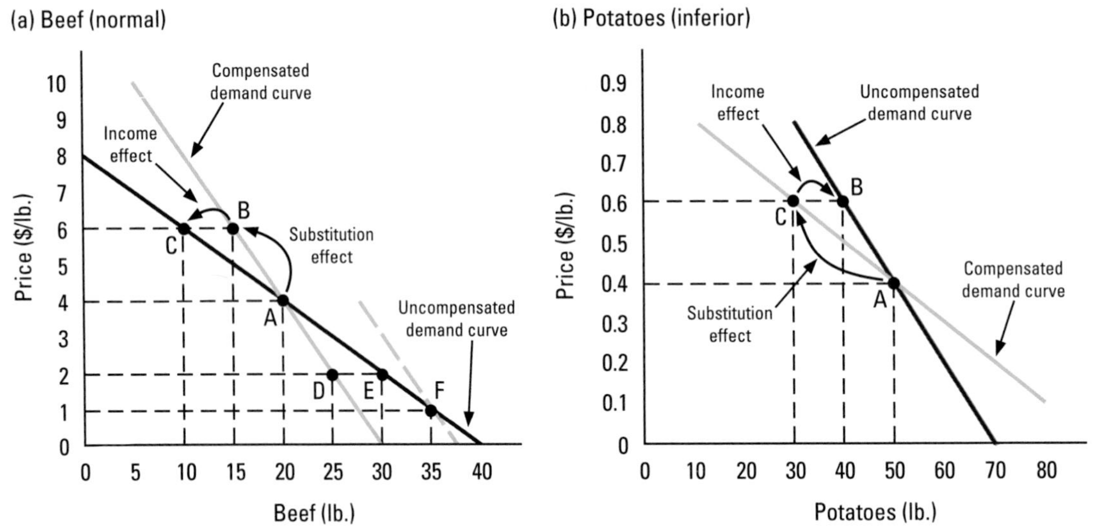

A **compensated demand curve**, or **Hicksian demand curve**, shows the effect of a compensated change in a good's price on the amount consumed. In other words, it describes the relationship between the price and the amount consumed holding the consumer's well-being fixed and allowing his income to vary.

pensated price change—from $4 per pound to any other price. This is called a **compensated demand curve**. It describes the relationship between the price of a good and the amount consumed, holding the consumer's well-being fixed and allowing his income to vary. Compensated demand curves are also known as **Hicksian demand curves**, in recognition of Nobel laureate John R. Hicks.

Unlike uncompensated demand curves, compensated demand curves *always* slope downward. Why? As we explained in Section 6.1, substitution effects always reduce the consumption of a good when its price rises, and increase its consumption when its price falls. A compensated demand curve shows these effects.

As we explained in Section 5.5, the level of a consumer's income determines the location of his uncompensated demand curve. Similarly, the level of his well-being determines the location of his compensated demand curve. To illustrate, let's suppose that the price of beef starts out at $1 per pound instead of $4 per pound. With the same level of income, the consumer is better off. According to the blue uncompensated demand curve in Figure 6.14(a), he buys 35 pounds of beef (point F). The dashed yellow curve that runs through point F shows the effect of a compensated price change from $1 per pound to any other price. Like the solid yellow curve that runs through point A, it is a compensated demand curve—one that corresponds to a higher level of well-being.

The Relationship between the Two Types of Demand Curves

For a normal good, the income and substitution effects work in the same direction, as in Figure 6.14(a).[9] A price change therefore produces a larger change in uncompensated demand than in compensated demand. As a result, wherever a compensated demand curve intersects an uncompensated demand curve, the uncompensated demand curve is necessarily flatter, as shown.

For an inferior good, the income and substitution effects work in opposite directions. As a result, wherever a compensated demand curve intersects an uncompensated demand curve, the uncompensated demand curve is either steeper or upward sloping.

Figure 6.14(b) illustrates the case of an inferior good. The blue line is the uncompensated demand curve for potatoes, which we assume are inferior. An uncompensated price increase from $0.40 to $0.60 per pound reduces consumption from 50 to 40 pounds, moving the consumer from point A to point B. According to the figure, the substitution effect of this price change reduces potato consumption from 50 to 30 pounds, while the income effect increases it from 30 to 40 pounds. Since the substitution and income effects work in opposite directions, the uncompensated demand curve (which runs through points A and B) is steeper than the compensated demand curve (which runs through points A and C).

What if a good is neither normal nor inferior? In that case, the compensated and uncompensated effects of a price change are the same. Therefore, the compensated and uncompensated demand curves coincide with each other.

For a more detailed and technical discussion of the relationship between the compensated and uncompensated demand curves, read the appendix to this chapter.

Sir John R. Hicks (1904–1989) won the 1972 Nobel Prize in Economics.

Application 6.5

Discount Warehouse Clubs and Two-Part Tariffs

Millions of Americans do the bulk of their shopping at discount warehouse clubs. The typical club charges an annual membership fee and sells a variety of products at discounted prices. Perhaps the most familiar warehouse club is Costco, which charges an annual membership fee of $45. Wal-Mart, a conventional retailer, owns a chain of warehouse stores known as Sam's Club, which charges $35 per year for a membership. Sam's Club accounts for roughly 13 percent of Wal-Mart's total revenues—an impressive figure considering that, in 2003, Wal-Mart was the top-ranked U.S. company in terms of total sales.

Let's think about how a discount club might set prices and a membership fee. To keep the analysis simple, let's divide all the products into two categories, groceries and other goods. Figure 6.15(a) illustrates the consumer's potential choices. The horizontal axis shows the quantity of groceries and the vertical axis, the quantity of other goods purchased. If the consumer chooses not to join the discount club, he purchases groceries and other goods at regular prices. His budget line is the steepest green line, L_1, and he chooses bundle A.

The discount club sells groceries at a discounted price in return for a membership fee. The discount rotates his budget constraint, making it flatter, while the membership fee shifts it toward the origin. In the figure, the parallel budget lines labeled L_2 and L_3 correspond to the same grocery discount; L_2 involves no membership fee, while L_3 involves a positive fee.

[9]We assume throughout this section that the consumer initially owns less of the good than he consumes. This contrasts with our discussion of leisure demand in Section 6.4.

Fixing the grocery discount, how high can the club set its membership fee? As we've drawn the figure, the club can set the fee as high as F_1, but no higher. With this fee, the consumer is willing to join the club. As a member, his budget line is L_2 and he chooses bundle B, which he likes exactly as well as bundle A. With any higher fee, his best choice would be worse than bundle A, and he would not join.

Now suppose the club offers an even larger discount on regular grocery prices. Membership becomes more attractive, so that the club can charge a higher membership fee. As before, it can increase the fee to the point where the consumer is just willing to join. In Figure 6.15(b), the club increases the fee, F_2, to the point where the resulting budget constraint, L_4 (which is flatter than L_3 due to the steeper grocery discount), is again tangent to the indifference curve. After joining the club the consumer selects bundle C.

To make sound business decisions, managers of the warehouse club need to understand the relationship between their pricing strategy and sales. In Figure 6.15(b), we see that as the club changes the discounted price, it should alter the membership fee to keep the consumer on the same indifference curve. The amount the consumer would purchase at each possible discounted price is given by his compensated demand curve for groceries!

Pricing is, of course, more complicated than this in practice. Because different consumers have different preferences, setting a single fee that makes them all just willing to join is impossible. Nevertheless, steeper discounts always permit clubs to charge a higher membership fee, at least partly to compensate for the resulting price differential. We will discuss these types of pricing strategies at greater length in Chapter 18.

Figure 6.15

Discount Clubs and Compensated Demand. As shown in figure (a), if the consumer decides not to become a member of the discount club, his budget constraint is L_1 and he chooses bundle A. The figure also shows the largest membership fee, F_1, for which the customer will join the club for a fixed grocery discount. Figure (b) shows that the club can increase the membership fee to F_2 when it increases its grocery discount.

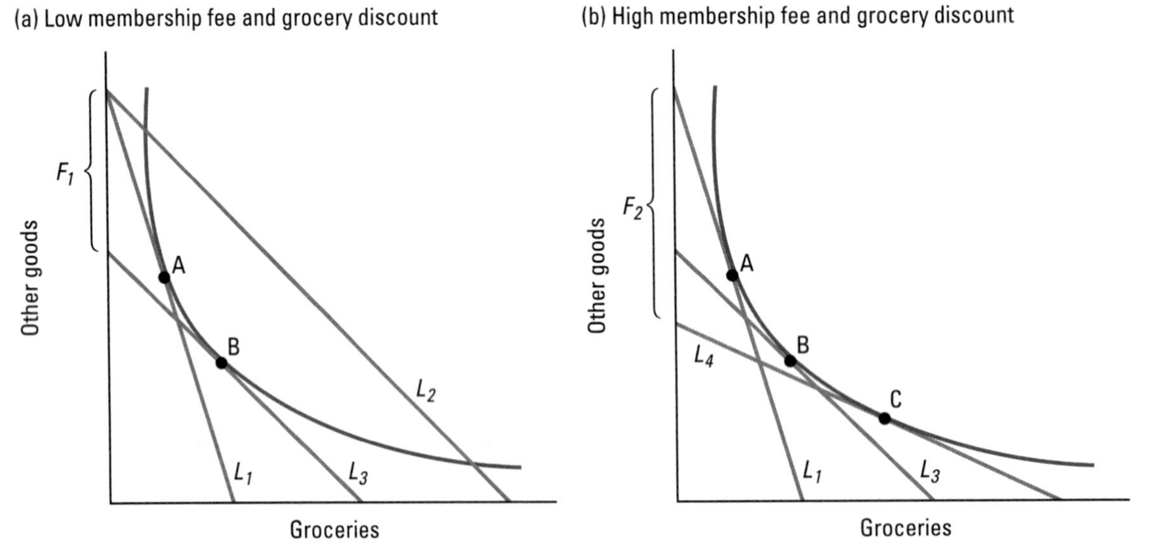

WORKED-OUT PROBLEM 6.4

The Problem Using the information in Figure 6.1 (page 168), plot three points on the uncompensated soup demand curve (assuming that the consumer's income is \$10 and that the price of bread is \$0.25 per ounce). Also plot three points on a compensated soup demand curve. Sketch the curves.

The Solution The consumer purchases 5 pints of soup when the price is \$1 per pint (bundle B in Figure 6.1(a)), 13 pints when the price is \$0.50 per pint (bundle A in Figures 6.1(a) and (b)), and 22 pints when the price is \$0.25 per pint (bundle D in Figure 6.1(b)). We have plotted these points in Figure 6.16(a) using the same labels. The uncompensated demand curve is shown in blue.

We will plot the compensated demand curve that runs through point A in Figure 6.16(a). A compensated price change from \$0.50 to \$1 per pint leads the consumer to buy 8 pints of soup (bundle C in Figure 6.1(a)). A compensated price change from \$0.50 to \$0.25 leads the consumer to buy 18 pints of soup (bundle E in Figure 6.1(b)). We have plotted these points in Figure 6.16(a) using the same labels. The compensated demand curve is shown in yellow.

Figure 6.16

Compensated and Uncompensated Demand Curves for Worked-Out Problems 6.4 and 6.5. In figure (a), we've plotted an uncompensated demand curve (blue) and a compensated demand curve (yellow) for soup, using the information in Figure 6.1, as required for worked-out problem 6.4. In figure (b), we've plotted an uncompensated demand curve (blue) and a compensated demand curve (yellow) for film tickets, using the formulas obtained in the solution to worked-out problem 6.5.

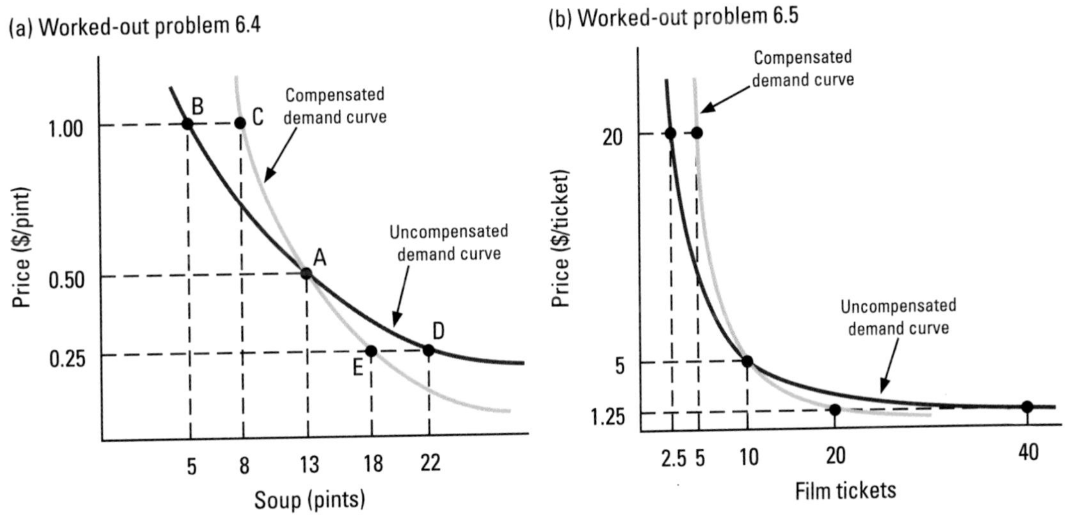

IN-TEXT EXERCISE 6.4 **Using the information in Figure 6.4 (page 174), plot two points on the uncompensated potato demand curve (assuming that the consumer's income is \$36 and that the price of beef is \$3 per pound). Also plot two points on a compensated potato demand curve. Sketch the curves.**

WORKED-OUT PROBLEM 6.5

The Problem As in worked-out problem 6.1 (page 171), Natasha's marginal rate of substitution for concerts with films, MRS_{CF}, is F/C, where C stands for the number of concert tickets and F stands for the number of film tickets. The formula for her indifference curves is $F = U/C$. Her income is \$100 per month. As we discovered in the solution to worked-out problem 5.5 (page 146), when concert and film prices are both \$5 per ticket, she buys 10 of each. Find the compensated demand curve for films that passes through this point and graph it. How does it compare to her uncompensated demand curve?

The Solution First we'll solve for Natasha's compensated demand curve. With a compensated change in the price of film tickets, her best choice must satisfy the tangency condition and lie on the indifference curve through the bundle $(C, F) = (10, 10)$. As in the solution to worked-out problem 6.1, the formula for the tangency condition is $F/C = P_C/P_F$. With $P_C = 5$, we can rewrite this formula as follows:

$$C = FP_F/5$$

As in worked-out problem 6.1, the formula for the indifference curve that runs through the bundle $(C, F) = (10, 10)$ is $F = 100/C$, which we will rewrite as:

$$C = 100/F$$

A bundle can satisfy both the tangency condition formula and the indifference curve formula at the same time only if $FP_F/5 = 100/F$. This requires $F^2 = 500/P_F$, or $F = \sqrt{500/P_F}$. This expression represents the number of tickets Natasha will buy following a compensated change in the price of film tickets from \$5 to any other price P_F. In other words, it is the formula for her compensated demand curve.

Our answer to worked-out problem 5.5 provided a formula for Natasha's uncompensated demand curve: $F = M/(2P_F)$. With $M = \$100$, the formula becomes $F = 50/P_F$.

We've graphed Natasha's compensated and uncompensated demand curves in Figure 6.16(b), plotting the amounts purchased for three film ticket prices: $P_F =$ \$1.25, \$5, and \$20. Notice that the compensated demand curve is steeper than the uncompensated demand curve. In this example, film tickets are normal goods.

IN-TEXT EXERCISE 6.5 **As in in-text exercise 6.1, Keiko's marginal rate of substitution for gasoline with wireless minutes, MRS_{GW}, is $10/\sqrt{G}$, where G stands for gallons of gasoline. The formula for her indifference curves is $W = U - 20\sqrt{G}$, where W stands for the number of wireless minutes. Keiko's income is \$125 and gasoline costs \$1 per gallon. How many wireless minutes will Keiko purchase if the price is \$0.50 per minute? Find the compensated demand**

curve for wireless service that passes through this point and graph it. How does it compare to her uncompensated demand curve? Will her compensated and uncompensated demand curves for gasoline differ? (Hint: You should be able to answer this last question without solving for the curves. Apply what you learned about Keiko's income effects for gasoline in worked-out problem 5.6, page 156.)

Exact Consumer Surplus

As we've mentioned, the method of computing consumer surplus described in Section 6.2 is actually an approximation rather than an exact measure of the compensating variation associated with the loss of access to a market. To understand the problem, look again at Figure 6.6(a). According to our calculation, the household receives $4,500 in consumer surplus from the computer market. If we abolished the computer market and compensated this household by paying it $4,500, its income would be $4,500 higher. As we noted in Section 5.5, a change in income shifts the demand curve. If computers are normal goods, the demand curve would shift outward, expanding the green-shaded area and increasing our measure of the household's consumer surplus beyond $4,500. In other words, when the household receives $4,500 as compensation for the ability to buy computers, the value of that ability grows beyond $4,500!

To overcome this problem, we compute consumer surplus following the same procedure as in Section 6.2 (recall Figure 6.6), except we use a compensated demand curve instead of an uncompensated demand curve. For an illustration, look at Figure 6.17(a), which reproduces the blue uncompensated computer demand curve from Figure 6.6(a). As before, computers sell for $1,500 each, and the consumer buys three. We've added a yellow curve, which shows the effects of compensated price changes starting from a price of $1,500. This is a compensated demand curve. (Where the compensated and uncompensated demand curves overlap, we use a dashed line that alternates blue and yellow segments.)

How much would we have to compensate the consumer for the loss of access to the computer market? To answer this question, let's imagine taking the computers away from him one by one, and calculate the required compensation for each. Let's start with the third computer. From either demand curve, we know that it's worth $2,000 to the consumer. He buys it for $1,500, so his net benefit is $500. If we pay him $500, he should be willing to give it up. In the figure, that payment equals the area of the green-shaded rectangle labeled C.

How much must we pay the consumer to compensate him for the loss of the second computer? According to the uncompensated (blue) demand curve, the net economic benefit of that computer is $1,500; according to the compensated (yellow) demand curve, it's $2,000. Which number is correct? To compensate the consumer for the loss of the second computer, we need to know its worth to him *after compensating him for the loss of the third computer*. The height of the compensated demand curve indicates the consumer's willingness to pay for the second computer after receiving this compensation, while the height of the uncompensated demand curve does not. Therefore, we must use the compensated demand curve. In this example, after receiving compensation for the third computer, the consumer is just willing to give up the second computer for a payment of $2,000 (the area of the green-shaded rectangle labeled B).

Through almost identical reasoning, we learn that, after receiving compensation for the second and third computers, the consumer should be willing to give up the first computer for a payment of $3,500 (the area of the green-shaded rectangle labeled A). To

Figure 6.17

Measuring Exact Consumer Surplus and Compensating Variations Using Compensated Demand Curves. In figure (a), the payments required to compensate the consumer for the loss of the third, second, and first computers in succession equal the areas of the green-shaded rectangles labeled C (for the third computer), B (for the second computer), and A (for the first computer). The consumer surplus for computers is therefore equal to the total green-shaded area. In figure (b), the compensating variation for an increase in the price of gasoline from $2 to $4 per gallon equals the green-shaded area (which compensates for reduced consumption) plus the red-shaded area (which compensates for the higher price paid on gallons purchased at $4 per gallon).

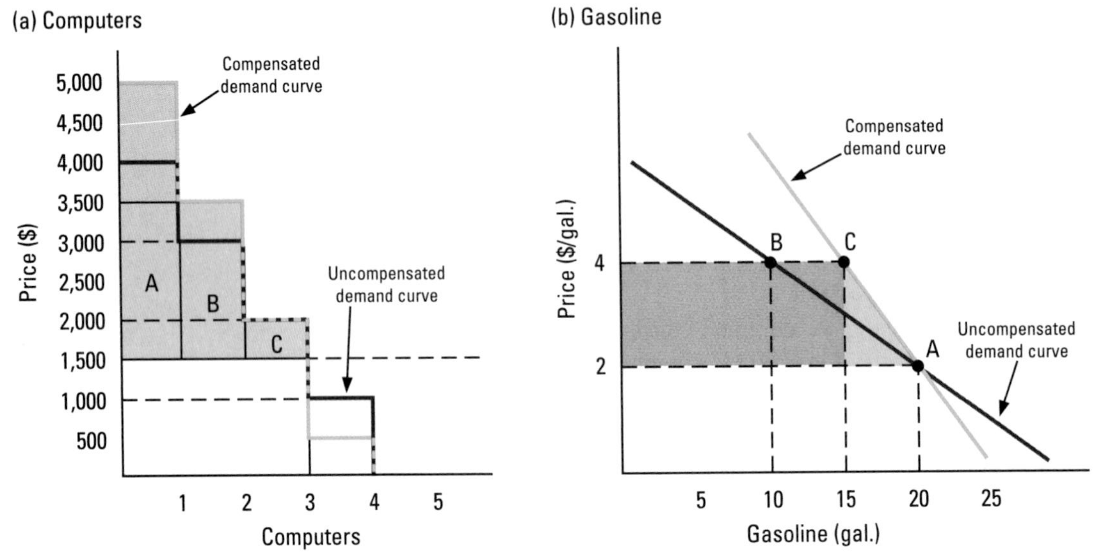

compensate him for the loss of all of his computers, we therefore have to pay him $6,000. Notice that this compensating variation equals the area between the compensated demand curve and a horizontal line drawn at the market price.

Exact Changes in Consumer Surplus In Section 6.3, we explained how to use an uncompensated demand curve not only to measure consumer surplus, but also to determine the change in welfare that results from a change in price (recall Figure 6.7). We now know that this procedure is actually an approximation. To compute the change in consumer surplus exactly rather than approximately, we follow the same procedure as in Section 6.3, except that we use a compensated demand curve instead of an uncompensated demand curve.

Suppose, for example, that a proposed gasoline tax will increase the price of gas from $2 to $4 per gallon. What is the economic cost to any given consumer? Look at Figure 6.17(b). The blue line is the consumer's uncompensated demand curve. At $2 per gallon, he would buy 20 gallons (point A); at $4 per gallon, he would buy only 10 gallons (point B). The yellow line is a compensated demand curve—it shows the effect of compensated prices changes starting from a price of $2 per gallon.

To compute the compensating variation for the price increase, we start at point A, which the consumer chooses without the tax. Then we take away gasoline little by little, compensating him as we go. As shown in the figure, the compensated increase in the price of gasoline from $2 to $4 reduces the consumer's gasoline purchases to 15 gallons (point C). The required rate of compensation for the last unit of gasoline always equals the height of the compensated demand curve, minus the original price, \$2. So the total payment required to compensate the consumer for the reduction in gasoline consumption from 20 to 15 gallons equals the area of the green-shaded triangle. The consumer also loses \$2 on each of the 15 gallons he continues to purchase. To compensate him for this loss, we have to pay him an additional \$30, the area of the red rectangle. The compensating variation therefore equals the area of the green triangle plus the area of the red rectangle. Had we used the uncompensated demand curve rather than the compensated demand curve, we would have understated the compensating variation.

Approximate Versus Exact Consumer Surplus Suppose for the moment that computers are neither normal nor inferior—in other words, that there are no income effects. In that case, the compensated and uncompensated demand curves for computers are identical, and we can compute exact consumer surplus using either one. Intuitively, with no income effects, compensating the consumer for the loss of a computer doesn't change his willingness to pay for the remaining computers.

When income effects are small, the uncompensated demand curve lies close to the compensated demand curve. If we compute consumer surplus using the uncompensated demand curve, we won't measure consumer surplus with complete accuracy, but we won't be far off. Consequently, the procedure for measuring consumer surplus described in Section 6.2 will yield a good approximation. This makes intuitive sense. Suppose, for example, that a consumer receives \$50 in consumer surplus annually from the butter market, and that his income is \$50,000. If he were to receive \$50 as compensation for losing the ability to buy butter, his income would be \$50,050, and his demand curve for butter would barely move. Adjusting for this movement would make little difference.

Sometimes, however, the approach described in Section 6.2 does not closely approximate consumer surplus. Suppose, for example, that a consumer receives \$30,000 in consumer surplus annually from leisure. If he gives up \$30,000 to gain access to the labor market, his uncompensated demand curve for leisure may shift dramatically. To compute his consumer surplus accurately, we must therefore use his compensated leisure demand curve.

WORKED-OUT PROBLEM 6.6

The Problem Repeat worked-out problem 6.2 (page 178), but compute Keiko's compensating variation using a compensated demand curve. Is the answer the same as in worked-out problem 6.2?

The Solution To compute the compensating variation, we use the compensated demand curve for wireless minutes that describes the effects of compensated changes in the price of minutes starting from the market price (\$0.50 per minute). If you solved in-text exercise 6.5 (page 198) correctly, you know that the formula for this compensated demand curve is $W = 300 - 200P_W$. Notice that this is the same as Abigail's uncompensated demand curve for wireless minutes in worked-out problem 6.3 (page 182). Figure 6.8 is therefore also a graph of one of Keiko's compensated demand curves. The compensating variation for the loss of her wireless phone is the area of the green triangle. We already determined that the area of this triangle is \$100. Therefore, Keiko's compensating variation is \$100. Notice that we obtained exactly the same answer in worked-out problem 6.2.

IN-TEXT EXERCISE 6.6 **Suppose the price of wireless service rises from \$0.50 per minute to \$1 per minute. What is Keiko's compensating variation? Show the lost consumer surplus on a graph.**

CHAPTER SUMMARY

1. **Dissecting the effects of a price change**
   a. The effect of an uncompensated change in the price of a good equals the effect of a compensated change in the price of the good (the substitution effect), plus the effect of removing the compensation (the income effect).
   b. The substitution effect is negative for a price increase and positive for a price reduction. If a good is normal, the income effect is negative for a price increase and positive for a price reduction. If a good is inferior, the income effect is positive for a price increase and negative for a price reduction.
   c. For a normal good, the income effect reinforces the substitution effect, so the demand curve slopes downward.
   d. For an inferior good, the income effect and the substitution effect work in opposite directions.
   e. If a good is sufficiently inferior, and if it accounts for a sufficiently large fraction of the consumer's spending, its demand curve may slope upward.
2. **Measuring changes in consumer welfare using demand curves**
   a. Economists often evaluate the gains or losses that consumers experience when economic circumstances change by computing compensating variations.
   b. Consumer surplus is the compensating variation associated with the loss of access to a market.
   c. The height of a good's demand curve indicates the consumer's willingness to pay for another unit of the good.
   d. One common method of calculating the consumer surplus derived from a good is to determine the area below the good's demand curve and above a horizontal line drawn at the good's price.
   e. The compensating variation for a price change equals the resulting change in consumer surplus. Therefore, economists use the change in consumer surplus as a measure of the change in the consumer's well-being.
3. **Measuring changes in consumer welfare using cost-of-living indexes**
   a. A cost-of-living index allows us to approximate changes in a consumer's well-being caused by changes in prices without knowing preferences or demand elasticities.
   b. With a perfect cost-of-living index, the consumer would be better off when real income rises according to the index, and worse off when real income falls according to the index.
   c. In theory, it's possible to construct a perfect price index by computing compensating variations. In practice, doing so requires knowledge of consumer preferences, which vary across the population.
   d. Most price indexes indicate the change in the cost of a fixed bundle of goods.
   e. Laspeyres price indexes suffer from substitution bias because they fail to capture the consumer's tendency to moderate the impact of a price increase by substituting away from goods that have become more expensive. As a result, they tend to overstate increases in the cost of living.
   f. Inflation is the change in the cost of living over time. A common official measure of inflation is based on the Consumer Price Index (CPI), which is a Laspeyres index. Recent estimates suggest that the CPI significantly exaggerates the rate at which the cost of living increases.
4. **Labor supply and the demand for leisure**
   a. To understand the supply of labor, we study the demand for leisure, treating the wage rate as the price of leisure.
   b. The substitution effect of an increase in the wage rate decreases leisure demand and increases labor supply.
   c. Since consumers are sellers of their time rather than buyers, income effects are reversed. When leisure is a normal good, the income effect and the substitution effect work in opposite directions. As a result, labor supply curves may bend backwards. There is evidence that, for many prime-age men, labor supply usually does not change much and may even decline as the wage rate rises.
   d. An increase in the wage rate should increase labor force participation. This principle helps to explain the dramatic increase in female labor force participation during the second half of the last century.

***5. Another type of demand curve**

a. Compensated demand curves always slope downward.

b. Different compensated demand curves correspond to different levels of the consumer's well-being.

c. For a normal good, wherever a compensated demand curve intersects an uncompensated demand curve, the uncompensated demand curve is necessarily flatter. For an inferior good, wherever a compensated demand curve intersects an uncompensated demand curve, the uncompensated demand curve is either steeper or upward sloping. If a good is neither normal nor inferior, the compensated and uncompensated demand curves coincide with each other.

d. To compute consumer surplus exactly, we must use compensated demand curves. If we calculate consumer surplus using uncompensated demand curves, we obtain an approximation of consumer surplus. This approximation will be good if income effects are small.

ADDITIONAL EXERCISES

Exercise 6.1: Nuts and bolts are perfect complements; a nut is valuable only when paired with a bolt, and vice versa. Ted spends all his money on nuts and bolts. On a graph, illustrate the effect of a compensated change in the price of nuts. Does this change alter the consumption of nuts or bolts? What does your answer tell you about the size of substitution effects resulting from changes in the price of nuts?

Exercise 6.2: Regular- and extra-strength pain killers are perfect substitutes; one extra-strength tablet is equivalent to two regular-strength tablets. In each of the following cases, show graphically the effect of a compensated increase in the price of regular-strength tablets. Does this change alter the consumption of regular- or extra-strength tablets? What do your answers tell you about the size of the substitution effects resulting from increases in the price of regular-strength tablets?

a. The price of an extra-strength tablet is more than twice the final price of a regular-strength tablet.

b. The price of an extra-strength tablet is more than twice the initial price of a regular-strength tablet, but less than twice the final price.

c. The price of an extra-strength tablet is less than twice the initial price of a regular-strength tablet.

Exercise 6.3: Figure 6.4 (page 174) shows the income and substitution effects associated with a reduction in the price of an inferior good. Draw a similar graph showing the income and substitution effects associated with an increase in the price of an inferior good.

Exercise 6.4: Figure 6.5 (page 175) shows the income and substitution effects associated with a reduction in the price of a Giffen good. Draw a similar graph showing the income and substitution effects associated with an increase in the price of a Giffen good.

Exercise 6.5: Can every good be a Giffen good? Why or why not?

Exercise 6.6: Think about your own preferences. What is your compensating variation for each of the following changes in your plans or expectations?

a. Listening to your economics professor perform a one-hour poetry reading.

b. Meeting your favorite musician.

c. Adding a week to the length of your spring break.

d. Majoring in economics if you plan to major in something else; majoring in something else if you plan to major in economics.

Exercise 6.7: Sam currently earns $30,000 a year. The government is considering a policy that would increase Sam's income by 12 percent, but raise all prices by 8 percent. What is Sam's compensating variation for the proposed policy? Can you compute it without knowing his preferences? Why or why not?

Exercise 6.8: Suppose policymakers are considering two potential projects that are mutually exclusive. Should they always pick the one for which the compensating variation is the largest negative number (in other words, the one for which the individual is willing to pay the most)? Why, or why not? If not, is there a way to compare the benefits of these projects using the concept of compensating variation? (Hint: Think about the compensating variation of reversing each policy.)

Exercise 6.9: The formula for Albert's demand curve for music downloads is $M = 150 - 60P_M$, where M is the number of downloads and P_M is the price of a download. Suppose the price of a music download falls from \$2 to \$1. Using the method described in Section 6.2, calculate the change in Albert's consumer surplus.

Exercise 6.10: Beatriz enjoys writing and uses a large amount of paper. Currently, paper costs \$2 for 100 sheets. The formula for her demand curve is $S = 525 - 50P$, where P_S is the price of 100 sheets and S is the number of sheets purchased. The governor of her state has proposed taxing paper at the rate of $0.50 for each 100 sheets. Assume that this policy would increase the price of paper to $2.50 (including tax).

a. Draw Beatriz' demand curve. Using the method described in Section 6.2, compute the change in her consumer surplus for the proposed tax increase.

b. How much revenue will the government raise by taxing Beatriz? How does that revenue compare to her economic losses? Does the new tax raise enough revenue for the government to compensate her for her loss?

Exercise 6.11: Arnold spends all his money on sunscreen and lemonade. In June he bought 5 ounces of sunscreen at $1 per ounce and 20 gallons of lemonade at $1.30 per gallon. In July he bought 7 ounces of sunscreen at $1.10 per ounce and 18 gallons of lemonade at $1.70 per gallon. In August he bought 3 ounces of sunscreen at $1.40 per ounce and 23 gallons of lemonade at $1.80 per gallon.

a. Create a Laspeyres price index using June as the base period (that is, use Arnold's consumption bundle for June to create the fixed weights). How did his cost of living change according to this measure?

b. Repeat part (a) first using July as the base period and then using August as the base period.

c. Do the Laspeyres price indexes you obtained in parts (a) and (b) imply the same percentage increases in Arnold's cost of living over time? If not, by how much do they differ?

Exercise 6.12: Is it possible for the true cost of living to rise for one consumer and fall for another in response to the same change in prices? If so, explain why, and give an example using graphs. If not, explain why not.

Exercise 6.13: Sheryl spends all of her leisure time and all of her money on sailing. She doesn't value leisure time if she can't sail, and she can only sail if she has leisure time. Sailboat rentals cost $10 per hour, and Sheryl earns W per hour. She has to decide how to allocate 15 hours per day between work and leisure. How many hours will she work if she earns $20 per hour? Find a formula for her labor supply curve. Is it upward or downward sloping? Why?

***Exercise 6.14:** For Alejandro, concert tickets and film tickets are perfect complements—he does not enjoy additional concerts when he has attended more concerts than films, or additional films when he has attended more films than concerts (as in in-text exercise 5.7, page 147). Initially, he can spend $200, film tickets cost $8 per ticket, and concert tickets cost $8 per ticket. Solve for a compensated demand curve for film tickets, showing the effects of compensated price changes starting from the initial film ticket price of $8 per ticket. How does this curve compare to his uncompensated demand curve for film tickets, found in the solution to in-text exercise 5.7?

***Exercise 6.15:** How would you measure consumer surplus if the demand curve is upward sloping? Warning: this is a trick question.

APPENDIX

THE SLUTSKY EQUATION

The relationship between compensated and uncompensated demand is summarized by an important formula known as the **Slutsky equation**. This equation is a precise statement of the principle, stated earlier as formulas (1) and (2), that the effect of an uncompensated price change equals the effect of a compensated price change (the substitution effect) plus the effect of removing the compensation (the income effect):

The **Slutsky equation** is a precise mathematical statement of the principle that the effect of an uncompensated price change equals the effect of a compensated price change (the substitution effect) plus the effect of removing the compensation (the income effect).

$$\left(\frac{\Delta Q}{\Delta P}\right)^{Uncomp} = \left(\frac{\Delta Q}{\Delta P}\right)^{Comp} - Q \times \left(\frac{\Delta Q}{\Delta Y}\right) \quad \textbf{(3)}$$

The symbol $(\Delta Q/\Delta P)^{Uncomp}$ stands for the uncompensated price effect. It is the change (per dollar) in the amount purchased resulting from a small uncompensated price change. The symbol $(\Delta Q/\Delta P)^{Comp}$ stands for the change (per dollar) in the amount purchased resulting from a small compensated price change. That term is the substitution effect. Finally, $\Delta Q/\Delta Y$ stands for the change (per dollar) in the amount purchased resulting from a small change in income. That term, multiplied by $-Q$, is the income effect.

Why do we need to multiply $\Delta Q/\Delta Y$ by $-Q$? The income effect equals $\Delta Q/\Delta Y$—the change in the amount purchased per dollar of income—times the change in purchasing power resulting from the price increase. As it turns out, the change in purchasing power is $-Q$. Why? Suppose a consumer purchases Q pounds of beef at a price of \$$P$ per pound, spending \$$PQ$. If the price increases by \$1 per pound, the same amount of beef costs \$$(P + 1)Q$, so he needs an additional \$$Q$ to purchase it. If his income hasn't changed and he attempts to buy the same bundle as before, he finds himself \$$Q$ short. So roughly speaking, he has lost \$$Q$ worth of purchasing power.

We can also write the Slutsky equation in terms of elasticities:[10]

$$E_P^{Uncomp} = E_P^{Comp} - S \cdot E_Y \quad \textbf{(4)}$$

In this equation, E_P^{Uncomp} stands for the elasticity of demand along the uncompensated demand curve (previously written simply as E_P). E_P^{Comp} stands for the elasticity of demand along the compensated demand curve. S is the good's budget share (that is, the fraction of income spent on it), and E_Y is the good's income elasticity.

[10]To get from equation (3) to equation (4), multiply both sides of (3) by P/Q. The term to the left of the equals sign becomes $(P/Q)(\Delta Q/\Delta P)^{Uncomp}$. You should recognize this expression as the price elasticity of demand for the uncompensated demand curve. The first term to the right of the equals sign becomes $(P/Q)(\Delta Q/\Delta P)^{Comp}$, the price elasticity of demand for the compensated demand curve. Finally, the second term to the right of the equals sign becomes $-(P/Q) \times Q \times (\Delta Q/\Delta Y)$, which is equivalent to $-(PQ/Y) \times (Y/Q) \times (\Delta Q/\Delta Y)$. The first part of that expression, PQ/Y, is the good's budget share. You should recognize the second part, $(Y/Q) \times (\Delta Q/\Delta Y)$, as the income elasticity of demand. Substituting these definitions into equation (3) gives us equation (4).

Using the Slutsky Equation to Determine Consumers' Preferences

Since a consumer's well-being is not observable, we can't measure the compensated elasticity of demand for a good directly. However, using the Slutsky equation, we can determine it indirectly. Since prices, income, and purchases are observable, we can measure the good's uncompensated elasticity of demand, its income elasticity, and its budget share. We can then compute the compensated price elasticity of demand simply by rearranging the Slutsky equation:

$$E_P^{Comp} = E_P^{Uncomp} + S \cdot E_Y \qquad \textbf{(5)}$$

With this equation, we can easily reconstruct the compensated demand curve for a good by observing a consumer's response to changes in prices and income. This allows us to measure consumer surplus exactly, rather than approximately, using the approach described earlier in this section. Since compensated price changes keep the consumer on the same indifference curve, we can, if necessary, also use the Slutsky equation to reconstruct the shape of the indifference curves.

Are Income Effects Important?

The Slutsky equation also tells us that the income effect is relatively unimportant when either a good's budget share (S) or its income elasticity (E_Y) is small. This observation is useful because, with small income effects, the discrepancies between the compensated and uncompensated demand curves are minor. In that case, we can compute consumer surplus using standard (uncompensated) demand curves without introducing much error.

For the vast majority of products, the budget share is very small, simply because people buy so many different things. As a result, income effects are usually tiny. This observation may help to explain why there are so few exceptions to the Law of Demand.

Let's take cheese as an example. According to recent estimates for the United Kingdom, the uncompensated price elasticity of cheese is -0.350 and its income elasticity is 0.23. The budget share is 0.0046, which means that an individual with an annual income of \$30,000 spends about \$138 per year on cheese. Multiplying the budget share by the income elasticity and rounding off the answer gives us 0.001. From equation (5), we see that the compensated price elasticity must be -0.349, practically the same as the uncompensated price elasticity.

This makes sense. Suppose that Nigel earns \$30,000 annually and spends \$138 per year on cheese. If the price of cheese increases by 20 percent, he needs an additional \$27.60 to make the same purchases. If his income hasn't changed and he attempts to buy the same consumption bundle as before, he finds himself \$27.60 short. So roughly speaking, his purchasing power has fallen by \$27.60. Nigel will spread this tiny reduction in purchasing power over everything he purchases. Its impact on his cheese consumption will be almost negligible compared to the direct impact of the price increase via the substitution effect.

Though income effects are typically small, there are exceptions. Generally, the exceptions involve goods with large budget shares. For example, the income effects of a change in the price of potatoes were undoubtably important for many 19th-century Irish households, who spent much of their incomes on potatoes. Similarly, the income effects of a change in the price of housing may be large for many contemporary consumers. For such goods, compensated and uncompensated demand curves may diverge significantly, and measures of consumer well-being that are derived from standard (uncompensated) demand curves, as described in Section 6.2, may be highly inaccurate.

IN-TEXT EXERCISE 6.7 **Rico spends 3 percent of his income on CDs. His uncompensated (standard) price elasticity of demand for CDs is 1.5, and his income elasticity of demand is 2. What is Rico's compensated price elasticity of demand?**

part

IIB

Production Decisions

In Part IIA, we studied how consumers decide which products to purchase. In the next three chapters, we'll see where the supply of those products comes from. In a free market economy, most goods are produced by *firms*—privately owned companies whose owners keep the profits generated by the sale of their products. The people who run firms decide what to produce and how to produce it. Our discussion of firms' choices is broken into three parts. First, in Chapter 7, we'll discuss production technology—that is, what firms are able to produce. Then in Chapter 8, we'll see how a firm can produce its products at the lowest possible cost. Finally, in Chapter 9, we'll study how a firm that wants to maximize its profit chooses the amount of its product to sell and its price.

chapters

7

Technology and Production

Learning Objectives

After reading this chapter, students should be able to:

- Describe a firm's efficient production methods.
- Identify average product and marginal product as two key measures of a firm's productivity.
- Define input substitution in production with two variable inputs.
- Understand the concept of returns to scale and its causes.
- Discuss various productivity differences across firms and over time.

In January 1907, Henry Ford was preparing to introduce the Model T, the car that would change automobile history. At that time, the automobile was an exciting new product that many entrepreneurs were trying to develop and sell. Yet, few individuals could afford to buy one. Cars were assembled by small numbers of workers using custom-fitted parts; the high cost of production made them a product only for the wealthy.

Ford dreamed of changing that with the Model T but faced a number of crucial questions. How should he produce the Model T? Was the production method his competitors used the right choice? Could he employ machines or use labor more effectively to lower the cost of production and expand sales? Ford's novel answers to these questions revolutionized the automobile industry, making him a rich man. In 1917, 1.7 million cars were sold in the United States, up from only 43,000 in 1906. Nearly 50 percent were Fords.

In a free market economy, most goods are produced by *firms*—privately owned companies whose owners keep the profits generated by the sale of their products. In this chapter, we'll begin our discussion of firms' production decisions by examining what firms are able to produce and how they can produce it.[1]

We'll cover five topics:

1. *Production technologies*. Firms can use many different methods to make their products. A firm's owner or manager should focus on the ones that are efficient, in the sense that they get the most output possible from the firm's available inputs. We'll see how to describe a firm's efficient production methods.
2. *Production with one variable input*. In the short-run, a firm may not be able to adjust its use of many of its inputs. We'll discuss the simplest case of short-run production, in which the firm has a single input whose use it can vary. We'll discuss two key measures of a firm's productivity, average product and marginal product.
3. *Production with two variable inputs*. In most cases, firms use many inputs to produce a product and, in the long-run, have the ability to substitute the use of one input for another. We'll study input substitution in the simplest case, in which the firm can choose how much to use of two inputs.
4. *Returns to scale*. As a firm produces more output, it may become more or less effective at transforming inputs into outputs. We'll discuss this concept, known as returns to scale, and the factors leading to it. The degree of returns to scale in the technology for producing a product can have important consequences for market structure and public policy.
5. *Productivity differences and technological change.* Firms within an industry can differ in their technologies and a single firm's technology can change over time. We'll discuss what it means for one firm to be more productive than another, or for a given firm to become more or less productive over time. We'll also discuss the sources of these productivity differences and changes.

7.1 PRODUCTION TECHNOLOGIES

Outputs are the physical products or services a firm produces. **Inputs** are the materials, labor, land, or equipment that firms use to produce their outputs.

Firms try to produce products or services that they can sell profitably. Whether they produce physical products, such as a Dell computer, or services, such as McKinsey's management consulting advice, economists refer to those products or services as **outputs**. Economists refer to the materials, labor, land, and equipment firms use to produce those outputs as **inputs**. For example, Dell uses various materials (memory chips, hard drives, shipping boxes), capital equipment (conveyor belts, testing equipment, trucks), labor (computer assemblers, advertising executives, truck drivers), and land (for its factories) to produce direct-to-home-or-office personal computers.

While most firms produce multiple outputs (Dell, for example, produces a range of desktop and laptop computers, televisions, and other products), in this chapter we'll focus on the simpler case in which a firm produces a single output. The basic lessons you'll learn, however, apply as well to the multiple-output case.

The first thing a firm's owner or manager needs to know is *how* she can produce the products she wants to sell. This involves understanding the firm's **production technology**.

A firm's **production technology** summarizes all of its possible methods for producing its output.

[1]Although most of our discussion will focus on profit-maximizing firms, it also applies to other types of organizations that produce goods. For example, our study of production technologies in this chapter is relevant for *any* producer, including nonprofit organizations and government agencies.

A firm's technology summarizes all of its possible methods for producing its output. Different methods can use the same amounts of inputs but produce different amounts of output.

Economists say that a production method is **efficient** if there is no other way for the firm to produce a larger amount of output using the same amounts of inputs. Owners and managers of firms should try to produce outputs efficiently. In practice, identifying efficient production methods is often a difficult task; good managers devote a great deal of time and effort to it.

A production method is **efficient** if there is no other way for the firm to produce a larger amount of output using the same amounts of inputs.

Let's look at an example.

Example 7.1

Building Garden Benches

Noah and Naomi want to start a company in their 1,000-square-foot garage that assembles garden benches from pre-cut bench "kits" that customers provide. Naomi will take charge of the production process; Noah will keep track of the firm's revenues and costs. They will also need to hire some workers to assemble the benches.

Assembling a bench involves three basic steps. The trickiest step is assembling the back section; assembling the frame (including the seat) and attaching the back section to the frame are easier.

A single worker can assemble 33 benches a week by herself. This possibility is labeled production method A in Table 7.1, which describes the number of assembly workers (the input) used and the number of garden benches (the output) produced. (Their garage space is also an input, but we'll assume for now that it cannot be varied.)

What can two workers produce? That depends on how they divide up their tasks. There are several possibilities. They could work by themselves, producing 66 benches a week—twice what a single worker could produce. This method is labeled production method B in Table 7.1. However, there are two other attractive possibilities. First, the workers could help each other in assembling the back sections. Because having a second set of hands makes the assembly of the back section much easier, their output increases to 70 benches a week. This method is labeled production method C in the table. Second, besides helping each other produce back sections, the workers could specialize in the other tasks—one of the workers could assemble the frames, while the other could attach the back sections to the frames. Because the workers would then not need to keep changing what they were doing, they would be able to produce more—in this case, 74 benches per week. (See Application 7.1 to

Table 7.1
Inputs and Output for Various Methods of Producing Garden Benches

Production Method	Number of Assembly Workers	Garden Benches Produced per Week	Efficient?
A	1	33	Yes
B	2	66	No
C	2	70	No
D	2	74	Yes
E	4	125	No
F	4	132	Yes

learn more about the specialization of labor.) This method is labeled method D. Other methods of using two workers not listed in the table produce less output than methods B–D.

For Noah and Naomi, methods A and D are efficient. Method A is efficient because it is the only way to produce benches with one assembly worker. Method D is efficient because it yields the largest output of all possible production methods using two assembly workers.

Noah and Naomi could hire still more workers. With four workers, for example, there would be numerous ways to produce the benches. One possibility would be to form two teams, each of which operates like the two workers in production method D. Unfortunately for Noah and Naomi, however, their garage is fairly small, so that the two teams of workers would sometimes get in each other's way. As a result, this production method would produce only 125 benches per week, less than double the output from method D, the efficient method with two assembly workers. This method is labeled method E in the table. The efficient method with four workers uses three teams: Two workers who work together assembling only back sections, one worker who assembles only frames, and one worker who attaches back sections to the frames. This approach—labeled method F—produces 132 benches a week. Though it is better than two teams, the workers still sometimes get in each other's way, so they fail to produce double the output of method D.

IN-TEXT EXERCISE 7.1 **Suppose that Noah and Naomi decide instead to produce garden chairs. There are two different methods for producing garden chairs with two assembly workers: A and B. There are three methods with three assembly workers: methods C, D, and E. The weekly output of each method is: 24 from A, 36 from B, 30 from C, 44 from D, and 24 from E. Which of these production methods are efficient?**

Application 7.1

The Specialization of Labor from Adam Smith to Simba

The specialization of labor is one of the most important methods for increasing workers' productivity. The Scottish economist and philosopher Adam Smith, in his famous book *The Wealth of Nations* (1776), first discussed its effects, describing the operations of a pin factory:

> To take an example, therefore, from a very trifling manufacture; but one in which the division of labour has been very often taken notice of, the trade of the pin-maker; . . . it is divided into a number of branches. . . . One man draws out the wire, another straights it, a third cuts it, a fourth points it, a fifth grinds it at the top for receiving, the head; to make the head requires two or three distinct operations; to put it on is a peculiar business, to whiten the pins is another; it is even a trade by itself to put them into the paper; and the important business of making a pin is, in this manner, divided into about eighteen distinct operations. . . . I have seen a small manufactory of this kind where ten men only were employed, and where some of them consequently performed two or three distinct operations. . . . [T]hose ten

Adam Smith (1723–1790)

persons . . . could make among them upwards of forty-eight thousand pins in a day. Each person, therefore, making a tenth part of forty-eight thousand pins, might be considered as making four thousand eight hundred pins in a day. But if they had all wrought separately . . . they certainly could not each of them had made twenty. . . .

One hundred thirty years later, Henry Ford put exactly the same principle to work in organizing the production of the Model T. His efforts at achieving an efficient production method culminated in 1913 with the introduction of the moving assembly line on which each worker performed a single specialized operation. As Ford put it: "The man who places a part does not fasten it. The man who puts in a bolt does not put on the nut; the man who puts on the nut does not tighten it." This arrangement greatly increased workers' productivity, because they could become more proficient at their specialized tasks and did not waste time switching between tasks. As a result, the time required to assemble an automobile chassis fell from over 12 hours to 93 minutes, and the price of the Model T fell from $850 when it was introduced to $440 in 1915. These advances made cars affordable to a broad range of Americans, greatly expanding Ford's sales.

Moving assembly line at Ford Motor Company's Michigan plant

The specialization of labor is no less important today. A look at the credits for Disney's classic animated film *The Lion King* reveals that the artists who worked on the film had highly specialized jobs. Many worked only on a single character, such as Simba; others worked only on scene backgrounds. Specializing in this way not only ensures continuity in the artistic representations; it also saves the artists from having to switch between numerous tasks, making them more efficient. For the same reason, new houses are built by teams of specialized workmen—carpenters, plumbers, and electricians—and large law firms contain lawyers who work in well-defined specialties, such as corporate law, tax law, and litigation.

The Production Possibilities Set and the Efficient Production Frontier

A firm's **production possibilities set** contains all the input and output combinations that are possible given the firm's technology. In Example 7.1, Noah and Naomi's production possibilities set includes the input-output combinations for methods A–F, plus those for any other possible production methods. Figure 7.1 shows Noah and Naomi's weekly bench output and the number of assembly workers for methods A–F. The horizontal axis measures the number of assembly workers they employ, while the vertical axis measures the number of garden benches produced per week. Each labeled point represents the inputs used and the output produced for one production method. Figure 7.1 also shows the output levels for the two best production methods involving three assembly workers, which are labeled methods G and H. Method G produces 111 garden benches per week, while method H produces 99 benches per week. The eight points shown in the figure are part of Noah and Naomi's production possibilities set.

A firm's **production possibilities set** contains all combinations of inputs and outputs that are possible given the firm's technology.

In Figure 7.1, the efficient production method for each number of assembly workers corresponds to the highest point on the vertical line at a given input level. For example, method D is the highest point on the dashed vertical line at two assembly workers in the figure. A firm's **efficient production frontier** contains the input-output combinations from all

A firm's **efficient production frontier** contains the combinations of inputs and outputs that the firm can achieve using efficient production methods.

of its efficient production methods. Noah and Naomi's efficient production frontier in Figure 7.1 consists of the points in blue circles, representing the efficient methods A, D, G, and F.

If Noah and Naomi can hire workers for any part of a week, their labor input becomes finely divisible. For example, Noah and Naomi might hire three workers for 40 hours a week and one worker for 16 hours a week, in which case they have hired 3.4 workers. Figure 7.2 shows Noah and Naomi's production possibility set when they can hire workers for any part of a week and their output is also finely divisible.[2] Their many possible

Figure 7.1

The Production Possibilities Set and Efficient Production Frontier for Producing Garden Benches. The labeled points are the input-output combinations for production methods A–H. These points are part of Noah and Naomi's production possibilities set. The points circled in blue are the input-output combinations for the efficient production methods A, D, F, and G. They are each part of Noah and Naomi's efficient production frontier.

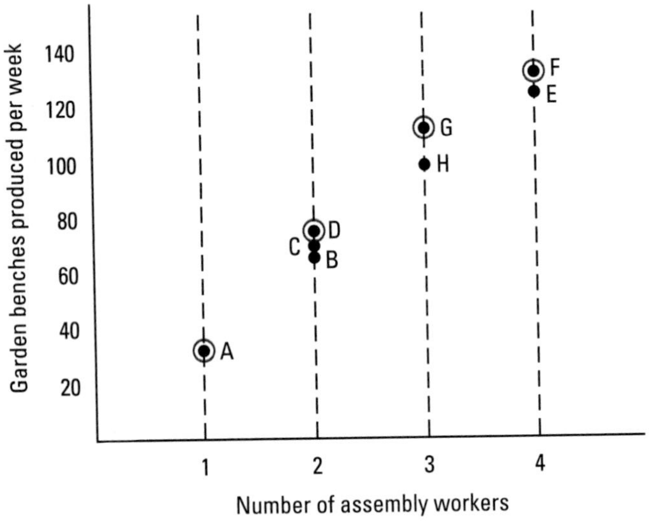

Figure 7.2

The Production Possibility Set and Efficient Production Frontier for Garden Benches When Workers Can be Hired for Part of a Week. When workers can be hired for part of a week, so that their inputs are finely divisible, Noah and Naomi's production possibility set will look like the shaded region in the figure. Their efficient production frontier is the upper (northwest) boundary of these points, represented by the blue curve in the figure. The input-output combinations for methods A, D, G, and F are shown as blue dots lying along this curve.

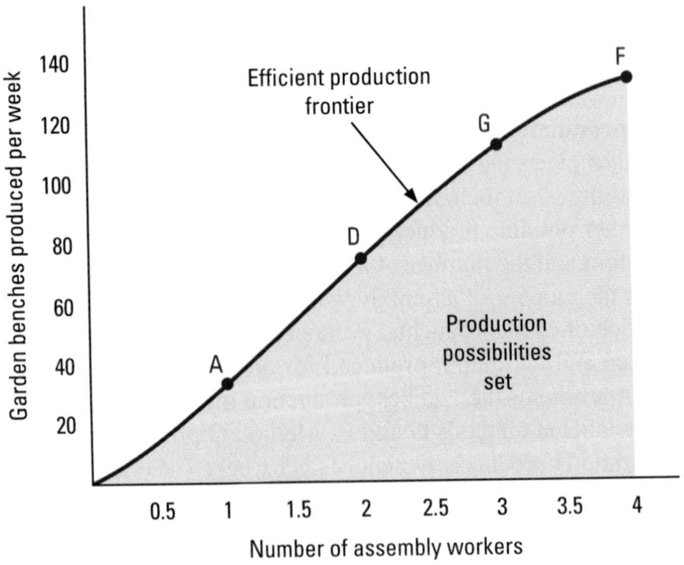

[2]The number of garden benches is finely divisible if, for example, part of a bench can be carried over for completion the next week.

input-output combinations appear as the shaded production possibility set in the figure. Their efficient production frontier is the upper (northwest) boundary of this production possibilities set, which is drawn in blue. Methods A, D, G, and F are just four of the many points on this blue curve.

Production Functions

A **production function** is a function of the form *Output* = *F*(*Inputs*), giving the amount of output a firm can produce from given amounts of inputs using efficient production methods.

We can describe the efficient production frontier mathematically by means of a **production function**. This is a function of the form *Output* = *F*(*Inputs*) that describes the amount of output that a firm can produce from given amounts of inputs using efficient production methods.

For example, the production function of a firm whose only input is labor might be $Q = F(L) = 10L$, where Q is the amount of output the firm produces and L is the amount of labor the firm hires. By substituting different amounts of labor for L, we see that the firm can produce 10 units of output if it hires one worker ($L = 1$); 20 units of output if it hires two workers ($L = 2$); and 30 units of output if it hires three workers ($L = 3$).

In Figure 7.2, Noah and Noami's efficient production frontier is described (for up to four workers) by the production function

$$Q = F(L) = -2L^3 + 10L^2 + 25L$$

For example, substituting different values for L we see that output is 33 benches with one worker; 74 benches with two; 111 benches with three, and 132 benches with four. If we graph these combinations of inputs and outputs we get points A, D, G, and F in Figure 7.2. (Noah and Naomi may have discovered that this production function describes the relationship between their labor input and their garden bench output for efficient production methods by using statistical regression techniques, like those we mentioned in the Appendix of Chapter 2.[3])

IN-TEXT EXERCISE 7.2 **Suppose that Noah and Naomi's production function is $Q = F(L) = 25L$. How many garden benches can they produce with one worker? With two workers? With three workers? With four workers? Graph their production function for up to four workers. Suppose now that the number of workers they hire is finely divisible (that is, they can hire workers for a fraction of a week). Graph their production function in this case. What if instead their production function is $Q = F(L) = \sqrt{L}$?**

Notice that Noah and Naomi's production function, drawn in Figure 7.2, slopes upward. The amount of output never falls when the amount of labor increases. The same is true of the production functions you examined in in-text exercise 7.2. Why is this so? Remember that a production function gives the output produced for *efficient* production methods. Suppose that with eight workers, a firm can produce 15 units of output. With nine workers, the firm certainly can produce *at least* that much: one worker could just be told to read magazines at home (and thereby not get in any others' way)! And there may be some way to organize the nine workers that produces even more output. Thus, the most efficient production method with nine workers has to produce at least as much output as

[3] In Chapter 2 we discussed how to learn about the relationship between the amount of a good that consumers demand (the dependent variable) and its price and other factors (the explanatory variables). Here, instead, the dependent variable would be the amount of output Noah and Naomi produce, while the explanatory variable would be the amount of labor they use.

the most efficient method with eight workers. (Of course, if the best way to use nine workers is to have one sit at home, the firm will never actually want to hire a ninth worker.) More generally, as long as a firm can freely dispose of any extra inputs it may have, such as by sending a worker home, it's production function must slope upward.

When a firm uses more than one input, the basic concept of a production function is the same as for the case with a single input, but the amount of output produced depends on the firm's use of all of these inputs. In the rest of the chapter, for example, we'll often consider a firm that uses two inputs, labor (L) and capital equipment (K). Its production function takes the form $Q = F(L, K)$. For instance, the firm's production function might be $Q = F(L, K) = 10\sqrt{L}\sqrt{K}$. In this case, if the firm hires 10 workers and employs 10 units of capital, it can produce 100 units of output (since $10\sqrt{10}\sqrt{10} = 100$).

Production in the Short Run and the Long Run

A **variable input** can be adjusted over the time period being considered, while a **fixed input** cannot.

The **short run** is a period of time over which one or more inputs is fixed. The **long run** is a period of time over which all inputs are variable.

Most firms use many inputs to produce their output. Some of these may be freely varied at any time. Others may take quite a while to be changed. When considering production over any given time period, an input is **fixed** if it cannot be adjusted and is **variable** if it can be. For example, in Example 7.1, Noah and Naomi's garage space was a fixed input, while their number of assembly workers was a variable input.

Economists often distinguish between production in the short run and the long run. The **short run** is a period of time over which one or more inputs is fixed. The **long run** is a period of time over which all inputs are variable. For example, in the long run, Noah and Naomi will be able to change their garage space. They could build an addition onto their garage or rent a new larger garage down the street. Using efficient production methods, they might then have the production possibilities shown in Table 7.2. The table shows the number of benches they produce each week for each number of assembly workers and amount of garage space, using efficient production methods. Each row in the table corresponds to the number of assembly workers they hire, while each column corresponds to the amount of garage space they use. For example, Noah and Naomi can produce 140 garden benches a week by hiring three assembly workers and using 1,500 square feet of garage space. Noah and Naomi's short-run production possibilities in Example 7.1 correspond to the second column in this table, where their garage space is fixed at 1,000 square feet.

What constitutes the long run depends on the production process being considered. For example, it may take an automobile manufacturer several years to build a new production facility, while Noah and Naomi may need only a month or two to rent and move into

Table 7.2
Weekly Output of Garden Benches for Various Combinations of Labor and Garage Space (Using Efficient Production Methods)

Number of Assembly Workers	Amount of Garage Space (Square Feet)				
	500	1,000	1,500	2,000	2,500
1	20	33	45	55	60
2	42	74	105	130	140
3	70	111	140	167	189
4	88	132	170	205	220

a new garage. And for a few production processes, there may literally be no short run: for example, a management consultant's only input may be the amount of time she spends talking to her clients and thinking, which she may be able to vary at will.

In reality, of course, the flexibility of input choices is a matter of degree. A given input may become flexible in a gradual way over time. Also, different inputs may become flexible at different rates over time. Nonetheless, as we'll see in Chapter 8, the short-run versus long-run distinction is useful and has important implications about the ways in which firms adjust to changes in their markets.

As Table 7.2 suggests, a firm's short-run and long-run production functions are closely related. In Sections 7.2 and 7.3, for example, we'll focus for simplicity on the case of a firm that uses only two inputs, labor and capital, one of which—capital—is fixed in the short run. The firm's long-run production function is $F(L, K)$. Its production function in the short run, when its capital is fixed at $\bar{K}$, is $F(L, \bar{K})$. Often, for simplicity, we'll write the firm's short-run production function given a level of capital simply as $F(L)$, as we did earlier in this section.

IN-TEXT EXERCISE 7.3 **Suppose that a firm uses both labor (L) and capital (K) as inputs and has the long-run production function $Q = F(L, K) = 10\sqrt{L}\sqrt{K}$. If its capital is fixed at $K = 10$ in the short run, what is its short-run production function? How much does it produce in the short run (using efficient production methods) if it hires one worker? Two workers? Three?**

7.2 PRODUCTION WITH ONE VARIABLE INPUT

In this section, we look in more detail at production technology for the case in which a firm uses a single variable input. As we discussed in Section 7.1, we can think of this situation as describing the production possibilities of a firm whose other inputs are fixed in the short run.[4] For example, in Example 7.1, Noah and Naomi used garage space and assembly workers to produce garden benches. While they could add assembly workers, they couldn't enlarge their garage—at least, not in the time frame we considered. For convenience, throughout this section we'll refer to the firm's single variable input as *labor*, which we will assume is perfectly homogeneous (different workers are equally productive).

Average and Marginal Products

For a firm that uses labor as an input, two useful measures of its workers' productivity are the average and marginal products of labor. The **average product of labor**, denoted AP_L, is the amount of output that is produced per worker. We calculate it using the formula

The **average product of labor**, denoted AP_L, equals the amount of output divided by the number of workers employed.

$$AP_L = \frac{Q}{L} = \frac{F(L)}{L}$$

Noah and Naomi's AP_L for up to four workers, when their garage space is fixed at 1,000 square feet, is shown in the last column of Table 7.3, which describes the production

[4]It also describes the long-run production possibilities of those firms which only have one input (such as the management consultant mentioned in Section 7.1).

technology for garden benches. For each number of workers, AP_L equals the second column (output) divided by the first column (labor input). In general, the average product of labor will depend on the number of workers. For Noah and Naomi's production process, AP_L first rises (from 33 with one worker to 37 with two workers) and then falls (beyond three workers). It rises when we add a second worker because the workers can help each other in assembling back sections and can specialize in the other tasks. It falls when the number of workers increases beyond three because of crowding in the garage.

The *marginal* product of labor, denoted MP_L, measures how much extra output is produced when the firm changes the amount of labor it uses by a little bit. This measure of productivity will be very useful when we ask whether a firm should change the amount of labor it uses. (In worked-out problem 7.1, for example, we'll consider how a firm should assign workers between two production plants.)

When we say a *little bit*, we mean the smallest amount of labor a firm can add or subtract. We'll call this ΔL. If only full-time workers are available, then $\Delta L = 1$. If half-time workers are available, then $\Delta L = 1/2$. If the firm can hire temporary workers by the day, and we measure labor in worker weeks, then $\Delta L = 0.2$ (since there are five days in a week).

The **marginal units of labor** are the last ΔL units hired, where ΔL is the smallest amount of labor an employer can add or subtract.

The **marginal product of labor** with L workers, denoted MP_L, equals the extra output produced by the ΔL marginal units of labor, per unit of labor added.

When L workers are employed, we call the last ΔL units of labor hired the **marginal units of labor**. The marginal product of labor measures how much extra output we get by hiring these marginal units of labor, per unit of labor added. (The idea is the same as the marginal benefit concept that we discussed in Chapter 3.) Starting with L units of labor, the change in output due to the marginal units is $\Delta Q = F(L) - F(L - \Delta L)$. Dividing by the amount of labor added, ΔL, gives us the **marginal product of labor**:

$$MP_L = \frac{\Delta Q}{\Delta L} = \frac{F(L) - F(L - \Delta L)}{\Delta L}$$

By dividing the change in output by ΔL, we make the marginal product of labor measure the output change on a per-unit basis. We do this because it turns our measure of output change into something we can interpret. For example, if you are told that the marginal units of labor increased Noah and Naomi's output by three benches, you wouldn't know anything about the marginal workers' productivity. But if you are told that the marginal units of labor added 1.5 benches per worker, that tells you those marginal workers' productivity.

For Noah and Naomi's production function, the marginal product of labor is shown in the third column of Table 7.3. Since Noah and Naomi must hire workers by the week,

Table 7.3

Output, Marginal Product of Labor, and Average Product of Labor for Producing Garden Benches, Given Various Amounts of Labor Input

Number of Assembly Workers	Garden Benches Produced per Week	MP_L	AP_L
0	0	—	—
1	33	33	33
2	74	41	37
3	111	37	37
4	132	21	33

$\Delta L = 1$ and the marginal product of labor is simply equal to $MP_L = F(L) - F(L - \Delta L)$. For example, their MP_L with two workers is equal to the extra output that results from their second worker, which is $F(2) - F(1) = 74 - 33 = 41$. In the table, dashed arrows show graphically the output levels whose difference is equal to MP_L.

Noah and Naomi's MP_L first increases (from $L = 1$ to $L = 2$) and then declines as the number of workers rises above two. The marginal product of labor eventually decreases because workers begin to crowd each other in the garage. We expect a similar effect to occur in most short-run production processes. The expectation that an input's marginal product will eventually decline as its use increases, holding all other inputs (such as garage space) fixed, is known as the **Law of Diminishing Marginal Returns.**

The **Law of Diminishing Marginal Returns** states the general tendency for the marginal product of an input to eventually decline as its use is increased holding all other inputs fixed.

The Relationship between Average and Marginal Product

The average and marginal products of an input are closely related. By comparing the marginal product to the average product, we can tell whether the average product rises or falls as more input is added. The marginal product tells us how much output the marginal worker adds. If he is more productive than average, he brings the average up. If he is less productive than average, he drives the average down.

Table 7.3 illustrates this point. With two workers, the marginal product of labor (41) is *greater than* the average product (37), and the average product *rises* when the marginal (second) worker is added (from 33 to 37). In contrast, with four workers, the marginal product (21) is *less than* the average product (33), and the average product *falls* (from 37 to 33) when the marginal worker is added. With three workers, the marginal and average products are the same (37), and the average product does not change when the marginal (third) worker is added.

You've seen the same principle at work in other contexts. Think about your grade point average (GPA). If your GPA last semester (your marginal product) is higher than your overall grade point average, then last semester's grades pulled your GPA up. If instead they are lower, then they pulled your GPA down. If they are the same, then they left your GPA unchanged.

We can summarize this relationship as follows:

The Relationship between a Firm's Average and Marginal Product When the marginal product of an input is (larger/smaller/the same as) the average product, the marginal units of the input (raise/lower/do not affect) the average product.

Average and Marginal Product Curves with Finely Divisible Inputs

When labor is finely divisible, we can graph the average and marginal products as curves to show how they vary with the amount of labor hired. Let's start with the average product of labor. The curve shown in Figure 7.3(a) represents a typical short-run production function. Pick any point on the curve and draw a straight line connecting it to the origin. The slope of this line equals the output at this point (*rise*) divided by the amount of labor used to produce this output (*run*). By definition, that's the average product. The figure illustrates the calculation of the average product at three different levels of labor: 10, 20, and

Figure 7.3

A Production Function (a) and Its Average Product Curve (b). Figure (a) shows a typical short-run production function. If we pick any point on the curve and draw a straight line connecting it to the origin, the slope of the line equals the average product of labor. The graph shows the average product at three different input levels ($L = 10$, $L = 20$, $L = 30$). Figure (b) shows how the average product of labor varies with the amount of labor.

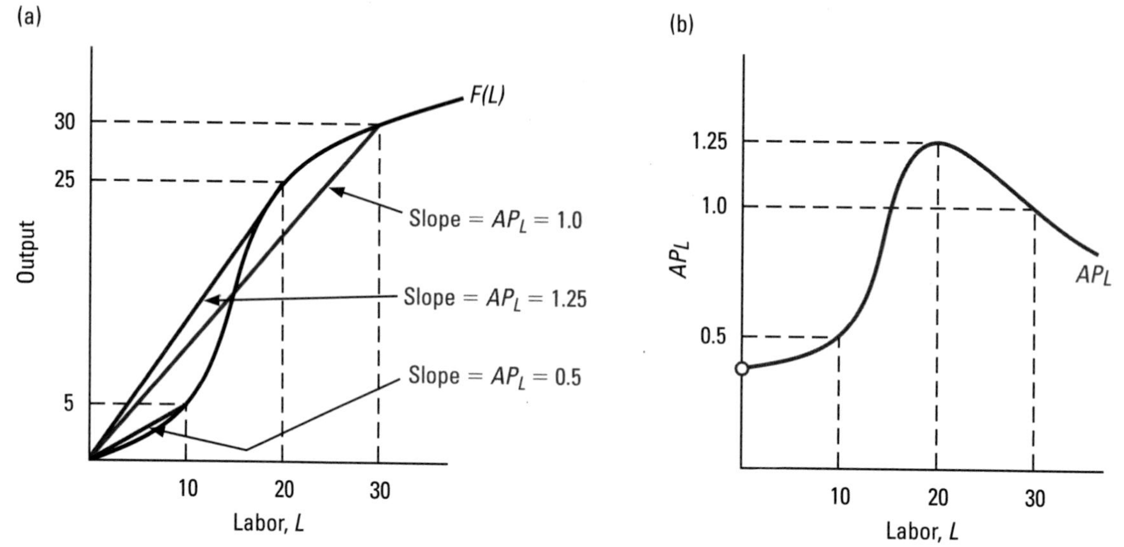

30 workers. For example, with 20 workers, the average product is 25/20 = 1.25. Figure 7.3(b) shows how the average product varies with the amount of labor. As in Table 7.3, the average product of labor for this production function first rises and then falls as labor increases. Note that an average product cannot be calculated when $L = 0$ (since there are then no workers); this is indicated in the figure by the little blue circle at $L = 0$.

Now let's think about the marginal product of labor. When labor inputs are finely divisible, the smallest amount of labor a firm can add or subtract is very tiny. In this case, with L units of labor, the marginal product of labor equals the slope of the dark red line tangent to the production function at point A in Figure 7.4. Why? The logic parallels our discussion of marginal benefit with finely divisible actions in Section 3.2, but we'll repeat it here for completeness.

Whatever the size of the smallest possible change in labor, the marginal product of labor equals rise over run along the production function. Suppose the smallest possible change is $\Delta L'$. Adding the last $\Delta L'$ units of labor involves a movement along the production function from point B to point A in Figure 7.4. This change increases output by the amount $\Delta Q' = F(L) - F(L - \Delta L')$, shown along the vertical axis in the figure. The marginal product of labor, $MP_L = \Delta Q'/\Delta L'$, therefore equals rise over run along the production function between points B and A; it is the slope of the straight light red line connecting these two points. Similarly, if the size of the marginal change is instead the smaller amount $\Delta L''$ (see the figure), the marginal product of labor would then be $\Delta Q''/\Delta L'' = [F(L) - F(L - \Delta L'')]/\Delta L''$, which equals rise over run along the total benefit

Figure 7.4

The Marginal Product of Labor When Labor Is Finely Divisible. When labor input is finely divisible, the marginal product of labor with L units of labor equals the slope of the dark red line tangent to the production function at point A, also known simply as the "slope of the production function" at point A. The light and medium red lines connecting points A and B and points A and C, respectively, show why this is so. Their slopes equal the marginal product of labor for two different numbers of marginal units of labor, $\Delta L'$ and $\Delta L''$, that are not tiny. As labor becomes finely divisible, so that the number of marginal units grows small, their slopes get closer and closer to the slope of the dark red line.

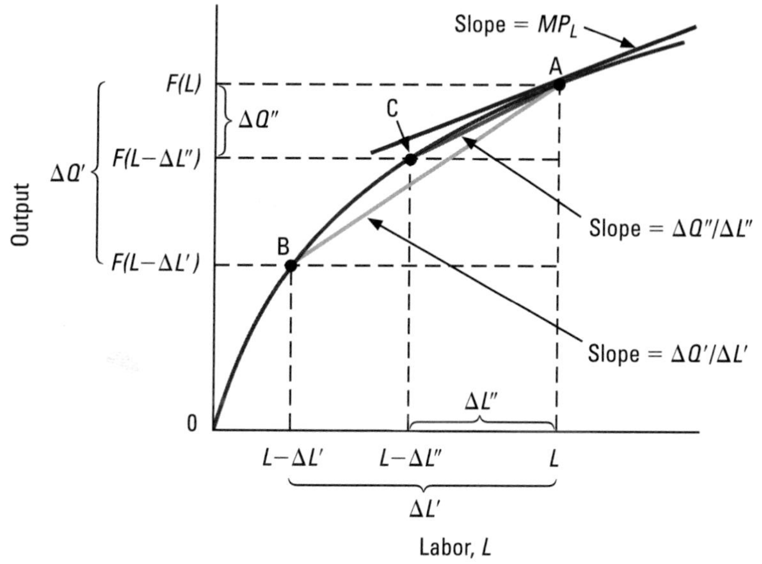

curve between points C and A. In other words, the marginal product of labor is then the slope of the straight medium red line connecting points C and A.

In Figure 7.4, the slope of the straight dark red line through point A equals rise over run—equivalently, the marginal product of labor—for very tiny changes in labor input, starting from point A. (Notice that the straight light and medium red lines would become closer and closer to the straight dark red line if we considered smaller and smaller changes in hours.) That dark red line is said to be tangent to the production function at point A.[5] Accordingly, when labor is finely divisible, the marginal product of labor at any given amount of labor equals the slope of the straight line that is tangent to the production function at that level of labor input. A common short-hand expression, which we'll often use, says that the slope of the line tangent to a curve at a point is "the slope of the curve" at that point. Using this language, we can restate our conclusion in this simple way: the marginal product of labor with L units of labor input in Figure 7.4 equals the slope of the production function at point A.[6]

---

[5]In mathematics, a line is said to be tangent to a curve at a point if its slope equals the rise over the run for very small changes along the curve starting at the point.

[6]If you have had calculus, you should recognize that the marginal product of labor, MP_L, equals $F'(L)$, the derivative of the production function at L.

Figure 7.5

A Production Function (a) and Its Marginal Product Curve (b). Figure (a) shows the same production function as in Figure 7.3(a). Here we have drawn straight lines tangent to the production function at three levels of labor input ($L = 10$, $L = 20$, $L =$ 30). Their slopes equal the marginal product of labor at those levels of labor. Figure (b) shows how the marginal product of labor varies with the amount of labor.

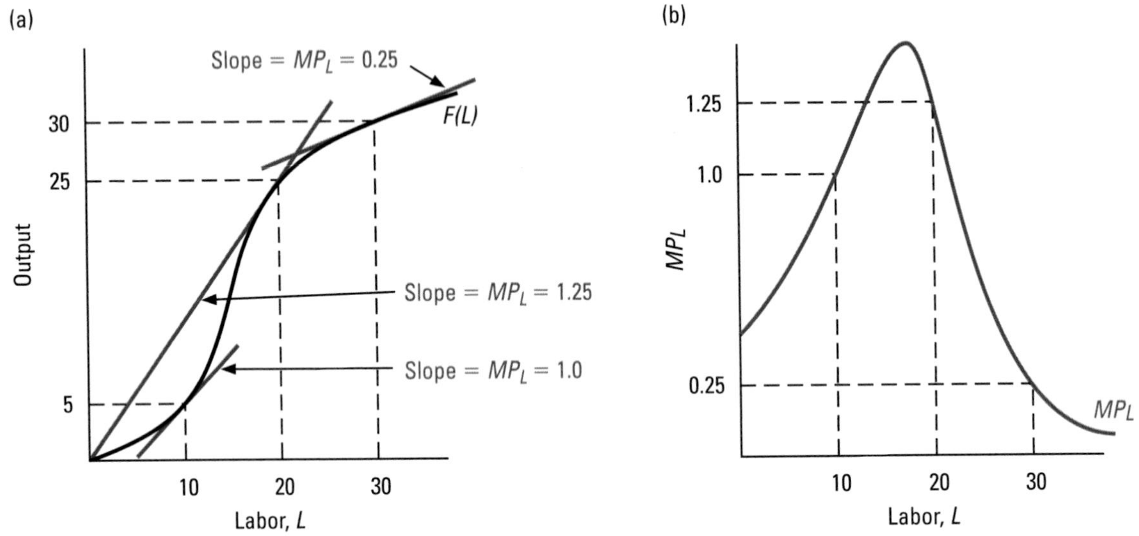

We can now graph the marginal product of labor curve for the production function in Figure 7.3(a), which is reproduced in Figure 7.5(a). There, we've drawn straight lines tangent to the production function at three different levels of labor. The slope of each line tells us the corresponding marginal product of labor. We've plotted the value of the marginal product for these levels of labor and others in Figure 7.5(b). Just as for Noah and Naomi's production function, the marginal product of labor curve in Figure 7.5(b) satisfies the Law of Diminishing Marginal Returns. Notice that in Figure 7.5(a), the tangent line at $L = 20$ goes through the origin, which means that the marginal and average products are equal at that point.

Figure 7.6 shows the average and marginal product of labor curves together. Notice that the average product curve slopes upward when it's below the marginal product curve and downward when it's above the marginal product curve. It is flat where it crosses the marginal product curve. This reflects the same principle we saw at work before, applied now to the case in which inputs are finely divisible.[7,8]

---

[7]Observe also that the AP_L and MP_L curves approach each other as the number of workers gets close to zero. The reason can be seen by looking again at Figures 7.3(a) and 7.5(a), where straight lines whose slopes are equal to AP_L and MP_L would have almost the same slope near $L = 0$. Intuitively, when there are very few workers, the productivity of all workers is very close to the productivity of the marginal workers.

[8]If you have had calculus, you can see this point by noting that the derivative of the average product function $\frac{F(L)}{L}$ equals $\left(\frac{1}{L}\right)\left[F'(L) - \frac{F(L)}{L}\right]$. Thus, the average product is increasing at L if and only if the marginal product at L, $F'(L)$, is greater than the average product at L, $\frac{F(L)}{L}$.

The Relationship between a Firm's Average and Marginal Product Curves
When labor inputs are finely divisible, the average product of labor curve is (upward sloping/downward sloping/neither rising nor falling) at *L* if the marginal product is (above/below/equal to) the average product.

IN-TEXT EXERCISE 7.4 **Consider again the production function $Q = F(L) = 25L$. Suppose that labor is finely divisible. Draw graphs like those in Figures 7.3, 7.5, and 7.6: one pair of graphs to derive the average product curve, one pair of graphs to derive the marginal product curve, and one graph showing both curves. How does the last graph reflect the relationship between a firm's average and marginal product?**

Using the Marginal Product of Labor to Make Production Decisions

The average and marginal products of labor are useful in practical applications. Here we'll discuss an example; others appear later in this book.

Consider a firm that has 100 workers and two production plants, whose production functions are shown in Figures 7.7(a) and (b). In each plant, the marginal product of labor declines as the amount of labor increases. How should the firm allocate its workers between the plants to maximize the amount it produces? When labor is finely divisible, we can use marginal product of labor curves to answer this question.

Figure 7.7(c) shows the plants' marginal products as a function of the amount of labor used in plant 1, which is measured along the lower horizontal axis. The marginal product of labor curve for plant 1, labeled MP_L^1, is drawn in red; it falls as the amount of labor used in plant 1 increases.

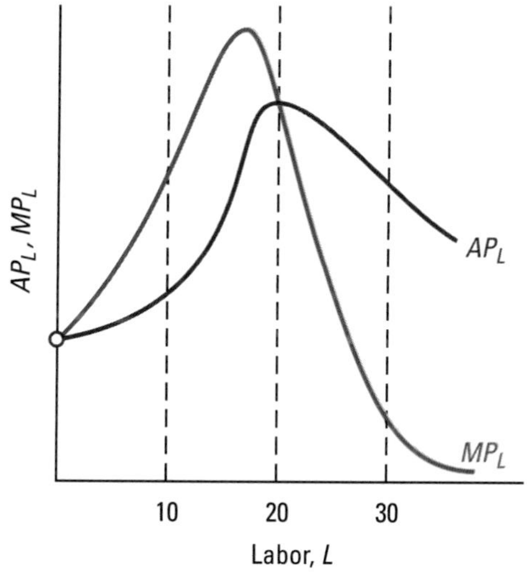

Figure 7.6
The Average and Marginal Product Curves. The figure shows together the average and marginal product curves from Figures 7.3(b) and 7.5(b). The average product slopes upward when it is below the marginal product curve and downward when it is above the marginal product curve. It is neither rising nor falling where the two curves cross.

Figure 7.7

The Optimal Assignment of Workers between Two Plants with Decreasing Marginal Products of Labor. Figures (a) and (b) show the production functions for the two plants. Figure (c) shows the marginal products of labor for the two plants as functions of the amount of labor assigned to plant 1, L_1 (measured from left to right along the lower horizontal axis) and the amount of labor used in plant 2, L_2(measured from right to left along the upper horizontal axis). At L_1' the marginal product is greater at plant 1 than at plant 2, and so we can increase output by shifting some labor from plant 2 to plant 1. At L_1'' the marginal product is greater at plant 2 than at plant 1, and so we can increase output by shifting some labor from plant 1 to plant 2. The best assignment of workers is the point at which the two marginal product curves cross, resulting in L_1^* workers being assigned to plant 1, and $100 - L_1^*$ workers being assigned to plant 2.

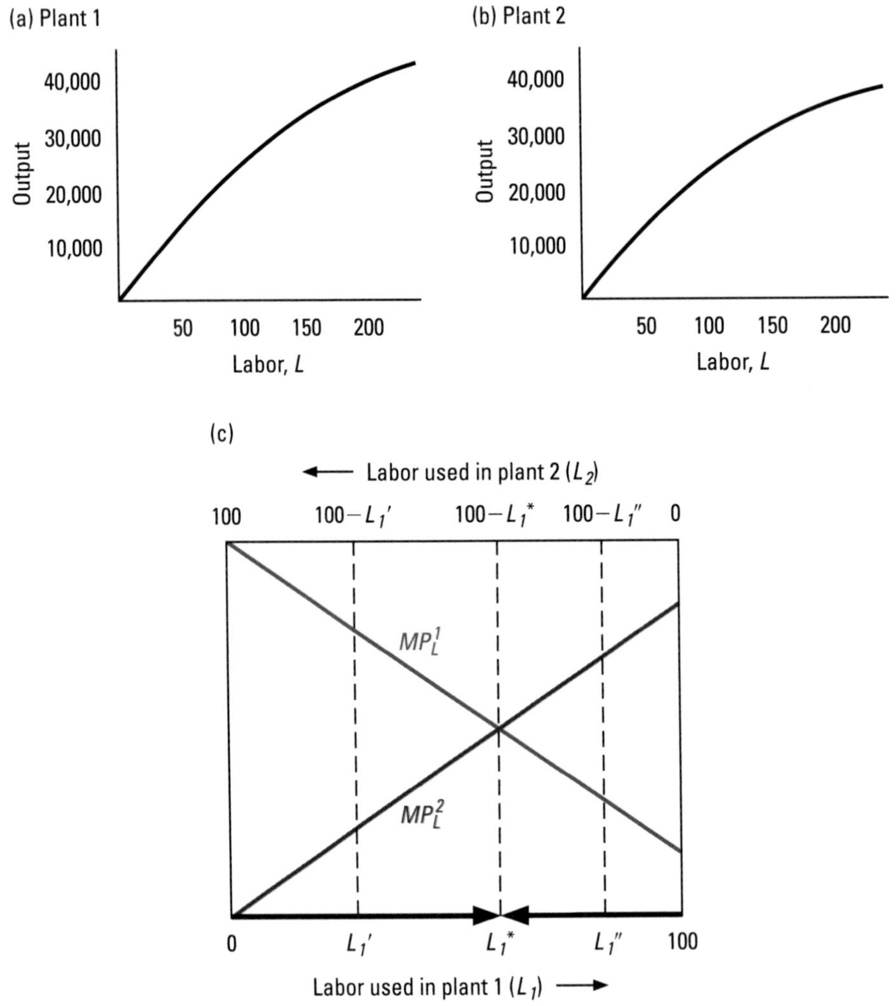

Drawing the marginal product of labor curve for plant 2, labeled MP_L^2, as a function of how much labor is used in plant 1 is a little trickier. If L_1 units of labor are used in plant 1, then $100 - L_1$ units of labor are used in plant 2. In Figure 7.7(c) we can therefore track the amount of labor used in plant 2 by measuring it *backward* (from right to left) along the upper horizontal axis. For example, all the way to the left of the graph, where the lower horizontal axis records that zero units of labor are assigned to plant 1, the upper horizontal axis records that 100 units are assigned to plant 2. The opposite is true all the way to the right of the graph. Once we have measured the number of workers assigned to plant 2 in this way, we can draw the marginal product curve for plant 2 in blue. Note that because the marginal product in plant 2 falls when the amount of labor used there increases, the curve rises as we move from left to right in the graph. That is, MP_L^2 increases with the amount of labor used in plant 1.

Now let's figure out how many workers to assign to plant 1. This number, L_1^*, is the point at which the two marginal product curves cross. Why? If we were to assign fewer than L_1^* workers to plant 1—such as the amount L_1' in the figure—then the marginal product of labor would be greater in plant 1 than in plant 2 and it would be better to move some units of labor from plant 2 to plant 1. The gain in output is MP_L^1 at plant 1, and the loss is MP_L^2 at plant 2, so there is a net gain of $MP_L^1 - MP_L^2 > 0$ (this is shown by in the rightward-pointing arrow on the horizontal axis). Likewise, if we were to assign more than L_1^* workers to plant 1—such as the amount L_1'' in the figure—then the marginal product of labor would be greater in plant 2 than in plant 1, and it would be better to move some units of labor from plant 1 to plant 2 (this is shown by the leftward-pointing arrow on the horizontal axis).

This conclusion reflects a general principle: if labor is finely divisible and workers are best assigned to both plants, the marginal product of labor at each plant must be *equal.* Otherwise, we could do better by changing the assignment of labor a little bit, shifting labor to the plant with the higher marginal product.

The problem of allocating labor between two plants is an example of maximizing benefits less costs, which we studied in Chapter 3. When we assign more workers to plant 1, the benefit is that plant 1 produces more output, so the marginal benefit is $MB = MP_L^1$. The cost of assigning more workers to plant 1 is an opportunity cost: plant 2 produces less. So the marginal cost is $MC = MP_L^2$. Thus, assigning inputs to equalize marginal products across the two plants is just an example of equating marginal benefit and marginal cost.[9]

Worked-out problem 7.1 shows how to determine the best assignment of workers across plants using algebra.

---

[9]In some cases, there is no assignment of workers at which the marginal products of the two plants are equal. If so, it's best to assign all the workers to just one plant, the one with the higher marginal product, and close the other plant. In other cases, the marginal product of labor may not be decreasing in the amount of labor used in a plant, and there could be more than one assignment of workers at which the marginal products of the plants are equal. To see how to find the best assignment in such cases you can apply the approach discussed in the appendix of Chapter 3.

WORKED-OUT PROBLEM 7.1

The Problem John, April, and Tristan own JATjuice, a firm that produces freshly squeezed orange juice. Oranges are their only variable input. They have two production facilities. Suppose the marginal product of oranges in plant 1 is $MP_O^1 = 1{,}000 - O_1$, where O_1 is the number of crates of oranges allocated to plant 1. The marginal product of oranges in plant 2 is $MP_O^2 = 1{,}200 - O_2$, where O_2 is the number of crates of oranges assigned to plant 2. Suppose that John, April, and Tristan have a total of 600 crates of oranges. What is the best assignment of oranges to the two plants?

The Solution Start by writing the marginal product in plant 2 as a function of the number of crates of oranges assigned to plant 1, O_1:

$$MP_O^2 = 1{,}200 - (600 - O_1) = 600 + O_1$$

Now find the level of O_1 that equates the marginal product of oranges in the two plants. We can do so with algebra by setting $MP_O^1 = MP_O^2$ and solving:

$$1{,}000 - O_1 = 600 + O_1 \Rightarrow O_1^* = 200$$

John, April, and Tristan should assign 200 crates to plant 1 and the rest (400) to plant 2.

IN-TEXT EXERCISE 7.5 **Suppose that John, April, and Tristan have a total of 700 crates of oranges and that the marginal product of oranges in plant 1 is $MP_O^1 = 1{,}000 - O_1$ and in plant 2 is $MP_O^2 = 1{,}200 - 2O_2$. What is the best assignment of oranges between the two plants?**

7.3 PRODUCTION WITH TWO VARIABLE INPUTS

Few production processes use only a single variable input. Indeed, most require many. Economists often divide inputs into four categories: labor, capital, materials, and land. Capital inputs are long-lived assets, such as the physical plant, operating machinery, and vehicles that are used in the production process. Materials are inputs that are fully used up in the production process. Labor includes all human services. And land is, well . . . land.

As we've discussed in Section 7.1, in the long run, all of a firm's inputs are variable. In this section, we'll study the problem faced by a firm that uses two (variable) inputs in the long run. For simplicity, in most of our discussion we will call these two inputs labor (L) and capital (K). We'll assume that each of these inputs is homogeneous—that is, all capital is equally productive as is all labor. (If this were not true, we would need to treat each type of labor or capital as a distinct input, so we would have more than two variable inputs.) In this case, the firm's production function is written $Q = F(L, K)$.

When a firm has more than one variable input, it can usually produce a given amount of output with many different combinations of inputs. Ford's assembly line, for example, not only specialized workers' tasks; it also substituted capital for labor. The assembly line provided a mechanized way to move the car between workers' stations, which meant that fewer workers were needed to produce any given amount of output. The following example illustrates input substitution in more detail.

Example 7.2

Building Garden Benches, Part 2

Table 7.4 shows how much Noah and Naomi can produce in the long run when they use different combinations of assembly workers and garage space. For up to four workers, the information in the table is exactly the same as in Table 7.2 on page 216, but to make things look more like the graphs we'll soon draw, we've presented it in a slightly different way: Now the rows correspond to the amount of garage space, while the columns—labeled on the bottom of the table—correspond to the numbers of workers. (The idea is the same as when we did this when studying consumption in Chapters 4 and 5.) We've also added information on their output if they have five or six workers. Each entry tells us the most output that can be produced from a particular combination of labor and garage space.

As more of either input is added, Noah and Naomi's production increases if they hold the other input fixed. This means that, if they want to keep their output unchanged, they can lower the amount they use of the other input. For example, the table shows that there are three different input combinations that each produce 140 garden benches a week (these are circled). The larger is the amount of garage space in one of these input combinations; the smaller is the required number of assembly workers.

Table 7.4

Three Input Combinations that Produce 140 Garden Benches per Week (Using Efficient Production Methods)

Amount of garage space (square feet)						
2,500	60	(140)	189	220	241	255
2,000	55	130	167	205	220	230
1,500	45	105	(140)	170	182	188
1,000	33	74	111	132	(140)	145
500	20	42	70	88	95	100
Number of assembly workers	1	2	3	4	5	6

As in the case of a single variable input, a production function with more than one variable input cannot produce less output when the amount of any input is increased, as long as the firm can freely dispose of any extra inputs. In fact, for most production processes, increasing *all* inputs leads to a *strictly greater* amount of output. In what follows, we will therefore assume the following:

The Productive Inputs Principle Increasing the amounts of all inputs strictly increases the amount of output the firm can produce (using efficient production methods).

Isoquants

Suppose a firm wants to produce a certain amount of output using capital and labor. What is the best way to do this? Should it use a lot of capital and not much labor, or a lot of labor and not much capital? We will provide a complete answer to this question in Chapter 8.

The first step, though, is to identify the possible choices. That is, what combinations of inputs can produce the desired amount of output?

An **isoquant** identifies all the input combinations that efficiently produce a given amount of output.

An **isoquant** identifies all of the input combinations that efficiently produce a given level of output. For example, Noah and Naomi can use the circled combinations of labor and garage space in Table 7.4 to produce 140 garden benches per week. We have plotted these input combinations in blue in Figure 7.8. The horizontal axis measures the number of assembly workers; the vertical axis measures the amount of garage space. The three blue points in Figure 7.8 are therefore part of Noah and Naomi's isoquant for 140 units of output. If Noah and Naomi's inputs are finely divisible, there will probably be many input combinations that efficiently produce 140 garden benches a week. If so, their isoquant for producing 140 garden benches a week might look like the solid black curve in Figure 7.8.

There is a close parallel between isoquants and consumer indifference curves. An isoquant identifies the input combinations that efficiently produce a given output level; an indifference curve identifies the different consumption good combinations that produce a given level of well-being. Recall that we can think of indifference curves as being like topographic contour lines. Similarly, we can think of isoquants as contour lines for the "hill" created by the production function.[10] Figure 7.9 shows the contour lines for a hypothetical production function with two inputs, labor and capital. The amount of output at any given input combination is measured by the height of the function. The light blue curve shows all of the points on the production function that result in 100 units of output. The dark blue curve directly below (at ground level) shows the combinations of labor and capital that are associated with the points on the light blue curve. This dark blue curve is the isoquant for 100 units of output.

A firm's **family of isoquants** consists of the isoquants corresponding to all of its possible output levels.

A firm's **family of isoquants** consists of the isoquants corresponding to all of its possible output levels. Let's discuss some of the properties of isoquants and families of isoquants.

Figure 7.8

The Isoquant For Producing 140 Garden Benches per Week. The blue points graph the combinations of labor and garage space from Table 7.4 that produce 140 garden benches per week. These input combinations are part of Noah and Naomi's isoquant for 140 units of output. If labor and garage space are finely divisible, there will be many input combinations that produce 140 garden benches per week. In this case, the isoquant for 140 units of output might look like the black curve in the figure.

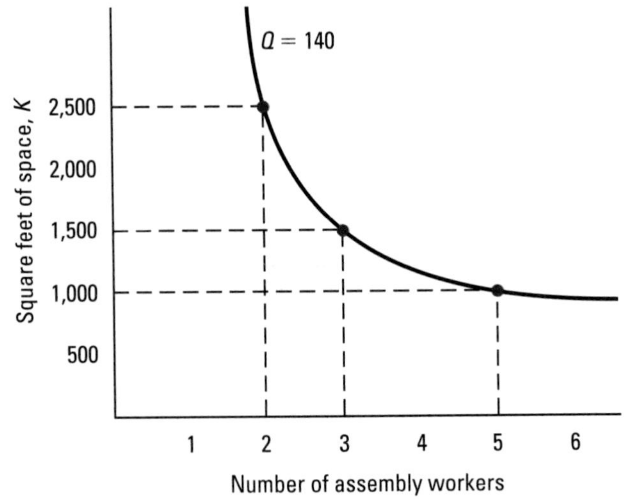

[10]One difference from consumer theory, however, is that here the height of the hill has real meaning. That is, outputs levels are *cardinal*, unlike utility levels, which are only ordinal (see Chapter 4).

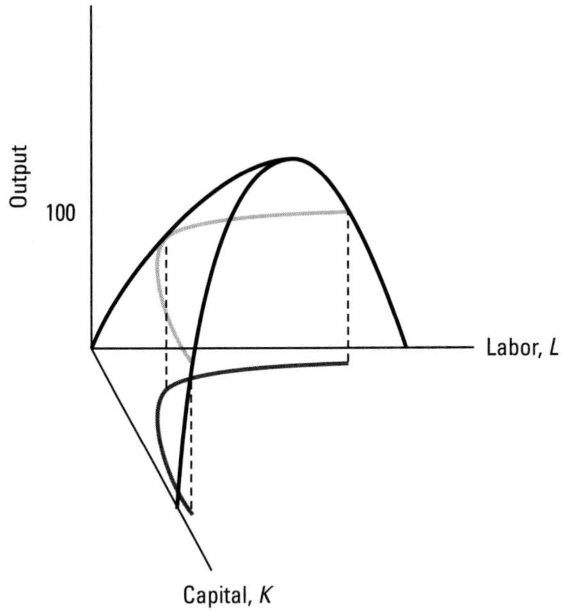

Figure 7.9
A Two-Input Production Function and One of Its Isoquants. Isoquants are the contour lines for the "hill" created by the production function. In the figure, the light blue curve shows all the points on the production function that yield 100 units of output. The dark blue curve directly below it (at "ground level") is the isoquant for 100 units of output; it shows the input combinations that produce that level of output.

The Productive Inputs Principle implies that isoquants and families of isoquants have several properties:

1. *Isoquants are thin.* To see why, consider Figure 7.10(a). If an isoquant was thick, then there would be two input combinations on the same isoquant, such as A and B, with one having more of every input than the other. This can't happen according to the Productive Inputs Principle.
2. *Isoquants do not slope upward.* The isoquant in Figure 7.8 slopes downward, from northwest to southeast. Thus, if we compare two points on this isoquant and one uses more assembly workers, then the other uses less garage space. Figure 7.10(b) shows why isoquants can't instead slope upward. There would then be two different input combinations on the isoquant, such as A and B, with one having more of every input than the other. The Productive Inputs Principle implies that this can't happen.
3. *An isoquant is the boundary between input combinations that produce more and less than a given amount of output.* The input combinations that produce more than Q lie above and to the right of the isoquant for output level Q. Those that produce less lie below and to the left of that isoquant.
4. *Isoquants for the same technology do not cross.* Suppose two isoquants for different production levels crossed, as in Figure 7.10(c). Then there would be two points A and B, one of which (A) has more of all inputs than the other, but produces less output, which can't happen according to the Productive Inputs Principle.
5. *Higher-level isoquants lie farther from the origin.* Since using more of all inputs leads to more output, isoquants for higher output levels lie farther from the origin, as Figure 7.10(d) shows.

In sum:

Five Properties of Isoquants and Families of Isoquants

1. Isoquants are thin.
2. Isoquants do not slope upward.
3. An isoquant is the boundary between input combinations that produce more and less than a given amount of output.
4. Isoquants from the same technology do not cross.
5. Higher-level isoquants lie farther from the origin.

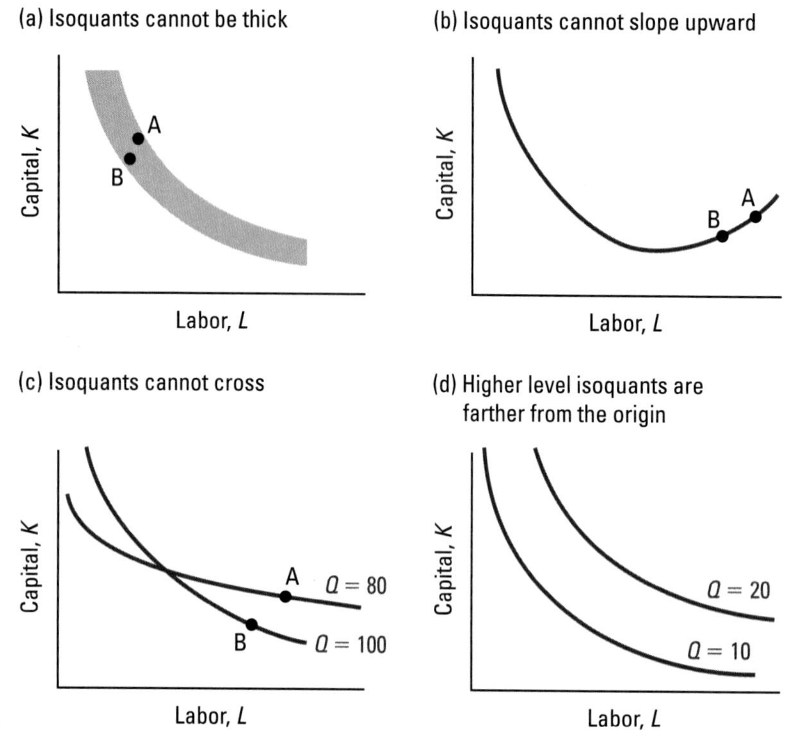

Figure 7.10

Some Properties of Isoquants and Families of Isoquants. Figure (a) shows that isoquants are thin. If an isoquant was thick, as in figure (a), there would be two points like A and B that produce the same output using efficient production methods, even though one uses more of all inputs than the other. That is inconsistent with the Productive Inputs Principle. Figures (b) and (c) show that an upward-sloping isoquant or isoquants that cross are also inconsistent with the Productive Inputs Principle. Figure (d) shows that isoquants for higher output levels lie farther from the origin.

Application 7.2

A Pressing Need for Labor and Capital

Greg Spina is the production manager of the Cold Hollow Cider Mill, located in Waterbury Center, Vermont. Cold Hollow, one of the most visited tourist attractions in the area, has been producing apple cider since 1974. During the peak months of cider production in the fall, the firm produces about 10,000 gallons of cider a day. Soon after starting at his job, Spina began thinking about the best way to organize Cold Hollow's production.

Making apple cider is a relatively simple process. Ground-up apples are squeezed, or pressed, and the juice is bottled. It takes 10 pounds of apples to make one gallon of cider. Three types of machines can be used in the pressing

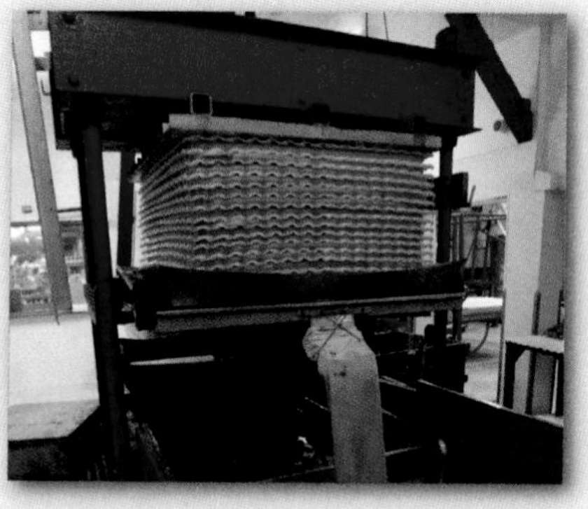

Cold Hollow's rack-and-cloth vertical press

process. They differ in cost, in daily capacity, and in the amount of labor they require.

The oldest type of machine is the rack-and-cloth vertical press. The rack is a lasagna-like structure with cloth layers, between which workers carefully spread mashed apples. The rack is then rolled over a hydraulic press (like the one that raises your car when a mechanic works on it), which squeezes the juice from the apples. The juice filters through the cloth into a collection tank. Workers then roll the rack back, clean out the mashed apples, and begin the process again. The two other types of machine, the belt press and the rack-and-bag horizontal press, are more modern and use less labor than the rack-and-cloth vertical press.

A single rack-and-cloth vertical press can make 5,000 gallons of cider in an eight-hour day using two and a half workers. (Workers can be hired part-time or assigned to other tasks when they are not needed to run the machine.) A single belt press can make 6,500 gallons a day using one and a half workers. A single rack-and-bag horizontal press can make 8,000 gallons a day using just one worker.

In considering his production options, Spina faces one important constraint. Because of Cold Hollow's tourist business, he must use at least one rack-and-cloth vertical press, since tourists want to see how a traditional cider mill works.

Let's look at Cold Hollow's isoquant for producing 10,000 gallons a day. Table 7.5 lists the labor and capital requirements for three possible ways of producing 10,000 gallons a day.[11] The first method (A) uses two rack-and-cloth vertical presses up to their capacity. Let's measure capital according to its cost. The cheapest machine is the rack-and-cloth vertical press. We'll count one of those machines as one unit of capital. The belt press costs four times as much as the rack-and-cloth vertical press, so we'll count it as four units of capital. And the rack-and-bag horizontal press costs 10 times as much, so we'll count it as 10 units of capital. As the table shows, method A uses 40 hours of labor and two units of capital each day (five workers over an eight-hour day equals 40 hours of labor).

The second method (B) uses one belt press up to its full 6,500 gallon capacity and one rack-and-cloth vertical press for the remaining 3,500 gallons.[12] This method involves five units of capital and requires a total of 26 hours of labor, 12 hours for the belt press and 14 hours for the rack-and-cloth vertical press. [The rack-and-cloth vertical press will run for $(3{,}500/5{,}000) \times 8 = 5.6$ hours a day, so its total labor use is $5.6 \times 2.5 = 14$ hours.]

The third method (C) uses one rack-and-bag horizontal press up to its full 8,000 gallon capacity and one rack-and-cloth vertical press for the remaining 2,000 units. It uses 11 units of capital and requires 16 hours of labor, 8 hours for the rack-and-bag horizontal press, and 8 hours for the vertical rack-and-cloth press. [In this case the rack-and-cloth vertical press runs for 3.2 hours each day, so its total labor use equals $3.2 \times 2.5 = 8$ hours.][13]

Figure 7.11 shows the three labor and capital combinations. Together the three points form Cold Hollow's isoquant for producing 10,000 gallons of cider a day. If Cold Hollow could (unrealistically, perhaps) rent its capital for part of a day, it could use the combinations of labor and capital on the dashed lines that connect the three points in the figure. For example, Cold Hollow could produce 10,000 gallons a day by using method A in the morning and method B in the afternoon, which would correspond to using 3.5 units of capital and 33 hours of labor each day. If many different types of machines were available instead of just three, Cold Hollow's isoquant would instead include many points like A, B, and C, and would look more like a smoothly rounded curve.

Table 7.5
Three Production Methods for Producing 10,000 Gallons/Day of Apple Cider

	Types of Presses				
Method	Rack-and-Cloth Vertical Press	Belt Press	Rack-and-Bag Horizontal Press	Hours of Labor/Day	Units of Capital
A	2	0	0	40	2
B	1	1	0	26	5
C	1	0	1	16	11

[11] We will ignore the number of apples Cold Hollow uses since it is the same (100,000 pounds) for all machines. Energy costs for the three machines are also roughly equal.

[12] There are other methods that use one belt press and one rack-and-cloth vertical press, with each type of machine producing different amounts of cider than in method B. But method B uses the least labor of all of those possibilities.

[13] Again, method C uses the least labor of any method that uses one rack-and-bag horizontal press and one rack-and-cloth vertical press.

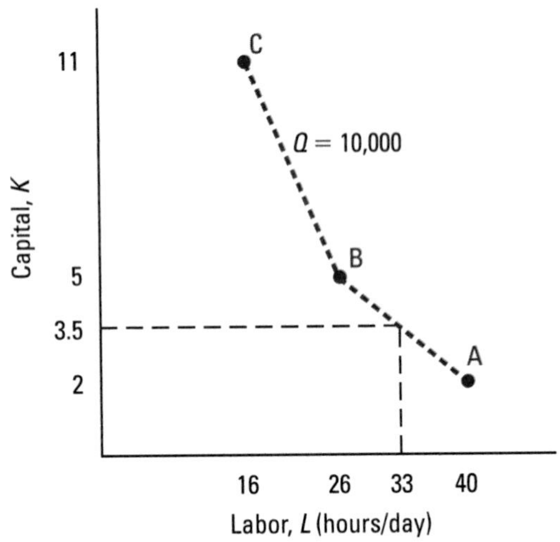

Figure 7.11
Cold Hollow's Isoquant for 10,000 Gallons of Cider per Day. The three labeled points show the input combinations for methods A, B, and C in Table 7.5. These three points form Cold Hollow's isoquant for 10,000 gallons/day. If Cold Hollow could rent its capital for part of a day, it could also use the input combinations on the dashed lines by employing different methods during different parts of the day.

Average and Marginal Products with More than One Input

When a firm's production technology uses more than one input, we can define the marginal and average products of any particular input just as we did in Section 7.2. Just as we did there, we do so holding the levels of other inputs fixed. We then speak of the average and marginal products of labor (still denoted AP_L and MP_L) given 1,500 square feet of space, or of the average and marginal product of capital (denoted AP_K and MP_K) given 5 workers. The average and marginal products of labor in Table 7.3, for example, are the levels of those measures given 1,000 square feet of garage space.

The Law of Diminishing Marginal Returns tells us to expect that holding other inputs fixed, the marginal product of an input will eventually decline as more of that input is used. What happens to the marginal product of an input as more of other inputs are added? Often, it increases. For example, with more space, each of Noah and Naomi's workers may be more productive. But sometimes the marginal product decreases—for example, when the inputs are close substitutes. To take an extreme example, imagine that in Section 7.2 we had decided to measure labor inputs as "workers named Bob," "workers named Jim," and so on, and that these workers are equally productive. If the marginal product of labor decreases as more workers are added, then the marginal product of workers named Bob will fall when we add more workers named Jim.

IN-TEXT EXERCISE 7.6 **How does Noah and Naomi's marginal product of labor with three workers change in Table 7.4 on page 227 as the amount of garage space increases from 1,000 to 1,500 square feet (assuming workers must be hired by the week, so that $\Delta L = 1$)? To 2,000? What is Noah and Naomi's marginal product of capital with 1,500 square feet of garage space and four workers if garage space can be changed in increments no smaller than 500 square feet (so that $\Delta K = 500$)?**

Substitution between Inputs

An important factor for a manager in choosing her firm's best mix of inputs is the rate at which one input can be substituted for another. This information is captured in the shape of the firm's isoquants. Figure 7.12 shows a firm's isoquant for producing 100 units of output from labor and capital, measured in hours of labor and machine time per week. Suppose the firm starts with 250 hours of labor and 1,000 hours of capital, labeled as point A in the figure. How much capital must the firm add to make up for a reduction of 50 hours of labor per week? From the isoquant we see that when it moves from 250 to 200 hours of labor the firm must add 50 hours of machine time to continue producing 100 units of output. The new input combination is point B.

For this change, the rate of substitution for labor with capital is measured by the ratio $-\frac{\Delta K}{\Delta L}$, which tells us how many machine hours of capital we must add per hour of labor that we eliminate. Because isoquants slope down, the ratio $\frac{\Delta K}{\Delta L}$ without the minus sign is a negative number. Including the minus sign in front of the ratio converts our measure of the rate of substitution into a positive number, making it easier to interpret (since a bigger positive number then indicates that more capital is required to compensate for a fixed reduction in labor).

Figure 7.12

Substitution between Labor and Capital Along an Isoquant and the Marginal Rate of Technical Substitution (MRTS). If we start at input combination A and reduce labor by 50 hours, moving to point B, we must add 50 hours of machine time to keep output unchanged. The rate of substitution for labor with capital for this change equals 1, which equals the slope of the line connecting points A and B, times negative one. If we instead reduce labor by 20 hours, moving to point C, we must add 10 hours of machine time to keep output constant. The rate of substitution for this change, 1/2, equals the slope of the line connecting points A and C, times negative one. If we consider smaller and smaller changes, the rate of substitution comes to equal negative one times the slope of the dark red line that is tangent to the isoquant at point A, also known as the *slope of the isoquant at point A*. This slope, times negative one, is the marginal rate of technical substitution for labor with capital at input combination A.

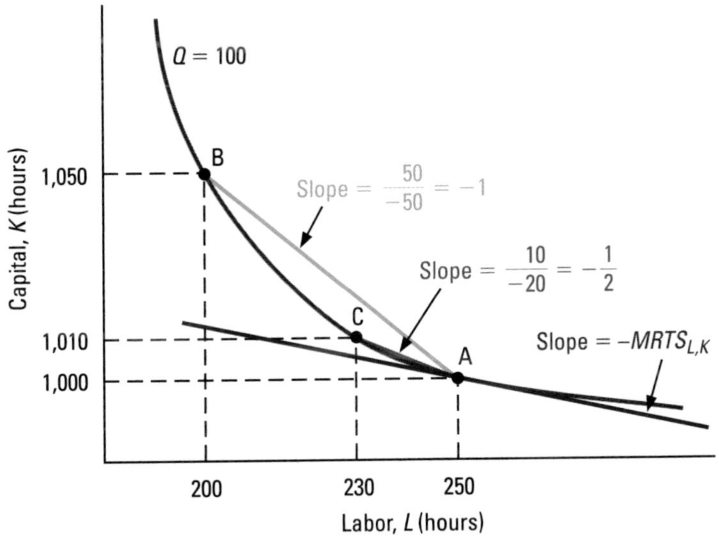

When we move from point A to point B in Figure 7.12, the change in labor is $\Delta L = -50$, and the required compensating change in capital is $\Delta K = 50$. The rate of substitution for labor with capital for this change is therefore $-\frac{\Delta K}{\Delta L} = -\frac{50}{-50} = 1$, which equals the slope of the light red line connecting points A and B, times negative one (its rise is $\Delta K = 50$ and its run is $\Delta L = -50$).

Suppose instead that we reduce labor by only 20 hours, from 250 to 230. To keep output unchanged, we must move from point A to point C in Figure 7.12. For this change, the rate of substitution between labor and capital is $-\frac{\Delta K}{\Delta L} = -\frac{10}{-20} = \frac{1}{2}$, which equals the slope of the medium red line connecting points A and C, times negative one.

From Figure 7.12 we can see that if we consider smaller and smaller changes in labor, the slope of the lines connecting the original and new input combinations will come closer and closer to the slope of the dark red line tangent to the isoquant at point A, often called simply the "slope of the isoquant" at point A. Thus, for *very small* (*marginal*) changes, the rate of substitution for labor with capital at a given input combination—which we call the **marginal rate of technical substitution (MRTS) for labor with capital**, written as $MRTS_{LK}$—equals the slope of the isoquant at that point, times negative one.[14] (Recall seeing the same point when we discussed the marginal rate of substitution in Chapter 4.)

The marginal rate of technical substitution (MRTS) for input *X* with input *Y*, written as $MRTS_{XY}$, is the rate $(-\frac{\Delta Y}{\Delta X})$ at which a firm must replace units of *X* with units of *Y* to keep output unchanged starting at a given input combination, when the changes involved are tiny. It equals the slope of the firm's isoquant at this input combination, times negative one.

This measure is closely related to that of a consumer's marginal rate of substitution, introduced in Chapter 4. The MRS is the rate at which a consumer can substitute one good for another without changing well-being; the MRTS is the rate at which a firm can substitute one input for another without changing output.

The MRTS and Marginal Products

How does $MRTS_{LK}$ relate to the productivity of labor and capital? Recall that the marginal product of an input captures how much additional output we can get for each additional unit of input when we increase the input by the smallest possible amount. Imagine that we change slightly the amount of labor by ΔL and the amount of capital by ΔK. Multiplying the marginal product of labor, MP_L, by the amount of labor added or removed, ΔL, gives us the change in output due to the adjustment in labor, $MP_L \times \Delta L$. Likewise, multiplying the marginal product of capital, MP_K, by the amount of capital added or removed, ΔK, gives us the change in output due to the adjustment in capital, $MP_K \times \Delta K$. If we choose ΔK and ΔL to keep output unchanged (that is, stay on the same isoquant), these two effects must sum to zero. Using symbols,

$$(MP_L \times \Delta L) + (MP_K \times \Delta K) = 0$$

Rearranging this expression gives us $-\Delta K/\Delta L = MP_L/MP_K$. Therefore,

$$MRTS_{LK} = \frac{MP_L}{MP_K}$$

This formula tells us that $MRTS_{LK}$ at a given input combination is equal to the ratio formed when we divide the marginal product of labor by the marginal product of capital. The more productive labor is relative to capital, the more capital we must add to make up for any given reduction in labor, so the larger the marginal rate of substitution.

[14] Note that the marginal rate of technical substitution for labor with capital, $MRTS_{LK}$, is *not* the same as the marginal rate of technical substitution for capital with labor, $MRTS_{KL}$. The former measures how much capital we must add to keep output unchanged per unit of labor that is taken away; the latter measures how much labor we must add to keep output unchanged per unit of capital that is taken away. In fact, one is the reciprocal of the other: $MRTS_{LK} = 1/MRTS_{KL}$.

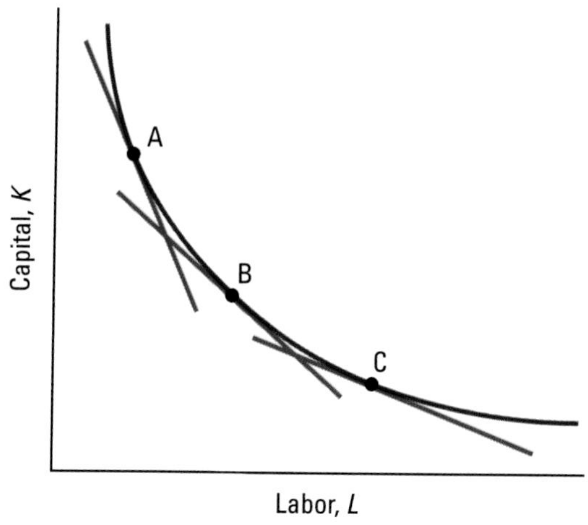

Figure 7.13

A Declining Marginal Rate of Technical Substitution. This figure shows the $MRTS_{LK}$ at three different points on an isoquant, with tangent lines drawn at each of those points. The $MRTS_{LK}$ falls as we move to the southeast along the isoquant, increasing labor and decreasing capital. If all of the firm's isoquants have this feature, then the firm's technology has a declining marginal rate of technical substitution.

Figure 7.13 shows the $MRTS_{LK}$ at three points (A, B, and C) on an isoquant. The $MRTS_{LK}$ declines as we increase L and decrease K (moving to the southeast) so that it has a **declining marginal rate of technical substitution**. We will often assume that a firm's isoquants have this property when we study cost minimization in Chapter 8. It will hold whenever (a) an increase in the amount of one of the inputs raises the marginal product of the other, and (b) an increase in the amount of one of the inputs lowers the marginal product of that input (as it does when the Law of Diminishing Marginal Returns holds). Why? MP_L falls as we move to the southeast both because L is bigger [by (b)] and because K is smaller [by (a)]. Using similar reasoning, we can see that MP_K rises. Together, these changes in marginal products cause $MRTS_{LK}$ to fall.[15]

An isoquant for a production process using two inputs, X and Y, has a **declining marginal rate of technical substitution** if $MRTS_{XY}$ declines as we move along the isoquant, increasing input X and decreasing input Y.

Input Substitution for Three Special Production Technologies

Technologies differ in how much the MRTS changes as a firm alters the inputs it uses to produce a given amount of output. At one extreme, two inputs may be perfectly substitutable for one another. At another extreme, a firm may have to use two inputs in fixed proportions, so that no substitution is possible. Let's look at these two extreme cases in more detail, as well as at an intermediate case known as the Cobb-Douglas production function.

1. Perfect Substitutes. Two inputs are **perfect substitutes** if their functions are identical, so that a firm is able to exchange one for another at a fixed rate. For example, suppose there are two types of workers, those with a college education and those without. We'll use the symbol C for the amount of college-educated labor and H for the amount of high-school educated labor. For some jobs (like janitor), the amount of education is unimportant, so the two types of worker are perfectly substitutable. In this case, as Figure 7.14(a) shows, each isoquant is a straight line with a slope of -1, so that $MRTS_{HC} = 1$ for all combinations of H and C. For inputs to be perfect substitutes, they need not be equally

Two inputs are **perfect substitutes** if their functions are identical, so that a firm can exchange one for another at a fixed rate.

[15]While (a) and (b) ensure that the firm's technology has a declining marginal rate of technical substitution, this property can still hold if either (a) or (b) is not satisfied.

Figure 7.14

Isoquants for Inputs That Are Perfect Substitutes. In figure (a), a high-school educated worker and a college-educated worker are equally productive. In figure (b), a college-educated worker is twice as productive as a high-school educated worker. In both cases, the $MRTS_{HC}$ is always the same, regardless of the amounts of inputs the firm uses. The two inputs are therefore perfect substitutes.

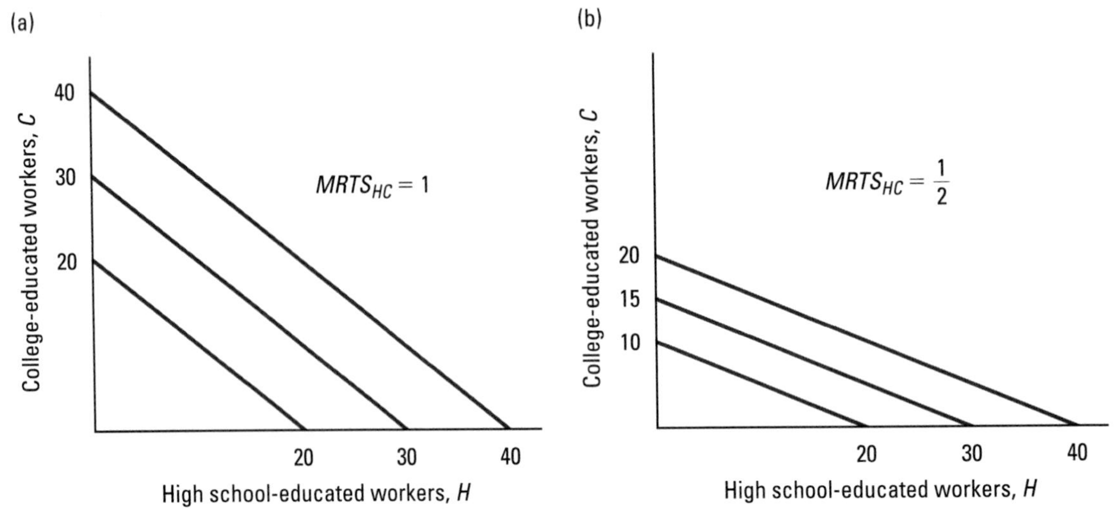

productive. If, for example, college-educated workers are exactly twice as productive as high-school educated workers, then a college-educated worker is perfectly substitutable for *two* high school educated workers. In that case, isoquants are still straight lines, as shown in Figure 7.14(b), but $MRTS_{HC} = 1/2$ for all combinations of inputs.

Two inputs are used in **fixed proportions** when they must be combined in a fixed ratio. They are then known as **perfect complements.**

2. Perfect Complements (Fixed Proportions). In some cases, a firm must combine inputs in **fixed proportions**. Those inputs are then **perfect complements**. For example, consider a manufacturer of salt. To make pure salt involves a chemical reaction between sodium and chlorine. The reaction uses 1.54 grams of chlorine per gram of sodium. If any extra sodium or extra chlorine is used, the extra amount is left over at the end of the reaction. Figure 7.15 shows a family of isoquants for making salt. The combinations of sodium and chlorine that are in this ratio lie on the dashed line drawn through the origin. The isoquants are L-shaped, with their kinks lying along the dashed line. Why?

Suppose the firm starts at the point labeled A and gets one extra gram of chlorine but no sodium, moving to point B. The extra chlorine is of no help in making more salt since there is no extra sodium to go with it. Similarly, if the firm has extra sodium without any extra chlorine, moving to point C, the firm also can't make any more salt. Since all these points and any others that involve an increase in just one of the inputs produce the same amount of output, the isoquant is L-shaped, with a kink at point A.

3. The Cobb-Douglas Production Function. Many analyses in economics use a particular type of production function first introduced by mathematician Charles Cobb

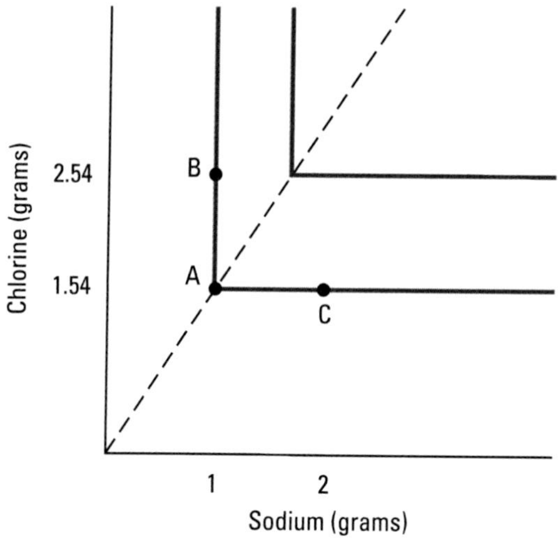

Figure 7.15

Isoquants for Inputs That Must Be Used in Fixed Proportions. The dashed line from the origin represents the input combinations in which sodium and chlorine are combined in a 1:1.54 ratio. Starting at point A in the figure, adding only more chlorine (such as point B) or only more sodium (such as point C) does not yield more salt. All such points lie on the same isoquant, which is L-shaped, with a kink at the 1:1.54 ratio line.

and economist (and U.S. Senator) Paul Douglas. The **Cobb-Douglas production function** is

The **Cobb-Douglas production function** is $Q = F(L, K) = AL^{\alpha}K^{\beta}$.

$$Q = F(L, K) = AL^{\alpha}K^{\beta}$$

where A, α, and β are parameters that take specific values for a given firm. For example, if $A = 10$ and $\alpha = \beta = 0.5$ then we get the production function $Q = F(L, K) = 10\sqrt{L}\sqrt{K}$ that we introduced in Section 7.2. The variable A captures the firm's general productivity level. For example, if A doubles, the firm produces twice as much for every combination of inputs. The parameters α and β affect the *relative* productivities of labor and capital. In particular, for this production function, the marginal product of labor is[16]

$$MP_L = \alpha AL^{\alpha-1}K^{\beta}$$

and the marginal product of capital is

$$MP_K = \beta AL^{\alpha}K^{\beta-1}$$

Therefore, the marginal rate of technical substitution between capital and labor is

$$MRTS_{LK} = \left(\frac{\alpha}{\beta}\right)\left(\frac{K}{L}\right) \quad \textbf{(1)}$$

The $MRTS_{LK}$ depends on the parameters α and β, which capture the relative productivities of labor and capital, but does not depend upon A, the firm's general productivity level. Increases in α increase labor's productivity and raise $MRTS_{LK}$, since more capital is required to compensate for any loss of labor. In contrast, increases in β increase capital's productivity and lower $MRTS_{LK}$. The $MRTS_{LK}$ also depends on the ratio of capital to labor—the lower the ratio of capital to labor, the smaller is $MRTS_{LK}$. Isoquants for Cobb-Douglas production functions therefore have a declining marginal rate of technical substitution.

[16]If you know calculus, you can derive these marginal products by taking the derivatives of the production function with respect to L and K, respectively.

Figure 7.16

Isoquants for Two Cobb-Douglas Production Functions. Figure (a) shows the isoquants for a Cobb-Douglas production function with A = 10 and $\alpha = \beta = 1/2$. In figure (b), A = 10, $\alpha = 3/2$, and $\beta = 1/2$. The dashed line from the origin represents combinations of equal amounts of labor and capital. The red tangent lines show that at these equal input combinations, the $MRTS_{LK}$ in figure (b) is larger than the one in figure (a).

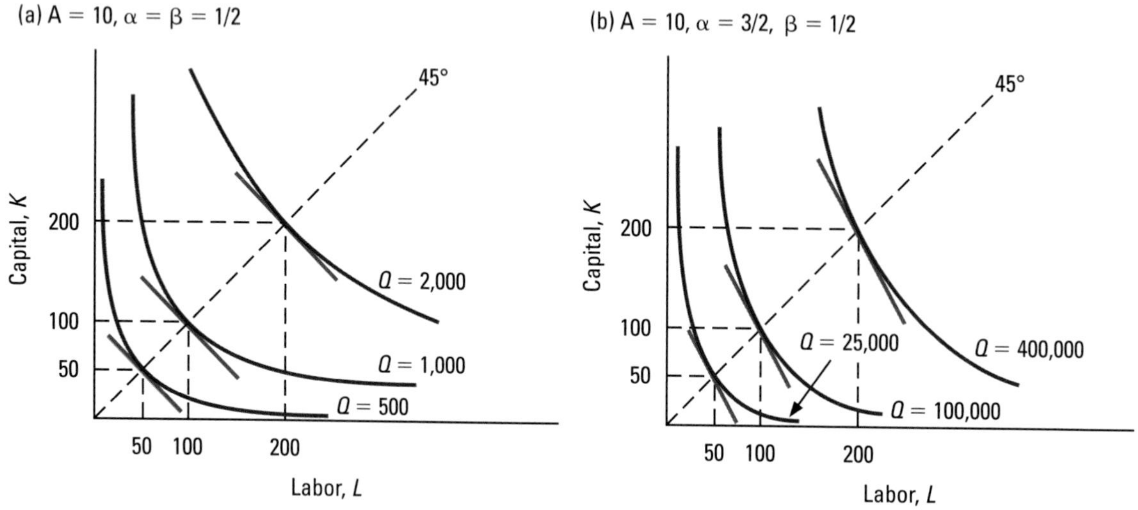

Figure 7.16 shows families of isoquants for two Cobb-Douglas production functions. In Figure 7.16(a), $A = 10$ and $\alpha = \beta = 1/2$; in Figure 7.16(b), $A = 10$, $\alpha = 3/2$, and $\beta = 1/2$. In each of the figures the 45-degree line drawn from the origin shows points along which the amounts of labor and capital are equal. The lines drawn tangent to the isoquants where they cross the 45-degree line show that the $MRTS_{LK}$ for production function (b) is larger than the one for production function (a) at those input combinations.

7.4 RETURNS TO SCALE

Some markets are served by many small firms: think of shoe repair stores, flower shops, and convenience stores. Other markets are dominated by a few very large firms: think of airplane manufacturing, pharmaceuticals, express package delivery. Why is this so? In Chapters 14, 17, and 19 we'll see that part of the explanation involves technological differences. When large producers in a market can produce at lower cost than small ones, small producers will have a hard time surviving.

Economists determine whether larger firms produce more effectively by examining **returns to scale**. To do so, they ask: What would happen if the firm increased the amounts of all its inputs by the same proportion? There are three possibilities:

A firm has **constant returns to scale** if a proportional change in all inputs produces the same proportional change in output.

1. The firm has **constant returns to scale**: a proportional change in the use of all inputs produces the same proportional change in output. For example, for a firm using only capital and labor, doubling the amount of both inputs doubles its output.

2. The firm has **increasing returns to scale**: a proportional change in the use of all inputs produces a more than proportional change in output. For example, for a firm using only capital and labor, doubling the amount of both inputs more than doubles its output.
3. The firm has **decreasing returns to scale**: a proportional change in the use of all inputs produces a less than proportional change in output. For example, for a firm using only capital and labor, doubling the amount of both inputs less than doubles its output.

A firm has **increasing returns to scale** if a proportional change in all inputs produces a more than proportional change in output.

A firm has **decreasing returns to scale** if a proportional change in all inputs produces a less than proportional change in output.

Suppose a firm uses two inputs, labor and capital, to produce its output. Figure 7.17(a) shows a case of constant returns to scale. If the firm initially is using 50 hours of labor and 25 hours of capital to produce 100 units of output, doubling its labor and capital to 100 and 50, respectively, doubles its output to 200. Doubling labor and capital again to 200 and 100, doubles output again to 400. Figure 7.17(b) shows a case of increasing returns to scale: each doubling of labor and capital now more than doubles output, increasing it by 150 percent. Figure 7.17(c) shows decreasing returns to scale: each doubling of labor and capital increases output by only 50 percent.

To see an example of production functions that have constant, increasing, and decreasing returns to scale, let's take another look at the Cobb-Douglas production function, $Q = F(L, K) = AL^{\alpha}K^{\beta}$, introduced in Section 7.3. For this production function, returns to scale are constant whenever $\alpha + \beta = 1$. How do we know this? With $2L$ units of labor and $2K$ units of capital, output is

$$F(2L, 2K) = A(2L)^{\alpha}(2K)^{\beta} = 2^{\alpha+\beta}(AL^{\alpha}K^{\beta}) = 2^{\alpha+\beta}F(L, K)$$

Thus, output exactly doubles if $\alpha + \beta = 1$ (since then $2^{\alpha+\beta} = 2$). By similar reasoning, when $\alpha + \beta < 1$, the Cobb-Douglas production function has decreasing returns to scale; when $\alpha + \beta > 1$, it has increasing returns to scale.

Figure 7.17

Constant, Increasing, and Decreasing Returns to Scale with Two Inputs. Figure (a) shows a case of constant returns to scale in which doubling of labor and capital exactly doubles output. In figure (b) each doubling of labor and capital more than doubles output, a case of increasing returns to scale. In figure (c), each doubling of labor and capital raises output by only 50 percent, a case of decreasing returns to scale.

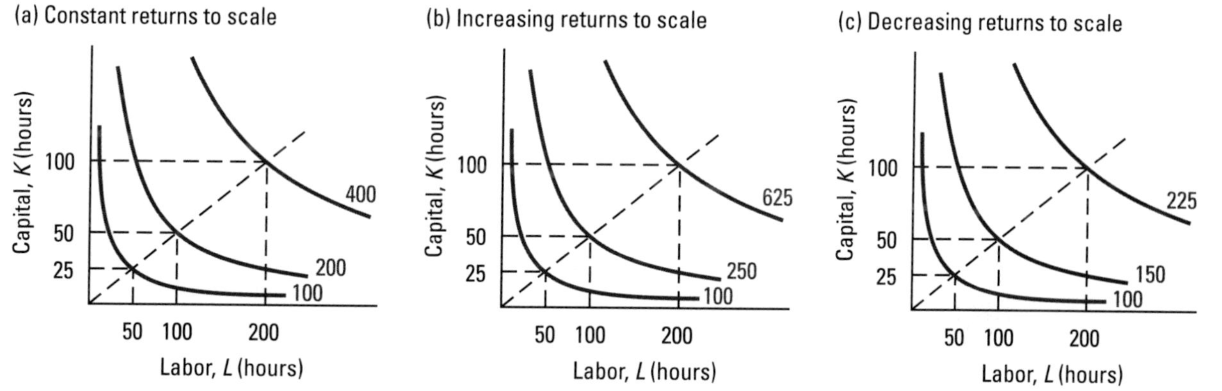

So far we have talked as if a technology has either constant, increasing, or decreasing returns to scale. But, in reality, a technology's returns to scale may vary, having increasing returns to scale in some ranges of output and decreasing returns to scale in others.

WORKED-OUT PROBLEM 7.2

The Problem Robert runs a cleaning company that uses labor, L, and capital, K, as inputs. If he hires L workers on a given day and uses K units of capital, he can clean $F(L, K) = \sqrt{L + K}$ houses. Does his technology have increasing, decreasing, or constant returns to scale?

The Solution If Robert doubles the inputs he uses from L workers and K units of capital to $2L$ workers and $2K$ units of capital his output will be

$$F(2L, 2K) = \sqrt{2L + 2K} = \sqrt{2(L + K)} = \sqrt{2}\sqrt{L + K} = \sqrt{2}\,F(L,K)$$

Since $\sqrt{2}$ is less than 2, output less than doubles when he doubles his inputs.

IN-TEXT EXERCISE 7.7 **Suppose that Robert's production function is instead $F(L, K) = (L + K)^2$. Does his production function have constant, increasing, or decreasing returns to scale?**

Application 7.3

Returns-to-Scale in Express Package Delivery

It's 4 p.m. and your graduate school applications are due at 10 a.m. the next morning. Like many other applicants, you'll probably call an express package delivery service, such as Federal Express (FedEx) or United Parcel Service (UPS). They will send a truck to pick up your application, take it to a nearby airport, fly it to a sorting facility somewhere in the middle of the country, transport it to the city where the school is located, load it onto another truck, and deliver it to the school's admissions office—all by 10 a.m. the next morning. Guaranteed.

In the second quarter of 2002, three companies and the U.S. Post Office accounted for essentially all of the approximately 260 million overnight package deliveries in the United States. FedEx and UPS together accounted for nearly 75 percent; Airborne Express, for about 20 percent; and the post office, for most of the rest. Why are there so few choices for express package delivery?

The answer to the question is that there are significant increasing returns to scale in express package delivery. Think about local pickup and delivery. When the number of packages doubles, fewer than double the number of trucks and drivers can do the job. The reason is that delivery routes can become more specialized. For example, a single truck would need to make deliveries all over town. With two trucks, the company will not need to send both trucks all over town. Instead, it might assign one truck to deliver to the northern half of town, and the other to deliver to the southern half. The amount of time spent driving from one delivery stop to another falls, and the number of packages that can be delivered by a truck in one day rises. This effect continues as the number of packages increases. If it gets large enough, each fully loaded truck may be able to make just one stop, delivering to a single business or apartment building.

The presence of increasing returns to scale makes it difficult for new express package delivery companies to enter the market. Their per-unit delivery costs would initially be much higher than those of FedEx and UPS, which have much larger scales of operation.

Reasons for Increasing and Decreasing Returns to Scale

The factors that produce increasing returns to scale are varied. One is the specialization of inputs as scale increases. We have seen in Example 7.1 how the specialization of labor can cause the average product of labor to rise with the number of workers. This effect can lead to increasing returns to scale. Application 7.5 shows how specialization of trucks' delivery routes produces increasing returns in express package delivery. In other cases, physical laws generate increasing returns. For example, doubling the square footage of a building does not double its construction cost.[17] Similar effects arise with oil tanker ships. For example, a tanker that can carry 200,000 deadweight tons of oil costs only a little more than three times as much to build as a tanker that carries only 20,000 deadweight tons.

The factors that produce *decreasing* returns to scale are somewhat harder to understand. Think about a manufacturer that currently uses L units of labor and K units of capital. Suppose the firm doubles both inputs. Certainly, *one* option is to simply replicate current operations, opening a new factory exactly like the current one and hiring the same number of workers to staff it. This approach should double output, achieving constant returns to scale. Possibly the firm can do even better by using its inputs in some other way to achieve increasing returns to scale (perhaps by expanding its current factory). However, as long as replication is possible, it can't do worse than doubling its output. So we should never see decreasing returns to scale.

In practice, though, we *do* see firms that appear to have decreasing returns to scale. Why? One possibility is that there is some fixed input that isn't being considered. For example, when Noah and Naomi double their assembly workers and garage space, they do not double Noah and Naomi themselves. Their limited managerial capacity is a fixed input. Decreasing returns may set in because they manage a larger firm less effectively. Of course, if Noah and Naomi could hire another equally qualified pair of managers, then doubling all three inputs—assembly workers, garage space, and managerial attention—should in principle increase output by a factor of two or more.

Replicating a firm's managerial team, however, may run into some problems. Suppose, for example, that Noah and Naomi decide to bring in another pair of managers to run a second identical plant. If those managers are given complete autonomy, Noah and Naomi may worry that they will misuse the company's resources, not work hard enough, or make less than ideal decisions. Someone has to oversee them. Noah and Naomi are likely to find themselves reviewing and intervening in the managers' decisions. This need for oversight leads to increased bureaucratic costs, which may prevent the firm from doubling its output when it opens the second plant.

Implications of Returns to Scale

We've already mentioned that returns to scale can have important consequences for a market's structure, a topic we'll return to later in the book. It can also create conflicts in public policy. With increasing returns to scale, production is most efficient if there is a single producer. Without the discipline of competition, however, a single producer may not operate as we would like. For example, as we will see in Chapter 17, it may set its

[17] To see why, observe that if the square footage of a building is F square feet, the building's perimeter is $4\sqrt{F}$ feet in length. So when the square footage of the building doubles, the amount of material required to build the walls less than doubles. (In contrast, the amount of material required to build a flat roof approximately doubles.)

price too high. In some cases, policymakers have resolved this tension by regulating a single producer (for example, local telephone companies), or by having the government take over production (for example, the U.S. Postal Service). We'll discuss this subject further in Chapter 17.

7.5 PRODUCTIVITY DIFFERENCES AND TECHNOLOGICAL CHANGE

Technological change occurs when a firm's technology changes over time.

A firm is **more productive** or has **higher productivity** when it can produce more output using the same amounts of inputs. Equivalently, its production function shifts upward at each combination of inputs.

Firms producing a given good often differ in their abilities to turn inputs into output (we'll discuss an example in Application 7.4). Likewise, a given firm's technology may change over time, making it more or less effective at turning inputs into output, a process known as **technological change**.

When economists say that one firm has **higher productivity** than another, or that a firm has become **more productive**, they mean that it can produce more from the same amounts of inputs. An improvement in productivity shifts a firm's efficient production frontier upward at each combination of inputs. This corresponds to an increase in its production function at each possible combination of inputs.

For example, suppose that Noah and Naomi have recently discovered how to produce garden benches more effectively, changing their production function given 1,000 square feet of garage space to $Q = F(L) = -2L^3 + 10L^2 + 30L$ from $Q = F(L) = -2L^3 + 10L^2 + 25L$. Their new short-run production function gives a larger level of output than their old one for every positive amount of labor they might use. For example, with four workers they can now produce 152 garden benches a week instead of 132. In Figure 7.18 we show their original efficient production frontier in blue and their new one in red. For each amount of labor used, the red technology produces more output than the blue one.

Figure 7.18

A Productivity Improvement. The red technology is more productive than the blue one because it results in more output at every positive level of input.

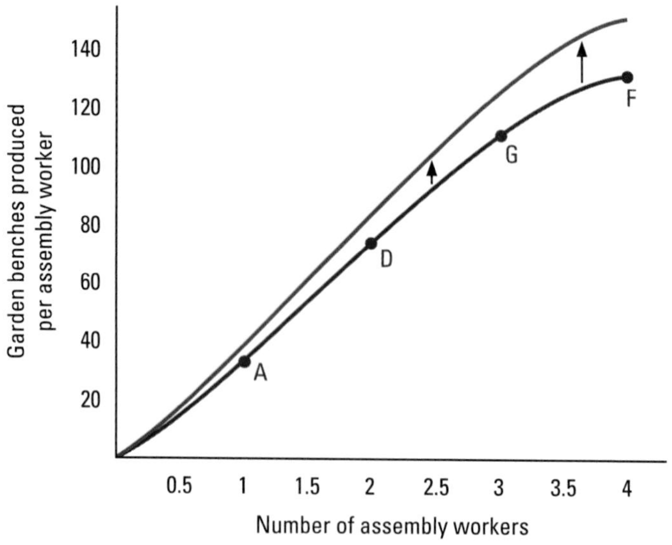

Productivity Differences and Technological Change with Two Inputs

"Things were done very differently on the farm when I was your age, Kenny."

With more than one input, a difference in productivity between two firms or a change in productivity in a given firm over time may be either general or specifically linked the use of one input. As an illustration, consider again the case of a Cobb-Douglas technology, $Q = F(L, K) = AL^{\alpha}K^{\beta}$. If the variable A increases, say from 10 to 15, this will increase the amount the firm produces by the same proportion (in this case, 50 percent) for every combination of inputs. As a result, if two different input combinations produced the same amount before the change, they will also produce the same amount after the change. This means that the firm's isoquants do not change in appearance, there is just a larger output level associated with each isoquant. For example, if A changes from 10 to 15 in Figure 7.16(a) on page 238, the isoquants would just be labeled 750, 1,500, and 3,000 instead of 500, 1,000, and 2,000. The firm's marginal rate of technical substitution at each input combination would not change.[18] More generally, a productivity improvement that keeps the MRTS unchanged at every input combination is called a **factor-neutral technical change.**

A **factor-neutral technical change** has no effect on the MRTS at any input combination. It simply changes the output level associated with each of the firm's isoquants.

In contrast, technological differences or changes sometimes involve changes in the relative productivities of different inputs. For example, the technology depicted in Figure 7.16(b) is more productive than the technology in Figure 7.16(a) because it has a larger value of α. Because labor is more productive with the technology in Figure 7.16(b) it takes more capital to substitute for any given reduction in labor with that technology.

Application 7.4

A Concrete Example of Productivity Differences

Ready-mix concrete is used in a wide range of construction projects including highways, sidewalks, swimming pools, and new home foundations. The product itself varies little across different firms and is made using a common method. You might expect that no firm would have a significant productivity advantage over others. But this is not the case.

Economist Chad Syverson used statistical methods to estimate plant-level production functions for ready-mix concrete firms using data on output, labor, and capital obtained from the U.S. Census Bureau. He found large differences in productivity across plants within local markets.[19] According to his estimates, a plant at the 75th percentile of the efficiency distribution (the 25th most efficient plant out of every 100) can produce approximately 37 percent more output from the same inputs than a plant at the 25th percentile (the 75th most efficient plant out of every 100).

What accounts for such large differences in measured productivity across firms in the same market that use the same basic technology? Part of the explanation is that there is undoubtedly variation in the quality of firms' inputs that is not captured well in the Census data. For example, the productivity of firms' capital (machines, trucks, etc.) is likely to differ depending on how well the firms have maintained

[18] You can also see this by recalling that formula (1) for the MRTS does not depend on A.

[19] Chad Syverson, "Market Structure and Productivity: A Concrete Example," *Journal of Political Economy* 112, December 2004, pp. 1181–1222.

it. Workers may also differ in their abilities, experience, and training. If so, then part of the explanation does not involve true differences in productivity, which are about producing different levels of output with the *same* inputs. But an equally important part of the story is likely to be that owners' and managers' of these firms differ in their knowledge of how to efficiently organize production and motivate workers. Such knowledge differences lead to true productivity differences across seemingly similar firms.

Productivity Comparisons

In asking whether one firm is more productive than another, or whether a given firm has become more productive, it is important to distinguish differences between and changes in firms' production functions from differences and changes caused by movements along a given production function. Sometimes, for example, one sees comparisons of different firms' labor productivity, measured by their average product of labor. One reason for one firm's average product of labor to be higher than another's is that the first firm is truly more productive in the sense just discussed. Another, however, is that it has chosen a different input mix for producing its output or is producing a different amount of output. Since the average product of an input can vary with both the input mix and the output level, the firm with the higher average product of labor is not necessarily more productive.

Reasons for Productivity Differences

Why might the productivity of two firms, or a given firm at two points of time, differ? First, firms may be subject to different regulations or market circumstances. These differences can involve labor laws, union contracts, and restrictions on hours of operation, among others. For example, airlines' labor contracts differ in the work rules that govern employees, such as the maximum number of hours a pilot can be on duty in one day. Such differences in work rules result in different productivity levels.

In addition, firms may have different levels of technical and organizational knowledge. One firm may have discovered a better production method than its rivals, or its managers may have figured out a better way of training, motivating, or organizing its workforce. This may come about through research and development, such as Henry Ford's efforts to develop assembly line production, or from the learning that results from the accumulation of production experience, a process known as "learning-by-doing" (see Application 7.5).

Productivity improvements by individual firms are a key factor leading to economy-wide productivity growth. (For a discussion of recent U.S. output and productivity growth see Add-On 7A.) These gains arise from investments in research and development (R&D), as well as learning by doing. R&D and the intellectual property (knowledge) that it generates are playing an increasingly important role in the economy. Industries in which research and development are critical to a firm's success—the so-called new economy—are now among the U.S. economy's most important industries. Economists David Evans and Richard Schmalensee report that in 1950 not one of the 100 highest-valued firms in the United States spent more than 5 percent of their revenues on R&D; in 1970, only 9 of the top 100 exceeded that level.[20] But, in 1999, 38 out of the 100 highest-valued firms spent at least 5 percent of their revenue on R&D; 22 firms spent more than 10 percent.

Policies that stimulate firms to make those investments play an important role in fostering continued economic growth. Intellectual property protection, such as patent rights, helps ensure that a firm that makes a discovery will not see it immediately copied by rivals. By doing so, it can provide an incentive for firms to innovate. At the same time, by granting sole use of an innovation to the innovator, these policies can create the kinds of monopoly losses that we'll study in Chapter 17. The optimal policy for encouraging innovation must therefore balance these concerns.

Application 7.5

Learning-by-Doing in Producing the Lockeed Tristar L-1011

In cases where firms make complex products, productivity can increase dramatically with experience. Producing a commercial airliner, for example, is an involved process. Once a design is set and a production facility is built, workers engage in a complex process of assembling the aircraft. Workers engaged in this process often become substantially more efficient as they gain experience with the tasks required for a given aircraft model.

The Lockheed TriStar L-1011

Using data on Lockheed's production of the L-1011 airplane from 1970–1984, economist C. Lanier Benkard found that Lockheed's productivity changed as the company gained experience producing the airplane.[21] According to his estimates, over the first 112 planes Lockheed produced, workers became roughly 42 percent more productive with each doubling of cumulative output (so that Lockheed would need roughly 30 percent fewer man-hours to complete assembly of a plane). Benkard also showed that those gains were partially lost when production was temporarily scaled back (probably because this led to worker turnover) and when the plane's design changed. Firms involved in such production processes can therefore gain significant cost advantages by trying to insure stability in their product designs and production levels.

[20]David S. Evans and Richard Schmalensee, "Some Economic Aspects of Antitrust in Dynamically Competitive Industries," Chapter 1 in A.B. Jaffe, J. Lerner, and S. Stern, eds., *Innovation Policy and The Economy* 2, 2002, Cambridge, MA: MIT Press and NBER.

[21]C. Lanier Benkard, "Learning and Forgetting: The Dynamics of Aircraft Production," *American Economic Review* 90, September 2000, pp. 1034–1054.

CHAPTER SUMMARY

1. **Production technologies**

   a. A firm's production possibilities set contains all of the input-output combinations that are possible given the firm's technology.

   b. A production method is efficient if there is no way to produce larger amounts of outputs using the same amounts of inputs. A firm's efficient production frontier contains all of the input-output combinations that can be achieved using efficient production methods. It can be described using a production function, a function of the form *Output* = *F(Inputs)*.

2. **Production with one variable input and one output**

   a. The average product of labor is equal to the amount of output divided by the number of workers employed, $Q/L = F(L)/L$.

   b. The marginal product of labor is equal to the extra output produced by adding the marginal units of labor ΔL—the smallest amount of labor the firm can add or subtract—divided by the number of units added, $[F(L) - F(L - \Delta L)]/\Delta L$.

   c. When the marginal product of labor is (bigger than/less than/equal to) the average product of labor, the average product is (increased by/decreased by/unchanged by) the marginal units of labor.

   d. A multiplant firm can use the marginal product of labor to assign workers to its plants to maximize the amount it produces from any given amount of labor. If at each plant the marginal product of labor falls when more workers are assigned to the plant, then the best assignment of workers equalizes the plants' marginal products, if such a point exists, and otherwise assigns all labor to the plant with the higher marginal product.

3. **Production with two variable inputs and one output**

   a. An isoquant contains all of the input combinations that produce a given amount of output.

   b. Isoquants are thin and slope downward. They separate input combinations that produce larger and smaller amounts of output than the combinations on the isoquant. Isoquants from the same technology do not cross and higher level isoquants lie farther from the origin.

   c. The marginal rate of technical substitution for input X with input Y ($MRTS_{XY}$) is the rate ($-\Delta Y/\Delta X$) at which the firm must add units of Y to keep output unchanged when the amount of input X is reduced by a small amount. It is equal to the marginal product of X divided by the marginal product of Y, $MRTS_{XY} = MP_X/MP_Y$.

   d. A technology using inputs X and Y has a diminishing marginal rate of technical substitution if $MRTS_{XY}$ declines as we move along an isoquant increasing input X and decreasing input Y.

   e. Technologies differ in how much the MRTS changes as we move along an isoquant. At one extreme, inputs may be perfect substitutes, at another extreme, perfect complements. An intermediate case is the Cobb-Douglas production function $Q = F(L, K) = AL^{\alpha}K^{\beta}$, whose MRTS changes gradually as we move along an isoquant.

4. **Returns to scale**

   a. Economists determine whether large or small firms produce more effectively by examining returns to scale.

   b. A firm has (constant/increasing/decreasing) returns to scale if a proportional change in all inputs leads to (the same/a greater than/a less than) proportional change in output.

   c. Increasing returns to scale arise because of the specialization of inputs as well as certain physical laws. The reasons we observe decreasing returns to scale are more elusive. They include the presence of implicitly fixed inputs, and bureaucratic costs.

5. **Productivity differences and technological change**

   a. A firm is more productive, or has higher productivity, when it can produce more output using the same amount of inputs. Higher productivity corresponds to an upward shift in a firm's efficient production frontier, and an increase in its production function at every input combination.

   b. Intellectual property protection (patents) helps provide incentives for firms to innovate, although at the cost of creating monopoly power.

ADDITIONAL EXERCISES

Exercise 7.1: The law firm of Dewey, Cheetham, and Howe files claims against unscrupulous car repair shops that take advantage of consumers who know nothing about cars. A lawyer who takes a 20-minute break after every two hours of work can process one claim with six hours of work. If the lawyer takes a 20-minute break after every four hours of work she can process one claim with eight hours of work. If she takes a 20-minute break after every hour of work, she is a claim superwoman and can process one claim with just five hours of work. What is the efficient method of production for Dewey, Cheetham, and Howe? Graph its production possibilities set. What is its production function?

Exercise 7.2: Pete and Mary run a firm that packs coffee beans. The number of pounds of coffee they pack depends on the number of workers they hire. They are able to hire workers for a fraction of a day. The number of pounds of coffee they pack in a day is given by the production function $Q = F(L) = 10L$, where L is the number of hours of labor they hire. Graph their production function.

Exercise 7.3: Suppose that in Table 7.3 (page 218) the number of garden benches produced by 0, 1, 2, 3, and 4 workers is instead 0, 35, 70, 99, and 112. Calculate the marginal and average products of labor that would have resulted. Check that the relation between these average and marginal products satisfies the properties that we discussed in Section 7.2.

Exercise 7.4: Emily draws cartoons that she sells to her classmates. Her average product of labor is five cartoons per hour if she works for one hour, four per hour if she works for two hours, three per hour if she works for three hours, and two-and-a-half per hour if she works for four hours. What is her marginal product of labor at one, two, three, and four hours of work?

Exercise 7.5: "The marginal product of labor can never be negative." Is this statement correct? What does it assume?

Exercise 7.6: Suppose that a firm uses both labor (L) and capital (K) as inputs and has the long-run production function $Q = F(L, K) = L \times \sqrt{L + K}$. If its capital is fixed at $K = 10$ in the short run, what is its short-run production function? How much does it produce in the short run (using efficient production methods) if it hires one worker? Two workers? Three?

Exercise 7.7: Suppose that a firm's production function is $Q = F(L) = L^3 - 200L^2 + 10{,}000L$. It's marginal product of labor is $MP_L = 3L^2 - 400L + 10{,}000$. At what amount of labor input are the firm's average and marginal product of labor equal? Confirm that the average and marginal product curves satisfy the relationship discussed in the text.

Exercise 7.8: Suppose that John, April, and Tristan have two production plants for producing orange juice. They have a total of 850 crates of oranges and the marginal product of oranges in plant 1 is $MP_O^1 = 1{,}000 - O_1$ and in plant 2 is $MP_O^2 = 1{,}200 - 2O_2$. What is the best assignment of oranges between the two plants?

Exercise 7.9: Is the following statement true or false?: "If a firm has two plants for producing output using only labor and plant B is more productive than plant A, a manager who wants to get the most output from a fixed amount of labor should always assign more labor to plant B." If you think this is true, say why. If you think it is false, give an example to prove your point.

Exercise 7.10: You have an economics test in two weeks. It will cover both micro and macroeconomics. Each part will be worth 50 points. You have a total of 100 hours that you can spend studying for this exam. For the first 25 hours you spend studying microeconomics, you will get 1 point more for each hour of studying. After that, you will get 1 point more for each 3 hours you spend studying, up to the maximum possible of 50 points. Macroeconomics is different. For your first 15 hours of studying you will get 1 point for each 45 minutes you spend studying. After that, you will get 1 point for each 1.5 hours you spend up to the maximum of 50 points. How should you allocate your studying time to get the best grade? Why?

Exercise 7.11: Beta Inc. has two production plants that use finely divisible labor to produce its output. The marginal product of labor at plant 1 is $MP_L^1 = 100/L_1$, and the marginal product of labor at plant 2 is $MP_L^2 = 50/L_2$. Beta Inc. wants to find the best assignment of 90 workers between the two plants. What is it?

Exercise 7.12: A supermarket is considering adding self-scan checkout machines. Currently the supermarket checks out 200 customers an hour using 10 checkout clerks. Customers differ in their abilities to use these machines. Market research suggests that 20 percent of the store's customers can check themselves out using these machines in three minutes (on average), 30 percent can check themselves out in five minutes, and 50 percent will refuse to use the new machines. One employee can monitor up to four self-scan machines. If there are fewer than four machines, this employee can use her extra time in other productive ways. Draw an isoquant for checking out 200 customers an hour where the variable inputs are checkout clerks and self-scan checkout machines.

Exercise 7.13: You run a firm that has two plants in the same city. The two plants use the same two inputs to produce your output. A consulting firm just told you that the MRTS is different in your plants. Are you assigning your inputs correctly? [*Hint:* Look back at Example 4.3's discussion of gains from trade on page 111.]

Exercise 7.14: Jason has a boat-building firm. It uses labor L, capital K, and materials M, to build its boats. Its production function is $Q = F(L, K, M) = AL^{\alpha}K^{\beta}M^{\gamma}$. For what values of α, β, and γ does Jason's technology have constant returns to scale? Increasing returns to scale? Decreasing returns to scale?

Exercise 7.15: Suppose that because of a technological breakthrough a firm that uses labor and capital to produce its output is able to double its production for any given amounts of inputs. What happens to the firm's MRTS at any given input combination?

Exercise 7.16: Suppose that because of a technological breakthrough a firm that uses a single input to produce its output is able to double its production for any given amounts of inputs. What happens to the firm's average product of labor? What about its marginal product of labor?

Exercise 7.17: You are the manager of a new firm that can choose between two technologies for producing output using only labor. Technology A can produce two units of output for each hour of labor input. Technology B can produce three units of output for each hour of labor input up to 100 hours, and β units of output for each hour of labor above 100 hours. For what values of β is technology B more productive than technology A?

8

COST

LEARNING OBJECTIVES

After reading this chapter, students should be able to:

- Describe various types of cost and the characteristics of each.
- Identify a firm's least-cost input choice, and the firm's cost function, in the short- and long-run.
- Understand the concepts of average and marginal cost.
- Describe the effect of an input price change on the firm's least-cost input combination.
- Explain the relationship between short-run and long-run cost with one or more variable inputs.
- Define economies and diseconomies of scale and explain their relationship to the concept of returns to scale.

Michael Dell began selling personal computers out of his dorm room as an undergraduate at the University of Texas at Austin. In 1984, with $1,000 in start-up funds, he founded Dell Computer Corporation.

Dell saw great inefficiencies in the operations of giant rivals like IBM and Compaq. In response, he pioneered direct-to-consumer marketing of computers. Cutting out middlemen such as wholesalers and retailers, he pushed his company to produce PCs at the lowest possible cost. This strategy required some gutsy and insightful decisions, which we'll examine later in the chapter.

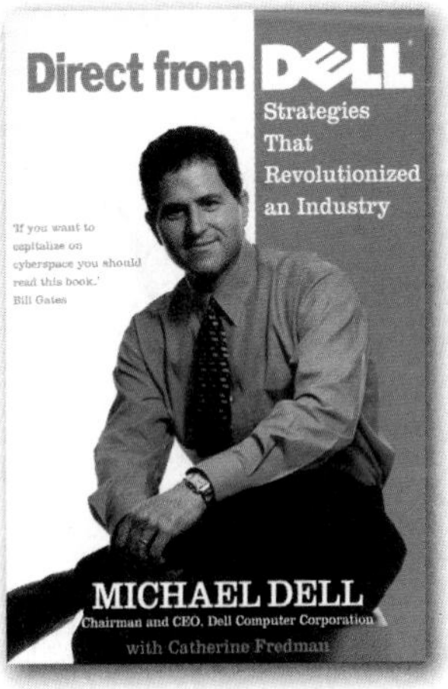

Michael Dell

Today, success in the PC market requires high-quality manufacturing at costs that are at or below those of competitors. Because Dell understood this point early on, his company profited handsomely. In 2004 Dell Computer Corporation's sales totaled $49.2 billion, and Michael Dell's personal net worth was more than $14 billion.

In Chapter 7, we studied technology and production. Once managers understand how they can produce their products, like Dell they need to figure out how to do so in the most economical way. In this chapter we'll study this problem by covering nine topics:

1. *Types of cost.* Some costs vary with the amount produced, while others do not. In addition, some costs may be avoided by shutting down production, while others are unavoidable. We'll discuss these distinctions and introduce the notion of a firm's cost function.

2. *What do economic costs include?* Sometimes the costs a firm incurs aren't immediately obvious. A firm's true costs include not only its out-of-pocket expenditures, but also the costs it incurs by forgoing opportunities to use resources in other ways.
3. *Short-run cost: one variable input.* In the simplest case, a firm uses only a single variable input to produce its output in the short run. We'll show how to determine a firm's cost function from its production function in this case.
4. *Long-run cost: cost minimization with two variable inputs.* In most cases, firms use many inputs to produce their product. In the long run, a firm can produce a given level of output using many technologically efficient methods, each involving different inputs and costs. We'll show how to find the method that results in the lowest possible cost and derive the firm's cost function, focusing on the simplest case in which the firm uses just two inputs.
5. *Average and marginal costs.* Just as average and marginal products are useful measures of a firm's productivity (see Chapter 7), average and marginal costs are useful measures of a firm's costs. We'll define these notions and discuss their relationships with one another.
6. *Effects of input price changes.* Changes in a firm's input prices generally lead to changes in its least-cost input combination. We'll study the directions of those effects.
7. *Short-run versus long-run costs.* We'll discuss the relationship between a firm's long-run and short-run costs.
8. *Economies and diseconomies of scale.* In Chapter 7 we discussed the notions of increasing and decreasing returns to scale. Here we'll examine the cost implications of returns to scale. This leads to the notions of economies and diseconomies of scale.

*9. *Multiproduct firms and economies of scope.* Most firms produce many products. One reason involves the presence of economies of scope, which arise when the cost of producing products together is lower than the cost of producing them separately. Sometimes diseconomies of scope discourage firms from producing multiple products. We'll define these concepts and discuss the reasons for their existence.

8.1 TYPES OF COST

A firm's **total cost** of producing a given level of output is the expenditure required to produce that output in the most economical way.

A firm's **total cost** of producing a particular level of output is the expenditure required to produce that output in the most economical way. We'll see in Chapter 9 (and later, again, in Chapters 14, 17, and 19) that to make good pricing and output decisions, managers need to know the total cost of producing different levels of output.

To illustrate, suppose the manager of an oil refinery is trying to decide how much gasoline to produce and sell at the going market price of $3 a gallon. She can sell either 1.5 or 1.2 million barrels of high-octane gasoline this month. To determine which is best (a decision that we'll study in Chapter 9), one thing she definitely needs to know is how much it costs to produce these two different amounts of gasoline.

How can she determine this? To produce 1.5 million barrels a month, the manager can use various combinations of crude oil, additives, and refining equipment. (In the terms of Chapter 7, these different input combinations correspond to her isoquant for 1.5 million gallons.) Gasoline additives, such as MTBE (methyl tertiary butyl ether), are costly. An alternative is to use catalytic reforming equipment, which requires expenditures on machinery. It also reduces yields, which means it requires more crude oil. Which method is cheaper, and what is its cost? And how does the answer change if she produces only 1.2 million barrels?

In this chapter, we'll show how to answer these questions. Specifically, taking the amount the firm wishes to produce as given (this choice will be the subject of Chapters 9, 14, 17, and 19), we'll ask how the firm can most economically produce that level of output, and what is its total cost of doing so. As in Chapter 7, for simplicity, we will mostly focus on the case of a firm that produces a single product. (An exception is Section 8.9.)

First, though, we need to introduce a few concepts.

We can break total cost into two types of costs. **Variable costs** are the costs of inputs that vary with the firm's output level. These costs typically include inputs like labor and materials. **Fixed costs** are the costs of inputs whose use does not vary as the firm's level of output changes, with the possible exception that the firm might not incur the cost if it decides to produce nothing.

Variable costs are the costs of inputs that vary with the firm's output level.

Fixed costs are the costs of inputs whose use does not vary as the firm's output changes, with the possible exception that the cost might not be incurred if the firm decides to produce nothing.

For example, a New York City taxicab owner needs to purchase a single taxicab medallion from the city regardless of how many hours he drives the taxi. That is a fixed cost. In contrast, the gasoline he needs to run his cab is a variable cost.

A fixed cost is **avoidable** if the firm doesn't incur the cost (or can recoup it) if it produces no output. For example, if the owner of the taxi cab can sell the medallion and recoup his initial expenditure, then the medallion cost is an avoidable fixed cost. A cost that is incurred even if the firm decides not to operate is **sunk**. For example, if New York City were to prohibit the resale of taxi medallions, then the taxicab owner's expenditure on the medallion, once incurred, is a sunk cost. Whether a fixed cost is avoidable or sunk can have important implications for decision making. (We've discussed this point in Section 3.3 and Add-On 3A.) Which it is (avoidable or sunk) can depend on the time frame we are considering. For example, if the taxi commission instead sells annual nontransferable taxi medallions, then the cost is sunk within the time frame of a year but avoidable over longer periods.

A fixed cost is **avoidable** if it is not incurred when the firm decides to produce no output. It is **sunk** if it is incurred even when the firm produces no output.

How do these distinctions (variable versus fixed costs, and avoidable versus sunk costs) relate to the concepts of variable and fixed inputs discussed in Chapter 7? The cost of an input that is fixed in the sense introduced in Chapter 7 is a sunk fixed cost; it does not vary with the firm's output level and can't be avoided. On the other hand, although the terminology is a little confusing, the cost of an input that is variable in the sense introduced in Chapter 7 can be an avoidable fixed cost. Consider, for example, the case of annual nontransferable taxi medallions. In the long run a taxi owner can decide to buy one or not; it is a variable input into his production process. But it is an (avoidable) fixed cost because its use is lumpy: to operate at all the owner needs a medallion, but he needs just one regardless of the number of hours he drives his cab.

The total cost of producing different levels of output is summarized in the firm's **cost function**, a function of the form *Total cost* = *C(Output)*. The firm's **variable cost function** gives the firm's variable cost at each possible combination of outputs. It is a function of the form *Variable cost* = *VC(Output)*. Since total cost equals fixed cost (*FC*) plus variable cost, we can write the firm's cost function as *C(Output)* = *FC* + *VC(Output)*.

A firm's **cost function** describes the total cost of producing each possible level of output. It is a function of the form *Total cost* = *C(Output)*.

A firm's **variable cost function** describes the variable cost of producing each possible level of output. It is a function of the form *Variable cost* = *VC(Output)*.

Let's look at an example.

Example 8.1

The Cost of Producing Garden Benches

In Example 7.1 (page 211) we determined Noah and Naomi's efficient production methods for assembling garden benches with up to four workers. Recall that Noah and Naomi produce their garden benches in a 1,000-square-foot garage. Let's suppose they've rented the garage for $1,000 a week, a cost they cannot avoid in the short run. The weekly wage of an assembly worker is $500. Table 8.1 shows the fixed, variable, and total costs of producing 33, 74, and 132 benches a week using the efficient production methods A, D, and F from Table 7.1 (page 211). Noah and Naomi's fixed cost is simply the cost of renting the garage. Their variable cost is the cost of hiring the assembly workers. Their total cost is the sum of the fixed and variable costs. Because these methods are efficient, they offer the lowest possible labor costs for producing those output levels. The table also shows the total, fixed, and variable costs of producing no output. Since the rental cost of the garage is sunk, producing nothing costs Noah and Naomi $1,000.

Table 8.1

Fixed, Variable, and Total Costs of Producing Garden Benches

Number of Garden Benches Produced per Week	Fixed Cost (per Week)	Variable Cost (per Week)	Total Cost (per Week)
0	$1,000	$0	$1,000
33	1,000	500	1,500
74	1,000	1,000	2,000
132	1,000	2,000	3,000

Application 8.1

Taking Flight: Variable and Fixed Costs at JetBlue

JetBlue Airways took to the air on February 11, 2000, with the inauguration of service between New York and Fort Lauderdale, Florida. CEO David Neeleman's vision was to offer a high-quality experience at a low price, and bring "humanity back to air travel." New planes, leather seats, live satellite TV—all would be part of the JetBlue experience. Within three years the airline was serving 27 cities around the country, making it one of the most successful new airline launches ever.

While Neeleman had a vision of what would make his new airline special, he also needed a keen understanding of his airline's costs. As a veteran in the airline industry, he knew all too well that a firm's ability to keep costs low can make the difference between success and bankruptcy court.

Let's examine JetBlue's costs. JetBlue produces air travel services—literally, leather seats flying through the air from one place to another, along with accompanying services like luggage transfer and satellite TV. When JetBlue's managers think about the cost of providing air travel service, they face both variable and fixed costs. One important variable cost is labor. Managers can adjust the number and

JetBlue CEO David Neeleman and one of his planes.

hours of the airline's flight attendants, ground crew, and ticket counter staff, depending on how many flights they plan to offer. Unlike managers at many traditional carriers (United, Delta, American), they can also adjust the number and hours of the airline's pilots, who are not unionized. Another important variable cost is jet fuel, which varies directly with the number of flights that managers schedule.

JetBlue also needs counter and gate space at airports. The airline has a 10-year lease with the Port Authority of New York for Terminal 6 at Kennedy Airport, JetBlue's hub. This cost is fixed: it cannot be adjusted if JetBlue alters the number of flights. Moreover, given the 10-year commitment (and assuming they cannot sublease it to another airline), it is a sunk cost: JetBlue must pay for the terminal even if it ceases to operate at Kennedy Airport.

JetBlue also rents gate and counter space on a monthly basis at other airports it serves. At some of these airports, JetBlue can rent this gate and counter space for just part of each day. Over periods longer than a month, this rental cost is fully variable, since JetBlue need only rent the gate for the period of the day when it has flights departing or arriving. At other airports, JetBlue must rent the gates for the entire day, so its rental cost is independent of the number of departures and arrivals (at least up to the gate capacity, which is beyond what JetBlue would schedule in most cities). At these airports, JetBlue's gate rental costs are a fixed cost. However, over periods longer than a month, they are avoidable: if managers decide not to serve these airports, they can simply stop renting the gates.

Another cost that is (mostly) fixed is the wages of the airline's administrative staff, including JetBlue's CEO, David Neeleman. Regardless of the number of flights, JetBlue needs a CEO and managers to head its finance, operations, and human resource departments. Since its contracts with all administrative personnel are short term, however, these are avoidable fixed costs.

What about the costs of the planes JetBlue flies? This cost is a bit more complicated. JetBlue owns some of its planes and leases others. Since we won't discuss the cost of owned durable goods until Section 8.2, let's focus on the leased planes. Whether those costs are fixed or variable depends on whether managers can alter the number of planes should they decide to alter the number of flights. Certainly, they can increase the number of leased planes whenever they want to. But what if they want to decrease that number? If the leases have opt-out clauses, can be renegotiated, or can be transferred to other airlines, then JetBlue's plane costs are variable costs. If not, they are fixed and sunk for the term of the lease.

8.2 WHAT DO ECONOMIC COSTS INCLUDE?

When you think of a firm's costs, its out-of-pocket expenditures on labor, materials, and rental of land and capital come readily to mind. But some of its costs are harder to identify. These do not involve out-of-pocket payments to others, but rather are hidden costs associated with lost opportunities to use resources to earn profits in other ways. Another tricky issue concerns the costs associated with capital equipment that the firm has previously purchased. In this section, we'll explain how to properly think about both of these kinds of costs.

Opportunity Costs

To produce their garden benches, Noah and Naomi hired workers and rented garage space. Were those their only costs? Not if they were spending their own time running their company. While the time they devoted to the business would not show up in their firm's accounts, it is still an economic cost of production, because Noah and Naomi could have been earning money doing something else. By spending their time running their firm, they are giving up the opportunity to earn a salary elsewhere. This forgone opportunity is an example of an opportunity cost. In general, an **opportunity cost** is the cost associated with forgoing the opportunity to employ a resource in its best alternative use (see also Section 3.1).

An **opportunity cost** is the cost associated with forgoing the opportunity to employ a resource in its best alternative use.

"And to think if I hadn't been home having dinner I might have missed this wonderful investment opportunity."

To give another example, suppose a firm has stored some materials. What is the true economic cost it incurs when it uses those materials in production? Since the firm incurs no out-of-pocket expenses in using these inputs, should it behave as if they are free? Alternatively, should the firm use some standard accounting rule for determining the cost of the inputs, based on their original purchase price?

If a well-functioning market exists for these inputs, the correct answer is that the cost of using a stored input equals the price the firm could sell it for. That is the firm's opportunity cost. By using the inputs, the firm forgoes the opportunity to sell them.

When managers make decisions, then, they must consider not only the costs that show up in the firm's accounting statements, but also its unstated opportunity costs, which are part of its true economic costs of production.

Application 8.2

The Cost of a Coors

Adolph Coors, Sr., opened the doors of his brewery in Golden, Colorado, in 1873. Today, Coors is one of the largest brewers in the United States, ranking third in sales behind Anheuser-Busch and Miller.

Coors' production strategy is unusual in that it makes most of its own inputs, a strategy known as *vertical integration*. Over the years, Coors has supplied its own rice, cans, coal, machinery, and trucking service. The company also owns the springs from which its "Rocky Mountain Spring Water" flows.[1] Why would Coors follow this strategy?

One often-cited reason for vertical integration is the desire to protect a firm's competitive position against cost increases due to input price fluctuations. Does this reasoning make sense? If the rice Coors grows is available for purchase elsewhere, the opportunity cost of using the company's rice supplies is exactly the market price. After all, instead of using a pound of that rice, managers could have sold it at the market price. This logic tells us that if the input in question is available in the marketplace, pursuing integration to protect Coors' competitive position against cost increases doesn't make sense.

A company may have other legitimate motives for integration. For example, if Coors needs a special kind of rice tailored specifically to its own needs, procuring it through market transactions may sometimes be difficult. To ensure the availability of a key ingredient, managers may decide to produce their own. Another possibility is that a firm's managers or owners may be risk-averse and want to stabilize the firm's cash flow. (We'll discuss risk aversion in Chapter 11.) Investments whose payoffs rise when the firm's profit falls can do this. Coors' vertical integration is an example of such an investment, since when input price increases cause Coors' true economic cost of beer production to rise, and beer profit therefore to fall, the payoff from production of the input rises (even if it is sold to other firms).

[1]To read more about Coors' vertical integration see "Adolph Coors in the Brewing Industry," Harvard Business School Case No. 9-388-014.

The User Cost of Capital

Most firms own much of the capital they use in production. Once the firm has paid for that capital, it may incur little or no additional out-of-pocket cost. But what is the true economic cost associated with using that capital? Thinking about opportunity costs provides the answer. If a well-functioning rental market for capital exists, then the cost of using the capital is equal to the market rental price. This is the amount of money the firm forgoes by using its own capital instead of renting it to another firm. For example, if a firm owns a five-year-old truck, the cost of using the truck for a year is simply the market rental price for a five-year-old truck.[2]

This cost typically differs from the costs shown in a firm's financial accounts. Sometimes long-lived assets are *expensed*, meaning that the firm records the full amount of the purchase in the year it occurs and nothing in later years. More often, a firm *amortizes* the purchase cost of a long-lived asset, recording part of the price as an expense in each year of the asset's lifetime using a standard depreciation schedule. Neither of these methods reveals the true cost of using the asset, however, which is the market rental price.

8.3 SHORT-RUN COST: ONE VARIABLE INPUT

In Chapter 7 we distinguished between production in the short run, where some inputs are fixed, and the long run, where all inputs are variable. We then studied production in a simple case in which a firm used two inputs in the long run, one of which is fixed in the short run. For Noah and Naomi's garden bench company, for example, the amount of garage space was fixed in the short run, but variable in the long run, while the number of assembly workers was variable in both the long and the short run. In Sections 8.3 and 8.4 we'll investigate such a firm's short-run and long-run costs. Here we'll focus on the short run.

Determining a firm's short-run cost function with only one variable input is simple. Once we have identified the efficient method for producing a given level of output, we know immediately how much of the variable input the firm must use. The firm's variable cost is equal to the cost of that amount of input; its total cost is the variable cost plus any fixed costs.

To illustrate, let's return to Noah and Naomi's garden bench company.

Example 8.2

The Cost of Producing Garden Benches, Part 2

To derive Noah and Naomi's variable cost curve, we'll start with their production function. Figure 8.1(a) shows the production function for using up to four assembly workers when workers can be hired for part of the week and output is finely divisible, reproduced from Figure 7.2 (page 214). We've also written the cost of the labor hired (at $500 per week) in dark red on the horizontal axis. This is Noah and Naomi's variable cost. Figure 8.1(b) shows Noah

[2]Sometimes there is no well-functioning rental market for a capital good. What's the cost of using the truck then? We'll return to this question in Chapter 10.

and Naomi's variable cost curve. Note that we've flipped the production function in Figure 8.1(a) by switching the two axes, recording the number of garden benches produced on the horizontal axis and the variable (labor) cost on the vertical axis. The variable costs of points A, D, and F correspond to the amounts listed in the third column of Table 8.1 (page 252).

Figure 8.2 shows this variable cost curve in dark red (labeled *VC*), along with Noah and Naomi's fixed and total cost curves in green and medium red, respectively (labeled *FC* and *C*). The fixed cost curve is a straight line at $1,000.[3] The total cost curve is the vertical sum of the fixed and variable cost curves. For example, the height of the total cost curve at $Q = 33$ is $1,500, which equals the height of the fixed cost curve ($1,000) plus the height of the variable cost curve ($500) at that output level.

Example 8.2 showed how to determine a firm's short-run costs graphically. We can also find a firm's short-run cost function using algebra. To do so, we'll use the firm's production function to find the amount of input needed to produce a given amount of output. For example, suppose a firm's short-run production function is $Q = F(L) = 2L$. This formula means that each worker produces two units of output. Solving for the quantity of labor L needed for any quantity of output Q tells us that $L = Q/2$. In other words, the firm

Figure 8.1

Deriving Noah and Naomi's Variable Cost Function from Their Production Function. Figure (a) shows Noah and Naomi's production function from Figure 7.2, in which the only variable input is the number of assembly workers. Here we've added the cost of hiring various numbers of workers in dark red on the horizontal axis. Figure (b) shows Noah and Naomi's variable cost function. We've flipped the production function in figure (a) putting variable (labor) cost on the vertical axis and the number of benches produced on the horizontal axis.

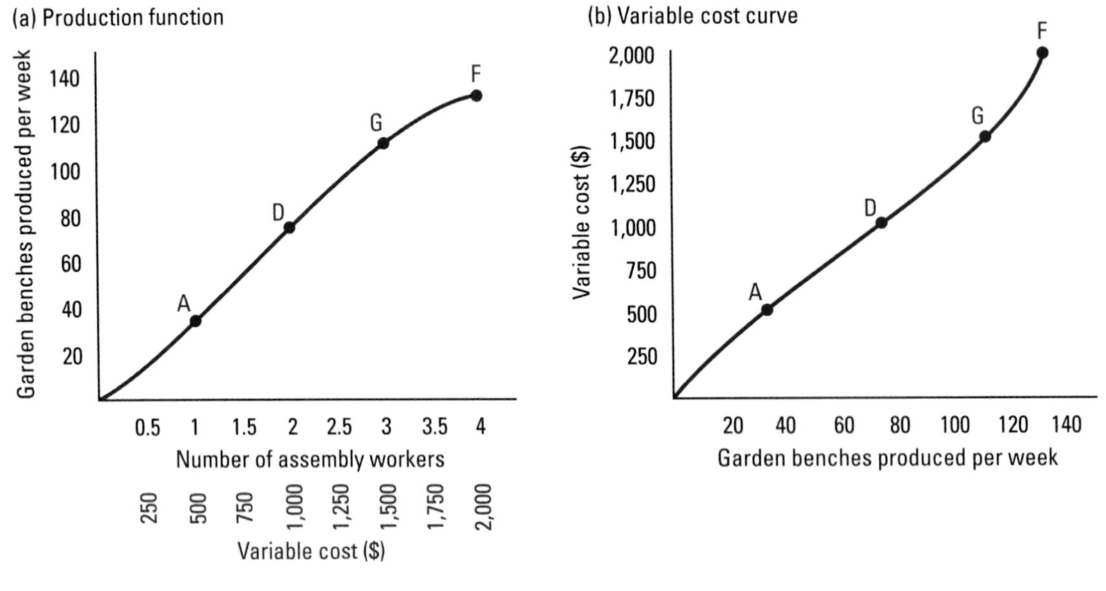

[3]Here we are supposing that Noah and Naomi's only fixed cost is the cost of their garage space (we ignore, for simplicity, any opportunity cost of their time).

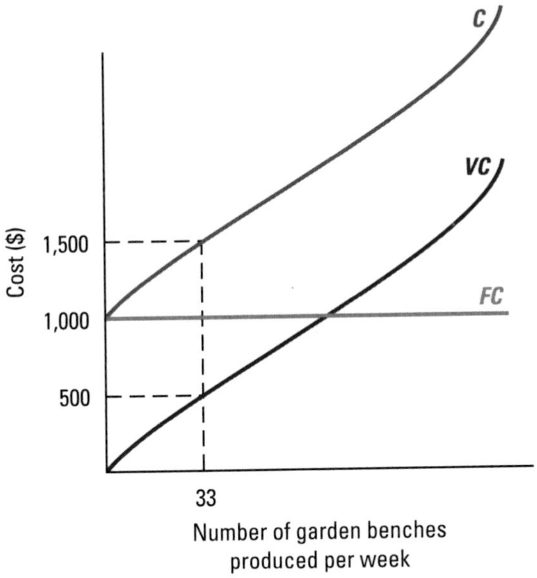

Figure 8.2

Noah and Naomi's Fixed, Variable, and Total Cost Curves. The dark red curve is Noah and Naomi's variable cost function, from Figure 8.1(b). The green curve is their fixed cost function, which is $1,000 at every output level. The medium red curve is Noah and Naomi's total cost function, which equals the vertical sum of their fixed and variable cost curves.

needs $Q/2$ units of labor to produce Q units of output. The firm's variable cost function for producing Q units of output is simply this labor requirement times the wage rate W. For example, if the wage rate is \$15 per hour, the variable cost function is $VC(Q) = (15/2)Q$. If the firm has sunk fixed costs associated with its fixed inputs of \$100 per week, then its cost function is $C(Q) = 100 + (15/2)Q$.

WORKED-OUT PROBLEM 8.1

The Problem Noah and Naomi have decided to start a firm to produce garden tables. Their short-run weekly production function is $Q = F(L) = \sqrt{L}$, where L is the amount of labor they hire, in hours. The wage rate is \$12 an hour. Noah and Naomi have committed to a long-term lease of their production facility, which costs them \$250 a week. This is a sunk cost. What is their short-run weekly cost function for producing garden tables? Graph it.

The Solution The relationship between Noah and Naomi's labor input and their garden table output is described by the formula $Q = \sqrt{L}$. Squaring both sides of this formula, we can solve for the number of hours of labor needed to produce Q tables per week: $L = Q^2$. Multiplying by the wage rate, we get the variable cost function $VC(Q) = 12Q^2$. The short-run cost function is therefore $C(Q) = 250 + 12Q^2$, shown in Figure 8.3.

IN-TEXT EXERCISE 8.1 **Suppose Noah and Naomi's short-run weekly production function is $Q = F(L) = 2\sqrt{L}$ and the wage rate is \$12 an hour. Suppose also that the sunk cost (for their fixed garage-space input) is \$500 a week. What is their short-run weekly cost function? Graph this cost function.**

Figure 8.3
Cost Function in Worked-Out Problem 8.1. The figure shows Noah and Naomi's short-run cost function; their fixed cost, a long-term lease, is sunk.

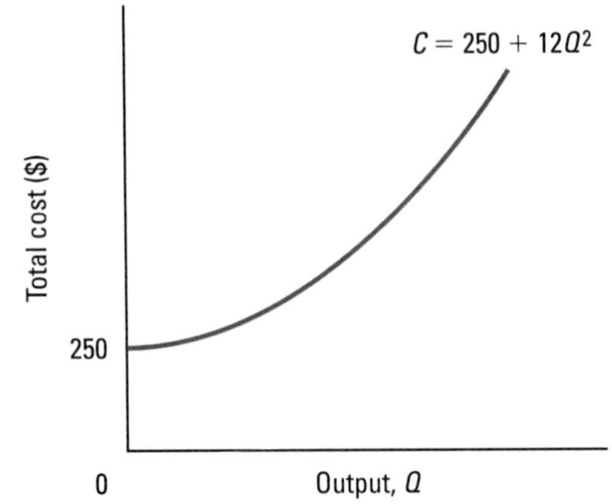

Application 8.3

Variable Costs for an Electric Utility

Usually we don't think much about where our electricity comes from or what it costs. All that changes rapidly, however, when costs rise suddenly or continued service is threatened. In October 2003, for example, former Governor Gray Davis of California lost his job to actor Arnold Schwarzenegger in large part because California's botched deregulation of the electric utility market led to blackouts throughout the state.

Electricity can be produced using a variety of technologies and inputs, including coal, natural gas, wind, water, and nuclear reactions. Different firms use different mixes of these inputs. Some have invested only in technologies that use natural gas. In the short run, when the capital of these technologically specialized firms is fixed, natural gas is essentially their only variable input.

One such firm is Calpine, which generates approximately 30,000 megawatts of electricity per hour across the United States, Mexico, and the United Kingdom—enough to meet the needs of more than 22 million households. In Texas, Calpine operates only gas-fired generating units. These units differ in efficiency. Most but not all of Calpine's generating capacity in Texas comes from modern combined-cycle units which are more efficient at turning gas into electricity than are older units.

What is Calpine's daily variable cost function in Texas? For any amount of electricity it produces in Texas, Calpine's efficient production method is simple. First use the most efficient generating unit until it hits capacity, then use the second most efficient unit, and so on until the desired output level is reached. Calpine's variable cost function is the cost of the natural gas used in this efficient production method.

Calpine's Freestone Energy Center in Fairfield, Texas.

Each of Calpine's 10 generating units has a different level of efficiency, resulting in 10 different cost levels. Table 8.2 lists these costs per megawatt hour on August 6, 2002, along with Calpine's capacity at each cost level. Most of its units have similar costs, ranging from about $23 to $26 per megawatt hour. The least efficient units, however, have costs of about $36 per megawatt hour.

Figure 8.4 shows Calpine's variable cost curve. Notice that this curve is a series of ten line segments. The slope of each line segment is equal to the cost per megawatt-hour of the corresponding generating unit in Table 8.2. If you lay a ruler along these segments, you'll see that they grow progressively steeper (if only slightly so), reflecting the fact that Calpine uses its most efficient generating units first. This is most pronounced for the last two steps, which are shown at a larger scale in the magnified box.

Table 8.2
Calpine's Costs for Various Generating Units in Texas (August 6, 2002)

Cost per Megawatt Hour	Capacity (Megawatt Hours)
$22.893	982
23.336	545
23.516	455
23.886	381
24.117	1,151
24.258	150
24.448	262
24.497	302
26.176	524
36.047	115

Figure 8.4
Calpine's Variable Cost Curve for Generating Electricity in Texas

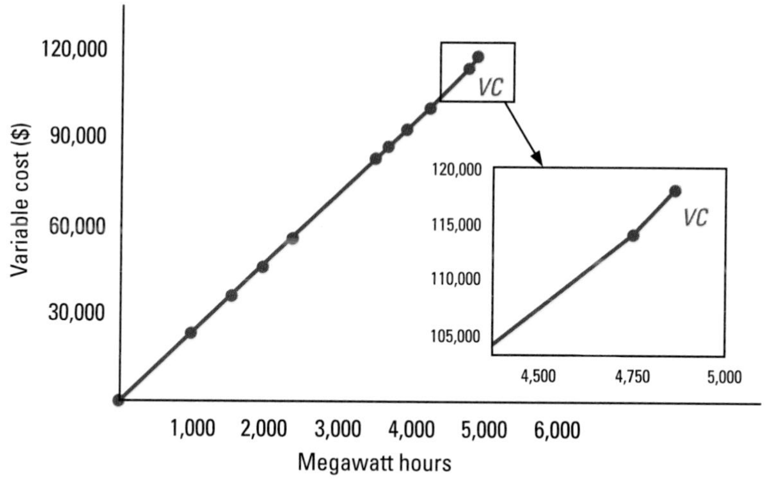

8.4 LONG-RUN COST: COST MINIMIZATION WITH TWO VARIABLE INPUTS

Let's turn now to the long run, in which all of the firm's inputs are variable. As we saw in Section 7.3, in this case a firm will usually have many efficient ways to produce a given amount of output, each with a different input combination. Which of these is cheapest?

For simplicity, we'll suppose as we did in Section 7.3 that the firm has only two variable inputs, labor (L) and capital (K). We'll also assume through most of our discussion that the firm's output and inputs are finely divisible. We'll return to this point at the end of the section to discuss the case of a lumpy input, which gives rise to an avoidable fixed cost.

Before we start, we should note that, in reality, most firms have many inputs that are variable in the short run. The lessons of this section apply as well to such a firm's problem of minimizing its cost of production in the short run.

Let's start with an example.

Example 8.3

The Cost of Producing Garden Benches, Part 3

Suppose Noah and Naomi can vary both the amount of garage space they rent and the number of assembly workers they hire per week. Both these inputs and their output are finely divisible. As in Example 8.1, an assembly worker earns $500 per week. Garage space rents for $1 per square foot per week. (In Example 8.1, a 1,000-square-foot garage rented for $1,000.) These are Noah and Naomi's only inputs.

Figure 8.5 reproduces Figure 7.8 (page 228). Each point on the isoquant represents the labor and capital required to produce 140 garden benches per week efficiently. While all those input combinations are associated with efficient production methods, their costs are not equal. For example, one efficient method (labeled A in the figure) uses two workers and a 2,500-square-foot garage at a cost of $3,500 per week. Another one (B) uses five workers and a 1,000-square-foot garage, also at a cost of $3,500 per week. Yet another efficient method (D) uses three workers and a 1,500-square-foot garage at a cost of $3,000 per week. Methods A and B are equally costly and more costly than D. Are there any less expensive input combinations than these three on the isoquant? Which is the least expensive one, and what is its cost? We'll see how to answer this last question next.

Figure 8.5
Isoquant for Producing 140 Garden Benches per Week. This isoquant shows the combinations of assembly workers and garage space that Noah and Naomi can use to produce 140 garden benches a week given efficient production methods. Different points on the isoquant involve different costs. For example, since a worker earns $500 per week and garage space rents for $1 per square foot per week, the costs of input combinations A and B are both $3,500 per week, while the cost of input combination D is $3,000 per week.

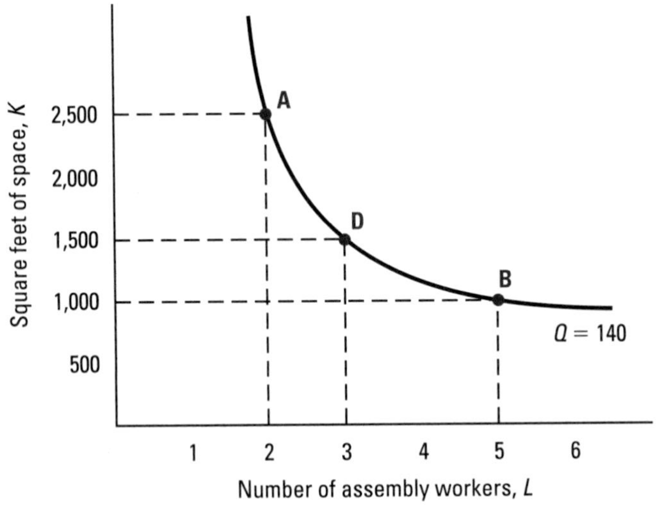

Isocost Lines

Let's begin by finding the least-costly method of production graphically. To do so, we start by identifying all possible input combinations with the same cost. Together they form an **isocost line**. Figure 8.6(a) shows Noah and Naomi's isocost line for a total expenditure of \$3,500 a week when, on a weekly basis, workers earn \$500 and garage space rents for \$1 per square foot. Input combinations A and B in Example 8.3 lie on this line. But so do other points, like input combination E with three workers and a 2,000-square-foot garage.

An **isocost line** contains all the input combinations with the same cost.

In general, if W is the cost of a unit of labor and R is the cost of a unit of capital, the isocost line for total cost C satisfies the formula:

$$WL + RK = C$$

Rearranging this formula, we can solve for the level of capital K that is associated with each level of labor L on this line:

$$K = \left(\frac{C}{R}\right) - \left(\frac{W}{R}\right)L$$

For example, the isocost line in Figure 8.6(a) can be represented as

$$K = \left(\frac{3{,}500}{1}\right) - \left(\frac{500}{1}\right)L = 3{,}500 - 500L$$

The slope of an isocost line is equal to $-(W/R)$, the negative of the ratio of input prices.

There is a close relationship between firms' isocost lines and consumers' budget lines, discussed in Section 5.1. In each case, the line shows the bundles (of inputs or goods) that

Figure 8.6

Isocost Lines for Producing Garden Benches. Figure (a) shows Noah and Naomi's isocost line for a total cost of \$3,500 per week. This line contains all the input combinations whose total cost is \$3,500. It includes the input combinations A and B, as well as many others such as E. Figure (b) shows several isocost lines (corresponding to total costs of \$2,500, \$3,500, and \$4,500) in Noah and Naomi's family of isocost lines. These lines lie parallel to one another, with slope equal to $-(\frac{W}{R}) = -(\frac{500}{1}) = -500$. Lines that lie farther from the origin correspond to higher levels of total cost.

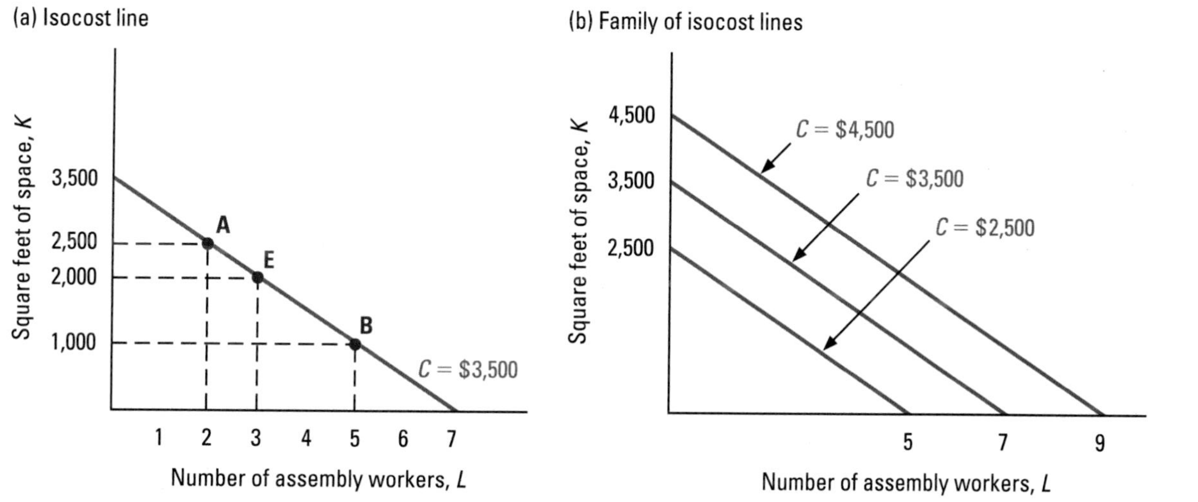

have the same cost, and its slope is the negative of the price ratio. Like a consumer's budget line, an isocost line separates the points that cost less than C, all of which lie below the isocost line, from the points that cost more than C, all of which lie above it.

A family of isocost lines contains, for given input prices, the isocost lines for all of the possible cost levels of the firm.

Each level of cost C has its own isocost line. If we were to draw an isocost line for every cost level C, we would have a **family of isocost lines**. All members of a family of isocost lines are parallel, because all have a slope that is equal to the negative of the same price ratio, $-(W/R)$. Isocost lines associated with a lower total cost lie closer to the origin. Figure 8.6(b), for example, shows three of Noah and Naomi's isocost lines, corresponding to the cost levels \$2,500, \$3,500, and \$4,500.

Least-Cost Production

How do we find the least-cost input combination for a given level of output? We do so by finding the lowest isocost line that touches the isoquant for producing that level of output. Let's look at an example. Figure 8.7 shows again Noah and Naomi's isoquant for 140 garden benches a week. It also shows two isocost lines, one of them for a total cost of \$3,500. Note that this line intersects the isoquant at two points, point A (with two workers and 2,500 square feet of garage space) and point B (with five workers and 1,000 square feet of garage space). Neither of these points is the least-cost input combination, because this isn't the lowest isocost line that touches the isoquant. The least-cost input combination is point D, which uses three workers and 1,500 square feet of garage space. It lies on the dark red isocost line representing the cost level $C =$ \$3,000. No lower isocost line touches the 140-bench isoquant.

We can easily recognize a least-cost input combination for producing Q units by applying the following simple rule:

The No-Overlap Rule The area below the isocost line that contains the firm's least-cost input combination for producing Q units does not overlap with the area above the Q-unit isoquant.

In Figure 8.7, for example, the area below the isocost line that contains input combination A overlaps with the area above the 140-bench isoquant; A is therefore not the least-cost input combination. In contrast, the area below the isocost line that contains input combination D does not overlap with the area above the 140-bench isoquant; D is a least-cost input combination.

Figure 8.7 looks a lot like the figures we saw when we studied consumer choice in Chapter 5, and the no-overlap rule for least-cost production is a lot like the no-overlap rule for consumer choice. This is no accident. There, the consumer was trying to reach the highest possible indifference curve while remaining on the budget line. Here, the firm is trying to reach the lowest possible isocost line while remaining on the isoquant. In each case, a decision maker is trying to spend money in an economically efficient way—in one case, to maximize well-being given a fixed budget; in the other, to minimize cost given a fixed production level.

Example 8.4 illustrates a particularly easy application of the no-overlap rule: the case in which production involves fixed proportions.

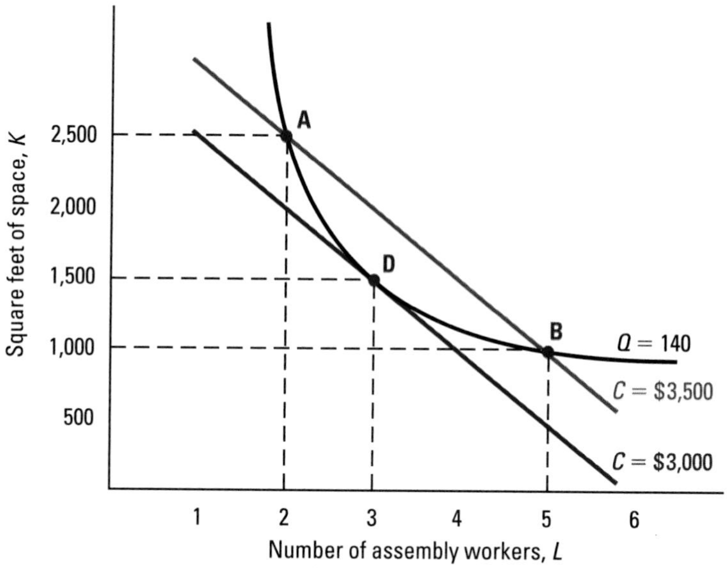

Figure 8.7

Noah and Naomi's Least-Cost Method for Producing 140 Garden Benches per Week. The least-cost method for producing 140 garden benches per week is the point on the 140-unit isoquant that lies on the lowest isocost line. In this figure, the lowest isocost line, shown in dark red, represents a cost of $3,000 per week. The least-cost input combination is point D, representing the input combination with three workers and 1,500 square feet of space.

Example 8.4

The Least-Cost Input Combination for Salt

Recall the technology for producing salt, described in Section 7.3 on page 236. Figure 8.8 shows an isoquant for producing 254 grams of salt, which requires 154 grams of chlorine and 100 grams of sodium. Also shown in red are several isocost lines corresponding to some given prices of chlorine and sodium. The least-cost input combination is point A, which is the only point on the isoquant that satisfies the no-overlap rule. To minimize production costs requires purchasing inputs in exactly the required ratio. Any other choice on the isoquant would involve purchasing more of some input than is necessary.

Interior Solutions

Let's look at this issue in a little more detail. An input combination is an **interior choice** if it uses at least a little bit of every input. When the least-cost input combination is an interior choice, we call it an **interior solution**. We'll consider these first.

An input combination is an **interior choice** if it uses at least a little bit of every input. When the least-cost input combination is an interior choice, we call it an **interior solution.**

Input combination D in Figure 8.7 is an interior solution. Notice that Noah and Naomi's 140-bench isoquant has the same slope at input combination D as does their $3,000-isocost line through this point. That is, at input combination D, the isocost line is tangent to the isoquant.[4] For this reason, we say that input combination D satisfies the **tangency condition**. In fact, interior solutions *always* satisfy the tangency condition: if the isocost line were *not* tangent to the isoquant, as at point A, then the isocost line would cross the isoquant, creating an overlap between the area under the isocost line and the area above

An input combination satisfies the **tangency condition** if, at that input combination, the isocost line is tangent to the isoquant.

[4] Recall that a line is tangent to a curve at a point if the line and the curve have the same slope at that point.

Figure 8.8

The Least-Cost Method of Making Salt. This figure shows the isoquant for making 254 grams of salt, a fixed-proportion production process that requires that sodium and chlorine be combined in a 1:1.54 ratio. The least-cost production method lies at point A where the dark red isocost line touches the isoquant; it represents 100 grams of sodium and 154 grams of chlorine.

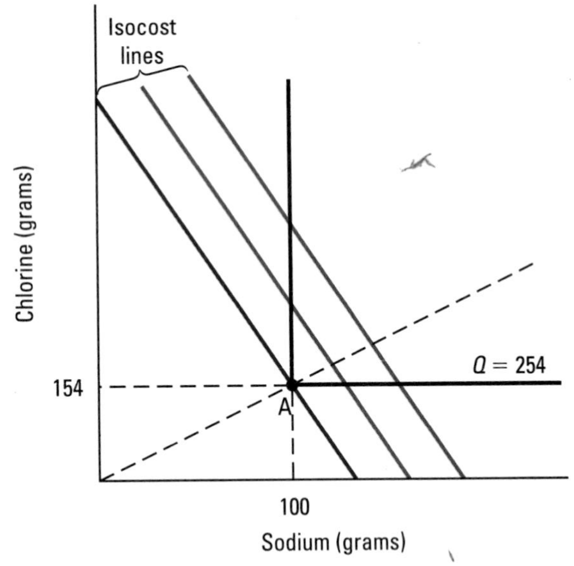

the isoquant. According to the no-overlap rule, such input combinations don't minimize the cost of production.

Notice again the parallel with our study of consumer choice in Chapter 5. At an interior solution to a consumer's choice problem, the consumer's budget line is tangent to her indifference curve; here, at an interior solution to a firm's cost minimization problem, the firm's isocost line is tangent to its isoquant.

An Implication of the Tangency Condition The tangency condition can be restated in terms of a relationship between the ratio of the firm's marginal products and the ratio of its input prices. To derive this relationship, recall from Section 7.3 that the slope of the firm's isoquant is equal to the firm's marginal rate of technical substitution for labor with capital ($MRTS_{LK}$) times negative one. In turn, the $MRTS_{LK}$ is equal to the ratio of the firm's marginal product of labor to its marginal product of capital:

$$MRTS_{LK} = \frac{MP_L}{MP_K}$$

The slope of the firm's isocost lines, on the other hand, equals $-(W/R)$. The tangency condition is therefore equivalent to the statement that the ratio of marginal products equals the ratio of input prices:

$$\frac{MP_L}{MP_K} = \frac{W}{R} \qquad (1)$$

Formula (1) has many important implications and applications. For example, in worked-out problem 8.2, we'll see that it can provide an easy way to identify a firm's least-cost input combination.

The formula can be interpreted as another example of the general principle that marginal benefit should equal marginal cost at a best choice (see Section 3.2). As we move from northwest to southeast along an isoquant, the amount of labor used increases. The manager's choice can therefore be thought of as a decision of how much labor to use. The marginal cost of using one more unit of labor is W; the marginal benefit equals the resulting reduction in expenditures on capital. This saving equals the resulting reduction in capital—which equals $MRTS_{LK}$—times the cost of capital R. When the firm's best choice is interior, this marginal benefit must equal the marginal cost, so that

$$R \times MRTS_{LK} = W$$

Since $MRTS_{LK}$ equals the ratio of the inputs' marginal products, this implies that

$$R\left(\frac{MP_L}{MP_K}\right) = W$$

Dividing both sides of this expression by R gives us formula (1).

We can also write formula (1) as

$$\frac{MP_L}{W} = \frac{MP_K}{R} \qquad \textbf{(2)}$$

The left-hand side of formula (2) can be interpreted as the increase in output for each extra dollar the firm spends on labor. To see why, observe that the firm can hire $(1/W)$ additional units of labor by spending one dollar more on labor. Multiplying this extra amount of labor by MP_L gives the amount of extra output this extra labor produces. For similar reasons, the right-hand side can be interpreted as the increase in output for each extra dollar the firm spends on capital.

Formula (2) nicely captures the idea of least-cost production: if the firm is using a least-cost input combination, then the marginal product of a dollar spent on labor must equal the marginal product of a dollar spent on capital. If that were not the case, the firm could produce more by shifting a dollar of its expenditure from the input with a lower marginal product per dollar to the one with a higher marginal product per dollar. It could then reduce both inputs, producing the original output at lower cost.[5]

Boundary Solutions

A firm's least-cost input combination may not be an interior solution, however. Some inputs may not be used at all. This will happen when a particular input is not very productive compared to its cost. (In fact, there is *no* firm that uses *every* conceivable input!)

When the least-cost input combination excludes some inputs it is called a **boundary solution**. In Section 7.3, for example, we saw that for some jobs (like janitors), high school and college-educated workers, denoted H and C, are perfect substitutes. The isoquant for producing 100 units of output is then a straight line with the slope -1, as shown in black in Figure 8.9. The wage rate, however, is higher for college-educated workers. This discrepancy implies that the firm's isocost lines, shown in red in Figure 8.9, are everywhere flatter than its isoquant [their slope is $-(W_H/W_C)$, which is closer to zero than -1]. As a result, the firm's least-cost input combination, point A, involves hiring only high school–educated workers (that is the only point on the isoquant at which the no-overlap rule holds). Notice, though, that the tangency condition does not hold at point A. Rather, $(MP_H/MP_C) > (W_H/W_C)$ at this point—that is, the marginal rate of technical substitution for labor with capital exceeds the input price ratio. More generally, for the least-cost input combination to use no college-educated labor, it must be that $(MP_H/W_H) \geq (MP_C/W_C)$—a

If the least-cost input combination excludes some inputs it is a **boundary solution.**

[5]As this logic suggests, if the firm has more than two inputs, the tangency condition must hold for any two inputs that the firm uses in positive amounts. To see this, observe that holding all other inputs fixed, the firm must be choosing those two inputs in a way that minimizes the firm's cost.

dollar spent on the marginal high school-educated worker must produce at least as much output as a dollar spent on the marginal college-educated worker, or else the firm would do better producing its output with at least some college-educated workers. That is, it must be that $(MP_H/MP_C) \geq (W_H/W_C)$.[6]

By similar reasoning, if a firm's least-cost input combination uses only college–educated workers, then it must be that $(MP_H/MP_C) \leq (W_H/W_C)$ at that point.

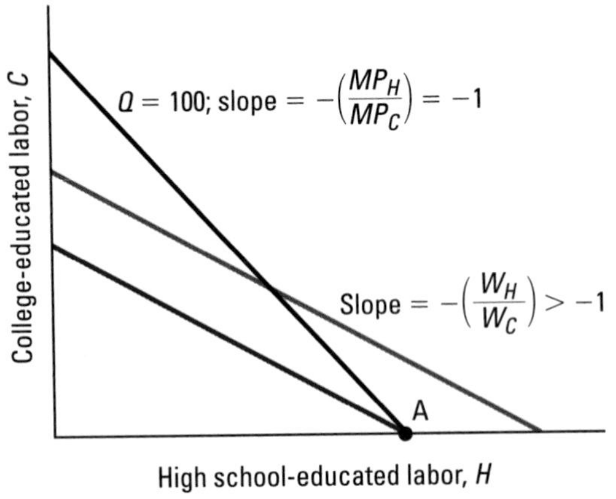

Figure 8.9

A Boundary Solution when High School and College Graduates are Perfect Substitutes. This figure shows a case in which high school (H) and college (C) graduates are equally productive, and therefore perfect substitutes. Since the wage rate of college graduates is higher, the least-cost method of production involves hiring only high school graduates. At the firm's least-cost input combination, point A, $(MP_H/MP_C) > (W_H/W_C)$.

Application 8.4

Input Substitution at Dell Computer Corporation

In 1984 Michael Dell noticed that computer manufacturers produced their products long before consumers bought them. A personal computer manufacturer such as IBM or Compaq would order large inventories of parts, use them to produce many computers, and ship the computers to retailers, where they would sit on the shelf until purchased. The process would start many months before a computer was actually sold to a consumer.

Dell organized his production process in a very different way. Rather than build his computers before consumers made their purchases, he built them only after an order was placed. He also implemented a production method known as *just-in-time manufacturing,* in which a firm purchases inputs only as they are needed, rather than keeping large inventories of parts.

Delaying the assembly of computers and purchase of parts can lower production costs significantly. The price of computer parts falls quickly over time, sometimes 10 percent in just a couple of months. By producing only after an order is in hand and buying parts just before assembly, Dell delays its purchases, buying at lower prices. This strategy also allows Dell to keep its money in the bank longer where it earns interest (the loss of interest is an important opportunity cost in manufacturing).[7]

Implementing this production system, however, required an investment in capital. Consumers would be happy only if Dell could assemble their computers quickly and reliably. To do so, Dell needed to invest in manufacturing equipment that would speed production and in information technology that would ensure the availability of parts in the right place at the right time. So Dell's manufacturing strategy relied on input substitution: it substituted manufacturing equipment and information technology for inventories of parts and finished goods.

[6]The inequality reflects the same properties of boundary choices that we encountered in our discussion of marginal benefit, marginal cost, and the No Marginal Improvement Principle in the appendix of Chapter 3. Here, at point A the number of high school-educated workers cannot be increased any further along the isoquant. So the marginal benefit of a high school-educated worker, $W_C \times (MP_H/MP_C)$, must not be less than the marginal cost, W_H, which is equivalent to saying that $(MP_H/MP_C) \geq (W_H/W_C)$.

[7]See Chapter 10 for a discussion of interest and the time value of money.

Finding the Least-Cost Input Combination

How can we find a firm's least-cost input combination? The tangency condition leads to a useful method for doing so. In parallel to our study of consumer choice, matters are particularly easy when the firm's isoquant for the desired level of output has a declining MRTS. In that case, if we find an interior input combination at which formula (1) (and, hence, the tangency condition) holds, that input combination must also satisfy the no-overlap rule and so must be the least-cost input combination. You can see why in Figure 8.7: since the tangency condition holds at point D and the isoquant has a declining MRTS, the isoquant becomes steeper to the left of point D and flatter to the right. In either direction, it veers away from and remains above the isocost line, as shown. So input combination D must satisfy the no-overlap rule and therefore be the least-cost input combination.

Worked-out problem 8.2 illustrates how to use this method to find a least-cost input combination using algebra.

WORKED-OUT PROBLEM 8.2

The Problem Hannah and Sam run Moretown Makeovers, a home remodeling business. The number of square feet they can remodel in a week is described by the Cobb-Douglas production function $Q = F(L, K) = 10L^{0.5}K^{0.5}$ (see Section 7.3), where L is their number of workers and K is units of capital. The wage rate is \$1,000 per week, and a unit of capital costs \$250 per week. What is their least-cost input combination for remodeling 100 square feet a week? What is their total cost?

The Solution In Section 7.3 we saw that the $MRTS_{LK}$ for the Cobb-Douglas production function $Q = F(L, K) = 10L^{\alpha}K^{\beta}$ is

$$MRTS_{LK} = \left(\frac{\alpha}{\beta}\right)\left(\frac{K}{L}\right)$$

which has a declining MRTS. Let's look for an interior input combination at which formula (1) holds. To locate this point, we need to set $MRTS_{LK}$ equal to the input price ratio:

$$\left(\frac{\alpha}{\beta}\right)\left(\frac{K}{L}\right) = \left(\frac{W}{R}\right) \qquad \textbf{(3)}$$

Substituting the values $\alpha = 0.5$, $\beta = 0.5$, $W = 1{,}000$, and $R = 250$ tells us that

$$\left(\frac{K}{L}\right) = 4$$

That is, the tangency condition holds at the point on the 100-square-foot isoquant at which the capital-labor ratio equals 4 (meaning that the number of units of capital is four times the number of workers). When Hannah and Sam use L units of labor and $4L$ units of capital, output is

$$F(L, 4L) = 10L^{0.5}(4L)^{0.5} = 10L^{0.5}2L^{0.5} = 20L$$

So to remodel 100 square feet a week requires $L = 5$. Their least-cost input combination therefore uses five workers and 20 units of capital. Their total cost is \$10,000 per week [$= (5 \times 1{,}000) + (20 \times 250)$].

IN-TEXT EXERCISE 8.2 **Suppose instead that Hannah and Sam need to remodel 200 square feet a week. Their production function and input prices are the same as in worked-out problem 8.2. What is their least-cost input combination? What is their total cost?**

When the firm's isoquant for the desired level of output does not have a declining MRTS, we can still use the tangency condition to find the least-cost input combination, but matters are a little more complicated. We can now use a procedure like the one developed in Section 3.2 (see also the two-step procedure in the appendix of Chapter 3). We first identify interior input combinations that satisfy the tangency condition, if any. We then compare the costs of those input combinations to the costs of any input combinations that use none of some inputs (boundary solutions).

The Firm's Cost Function

Recall that the firm's cost function summarizes how total cost varies with the firm's output level, for fixed input prices. To determine the firm's cost function, we therefore need to find its least-cost input combination for every output level.

Figure 8.10 shows a firm's least-cost input combinations at 100, 200, and 300 units of output, for fixed input prices. They are points D, E, and F, respectively. If we were to compare many different output levels, the least-cost points would form a curve, like the one shown in blue. That curve is called the firm's **output expansion path.**

A firm's **output expansion path** shows the least-cost input combinations at all possible levels of output for fixed input prices.

Sometimes the output expansion path is a straight line. In that case, the capital-labor ratio does not change as the firm produces more. For example, if you look back at worked-out problem 8.2, you'll see that the capital-labor ratio at the least-cost input combination does not depend on the level of output for a Cobb-Douglas technology. Sometimes, though, the output expansion path bends. In Figure 8.10(a), for example, the firm's capital-labor ratio shrinks as its output increases.

We're now ready to determine the firm's cost function given fixed input prices and to graph the firm's total cost curve. Figure 8.10(b) graphs the total cost of 100, 200, and 300 units of output by plotting the cost of input combinations D, E, and F in Figure 8.10(a). Those costs—\$1,250, \$3,000, and \$5,000—give us three points on the firm's cost function: $C(100) = 1{,}250$, $C(200) = 3{,}000$, and $C(300) = 5{,}000$. We can find other points on the total cost curve in a similar way.

WORKED-OUT PROBLEM 8.3

The Problem Consider again Hannah and Sam's remodeling business in worked-out problem 8.2 (page 267). What is their cost function?

The Solution The solution to worked-out problem 8.2 tells us that to produce Q garden benches Hannah and Sam need the amount of labor L that solves the formula

$$Q = 20L$$

and they need four times that amount of capital. So they need $(Q/20)$ workers and $(4Q/20)$ units of capital. Their cost of producing Q units is therefore

$$C(Q) = 1{,}000(Q/20) + 250(4Q/20) = 100Q$$

Figure 8.10

A Firm's Output Expansion Path and Total Cost Curve. Given fixed input prices, a firm's output expansion path, shown in figure (a), contains the least-cost input combinations at all possible levels of output. The firm's total cost curve, shown in figure (b), shows how its total cost changes with its output level, given fixed input prices. Each point on the firm's total cost curve corresponds to the cost level associated with a point on its output expansion path.

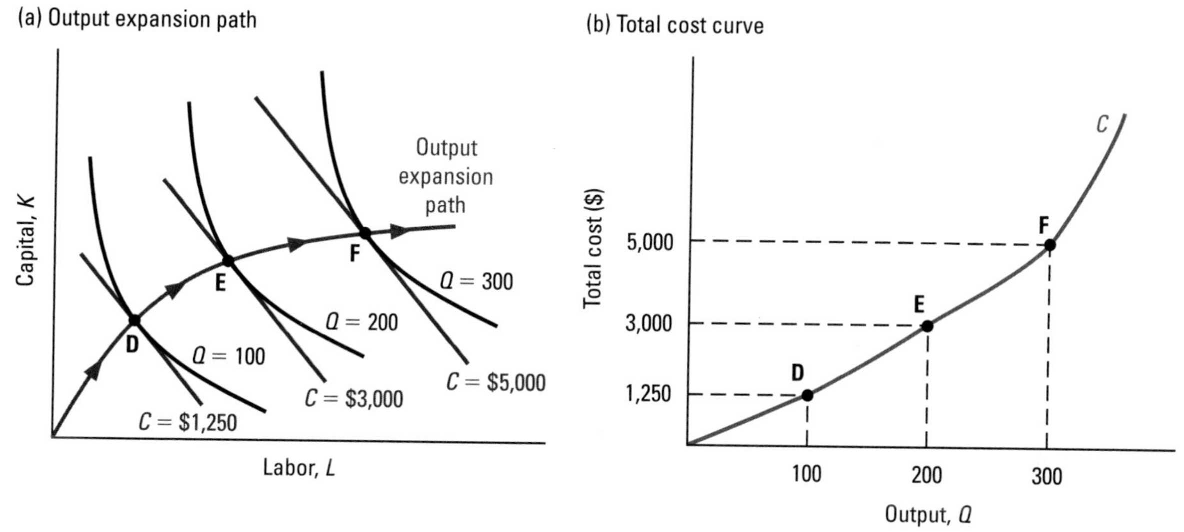

IN-TEXT EXERCISE 8.3 **Suppose that a unit of capital instead costs Hannah and Sam $1,000 per week. (Their production function is the same as in worked-out problems 8.2 and 8.3.) What is their cost function?**

Lumpy Inputs and Avoidable Fixed Costs Firms can vary all of their inputs in the long run, but sometimes some of those inputs are lumpy. Either the input isn't finely divisible, so that at least some minimum amount must be used, or the production process is such that producing any output requires a minimum amount of the input. As an example, think of a hospital that wants to perform CT scans. The lowest capacity scanner might be able to scan five patients a day. Even if the hospital is in a small town and needs to scan only one patient a day, it still must buy or rent this scanner.[8]

Lumpy inputs face firms with avoidable fixed costs in the long run (see Section 8.1). Figure 8.11 illustrates this situation. There capital costs $1,000 per unit. Figure 8.11(a) shows the isoquants for a firm that must use at least one unit of capital to produce any output. The yellow-shaded area represents the input combinations that produce no output

[8]Because of the time involved in moving a scanner, the hospital can't rent it for just part of a day.

Figure 8.11

A Firm's Output Expansion Path and Total Cost Curve with a Lumpy Input. Figure (a) shows the output expansion path for a firm that must use at least one unit of capital to produce any output, but never finds it worthwhile to use more than one unit. Its capital cost is therefore an avoidable fixed cost of $1,000, which gives rise to the total cost function shown in figure (b). Total cost is zero when no output is produced, but jumps up to approximately $1,000 as soon as the firm's output is positive. This jump is indicated by the little circle at $Q = 0$.

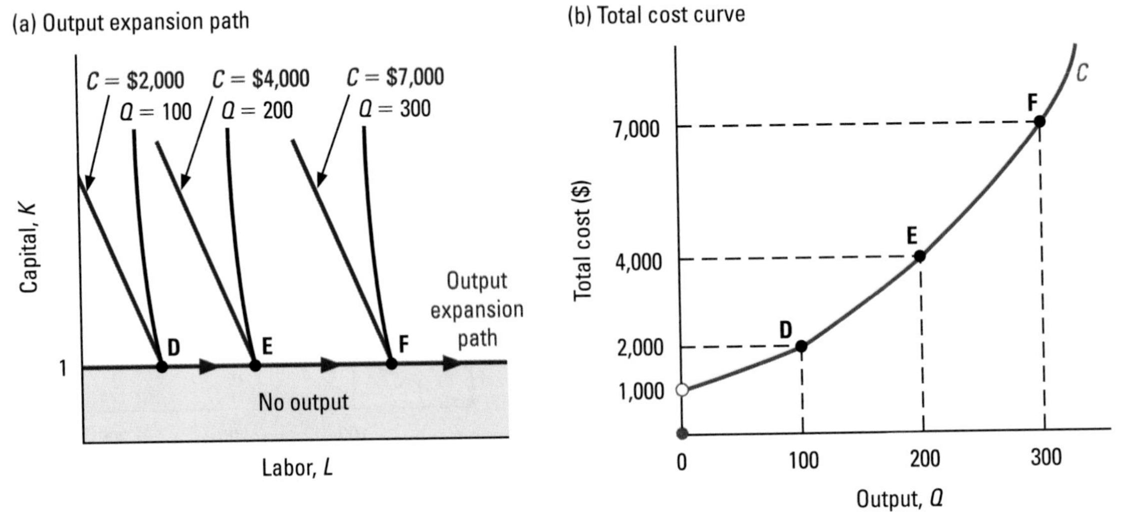

because they do not include at least one unit of capital. But having more than one unit of capital isn't very useful: the firm's $MRTS_{LK}$ is very large when K is at least one.[9] The firm therefore minimizes its costs of producing any given level of output by using exactly one unit of capital. Its output expansion path is shown in blue.

Figure 8.11(b) shows the firm's total cost function. Cost is zero when no output is produced. But to produce any positive output, the firm must acquire one unit of capital at a cost of $1,000. That $1,000 is therefore an avoidable fixed cost; the firm incurs it regardless of how much it produces as long as production is positive but can avoid it by shutting down and producing nothing. It causes the cost function to jump up as soon as output is positive, which is indicated by the little circle in Figure 8.11(b) at $Q = 0$.

[9] In an extreme case, in which having more than one unit of capital isn't useful at all—such as the New York City taxicab owner who needs one, and only one, medallion to operate his taxi—the firm's isoquants would be perfectly vertical for K greater than one.

WORKED-OUT PROBLEM 8.4

The Problem Noah and Naomi have decided to start a firm to produce garden tables. If Noah and Naomi have at least 500 square feet of garage space their weekly production is $Q = F(L) = \sqrt{L}$, where L is the amount of labor they hire, in hours. Additional garage space beyond 500 square feet does not increase their production. The wage rate is \$12 an hour, and a 500-square-foot garage rents for \$250 per week. What is their long-run weekly cost function for producing garden tables? Graph it.

The Solution The relationship between Noah and Naomi's labor input and their garden table output is the same as in worked-out problem 8.1 (page 257). So their cost function is

$$C(Q) = \begin{Bmatrix} 0 & \text{if } Q = 0 \\ 250 + 12Q^2 & \text{if } Q > 0 \end{Bmatrix}$$

which is shown in Figure 8.12. In the figure, costs for $Q = 0$ are represented by the solid dot at the origin. The total cost curve jumps upward as soon as Noah and Naomi begin to produce a positive amount of output, since they must then incur the garage rental cost of \$250.

IN-TEXT EXERCISE 8.4 **Noah and Naomi have decided to start a firm to produce garden tables. If Noah and Naomi have at least 500 square feet of garage space their weekly production is $Q = F(L) = 2\sqrt{L}$, where L is the amount of labor they hire, in hours. Additional garage space beyond 500 square feet does not increase their production. The wage rate is \$12 an hour, and a 500-square-foot garage rents for \$500 per week. What is their long-run weekly cost function for producing garden tables? Graph it.**

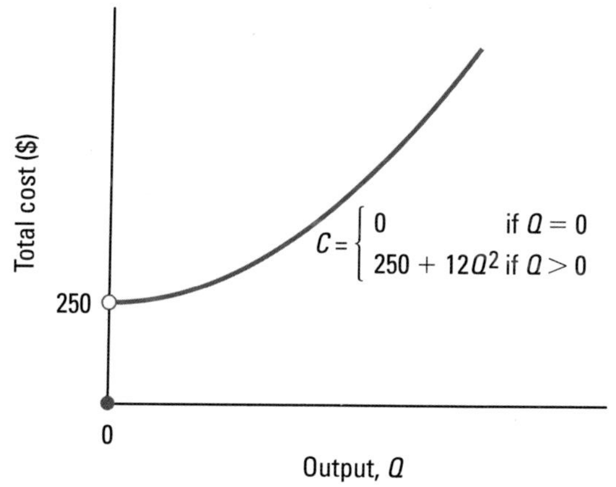

Figure 8.12
Total Cost Curve in Worked-Out Problem 8.4.

Application 8.5

Variable Costs for An(other) Electric Utility

The same methods we have just studied can be used to find the least-cost input combination for a firm that has a fixed level of capital and two variable inputs in the short run. In Application 8.3, it was easy to derive Calpine's short-run variable cost function for generating electricity in Texas because Calpine used only one type of fuel, natural gas. Unlike Calpine, West Texas Utilities (WTU), another generator of electric power, uses both coal and natural gas. WTU can generate up to 658 megawatts of electricity an hour in its coal-fired plants, and up to 420 megawatts an hour in its gas-fired plants. Typically, coal plants are much cheaper to run than gas plants. WTU's coal plant requires 10.58 million BTUs (British thermal units) of coal for each megawatt hour produced. On August 6, 2002, coal cost \$1.40 per million BTUs. So a megawatt hour produced with coal cost \$14.81. In contrast, WTU's gas-fired plants require 10.21 million BTUs of natural gas for each megawatt hour produced. On August 6, 2002, natural gas cost \$2.86 per million BTUs, so a megawatt hour produced with gas cost \$29.20.

Since each megawatt produced with coal costs less than each megawatt produced with gas, WTU will use only its coal-fired plants until they reach capacity, and then use its gas-fired plants until their capacity is also reached. Figure 8.13(a), which measures the amount of coal and natural gas used per hour in millions of BTUs, shows WTU's output expansion path as a blue line.

The figure also shows some of WTU's isoquants up to its capacity of 1,078 megawatt hours. WTU can choose any input combination that does not exceed its coal and gas-fired generating capacities. When run at full capacity, its coal generating plant uses $658 \times 10.58 = 6{,}962$ million BTUs of coal and its gas plants use $420 \times 10.21 = 4{,}288$ million BTUs of natural gas. So WTU's feasible input choices are shown as the green-shaded area in the figure.

WTU's isoquants are shown in black and are less steeply sloped than are its isocost lines, which are shown in dark red. Why? The isoquants' slopes are $-(10.21/10.58) \approx -0.96$ (the marginal product of coal is 1/10.58 megawatts per million BTUs, since 10.58 million BTUs of coal are needed to generate one megawatt hour of electricity, while the marginal product of gas is 1/10.21 megawatts per million BTUs). WTU's isocost lines have slope $-(1.40/2.86) \approx -0.49$, the ratio of the price of coal to the price of gas, times negative one. Observe that only points on the lower and right-hand borders of the green-shaded region satisfy the no-overlap rule.

Figure 8.13(b) shows WTU's variable cost curve up to its capacity. (WTU's fixed costs are not included in the figure.) It consists of two line segments. The slope of the first segment is \$14.81, the cost per megawatt hour of its coal-fired plant. The slope of the second is \$29.20, the cost per megawatt hour of its gas-fired plant.

8.5 AVERAGE AND MARGINAL COSTS

In Sections 8.3 and 8.4 we saw how to derive a firm's cost function, $C(Q)$. Just as the average and marginal product, discussed in Chapter 7, are useful measures of a firm's productivity, average and marginal cost are useful measures of a firm's costs.

A firm's **average cost,** $AC = C/Q$, is its cost per unit of output produced.

A firm's **average cost,** AC, is its cost per unit of output produced. We calculate it by dividing the firm's total cost, C, by the number of units the firm produces, Q:

$$AC = \frac{C}{Q}$$

A firm's marginal cost, MC, captures how much extra cost is incurred when the firm changes the amount of output it produces a little bit. We've discussed marginal cost already in Section 3.2; let's review that discussion briefly. (The basic ideas are also the same as in our discussion of marginal product in Section 7.2.) As in Section 3.2, when

Figure 8.13

WTU's Output Expansion Path and Variable Cost Curve. WTU's least-cost production method is to use its coal-fired generating plants until their capacity has been reached, then add its gas-fired generating units. This strategy results in the output expansion path shown in blue in figure (a). WTU's variable cost curve can be determined from the cost levels along its output expansion path. The curve, shown in figure (b), consists of two line segments. The slope of the first segment is \$14.81, the cost per megawatt hour of its coal-fired plants; the slope of the second is \$29.20, the cost per megawatt hour of its gas-fired plants.

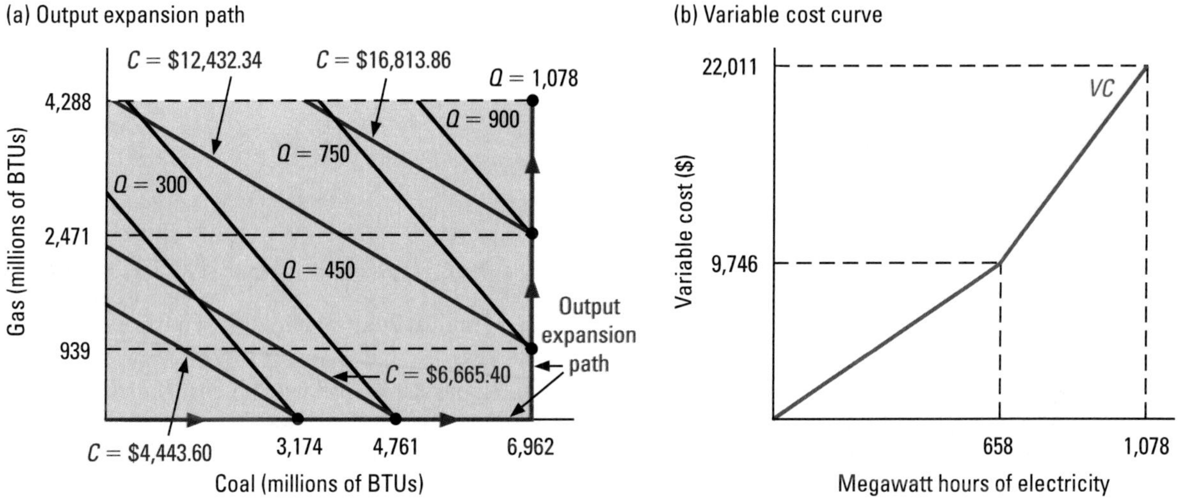

we say a "little bit," we mean the smallest amount of output the firm can add or subtract. We'll call this amount ΔQ. When the firm produces Q units, we say that the last ΔQ units are the **marginal units of output.** If the firm can produce its output only in one-gallon batches and output is measured in ounces, then $\Delta Q = 128$ (since there are 128 ounces in a gallon). If the firm can produce output in one-quart batches, then $\Delta Q = 32$; in one-ounce batches, then $\Delta Q = 1$. In some cases, there may be virtually no limit to how finely a firm's output level can be adjusted.

The **marginal units of output** are the last ΔQ units, where ΔQ is the smallest amount of output the firm can add or subtract.

The firm's **marginal cost** measures how much extra cost the firm incurs to produce the marginal units of output, per unit of output added. When the firm produces Q units of output, the change in cost due to the marginal units is $\Delta C = C(Q) - C(Q - \Delta Q)$. Dividing by the amount of output added, ΔQ (to express this change on a per unit basis) gives us the marginal cost:

A firm's **marginal cost**, *MC*, measures how much extra cost the firm incurs to produce the marginal units of output, per unit of output added.

$$MC = \frac{\Delta C}{\Delta Q} = \frac{C(Q) - C(Q - \Delta Q)}{\Delta Q}$$

Table 8.3 illustrates the costs for a firm that can produce output in one-ton increments, so that $\Delta Q = 1$. The first column shows the level of output per day in tons. The second column shows the total cost per day at each output level. The third and fourth columns show the firm's marginal and average costs per ton at each output level. The dashed arrows show the change in cost that corresponds to marginal cost. Note that as output increases, marginal cost first falls and then rises. Average cost follows the same pattern.

Table 8.3

Cost, Average Cost, and Marginal Cost for a Hypothetical Firm

Output, *Q* (tons per day)	Total Cost, C ($ per day)	Marginal Cost, MC ($ per ton)	Average Cost, AC ($ per ton)
0	$0	—	—
1	1,000	$1,000	$1,000
2	1,800	800	900
3	2,100	300	700
4	2,500	400	625
5	3,000	500	600
6	3,600	600	600
7	4,300	700	614
8	5,600	1,300	700

Average and Marginal Cost Curves with Finely Divisible Output

When output is finely divisible, we can graph average and marginal cost as curves to show how they vary with the firm's output.

Let's start with the average cost. Figure 8.14(a) shows the cost function for another new venture of Noah and Naomi's, producing garden hoses. The horizontal axis shows the firm's output of garden hoses, measured in feet; the vertical axis shows the total cost of production per week. If we pick any point on the cost curve and draw a straight line connecting it to the origin, the slope of that line will equal the cost (the rise) divided by

Figure 8.14

Average Cost. Figure (a) shows that at any output level, average cost equals the slope of a line running from the origin to the point on the firm's total cost curve that corresponds to that output level. Figure (b) shows the firm's average cost at each output level.

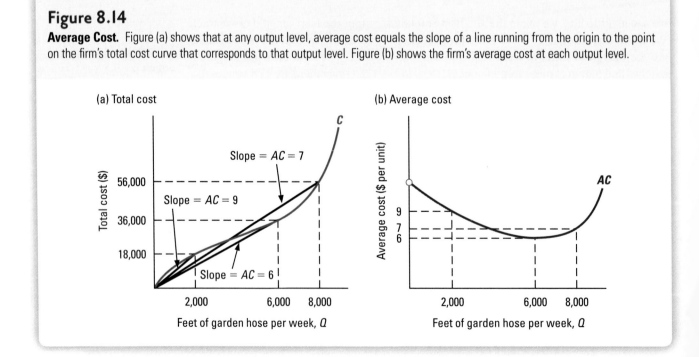

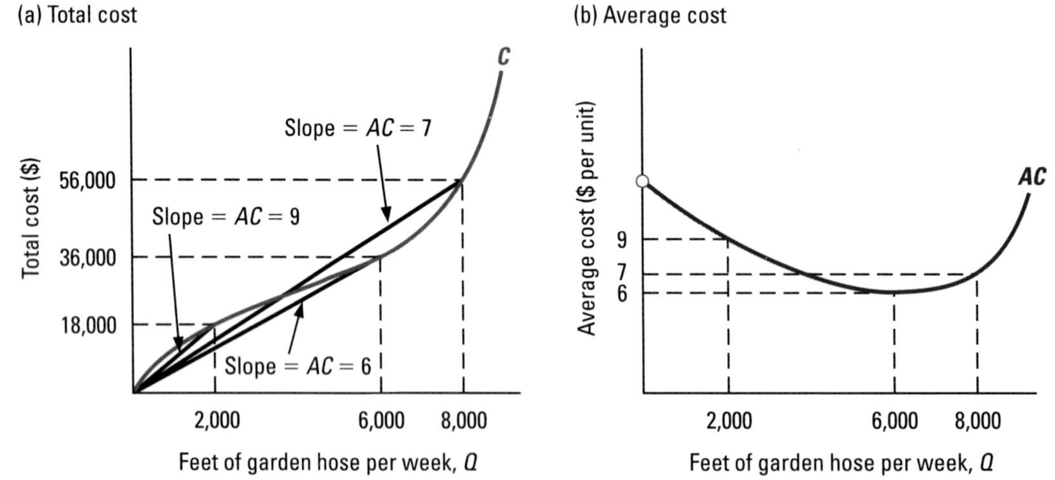

the amount of output produced (the run). By definition, that's the average cost. The figure illustrates the calculation of the average cost at three different levels of output: 2,000, 6,000, and 8,000 feet of hose per week. For example, when output is 2,000 feet, the average cost is \$9 per hose. Figure 8.14(b) shows the average cost curve. As in Table 8.3, average cost first falls and then rises as output increases. (Average cost is only defined for positive output levels; this is indicated by the little circle at $Q = 0$.)

Note that the average cost of production is lowest when the firm produces 6,000 feet per week. This level of output is known as the firm's **efficient scale of production**. Its name does *not* mean that the firm should always try to produce at this level of output, however. Rather, it tells us that if we want to produce a large amount of output at the lowest possible cost, we should try to divide it up among a number of firms, each of which produces at the efficient scale of production. For example, the cheapest way to produce 180,000 feet of hose a week would be to have 30 firms produce 6,000 feet each. This observation will play an important role in Chapter 14, when we study long-run competitive equilibrium.

A firm's **efficient scale of production** is the output level at which its average cost is lowest.

Now let's think about marginal cost. When output is finely divisible, the smallest amount of output that a firm can add or subtract, ΔQ, is very tiny. In this case, when a firm produces Q units of output, its marginal cost is equal to the slope of its cost function at output level Q. (The logic is the same as in our discussions of marginal product in Section 7.2, and of marginal benefit and marginal cost in Section 3.2.)

We can now graph Noah and Naomi's marginal cost curve for producing garden hoses. Figure 8.15(a) shows lines drawn tangent to the total cost curve at the same three levels of output as in Figure 8.14: 2,000, 6,000, and 8,000 feet per week. The slope of each line tells us the corresponding marginal cost. For example, the marginal cost at $Q =$ 2,000 is \$7 per unit. We've plotted the marginal cost at these levels of output and others

Figure 8.15

Marginal Cost. Figure (a) shows that at any output level, the firm's marginal cost equals the slope of the total cost curve at that output level. Figure (b) shows the firm's marginal cost at each output level.

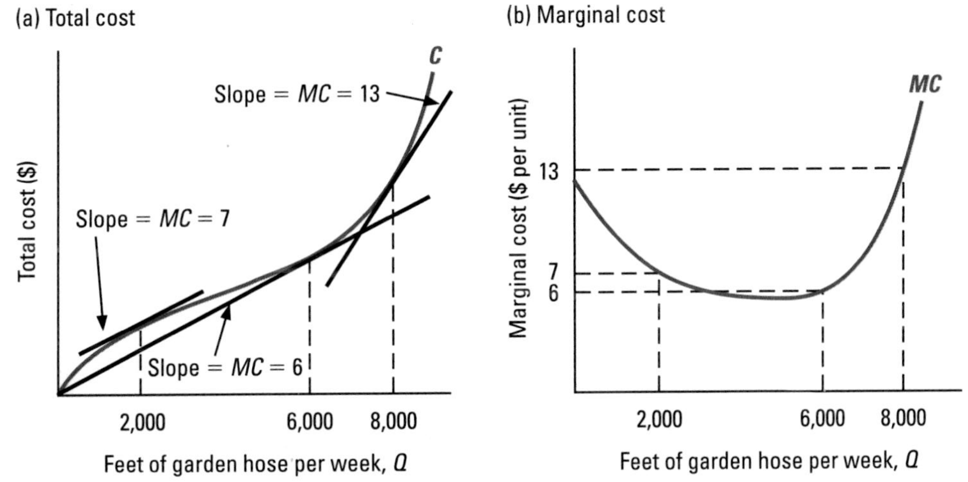

in Figure 8.15(b), which shows the firm's marginal cost curve. Notice that the tangent line at $Q = 6{,}000$ runs through the origin, indicating that the marginal and average costs are equal at that output level.

Figure 8.16 shows Noah and Naomi's average and marginal cost curves together. Notice that the average cost curve slopes downward where it lies above the marginal cost curve and upward where it lies below the marginal cost curve. Where the average and marginal cost curves cross, the average cost curve is neither rising nor falling. This reflects the same relationship between averages and marginals we've seen before.

This relationship between average and marginal cost means that the marginal cost curve always crosses the average cost curve at its lowest point, the efficient scale of production, since the average cost curve is neither rising nor falling at that output level (see Figure 8.16). Moreover, this crossing must be from below. Why? At output levels a little below the efficient scale of production, average cost must be declining, which means that marginal cost must be below average cost. At output levels a little above the efficient scale of production, average cost must be rising, which means that marginal cost is above average cost.

The Relationship between the Average and Marginal Cost Curves When output is finely divisible, the average cost curve is upward sloping at Q if marginal cost is above average cost. It is downward sloping if marginal cost is below average cost, and neither rising nor falling if marginal cost equals average cost. Moreover, the marginal cost curve always crosses the average cost curve from below at the efficient scale of production.

In Chapters 9, 14, 17, and 19 marginal and average costs will play central roles in our discussions of profit-maximizing sales quantities or prices. Worked-out problem 8.5 shows another way that the concept of marginal cost is useful.

Figure 8.16

The Relationship between Average and Marginal Cost. This figure shows the average and marginal cost curves from Figures 8.14(b) and 8.15(b). At output levels at which marginal cost is less than average cost, the average cost curve is downward sloping; it is upward sloping at output levels at which marginal cost exceeds average cost. The marginal cost curve crosses the average cost curve from below at the efficient scale of production ($Q = 6{,}000$). At that point, average cost is at its lowest level, and the average cost curve is neither rising nor falling.

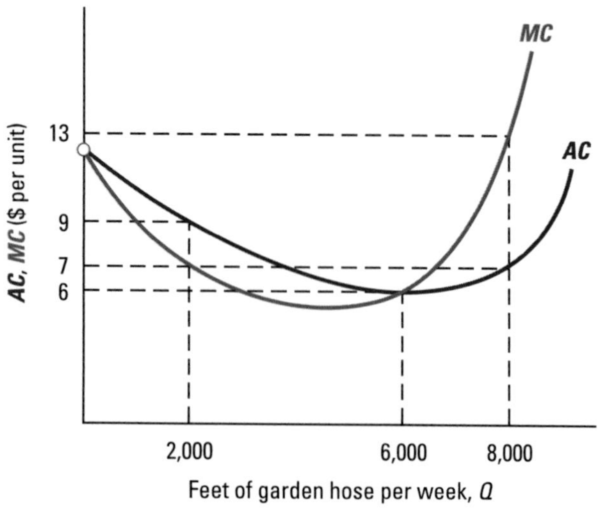

WORKED-OUT PROBLEM 8.5

The Problem Suppose Noah and Naomi have just acquired a second garden bench production plant. As with their first plant, they can adjust both the square footage and the number of workers in this second facility. Suppose production costs are $C_1 = 3(Q_1)^2$ at plant 1 and $C_2 = 2(Q_2)^2$ at plant 2, where Q_1 and Q_2 are the number of benches produced at each plant per week. The corresponding marginal costs at the two plants are $MC_1 = 6Q_1$ and $MC_2 = 4Q_2$. If Noah and Naomi plan to produce 100 garden benches per week and want to do it as economically as possible, how many benches should they produce at each plant?

The Solution The basic principle behind the solution to this problem is the same as in worked-out problem 7.1 (page 226). With a least-cost plan that assigns a positive amount of output to each plant, *marginal cost must be the same at both plants.* If that were not true, the total cost could be lowered by reassigning a little bit of output from the plant with the higher marginal cost to the plant with the lower marginal cost.

Noah and Naomi need to divide production between the two plants so that their marginal costs are equal. Doing so means choosing Q_1 and Q_2 so that $MC_1 = MC_2$. Since total output equals 100, we know that $Q_2 = 100 - Q_1$, so we can express the marginal cost in plant 2 as a function of the amount of output produced in plant 1: $MC_2 = 4(100 - Q_1)$. We can then find the output assignment that equates marginal costs in the two plants by solving the formula $MC_1 = MC_2$, which is equivalent to

$$6Q_1 = 4(100 - Q_1)$$

The solution is $Q_1 = 40$. Noah and Naomi should produce 40 garden benches a week in their first facility and 60 garden benches a week in their second facility. Their total production costs will then be

$$C = 3(40)^2 + 2(60)^2 = \$12{,}000$$

IN-TEXT EXERCISE 8.5 **Repeat worked-out problem 8.5, but assume instead that the cost and marginal cost at plant 1 are $C_1 = 6(Q_1)^2$ and $MC_1 = 12Q_1$, respectively.**

Marginal Cost, Marginal Products, and Input Prices

Intuitively, a firm's costs should be lower the more productive it is and the lower are the input prices it faces. This observation suggests that there should be a relationship between a firm's marginal cost and its marginal products and input prices. To derive this relationship, consider a firm that is producing 100 units of output. If it wants to increase its output by 1 unit, one possibility is that it can use only more labor. This requires $(1/MP_L)$ additional units of labor and costs $W \times (1/MP_L) = W/MP_L$. Alternatively, it could use only capital, which would cost $R \times (1/MP_K) = R/MP_K$. But formula (2) tells us that these two amounts are equal. So the firm's marginal cost equals each input's price divided by its marginal product at the firm's least-cost input combination; that is:

$$MC = \frac{R}{MP_K} = \frac{W}{MP_L}$$

Marginal Costs and Variable Cost

Marginal cost measures the incremental cost of each additional unit the firm produces. A firm's variable cost is therefore equal to the sum of the marginal costs of the individual units it produces. To see this point, look at Figure 8.17(a), which shows the marginal cost curve for a firm that is producing 50 units. If the firm's output were lumpy so that it could produce only in batches of 10 units each, the extra cost from producing each batch of 10 units would be the series of red-shaded steps. The firm's variable cost would equal the sum of these steps; that is, the total red-shaded area. When the firm's output is finely divisible, these steps become very small, and variable cost comes to equal the area under the marginal cost curve, as Figure 8.17(b) shows. This relationship also means that the change in variable cost between any two output levels is equal to the area under the marginal cost curve between those output levels.

More Average and Marginal Costs

We can also apply the notions of average and marginal cost to a firm's variable and fixed costs. A firm's average variable cost, AVC, is

$$AVC = \frac{VC}{Q}$$

while its average fixed cost, AFC, is

$$AFC = \frac{FC}{Q}$$

Figure 8.17

Variable Cost Equals the Area Under the Marginal Cost Curve. Figure (a) shows that when output is lumpy and can be produced only in 10-unit batches, variable cost for a firm producing 50 units equals the sum of the red-shaded rectangles, representing the marginal costs of the five 10-unit batches the firm produces. Figure (b) shows that when output is finely divisible, variable cost equals the area under the marginal cost curve up to 50 units.

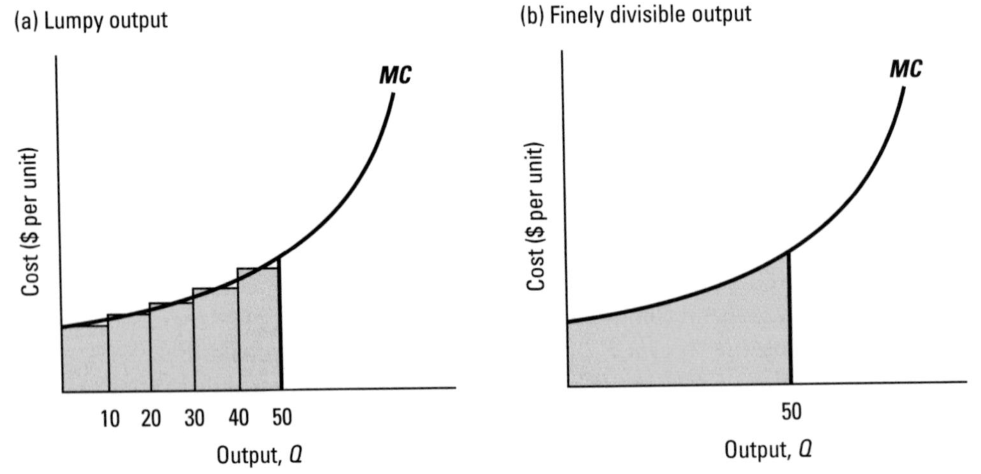

Since total cost is equal to the sum of variable and fixed costs, average cost is equal to the sum of the average variable and average fixed costs:

$$AC = \frac{C}{Q} = \frac{VC + FC}{Q} = \frac{VC}{Q} + \frac{FC}{Q} = AVC + AFC$$

Figure 8.18 shows a hypothetical firm's average variable cost curve (in black), average fixed cost curve (in green), and average cost curve (in red). Since a firm's fixed cost, FC, is a fixed number, its AFC curve is always downward sloping (as the output level increases, we are dividing the same fixed cost among more and more units). At each level of output the AC curve is the vertical sum of the AVC and AFC curves. Thus, the average cost curve lies above both the average variable and average fixed cost curves at every output level.

Notice that the efficient scale of production, Q^e (the output level at which average cost is lowest), exceeds the output level where AVC is lowest, labeled Q^e_{VC}. In fact, the output level that minimizes AC can *never* be below Q^e_{VC}. Why not? First, since both AVC and AFC are lower at Q^e_{VC} than at any lower quantity, this must also be true of AC (which is the sum of AVC and AFC). Next, observe that the AVC curve is neither rising nor falling right at Q^e_{VC} (see Figure 8.18), while the AFC curve is downward sloping. Since the AC curve is the sum of those two curves, it must slope downward at Q^e_{VC}, which implies that there are larger outputs than Q^e_{VC} that have a lower average cost.

Now let's think about marginal costs. Because fixed cost is a fixed number, marginal units of output always add zero fixed cost. So *all* the costs of producing marginal units are variable costs. That means there is no difference between marginal cost and marginal variable cost. Figure 8.19 illustrates this point. The figure shows a firm's total cost and variable cost curves. Since total cost at each output level is just the variable cost curve shifted up by the constant fixed cost, the slope of the two curves is the same at each output level and is equal to MC. The figure demonstrates this fact at two output levels, Q' and Q''.

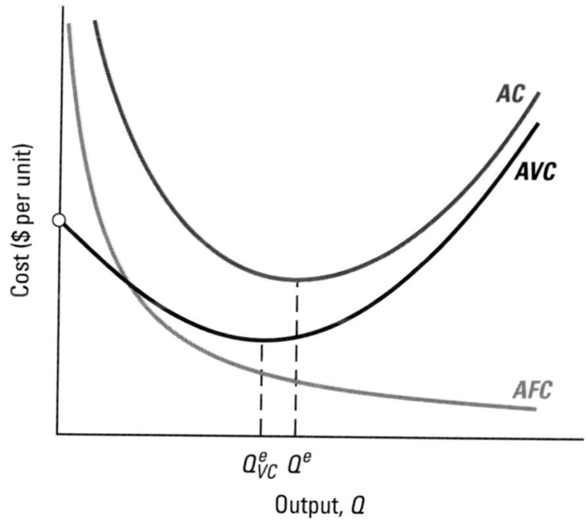

Figure 8.18

Average Fixed Cost, Average Variable Cost, and Average Cost. At each output level, the average cost (AC) curve is the sum of the average fixed cost (AFC) and average variable cost (AVC). Thus, at every output level the AC curve lies above the AFC and AVC curves. The average fixed cost curve is downward sloping at all output levels. The output level at which AC is lowest, the efficient scale Q^e, is never below Q^e_{VC}, the output level at which AVC is lowest.

Finally, what about the relationship between average variable cost and marginal cost? The usual relationship between averages and marginals applies. Average variable cost increases, decreases, or remains constant where it is less than, more than, or equal to marginal cost (this follows from the fact that MC equals marginal variable cost). Figure 8.20 shows this relationship.

Figure 8.19

Marginal Variable Cost Equals Marginal Cost. At every output level the slopes of the variable cost and total cost curves are the same, since the total cost curve is simply the variable cost curve shifted up by the constant amount of fixed cost.

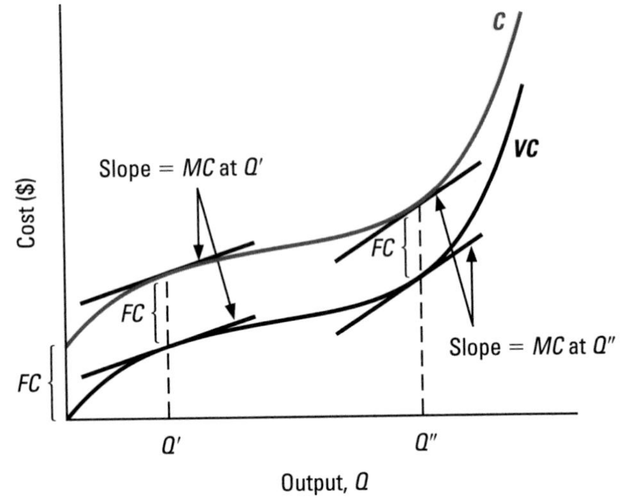

Figure 8.20

Relationship between Average Cost, Average Variable Cost, and Marginal Cost. The marginal cost curve crosses both the average and average variable cost curves from below at their minimums. It lies below each of these curves where they are downward sloping and is above them where they are upward sloping.

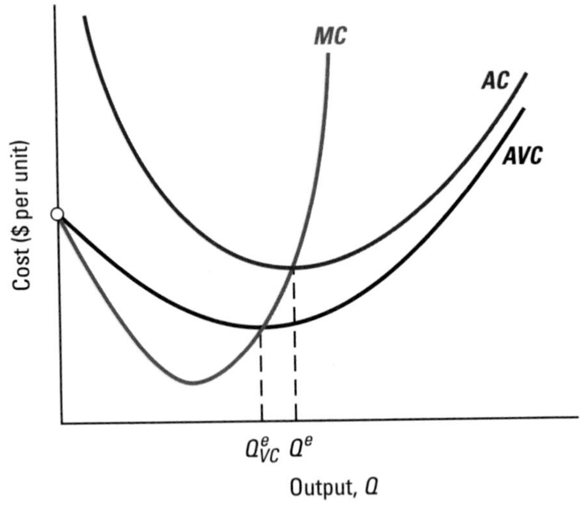

8.6 EFFECTS OF INPUT PRICE CHANGES

Changes in a firm's input prices generally lead to changes in its least-cost production method. Intuitively, if an input becomes more expensive, we would expect the firm to use less of it, substituting toward the use of other inputs in its place. To illustrate, let's look again at worked-out problem 8.2 (page 267). There we solved for Hannah and Sam's least-cost input combination for remodeling 100 square feet per week with a wage rate of $1,000 per week and capital cost of $250 per unit. That least-cost input combination, labeled point A in Figure 8.21, was five workers and 20 units of capital.

What if the cost of capital were instead $1,000 per week? If you've solved in-text exercise 8.3 (page 269), you've seen that the new least-cost input combination, shown as point B in Figure 8.21, is 10 workers and 10 units of capital (if you haven't, check this now.) So when the price of capital increases, the least-cost production method uses less capital and more labor.

Can we draw any general conclusions about the effects of input price changes on the least-cost input combination? The answer is *yes*. After an increase in the price of an input, a firm *never* uses more of that input in its least-cost input combination, and usually employs less. Likewise, after a decrease in the price of an input, a firm *never* uses less of that input in its least-cost input combination, and usually employs more.

Figure 8.22 demonstrates this point for an input price increase. The dark red isocost line labeled R reflects the initial prices of labor and capital, W and R. Suppose that the least-cost input combination at those input prices is point A. (The figure deliberately omits the firm's isoquant.) Now suppose the price of capital increases to $R' > R$, resulting in a flatter isocost line. The new isocost line that contains point A is shown in light red. Where will the new least-cost input combination lie? The answer is that it must lie somewhere in the green-shaded region, like point B. Why? Since B was not cheaper than A at the old prices, it must lie on or above the original isocost line through A. On the other hand, since B is no more expensive than A at the new prices (since it is the least-cost input

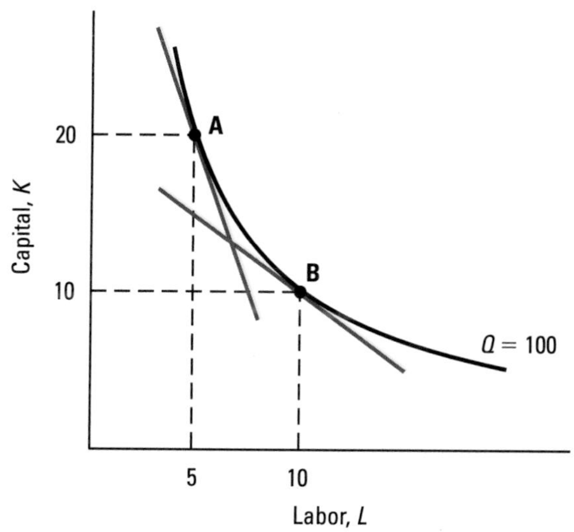

Figure 8.21

The Effect of an Input Price Change on the Least-Cost Production Method for a Cobb-Douglas Production Function. Point A is the least-cost input combination when the price of labor is four times more than the price of capital. When capital and labor are equally costly, the least-cost input combination is point B, where the firm uses less capital and more labor.

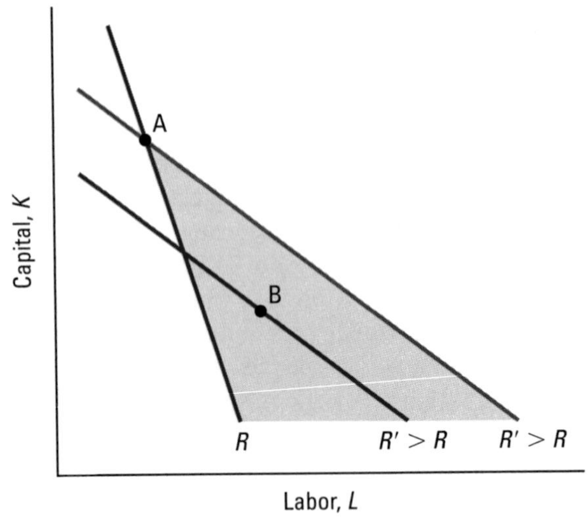

Figure 8.22
Effects of an Input Price Change. In the figure, the least-cost combination when capital costs R per unit is A. When the price of capital rises to R', the new least-cost input combination must lie in the green-shaded region, such as point B. This means that it uses no more capital than does input combination A.

combination at the new prices) it must lie on or below the new isocost line through A. The result follows since *all* of the points in the green-shaded region require no more capital than input combination A.

The same argument works for *any* change in *any* input price (check this for an input price decrease on your own). The only caveat is that sometimes (as illustrated in Application 8.6) the firm's input choice does not change when an input price changes.

In sum:

Responses to a Change in an Input Price When the price of an input decreases, a firm's least-cost production method never uses less of that input, and usually employs more. Likewise, when the price of an input increases, a firm's least-cost production method never uses more of that input, and usually employs less.

Application 8.6

Least-Cost Production at Cold Hollow Cider Mill

In Application 7.2 (page 230) we derived Cold Hollow Cider Mill's isoquant for producing 10,000 gallons of apple cider per day. Recall that Cold Hollow can use three different machines to produce its cider: a traditional rack-and-cloth vertical press, a belt press, and a rack-and-bag horizontal press. If Cold Hollow's production manager, Greg Spina, anticipates producing 10,000 gallons a day, what is his least-cost production method? How does it depend on the wage rate?

To answer this question, we need to know Cold Hollow's input costs. Suppose a unit of capital costs \$10 per day, while workers earn \$8.50 an hour. Figure 8.23 shows its isoquant for producing 10,000 gallons of cider per day along with three isocost lines, corresponding to three different prices of capital, R. The isocost line labeled $R = \$10$ has a slope of $-(8.5/10)$. As the figure shows, the least-cost input combination when $R = \$10$ is point C, which uses one rack-and-bag horizontal press, one rack-and-cloth vertical press, and 16 hours of labor (see Table 7.5 on page 231). The total cost of production is $[(11)(\$10) + (16)(\$8.50)] = \$246$ per day.

Since Cold Hollow's isoquant is kinked, its least-cost input combination will remain the same over a range of input prices. For example, an increase in the price of a unit of capital to \$12 will flatten Cold Hollow's isocost lines but leave its least-cost input combination unchanged, as shown in the figure by the isocost line labeled $R = \$12$. However, as is also shown in the figure, if the price of a unit of capital rises to \$25 per day ($R = \$25$), then Cold Hollow's least-cost input combination would be B, which uses less capital and more labor.

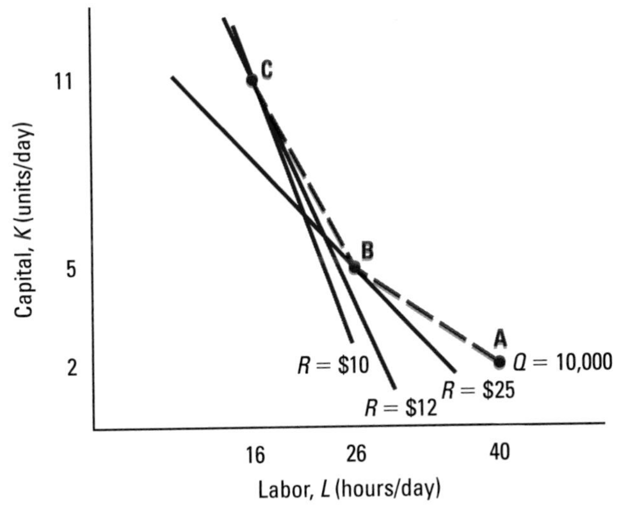

Figure 8.23

Cold Hollow Cider Mill's Least-Cost Method of Producing 10,000 Gallons of Cider per Day. This figure shows Cold Hollow's isoquant for producing 10,000 gallons of cider per day, reproduced from Figure 7.11. When the price of capital is \$10 per unit per day and the wage rate is \$8.50 per hour, Cold Hollow's least-cost input combination is point C. It is the same if the price of capital increases to \$12 per unit per day, but switches to point B if the price of capital increases to \$25 per unit per day.

8.7 SHORT-RUN VERSUS LONG-RUN COSTS

What is the relationship between a firm's short-run and long-run costs? To answer this question, Figure 8.24 shows three of Noah and Naomi's isoquants for producing garden benches: $Q = 120$, $Q = 140$, and $Q = 160$ benches per week. Imagine that the wage rate is \$500 per week and garage space rents for \$1 per square foot. In the long run, Noah and Naomi can vary both these inputs. At each of the three output levels, they will choose the least-cost input combination, which occurs at the tangency of the isoquant with an isocost line. In the figure, these least-cost input combinations are labeled A, B, and D, respectively.

Now suppose Noah and Naomi are producing 140 garden benches a week (point B) when the demand for garden benches suddenly increases, raising the amount of output they want to produce to 160 benches a week. Suppose, too, that over the short run, they can't vary their garage space which is fixed at 1,500 square feet. How will they produce

Figure 8.24

Input Responses over the Long and Short Run. Noah and Naomi are producing 140 garden benches per week at input combination B. If they decide to increase their output to 160 benches per week they will shift to input combination F over the short run, when they cannot adjust their garage space. In the long run, when they can adjust their garage space, they will shift to input combination D. Thus, their cost is lower in the long run. Likewise, if they decide to decrease their output to 120 garden benches a week, they will shift to input combination E in the short run, and to input combination A in the long run. Again, their cost is lower in the long run.

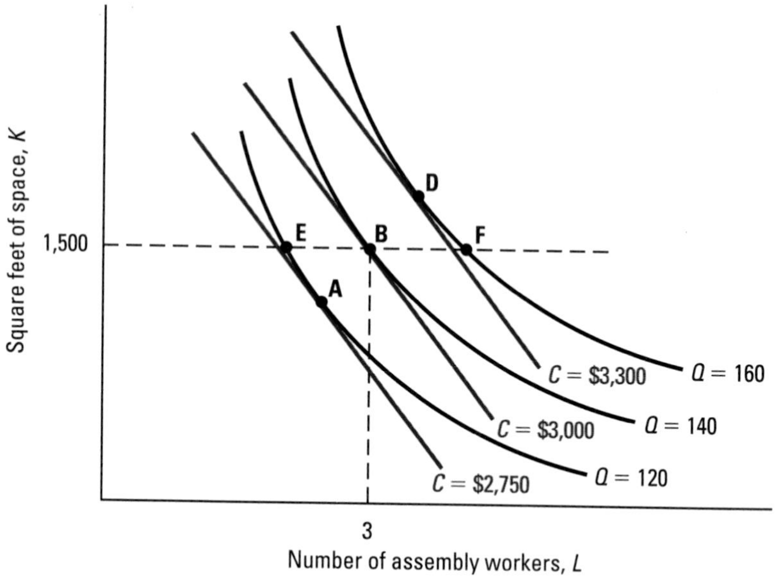

the extra output? The only way to do it is to increase the number of workers. The required input combination is point F, which has the same amount of garage space as point B, but a greater number of workers. Notice that the cost of production at point F is greater than at point D, the least-cost input combination at $Q = 160$.

Similarly, if Noah and Naomi unexpectedly needed to reduce their output to 120 benches a week, they would use the input combination labeled E. Again, point E involves a greater cost than point A, the least-cost input combination over the long run at $Q = 120$.

Figure 8.25(a) shows the resulting long-run and short-run total cost curves, labeled C_{LR} and C_{SR}^{140}. At 140 garden benches a week the two curves coincide, since Noah and Naomi are at point B in either case. But at all other output levels, the short-run cost curve lies above the long-run cost curve because the extra flexibility Noah and Naomi have over the long run allows them to produce at a lower cost.

Figure 8.25(b) shows the long-run and short-run average cost curves, labeled AC_{LR} and AC_{SR}^{140}. Since short-run cost is greater than long-run cost at all positive output levels other than 140, the same is true of short-run and long-run average cost.

Figure 8.26 shows what happens when we look at Noah and Naomi's short-run average cost curves starting at various output levels. For example, AC_{SR}^{40} is their short-run average cost curve when they start off using the least-cost input combination for producing 40 garden benches a month. AC_{SR}^{100} corresponds to initially producing 100 garden benches a month. The figure shows that their long-run average cost curve is the *lower envelope* of their various short-run average cost curves. (This lower envelope is the highest curve that lies below all of the short-run curves.) At each output level Q, the long-run average cost curve just touches the short-run average cost curve AC_{SR}^{Q}, and it lies below that short-run average cost curve everywhere else.

What about short-run and long-run marginal cost? Look back at Figure 8.25(a). The slopes of the short-run and long-run cost functions are equal at $Q = 140$; thus, short-run marginal cost equals long-run marginal cost at that output level. Just above $Q = 140$, short-run cost rises more quickly than long-run cost, so short-run marginal cost is greater than

Figure 8.25

Long-Run and Short-Run Costs. Figure (a) shows Noah and Naomi's long-run and short-run cost curves, labeled as C_{LR} and C_{SR}^{140}, respectively, when they are initially producing 140 garden benches per week. The two curves coincide at $Q = 140$; elsewhere, the long-run cost curve lies below the short-run cost curve for the reasons shown in Figure 8.24. Figure (b) shows the long- and short-run average cost curves. Again, they coincide at $Q = 140$; elsewhere, the long-run average cost curve lies below the short-run average cost curve.

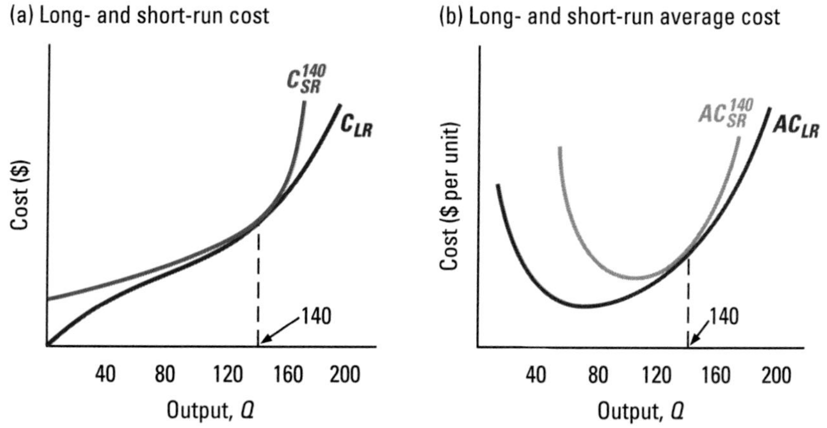

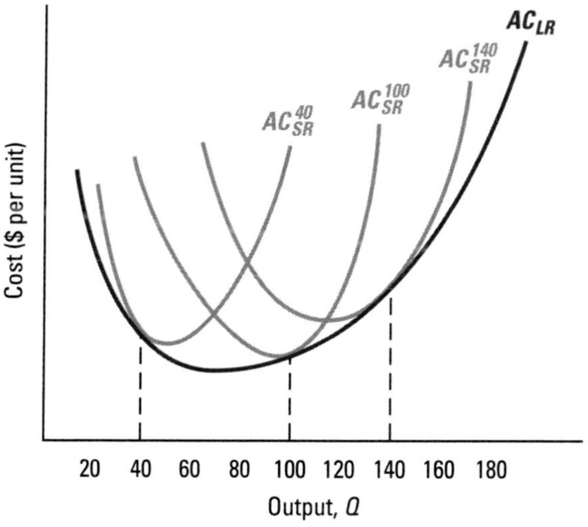

Figure 8.26

Long-Run and Short-Run Average Cost Curves. The long-run average cost curve AC_{LR} is the lower envelope of the various short-run average cost curves. At each output level Q, the long-run average cost curve touches the corresponding short-run average cost curve AC_{SR}^{Q}, and it lies below it everywhere else.

long-run marginal cost. Just below $Q = 140$, short-run cost rises more slowly than long-run cost, so short-run marginal cost is lower than long-run marginal cost. Thus, if Noah and Naomi are producing 140 garden benches a week at point B, their short-run and long-run marginal cost curves have the relationship shown in Figure 8.27. In Chapter 9, we'll see that this relationship has an important implication: competitive firms will respond more to changes in output prices over the long run than they will over the short run.

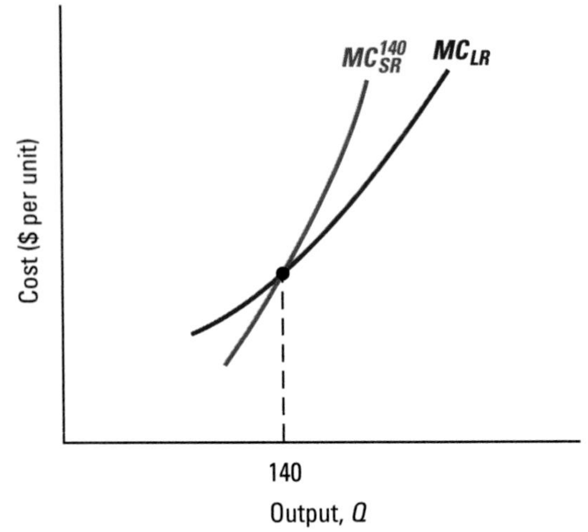

Figure 8.27
Long-Run and Short-Run Marginal Cost. This figure shows Noah and Naomi's long-run and short-run marginal cost curves when they are initially producing 140 garden benches per week. The short-run marginal cost curve is steeper than the long-run marginal cost curve, and the two curves cross at $Q = 140$.

WORKED-OUT PROBLEM 8.6

The Problem Consider again Hannah and Sam's remodeling business in worked-out problems 8.2 and 8.3 (pages 267 and 268). Suppose that they are initially remodeling 100 square feet per week. What are their short-run and long-run cost functions?

The Solution The solution to worked-out problem 8.2 tells us that they initially use 20 units of capital. So, if their capital is fixed at 20 units, to remodel Q square feet Hannah and Sam need the amount of labor L that solves the formula

$$10\sqrt{L}\sqrt{20} = Q$$

which means that $L = (Q^2/2{,}000)$. So, their short-run cost function is

$$C_{SR}^{100}(Q) = (250)(20) + (1{,}000)\left(\frac{Q^2}{2{,}000}\right)$$

or equivalently,

$$C_{SR}^{100}(Q) = 5{,}000 + \left(\frac{Q^2}{2}\right)$$

In contrast, the solution to worked-out problem 8.3 tells us that Hannah and Sam's long-run cost function is

$$C_{LR}(Q) = 100Q$$

Observe, though, that their short-run and long-run costs are equal when $Q = 100$ [since $C_{SR}^{100}(100) = C_{LR}(100) = 10{,}000$], just as our discussion indicated they should.

IN-TEXT EXERCISE 8.6 **Suppose that a unit of capital instead costs Hannah and Sam $1,000 per week. (Their production function is the same as in worked-out problems 8.2 and 8.3.) They are initially remodeling 100 square feet per week. What are their short-run and long-run cost functions?**

8.8 ECONOMIES AND DISECONOMIES OF SCALE

In Section 7.4 we introduced the concept of returns to scale. We learned that a firm has constant, increasing, or decreasing returns to scale depending on whether an increase in its inputs increases its output proportionately, more than proportionately, or less than proportionately. In this section we'll look at the cost implications of returns to scale.

A firm experiences **economies of scale** when its average cost falls as it produces more. This occurs when cost rises less, proportionately, than the increase in output. For example, suppose a firm increases its output from Q to $2Q$. If costs less than double, then $C(2Q) < 2C(Q)$; dividing both sides by $2Q$ tells us that $C(2Q)/2Q < C(Q)/Q$, so average cost is lower at $2Q$ than at Q. When the production technology for a good creates economies of scale, small producers will have a hard time surviving, because their average cost will be higher than that of larger competitors.

A firm experiences **economies of scale** when its average cost falls as it produces more.

A firm experiences **diseconomies of scale** when its average cost rises as it produces more. Diseconomies occur when cost rises more, proportionately, than the increase in output.

A firm experiences **diseconomies of scale** when its average cost rises as it produces more.

What is the relationship between returns to scale and economies of scale? When a firm's input prices do not vary with the amount it produces, it experiences economies of scale if its technology has increasing returns to scale, and experiences diseconomies of scale if its technology has decreasing returns to scale.

Figure 8.28 illustrates why. Let's first consider a firm that has increasing returns to scale in Figure 8.28(a). Suppose the firm begins by producing 100 units of output per month using input combination A. If the firm decides to double its output to 200 units by increasing its use of all inputs in the same proportion, it must use input combination C. Because the firm has increasing returns to scale, C will use less than double the amount of inputs used in A, so it will be less than twice as costly (the input combination that uses double the inputs in A is labeled 2A in the graph). Since the least cost bundle for producing 200 units, bundle B, is less costly than bundle C, it must also cost less than twice as much as bundle A. This means that the firm's average cost of producing 200 units is less than its average cost of producing 100 units; it has economies of scale.

Now consider a firm that has decreasing returns to scale in Figure 8.28(b). Suppose the firm starts by producing 200 units a month using input combination B. If it decides to cut its production in half to 100 units by reducing its use of all inputs in the same proportion, it must use input combination D. Because the firm has decreasing returns to scale, D will use *less* than half of the amount of inputs as B, so it will be less than half as costly (the input combination that uses half the inputs in B is labeled B/2 in the graph). Since the least cost bundle for producing 100 units, bundle A, is less costly than D, it must also

Figure 8.28

Returns to Scale and Economies of Scale. The figures illustrate that increasing returns to scale implies economies of scale and that decreasing returns to scale implies diseconomies of scale. In figure (a) with increasing returns to scale, input combination C costs less than twice as much as A. So B, which costs less than C, must also cost less than twice as much as A. In figure (b) with decreasing returns to scale, input combination D costs less than half as much as B. So A, which costs less than D, must also cost less than half as much as B.

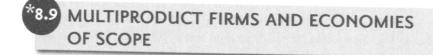

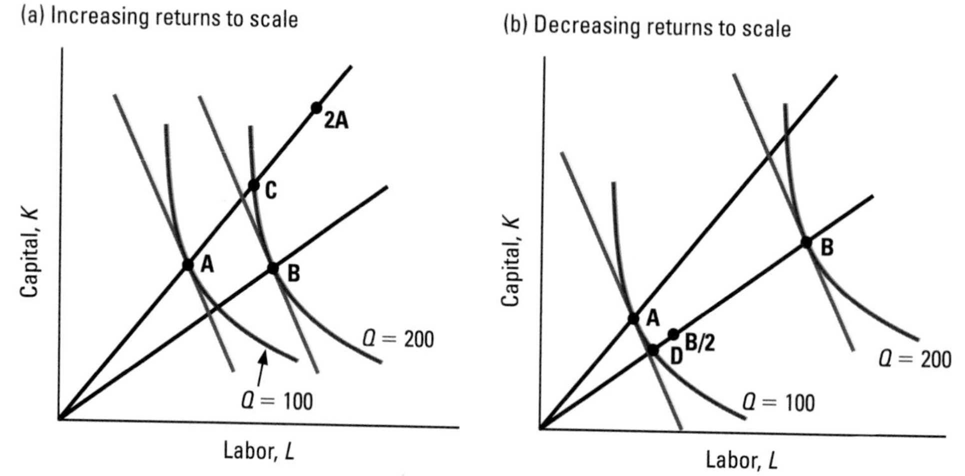

be less than half as costly as B. This means that the firm's average cost for producing 100 units is less than the average cost of producing 200 units; it has diseconomies of scale.[10]

We have discussed situations in which a firm's cost function has either economies of scale, diseconomies of scale, or a constant average cost. However, a firm's cost function may have economies of scale over a particular range of output, and diseconomies of scale over another range of output. The cost function shown in Figure 8.14 (page 274) is one example.

*8.9 MULTIPRODUCT FIRMS AND ECONOMIES OF SCOPE

In most of this chapter we have focused, for simplicity, on firms that produce a single product. Yet few firms actually do so. Hewlett Packard produces notebook computers, printers, and printer cartridges; Microsoft produces Windows, Office, and computer

[10]Sometimes a firm's input prices vary with the amount it produces. For example, the firm may get a quantity discount or face a quantity penalty (see Add-On 5D), so that its input price changes when it uses more or less of the input. In that case, there is a factor in addition to the firm's technology that contributes to economies or diseconomies of scale. For example, a firm facing a quantity discount for its inputs could have economies of scale even though it has decreasing returns to scale. Similarly, a firm that faces a quantity penalty for its inputs could have diseconomies of scale even though it has increasing returns to scale.

games. Even the corner gas station sells multiple grades of gasoline—"regular," "super," and "premium."

Fortunately, the basic concepts we've studied apply equally well to firms that produce many products. Suppose you're the manager of a firm that sells two products, whose output levels are Q_1 and Q_2. To make sound decisions, you need to determine your firm's cost function, which takes the form $C(Q_1, Q_2)$. This function tells you the total cost of producing each possible bundle of outputs. To derive it, you need to find the least-cost production method for each possible output bundle (Q_1, Q_2). Just as with a single product, there is an isoquant that gives the combinations of inputs that will allow you to produce this bundle of outputs using efficient production methods. Least-cost production involves finding the least costly point on that isoquant.

Why do firms produce multiple products? Just as economies of scale determine whether small or large firms are more effective competitors in a single-product market, the nature of technology and input costs help to determine whether single-product or multi-product firms are more effective competitors. **Economies of scope** occur when a single firm can produce two or more products more cheaply than two separate firms. For example, a single firm can produce the output bundle (Q_1, Q_2) more cheaply than two separate firms if

Economies of scope occur when a single firm can produce two or more products more cheaply than two separate firms.

$$C(Q_1, Q_2) < C(Q_1, 0) + C(0, Q_2)$$

Diseconomies of scope occur when producing two products in the same firm is more expensive than producing them separately, in different firms, so that $C(Q_1, Q_2) > C(Q_1, 0) + C(0, Q_2)$.

Diseconomies of scope occur when producing two products in a single firm is more expensive than producing them separately, in different firms.

Economies of scope arise for many of the same reasons as increasing returns to scale (see Section 7.4). If Noah and Naomi produce both garden benches and garden chairs, for example, workers may be able to specialize even further (perhaps by assembling similar portions of both products). Likewise, delivery routes may become more efficient when a truck delivers more than one product, perhaps by delivering both to the same address. Sometimes physical processes create opportunities for joint production. Many manufacturing firms now sell electricity generated from the heat produced as a by-product of their production processes.

Another reason for economies of scope, at least over some range of production, is the more intensive utilization of lumpy, indivisible inputs. The top executives of a firm that produces only one product may find they have the time and ability to manage the production of second, related product. A similar effect comes from the transfer of knowledge. For example, Xerox invested a great deal in learning how to design paper-feeding mechanisms for copy machines. That same knowledge can be used for printers.

As in our discussion of returns to scale in Section 7.4, it's harder to see why a firm might have diseconomies of scope. Couldn't the firm always set up a separate facility to produce each product, thereby producing just as cheaply as separate firms? Not necessarily. Indeed, in the 1990s, many firms decided that some of their divisions would be more efficient if they were run as separate firms; they sold off those divisions to other firms or to division managers. One of the motives behind these sales was to overcome the kinds of bureaucratic costs we discussed as a reason for decreasing returns to scale. When a firm has many divisions, the CEO can't run all of them; she relies on other managers. But the CEO often maintains some oversight of those managers, sometimes intervening in their decisions or controlling their access to capital. This lack of autonomy can make such divisions less efficient than separate firms.

Application 8.7

FedEx Ground

In 1965, Yale University undergraduate Frederick Smith wrote a term paper about the passenger route systems most air freight shippers used, which he viewed as economically inefficient. Smith emphasized the need for a system designed specifically for air freight which could accommodate time-sensitive shipments such as medicines, computer parts, and electronics. In 1973 he founded Federal Express, which would soon become the dominant provider of express package delivery.

In January 2000 Smith launched FedEx Ground, which aimed to compete with archrival United Parcel Service (UPS) in five-to-seven-day package deliveries via truck transport. Unlike Federal Express, UPS had started out as a ground shipping company and for years it enjoyed a virtual monopoly in five-to-seven-day ground package delivery. UPS entered the air-based express delivery market in the mid-1980s, after FedEx had established itself. Now Federal Express would be going head-to-head with UPS in UPS's core market.

A FedEx Ground truck

Why would FedEx be a good competitor for UPS in the five-to-seven-day ground market? Might it have lower costs than a separate ground-based shipping company? That is, might FedEx profit from economies of scope between express and five-to-seven-day ground delivery?

You might think that FedEx would benefit from economies of scope by using the same local trucks and delivery routes for its express and ground-based services. In fact, the company maintains two separate delivery fleets. So where might the economies of scope have come from? One possible source was the many existing FedEx offices, which could accept ground packages as well as express packages.[11] FedEx also had a lot of accumulated experience in the efficient organization of transportation systems, which was applicable to ground shipping. Finally, FedEx also had its excellent brand name and reputation. By leveraging its existing reputation for high quality service in express package delivery, FedEx may have avoided some of the costs of developing brand recognition.

Although our focus is on costs, demand factors may also have made FedEx a natural entrant into the ground shipping market. If existing FedEx customers valued the opportunity to use just one shipper for all of their shipping needs, FedEx could offer more value to those customers than a stand-alone ground shipping company.

CHAPTER SUMMARY

1. **Types of cost**

   a. A firm's total cost of producing a given level of output is the expenditure required to produce that output in the most economical way.

   b. Costs can be either variable or fixed. Variable cost is the cost of inputs that vary as the firm's output changes. Fixed cost is the cost of inputs that do not vary as the firm's output changes.

   c. Fixed costs can be either avoidable or sunk. A firm will not incur an avoidable fixed cost if it decides to produce no output, but it cannot avoid a cost that is sunk.

[11] There's also a downside, however, as one of us discovered when we had to send a draft of this chapter out quickly for overnight delivery—and found ourselves at the end of a long line of ground customers shipping their college belongings home at the end of the school year!

2. **What do economic costs include?**

   a. A firm's true economic costs of production include not only its out-of-pocket expenditures, but the opportunity costs it incurs when it forgoes opportunities to use resources in their best alternative use.

   b. When a firm owns some of the long-lived capital used in production, the true economic cost of its use is an opportunity cost. This cost equals the amount the firm could have received by renting the capital to someone else.

3. **Short-run cost: one variable input**

   a. In the short run, if a firm has just one variable input, we can find the firm's short-run variable cost curve by "flipping" the production function, plotting output on the horizontal axis and variable cost (the input price times the input level) on the vertical axis.

   b. The short-run variable cost function can be determined mathematically by using the production function to solve for the amount of variable input needed at each level of output and multiplying by the input's price. The firm's total cost is equal to this variable cost plus its fixed cost.

4. **Long-run cost: cost minimization with two variable inputs**

   a. When a firm has more than one variable input, the least-cost production method for producing Q units is the point on the Q-unit isoquant that lies on the lowest possible isocost line, which is equivalent to satisfying the no-overlap rule.

   b. If the least-cost production method is an interior solution, it must satisfy the tangency condition, at which point the MRTS—the ratio of marginal products—equals the input price ratio.

   c. If the least-cost input combination is a boundary solution, then the relationship between the MRTS and the input price ratio may instead satisfy an inequality condition.

   d. If the firm's isoquants have a declining MRTS, then any interior input combination that satisfies the tangency condition (so that the ratio of marginal products equals the input price ratio) is a least-cost input combination.

   e. The firm's output expansion path contains the least-cost input combinations at various levels of output at given input prices. The firm's cost function gives the cost of the input combinations along the firm's output expansion path.

5. **Average and marginal costs**

   a. Average cost is total cost divided by the number of units produced: $AC = C/Q$.

   b. Marginal cost is the extra cost associated with the ΔQ marginal units of output, measured on a per-unit basis: $MC = [C(Q) - C(Q - \Delta Q)]/\Delta Q$.

   c. When output is finely divisible, marginal cost at Q units of output is equal to the slope of the line drawn tangent to the cost curve at Q.

   d. A firm's average cost curve is downward sloping where marginal cost is less than average cost; upward sloping where marginal cost is greater than average cost; and neither rising nor falling where marginal cost equals average cost. The marginal cost curve crosses the average cost curve from below at the efficient scale of production. The same is true of the relationship between marginal cost and average variable cost.

6. **Effects of input price changes**

   When the price of an input increases (decreases), the least-cost production method uses less (more) of that input, or remains unchanged.

7. **Short-run versus long-run costs**

   a. If a firm cannot adjust one of its inputs in the short run but can do so over the long run, its costs when its output level changes will be higher in the short run than in the long run.

   b. The long-run average cost curve is the lower envelope of the firm's short-run average cost curves.

   c. Starting at any initial output level, the firm's short-run marginal cost curve is steeper than its long-run marginal cost curve. It crosses the long-run marginal cost curve at the initial output level.

8. **Economies and diseconomies of scale**

   a. A firm enjoys economies of scale if its average cost decreases as the quantity produced increases. It suffers diseconomies of scale if its average cost increases as the quantity produced increases.

   b. A firm whose technology has increasing returns to scale will enjoy economies of scale, while a firm with decreasing returns to scale will have diseconomies of scale.

*9. **Multiproduct firms and economies of scope**

   a. Most firms produce many products. One reason they do so is to take advantage of economies of scope, which arise when the cost of producing products together is lower than the cost of producing them in separate firms.

   b. When firms experience diseconomies of scope, it is cheaper to produce different products in separate firms.

Exercise 8.1: Economist Milton Friedman is famous for remarking that "There is no such thing as a free lunch." Interpret this comment in light of the discussion in Section 8.2.

Exercise 8.2: Many resort hotels remain open in the off season, even though they appear to be losing money. Why would they do so?

Exercise 8.3: Suppose Noah and Naomi's short-run weekly production function for garden benches is $F(L) = (3/2)L$, where L represents the number of hours of labor employed. The wage rate is \$15 an hour. What is their short-run cost function?

Exercise 8.4: Suppose Noah and Naomi's short-run weekly production function for garden benches is $F(L) = \min\{0, L - 2\}$, where L represents the number of hours of labor employed. The wage rate is \$15 an hour. What is their short-run cost function?

Exercise 8.5: "A production method must be efficient to be a least-cost method of producing Q units of output, but an efficient method need not be a least-cost method." True or false? Why?

Exercise 8.6: Johnson Tools produces hammers. It has signed a labor contract that guarantees workers a minimum of 30 hours per week of work. The contract also doubles the regular \$20 per hour wage for overtime (more than 30 hours per week). Johnson's production technology uses only one variable input, labor. The company can produce two hammers per hour of employed labor. What is its variable cost function? Graph its variable cost curve.

Exercise 8.7: Suppose college graduates earn \$25 an hour and high school graduates earn \$15 an hour. Suppose too that the marginal product of college graduates at Johnson Tools is five hammers per hour, while the marginal product of high school graduates is four hammers per hour (regardless of the number of each type of worker employed). What is the least-cost production method for producing 100 hammers in an eight-hour day? What if the marginal product of high school graduates were instead two hammers per hour? What is the critical difference in productivity (in percentage terms) at which the type of worker hired changes?

Exercise 8.8: Suppose that the production function for Hannah and Sam's home remodeling business is $Q = F(L, K) = 10L^{0.2}K^{0.3}$. If the wage rate is \$1,500 per week and the cost of renting a unit of capital is also \$1,000 per week, what is the least-cost input combination for remodeling 100 square feet each week? What is the total cost?

Exercise 8.9: Suppose that XYZ Corporation's total wages are twice the company's total expenditure on capital. XYZ has a Cobb-Douglas production function that offers constant returns to scale. What can you deduce about parameters α and β of this production function?

Exercise 8.10: Suppose that in worked-out problem 8.4 (page 271) Noah and Naomi wanted to produce 200 garden benches a week. What would be the best assignment of output to their two plants?

Exercise 8.11: Suppose that in worked-out problem 8.5 (page 277), the cost function at plant 2 was $C_2 = 650Q_2 + 2(Q_2)^2$, and marginal cost at that plant was $MC_2 = 650 + 4Q_2$. What would be the best assignment of output between the two plants?

Exercise 8.12: Noah and Naomi want to produce 100 garden benches per week in two production plants. The cost functions at the two plants are $C_1 = 600Q_1 - 3(Q_1)^2$ and $C_2 = 650Q_2 - 2(Q_2)^2$, and the corresponding marginal costs are $MC_1 = 600 - 6Q_1$ and $MC_2 = 650 - 4Q_2$. What is the best assignment of output between the two plants?

Exercise 8.13: Consider again worked-out problem 8.6 (page 286) but assume that Hannah and Sam are initially remodeling 200 square feet per week. What are their short-run and long-run cost functions?

Exercise 8.14: Consider again worked-out problem 8.6 (page 286) but assume that a unit of capital costs \$1,000 per week and that Hannah and Sam are initially remodeling 200 square feet per week. What are their short-run and long-run cost functions?

Exercise 8.15: Suppose that Hannah and Sam have the Cobb-Douglas production function $Q = F(L, K) = 10L^{0.25}K^{0.25}$. Both a worker and a unit of capital cost \$1,000 per week. If Hannah and Sam begin by remodeling 100 square feet per week, and if their capital is fixed in the short run but variable in the long run, what are their long-run and short-run cost functions? What are their long-run and short-run average cost functions for positive output levels?

Exercise 8.16: Does a firm with the cost function $C(Q) = Q^2$ experience economies of scale, diseconomies of scale, or neither?

Exercise 8.17: Many airlines operate a hub-and-spoke system in which passengers headed for different destinations fly into the hub on the same plane, then switch planes to reach their final destinations. How does this system reflect the presence of economies of scope?

9

PROFIT MAXIMIZATION

LEARNING OBJECTIVES

After reading this chapter, students should be able to:

- Describe the relationship between a firm's profit-maximizing sales quantity and the firm's marginal revenue and marginal cost.
- Demonstrate how price-taking firms should determine their profit-maximizing sales quantities.
- Determine a price-taking firm's supply function.
- Explain why price-taking firms usually respond more over the long run than they do over the short run.
- Define producer surplus and describe its measurement.

In 1992, Phillip Morris made over $5 billion from cigarette sales in the United States, and much more worldwide. More than 60 percent of that profit came from its Marlboro brand, one of the most successful brands ever created. Indeed, in 1992, almost a quarter of all cigarettes sold in the United States were Marlboros. The company had successfully imprinted the image of the rugged and independent Marlboro cowboy in consumers' minds.

Early in 1993, however, the Marlboro cowboy seemed to be circling his wagons. Sales of discount cigarettes were growing rapidly, reaching a market share of 30 percent in 1992—up from less than 20 percent only two years earlier. During the same period, Marlboro's market share had dropped from 26 percent to 24 percent. Combined with increased restrictions and taxes on cigarette smoking and a general decline in the number of smokers, this drop in market share spelled trouble in "Marlboro Country."

The Marlboro Cowboy

Executives at Phillip Morris needed to decide what to do. They faced a difficult choice. If things kept going as they were, discount cigarettes were likely to further erode Marlboro's sales. On the other hand, Phillip Morris might be able to regain market share by reducing prices. Yet taking that step would be costly, reducing the company's profits on each pack of cigarettes sold. Which choice would maximize Phillip Morris's profit? (We'll see what executives did later in Application 9.2.)

A firm that understands its technology and knows how to produce its output in the most economical way possible—the topics of Chapters 7 and 8—has taken the first steps toward maximizing its profit. But other decisions the firm faces can have an important influence on its profitability. In this chapter we'll provide a first discussion of the most central of these decisions, the firm's choice of the amount to sell or its product's price.

Here we'll introduce some general concepts and then focus on the special case of a firm that takes the price at which it can sell its product as given, as in the competitive markets we'll study in detail in Chapters 14 and 15 (and already discussed in Chapter 2). We'll consider cases in which firms are not price takers in Chapters 17–19 when we study monopoly and oligopoly.

In this chapter, we'll cover six topics:

1. *Profit-maximizing quantities and prices.* We'll explain that a manager who wants to maximize profit, the difference between revenue and cost, can equivalently think of her choice of finding the best price as one of finding the best sales quantity.

2. *Marginal revenue, marginal cost, and profit maximization.* In Chapter 3, we learned how to use the concepts of marginal benefit and marginal cost to find a best choice. Here we'll apply those lessons to the problem of finding the price or sales quantity that maximizes the firm's profit.

3. *Supply decisions by price-taking firms.* In Chapters 14–16 we'll continue our study of competitive markets in which firms take the market price for their product as given. Here we'll apply lessons learned in the preceding sections to show how price-taking firms should determine their profit-maximizing sales quantities.

4. *Short-run versus long-run supply by price-taking firms.* In Section 8.7 we discussed ways that a firm's cost function may differ over the short and long run. Those differences can affect the firm's short-run and long-run responses to a change in the price at which they can sell their output. We'll see why firms typically respond more over the long run than they do in the short run.

5. *Producer surplus.* We'll discuss a measure of a firm's profit that focuses on its avoidable costs and can be measured in a very convenient way using demand and supply curves. We'll use this measure frequently in later chapters when discussing the effects of policies.

*6. *Supply by multiproduct price-taking firms.* Most firms produce and sell more than one product. We'll discuss how a price-taking firm that sells more than one product can determine its profit-maximizing sales quantities. We'll also see how a change in the price of one product affects the amounts the firm sells of its other products.

9.1 PROFIT-MAXIMIZING QUANTITIES AND PRICES

A firm's **profit**, which we'll write as the Greek letter Π (pronounced "pie"), equals its revenue R less its cost C: that is, $\Pi = R - C$. The firm's profit maximization problem is to find the quantity or price that results in the largest possible profit.[1]

A firm's **profit,** Π, is equal to its revenue R less its cost C: that is, $\Pi = R - C$.

Do firms really try to maximize their profits? Certainly there are some cases in which they don't. A family-owned business might employ a family member even if she is not the best candidate for the job. And as the headlines show, sometimes a firm's managers seek to enrich themselves at the expense of the firm's shareholders. Nevertheless, the typical family business makes most of its decisions with an eye toward maximizing the family's income. Similarly, in large corporations, a number of mechanisms help to ensure that managers act primarily in the interest of shareholders. Those mechanisms include managerial incentives, corporate oversight, and the risk that an underperforming firm will be acquired, and its managers replaced. Moreover, in very competitive industries, a firm that does not maximize profit will simply fail to survive. Despite the exceptions, economists have found the assumption that firms will maximize their profit both useful and reasonably accurate.

Choosing Price versus Choosing Quantity

Before they attempt to sell a product, managers need to think about how many units they can sell and at what price.[2] This information is captured in the demand function and demand curve for the firm's product. As we saw in Chapter 2, a product's demand function states how many units buyers will demand at each price. It takes the form Quantity demanded = D(Price). Here we are implicitly holding all of the factors other than price that might affect demand for the product—consumer tastes, consumer income, the prices of substitutes, et cetera—fixed.

Figure 9.1 shows a typical demand curve, with the price P measured on the vertical axis and the quantity demanded, Q, measured on the horizontal axis. It shows how many units the firm will sell at each price. The lower the price, the more units it sells. Notice, however, that the manager could equally well think in terms of how many units she wants to sell. In that case, reading the demand curve in reverse tells her the price she needs to charge, $P(Q)$, to sell quantity Q (see Figure 9.1). This relationship is known as the product's **inverse demand function**, a function of the form Price = P(Quantity demanded).

The **inverse demand function** for a firm's product describes how much the firm must charge to sell any given quantity of its product. It takes the form *Price* = *P*(*Quantity demanded*).

[1]In this chapter we'll focus on pricing and output decisions. For decisions that have long-run effects, such as advertising or research and development, the firm will want to make a choice that maximizes its profit over time. We'll explain how to measure long-run profit in Chapter 10.

[2]In most of this chapter, we'll focus for simplicity on firms that sell a single product. In Section 9.6, we'll extend the analysis to a firm that sells many products.

Figure 9.1

The Demand Curve for a Firm's Product. The demand for the firm's product at any price *P* is given by the firm's demand curve, shown here. Alternatively, we can use the demand curve to determine the price *P*(*Q*) the firm must charge to sell a given quantity *Q*.

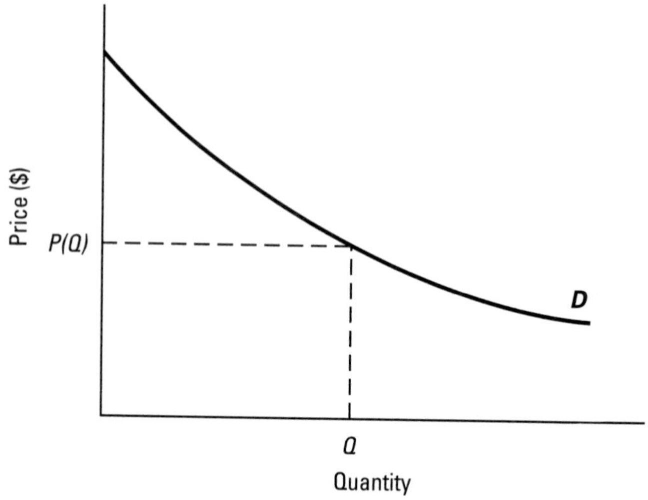

WORKED-OUT PROBLEM 9.1

The Problem The weekly demand for Noah and Naomi's garden benches is described by the demand function $Q^d = D(P) = 200 - P$. What price must Noah and Naomi charge if they want to sell 50 garden benches per week? What is Noah and Naomi's inverse demand function?

The Solution We want to solve for the price at which $Q^d = 50$. That is, we want to solve for P such that

$$200 - P = 50$$

The solution is $P = 150$. More generally, we can find the inverse demand function $P(Q)$ by solving the formula

$$200 - P = Q$$

for P, which gives us

$$P(Q) = 200 - Q$$

IN-TEXT EXERCISE 9.1 **Suppose the weekly demand for Noah and Naomi's garden benches is $Q^d = D(P) = 450 - 2P$. What price must they charge if they want to sell 100 benches per week? If they want to sell 150 benches per week? What is Noah and Naomi's inverse demand function?**

Maximizing Profit

Let's think about the firm's choice in terms of the quantity it sells. Recall that the firm's profit, Π, is equal to its revenue R less its total costs C; that is, $\Pi = R - C$. (In what follows, where it creates no confusion, we will just refer to the firm's total costs as its costs.)

Consider first the firm's revenue. If the firm wants to sell Q units, it must charge price $P(Q)$. Its revenue R when it sells Q units is therefore

$$R = P(Q) \times Q$$

To earn the greatest possible profit, the firm should choose the sales quantity that maximizes revenue less cost, where both revenue and cost depend on how much the firm decides to sell:

$$\Pi = R(Q) - C(Q)$$
$$= [P(Q) \times Q] - C(Q)$$

This problem is another example of finding a best choice by balancing benefits and costs, a topic we studied in Chapter 3. The *benefit* of selling quantity Q is the firm's revenue $R(Q) = P(Q) \times Q$. The *cost* of selling quantity Q is the firm's cost of production $C(Q)$.

Example 9.1

The Profit-Maximizing Price of Garden Benches

Suppose Noah and Naomi can produce up to 100 garden benches a week in batches of 10. Of all their possible production quantities (0, 10, 20, et cetera), which will yield the highest profit? What price should they charge?

To start, we need to know the weekly demand function for Noah and Naomi's garden benches. Let's suppose that it is $Q^d = D(P) = 200 - P$. Worked-out problem 9.1 shows that their inverse demand function is $P(Q) = 200 - Q$. That is, to sell Q garden benches a week, Noah and Naomi need to set their price equal to $200 - Q$.

The second thing we need to know is Noah and Naomi's weekly cost function for producing garden benches. Let's suppose that it is $C(Q) = Q^2$.

Table 9.1 contains the information we need to find Noah and Naomi's best choice. The first column lists their possible sales quantities. The second column records the price Noah

Table 9.1
Profits from Garden Bench Sales

	Sales Quantity	Price (per Unit)	Revenue	Cost	Profit
	0	$200	$0	$0	$0
	10	190	1,900	100	1,800
	20	180	3,600	400	3,200
	30	170	5,100	900	4,200
	40	160	6,400	1,600	4,800
Best choice →	(50)	150	7,500	2,500	(5,000)
	60	140	8,400	3,600	4,800
	70	130	9,100	4,900	4,200
	80	120	9,600	6,400	3,200
	90	110	9,900	8,100	1,800
	100	100	10,000	10,000	0

and Naomi must charge to sell each possible quantity Q of garden benches. The third column shows the revenue R from each choice, which is the product of columns 1 and 2. The fourth column gives the cost C of each choice. Finally, the fifth column shows the profit from each choice, equal to the revenue (column 3) minus the cost (column 4). Noah and Naomi's profit-maximizing choice is to sell 50 garden benches a week at a price of $150, which gives them a profit of $5,000 per week.

Figure 9.2(a) shows this solution graphically. The revenue at each possible quantity is plotted in blue and the cost in red. The best choice is 50 benches per week, at which point the vertical distance between the blue revenue points and the red cost points is greatest.

When output is finely divisible, we can find a firm's profit-maximizing sales quantity by graphing its revenue and cost curves. Let's now suppose that Noah and Naomi's garden bench output is finely divisible. Figure 9.2(b) shows Noah and Naomi's revenue and cost curves. The profit-maximizing quantity, $Q = 50$, is located where the vertical distance between the revenue and cost curves is greatest and their profit is $5,000 per week.

Figure 9.2

The Profit-Maximizing Sales Quantity of Garden Benches. Noah and Naomi's profit is maximized when they sell 50 garden benches per week, the quantity at which the vertical distance between their revenue (in blue) and their cost (in red) is greatest. At this sales quantity, their profit is $5,000 per week. Figure (a) shows the case where benches must be produced in batches of 10. Figure (b) shows the case where their output is finely divisible.

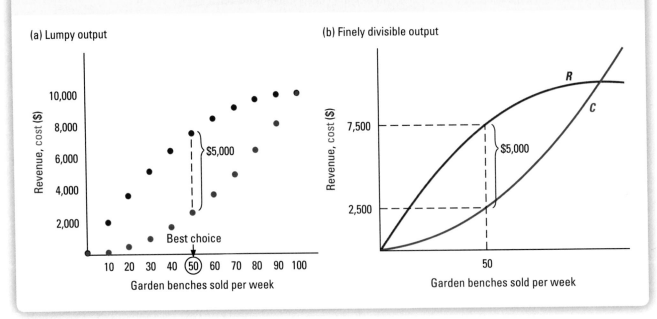

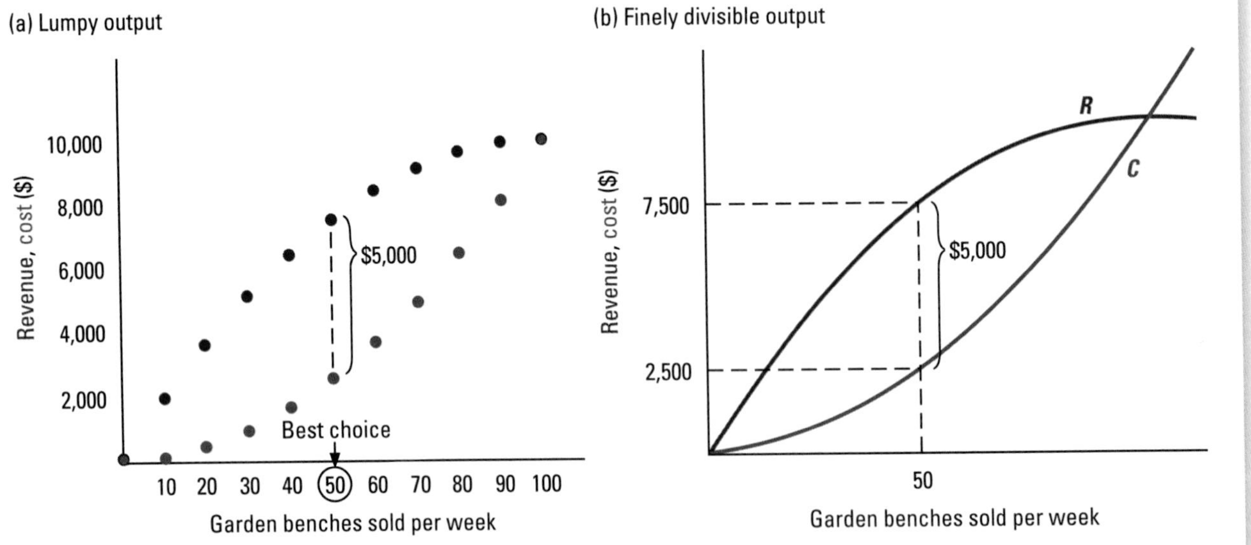

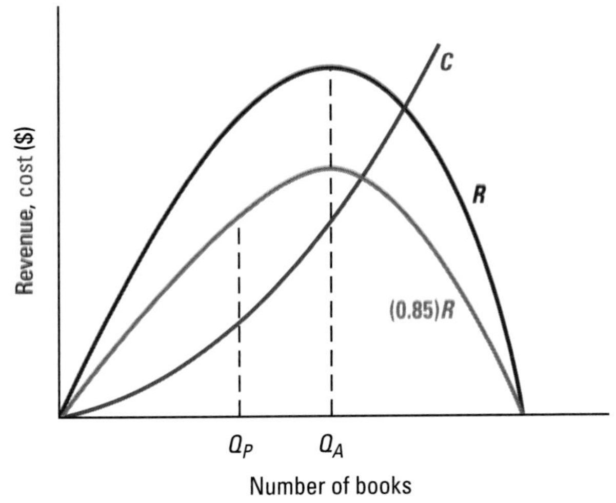

Figure 9.3

The Profit-Maximizing Sales Quantity for a Textbook's Author versus the Textbook's Publisher. If a textbook author receives 15 percent of revenue, (0.15)R, her profit is maximized when Q_A books are sold. The textbook's publisher receives the remainder of revenue and pays all costs, earning the profit (0.85)$R - C$. The publisher's profit is therefore maximized at Q_P books, which is less than Q_A. Thus, the publisher wants to charge a higher price for the book than does the author.

Application 9.1

A Textbook-Pricing Example

Setting the right price for a textbook can have an important effect on the profits it generates. But who sets the price, the authors or the publisher, and does the answer to this question affect the price you pay?

Typically, the publisher of a book sets the price, not the author or authors (that is, not us!). This fact can have an important effect on the book's price. An author's income from a book's sales is usually a fixed percentage of the revenue. For example, an author might receive 15 percent of revenue so that her profit is (0.15)R. In contrast, the publisher's profit from a book's sales is the remaining revenue less the book's production costs, all of which are borne by the publisher. So if the author gets (0.15)R, the publisher's profit is (0.85)$R - C$.

This difference in earnings means that the publisher and the author will prefer different prices. Figure 9.3 illustrates the difference. An author, who bears none of the production costs, wants to set a price (or, equivalently, a sales quantity) that maximizes the revenue R. Thus, the author's best sales quantity is Q_A, the quantity at which the dark blue revenue curve is highest. The publisher's revenue curve, (0.85)R, is shown in light blue, and the publisher's cost curve in red. The publisher's profit-maximizing sales quantity, Q_P, is the quantity at which the distance between those two curves is greatest.

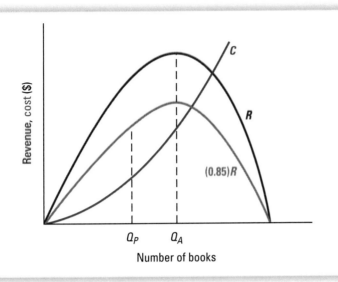

"I don't have a title yet, or even a subject. All I have is the price: twenty-three ninety-five in hardcover."

Note that Q_P, the publisher's profit-maximizing quantity, is less than Q_A, the author's profit-maximizing quantity. Thus, the author wants to set a lower price than the publisher (to sell the higher quantity). Intuitively, the author finds selling additional books a more attractive proposition than the publisher does, because the author doesn't bear the cost of producing those extra books.[3] In fact, it is common for authors to urge their publishers to set a lower price.

[3]Another reason why authors prefer a lower price is that they usually care about how many people read their book. The publisher, in contrast, cares mainly about profit.

9.2 MARGINAL REVENUE, MARGINAL COST, AND PROFIT MAXIMIZATION

In Section 3.2, we saw how marginal benefit must equal marginal cost at a decision maker's best choice whenever a small increase or decrease in her action is possible. We can apply the same ideas to the firm's profit maximization problem.

Marginal Revenue

A firm's **marginal revenue** at Q units equals the extra revenue produced by the ΔQ marginal units sold, measured on a per unit basis.

Here revenue is the benefit, so the firm's marginal benefit is its **marginal revenue**, denoted MR. The firm's marginal revenue captures the additional revenue it gets from the marginal units it sells (the smallest possible increment ΔQ in sales quantity), measured on a per unit basis. So if the firm is selling Q units of its product, its marginal revenue is

$$MR = \frac{\Delta R}{\Delta Q} = \frac{R(Q) - R(Q - \Delta Q)}{\Delta Q}$$

Table 9.2 shows the quantity, price, revenue, and marginal revenue for Noah and Naomi's business, whose revenues and costs were shown in Table 9.1. Arrows indicate the change in revenue captured with each change in quantity (note that here $\Delta Q = 10$).

Notice in Table 9.2 that Noah and Naomi's marginal revenue is equal to the price at $Q = 10$ but is less than the price at all sales levels above 10. Why? Think about how much revenue their last ΔQ units contribute. The increase in their sales quantity from $Q - \Delta Q$ to Q changes their revenue in two ways. The first is obvious: they sell ΔQ additional units, each at a price of $P(Q)$. We'll call this the *output expansion effect*. The second is more subtle: the increase in their sales quantity requires that they lower their price from $P(Q - \Delta Q)$ to $P(Q)$, which reduces the revenue they earn from the $Q - \Delta Q$ units that are *not* marginal, known as **inframarginal units**. This is the *price reduction effect*.

The **inframarginal units** are the units the firm sells other than the ΔQ marginal units.

Table 9.2

Revenue and Marginal Revenue from Garden Bench Sales

Sales Quantity	Price (per Unit)	Revenue	Marginal Revenue (per Unit)
0	$200	$0	—
10	190	1,900	$190
20	180	3,600	170
30	170	5,100	150
40	160	6,400	130
50	150	7,500	110
60	140	8,400	90
70	130	9,100	70
80	120	9,600	50
90	110	9,900	30
100	100	10,000	10

Figure 9.4

The Relationship between Marginal Revenue and Price. When the firm expands its sales from $Q - \Delta Q$ to Q, it earns $P(Q) \times \Delta Q$ in revenue on the extra units it sells, equal to the green-shaded rectangle in both figures. Were that the only change in its revenue, as in figure (a), its marginal revenue—the extra revenue earned per marginal unit sold—would exactly equal the price. However, when the demand curve is downward-sloping, the firm also suffers a loss in revenue on the $Q - \Delta Q$ inframarginal units because it must lower its price by the amount $P(Q - \Delta Q) - P(Q)$ to sell the extra units. This revenue loss equals the yellow-shaded rectangle in figure (b). The firm's marginal revenue in that case is less than the price $P(Q)$.

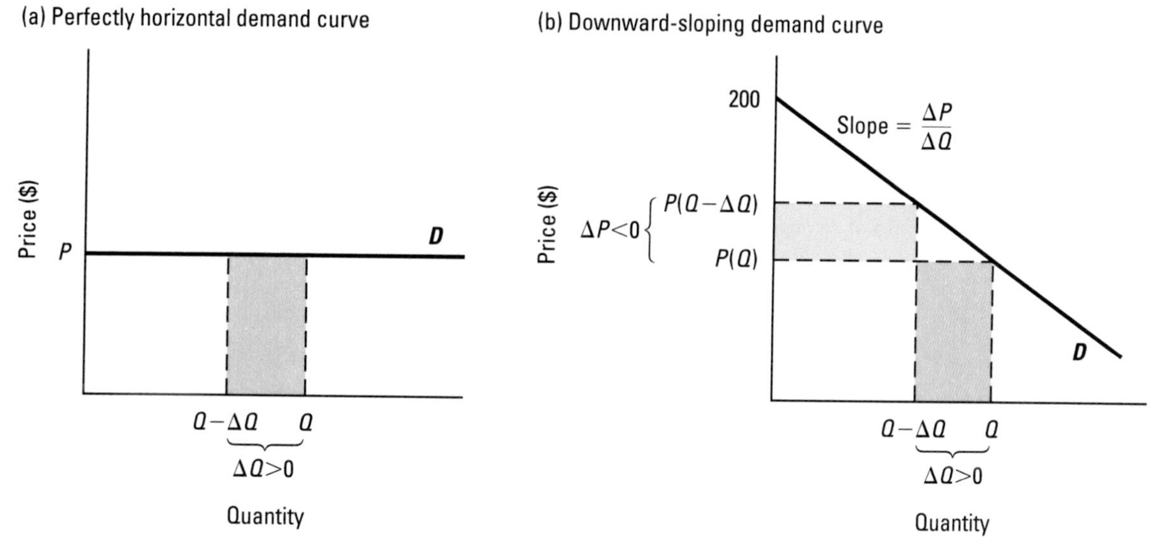

To explore these two effects further, consider first the case in which the firm's demand curve is perfectly horizontal at price P, illustrated in Figure 9.4(a). In that case, the firm can sell as much as it wants at the price P, but nothing at any higher price. Such a firm is called a **price taker**. (For example, a firm in a perfectly competitive market is a price taker since it can sell as much as it wants at the market price, but nothing at any higher price.) In this case, only the output expansion effect is present, because increasing the firm's sales quantity does not require a reduction in price. The firm's extra revenue is the area of the green-shaded rectangle in the figure [with a height of P and a width of ΔQ], equal to $P \times \Delta Q$. So, dividing that revenue change by ΔQ, marginal revenue is exactly P per unit.

A firm is a **price taker** when it can sell as much as it wants at some given price *P*, but nothing at any higher price.

Figure 9.4(b) shows a case in which demand is downward sloping. The extra ΔQ sales at price $P(Q)$ contribute additional revenue of $P(Q) \times \Delta Q$, equal to the area of the green-shaded rectangle in the figure. That's the output expansion effect. To sell the ΔQ marginal units, Noah and Naomi must reduce their price from $P(Q - \Delta Q)$ to $P(Q)$. They lose the difference, $P(Q - \Delta Q) - P(Q)$, on each inframarginal unit. Notice that this price difference equals the height of the yellow rectangle in Figure 9.4(b). Since there are $Q - \Delta Q$ inframarginal units (the width of the yellow rectangle), Noah and Naomi's revenue falls by $[P(Q - \Delta Q) - P(Q)](Q - \Delta Q)$, the area of the yellow rectangle. This is the price reduction effect. The overall change in revenue equals the green-shaded area less the yellow-shaded area, which together is less than $P(Q) \times \Delta Q$. Dividing by ΔQ, marginal revenue is less than $P(Q)$.

Notice also that when sales are very small, the second effect—the revenue loss on the inframarginal units—will be small. Indeed, when the firm sells its first ΔQ units, there are no inframarginal units, so marginal revenue equals the price.

Figure 9.5 shows the relationship between marginal revenue and price when output is finely divisible. The same principles hold (the logic above did not depend on whether output is finely divisible). Figure 9.5(a) shows the case of a firm that is a price taker, whose demand curve is perfectly horizontal. In that case, the marginal revenue and demand curves coincide. Figure 9.5(b) shows the case of a downward-sloping demand curve. In that case, marginal revenue is equal to price when sales (and, hence, inframarginal units) are zero, and is below price at every positive sales quantity.

Figure 9.5

Marginal Revenue and Demand Curves. Figure (a) shows that the marginal revenue curve coincides with the demand curve when the demand curve is perfectly horizontal. With a downward-sloping demand curve, as in figure (b), the marginal revenue curve lies below the demand curve at all positive sales quantities, and coincides with it at a quantity of zero.

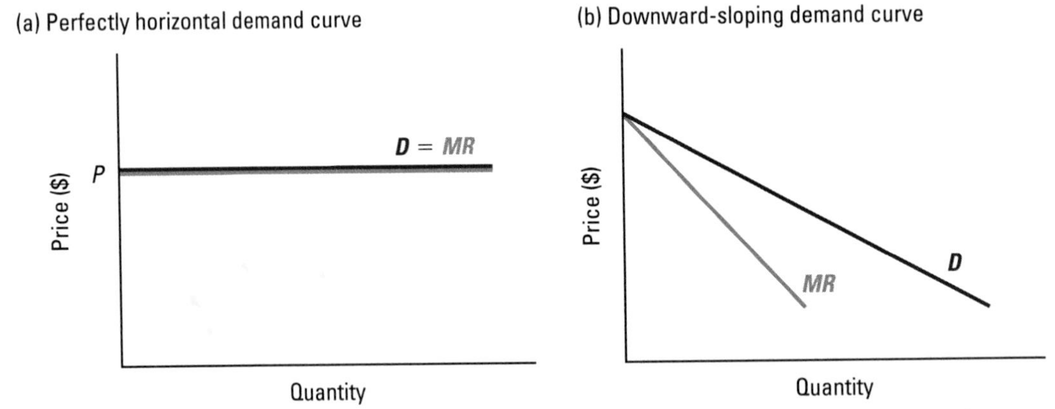

Application 9.2

Marlboro Friday

On Friday April 2, 1993, executives at Phillip Morris made a bold move, announcing a reduction of approximately 20 percent in the price of Marlboros. The retail price dropped from \$2.20 to \$1.80 a pack. The announcement sent shock waves through the cigarette industry. The reaction in the stock market was swift and punishing: Phillip Morris's stock price dropped 23 percent in a single day, erasing \$13.4 billion in stockholder value. That day was immediately dubbed "Marlboro Friday."

Was the price reduction really such a bad idea for Phillip Morris? That depends crucially on two things: (a) how much Marlboro sales would increase after the price reduction and (b) how much it would cost Phillip Morris to produce the extra cigarettes. Let's denote Marlboro sales before the price reduction Q_B, and sales afterward Q_A. Then the price reduction would raise profit if

$$(1.80)Q_A - C(Q_A) > (2.20)Q_B - C(Q_B)$$

Another way to put this is that overall profit would increase if the profit earned on the extra sales exceeded the revenue lost on existing sales:

$$(1.80)(Q_A - Q_B) - [C(Q_A) - C(Q_B)] > (0.40)Q_B$$

Without access to Phillip Morris's proprietary information, we cannot know the cost of the extra units. But we can try to get a rough sense of the cost by looking at published estimates of the industry's average variable cost. In 1992 that cost was \$1 per pack.[4] If the extra packs Phillip Morris sold as a result of the price reduction each cost \$1 to produce, so that $C(Q_A) - C(Q_B) = Q_A - Q_B$, then the price reduction would be a good idea if:

$$(0.80)(Q_A - Q_B) > (0.40)Q_B$$

Dividing by Q_B and rearranging terms, this expression tells us that the price reduction would raise profit if

$$\frac{Q_A - Q_B}{Q_B} > \frac{0.40}{0.80} = 0.50$$

That is, if we are using the correct cost for the extra packs, then the 20 percent price reduction would increase profit if Marlboro sales increased more than 50 percent.

Sales of Marlboros did increase after Marlboro Friday. By the beginning of 1995, Marlboro's market share had climbed to over 30 percent, an increase of roughly 36 percent over its March 1992 market share of 22 percent, but still less than the 50 percent gain that we calculated above was necessary for profits to increase. Given the uncertainties in our calculation of that threshold, however, it is nonetheless possible that the price cut may have increased Phillip Morris's profit.[5] Indeed, by early March 1995, Phillip Morris's share price had reached \$61, nearly its level just before Marlboro Friday.[6]

The Profit-Maximizing Sales Quantity

In Section 3.2 (and the appendix to Chapter 3), we saw that a best choice must satisfy the No Marginal Improvement Principle, which says that no marginal increase or decrease in the choice can produce an increase in net benefit. To review: when actions are finely divisible, marginal benefit (MB) equals marginal cost (MC) at an interior best choice (one at which the action can be both slightly increased or slightly decreased): if $MB > MC$, then it would be better to increase the action a little bit because the extra benefit would be larger than the extra cost. If, instead, $MB < MC$, then it would be better to slightly decrease the action because the cost savings would be larger than the lost benefits.

This fact helped us to devise a convenient method for finding a best choice. This method had two steps:

Step 1: Identify any interior actions at which $MB = MC$. If more than one interior action satisfies $MB = MC$, determine which produces the highest net benefit.

Step 2: Compare the net benefits at any boundary actions to the net benefit at the best interior action. The best choice is the action with the highest net benefit.

---

[4]This includes variable production costs, taxes, and retail markups.

[5]We are omitting some other factors as well. First, Phillip Morris also produced other cigarettes, including discount brands. (In fact, Phillip Morris also changed the prices on those other brands.) Some of the increased sales of Marlboros may have come from consumers who switched from those other Phillip Morris brands. Another issue is that we have assumed that absent the price reduction, Marlboro sales would have continued at their 1992 level, rather than eroding further.

[6]To read more about Phillip Morris's decision, see "Phillip Morris: Marlboro Friday (A) and (B)," Harvard Business School Case Studies 9–596–001 and 9–596–002.

We can apply the same principles here to the firm's profit maximization problem by comparing marginal revenue and marginal cost. For the firm's profit maximization problem, any positive sales quantity is interior. So, if the firm's profit-maximizing sales quantity is positive, marginal revenue equals marginal cost at that quantity. For the second step, the only possible boundary choice involves selling nothing (shutting down). The two-step procedure becomes:

Finding the Profit-Maximizing Sales Quantity using Marginal Revenue and Marginal Cost

Step 1: Quantity rule. Identify any positive sales quantities at which $MR = MC$. If more than one positive sales quantity satisfies $MR = MC$, determine which one is best (which produces the highest profit).

Step 2: Shut-down rule. Check whether the most profitable positive sales quantity from Step 1 results in greater profit than shutting down. If it does, that is the profit-maximizing choice. If not, then selling nothing is the best option. If they are the same, then either choice maximizes profit.

In the remainder of this chapter, we'll use this procedure to study profit maximization by firms that are price takers. In Chapters 17–19 we'll use it again to look at the behavior of firms that face downward-sloping demand curves.

9.3 SUPPLY DECISIONS BY PRICE-TAKING FIRMS

The rest of this chapter is devoted to the supply decisions of firms that are price takers. Recall that these are firms that can sell as much as they want at some price P, but nothing at any higher price. A firm that is a price taker faces a perfectly horizontal demand curve for its product as in Figures 9.4(a) and 9.5(a). Firms in perfectly competitive markets, which we've examined briefly in Chapter 2 and will return to study in Chapters 14–16, take the market price as given when deciding how much to sell.

The methods we'll discuss in this section apply for any cost function the firm may be facing. As a result, they apply whether we are considering the short run or the long run. In Section 9.4, we'll examine the implications they have for differences in a firm's behavior in the short run and long run.

The Profit-Maximizing Sales Quantity of a Price-Taking Firm

In Section 9.2 we saw that profit maximization means selling the quantity at which marginal revenue equals marginal cost if that quantity yields a positive profit, and selling nothing otherwise. Here, we'll apply this general principle to the case of a price-taking firm.

When a firm is a price taker, changes in its sales quantity have no effect on the price P it can charge. In Section 9.2, we saw that this implies that a price-taking firm's marginal revenue (MR) equals the price of its output (P). As a result, the firm's price must equal its marginal cost at its profit-maximizing sales quantity (also called its profit-maximizing output level): that is, since $MR = MC$ at a firm's profit-maximizing quantity, and since $MR = P$ for a price-taking firm, we must have $P = MC$. Moreover, the two-step procedure for finding the firm's profit-maximizing sales quantity that we discussed in Section 9.2 can be adapted as follows:

Finding the Profit-Maximizing Sales Quantity (or Output Level) for a Price-Taking Firm

Step 1: Quantity rule. Identify any positive sales quantities at which $P = MC$. If more than one positive sales quantity satisfies $P = MC$, determine which one is best (which produces the highest profit).

Step 2: Shut-down rule. Check whether the most profitable positive sales quantity from Step 1 results in greater profit than shutting down. If it does, that is the profit-maximizing choice. If not, then selling nothing is the best option. If they are the same, then either choice maximizes profit.

If a firm has no sunk costs, then the profit from shutting down is zero. The shut-down rule then amounts to checking whether profit is nonnegative at the best positive sales quantity ($PQ - C \geq 0$) or, equivalently, whether the price is at least as large as the firm's average cost ($P \geq AC$).

Figure 9.6 illustrates this procedure. The firm in Figure 9.6(a) faces a perfectly horizontal demand curve for its product at price P. Applying the quantity rule, the best positive sales quantity is Q^*, the quantity at which marginal cost equals the price P. Figure 9.6(b) adds the firm's average cost curve to illustrate the shut-down rule. Since the firm's average cost curve is below the price P at Q^*, the firm's profit from selling Q^* units is positive and equals the area of the green-shaded rectangle, which is $(P - AC)Q$. (Notice that $(P - AC)Q = [P - (C/Q)]Q = PQ - C$, which is the firm's profit.) Assuming the firm has no sunk costs, the firm is better off selling Q^* units than it would be if it shut down.

In fact, for a price-taking firm without sunk costs, the shut-down rule takes a particularly simple form. Let's use AC_{min} to stand for the firm's average cost at its efficient scale Q^e—the lowest point on its average cost curve [see Figure 9.6(b)]. If the price P exceeds AC_{min}, then the firm could make a positive profit by selling Q^e units. Its profit at its best sales quantity is therefore surely positive. On the other hand, if P is less than AC_{min} then AC is greater than the price at every possible sales quantity. The firm can't make a positive profit in that case. So an equivalent way to state the shut-down rule for a price-taking firm without sunk costs is:

The Shut-Down Rule without Sunk Costs If P exceeds AC_{min}, the best positive sales quantity maximizes profit. If P is less than AC_{min}, shutting down maximizes profit. If P equals AC_{min}, then both the best positive sales quantity and shutting down yield zero profit, which is the best the firm can do.

Figure 9.6

The Profit-Maximizing Sales Level for a Price-Taking Firm. Figure (a) illustrates the quantity rule: The most profitable positive sales quantity is the quantity Q^* at which price equals marginal cost. Figure (b) illustrates the shut-down rule: Since the profit at sales quantity Q^* is positive (the green-shaded area), selling quantity Q^* is better than shutting down. Note that the price is greater than average cost at quantity Q^*.

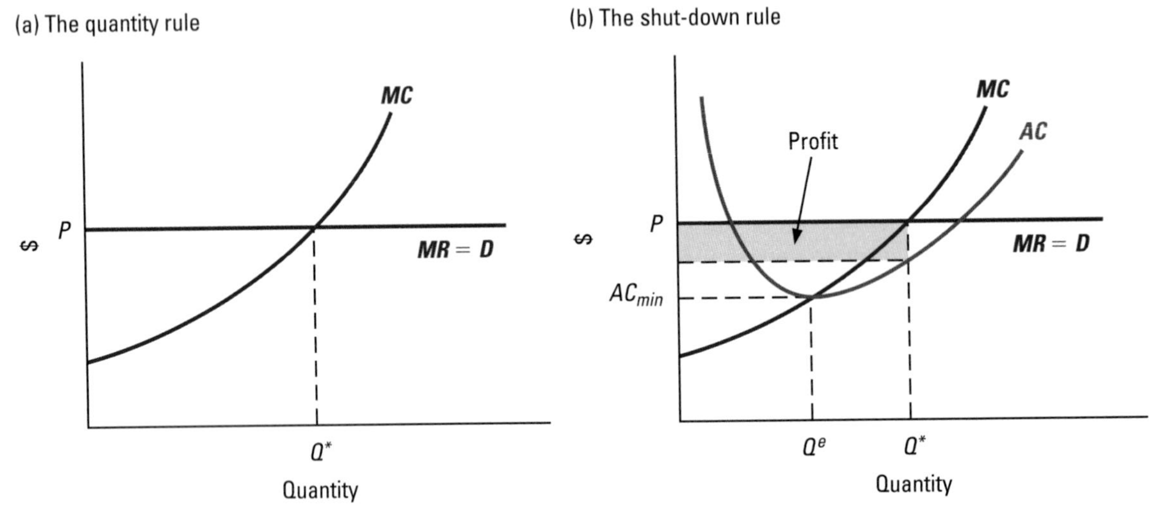

What if the firm does have sunk costs, so that its profit should it shut down is negative (equal to those sunk costs)? One very simple way to proceed is to simply ignore sunk costs entirely. Since, as we discussed in Section 3.3, the level of sunk costs doesn't effect a decision maker's best choice (sunk costs are "water under the bridge"), we can just ignore them in calculating costs and proceed exactly as above. This amounts to comparing the price P not to average cost in making the shut-down decision but to average cost excluding any sunk costs; that is, to *average avoidable cost.*[7]

Worked-out problem 9.2 shows how to solve for a price-taking firm's profit-maximizing sales quantity using algebra.

WORKED-OUT PROBLEM 9.2

The Problem Dan loves pizza. His company, Dan's Pizza Company, makes frozen pizzas. The market price of a pizza is \$10, and Dan is a price taker. His daily cost of making pizzas is $C(Q) = 5Q + (Q^2/80)$, and his marginal cost is $MC = 5 + (Q/40)$. How many pizzas should Dan sell each day? What if he also has an avoidable fixed cost of \$845 per day?

[7]Another way to see that this is the right comparison is as follows: The firm wants to operate provided that its profit is no less than its profit if it shuts down, or Profit $\geq -$(Sunk cost). Since profit equals (PQ—Avoidable cost—Sunk cost), adding sunk costs to both sides of the inequality tells us that this is equivalent to saying that the firm wants to operate if $PQ -$ Avoidable cost ≥ 0. This is equivalent to saying that $P \geq$ Average avoidable cost.

The Solution Applying the quantity rule, Dan's best positive sales quantity solves the formula $P = MC$, or

$$10 = 5 + \frac{Q}{40}$$

The solution is $Q = 200$. Now let's consider the shut-down rule. We can verify that the profit from producing 200 pizzas a day is positive in several ways: (a) By directly calculating that the profit is $\Pi = (10 \times 200) - (5 \times 200) - (200^2/80) = \$500$; (b) By observing that average cost when $Q = 200$ [\$7.50 per pizza, since $AC(Q) = 5 + (Q/80)$] is less than the price (\$10); or (c) By observing that the price (\$10) is greater than AC_{min} (\$5). (To find AC_{min}, note that Dan's average cost $AC(Q) = 5 + (Q/80)$ increases as his output increases, so it is lowest when his output is very close to zero, where it equals \$5.)

If Dan also has an avoidable fixed cost of \$845 per day, his profit at $Q = 200$ would be −\$345, and the shut-down rule would tell us that he should stop selling frozen pizzas altogether. [Alternatively, we could see that the price (\$10) is now less than the average cost at 200 pizzas, which is \$11.73, rounded to the nearest penny.]

IN-TEXT EXERCISE 9.2 **Suppose the price of a pizza rises to \$15. What will be Dan's profit-maximizing sales quantity? What if he also has an avoidable fixed cost of \$750?**

The Supply Function of a Price-Taking Firm

The **supply function** of a price-taking firm tells us how much the firm wants to sell at each possible price P. It is a function of the form *Quantity supplied* = *S(Price)*. To find a firm's supply function, we can apply the quantity and shut-down rules. At each price above the lowest level of average cost, AC_{min}, the firm's profit-maximizing quantity is positive and equates price with marginal cost. At each price below the lowest level of average cost AC_{min}, the firm supplies nothing. When the price exactly equals AC_{min}, the firm is indifferent between producing nothing and producing at its efficient scale Q^e, the quantity at which its average cost is lowest, if that is different from zero.

The **supply function** of a price-taking firm tells us how much the firm wants to sell at each possible price P. It is a function of the form *Quantity Supplied* = *S(Price)*.

Figure 9.7 shows two examples of a price-taking firm's supply curve. In Figure 9.7(a), average cost increases as the firm's output rises, so AC is smallest at $Q = 0$ and marginal cost is everywhere above average cost. In Figure 9.7(b), average cost first falls and then rises, so the firm's efficient scale Q^e is positive. In both cases, when the price exceeds AC_{min}, the firm's supply curve (shown in green) coincides with its marginal cost curve. For example, at the price P' (shown in both figures), the firm supplies the quantity $S(P')$. At prices below AC_{min}, the firm supplies nothing. [Whenever the part of a firm's supply curve that coincides with its marginal cost curve hits the vertical axis, as in Figure 9.7(a), we won't draw the portion of the supply curve below that point. Supply is zero for all lower prices. However, whenever a firm's supply jumps upward when the price reaches AC_{min}, as in Figure 9.7(b), we will draw the portion of the supply curve that lies along the vertical axis, indicating zero supply, to avoid any confusion.] Notice also that in Figure 9.7(b), both zero and Q^e are part of the firm's supply curve when the price equals AC_{min}.

Figure 9.7

The Supply Curve of a Price-Taking Firm. Figures (a) and (b) show the supply curve of a price-taking firm when the firm's efficient scale of production Q^e—the quantity at which average cost is smallest—is zero [in Figure (a)] and positive [in Figure (b)]. In each case, the supply curve coincides with the firm's marginal cost curve at prices above the lowest level of average cost, AC_{min}, and involves zero supply at prices below the minimum average cost.

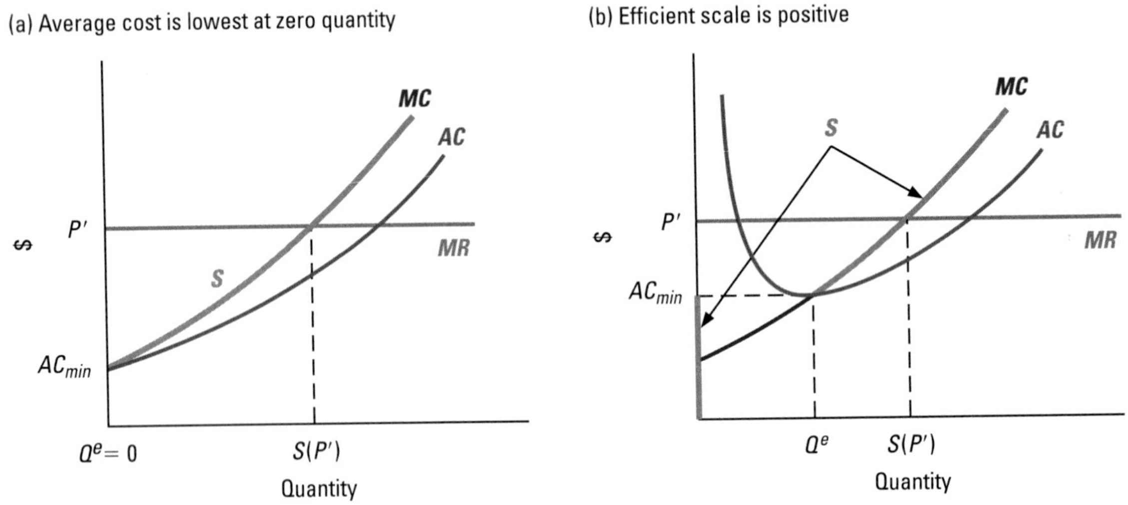

Worked-out problem 9.3 shows how to find a firm's supply function using algebra.

WORKED-OUT PROBLEM 9.3

The Problem Recall Dan's Pizza Company from worked-out problem 9.2. What is Dan's supply function if he has no avoidable fixed cost? What if his avoidable fixed cost is \$845 per day?

The Solution Using the same logic as in the solution to worked-out problem 9.2, the best positive sales quantity Q when the price is P sets price equal to marginal cost, so that

$$P = 5 + \frac{Q}{40}$$

Solving this expression for Q, we find that

$$Q = 40P - 200$$

Recall that when Dan has no avoidable fixed cost, AC_{min} = \$5. So using the shut-down rule, Dan's supply function is

$$S(P) = \begin{cases} 40P - 200 \text{ if } P \geq 5 \\ 0 \text{ if } P \leq 5 \end{cases}$$

Figure 9.8(a) shows this supply curve.

When we add an avoidable fixed cost of \$845 per day, the implications of the quantity rule do not change (the avoidable fixed cost changes neither marginal revenue nor marginal cost). However, the desirability of staying in business does change, so we need to determine the new level of AC_{min}. Let's first find the new efficient scale of production by determining the output level at which marginal cost equals average cost. It is the quantity Q^e at which

$$MC = 5 + \frac{Q^e}{40} = \frac{845}{Q^e} + 5 + \frac{Q^e}{80} = AC$$

Solving, we find that $Q^e = 260$. Substituting this quantity into the expression for average cost tells us that

$$AC_{min} = \frac{845}{260} + 5 + \frac{260}{80} = \$11.50$$

So Dan's supply function is now

$$S(P) = \begin{Bmatrix} 40P - 200 \text{ if } P \geq 11.50 \\ 0 \text{ if } P \leq 11.50 \end{Bmatrix}$$

Figure 9.8(b) shows this supply curve.

IN-TEXT EXERCISE 9.3 **Consider again Dan's Pizza Company from worked-out problem 9.2. What is Dan's supply function if he has a daily variable cost of $VC = Q^2/2$, a marginal cost of $MC = Q$, and an avoidable fixed cost of \$50 per day?**

Figure 9.8

Dan's Supply Curves. Figure (a) shows Dan's supply curve when he has no avoidable fixed cost. Figure (b) shows Dan's supply curve with an avoidable fixed cost of \$845 per day.

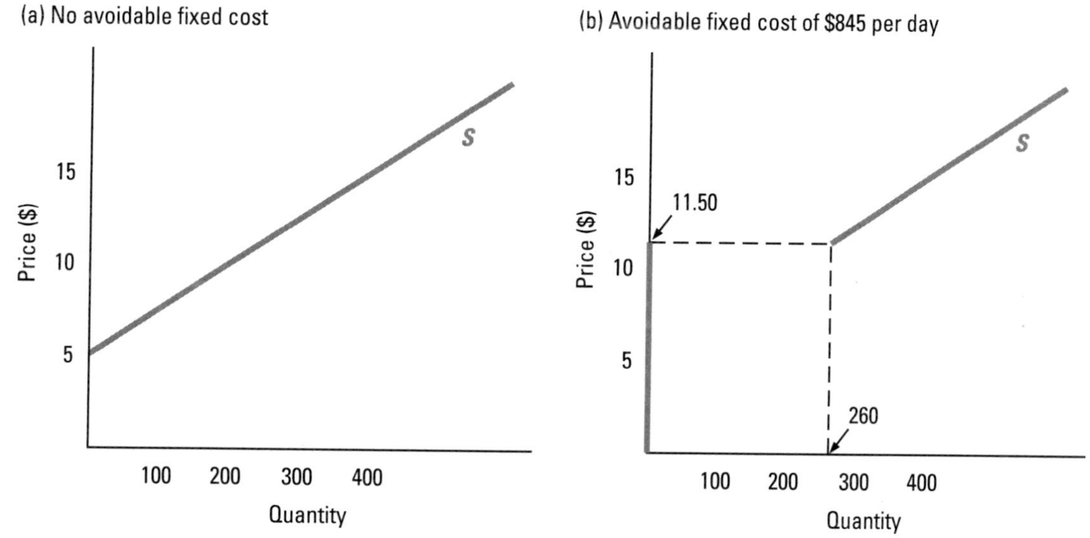

The Law of Supply

The **Law of Supply** says that when the market price increases, the profit-maximizing sales quantity for a price-taking firm never decreases.

You may have noticed that all the supply functions we've derived have had the property that a competitive firm's sales quantity either increases or remains unchanged when the market price rises. That is not an accident. The **Law of Supply** says that is the way things always work. Indeed, unlike the Law of Demand for consumers (which, as we saw in Chapter 5, need not hold if the good is inferior and income effects are sufficiently large), the Law of Supply always holds for price-taking firms.

To see why, look at Figure 9.9. There we've drawn a price-taking firm's revenue curve at the initial price $\bar{P}$, $R(Q) = \bar{P}Q$, in dark blue. It's a straight line with a slope of $\bar{P}$ that runs through the origin. The firm's cost function is shown in red. We've deliberately drawn it with a fixed cost (total cost jumps from \$0 to a positive number when the firm produces a very small amount) and an odd shape to emphasize that the Law of Supply holds for *any* cost function. The profit-maximizing sales quantity at price $\bar{P}$ is Q^*, where the vertical distance between the revenue and cost curves is greatest (and the slopes of the revenue and cost curves are equal since $MR = MC$).

Now suppose the price rises to $\hat{P}$, shifting the firm's revenue curve to $R(Q) = \hat{P}Q$, the light blue line running through the origin. The firm's revenue rises at each sales level. The size of the increase is given by the length of the arrows pointing from the old revenue curve to the new one. Notice that the arrows become longer as we move from left to right, so that the increase in revenue at Q^* is greater than the increase in revenue at any quantity below Q^*. Since selling Q^* units was more profitable than selling any smaller number of units before the price increase, it must still be better after the price increase. This analysis implies that a competitive firm's profit-maximizing sales quantity *cannot decrease* when the market price increases. (In fact, it will usually increase. For example, in Figure 9.9, the new quantity that maximizes the distance between the revenue and cost curves lies to the right of Q^*.)

Figure 9.9

The Law of Supply. This figure shows why the Law of Supply, which says that a price-taking firm never decreases its supply when the market price rises, holds. Quantity Q^* maximizes the distance between the firm's revenue and cost curves at price $\bar{P}$. When the market price rises to $\hat{P}$, revenue rises more at quantity Q^* than at any smaller quantity. As a result, since quantity Q^* was better than any smaller quantity before the price increase, it must still be better than any smaller quantity after the price increase. This analysis implies that the firm's most profitable sales quantity after a price increase cannot be lower than Q^*.

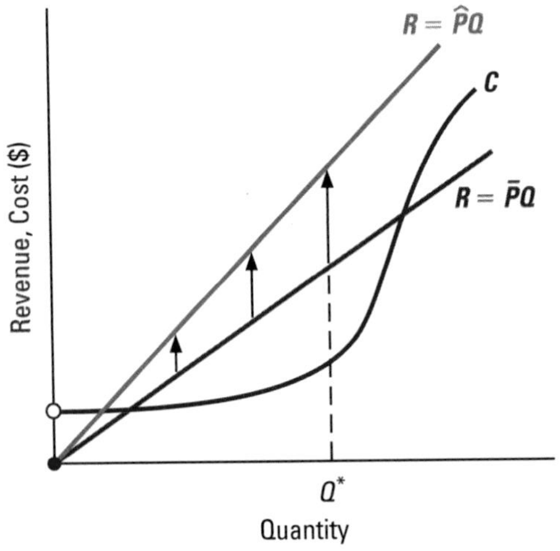

Changes in Input Prices and Shifts in the Supply Function

How does a change in an input price affect a firm's supply function? Imagine that a wheat farmer faces an increase in the price of water, raising her cost by \$5 for each bushel she produces. Figure 9.10(a) shows her marginal and average cost curves before the change, labeled MC_B and AC_B. Her supply curve before the change, labeled S_B, is shown in green. Figure 9.10(b) shows the average and marginal cost curves after the change, labeled MC_A and AC_A. Both curves have shifted up by exactly \$5 at every quantity. The new supply curve, S_A, has also shifted up by \$5. In essence, if the farmer receives exactly \$5 more per bushel, she is willing to supply the same amount of wheat as before.

Figure 9.11 shows how the farmer's supply curve changes with an increase in avoidable fixed cost. Figure 9.11(a) shows the farmer's marginal and average cost curves and the supply function before the change, labeled MC_B, AC_B, and S_B. Figure 9.11(b) shows these same curves after the change, labeled MC_A, AC_A, and S_A. AC_{min} has gone up from \$5 to \$10. Notice that the average cost curve shifts upward, but the marginal cost curve is unaffected. As a result, the farmer sells exactly the same quantity as before, provided she doesn't shut down. Now, however, it requires a higher price—at least \$10 instead of \$5—to stay in business.

Determining the change in a firm's supply function using algebra is just a matter of finding its supply function twice, once for before the change and once after. In essence,

Figure 9.10

A Change in a Wheat Farmer's Supply Curve. Figure (a) shows a wheat farmer's initial situation and supply curve. Figure (b) shows the change in the farmer's supply curve when her cost rises by \$5 per bushel, shifting the supply curve upward by \$5 at every quantity.

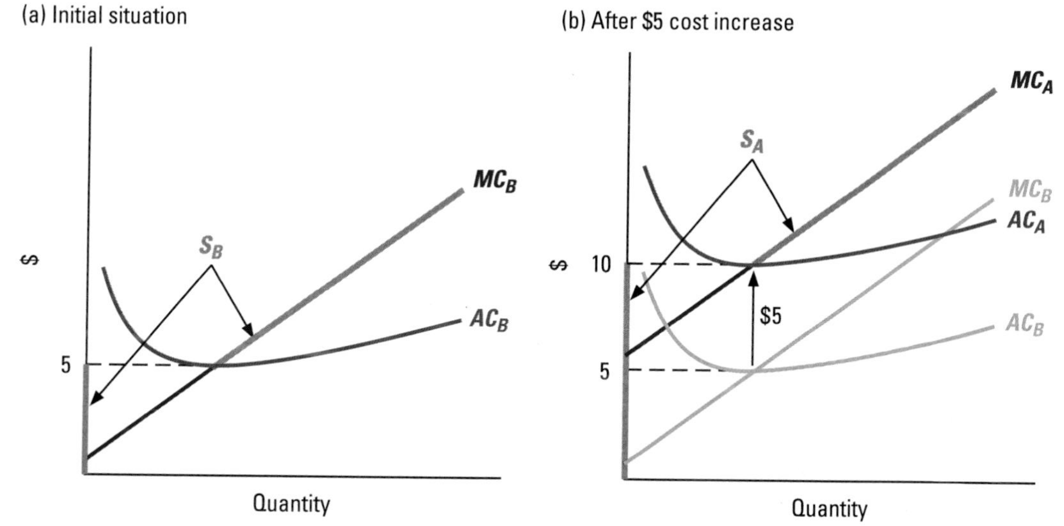

this is what we did in in-text exercise 9.2, where we found Dan's supply function both with and without an avoidable fixed cost of $850.

Changes in a firm's input prices change not only the firm's profit-maximizing sales quantity, but also its input (or factor) demands. In Add-On 9A we discuss the direction of those effects.

Figure 9.11

Another Change in a Wheat Farmer's Supply Curve. The farmer's initial situation, shown in figure (a), is the same as in Figure 9.10(a). This time, the farmer experiences an increase in avoidable fixed cost. Figure (b) shows the shift in average cost and the resulting supply curve. Note that the marginal cost curve does not change so the farmer's supply is unchanged if she doesn't shut down.

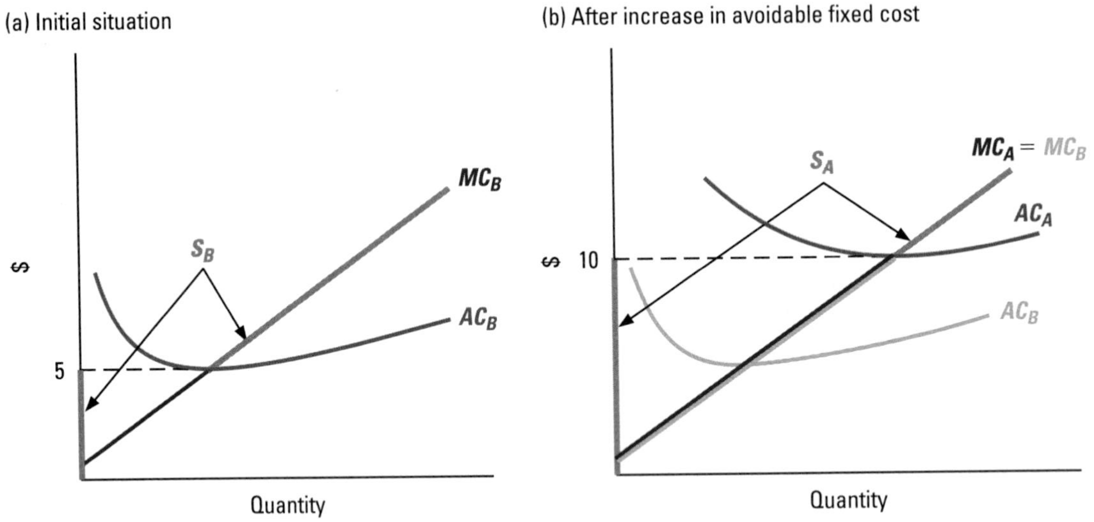

Application 9.3

Canadian Softwood Exports and the U.S.-Canada Softwood Lumber Agreement of 1996–2001

Softwood lumber is one of Canada's largest exports to the United States, with over 19 billion board feet (worth $6.8 billion) shipped in 2003 alone. It is also one of the biggest headaches in U.S.-Canadian relations. While the North American Free Trade Agreement (NAFTA) eliminated most trade restrictions between the two countries, softwood lumber is a notable exception. For years, a dispute has raged over the product. In the United States, the main proponents of limited Canadian imports are U.S. lumber producers, who have often successfully lobbied the U.S. government for protection.

Under a binational agreement that was in effect from 1996 to 2001, lumber producers in the provinces of Alberta, British Columbia, Ontario, and Quebec faced penalties for exceeding certain limits on exports. Producers could export up to a "fee-free limit" without penalty. Above the limit, they had to pay a penalty of $50 per 1,000 board feet up to another limit (the "low-fee limit"), and above that a penalty of $100 per 1,000 board feet. (In 1995, the average softwood lumber price was $337 per 1,000 board feet, so the penalties were substantial.)

Figure 9.12 shows the effect of the penalties on the supply curve of a typical Canadian softwood lumber producer. Figure 9.12(a) shows the producer's average and marginal costs before the agreement, labeled *AC* and *MC*. Without the agreement, the supply curve coincides with the *MC* curve at prices above AC_{min}, and with the vertical axis (zero supply) at prices below AC_{min}.

Figure 9.12(a) also shows the average and marginal cost curves with the agreement, labeled AC_A and MC_A. The fee-free limit is Q_0; the low-fee limit is Q_1. At all quantities between Q_0 and Q_1 the Canadian producer must pay a penalty of $50 per 1,000 board feet, which shifts the marginal cost curve up by $50. At all quantities above Q_1 the Canadian producer must pay a penalty of $100 per 1,000 board feet, which shifts the marginal cost curve up by another $50. As a result, the curve MC_A jumps up by $50 at Q_0 and Q_1 (the jumps at those quantities are indicated by dashed vertical lines).

Average cost is also higher at each output level over Q_0. However, at each such output level, the difference between the two average cost curves is smaller than the change in marginal cost because in calculating average cost the penalties are averaged over all units, including those for which there is no penalty.

Figure 9.12(b) shows the firm's supply curve after the agreement in green. As usual, it coincides with the MC_A curve at prices above AC_{min}, and with the vertical axis (zero supply) at prices below AC_{min}. The only tricky parts are the vertical segments of the supply curve at Q_0 and Q_1. Suppose the price is between $\underline{P}_0$ and $\overline{P}_0$. In that case, the firm's (horizontal) demand curve passes through the jump in the marginal cost curve at Q_0. There is therefore no positive quantity at which *P* equals *MC*. Nonetheless, Q_0 is the firm's most profitable choice. To see why, observe that at quantities below Q_0, the price exceeds marginal cost, so it pays to increase output. At all quantities above Q_0, the price is less than marginal cost, so it pays to reduce output.[8] So the supply curve in Figure 9.12(b) shows that for all such prices the firm will export exactly Q_0 thousand board feet of lumber. Similarly, at all prices between $\underline{P}_1$ and $\overline{P}_1$, the firm will export exactly Q_1 thousand board feet of lumber.

9.4 SHORT-RUN VERSUS LONG-RUN SUPPLY BY PRICE-TAKING FIRMS

In Section 8.7 we saw that a firm's marginal and average costs may differ in the long and short run because, in the short run, some inputs are fixed rather than variable. Those differences affect the way the firm responds over time to a change in the price it faces for its product.

Figure 9.13 shows what happens with a price-taking firm when the price at which it can sell its product rises suddenly from $\overline{P}$ to $\hat{P}$ and remains at that new level. Figure 9.13(a) shows the firm's short-run and long-run marginal cost curves, labeled MC_{SR} and MC_{LR} respectively. These curves reflect the relationship between short-run and long-run marginal cost discussed in Section 8.7: the curves cross at the initial price $\overline{P}$, and the short-run marginal cost curve is steeper than the long-run curve. These curves can be used to apply the quantity rule. In the short run, the firm's best positive quantity is Q^*_{SR}, but in the long run the firm's best positive quantity is the larger amount Q^*_{LR}.

[8]The two-step procedure in the text assumes that the firm's MC curve has no jumps. When the marginal cost curve has jumps, as here, the No Marginal Improvement Principle (see Section 3.2) requires us to check in step 1 of the two-step procedure whether a small increase or decrease in output would raise profit at the output levels at which marginal cost jumps. An increase doesn't raise profit if $P \leq MC$ at slightly higher outputs; a decrease doesn't raise profit if $P \leq MC$ at slightly lower outputs. For example, at prices between $\underline{P}_0$ and $\overline{P}_0$, quantity Q_0 is the only output level that satisfies the test in this amended step 1.

Figure 9.12

The Effect of the U.S.-Canadian Softwood Lumber Agreement on the Supply Curve of a Canadian Lumber Producer. Figure (a) shows the effect of the agreement on the producer's marginal and average costs. The original marginal and average cost curves, in light red, are labeled *MC* and *AC*; the new marginal and average cost curves are labeled MC_A and AC_A. At export quantities between the fee-free limit Q_0 and the low-fee limit Q_1, the penalty shifts the producer's marginal cost curve up by \$50. Above Q_1, the marginal cost curve shifts up by \$100. The firm's supply curve with the agreement, shown in figure (b), coincides with its new marginal cost curve at all prices above AC_{min}, and also includes the vertical segments where the MC_A curve jumps upward at Q_0 and Q_1.

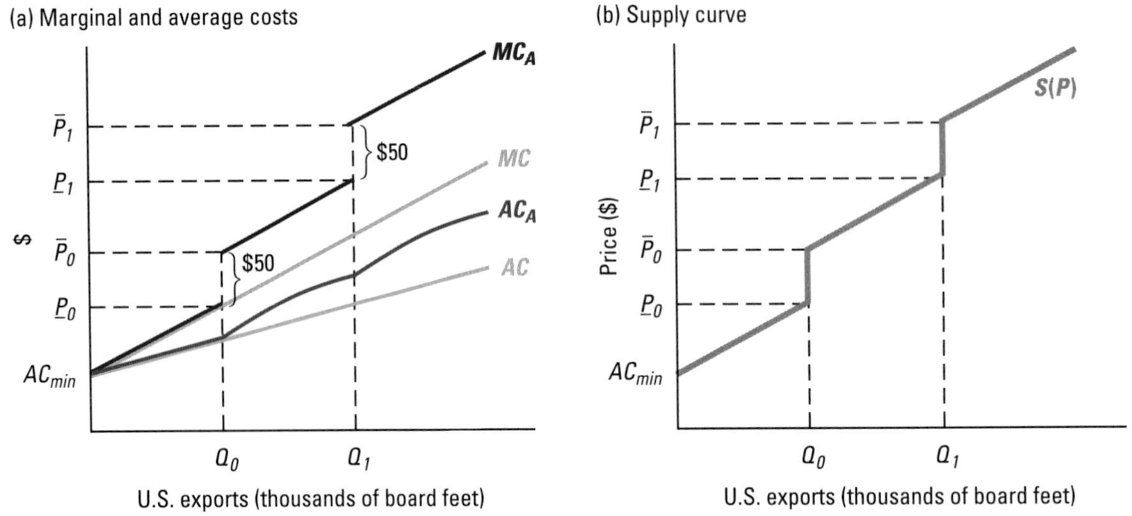

Figure 9.13(b) adds average cost curves to the picture to consider the shut-down rule. The figure shows three average cost curves. AC_{LR} is the firm's long-run average cost curve. The long-run marginal cost curve crosses the AC_{LR} curve at its lowest point. AC_{SR} is the firm's short-run average cost curve, including the sunk cost of its fixed inputs. It reflects the relation to the firm's long-run average cost curve we discussed in Section 8.7: it touches the long-run average cost curve at the firm's initial output level Q^*, and lies above it everywhere else. Finally, the curve Avoidable AC_{SR} is the firm's avoidable average cost. It includes only the firm's avoidable costs, and so lies below the curve AC_{SR}. The short-run marginal cost curve crosses both of these short-run average cost curves at their lowest points. Since the new price $\hat{P}$ is above the avoidable short-run average cost at Q^*_{SR} and the long-run average cost at Q^*_{LR}, the firm prefers to operate in both the short run and the long run.

Figure 9.13

Long-Run and Short-Run Supply Responses to a Price Increase. The figure shows the long-run and short-run increases in the quantity supplied for a price-taking firm in response to a price increase from $\bar{P}$ to $\hat{P}$. Figure (a) considers the quantity rule. It shows the firm's short-run and long-run marginal cost curves. They cross at Q^*, with the short-run curve steeper than the long-run curve, for the reasons discussed in Section 8.7. In the short run, the firm's best positive output level is Q^*_{SR}, while in the long run it is Q^*_{LR}. Figure (b) considers the shut-down rule. The firm prefers to operate in both the short run and the long run.

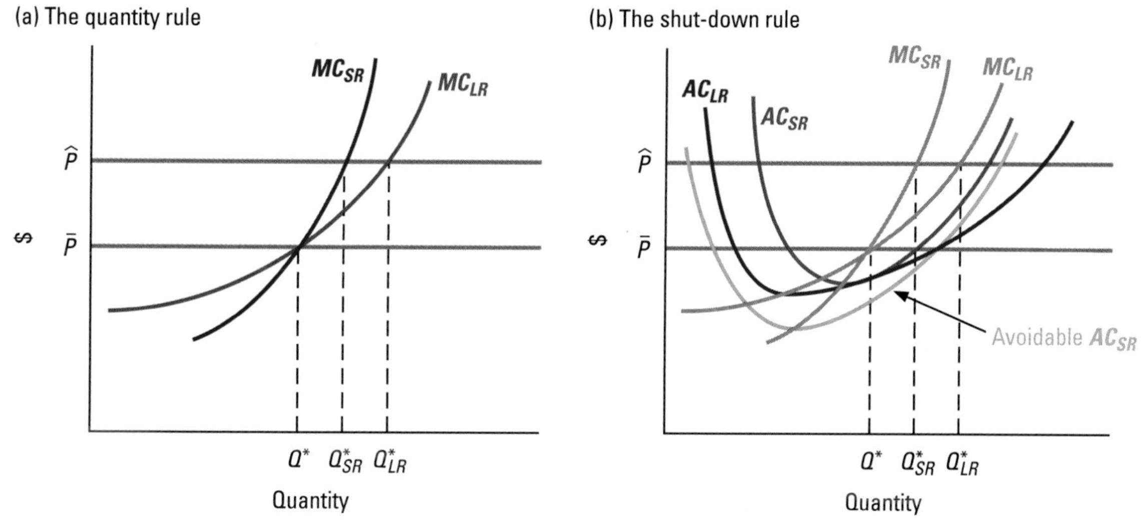

Combining the quantity rule and shut-down rule, we see that the firm will increase its output to Q^*_{SR} in the short run, and increase it further to Q^*_{LR} in the long run.[9]

IN-TEXT EXERCISE 9.4 **Suppose that the price at which a price-taking firm can sell its product decreases. Use a figure like Figure 9.13 to show how the firm's profit-maximizing sales quantity adjusts in the short run and the long run. Is the firm more likely to shut down in the short run or the long run?**

[9]The situation shown in Figure 9.13 is the typical one, in which a competitive firm's long-run response to a price change exceeds its short-run response. Sometimes, however, the reverse can happen. Such cases can arise when a firm's short-run marginal costs are interrelated across time. For example, imagine that a firm's workforce is more rested and productive—and the firm's marginal cost of production consequently lower—the less the firm produced the preceding month. To be specific, imagine that the price of the firm's product suddenly increases on January 1. The price increase will lead the firm to increase its output from its December level. That increase in January's output, however, will increase February's marginal cost and lead the firm to sell less in February than in January.

Application 9.4

Short-Run and Long-Run Supply Responses by U.S. Crude Oil Producers

Jed Clampet, the lead character on the 1960s TV sitcom *Beverly Hillbillies,* struck it rich one day when he missed his target while hunting. Up from the ground bubbled crude—"oil that is, black gold, Texas tea." Clampet sold his land to the OK Oil Company and moved to Beverly Hills. The rest is TV history.

The Beverly Hillbillies

Making money in the oil business isn't always so easy. Oil companies need to spend considerable resources to find oil and then extract it. U.S. oil producers supply only about 10 percent of the world's oil. Because individual producers supply only a tiny fraction of that amount, many economists would regard them as price takers.

The price that a U.S. producer receives for a barrel of oil has fluctuated dramatically over the last 30 years, due to changes in both U.S. oil regulations and the world oil market. Figure 9.14 shows the nominal and real prices per barrel that U.S. crude oil producers received from 1970 to 2002. The "real" prices are adjusted for inflation, and are stated in year 2000 dollars (see Section 6.3). Two price changes are particularly noticeable. First, the price increased more than 150 percent between 1978 and 1981, due to the combined effect of the Iran-Iraq war, which reduced world oil supplies and raised oil prices, and the deregulation of domestic crude oil prices. (The Arab oil embargo of 1973 led to a much smaller price increase, 60 percent.) Second, in 1985–1986, crude oil prices plunged, falling about 50 percent, when OPEC (the Organization of Petroleum Exporting Countries), the cartel that had helped to elevate oil prices since the 1973 embargo, lost its ability to control its members' production.

The responses of U.S. oil producers to these dramatic price changes illustrate the difference between long-run and short-run supply by price-taking firms. While data on individual producers' output is not publicly available, we can examine production data at the state level.[10] Figure 9.15 shows the number of active oil wells (in red) and annual production (in blue) in the state of New Mexico from 1970 to 2002. (The number of wells is measured on the left vertical axis; the number of barrels produced on the right vertical axis.) The period of sharp price changes, 1978–1988, is highlighted in green with dashed vertical lines distinguishing three periods: 1978–1981 (when prices rose sharply), 1981–1985 (when prices fell gradually), and 1985–1988 (after the sharp price decline in 1985–1986).

Over 32 years, New Mexico's oil production declined almost every year. A notable exception to this trend, however, occurred in 1981–1985, when production increased almost 15 percent at the same time that crude oil prices were falling. How could supply rise while the price fell? The explanation lies in the large rise in the number of active wells during this time period, stimulated by the price increases of 1978–1981. The response to the price increases, which led firms to increase the amount of two critical inputs, oil wells and drilling machinery, took some time. Companies needed to identify new oil locations and drill new wells. By 1985, the number of active wells had increased almost 30 percent over its 1978 level. As the new wells became active, they led New

[10] This information can be found at www.eia.doe.gov.

Mexico producers to supply more oil than before, even after prices dropped.[11]

In 1985–1986 real crude oil prices dropped back to their 1975 level. Over the next two years the number of active wells declined, as producers shut down older more costly wells and drilled few new ones. As a result, production fell during those years.

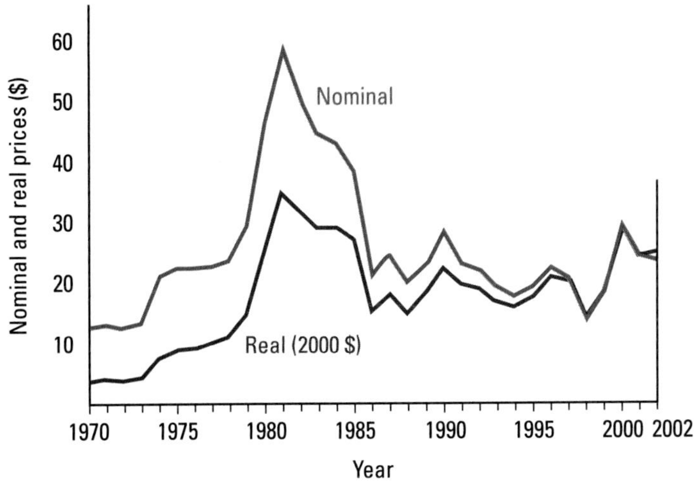

Figure 9.14

Nominal and Real Prices Received by U.S. Crude Oil Producers, 1970–2002. The figure shows the average nominal and real prices received by U.S. crude oil producers each year from 1970 to 2002. Real prices are shown in year 2000 dollars. Oil prices increased more than 150 percent from 1978 to 1981 and fell dramatically from 1985 to 1986.

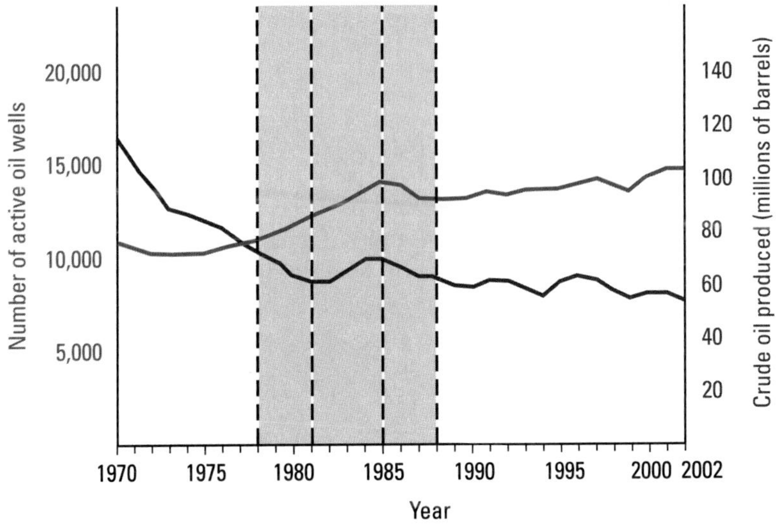

Figure 9.15

The Number of Active Oil Wells and Crude Oil Production in New Mexico, 1970–2002. This figure shows the number of active oil wells (in red) and total crude oil production (in blue) in New Mexico from 1970 to 2002. The number of oil wells and production increased for several years following the 1979–1981 price increase, and continued to increase even after prices started to decline, reflecting the time needed to find suitable sites and drill new oil wells. After the 1985–1986 price decline, the number of active oil wells and total production fell.

[11]The fact that supply increased as prices fell does *not* contradict the Law of Supply (see Section 9.3), which says that supply never decreases in response to a price increase provided that the firm's cost function *stays unchanged.* Here, the firm's short-run cost function changes over time as fixed inputs become variable. The fact that the number of active wells continued to increase for a while after prices started falling (see Figure 9.15) probably reflects the fact that producers had already sunk much of the costs of their development.

WORKED-OUT PROBLEM 9.4

The Problem Suppose that Hannah and Sam's short-run and long-run cost functions are $C_{SR}(Q) = 5{,}000 + (Q^2/2)$ and $C_{LR}(Q) = 100Q$. [These are the short-run and long-run cost functions derived in worked-out problem 8.6 (page 286).] Given these cost functions, their short-run marginal cost is $MC_{SR} = Q$ and their long-run marginal cost is $MC_{LR} = 100$. What are their short-run and long-run supply functions?

The Solution Let's consider their long-run supply function first. If the price is above 100, there is no quantity at which $P = MC$: we have $P > MC$ at every output level. Since they make a positive profit on every unit they sell, they will want to sell an infinite amount. If the price is below 100, they want to sell nothing, and if the price is exactly 100 they are willing to supply any amount, since they earn zero regardless of how much they sell.

Now consider the short run. Applying the quantity rule, the sales quantity at which $P = MC$ solves the formula $P = Q$. So the most profitable positive sales quantity given price P is $Q = P$. Since, at this quantity, Hannah and Sam's revenue is P^2 and their avoidable costs are $P^2/2$, they will produce in the short run as long as the price is positive. Thus, their short-run supply function is $S_{SR}(P) = P$.

IN-TEXT EXERCISE 9.5 **Suppose that Hannah and Sam's short-run and long-run cost functions are $C_{SR}(Q) = 10{,}000 + Q^2$ and $C_{LR}(Q) = 200Q$. [These are the short-run and long-run cost functions in the situation you were asked to study in in-text exercise 8.6 (page 287).] Given these cost functions, their short-run marginal cost is $MC_{SR} = 2Q$, and their long-run marginal cost is $MC_{LR} = 200$. What are their short-run and long-run supply functions?**

9.5 PRODUCER SURPLUS

A firm's **producer surplus** equals its revenue less its avoidable costs.

Profit is the excess of revenue over total cost. At times it will be convenient to work with a related concept, called producer surplus. **Producer surplus** equals the firm's revenue less its avoidable cost, which includes both its variable cost and its avoidable fixed cost, but does not include its sunk costs. So

$$\text{Profit} = \text{Producer surplus—Sunk cost}$$

Since sunk costs are incurred no matter what, they can generally be ignored in making economic decisions (see Section 3.3). So, it is often the case that we can just focus on producer surplus rather than profit. For example, another way of stating the shut-down rule is to say that the firm will shut down if its producer surplus from producing its most profitable positive quantity would be negative. Likewise, in later chapters we'll frequently investigate the welfare implications of various policies. When we consider how firms are affected by these policies, it often suffices to focus on their effects on firms' producer surplus because such policies often don't have any effects on sunk costs. If so, the change in a firm's profit will be the same as the change in its producer surplus.

One advantage of focusing on producer surplus when we consider policy changes is that it can be measured in a very convenient way using supply curves.

Figure 9.16 shows that producer surplus for a firm selling Q units can be represented by the area between a horizontal line drawn at the level of the firm's price P and the firm's supply curve. Why? Consider, first, Figure 9.16(a), which considers a case where the firm has no avoidable fixed costs and its supply curve has no jumps. Recall from Section 8.5 that the firm's variable cost equals the area under its marginal cost curve up to Q units. This is the red-shaded area in Figure 9.16(a). The firm's revenue, on the other hand, equals its price P times the amount it produces. Its revenue therefore equals the area of rectangle ABCD. If we subtract the red-shaded variable cost area from that revenue rectangle we are left with the yellow-shaded area, which is the firm's producer surplus.

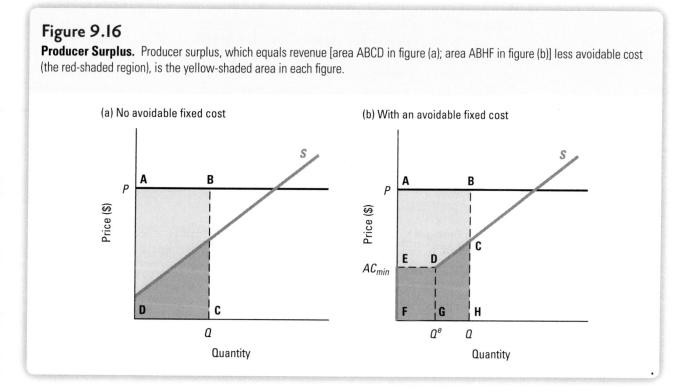

Now consider the case with an avoidable fixed cost, shown in Figure 9.16(b). With an avoidable fixed cost, the firm's supply curve jumps from 0 to Q^e when the price equals AC_{min}. Nonetheless, just as in Figure 9.16(a), the firm's producer surplus equals the yellow-shaded area between the horizontal line drawn at the level of the firm's price P and the firm's supply curve (here we fill in the horizontal jump in the supply curve to define that area). Why? Recall that the firm's profit producing quantity Q^e when the price equals AC_{min} exactly equals it's profit from producing zero. This means that the firm's added cost from producing quantity Q^e rather than 0 must exactly equal its revenue from selling Q^e units at a price of AC_{min}, which is the area of rectangle DEFG. To get its avoidable costs of producing Q units, we then need to add to this amount the additional cost of increasing output from Q^e to Q. That additional cost equals the area under its supply curve between

Figure 9.16

Producer Surplus. Producer surplus, which equals revenue [area ABCD in figure (a); area ABHF in figure (b)] less avoidable cost (the red-shaded region), is the yellow-shaded area in each figure.

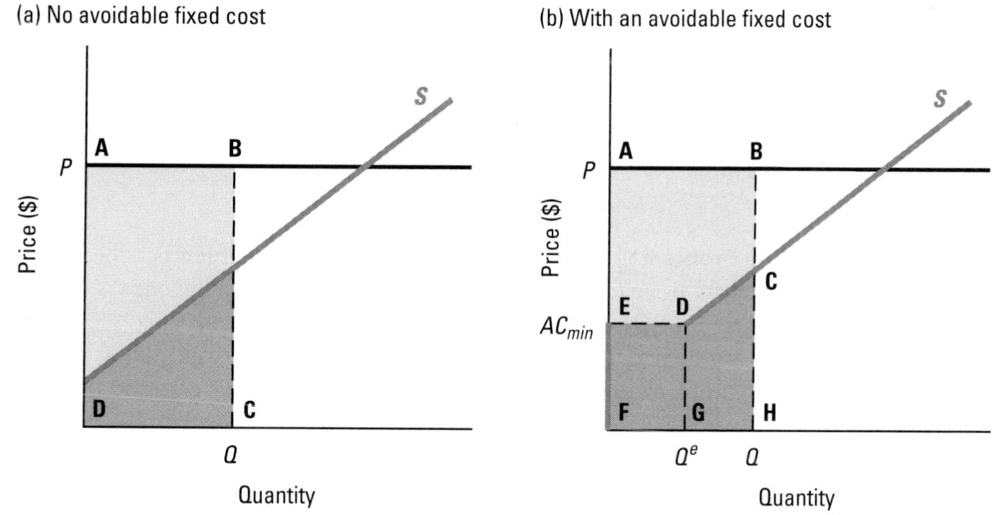

Q^e and Q. Thus, the firm's avoidable cost of producing quantity Q is equal to the red-shaded area. Its producer surplus, equal to its revenue at price P (rectangle ABHF) less its avoidable costs (the red-shaded area), therefore equals the yellow-shaded area.

There is also a second way to measure the firm's producer surplus when it has an avoidable fixed cost. In this approach we use the firm's marginal cost curve rather than its supply curve: measure the firm's revenue less its variable cost by measuring the area between a horizontal line drawn at the level of its price P and its marginal cost curve [just as in Figure 9.16(a), where there were no avoidable fixed costs so the marginal cost and supply curves coincide]. Then, subtract its avoidable fixed cost to get its producer surplus.

*9.6 SUPPLY BY MULTIPRODUCT PRICE-TAKING FIRMS

Most firms produce more than one product. As we discussed in Section 8.9, the firm's cost function then depends on its output of all of its products. For example, a firm that produces two outputs, Q_1 and Q_2, will have a cost function of the form $C(Q_1, Q_2)$. In these cases, the marginal cost of producing one product often depends on the production levels of other products. Oil refineries produce many different products, including high-octane gasoline, low-octane gasoline, and heating oil. If a refinery increases the production of one product, the marginal cost of producing the others can change.

Sometimes the marginal cost of a product increases when the firm produces more of another good; sometimes it decreases. For example, if Noah and Naomi produce both garden benches and garden chairs, the more garden chairs they produce, the more crowded their production facility becomes, increasing their marginal cost of producing benches. On the other hand, if they are producing a lot of benches, they may decide to invest in equipment that lowers the marginal cost of producing chairs as well.

To find the profit-maximizing sales quantities and prices for two products, we need to extend the quantity and shut-down rules. The new quantity rule says to find the most profitable pair of positive sales quantities at which price equals marginal cost for *both* products. The new shut-down rule compares the profit from those quantities to three alternatives: (a) shutting down the first product while continuing to sell the second; (b) shutting down the second product while continuing to sell the first; and (c) shutting down both products. Worked-out problem 9.5 shows how this procedure works.

WORKED-OUT PROBLEM 9.5

The Problem Noah and Naomi produce both garden benches and garden chairs. They are price takers. Their cost function for garden benches is $C_B(Q_B, Q_C) = 50Q_B + Q_B^2 - Q_BQ_C$ and their marginal cost is $MC_B = 50 + 2Q_B - Q_C$, where Q_B and Q_C are their output levels of benches and chairs respectively. Their cost function for garden chairs is $C_C(Q_B, Q_C) = 25Q_C + Q_C^2 - Q_CQ_B$, and their marginal cost is $MC_C = 25 + 2Q_C - Q_B$. The price of a garden bench, P_B, is \$140; the price of a garden chair, P_C, is \$55. What are Noah and Naomi's profit-maximizing sales quantities?

The Solution Applying the quantity rule, we find the sales quantities for both benches and chairs at which price equals marginal cost, which means finding Q_B and Q_C such that

$$140 = 50 + 2Q_B - Q_C$$

and

$$55 = 25 + 2Q_C - Q_B$$

Doing so gives us two formulas for the two unknowns Q_B and Q_C. Solving, we find that the best positive quantities are $Q_B = 70$ and $Q_C = 50$. (You can solve these by using the first formula to determine that $Q_C = 2Q_B - 90$, and then substitute this expression for Q_C into the second formula and solve it for Q_B. This yields $Q_B = 70$. Since $Q_C = 2Q_B - 90$, this implies that $Q_C = 50$.) Noah and Naomi's profit is \$7,400.

Applying the shutdown rule, we compare this profit not just to the profit Noah and Naomi earn if they shut down completely (zero) but to their profit if they stop producing one of the two products. If they stop producing garden chairs, so that $Q_C = 0$, their cost function for benches becomes $C_B(Q_B) = 50Q_B + Q_B^2$ (because $Q_C = 0$) and their marginal cost is $MC_B = 50 + 2Q_B$. The best sales quantity of benches is then $Q_B = 45$, which yields a profit of \$2,025 (you should check this). That is less than Noah and Naomi will make by producing both products.

If instead Noah and Naomi stop producing garden benches, so that $Q_B = 0$, their cost function for chairs becomes $C_C(Q_C) = 25Q_C + Q_C^2$, and their marginal cost is $MC_C = 25 + 2Q_C$. The best sales quantity for garden chairs is then $Q_C = 15$, which yields a profit of \$225 (you should also check this). Again, this is less than they would make by producing both products, so Noah and Naomi's profit-maximizing sales quantities are $Q_B = 70$ and $Q_C = 50$.

IN-TEXT EXERCISE 9.6 **In worked-out problem 9.5, how would Noah and Naomi's profit-maximizing sales quantities change if the price of garden benches were \$110?**

For a multiproduct firm that is a price taker, a change in the price of one product can affect the profit-maximizing sales quantities of other products. The direction of the effect depends on how the production of one product affects the marginal cost of another. Suppose the marginal cost of a product decreases when the firm sells more of a second product. If the price of the second product increases, the firm will increase sales of that product (in accord with the Law of Supply, which remains true for multiproduct firms). Since this change also decreases the marginal cost of the first product, it will *increase* sales of that product. The solution to in-text exercise 9.6, compared with the solution of worked-out problem 9.4, illustrates this case. If instead the marginal cost of one product increases with increased sales of another, then an increase in the price of the second product will reduce the sales of the first.

CHAPTER SUMMARY

1. **Profit-maximizing quantities and prices**
   a. The relationship between a firm's price and sales quantity is described by the demand curve for its product.
   b. A firm's manager can think in terms of finding either the profit-maximizing price or the profit-maximizing sales quantity.
2. **Marginal revenue, marginal cost, and profit maximization**
   a. Marginal revenue measures the extra revenue produced by the ΔQ marginal units sold, measured on a per-unit basis: $MR = \Delta R/\Delta Q = [R(Q) - R(Q - \Delta Q)]/\Delta Q$.
   b. When a firm's demand curve is downward sloping, its marginal revenue at any positive sales quantity is less than its price, because selling the marginal units reduces the amount the firm receives on inframarginal sales. A price-taking firm, however, need not lower its price to sell more, so its marginal revenue always equals its price.
   c. When a firm's profit-maximizing sales quantity is positive, its marginal revenue equals its marginal cost at that quantity.
   d. We can follow a two-step procedure to find the firm's profit-maximizing sales quantity: In the first step, the quantity rule, identify the best positive sales quantity, at which $MR = MC$. In the second step, the shut-down rule, check whether the profit from that sales quantity is at least as large as the profit from shutting down.
   e. If the firm has no sunk costs, or if these are ignored in calculating its cost, the shut-down rule is equivalent to checking whether the profit from the best positive sales quantity is nonnegative ($PQ - C(Q) \geq 0$) or, equivalently, if the firm's price is at least as large as its average cost ($P \geq AC$).
3. **Supply decisions by price-taking firms**
   a. A price-taking firm can use the two-step procedure to find its best sales quantity. Doing so involves identifying sales quantities at which marginal cost equals the price in applying the quantity rule.
   b. The Law of Supply tells us that a competitive firm's supply never decreases when the market price increases.
   c. When a firm's marginal cost curve is upward sloping, its supply curve coincides with its marginal cost curve at prices above AC_{min}; it coincides with the vertical axis (representing zero supply) at prices below AC_{min}.
4. **Short-run versus long-run supply by price-taking firms**
   The fact that a firm's short-run marginal cost curve is steeper than its long-run marginal cost curve means that a competitive firm responds more to a price change in the long run than it does in the short run.
5. **Producer surplus**
   a. A firm's producer surplus equals its revenue less its avoidable costs. Therefore, the firm's profit equals its producer surplus less its sunk costs.
   b. A firm's producer surplus equals the area between a horizontal line drawn at the level of its price P and its supply curve.
6. **Supply by multiproduct price-taking firms**
   When a firm's marginal cost of production for one product changes with the quantity of a second product it produces, an increase in the price of the second product can change the firm's supply of the first product.

ADDITIONAL EXERCISES

Exercise 9.1: If the demand function for Noah and Naomi's garden benches is $Q^d = D(P) = 1{,}000/\sqrt{P}$, what is their inverse demand function?

Exercise 9.2: Consider the preferred prices of the author and the publisher of an electronic book, whose marginal cost of production is close to zero. Would the two disagree about the price to be charged for the book?

Exercise 9.3: Reconsider the textbook pricing issue in Application 9.1 (page 299). Show why the publisher wants a higher price using MR and MC.

Exercise 9.4: How does the price preferred by an author who gets a 25 percent royalty compare to that preferred by an author who gets a 15 percent royalty?

Exercise 9.5: Consider again Phillip Morris's decision in Application 9.2 (page 302). How much would Marlboro sales have had to increase in response to a price reduction to \$2 for that price reduction to increase profit?

Exercise 9.6: A price-taking firm's variable cost function is $VC = Q^3$, where Q is its output per week. It has a sunk fixed cost of \$3,000 per week. Its marginal cost is $MC = 3Q^2$. What is it's profit-maximizing output when the price is $P = \$243$? What if the fixed cost is avoidable?

Exercise 9.7: In exercise 9.6, what is the firm's supply function when the \$3,000 fixed cost is sunk? When it is avoidable?

Exercise 9.8: Suppose Dan's cost of making pizzas is $C(Q) = 4Q + (Q^2/40)$, and his marginal cost is $MC = 4 + (Q/20)$. Dan is a price taker. What is Dan's supply function? What if Dan has an avoidable fixed cost of \$10?

Exercise 9.9: Consider again exercise 9.8. If Dan's cost increases by \$2 per pizza, so that his cost function becomes $C(Q) = 6Q + (Q^2/40)$ and his marginal cost becomes $MC = 6 + (Q/20)$, how will his supply function change?

Exercise 9.10: Consider again exercise 9.8. If Dan's avoidable fixed cost increases from \$10 to \$22.50, how will his supply function change?

Exercise 9.11: Suppose that it costs a firm \$2 to produce each unit of its output. What is its supply function? Graph it.

Exercise 9.12: In exercise 8.14 (page 292) you derived Hannah and Sam's long-run and short-run cost function when they have the Cobb-Douglas production function $Q = F(L, K) = 10L^{0.5}K^{0.5}$, both a worker and a unit of capital cost \$1,000 per week, and they initially remodel 200 square feet per week. Their capital is fixed in the short run but variable in the long run. What are their long-run and short-run supply functions? Graph them.

Exercise 9.13: In exercise 8.15 (page 292) you derived Hannah and Sam's long-run and short-run cost function when they have the Cobb-Douglas production function $Q = F(L, K) = 10L^{0.25}K^{0.25}$, both a worker and a unit of capital cost \$1,000 per week, and they initially remodel 100 square feet a week. Their capital is fixed in the short run but variable in the long run. What are their long-run and short-run supply functions? Graph them.

Exercise 9.14: Noah and Naomi produce both garden benches and garden chairs; they are price takers in both markets. The cost function for garden benches is $C_B(Q_B, Q_C) = 50Q_B + Q_B^2 + Q_BQ_C$, and the marginal cost is $MC_B = 50 + 2Q_B + Q_C$. The cost function for garden chairs is $C_C(Q_B, Q_C) = 25Q_C + Q_C^2 + Q_CQ_B$, and the marginal cost is $MC_C = 25 + 2Q_C + Q_B$. The price of a garden bench, P_B, is \$120; the price of a garden chair, P_C, is \$75. What are Noah and Naomi's profit-maximizing sales quantities of benches and chairs? What happens if the price of benches increases to \$135?

Exercise 9.15: Argue that another way to represent a firm's producer surplus is as the area between its marginal revenue curve and its supply curve. Use this fact to show why $MR = MC$ at any positive profit-maximizing sales quantity.

part

IIC

Additional Topics Concerning Decisions

The next four chapters extend and enrich the theory of decision making developed in Chapters 4 through 9. In Chapter 10, we'll examine decisions involving time, such as saving and investment. In Chapter 11, we'll turn to decisions involving uncertainty, such as gambling, insurance, and risk management. As we'll see, it's possible to understand decisions involving time and uncertainty by applying the tools that we've already developed. In Chapter 12, we'll develop new tools for thinking about decisions involving strategy. Finally, in Chapter 13, we'll survey a field known as behavioral economics, which attempts to modify, supplement, and enrich economic theories of decision making by incorporating insights from psychology.

chapters

Choices Involving Time

10

Learning Objectives

After reading this chapter, students should be able to:

- Explain how consumers and firms move cash from one point in time to another by borrowing and lending.
- Calculate the present discounted value of a claim on future resources.
- Understand consumers' decisions regarding saving and borrowing.
- Analyze the profitability of investment projects with future cash flows.
- Explain how saving, borrowing, and investment depend on the interest rate.

Interior (above) and exterior (below) of Volkswagen's Phaeton production plant in Dresden, Germany

In the 1990s, Volkswagen executives set their sights on the market for luxury automobiles. They conceived both a new car—the Phaeton—and a state-of-the-art production facility in Dresden, Germany. Eager to impress well-heeled customers, they located the new plant along the banks of the historic Elbe River, on more than 20 acres of manicured parkland. With walls of glass—roughly 290,000 square feet in all—and floors of polished Canadian maple, it was easily mistaken for an art gallery. In fact, after the Dresden Opera House flooded, 17 performances of the opera *Carmen* were held in the factory's sumptuous visitor's center.

Like Rome, the Phaeton plant wasn't built in a day. The first Phaeton didn't hit the streets of Europe until 2002. Volkswagen sank more than $200 million into the project years before the plant began generating revenue.

Designing, producing, and selling products, be they Volkswagen Phaetons or garden benches, *always* requires time. Companies often invest substantial sums of money long before they receive any revenue, particularly when, as in the case of the Phaeton, new designs and production facilities are needed. How should companies evaluate investments when production isn't instantaneous? How do they obtain the necessary cash to cover their up-front expenses? Why are lenders and investors willing to part with their cash, forgoing consumption goods today in exchange for some future benefit?

In this chapter, we provide some answers to these and other questions concerning economic decisions involving time. We organize our discussion around three topics:

1. *Transactions involving time.* By lending and borrowing, people can move resources from one point in time to another. As we'll see, these financial transactions allow consumers and firms to make sure cash is available when it's needed.
2. *Saving and borrowing.* Consumers don't usually earn money at the same time they want to spend it. After retirement, for example, their needs remain basically the same even though their incomes plummet. We'll examine how people can provide for their needs later in life by saving when they're young.
3. *Investment.* Before producing anything, a company must usually invest in plant and equipment. We'll explain how to distinguish between investments that are profitable and those that aren't. The same principles apply to other types of investment, such as the decision to go to college.

10.1 TRANSACTIONS INVOLVING TIME

Consumers and firms often need to move cash from one point in time to another. Various types of financial transactions help them to do so. For example, by temporarily lending someone money or depositing it in a bank account, they can move their resources from the present to the future. Alternatively, by borrowing money, they can move resources from the future to the present. To understand economic decisions involving time, we must begin with a careful examination of these transactions and the trade-offs they imply.

To keep the analysis reasonably concrete, we'll focus primarily on the use of bank accounts. As we explain below, a bank account is simply a loan from a depositor to a bank. Keep in mind, however, that similar principles apply regardless of whether we are borrowing or lending, or of the particular financial vehicle we're using.

Principal is the amount borrowed when one person (or firm) lends money to another.

Interest is the amount of money a borrower is obliged to pay a lender, over and above the principal.

Interest Rates and Compound Interest

When one person (or firm) lends money to another, the amount borrowed is known as the lender's **principal**. The borrower is usually obliged to repay the principal at some particular point (or points) in time, along with compensation for the privilege of holding and using the lender's money. This compensation is known as **interest**.

It's useful to think about bank accounts in the same terms. That is, the bank is the borrower, the depositor is the lender, and the amount deposited is the principal. Many bank accounts pay interest; that is one reason bank accounts are better than stuffing money in a mattress. Some accounts allow the depositor to withdraw money at will, which means the bank must repay the loan on demand. Others require the funds to remain on deposit for a fixed period.

The **interest rate** is the amount of interest paid on a loan during a particular time period (usually a year), stated as a percentage of the principal. So if a bank account pays an interest rate of 3 percent per year, a \$100 deposit generates \$3 in interest over the course of a year.

The **interest rate** is the amount of interest paid on a loan during a particular period (usually a year), stated as a percentage of the principal.

For some loans, the interest obligation is simply added to the loan balance and remains unpaid until the principal comes due. At any point in time, the lender earns interest on the total loan balance, which includes all of the interest he has earned prior to that point. Since the amount of interest earned during any fixed time interval rises proportionately with the growing loan balance, the balance grows faster as time passes. This process is known as **compounding**.

Compounding refers to the payment of interest on loan balances that include interest earned in the past, a practice that causes the loan balance to grow faster as time passes.

To illustrate, let's suppose you deposit \$100 into an account that pays 10 percent interest per year.[1] Rather than withdrawing the interest, you allow it to accumulate within the account.

- Since your balance at the start of the first year is \$100, you receive \$10 in interest over the course of the first year (10 percent of \$100), finishing with \$110.
- Since your balance at the start of the second year is \$110, you receive \$11 in interest over the course of the second year (10 percent of \$110), finishing with \$121.
- Since your balance at the start of the third year is \$121, you receive \$12.10 in interest over the course of the third year (10 percent of \$121), finishing with \$133.10.

In Figure 10.1, the blue line shows the growth of your account balance over time, and the red line shows the growth of the interest payments you receive. Since the amount of interest received increases each year, your balance grows faster as time passes. This accelerating growth is a consequence of compound interest.

We can describe the effects of compound interest on your account balance with a simple formula. Let's use the symbol R to stand for the rate of interest, expressed as a decimal rather than a percentage. For example, at an interest rate of 10 percent, $R = 0.10$. If your balance is B dollars at the start of the year, you receive BR dollars in interest over the course of the year, finishing with a balance of $(B + BR) = B(1 + R)$ dollars. Let's say your initial deposit is D dollars. Then:

- Since your balance at the start of the first year is D dollars, you finish the first year with $D(1 + R)$ dollars.
- Since your balance at the start of the second year is $D(1 + R)$ dollars, you finish the second year with $D(1 + R)^2$ dollars.
- Since your balance at the start of the third year is $D(1 + R)^2$ dollars, you finish the third year with $D(1 + R)^3$ dollars.

[1]To keep things simple, we will assume throughout this chapter that interest *compounds annually*. That is, the interest earned during a year is included in the account balance used to calculate additional interest only in *subsequent* years. Interest compounds monthly if it is included in the account balance used to calculate additional interest only in subsequent months; it compounds daily if it is included in the account balance used to calculate additional interest only on subsequent days, and so forth.

Figure 10.1
The Effects of Compound Interest. $100 deposited in a bank account at 10 percent interest for 25 years grows faster over time, as the blue line shows. The amount of interest paid during each year grows in proportion to the total balance, as the red line shows.

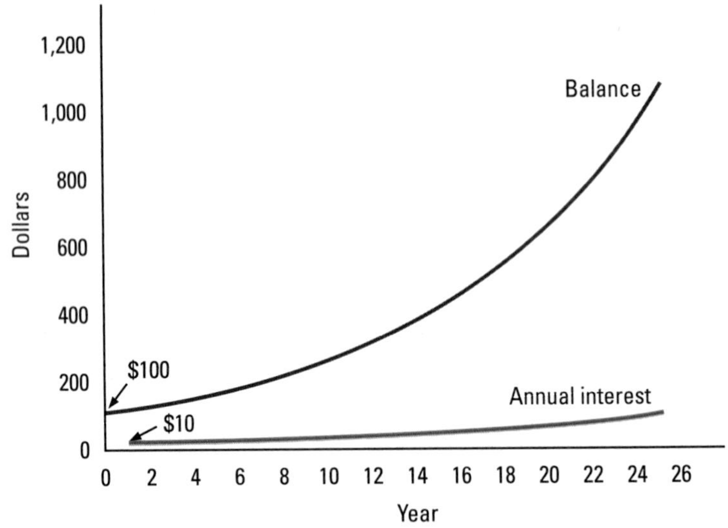

By repeating this calculation, we discover that at the end of T years, your account balance, B_T, is:

$$B_T = D(1 + R)^T \quad \textbf{(1)}$$

Table 10.1 shows how account balances grow over time at a range of interest rates. In each case, we start with an initial deposit of $100. From the numbers in the table, we can see that higher interest rates magnify the importance of compounding. For example, at an interest rate of 5 percent, the account earns $332.19 in interest over 30 years (the final balance of $432.19 minus the initial deposit of $100). In contrast, at an interest rate of 10 percent, it earns $1,644.94 in interest over the same period. So doubling the interest rate from 5 percent to 10 percent produces a nearly five-fold increase in total interest earned over 30 years!

Table 10.1
Growth in Account Balances at Various Interest Rates

	Interest rate				
Years	1%	3%	5%	10%	15%
1	101.00	103.00	105.00	110.00	115.00
5	105.10	115.93	127.63	161.05	201.14
10	110.46	134.39	162.89	259.37	404.56
15	116.10	155.80	207.89	417.72	813.71
20	122.02	180.61	265.33	672.75	1,636.65
30	134.78	242.73	432.19	1,744.94	6,621.18

Present Value and the Price of a Future Dollar

At first, depositing money in a bank account may seem a very different kind of transaction than, say, buying apples at a grocery store. But in fact, these two transactions have much in common.

Suppose a grocery store sells apples for 30 cents each. The price tells customers the rate at which they can trade money for apples. For example, a customer can trade \$3.60 for a dozen apples.

Now think about a bank that accepts deposits, returning customers' cash one year later with interest. The bank is like the grocery store, except that instead of apples, it's selling a product called *future cash.* Like a price, the interest rate tells customers the rate at which they can trade cash-in-hand for the bank's product (future cash). At an interest rate of 10 percent, a customer can trade \$3.60 of cash-in-hand for \$3.96 of cash delivered a year from now.

Let's explore the similarity between interest rates and prices a bit further. What is the price today of \$1 delivered a year from now? In other words, how much must you "pay" a bank today (by depositing money in an account) to "purchase" (withdraw) \$1 a year from now? Let's say the interest rate is 25 percent. In that case, the answer is 80 cents. Why? If you put 80 cents in the bank today, you'll earn 20 cents in interest over the course of the next year (25 percent of 80 cents), leaving you with exactly \$1 at the end of the year.

Given any interest rate R, we can find today's price for \$1 delivered in a year. If you deposit D dollars today, we know you'll have $D(1 + R)$ dollars at the end of the year. If you want to have exactly one dollar at the end of the year, you need to choose your deposit, D dollars, so that $D(1 + R) = 1$. Solving for D, we see that $D = 1/(1 + R)$. So the price that you must pay today to receive \$1 delivered one year from now is $1/(1 + R)$ dollars.

Present discounted value (or PDV) of a claim on future resources is the monetary value of that claim today.

The **present discounted value** (or PDV) of a claim on future resources is the monetary value of that claim today.[2] The expression $1/(1 + R)$ is the present discounted value of \$1 received a year in the future. We use the word *value* because $1/(1 + R)$ is the price of a future dollar, and price is one measure of economic value. We use the word *present* because we're measuring *today's* price for the future dollar. And we use the word *discounted* because at a positive interest rate, \$1 received in the future sells for less than a dollar today. In other words, *present discounted value* means *today's lower price*—it tells us how much we must pay today for a claim on future resources.

Given a choice between receiving \$1 a year from now, or the PDV of that dollar immediately, you should be indifferent. Why? Even after you pick one of those alternatives, you can always swap it for the other. Say the interest rate is 25 percent, so that the PDV is 80 cents. Suppose you choose one dollar a year from now. You could still swap this for 80 cents today—just borrow 80 cents, and after a year, use the dollar to pay off your loan, with interest. Suppose you choose 80 cents today. You can still swap it for \$1 in a year—just put the 80 cents in a bank account and let the interest accumulate.

Figure 10.2 shows the PDV of \$1 received a year from now at various rates of interest. Notice that as the interest rate rises, PDV declines—that is, future dollars become less expensive. This makes sense—at a higher interest rate, you don't need to deposit as much to reach the \$1 target. So, rounding to the nearest penny, when the interest rate is 3 percent, the PDV of \$1 a year from now is 97 cents; when the interest rate is 10 percent, the PDV is 91 cents; and when the interest rate is 15 percent, the PDV is 87 cents.

---

[2]This concept is also known more simply as *present value.*

Figure 10.2

The PDV of $1 Received in One Year. The blue line shows the PDV of $1 received in one year—in other words, the price that you must pay today to receive $1 one year from today—at various interest rates.

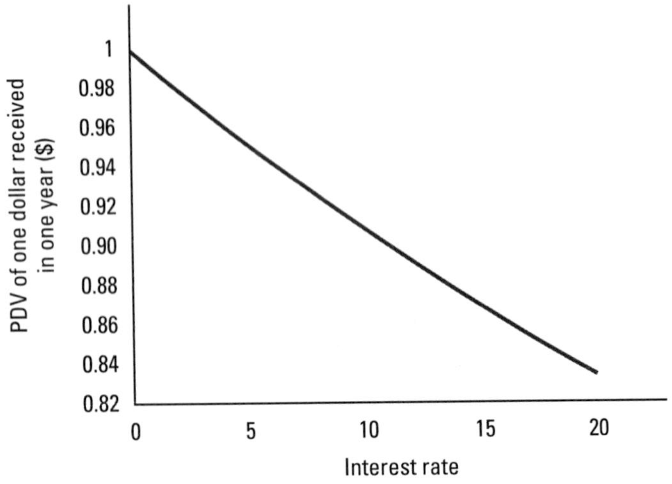

By making deposits in bank accounts, people can trade cash today for cash at any point in the future. Suppose you want to have exactly one dollar available in T years. How much can you "buy" it for today? From formula (1), we know that if you deposit D dollars today, you'll have $D(1 + R)^T$ dollars after T years. To end up with exactly $1, you need to choose D so that $D(1 + R)^T = 1$. Solving for D, we see that $D = 1/(1 + R)^T$. In other words, the price that you must pay today to receive one future dollar delivered T years from now is $\$1/(1 + R)^T$. Since present discounted value is the equivalent of today's lower price, we have:

$$\text{PDV of \$1 delivered in } T \text{ years} = \$1/(1 + R)^T \quad \textbf{(2)}$$

Table 10.2 shows how the PDV of a dollar delivered in T years changes with T and with the interest rate. Note that the PDV is smaller when the number of years is larger, and when the interest rate is higher. This makes sense: in both cases, any initial deposit accumulates to a larger balance, so you don't need to deposit as much to reach the $1 target. At

Table 10.2

The PDV of $1 Received at Various Points in the Future, at Various Interest Rates

(Note: The amounts listed in this table are in cents)

	Interest rate				
Years	**1%**	**3%**	**5%**	**10%**	**15%**
1	99.01	97.09	95.24	90.91	86.96
5	95.15	86.26	78.35	62.09	49.72
10	90.53	74.41	61.39	38.55	24.72
15	86.13	64.19	48.10	23.94	12.29
20	81.95	55.37	37.69	14.86	6.11
30	74.19	41.20	23.14	5.73	1.51

an interest rate of 5 percent, for example, $1 delivered next year costs 95.24 cents today, while $1 delivered in 30 years costs only 23.14 cents today. Likewise, at an interest rate of 1 percent, you can "buy" $1 delivered 30 years from now for 74.19 cents today. But if the interest rate is 15 percent, the same dollar costs only 1.51 cents!

IN-TEXT EXERCISE 10.1 **Calculate the PDV of: (a) $1 delivered 7 years from now if the interest rate is 5 percent; (b) $1 delivered 12 years from now if the interest rate is 7 percent; (c) $1 delivered 100 years from now if the interest rate is 2 percent.**

Once we know the price today of future dollars, we can determine the PDV of any amount of money at any point in the future. To illustrate, let's compute the PDV of $100 delivered in 30 years, assuming the interest rate is 5 percent. If we were talking about 100 apples, we would take the price per apple (say 30 cents) and multiply it by 100 to find the total cost (30 cents × 100 = $30). The same principle applies here. According to Table 10.2, each dollar delivered 30 years from now costs 23.1 cents. Today, you can buy 100 future dollars for 100 × 23.1 cents = $23.10.[3] The PDV of $100 delivered in 30 years is therefore $23.10.

In thinking about decisions involving time, it's useful to have a general formula for PDV. Formula (2) tells us that a dollar delivered T years from now costs $1/(1 + R)^T$ dollars today. So a claim on F dollars in T years (the future value) costs $F/(1 + R)^T$ dollars today.[4] In other words,

$$\text{PDV} = \frac{\text{Future value } (\$F)}{(1 + R)^T} \tag{3}$$

So far we've focused on the PDV of money *received* in the future. The same principles apply to an obligation to *pay* money in the future. That is, formula (3) works even when F is a negative number. For example, at an interest rate of 25 percent, there is no difference between owing someone a dollar a year from now and owing 80 cents today. If you owe $1 a year from now, you can pay the debt off today with 80 cents—just deposit 80 cents in a bank account, let it sit for a year, and then use the principal and interest to meet your obligation. Likewise, if you owe 80 cents today, you can pay the obligation off with $1 a year from now—just borrow 80 cents to pay the obligation today, and then use $1 to pay off the new loan plus interest in a year.

Valuing Streams of Future Payments or Receipts

Many economic decisions require us to evaluate streams of future payments or receipts, rather than a single payment or receipt at a fixed point in the future. Let's say you need to buy a washing machine, for example. Sears sells it for $600. CostCo charges $625 for the same machine but doesn't require you to make any payments for a year. Best Buy charges $640, but offers an installment plan: you pay $200 up front, then $110 per year for the next four years. The interest rate is 5 percent. In this hypothetical example, which store offers the best deal?

---

[3] To do so, you would deposit $23.10 in a bank account paying 5 percent interest, and allow the balance to accumulate for 30 years, at which point you would have exactly $100.

[4] To buy this claim, you would deposit $F/(1 + R)^T$ dollars in a bank account that pays interest at the rate R, and allow the balance to accumulate for T years, at which point you would have exactly $(1 + R)^T F/(1 + R)^T = F$ dollars.

To compare these choices, we have to figure out what each washing machine costs in today's dollars. For Sears, the answer is obvious: \$600. What about CostCo? From Table 10.2, we know that a dollar delivered one year from now costs 95.2 cents today. Since we need \$625 delivered one year from now, the total cost is \$625 × \$0.952 = \$595.24. In other words, if you deposit \$595.24 in a bank account paying 5 percent interest today, you'll have just enough to make the \$625 payment in one year. CostCo's deal is better than Sears's, even though its price appears to be higher!

Best Buy's deal involves a stream of payments; Table 10.3 computes the cost in today's dollars. The \$200 payment up front obviously costs \$200. The four installment payments cost \$104.76, \$99.77, \$95.02, and \$90.50 respectively in today's dollars (in each case, we multiply the number of future dollars required, 110, by the cost of buying one future dollar today).[5] In total, Best Buy's washer costs \$200 + \$104.76 + \$99.77 + \$95.02 + \$90.50 = \$590.05 today. The washing machine is therefore cheaper at Best Buy than at either Sears or CostCo, even though Best Buy appears to charge the highest price!

In this example, we've computed the PDV of a particular stream of payments. We can do the same for any stream of payments or receipts occurring over any period of time, and for any interest rate. Suppose you are obliged to pay someone F_0 dollars today, F_1 dollars one year from now, F_2 dollars two years from now, and so forth, with the final payment, F_T dollars, due T years from now. How much do you owe in today's dollars? The answer is

$$\text{PDV of stream} = F_0 + \frac{F_1}{1+R} + \frac{F_2}{(1+R)^2} + \cdots + \frac{F_T}{(1+R)^T} \qquad \textbf{(4)}$$

We can also use formula (4) to calculate the PDV of a stream of future receipts rather than payments, or a stream that includes both payments and receipts.

To understand formula (4), consider an analogy. Suppose apples cost 25 cents each and oranges cost 20 cents each. You are obliged to give someone four apples and six oranges. To determine the total cost of this obligation, you multiply the prices times the quantities (\$0.25 × 4 = \$1.00 for apples and \$0.20 × 6 = \$1.20 for oranges), and then add (\$1.00 + \$1.20 = \$2.20). Formula (4) involves the same type of calculation. To meet your entire obligation immediately, you need to come up with F_0 dollars today, which cost a dollar each; plus F_1 dollars delivered one year from now, which cost $\$1/(1+R)$ each today; plus F_2 dollars delivered two years from now, which cost $\$1/(1+R)^2$ each today;

Table 10.3
The True Cost of a Washing Machine Purchased on an Installment Plan

	Now	One Year	Two Years	Three Years	Four Years	Total
Number of dollars needed	200.00	110.00	110.00	110.00	110.00	**640.00**
Price of a dollar, from today's perspective	1.00	0.952	0.907	0.864	0.823	
Cost in today's dollars	200.00	104.76	99.77	95.02	90.50	**590.05**

[5]If you put \$104.76 in the bank today, you'll have just enough to make the first installment payment in one year; if you add \$99.77 today, you'll have just enough to make the second payment in two years, and so forth.

and so forth. The formula simply tells us to multiply prices by quantities and then add up the results.

Some transactions involve streams of payments or receipts that don't change over time. For example, to repay a typical car loan, the borrower has to make the same payment month after month for several years. When the payment stream is constant, there's an easier way to calculate the PDV. Let's say you are obliged to pay someone F dollars annually, starting one year from today, with the final payment to be made in T years. How much do you owe in today's dollars? The answer is:[6]

$$\text{PDV of constant stream} = \frac{F}{R}\left(1 - \frac{1}{(1 + R)^T}\right) \tag{5}$$

As we'll see, formula (5) is often useful.

Here's an easy way to understand why formula (5) holds. Suppose you put F/R dollars in a bank account. During the first year, you'll earn F dollars of interest, which you can use to make your first payment, leaving you with F/R dollars in your account at the start of the second year. Likewise, during the second year, you'll earn F dollars of interest, which you can use to make your second payment, leaving you with F/R dollars in your account at the start of the third year. If you continue in this way, you'll make all of your required payments over the course of T years, and you'll have F/R dollars left in your account. Since you have something left over, your original deposit was larger than it had to be to cover your obligations. How much larger? Since the PDV of your ending balance is $(F/R)/(1 + R)^T$ dollars, you deposited $(F/R)/(1 + R)^T$ dollars too much. You could have covered all of the required payments with an initial deposit of $F/R - (F/R)/(1 + R)^T = F/R(1 - 1/(1 + R)^T)$ dollars. According to formula (5), this is indeed the PDV of your payments.

If you're obliged to make the same payment periodically for a very long time, the PDV of your future payments is approximately F/R dollars. Why? When T is a very large number, the last term in formula (5), $1/(1 + R)^T$, is close to zero. (For example, remember that, with an interest rate of 15 percent, the PDV of \$1 received 30 years from now is 1.5 cents). As a result, formula (5) delivers a value very close to F/R dollars.

Application 10.1

Interest Rates and Bond Prices

Depositing money in a bank account is just one way to swap current dollars for future dollars. Another is to buy a *bond*, a legally binding promise to make specific future payments. In other words, a bond is an I.O.U. Corporations and governments create (or issue) bonds to borrow money from the public. They sell them on the open market at whatever prices investors are willing to pay and must then make the promised payments to the bonds' owners. The purchaser of a bond is usually free to sell it to another investor. When the bond changes hands, the new owner is entitled to the remaining payments.

In the United States, the value of all outstanding bonds exceeded \$25 trillion in 2005. That figure includes more than \$4 trillion of U.S. Treasury securities, nearly \$6 trillion of

[6]Here's one way to derive formula (5). Let's use X to stand for the PDV of the promised payments. That is, $X = F/(1 + R) + F/(1 + R)^2 + F/(1 + R)^3 + \cdots + F/(1 + R)^T$. Multiplying both sides of this formula by $(1 + R)$ tells us that $(1 + R)X = F + F/(1 + R) + F/(1 + R)^2 + \cdots + F/(1 + R)^{T-1}$. Subtracting the first formula from the second, we obtain $RX = F - F/(1 + R)^T$, which we can rewrite as $RX = F[1 - 1/(1 + R)^T]$. Dividing both sides by R produces formula (5).

mortgage-related securities, roughly $5 trillion of corporate debt, and more than $2 trillion of municipal government debt.

Some people buy bonds as long-term investments. Others try to make money by anticipating changes in bond prices, buying right before prices rise, and selling right before they fall. The high-stakes business of bond trading requires a thorough knowledge of the economic factors that influence bond prices.

Listen to a few financial reports, and you'll quickly learn that bond prices rise when interest rates fall and fall when interest rates rise. For example, in Figure 10.3, we've plotted the price of a particular type of bond—a six-month U.S. Treasury bill—against the prime interest rate (that is, the interest rate that banks charge their most creditworthy customers). The figure includes a data point for each month between January 1982 and August 2006. These data clearly show that the bond price and the interest rate move in opposite directions.

What accounts for this pattern? Unlike a bank account, a bond contract usually describes future payments in dollar amounts rather than as rates of interest. When the interest rate rises, the present discounted value of the promised future payments declines. Since the promised payments are worth less in current dollars, the bond's price falls.

Many bonds provide a regular, constant payment known as the *coupon*, for a fixed period, known as the *maturity*. Usually, the issuer promises to make a larger payment, known as the *face value*, with the final coupon payment. For example, a bond might pay $100 per year for 30 years, with a $1,000 payment at maturity. Using the symbols C for the coupon, M for the maturity, V for the face value, and R for the rate of interest, we can write a formula for the PDV of the promised future payments as follows:

$$\text{PDV of promised bond payments} = \frac{C}{1+R} + \frac{C}{(1+R)^2} + \cdots + \frac{C+V}{(1+R)^M}$$

Equivalently, we can use formula (5) to compute the PDV of the constant coupon payments, and then add the PDV of the face value payment:

$$\text{PDV of promised bond payments} = \frac{C}{R}\left(1 - \frac{1}{(1+R)^M}\right) + \frac{V}{(1+R)^M} \quad \textbf{(6)}$$

(Since this expression is the amount people are willing to pay for the bond, it is also the price at which the bond will trade.)

Using these formulas, we can calculate the PDV of the promised payments for any bond at any interest rate. As an example, let's examine six-month U.S. Treasury bills. These *zero coupon* bonds are usually issued with a face value of $1,000, which is paid upon maturity six months later. In other words, $C = 0$, $V = 1{,}000$, and $M = 1/2$ (since six months is half of a year). By plugging these values into formula (6), we learn that the PDV of a six-month U.S. Treasury bill is $1{,}000/\sqrt{1+R}$ dollars. Clearly, as the interest rate rises, the PDV must fall. For instance, the PDV falls from $976 to $953 as the interest rises from 5 percent to 10 percent.[7]

Figure 10.3

The Price of a Bond versus the Prime Interest Rate. In this figure, we've plotted the the price of a particular type of bond—a six-month U.S. Treasury bill—against the prime interest rate (that is, the interest rate that banks charge their most creditworthy customers), using monthly data from January 1982 and August 2006. The bond price and the interest rate move in opposite directions.

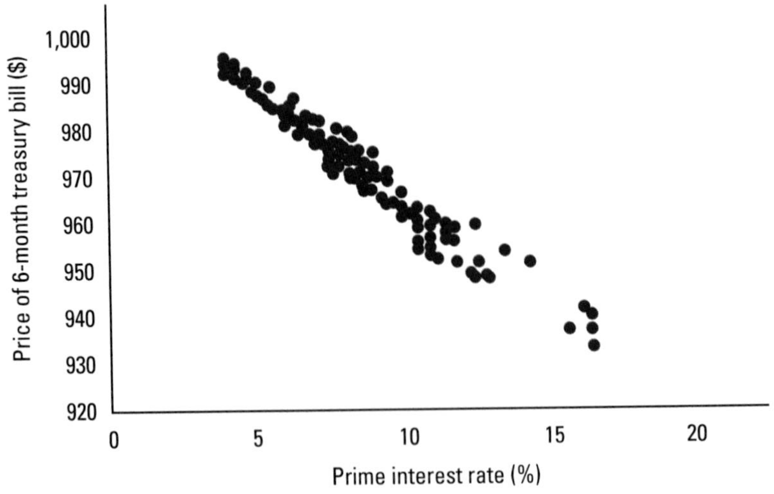

[7]The Treasury bill prices shown in Figure 10.3 are slightly higher than those PDVs. That's because the prime rate isn't quite the right interest rate to use when valuing U.S. Treasury securities. Since the Treasury is more reliable than even the most creditworthy bank customer, it pays interest at a rate below the prime rate.

WORKED-OUT PROBLEM 10.1

The Problem Calculate the PDV of promised payments for a 30-year bond with a \$100 coupon and a face value of \$1,000 at interest rates of 5 percent, 10 percent, and 15 percent. Assume that the coupon payments are made at the end of each year.[8]

The Solution For this bond, we have $C = 100$, $M = 30$, and $V = 1{,}000$. According to formula (6), the PDV of the promised payments is therefore

$$\frac{100}{R}\left(1 - \frac{1}{(1+R)^{30}}\right) + \frac{1{,}000}{(1+R)^{30}}$$

By plugging in different interest rates, we find that the PDV is \$1,768.62 at 5 percent, \$1,000 at 10 percent, and \$671.70 at 15 percent.

IN-TEXT EXERCISE 10.2 **Calculate the PDV of promised payments for a 15 year bond with a \$4,000 coupon and a face value of \$50,000 at interest rates of 5 percent, 10 percent, and 15 percent. What if the interest rate is 0 percent?**

Why Do Interest Rates Differ?

So far, we've assumed that there is a single rate of interest, but in fact, there are many. For consumers, interest rates on bank deposits differ across banks and account types. For example, a certificate of deposit (or CD)—which places restrictions on deposits and withdrawals for a fixed period—typically pays a higher interest rate than a money market checking account.

Consumers also pay interest when they borrow money. And again different types of loans carry different interest rates. The interest rates for credit card balances, for example, are typically much higher than home mortgage rates. The maturity of a loan also has a significant effect on the interest rate. In 2006, rates were lower for 15-year mortgages than for 30-year mortgages.

Why do interest rates differ? Risk plays an important role. Sometimes individuals, corporations, and even governments **default**—that is, they fail to pay back the money they've borrowed. To compensate for this risk, lenders demand higher interest payments. The interest rates on credit cards are high in part because a sizable fraction of cardholders are somewhat unreliable. In contrast, the U.S. Treasury can borrow at a low interest rate because almost everyone expects the federal government to honor its obligations.[9] (We'll discuss risk at greater length in Chapter 11.)

Default is the failure to pay back borrowed money.

Interest rates also depend on some specific features of the agreement between a borrower and a lender. For example, banks must pay higher rates on CDs than on money market checking accounts to compensate their customers for the loss of financial flexibility.

[8] Many bonds promise payments at other intervals, such as semiannually.

[9] Even if a government never defaults, it can still choose to pay less in real terms by adopting policies that lead to higher rates of inflation. In that case, we say that the government has *monetized* a portion of its debt.

The timing of repayment is also important. Lenders charge different rates for short-term loans than for long-term loans. These advanced topics aren't covered in this book, but you'll learn more about them if you go on to study finance or money and banking.

In computing the present value of some future payment, it's important to use an interest rate for an obligation that has similar characteristics. When the future payment involves little or no risk (as we assume throughout this section), we can use the rate paid by an extremely reliable borrower, like the U.S. Treasury. When the future payment is risky, we need to use the rate paid by a less reliable borrower. Likewise, in valuing dollars delivered, say, 30 years in the future, it's appropriate to use a long-term interest rate. A short-term rate is useful in valuing a dollar delivered within, say, three months.

Real versus Nominal Interest

Whenever we lend or borrow money, it's important to remember that future dollars may not carry the same purchasing power as current dollars. (Recall our discussion of inflation in Section 6.3). If the interest rate is 10 percent, we can trade \$10 today for \$11 next year. From that perspective, we appear to come out ahead. But if Donald spends all of his money on beef, and if the price of beef is expected to increase by 10 percent over the next year from \$5 to \$5.50, then trading \$10 today for \$11 next year amounts to trading two pounds of beef this year for two pounds of beef next year. Donald may come out ahead in terms of dollars, but not in terms of beef.

Nominal interest is the compensation received by the lender over and above the principal, measured in nominal dollars (that is, without adjusting for inflation).

Real interest is the compensation received by the lender over and above the principal, measured in real dollars (that is, adjusted for inflation).

For this reason, economists distinguish between **nominal interest** and **real interest**, a distinction that parallels the one between nominal income and real (inflation-adjusted) income, discussed in Section 6.3. Nominal interest is the compensation received by the lender over and above the principal, measured in nominal dollars (that is, without adjusting for inflation). Real interest is the compensation received by the lender over and above the principal, measured in real dollars (that is, adjusted for inflation). When a bank or a lender quotes an interest rate, it's usually a nominal rate.

To calculate the annual real interest rate earned on money deposited in a bank account, R^{real}, we express the change in the real account balance over a year as a fraction of the real dollars deposited:

$$R^{real} = \frac{\text{Real dollars next year} - \text{Real dollars deposited}}{\text{Real dollars deposited}}$$

Let's suppose the deposit is one real dollar. Over one year, that deposit will grow to $1 + R^{nominal}$ dollars, where $R^{nominal}$ is the nominal interest rate. However, due to inflation, those $1 + R^{nominal}$ dollars will be worth only $(1 + R^{nominal})/(1 + INFL)$ real dollars, where $INFL$ is the rate of inflation (see Section 6.3). When we substitute this expression into the previous formula, and remember that the original deposit is one real dollar, we discover that

$$R^{real} = \frac{(1 + R^{nominal})/(1 + INFL) - 1}{1} = \frac{R^{nominal} - INFL}{1 + INFL} \quad (7)$$

Using formula (7), we can calculate the real interest rate from the nominal interest rate and the inflation rate. For example, in Donald's case, the nominal interest rate and the inflation rate (the expected change in the price of beef) are both 10 percent, so the real rate of interest is 0 percent (because $(0.10 - 0.10)/(1 + 0.10) = 0$). This rate reflects the fact that Donald can trade a pound of beef today for a pound of beef next year, no more and no less.

If the rate of inflation is low, dividing by $1 + INFL$ in formula (7) doesn't make much of a difference. As a result, the real interest rate is roughly equal to the difference between the nominal interest rate and the inflation rate:

$$R^{real} \approx R^{nominal} - INFL \qquad \textbf{(8)}$$

For example, if the nominal interest rate is 5 percent and the inflation rate is 3 percent, formula (7) implies that the real interest rate is 1.942 percent ($R^{real} = 0.02/1.03 = 0.01942$). Formula (8) tells us that it's approximately 2 percent, which is off by only six one-hundredths of a percentage point. However, formula (8) is sometimes less reliable. If the nominal interest rate were 30 percent and the inflation rate were 25 percent, formula (7) tells us that the real interest rate would be 4 percent. Formula (8) yields an answer of approximately 5 percent, a full percentage point off.

In the last section, we didn't say explicitly whether we were dealing with real interest rates or nominal interest rates. Does it matter? The answer is no, as long as we're consistent. That is, we can calculate the PDV of a *nominal* future cash flow using a *nominal* interest rate, or we can calculate the PDV of a *real* future cash flow using a *real* interest rate. Either way, we'll get the same answer.[10]

WORKED-OUT PROBLEM 10.2

The Problem If the real interest rate is 5 percent and the inflation rate is 3 percent, what is the nominal interest rate?

The Solution Rearranging formula (7), we see that $R^{nominal} = INFL + R^{real}(1 + INFL)$. When we substitute $R^{real} = 0.05$ and $INFL = 0.03$, we find that $R^{nominal} = 0.0815$. So the nominal interest rate is 8.15 percent.

IN-TEXT EXERCISE 10.3 **Suppose the nominal interest rate is 4 percent and the inflation rate is 1 percent. What is the real interest rate? What if the nominal interest rate is 5 percent and the inflation rate is 2 percent? In general, if the nominal interest rate and the inflation rate both rise by one percentage point, does the real interest rate change? What about the approximate value of the real interest rate given by formula (8)?**

[10]Suppose you expect to receive \$1 one year from now. Using the nominal cash flow and the nominal interest rate, the PDV is $1/(1 + R^{nominal})$. Using the real cash flow and the real interest rate, the PDV is $(1/(1 + INFL))/(1 + R^{real})$. By adding one to both sides of formula (7), we learn that $1 + R^{real} = (1 + R^{nominal})/(1 + INFL)$. Substituting this formula into the previous expression, we discover that the $(1/(1 + INFL))/(1 + R^{real}) = 1/(1 + R^{nominal})$.

Application 10.2

Now That You've Won the Lottery . . .

On February 12, 2005, Vera Olds of Baton Rouge, Louisiana, learned that she was the winner of a $40.6 million Powerball jackpot. Yet the lottery paid her "only" $23.04 million. Why the difference?

State lotteries usually pay out people's winnings in annual installments, over a period of 20 years or more. The size of the advertised jackpot refers to the total nominal amount paid and not to the PDV of those earnings. For example, a $10 million prize might yield annual nominal payments of $500,000 per year for 20 years. The states spread the payments out over time precisely so they can advertise a larger prize without actually giving up more money.

Many states allow winners to claim their prizes in the form of an immediate lump-sum payment. However, the amount paid out in that form is typically around half the total jackpot. Ms. Olds received $23.04 million instead of $40.6 million because she chose the lump-sum payment.

Was Ms. Olds foolish to give up more than $17 million for the sake of gaining instant access to her prize? Not necessarily. Since the $40.6 million was a claim on future nominal dollars, it was worth considerably less than $40.6 million on February 12, 2005. The question is whether it was worth more or less than $23.04 million.[11]

To answer this question, it's helpful to understand how lottery jackpots are determined. Let's take California as an example. For every drawing, the California Lottery allocates some fixed amount of money to a grand prize. That amount is what a winner receives upon choosing the lump-sum option. It differs from the advertised jackpot, which is the sum of winnings paid out in 26 annual installments. The size of the advertised jackpot is chosen so that the PDV of those installments, using the prevailing nominal interest rates, exactly equals the amount of money allocated to the prize. If a winner chooses to receive the prize in installments, the state uses the allocated prize money to purchase a collection of zero-coupon Treasury bonds which at maturity will provide just enough funds to cover the promised installments. That way, the state pays out exactly the same amount of money regardless of whether the winner chooses the installments or the lump sum.

As long as the lump sum equals the PDV of the nominal installment payments, it is neither a good deal nor a bad one. It simply reflects the jackpot's current value.

10.2 SAVING AND BORROWING

To keep matters as simple as possible while introducing the basic principles of consumer decision making, we assumed throughout Chapters 5 and 6 that consumers could neither save current income nor borrow against future income. This assumption is obviously unrealistic. In this section, we'll see how the theory of consumer choice accounts for saving and borrowing.

The Timing of Consumption

You might think that adding saving and borrowing to the mix would significantly complicate our analysis of consumer choice. If so, you're in for a pleasant surprise! You've already learned all the basic concepts required to understand saving and borrowing. For

[11]In part, the answer to this question depends on the income tax treatment of lottery winnings. Here, we'll keep the analysis simple by ignoring taxes. If you ever win the lottery, we recommend consulting a reliable financial planner before deciding whether to take your prize as a lump sum or a series of installments!

the most part, all you need to do is apply what you learned in Chapters 4 through 6, using some of the tools developed in the last section.

Before we proceed, let's first address a basic question: When are two consumable items different goods and when are they the same good? In some cases, the answer is obvious. For example, a gallon of water and a gallon of gasoline are plainly different goods. Why? They serve different purposes and meet different needs. You drink the water and put the gasoline in your car's gas tank. Disastrous consequences follow if you drink the gasoline and put water in your gas tank.

Now think about two separate gallons of water, gallon A and gallon B, with identical chemical profiles. Are they examples of the same good? If you're like most people, you're probably tempted to say yes (unless you sense, correctly, that this is a trick question). The two gallons appear to serve the same purposes and meet the same needs. Both are equally well suited for drinking, watering plants, and washing hands.

Or are they? What if gallon A is available today and gallon B is available a year from now? In that case, they no longer meet the same needs. If I'm thirsty today, I can satisfy my need for water only by drinking from gallon A, but not by drinking from gallon B. This means we should think of them as *different* goods. In contrast, if gallon A and gallon B are both available at the same moment in time, at the same place, and under the same conditions, then they do indeed serve the same needs and are examples of the same good.

To study consumption decisions involving time, then, we simply think of a good's time of availability as a physical characteristic, just like size, color, or function. We treat identical physical objects (or services) as distinct goods if they are available at different points in time. Otherwise, we proceed as we did in Chapters 4 through 6.

Preferences for the Timing of Consumption In Section 4.2, we began by describing the consumer's preferences for consumption bundles. Remember that a consumption bundle lists the amount of each good consumed. Since we must distinguish among goods according to the time at which they are available, our list must itemize separately goods consumed now and goods consumed at particular points in the future. For real consumers, the list will be quite long.

To keep the analysis relatively simple, we'll examine a case in which the consumer, whom we'll call Brian, cares only about two goods, food this year and food next year (both measured in kilograms). Figure 10.4(a) shows Brian's set of potential consumption bundles graphically. Each point on the graph corresponds to a different bundle. For example, point A represents the consumption bundle consisting of 300 kg of food this year and 300 kg of food next year. At all points lying on the 45-degree line through the origin, like point A, Brian eats the same amount of food this year and next. For all points above the 45-degree line, like point B, Brian eats less food this year than next. And at all points below the 45-degree line, like point C, Brian eats more food this year than next.

We've illustrated Brian's preferences for these bundles by drawing the red indifference curves in Figure 10.4(a). Note that they have the same general shape as the indifference curves in Sections 4.2 and 4.3, for essentially the same reasons. Since we can compensate Brian for a reduction in food this year by providing him with more food next year (and vice versa), the curves slope downward. And since having extra food is relatively more important when food is scarce, each indifference curve has a declining marginal rate of substitution.

Figure 10.4(b) shows a family of indifference curves (in blue) for a second consumer, Ryan. At any particular point, like point E in both figures, Ryan's indifference curve is

Figure 10.4

Consumer Preferences for the Timing of Consumption. Each point on these graphs corresponds to a consumption bundle consisting of food this year and food next year. At points on the 45-degree line, like point A in figure (a), consumption is the same in both years. At points above the 45-degree line, like point B in figure (a), consumption is lower this year than next. At points below the 45-degree line, like point C in figure (a), consumption is higher this year than next. At any particular point, like point E in both figures, Ryan's indifference curve (in figure (b)) is steeper than Brian's (in figure (a)), which means that Ryan's marginal rate of substitution for food this year with food next year is larger. The greater steepness of Ryan's indifference curves therefore indicates greater impatience.

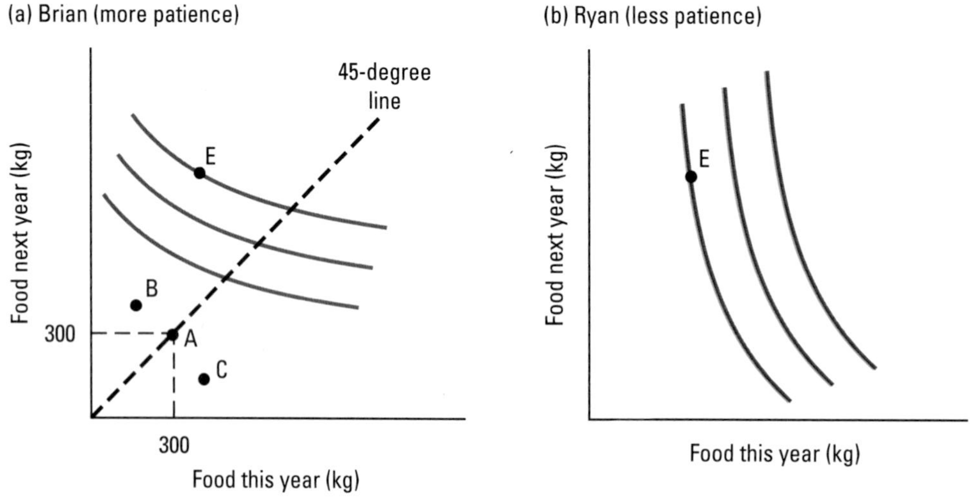

steeper than Brian's, which means that Ryan's marginal rate of substitution for food this year with food next year is larger. To compensate for the loss of a kilogram of food this year, Ryan would require a larger increase in food next year than Brian. The greater steepness of Ryan's indifference curves therefore indicates greater impatience.

Affordable Consumption Bundles As in Section 5.1, the next step is to identify affordable consumption bundles. Let's start with an example. Suppose that Brian expects to earn \$380 this year and \$220 next year. The interest rate is 10 percent and the price of food is \$1 per kilogram both this year and next. Which bundles can Brian afford?

Clearly, Brian can afford the bundle A in Figure 10.5(a), which contains 380 kg of food this year and 220 kg of food next year. To purchase this bundle, he simply spends his income when he receives it.

Brian can also purchase any bundle on the green line that runs through bundle A in Figure 10.5(a). For bundles on this line to the left of point A, income exceeds spending this year, and spending exceeds income next year. Brian can obtain these bundles by saving. For example, if he puts \$180 in a bank account this year (leaving him with \$200 to spend on food), he'll be able to spend \$418 next year (his income, \$220, plus the amount he saved, \$180, plus interest on his saving, \$18). This possibility corresponds to bundle B in Figure 10.5(a). For bundles on the green line to the right of point A, spending exceeds

Figure 10.5

Affordable Alternatives with Saving and Borrowing. Brian earns $380 this year and $220 next year. If he spends his money when he receives it, he consumes the bundle labeled A in both figures. Figure (a) shows that he can reach point B by saving $180 this year, which will give him an extra $198 next year. Figure (b) shows that he can reach point C by borrowing $100 this year and repaying $110 next year.

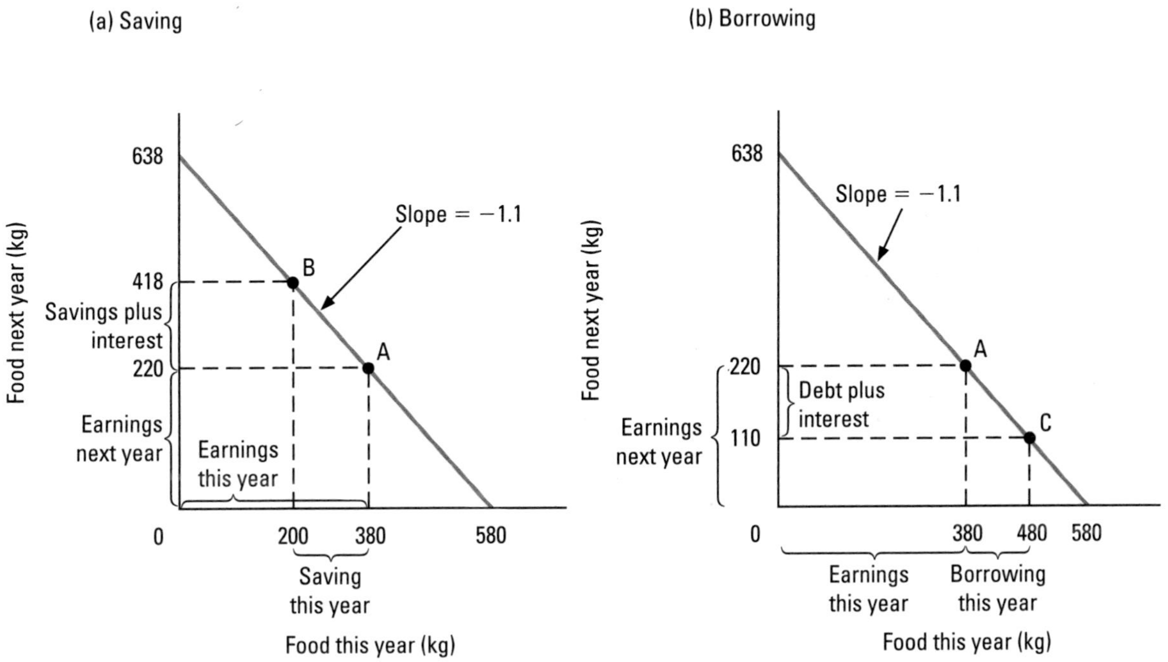

income this year, and income exceeds spending next year. Brian can obtain these bundles by borrowing. For example, if he borrows $100 this year and spends $480 on food, he'll be able to spend $110 next year (his income, $220, minus the amount he borrowed, $100, minus interest on his debt, $10). This possibility corresponds to bundle C in Figure 10.5(b).

Notice that the slope of the green line is −1.1. If Brian reduces his consumption this year by one kilogram, he can either increase his saving by $1, in which case he will earn 10 cents more interest, or reduce his borrowing by $1, in which case he will pay 10 cents less interest. In either case, he will have an extra $1.10 next year, which buys 1.1 kg of food.

More generally, a consumption bundle is affordable if, through borrowing and lending, the consumer can make all the required payments as they come due. That is possible as long as the PDV of the consumption stream doesn't exceed the PDV of the income stream. When the More-Is-Better Principle holds, the best choice leaves no income unspent, so

$$\text{PDV of consumption stream} = \text{PDV of income stream} \quad \textbf{(9)}$$

Let's apply this formula to Brian's problem. We'll use P_0 to stand for the price per kilogram of food this year, P_1 for the price per kilogram of food next year, and R for the interest rate. Formula (9) implies that

$$\text{Food this year (kg)} \times P_0 + \text{Food next year (kg)} \times \left(\frac{P_1}{1+R}\right)$$

$$= \text{Income this year} + \frac{\text{Income next year}}{1+R} \qquad \textbf{(10)}$$

Using the same numerical values as above ($P_0 = P_1 = 1$, $R = 0.10$, income this year is \$380, and income next year is \$220), formula (10) simplifies as follows:

$$\text{Food this year (kg)} + \text{Food next year (kg)} \times \left(\frac{1}{1.1}\right) = 580$$

The consumption bundles that satisfy this formula lie on the green line in Figures 10.5(a) and (b). (Check this!)

The expression $P_1/(1 + R)$, which appears in formula (10), is the PDV of the price-per-kilogram of food next year. We can also interpret $P_1/(1 + R)$ as the price of food next year *from today's perspective.* Why? The price of a good is the amount of money you need to give up in exchange for it. If you give up $P_1/(1 + R)$ dollars today by putting it in the bank, you'll have just enough money to buy a kilogram of food a year from now (P_1 dollars).

With this interpretation of $P_1/(1 + R)$ in mind, we see that formula (10) describes a budget line, just like the ones introduced in Section 5.1. In the first line of this formula, we multiply the amount of food purchased in each year times its price from today's perspective; then we add these numbers up to find total spending. The second line tells us that total spending equals total income—again valued from today's perspective.

In Section 5.1, we saw that the slope of a budget line equals the ratio of the goods' prices, times negative one. In the context of Brian's problem, the price of food this year is P_0 and the price of food next year (from today's perspective) is $P_1/(1 + R)$. We therefore have the following formula for the slope of the budget line:

$$\text{Slope of budget line} = -\frac{P_0}{P_1/(1+R)} = -(1+\text{R})\left(\frac{P_0}{P_1}\right) \qquad \textbf{(11)}$$

In our numerical example, we assumed that food costs \$1 per kilogram in each year ($P_0 = P_1 = 1$), and that the interest rate is 10 percent ($R = 0.10$). Therefore, formula (11) tells us that the slope of Brian's budget line is $-(1 + 0.10)(1/1) = -1.1$, just as we determined above.

Consumption Choices To determine Brian's best choice, we apply the no-overlap rule (which we introduced in Section 5.2). When Brian's preferences correspond to the family of red indifference curves in Figure 10.4(a), he chooses point B in Figure 10.6(a). Since point B is to the left of point A, we know he saves something this year so he can consume more food next year.

Figure 10.6(b) examines Ryan's best choice assuming that his preferences correspond to the blue family of indifference curves in Figure 10.4(b). Since the blue indifference curves are steeper than the red curves, the blue curve that runs through point B crosses the budget line, as shown. Ryan can do better than point B by moving along the budget

Figure 10.6

Best Choices with Saving and Borrowing. Based on his earnings, Brian starts out at point A in figure (a). His best choice with the red indifference curves is point B. Since point B is to the left of point A, he saves. With the blue indifference curve in figure (b), which reflects greater impatience, Ryan's best choice is point C. Since point C is to the right of point A, he borrows.

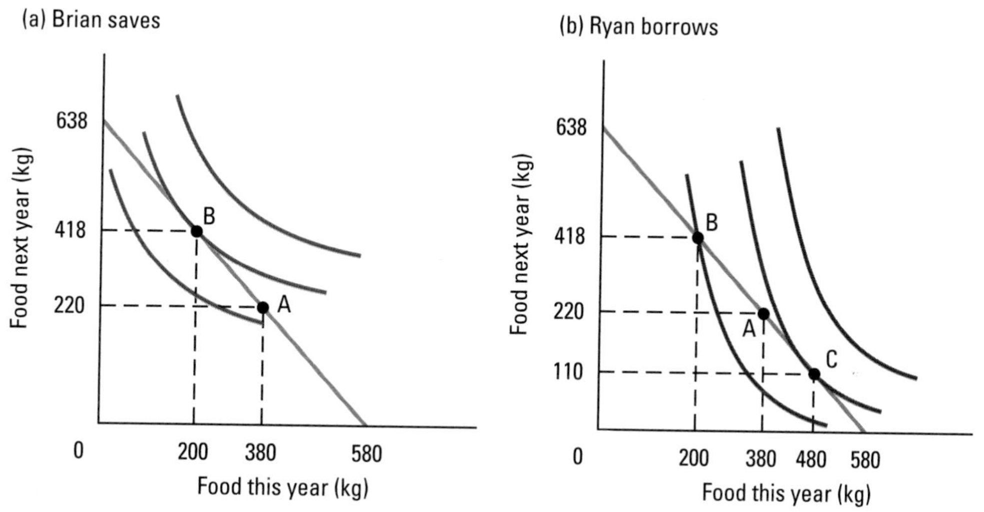

line to the southeast. His best choice is point C. Since point C is to the right of point A, we know that Ryan borrows money this year so he can consume more food than his current income would allow. There is nothing necessarily wrong with that—compared with Brian, he simply prefers to consume more this year and less next year.

Saving, Borrowing, and the Interest Rate

When the interest rate rises, saving becomes more rewarding and borrowing becomes more costly. It's natural to think that people would respond to a rise in the interest rate by saving more and borrowing less. However, the truth is not quite so straightforward. Suppose, for example, that your objective is to accumulate $30,000 over the next five years so you can buy a nice car. If the interest rate rises, you'll earn more interest on each dollar saved, which means you won't need to save as much to reach your target. Therefore, you might decide to save *less*.

To understand how saving and borrowing respond to changes in the interest rate, we first need to study how those changes affect consumers' budget constraints. Let's assume that point A in Figure 10.7(a) is the bundle Brian can afford if he spends all of his income when he receives it. Let's also assume that he can purchase any bundle on the line labeled L_1 at the prevailing interest rate. An increase in the interest rate rotates his budget line to L_2, pivoting it around point A. Why? He can still spend all of his income when he receives it, so bundle A remains affordable. However, according to formula (11), the budget line becomes steeper. Intuitively, an increase in the interest rate reduces the amount of money

Figure 10.7

The Effect of a Change in the Interest Rate on Saving. In figure (a), Brian initially chooses point B. When the interest rate rises, he picks point D. Figure (b) breaks this change up into a substitution effect (the movement from B to E) and an income effect (the movement from E to D). Assuming food this year is a normal good, these effects work in opposite directions. Food this year can therefore rise or fall. This means that, in response to an increase in the interest rate, saving can rise or fall.

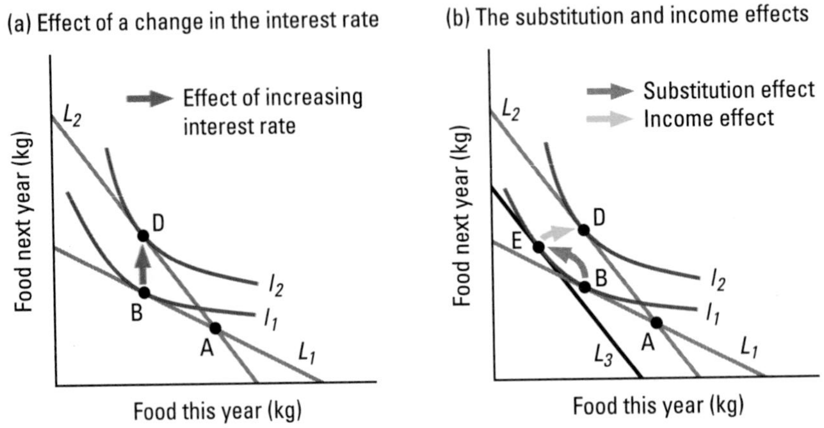

Brian must set aside today to purchase a kilogram of food next year. This allows him to exchange food this year for food next year at a more favorable rate.

How is Brian's saving affected by this change in the interest rate? To answer this question, we examine the resulting change in food consumption this year. If food consumption this year rises, Brian must save less if he is a saver, or borrow more if he is a borrower. If food consumption this year falls, Brian must either save more if he is a saver, or borrow less if he is a borrower.

In Figure 10.7(a), we reproduce Brian's indifference curves (shown in red) from Figure 10.4(a). At the lower interest rate he faces the budget line labeled L_1 and picks point B, which involves saving. If the interest rate rises, changing his budget line to L_2, his best choice shifts to point D.

Will Brian's food consumption this year rise or fall? In Figure 10.7(a), it declines slightly; more generally, the answer is unclear. Why? In Section 6.1 we learned that a change in the price of a good creates both a substitution effect and an income effect. We illustrate these effects in Figure 10.7(b). The substitution effect involves a movement along indifference curve I_1 from point B to point E (budget line L_3 runs parallel to L_2 and is tangent to I_1 at point E). Since point E lies to the left of B, consumption this year falls and saving rises. Intuitively, Brian substitutes away from food this year because food next year has become comparatively less expensive. What about the income effect? Since Brian is a saver, the higher interest rate *increases* his purchasing power. The income effect therefore involves an *outward* shift of the budget line, from L_3 to L_2, which moves him

Figure 10.8

The Effect of a Change in the Interest Rate on Borrowing. In figure (a) Ryan chooses point C. When the interest rate rises, he picks point F. Figure (b) breaks this change up into a substitution effect (the movement from C to G) and an income effect (the movement from G to F). Assuming food this year is a normal good, these effects work in the same direction, and food this year necessarily falls. This means that, in response to an increase in the interest rate, borrowing necessarily falls.

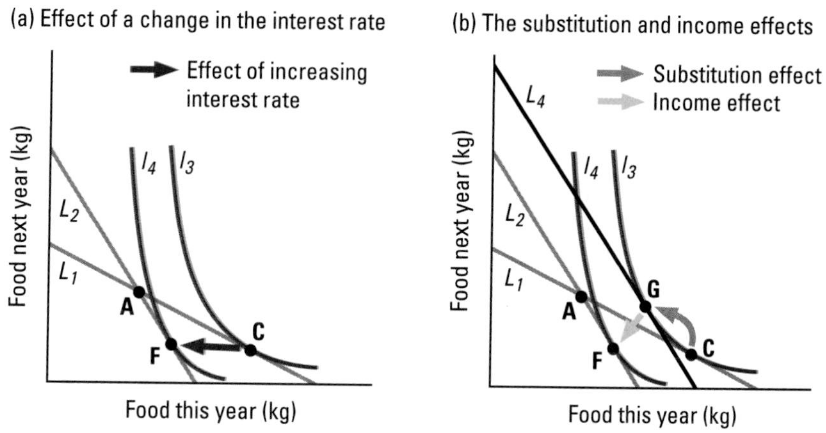

from point E to point D. As long as food this year is a normal good, Brian will consume more of it as a result of the income effect, and save less. So just as in our analysis of labor supply decisions (Section 6.4), the income and substitution effects work in opposite directions. Brian's food consumption this year, and therefore his saving, can either rise or fall, depending on which effect is larger.

How does an increase in the interest rate affect borrowing? In Figure 10.8(a), we reproduce Ryan's indifference curves (shown in blue) from Figure 10.4(b). At the lower interest rate, he faces the budget line labeled L_1 and picks point C, which involves borrowing. The change in the interest rate shifts his budget line to L_2 and his best choice to point F. Because point F lies to the left of point C, Ryan's borrowing falls. Ryan's response involves an income effect and a substitution effect, which we illustrate in Figure 10.8(b). Like Brian in Figure 10.7(b), Ryan consumes less food this year as a result of the substitution effect, which moves him along indifference curve I_3 from point C to point G (budget line L_4 is parallel to L_2 and tangent to I_3 at point G). In this case, Ryan is a borrower, so the higher interest rate *reduces* his purchasing power. The income effect therefore involves an *inward* shift of the budget line, from L_4 to L_2, which moves Ryan from point G to point F. As long as food this year is a normal good, Ryan will consume less of it as a result of the income effect. So the income and substitution effects push food consumption this year in the *same* direction. Therefore, borrowing will definitely fall.

In sum, if we assume that consumption at each point in time is a normal good, then among savers, an increase in the interest rate can either raise or lower saving, but among borrowers, an increase in the interest rate definitely reduces borrowing.

WORKED-OUT PROBLEM

The Problem Angela cares only about food this year and food next year. Let's use F_0 to stand for food this year (in kilograms) and F_1 to stand for food next year (also in kilograms). Assume that Angela's marginal rate of substitution between food this year and food next year is F_1/F_0. Suppose she earns \$100 this year and nothing next year. Food costs \$1 per kg in both years and the interest rate is 10 percent. How much does she consume this year and how much does she save? Write a formula for her saving as a function of the interest rate, R. Does she save more, less, or the same amount when the interest rate rises?

The Solution First, let's identify bundles that satisfy the tangency condition. The slope of Angela's indifference is $-F_1/F_0$ (her marginal rate of substitution for food this year with food next year, times negative one), and the slope of her budget line is $-(1 + R)$. At her best choice, her indifference curve and her budget line must have the same slope, which requires $F_1/F_0 = 1 + R$, or equivalently $F_1 = F_0(1 + R)$. This tangency condition formula tells us that Angela eats $1 + R$ times as much food next year as this year.

The formula for Angela's budget line is $F_0 + F_1/(1 + R) = 100$. To find a bundle satisfying both the tangency condition formula and the budget line formula, we substitute for F_1 in the budget line formula using the tangency condition formula. This substitution yields the formula $F_0 + F_0(1 + R)/(1 + R) = 100$, which simplifies to $2F_0 = 100$, or $F_0 = 50$. So, this year Angela spends \$50 and saves \$50; next year she spends \$50$(1 + R)$. Because the interest rate is 10 percent, she consumes 50 kg of food this year and 55 kg next year.

The formula for saving, S, is simply $S = 50$. Angela's saving doesn't depend on the interest rate.

IN-TEXT EXERCISE 10.4 **Assume that Angela earns nothing this year and \$100 next year. To consume food this year, she must borrow. Repeat worked-out problem 10.3. This time, write a formula for her borrowing as a function of the interest rate. According to your formula, does she borrow more or less as the interest rate rises? Why does the interest rate affect borrowing in this exercise, even though it didn't affect saving in worked-out problem 10.3?**

Saving and Consumption over the Life Cycle

In practice, decisions involving saving are a good deal more complicated than Brian's simple problem. Among other things, if we expect to live for many years, we have to provide resources not merely for next year, but for the year after that, and the year after that.

In the 1950s and 1960s, economists Franco Modigliani (who later received the Nobel Prize), Richard Brumberg, and Albert Ando developed a theory of consumption and saving known as the Life Cycle Hypothesis, which describes the choices of consumers who live for a long time. Today, their theory is widely applied and is one of the most important tools economists use.

The Life Cycle Hypothesis applies the same logic we used to solve Brian's problem, but it adds two assumptions. The first, concerning earnings, holds that the typical person's adult life has two main stages. In the first stage, he or she is gainfully employed. Earnings rise with experience, level off in middle age, and then may decline a bit. In the second stage, the person is retired and earns nothing.[12]

The second assumption, concerning preferences, is that people like stability. That is, they prefer a constant or slowly changing lifestyle to a feast-or-famine roller-coaster ride. Of course, in comparing two stable alternatives, they favor the one that offers the higher living standard.

To see where these assumptions lead, look at Figure 10.9(a), which presents a more realistic version of Brian's problem. The blue curve shows his earnings rising steadily through middle age, falling a bit as retirement nears, and dropping to zero after retirement—a fairly typical pattern. The light and dark red lines show three possible consumption levels. In each of these cases, Brian's living standard is completely stable—consumption

Figure 10.9

The Life Cycle Hypothesis. As figure (a) shows, earnings usually rise with experience, level off in middle age, and then decline a bit before disappearing after retirement. Assuming that the consumer prefers a stable living standard, he'll choose a consumption path that doesn't vary with age, like C_1, C_2, or C_3. Of these choices, C_2 is the best feasible alternative: C_1 isn't feasible, and C_3 doesn't exhaust the consumer's lifetime resources. C_2 is also better than the wavy green consumption path, because it avoids ups and downs. Figure (b) shows how the consumer's saving and wealth changes with age when he follows consumption path C_2. After retirement, he will spend down his wealth to maintain his living standard.

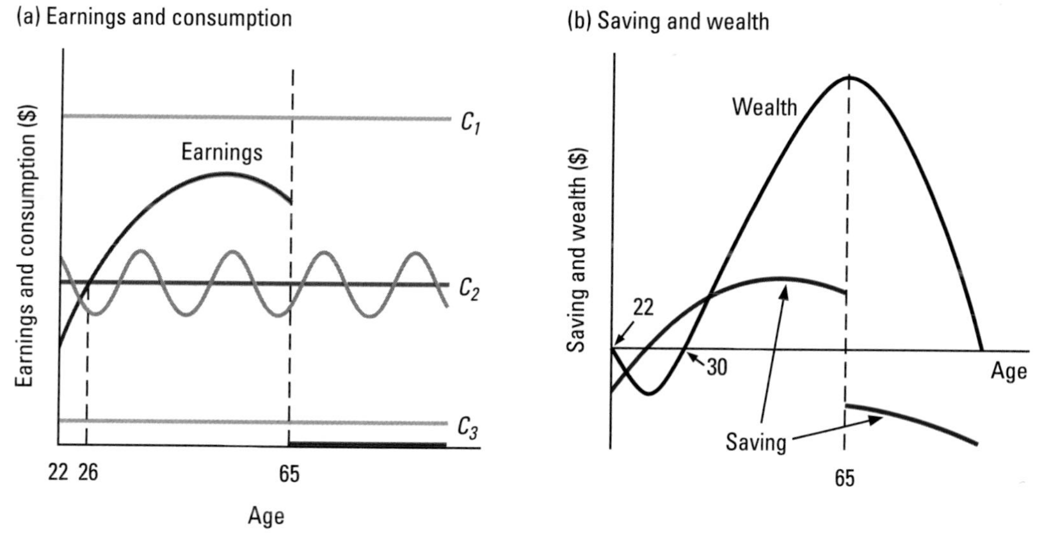

[12]The theory also allows for the possibility that people may partially retire or receive pension income after retirement. In either case, their cash income from employment falls after retirement, but not necessarily to zero. Economists have explored many other variations of the basic theory, including situations in which people are uncertain about how long they'll live and in which they invest in risky assets.

doesn't change at all with his age. Naturally, the line labeled C_1 is the best of the three, and the line labeled C_3 is the worst.

To determine whether any particular consumption path is feasible, we need to make sure its PDV doesn't exceed the PDV of Brian's earnings. The light red consumption path C_1 isn't feasible because it lies above the blue earnings line at every age; Brian doesn't earn enough money over his lifetime to pay for it. The light red consumption path C_3 is feasible but not particularly desirable, since it doesn't even begin to exhaust his earnings. Somewhere between these two possibilities lies a line like C_2 (shown in dark red) for which the PDV of consumption equals the PDV of Brian's earnings. Paying for this consumption stream will just exhaust Brian's lifetime earnings. This is the best available choice—better, for example, than living hand-to-mouth, spending income as it is earned, because it avoids an enormous drop in living standard at retirement. It is also better than following the wavy green curve, because it avoids ups and downs.[13]

Figure 10.9(b) shows how Brian's saving and his wealth (that is, his accumulated savings minus his accumulated debt) changes as he ages. When Brian follows consumption path C_2, he spends more than he earns from ages 22 through 26. To make up the vertical gap between the red and blue curves in Figure 10.9(a), he has to borrow.[14] That means his saving is negative, as shown by the brown line in Figure 10.9(b). Since he accumulates debt, his wealth also becomes negative, as shown by the black line. Fortunately, Brian's earnings rise with experience. After age 26, his income is sufficient to pay for his consumption. The vertical gap between the blue and red curves represents extra funds, which he uses to pay the interest on his debt. If anything is left over after interest payments, he repays part of the balance on his debt. At that point, his saving becomes positive and his wealth—though still negative—begins to rise.

According to Figure 10.9(b), Brian pays off all of his debts by age 30. Then he begins to accumulate positive wealth. As time passes, his saving increases, reflecting both the growing difference between his earnings and his spending, and the rising interest on his wealth. At retirement, however, his earnings disappear. To maintain the same living standard, he has to pay his living expenses out of his interest income and his wealth. His wealth therefore declines steadily, which means his saving is negative, as in his youth. With less wealth, he earns less interest income, and is forced to pay more expenses out of his wealth. This is why the brown curve (saving) declines after retirement, and why the black curve (wealth) declines at an increasing rate. If Brian times this drawdown perfectly, he will die with just enough money left to cover his funeral expenses.[15]

The Life Cycle Hypothesis has many important implications. For example, it helps us to understand and predict how changes in the age structure of a country's population will affect its overall rate of saving. Saving tends to be low in developing countries which have high concentrations of young people. Overall saving is also projected to decline in many developed countries because a significant proportion of their population is shifting steadily toward retirement ages.

[13] Though we've drawn flat consumption lines, most people seem to prefer a gradually rising living standard. The Life Cycle Hypothesis easily accommodates this preference.

[14] In addition to the difference between his planned consumption and his earnings, Brian also needs to borrow enough money to pay the interest on his outstanding debt. In practice, many young people have difficulty finding lenders from whom to borrow at reasonable terms, due mostly to informational problems (see Chapter 21). Some versions of the Life Cycle Hypothesis include these types of restrictions.

[15] In practice, people don't know how long they'll live, and many wish to leave bequests. In versions of the Life Cycle Hypothesis that allow for these possibilities, people die with some positive wealth.

Application 10.3

Stimulating Saving for Retirement

Many economists and policymakers think Americans save too little for retirement. Some attribute this tendency, at least in part, to the income tax system, which reduces the economic rewards of saving by, for example, taxing interest income. To illustrate, suppose the interest rate is 5 percent, and individuals must pay the government 20 percent of each additional dollar earned. If a taxpayer puts away \$1 today, he'll have only \$1.04 a year from now instead of \$1.05; the extra penny will go to the government. In other words, the after-tax interest rate is only 4 percent.

To stimulate saving, the U.S. government offers taxpayers the opportunity to open Individual Retirement Accounts (IRAs). Funds in an IRA account earn interest tax-free until withdrawal, and under some circumstances, contributions are tax-deductible. As a result, the after-tax return on IRA savings is significantly higher than it is on normal saving.

The effect of IRAs on household saving is the subject of considerable disagreement and debate, however. Opponents of the policy emphasize three concerns. First, as we've seen in this chapter, there is no reason to think saving *necessarily* rises with the interest rate. An increase in the interest rate creates both a substitution effect, which reduces current consumption, and an income effect, which can increase consumption. Overall, saving could remain constant or even decline. Historically, higher-than-normal rates of saving have not coincided with higher-than-normal real interest rates.

The second concern emphasized by IRA opponents is that IRA contributions are limited by law. Someone who wants to save more than the limit receives no tax relief on the last dollar saved, and therefore has no incentive to save more.

Figure 10.10 illustrates this second concern. The consumer allocates his resources between consumption before retirement and consumption after retirement. He starts out at point A, with positive earnings before retirement and nothing after retirement. Given his after-tax rate of return, he can choose any point on the line labeled L_1.

Now suppose the government allows him to save up to some fixed amount in an IRA, and taxes interest on IRA savings at a lower rate. In that case, the consumer can choose any point on the kinked line labeled L_2. As he starts to save, he is able to trade consumption before retirement for consumption after retirement at a more attractive rate. That is why L_2 is steeper than L_1 between points A and B. However, once the consumer reaches the contribution limit, he goes back to earning the original interest rate on each additional dollar saved. That is why L_2 is parallel L_1 to the left of point B.

"Remember, son, it's never too early to start saving for retirement."

How does the IRA affect saving? The consumer with the blue indifference curves picks point C without an IRA and point D with an IRA, in each case saving *less* than the contribution limit. Since the shift from point C to point D involves both an income effect and a substitution effect, his saving can either rise or fall. In contrast, the consumer with the red indifference curves picks point E without an IRA and point F with an IRA, in each case saving *more* than the contribution limit. The shift from point E to point F involves an income effect but no substitution effect. Ordinarily, therefore, point F involves more consumption and *less* saving before retirement.

The third concern emphasized by IRA opponents is that people sometimes borrow to make their IRA contributions. Once we factor in borrowing, the consumer can choose any point on the straight line running through points B and F in Figure 10.10, including the dashed segment. For example, starting from point A, he can reach point G in two steps. The first step is to move from point A to point B by making the largest allowable contribution to his IRA account. The second step is to move from point B to point G by taking out a loan that replaces the money he contributed to his IRA. The consumer comes out ahead, in effect, by lending money at a high (before-tax) rate of interest while borrowing money at a low (after-tax) rate of interest.[16] Thus, the availability of IRAs simply shifts L_1 outward without changing its slope, producing an income effect but no substitution effect. As a result, saving ordinarily falls, regardless of whether the consumer would save more or less than the contribution limit without an IRA.

Proponents of IRAs respond that many people save less than the contribution limit, and that few replace contributed funds by borrowing. They also contend that opponents ignore various indirect effects of IRAs. For example, the program may focus the public's attention on retirement, and it may induce financial institutions to advertise and market retirement savings products aggressively.

Unfortunately, the available evidence on the effects of IRAs is mixed.[17] Some studies have found that each dollar contributed to an IRA account adds one dollar to total saving; others have concluded that IRA contributions are completely offset by a combination of increased borrowing and reduced saving in other forms. Research continues, as economists look for a definitive answer.

Figure 10.10

The Effect of IRAs on Saving. Without an IRA, the consumer's budget line is L_1. With an IRA, his budget line, L_2, is kinked at point B where his saving reaches the contribution limit. For someone who is saving less than the contribution limit (the blue indifference curves), an IRA creates both an income and a substitution effect, so that saving can either rise or fall. For someone who is saving more than the contribution limit (the red indifference curves), an IRA creates only an income effect, so that saving falls.

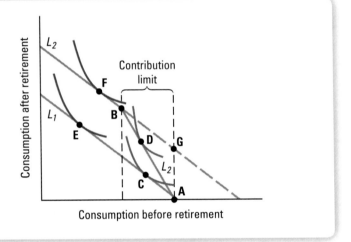

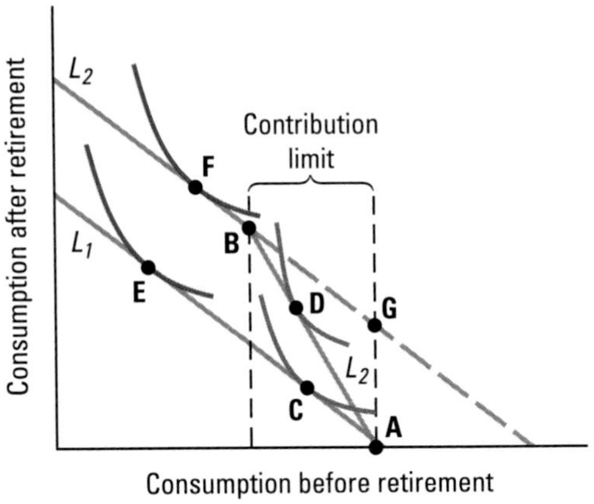

10.3 INVESTMENT

Time is almost always an important consideration in decisions involving production. Why? Production usually requires capital, and most types of capital—factories, office buildings, machines, tools, and so forth—are reasonably durable. Machines can last for years, factories often remain productive for decades, and buildings are sometimes used for centuries. In addition, some capital inputs take time to assemble. While companies can purchase many common tools and machines without delay, complex factories (like Volkswagen's Phaeton plant) often require many years of planning and construction.

[16]Interest payments on debts are assumed to be tax deductible.

[17]For a good summary of the evidence on both sides, see James Poterba, Stephen Venti, and David Wise, "How Retirement Saving Programs Increase Saving," as well as Eric Engen, William Gale, and John Karl Sholz, "The Illusory Effects of Saving Incentives on Saving," both of which appeared in the Fall 1996 issue of *Journal of Economic Perspectives* 10, no. 4, pp. 91–138.

When a company acquires capital, it incurs up-front costs with the expectation of generating future profits. This type of transaction is known as **investment**.[18] A firm's economic performance is tied closely to the types and levels of investment it makes. Thus, knowing how to distinguish between a good investment and a bad one is an essential management skill.

Investment refers to up-front costs incurred with the expectation of generating future profits.

Let's examine a simple hypothetical investment opportunity for a company called Snow Stuff, Inc., which specializes in winter recreation products. After studying trends in demand, one of the company's managers has proposed launching a line of snowboards. None of Snow Stuff's existing facilities are suited for manufacturing snowboards, so the new product would require a new factory. Careful research indicates that Snow Stuff could construct a factory with a capacity of 1,200 snowboards per year at a cost of $300,000 the first year and an additional $100,000 the second year. The factory would have limited production capacity during the second year (only 200 units), but would be fully operational at the start of the third year.

Table 10.4 shows the required investments, along with the related sales, revenue, and cost forecasts. As the market grows, sales are expected to rise steadily from 200 units in the second year to 1,200 in the sixth year. Until the sixth year, demand will be too low to run the plant at capacity. Snow Stuff expects to sell the boards to retail outlets for $400 each. Rent on the land will run $50,000 per year (listed as a fixed cost). All other costs (labor, materials, *et cetera*) are variable; they total $275 per board. At the end of 10 years the factory will be obsolete, and Snow Stuff expects to sell its old equipment for $50,000 (listed in the table as scrap value). It does not plan to replace the factory.

In the next few sections, we'll consider whether this investment is a good idea.

Table 10.4

Data for Snow Stuff's Proposed Factory

Calendar Year (Project Year)	Investment	Units	Revenue	Fixed Cost	Variable Cost	Scrap Value
2008 (1)	300,000	0	0	50,000	0	0
2009 (2)	100,000	200	80,000	50,000	55,000	0
2010 (3)	0	400	160,000	50,000	110,000	0
2011 (4)	0	800	320,000	50,000	220,000	0
2012 (5)	0	1,000	400,000	50,000	275,000	0
2013 (6)	0	1,200	480,000	50,000	330,000	0
2014 (7)	0	1,200	480,000	50,000	330,000	0
2015 (8)	0	1,200	480,000	50,000	330,000	0
2016 (9)	0	1,200	480,000	50,000	330,000	0
2017 (10)	0	1,200	480,000	50,000	330,000	0
2018 (11)	0	0	0	0	0	50,000

[18]Economists sometimes distinguish between *physical* investment, such as the construction of plant and equipment, and *financial* investment, such as the purchase of a bond, or shares of a company's stock. Financial investment is closely related to saving; however, the two concepts are not identical. To illustrate the difference, suppose someone borrows $1,000 to purchase $1,000 worth of a company's stock. Together, these transactions involve financial investment, but no saving (since current consumption is unaffected).

Measuring the Profitability of Investments: Net Present Value

In Section 9.1 we learned that a well-functioning firm seeks to maximize its profits, defined as the difference between its total revenue and total cost. To evaluate Snow Stuff's investment, we apply the same principle with a new twist: in computing profit, we need to remember that a dollar in the future is worth less than a dollar today.

Before grappling with Snow Stuff's relatively complex problem, let's start with a much simpler example. Jennifer has an opportunity to buy a case of fine cabernet sauvignon from a Napa Valley winery for $500. She doesn't like wine, so she is thinking about this transaction as an investment. The wine is freshly bottled and not yet drinkable, but experts expect it to become exceptional in five years, at which point the case will be worth $1,000.

Is this purchase a profitable investment? Revenue consists of $1,000 received in five years. In terms of PDV, that revenue is worth $\$1{,}000/(1 + R)^5$ today. The cost is $500 today. From today's perspective, profit is therefore $\$1{,}000/(1 + R)^5 - \$500$. So, if the interest rate is 10 percent, Jennifer clears a profit of $\$1{,}000/(1 + 0.01)^5 - \$500 = \$121$.

More generally, to assess the profitability of any investment project, we compute the difference between the PDV of the revenue stream and the PDV of the cost stream. This difference is known as the project's **net present value** (abbreviated NPV). An investment project is profitable when its NPV is positive, and unprofitable when its NPV is negative. This important principle is known as the **NPV criterion.**

The **net present value (NPV)** of an investment project is the difference between the PDV of the revenue stream and the PDV of the cost stream.

The **NPV criterion** states that an investment project is profitable when its NPV is positive, and unprofitable when its NPV is negative.

A **net cash flow (NCF)** is the difference between revenue and cost during a single year of a project's life.

The definition of NPV suggests a two-step procedure for determining an investment's profitability. First, we separately discount the project's revenue and cost streams. Second, we find the project's NPV by netting the PDV of the cost stream against the PDV of the revenue stream. In practice, investors often use a different procedure. First, they compute the project's net cash flows. A **net cash flow (NCF)** is the difference between revenue and cost during any single year of the project's life. We'll use NCF_t to stand for the net cash flow received (or paid) in t years. Second, they determine the project's NPV by computing the PDV of its net cash flows:

$$NPV = NCF_0 + \frac{NCF_1}{1 + R} + \frac{NCF_2}{(1 + R)^2} + \cdots + \frac{NCF_T}{(1 + R)^T}$$

These two procedures involve the same calculations, performed in a different orders. Since the order doesn't matter, they always produce the same answer.

Let's compute the NPV of Snow Stuff's proposed investment in a snowboard factory. First we add up costs and revenues listed in Table 10.4 to obtain a net cash flow for each year. Table 10.5 shows the results. The last column of the table lists the PDV of each year's net cash flow, assuming an interest rate of 5 percent. Adding up these numbers, we discover that the project's NPV is $22,730. Since this figure is positive, the project is profitable.

That is not the way an accountant thinks about profit. To an accountant, *profit* refers to net gain within some fixed period, such as a year. To an economist, it refers to the economic gain from the entire project. Since this difference can cause confusion, it is important to remember that we are concerned with economic profits, not accounting profits.

Net Present Value as Instant Cash Here's another way to see that NPV is the correct measure of a project's profit. In Section 10.1, we learned that the present discounted value of a stream of future payments represents the amount of money you would have to

Table 10.5

PDV of Snow Stuff's Proposed Factory

(Calculations assume an interest rate of 5%)

Calendar Year (Project Year)	Net Cash Flow	PDV of $1	PDV of NCF
2008 (1)	−350,000	1.000	−350,000
2009 (2)	−125,000	0.952	−119,048
2010 (3)	0	0.907	0
2011 (4)	50,000	0.864	43,192
2012 (5)	75,000	0.823	61,703
2013 (6)	100,000	0.784	78,353
2014 (7)	100,000	0.746	74,622
2015 (8)	100,000	0.711	71,068
2016 (9)	100,000	0.677	67,684
2017 (10)	100,000	0.645	64,461
2018 (11)	50,000	0.614	30,696
Total	**200,000**		**22,730**

set aside immediately to cover all of the payments as they come due. A similar principle applies to investments. Suppose a project has a stream of net cash flows with an NPV of X dollars. By saving and borrowing, an investor can rearrange the timing of the project's cash flows so that he receives X dollars instantly if X is positive or pays $-X$ dollars instantly if X is negative, and neither receives nor pays anything in the future. The project is therefore just as good as X dollars of instant cash.

To illustrate, let's return to Jennifer's investment decision. If she wanted to, Jennifer could borrow $621 today (at 10 percent interest), use $500 to buy the wine, and keep the remaining $121 (the project's NPV) as instant cash profit. After five years, she would owe exactly $1,000 ($621 $\times$ 1.1^5), which she could pay off with the proceeds from selling the wine. In other words, after taking her $121 in the form of an instant cash profit, she would receive zero net cash flow from the project every year after that.

Net Present Value and the Opportunity Cost of Funds In Sections 3.1 and 8.2, we learned that our actions often have *opportunity costs,* meaning the benefits we sacrifice by forgoing other attractive alternatives. Every investment project excludes at least one reasonably attractive alternative—lending the required cash at the prevailing interest rate (for example by putting it in the bank or buying a bond). Positive NPV means that the project is better than that alternative; negative NPV means that it's worse. By computing NPV, we're simply netting out the opportunity cost of the interest we would have earned had we lent the money at the prevailing interest rate. Economists sometimes call this cost the **time value of money**, or the **opportunity cost of funds**.

The **time value of money** (also called the **opportunity cost of funds**) is the opportunity cost associated with the economic benefit an investor could receive by lending money at the prevailing interest rate.

To illustrate, let's return to Jennifer's problem. If instead of buying the wine for $500, she chose to deposit the same sum in a bank account that earns 10 percent interest, she would have $805 in five years. The wine is a good investment because it beats the bank account: in five years, it gives her $1,000, which is $195 more than she receives from the bank account. What is the extra $195 worth today? At a 10 percent interest the PDV of $195 received in five years is $121, the investment's NPV.

The Internal Rate of Return

A project's **internal rate of return** (or **IRR**) is the rate of interest at which its NPV is exactly zero.

Every project's NPV depends on the interest rate. Usually, there's an interest rate at which the NPV is exactly zero. This is known as the project's **internal rate of return (IRR)**. For example, the IRR of Jennifer's wine investment is 14.9 percent. We can confirm this by checking that the NPV of her investment is zero at an interest rate of 14.9 percent: $1{,}000/(1 + 0.149)^5 - 500 = 0$.

Why is it useful to know a project's IRR? Suppose that a project's cash inflows (negative values of NCF) occur before its cash outflows (positive values of NCF). In that case, we can determine whether the investment is profitable simply by comparing its IRR to the interest rate. The project is profitable when the rate of interest is less than its IRR, and unprofitable when the rate of interest is greater than its IRR.[19] For example, the NPV of Jennifer's project is positive when the interest rate is less than 14.9 percent, and negative when it's greater than 14.9 percent. (Check this by calculating the project's NPV at other interest rates.) In effect, the investor should choose between putting cash into a project or into a bank account based on which of the two investments yields the higher rate of return.

For a two-period investment (one with all cash flows concentrated in periods 0 and 1), the IRR is easy to calculate. The investment's NPV is $NCF_0 + NCF_1/(1 + R)$. Setting this expression equal to zero and solving for R, we discover that $R = -(NCF_1 + NCF_0)/NCF_0$.[20] For example, if a project requires an investment of $1,000 in period 0 ($NCF_0 = -1{,}000$) and returns of $1,200 in period 1 ($NCF_1 = 1{,}200$), its IRR is 0.2, or 20 percent.

For investments lasting more than two periods, the IRR is more difficult to calculate. For example, the NPV of a three-period investment is $NCF_0 + NCF_1/(1 + R) + NCF_2/(1+R)^2$. As in the two-period case, we can set this expression equal to zero and solve for R. But to find the solution, we need to use the quadratic formula. For longer term investments, we usually solve for IRRs numerically, using spreadsheets or other computer programs.

Here's an example. Figure 10.11 shows the NPV of Snow Stuff's proposed factory at interest rates ranging from 0 to 10 percent. At 0 percent, the NPV is $200,000. At 10 percent, it's −$96,652. Between those two extremes, NPV declines as the interest rate rises. At 5 percent (the rate assumed in Snow Stuff's NPV calculations), it's $22,730. At roughly 5.8 percent, NPV passes from positive to negative. The IRR for Snow Stuff's project is therefore 5.8 percent. As the figure shows, the project is profitable when the interest rate is below 5.8 percent, and unprofitable when it's above 5.8 percent.

Investment and the Interest Rate

The interest rate plays a key role in determining the amount of investment undertaken by a single company, or by a group of companies (for example, all the companies located in a country). When interest rates rise, most potential projects become less profitable. Some become unprofitable, which causes the total amount of investment to fall. Falling interest rates have the opposite effect.

---

[19]Sometimes, an investment project requires net cash inflows (negative values of NCF) *after* generating net cash outflows (positive values of NCF). For example, a factory with a service life of 30 years may require not only substantial up-front investment, but a costly refurbishment after 15 years of profitable operation. In such cases, NPV may *increase* with the interest rate over some ranges, and may even equal zero at several different interest rates (that is, the project may have several IRRs). In some cases, a project may be unprofitable—that is, it may have negative NPV—even when its IRR exceeds the interest rate. For a numerical illustration, see exercise 10.14 at the end of the chapter.

[20]Similarly, we determined the IRR for Jennifer's wine investment by writing down the formula for its NPV as a function of the interest rate: $NPV = 1{,}000/(1 + R)^5 - 500$. By setting this expression equal to zero and solving for R, we discovered that $R = 2^{1/5} - 1 = 0.149$.

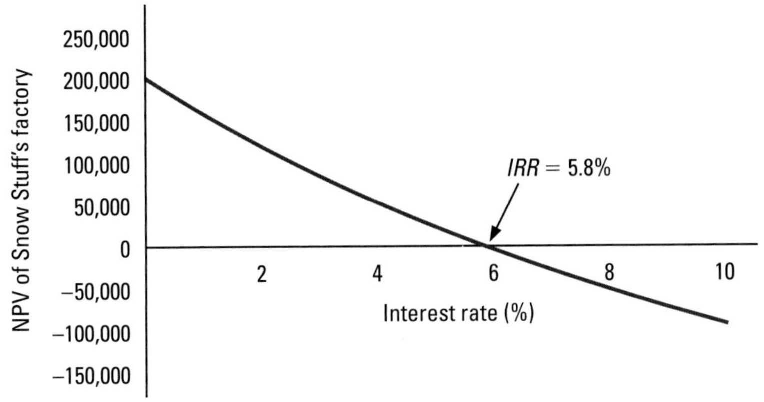

Figure 10.11

The NPV of Snow Stuff's Proposed Factory. The blue line shows the NPV of Snow Stuff's proposed factory as a function of the interest rate. The line crosses the horizontal axis at a rate of 5.8 percent, which means that the factory has an IRR of 5.8 percent. The factory's NPV is positive if the interest is less than 5.8 percent, and negative if the interest rate is greater than 5.8 percent.

Here are two different ways to understand why an increase in the interest rate usually makes investment projects less attractive:

1. At a higher interest rate, future dollars are worth less compared to current dollars. Since the typical investment project incurs a disproportionate fraction of its cost early in its life and generates a disproportionate fraction of its revenue later in its life, a higher interest rate reduces the value of its revenue relative to its cost.
2. At a higher interest rate, putting money in the bank becomes more attractive (and borrowing becomes less attractive). Thus, the opportunity cost of funds is greater. Net of the opportunity cost, profit is lower.

Projects with different IRRs are profitable at different ranges of the interest rate. As the interest rate rises, it exceeds the IRRs of more and more projects, and the overall level of investment falls. When the interest rate is 4 percent, for example, Snow Stuff's factory and Jennifer's wine investment are both profitable. If the interest rate rises to 12 percent, it's still lower than Jennifer's IRR, but higher than Snow Stuff's. So Jennifer's project is still profitable, but Snow Stuff's isn't. If the interest rate climbs to 18 percent, it exceeds the IRRs of both projects, so neither is profitable.

Application 10.4

Bond Yields

When someone buys a bond, he gives up the bond's price in exchange for future income. The IRR for this financial investment is known as the bond's *yield to maturity* (often abbreviated as either *yield*, or *YTM*). If a bank account paid interest at a rate equal to the bond's yield, a depositor could reproduce the bond's promised payments, given an initial deposit equal to the bond's price.

Consider a bond with a face value of V dollars and a coupon of C dollars that matures in M years. If the bond sells for P dollars, its yield to maturity is the interest rate R that satisfies the following formula:

$$\frac{C}{R}\left(1-\frac{1}{(1+R)^M}\right)+\frac{V}{(1+R)^M}=P \tag{12}$$

Why? We learned earlier that the expression to the left of the equals sign in formula (12) is the PDV of the bond's future payments [look again at formula (6)]. When we subtract the bond's price from the PDV of its future payments, we obtain the investment's NPV. Any interest rate that results in an NPV of zero (in other words, any IRR) must therefore also result in equality between the bond's price and the PDV of its future payments, which is what formula (12) requires.

To illustrate, suppose that a 10-year bond with a $100 coupon and a $1,000 face value sells for $749 dollars. At an interest rate of 15 percent, the PDV of the bond's promised payments is exactly $749 (to check this, plug those numbers into the expression to the left of the equals sign in formula (12)). That means the bond's yield to maturity is 15 percent. The larger the promised payments and the lower the bond's price, the greater the yield. For example, if the same bond sells for $581, its yield to maturity is 20 percent. (Check this!)

Investors evaluate bonds in part by examining their yields. If a bond's yield is too low, investors won't be willing to buy it. Supply will exceed demand, causing the bond's price to fall. At a lower price, the bond will have a higher yield, making it more attractive to investors. The bond's price continues to fall until its yield is high enough to compensate investors for the opportunity cost of their funds.

Table 10.6 provides information on the prices and yields of U.S. Treasury bonds of various maturities, as of March 11, 2005. The information in this table appears much as it would in the financial section of a newspaper. The first column lists the type of bond, based on the total time between issuance and maturity. The bond's coupon, expressed as a percentage of face value, appears in the second column, and its date of maturity in the third column. The fourth column tells us the price at which the bond traded, expressed as a percentage of its face value (the number to the right of the hyphen stands for 32nds of a percentage point). The final column lists the yield to maturity. So, for example, a 10-year Treasury bond with a 4 percent coupon maturing on February 15, 2015, sold for $95^{23}/_{32}$ percent of its face value, implying a yield to maturity of 4.54 percent.

Table 10.6

Prices and Yields on U.S. Treasury Bonds of Various Maturities

(Coupon and price are expressed as a percentage of face value. For price, the number to the right of the hyphen stands for 32nds of a percentage point.)

Type	Coupon	Date of Maturity	Price	Yield to Maturity
2-year	3.375	2/28/2007	99-11	3.72%
3-year	3.375	2/15/2008	98-15	3.93%
5-year	4.000	3/15/2010	99-00	4.22%
10-year	4.000	2/15/2015	95-23	4.54%
30-year	5.375	2/15/2031	108-08	4.81%

Choosing between Mutually Exclusive Projects

The mere fact that a project is profitable doesn't necessarily mean that a firm should invest in it. Sometimes profitable projects are mutually exclusive. For example, a firm might have to choose between several locations for a new factory. As in Chapter 9, the best choice among mutually exclusive alternatives is the one that yields the greatest profit. For investment projects, that means the one with the highest NPV.[21]

Let's revisit Snow Stuff's investment problem. Imagine that another manager suggests a different location for Snow Stuff's new factory—Stockton instead of Fresno—on the grounds that labor costs are lower in Stockton. After careful analysis, the company concludes that the NPV of the Stockton project is $28,200. Since that amount exceeds the NPV of the Fresno project, $22,730, Snow Stuff should build the factory in Stockton.

Other Criteria for Choosing between Mutually Exclusive Projects Companies sometimes compare mutually exclusive projects using criteria other than NPV. This can lead to poor decision making. There is no guarantee that any other criteria will correctly identify the most profitable project.

[21]This statement assumes that projects involving facilities with different operational lifetimes are evaluated over the same time horizon. For example, to compare a project involving a facility with a 30-year lifetime to one involving a facility that would require replacement after 15 years, we would include the cash flows from the replacement facility.

For example, it's usually inappropriate to choose between two mutually exclusive projects by selecting the one with the higher IRR. Comparing IRRs, Jennifer's wine investment looks better than Snow Stuff's factory. Yet if an investor were forced to choose between the two, the correct choice, based on a comparison of their NPVs, would hinge on the interest rate. At an interest rate between 5.8 and 14.9 percent, Jennifer's investment is clearly the better one because it's profitable and the factory isn't. But if the interest rate is 3 percent, the factory provides an NPV of $85,140, while the wine provides an NPV of only $363.

The **payback period** is the amount of time required before a project's total inflows match its total outflows.

Another commonly used criterion is the **payback period**, the amount of time required before a project's total inflows match its total outflows. For example, in the case of Snow Stuff's investment, $475,000 flows out of the firm before any money flows back in (see Table 10.5). Total inflows reach $425,000 in year 8 and $525,000 in year 9, so the payback period is roughly $8^1/_2$ years. Companies sometimes look for projects with short payback periods; some even establish fixed payback requirements (for example, payback within five years).

The payback period provides sound investment guidance only when by chance it happens to coincide with the maximization of NPV. Often it doesn't. For example, which would you prefer, a $1,000 investment that returns $1,001 in one year and nothing thereafter, or a $1,000 investment that returns $300 per year for the next 50 years? Unless the interest rate is near 30 percent, the second investment has a much higher NPV than the first. But judged by the payback period, the first investment looks far better—it breaks even after a single year, compared with more than three years for the second investment.

One possible justification for looking at payback periods is that investors are less certain about net cash flows that occur further into the future. In that case, insisting on a quick payback is one way to express an aversion to uncertainty. As we'll see in the next chapter, however, there are better ways to handle uncertainty. Another possible justification is that a company with limited credit might need to generate cash quickly to pay for other investment projects. While it's useful to take these kinds of concerns into account, the payback period is at best only a rough rule of thumb.

Investing Now or Later Every investment project excludes at least one other alternative: waiting. A company shouldn't start a project immediately just because its NPV is positive, even if it doesn't preclude other projects. Why not? Unless the company expects the opportunity to evaporate, it may achieve an even greater NPV by starting at a later date.

To illustrate, suppose Snow Stuff has the option of waiting a year before starting work on its factory in Fresno. As Table 10.7 shows, investment, production, and cash flows during the project's first and second years will not change. In the project's third year, the company will produce 800 snowboards instead of 400, because the year will be 2011 instead of 2010, and the demand for snowboards will be higher. For the same reason, the company will produce 1,000 snowboards instead of 800 in the project's fourth year, and 1,200 instead of 1,000 in its fifth year. Thereafter, the factory will operate at capacity, whether or not the project is delayed.

To compare Snow Stuff's two alternatives—starting the factory immediately and starting it after one year—we must discount net cash flows for both alternatives to the *same point in time.*[22] Discounting net cash flows to the beginning of 2008, we find that the NPV of the delayed project is $104,995. Since this amount is far greater than the NPV of the project if it begins immediately, $22,730, the company is better off waiting a year. The

[22]If we discounted the cash flows for each alternative to the project's start date—2008 for the first alternative and 2009 for the second—the two figures would not be comparable; they would refer to dollars at different points in time.

Table 10.7

The Value of Delaying Construction of Snow Stuff's Factory

(Calculations assume an interest rate of 5%.)

Calendar Year (Project Year)	Investment	Units	Revenue	Fixed Cost	Variable Cost	Scrap Value	Net Cash Flow	PDV of $1	PDV of NCF
2008	0	0	0	0	0	0	0	1.000	0
2009 (1)	300,000	0	0	50,000	0	0	−350,000	0.952	−333,333
2010 (2)	100,000	200	80,000	50,000	55,000	0	−125,000	0.907	−113,379
2011 (3)	0	800	320,000	50,000	220,000	0	50,000	0.864	43,192
2012 (4)	0	1,000	400,000	50,000	275,000	0	75,000	0.823	61,703
2013 (5)	0	1,200	480,000	50,000	330,000	0	100,000	0.784	78,353
2014 (6)	0	1,200	480,000	50,000	330,000	0	100,000	0.746	74,622
2015 (7)	0	1,200	480,000	50,000	330,000	0	100,000	0.711	71,068
2016 (8)	0	1,200	480,000	50,000	330,000	0	100,000	0.677	67,684
2017 (9)	0	1,200	480,000	50,000	330,000	0	100,000	0.645	64,461
2018 (10)	0	1,200	480,000	50,000	330,000	0	100,000	0.614	61,391
2019 (11)	0	0	0	0	0	50,000	50,000	0.585	29,234
Total							**200,000**		**104,995**

reason is simple: if Snow Stuff waits for demand to grow, it won't waste as much money maintaining idle production capacity.

WORKED-OUT PROBLEM 10.4

The Problem Managers at Investments R Us, Inc., must choose between three mutually exclusive projects, A, B, and C. They can also decide to skip all three projects. Each project requires an investment in the first year and produces a positive net cash flow for the next four years. The top half of Table 10.8 shows the net cash flows, by year, for each project. Assuming that the interest rate is 5 percent, what is the NPV of the cash flows from each project? Which one should the company choose? Does the best project have the highest total net cash flow? The shortest payback period? The highest internal rate of return?

The Solution The lower half of Table 10.8 shows the PDV of the annual net cash flows for each project, and then sums them to obtain the NPV of each project. The NPV of project A is $4,004; the NPV of project B is $4,685; and the NPV of project C is $4,595. The company should choose project B.

Project B also has the highest total nominal net cash flow ($8,750 compared to $8,000 for project C and $6,750 for project A). However, it has the longest payback period (total net cash flow doesn't become positive until year 5, compared to year 4 for the other two projects).

To compute the internal rate of return for each project, we find the interest rate at which the project's NPV is zero. One way to do this is to create a spreadsheet that computes the NPV for different interest rates, and search systematically for the IRR.[23] Take project A as an example. To start, we would compute the NPV at whole interest rates (1 percent, 2 percent, etc.). We'd discover that the NPV is positive at an interest rate of 14 percent but negative at an interest rate of 15 percent. This means that the IRR is between 14 and 15 percent. Next we'd compute the NPV at interest rates of 14.1 percent, 14.2 percent, and so forth, up to 14.9 percent. We'd learn that the IRR is between 14.2 percent (at which the NPV is positive) and 14.3 percent (at which it is negative). Finally, we'd compute the NPV at interest rates of 14.21 percent, 14.22 percent, and so forth, up to 14.29 percent. We'd find that the NPV is approximately zero at an interest rate of 14.26 percent. While we could pin the IRR down even more precisely, that is close enough.

Table 10.9 lists the IRRs for projects A, B, and C, and verifies that the project's NPV is zero in each case. Project B, the best alternative at an interest rate of 5 percent, has the lowest IRR of the three projects, 12.34 percent, while project A has the highest, 14.26 percent. Therefore, using the IRRs to decide between those projects would lead to the wrong decision.

IN-TEXT EXERCISE 10.5 **Compute the NPVs for the projects described in worked-out problem 10.4 at the following interest rates: 8 percent, 12 percent, 16 percent.**

Investing in Human Capital

Not all investments involve buildings, machines, inventories, and other forms of physical capital. Sometimes companies invest in knowledge through research and development. Sometimes they invest in reputation through advertising and public relations. The same investment principles apply to any situation in which the costs and benefits of a project occur at different points in time.

Table 10.8

Data for Worked-Out-Problem 10.4

Net Cash Flows and NPVs for Three Mutually Exclusive Investments

(Calculations assume an interest rate of 5%.)

Year	1	2	3	4	5	Total
Net Cash Flow for:						
Project A	−21,250	10,000	8,000	6,000	4,000	6,750
Project B	−23,250	5,000	7,000	9,000	11,000	8,750
Project C	−22,000	7,500	7,500	7,500	7,500	8,000
PDV of \$1	1.000	0.952	0.907	0.864	0.823	
PDV of Net Cash Flow for:						
Project A	−21,250	9,524	7,256	5,183	3,291	4,004
Project B	−23,250	4,762	6,349	7,775	9,050	4,685
Project C	−22,000	7,143	6,803	6,479	6,170	4,595

[23]With some spreadsheet programs, the user can set up the NPV calculation and then instruct the program to search automatically for an interest rate that produces an NPV of zero.

Table 10.9

Data for Worked-Out Problem 10.4

Internal Rates of Return for Three Mutually Exclusive Investments

Year	1	2	3	4	5	Total
Project A with interest rate of 14.26%						
NCF	−21,250	10,000	8,000	6,000	4,000	6,750
PDV of $1	1.000	0.875	0.766	0.670	0.587	
PDV of NCF	−21,250	8,752	6,128	4,023	2,347	0
Project B with interest rate of 12.34%						
NCF	−23,250	5,000	7,000	9,000	11,000	8,750
PDV of $1	1.000	0.890	0.792	0.705	0.628	
PDV of NCF	−23,250	4,451	5,546	6,348	6,906	0
Project C with interest rate of 13.67%						
NCF	−22,000	7,500	7,500	7,500	7,500	8,000
PDV of $1	1.000	0.880	0.774	0.681	0.599	
PDV of NCF	−22,000	6,598	5,804	5,106	4,492	0

Human capital consists of marketable skills acquired through investments in education and training.

Education (including occupational training) is also an investment. A student incurs up-front costs in the hope of acquiring durable, marketable skills that will generate higher income. Indeed, economists often refer to these skills as **human capital**. But education isn't always worthwhile (remember Application 3.1 from Chapter 3, page 69). Standard investment principles allow us to determine whether education makes sense from a purely financial perspective in a particular instance.[24]

To illustrate, let's examine a typical educational decision in detail. Thomas took a job after graduating college at age 22. He's turning 26 next year and is thinking about going to business school full time for two years to improve his earnings potential. If he receives a business degree, Thomas expects to earn an extra $15,000 a year through his retirement at age 65. Unfortunately, business school is expensive. He'll have to come up with $20,000 per year to cover tuition, plus an additional $2,000 for books and supplies.

To evaluate this option, we need to compute the NPV of the financial costs and benefits. Have we listed all the relevant costs? Not yet. To attend business school full time, Thomas would have to give up his current job, which pays $45,000 per year. This sacrifice is an important opportunity cost. In fact, it's significantly larger than the costs of tuition, books, and supplies combined. If Thomas ignores this cost, he's likely to make a faulty decision.

Table 10.10 calculates the NPV of attending business school, assuming an interest rate of 8 percent. As the table shows, Thomas gives up a total of $67,000 per year while he's in school in return for an extra $15,000 per year after he finishes. Simply adding up the costs and benefits yields a net gain of $436,000. But because that figure makes no adjustment for the fact that the costs are incurred up front while the benefits are delayed, it exaggerates the true gains. The last column of the table lists the PDV of the net cash flow in each year. For simplicity, we've assumed that all payments are made and all income is received at the beginning of each year. (We've used formula (5) to compute the PDV

[24]Nonfinancial concerns may also influence decisions concerning education and training. Completing a degree confers greater social status, and is also a direct source of satisfaction to many people, some of whom also find education more pleasant than work.

Table 10.10

The PDV of Attending Business School

(Hypothetical data, 8% interest rate)

Age	Tuition	Books and Supplies	Increase in Earnings	Opportunity Cost	Total Net Change	PDV
26	20,000	2,000	0	45,000	−67,000	−67,000
27	20,000	2,000	0	45,000	−67,000	−62,037
28–65	0	0	15,000/yr	0	15,000/yr	164,290
Total					**436,000**	**35,253**

at age 27 of the increase in earnings between ages 28 and 65, then we've discounted the result back to age 26.) Adding up these discounted cash flows, we find that the NPV is $35,253. Though this is far less than $436,000, the investment is still justified.

Economists often summarize the financial returns to education by calculating an internal rate of return. For Thomas, the IRR of attending business school is 10.4 percent. As long as the interest rate is less than 10.4 percent, an MBA would be a good deal for him.

Application 10.5

The Economic Value of Education

In 1958, an economist named Jacob Mincer pioneered a method for measuring the effects of schooling on wages, while simultaneously estimating the rate of return earned on investments in human capital. Mincer's method has been refined and extended over nearly 50 years through a long sequence of scholarly papers. At its core, the refined method involves a comparison of the wages earned by people with different levels of education and experience.

A recent study by economists James Heckman, Lance Lochner, and Petra Todd estimates separate internal rates of return for each two-year increment in schooling from sixth grade through college.[25] According to this study, after factoring in the effects of tuition and progressive taxation, the internal rate of return for completing the last two years of high school in 1990 was somewhere between 30 and 50 percent for white males and between 40 and 65 percent for black males. In contrast, the return on a college education was only 12 to 14 percent for white males and 15

"They may be your grades, but they're the return on my investment."

[25] James J. Heckman, Lance J. Lochner, and Petra E. Todd, "Fifty Years of Mincer Earnings Regressions," *Handbook of Education Economics*, forthcoming.

to 17 percent for black males—not nearly as high, but still an excellent investment. Comparisons with earlier decades suggest that the returns to education have risen steeply over time. This trend is not surprising, given that high-paying jobs increasingly require technical skills and specialized knowledge.

One difficulty with this approach, however, is that it fails to recognize the strong correlation between education and ability. More talented people tend both to stay in school longer and to earn higher incomes. Unfortunately, it isn't clear whether their greater earnings reflect their schooling or their talent.

To address this problem, economists have searched for characteristics that influence the amount of schooling received, but are unrelated to talent. One study by economists Joshua Angrist and Alan Krueger notes that people born earlier in the calendar year tend to receive slightly less schooling than people born later in the calendar year.[26] One possible explanation for this pattern involves compulsory schooling laws: those who are born earlier in the year tend to be older for their grade levels and are therefore eligible to drop out of school at lower grade levels. Those who are born later in the year also earn more, on average, than those born earlier in the year, which suggests that forcing students to remain in school does raise their earnings. Other studies have attempted to infer the effects of schooling on earnings from differences in educational attainment that are attributable to factors such as the distance from an individual's home to the nearest two-year or four-year college, the disruption of schooling due to war, changes in compulsory schooling laws, and changes in rules governing eligibility for educational subsidies.

CHAPTER SUMMARY

1. **Transactions involving time**

   a. Consumers and firms often need to move cash from one point in time to another. They do so by borrowing and lending.

   b. For any interest-bearing account or loan, compounding of interest causes the account or loan balance to grow faster as time passes.

   c. The PDV of a claim on future resources represents the price at which someone could buy or sell that claim today.

   d. The longer the delay until payment and the higher the interest rate, the smaller the PDV of $1.

   e. To find the PDV of a stream of payments, we take the PDV of each payment and then total them.

   f. Interest rates differ because of variations in default risk, lender flexibility, and the timing of payments. When computing the PDV of some future payment, it's important to select an interest rate for an obligation with similar characteristics.

   g. The real interest rate is approximately equal to the nominal interest rate minus the rate of inflation. This approximation works well when interest and inflation rates are low. When a bank or lender quotes an interest rate, it's usually a nominal rate.

2. **Saving and borrowing**

   a. Saving reflects decisions about the timing of consumption. To analyze saving, we can apply the theory developed in Chapters 4 through 6, treating a good's "time of availability" as a physical characteristic. We use indifference curves to represent a consumer's preferences for consumption at different points in time, and a budget line to represent the available opportunities. In constructing the budget line, we use the price of each good from today's perspective—that is, the PDV of the future price.

   b. Sufficiently patient consumers save and sufficiently impatient consumers borrow. Among savers, an increase in the interest rate can either raise or lower saving, because the income and substitution effects work in opposite directions. In contrast, among borrowers, an increase in the interest rate typically reduces borrowing, because the income and substitution effects usually work in the same direction.

   c. The Life Cycle Hypothesis relies on two additional assumptions: first, that earnings tend to rise with experience, level off in middle age, and fall sharply at retirement; and second, that people like stability. The theory implies that people smooth consumption over their lifetimes, borrowing when they are young, saving during middle age, and spending down their wealth in retirement. The theory helps us to understand why saving rates differ from one country to another.

[26] Joshua D. Angrist and Alan B. Krueger, "Does Compulsory School Attendance Affect Schooling and Earnings?" *Quarterly Journal of Economics*, 1992, 106:979–1014.

3. **Investment**

a. NPV is a measure of profitability—it is the difference between the value of a project's outputs and the value of its inputs, from today's perspective. An investment project is profitable when its NPV is positive and unprofitable when its NPV is negative.

b. By saving and borrowing, an investor can rearrange the timing of the project's cash flows so that he receives its NPV instantly if the NPV is positive, or pays its NPV instantly if the NPV is negative, and neither receives nor pays anything in the future. The project's NPV therefore tells us what it is worth in terms of instant cash.

c. When we compute the NPV of a project, we are netting out the opportunity cost of funds.

d. When faced with a choice between two or more mutually exclusive projects with positive NPVs, a company should pick the one with the highest NPV.

e. Every investment project excludes waiting as an alternative. Even when a project's NPV is positive, waiting may be better than starting the project immediately.

f. When interest rates rise, most potential projects become less profitable, and the general level of investment falls. Falling interest rates have the opposite effects.

g. As long as cash inflows occur before cash outflows, a project is profitable when the rate of interest is less than its internal rate of return (IRR), and unprofitable when the rate of interest is greater than its IRR. It is not usually appropriate to choose between mutually exclusive projects based on their IRRs, however.

h. The payback period is the amount of time required before a project's total inflows match its total outflows. In general, the payback period is not a reliable criterion for evaluating investment projects.

i. Human capital consists of marketable skills acquired through investments in education and training. Standard investment principles allow us to determine whether, in a particular instance, acquiring an education makes sense from a purely financial perspective.

ADDITIONAL EXERCISES

Exercise 10.1: In each of the following cases, calculate the balance in a bank account after the specified number of years, given the specified initial deposit and rate of interest.

a. \$300 deposited at 8 percent interest for 15 years.

b. \$4,200 deposited at 3 percent interest for 40 years.

c. \$525 deposited at 6 percent interest for 5 years.

Exercise 10.2: During the 1984 presidential election campaign, Democratic hopeful Walter Mondale criticized the Reagan administration's economic record by arguing that high real interest rates were choking off investment and consumer spending. Vice-President George H.W. Bush responded famously that interest rates had fallen dramatically from a peak of 21 percent at the end of the Carter administration, and that "the real interest rate is what you pay when you go down and try to buy a TV set or buy a car." Evaluate the logic of Mr. Bush's argument.

Exercise 10.3: In each of the following cases, calculate the PDV of the specified amount under the specified circumstances.

a. \$6,300 received in eight years, at an interest rate of 4 percent.

b. \$115,000 received in two years, at an interest rate of 18 percent.

c. \$45,000 received in 100 years, at an interest rate of 1 percent.

Exercise 10.4: Calculate the PDV of the following bonds.

a. A 5-year bond with an annual coupon payment of \$200, and a principle payment at maturity of \$5,000, at an interest rate of 4 percent.

b. A 15-year bond with an annual coupon payment of \$50, and a principle payment at maturity of \$600, at an interest rate of 10 percent.

Exercise 10.5: Consider a bond with a face value of \$1,000 and a coupon of \$100. Suppose the interest rate is 10 percent. Does the PDV of the promised payments depend on the bond's maturity? Why or why not? (Hint: Think about putting \$1,000 in a bank account that pays 10 percent interest. If you withdraw \$100 at the end of each year, what do you always have left?)

Exercise 10.6: Repeat worked-out problem 10.3 (page 346), but assume that Angela earns \$70 this year and \$30 next year.

Exercise 10.7: Repeat worked-out problem 10.3 (page 346), but assume that in Angela's view, one kg of food this year is the perfect complement to one kg of food next year. In other words, assume that her indifference curves are L-shaped, and that the corner of the L in each curve lies on the 45-degree line. How would you interpret her preferences?

Exercise 10.8: People like to have a stable living standard from one year to the next. Yet studies show that the level of consumption drops suddenly, predictably, and significantly at retirement [contrary to Figure 10.9(a)]. Why? Can you think of an explanation that is consistent with the approach to saving taken in Section 10.2?

Exercise 10.9: The net cash flows from an investment project are −\$15,000 in the first year, −\$11,000 in the second year, +\$5,000 in the third year, +\$1,800 in the fourth year, +\$7,000 in the fifth year, +\$6,400 in the sixth year, +\$4,300 in the seventh year, and +\$6,200 in the eighth year. Compute the NPV of this project at the following interest rates: 2 percent, 5 percent, 8 percent.

Exercise 10.10: For each of the following investments, compute the IRR.

a. The net cash flows are −\$12,000 in the first year and +\$15,000 in the second year. (Use the formula for two-period investments given in the text.)

b. The net cash flows are −\$10,000 in the first year, +\$5,000 in the second year, and +\$6,000 in the third year. (Use the quadratic formula.)

c. The net cash flows are the same as in exercise 10.9. (Use either the search method illustrated in worked-out problem 10.4 (page 358), or the automatic search feature of a spreadsheet program.)

Exercise 10.11: The net cash flows from an investment are $-X$ dollars in the first year, positive Y dollars in year T, and zero in all other years. Write a formula for the NPV. Set the NPV equal to zero, and solve for the IRR in terms of X and Y.

Exercise 10.12: Calculate the yield to maturity for each of the following bonds.

a. A 20-year bond with a coupon of \$100, principle payment at maturity of \$2,000, and a current price of \$2,000.

b. A 5-year bond with a coupon of \$500, principle payment at maturity of \$10,000, and a current price of \$8,000.

Exercise 10.13: Two mutually exclusive projects, A and B, require the same up-front investment in the first year. Project A generates positive net cash flows in years 2 through 5 and nothing after that. Project B generates nothing in years 2 through 5; positive net cash flows in years 6 through 10; and nothing after that. At an interest rate of 10 percent, project A is a better investment than project B. Explain intuitively why project A must be better than project B at higher interest rates as well.

Exercise 10.14: A project that requires an investment of \$6,000 in the first year generates a positive net cash flow of \$15,000 in the fourth year. It leaves the investor with an obligation to pay \$10,000 in the eighth year, and yields no net cash flow in any other year.

a. Find the NPV of this investment at the following interest rates: 0 percent, 5 percent, 10 percent, 15 percent, 20 percent.

b. This investment has two different IRRs. Find them, using the method illustrated in worked-out problem 10.4.

c. At what interest rates is this project profitable? (Use the graph from part b.) Is it always profitable when one of the IRRs exceeds the interest rate? What if both of the IRRs exceed the interest rate?

d. Why does this example produce two IRRs? How does it differ from the examples presented in this chapter? (Hint: Using a spreadsheet, graph the NPV against the interest rate. How does this graph change when you reduce the value of the payment in the eighth year from \$10,000 to some smaller number? What happens to the IRRs?)

Exercise 10.15: A project requires a cash investment in the first year and generates a positive net cash flow in all future years. Knowing only that Janet is more patient than Michael, would you say she is more likely to undertake the project than Michael? Justify your answer.

Exercise 10.16: Make your best guess about the various financial costs and benefits of attending your current educational institution (assuming that you complete your degree). Think about your likely earnings with and without the degree, the cost of tuition and books, and any other factors you consider relevant. Based on your estimates, compute the PDV and the IRR of your investment in human capital.

11

Choices Involving Risk

Learning Objectives

After reading this chapter, students should be able to:

- Define and measure economic risk.
- Illustrate an individual's risk preferences graphically.
- Explain why people purchase insurance policies.
- Analyze why people take certain risks and avoid others.
- Identify and explain several strategies for managing risk.

Early in 1996, two graduate students at Stanford University, Larry Page and Sergey Brin, began developing a new technology for retrieving information from huge databases. With no business experience to speak of, they tried but failed to convince investors of their technology's commercial potential. Reluctantly, they set up operations in Page's dorm room, where they cobbled together a patchwork data center made of surplus computer memory acquired at bargain prices. Over the next two years, they managed to raise just under $1 million from interested investors, which they used to launch a company. By September 1998, Google Inc. was officially open for business. Six years later, on August 19, 2004, the company held an initial public offering (IPO) in which for the first time members of the general public were allowed to buy shares. Page and Brin both collected more than $40 million in cash, retaining shares valued at more than $3.2 billion each! They (and their investors) had taken a big chance—one that had paid off beyond their wildest expectations.

Google, Inc. founders Larry Page and Sergey Brin

During the dot-com mania of the late 1990s, thousands of bright young entrepreneurs with clever ideas launched risky new ventures. Unlike Page and Brin, most came up empty handed. A grocery delivery service

called Webvan went belly-up in 2001 with accumulated losses of $830 million. Clothing outlet Boo.com blew through $225 million of investors' money, only to be acquired for well under $1 million by Fashionmall.com. Web sites like "The Museum of E-Failure" were created just to keep track of the duds. Some of them, like "Dot-Com Flop Tracker," flopped themselves. For an investor, the trick was to distinguish the Googles from the Webvans. Many of those who guessed right became wealthy; others lost their shirts. Still others watched from the sidelines, unwilling to gamble their hard-earned savings on such risky prospects.

Though most people aren't dot-com entrepreneurs, everyone takes risks. Obviously, buying a lottery ticket is a risky proposition, as are going to college (since jobs aren't guaranteed), lending money to a friend (since default is possible), and driving a car (since accidents do happen). Risk is the rule, not the exception.

In this chapter, we'll examine four topics related to risky economic decisions.

1. *What is risk?* Common sense tells us when a decision involves risk. Economics and statistics show us how to gauge the amount of risk with some precision.
2. *Risk preference.* In Chapter 4, we learned how to describe an individual's consumption preferences. Here, we'll apply the same concepts to situations in which the outcome is uncertain.
3. *Insurance.* Much of life is unavoidably risky. People address a wide range of financial risks by purchasing insurance policies. We'll see why insurance makes them better off.
4. *Other methods of managing risk.* Most people avoid some risks but voluntarily accept others. For example, they reduce risk by purchasing insurance, but then introduce new risks by investing in the stock market. We'll see why doing so makes sense. We'll also study the steps people take to moderate the risks they accept.

11.1 WHAT IS RISK?

Risk exists whenever the consequences of a decision are uncertain. In this section, we'll explain how economists analyze risks and gauge their magnitude.

Possibilities

A **state of nature** is one possible way in which events relevant to a risky decision can unfold.

The consequences of any risky decision depend on events outside the decision maker's control. Usually, events can unfold in many different ways. Economists and statisticians refer to each possible unfolding of events as a **state of nature**, or *state* for short.

To illustrate, suppose that Alberto is trying to decide whether to buy tickets to a baseball game. His enjoyment of the game will depend on two uncertain events that are beyond his control: whether it rains and whether his team wins. He will be happiest if it doesn't rain and his team wins. That is one possible state of nature.

To analyze a risky decision, economists begin by describing every possible state of nature. In Alberto's case, events can unfold in four different ways: it rains and his team wins; it rains and his team loses; it doesn't rain and his team wins; or it doesn't rain and his team loses. Each item on this list is a state of nature.

Once someone makes a choice, he experiences one and only one state of nature. For example, Alberto will experience one of the four states listed in the last paragraph, because we haven't left out any possibilities. He can't experience more than one state, however, because we've described each one in a way that rules out the others.

Probability

Some states of nature are more likely than others. For example, if Alberto lives in San Diego (where it rarely rains during baseball season), states of nature involving rain are relatively unlikely.

Probability is a measure of the likelihood that a state of nature will occur. It's usually written either as a number between 0 and 1 or as a percentage. A probability of 0 (or 0%) means that a state is impossible; a probability of 1 (or 100%) means that it's certain. A probability of, say, 3/4 (or 75%) means that the odds of the state in question occurring are three out of four.

Probability is a measure of the likelihood that a state of nature will occur.

By adding the probabilities of two states of nature, we obtain the probability that one of those two states will occur. For example, let's suppose the odds are 3 in 10 (30%) that it will rain and Alberto's team will win, and 4 in 10 (40%) that it will rain and Alberto's team will lose. Then the odds of it raining (with Alberto's team either winning or losing) must be 7 in 10 (70% = 30% + 40%). The probabilities of *all* states of nature always add up to 1 (or 100%), because it's certain that *something* will happen.

Sometimes we can measure the probability of a state of nature by determining the frequency with which it has occurred in the past, under comparable conditions. Such measure are known as **objective probabilities**. For example, if we flip a coin thousands of times, we'll find that it comes up heads and tails with roughly equal frequency. Thus, we conclude that the probability of each outcome is the same—in each case, 1/2 (or 50%). Likewise, Alberto might estimate the probability of each state of nature based on the historical frequency of rain and his team's won-lost record.

An **objective probability** is a measure of the likelihood that a state of nature will occur based on the frequency with which it has occurred in the past, under comparable conditions.

Sometimes we can measure the probability of a state of nature, at least in part, by exercising our own judgment. While this type of assessment, known as **subjective probability**, may be informed by facts, it may also reflect "instinct" or a "gut feeling." Naturally, different people may come to very different subjective judgments. For example, if the Yankees play the Giants in the World Series, their fans may harbor radically different views concerning the likely outcome, even based on the same information (see Application 11.2 on page 380).

A **subjective probability** is a measure of the likelihood that an event will occur based on subjective judgment.

Uncertain Payoffs

Risky choices often have financial consequences, also known as *payoffs*. Payoffs can be either positive (gains) or negative (losses). To evaluate a choice, we need to know the **probability distribution** of the payoffs—that is, the likelihood of each possible payoff occurring. Like other consequences, payoffs depend on unfolding events, in other words, on the state of nature. As long as we know the probability of each possible state of nature, we can determine the probability of each possible payoff.

The **probability distribution** of a set of payoffs tells us the likelihood that each possible payoff will occur.

Here's an example. The managers of New Stuff, Inc., are thinking about building a factory to make a new product called a thingamajig. A competitor has already started producing a similar product and has filed for patent protection. If approved, the patent would prevent New Stuff from making thingamajigs. In addition, the market for thingamajigs is untested. Eventually, demand will turn out to be either high or low. If it's low, New Stuff will have to shut its factory down, whether or not the competitor's patent is approved.

In this example, there are four possible states of nature: the competitor's patent is approved and demand is low; the competitor's patent is approved and demand is high; the competitor's patent is not approved and demand is low; or the competitor's patent is not approved and demand is high. Based on both objective evidence and subjective judgment, New Stuff's managers arrive at the probabilities shown in the second column of Table 11.1.

Unsure of their best course of action, the managers have drawn up two sets of plans, one for a large factory and the other for a small one. If the competitor's patent is not approved and demand is high, New Stuff expects to make $8.5 million from the large factory and $4.5 million from the small one, net of investment costs. With all other states of nature, they expect to lose their investment ($1.5 million for the large factory and $0.5 million for the small one). All of these figures refer to net present values, defined in Section 10.3. New Stuff's payoffs are shown in the third and fourth columns of Table 11.1.

Table 11.2 shows the probability distributions of the payoffs from the two factories. (For the moment, ignore the last column in the table, as well as the rows labeled *expected*

Table 11.1

States of Nature, Probabilities, and Payoffs for New Stuff's Thingamajig (Hypothetical Figures)

		Payoff (NPV, $ million)	
State of Nature	Probability	Large Factory	Small Factory
Patent approved, low demand	30%	−1.5	−0.5
Patent approved, high demand	20	−1.5	−0.5
Patent not approved, low demand	30	−1.5	−0.5
Patent not approved, high demand	20	+8.5	+4.5

Table 11.2

Expected Value of New Stuff's Profits on the Thingamajig (Hypothetical Calculation)

Large Factory	Payoff ($)	Probability	Probability × Payoff
	8,500,000	20%	1,700,000
	−1,500,000	80	−1,200,000
Expected payoff			**500,000**
Small Factory	**Payoff ($)**	**Probability**	**Probability × Payoff**
	4,500,000	20%	900,000
	−500,000	80	−400,000
Expected payoff			**500,000**

payoff.) With the large factory, New Stuff receives a payoff of \$8.5 million with 20 percent probability, which is the probability that the competitor's patent is not approved and demand is high, and a payoff of −\$1.5 million with 80 percent probability, which is the total probability of all other states of nature. Similarly, with the small factory, New Stuff receives a payoff of \$4.5 million with 20 percent probability and a payoff of −\$0.5 million with 80 percent probability (as shown in the lower half of Table 11.2).

Histograms can help us to visualize probability distributions. The one in Figure 11.1(a) summarizes the possible consequences of New Stuff's large factory. The horizontal axis measures the payoff, and the vertical axis measures probability. The taller of the two red bars tells us that New Stuff loses \$1.5 million (the horizontal coordinate) with 80 percent probability (the vertical coordinate). The shorter bar tells us that the company gains \$8.5 million (the horizontal coordinate) with 20 percent probability (the vertical coordinate). The histogram in Figure 11.1(b) summarizes the smaller factory's possible consequences. The two blue bars tell us that New Stuff loses \$0.5 million with 80 percent probability and gains \$4.5 million with 20 percent probability.

To evaluate a choice with risky financial prospects, we usually begin with two simple questions. First, what do we expect to gain or lose, on average? Second, do we expect the actual gain or loss to be close to that average or far from it? We'll tackle these two questions in turn.

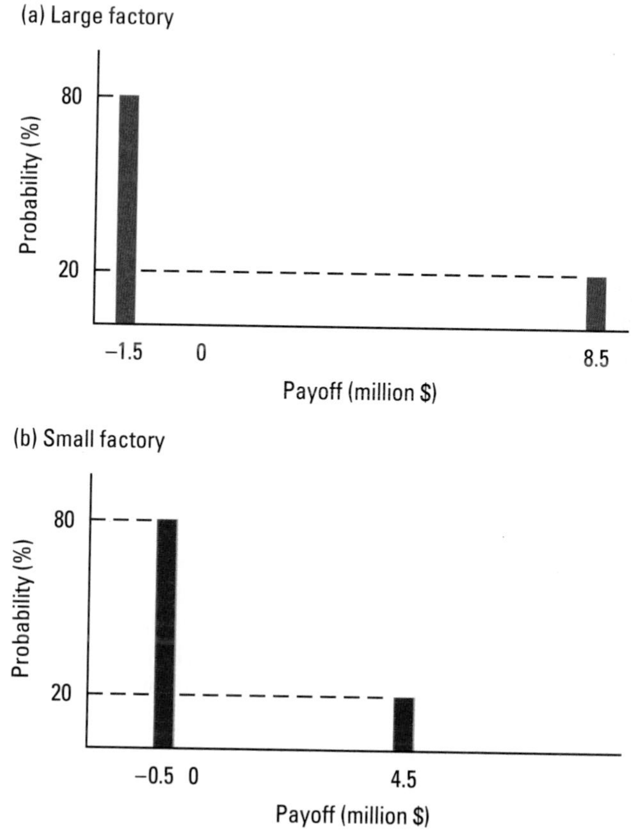

Figure 11.1

Possible Consequences of New Stuff's Investment in the Thingamajig. New Stuff's large factory [figure (a)] results in a loss of \$1.5 million with 80 percent probability and a gain of \$8.5 million with 20 percent probability. The small factory [figure (b)] results in a loss of \$0.5 million with 80 percent probability and a gain of \$4.5 million with 80 percent probability.

Expected Payoff

The **expected payoff** of a risky financial choice is a weighted average of all the possible payoffs, using the probability of each payoff as its weight.

To determine the average gain or loss from a risky financial choice, we can calculate its **expected payoff**. The expected payoff is a weighted average of all the possible payoffs, using the probability of each payoff as its weight.

To illustrate, suppose Ilya and Napoleon bet $5 on the flip of a coin. If the outcome is heads (H), Napoleon pays Ilya $5; if tails (T), Ilya pays Napoleon $5. We compute Ilya's expected payoff as follows:

$$\text{Ilya's expected payoff} =$$
$$(\text{Probability of H}) \times (\text{Ilya's payoff if H}) + (\text{Probability of T}) \times (\text{Ilya's payoff if T})$$
$$= (^1/_2) \times (5) + (^1/_2) \times (-5) = 0$$

Using the same logic, we see that Napoleon's expected payoff is also zero.

More generally, suppose the payoff from a risky choice can take on one of N different values, $P_1, P_2, \ldots, P_N$, and that it turns out to be P_n with the probability Π_n (the Greek letter *pi*). We can calculate the expected payoff, abbreviated *EP*, using the following formula:

$$EP = \Pi_1 \times P_1 + \Pi_2 \times P_2 + \cdots + \Pi_N \times P_N \qquad (1)$$

The final column of Table 11.2 applies this formula to New Stuff's proposed factories. As indicated, the two factories have exactly the same expected payoff, $500,000.

Notice that in these examples, the actual payoff *never* equals the expected payoff. In general, the expected payoff from a risky choice is *not* necessarily the most likely outcome, and need not even be remotely likely. Rather, it's the amount you would earn, on average, if you were to make the same risky choice many times. To illustrate, take Ilya and Napoleon's coin flip. Were they to make the same bet, say, 10,000 times, the frequency of heads and tails would be very close to 50 percent, so their average payoff would be very close to zero.

Application 11.1

The Development of New Drugs

Pharmaceutical manufacturers have drawn widespread criticism by charging high prices for life-saving drugs. For example, the drugs used to treat HIV, the virus that causes AIDS, can cost a patient tens of thousands of dollars a year, placing treatment beyond the reach of many, including millions in third world countries. Critics point out that manufacturers could make these drugs available at lower prices and still cover their costs of production.

The companies respond that drug prices must be high enough to cover the costs not only of production, but of development, including expensive clinical trials. Otherwise, they would have no incentive to develop new drugs. In evaluating the cost of development, they emphasize, it's essential to account for the fact that success isn't assured. Only a minority of experimental drugs eventually win approval by the Food and Drug Administration (FDA) and only after clinical testing. Companies won't develop new drugs unless, on average, their profits cover their development costs.

How much does the typical approved drug need to earn to cover a company's development costs? Let's say that a company has to spend an average of $50 million on development costs for each experimental drug, and that the probability of approval by the FDA is 20 percent. If each approved drug generates *A* dollars in profits (ignoring development costs), then using formula (1), the expected payoff from each experimental drug is:

$$\text{Expected payoff} = (0.2 \times \$A + 0.8 \times \$0) - \$50 \text{ million}$$

Setting $A = 250$ million, we find that the expected payoff is exactly zero. So on average, a successful drug has to generate a profit of at least $250 million after its approval to justify the company's development of experimental drugs. Merely covering the $50 million in development costs for the approved drug isn't enough.

Experts disagree sharply about the costs of drug development. According to one controversial study by economists Joseph DiMasi, Ronald Hansen, and Henry Grabowski, the average successful drug must generate $802 million in profits after the FDA's approval to cover a company's development costs.[1] Other studies have arrived at lower figures.[2]

Variability

Economists gauge financial risk by measuring the **variability** of gains and losses. Roughly speaking, variability is low when the range of likely payoffs is narrow, and high when the range is wide. With little variability, the actual payoff is almost always close to the expected payoff. With substantial variability, the two amounts often differ significantly.

The **variability** of payoffs is an indication of risk. With little variability, the actual payoff is almost always close to the expected payoff. With substantial variability, the two amounts often differ significantly.

Histograms can help us to visualize variability. For example, look again at Figure 11.1, which summarizes the possible financial consequences of New Stuff's proposed factories. Notice that the blue bars in Figure 11.1(b) are closer together—and closer to the expected payoff of $0.5 million—than the red bars in Figure 11.1(a). That means the payoffs from the small factory are less variable than the payoffs from the large one.

The difference between the actual payoff and the expected payoff is called a **deviation**. Greater variability is associated with larger deviations. Figures 11.2(a) and (b) illustrate the possible deviations from expected payoff for New Stuff's proposed factories. We've indicated the expected payoff for each of the proposed factories, $0.5 million, on the horizontal axes. As Figure 11.2(a) shows, for the large factory there is an 80 percent chance that the deviation will be −$2 million (the horizontal distance between the tall red bar and a vertical line drawn at the expected payoff), and a 20 percent chance that the deviation will be +$8 million (the horizontal distance between the short red bar and a vertical line drawn at the expected payoff). In contrast, for the small factory there is an 80 percent chance that the deviation will be −$1 million, and a 20 percent chance that it will be +$4 million.

A **deviation** is the difference between the actual payoff and the expected payoff.

Often, economists measure the variability of a risky financial payoff by calculating either its variance or its standard deviation. The **variance** is the expected value of a squared deviation. The calculation of variance involves three steps: first, compute the deviations for all possible outcomes; second, square each deviation; third, find the weighted average of all the possible squared deviations, using the probability of each squared deviation as its weight. The **standard deviation** is the square root of the variance. Both the variance and the standard deviation tell us something about the size of the typical deviation.

The **variance** is the expected value of a squared deviation.

The **standard deviation** is the square root of the variance.

[1]Joseph A. DiMasi, Ronald W. Hansen, and Henry G. Grabowski, "The Price of Innovation: New Estimates of Drug Development Costs," *Journal of Health Economics* 22, 2003, pp. 151–185.

[2]For example, a study by the Global Alliance for TB Drug Development (*The Economics of TB Drug Development*, October 2001) concludes that the average successful tuberculosis drug must generate between $115 and $250 million in profits to cover develpment costs.

Figure 11.2

Expected Payoff and Deviations for New Stuff's Investment in the Thingamajig. The expected payoff from each of New Stuff's proposed factories is $0.5 million. However, the histograms show that the large factory's payoff is more variable—its distribution is wider, and the deviations are larger.

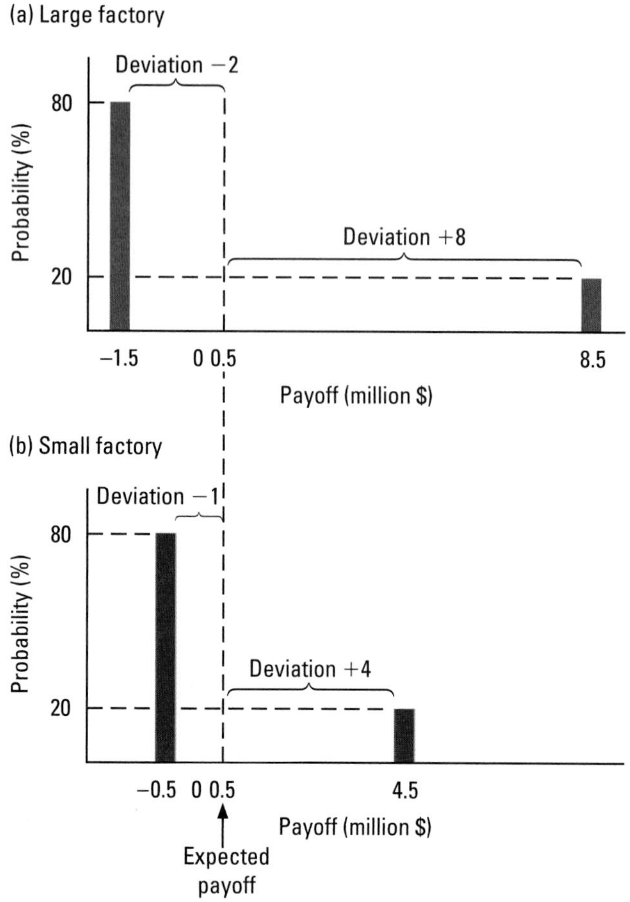

Table 11.3 calculates the variance and standard deviation of the payoffs for each of New Stuff's proposed factories. For the large factory, the variance is 16 trillion dollars squared, and the standard deviation is $4 million. For the small factory, the variance is 4 trillion dollars squared, and the standard deviation is $2 million. These numbers confirm what we saw in Figure 11.2; the payoffs for the large factory are much more variable than the payoffs for the small one.

11.2 RISK PREFERENCES

Fortunately, we don't need to develop an entirely new theory to analyze decisions involving risk. We can simply apply the basic theory of consumer decision making that we learned in Chapters 4 through 6.

Table 11.3
Variability of New Stuff's Profits on the Thingamajig

Large Factory	Probability	Deviation (million $)	Squared Dev. (trillion $²)	Probability × Squared Dev. (trillion $²)
	20%	8	64	12.8
	80	−2	4	3.2
Variance (trillion $²)				16
Standard dev. (million $)				4
Small Factory	**Probability**	**Deviation (million $)**	**Squared Dev. (trillion $²)**	**Probability × Squared Dev. (trillion $²)**
	20%	4	16	3.2
	80	−1	1	0.8
Variance (trillion $²)				4
Standard dev. (million $)				2

Consumption Bundles

In Section 10.2 we learned how to apply that theory to decisions involving time. The key was to think of a consumption bundle as a list of the quantities of each good consumed at each point in time. (If you skipped Chapter 10, take a moment to read the short section titled the Timing of Consumption, which begins on page 338.) We can handle risk in much the same way. That is, we can think of a consumption bundle as a list of the quantities of each good consumed in each possible state of nature.

To illustrate, let's start with a simple problem. A consumer, whom we'll call Maria, is uncertain about the weather. There are only two possible states of nature, "sun" and "hurricane." We'll assume that Maria is familiar with the probability of each state from past experience.

To keep the analysis simple, we'll assume that Maria consumes only one good, called "food," which is measured in kilograms. Maria needn't consume the same amount of food when it's sunny and when there's a hurricane. Indeed, if a hurricane were to destroy some of her property, forcing her to spend some of her money on repairs, she would most likely consume less. Therefore, her consumption bundle must list both the amount of food she eats when it's sunny and the amount she eats when there's a hurricane.

Figure 11.3 illustrates Maria's potential consumption bundles. The horizontal axis measures her consumption if it's sunny, and the vertical axis measures her consumption if there's a hurricane. Each point on the graph corresponds to a distinct alternative. For example, point B represents the consumption bundle consisting of 600 kg of food if it's sunny and 300 kg of food if there's a hurricane.

Figure 11.3

Consumption Bundles. Each point on this graph corresponds to a different risky alternative. Point B, for example, means that Maria eats 600 kg of food if it's sunny and 300 kg if there's a hurricane. For points like A on the 45-degree line (also called the *guaranteed consumption line*), she eats the same amount, rain or shine. Maria's expected consumption is the same (500 kg) for all points on the green line (also called a *constant expected consumption line*). As Maria moves away from point A in either direction along the green line, variability (risk) increases.

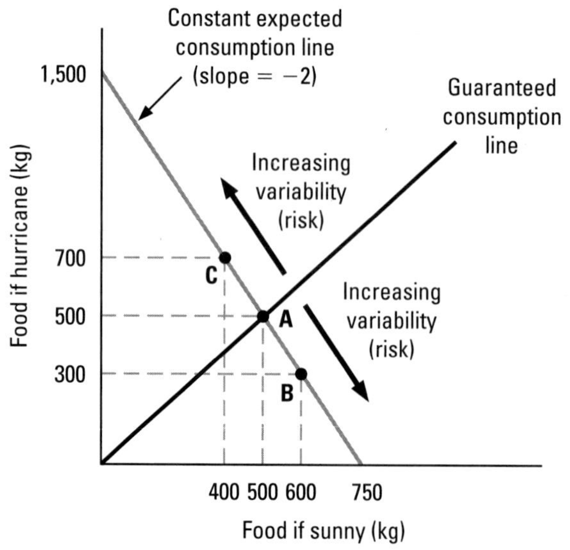

The **guaranteed consumption line** shows the consumption bundles for which the level of consumption does not depend on the state of nature.

Guaranteed Consumption For some bundles, the level of consumption is guaranteed in the sense that it does not depend on the state of nature. In Figure 11.3, those bundles all lie along the 45-degree line through the origin, also known as the **guaranteed consumption line**. Notice, for example, that point A provides Maria with the same amount of food, 500 kg, if it's sunny and if there's a hurricane. At all points below the guaranteed consumption line, like point B, Maria eats more food if it's sunny; at all points above that line, like point C, she eats more food if there's a hurricane.

Expected Consumption and Variability For bundles that don't lie on the guaranteed consumption line in Figure 11.3, Maria's payoff (the amount of food she consumes) is uncertain. Given any particular bundle, we can compute her expected consumption (abbreviated EC) by applying formula (1). Let's use F_S to stand for the amount of food she consumes if it's sunny, F_H for the amount she consumes if there's a hurricane, and Π for the probability of sun (so that the probability of a hurricane is $1 - \Pi$). Then

$$EC = \Pi \times F_S + (1 - \Pi) \times F_H \qquad \textbf{(2)}$$

For example, if the probability of sun is $2/3$, F_S is 600 kg, and F_H is 300 kg, then expected consumption is 500 kg.

Many of the bundles in Figure 11.3 share the same level of expected consumption. Which ones? Let's rearrange formula (2) as follows:[3]

$$F_H = \frac{EC}{1 - \Pi} - \left(\frac{\Pi}{1 - \Pi}\right)F_S \qquad \textbf{(3)}$$

A **constant expected consumption line** shows all the risky consumption bundles with the same level of expected consumption.

Formula (3) implies that risky consumption bundles with the same level of expected consumption (that is, the same value of EC) lie along a straight line with a slope of $-\Pi/(1 - \Pi)$. We call this a **constant expected consumption line**.

[3] To obtain formula (3) from formula (2), first subtract $\Pi \times F_S$ from both sides, and then divide through by $1 - \Pi$.

To illustrate, let's suppose that $\Pi = {}^2/_3$. For all of the bundles on the green line in Figure 11.3, expected consumption is 500 kg. Therefore, this is a constant expected consumption line. Notice that the slope of this line is $-\Pi/(1 - \Pi) = -2$. The line would be steeper for a higher value of Π and flatter for a lower value.

Although every point on the green line in Figure 11.3 has the same level of expected consumption, the *variability* of consumption differs. At point A, consumption doesn't depend on the weather, so there is no variability. As Maria moves away from point A in either direction along the constant expected consumption line, her consumption becomes increasingly variable. (Pick a point on this line and draw the histogram for the probability distribution of Maria's consumption. Notice that, as your chosen point moves farther away from point A, the bars corresponding to sun and hurricane move farther apart.)

Preferences and Indifference Curves

If one consumption bundle guarantees more of every good than a second bundle, a consumer should prefer the first bundle to the second. This assumption reflects the More-Is-Better Principle, which we introduced in Chapter 4. Notice that a consumption bundle does not have to guarantee a particular level of consumption to guarantee more consumption than a second bundle. For example, point D in Figure 11.4(a) guarantees a higher level of food consumption than point B: with point D, consumption is higher in every state of nature—both if it's sunny (700 kg vs. 500 kg) and if there's a hurricane (400 kg vs. 300 kg). Maria must therefore prefer point D to point B.

Assuming that more is better, we can illustrate Maria's preferences for consumption bundles by drawing indifference curves, exactly as we did in Chapter 4. For the reasons

Figure 11.4

Maria's Preferences for Risky Consumption Bundles. The indifference curves show Maria's preferences for risky consumption bundles. A high probability of a hurricane leads to relatively flat indifference curves, like the red ones shown in figure (a), and a low probability leads to relatively steep indifference curves, like the blue ones shown in figure (b).

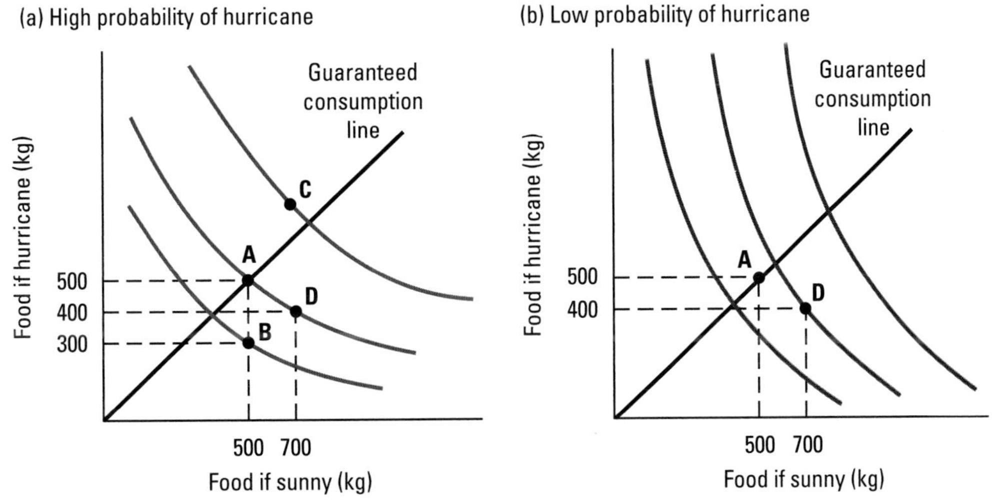

discussed in Section 4.2, her indifference curves must be downward sloping lines, and those that are farther from the origin must correspond to higher levels of well-being. For example, the indifference curves in Figure 11.4(a) show that Maria prefers point C to point A, and point A to point B. She is indifferent between points A and D. Given a choice between these four alternatives, she'll pick point C.

The slope of an indifference curve indicates the consumer's willingness to shift consumption from one state of nature to another. For example, Maria's indifference between points A and D in Figure 11.4(a) implies that, starting from point D, she is willing to give up 200 kg of food if it's sunny in order to secure an additional 100 kg if there's a hurricane.

Usually, a consumer's willingness to shift consumption from one state of nature to another depends on the probabilities of those states. Therefore, a change in probabilities changes the slopes of the consumer's indifference curves. In Maria's case, a high probability of a hurricane leads to relatively flat indifference curves, like the red ones shown in Figure 11.4(a), and a low probability leads to relatively steep indifference curves, like the blue ones shown in Figure 11.4(b). To understand why, suppose that Maria starts out with point D. When the probability of a hurricane is high [Figure 11.4(a)], she is indifferent between points A and D, and willing to swap 200 kg of food if it's sunny for an additional 100 kg if there's a hurricane. When the probability of hurricane falls, she becomes less concerned about consumption if there's a hurricane and more concerned about consumption if it's sunny. Therefore, as shown in Figure 11.4(b), the same swap makes her worse off; she prefers point D to point A. Since she now requires *more* than 100 kg of food if there's a hurricane to compensate for the loss of 200 kg of food if it's sunny, her indifference curve is steeper. In other words, reducing the probability of a hurricane increases her marginal rate of substitution for food if it's sunny with food if there's a hurricane.

The Concept of Risk Aversion

Most people don't like uncertainty. They pay money to eliminate or reduce risk—for example, by purchasing an insurance policy. They also avoid accepting a new risk unless they're adequately compensated. We say that a person is **risk averse** if, in comparing a riskless bundle to a risky bundle with the same level of expected consumption, he prefers the riskless bundle. This definition captures the idea that, by itself, variability is a bad thing.

A person is **risk averse** if, in comparing a riskless bundle to a risky bundle with the same level of expected consumption, he prefers the riskless bundle.

What does risk aversion imply about the shape of an indifference curve? Figure 11.5 reproduces the constant expected consumption line from Figure 11.3. This line crosses the guaranteed consumption line at point A. Therefore, point A is the only riskless bundle on the constant expected consumption line. If Maria is risk averse, she will prefer point A to all other points on this line. This implies that one of her indifference curves lies tangent to the constant expected consumption line at point A, and above all other points on that line, as shown.

Risk-averse individuals do not avoid risk at all costs. Starting from a riskless position, they are usually willing to accept some risk, provided that they receive adequate compensation in the form of higher expected consumption. For example, in Figure 11.5, Maria will prefer bundle B to bundle A, even though bundle B involves more variability, and in the event of a hurricane, lower consumption than bundle A.

The **certainty equivalent** of a risky bundle is the amount of consumption which, if provided with certainty, would make the consumer equally well off.

Certainty Equivalents and Risk Premiums For risk-averse individuals, exposure to risk reduces well-being. How do we measure that cost? To answer this question, we'll introduce the concept of a **certainty equivalent**. The certainty equivalent of a risky bun-

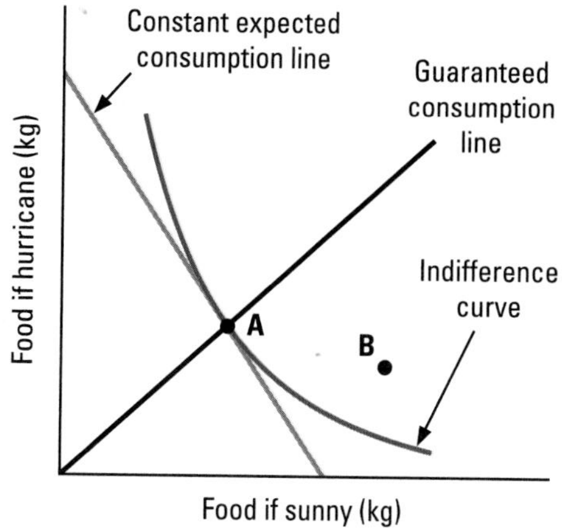

Figure 11.5

Risk Aversion. The constant expected consumption line crosses the guaranteed consumption line at point A. Therefore, point A is the only riskless bundle on the constant expected consumption line. If Maria is risk averse, she must prefer point A to all other points on this line. This implies that her indifference curve lies tangent to the constant expected consumption line at point A, and above all other points on this line, as shown.

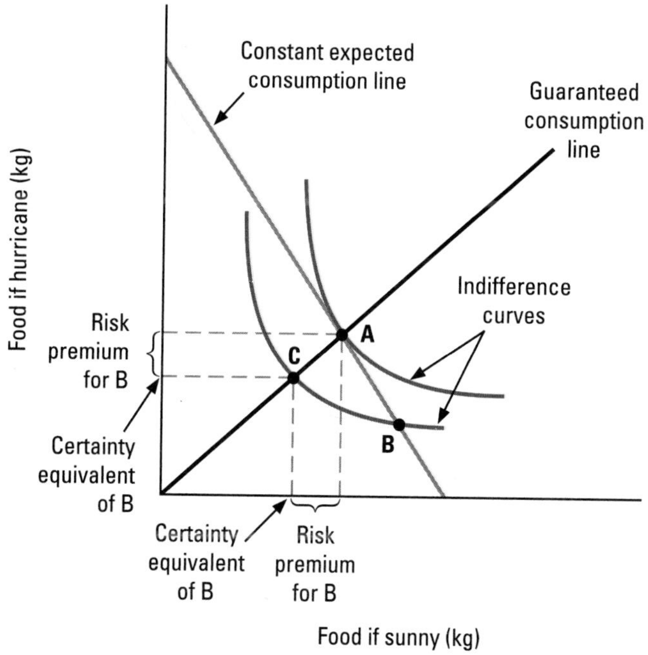

Figure 11.6

The Certainty Equivalent and the Risk Premium. The fixed level of food consumption associated with point C is the certainty equivalent of the risky consumption bundle B. The risk premium for bundle B is the difference between the expected level of consumption at B and B's certainty equivalent. It's also the amount by which the consumer is willing to reduce expected consumption to eliminate all risks. Since the expected level of consumption is the same at points A and B, the risk premium for bundle B equals the horizontal distance (also the vertical distance) between points C and A.

dle is the amount of consumption which, if provided with certainty, would make the consumer equally well off. Figure 11.6 illustrates this concept. Let's take any risky bundle, like bundle B, and draw the consumer's indifference curve through it. This curve intersects the 45-degree line at point C, which guarantees a fixed level of consumption. This guaranteed level, which we can read from either the horizontal or vertical axis (as shown in the figure), is the certainty equivalent of bundle B.

A risky bundle's certainty equivalent tells us exactly what it's worth to the consumer. When faced with a choice between two risky bundles, the consumer always chooses the one with the higher certainty equivalent. So if one risky bundle is worth \$5 for sure and another is worth only \$4 for sure, the first is plainly better than the second.

For a risk-averse individual, the certainty equivalent of a risky bundle is always less than expected consumption. Why? Providing the same expected consumption with no risk would clearly make the individual better off. In the figure, Maria prefers point A to point B. To make Maria indifferent between bundle B and a riskless bundle, we have to *reduce* her guaranteed consumption from the level associated with point A to the level associated with point C.

The **risk premium** of a risky bundle is the difference between its expected consumption and the consumer's certainty equivalent.

The **risk premium** of a risky bundle is the difference between its expected consumption and the consumer's certainty equivalent. In other words, it's the amount by which the consumer is willing to reduce expected consumption to eliminate all risk. In Figure 11.6, the risk premium corresponds to the horizontal distance (equivalently, the vertical distance) between point A (which has the same expected level of consumption as the risky bundle B) and point C. The size of the risk premium reflects the psychological cost of risk.

WORKED-OUT PROBLEM 11.1

The Problem Suppose Maria's indifference curves are given by the following formula:

$$\frac{2}{3}\sqrt{F_S} + \frac{1}{3}\sqrt{F_H} = C$$

where C is a constant (the value of which differs from one indifference curve to another). Maria receives 36 kg of food when it's sunny and 81 kg when there's a hurricane. If the probability of sunshine, Π, equals $2/3$, what is her expected food consumption? What is the certainty equivalent of this risky bundle? What is the risk premium?

The Solution Expected consumption is $2/3 F_S + 1/3 F_H = 2/3 \times 36 + 1/3 \times 81 = 51$. To compute the certainty equivalent, we need to find a level of guaranteed food consumption, F, that places Mary on the same indifference curve as the risky bundle:

$$\frac{2}{3}\sqrt{36} + \frac{1}{3}\sqrt{81} = \frac{2}{3}\sqrt{F} + \frac{1}{3}\sqrt{F}$$

Simplifying, we get $4 + 3 = \sqrt{F}$, or $F = 49$. So the certainty equivalent is 49 kg. Since $51 - 49 = 2$, the risk premium is 2 kg.

IN-TEXT EXERCISE 11.1 **Repeat the calculation in worked-out problem 11.1 for each of the following risky consumption bundles.**

(a) 81 kg when it's sunny, and 36 kg when it rains.
(b) 225 kg when it's sunny, and 144 kg when it rains.
(c) 9 kg when it's sunny, and 900 kg when it rains.

Degrees of Risk Aversion Some people need relatively little encouragement to take a risk. Others prefer safe alternatives unless the cards are heavily stacked in their favor. What do these differences imply about the shapes of their indifference curves?

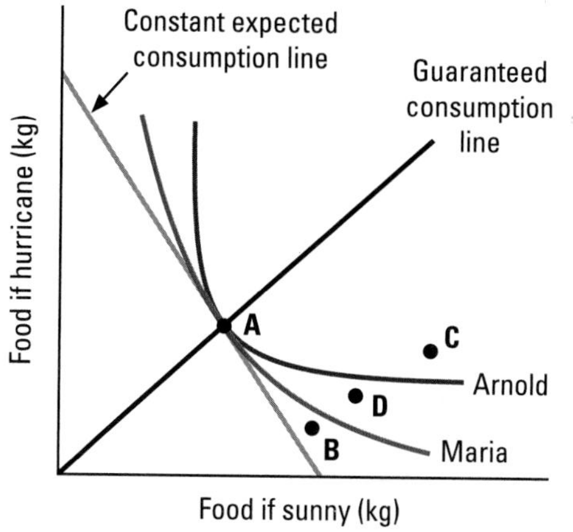

Figure 11.7

Degrees of Risk Aversion. The red indifference curve belongs to Maria; the blue one belongs to Arnold. Maria is less risk averse than Arnold. Neither would trade the riskless consumption bundle A for risky alternatives that lie below their indifference curves, like bundle B. Both would trade bundle A for risky alternatives above their indifference curves, like bundle C. However, Maria will trade bundle A for risky bundles between the two indifference curves, like bundle D, while Arnold will not.

Figure 11.7 reproduces Maria's indifference curve (shown in red), along with an indifference curve for another consumer, Arnold (shown in blue). Since Maria and Arnold are both risk averse, both curves lie tangent to the constant expected consumption line at point A. However, Arnold's curve bends more sharply at the 45-degree line, and it lies above Maria's everywhere else. That means Arnold is more risk averse than Maria, starting from point A.

To understand why, notice that the two indifference curves divide the set of possible alternatives into three parts. First, there are points below Maria's indifference curve, like point B. Neither Maria nor Arnold will swap bundle A for any risky bundle in this part of the figure. Second, there are points above Arnold's indifference curve, like point C. Both Maria and Arnold will swap bundle A for any risky bundle in this part of the figure. Finally, there are points between the two indifference curves, like point D. Maria will exchange bundle A for a risky bundle in this part of the figure, but Arnold will not. Since Maria is willing to take on a wider range of risk than Arnold, she's less risk averse.

Greater risk aversion implies that for any risky bundle, the certainty equivalent is lower and the risk premium higher than it is for less risk-averse consumers. In other words, the psychological cost of risk exposure is greater for more risk-averse consumers. As an example, take point D in Figure 11.7. Since Maria prefers point D to point A, her certainty equivalent for point D must be *larger* than the level of consumption that point A guarantees. Since Arnold prefers point A to point D, his certainty equivalent for point D must be *smaller* than the level of consumption that point A guarantees. Maria's certainty equivalent is therefore larger than Arnold's, and her risk premium is smaller.

Alternatives to Risk Aversion

Some people actually like to take risks, at least in some situations. We say that a person is **risk loving** if, in comparing a riskless bundle to a risky bundle with the same level of expected consumption, he prefers the risky bundle. This definition captures the idea that variability is in itself a good thing. A risk-loving individual will voluntarily accept higher variability even if it isn't associated with a higher level of expected consumption.

A person is **risk loving** if, in comparing a riskless bundle to a risky bundle with the same level of expected consumption, he prefers the risky bundle.

What would Maria's indifference curves look like if she were risk loving? Figure 11.8 reproduces the constant expected consumption line from Figure 11.3. Recall that point A

Figure 11.8
A Risk Loving Consumer. As before, point A is the only riskless bundle on the constant expected consumption line. If Maria is risk loving, she must prefer all other points on this line to point A. This implies that her indifference curve lies tangent to the constant expected consumption line at point A and below all other points on this line, as shown.

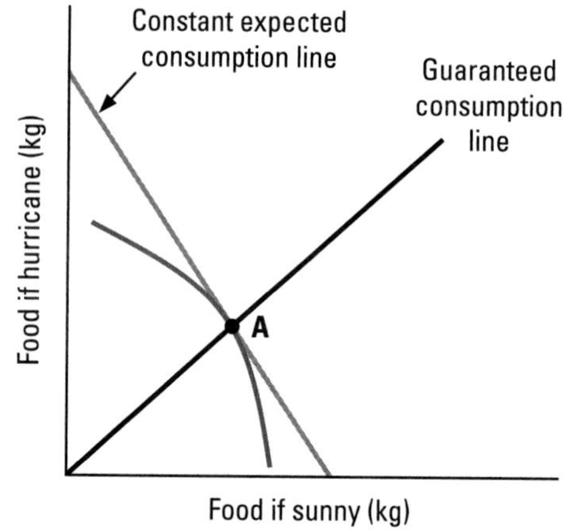

is the only riskless bundle on this line. If Maria is risk loving, she will prefer every other point on this line to point A. This implies that one of her indifference curves lies tangent to the constant expected consumption line at point A, and below all other points on that line, as shown.

A person is **risk neutral** if he is indifferent between all bundles with the same level of expected consumption.

Conceivably, some consumers may not care about risk one way or the other. As a result, they are indifferent between all bundles with the same level of expected consumption. In comparing two risky bundles, they simply select the one with the highest level of expected consumption. The indifference curves of these **risk neutral** consumers therefore coincide with the constant expected consumption lines.

Application 11.2

Betting on Sports

Though sports betting is illegal in 48 states, it is widespread. According to some estimates, Americans may have wagered as much as $380 billion on sporting events in 1999.[4] This figure is expected to rise with the explosive growth of Internet gambling.

Why is sports betting so popular? Evidence shows that most people are risk averse: for example, they buy insurance. Two risk-averse individuals will never bet against each other if they agree on the probabilities of the outcomes. Being risk averse, neither will bet unless he thinks the wager yields a positive expected payoff. But since their payoffs always add up to zero (one wins what the other loses), any wager that has a positive expected payoff for one person has a negative expected payoff for the other.

In contrast, if two risk-averse people disagree about the probabilities of the outcomes, they may want to bet against each other. Let's say Germany is playing Brazil for the world soccer championship. Helga and Luiz disagree about Germany's likelihood of winning; Helga thinks it's 70 percent, while Luiz thinks it's 30 percent. What if they bet $100 on the outcome, with Helga taking Germany and Luiz taking Brazil? From Helga's perspective, her expected payoff is $40 (since

[4]This estimate appears in the *1999 Final Report of the National Gambling Impact Study Commission*. Of course, since most gambling is unreported, the true figure is unknown. Other estimates place total sports betting as low as $80 billion—still a hefty sum.

0.7 × 100 − 0.3 × 100 = 40). From Luiz's perspective, his expected payoff is also $40. Both think they're getting a positive expected payoff.

Is this a good explanation for sports betting? Not necessarily. It begs the question of *why* Helga and Luiz disagree about the likely outcome. Certainly, they could come to different objective conclusions if they had different information. However, two rational, risk-averse people should never be willing to wager with each other for that reason alone.

To see why, let's change the example. Suppose Helga and Luiz agree that Germany has a 30 percent chance of beating Brazil. The day after the game, Helga picks up the sports section of the newspaper while having coffee with Luiz and reads that, despite the odds, Germany has won. Assuming that Luiz hasn't yet heard the result, they now have different beliefs that reflect different information. Even so, Luiz should refuse to take any gamble that Helga proposes. Suppose she says, "I'll bet you $100 that Germany beat Brazil yesterday." Her willingness to make this bet after reading the paper should convince Luiz that Germany did indeed win. By proposing the gamble, Helga effectively reveals her information, thereby eliminating the difference in beliefs that might have sustained a wager.

Even after considering what they might learn from the other's willingness to make the bet, Helga and Luiz could both think they're getting a better-than-fair deal if they start out with different **subjective** beliefs. Maybe Helga has a gut feeling that Germany will win, or Luiz is feeling lucky. In other words, differences in feelings—unlike differences in hard information—could explain sports betting.[5]

Of course, many people also gamble for entertainment. For example, some think that placing a bet heightens the excitement they feel when watching a game. But while that is certainly part of the explanation, it isn't the whole story. People also place bets on the outcomes of games they don't watch, and many regular gamblers are convinced they can consistently pick winners.

Expected Utility

In Chapter 4 we learned that it's possible to represent a consumer's indifference curves with a utility function, which assigns a numerical index of well-being to each consumption bundle. In Maria's case, a consumption bundle consists of the amount of food she eats if it's sunny, F_S, and the amount of food she eats if there's a hurricane, F_H. Thus, we can represent her indifference curves, like the ones in Figure 11.4(a) or (b), with a utility function of the form $U(F_S, F_H)$.

When we write a utility function like $U(F_S, F_H)$, we are allowing for a very wide range of possibilities. That flexibility may make it difficult to determine consumers' preferences by observing their choices. To narrow down the range of possibilities, economists usually make some additional assumptions.

Expected Utility Functions Let's assume that the benefit Maria derives from food depends only on the amount she eats, and not on the weather. The function $W(F)$ will tell us the size of that benefit. When it's sunny, Maria eats F_S kilograms and receives a benefit of $W(F_S)$. When there's a hurricane, she eats F_H kilograms and receives a benefit of $W(F_H)$. It is then natural to assume that Maria's utility is simply her expected benefit:

$$U(F_S, F_H) = \Pi \times W(F_S) + (1 - \Pi) \times W(F_H) \quad \textbf{(4)}$$

(Recall that Π is the probability of sun and 1 − Π is the probability of a hurricane.)

Formula (4) is an example of an **expected utility function.**[6] It assigns a benefit level to each possible state of nature based only on what is consumed, and then takes the

An **expected utility function** assigns a benefit level to each possible state of nature based only on what is consumed, and then takes the expected value of those benefits.

[5]Another possibility is that each thinks the other may not understand the implications of the information they possess.

[6]More than 60 years ago, a mathematician named John von Neumann and an economist named Oskar Morgenstern proved an important theorem concerning expected utility: as long as someone's choices satisfy a few simple assumptions (also known as the von Neumann-Morgenstern *axioms*), they will behave as if they maximize an expected utility function when making choices involving risk. Many economists think von Neumann and Morgenstern's assumptions are reasonable; others disagree. We describe some alternatives in Section 13.4.

expected value of those benefits. In other words, it's a weighted average of all the possible benefit levels, using the probability of each benefit level as its weight.

What if Maria's enjoyment of food depends on the weather? For example, what if she tends to have a larger appetite when it's sunny (perhaps because she gets more exercise)? In that case, we may not be able to represent her indifference curves with an expected utility function like formula (4). Most (but certainly not all) economists nevertheless think that the assumptions behind expected utility functions are reasonably accurate in most circumstances.

WORKED-OUT PROBLEM 11.2

The Problem Suppose we can represent Maria's preferences with an expected utility function, and that $W(F) = \sqrt{F}$. Suppose also that the probability of sun is 2/3, and the probability of a hurricane is 1/3. Plot the indifference curve that runs through the point $(F_S, F_H) = (400, 400)$. Plot the constant expected consumption line that runs through this same point. Is Maria risk averse, risk loving, or risk neutral?

The Solution Maria's expected utility function is

$$U(F_S, F_H) = \frac{2}{3}\sqrt{F_S} + \frac{1}{3}\sqrt{F_H}$$

Using this formula, we see that $U(400, 400) = 20$. So points on the indifference curve through the point $(F_S, F_H) = (400, 400)$ satisfy the formula $\frac{2}{3}\sqrt{F_S} + \frac{1}{3}\sqrt{F_H} = 20$. After multiplying through by 3, subtracting $2\sqrt{F_S}$ from both sides, and squaring, we can rewrite this formula as:

$$F_H = (60 - 2\sqrt{F_S})^2$$

We've plotted this indifference curve in Figure 11.9 by plugging in several numerical values: for $F_S = 300$ we have $F_H = 643$; for $F_S = 350$ we have $F_H = 510$; for $F_S = 400$ we have $F_H = 400$; for $F_S = 450$ we have $F_H = 309$; and for $F_S = 500$ we have $F_H = 233$.

Points on the constant expected consumption line that runs through the point $(F_S, F_H) = (400, 400)$ satisfy the formula $\frac{2}{3}F_S + \frac{1}{3}F_H = 400$, which we can rewrite as $F_H = 1{,}200 - 2F_S$. We've also plotted that line in Figure 11.9. Notice that the indifference curve lies tangent to the constant expected consumption line at the point $(F_S, F_H) = (400, 400)$, and above all other points on that line. Maria is therefore risk averse.

IN-TEXT EXERCISE 11.2 **Repeat the calculation in worked-out problem 11.2, but assume that $W(F) = F^2$.**

Expected Utility and Risk Aversion Assuming that it's possible to represent Maria's preferences with an expected utility function, we can determine her attitude toward risk from the shape of her benefit function, $W(F)$. If $W(F)$ is concave (that is, if it flattens as F increases), she's risk averse; if it's convex (that is, if it steepens as F increases), she's risk loving; and if it's linear (that is, a straight line), she's risk neutral.

Let's examine the case where the benefit function $W(F)$ is concave. Look at Figure 11.10, in which we've graphed the benefit function from worked-out problem 11.2,

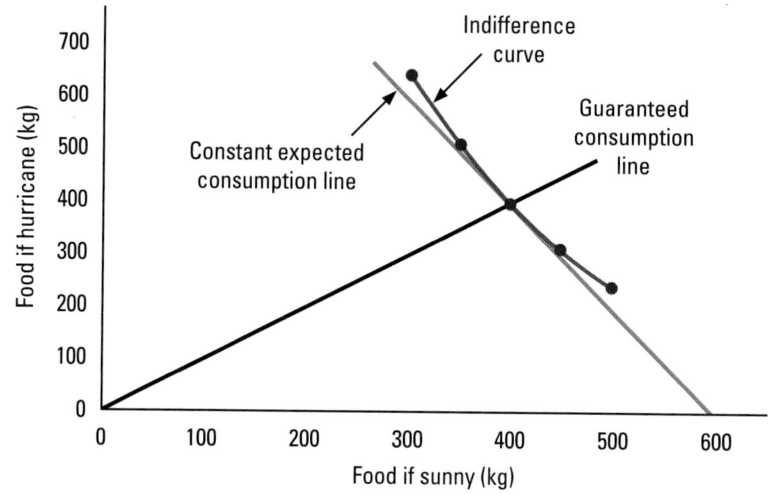

Figure 11.9
Solution to Worked-Out Problem 11.2. Maria's indifference curve is shown in red. The constant expected consumption line is shown in green. Since her indifference curve lies tangent to the constant expected consumption line where it crosses the guaranteed consumption line, and above the constant expected consumption line at all other points, Maria is risk averse.

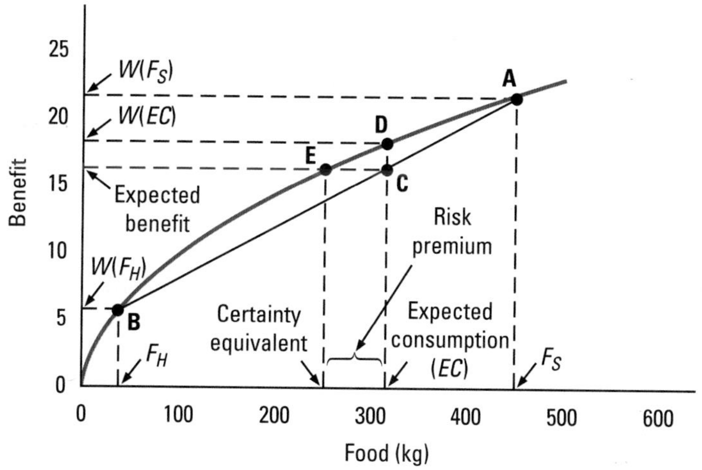

Figure 11.10
Expected Utility for a Risk-Averse Consumer. If Maria's benefit function is concave, she is risk averse. Consider a consumption bundle consisting of F_S kg of food if it's sunny, yielding a benefit of $W(F_S)$, and F_H kg of food if there's a hurricane, yielding a benefit of $W(F_H)$. The coordinates of point C, which lies on the straight line between points A and B, correspond to expected consumption and expected benefit. Since the concave benefit function bows upward, a riskless bundle with the same level of expected consumption yields a larger benefit (point D). Therefore, Maria prefers it to the risky bundle.

$W(F) = \sqrt{F}$. This is a typical concave function; as F increases, it becomes flatter. As we have already seen in worked-out problem 11.2, this benefit function implies risk aversion. Figure 11.10 shows that this is a consequence of the function's concavity.

Let's consider a consumption bundle consisting of F_S kg of food if it's sunny and F_H kg of food if there's a hurricane. In the event of sun, Maria's benefit is $W(F_S)$, shown as point A in Figure 11.10. In the event of a hurricane, her benefit is $W(F_H)$, shown as point B in the figure. Now consider point C. Its horizontal coordinate is the level of expected consumption, and its vertical coordinate is the expected benefit. By definition, the coordinates of point C are weighted averages of the coordinates of points A and B, where the probabilities of sun and hurricane are used as the weights. Therefore, point C must lie on the straight line that connects points A and B, as shown.

Now let's consider a second consumption bundle with the same level of expected consumption, but no risk. The benefit that Maria receives from this bundle is the vertical coordinate of point D. Point D has the same horizontal coordinate as point C. However, since the concave function $W(F)$ bows upward between points A and B, point D's vertical coordinate is larger than point C's. Maria is therefore risk averse: she prefers the safe bundle, which provides a benefit equal to point D's vertical coordinate, to the risky one, which provides an expected benefit equal to point C's vertical coordinate.

Let's check this conclusion numerically. In the figure, $F_S = 441$, $F_H = 36$, $\Pi = 2/3$, and $W(F) = \sqrt{F}$. You can verify that $W(F_S) = 21$, $W(F_H) = 6$. Expected consumption (EC) is 306, and Maria's expected benefit is 16. For a riskless bundle providing 306 kg of food in both states of nature, her benefit is approximately 17.5. Since 17.5 exceeds 16, Maria prefers the riskless bundle.

Concavity of the benefit function is linked to the idea that scarcity makes a commodity more valuable. For instance, the marginal benefit of extra food in Figure 11.10 (equivalently, the slope of the benefit function) is greater at a low level of consumption like F_H than at a high level of consumption like F_S. That is precisely why Maria is risk averse. Starting with a risky consumption bundle, she is willing to give up some food in a state of nature where food has low incremental value because it's plentiful, for extra food in a state of nature where food has high incremental value because it's scarce.

Now let's consider the case where the benefit function $W(F)$ is convex. We can evaluate a risky bundle using a diagram similar to Figure 11.10. With a convex benefit function, the red curve would bow downward rather than upward. As a result, point D would be lower than point C, rather than higher. (Check your understanding by drawing the figure.) This configuration implies a preference for the risky bundle over a riskless one with the same level of expected consumption. In other words, the consumer is risk loving. You have already seen an example of this principle: the consumer from in-text exercise 11.2 is risk loving because the benefit function $W(F) = F^2$ is convex (check this by graphing the function).

What if the benefit function $W(F)$ is linear? Once again, we can evaluate a risky bundle using a diagram similar to Figure 11.10. With a linear benefit function, the red curve would be a straight line. As a result, point D would be the same as point C. (Check your understanding by drawing the figure.) This configuration implies indifference between the risky bundle and a riskless one with the same level of expected consumption. In other words, the consumer is risk neutral.

Certainty Equivalents, Risk Premia, and Degrees of Risk Aversion Figure 11.10 illustrates another way to find the certainty equivalent and risk premium for a risky consumption bundle. The horizontal line between point C and the vertical axis intersects the function $W(F)$ at point E. The horizontal coordinate of point E is the certainty equivalent of the risky bundle. Why? If Maria consumes that amount of food with certainty, her benefit will be the same as her expected benefit from the risky bundle. As shown in the figure, Maria's risk premium, which we defined previously as the difference between expected consumption and the certainty equivalent, corresponds to the horizontal gap between points C and E. Returning to our numerical example, we see that Maria's certainty equivalent, CE, solves the formula $W(CE) = 16$. This implies that $CE = 16^2 = 256$ kg. Since expected consumption is 306 kg, Maria's risk premium is 50 kg.

How does the shape of the benefit function $W(F)$ relate to the degree of risk aversion? Since concavity implies risk aversion, you won't be surprised to learn that the greater the concavity, the greater the risk aversion. To see why, look at Figure 11.11, which analyzes

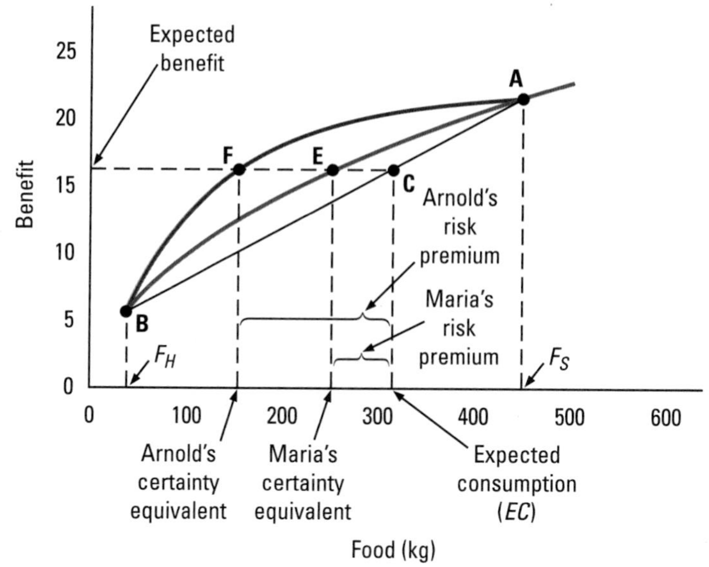

Figure 11.11

Expected Utility and the Degree of Risk Aversion. The red benefit function is for Maria, and the blue benefit function is for Arnold. The blue curve is more bowed than the red curve; it's more concave. Maria's certainty equivalent is the horizontal coordinate of point E and Arnold's is the horizontal coordinate of point F. Maria's risk premium is the horizontal gap between points C and E; Arnold's is the horizontal gap between points C and F. Since Arnold's certainty equivalent is smaller and his risk premium larger than Maria's, he is more risk averse.

the same risky bundle as Figure 11.10. We've reproduced a number of elements from Figure 11.10, including Maria's benefit function (in red), certainty equivalent, and risk premium. The preferences of a second consumer, Arnold, correspond to the blue benefit function. Notice that the blue curve is more bowed than the red curve; it's more concave. Using the same logic as before, we see that Arnold's certainty equivalent is the horizontal coordinate of point F, and his risk premium is the horizontal gap between points C and F. Since Arnold's certainty equivalent is smaller and his risk premium larger than Maria's, he is more risk averse.

11.3 INSURANCE

Much of life is inherently risky. While we can take some measures to improve the odds of staying safe, secure, and healthy, many events are outside our control. To protect ourselves against the financial consequences of these risks, we sometimes purchase insurance.

An **insurance policy** is a contract that reduces the financial loss associated with some risky event, like a burglary, an accident, an illness or death.

The Nature of Insurance

People address a wide range of risks by purchasing **insurance policies**. An insurance policy is a contract that reduces the financial loss associated with some risky event, like a burglary, an accident, an illness, or death. The simplest type of insurance policy specifies a **premium**, which is the amount of money the policyholder pays for the policy, and a **benefit**, which is the amount the policyholder receives if a specific loss occurs.

An insurance **premium** is the amount of money the policyholder pays for the insurance policy.

An insurance **benefit** is the amount of money a policyholder receives if a specific loss occurs.

The purchaser of an insurance policy is essentially placing a bet. Let's use the symbol M to stand for the size of the premium, and the symbol B to stand for the size of the promised benefit. Having paid M, the policyholder receives B if a loss occurs, for a net gain of

$B - M$. If a loss doesn't occur, he loses the premium, M. Since the policy pays off only when a loss occurs, in a sense the consumer is betting that the loss will happen.

An insurance policy is **actuarially fair** if it's expected net payoff is zero.

When the expected net payoff from an insurance policy is zero, we say that it's **actuarially fair**. Sometimes we simply call it *fair insurance*. Purchasing an actuarially fair insurance policy does not change the purchaser's expected consumption; it simply raises consumption in some states of nature and reduces it in others. Let's use the Greek symbol Π to stand for the probability of avoiding a loss, in which case the probability of sustaining a loss is $1 - \Pi$. Actuarial fairness requires that

$$\Pi \times (-M) + (1 - \Pi) \times (B - M) = 0$$

which implies that $M = B(1 - \Pi)$. That is, an actuarially fair insurance premium equals the promised benefit times the probability of a loss.

Insurance policies are usually less than actuarially fair. That is, the premium typically exceeds the promised benefit times the probability of a loss ($M > B(1 - \Pi)$). This is because insurance companies must come out ahead to cover their costs of operation. On average, then, policyholders lose money; purchasing an actuarially unfair policy reduces the purchaser's expected consumption.

The Demand for Insurance

Considered in isolation, the typical insurance policy seems unattractive. Its payoff is uncertain, and it reduces expected consumption. Risk-averse consumers are nevertheless willing to make actuarially unfair bets by purchasing insurance because an insurance policy cancels out other risks.

To illustrate, let's suppose Maria earns \$500 and would like to spend as much as possible on food, which costs \$1 per kilogram. As before, the weather is uncertain; the probability of sun (Π) is two-thirds, and the probability of a hurricane ($1 - \Pi$) is one-third. If it's sunny, Maria spends all \$500 on food. If there's a hurricane, she sustains a loss of \$300 due to property damage from flooding, and can spend only \$200 on food. Thus, she starts out with the risky consumption bundle labeled A in Figure 11.12. She can protect herself from this serious risk by purchasing flood insurance (which pays off in the event of a hurricane). Let's see how the process works.

The Demand for Fair Insurance In Figure 11.12, we've drawn the constant expected consumption line through point A, and labeled it L. (From formula (3), we know that the slope of L is $-\Pi/(1 - \Pi) = -2$.) Since a fair insurance policy doesn't change Maria's expected consumption, it moves her from point A to some other bundle on L.

We've marked the point where L crosses the guaranteed consumption line as point B. To reach point B, Maria can purchase an insurance policy with a benefit level of \$300 for a premium of \$100.[7] In that case, the promised benefit equals the potential loss, giving Maria **full insurance**. With full insurance, consumption is the same regardless of whether a loss occurs. Here, Maria spends \$400 on food—the amount she has left after paying her insurance premium—regardless of the weather.

With **full insurance**, the promised benefit equals the potential loss.

To reach any other point on the solid line connecting points A and B, Maria can buy an insurance policy with a benefit that's smaller than her potential loss. For example, she might pay \$50 for a policy that promises a \$150 benefit, obtaining the midpoint between

[7] We've seen that $M = B(1 - \Pi)$ with actuarially fair insurance. Here, $B = \$300$ and $\Pi = 2/3$, so the actuarially fair insurance premium is $\$300 \times (1 - 2/3) = \$100$.

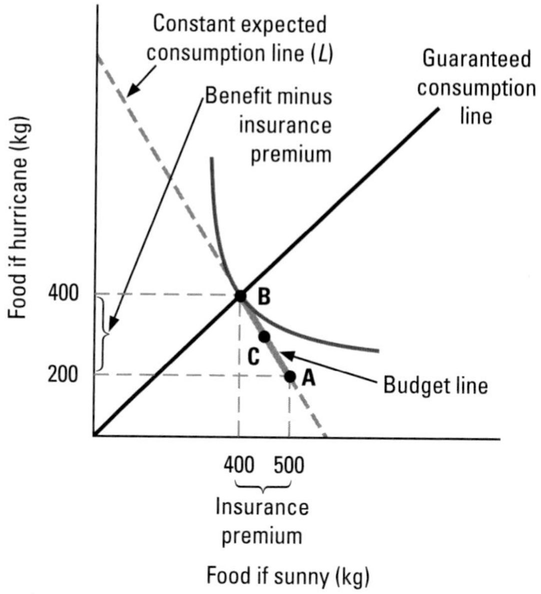

Figure 11.12
The Demand for Fair Insurance. Maria starts out with a risky consumption bundle, at point A. By purchasing actuarially fair insurance, she can reach any point on the solid green line segment connecting points A and B. If she's risk averse, she'll choose point B, representing full insurance.

A and B, marked as C in the figure. Because the promised benefit is less than the potential loss, this type of policy is called **partial insurance**. With partial insurance, Maria's consumption still depends on the weather, but it varies less. At point C, she consumes 450 kg of food if it's sunny (spending her \$500 income minus the \$50 insurance premium) and 300 kg when there's a hurricane (spending her \$500 income minus the \$50 premium, minus the \$300 loss, plus the \$150 benefit).

With **partial insurance**, the promised benefit is less than the potential loss.

Maria cannot obtain any point on L to the left of point B or the right of point A. Points to the left of point B would require an insurance contract that promises benefits in excess of losses. Generally, insurance policies cover policyholders only up to the amount of the actual loss; we'll discuss some reasons for this rule in Chapter 21. Points to the right of point A would require Maria to pay the insurance company in the event of a flood, which is contrary to the definition of flood insurance.

Through fair insurance, Maria can therefore obtain any risky bundle on the solid green line connecting points A and B. Consequently, that is her budget line.

If Maria is risk averse, she will purchase full insurance. To understand why, remember that for risk-averse consumers, points of tangency between indifference curves and constant expected consumption lines lie on the guaranteed consumption line (as in Figure 11.5). In Figure 11.12, we've drawn Maria's indifference curve through point B. Since point B is her most preferred point on L, it is certainly her best choice on the solid portion of L between points A and B.

Notice that this conclusion doesn't depend on the degree of Maria's risk aversion. Whether she's slightly or severely risk averse, point B is her best choice on the constant expected consumption line through point A, so she fully insures.

The Demand for Less-than-Fair Insurance What if insurance is less than actuarially fair? Let's suppose that the insurance company charges a premium of R dollars per dollar of coverage (in other words, $M = BR$), where $R > 1 - \Pi$. If Maria increases B by one dollar, her consumption falls by R dollars if it's sunny and rises by $1 - R$ dollars if there's a hurricane. Therefore, by purchasing insurance, Maria can obtain bundles on a straight line through her starting point, A, with a slope of $-(1 - R)/R$.

To illustrate, let's assume that Maria pays 50 cents for each dollar of promised benefit (that is, $R = 0.5$), rather than the actuarially fair price of 33 $^1/_3$ cents. Then $-(1 - R)/R = -1$. In Figure 11.13, we've drawn a straight green line with a slope of -1 between points A and D. That is Maria's budget line. To reach point D, she must fully insure by purchasing a policy with a benefit level of \$300. She pays a premium of \$150, or \$50 more than her premium for fair insurance. As a result, her food consumption is 50 kg lower, regardless of the state of nature (350 kg instead of 400 kg). To reach any consumption level between points A and D, she must partially insure. For example, she can achieve point E by spending \$100 to purchase a policy with a promised benefit of \$200.

With less-than-fair insurance, Maria definitely won't insure fully. Why not? The constant expected consumption line that runs through point D, shown as a broken green line in the figure, has a slope of -2, so it's steeper than the budget line. Because the indifference curve that runs through point D is tangent to this constant expected consumption line, it passes below the budget line to the right of point D. So Maria's best choice on that line must lie to the right of point D. Point E is the best choice. Maria partially insures by purchasing a policy with a benefit equal to two-thirds of her potential loss.

In contrast to fair insurance, the amount of less-than-fair insurance purchased *does* depend on the policyholder's degree of risk aversion. For example, a risk neutral consumer will buy no insurance. Why? His indifference curves coincide with the constant expected consumption lines in Figure 11.13. Point A is therefore his best choice. Even if the consumer is slightly risk averse, his indifference curves will still be steeper than the budget line (since they will bend only slightly as they move away from the guaranteed consumption line), so point A will remain the best choice.

Figure 11.13

The Demand for Unfair Insurance. Maria starts out with a risky consumption bundle, at point A. By purchasing actuarially unfair insurance, she can reach any point on the solid green line connecting points A and D. Her best choice, point E, lies to the right of point D, which means she partially insures.

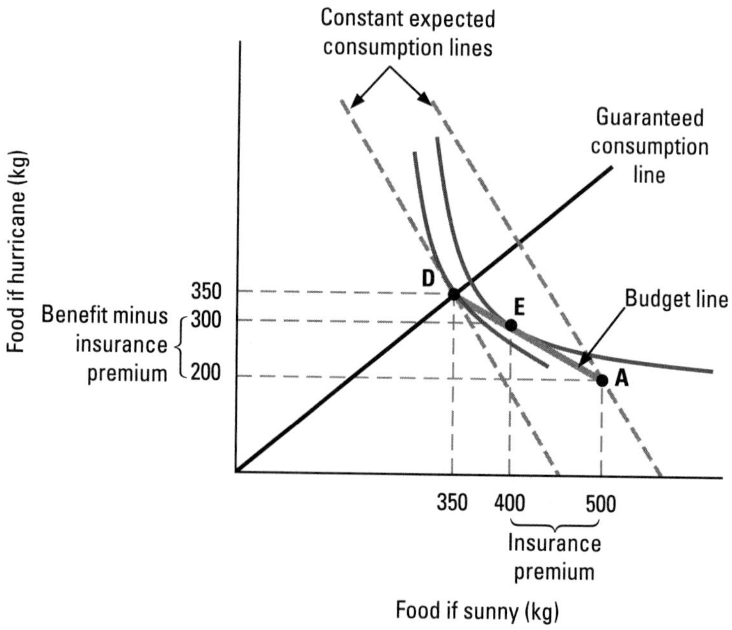

The Value of Insurance

Insurance makes people better off by protecting them from the consequences of a loss. One way to measure the benefits it offers is to compare certainty equivalents.

Let's start with fair insurance. Figure 11.14 reproduces points A and B from Figure 11.12, along with the budget line that runs between them. With fair insurance, Maria chooses point B. Since this bundle involves no risk, its certainty equivalent is the same as the amount consumed, 400 kg. Without insurance, Maria is stuck with point A. We've drawn the indifference curve that runs through point A and marked its intersection with the 45-degree line as point G. The certainty equivalent of point A is the horizontal (equivalently, vertical) coordinate of G, 300 kg. Fair insurance raises the certainty equivalent of Maria's best choice from 300 kg to 400 kg. The difference between these two numbers, 100 kg, is the net value of fair insurance, considering both the benefits and the premiums.

Now let's turn to less-than-fair insurance. Figure 11.14 also reproduces points A, D, and E from Figure 11.13, along with the budget line that runs between points A and D, and the indifference curve that runs through point E. We've marked the point where this indifference curve crosses the 45-degree line as point H. Maria chooses the risky bundle E by partially insuring. The certainty equivalent of point E is the horizontal (equivalently, vertical) coordinate of point H, 375 kg. As before, without insurance, Maria is stuck with point A, which has a certainty equivalent of 300 kg. Less-than-fair insurance raises the certainty equivalent of her best choice from 300 kg to 375 kg. The difference between these two numbers, 75 kg, is the net value of less-than-fair insurance. It isn't as great as the value of fair insurance, but it contributes significantly to Maria's well-being.

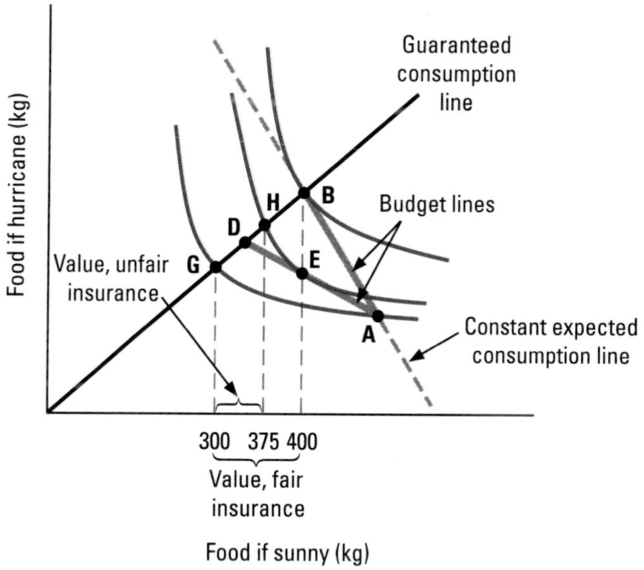

Figure 11.14

The Value of Insurance. Maria starts out with a risky consumption bundle at point A. The certainty equivalent of this risky bundle, given by the level of consumption at point G, is 300 kg. With actuarially fair insurance, Maria obtains point B, which has a certainty equivalent of 400 kg. The value of actuarially fair insurance is therefore 400 kg – 300 kg = 100 kg. With actuarially unfair insurance, Maria obtains point E. The certainty equivalent of this risky bundle, given by the level of consumption at point H, is 375 kg. The value of actuarially unfair insurance is therefore 375 kg – 300 kg = 75 kg.

Application 11.3

The Value of Life Annuities

None of us knows how long we'll live. This uncertainty is the source of significant financial risk. Most obviously, the unexpected death of a family's primary breadwinner can have major financial consequences. That is why people buy life insurance.

But uncertainty concerning the length of one's life also creates a second type of risk: the possibility that a person will outlive his resources. Imagine for the moment that you're 65 years old and newly retired. How well can you afford to live? The answer depends on how long you'll end up living. If you expect to live a long time, you'll have to watch your spending to make sure you won't run out of money. Even then you may find yourself in trouble. For example, you might plan your spending at age 65 on the assumption that you'll probably die by age 90. But what if you live to 95? Will you have enough money to get by in those final years? Alternatively, you could be extremely conservative and plan your spending at age 65 on the assumption that you'll live forever. But you probably won't get to spend a large chunk of your wealth in that case.

To address the risk of living "too long," people can purchase an insurance policy called a *life annuity*. The policyholder pays a premium (either in a lump sum or in installments), and in return receives a constant income for the rest of his life starting at some specified age. If he dies quickly, his premium exceeds the present value of the benefits received. But if he lives to a ripe old age, the present value of the benefits received exceeds his premium. So in effect, he is betting on living a long life. (With life insurance, he is betting on dying quickly.)

Life annuities make planning easier. A new retiree can lock in a living standard without worrying about outliving his resources. And he can achieve a higher living standard than if he conservatively planned his spending based on the assumption that he'll live forever.

How valuable is this form of insurance? According to economists Olivia Mitchell, James Poterba, Mark Warshawsky, and Jeffrey Brown, people who behave according to the Life Cycle Hypothesis (discussed in Section 10.2) would give up 30 to 38 percent of their wealth at age 65 in exchange for the ability to purchase actuarially fair life annuities![8]

Most of us end up relying heavily on life annuities, because Social Security and many private pension plans provide benefits in that form. However, relatively few people buy life annuities directly. In light of the enormous potential value of these policies, their lack of popularity is something of a puzzle. A number of explanations have been proposed. First, annuities aren't actuarially fair. Second, since Social Security and pensions partially insure people against living too long, additional insurance is less valuable than the figures in the previous paragraph would suggest. Third, since benefits are usually paid in nominal terms, the policyholder is exposed to inflation risk. Fourth, people may be reluctant to lock up their funds in annuities. Once money is invested in an annuity, it becomes unavailable to heirs (since income is received only while the investor lives), and the investor usually can't withdraw funds to cover unplanned expenses like uninsured nursing home care. Consequently, the demand for annuities may be low among those who want to leave bequests, or who are concerned about large uninsured expenses.

Mitchell and her coauthors found that the first two explanations are reasonably important, but fail to tell the whole story. Because annuity premiums are actuarially unfair, the typical person can expect to receive 15 to 20 percent less in benefits than he pays in premiums. However, that gap would have to be significantly larger (23 to 31 percent) to offset the advantages of annuity insurance, even taking Social Security and pensions into account. Mitchell et al. also conclude that the third consideration—inflation risk—is of little importance. Other evidence suggests that the fourth explanation plays a more central role.[9]

---

[8] Olivia S. Mitchell, James M. Poterba, Mark J. Washawsky, and Jeffrey R. Brown, "New Evidence on the Money's Worth of Individual Annuities," *American Economic Review* 89, December 1999, pp. 1299–1318.

[9] See B. Douglas Bernheim, "How Strong Are Bequest Motives? Evidence Based on the Demand for Life Insurance and Annuities," *Journal of Political Economy* 99, no. 5, October 1991, pp. 899–927.

WORKED-OUT PROBLEM 11.3

The Problem The probability of sun is two-thirds, and the probability of a hurricane is one-third. Maria's indifference curves are given by the following formula:[10]

$$F_H F_S^2 = C$$

where F_S is the amount of food she consumes if it's sunny, F_H is the amount of food she consumes when there's a hurricane, and C is a constant (the value of which differs from one indifference curve to another). For indifference curves in this family, the marginal rate of substitution for food if it's sunny with food if there's a hurricane is:

$$MRS_{SH} = 2\frac{F_H}{F_S}$$

Without insurance, Maria can spend \$400 if it's sunny but only \$75 if there's a hurricane (due to property losses from flooding). Food costs one dollar per kilogram. She can purchase flood insurance for a premium of 40 cents for each dollar of promised benefit. How much insurance will she purchase? What will she pay for it? What is its value?

The Solution Maria's available choices lie on a budget line like the one connecting points A and D in Figure 11.14. In this case, $R = 0.4$, so the slope of the budget line, $-(1 - R)/R$, is -1.5. The formula for the budget line is therefore $F_H = C - 1.5F_S$, where C is a constant. Since the budget line must pass through Maria's starting point, $(F_S, F_H) = (400, 75)$, we know that $75 = C - 1.5 \times 400$, so $C = 675$.

Maria's best choice is a point of tangency between the budget line and an indifference curve, like point E in Figure 11.14. At any such point, the slope of the budget line is the same as the slope of her indifference curve. Thus,

$$-1.5 = -MRS_{SH} = -2\frac{F_H}{F_S}$$

From this formula, we can conclude that at any point of tangency, $F_H = 0.75F_S$.

We know that Maria's best choice satisfies both $F_H = 675 - 1.5F_S$ (it's on the budget line) and $F_H = 0.75F_S$ (it's a point of tangency), so we can solve for it algebraically. Substituting the second expression into the first, we get $0.75F_S = 675 - 1.5F_S$, so $F_S = 675/2.25 = 300$. In other words, she consumes 300 kg of food if it's sunny, at a cost of \$300. Since Maria starts with \$400 if it's sunny, she must spend \$100 on insurance. That means her insurance benefit must be \$250 (since $0.4 \times 250 = 100$). If there's a hurricane, she consumes $F_H = 75 + 250 - 100 = 225$ kg of food.

After purchasing insurance, Maria's risky bundle is $(F_S, F_H) = (300, 225)$. Points on the indifference curve that runs through this bundle satisfy the formula $F_H F_S^2 = 225 \times 300^2 = 20{,}250{,}000$. To find a riskless bundle on this indifference curve (one for which F_S and F_H have the same value), we solve the formula $F^3 = 20{,}250{,}000$. The solution is $F = 272.6$. This is the certainty equivalent of Maria's risky bundle after purchasing insurance.

[10] These are Maria's indifference curves when her preferences correspond to an expected utility function of the form $\frac{2}{3}\log(F_S) + \frac{1}{3}\log(F_H)$ [that is, $W(F) = \log(F)$].

Maria's initial bundle is $(F_S, F_H) = (400, 75)$. Points on the indifference curve that runs through this bundle satisfy the formula $F_H F_S^2 = 75 \times 400^2 = 12{,}000{,}000$. To find a riskless bundle on this indifference curve, we solve the formula $F^3 = 12{,}000{,}000$. The solution is $F = 228.9$. This is the certainty equivalent of Maria's initial risky bundle. Since $272.6 - 228.9 = 43.7$, the value of insurance is \$43.70.

IN-TEXT EXERCISE 11.3 **Repeat worked-out problem 11.2 assuming that flood insurance costs 50 cents for each dollar of promised benefit. Repeat it again assuming that flood insurance costs \$8/11 for each dollar of promised benefit. What happens if the premium is higher than that amount?**

11.4 OTHER METHODS OF MANAGING RISK

People often take risks voluntarily. For example, they invest in the stock market, start new businesses, take jobs in start-up companies, and try out new products. Companies invest in research and development, build new factories despite uncertain demand, and bring new, untried products to market. In these cases, the expected reward is high enough to justify risk-taking.

The object of **risk management** is to make risky activities more attractive by taking steps to moderate the potential losses while preserving much of the potential gains.

Often, we can make risky activities more attractive by taking steps to moderate potential losses while preserving much of our potential gains. Such steps are known as **risk management**. As we've seen, one way to manage risks is to purchase insurance. When a company builds a factory, for example, managers buy insurance to guard against losses due to fire, theft, lawsuits, and other unforseen events. In this section, we'll investigate four other strategies for managing risk: risk sharing, hedging, diversification, and information acquisition. We'll see how each of these strategies influences the demand for risky assets. To learn more about the demand for risky assets, read Add-On 11A.

Risk Sharing

Risk sharing involves dividing a risky prospect among several people.

One way to make a risky prospect more attractive is to divide it among several people, a strategy known as **risk sharing**. A simple example will illustrate.

Suppose Maria earns \$600 regardless of the weather, which she's free to spend on food. In other words, she starts out at point A in Figure 11.15 (we'll continue to assume that one kg of food costs \$1). Suppose she's offered the opportunity to acquire a sunscreen concession at the local beach for an investment of \$300. If it's sunny, she makes \$600 (net of her investment), which means she can spend \$1,200 on food (her earnings, \$600, plus her net profit, \$600). If there's a hurricane, she sells nothing and loses her investment. In that case, she can spend only \$300 on food (her earnings, \$600, minus her investment, \$300). So if Maria makes the investment, she obtains the risky consumption bundle labeled B in the figure.

If the probability of sun is two-thirds, this investment has an expected payoff of \$300 (Maria comes out ahead by \$600 with a probability of two-thirds, and behind by \$300 with a probability of one-third). Since this expected return is positive, point B lies above the constant expected consumption line that runs through point A, shown as the broken green line in Figure 11.15. So while the investment would expose Maria to risk, it would also provide her with a higher level of expected consumption.

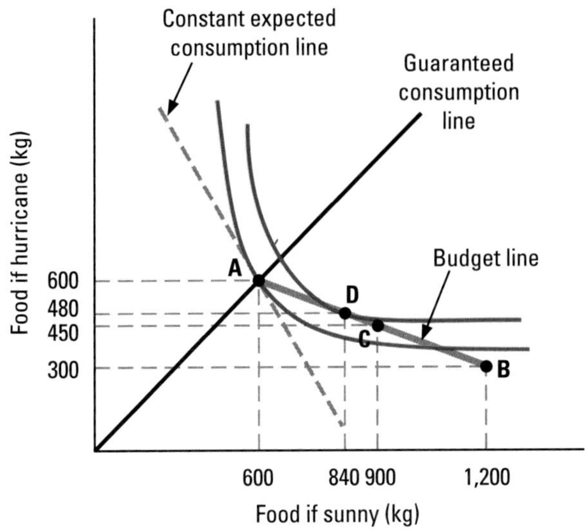

Figure 11.15

Risk Sharing. Maria starts out with a riskless consumption bundle at point A. By making an investment, she can swap bundle A for bundle B, which provides higher expected consumption. Given her preferences, however, she prefers bundle A. If she can find partners to split the investment and the profits, she can reach points on the solid green line. In that case, she would want to take a share. Point D would be her best choice.

Even so, Maria does not want to make the investment. As her indifference curves show, she prefers bundle A to bundle B. The higher expected consumption offered at point B is simply not enough to offset the risk of having little to eat if there's a hurricane. In other words, the investment looks attractive from the perspective of expected profit, but it's just too big a risk for Maria to take on alone.

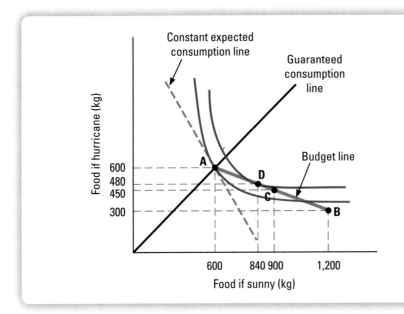

"I was spreading some risk around, and apparently it all wound up in your portfolio."

Now let's suppose Maria has a friend, Arnold, who has the same earnings and the same preferences. What if the two of them make the investment as equal partners? That is, each invests \$150 and receives \$300 in net profit if it's sunny. This strategy allows both Maria and Arnold to reach point C in Figure 11.15 (\$600 + \$300 = \$900 if it's sunny, and \$600 − \$150 = \$450 if there's a hurricane), which lies above the indifference curve that runs through point A. Both Maria and Arnold prefer point C to point A. Risk sharing allows both to benefit from an investment that neither would find attractive alone.

By taking on more partners, Maria can create more opportunities for risk sharing. With three equal partners, she would invest \$100 and receive \$200 in net profit if it's sunny; with four equal partners, she would invest \$75 and receive \$150 if it's sunny; and so forth. Maria could also take on unequal partners. For example, she could arrange a 60-40 split of the investment and net profits with Arnold.

An **equity share** is a proportional claim on the ownership of a company.

In practice, owners of companies often take on partners by issuing **equity shares**. An equity share is a proportional claim on the ownership of a company. As an example, suppose the sunscreen concession has issued 1,000 shares, each of which sells for 30 cents and gives its owner a claim on 1/1,000 of any profit earned. Maria could buy the entire concession by acquiring all 1,000 shares for \$300, which would place her at point B. Or she could buy half of the concession by acquiring 500 shares for \$150, which would put her at point C. In fact, by purchasing the appropriate number of shares, Maria could come very close to any point on the green line connecting points A and B in Figure 11.15. In effect, that line becomes Maria's budget line. Her best choice is point D where she spends \$120 on 400 shares to acquire 40 percent of the concession (leaving her with $\$600 + 0.4 \times \$600 = \$840$ if it's sunny and $\$600 - \$120 = \$480$ if there's a hurricane).

The logic of Figure 11.15 leads us to a remarkable conclusion. Even if Maria is extremely risk averse and the expected profit from the investment is very small, she will still want to invest *something* in it. Why? First, as long as Maria is risk averse, her indifference curve will lie tangent to the expected consumption line at point A. Increasing her risk aversion will only cause her indifference curve to bend more sharply at that point. Second, as long as the investment's expected profit is positive, Maria's budget line will extend above the expected consumption line through point A. Combining these two observations, we see that the budget line must always pass above the indifference curve, just as in the figure. A small enough investment therefore necessarily makes Maria better off.

Application 11.4

Insurance Coverage for Satellites

Every time someone reduces his exposure to financial risk by purchasing an insurance policy, someone else (usually an insurance company) accepts a new risk by selling the policy. Why is the insurance company willing to take on the policyholder's risk? As long as the policy is less-than-actuarially fair, the company comes out ahead on average.[11] If the risk is sufficiently small, the company may be willing to absorb all of it at terms that are only slightly worse than actuarially fair.

But what if the risk is extremely large? Take the case of commercial satellites. The costs of building and launching a single satellite regularly exceed \$250 million, and satellite owners have been known to seek more than \$400 million in coverage. Historically, roughly 1 out of every 10 satellites is either destroyed on launch or fails within a year of reaching orbit, so these ventures are extremely risky propositions for insurers. For example, estimates place satellite insurers' collective losses for 1998 at \$1.9 billion, against only \$860 million in premiums.

Not surprisingly, individual insurers are generally unwilling (and often simply unable) to accept responsibility for such catastrophic losses. Nevertheless, insurance for satellites is readily available, and the premiums do not appear to be wildly out of line with the expected benefits.[12] Insurance companies manage to provide satellite coverage at reasonably attractive rates by sharing risks. Even if a company is unwilling to take on a 10 percent risk of losing \$250 million for a premium of \$40 million, it might be perfectly content with 1/25 of that policy—that is, a 10 percent risk of losing \$10 million for a premium of \$1.6 million. If 25 companies will accept these terms, the satellite owner can piece together the desired coverage.

In practice, insurance companies often save satellite owners the trouble of making these arrangements. Sometimes they form syndicates to insure large-scale projects. Sometimes one company takes on a large policy and then sells interests in it to others through "reinsurance" agreements. These types of arrangements allow insurers to spread the risk more evenly through the industry, so that no single insurer faces the prospect of a catastrophic loss.

---

[11] The seller may also care less about absorbing the risk than the policyholder, for two reasons. First, by insuring many unrelated risks, the seller can benefit from diversification, discussed in the next section. Second, the seller may be less risk averse to begin with. Of course, sellers must also cover operating costs.

[12] Historically, 7 percent of launches fail. Between 1995 and 2002, average premiums for launch insurance ranged from 7 to 15 percent of the covered amount.

Hedging and Diversification

Another way to make risky activities more attractive is to combine them appropriately with other risky activities. We'll discuss two versions of this strategy, hedging and diversification.

First, we need to introduce the statistical concept of correlation. Two variables are **positively correlated** if they tend to move in the same direction. For example, the number of minutes of sunshine per day is positively correlated with average temperature. Two variables are **negatively correlated** if they tend to move in the opposite directions. The number of minutes of sunshine per day is negatively correlated with rainfall. Two variables are **uncorrelated** if their movements tend to be unrelated. The number of minutes of sunshine per day is uncorrelated with earthquake activity. Finally, two variables are **perfectly correlated** if one is simply a multiple of the other. The number of inches of rain and the number of millimeters of rain are perfectly correlated.

Two variables are **positively correlated** if they tend to move in the same direction. Two variables are **negatively correlated** if they tend to move in the opposite direction. Two variables are **uncorrelated** if their movements tend to be unrelated. Finally, two variables are **perfectly correlated** if one is simply a multiple of the other.

Hedging

Hedging refers to the practice of taking on two risky activities with negatively correlated financial payoffs. We'll illustrate this strategy by adding a new twist to the example we discussed in the last section.

Hedging is the practice of taking on two risky activities with negatively correlated financial payoffs.

As before, we'll assume Maria has the opportunity to buy the entire sunscreen concession, allowing her to reach point B in Figure 11.16. In addition, we'll assume that Maria can invest \$300 in a portable generator distributorship. In the event of a hurricane, the generator distributorship will turn a net profit of \$600. In the event of sun, Maria will lose her investment. Assuming as before that the probability of sun is two-thirds, the expected payoff from this investment is zero ($^1/_3 \times \$600 - {^2/_3} \times \$300 = \$0$). If Maria invests in the generator distributorship but not the sunscreen concession, she obtains point E in Figure 11.16.

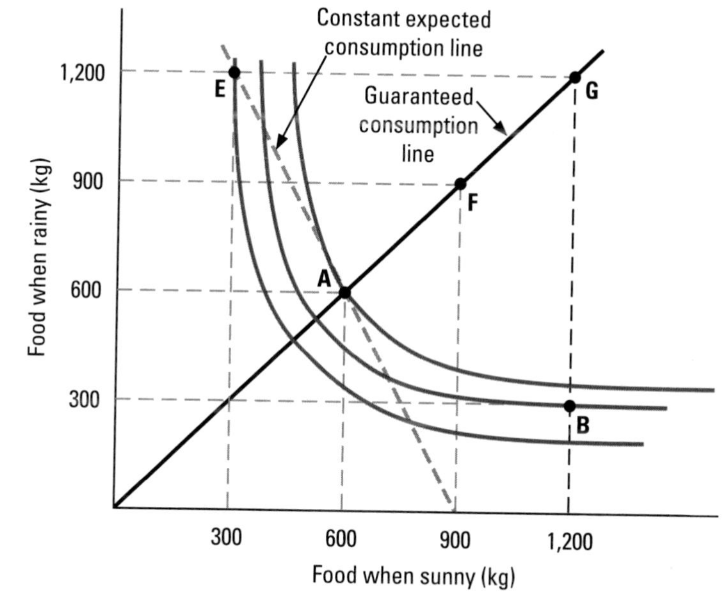

Figure 11.16
Hedging a Risky Venture. Maria starts out with a riskless consumption bundle at point A. By making an investment, she can swap point A for point B, which provides a higher level of expected consumption, or point A for point E, which provides the same level of expected consumption. Neither investment is attractive by itself. However, since each succeeds when the other fails, Maria can hedge her bets by making both investments. That strategy allows her to reach point F, which is better than point A. With perfect information concerning the weather, she could reach point G.

Taken individually, both these investments look unattractive to Maria (in Figure 11.16 points B and E lie on lower indifference curves than point A). Both investments are associated with substantial risk premiums. Being risk averse, Maria would certainly never consider the generator investment, which creates risk without offering her a higher expected level of consumption.

Yet what if Maria bought *both* concessions? Doing so would require an investment of \$600, but would *guarantee* an overall net profit of \$300 (\$600 from the successful project minus \$300 from the unsuccessful one). Regardless of the weather, Maria would be able to spend \$900 on food (the \$600 she earns plus \$300 in net profit). In other words, Maria would be able to reach point F in the figure, which is obviously better than point A. Taken together, these investments are *riskless*: When Maria combines them, their risk premiums disappear!

The critical feature of this example is that the profits from the two concessions are perfectly negatively correlated. Maria hedges her bet on the sunscreen concession by investing in the generator distributorship, and vice versa. That way, bad news on one investment is always more than offset by good news on the other, so that she comes out ahead.

Insurance is actually a form of hedging. That is, the benefit paid by a flood insurance policy is perfectly negatively correlated with a loss from flooding. If Maria buys flood insurance, she is hedging against the possibility of a flood.

Diversification is the practice of undertaking many risky activities, each on a small scale, rather than a few risky activities (or just one) on a large scale.

Diversification **Diversification** refers to the practice of undertaking many risky activities, each on a small scale, rather than a few risky activities (or just one) on a large scale. The simplest argument for diversification is the old adage that it's unwise to put all your eggs in one basket. Dividing them among many baskets reduces risk.

To illustrate, let's suppose that Maria wants to invest \$300. She is thinking about two start-up companies, Go for Broke, Inc., and Shoot the Moon, Inc. An investment in Go For Broke, Inc., triples in value with 50 percent probability and becomes worthless with 50 percent probability. The same is true of an investment in Shoot the Moon, Inc. However, the payoffs for these investments are uncorrelated.

One alternative is for Maria to invest all of her money (\$300) in a single company. The histogram in Figure 11.17(a) shows the probability distribution of her payoff. Her expected payoff is \$450 ($^1/_2 \times \$900 + ^1/_2 \times \$0 = \$450$), which exceeds her investment by \$150. However, the risk is considerable—there's a 50 percent chance that she'll lose everything. The standard deviation of her payoff is \$450 (the square root of the expected squared deviation, $^1/_2 \times 450^2 + ^1/_2 \times 450^2$).

Alternatively, Maria could diversify, investing half of her money (\$150) in each company. If both companies succeed, her payoff will be \$900. Since each company succeeds with 50 percent probability, the probability that both succeed at the same time is $^1/_2 \times ^1/_2 = ^1/_4$. If both companies fail, Maria's payoff will be zero. Since each company fails with 50 percent probability, the probability that both fail at the same time is $^1/_2 \times ^1/_2 = ^1/_4$. If one company succeeds and the other fails, Maria's payoff will be \$450, an outcome that occurs with a probability of $^1/_2$. (The probability that Go for Broke succeeds while Shoot the Moon fails is $^1/_4$, as is the probability that Shoot the Moon succeeds while Go for Broke fails.) Maria's overall expected payoff is still \$450 ($^1/_4 \times \$900 + ^1/_2 \times \$450 + ^1/_4 \times \$0 = \$450$), but the standard deviation is lower, \$318 (the square root of $^1/_4 \times 450^2 + ^1/_4 \times 450^2$).

The histogram in Figure 11.17(b) shows this information graphically. Compared with Figure 11.17(a), the payoff is less variable. Investing in two companies instead of one

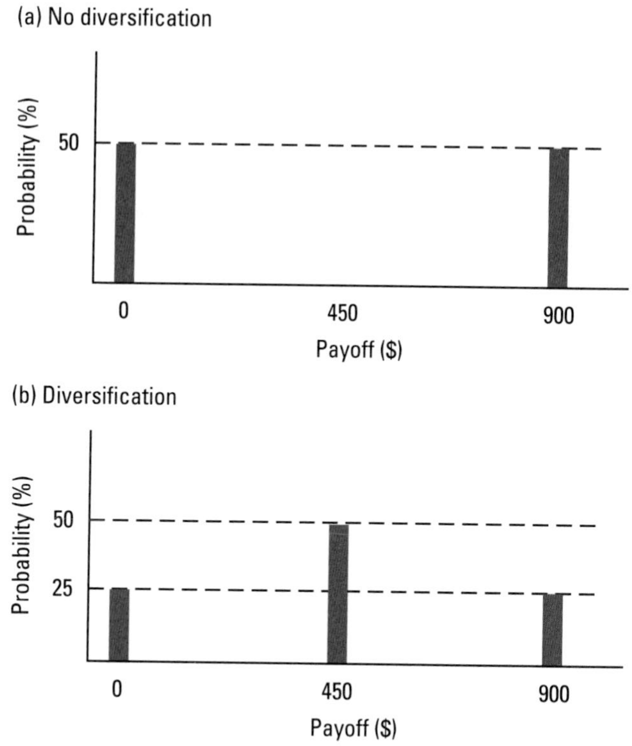

Figure 11.17

Diversification of Risk. If Maria invests $300 in Go for Broke, Inc., her payoff will be $900 with 50 percent probability, and $0 with 50 percent probability, as shown in figure (a). If she diversifies by investing $150 in Go for Broke, Inc., and $150 in Shoot the Moon, Inc., she shifts probability to an intermediate payoff ($450), reducing variability without changing her expected payoff, as shown in figure (b).

moves half the bar at $0 to $450, and half the bar at $900 to $450. Extreme outcomes become less likely, and a moderate outcome becomes more likely. So diversification reduces risk without changing the expected payoff.

In this example, the payoffs from the two investments are uncorrelated. What if they were perfectly positively correlated? In that case, Shoot the Moon would succeed when Go for Broke succeeds and fail when Go for Broke fails. Investing $150 in each company would then be equivalent to investing $300 in one of the companies. With perfect positive correlation, there's no benefit to diversification.

What if the payoffs from the two investments were perfectly negatively correlated? In that case, Shoot the Moon would succeed when Go for Broke fails and fail when Go for Broke succeeds. By investing in both companies, Maria would perfectly hedge her bets. The risks would cancel out, delivering a payoff of $450 with certainty.

Comparing these three cases (no correlation, perfect positive correlation, and perfect negative correlation), we see that as the correlation between the payoffs increases, the risk-reducing effect of diversification decreases. Intuitively, diversification reduces risk because a gain sometimes offsets a loss, leading to an intermediate outcome. When the correlation is lower, offsetting outcomes are more likely, so diversification is more valuable. Hedging is simply a case in which diversification is particularly effective at reducing risk because the payoffs from the hedged activities are negatively correlated, so that gains usually offset losses.

This discussion underscores the point that it's dangerous to evaluate risky activities in isolation. The desirability of undertaking a risky project depends on *other* actual and potential risks, including opportunities for hedging and diversification. One of the most important functions of the stock market, in fact, is that it allows people to diversify their risky investments by purchasing small interests in many companies, instead of betting everything on a single business. Application 11.5 describes one easy way to diversify.

Application 11.5

Diversification through Mutual Funds

In principle, diversification through the stock market seems like a good idea. But in practice, many small investors find it rather difficult. Picking the right companies requires a good deal of research. Each investment has to be monitored and adjusted as prices rise and fall. Brokerage fees can add up, particularly if transactions involve only a few shares. For someone who is putting, say, \$10,000 in the stock market, these costs are potentially prohibitive.

Mutual funds make diversifying investments easy. A mutual fund raises money from investors by selling shares in the fund and then invests the proceeds. Investors share in the fund's gains and losses until they either redeem their shares from the fund or sell them to other investors.

There are several different types of mutual funds. For example, equity funds invest only in common stocks, bond funds invest only in bonds, and balanced funds invest in both. Some funds specialize in certain types of stocks or bonds, while others do not. Some funds are actively managed, which means that the manager tries to choose investments that will outperform some recognized index, like the S&P 500 (which is published by Standard and Poor's and tracks the performance of 500 prominent companies). Other funds, known as index funds, try to match the performance of an index, usually by holding the stocks that make up the index.

During the 1990s, total U.S. mutual fund investments exploded, growing from \$1.07 trillion to \$6.85 trillion by the end of the decade. In large part, that growth resulted from the increased popularity of 401(k) pension plans and other similar types of retirement savings accounts, which typically require individual investors to allocate their savings among particular mutual funds. As of year-end 2003, the mutual fund industry served more than 260 million separate accounts, with a total balance of \$7.41 trillion. More than three-quarters of that total was held in accounts owned directly by households, and those accounts contained more than 18 percent of all U.S. household financial assets. Nearly 48 percent of U.S. households had at least one mutual fund account. Overall, mutual funds held 22 percent of all U.S. corporate equity.

While mutual fund companies tout a long list of advantages over direct investment, some of their claims are disputed. For example, there is little evidence that active management improves investment outcomes. Actively managed funds do outperform index funds some of the time, but we would expect this to occur purely by chance, and there is little evidence that anything more than chance is involved. Nevertheless, mutual funds do offer individual investors at least one indisputable advantage: convenient, low-cost diversification.

WORKED-OUT PROBLEM 11.4

The Problem Suppose Maria starts out with \$300, and that she seeks to maximize her expected benefit, $\sqrt{X}$, where X measures her resources in dollars. She has three options: keep the \$300, invest it all in Go for Broke, Inc., or invest \$150 each in Go for Broke, Inc., and Shoot the Moon, Inc. Compute the certainty equivalent of each option. Which is best? What is the benefit of diversification?

The Solution Keeping \$300 guarantees a benefit of 17.3 (the square root of 300); the certainty equivalent is clearly \$300. Investing \$300 in Go for Broke produces an expected benefit of

$$\frac{1}{2}\sqrt{0} + \frac{1}{2}\sqrt{900} = 15$$

Her certainty equivalent solves $\sqrt{X} = 15$, so $X = 225$. Investing in both companies produces an expected benefit of

$$\frac{1}{4}\sqrt{0} + \frac{1}{2}\sqrt{450} + \frac{1}{4}\sqrt{900} = 18.1$$

Her certainty equivalent solves $\sqrt{X} = 18.1$, so $X = 328$.

Maria's best choice is to invest in both companies. Her second best choice is not to invest. The benefit of diversification is \$103 (\$328 − \$225) compared with no diversification, and \$28 (\$328 − \$300) compared with the next best choice (no investment).

IN-TEXT EXERCISE 11.4 **Repeat worked-out problem 11.4 assuming that Maria seeks to maximize the expected value of $2{,}000X - X^2$ (for values of X less than 1,000).**

Information Acquisition

People often try to reduce or eliminate risk by acquiring information. Because better information about probable events leads to better decisions, it can reduce the likelihood of undesirable outcomes.

To illustrate this point, let's return to the example we used in our discussion of hedging. As before, Maria can invest in a sunscreen concession, a generator distributorship, or both. She starts out at point A in Figure 11.16 (page 395); her investment options allow her to reach points B, E, and F. As we've said, her best choice is to buy both concessions (point F), yet that isn't the ideal solution. Because the sunscreen concession does poorly if there's a hurricane and the generator distributorship does poorly if the sun shines, one concession or the other will always do poorly, so Maria wastes the \$300 she invests in it. Can she do better?

If Maria could predict the weather perfectly, she would always make the right investment, investing in the sunscreen concession only when the sun is about to shine and the generator distributorship only when a hurricane is about to hit. Rain or shine, she would earn a net profit of \$600, leaving her with \$1,200 (including her earnings) to spend on food. In other words, with perfect information, Maria would reach point G in Figure 11.16, which is significantly better than point F. Clearly, Maria has a strong incentive to gather information about likely weather patterns.

Suppose Maria knows of a meteorological consultant who can predict the weather perfectly. How much would she pay for his services? We know she ends up with \$1,200 for sure if she can predict the weather, and only \$900 for sure (through hedging) if she can't. That means she should be willing to pay up to \$300 for perfect weather prediction. In this example, the value of information is \$300.

CHAPTER SUMMARY

1. **What is risk?**

   a. Sometimes we can assess the probability of a state of nature by determining the frequency with which it has occurred in the past. This concept is known as *objective probability.* At other times, we may assess the probability of a state of nature by using subjective judgment, a concept known as *subjective probability.*

   b. If we know the probability and payoff associated with each state of nature, we can find the probability distribution of the payoffs. We can also calculate the expected payoff, as well as the standard deviation and the variance, two measures of variability.

2. **Risk preferences**

   a. To analyze decisions involving risk, we can apply the theory developed in Chapters 4 through 6, thinking of a consumption bundle as a list of the amount of each good consumed in each state of nature. Indifference curves represent the consumer's preferences for consumption in different states of nature.

   b. With only two possible states of nature, a risk-averse consumer's preferred point on any constant expected consumption line lies on the guaranteed consumption line.

   c. With only two possible states of nature, we can find the certainty equivalent of a risky consumption bundle by identifying the indifference curve that runs through the bundle and determining the level of consumption that corresponds to the point where the curve crosses the guaranteed consumption line.

   d. The difference between a bundle's expected level of consumption and its certainty equivalent, known as the *risk premium*, reflects the psychological cost of exposure to risk.

   e. At greater levels of risk aversion, indifference curves bend more sharply where they cross the guaranteed consumption line. The certainty equivalent of any risky bundle is lower and the risk premium higher with greater levels of risk aversion.

   f. With only two possible states of nature, a risk-loving consumer's least preferred point on any constant expected consumption line lies on the guaranteed consumption line. For risk-neutral consumers, indifference curves coincide with the constant expected consumption lines.

   g. Under some conditions, we can use an expected utility function to describe a consumer's risk preferences.

   h. For expected utility, a concave benefit function implies risk aversion; a convex function implies risk-loving preferences. A linear benefit function implies risk neutrality.

3. **Insurance**

   a. If insurance is actuarially fair, a risk-averse consumer will purchase full insurance.

   b. If insurance is less than actuarially fair, a risk-averse consumer will purchase partial insurance or no insurance at all. The amount of insurance purchased will depend on the degree of risk aversion. Those who are not very risk averse will purchase no insurance.

   c. The value of insurance equals the difference between the certainty equivalent of the consumer's consumption bundle after purchasing insurance and the certainty equivalent of the bundle before purchasing insurance. The greater the risk aversion, the higher the value of the insurance.

4. **Other methods of managing risks**

   a. One way to make a risky investment more attractive is to share the risk by dividing it among several people. Companies can expand the opportunities for risk sharing by issuing equity shares. As long as an investment's expected payoff is positive, even an extremely risk-averse person will benefit from taking a small share of it.

   b. Hedging reduces risk, because when the payoffs from two activities are negatively correlated, the gains offset the losses.

   c. Diversification reduces risk because it creates opportunities for gains to offset losses, raising the likelihood of intermediate outcomes. The risk-reducing effects of diversification are smaller when the payoffs are more positively correlated, making offsetting gains and losses less likely. One of the most important functions of the stock market is to allow people to diversify their risky investments by purchasing small interests in many companies, instead of betting everything on the performance of a single business.

   d. Better information about probable events leads to better decisions, reducing the likelihood of a loss. The value of information equals the difference between the certainty equivalent of the risky outcome when an individual is informed and the certainty equivalent of the risky outcome when he is uninformed.

Exercise 11.1: List as many types of financial risk as possible for each of the following activities: driving a car; going to college; trying out a new brand of breakfast cereal; taking a vacation in Europe; hiring a new employee.

Exercise 11.2: Compute the expected payoff and the standard deviation for each of the following probability distributions:

a. A payoff of 200 with a probability of 0.4 and 500 with a probability of 0.6.

b. A payoff is 110 with a probability of 0.2; 130 with a probability of 0.3; 150 with a probability of 0.1; and 170 with a probability of 0.4.

c. Every possible payoff that's a whole number between (and including) 100 and 200, each with the same probability. (Use a spreadsheet.)

Exercise 11.3: As in Figure 11.3, draw the constant expected consumption line through point A under the assumption that the probability of rain is:

a. 50 percent

b. 25 percent

c. 75 percent

Exercise 11.4: Suppose that consumption when it's sunny and consumption when there's a hurricane are perfect complements. The investor's indifference curves are L-shaped, and the corner of each L lies on the 45-degree line. Using graphs, explain why these assumptions imply infinite risk aversion.

Exercise 11.5: Repeat worked-out problem 11.1 (page 378), assuming that the indifference curves are L-shaped, as in exercise 11.4.

Exercise 11.6: The risk premium for a risky consumption bundle is never larger than the difference between expected consumption and the lowest payoff that occurs with a positive probability. Explain why this statement is true. Assuming there are only two possible outcomes, illustrate with a graph.

Exercise 11.7: Using a graph like the one in Figure 11.6, show the risk premium and certainty equivalent for a risky consumption bundle, assuming that the consumer is risk-loving. Explain why the certainty equivalent exceeds the expected level of consumption, and why the risk premium is negative.

Exercise 11.8: Suppose that Maria seeks to maximize the expected value of the benefit function $W(F) = 1{,}000F - F^2$ (for values of F below 100). Maria consumes 50 kg of food when it's sunny and 30 kg when there's a hurricane. There's a 25 percent chance of a hurricane. Compute her expected payoff, her expected utility, the certainty equivalent of her risky consumption bundle, and the risk premium.

Exercise 11.9: Show graphically that a risk-loving consumer would never purchase actuarially fair insurance.

Exercise 11.10: You've seen that the consumer's degree of risk aversion doesn't affect the quantity of actuarially fair insurance purchased (since all risk-averse consumers will fully insure). Using graphs, show that the degree of risk aversion does affect the *value* of insurance. Is the value of fair insurance smaller or larger to a more risk-averse consumer?

Exercise 11.11: Initially, Maria consumes 400 kg of food when it's sunny and 75 kg of food when there's a hurricane (due to property losses from flooding). Her indifference curves are L-shaped, as in exercise 11.4. Suppose that flood insurance is available, and that the premium, M, for each dollar of promised benefit is less than a dollar (but greater than zero). Solve for Maria's best choice as a function of M. How much insurance will she buy, and how much food will she consume? (Hint: Draw a graph. Does she partially insure or fully insure?) Does your answer depend on the probability of rain? Explain.

Exercise 11.12: Why might it make sense for the same risk-averse person to both eliminate risk by purchasing insurance and take on new risk by investing in the stock market?

Exercise 11.13: Recall the risk-sharing problem illustrated in Figure 11.15. Show graphically that if Maria is less risk averse, she'll want to buy a larger fraction of the sunscreen concession (represented by a point to the right of point D).

Exercise 11.14: Consider again the risk-sharing problem illustrated in Figure 11.15. If the sunscreen concession becomes more profitable when the sun shines, what happens to Maria's best choice? Show your answer graphically. Can you say whether she will want to own a larger or smaller share of the concession?

Exercise 11.15: Suppose a consumer can buy equity shares in any of several risky projects, all of which have the same net expected payoff and the same variability. Suppose too that the payoffs from the various projects are uncorrelated. If the consumer is risk loving, should she diversify? What if she's risk neutral? Explain.

Exercise 11.16: Jeffrey, who is risk neutral, is thinking about investing in one of two mutually exclusive projects. Project A requires an investment of \$200 up front. It pays \$600 if it rains, \$800 if it snows, \$400 if it hails, and \$0 if it's sunny. Project B requires an investment of \$300 up front. It pays \$200 if it rains, \$0 if it snows, \$600 if it hails, and \$700 if it's sunny. The probability of each outcome is 0.1 for rain, 0.3 for snow, 0.2 for hail, and 0.4 for sun.

a. What is the net expected payoff from each project? Which is better for Jeffrey, and by how much?

b. Suppose that a meteorologist can forecast the weather with perfect accuracy. How much will Jeffrey pay for the information?

12 Choices Involving Strategy

Learning Objectives

After reading this chapter, students should be able to:

- Explain what an economist means by a game, and distinguish between one-stage and multiple-stage games.
- Describe methods for reasoning out the likely choices of opponents, and understand their limitations.
- Explain the concept of a Nash equilibrium, and apply it in simple games.
- Understand the benefits of playing unpredictably in certain games.
- Recognize whether threats are credible, and whether cooperation is achievable, in multiple-stage games.

On June 6, 1944, the Western Allies invaded Nazi-occupied France, pitting more than 150,000 men, 5,000 ships, and 11,000 aircraft against German defenses along the beaches of Normandy. Hitler was aware of the impending invasion, but thought it would more likely occur at Calais, not Normandy. Calais required shorter supply lines from England. It also offered access to an extensive road network, which would permit more rapid troop deployment toward Germany.

On the advice of his strategists, General Dwight D. Eisenhower, Supreme Commander of the Allied Expeditionary Force, reinforced Hitler's preconceptions through deception and misdirection. The Allies stationed squadrons of plywood airplanes and inflatable tanks near the port of Dover, directly across the English Channel from Calais. They located a fleet of rubber landing craft nearby, at the mouth of the Thames River. Allied operatives passed the Germans false information through known enemy agents and coded radio transmissions intended for interception. To reinforce the misinformation, Allied commanders held actual military maneuvers near the decoy forces and dropped more bombs on Calais than on Normandy. As a result, Hitler ordered his generals to fortify German defenses at Calais, leaving Normandy comparatively vulnerable. According to General Alfred Jodl, Hitler's chief of staff, this was Germany's fatal strategic error.

Eisenhower's attempt to mislead Hitler prior to D-day is an example of strategic decision making. A choice involves strategy whenever its effects depend on the actions and reactions of other people. Even in nonmilitary situations, sound decision making frequently requires careful strategic thought. People often mull over strategies for getting dates, obtaining extensions on their assignments, securing jobs, and achieving a host of other objectives in which success or failure hinges on others' choices. Strategy is particularly important in business because the outcome of choices regarding investment, research and development, product design, pricing, and marketing depends critically on the decisions of other companies in the same line of business. For example, investing heavily in the development of a new product can turn out to be wildly profitable if your company is the first to market, or disastrous if another company beats yours to it.

In examining strategic decisions, economists rely on tools taken from a field called *game theory*. This chapter provides an introduction to the theory of games, particularly with respect to economic decisions. We'll study five topics:

1. *What is a game?* We'll introduce the concept of a game, and distinguish between one-stage games and multiple-stage games.
2. *Thinking strategically in one-stage games.* Strategic situations require us to think about what other people will do. We'll see that it's sometimes possible to reason out the likely choice of a sensible opponent by thinking about the game from your opponent's perspective.
3. *Nash equilibrium in one-stage games.* In Chapter 2, you learned that competitive markets have equilibria that balance supply and demand. Games have equilibria of a different kind. We'll introduce and explore an important notion of strategic equilibrium, and explain why a decision maker might choose an equilibrium strategy.
4. *Games with multiple stages.* When a game involves a sequence of decisions, people have opportunities to reward and punish each others' choices. By studying those games, we'll learn how to determine whether a threat is credible. We'll also see how people with competing interests manage to cooperate with each other.

*5. *Games in which different people have different information.* When people have different information, their choices often reveal something about what they know. We'll explain how someone can learn from the choices of other decision makers, and we'll see how this affects their behavior.

12.1 WHAT IS A GAME?

A **game** is a situation in which each member of a group makes at least one decision, and cares both about his own choice and about others' choices. This definition isn't limited to recreational games and sports, like poker and baseball; it includes any situation in which strategy plays a role, from military planning to dating.

> A **game** is a situation in which each member of a group makes at least one decision, and cares both about his own choice and about others' choices.

Economists study an enormous variety of games. For example, game theory provides the foundation for understanding competition in industries with only an few producers. We devote Chapter 19 to that topic. Auctions, which we discuss at various points in this chapter, are games. Every negotiation—such as a buyer and a seller haggling over price, an entrepreneur and a venture capitalist arranging financing for a start-up company, or two countries bargaining over trade restrictions—is a game. There are many other examples. We devote a separate chapter to game theory because it has become such a central and broadly applicable component of the modern economist's toolkit.

Two Types of Games

In a **one-stage game,** each participant makes all of his choices before observing any choice by any other participant.

Some games are easier to analyze than others. In the simplest games, known as **one-stage games**, each participant makes all of his choices before observing any choice by any other participant. Rock Paper Scissors—a game familiar to most schoolchildren—is a good example. Two players face off with one fist extended toward each other. Together, they raise and lower their forearms three times. As a player's fist descends for the third time, he forms it into one of three shapes: rock, paper, or scissors. Ideally, the two players make their choices at the same moment. The winner depends on the choices: rock smashes scissors, scissors cut paper, and paper covers rock.

In a **multiple-stage game,** at least one participant observes a choice by another participant before making some decision.

In contrast, in a **multiple-stage game**, at least one participant observes a choice by another participant before making some decision. Complex multiple-stage games allow for elaborate sequences of moves and countermoves. Tic-tac-toe, chess, and poker are all examples of multiple-stage games.

In economics, multiple-stage games are much more common than one-stage games. For example, when companies compete with one another, each learns about its competitors' choices over time (prices, advertising expenditures, and so forth) and adjusts it own choices in response. That form of competition is therefore a multiple-stage game. Even so, as we'll see in Chapter 19, we can still learn a great deal about competitive strategy by examining simplified one-stage games.

The World RPS Society, based in Toronto, Canada, sponsors an annual Rock Paper Scissors world championship, at which more than a thousand screaming fans watch the master players showcase techniques such as "paper clipping" and "priming the chump" while competing for a cash prize (7,000 Canadian dollars in 2006).

For a practical illustration of the distinction between one-stage and multiple-stage games, let's compare two different types of auctions: the open-outcry auction, and the sealed-bid auction. When people think about auctions, they usually picture the open-outcry format in which an auctioneer solicits bids from a crowd and pounds a gavel to declare the winner. These auctions are multiple-stage games, as they involve sequences of bids and counterbids. In contrast, the less flashy sealed-bid format, which calls for each potential buyer to submit a single bid privately and provides no opportunity for rebidding or counterbids, is a one-stage game.

Though multiple-stage games are often more complex than single-stage games, we'll see that many of the same principles apply in both contexts. To keep things simple, we'll start with one-stage games and then move to multiple-stage games.

How to Describe a Game

To teach someone how to play a game, we typically start by explaining the rules and the players' objectives. Sometimes there are written rules. For example, organized sports have rule books; recreational games have instruction manuals. The decision-making meetings of many clubs and civic organizations are governed by *Robert's Rules of Order*, and attorneys must abide by the *Federal Rules of Evidence* when introducing evidence in U.S. Federal courts. In other contexts, however, the rules governing social interaction are informal and unwritten; we learn the ropes from others and through experience.

To analyze a game, we also start with a description of the game's rules and the players' objectives. However, our description usually involves fewer details than someone would need if they intended to play the game. For example, to analyze Rock Paper Scissors, we need to know that each participant chooses one of three alternatives, and that they make their decisions simultaneously. We don't need to know that they raise and lower their forearms three times before choosing.

We'll explain how to describe multiple-stage games in Section 12.4; here, we'll focus on one-stage games. To describe the essential features of a one-stage game, we follow two steps. First, we identify the players and list the actions available to each. For one-stage games, we use the words *action* and *strategy* interchangeably; however, this will not be the case for multiple-stage games (see Section 12.4). Second, for every possible combination of strategies (one for every player), we identify each player's payoff, be it a reward or penalty. As Example 12.1 illustrates, we can usually summarize all of the relevant information in a simple table.

Example 12.1

The Battle of Wits, Part 1

In the classic children's novel *The Princess Bride* by S. Morgenstern (known to many from the 1987 movie of the same title), the hero, Wesley, disguised as "the man in black," attempts to rescue his sweetheart, Buttercup, from a clever kidnapper named Vizzini. In a battle of wits, Wesley presents Vizzini with two goblets of wine, explaining that one contains an odorless, tasteless, and lethal poison called iocane powder. Then he challenges Vizzini to a toast.

"Your guess," says Wesley. "Where is the poison?"

"*Guess?*" Vizzini cries. "I don't guess. I think. I ponder. I deduce. Then I decide. But I never guess."

"The battle of wits has begun," says Wesley. "It ends when you decide and we drink the wine and find out who is right and who is dead . . ."

The Battle of Wits is a one-stage game: though Vizzini chooses after Wesley, he can't observe Wesley's choice. Figure 12.1 summarizes the game's essential features. Wesley has two choices: put the poison in the goblet on the left or put it in the goblet on the right. The table contains one row for each strategy. Vizzini also has two choices: drink from the goblet on the left or drink from the goblet on the right. The table contains one column for each of these strategies. Each of the four cells represents a pair of strategies. For example, the yellow-shaded cell lies in the "left goblet" row and the "right goblet" column, so it means that Wesley places the poison in the left goblet, while Vizzini drinks from the right goblet.

We've divided each cell into two halves. The number in the southwest half indicates Wesley's prize (or penalty); the number in the northeast half indicates Vizzini's. The numbers in the yellow-shaded cell, for example, tell us that, when Wesley puts the poison in the left goblet and Vizzini drinks from the right goblet, Wesley's payoff is −1 (he dies), while Vizzini's payoff is 1 (he survives and keeps Buttercup). The magnitudes of these payoffs are unimportant; they simply indicate a preference for surviving over dying.

This example, though whimsical, captures the essence of many important strategic problems. With a bit of relabeling, for example, we can view it as a simple version of the game that preceded D-Day. Think of Wesley as Eisenhower. Putting the poison in the left goblet corresponds to invading Normandy; putting it in the right goblet corresponds to invading Calais. Now think of Vizzini as Hitler. Drinking from the left goblet corresponds to defending Calais; drinking from the right goblet corresponds to defending Normandy. If the same location is attacked and defended, Hitler wins; otherwise, Eisenhower wins.

Figure 12.1

The Battle of Wits. This table contains one row for each of Wesley's alternatives and one column for each of Vizzini's. Each cell corresponds to a pair of strategies. In the yellow cell, for example, Wesley chooses the left goblet and Vizzini chooses the right one. The number in the southwest half of each cell indicates Wesley's prize (or penalty); the number in the northeast half indicates Vizzini's.

Wesley \ Vizzini	Drink from left goblet	Drink from right goblet
Poison in left goblet	Wesley: 1, Vizzini: −1	Wesley: −1, Vizzini: 1
Poison in right goblet	Wesley: −1, Vizzini: 1	Wesley: 1, Vizzini: −1

IN-TEXT EXERCISE 12.1 **Bob and Brian square off for the World Rock Paper Scissors Championship. The winner will take home $7,000, the loser receives nothing, and they split the prize in the event of a tie. Draw a table (like Figure 12.1) showing the players' possible choices, and the payoffs that result from each pair of actions.**

12.2 THINKING STRATEGICALLY IN ONE-STAGE GAMES

How should someone go about making a strategic decision? For example, let's think about how Vizzini might make his choice in the Battle of Wits. He knows his payoff will depend in part on what Wesley does. That suggests he should start by putting himself in Wesley's shoes, so he can figure out what Wesley might do. Then he can think about his own choice, taking Wesley's view into account.

What happens when Vizzini puts himself in Wesley's shoes? He quickly notices that Wesley's payoff depends in part on what Vizzini does. The implication dawns on him: Wesley will start by putting himself in Vizzini's shoes so that he can form a view of what Vizzini will do. That means Vizzini has to think about what will run through Wesley's mind when Wesley puts himself in Vizzini's shoes.

It gets worse. Vizzini realizes that when Wesley puts himself in Vizzini's shoes, he will recognize that Vizzini starts out by putting himself in Wesley's shoes. So Vizzini has to think about what will run through Wesley's mind when Wesley thinks about what will run through Vizzini's mind when Vizzini thinks about Wesley's choice.

It doesn't stop there. In fact, it doesn't stop *anywhere*. Vizzini can always take this line of reasoning to the next level.

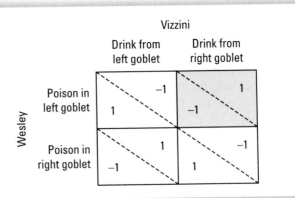

Not surprisingly, thinking through strategic choices in this way is often a dead end. If, in the Battle of Wits, Wesley can reason out what Vizzini will choose by putting himself in Vizzini's shoes, then Wesley must win. Likewise, if Vizzini can reason out what Wesley has done by putting himself in Wesley's shoes, then Vizzini must win. Since they can't both win, it must not be possible to reason out each others' choices in this way. Let's see what happens, according to S. Morgenstern, when Vizzini tries:

> "It's all so simple," says Vizzini. "All I have to do is deduce, from what I know of you, the way your mind works. Are you the kind of man who would put the poison into his own glass, or into the glass of his enemy?
>
> "Now a great fool," he continues, "would place the poison in his own goblet, because he would know that only another great fool would reach first for what he was given. I am clearly not a great fool, so I will clearly not reach for your wine."
>
> "That's your final choice?"
>
> "No. Because you knew I was not a great fool, so you would know that I would never fall for such a trick. You would count on it. So I will clearly not reach for mine either."
>
> "Keep going," says Wesley.
>
> "I intend to." After reflecting for a moment, Vizzini continues. "We have now decided the poisoned cup is most likely in front of you. But the poison is powder made from iocane and iocane comes only from Australia and Australia, as everyone knows, is peopled with criminals and criminals are used to having people not trust them, as I don't trust you, which means I can clearly not choose the wine in front of you. But again, you must have suspected I knew the origins of iocane, so you would have known I knew about the criminals and criminal behavior, and therefore I can clearly not choose the wine in front of me."
>
> "Truly you have a dizzying intellect," whispers Wesley.

Vizzini's two contradictory conclusions—that he "will clearly not reach for your wine" and that he "will clearly not reach for mine either"—underscore the limitations of reasoning strategically by putting oneself in another's shoes—at least in the context of the Battle of Wits.

Fortunately, the problem isn't as hopeless as it might appear. The problem of strategic thinking may be a thorny one, but we can still make useful progress. Next we'll examine some special cases in which the issues are more straightforward.

Dominant Strategies

Sometimes, there's no need for one player to think through what another will do. To explain why, we need to introduce two new concepts. The first is known as a **best response**. This term refers to a strategy that provides a player with the highest possible payoff, assuming that other players behave in a specified way. For example, if Vizzini assumes that Wesley put the poison in the left goblet, his best response is to drink from the right goblet. The second concept is known as a dominant strategy. A strategy is **dominant** if it is a player's only best response, regardless of other players' choices.

A player's **best response** is a strategy that provides him with the highest possible payoff, assuming that other players behave in a specified way.

A strategy is **dominant** if it is a player's only best response, regardless of other players' choices.

In discussing Vizzini's thought process (page 406), we said that Vizzini should start by putting himself in Wesley's shoes so he could form an idea of what Wesley might do. Strictly speaking, that is only necessary because Vizzini doesn't have a dominant strategy;

his best response depends on what Wesley does. (Check this!) If Vizzini and Wesley were playing a game in which Vizzini had a dominant strategy, then Vizzini wouldn't need to forecast Wesley's decision. Every conceivable forecast would lead him to the same conclusion: play the dominant strategy. To illustrate this point, we consider a new game, known as the Prisoners' Dilemma (Example 12.2).

Example 12.2

The Prisoners' Dilemma

Oskar and Roger are both enrolled in Microeconomics. While grading the midterm, Professor Getalife notices suspicious similarities between their answers. They truthfully attribute this coincidence to the fact that they always study together, but Getalife is unconvinced. Though they are actually innocent, he accuses them of cheating and asks for a disciplinary review.[1]

The disciplinary committee meets with Oskar and Roger separately, forbidding them to speak with each other until the process is complete. In each meeting, the head of the committee, Dean Windbag, presents the student with a simple choice. He explains that the college would like to send a clear message to the student body by making an example of a cheater. He says that the circumstantial evidence against them is strong enough to suspend them for only two quarters, which in his mind does not send a sufficiently powerful message. So he offers each a deal: squeal on your friend so that we can suspend him for six quarters, and we'll reduce your suspension by one quarter. If your friend denies cheating, you'll get off with one quarter instead of two; if he also squeals on you, you'll get off with five quarters instead of six.

Figure 12.2 summarizes the crucial features of this game. Oskar has two choices, deny or squeal; the table contains a row for each. Roger has the same two choices; the table contains a column for each. All together there are four cells, each of which represents a pair of actions. The yellow-shaded cell, for example, lies in the "squeal" row and the "deny" column, so it represents the pair of choices (squeal, deny), meaning that Oskar squeals and Roger denies. Again, we've divided each cell into two halves. The number in the southwest half indicates Oskar's payoff; the number in the northeast half indicates Roger's. The numbers in the yellow-shaded cell tell us that Oskar is suspended for one quarter (a payoff of −1) and Roger is suspended for six (a payoff of −6).

In Figure 12.3(a) we investigate whether Oskar's best response depends on Roger's decision. First, assume that Roger will definitely deny cheating. In that case, only the first column is relevant. For Oskar, denial results in a penalty of −2, while squealing results in a penalty of −1. Clearly, −1 is a better outcome than −2, so squealing is his best response. We've used green shading to show that −1 is Oskar's highest payoff in the first column.

Next, assume that Roger will definitely squeal. In that case, only the second column is relevant. For Oskar, denying results in a penalty of −6, while squealing results in a penalty of −5. Clearly, −5 is a better outcome than −6, so squealing is again his best response. We've used green shading to show that −5 is Oskar's highest payoff in the second column.

Notice that Oskar's best response doesn't depend on Roger's decision. Even without knowing Roger's choice, he knows he's better off squealing. Roger is in the same boat. In Figure 12.3(b), we've used red shading to indicate that squealing is Roger's best response to each of Oskar's choices. (To check this, notice that squealing, the second column, delivers Roger's highest payoff in each row.) Even without knowing Oskar's choice, Roger is clearly better off squealing. For both students, squealing is a dominant strategy.

[1] Usually, descriptions of this game involve two individuals who stand accused of committing a crime, which is why it's called the "Prisoners' Dilemma."

Our analysis leads to a rather startling conclusion: despite their innocence, Oskar and Roger will both squeal on each other, and each will be suspended for five quarters. If they both denied cheating, both would be better off. Unfortunately, they can't achieve that preferred outcome because each has a strong incentive to sell the other out.

Is this rather nasty outcome likely in practice? Undoubtedly, you can think of many reasons why one student might be reluctant to squeal on another—concern for a friend, fear of retribution, loss of face among fellow students. That doesn't mean we've made a mistake in solving the game. Rather, it means that in an actual disciplinary situation, there is usually more going on. To capture this complexity, we would have to construct a more elaborate game. You'll see how this is done in Section 12.4.

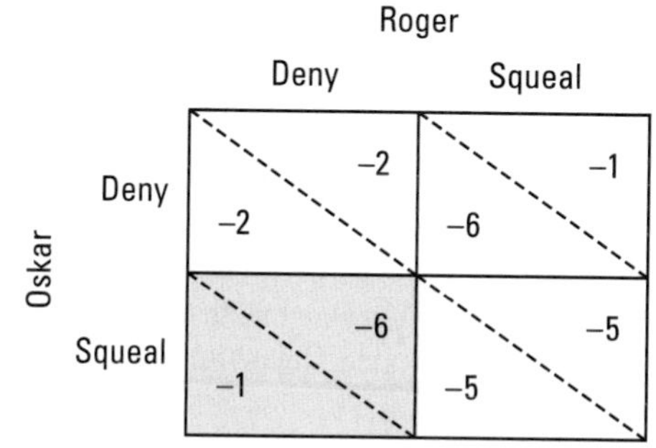

Figure 12.2

The Prisoners' Dilemma. This table contains one row for each of Oskar's alternatives and one column for each of Roger's. Each cell corresponds to a pair of strategies. In the yellow cell, for example, Oskar squeals and Roger denies. The number in the southwest half of each cell indicates Oskar's payoff; the number in the northeast half indicates Roger's.

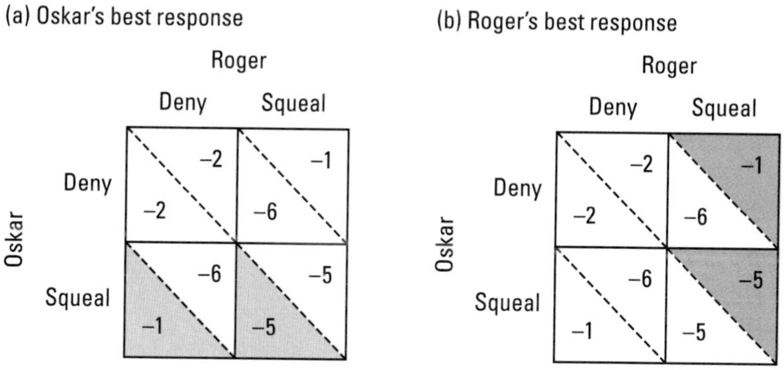

Figure 12.3

Best Responses in the Prisoners' Dilemma. In figure (a), the green shading indicates Oskar's highest payoff in each column. We see that Oskar's best response is to squeal, regardless of what he thinks Roger will do. In figure (b), the red shading to indicates Roger's highest payoff in each row. We see that Roger's best response is to squeal, regardless of what he thinks Oskar will do. Squealing is therefore a dominant strategy for both students.

When a player has a dominant strategy, as Oskar and Roger do, he doesn't need to think about what others will choose. But what if he doesn't have a dominant strategy? In that case, he *does* need to think about what others will choose because his best choice depends on their decisions. Even so, there are some situations in which his ideal strategy is obvious. For example, if *everyone else* has a dominant strategy, their choices are predictable. In that case, a player should simply assume that everyone else will play their dominant strategies, and choose his best response accordingly. Our next example illustrates this point.

Figure 12.4

The Provost's Nephew. The choices and payoffs in the Provost's Nephew are the same as in the Prisoners' Dilemma, except that Oskar receives a payoff of 0 (instead of –2) if both students deny cheating.

Oskar \ Roger	Deny	Squeal
Deny	0, –2	–6, –1
Squeal	–1, –6	–5, –5

Example 12.3

The Provost's Nephew

Let's modify the preceding example ever so slightly by imagining that Oskar is the provost's nephew. As long as no one confesses, he's untouchable. However, if he confesses or if Roger squeals, his uncle can't protect him.

Figure 12.4 illustrates this game. Notice that it's exactly the same as Figure 12.2, except for one detail. We've changed Oskar's payoff in the upper-left-hand cell from −2 to 0, signifying that if both students deny cheating, Oskar will avoid suspension.

Figure 12.5(a) shows Oskar's best responses. Notice that 0 is his highest payoff in the first column (indicated by the green shading). So assuming that Roger denies cheating, denial is Oskar's best response. As before, −5 is Oskar's highest payoff in the second column (indicated again by green shading). So assuming that Roger squeals, squealing is Oskar's best response.

In this case, Oskar doesn't have a dominant strategy. His best response depends on Roger's choice. Even so, we can still identify Oskar's best strategic choice because Roger's decision is predictable.

To understand why, look at Figure 12.5(b), which shows Roger's best responses. Since we haven't changed Roger's payoffs, the red shading is the same as in Figure 12.3(b). Squealing is Roger's best response regardless of what Oskar does—it's his dominant strategy. So Roger necessarily squeals.

We know that Oskar would be willing to deny cheating if he thought Roger would do likewise. But in fact, he knows that Roger will squeal, which means his best choice is to squeal as well. Though squealing isn't a dominant strategy for Oskar, it's his only sensible choice. Therefore, despite their innocence and despite Oskar's connection to the provost, both students will end up with a five-quarter suspension.

Dominated Strategies

Example 12.3 shows that we can make some headway as long as at least one player has a dominant strategy. But what if no one has a dominant strategy? Even when we can't

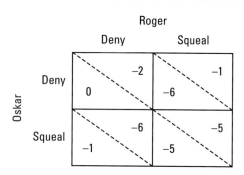

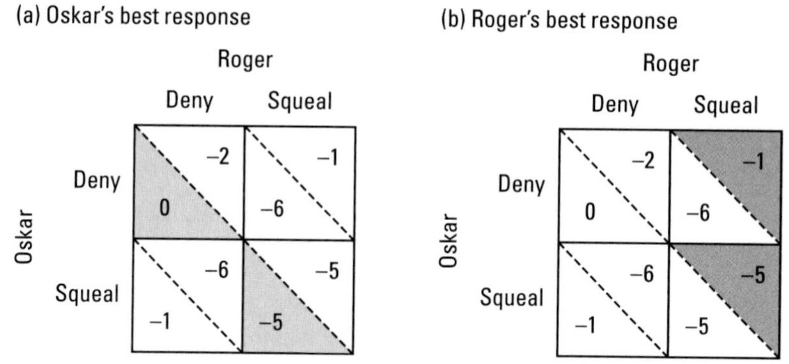

Figure 12.5

Best Responses in the Provost's Nephew. In figure (a), the green shading indicates Oskar's highest payoff in each column. We see that Oskar's best response is to deny if he expects Roger to deny, and to squeal if he expects Roger to squeal. Neither choice is a dominant strategy. In figure (b), the red shading indicates Roger's highest payoff in each row. We see that Roger's best response is to squeal, regardless of what he thinks Oskar will do. Squealing is therefore Roger's dominant strategy.

immediately say which strategies players *will* choose, we can often make progress by identifying strategies they definitely *won't* choose.

We say that a strategy is **dominated** if there is some other strategy that yields a strictly higher payoff regardless of others' choices.[2] This second strategy need not be a *dominant* strategy—that is, it may not be the player's best response in all instances (or even in any single instance). It is always better than the strategy it dominates, however. When a player does have a dominant strategy, all other strategies are dominated.

A strategy is **dominated** if there is some other strategy that yields a strictly higher payoff regardless of others' choices.

No sane player would ever select a dominated strategy. Why not? If the player switched to the strategy that dominates it, he would definitely end up with a higher payoff, regardless of how anyone else played. Thus, dominated strategies are completely irrelevant. A player with access to a dominated strategy will never choose it, and everyone else knows that he will never choose it. Nothing is lost by simply removing that strategy from the game.

Once we've removed a dominated strategy, we have a new, simpler game. Of the remaining strategies, some that weren't dominated in the original game may be dominated in the new game. (We'll provide an example of this in the next paragraph.) If so, we should remove them as well, because everyone knows they will never be played. Doing so leaves us with an even simpler game. We can repeat this procedure until there are no more dominated strategies left to remove, a process known as **iterative deletion of dominated strategies**.

The **iterative deletion of dominated strategies** refers to the following process: Remove the dominated strategies from a game. Inspect the simplified game to determine whether it contains any dominated strategies. If it does, remove them. Repeat this procedure until there are no more dominated strategies left to remove.

In essence, we solved the game in Example 12.3 by iteratively deleting dominated strategies. To see why, look at Figure 12.6(a), which starts on the left by replicating Figure 12.4. As we've said, squeal is a dominant strategy for Roger, which means that deny is dominated. Roger won't choose deny, and Oskar knows it, so that strategy is irrelevant; we might as well remove it from the game. Doing so leaves the simpler game shown in Figure 12.6(b). Roger actually has no choice in this game; only Oskar makes a decision. In this simplified game, deny is a dominated strategy for Oskar (it yields a lower payoff

[2] Technically, a strategy is also dominated if there is a way of randomizing over other strategies that yields a higher expected payoff regardless of others' choices. To keep the analysis simple, we'll avoid discussing randomizations here. The same qualification applies to the notion of weak dominance, introduced later in this section.

Figure 12.6

Deletion of Dominated Strategies in the Provost's Nephew. In figure (a), deny is a dominated strategy for Roger, so we can remove it from the game, leaving the simpler game in figure (b). In figure (b), deny is a dominated strategy for Oskar, so we can remove it from the game, leaving only one choice for each student in figure (c).

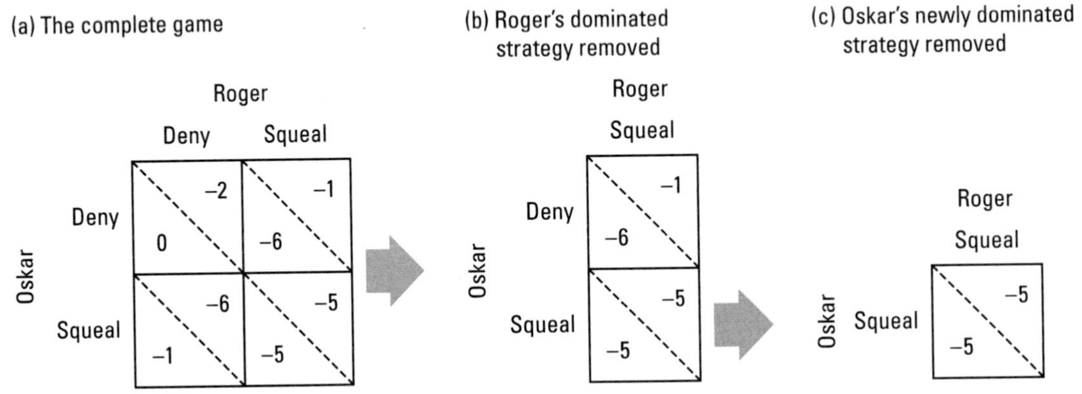

than squeal, given the only choice Roger can make). Oskar won't choose deny, so it's irrelevant; we might as well remove it, leaving the game shown in Figure 12.6(c). Now there is only one possible outcome: both students squeal.

In Example 12.3, one of the players had a dominant strategy. As Example 12.4 shows, the iterative deletion of dominated strategies sometimes allows us to solve strategic problems even when *no player* has a dominant strategy.

Example 12.4

Guessing Half the Median

Imagine that five people are playing a one-stage guessing game. Each is asked to choose a number between 1 and 8 (inclusive), with the object of coming as close as possible to half the median choice. (The median is the middle value—here, the third highest choice.) After the players privately select their numbers, a referee finds the median and divides by two. Each player pays a penalty (in dollars) equal to the gap between this number and his own guess.

To illustrate, suppose the chosen numbers are 2, 3, 6, 7, and 7. The median is 6, so half the median is 3. The player who chose 2 pays a penalty of $1 (having missed the target by one unit), the player who chose 3 pays no penalty (having hit the target). The player who chose 6 pays a penalty of $3 (having missed the target by three units), and the players who chose 7 pay a penalty of $4 (having missed the target by four units).

Before reading further, think a bit about this game. If you were a player, what number would you choose?

Notice that in this game, no player has a dominant strategy. Why? Each player's best response depends on others' choices. For example, if everyone else chooses 6, the best choice is 3 (the median is 6, so half the median is 3). But if everyone else chooses 4, the best choice is 2 (the median is 4, so half the median is 2). No single choice is always best regardless of what others do.

Even though no player has a dominant strategy, every player has some dominated strategies. Since the median choice can be no higher than 8, half the median can be no higher than 4. Therefore, choosing 4 dominates any number greater than 4. No one should choose any number greater than 4, and everyone knows it. Those choices are irrelevant, so we might as well remove them from the game. When we do, we end up with the same guessing game as before, except that now each player must choose a number between 1 and 4.

Now let's think about the game in which each player chooses a number between 1 and 4. Again, no player has a dominant strategy. For example, if everyone else selects 4, the best choice is 2. But if everyone else chooses 2, the best choice is 1. Even so, every player has some dominated strategies. Since the median choice can be no higher than 4, half the median can be no higher than 2. Therefore, choosing 2 dominates any choice greater than 2. No one should choose any number greater than 2, and everyone knows it. Those choices are irrelevant, so we might as well remove them, just as we removed the numbers 5 through 8. When we do, we end up with the same guessing game as before, except that now each player must choose a number between 1 and 2.

Now let's think about the game in which each player chooses either 1 or 2. Since the median choice can be no higher than 2, half the median can be no higher than 1. Choosing 1 is therefore the best available alternative, regardless of what others do. In other words, in this simplified game, 1 is the dominant strategy.

In sum, iteratively deleting dominated strategies has led us to a clear and unambiguous conclusion: *All players should choose the number 1.* The same logic will lead to the same conclusion when the range of potential choices is 1 to 100, 1 to 1,000, or even 1 to 1,000,000, regardless of the number of players.

Weakly Dominated Strategies

We've had some success in reasoning out strategic decisions by identifying strategies that players definitely won't select. So far, we've focused on dominated strategies. Arguably, we can go further and rule out strategies that are *weakly* dominated. We say that a strategy is **weakly dominated** if there is some other strategy that yields a strictly higher payoff in some circumstances, and that never yields a lower payoff regardless of others' choices.

A strategy is **weakly dominated** if there is some other strategy that yields a strictly higher payoff in some circumstances, and that never yields a lower payoff regardless of others' choices.

To see an illustration of this concept, look at Figure 12.7, which shows a game played by Susan, who chooses up or down, and Myrna, who chooses left or right. The green shading indicates Susan's highest payoff in each column. Notice that down is a best response for Susan no matter what Myrna does, but it isn't the only best response when Myrna plays left. Also notice that for each of Myrna's choices, Susan's payoff is at least as large when playing down as when playing up. Since both choices yield the same payoff when Myrna selects left, down doesn't dominate up. However, since Susan is strictly better off with down than with up when Myrna chooses right, down weakly dominates up.

Figure 12.7

A Weakly Dominant Strategy. Myrna chooses left or right and Susan chooses up or down. For Susan, down is just as good as up when Myrna picks left; it is better than up when Myrna picks right. That is, for Susan, down weakly dominates up. The green shading indicates Susan's highest payoff in each column. Notice that down is a best response for Susan no matter what Myrna does, but it isn't the only best response when Myrna chooses left.

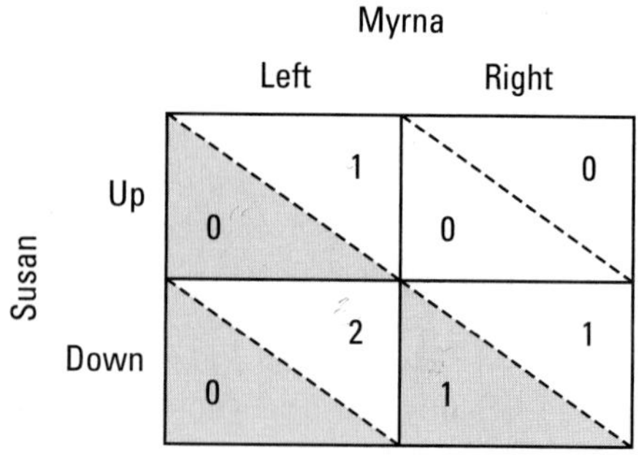

It may be a stretch to claim that no sane player would ever select a weakly dominated strategy. If, for example, Susan is sure that Myrna will play left, up is a perfectly reasonable choice. Even though it is weakly dominated, Susan can't improve her payoff by switching to down. Even so, down seems a safer choice. If Susan is right about Myrna, she won't end up any worse off; if she's wrong, she'll fare better. This reasoning suggests that it's usually wise to avoid weakly dominated strategies.

Example 12.5

Voting by Secret Ballot under Plurality Rule

Three candidates, Mr. Left, Ms. Right, and Ms. Maverick, are running for the same public office. There are 1,000 voters, each of whom either casts a secret ballot naming one of the candidates or abstains. The candidate with the most votes wins, even if he or she does not receive a majority of the votes. For example, if 400 ballots name Ms. Right, 350 name Mr. Left, and 250 name Ms. Maverick, then Ms. Right wins. In the event of a tie, a coin flip determines the winner. This procedure is known as *plurality rule*. It is also a simple one-stage game. What does game theory tell us about how people ought to vote?

Notice that there are no dominant strategies in this game, nor are there any dominated strategies. For example, if every other citizen votes for Mr. Left, then Mr. Left will win regardless of how you vote. Therefore, all of your strategies are best responses.

However, voting for your least favorite candidate is weakly dominated by abstention. Switching to abstention reduces the vote total for your least favorite candidate. This can't make you worse off, and in some situations you're better off, because your vote makes the difference. Similarly, abstention is weakly dominated by voting for your favorite candidate. (Why?)

However, voting for your second favorite candidate is not weakly dominated. In fact, it can be a perfectly reasonable choice. To illustrate, suppose you prefer Ms. Maverick to Mr. Left, and Mr. Left to Ms. Right. Assume that 496 of your fellow citizens will vote for Mr. Left, 496 for Ms. Right, and only 7 for Ms. Maverick. In that case, you're better off breaking the tie by voting for Mr. Left, even though you prefer Ms. Maverick. In real elections involving three or more candidates, people are indeed frequently reluctant to cast their votes for a favored candidate with little or no chance of victory.

Application 12.1

Second-Price Sealed-Bid Auctions

At the beginning of this chapter, we mentioned that sealed-bid auctions—in which each potential buyer submits a single bid privately, and there is no opportunity for rebidding or counterbids—are one-stage games. Typically, the object for sale is awarded to the highest bidder, but different sealed-bid auction formats have different rules for determining how much the winner pays. In a first-price sealed-bid auction, the selling price is the winning bid. In a second-price sealed-bid auction, the selling price is the *second* highest bid. This arrangement is also known as a *Vickrey auction*, named for William S. Vickrey, who received the 1996 Nobel Prize in Economics for his work on this topic.

William Vickrey (1914–1996) received the 1996 Nobel Prize in Economics in part for his pioneering work on the theory of auctions.

The first known second-price sealed-bid auction was held in 1893 for the purpose of selling a collection of U.S. and foreign postal stamps. During the first half of the 20th century, the format came into widespread use among companies that organized postage stamp auctions. Today, second-price auctions are less common than their first-price cousins, but they have gained popularity with the growth of eBay and other Internet auction services. At first blush, most of these services appear to use a format called the *English* or *ascending-price* auction, in which potential buyers best each others' bids until only one bidder is left. In many cases, however, buyers can make proxy bids. On eBay, for example, the customer can enter a maximum bid, and eBay will bid on his behalf up to his maximum. If you submit a maximum bid and win, you pay the price at which the next highest bidder drops out—in other words, the second highest bid (plus the minimum bid increment). Consequently, an ascending-price English auction with proxy bids amounts to a second-price sealed-bid auction.

Suppose you're participating as a buyer in a second-price sealed-bid auction. How much should you bid? It turns out that bidding the maximum amount you're willing to pay weakly dominates all your other possible choices. That is, if you're willing to pay $100 for an object but not a penny more, you should bid exactly $100. The same principle holds for proxy bids submitted on eBay. Why?

Let's think about what happens if you submit a lower bid—say $95—instead of $100. If your competitors' bids are all less than $95, you'll win and pay the same price—the second highest bid—bidding either $95 or $100. If at least one of your competitors bids more than $100, you'll lose in both cases. But if none of your competitors bids more than $100 and at least one bids more than $95, your $95 bid will lose while your $100 bid will win the object at a price below its value to you. So bidding $95 instead of $100 can't make you better off, and sometimes makes you worse off.

Now let's think about what happens if you submit a higher bid—say $105—instead of $100. If your competitors' bids are all less than $100, or if at least one bids more than $105, you fare equally well bidding either $100 or $105. (Why?) But if none of your competitors bids more than $105 and at least one bids more than $100, your $100 bid loses, while your $105 bid wins the object at a price above its value to you. So bidding $105 instead of $100 can't make you better off, and sometimes makes you worse off.

Why might a *seller* prefer a second-price sealed-bid auction to a first-price sealed-bid auction? Wouldn't he collect more money by requiring the winner to pay the highest bid instead of the second highest bid? The answer is, not necessarily, because bids tend to be lower in first-price auctions than in second-price auctions. As we've seen, in a second-price auction, each potential buyer should bid the maximum price he is willing to pay. But in a first-price auction, that same strategy is weakly dominated. It guarantees that the bidder won't come out ahead—even if he wins, he'll give up as much value as he gets. If instead he submits a lower bid, he may be able to buy the good for less than it's worth to him.

The life of John Nash (1928–), was the subject of the critically acclaimed film *A Beautiful Mind,* which received four Academy Awards.

In a **Nash equilibrium**, the strategy played by each individual is a best response to the strategies played by everyone else.

12.3 NASH EQUILIBRIUM IN ONE-STAGE GAMES

To this point, we've managed to reason out strategic decisions in some special situations by thinking about dominance. Unfortunately, that line of attack will only take us so far. In many one-stage games, no choice dominates any other, even weakly. What happens in those games?

The Concept of Nash Equilibrium

In 1950, a 22-year-old mathematician named John Nash published an article based on his Princeton PhD thesis, for which he later received the Nobel Prize in Economics. His article proposed a new tool for thinking about strategic decisions, known today as Nash equilibrium. While the idea took a while to catch on, over the last three decades it has become one of the most central and important concepts in microeconomics.

In a **Nash equilibrium**, the strategy played by each individual is a best response to the strategies played by everyone else. In other words, everyone correctly anticipates what everyone else will do and then chooses the best available alternative.

Let's look for a Nash equilibrium in the Prisoners' Dilemma. Figure 12.8 combines the red and green shading from the two parts of Figure 12.3. Remember that green shading indicates Oskar's best response within each row, while red shading indicates Roger's best response within each column. Notice that the southeast cell is shaded half red and half green. The two-tone shading implies that this cell is a Nash equilibrium: since the cell is half green, the row choice is Oskar's best response to Roger's column choice; since it is also half red, the column choice is Roger's best response to Oskar's row choice. In this equilibrium, both players squeal. Squealing is Oskar's best response if Roger squeals, and it's Roger's best response if Oskar squeals. Because there are no other two-tone cells, the southeast cell is the *only* Nash equilibrium.

IN-TEXT EXERCISE 12.2 **Using a diagram like Figure 12.8, explain why the pair of choices (squeal, squeal) is the only Nash equilibrium in the Provost's Nephew.**

Justifications for Nash Equilibrium Why are Nash equilibria of interest? The combination of strategies chosen in a Nash equilibrium is stable. Every participant is content

Figure 12.8

Nash Equilibrium in the Prisoners' Dilemma. As in Figure 12.3, green shading indicates Oskar's best responses and red shading indicates Roger's. The Nash equilibrium is the cell that is shaded both red and green. In this equilibrium, both Oskar and Roger squeal.

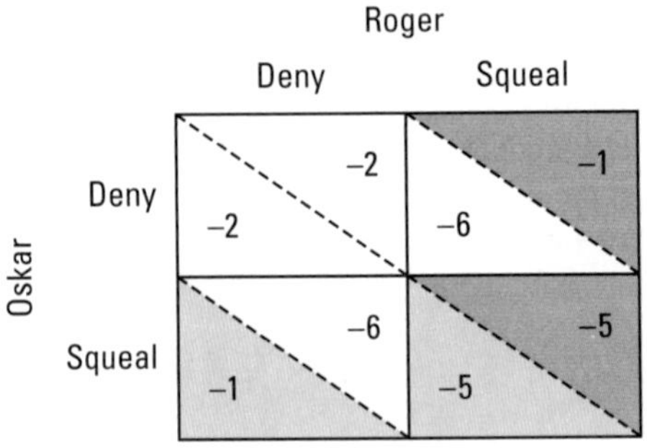

with his choice; no one wants to play anything else. All other outcomes are unstable, in the sense that at least one participant would want to change his strategy. As you learned in Chapter 2, we study the equilibria of competitive markets for a similar reason: the competitive price is stable, in the sense that there is no pressure for it to either rise or fall.

Why would we necessarily expect a group of people to settle on a stable combination of strategies? One explanation has to do with the effect of experience on the accuracy of participants' expectations. When people play games, they try to guess what their opponents will do and then play their best responses. As they gain experience (possibly with different opponents), they learn how others tend to play. If they eventually learn to make accurate guesses, they will choose best responses to their opponents' actual decisions. If in addition all players are experienced, then each will have reasonably accurate expectations and each will tend to make the best responses to the others' choices. In short, they'll play a Nash equilibrium. In fact, laboratory experiments have confirmed that, for certain types of games, experienced players do tend to select Nash equilibrium strategies.

Some economists prefer to think of Nash equilibria as **self-enforcing agreements**. An agreement is self-enforcing if each party to the agreement has an incentive to abide by it, assuming that others do the same. The strategies that make up a Nash equilibrium have this property. That is, if the parties agree to play Nash equilibrium strategies, no one has an incentive to break the agreement. In some situations, people can formalize agreements by writing contracts and rely on the courts for enforcement. In those cases their agreements don't have to be self-enforcing. When that isn't possible, however, agreeing to an arrangement is pointless unless it's self-enforcing.

In a **self-enforcing agreement**, every party to the agreement has an incentive to abide by it, assuming that others do the same.

Take the Provost's Nephew, for example. Imagine for the moment that Oskar and Roger have a chance to speak with each other immediately before their disciplinary hearings. Although they would like to agree not to squeal, that isn't self-enforcing. Oskar knows that Roger has a strong incentive to break their agreement. Knowing this, he'll probably squeal as well.

Why Nash Equilibrium Is a Useful Concept The concept of a Nash equilibrium doesn't lead to any new conclusions in the Prisoners' Dilemma or the Provost's Nephew. By thinking about dominance, we've already figured out that both players will squeal in those games. In many other games, however, we can say a great deal more about strategic behavior by studying Nash equilibria than by examining dominance. That is why Nash equilibrium is a useful concept. Example 12.6 and Application 12.2 illustrate this point.

Example 12.6

The Battle of the Sexes

Tony and Maria are planning an evening at the movies. Tony wants to see an action-adventure film, *Revenge of Chomp and Chew,* while Maria favors a romantic comedy, *Chickflick: The Sequel.* Neither cares much for the other's suggestion, and neither can force the other to attend a particular movie, but both want to spend the evening together, even if it means suffering through the other's preferred film.

Figure 12.9(a) shows Tony and Maria's possible choices and payoffs. The table contains two rows, one for each of Maria's choices—see the action-adventure film or see the romantic comedy. It also contains two columns, one for each of Tony's choices. The northwest cell represents attending the action-adventure film together, which makes Tony happy (a payoff of 5) and Maria more or less content (a payoff of 2). The southeast cell represents attending the romantic comedy together, which makes Maria happy and Tony more or less content. In the southwest corner, each attends his or her preferred movie alone, which isn't much fun (a payoff of 1 for both). In the northeast corner, each attends the other's preferred movie alone, which is downright unpleasant (a payoff of −1 for both).

Figure 12.9(b) uses green shading to indicate Maria's best response within each column and red shading to indicate Tony's best response within each row. Notice that each prefers to go wherever he or she believes the other will go. As a result, no choice is dominated, and we learn nothing about strategic behavior in this game by examining dominance.

What about Nash equilibria? In Figure 12.9(b), the northwest and southeast cells are shaded half red and half green. Seeing either film together is therefore a Nash equilibrium—Tony's film choice is a best response to Maria's and Maria's is a best response to Tony's. Both equilibria are self-enforcing agreements: If Tony and Maria agree to meet at the action-adventure film, each can count on the other to follow through, and likewise if they agree to meet at the romantic comedy. Since there are two equilibria, the concept of Nash equilibrium can't pin down which film the couple will see, but it does tell us they'll attend a film together.

Figure 12.9

The Battle of the Sexes. Figure (a) contains one row for each of Maria's alternatives and one column for each of Tony's. The number in the southwest half of each cell indicates Maria's payoff; the number in the northeast half indicates Tony's. In figure (b), the green shading indicates Maria's best respones in each column, and the red shading indicates Tony's best response in each row. We see that their best responses depend on each others' choices. The two cells that are shaded half red and half green are Nash equilibria.

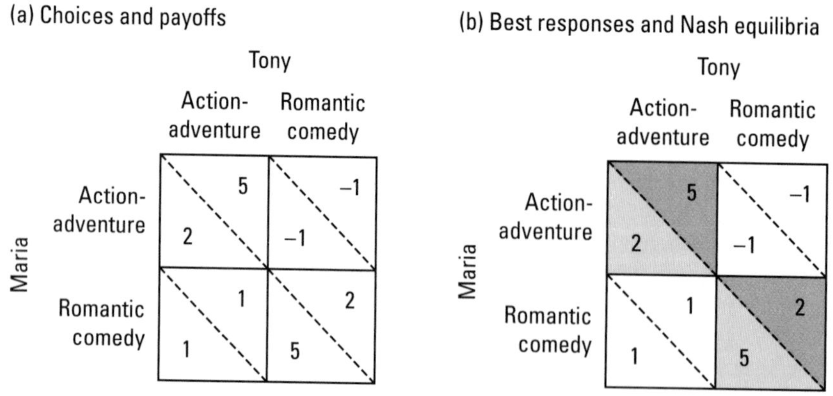

"As a matter of fact, you did catch us at a bad time."

Application 12.2

Comparing First-Price and Second-Price Auctions

At the end of Application 12.1 (page 415), we asked whether first-price or second-price auctions will tend to generate more revenue for sellers. Using the concept of weak dominance, we can figure out what people will bid (and therefore what the seller will earn) in a second-price auction, but not in a first-price auction. The concept of Nash equilibrium is useful here because it allows us to project the outcome of a first-price auction and thus to compare the revenues generated by the two auction formats.

To illustrate, suppose there are three potential buyers, William, Eva, and Paul. The object they want is worth $103 to William, $100 to Eva, and $95 to Paul. For now, let's assume that everyone knows everyone else's valuation. Bids must be made in even pennies. In the event of a tie, the winner is determined at random (possibly by a coin flip).

Suppose first that the object is sold through a second-price sealed-bid auction. From Application 12.1, we know that each potential buyer should bid his actual valuation.[3] William bids $103, Eva bids $100, and Paul bids $95. William wins and pays the seller $100 (Eva's bid).

Next suppose that the object is sold through a first-price sealed-bid auction. Here's one Nash equilibrium: William bids $100, Eva bids $99.99 (a penny less than her valuation), and Paul bids $94.99 (a penny less than his valuation). William wins and pays the seller $100 (his own bid).[4] Let's check that each participant's bid is a best response to the others' bids. Given that Eva bids $99.99 and Paul bids $94.99, William can't do any better. If he bid higher, he would have to pay more; if he bid less, he would either lose for sure (by offering less than $99.99) or win with only 50 percent probability (by offering exactly $99.99). Given that William bids $100 and Eva bids $99.99, Paul can't buy the good for less than it's worth to him ($95), so he can't do any better. Similarly, given that William bids $100 and Paul bids $94.99, Eva can't buy the good for less than it's worth to her ($100), so she can't do any better.

Notice that the seller receives *exactly the same revenue* under the first-price and second-price formats. William is the winner in each case. He bids less in the first-price auction than in the second-price auction ($100 instead of $103), but pays the same amount ($100) regardless of the format.

We've assumed here that everyone knows everyone else's valuation. Usually that isn't realistic. At this point, we're not equipped to study auctions in which people don't know one another's valuations; we'll address that topic in Section 12.5. Under reasonably general conditions, however, the conclusion we've reached here remains valid: on average, first-price and second-price sealed-bid auctions should raise exactly the same amount of revenue. This conclusion is known as the *revenue equivalence theorem*.

---

[3]While some Nash equilibria lead to other outcomes, all of those involve weakly dominated strategies.

[4]This isn't the only possible Nash equilibrium. However, for any equilibrium in which the bidders avoid weakly dominated strategies, William buys the object for $100. See if you can figure out why.

Nash Equilibria and Welfare In both the Prisoners' Dilemma and the Provost's Nephew, the Nash equilibrium leads to a rather bad outcome: the players are worse off than they would be if both denied the allegations. Why does this unfortunate result happen? When comparing the desirability of squeal and deny, Oskar thinks about his own payoff, but ignores Roger's; likewise, Roger thinks about his own payoff, but ignores Oskar's. By choosing squeal, each player helps himself by doing greater harm to the other, with the result that both are worse off. (Similar problems will come up in Chapter 20, where we'll explain how "externalities" can lead to poor resource allocation.)

Keep in mind, however, that Nash equilibria can also lead to good outcomes. Think about the Battle of the Sexes. One Nash equilibrium produces the best possible outcome for Maria; the other produces the best possible outcome for Tony. Moreover, both Maria and Tony are better off in either equilibrium than they would be with the other two alternatives, which involve spending the evening apart. Therefore, depending on the game, Nash equilibrium can involve either good outcomes or bad ones.

Nash Equilibria in Games with Finely Divisible Choices

So far, we've studied games in which players have a small number of choices. Yet economists typically examine situations in which the number of choices is quite large. Indeed, strategic decisions often involve finely divisible quantities, like time or money. How do we find the Nash equilibria in these settings?

Let's address this question by examining a concrete economic problem. Businesses frequently assign tasks to teams of employees rather than to individuals. When the employer can't identify the separate contributions of each team member, the members' choices become strategic. Some individuals will seek to "free ride" on others' contributions. Suppose, for example, that two employees, Liz and Scott, are writing a report together. They have 24 hours to do background research. The quality of their research will affect their prospects for raises and promotions. The more time they spend on the research, the better, but each wants the other to do most of the work.

Let's assume that Liz and Scott must conduct their research simultaneously and separately. Neither will learn how hard the other has worked until both are finished. In that case, their task is a one-stage game. Each chooses the amount of time he or she devotes to research without observing the other's choice.

Figure 12.10(a) shows Liz and Scott's potential choices. The horizontal axis measures the number of hours Scott spends on research; the vertical axis measures the number of hours Liz spends. For example, at point A, Liz and Scott each spend 15 hours on research.

If we know Liz's objectives, then for each choice that Scott might make, we can figure out Liz's best response. Doing so allows us to plot the relationship between Scott's choices and Liz's best responses. (For an example of how this is done, see worked-out problem 12.1, below.) Let's suppose that relationship corresponds to the green line in Figure 12.10(a). For example, if Scott spends 5 hours on research, Liz's best choice is to put in 10 hours (follow the vertical arrow from point B to the green line and the horizontal arrow from the green line to point C). Notice that the green line is downward sloping; if Liz can count on Scott to work longer hours, she will "free ride" by working fewer hours.

Likewise, if we know Scott's objectives, we can plot his best responses to each of Liz's choices. Suppose that relationship corresponds to the red line in Figure 12.10(a).

Figure 12.10

Free Riding in Groups. In figure (a), the green line shows the relationship between Scott's hours and Liz's best response. The red line shows the relationship between Liz's hours and Scott's best response. In figure (b), point N is a Nash equilibrium because it lies on both the red line and the green line. In this Nash equilibrium, Scott and Liz both put in eight hours.

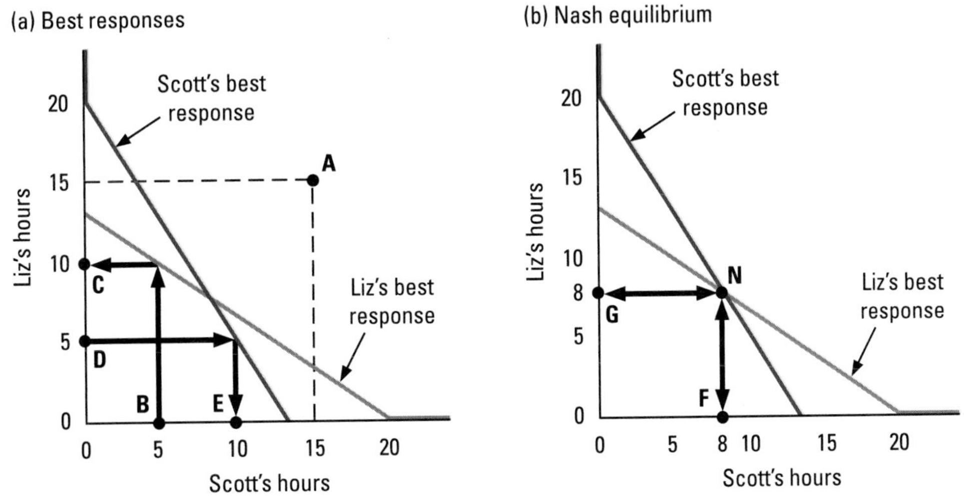

For example, if Liz spends 5 hours on research, Scott's best choice is to put in 10 hours (follow the horizontal arrow from point D to the red line, and the vertical arrow from the red line to point E). Since Scott would like to "free ride" on Liz's work, the red line is also downward sloping. The red and green curves are known as **best response functions** (or **reaction functions**); each one shows the relationship between one player's choice and the other's best response.

A **best response function**, also known as a *reaction function*, shows the relationship between one player's choice and the other's best response.

Notice that the layout of Figure 12.10(a) resembles that of Figure 12.9(b). Liz chooses the vertical coordinate in Figure 12.10(a), which is just like choosing a row in Figure 12.9(b). Likewise, Scott selects the horizontal coordinate in Figure 12.10(a), which is just like choosing a column in Figure 12.9(b). The main difference is that Figure 12.10(a) shows each pair of choices as a point rather than a cell. The green and red lines in Figure 12.10(a) play exactly the same role as the green and red shading in Figure 12.9(b). In both figures, green indicates one participant's best response and red indicates the other participant's best response. In Figure 12.9(b), a pair of choices is a Nash equilibrium if it corresponds to a cell that is shaded half red and half green. In Figure 12.10(a), a pair of choices is a Nash equilibrium if it corresponds to a point that lies on both the red line and on the green line. There is one such point, which we've labeled N (for "Nash equilibrium") in Figure 12.10(b).

As we've drawn the figure, the Nash equilibrium involves both employees spending eight hours on research. Let's confirm that this is indeed a Nash equilibrium. Suppose that Scott chooses eight hours. Following the vertical arrow in Figure 12.10(b) from point F to the green line and the horizontal arrow from the green line to point G, we see that Liz's best response is to put in eight hours. Now suppose that Liz chooses eight hours. Following the horizontal arrow from point G to the red line and the vertical arrow from the red line to point F, we see that Scott's best response is to put in eight hours. At point N, each employee makes a best response to the other's choice; therefore, point N is a Nash equilibrium.

WORKED-OUT PROBLEM 12.1

The Problem Let's use the symbol X to indicate the number of hours Scott spends on research and the symbol Y to indicate the number of hours Liz spends. Both these numbers must be positive and neither can exceed 24. Suppose we can measure Scott and Liz's costs and benefits on a utility scale (recall the discussion of utility in Section 4.4). When Scott works for X hours and Liz works for Y hours, each receives a total benefit of $40(X + Y) - (X + Y)^2$. That means the marginal benefit of spending extra time is $40 - 2(X + Y)$, regardless of who puts in the time. Notice that the marginal benefit of time declines as total time rises. Let's assume that the cost of their effort is $X^2/2$ for Scott and $Y^2/2$ for Liz. The marginal cost of extra time is then X for Scott and Y for Liz. Find the Nash equilibrium of this game. Is it a good outcome for Liz and Scott? Could they do better?

The Solution Suppose that Scott puts in X hours. To find Liz's best response, we need to set her marginal benefit equal to her marginal cost: $40 - 2(X + Y) = Y$. Solving for Y, we obtain a formula that describes the relationship between Scott's choices and Liz's best responses:

$$Y = \frac{40}{3} - \frac{2X}{3}$$

This is the formula for the green line in Figure 12.10. (Check this.)

Now suppose that Liz puts in Y hours. Through a similar calculation, we obtain a formula that describes the relationship between Liz's choices and Scott's best responses:

$$X = \frac{40}{3} - \frac{2Y}{3}$$

This is the formula for the red line in Figure 12.10. (Again, check this.)

To solve for the Nash equilibrium, we need to identify the point at which the red and green lines intersect. Doing so amounts to finding the values of X and Y that satisfy both best response formulas at the same time. Substituting the first formula into the second gives us

$$X = \frac{40}{3} - \frac{2}{3}\left[\frac{40}{3} - \frac{2X}{3}\right]$$

Solving for X, we find that $X = 8$. Plugging this value for X into the first formula, we discover that $Y = 8$. So in the Nash equilibrium, Liz and Scott each put in eight hours.

This result is not the best possible outcome. Liz and Scott would be happier if they both worked harder. Suppose, for example, that they each put in nine hours. In that case, each would receive a total benefit of $40(9 + 9) - (9 + 9)^2 = 396$, and would incur total costs of $9^2/2 = 40.5$, for a net payoff of 355.5. In contrast, when they both put in eight hours, each receives a total benefit of $40(8 + 8) - (8 + 8)^2 = 384$, and incurs a total cost of $8^2/2 = 32$, for a net payoff of only 352. Clearly, both would be better off if they worked for nine hours.

IN-TEXT EXERCISE 12.3 **Repeat worked-out problem 12.1, changing the assumptions as follows. When Scott works for X hours and Liz works for Y hours, each receives a total benefit of $60(X + 2Y) - (X + 2Y)^2$. The marginal benefit of Scott's extra time is $60 - 2(X + 2Y)$, while the marginal benefit of Liz's extra time is $120 - 4(X + 2Y)$. The cost of their effort is X^2 for Scott and $4Y^2$ for Liz, so the marginal cost is $2X$ for Scott and $8Y$ for Liz.**

Mixed Strategies

While the concept of a Nash equilibrium helps us understand strategic decision making in some games, it isn't always useful.[5] Figure 12.11 reproduces the Battle of Wits game from Figure 12.1, with green shading to indicate Wesley's best response in each column, and red shading to indicate Vizzini's best response in each row. Notice that no cell is shaded half red and half green. Consequently, if Wesley's choice is a best response to Vizzini's, then Vizzini's isn't a best response to Wesley's. For example, Wesley will poison the left goblet if he expects Vizzini to drink from the left goblet, but Vizzini will do so only if he thinks Wesley has poisoned the right goblet. We conclude that there is no Nash equilibrium in the Battle of Wits. Using a similar diagram, you should be able to explain why there is no Nash equilibrium in Rock Paper Scissors.

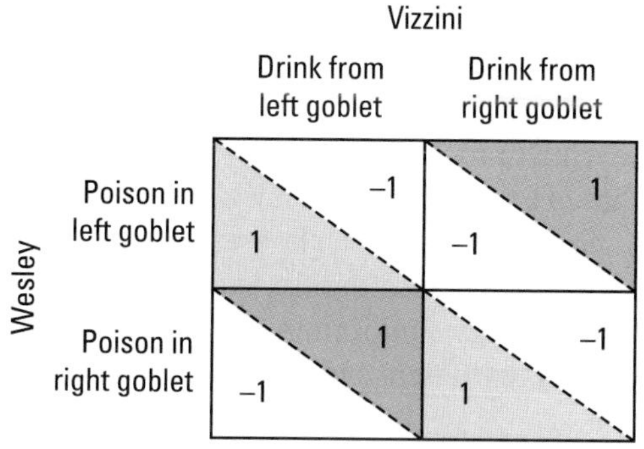

Figure 12.11
A Game with No Nash Equilibrium in Pure Strategies. We have reproduced the Battle of Wits from Figure 12.1. The green shading indicates Wesley's best response in each column and the red shading indicates Vizzini's best response in each row. No cell is shaded half red and half green, so there is no Nash equilibrium in pure strategies.

[5]Technically, this paragraph refers to Nash equilibria in which players do not randomize over their choices. As explained below, the problem described in this paragraph disappears if we assume that players can make random choices.

Playing Unpredictably How do we think about strategic decisions in games like the Battle of Wits and Rock Paper Scissors? The key to success in such games is unpredictability. As soon as a player's choices become predictable, he loses. How can a player become unpredictable? The most obvious way is to make choices randomly. (If you skipped Chapter 11, you should pause to read Section 11.1, in which we explained some basic concepts concerning probability, risk, and expected payoff.)

When a player chooses a strategy without randomizing, we say he is playing a **pure strategy.** When he uses a rule to randomize over the choice of a strategy, we say he is playing a **mixed strategy**.

When a player chooses a strategy without randomizing, we say that he is playing a **pure strategy**. When he uses a rule to randomize over the choice of a strategy, we say he is playing a **mixed strategy**. For example, in the Battle of Wits, a mixed strategy might call for Wesley to poison the left goblet with 60 percent probability and poison the right goblet with 40 percent probability. Technically, a pure strategy is a special kind of mixed strategy in which all probability is placed on a single choice.

In a **mixed strategy equilibrium**, players choose mixed strategies, and the mixed strategy chosen by each is a best response to the mixed strategies chosen by the others.

So far, we've studied Nash equilibria in which players use pure strategies. We've seen that not all games have equilibria of this type. This problem may have a simple solution. Since behaving unpredictably is sometimes an advantage, it makes sense to look for Nash equilibria in which players introduce a degree of randomness by playing mixed strategies. This kind of equilibrium is known as a **mixed strategy equilibrium.**[6] In such an equilibrium, the mixed strategy chosen by each player is a best response to the mixed strategies chosen by the others. As it turns out, virtually all games have mixed strategy equilibria.

Take the Battle of Wits, for example.[7] Suppose Wesley and Vizzini both make their choices randomly, selecting each alternative with 50 percent probability. This pair of mixed strategies is an equilibrium. To see why, first think about the problem from Wesley's perspective. Suppose Vizzini drinks from each goblet with 50 percent probability. No matter which goblet Wesley chooses, he receives a payoff of 1 half of the time, and -1 half of the time, so his expected payoff is 0:

$$\text{Expected payoff} = 0.5 \times 1 + 0.5 \times (-1) = 0$$

Even if he randomizes between the goblets, his expected payoff is still 0. Selecting each goblet with 50 percent probability is therefore one of many best responses to Vizzini's mixed strategy. For exactly the same reasons, Vizzini's mixed strategy is a best response to Wesley's. Since each player's mixed strategy is a best response to the other's, we have a mixed strategy equilibrium.

How to Find a Mixed Strategy Equilibrium How do we find mixed strategy equilibria? That is, how do we know which probabilities will work? If a player is willing to decide between two alternatives based on a coin flip, he must like them equally well; otherwise he'd simply pick the one he prefers. Thus, if he chooses a mixed strategy, his opponent must be behaving in a way that makes him indifferent between the strategies over which he's randomizing. In a mixed strategy equilibrium, his opponent's probabilities are therefore chosen to make sure that he's indifferent and consequently willing to randomize,

[6]A Nash equilibrium in mixed strategies is sometimes called a *mixed strategy Nash equilibrium*, while a Nash equilibrium in pure strategies is sometimes called a *pure strategy Nash equilibrium*.

[7]To keep the analysis simple, we'll assume here and throughout the rest of the chapter that players are risk neutral. Alternatively, we could assume that the players have expected utility functions, and that the payoffs correspond to the values of their utility indexes rather than to dollars (see the section titled "Expected Utility" starting on page 381).

while his own probabilities are chosen to make sure that his opponent is indifferent and consequently willing to randomize.

Let's see how this works in the Battle of Wits. Let's use P to stand for the probability that Wesley will poison the left goblet, in which case $1 - P$ is the probability that he will poison the right goblet. Similarly, let's use Q to stand for the probability that Vizzini will drink from the left goblet, which means that he will drink from the right goblet with a probability of $1 - Q$.

Since Wesley randomizes between the left and right goblets, he must be indifferent between them. Given how Vizzini randomizes, Wesley's expected payoff from poisoning the left goblet is $Q \times 1 + (1 - Q) \times (-1)$, and his expected payoff from poisoning the right goblet is $Q \times (-1) + (1 - Q) \times 1$. Since he's indifferent, we know these two expressions must be equal:

$$Q - (1 - Q) = -Q + (1 - Q).$$

The only solution to this formula is $Q = 1/2$. In other words, Wesley is indifferent between the two goblets only if he thinks Vizzini is equally likely to choose either of them.

Likewise, since Vizzini randomizes between the left and right goblets, he too must be indifferent between them. Given how Wesley randomizes, Vizzini's expected payoff from drinking out of the left goblet is $P \times (-1) + (1 - P) \times 1$, and his expected payoff from drinking out of the right goblet is $P \times 1 + (1 - P) \times (-1)$. These expressions are equal only if $P = 1/2$. In other words, Vizzini is indifferent between the two goblets only if he thinks Wesley is equally likely to choose either of them.

We conclude that the Battle of Wits has a single mixed strategy equilibrium. In effect, both Wesley and Vizzini choose between the goblets by flipping a coin (so that both goblets are equally likely to be chosen).

Of course, this solution to the Battle of Wits assumes that cheating is impossible. In *The Princess Bride*, Wesley was unwilling to trust to chance:

> [Vizzini] picked up his own wine goblet.
>
> The man in black [Wesley] picked up the one in front of him.
>
> They drank.
>
> "You guessed wrong," said the man in black.
>
> "You only *think* I guessed wrong," said [Vizzini], his laughter ringing louder. "That's what's so funny. I switched glasses when your back was turned . . ."
>
> He was quite cheery until the iocane powder took effect.
>
> The man in black stepped quickly over the corpse, then roughly ripped the blindfold from the Princess's eyes . . .
>
> "To think," she murmured, "all that time it was your cup that was poisoned."
>
> "They were both poisoned," said the man in black. "I've spent the past two years building up immunity to iocane powder."

IN-TEXT EXERCISE 12.4 **Solve for a mixed strategy equilibrium in Rock Paper Scissors.**

Application 12.3

Mixed Strategies in Sports

In most sports, predictability is a serious weakness, so contestants work hard to avoid it. In baseball, pitchers mix their pitches, alternating between fastballs, curves, and change-ups to keep batters guessing. In football, offenses set up the passing game with the running game—that is, they try to induce their opponents to defend against running plays so that passing plays will be more effective. In tennis, players vary the direction, speed, and spin of their serves so their opponents don't know what's coming. In soccer, players vary the direction of their penalty kicks so goalies won't know which way to dive.

When people make these decisions, are they in fact playing mixed strategy equilibria? How can we tell? As we've emphasized, in any mixed strategy equilibrium, every player must be indifferent between the choices over which he's randomizing. In some situations, we can actually check whether this condition holds.

Take tennis. When Roger Federer serves to Andy Roddick, each has a clear objective: win the next point. Federer can serve to the left or to the right. Roddick can prepare for a forehand return or a backhand return. Both mix up their choices to avoid becoming predictable. Could they be playing a mixed strategy equilibrium? If so, each must be indifferent toward his potential choices. That is, each choice must yield the same probability of winning the point; otherwise it would be better to pick the alternative with the highest probability of winning.

Two economists, Mark Walker and John Wooders, have tested this implication using data on 10 high-profile tennis matches between top professional players, held between 1974 and 1997.[8] Their analysis confirms the key feature of mixed strategy equilibria. While players served toward the left side of the court more frequently than toward the right (54 versus 46 percent overall), they won points with virtually the same frequency, regardless of their choices (64 percent when serving to the left and 65 percent when serving to the right).[9]

The same principles apply to penalty kicks in soccer. A team of three economists, Pierre-Andre Chiappori, Steven Levitt, and Timothy Groseclose, carefully examined data on virtually every penalty kick in the elite French and Italian leagues over a three-year period, with the object of determining whether contestants were playing mixed strategy equilibria.[10] Their results confirmed the key implications of the theory. Most notably, they found that kickers scored with roughly the same frequency whether aiming at the left, right, or center of the goal.

WORKED-OUT PROBLEM 12.2

The Problem Dorothy and Henry are playing the one-stage game shown in Figure 12.12. Dorothy has three possible choices (left, middle, and right), as does Henry (up, middle, and down). Assume that $A = 1$, $B = 0$, $C = 6$, and $D = 3$. Find all of the Nash equilibria in pure strategies and mixed strategies.

[8]Mark Walker and John Wooders, "Minimax Play at Wimbledon," *American Economic Review* 91, no. 5, December 2001, pp. 1521–1538.

[9]The data do not match the theory in all respects. Most servers change from left to right too frequently, making their choices somewhat predictable.

[10]Pierre-Andre Chiappori, Steven Levitt, and Timothy Groseclose, "Testing Mixed-Strategy Equilibria When Players are Heterogeneous: The Case of Penalty Kicks in Soccer," *American Economic Review* 92, no. 4, September 2002, pp. 1138–1151.

The Solution Focusing first on pure strategies, there are two Nash equilibria in this game: (1) Dorothy and Henry both pick middle and (2) Dorothy picks right and Henry picks down. In each case, the choices are best responses to each other. It is easy to check that no other cell is a Nash equilibrium. For example, (up, left) isn't a Nash equilibrium because Henry and Dorothy would both switch to middle.

Are there any mixed strategy equilibria in this game? In an equilibrium, no one ever uses a dominated strategy (it's never a best response). For Henry, up is dominated by middle; for Dorothy, left is dominated by right. Henry must therefore randomize over middle and down, and Dorothy must randomize over middle and right. Let's use P to stand for the probability Henry will choose middle, and Q to stand for the probability Dorothy will choose middle. Dorothy's expected payoff from choosing middle is $7P + 1(1 - P)$, while her expected payoff from choosing right is $5P + 3(1 - P)$. Since Henry's choice of P has to make Dorothy indifferent between middle and right (so that she's willing to randomize between the two), we know that $5P + 3(1 - P) = 7P + (1 - P)$, which means that $P = 1/2$. Henry's expected payoff from choosing middle is $8Q + 5(1 - Q)$, while his expected payoff from choosing down is $4Q + 6(1 - Q)$. Since Dorothy's choice of Q has to make Henry indifferent between middle and down (so that he's willing to randomize between the two), we know that $8Q + 5(1 - Q) = 4Q + 6(1 - Q)$, which means that $Q = 1/5$. The following is therefore a mixed strategy equilibrium: Henry chooses middle and down with 50 percent probability each (since $P = 1/2$); Dorothy chooses middle with 20 percent probability and right with 80 percent probability (since $Q = 1/5$).

IN-TEXT EXERCISE 12.5 **Repeat worked-out problem 12.2 using these values: $A = 3, B = 1, C = 4$, and $D = 0$.**

Henry \ Dorothy	Left	Middle	Right
Up	A, B	6, 2	3, 1
Middle	2, 4	8, 7	5, 5
Down	1, 2	4, 1	C, D

Figure 12.12

Worked-Out Problem 12.2. This table contains a column for each of Dorothy's choices (left, middle, and right) and a row for each of Henry's (up, middle, and down). The number in the southwest half of each cell is Henry's; the one in the northeast half is Dorothy's.

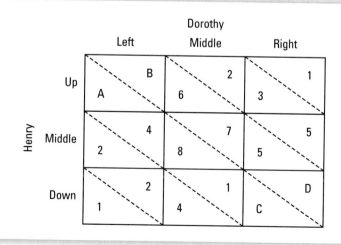

Reinhard Selten (1930–), who shared the Nobel Prize in Economics with John Nash, pioneered the study of credible behavior in multiple-stage games.

12.4 GAMES WITH MULTIPLE STAGES

In most strategic settings, events unfold over time, and actions can provoke responses and counter-responses. Even the simplest recreational games, like tic-tac-toe, have this feature. Clearly, then, we need to move beyond one-stage games. In this section, we provide an introduction to games with multiple stages. We focus on two important issues: how to recognize whether threats are credible, and how to establish and sustain cooperation between people with conflicting interests. To learn more about multiple-stage games, read Add-On 12A.

Credible Threats in Games with Perfect Information

How might you discourage someone from taking an action that's harmful to you? One possibility is to issue a threat. In other words, you could promise to deliver damaging consequences in return. Some threats are believable and effective, while others are empty and ineffective. What makes a threat credible?

In this section, we'll study the credibility of threats in simple multiple-stage games with **perfect information**. A game falls into this category if players make their choices one at time, and nothing is hidden from any player. Tic-tac-toe and chess are good examples of such games. Rock Paper Scissors is *not* a game of perfect information because the players make their choices at the same time. Neither is poker, because some information is hidden from each player—for example, which cards other players are dealt, and which ones they discard. To learn how to identify credible threats in more elaborate multiple-stage games, read Add-On 12A.

In a game with **perfect information**, players make their choices one at time, and nothing is hidden from any player.

Describing a Game with Perfect Information The simplest way to describe a multiple-stage game of perfect information is to draw a tree diagram that identifies the players and shows every possible sequence of decisions, along with the resulting payoffs. To illustrate this procedure, let's consider an example.

Earlier, we introduced a one-stage game called the Battle of the Sexes (see Example 12.6, page 417). We can turn the Battle of the Sexes into a two-stage game with perfect information by making one small change. We'll assume that Tony chooses a film before Maria, and that Maria learns what he chose before making her own decision (perhaps because he leaves her a note). For reasons that will become clear, we'll call this game the Lopsided Battle of the Sexes.

Figure 12.13 represents the Lopsided Battle of the Sexes graphically. The figure looks a bit like a tree turned on its side, growing from the left to the right. The tree is constructed from points and arrows. For the moment, ignore the fact that some arrows are black and some are green; we will explain the significance of these colors below. There is one unfilled point, labeled A. That's where the game starts. Tony's name appears next to point A because he chooses first. Two arrows run from point A, one for each of Tony's alternatives. The one labeled "action-adventure" ends at point B; the one labeled "romantic comedy" ends at point C. Maria's name appears next to points B and C, which means that she chooses next.

Two arrows, representing Maria's two alternatives should Tony pick the action-adventure film, run from point B. Two more arrows, representing Maria's two alternatives

Figure 12.13

The Lopsided Battle of the Sexes. This tree diagram describes a version of the Battle of the Sexes in which Tony chooses first and Maria learns what he did before making her own choice. Solving the game by reasoning in reverse, we identify the best choice (indicated by a green arrow) at each point. Our analysis tells us that Tony will choose the action-adventure film, and Maria will follow him wherever he goes.

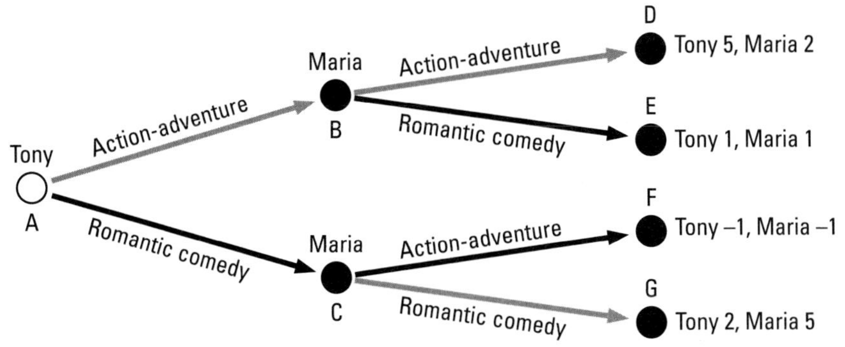

should Tony pick the romantic comedy, run from point C.[11] These four arrows end at the points D, E, F, and G. Tony and Maria's payoffs appear next to those points. So, for example, if Tony goes to the action-adventure film and Maria follows, play will progress from point A to point B to point D; Tony's payoff will be 5 and Maria's will be 2.

Figure 12.13 is a complete description of the Lopsided Battle of the Sexes. It identifies the players (Tony and Maria), all the possible sequences of decisions (paths from point A to point D, E, F, or G), and each player's objectives (payoffs). Everything we need to know about the game is contained in that figure.

Thinking Strategically in a Game with Perfect Information How should Tony go about making his decision in the Lopsided Battle of the Sexes? Clearly, his best choice depends on how he expects Maria to behave. Suppose for the moment that Maria phones Tony before the game starts and says, "You can watch whatever film you want, but I'm going to the romantic comedy no matter what." Then she hangs up without allowing Tony to reply. Tony would rather watch the romantic comedy with Maria than see the action-adventure film alone, so if he believes Maria's threat, he'll pick the romantic comedy. The question is, should he believe her?

To think strategically in a game with perfect information, a player should reason in *reverse*, starting at the *end* of the tree diagram and working back to the beginning. Why? Even before deciding what to do, an early mover (like Tony) can figure out how a late mover (like Maria) will *react* if actually confronted with a situation. Knowing those reactions, the early mover can then identify the best choice. The process of solving a strategic problem by reasoning in reverse is known as **backward induction**.

Backward induction is the process of solving a strategic problem by reasoning in reverse, starting at the end of the tree diagram that represents the game, and working back to the beginning.

[11] In this game, Maria's alternatives do not depend on Tony's choice. In other games, the choices of one player may affect the alternatives available to another player.

Let's use this technique to solve the Lopsided Battle of the Sexes. We'll start by determining Maria's reaction to each of Tony's possible choices. In Figure 12.13, we've used green arrows to indicate those reactions. First suppose Tony chooses the action-adventure film, placing Maria at point B. If Maria chooses the action-adventure film, her payoff will be 2 (at point D); if she chooses the romantic comedy, it will be 1 (at point E). The action-adventure film is a better choice. That is why the arrow that runs from point B to point D in Figure 12.13 is colored green. Next suppose Tony chooses the romantic comedy, placing Maria at point C. Here, the romantic comedy is Maria's better choice; it gives her a payoff of 5 (at point G), rather than -1 (at point F). That is why the arrow running from point C to point G in Figure 12.13 is colored green. As the figure shows, Maria will react to Tony's choices by following him wherever he goes.

Having determined Maria's reactions, let's turn to Tony's choice. Taking Maria's reactions into account, Tony knows he can achieve a payoff of 5 by choosing the action-adventure film (since this will lead to point D), versus a payoff of 2 by choosing the romantic comedy (since this will lead to point G). We've used a green arrow to show that the action-adventure film is Tony's best choice.

We conclude that Tony will go the action-adventure film and that Maria will follow him wherever he goes. Even if Maria has threatened to see the romantic comedy "no matter what," she'll recognize that she can't change Tony's decision after the fact. If Tony calls Maria's bluff by going to the action-adventure film, she won't follow through on her threat, because she prefers to be with him. Knowing that, Tony will ignore the threat and count on Maria to act in her own interest when the time comes.

At this point, you're probably thinking of reasons why Maria might follow through on her threat. For example, she might be concerned that if she gives in, Tony will take advantage of her in the future. That's a valid point, but it doesn't mean that our analysis of the game is wrong. Rather, it means that the game is too simple to capture many aspects of real relationships. Most significantly, in this game there is no future. To think about what Maria might do in a relationship with a future, we'd have to consider a more elaborate game.

Nash Equilibria in a Game with Perfect Information The concept of Nash equilibrium that we introduced in Section 12.3 applies equally well to single-stage and multiple-stage games. In fact, as we'll explain in this section, the behavior described in the previous section is a Nash equilibrium.

A **strategy** is one player's detailed plan for playing a game. For every situation that might come up during the course of play, it tells us what the player will do.

Before applying the concept of Nash equilibrium to a multiple-stage game, we first have to clarify the meaning of the word *strategy*. In game theory, a **strategy** is one player's detailed plan for playing the game. For every situation that might come up during the course of play, it tells us what the player will do. In a one-stage game, a strategy simply indicates a player's chosen action. But in a multiple-stage game, a strategy can prescribe different actions depending on what a player observes.

How would we describe the players' strategies in the Lopsided Battle of the Sexes? Since Tony chooses first, his strategy simply tells us what he chooses—either the action-adventure film, or the romantic comedy. What about Maria? Since she chooses second, two situations can come up during the course of play: either she'll learn that Tony has chosen the action-adventure film, or she will learn that Tony has chosen the romantic comedy. A strategy indicates what she will choose in each of these situations. For example, the following rule is a strategy:

> If Tony chooses the action-adventure film, then choose the action-adventure film. If Tony chooses the romantic comedy, then choose the action-adventure film.

Altogether, Maria has four strategies to choose from. Here are the other three:

> If Tony chooses the action-adventure film, then choose the action-adventure film. If Tony chooses the romantic comedy, then choose the romantic comedy.
>
> If Tony chooses the action-adventure film, then choose the romantic comedy. If Tony chooses the romantic comedy, then choose the action-adventure film.
>
> If Tony chooses the action-adventure film, then choose the romantic comedy. If Tony chooses the romantic comedy, then choose the romantic comedy.

A Nash equilibrium for the Lopsided Battle of the Sexes consists of a pair of strategies, one for Tony and one for Maria, such that Tony's strategy is a best response to Maria's and Maria's is a best response to Tony's. In the previous section, we concluded that Tony and Maria will play according to the following strategies:

> **Tony's strategy:** Choose the action-adventure film.
>
> **Maria's strategy:** If Tony chooses the action-adventure film, then choose the action-adventure film. If Tony chooses the romantic comedy, then choose the romantic comedy.

In other words, Tony picks his favorite film, knowing that Maria will follow him wherever he goes. As it turns out, this pair of strategies is a Nash equilibrium.

Let's check that each player's strategy in this equilibrium is a best response to the other's. We'll start with Tony. Knowing that Maria will follow him wherever he goes, Tony is clearly better off choosing the action-adventure film. Therefore, Tony's strategy is a best response to Maria's.

Is Maria's strategy a best response to Tony's? As we've seen, a strategy tells Maria what to do in two situations: when Tony chooses the action-adventure film, and when Tony chooses the romantic comedy. From Tony's equilibrium strategy, Maria knows that the first situation will definitely come up (that is, Tony will choose the action-adventure film). Therefore, if she changes her choice in the first situation from the action-adventure film to the romantic comedy, she'll be worse off—her payoff will be 1 instead of 2. From Tony's equilibrium strategy, Maria also knows that the second situation definitely won't come up (that is, Tony won't choose the romantic comedy). Therefore, if she changes her choice in the second situation from the romantic comedy to the action-adventure film, she'll be neither better off nor worse off. Because no change in Maria's strategy would make her better off, her strategy is a best response to Tony's. Since Tony's strategy is also a best response to Maria's, these strategies form a Nash equilibrium.

For a game with perfect information, we can *always* find a Nash equilibrium by reasoning in reverse, as in the previous section. As it turns out, this needn't be the game's only Nash equilibrium. In fact, for the Lopsided Battle of the Sexes, there are other equilibria. However, by reasoning in reverse, we always identify the most reasonable equilibrium—one in which no one makes the mistake of believing a threat that isn't credible. For an explanation of this point, read Add-On 12A.

Sometimes, games of perfect information are simply too complicated to solve by reasoning in reverse. Chess is a good example. Using powerful supercomputers, chess enthusiasts have applied the approach outlined here to solve endgames involving relatively few pieces. However, the number of possible configurations explodes exponentially as the number of pieces increases. While in principle it is possible to solve chess, no one has yet solved it in practice.

Even so, by solving simple games of perfect information in reverse, we can gain a great deal of practical insight into credible strategic behavior. Application 12.4 provides an illustration.

Application 12.4

British Satellite Broadcasting versus Sky Television

Until recently, television was a relatively staid affair in Great Britain. In 1988, British consumers were limited to four stations, two of them government-operated through the British Broadcasting Corporation. Cable TV was available to only 2 percent of households in the United Kingdom, compared with 60 percent in the United States.

Drawn by the opportunities associated with this virtually untapped market, a company called British Satellite Broadcasting (BSB) began developing plans to provide British consumers with satellite TV service. Then, in June 1988, the Australian media mogul Rupert Murdoch announced that his company, Sky Television, would follow suit.[12]

Unfortunately, as the two companies recognized, the market wasn't big enough for both of them. Unless one exited, neither would be able to cover the necessary costs. But which one would go, and how long would the shake-out take? Could Murdoch drive BSB from the market by credibly threatening to stick around at all costs? Could BSB credibly confront Sky with the same threat? Economists call this type of competition a *war of attrition*—a situation in which two rivals incur losses until one concedes, after which the survivor becomes profitable.

The two firms were in rather different positions. BSB planned to use a superior technology, and as a result projected higher costs and longer delays before launching its service, drawbacks that provided Sky Television with an edge. Table 12.1 displays the estimated profits and losses for both companies. As we saw in Chapter 10, investment decisions should depend on the net present value (NPV) of anticipated profits. The last column in the top half of the table shows the NPV of the profits each company expected to earn with the other as a competitor (losses of £747 million for BSB and losses of £117 million for Sky). The last column in the bottom half shows the NPV of the profits each expected to earn without a competitor (£137 million for BSB and £673 million for Sky). The table also shows the flow of profits and losses broken down between two periods, 1989–90 and after 1990. For example, without a competitor, Sky would lose £356 million in 1989–90, but would earn £1,029 million afterward, for a total gain of £673 million.

Table 12.1
British Satellite Broadcasting versus Sky Television

	1989–90	After 1990	All years
NPV of profits (million £) with competitor present			
BSB	−637	−110	−747
Sky	−363	246	−117
NPV of profits (million £) with no competitor			
BSB	−595	732	137
Sky	−356	1,029	673

Figure 12.14 represents the conflict between BSB and Sky as a multiple-stage game with perfect information. For the moment, ignore the fact that some arrows are black and others are green. Notice that a broken vertical line divides the tree diagram into two halves. Decisions to the left of this line took place in 1989; decisions to the right of it took place in 1991. In 1989, each firm had to decide whether to stay in the market or exit. We assume here that BSB went first, and Sky observed its choice. In 1991, the remaining firm or firms once again had to decide whether to stay or exit. If both were still active at the start of 1991, BSB would have once

[12]This application is based on the Harvard Business School Case "Sky Television versus British Satellite Broadcasting" # 9-792-039. See also www.vintagebroadcasting.org.uk/bsb.htm and www.museum.tv/archives/etv/B/htmlB/britishskyb/britishskyb/htm.

again moved first, and Sky would have observed its choice. We've computed the payoffs based on the data in Table 12.1; BSB's payoff appears first and Sky's second. For example, if BSB survived until 1991 but then dropped out, while Sky stayed in the market through the end of the game, BSB's payoff would be −£637 million (it would lose that amount competing against Sky in 1989–90), while Sky's payoff would be £666 million (it would lose £363 million competing against BSB in 1989–90 but earn £1,029 million after 1990).

We can identify credible strategies by solving this game in reverse. We'll use green arrows to indicate best choices at each point in the game. Let's start with Sky's decision in 1991. At point G, Sky will choose to stay, earning a payoff of −£117 million, compared to −£363 million if it exits. Sky will also choose to stay at points H (£666 million exceeds −£363 million) and F (£673 million exceeds −£356 million). In other words, having reached 1991, Sky will stay in the market regardless of whether BSB stays or exits. These decisions are shown by the green arrows.

Next, let's look at BSB's decision in 1991. Taking Sky's choices at points G and H into account, we see that BSB will choose to exit at point D (−£637 million exceeds −£747

Figure 12.14

British Satellite Broadcasting versus Sky Television. This figure represents the competition between BSB and Sky as a multiple-stage game with perfect information. Solving the game by reasoning in reverse, we identify the best choice (indicated by a green arrow) at each point. Our analysis tells us that BSB should exit in 1989 after which Sky can operate profitably as the only provider of Satellite TV service in Britain.

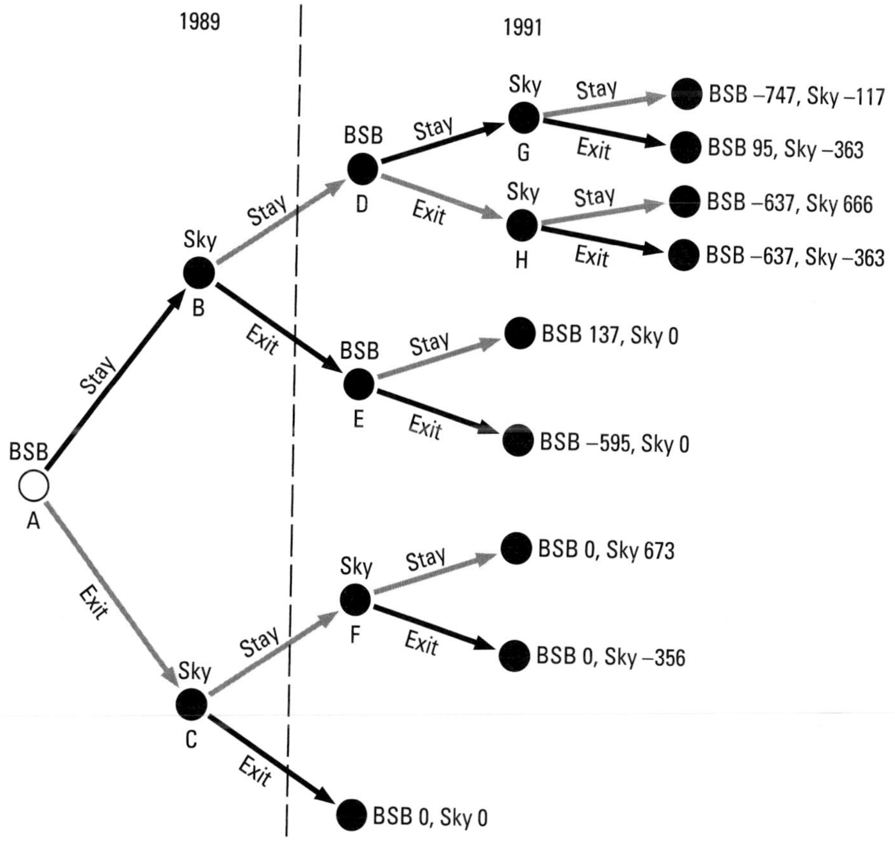

million). In contrast, BSB will choose to stay at point E (£137 million exceeds −£595 million). In other words, having reached 1991, BSB will drop out if Sky is still around, but will stay if Sky has exited. Again, these decisions are shown by the green arrows.

Now let's turn to 1989. We'll start with Sky's decision at point B. In light of BSB's choices at points D and E, as well as Sky's own choices at points G and H, Sky should stay in the market (£666 million exceeds 0). Sky knows that if it stays in, BSB will drop out. Similarly, at point C, Sky will anticipate its own choice at point F and choose to stay (£673 million exceeds zero). In other words, in 1989 as in 1991, Sky will stay in the market regardless of BSB's decision. Again, these decisions are shown by the green arrows.

Finally, we come to BSB's initial choice at point A. In light of everything we've learned about the firms' subsequent decisions, the best choice here is to exit and accept a payoff of zero (as shown by the green arrow running from point A to point C). If instead BSB remains in the market, Sky will stay, forcing BSB to exit in 1991, with a loss of £637 million.

By reasoning in reverse, we've arrived at a Nash equilibrium. Our analysis tells us that BSB should have exited in 1989, and that Sky should have operated profitably as the only provider of satellite TV services in Britain. A threat by Sky to stay in the market regardless of BSB's choices was credible, but a threat by BSB to stick around regardless of Sky's choices was not.

What actually happened? As we predicted, Sky was the eventual winner in this competition. To avoid serious losses, the two companies merged in November 1990, forming British Sky Broadcasting. The next year, Murdoch effectively shut down BSB, firing its staff and selling its satellites.[13]

WORKED-OUT PROBLEM 12.3

The Problem Agatha challenges Danielle to a game of matchsticks (which some readers may recognize as a simplified version of Nim). The game begins with four matchsticks in a pile; the players take turns removing them from the pile. On each turn they must remove either one or two matchsticks. The player who removes the last stick wins and receives one dollar from the loser. Danielle has the first move. Illustrate this game by drawing a tree and solve it by reasoning in reverse.

The Solution The tree for this game appears in Figure 12.15. We can solve it by reasoning in reverse, using green arrows to indicate the best choices at each point in the game. There is no decision to make at points E, F, or G—only one stick remains, so the next player to move must take it and win. At point D, two sticks are left, and Danielle wins by taking both of them. The same is true for Agatha at point C. At point B, with three sticks left, Agatha doesn't care whether she takes one or two sticks; in light of Danielle's decision at point D, Agatha will lose in either case, so both are best choices. Taking all this into account, Danielle knows that at point A, she'll win if she takes one matchstick, but lose if she takes two. She therefore takes one.

IN-TEXT EXERCISE 12.6 **Repeat worked-out problem 12.3, changing the rules as follows. To begin, there are six matchsticks in the pile. At each turn a player can remove one, two, or three matchsticks.**

[13]BSB's departure didn't occur quite as quickly as our analysis led us to expect. Uncertainty about the market's potential and BSB's own competitive position probably caused executives to keep it afloat a bit longer, in hopes of a better outcome.

Figure 12.15

A Game of Matchsticks. This figure represents the game of matchsticks described in worked-out problem 12.3. At the start, there are four matchsticks in a pile; players take turns removing either one or two of them on each turn. The player to take the last stick wins one dollar from the loser. Solving the game by reasoning in reverse, we identify the best choices (indicated by green arrows) at each point. Our analysis tells us that Danielle should start the game by taking one stick. Regardless of whether Agatha responds by taking one or two sticks, Danielle can then take all that remain.

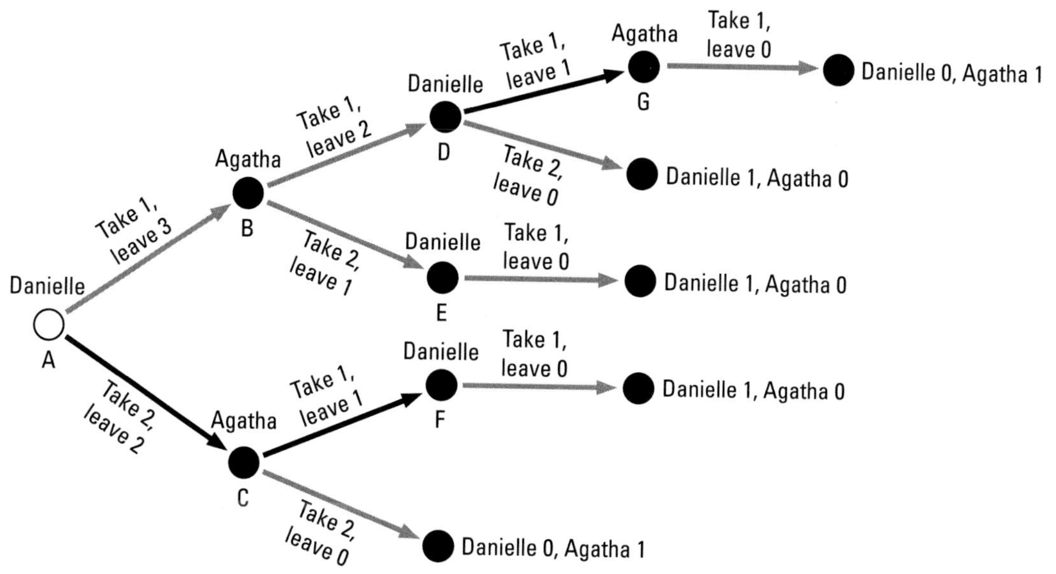

Cooperation in Repeated Games

Why do people make personal sacrifices to help others? Altruism certainly plays a role; sometimes we help people we like or for whom we feel compassion. But in other situations we recognize the benefits of mutual cooperation and help people out of self-interest.

Cooperation is usually sustained by the threat of a punishment for bad behavior or the promise of a reward for good behavior. Efforts to establish cooperation will fail unless those threats and promises are credible. To illustrate this point, we'll study an example involving a married couple, Marge and Homer. On any given day, each can choose to either clean the house or loaf. Figure 12.16 shows their payoffs for that day. Notice that both prefer loafing to cleaning, regardless of what the other chooses. However, when one of them cleans the house, the other is happier. Moreover, they are better off if both clean than if both loaf.

Let's consider a one-stage game in which Marge and Homer simultaneously choose between cleaning and loafing on a single day. This game is a variant of the Prisoners' Dilemma (Figure 12.2, page 409); we'll call it the Spouses' Dilemma. Because loafing is a dominant strategy for both spouses, no one cleans, and each receives a payoff of 1. If Marge and Homer could cooperate and clean the house together, both would be happier. But neither has a reason to cooperate in the one-stage game.

Nobel Laureate Robert Aumann (1930–) pioneered the study of cooperation and conflict in repeated games.

Figure 12.16

The Spouses' Dilemma. Marge and Homer simultaneously choose to clean the house or loaf. According to this table, both prefer loafing to cleaning, regardless of what the other chooses. However, when one of them cleans the house, the other is happier. Moreover, they are better off if both clean than if both loaf.

Homer \ Marge	Clean	Loaf
Clean	Homer: 2, Marge: 2	Homer: 0, Marge: 3
Loaf	Homer: 3, Marge: 0	Homer: 1, Marge: 1

Marriage is not, however, a one-stage game. (If you think it is, we recommend remaining single.) Spouses interact with each other repeatedly through time. They have ample opportunity to reward each other for considerate choices and punish each other for inconsiderate choices. Those opportunities foster cooperation.

To see how cooperation can emerge in a multiple-stage game, let's suppose that Marge and Homer play the Spouses' Dilemma repeatedly; each day, they simultaneously choose to clean or loaf. This is an example of a **repeated game**, one that's formed by playing a simpler game many times in succession. In some contexts, economists study games that are repeated a fixed number of times, and then end. These settings are known as **finitely repeated games**. In other contexts, economists study **infinitely repeated games**, in which the repetitions can continue indefinitely. When economists model strategic problems as infinitely repeated games, they don't literally mean that the players will interact with each other until the end of time. Rather, they simply mean that there isn't a known, fixed point in time at which the players will stop interacting with each other; instead, there is always a possibility of further interaction.

A **repeated game** is formed by playing a simpler game many times in succession.

A **finitely repeated game** is formed by repeating a simpler game a fixed number of times, after which the game ends. An **infinitely repeated game** is formed by repeating a simpler game indefinitely.

A Nash equilibrium in a repeated Spouses' Dilemma game is a pair of strategies, one for Marge and one for Homer, such that Marge's strategy is a best response to Homer's and Homer's is a best response to Marge's. As before, a strategy tells us what a player will do for every situation that might come up during the course of play. *Always clean* is a strategy. So is *loaf if my spouse loafed yesterday, otherwise clean*. In fact, any rule that specifies a choice based on the history of past choices can serve as a strategy.

An Equilibrium without Cooperation When a one-stage game is repeated, it's always possible that the participants will simply play the equilibrium of the one-stage game over and over. In fact, that method of playing is always a Nash equilibrium for the repeated game, regardless of whether the game is finitely or infinitely repeated.

We'll illustrate this point in the context of the Spouses' Dilemma. Without repetitions, the only Nash equilibrium in this game is for Marge and Homer to loaf. Consequently, there is a Nash equilibrium for the repeated Spouses' Dilemma in which Marge and Homer both choose the strategy, always loaf. If Homer chooses that strategy, then always loaf is a best response for Marge. Why? On any given day, loafing will give her a higher payoff than cleaning, and her choice won't affect Homer's future behavior. For the same reason, if Marge chooses the strategy always loaf, then always loaf is a best response for Homer. This equilibrium involves no cooperation.

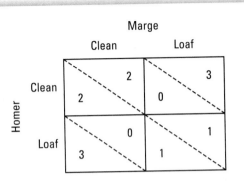

In a finitely repeated Spouses' Dilemma, there is no other reasonable equilibrium. The players can't cooperate because threats of punishment and promises of reward aren't credible. Suppose, for example, that Marge and Homer plan to part ways after 100 days. To determine what they will do, we reason in reverse, starting from the end of the game. On the last day, they'll both know that they have no future together. Since neither will have a chance to reward or punish the other, both will loaf. On the second-to-last day, they'll both know that they have one day left together, and that they'll spend it loafing. Since neither will choose to reward or punish the other when the final day arrives, both will loaf on the second-to-last day. On the third-to-last day, they'll both know that they have two days left together, and that they'll spend both days loafing. Since neither will choose to reward or punish the other when those final days arrive, both will loaf on the third-to-last day. Reasoning in this manner, we reach the conclusion that Homer and Marge will loaf every day. The same conclusion follows regardless of whether they plan to part after 10 days, 100 days, or 10,000 days. Any definite stopping point causes cooperation to unravel.

Equilibria with Cooperation Can Marge and Homer manage to cooperate if the game has no fixed stopping point? As long as they care enough about the future, the answer is yes. One relatively simple possibility is to use strategies that threaten *permanent* punishment for selfish behavior, also known as **grim strategies**. For the infinitely repeated Spouses' Dilemma, we'll examine the following grim strategies (one for Homer, one for Marge):

With **grim strategies**, the punishment for selfish behavior is permanent.

> Clean on the first day. On subsequent days, clean as long as my spouse and I have an unbroken history of cleaning on every previous day; otherwise loaf.

What happens when Marge and Homer both play these strategies? Obviously, they both clean on the first day. That means they will have an unbroken history of cleaning at the start of the second day, so they'll both clean again. The same thing happens at the start of the third day, and so forth. In other words, the couple will clean every day. However, if one of them ever departs from that plan and loafs, their history of cleaning will be broken, and neither will ever clean again. In that sense, the punishment for loafing is permanent.

Assuming Marge and Homer use these strategies, will either be tempted to loaf? Suppose they have an unbroken history of cleaning. According to their strategies, both are supposed to clean, receiving a payoff of 2 in every period moving forward. But what if Homer decides to loaf? He'll increase his payoff to 3 in the current round, but at a cost. Marge's strategy will tell her to retaliate by loafing on all subsequent days, reducing Homer's best available payoff from 2 to 1. Therefore, if Homer cares enough about his future interactions with Marge, he'll clean. Marge will reason the same way. Accordingly, we have a Nash equilibrium in which the threat of a punishment—mutual loafing—causes Homer and Marge to cooperate.

Does the equilibrium described in the last two paragraphs involve credible threats? The answer is yes. Suppose either Homer or Marge has loafed, setting off the punishment. In that case, according to their strategies, each will always loaf in the future, no matter what the other does. If Homer thinks Marge will follow this strategy, his best choice is to loaf, and vice versa. Consequently, each of them has incentive to follow through with the punishment.

The fact that Marge and Homer *can* cooperate doesn't mean that they *will* cooperate. Remember that there is also an equilibrium in which they both always loaf. But let's suppose that Marge and Homer can discuss their strategies before playing. In that case, we can interpret Nash equilibria as self-enforcing agreements. Marge and Homer have a mutual interest in reaching an agreement that produces cooperation. Therefore, they are likely to play a cooperative equilibrium.

Even so, Marge and Homer may not agree upon the cooperative equilibrium described above. In practice, the use of grim strategies is potentially risky. If the players have a misunderstanding—for example, if Marge becomes convinced that Homer has loafed, even though he has cleaned—cooperation can fall apart forever. For that reason, it may be better to reach a self-enforcing agreement that relies on *temporary* punishments. Homer and Marge might, for example, use strategies that tell them to punish selfish choices by loafing for a few days, and then to start cleaning again. Those strategies are less risky than grim strategies (in the sense that misunderstandings will only have temporary consequences), but they're also less powerful. The less Homer and Marge care about the future, the longer punishments must last to deter selfish choices.

Application 12.5

A Crude Cartel

Worldwide, the uneven geographic distribution of crude oil deposits has had a profound effect on the economic and political landscape. For countries with abundant petroleum resources, oil represents a critical source of wealth and economic prosperity. These exporters of petroleum have a strong interest in maintaining high oil prices, which creates conflict with nations that depend on imported oil.

Maintaining high oil prices is a challenging objective, however. Since the worldwide demand curve for oil is downward sloping, high prices require low output. But why should any single oil-exporting country restrict its production? Though the price of oil will go up, other oil exporters will reap much of the benefit, as they continue producing at high levels. In other words, even though all oil exporters would benefit if they reduced production, each may lack the incentive to do so unilaterally.

The simple one-stage game shown in Figure 12.17 captures the essence of the oil exporters' quandary. Let's focus on two large exporters, Saudi Arabia and Iran, ignoring other sources for the sake of simplicity. Each country has two strategies, a low production level and a high one. High production corresponds roughly to actual levels in 2004; 9 million barrels per day (bbl/day) for Saudi Arabia and 4 million bbl/day for Iran. Low production represents a 10 percent reduction, to 8.1 million bbl/day for Saudi Arabia and 3.6 million bbl/day for Iran. The figure includes a column for each of Saudi Arabia's choices and a row for each of Iran's. The number in the northeast half of each cell shows Saudi Arabia's profit from the corresponding strategies; the number in the southwest half of each cell is Iran's profit.[14]

According to these figures, both countries will be better off if they both choose low production than if they both choose high production. (Profits will rise from \$135 to \$138

[14]We've assumed that the cost of production is \$15 per barrel and that oil sells for \$30 per barrel at high production levels (for a profit margin of \$15 per barrel). Lower production raises prices and therefore profit margins. The price of oil rises by \$1.2 per barrel when Saudi Arabia reduces production unilaterally; by \$0.5 per barrel when Iran reduces production unilaterally; and by \$1.9 per barrel when both countries reduce production at the same time.

million per day for Saudia Arabia and from $60 to $61 million per day for Iran.) The resulting price increase will more than compensate for the reduction in volume.

Nevertheless, each country will unilaterally choose high production. Why? In Figure 12.17, we have used green shading to indicate Iran's best response, and red shading to indicate Saudi Arabia's. Notice that high production is a dominant strategy for both countries. For Iran, cutting production will reduce profit regardless of the Saudi production level. The price increase resulting from low production will not be enough to compensate Iran for the loss of volume, because Iran is ignoring the benefits to the Saudis. Similar reasoning applies to Saudi Arabia, though the numbers differ. In short, this game has essentially the same structure as the Prisoners' Dilemma (Figure 12.2, page 409) and the Spouses' Dilemma (Figure 12.16, page 436).

In practice, of course, Saudi Arabia and Iran don't play a one-stage game. They produce and sell oil month after month, year after year. Let's suppose they play the game in Figure 12.17 repeatedly. Can they achieve a more profitable outcome through cooperation? Our discussion of the Spouses' Dilemma suggests that they can, as long as they attach sufficient importance to their future interaction. In a cooperative Nash equilibrium, each will begin by choosing low production and will continue to do so unless one of them "cheats" by choosing high production. At that point, both will switch to high production. Though cheating increases current profits, it draws retaliation, which reduces future profits. Fear of retaliation keeps both countries in line.

What have oil-rich countries done in the past? In 1960, Iran, Iraq, Kuwait, Saudi Arabia, and Venezuela formed the Organization of Petroleum Exporting Countries (OPEC). Their object was to agree on mutually beneficial prices and production levels. Since then, they've been joined by six other countries—Algeria, Indonesia, Libya, Nigeria, Qatar, and the United Arab Emirates.

OPEC's efforts to maximize its members' profits have met with mixed success. The organization sets voluntary production targets (quotas) for its members, but compliance is imperfect. In the 1970s, oil exporters worked in concert to increase prices tenfold, precipitating an economic crisis in western countries. However, the high prices proved impossible to sustain. Cheating exploded during the second half of the 1980s, with actual production exceeding total quotas by as much as 25 percent. Oil prices plummeted, eliminating most of the gains from the 1970s. By the end of 1990, cheating on quotas subsided, but only because OPEC, acknowledging the inevitable, had allowed quotas to increase in 1989. Even so, most studies suggest that OPEC has been at least moderately successful at maintaining prices above levels that would otherwise prevail.

OPEC's checkered record illustrates the difficulties that people, companies, and countries encounter when they attempt to cooperate. Cooperation necessarily creates the temptation to cheat. When that temptation is sufficiently strong, a mutually beneficial course of action is unsustainable.

Iran \ Saudi Arabia	8.1 mil bbl/day	9.0 mil bbl/day
3.6 mil bbl/day	Saudi Arabia: $138 mil/day; Iran: $61 mil/day	Saudi Arabia: $140 mil/day; Iran: $56 mil/day
4.0 mil bbl/day	Saudi Arabia: $131 mil/day; Iran: $65 mil/day	Saudi Arabia: $135 mil/day; Iran: $60 mil/day

Figure 12.17

Cooperation among OPEC Nations. This game represents the interaction between oil producers Saudi Arabia and Iran as a Prisoners' Dilemma. Each nation chooses either low or high oil production. As the green shading indicates, high production is a dominant strategy for Iran. And as the red shading indicates, high production is a dominant strategy for Saudi Arabia. Yet if both chose low production, both would be better off. If both nations interact repeatedly and care enough about their future interaction, they can cooperate.

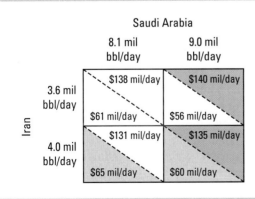

John Harsanyi (1920–), who shared the Nobel Prize in Economics with John Nash and Reinhard Selten, pioneered the study of games in which at least one party is uncertain about another's preferences, and consequently its objectives.

*12.5 GAMES IN WHICH DIFFERENT PEOPLE HAVE DIFFERENT INFORMATION

In many strategic settings, people have difficulty predicting each others' choices because they don't share the same information. For example, when a potential buyer negotiates the price of a used car, he typically knows less than the seller about the car's quality. When a new company enters a market, it usually has limited information about the production costs of existing firms. And when the leaders of two countries find themselves at odds, each may be unsure of the other's willingness to risk war.

Games in which different people have different information fall into two broad categories. The first category involves situations, such as the first two examples in the previous paragraph, in which objective information is available to one party, but not to another. The second category involves situations, such as the last example in the previous paragraph, in which at least one party is uncertain about another's preferences, and consequently its objectives.[15]

When people have different information, whether about objective facts or about their preferences, their choices can reveal something about what they know. Two important points follow. First, each participant in a game can potentially learn important information from the behavior of other participants. Second, when a participant knows that others are trying to learn from his choices, he may have an incentive to mislead others by acting contrary to his immediate interests. We will illustrate the first point by describing a phenomenon known as *the winner's curse*, and the second point by discussing the creation and maintenance of reputations.

The Winner's Curse

Olivia attends an automobile auction in the hope of purchasing a used car at a low price. After carefully examining a 2000 Ford Mustang convertible, she feels reasonably confident that the car is in good shape and worth at least $10,000, its blue book value. To her surprise, she comes out on top with a winning bid of $6,000. Her first reaction is delight. Her second reaction: what's wrong with the car?

The **winner's curse** is the tendency, in certain types of auctions, for unsophisticated bidders to overpay whenever they win.

Olivia's experience illustrates the principle that, in certain types of auctions, unsophisticated bidders tend to overpay whenever they win. This phenomenon, known as the **winner's curse**, potentially arises whenever the item's commonly perceived value depends on information that may become available to some but not all bidders. For example, in an automobile auction, some bidders may discover a mechanical problem that others overlook. Because the winner will tend to be a bidder who overlooked the problem, the winning bid will often be too high.

A sophisticated bidder—even one who potentially overlooks pertinent information—needn't fall prey to the winner's curse. For example, before bidding $6,000 for the Mustang, Olivia should ask herself: "If no one bids more than $6,000, does this mean they've noticed something that I've overlooked? If so, is the car really worth $6,000?" In other words, to avoid overpaying, Olivia should try to extract information from the anticipated

[15]These are known as *games of incomplete information*.

behavior of other bidders on the assumption that she will win. The following example shows how this is done.

Example 12.7

The Winner's Curse in a Second-Price Auction

A Ford Mustang is offered for sale through a second-price auction. There are three bidders, Melissa, Olivia, and Elvis. There's a 50 percent chance that the car has a serious mechanical problem, in which case it's worth $2,000 to all bidders, and a 50 percent chance that it's problem-free, in which case it's worth $10,000. Melissa has had an opportunity to inspect the car and knows whether or not it has a problem. Olivia and Elvis have had no such opportunity. Given their uncertainty, they are willing to pay only $6,000.

In this game, a strategy for Melissa must specify one bid if the car has a problem and another if it's problem-free. A strategy for Olivia or Elvis simply specifies a single bid.

For the same reasons as in Application 12.1, each participant should bid whatever he or she thinks the car is worth. Because Melissa is fully informed, her best strategy is to bid $2,000 if the car has a problem and $10,000 if it's problem-free. If neither Olivia nor Elvis accounts for the winner's curse, each will naively bid $6,000. Because the second highest bid will be $6,000 regardless of Melissa's bid, the car will sell for $6,000. When it is problem-free, Melissa will win and underpay for it. When it has a problem, either Olivia or Elvis will win and overpay for it.

To avoid the winner's curse, Olivia and Elvis must become more sophisticated. In light of Melissa's strategy, no bid between $2,000 and $10,000 can possibly win if the car is problem-free. Therefore, Olivia and Elvis both know that if they win with such a bid, the car will be worth only $2,000—in other words, less than their bid.

Suppose Olivia and Elvis bid $2,000 instead of $6,000, and Melissa bids as described above. That combination of strategies is a Nash equilibrium. When the car has a problem, all three participants bid $2,000. The car sells for $2,000, the buyer is selected at random, and everyone's net payoff is zero. When the car is problem-free, Melissa bids $10,000 while Olivia and Elvis bid $2,000. Melissa buys the car for $2,000 and receives a net payoff of $8,000. The payoff to Olivia and Elvis is again zero.

To confirm that this is a Nash equilibrium, let's make sure that no participant can do better. No matter what Olivia bids, she will either win or lose. If she loses, her payoff will be zero. If she wins, the second highest bid will necessarily be $2,000 if the car has a problem, and $10,000 if it's problem-free (given the strategies used by Elvis and Melissa). In either case, she will pay exactly what the car is worth and receive a net payoff of zero. Therefore, Olivia can't improve on her equilibrium payoff. The same reasoning applies to Elvis. What about Melissa? If she loses, her payoff will be zero. If she wins, the second highest bid will necessarily be $2,000 whether or not the car has a problem. Therefore, her net payoff cannot exceed zero when the car has a problem and $8,000 when it's problem free. Since this is what she receives in equilibrium, Melissa can't improve on her equilibrium payoff.

By avoiding the winner's curse, Olivia and Elvis achieve better results. Notice that Melissa benefits from their sophistication: when the car is problem-free, she pays a lower price. Because the car sells for $2,000 instead of $6,000 regardless of whether it's problem-free, the seller is worse off.

Application 12.6

The Winner's Curse in Auctions for Offshore Oil Leases

Companies that drill for oil and natural gas in U.S. waters lease the rights to particular territories, known as *tracts*, from the federal government. Historically, the government has sold these rights through auctions.

Sales of offshore drilling rights fall into two main categories, drainage sales and wildcat sales. In a drainage sale, the government auctions off tracts that are adjacent to areas with known deposits. A wildcat sale involves tracts in areas where no drilling has occurred. In either instance, potential bidders attempt to evaluate a tract's potential through seismic tests. However, in the case of a drainage sale, the firms that hold leases on adjacent tracks (which we'll call *neighbor firms*) can attempt to draw useful lessons from their experiences. In auctions for drainage leases, non-neighbor firms may therefore have inferior information, in which case they are potentially exposed to the winner's curse (just like Olivia and Elvis in Example 12.7).

Do neighbor firms in fact have better information about a tract's potential than non-neighbor firms? If so, are non-neighbor firms aware of their handicap? Do they adequately compensate for this disadvantage and avoid the winner's curse? A study by economists Kenneth Hendricks and Robert Porter addresses these questions by examining a collection of federal auctions for drainage leases that took place between 1959 and 1969.[16] The study contains a number of significant findings.

First, neighbor firms did indeed have better information than non-neighbor firms. We know this because the ultimate profitability of the typical tract was more highly correlated with the participation and bids of neighbor firms than of non-neighbor firms. Neighbor firms won most of the auctions for profitable drainage tracks, and they earned substantially higher profits than non-neighbor firms.

Second, Hendricks and Porter found evidence of the winner's curse. Notably, when the neighbor firms chose not to bid, the prevailing non-neighbor firm typically suffered significant losses.

Finally, there were strong indications that non-neighbor firms were aware of the winner's curse and that they attempted to compensate for it. Despite being at an informational disadvantage, non-neighbor firms managed to break even on average by behaving conservatively. Because they often declined to participate, the typical drainage tract auction had fewer competitors than the typical wildcat tract auction. Participating non-neighbor firms also bid conservatively, reducing competitive pressure on neighbor firms. As a result, the government collected only 66 percent of the typical drainage tract's value, compared with 77 percent for wildcat tracks.

Reputation

A **reputation** is a widely held belief about a characteristic of a person or company that predisposes them to act in a particular way.

A **reputation** is a widely held belief about a characteristic of a person or company that predisposes them to act in a particular way. Usually, reputations are acquired through consistent patterns of behavior. Recognizing this fact, people often choose to act in ways that build or maintain good reputations. For example, people act kindly toward others both because they are kind, and because they like to cultivate reputations for kindness.

Concerns over reputation influence a wide variety of important economic decisions. As an illustration, let's suppose you've finished your schooling and taken an entry-level position with a good company. You're hoping to stay with the company as you build a career. You know that your boss tries to promote the type of people who like to work hard.

[16]Kenneth Hendricks and Robert H. Porter, "An Empirical Study of an Auction with Asymmetric Information," *American Economic Review* 78, no. 5, December 1988, pp. 865–883.

As a result, you'd like to develop a reputation as someone who enjoys lots of challenging assignments.

To learn whether you like to work hard, your employer will pay attention to the number of hours you put in, the amount of effort you show, and your level of productivity. Consequently, you can try to enhance your reputation by working long hours, seeking difficult assignments, and making sure your contributions to team projects are visible. In fact, if career advancement would provide you with opportunities to take it easy, you may wish to follow that strategy even if, at heart, you're actually not such a hard worker.

Of course, sophisticated employers will not be completely fooled. They will understand that the same level of apparent devotion to work may reflect either a true love of challenges or a desire to disguise less productive tendencies. Even so, the ruse may succeed for some pretenders. By working hard to make visible contributions, they may prevent their bosses from discovering their true inclinations, and thereby secure desired promotions. This is why law firms sometimes worry that associates will become less productive after making partner, and some universities fear that faculty will publish fewer research papers after receiving tenure.

CHAPTER SUMMARY

1. **What is a game?**
   a. Some strategic situations correspond to one-stage games; other correspond to multiple-stage games. In economics, multiple-stage games are more common.
   b. To describe the essential features of a one-stage game, we follow two steps. First, we identify the players and list the actions available to each. Second, for every possible combination of actions (one for every player), we identify each player's payoff, be it a reward or penalty.
2. **Thinking strategically in one-stage games**
   a. Strategic situations require us to think about what other people will do. We can try to do so by putting ourselves into others' shoes, but that approach frequently leads to unproductive circular reasoning. Even so, in some situations it is possible to reason out the likely choice of a sensible opponent.
   b. If a player has a dominant strategy he ought to play it, regardless of what he thinks others might do. In some games, like the Prisoners' Dilemma, all players have a dominant strategy.
   c. Sometimes it is possible to reason out the likely choice of a sensible opponent by iteratively deleting dominated strategies.
   d. It's usually a good idea to avoid weakly dominated strategies. In some cases, this dictum leads to a clear choice. For example, it implies that people should bid their true valuations in second-price sealed-bid auctions.
3. **Nash equilibrium in one-stage games**
   a. Given a table that summarizes a one-stage game with two players, we can find a Nash equilibrium by looking for a cell that (a) gives the row player the highest payoff in the same column and (b) gives the column player the highest payoff in the same row.
   b. The combination of strategies chosen in a Nash equilibrium is stable. Every participant is content with his choice; no one wants to play anything else. All other outcomes are unstable, in the sense that at least one participant would want to change his strategy.
   c. One justification for focusing on Nash equilibria is that when all players are experienced, they should have reasonably accurate expectations of what the others will do, and should therefore tend to make their best responses to one anothers' choices.
   d. A Nash equilibrium is also a self-enforcing agreement—one in which every party to the agreement has an incentive to abide by it, assuming that others do likewise.
   e. In many games, no strategy dominates any other, even weakly. The concept of Nash equilibrium allows us to analyze strategic behavior in those games.

f. Depending on the game, Nash equilibrium can involve either good outcomes or bad ones.

g. In two-player games in which the choices are finely divisible, we can plot curves that show each player's best response as a function of the other's choice. To find the Nash equilibria, we then identify the points where the curves intersect.

h. In many games involving pure strategies, there are no Nash equilibria, but virtually all games have mixed-strategy equilibria.

i. Players are most likely to use mixed strategies in situations in which unpredictability is a key to success.

j. In any Nash equilibrium involving mixed strategies, each player must be indifferent among the choices over which he randomizes. This principle helps us to solve for the equilibria.

4. **Games with multiple stages**

a. We can describe a game with perfect information by drawing a tree diagram that shows the sequence of decisions and indicates the players' payoffs.

b. The best way to identify credible strategies and sensible Nash equilibria in a game with perfect information is to reason in *reverse*; that is, to start at the end of the tree diagram and work back to the beginning, identifying the choices that each player will make as we go.

c. For a finitely repeated game, punishments and rewards may not be credible, and cooperation may not be possible, in any reasonable Nash equilibrium.

d. For an infinitely repeated game, punishments and rewards are credible, and cooperation is possible, provided that the players care enough about the future.

5. **Games in which different people have different information**

a. In many strategic settings, people have difficulty predicting each others' choices because they don't share the same information. One player may receive objective information that is not available to some other player, or one player may be uncertain about another's preferences.

b. In certain types of auctions, unsophisticated bidders tend to overpay whenever they win. A sophisticated bidder anticipates this winner's curse and bids more conservatively.

c. Other people often learn things about us by observing our actions. As a result, a consistent pattern of behavior can create a reputation. Knowing this, people may intentionally adopt patterns of behavior that help to build or maintain desirable reputations.

ADDITIONAL EXERCISES

Exercise 12.1: Consider the game shown in Figure 12.7 (page 414). What are Myrna's best responses? Does she have a dominant strategy? What are the Nash equilibria in this game? If there is more than one, which do you think is the most plausible? Why?

Exercise 12.2: Paul and Susie each pick an integer between 1 and 5 (inclusive). They make their choices simultaneously. If they pick the same number, each receives a payoff (in dollars) equal to the number they named. If they pick different numbers, they receive nothing. Draw a table representing this game, showing the players' strategies and payoffs. Does either player have a dominant, weakly dominated, or dominated strategy? Identify all the Nash equilibria. Are all equally plausible? Why or why not?

Exercise 12.3: Fred and Barney are negotiating with each other to divide \$4. Simultaneously, each proposes an integer between 0 and 4 (inclusive) to represent the amount that Fred gets. If they propose the same number, Fred receives the proposed amount and Barney receives the rest. If they propose different numbers, neither gets anything. Does either player have a dominant, weakly dominated, or dominated strategy? Identify all the Nash equilibria. Is there an equilibrium in which Fred and Barney don't reach an agreement (that is, in which they make different proposals)? If such an equilibrium exists, is it reasonable? Why or why not?

Exercise 12.4: Repeat exercise 12.3, but change the problem as follows. Fred and Barney each have an additional option: to withdraw from the negotiation. If either one withdraws, he receives a payoff of \$1.50. Everything else is the same as in exercise 12.3.

Exercise 12.5: Two companies, Green, Inc. and Red, Inc., produce granfalloons. Each can produce 0, 1, 2, 3, or 4 granfalloons (they can't produce fractions of granfalloons). Let X be the number of units produced by Green, Inc., and Y be the number of units produced by Red, Inc. Given X and Y, granfalloons sell at a price equal to $\$(14 - X - Y)$. Every granfalloon costs $5 to produce. The companies choose X and Y simultaneously, each trying to maximize profits. Draw a table representing this one-stage game, showing the players' strategies and payoffs. Does either company have a dominated strategy? Can you solve this game by the iterative deletion of dominated strategies? Find the Nash equilibrium. Would the companies do better if they both reduced production (starting from the equilibrium point) by one unit? Why or why not?

Exercise 12.6: Alice and Tiffany are playing a simple one-stage game. Each simultaneously picks either 1 or 2. If they both pick 1, Alice pays Tiffany $1. If they both pick 2, Alice pays Tiffany $2. If they pick different numbers, Tiffany pays Alice $1. Draw a table showing the two players' strategies and payoffs. Are any strategies dominant, weakly dominated, or dominated? Indicate each player's best responses. Is there a Nash equilibrium? Solve for a mixed-strategy equilibrium.

Exercise 12.7: Wilma and Betty are contractors who are bidding for a job. The client will hire the contractor who submits the lower bid; if the bids are tied, he'll hire Wilma. The winning contractor will incur $900 in costs. The two contractors are allowed to submit bids of $1,000, $2,000, or $3,000. For the winner, profit equals the difference between the bid and cost; for the loser, profit is zero. Wilma and Betty submit their bids simultaneously. Draw a table representing this game, showing the players' strategies and payoffs. Are there any dominant, weakly dominated, or dominated strategies? Can you solve this game by the iterative deletion of dominated strategies? Find the Nash equilibrium.

Exercise 12.8: Consider the plurality rule election described in Example 12.5 (page 414). Suppose that *all* voters prefer Ms. Maverick to Ms. Right, and Ms. Right to Mr. Left. Is there a Nash equilibrium in which Ms. Maverick wins? Is there one in which Ms. Right wins? Is there one in which Mr. Left wins? In each case, either describe an equilibrium or explain why there isn't one. Also, for each equilibrium that you describe, say whether any voters use weakly dominated strategies.

Exercise 12.9: Suppose Wesley and Vizzini play the Battle of Wits according to the following rules: Wesley moves first, and Vizzini is allowed to watch what he does; then Vizzini drinks from a goblet. Illustrate this game by drawing a tree and solve it by reasoning in reverse.

Exercise 12.10: Suppose John and Reinhard play Rock Paper Scissors according to the following rules: John chooses first, and Reinhard is allowed to watch what he does before making his own decision. Illustrate this game by drawing a tree and solve it by reasoning in reverse.

Exercise 12.11: A firm has an unprofitable factory. Managers decide to close the factory, but only after operating it for an additional six months to meet existing contractual obligations. They can inform workers immediately or just prior to closure. If they tell workers immediately, the typical worker has a choice: try to line up a new job that will start when the factory closes or get a new job immediately.

If the typical worker gets a new job immediately, avoiding unemployment, the firm will have to use temporary employees, who are inefficient. The payoffs of this outcome are $40,000 for each worker and −$10 million for the firm.

If the typical worker lines up a new job that will start when the factory closes, the worker will experience a short period of unemployment, but the firm will be able to wind down its operations efficiently. The payoffs of this outcome are $38,000 for each worker and −$5 million for the firm.

If the firm closes the factory without warning, the typical worker will experience a long period of unemployment. The firm will be able to wind down its operations efficiently, but will create a costly public relations problem. The payoffs of this outcome are $30,000 for each worker and −$8 million for the firm.

Illustrate this game (between the firm and a typical worker) by drawing a tree and solve it by reasoning in reverse. Is there a better outcome? How might the firm and worker achieve it?

Exercise 12.12: Fred and Barney are playing the centipede game, which works as follows. Each player starts with a pile of money containing $2. Fred moves first; then they alternate turns. On each turn, a player says either stop or continue. If he says stop, the game ends and each player keeps the money in his own pile. If he says continue, $1 is removed from his own pile and $2 is added to the other player's pile, after which the next player takes his turn. The game must end when each player's pile contains $10 (which the players keep). Illustrate this game by drawing a tree and solve it by reasoning in reverse. Do you think people would actually play the game this way? Why or why not? How would your answer change if the game ended only when each pile contained $100?

Exercise 12.13: Wilma and Betty must split $10 by playing the ultimatum game, which works as follows. First, Wilma proposes an integer between 0 and 10 (inclusive), representing the amount she will keep for herself (Betty gets the rest). Second, Betty either accepts or rejects the proposal. If she accepts it, the money will be divided as proposed. If she rejects it, neither will receive anything. Illustrate this game by drawing a tree and solve it by reasoning in reverse (there may be more than one equilibrium). Do you think people would actually play the game this way? Why or why not?

Exercise 12.14: We know that chess has at least one Nash equilibrium. Even though we can't solve for it, we can still reach some conclusions. Specifically, if there is a Nash equilibrium in which the first-mover wins, then the first-mover wins in every Nash equilibrium. Likewise, if there is an equilibrium in which the second-mover wins, then the second-mover wins in every equilibrium. And if there is an equilibrium that results in a draw, then every equilibrium results in a draw. Can you figure out why?

Exercise 12.15: Suppose that Homer and Marge plan to play the Spouses' Dilemma on 10,000 consecutive days, and then part ways forever. Do you agree with the prediction that they'll be unable to cooperate? If not, how and why might they be able to sustain cooperation?

Exercise 12.16: Let's change Example 12.7 (page 441) as follows. With 20 percent probability, Melissa's examination of the car definitely reveals whether or not it's problem-free. With 80 percent probability, she learns nothing from her examination. In that case, given her uncertainty, she will be willing to pay $6,000, just like Olivia and Elvis. Neither Olivia nor Elvis knows whether Melissa learns anything from her examination. Does Melissa have a weakly dominant strategy? If so, what is it? If Olivia and Elvis bid naively, will they still suffer from the winner's curse?

13

BEHAVIORAL ECONOMICS

LEARNING OBJECTIVES

After reading this chapter, students should be able to:

- Describe the objectives and methods of behavioral economics.
- Summarize, interpret, and evaluate evidence of systematic departures from perfect rationality.
- Explain why some economists are calling for modifications to the standard theory of decisions involving time and uncertainty.
- Discuss why it may be important to account for social motives when analyzing strategic decisions.
- Describe the emerging field of neuroeconomics and explain what neuroeconomists hope to accomplish.

Britney Spears served as a spokesperson for PepsiCo products during 2001 and 2002.

Early in 2001, pop icon Britney Spears signed a deal with PepsiCo to serve as spokesperson for the company's products. Pepsi reportedly paid Spears tens of millions of dollars for television commercials and other promotional activities. The company clearly expected Spears's ads to boost sales—but why? Her endorsement provided consumers with little if any useful information. They certainly didn't learn anything about their own preferences for Pepsi. As it happens, they didn't learn anything about Spears's preferences, either. According to reports, a technical rider to the contract for Spears's 2000 World Tour required promoters to stock her dressing room with Coke, and tabloid journalists periodically spotted her with the product. But advertising speaks more often about psychology than about substance. Spears's endorsement wasn't intended to "prove" anything. Rather, in linking Pepsi to the pop star in consumers' minds, the company hoped to create a positive image by association.

Many economists seek to gain a better understanding of such phenomena by studying the psychology of decision making, a field of inquiry known as *behavioral economics*. Some behavioral economists view psychology as offering an alternative to the standard economic theory of decision making described in Chapters 3 through 12. However, most believe that economics and psychology are fundamentally compatible. These scholars use insights from psychology to modify, supplement, and enrich the economic approach.

Much like the field of behavioral economics, this chapter presents a collection of noteworthy observations concerning decision making and offers specialized theories to explain a number of them. In contrast to previous chapters, it does not build from a few fundamental principles to a single general theory. Some behavioral economists hope their field will become more unified over time as they gain new insights into decision making, while others expect it to remain compartmentalized.

This chapter provides an overview of some important research in behavioral economics. We'll address six topics:

1. *Objectives and methods of behavioral economics*. In seeking to enrich economic theory through insights drawn from psychology, behavioral economists use the same tools as other economists. However, as we'll see, they tend to rely more heavily on experiments with human subjects.
2. *Departures from perfect rationality*. No one is completely rational all of the time. Many behavioral economists believe that departures from perfect rationality tend to occur in certain types of circumstances and take certain forms. We'll discuss some of the evidence offered in support of these conclusions and discuss its implications. (This material complements Chapters 4 through 9.)
3. *Choices involving time*. In Chapter 10, we studied the standard economic theory of decisions involving time. Many behavioral economists see that theory as too restrictive, because it rules out certain patterns of behavior that are sometime observed in practice. We'll review some of the relevant evidence and discuss its implications.
4. *Choices involving risk*. In Chapter 11, we studied the standard economic theory of decisions involving risk. Many behavioral economists see that theory as requiring modification in light of evidence concerning the beliefs that people actually hold and the choices they actually make. Again, we'll review some of the relevant evidence and discuss its implications.
5. *Choices involving strategy*. In Chapter 12, we studied the field of game theory, which provides powerful tools for understanding choices involving strategy. Sometimes, strategic decisions appear to be motivated not only by material self-interest, but also by social concerns such as altruism, fairness, and prestige. We'll discuss the potential importance of accounting for these social motives when analyzing strategic decisions.
6. *Neuroeconomics: a new frontier*. Some economists believe that it may be possible to develop a new unified theory of decision making by studying the human neural system, including brain processes. We'll summarize some provocative findings in this emerging branch of economics.

13.1 OBJECTIVES AND METHODS OF BEHAVIORAL ECONOMICS

What is the need for behavioral economics? What are the field's objectives? How is it related to the standard economic approach to decision making, which we studied in Chapters 4 through 12? How is behavioral economics different from and similar to standard economics? This section provides brief answers to each of these questions.

Motivations and Objectives

There are two main motivations for research in behavioral economics, both of which concern apparent weaknesses in the standard economic theory of decision making. First, people sometimes make choices that are inconsistent with—or at least very difficult to reconcile with—standard economic theory. Second, in some situations, standard economic theory leads to seemingly unreasonable conclusions about consumer welfare.

Here's a hypothetical example that illustrates the first concern. Suppose that on any given night, Ethan's favorite restaurant serves two of the following three dishes: hamburgers, tacos, and pizza. On his way to the restaurant, Ethan thinks about the various possibilities. He concludes that between hamburgers and tacos, he'd choose tacos; between tacos and pizza, he'd choose pizza; and between pizza and hamburgers, he'd choose hamburgers. The preferences that are implied by these choices violate the Ranking Principle, which holds that consumers can rank their alternatives from best to worst (see Section 4.1).[1] To see why, look at Figure 13.1. The arrow between each pair of alternatives points to the one that Ethan chooses. With this circular configuration, there's no way to rank the choices from best to worst. As we'll see in Section 13.2, experimental evidence suggests that sometimes, problems like this may arise in everyday decision making.

With respect to the second concern, standard theory tells us to evaluate consumer welfare by applying the principle of *revealed preference* (see Section 5.6). In other words,

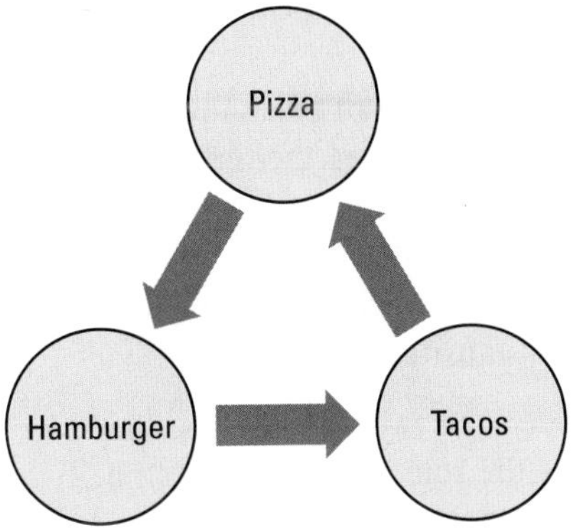

Figure 13.1
Inconsistent Choices. Between hamburgers and tacos, Ethan prefers tacos; between tacos and pizza, he prefers pizza; and between pizza and hamburgers, he prefers hamburgers. The preferences implied by these circular choices would violate the Ranking Principle, according to which consumers can rank their alternatives from best to worst.

[1]Technically, they violate the assumption of transitivity, which we defined in footnote 1 on page 93.

it assumes that the alternative the consumer chooses makes him at least as well off as any other alternative he could have chosen. But indiscriminate application of this principle sometimes leads to unreasonable conclusions. For example, American tourists in London suffer numerous injuries and fatalities because they often look only to the left before stepping into the street, even though they know traffic approaches from the right. Should we conclude that these people prefer to throw themselves into the path of oncoming cars? Obviously not. Their objective—to cross the street safely—is clear, but their choices are plainly mistakes. What about eating disorders? Should we assume that an anorexic's refusal to eat is an expression of valid preferences, or is it a medical problem that requires intervention? And what about addiction? Do addicts use addictive substances because they want to, or because they've lost the ability to control their own self-destructive tendencies?

The field of behavioral economics grew out of research in psychology. In a long succession of scholarly studies, researchers identified and investigated various puzzling forms of behavior, often with the objective of disproving key premises of economic theory. Today, however, most behavioral economists recognize that economic theory is remarkably powerful and flexible and has proved capable of accounting for behavior in a wide range of contexts. Their objective is to modify, supplement, and enrich the theory—not to overturn it—by adding insights from psychology.

In keeping with the two main motivations for behavioral economics listed at the beginning of this section, modifications of the standard theory usually take one of two forms. In some instances, behavioral economists suggest that people care about things that standard theory ignores, like fairness or status. In other instances, they allow for the possibility that certain actions—like the use of a highly addictive substance—can be mistakes.

Methods

Because behavioral economics is an extension of standard economics, for the most part it employs the same tools as standard economics within the same methodological framework. Behavioral economists have much in common with other economists:

- They usually assume that each individual has well-defined objectives, that there is a connection between an individual's objectives and actions, and that the actions chosen affect an individual's well-being.
- They rely heavily on mathematical models of behavior, which requires them to state their assumptions precisely, and discourages them from relying on incomplete or loose reasoning. This approach also allows them to answer important quantitative questions that arise in business and government.
- They subject their theories to careful, thorough empirical tests using objective data, replicable methods, and standard statistical tools.

Despite these similarities between the two approaches, there are also some differences. The most important concerns the role of experiments involving human subjects. In testing their theories, behavioral economists tend to rely primarily (though not exclusively) on experimental data, while standard economists tend to rely primarily (though not exclusively) on data drawn from the real world.

The Advantages of Experiments In a typical economic experiment, subjects make decisions with monetary consequences under conditions that the experimenter controls.

Compared to the analysis of real world data, experimental methods offer several advantages, some of which are particularly important for research in behavioral economics.

First, through laboratory experiments, it's easier to determine whether people's choices are consistent with standard economic theory.[2] The real world is extremely complex; numerous factors can influence every significant decision. Even when human behavior looks peculiar, economists can often come up with subtle explanations. Take the hypothetical example just discussed, in which Ethan's preferences violated the Ranking Principle. If the chef tends to overcook pizza while making hamburgers but not while making tacos, Ethan's preferences would make perfect sense. In a laboratory setting, in contrast, all the influences on decision making are potentially knowable and controllable. A good experiment can rule out alternative explanations (like systematic variation in the quality of pizza).

Second, with laboratory experiments, it's often easier to establish causality. For example, think about the problems we encounter in estimating a demand curve using real-world data on quantities and prices. As we discussed in the appendix to Chapter 2, such data reflect the interplay of supply and demand. Separating supply effects from demand effects is a tricky procedure that requires the use of subtle statistical techniques. In the laboratory, it's possible to avoid these difficulties altogether. The experimenter simply sets a price and measures the associated demand.

Third, with laboratory experiments, researchers can double check their assumptions and conclusions by testing and debriefing subjects. Careful questioning can reveal whether a subject has properly understood a task and interpreted options and outcomes as intended. It can also shed light on subjects' thought processes and their reasons for making particular choices.

Finally, in the laboratory, it's often possible to obtain information that isn't available in the real world. For example, experimentation offers reliable ways to measure subjects' plans and expectations.

The Disadvantages of Experiments Experiments aren't perfect. While the advantages of the experimental method are undeniable, there are also some disadvantages. First, decisions made in the laboratory differ from decisions made in the real world. In the laboratory, tasks and settings are usually artificial, and often somewhat unfamiliar. Since behavioral economists have limited research budgets, the subjects typically don't have much at stake. Some scholars argue that these differences are too large to justify generalizations to real-world decisions. Experimental economists have attempted to address these concerns in a number of ways. Some have run experiments with both small and large stakes to determine whether the size of the stakes matters. Others have conducted field experiments in which the tasks and settings are both natural and familiar, and the stakes meaningful. Some experimental results turn out to be representative of behavior outside the lab; others don't.

Second, laboratory experiments introduce influences on decision making that are difficult to measure or control. For example, there is strong evidence that subjects often try to conform to what they think are the experimenter's expectations. Psychologists frequently attempt to overcome this difficulty through deception. That is, they invent a false explanation for the experiment's purpose. Experimental economists rarely engage in deception,

[2]For example, in Application 2.1 (page 33), we described a famous laboratory experiment that was designed to determine whether the theory of supply and demand accurately predicts prices and the amounts bought and sold.

however. In a university setting, students quickly learn that experiments involve deception; as subjects, they begin to second-guess an experiment's purpose, introducing unknown and uncontrolled influences on their decision making. Instead of using deception, most experimental economists try to avoid telegraphing their expectations to subjects by describing the subjects' tasks in neutral terms.

Third, in most cases, experimental subjects are students at colleges and universities, which means that by and large, they are unrepresentative of the general population. They are also relatively inexperienced at making important economic decisions. To determine whether results obtained from student subjects are representative, economists sometimes repeat their experiments with subjects recruited from other settings (for example, the workplace).

Fourth, as a practical matter, the scale of any given experiment is limited by the available resources. As a result, the typical experimental trial involves a relatively small number of subjects, which makes it difficult to apply the results to economic behavior in very large groups. For example, an experiment involving a market consisting of fifteen buyers and fifteen sellers may not tell us much about markets with thousands of buyers and/or sellers.

How to Evaluate Behavioral Evidence

Much of behavioral economics is controversial. Some economists are convinced that certain aspects of the standard model are flawed; others think the evidence against it is weak and overstated. In evaluating behavioral research, we recommend a mix of open-mindedness and healthy skepticism. Each time we read about a pattern of behavior that is allegedly inconsistent with standard theory, we should ask ourselves the following critical questions.

- Is the evidence convincing? If it is from a laboratory study, for example, was the experiment well-designed? Were the subjects provided with clear instructions? Did they have appropriate incentives? Were they being guided (perhaps unintentionally) to select certain choices?
- Is the observed behavioral pattern robust? Does it show up in many studies, under a variety of conditions? Are there some conditions under which it *isn't* observed? For example, does the pattern appear with certain experimental procedures, and disappear with others?
- If the pattern is observed in the laboratory, how—if at all—would we expect it to translate to the real world? Did the experimental tasks involve common choices and familiar situations? Are the stakes usually different in the real world, and if so, does it matter? Does the pattern survive after people have gained experience and received feedback? Is it likely to survive in a market, where competition favors those who make better decisions?
- What are the possible explanations for the observed pattern? Can we reconcile the pattern with standard theory? For example, if an experimental subject appears to make a series of inconsistent choices, could it be that the experimenter unintentionally allowed some condition, like the quality of one of the alternatives, to vary?
- If evidence suggests that standard economic theory fails to account for a behavioral pattern in economically significant situations, how should we modify the theory?

Does the observed pattern reflect preferences or mistakes? Is it possible to tell the difference between the two? What are the larger implications for economic analysis?

We make no attempt to answer every one of these questions for every pattern we discuss. To do so would require a book, not a chapter. Rather, our object is to bring a collection of interesting and potentially important behavioral patterns to your attention, so that you can start the process of critical evaluation. Here you will find much food for thought, but few definitive answers.

13.2 DEPARTURES FROM PERFECT RATIONALITY

No one is completely rational all of the time. Psychologists and behavioral economists have identified some apparent departures from perfect rationality that tend to occur in certain types of situations, and take certain forms. In this section, we'll examine some of the pertinent behavioral evidence and discuss implications for economic analysis.

Incoherent Choices

The idea that choices reflect preferences is central to the theory of consumer decision making, described in Chapters 4 through 6. But do people actually make choices that reflect sensible preferences? According to some psychologists and behavioral economists, the answer is no, at least in some situations.

Choice Reversals If Ethan's preferences satisfy the Ranking Principle, he will not make the circular choices illustrated in Figure 13.1. Consequently, those choices do not reflect sensible preferences. Yet laboratory subjects sometimes display this type of incoherent behavior when confronted with certain types of choices.

In one series of experiments, subjects were asked to make decisions involving two different bets. The first involved a high probability of winning a small amount of money. For example, the subject might win $4 with 97 percent probability, or lose $1 with 3 percent probability. We'll call this type of bet the *low stakes bet*. The second bet involved a low probability of winning a larger amount of money. For example, the subject might win $16 with 30 percent probability, or lose $1.50 with 70 percent probability. We'll call this type of bet the *high stakes bet*.

Subjects were asked first to choose between a low stakes bet and a high stakes bet. Second, they were asked to state a dollar amount that was just as good as the low stakes bet—no better or worse.[3] Third, they were asked to state a dollar amount that was just as good as the high stakes bet—no better or worse.

Table 13.1 summarizes the results of a trial involving 46 subjects, each of whom considered six different pairs of low stakes bets and high stakes bets (for a total of 276 comparisons). As shown in the line labeled *low stakes bet*, in 99 comparisons subjects chose the low stakes bet over the high stakes bet. Yet for 69 of these, he or she assigned a higher dollar value to the high stakes bet than to the low stakes bet. In other words, in those

[3]In Chapter 11, we referred to this amount as the *certainty equivalent*.

Table 13.1
Choice Reversals

Chosen Alternative	Frequency	Value of Low Stakes Bet Is Higher	Value of High Stakes Bet Is Higher	Values Equal
Low stakes bet	99	26	69	4
High stakes bet	174	22	145	7
Indifferent	3			

Source: David M. Grether and Charles R. Plott, "Economic Theory of Choice and the Preference Reversal Phenomenon," *American Economic Review* 69, no. 4, September 1979, pp. 623–638. Subjects were all undergraduates at the California Institute of Technology.

cases, subjects selected the alternative regarded as less valuable.[4] Similar inconsistencies occurred in cases in which the subject chose the high stakes bet over the low stakes bet, though with much lower frequency (only 22 out of 174 cases, as shown in the line labeled *high stakes bet*).

Even though this experiment involved bets rather than dinners, the problem with the subjects' choices is exactly the same as in Figure 13.1. To see why, consider a subject who chose a low stakes bet over a high stakes bet. Assume he valued the high stakes bet at \$3.60 and the low stakes bet at \$3.40, which means that he preferred the high stakes bet (valued at \$3.60) to \$3.50, and \$3.50 to the low stakes bet (valued at \$3.40). Figure 13.2 illustrates these choices. Between each pair of alternatives, the arrow points to the one chosen. With this configuration, just as in Figure 13.1, there is no way to rank the three choices (the low stakes bet, the high stakes bet, and \$3.50) from best to worst.

Does this finding undermine the validity of standard economic theory? The answer to this question may depend on context. It seems unlikely that among people who would choose the Honda Prelude over the Toyota Camry, many would be willing to pay more for

Figure 13.2
A Choice Reversal. An experimental subject who chooses a low stakes bet over a high stakes bet, but who attaches a higher dollar value to the high stakes bet than to the low stakes bet, violates the Ranking Principle. In this illustration, we assume that he values the low stakes bet at \$3.40 and the high stakes bet at \$3.60. In that case, he chooses the high stakes bet over \$3.50, and \$3.50 over the low stakes bet. Yet he chooses the low stakes bet over the high stakes bet. As shown, his choices among these three options (the low stakes bet, the high stakes bet, and \$3.50) are circular.

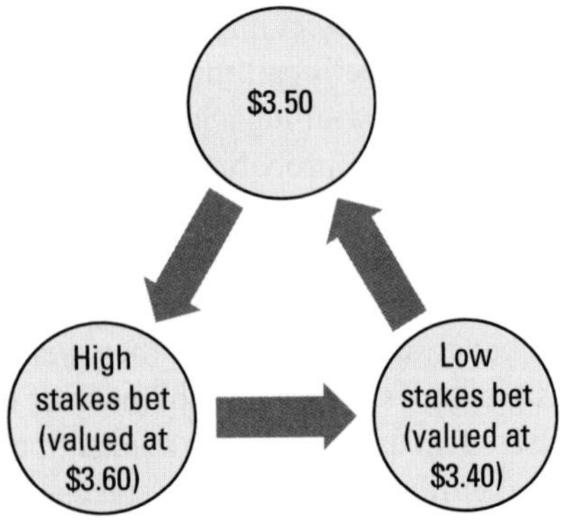

[4]This phenomenon was first reported by Sarah Lichtenstein and Paul Slovic, "Reversals of Preferences Between Bids and Choices in Gambling Decisions," *Journal of Experimental Psychology* 89, July 1971, pp. 46–55, and by H. R. Lindman, "Inconsistent Preferences Among Gambles," *Journal of Experimental Psychology* 89, August 1971, pp. 390–397.

the Camry than the Prelude. More likely, the reversal just described has something to do with the way people think about certain kinds of bets. There is also some evidence that the frequency of such reversals declines considerably when decisions are repeated in market settings, where people can learn from the consequences of their choices.[5] For these reasons, many economists question whether the phenomenon of choice reversal is relevant to familiar and significant economic choices.

Anchoring Another line of research suggests that some choices are fundamentally arbitrary, and therefore can't reflect meaningful preferences. Support for this view comes from experiments in which subjects' choices depended on prominent but patently irrelevant information, a phenomenon known as **anchoring**.[6]

Anchoring occurs when someone's choices are linked to prominent but patently irrelevant information.

In one study, 55 subjects were shown a series of six common products with an average retail price of about $70. For each product, the experiment involved two steps. First, the subject was asked if he would be willing to purchase the product at a price equal to the last two digits of his Social Security number. Second, the subject was asked to state the highest amount he would be willing to pay for the object. The experiment was designed so that each subject had an incentive to respond truthfully.

Table 13.2 shows subjects' average willingness to pay for each product in the second step. The table separates subjects into five groups of equal size based on the last two digits of their Social Security numbers. For example, if a subject's Social Security number ended in "02," he would be placed in the group labeled *lowest fifth*; if it ended in "98," he would be placed in the group labeled *highest fifth*. According to the table, the typical subject's willingness to pay in the second step was closely related to the last two digits of his Social Security number. For example, those in the lowest fifth were willing to pay an average of $11.73 for a rare bottle of wine, while those in the highest fifth were willing to pay an average of $37.55—more than three times as much. Obviously, the last two digits

Table 13.2
Anchoring Effects on Economic Valuation

Rank of SSN	Cordless Trackball	Cordless Keyboard	Average Wine	Rare Wine	Design Book	Belgian Chocolate
Lowest fifth	$8.64	$16.09	$8.64	$11.73	$12.82	$9.55
2nd lowest fifth	11.82	26.82	14.45	22.45	16.18	10.64
Middle fifth	13.45	29.27	12.55	18.09	15.82	12.45
2nd highest fifth	21.18	34.55	15.45	24.55	19.27	13.27
Highest fifth	26.18	55.64	27.91	37.55	30.00	20.64

Source: Dan Ariely, George Loewenstein, and Drazen Prelec, "'Coherent Arbitrariness': Stable Demand Curves Without Stable Preferences," *Quarterly Journal of Economics*, February 2003, 73–105. Subjects were all MBA students at MIT's Sloan School of Management.

[5]In one experiment involving involving auctions, choice reversals tended to disappear after five repetitions. See James C. Cox and David M. Grether, "The Preference Reversal Phenomenon: Response Modes, Markets, and Incentives," *Economic Theory* 7, 1996, pp. 381–405.

[6]Anchoring was first documented by Amos Tversky and Daniel Kahneman, "Judgment Under Uncertainty: Heuristics and Biases," *Science* 185, 1974, pp. 1124–1131.

of a person's Social Security number should have nothing to do with his preference for wine and are indeed unrelated to his willingness to pay for the wine when the first step of the experiment is omitted. But apparently, by calling attention to those digits in the context of a purchase decision (the first step), the experimenters created an anchor for the subjects' subsequent valuations (the second step).

In this experiment, subjects displayed extreme sensitivity to the power of suggestion. Skeptics note that the typical MBA student (the subject pool for this experiment) has relatively little experience purchasing or consuming the items listed in Table 13.2. They suggest that these same subjects might have been less sensitive to suggestion with respect to the value of familiar products, like soda or wireless phone service. The significance of anchoring effects for both everyday economic choices and major decisions calling for careful deliberation remains unclear.

Bias toward the Status Quo

In some situations, people exhibit a strong attachment to the status quo. From an economic point of view, there are two potentially important manifestations of this tendency. One is called the **endowment effect**, which refers to the observation that people tend to value something more highly when they own it than when they don't. The other is called the **default effect**, which refers to the fact that when confronted with a menu of alternatives, people sometimes avoid making a choice and end up with the option assigned as a default.

The **endowment effect** refers to the observation that people tend to value something more highly when they own it than when they don't.

The **default effect** refers to the fact that when confronted with many alternatives, people sometimes avoid making a choice and end up with the option that is assigned as a default.

The Endowment Effect Table 13.3 summarizes the results of an experiment illustrating the endowment effect. Forty-four students were gathered together in a classroom. Half (22) were given mugs, which were available at the campus bookstore for $6 each. The other half were allowed to examine the mugs. Each student who had a mug was asked to name the lowest price at which he or she would be willing to sell it (we'll call this amount the *owner valuation*). Each student who did not have a mug was asked to name the highest price at which he or she would be willing to buy it (we'll call this amount the *nonowner valuation*). The experimenter used the answers to construct supply and demand curves and identify the equilibrium price. Willing buyers actually purchased the mugs

Table 13.3
The Endowment Effect

Round	Equilibrium Price	Median Nonowner Value	Median Owner Value
1	$4.25	$2.75	$5.25
2	4.75	2.25	5.25
3	4.50	2.25	5.25
4	4.25	2.25	5.25

Source: Daniel Kahneman, Jack L. Knetsch, and Richard H. Thaler, "Experimental Tests of the Endowment Effect and the Coase Theorem," *Journal of Political Economy* 98, no. 6, December 1990, pp. 1325–1348. The subjects were undergraduates at Cornell University.

Figure 13.3

The Endowment Effect and the Shape of Indifference Curves. In figure (a), Angelica starts out at bundle A. The blue indifference curve running through bundle A is kinked at A because of the endowment effect. As a result, over a wide range of prices (for example, those corresponding to the green budget lines L_1 and L_2), Angela simply keeps her endowment. If the price of mugs falls far enough, however, she will trade T-shirts for mugs. For example, bundle B is her best choice on the budget line labeled L_3. After she adjusts to her trade psychologically, her indifference curve running through bundle B develops a kink at B [as shown in figure (b)]. She sticks with bundle B even when the price of mugs rises to its original level (rotating the budget line to L_4, which is parallel to the original budget line, L_1).

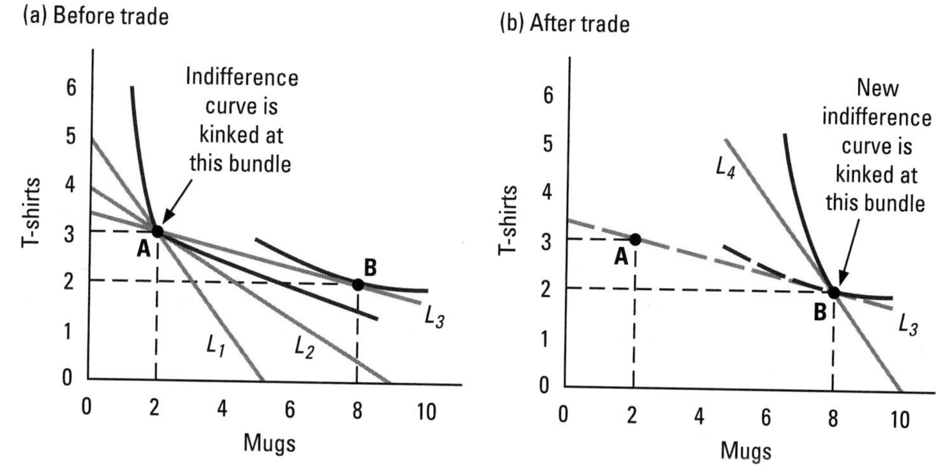

from willing sellers at that price.[7] Students repeated the exercise four times in succession (with one round selected at random as binding) to see if learning and market experience might affect their behavior.

Since the mugs were assigned randomly, standard economic theory would predict that the average owner valuation should be the same as the average nonowner valuation. But the results shown in Table 13.3 contradict this prediction. The median owner value was roughly twice as large as the median nonowner value. In other words, when a subject is randomly chosen to receive a mug, receipt of the mug appears to double his or her valuation of it. This result did not change much as subjects gained experience through successive rounds.

Some economists think the endowment effect reflects something fundamental about the nature of preferences. How might we incorporate it into consumer theory? Look at Figure 13.3(a). Let's suppose that Angelica likes to collect mugs and T-shirts. Initially, she has two mugs and three T-shirts, putting her at bundle A in Figure 13.3(a). The endowment effect implies that her indifference curve running through bundle A (the blue curve) is kinked at that point. Here's why:

- In moving southeast from bundle A, Angelica gives up T-shirts in exchange for mugs. Since she already owns the T-shirts but doesn't yet own the additional mugs, the

[7] With this procedure, subjects may not have had an incentive to tell the truth about their valuations, because a subject's reported valuation could affect the price. Even with procedures that provide an incentive for truth-telling, however, the same patterns still emerge.

T-shirts seem especially valuable to her compared to the mugs. Thus, it takes many new mugs to compensate for the loss of one T-shirt. That is why this portion of the curve is relatively flat.

- In moving northwest from bundle A, Angelica gives up mugs in exchange for T-shirts. Since she already owns the mugs but doesn't yet own the additional T-shirts, the mugs seem especially valuable to her compared to the T-shirts. Thus, it takes many new T-shirts to compensate for the loss of one mug. That is why this portion of the curve is relatively steep.

With these preferences, Angelica is reluctant to trade at all. For a wide range of prices, she simply hangs onto her endowment. Consider, for example, the budget lines labeled L_1 and L_2, which reflect different prices. Bundle A is her favorite alternative on both budget lines.

There are, of course, circumstances in which Angelica will trade away part of her endowment. If the price of mugs falls far enough, she will sell a T-shirt so she can buy some extra mugs. For example, suppose that a reduction in the price of mugs rotates Angelica's budget line from L_1 to L_3. Since L_3 crosses into the area above Angelica's indifference curve, she will swap point A (two mugs and three T-shirts) for some other alternative, like bundle B (eight mugs and two T-shirts).

By trading, Angelica changes what she owns, from bundle A to bundle B. Once she adjusts to the trade psychologically, her indifference curve running through bundle B develops a kink at that point, as shown in Figure 13.3(b). So even if the price of mugs rebounds to its original level, producing the budget line labeled L_4 (which is parallel to the original budget line L_1), she hangs onto her eight mugs. With the endowment effect, smooth fluctuations in price therefore produce "jerky" changes in consumption.

Some economists think that the endowment effect reflects systematic mistakes rather than actual preferences. In support of this view, they point to evidence showing that the effect can be switched on and off by varying the experimental procedure. According to one study, the effect disappears entirely when sufficient care is taken to make sure that the subjects fully understand those procedures.[8]

The Default Effect Experimental evidence suggests that people are sometimes less likely to make a choice and more likely to end up with a default option when they are confronted with several alternatives at once. In one study, 80 subjects were asked to fill out a short questionnaire in return for a payment of $1.50.[9] At the end of the experiment, half were offered the chance to swap the $1.50 for a Zebra pen, worth roughly $2. The other half were offered the chance to exchange the $1.50 for *either* a Zebra pen *or* two Pilot pens, also worth roughly $2.

According to standard economic theory, the introduction of a second option (the Pilot pens) should *reduce* the number of subjects who keep the $1.50. Why? Anyone who was willing to trade the $1.50 for a Zebra pen still has that option when the Pilot pens are available. In addition, some subjects who were unwilling to swap the $1.50 for the Zebra pen may be willing to trade for the Pilot pens. Therefore, fewer subjects overall should choose to keep the cash.

---

[8]See Charles R. Plott and Kathryn Zeiler, "The Willingness to Pay–Willingness to Accept Gap, the 'Endowment Effect,' Subject Misconceptions, and Experimental Procedures for Eliciting Values," *American Economic Review* 95, no. 3, June 2005, pp. 530–545.

[9]Amos Tversky and Eldar Shafir, "Choice Under Conflict: The Dynamic of Deferred Decision," *Psychological Science* 3, 1992, pp. 358–361. The subjects were undergraduate students.

Yet precisely the opposite pattern was observed in the laboratory. When the only choice was a Zebra pen, only 25 percent kept the cash. When the choice included either a Zebra pen or two Pilot pens, 53 percent kept the cash. One possible explanation is that, when many alternatives are available, decision making entails greater psychological costs, increasing the number of people who accept the default alternative.

Choices involving pens and small amounts of cash show only that the costs of decision making outweigh the benefits when relatively little money is at stake. Do people also avoid making choices when the stakes are high? Application 13.1 suggests that the answer is yes.

Application 13.1

Saving for Retirement by Default

Financial consultants typically advise workers that they will need 60 percent to 80 percent of their preretirement income after retirement. That income can come from three sources: personal saving, Social Security, and private pensions plans sponsored by employers. Historically, private pension plans didn't offer employees many choices. Today, employees have a great deal of control over their contribution levels and their pension investment portfolios. By 2003, U.S. employers offered roughly 400,000 401(k) plans to 42 million covered workers, who had accumulated $1.9 trillion in assets. The typical 401(k) plan allows each employee to contribute whatever she wants (up to a legal maximum) and to invest in a wide variety of mutual funds.

When people are free to choose among many complex alternatives, it's natural to wonder whether default options matter. In the vast majority of voluntary pension plans, nonparticipation is the default option, one many people end up with. Does their nonparticipation reflect intentional and deliberate choice, or are they simply overwhelmed by the wide range of saving and investment options available to them? To answer that question, two economists, Brigitte Madrian and Dennis Shea, studied field data on the effects of a change in the default provisions for the 401(k) plan of a Fortune 500 company. Prior to April 1, 1998, the default option was nonparticipation. After that date, all new employees were immediately enrolled in the plan at a 3 percent default contribution rate, and contributions were invested in money market funds unless the employee specified something else. Since the plan's other alternatives were unchanged, standard economic theory tells us that the new default provisions should have had no impact on employees' behavior.

What actually happened? Table 13.4 compares the contribution rates after 3 to 15 months of employment for two groups of workers: those hired during the year prior to the change (for whom the default provision was nonparticipation) and those hired during the year after the change (to whom the new default provisions applied). The new default provision reduced the rate of nonparticipation from 63 percent to 14 percent. It increased the fraction of workers choosing a 3 percent contribution rate from 4 percent to 65 percent. It also reduced the fraction of workers contributing *more* than 3 percent from 30 percent to 20 percent.

The study also documented the effects of the change in default provisions on employees' investment portfolios. Under the new default provisions, the fraction of assets invested in money market funds was 80 percent, compared to less than 10 percent under the old provisions. Roughly 75 percent of workers placed *all* their assets in money market funds under the new provisions, compared to 6.1 percent under the old provisions. Overall, 61.1 percent of employees followed all aspects of the new default provisions *exactly*, while less than 1 percent made those choices when the default was nonparticipation.

Can standard economic theory account for these patterns? Possibly. The typical employee may be roughly indifferent toward many of the choices available to him, simply because he doesn't have the expertise to determine whether one is better than another. If resolving this question requires a great deal of time or money (for example, to consult an expert advisor), going with the default provision may be the best choice.

Table 13.4

Default Effects in Pension Plan Choices

Contribution Rate	Fraction of Employees (default: no participation)	Fraction of Employees (default: participation)
0%	63%	14%
1–2	3	1
3	4	65
4–5	4	2
More than 5	26	18

Source: Brigitte C. Madrian and Dennis F. Shea, "The Power of Suggestion: Inertia in 401(k) Participation and Savings Behavior," *Quarterly Journal of Economics* 116, no. 4, November 2001, pp. 1149–1187.

Narrow Framing

To some extent, all the decisions we make are interrelated. Whenever we spend money or time on something, less remains to spend on everything else. At times, many of us seem to ignore these interrelationships, however. Instead, we sometimes simplify the process of decision making by compartmentalizing. When shopping for groceries, we may think only about our food purchases. When shopping for sweaters, we may think only about our clothing purchases. We tend to group related items into categories and draw artificial boundaries around those categories. In making certain types of choices, we tend to consider other items in the same category and may ignore items in different categories—a phenomenon known as **narrow framing**.

Narrow framing is the psychological tendency to group related items into categories, and, in making a choice, to consider other items in the same category while ignoring items in different categories.

In some situations, narrow framing can lead to behavior that is hard to justify objectively. For example, in one study, subjects were asked the following questions:[10]

> "Imagine that you have decided to see a play where admission is $10 per ticket. As you enter the theater you discover that you have lost a $10 bill. Would you still pay $10 for a ticket for the play?"

[10] Amos Tversky and Daniel Kahneman, "The Framing of Decisions and the Psychology of Choice," *Science* 211, no. 4481, January 30, 1981, pp. 453–458.

"Imagine that you have decided to see a play and paid the admission price of $10 per ticket. As you enter the theater you discover that you have lost the ticket. The seat was not marked and the ticket cannot be recovered. Would you pay $10 for another ticket?"

As long as additional tickets are available, there's no meaningful difference between losing $10 in cash before buying a ticket, and losing the $10 ticket after buying it. In both cases, you're out $10. Yet far more subjects say they would see the play in response to the first question than in response to the second (88% versus 56%).

The leading explanation for this pattern attributes it to narrow framing. In the first scenario, there is no immediate connection between the thing that is lost (a $10 bill) and the play. Because the loss of the money has nothing *directly* to do with the evening's entertainment, subjects unconsciously assign these items to different mental accounts. In the second scenario, there is an immediate connection between the lost ticket and the play. Because subjects assign these items to the same mental account, they see themselves as $10 poorer for the evening and are less likely to replace the ticket than they were to buy one in the first scenario.

Narrow framing can also influence how we evaluate the factors we *do* consider in making our decisions. For example, the same study posed the following two questions:

"Imagine that you are about to purchase a jacket for $125, and a calculator for $15. The calculator salesman informs you that the calculator you wish to buy is on sale for $10 at the other branch of the store, located 20 minutes drive away. Would you make the trip to the other store?"

"Imagine that you are about to purchase a jacket for $15, and a calculator for $125. The calculator salesman informs you that the calculator you wish to buy is on sale for $120 at the other branch of the store, located 20 minutes drive away. Would you make the trip to the other store?"

Objectively, these two scenarios are identical. You plan to spend a total of $140, and can save $5 by making a 20-minute trip to another store. Yet far more subjects say they would make the trip in the first scenario than in the second (68% versus 29%).

In each case, subjects should ask themselves the same question: does saving $5 justify a 20-minute trip? However, most people tend to think of savings in relative terms. They see a steep 33 percent discount ($5 off the $15 price) in the first scenario, compared to a modest 4 percent discount ($5 off the $125 price) in the second. In both cases, narrow framing links the potential savings to the calculator but not to the jacket.

Are some of the choices described here mistakes, or do all of them reflect the subjects' true preferences? The answer to this question isn't entirely obvious. Even if two situations are objectively identical, they may *feel* different. For example, the person who loses a $10 ticket to a play may become irritable (compared to the person who loses a $10 bill), and thus may not enjoy himself. If he ignores his reaction and tries to behave rationally by replacing his ticket, he may end up feeling worse off.

Is there some way to tell whether these choices are mistakes? One strategy is to make subjects aware of what they're doing (for example, by pointing out that losing a $10 bill is objectively identical to losing a $10 ticket) and then see whether they continue the pattern. If they change their behavior and eliminate the apparent inconsistencies, then it may be reasonable to conclude that some of their earlier choices were mistaken.

Application 13.2

Driving a Cab. . . One Day at a Time

In Section 6.4, we saw that an increase in the wage rate can either raise or lower the amount of labor supplied. The substitution effect is positive (leisure becomes more expensive, so people buy less of it), but the income effect is negative (with greater resources, people buy more leisure). Based on theory alone, there's no way to tell which effect is larger.

But what if someone's wage were to increase for only a *single day*? If she's free to vary her hours, she would definitely supply more labor on that day. Why? Since earnings on any given day are trivial in comparison to total lifetime resources, the income effect is very small. The overall impact of the wage increase is therefore determined almost entirely by the substitution effect. At a higher wage, leisure becomes more expensive *on that day*, so the worker buys less of it.

Do people actually behave that way? This question is surprisingly difficult to answer. Most people don't experience day-to-day variation in their wages, nor do they have the freedom to vary their hours on extremely short notice. However, taxicab drivers' hourly compensation varies considerably from day to day. If the weather is bad, a large convention has come to town, or transit workers are on strike, a cab driver knows that passengers will be easy to find. And the typical taxicab driver is free to shorten or lengthen his shift on any given day. According to standard economic theory, then, drivers should work longer shifts on busy days.

Is that how taxicab drivers actually behave? This question was the focus of a study by a team of four economists, Colin Camerer, Linda Babcock, George Loewenstein, and Richard Thaler.[11] The study examined roughly 2,000 trip sheets submitted by New York City cab drivers during 1988, 1990, and 1994. The authors found that on any given day, the length of the shift was *negatively* related to hourly compensation. In fact, much of their analysis suggested that the elasticity of hours worked with respect to hourly compensation was approximately -1.

For the reasons just discussed, a negative relationship between the labor supply and hourly compensation on a single day is inconsistent with the implications of standard economic theory. If cab drivers aren't following consumer theory, what are they doing? The estimated elasticity of labor supply may provide an important clue. It implies that a 1 percent increase in hourly compensation leads to a roughly 1 percent decrease in hours. As hourly compensation changes, then, total income—the product of the hours worked and hourly compensation—remains fixed. (See Section 2.4.) In other words, the typical cab driver appears to have a daily income target. When he reaches that target, he quits for the day.

Daily income targeting is highly inefficient. To see why, let's think about the following example. Martha works 20 days each month and needs to earn \$2,000, or an average of \$100 per day, to cover her expenses. On good days, she earns \$20 per hour; on bad days she earns \$10 per hour. Good and bad days occur with equal frequency. Suppose Martha sets a target of \$100 per day and works until she reaches it. She works 5 hours on good days and 10 hours on bad days, putting in a total of 150 hours over the course of the month. What if instead she worked 10 hours on good days and 5 hours on bad days? For the entire month, she would earn \$2,500—25 percent more than with daily targeting—without putting in any extra time. Alternatively, she could reach her monthly goal of \$2,000 by working 10 hours on good days and taking bad days off, putting in a total of only 100 hours per month rather than 150.

Cab drivers appear to ignore the sizable inefficiencies associated with daily income targeting. Why? According to the authors of the study, most approach their jobs one day at a time. That is, they make their decisions about how many hours to work within the narrow frame of a single day. This narrow frame prevents them from noticing that they would be better off over the course of a typical month if they worked longer hours on days when they earn more money per hour. This conclusion has been challenged by another study using different data, and remains controversial.[12]

[11]Colin Camerer, Linda Babcock, George Loewenstein, and Richard Thaler, "Labor Supply of New York City Cab Drivers: One Day at a Time," *Quarterly Journal of Economics* 112, no. 2, May 1997, pp. 407–441.

[12]Farber, Henry, "Is Tomorrow Another Day? The Labor Supply of New York City Cab Drivers," Working Paper #473, Industrial Relations Section, Princeton University, 2003.

Salience

The salience of any particular fact depends on the way it is presented. Some psychologists and behavioral economists argue that people are more likely to consider a fact when its presentation is more attention-grabbing. As a result, two different presentations of the same information can lead to different choices.

In one experiment, a group of randomly selected subjects answered the following policy question:[13]

> "Imagine that the U.S. is preparing for the outbreak of an unusual Asian disease, which is expected to kill 600 people. Two alternative programs to combat the disease have been proposed. Assume that the exact scientific estimates of the consequences of the programs are as follows:
>
> > If program A is adopted, 200 people will be saved.
> >
> > If program B is adopted, there is a 1/3 probability that 600 people will be saved, and a 2/3 probability that no people will be saved.
>
> Which of the two programs would you favor?"

A second randomly selected group answered the same question, with the following two alternatives replacing programs A and B:

> > "If program C is adopted 400 people will die.
> >
> > If program D is adopted there is a 1/3 probability that no one will die, and a 2/3 probability that 600 people will die."

Objectively, program A is identical to program C, and program B is identical to program D. Yet 72 percent of the first group said they preferred A to B, while 78 percent of the second group said they preferred D to C. What explains these results? The first presentation emphasizes lives saved, while the second emphasizes deaths. As a result, the salient information is different. Program A sounds attractive because it saves lives for sure; program C sounds unattractive because it guarantees deaths. But programs A and C are the same. Whether subjects love or hate this alternative depends on how they look at it.

Were some of the choices subjects made mistakes, or did they all reflect the subjects' true preferences? Once people have been made aware of their sensitivity to the presentation of information, they tend to correct for it, and their choices become much more consistent across objectively equivalent decision problems. This finding suggests that their earlier inconsistencies were probably mistakes.

Rules of Thumb

Many economic decisions are quite complex, so that thinking through all of the possible consequences for every alternative is extremely difficult. Most of us don't try. Instead, we often rely on simple rules of thumb that have served us or others reasonably well in the past.

Take the example of saving. The appropriate rate of saving for any particular person depends on a long list of factors—age, marital status, income, expected growth in income,

[13]Amos Tversky and Daniel Kahneman, "The Framing of Decisions and the Psychology of Choice," *Science* 211, no. 4481, January 30, 1981, pp. 453–458.

likelihood of unemployment, expected age at retirement, Social Security contributions, private pensions, number and ages of children, expected college expenses, potential medical expenses, and so forth. Even in simple economic models, finding the best rate of saving involves complex mathematical calculations. No wonder that most people take shortcuts. In a best-selling book on personal finance called *The Wealthy Barber* (Three Rivers Press, 1997), author David Chilton simply advises readers (through the sage musings of a fictitious barber named Roy) to "pay yourself first" by saving 10 percent of every paycheck.

In practice, people do seem to follow simple rules of thumb for saving. According to one survey, among Americans who actually try to save some of their income, 62 percent think about their saving target as a percentage of income. The vast majority of these (73.6%) report targets that are even multiples of 5 percent. Nearly one-third of them attempt to save *exactly* 10 percent of their income, just as Roy the barber recommends. Moreover, these simple targets appear to be insensitive to factors that standard economic theory indicates should significantly affect saving, such as expected future income.[14]

It's important to emphasize that a person who uses a rule of thumb isn't necessarily making a mistake. A good rule of thumb is arrived at through trial and error or by imitating other people who have made successful decisions. As a result, popular rules of thumb may represent choices that are *nearly* optimal for the decisions to which they're usually applied. Given the costs and difficulty of solving complex problems, further improvements may not be worth the effort.

Some economists think that the widespread tendency to rely on rules of thumb invalidates laboratory experiments that appear to document inconsistent or irrational behavior (including many of the ones discussed earlier). They argue that whenever we confront a new or unfamiliar task, we look for analogies to other problems we've faced in an effort to identify an applicable rule of thumb. According to this view, psychologists and behavioral economists may find evidence of irrational behavior in the laboratory because their experiments trick subjects into applying good rules of thumb to the wrong situations.

Application 13.3

Rules of Thumb in Portfolio Allocation

Add-On 11A provided a brief introduction to the economic and financial principles governing portfolio allocation. If you read that add-on, and if you're like most readers, you probably found the material challenging. In fact, it's one of the toughest topics in this book. That's why many people rely on trained financial consultants for advice and guidance and why others resort to simple rules of thumb.

A study by economists Gur Huberman and Wei Jiang examined the accounts of nearly 38,000 individuals who began contributing to a 401(k) plan in 2001. The study concluded

[14]B. Douglas Bernheim, "Personal Saving, Information, and Economic Literacy: New Directions for Public Policy," in Charles E. Walker, Mark Bloomfield, and Margo Thorning (eds.), *Tax Policy for Economic Growth in the 1990s*, American Council for Capital Formation, March 1994.

that rules of thumb frequently govern the allocation of 401(k) pension assets.[15] A majority of individuals (53.6%) invest their money in more than one but fewer than six mutual funds. Of those, nearly two out of five (38.3%) divide their contributions *equally* among the mutual funds to which they contribute. It is extremely unlikely that equal division would lead to the best portfolio for such a high fraction of investors. It is far more likely that equal division is a rough rule of thumb, which many investors adopt to simplify the complex problem of portfolio allocation.

13.3 CHOICES INVOLVING TIME

In Chapter 10, we studied the standard economic theory of decisions involving time. Many behavioral economists see that theory as too restrictive, because it rules out certain patterns of behavior that are sometime observed in practice. For example, some people may have difficulty following through on carefully formulated plans because of lapses in self-control. They may also make systematic errors in forecasting the future, and they may be reluctant to abandon projects after incurring substantial sunk costs, even when the chances of success are low. In this section, we review some of the evidence that points to these violations of the standard theory, and discuss their implications for economic analysis.

Maintaining Self-Control

From time to time, most people encounter situations in which they have difficulty maintaining self-control. Some of us start diets and then succumb to chocolate cake. Others draw up budgets and then splurge on new clothes. Still others swear off cigarettes, alcohol, or drugs and then fall off the wagon. How do behavioral economists think about such problems?

The Problem of Dynamic Inconsistency Standard consumer theory assumes that a person's preferences over the alternatives available at some future date don't change as the date approaches or once it arrives. This property is called **dynamic consistency**. A person with dynamically consistent preferences always wants to follow through on his plans and intentions. Lapses of self-control never occur. If a dynamically consistent consumer swears off alcohol, he'll feel the same way when the moment of truth arrives, and he'll never fall off the wagon.

A person is **dynamically inconsistent** if he changes his ranking of the alternatives available at some future date as the date approaches, or once it arrives. Dynamic inconsistency is usually thought to reflect a bias toward immediate gratification, known as **present bias**. A person with present bias often suffers from lapses of self-control. On any given day, for example, a dieter might prefer to eat small portions at his next meal, but might nevertheless choose large portions at mealtime.

A person is **dynamically consistent** if his preferences over the alternatives available at some future date don't change as that date approaches or once it arrives. When this condition doesn't hold, preferences are **dynamically inconsistent**.

Present bias is a form of dynamic inconsistency involving a bias toward immediate gratification.

Many laboratory experiments have documented the existence of present bias. In a typical study, subjects choose between receiving a small reward after some initial delay

[15]Gur Huberman and Wei Jiang, "Offerings vs. Choice in 401(k) Plans: Equity Exposure and Number of Funds," *Journal of Finance*, 2005, 2006, Vol. 61, no. 2, pp. 763–801.

and a large reward after some additional delay. To illustrate, suppose the subject chooses on Monday, the small reward is available on Thursday, and the large reward is available on Friday. Then the initial delay is three days (the time elapsed between Monday and Thursday), and the additional delay is one day (the time elapsed between Thursday and Friday). If subjects are dynamically consistent, their choices shouldn't depend on the length of the initial delay. As long as the same rewards remain available on Thursday and Friday, they will make the same choices on Monday (with an initial delay of three days), Tuesday (with an initial delay of two days), Wednesday (with an initial delay of one day), and Thursday (with no initial delay). But if subjects are present-biased, they will be more likely to pick the smaller reward if they choose on Thursday, when there is no initial delay and gratification is immediate, than if they choose on Monday, when gratification is delayed regardless of the subject's choice. Therefore, to determine whether subjects are dynamically consistent, the experimenter asks whether a change in the length of the initial delay affects choices, holding the size of the rewards and the length of the additional delay fixed.

In one classic study, 60 subjects were exposed continuously to a loud (90 decibel) noise, and were rewarded with intervals of silence.[16] The small reward lasted 60 seconds, the large reward 120 seconds. The initial delay (prior to the start of the small reward) was either 0, 7.5, or 15 seconds. The additional delay (between the end of the small reward and the start of the large reward) was held fixed at 60 seconds. Each subject repeated the task ten times.

Table 13.5 summarizes some of the experiment's results. The shorter the initial delay, the more often the subjects chose the small reward. This general pattern, which has been replicated in many experiments with both human and animal subjects and with different kinds of rewards, is evidence of present bias.

The Solution: Precommitment If people are dynamically inconsistent, unable to follow through on plans and intentions, what can they do about it? For an answer to this question, we turn to classical literature. In Homer's *Odyssey*, Odysseus sails his ship near the island of the Sirens, mythical creatures whose beautiful singing lures sailors to their deaths. Though he wants to hear the sirens' songs, he also wants to survive, and knows he

Table 13.5
Present Bias in Choosing Rewards

Initial Delay	Percent of trials in which the smaller, more immediate reward is chosen (median across subjects)
0 seconds	80%
7.5 seconds	40
15 seconds	10

Source: Jay V. Solnick, Catherine H. Kannenberg, David A. Eckerman, and Marcus B. Waller, "An Experimental Analysis of Impulsivity and Impulse Control in Humans," *Learning and Motivation* 11, 1980, pp. 61–77. The subjects were undergraduates at the University of North Carolina.

[16]To enhance the value of the rewards, subjects were asked to solve math problems during the experiment. See Jay V. Solnick, Catherine H. Kannenberg, David A. Eckerman, and Marcus B. Waller, "An Experimental Analysis of Impulsivity and Impulse Control in Humans," *Learning and Motivation* 11, 1980, pp. 61–77.

won't be able to resist their deadly call. So he instructs his men to block their ears with beeswax, to bind him to the ship's mast, and to ignore his demands for release until the siren's land is well out of sight.

Odysseus, lashed to the ship's mast, listens to the Sirens' songs.

Odysseus' decision to have himself bound to the ship's mast is an example of a **precommitment**—that is, a choice that removes future options. Precommitments are useful in situations in which, because of dynamic inconsistency, people don't trust themselves to follow through on their plans and intentions. Everyday life offers many illustrations. A smoker decides to quit and throws away her cigarettes. A student who wants to avoid driving while intoxicated hands his car keys to a friend before joining a party. A worker with a history of procrastination wants to avoid falling behind on a major project, so she promises a series of presentations showing her work in progress. In each case, the decision maker's object is to avoid "bad" choices by restricting future options.

A **precommitment** is a choice that removes future options.

Precommitments have been observed in the laboratory. Take the experiment described in the last section. Given the opportunity, will subjects who appear to be dynamically inconsistent choose to restrict their future options? Another version of the experiment examined this possibility.[17] Subjects were told that they would choose between the small and large rewards with no initial delay. Then, 15 seconds before making this choice, they were offered the chance to rule out the possibility of choosing the small reward. Overall, subjects took the opportunity 57 percent of the time, precommitting themselves to the large reward.

Implications for Saving People who suffer from present bias may have difficulty exercising the self-control required to save money. To study the effect of present bias on saving, economists have modified the tools discussed in Section 10.2. Their approach is to assume that a consumer applies one set of preferences when the alternatives under consideration involve only future consequences and another set of preferences when at least one of those alternatives involves an immediate consequence.

To illustrate, suppose Myra's employer sends her on a three-day trip, providing her with a \$60 meal allowance. As long as she sticks to the overall budget, she's free to spend as much or as little as she likes on each day. Assuming that Myra suffers from present bias, what will she do?

To make a choice on the first day of her trip (Monday), Myra has to figure out how she would spend any remaining balance on Tuesday and Wednesday. Figure 13.4 illustrates. The horizontal axis shows the amount of food she eats on Tuesday, and the vertical axis shows the amount she eats on Wednesday. The blue indifference curves (labeled I_1 and I_2) reflect Myra's preferences as of Monday; the red indifference curves (labeled I_3 and I_4) reflect her preferences as of Tuesday.

Myra's preferences change from Monday to Tuesday because Tuesday's meals provide her with immediate gratification on Tuesday but not on Monday. As we've drawn the figure, the red indifference curves are steeper than the blue ones wherever they intersect, implying that Myra suffers from present bias. Why? Suppose Myra starts out at bundle

[17]This version of the experiment involved 15 subjects. See Jay V. Solnick, Catherine H. Kannenberg, David A. Eckerman, and Marcus B. Waller, "An Experimental Analysis of Impulsivity and Impulse Control in Humans," *Learning and Motivation* 11, 1980, pp. 61–77.

Figure 13.4

Dynamic Inconsistency in Saving. Myra's dining preferences for Tuesday and Wednesday change from Monday to Tuesday. The blue indifference curves correspond to her preferences on Monday; the red ones correspond to her preferences on Tuesday. Wherever a blue curve crosses a red one, for example at bundle A, the red one is steeper, meaning that Myra shows less patience concerning Tuesday's dining on Tuesday than on Monday. If she has $40 to spend on Tuesday and Wednesday, and if food costs $0.50/oz., she can pick any bundle on the green budget line. From Monday's perspective, she would like to choose bundle B, but on Tuesday she will pick bundle D. Myra lacks the self-control to follow through on Monday's plan.

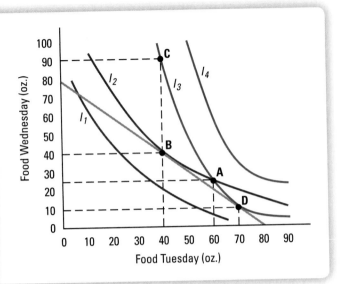

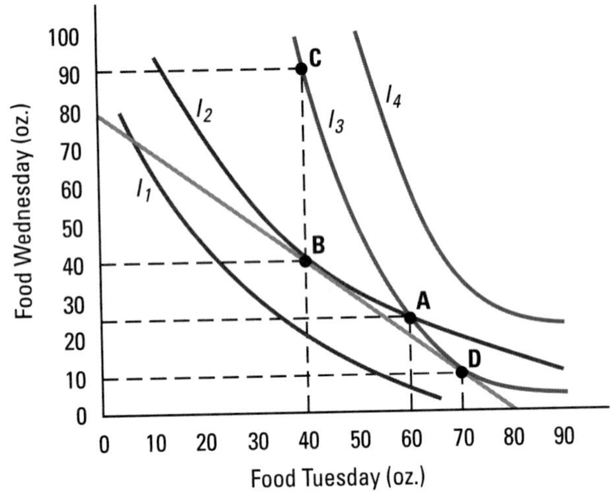

A (60 ounces on Tuesday and 25 ounces on Wednesday). According to Monday's preferences, she would require an extra 15 ounces on Wednesday—40 in total—to compensate for the loss of 20 ounces on Tuesday (because bundles A and B lie on the same blue indifference curve, I_2). But according to Tuesday's preferences, she would require an extra 65 ounces on Wednesday—90 in total—to compensate for the same loss (because bundles A and C lie on the same red indifference curve, I_3).

Now suppose food costs $0.50 per ounce, and that Myra spent $20 for 40 ounces of food on Monday, leaving her with $40 to spend on Tuesday and Wednesday. That means she can pick any bundle on the green budget line. According to her preferences on Monday, she'd like to pick bundle B, splitting her remaining allowance equally between Tuesday and Wednesday. On Tuesday, however, she prefers bundle D. Though her best plan as of Monday is to spend $20 on Tuesday and $20 on Wednesday, she ends up spending $35 on Tuesday (to purchase 70 ounces of food) and only $5 on Wednesday (enough for 10 ounces of food). From Monday's perspective, Tuesday's bias toward instant gratification causes her to save too little for Wednesday.

On Monday, present bias affects Myra's decisions in two ways. The first is obvious: as on Tuesday, consumption provides her with immediate gratification while saving doesn't, so Myra saves less than she would if she didn't suffer from present bias. The second consideration is a bit more subtle. Knowing that she will blow most of her remaining funds once Tuesday arrives, she may think that it's pointless to save much. Or she may feel the need to compensate for Tuesday's poor choices by saving more, to make sure she doesn't go hungry on Wednesday. In most models, present bias reduces saving overall.

From Myra's perspective on or before Monday, her employer provides her with too much flexibility. A precommitment to save more and spend less would improve her situation. Given the opportunity, for example, she might choose a meal allowance that provides $20 each day, rather than $60 for three days.

This simple example suggests some important lessons concerning retirement saving. People who suffer from present bias may save less for retirement than those who are time-consistent. They may indulge their whims when young and then regret it when they are old. If they're aware of their tendencies, they may look for ways to save automatically, to lock up funds for retirement. Many pension plans, including 401(k)s, provide such opportunities (see Applications 13.1 and 13.3). Employees fix their contributions in advance and aren't allowed to change them on short notice. In some cases, early withdrawals from these plans are not permitted; in other cases they are heavily penalized. These features may help to explain why most households do much of their saving through pensions.[18]

Application 13.4

Paying Not to Go to the Gym

For most people, relaxation provides immediate gratification; strenuous physical activity doesn't. Present bias therefore makes fitness objectives difficult to achieve. Many people who would like to maintain a regular exercise program lack the willpower to follow through.

We've seen that people often deal with present bias by making precommitments. Short of joining the armed services, there's no fool-proof way to guarantee that you'll exercise regularly. However, there are ways to make partial commitments that either reduce the marginal cost of exercise or create costs for skipping it. If you join a soccer team or schedule tennis games with your friends, for example, social pressure will help you to follow through.

Leo Cullum
"I'll be at lunch. If anyone calls say I'm at the health club."

Many people try to get fit by joining a health club. In January 2001, nearly 17,000 health clubs were operating in the United States, boasting more than 32 million members and annual industry revenues of $11.6 billion. Most health clubs offer monthly and annual membership contracts for a recurring fee. Some also require initiation fees. Many health clubs also allow nonmembers to use their facilities on a pay-per-visit basis. In some cases, customers can pay up front for a fixed number of visits.

Why do so many customers choose memberships rather than paying for actual visits? One possible explanation is that memberships can be less expensive, depending on the frequency of a customer's visits. If the recurring membership fee is $80/month and a single visit costs $10, a customer must exercise more than eight times a month to come out ahead with a monthly contract.

Another possible explanation has to do with present bias. A customer who suffers from present bias fears that, in the future, he will attach too much importance to the costs of exercise, most of which will be immediate, and not enough importance to the benefits, most of which will be delayed. Purchasing a membership can counteract that bias by reducing the marginal cost of future exercise. When the future arrives, a member will be more likely to go to the club than a nonmember because the member's visits cost nothing on the margin, rather than $10. Also, once a customer pays for a membership, skipping an exercise session may become psychologically costly. As a result, some customers may become members hoping that they'll exercise more often.

How do health club customers actually behave? Economists Stefano Della Vigna and Ulrike Malmendier studied the choices made by nearly 8,000 members of three

[18]Pensions plans also receive favorable tax treatment, and this is another reason for their popularity.

New England health clubs over a four-year period, starting in 1997.[19] Table 13.6 provides some information about costs and attendance for monthly members during each of the first six months after enrollment. In every single month, the average price per visit (final column) exceeded the pay-per-visit fee of $10 by a wide margin. Clearly, customers weren't choosing memberships because they were less expensive!

To some extent, this pattern could reflect excessive optimism at the time of enrollment. Were that the only explanation, however, we would expect to see cancellations by members with lower-than-expected attendance. As a result, the average attendance among continuing members would tend to rise with the passage of time after enrollment, and the average price per visit would fall. The data in Table 13.6 are not consistent with this prediction. Among those who remained members after six months, the average price per visit ($18.9) was nearly *double* the pay-per-visit price, and higher than during the first five months of membership.

Based on the evidence presented in their study, Della Vigna and Malmendier concluded that many people become health club members—and end up paying more per visit—at least in part because this strategy can counteract the effects of present bias.

Table 13.6
The Cost to Members of Going to the Gym

Months after Enrollment	Average Price per Month	Average Attendance per Month	Average Price per Visit
1	$55.1	3.45	$16.0
2	$80.5	5.45	$14.8
3	$70.0	4.97	$14.1
4	$81.7	4.61	$17.7
5	$81.9	4.43	$18.5
6	$81.9	4.32	$18.9
Nonmembers	—	—	$10

Source: Stefano Della Vigna and Ulrike Malmendier, "Paying Not to Go to the Gym," *American Economic Review*, 2006, forthcoming.

WORKED-OUT PROBLEM 13.1

The Problem It's Sunday and Matt is making plans for the week. He has to do an unpleasant chore by Thursday at the latest. On the day he does the chore, his payoff will be −4, but he will receive a benefit on the next day. If he does the chore on Monday, his payoff on Tuesday will be 12; if he does it on Tuesday, his payoff on Wednesday will be 10; if he does it on Wednesday, his payoff on Thursday will be 8; and if he does it on Thursday, his payoff on Friday will be 5. Matt behaves as follows. On any given day, he wants to maximize the utility function $2P_N + P_F$, where P_N is his payoff on that day, and P_F is the sum of his payoffs on future days. To illustrate, suppose he does the chore on Wednesday. Then his utility from Tuesday's perspective

[19]Stefano Della Vigna and Ulrike Malmendier, "Paying Not to Go to the Gym," *American Economic Review* 96, no. 3, 2006, pp. 694–719.

will be $2 \times 0 + (-4 + 8) = 4$, but his utility from Wednesday's perspective will be $2 \times (-4) + 8 = 0$. When deciding whether to do the chore on any given day, Matt correctly anticipates how he will behave on subsequent days. As of Sunday, when would Matt like to do the chore? When will he actually do the chore? Does he procrastinate? Is he dynamically consistent?

The Solution From Sunday's perspective, Matt's utility will be $12 - 4 = 8$ if he does the chore on Monday, $10 - 4 = 6$ if he does it on Tuesday, $8 - 4 = 4$ if he does it on Wednesday, and $5 - 4 = 1$ if he does it on Thursday. Therefore, as of Sunday, he would like to do it on Monday.

Now let's determine what Matt will actually do. Suppose he reaches Wednesday without having done the chore. He can either do it on Wednesday or delay until Thursday. If he does it on Wednesday, his utility (from Wednesday's perspective) will be $2 \times (-4) + 8 = 0$. If he delays until Thursday, his utility (from Wednesday's perspective) will be $5 - 4 = 1$. Since $0 < 1$, he won't do the chore on Wednesday.

Next, suppose Matt reaches Tuesday without having done the chore. He can either do it on Tuesday or delay. If he does it on Tuesday, his utility (from Tuesday's perspective) will be $2 \times (-4) + 10 = 2$. If he delays, he knows he will end up doing it on Thursday (as explained in the previous paragraph), so his utility (from Tuesday's perspective) will be $5 - 4 = 1$. Since $2 > 1$, he'll do the chore on Tuesday.

On Monday, Matt can either do the chore or delay. If he does it, his utility (from Monday's perspective) will be $2 \times (-4) + 12 = 4$. If he delays, he knows he will end up doing it on Tuesday (as explained in the previous paragraph), so his utility (from Monday's perspective) will be $10 - 4 = 6$. Since $4 < 6$, he won't do the chore on Monday.

Based on this reasoning, we conclude that Matt will procrastinate doing the chore until Tuesday. Since he won't follow through on Sunday's intention to do it on Monday, he is dynamically inconsistent.

IN-TEXT EXERCISE 13.1 **Repeat worked-out problem 13.1, but assume that Matt wants to maximize the utility function $3P_N + P_F$.**

Ignoring Sunk Costs

In Section 3.3, we saw that in making decisions, it's important to ignore sunk costs. This dictum is one of the most basic and fundamental principles in microeconomics. But do people always follow it?

Suppose that within a few days of buying a new pair of shoes, you discover they're extremely uncomfortable and stop wearing them. At that point, you can either throw them away or stow them in the back of your closet. Does your action depend on how much you paid for them? For example, are you less likely to throw the shoes away if you paid \$200 for them than if you paid \$30? According to standard microeconomic principles, the amount you paid is a sunk cost, so it shouldn't affect your decision. But some people would be less likely to throw the shoes away if they paid the higher price. Those people suffer from the incorrect belief that, if they paid more for something, it must be more valuable to them. That belief is known as the **sunk cost fallacy**.

The **sunk cost fallacy** refers to the belief that, if you paid more for something, it must be more valuable to you.

Table 13.7
Effect of Sunk Costs on Theater Attendance

Season Ticket Discount	Attendance, First 5 Plays	Attendance, Last 5 Plays
None	4.11	2.28
$2	3.32	1.84
$7	3.29	2.18
Difference statistically significant?	Yes	No

Source: Hal R. Arkes and Catherine Blumer, "The Psychology of Sunk Cost," *Organizational Behavior and Human Decision Processes* 35, 1985, pp. 124–140. The subjects were season ticket holders for the Ohio University Theater.

Experiments have confirmed that people are sometimes susceptible to the sunk cost fallacy. One study involved the first 60 people to approach the ticket window at Ohio University's Theater with the intention of buying 1982–83 season tickets.[20] One-third of the subjects were charged the normal ticket price ($15), a third unexpectedly received discounts of $2, and another third unexpectedly received discounts of $7. Once the tickets were purchased, the amount paid became a sunk cost. According to standard economic theory, the size of this sunk cost should have had no effect on whether customers subsequently chose to attend the plays. Yet Table 13.7 shows customers who paid more for their tickets, and who therefore incurred higher sunk costs, attended significantly more performances than others during the first half of the season. This pattern suggests that they valued the plays more highly simply because they paid more for their tickets. However, this difference had largely disappeared by the second half of the season, suggesting that while sunk costs do influence people's valuations, their effect shrinks over time.

Application 13.5

Do Investors Hang on to Losing Stocks?

Suppose you purchase some stock in a publicly traded company for $50 per share. After a month, the share price falls to $40. Should you sell your shares or hang on to them? Would your answer change if you had originally paid $30 per share, and the price *rose* to $40 after a month?

The amount you paid for the stock is a sunk cost. According to economic theory, it shouldn't affect your decision—at least not directly.[21] There are some indirect considerations involving taxes. Accounting for taxes, you actually have a strong incentive to sell your shares more quickly if your have losses than if you have gains.[22] For the example described in the previous paragraph, you should therefore be *more* willing to sell the stock if you bought it for $50 than if you bought it for $30. But if you suffer from the

[20]Hal R. Arkes and Catherine Blumer, "The Psychology of Sunk Cost," *Organizational Behavior and Human Decision Processes* 35, 1985, pp. 124–140.

[21]You might think that after a loss, further losses are more likely to occur, or alternatively, that losing stocks are more likely to rebound. In fact, there is almost no correlation between past returns and future returns.

[22]Because you pay taxes on your net investment income (the difference between gains and losses), you're better off using your losses to reduce your taxes as soon as possible.

sunk cost fallacy, you'll attach *more* value to the stock, and you'll therefore be *less* willing to sell it for $40, if you bought it for $50 than if you bought it for $30.

What do investors actually do? To answer this question, economist Terrance Odean examined trading data for 10,000 randomly selected customers of a nationwide discount brokerage firm.[23] He found that, on average, investors realize 14.8 percent of their gains (by selling the stock on which the gains were earned) but only 9.8 percent of their losses. In other words, the typical investor is more reluctant to let go of a stock if he paid more for it. This finding is consistent with the view that investors are susceptible to the sunk cost fallacy. In fact, it suggests that the sunk cost fallacy is so powerful that it overcomes the desire to reduce taxes by realizing losses. Odean considered and rejected a number of other explanations. He also found that the strategy of hanging on to losing stocks has significant costs. According to his calculations, the typical investor's after-tax return over the subsequent year would have been about 4.4 percentage points higher on average, if he had sold a losing stock rather than a winning one.

Forecasting Future Tastes and Needs

Whenever our actions have future consequences, the quality of our decisions will depend in part on the accuracy of our forecasts. Among other things, we need to forecast our own tastes and needs. For example, if we expect to be hungry, we'll favor alternatives that provide food; if we expect to be thirsty, we'll lean toward choices that provide water.

Evidence suggests that people sometimes have trouble forecasting how they'll feel about different outcomes in the future. Instead of making reasonable forecasts, they evaluate future consequences based on their tastes and needs at the moment of decision making. In other words, they *project* their current states of mind into the future. For example, when they're hungry, they may project their hunger into the future, causing them to favor alternatives that provide food in the future, even if there's no objective reason to think they'll still be hungry. This tendency is known as **projection bias**.

Projection bias is the tendency to evaluate future consequences based on tastes and needs at the moment of decision making.

When a consumer suffers from projection bias, a temporary mood or state of mind can exert a powerful influence on decisions that have only long-term consequences. For example, in controlled experiments that manipulate subjects' hunger prior to grocery shopping, those who are hungry have a greater tendency to stock up on supplies than those who are sated.[24]

Projection bias can also lead people to underestimate their adaptability. Experiments have shown that people tend to overestimate the intensity and duration of unhappiness caused by a wide variety of events, including a romantic breakup, failure to receive a promotion or to be hired by a potential employer, the defeat of a preferred political candidate, and negative feedback on their performance.[25] Before these events, the typical person tends to forecast his reaction based on his current state of mind. But after the events occur, he adjusts and comes to view them as much less disturbing.

---

[23]Terrance Odean, "Are Investors Reluctant to Realize Their Losses?" *Journal of Finance* 53, no. 5, October 1998, pp. 1775–1798.

[24]Daniel T. Gilbert, Michael J. Gill, and Timothy D. Wilson, "The Future Is Now: Temporal Correction in Affective Forecasting," *Organizational Behavior and Human Decision Processes* 88, no. 1, May 2002, pp. 430–444.

[25]Daniel T. Gilbert, Elizabeth C. Pinel, Timothy D.Wilson, Stephen J. Blumberg, and Thalia P. Wheatley, "Immune Neglect: A Source of Durability Bias in Affective Forecasting," *Journal of Personality and Social Psychology*, 75, no. 3, September 1998, pp. 617–638.

13.4 CHOICES INVOLVING RISK

In Chapter 11, we studied the standard economic theory of decisions involving risk. Many behavioral economists see that theory as requiring modification in light of evidence concerning the beliefs that people actually hold and the choices they actually make. For example, some people may have trouble assessing probabilities. Others may attach disproportionate significance to low-probability events, or to potential losses. In this section, we review some of the evidence that points to these violations of the standard theory, and discuss their implications for economic analysis.

Trouble Assessing Probabilities

In making risky choices, people tend to attach more importance to likely outcomes than to unlikely ones. In that sense, probabilities definitely factor into their decisions. But the laws of probability are complicated, and few of us are trained statisticians. Research suggests that people tend to make specific errors in assessing probabilities.

The **hot-hand fallacy** is the belief that once an event has occurred several times in a row, it is *more* likely to repeat.

The **gambler's fallacy** is the belief that once an event has occurred, it is *less* likely to repeat.

Two Common Fallacies When you flip a coin, the probability of heads is 50 percent. But suppose you flip the coin 10 times in a row and it comes up heads every time. What's the probability of heads on the 11th flip? Students of statistics know that the correct answer is exactly 50 percent. But some people suffer from the **hot-hand fallacy**, the belief that once an event has occurred several times in a row, it is *more* likely to repeat. This fallacy leads to the false conclusion that after you've flipped heads 10 times in a row, the probability of heads is greater than 50 percent because "you're on a run." Other people suffer from the **gambler's fallacy**, the belief that once an event has occurred, it is less likely to repeat. This fallacy leads to the false conclusion that after a streak of 10 consecutive heads, the probability of heads is less than 50 percent, because tails is "due."

Even if you understand probability in the context of coin flips, you may nevertheless fall prey to these two fallacies in other contexts. The hot-hand fallacy tends to arise in situations in which people can easily invent explanations for streaks. Take basketball. The overwhelming majority of fans, players, coaches, and commentators believe that from time to time, a player has "the hot hand"—in other words, he or she practically can't miss. Some players even develop reputations as "streak shooters." Those who believe in the hot-hand phenomenon attribute it to a variety of plausible factors, such as changes in a player's level of confidence. But we know that some streaks will occur purely by chance. For example, if the probability of making any given shot is 50 percent, the odds are 1 in 16 that a player will hit four in a row. Do players in fact run hot and cold, or are streaks just an illusion created by the luck of the draw?

Table 13.8 shows the shooting percentages for members of a professional basketball team, the Philadelphia 76ers, based on 48 home games played during the 1980–81 season.[26] The first row shows the frequency with which players made their shots ("hits") after missing three in a row; the second row shows the frequency of hits after missing two in a row, and so forth. The table reports results both for the team as a whole and for two players, Hall of Famer Julius Erving ("Dr. J") and notorious "streak shooter" Andrew Toney. If

[26] Thomas Gilovich, Robert Vallone, and Amos Tversky, "The Hot Hand in Basketball: On the Misperception of Random Sequences," *Cognitive Psychology* 17, 1985, pp. 295–314.

Table 13.8

The Myth of the "Hot Hand"

	Shooting Percentage on the Next Shot for:		
After a Run of:	Entire Team	Julius Erving	Andrew Toney
3 misses	56%	52%	52%
2 misses	53	51	53
1 miss	54	51	51
1 hit	51	53	43
2 hits	50	52	40
3 hits	46	48	34

Source: Thomas Gilovich, Robert Vallone, and Amos Tversky, "The Hot Hand in Basketball: On the Misperception of Random Sequences," *Cognitive Psychology* 17, 1985, pp. 295–314.

players run hot and cold, we would expect to see higher shooting percentages after runs of hits and lower shooting percentages after runs of misses. In fact, the table shows *precisely the opposite pattern* for the team as a whole and for Toney. A hit was *more* likely after a run of misses, and *less* likely after a run of hits. (Erving's shooting percentage was, for the most part, unrelated to his recent hits and misses.) A variety of other statistical tests failed to turn up any evidence of "the hot hand."

The gambler's fallacy tends to arise in situations in which people can't easily invent explanations for streaks. State lotteries provide good illustration. Several studies have shown that many people stop betting on a number right after it wins. This phenomenon occurs even in parimutuel lotteries, in which people have a strong incentive to bid on unpopular numbers (because multiple winners must split the prize). Take New Jersey's pick-three parimutuel lottery game. A study of nearly 1,800 daily drawings between 1988 and 1992 found that after a number came up a winner, bettors tended to avoid it. As a result, recent winning numbers were much better bets than other numbers. For two weeks after a win, a number's expected payoff was elevated by 33 percent; over the next two months, it gradually returned to normal.[27]

The hot-hand fallacy and the gambler's fallacy have potentially important implications for economic behavior. They are clearly relevant in the context of investing, for instance. Some investors assume that a rising stock will continue to rise (the hot-hand fallacy); others assume that a falling stock is due for a rebound (the gambler's fallacy). Investors may also make mistakes in evaluating financial analysts and advisors. For example, they may conclude that a broker who has recommended four or five good stocks in a row is "on a roll," and decide to invest a great deal on his or her next pick.

The Danger of Overconfidence Studies show that many people have overly inflated views of their own abilities. In a variety of studies, for example, researchers have asked people to evaluate themselves in relation to a reference group. If people were objective about themselves, 10 percent would say that they fall within the top 10 percent of the group, 20 percent would say that they fall within the top 20 percent, and so forth. But in

[27]D. Terrell, "A Test of the Gambler's Fallacy—Evidence from Parimutuel Games," *Journal of Risk and Uncertainty* 8, no. 3, 1994, pp. 309–317.

fact, on virtually every personal and professional characteristic, people rate themselves much more favorably. In one survey of U.S. students with an average age of 22, 82 percent ranked their driving ability among the top 30 percent of their age group.[28]

In the context of decisions involving risk, overconfidence causes people both to overstate the likelihood of favorable events and to understate the uncertainty involved. As Application 13.6 illustrates, this tendency has important implications for economic behavior.

Application 13.6

Overconfidence and Business Failure

Relatively few new businesses are successful. In the manufacturing sector, more than 60 percent of new entrants exit within five years; nearly 80 percent exit within 10 years. In most cases, their exit results from business failure.

There are many possible explanations for the high rate of business failure. In some cases, entrepreneurs may launch new businesses in response to temporary profit opportunities, intending to shut them down when the opportunities evaporate. In other cases, the profits from a successful start-up company may be so large that despite the high failure rate, the expected return on entry is still positive. But it is also possible that overconfidence causes new business owners to overestimate their chances of success.

Surveys of entrepreneurs suggest that overconfidence may indeed play a role. In one study, 81 percent of nearly 3,000 new business owners assessed their chances of success at more than 70 percent or better, though only 39 percent thought a business like theirs would be that likely to succeed.[29] One-third described their success as *certain.* Judging from actual experience, those expectations were wildly off the mark. In addition, entrepreneurs' self-assessed chances of success were largely uncorrelated with objective factors that might predict business survival, such as their education, prior experience, and initial capital.

Economists Colin Camerer and Dan Lovallo have investigated these issues using an experiment involving a simple game of entrepreneurship.[30] At the start of the game, each entrepreneur decides whether to enter a fictitious industry. Participating are told that their profits will depend on their position in some ranking relative to other entrants; a higher ranking implies higher profits. In one version of the game, those who enter are ranked randomly. In another, the ranking depends on the entrepreneur's skill at solving brain-teaser puzzles or answering trivia questions. In trials with random rankings, total payoffs per round averaged \$16.87. But in trials with skill-based rankings, considerably more entry occurred, causing the average subject to *lose* money (total payoffs averaged −\$1.56). Because overconfidence only comes into play when skill is a factor, it provides a natural explanation for this pattern. When potential subjects were told at the time of recruitment that their payoffs would be partly skill-based (which presumably discouraged participation by less confident students), the results were even more striking. Total payoffs per round averaged \$13.96 with random rankings and −\$13.13 with skill-based rankings. Apparently, overconfidence in one's skill leads to excessive optimism and, consequently, too much entry, causing the average entrant to lose money.

[28]O. Svenson, "Are we all less risky and more skillful than our fellow drivers?" *Acta Psychologica* 47, 1981, pp. 143–148.

[29]See A. Cooper, C. Woo, and W. Dunkelberg, "Entrepreneurs' perceived chances for success," *Journal of Business Venturing* 3, 1988, pp. 97–108.

[30]Colin Camerer and Dan Lovallo, "Overconfidence and Excess Entry: An Experimental Approach," *American Economic Review* 89, no. 1, March 1999, pp. 306–318. Subjects included 118 MBA and undergraduate students from the University of Pennsylvania's Wharton School and the University of Chicago.

Preferences toward Risk

In Section 11.2, we presented the standard economic theory of risk preferences. Some economists have expressed doubts that the standard theory can account adequately for observed behavior. To address its perceived shortcomings, they've also proposed modifications of the theory. One of the main alternatives is motivated primarily by two behavioral puzzles, one involving low probability events, and the other involving aversion to very small losses.

A Puzzle Involving Low Probability Events Experimental subjects definitely show an aversion to risk in gambles involving moderate odds. For example, most choose \$2,500 for sure over a 50 percent chance of winning \$5,000, coupled with a 50 percent chance of winning nothing. When gambles offer very high payoffs with very low probabilities, however, some subjects appear to become risk loving.

To illustrate, suppose someone offered you the following choice:

Option A: Win \$5 for sure.

Option B: Win \$5,000 with odds of 1 in 1,000; otherwise win nothing.

Which option would you pick? In laboratory experiments, a sizable majority of subjects say they would pick option B.[31] They prefer a small chance of winning a large sum to the certainty of receiving a very small sum. This choice is puzzling because options A and B have the same expected payoff (\$5), but option B clearly involves greater risk. If subjects are risk averse, they should pick option A.

This puzzle isn't confined to the laboratory. The expected payoff on a lottery ticket is only a fraction of its price, and the odds against winning a large prize are astronomical. Yet every year, millions of Americans spend billions of dollars on lottery tickets. Other evidence suggests that most of these people are risk averse; for example, they insure a wide variety of risks. So why are they so attracted to lotteries?

A Puzzle Involving Aversion to Very Small Risks Suppose you were offered the following gamble:

Option C: Win \$1,010 with 50 percent probability; otherwise, lose \$1,000 with 50 percent probability.

Would you be willing to take it? Most people say they wouldn't. Because the expected payoff is only \$5, risking \$1,000 doesn't seem worthwhile to them. However, in Section 11.4, you learned that a risk-averse individual will always be willing to accept a sufficiently small share of any gamble that provides a positive expected payoff. The following gamble is a 1/100 share of option C:

Option D: Win \$10.10 with 50 percent probability; otherwise, lose \$10 with 50 percent probability.

Would you be willing to take it? Again, most people say they wouldn't. Because the expected payoff is only 5 cents, risking \$10 doesn't seem worthwhile to them.

[31]In one experiment, 72 percent of subjects said they would choose option B. The subjects were all students at an Israeli university, and the amounts given referred to Israeli pounds rather than U.S. dollars. See Daniel Kahneman and Amos Tversky, "Prospect Theory: An Analysis of Decision Under Risk," *Econometrica* 47, no. 2, 1979, pp. 263–291.

As this example suggests, many people appear reluctant to take even very tiny shares of certain gambles that have positive expected payoffs. That reluctance implies a level of risk aversion so high that it becomes impossible to explain the typical person's willingness to take larger financial risks.

Prospect Theory: A Potential Solution In the late 1970s two psychologists, Daniel Kahneman (who later won the Nobel Prize in economics) and Amos Tversky, proposed an alternative to the standard economic theory of risk preference. Their approach, known as **prospect theory**, was intended to resolve a number of puzzles related to risky decisions, including the ones just mentioned.

Prospect theory is an alternative to expected utility theory that may resolve a number of puzzles related to risky decisions.

To explain the basic elements of prospect theory, we need a bit of mathematical notation. Suppose a consumer starts out with resources \$$R$. We'll focus our discussion on a gamble with two potential payoffs, \$$X_1$ and \$$X_2$, which may be positive or negative. Let's say the gamble pays out \$$X_1$ with probability P and \$$X_2$ with probability $1 - P$ (where P is greater than 0 and less than 1). Using expected utility theory (which we covered in Section 11.2), we'd assume that the decision maker takes this gamble when

$$U(R) < P \times U(R + X_1) + (1 - P) \times U(R + X_2), \quad (1)$$

where U is the expected utility function. The left-hand side of this is expression is the utility associated with the resource level R, while the right-hand side is the expected value of utility when the decision maker takes the gamble. Using prospect theory, however, we assume that the decision maker takes this gamble when

$$V(0) < W(P) \times V(X_1) + W(1 - P) \times V(X_2), \quad (2)$$

where W assigns a weight to each probability and V assigns a value to gains and losses.[32] The left-hand side of this expression is the value associated with the status quo (that is, neither a gain nor a loss), while the right-hand side is a weighted average of the values associated with the gamble's gains and losses.

Two pioneers in the field of behavioral economics, Nobel Laureate Daniel Hahneman (above, 1934–), and Amos Tversky (below, 1937–1996).

There are two differences between expressions (1) and (2). First, using expected utility theory, we evaluate an outcome based on total resources (that is, R, $R + X_1$, or $R + X_2$). Using prospect theory, we evaluate an outcome based on the *change* in total resources (that is, 0, X_1, or X_2). In other words, prospect theory holds that we judge alternatives according to the gains and losses they generate, relative to the status quo. Kahneman and Tversky justified this assumption as follows:

> "Our perceptual apparatus is attuned to the evaluation of changes or differences rather than to the evaluation of absolute magnitudes. When we respond to attributes such as brightness, loudness, or temperature, the past and present context of experience defines an adaptation level, or reference point, and stimuli are perceived in relation to this reference point."

The second difference between expressions (1) and (2) is that in expression (1), we multiply each valuation by its probability, whereas in expression (2), we multiply each valuation by the weight assigned to its probability. According to prospect theory, the weighting function has the shape shown in Figure 13.5(a). For low values of P, the weight $W(P)$ exceeds P; for high values of P, P exceeds the weight $W(P)$. In other words, people assign disproportionate weight to low-probability outcomes.

---

[32] If an alternative yields a payoff of \$X with certainty, expected utility theory tells us the decision maker ranks it against other alternatives according to the value $U(R + X)$; prospect theory tells us the decision maker ranks it according to the value of $V(X)$.

Figure 13.5

Prospect Theory. Figure (a) shows a hypothetical weighting function. The weight exceeds the probability when the probability is low; when the probability is high, it exceeds the weight. Figure (b) shows a hypothetical valuation function. Valuation depends on changes (gains and losses) starting from the origin, which represents the consumer's status quo. The kink at the origin generates loss aversion. The curve bows upward to the right of the origin and downward to the left, reflecting diminishing sensitivity to gains and losses.

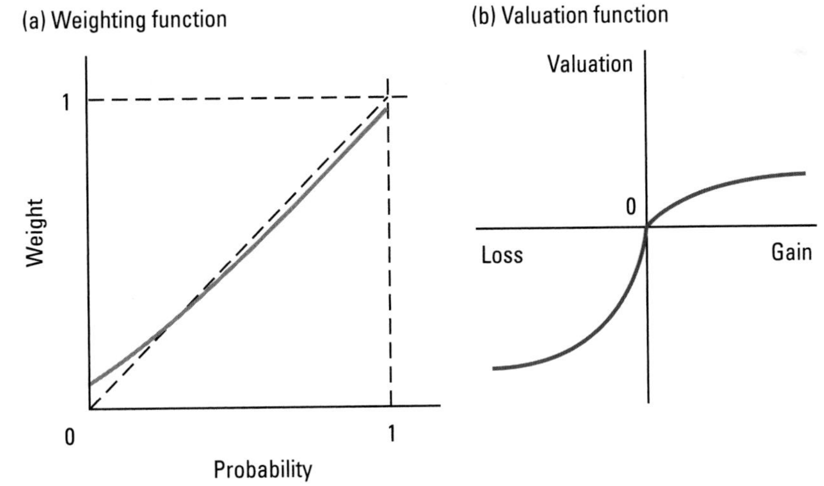

Prospect theory also makes some assumptions about the shape of the value function, $V(X)$; see Figure 13.5(b). First, there is a kink at zero, so that the function is steeper to the left of the origin than to the right. This kink means that people are more sensitive, per dollar, to small losses than to small gains, a feature of the theory known as **loss aversion**. The endowment effect can be seen as a form of loss aversion. In fact, the indifference curves in Figure 13.3 (page 457) and the value function in Figure 13.5(b) are kinked for similar reasons. Notice that in Figure 13.5(b), the value function bows upward to the right of the origin but downward to the left of the origin. In both directions—gain or loss—the marginal impact of enlarging a change from the status quo declines with the size of the change. This property is known as **diminishing sensitivity**. Think about buying and selling objects of different value. When you buy (or sell) a coffee mug, you probably care whether the price is \$5 or \$15, but when you buy (or sell) a car, do you really care whether the price is \$15,530 or \$15,540? In each case the difference is \$10, but in the second case you may be less sensitive to this difference because you're considering a larger change from the status quo.

Loss aversion occurs when the consumer's valuation of an outcome is more sensitive, per dollar, to small losses than to small gains.

The principle of **diminishing sensitivity** holds that the marginal impact of enlarging a change from the status quo declines with the size of the change.

Prospect theory can account for each of the puzzles described in this section. (See worked-out problem 13.2 and in-text exercise 13.2 on pages 481–2 for numerical examples of these points.)

- In the puzzle involving low-probability events (page 477), why do people prefer option B to option A? To evaluate option B using expected utility theory, we would assign a weight of 0.001 to the utility level associated with winning \$5,000, and a weight of 0.999 to the utility level associated with winning nothing. In contrast, to evaluate option B using prospect theory, we would assign a weight greater than 0.001

to the value associated with winning \$5,000, and a weight less than 0.999 to the value associated with winning nothing. Compared with expected utility theory, prospect theory makes option B look more attractive because it shifts weight toward the low probability outcome, winning \$5,000. Similarly, prospect theory implies that people buy lottery tickets because they attach disproportionate weight to prizes that are received with low probability. According to prospect theory, people who buy lottery tickets also demand insurance because they assign disproportionate weight to large losses that occur with low probability.

- Why are people averse to small gambles with positive expected payoffs? Prospect theory attributes this puzzle to loss aversion. Because of the kink in the value function, each dollar lost counts more than each dollar gained.

Prospect theory remains controversial. Some critics have challenged the evidence, arguing that despite a few puzzles, expected utility theory accounts rather well for most risky choices. Others suggest that the evidence reflects systematic mistakes that consumers might correct through experience and awareness. Still others complain that, instead of *explaining* behavioral puzzles, prospect theory merely *summarizes* them by cobbling together a collection of unrelated assumptions.

With respect to this last point, advocates of prospect theory point to success in explaining new puzzles discovered since the theory was proposed. Application 13.7 is sometimes offered as an example.

Application 13.7

The Equity Premium Puzzle

In the appendix to Chapter 11, we noted that stocks (corporate equities) are riskier than U.S. Treasury bonds. To compensate for their greater risk, investors demand a higher return on stocks than on safe bonds. The difference between the annual returns on a broad portfolio of stocks and safe bonds is known as the *equity premium.* For most of the 20th century, the equity premium averaged around 8 percentage points. In other words, when safe bonds pay 2 percent per year, the rate of return for stocks will be roughly 10 percent, on average.

In 1985, economists Edward C. Prescott (who later received the Nobel Prize in Economics) and Rajnish Mehra published a famous study in which they attempted to reach conclusions about investors' risk preferences based on historical asset returns.[33] To everyone's surprise, they discovered that only an absurdly risk-averse investor would demand an 8 percent equity premium. Someone with that level of risk aversion would be indifferent between flipping a coin for a payoff of either \$50,000 or \$100,000, and receiving \$51,209 for sure. Yet most people would strongly prefer the coin flip. This finding, known as the *equity premium puzzle,* suggests that standard economic models can account for the historical equity premium only if investors are absurdly risk averse.

Edward Prescott (1940–) received the Nobel Prize in Economics in 2004. He and Rajnish Mehra were the first economists to describe the equity premium puzzle.

The discovery of the equity premium puzzle sent shockwaves through the economics profession. For the last two decades, finding a good explanation for the

[33]Rajnish Mehra and Edward C. Prescott, "The Equity Premium: A Puzzle," *Journal of Monetary Economics* 15, 1985, pp. 145–161.

puzzle has been one of the central objectives of financial economists. Many explanations have been proposed. One of them involves loss aversion, a central feature of prospect theory. The idea is simple: unlike bond returns, annual stock returns are frequently negative. Loss-averse investors would demand compensation for exposure to such losses.

How much loss aversion is required to explain the equity premium puzzle? The answer depends on whether investors focus on short- or long-term returns. If investors are worried primarily about returns over the next year, moderate levels of loss aversion can produce an equity premium of 8 percent. Specifically, in Figure 13.5(b) (page 479), the slope of the valuation function slightly to the left of the origin must be 2.25 times as large as the slope slightly to the right of the origin.[34] Over longer time horizons, equity returns are less likely to be negative, so much greater loss aversion is required to produce an 8 percent equity premium. If investors focus on returns over, say, 20 or 30 years, loss aversion cannot explain the equity premium.

WORKED-OUT PROBLEM 13.2

The Problem Rosa evaluates risky alternatives based on prospect theory (see expression (2), page 478). For positive values of X (up to \$5,000), her valuation function is $V(X) = 20{,}000X - X^2$. For negative values of X (closer to zero than $-\$5{,}000$), it's $V(X) = 40{,}000X + 2X^2$. Rosa's probability weighting function is $W(P) = 0.001 + 0.998P$. By graphing these functions, you can see that they look like the ones shown in Figure 13.5.

A. With respect to the first puzzle described on page 477, show that Rosa prefers option B over option A.

B. There is a 0.2 percent chance Rosa will need automobile repairs costing \$2,000. She can buy insurance for \$5. Since her expected loss is \$4, the insurance is actuarially unfair. Rosa has just learned of this risk, and still thinks of the status quo as involving neither repairs nor insurance premiums. Show that she will buy this insurance.

The Solution To answer each of these questions, we need to solve for the expected valuation of each risky prospect using expression (2).

A. Option A provides a valuation of $V(5) = 99{,}975$. Option B provides a valuation of either $V(5{,}000) = 75{,}000{,}000$ or $V(0) = 0$. The weight attached to $V(5{,}000)$ is $W(0.001) = 0.001998$, while the weight attached to $V(0)$ is $W(0.999) = 0.998002$. The value Rosa attaches to option B is therefore $0.001998 \times 75{,}000{,}000 + 0.998002 \times 0 = 149{,}850$. Since $149{,}850 > 99{,}975$, Rosa picks option B.

B. Rosa's valuation for auto insurance is $V(-5) = -199{,}950$. No insurance provides a valuation of either $V(-2{,}000) = -72{,}000{,}000$ or $V(0) = 0$, depending on whether she has an accident. The weight attached to $V(-2{,}000)$ is $W(0.002) = 0.002996$, while the weight attached to $V(0)$ is $W(0.998) = 0.997004$. The value Rosa attaches to option B is therefore $-0.002996 \times 72{,}000{,}000 + 0.997004 \times 0 = -215{,}712$. Since $-199{,}950 > -215{,}712$, Rosa buys insurance.

[34] Shlomo Benartzi and Richard Thaler, "Myopic Loss Aversion and the Equity Premium Puzzle," *Quarterly Journal of Economics* 110, no. 1, 1995, pp. 73–92.

IN-TEXT EXERCISE 13.2 **Show that Rosa will not take the gamble labeled option C on page 477. Show that she will nevertheless risk losing $1,000 against winning $5,000 based on a coin flip.**

13.5 CHOICES INVOLVING STRATEGY

In Chapter 12, we studied the field of game theory, which provides powerful tools for understanding choices involving strategy. How well do those tools perform in practice? The evidence is mixed. However, as we will see in this section, some of game theory's apparent failures may be attributable to faulty assumptions about people's preferences, rather than to fundamental problems with the theory itself. Many applications of the theory assume that people are motivated only by material self-interest. But strategic decisions are inherently social, in the sense that they involve more than one person. When making strategic decisions, some people appear to be motivated in part by social concerns such as altruism, fairness, and prestige. In some situations, it may be important to account for these social motives when analyzing strategic decisions.

Possible Shortcomings of Game Theory

Game theory tends to predict behavior most accurately once players have gained some experience with a game, particularly if the rules are relatively simple. However, even experienced players of simple games sometimes make decisions that seem contrary to their own interests.

In a **voluntary contribution game**, each member of a group makes a contribution to a common pool. Each player's contribution benefits everyone.

To illustrate these points, we'll examine the types of choices that people tend to make in **voluntary contribution games**. In such a game, each member of a group receives a fixed number of tokens. Players are invited to contribute some or all of their tokens to a central pool. They choose their contributions simultaneously, then the game ends. The following formula determines each player's payoff:

$$\text{Player's payoff (\$)} = \text{Player's remaining tokens} + M \times \text{Tokens in common pool}$$

where M is some number between 0 and 1. So when a player contributes a token to the common pool, everyone else gains $\$M$. The contributor gains $\$M$ through the growth of the common pool, but loses $1 in the form of the donated token.

Problems like the voluntary contribution game come up in the real world all the time. Think of the common pool as a joint project, in which contributions can take the form of money or effort. Each person's contribution to the project benefits everyone else.

Before reading further, imagine yourself playing this game with three other people. Suppose everyone starts with 20 tokens, and $M = 0.4$. What would you do?

For each token you contribute to the central pool, your payoff changes by $\$(0.4 - 1)$, or $-\$0.60$. No matter what you expect others to do, your best choice is to contribute nothing. In other words, giving nothing is a dominant strategy. Standard game theory predicts that every player should keep all his tokens.

But what if *every* player were to contribute one token? In that case, everyone's payoff would change by $\$(4 \times 0.4 - 1)$, or $+\$0.60$. Everyone would come out ahead. If the players could reach a binding agreement with each other, they would no doubt decide to contribute *all* their tokens. That way, each would end up with $4 × 0.4 × 20, or $32, rather than $20.

In essence, the voluntary contribution game creates a conflict between individual interests and collective interests. Think of it as a multiple-player version of the Prisoners' Dilemma. Each player has a dominant strategy, but playing those strategies is bad for the group as a whole.

What do people do when they play this game for the first time? Many focus on their individual economic incentives and give nothing. Many others focus on the collective interest and give all of their tokens. Relatively few give something in between. The overall contribution rate is usually around 30 percent to 50 percent—rather far from what game theory would predict.

What happens, though, when people gain experience with this game? In one experiment, subjects played the voluntary contribution game described above 20 times in a row. Playing a game repeatedly can sometimes change the subjects' strategic opportunities and incentives—for example, by introducing the possibility of retaliation or reciprocation (recall Section 12.4). To avoid this possibility, the experimenters assigned players to a new group in each round, so that each round involved a group of "strangers." Subjects were not told what other members of their group had contributed in past rounds.

Figure 13.6 shows the average contributions by round. For the moment, let's focus on the results for the first 10 rounds. Note that contributions dropped steadily as players

Figure 13.6

Average Contributions in the Voluntary Contribution Game. In a voluntary contribution game, the amount given dropped steadily as players gained experience. By the 10th round, players contributed only about 10 percent of the their tokens (2 tokens), on average. As soon as punishments became available (round 11), the contribution rate leaped to nearly 40 percent (8 tokens). As players gained experience with punishments, the contribution rate continued to increase. By the 20th round, the average contribution rate was about 65 percent (13 tokens).

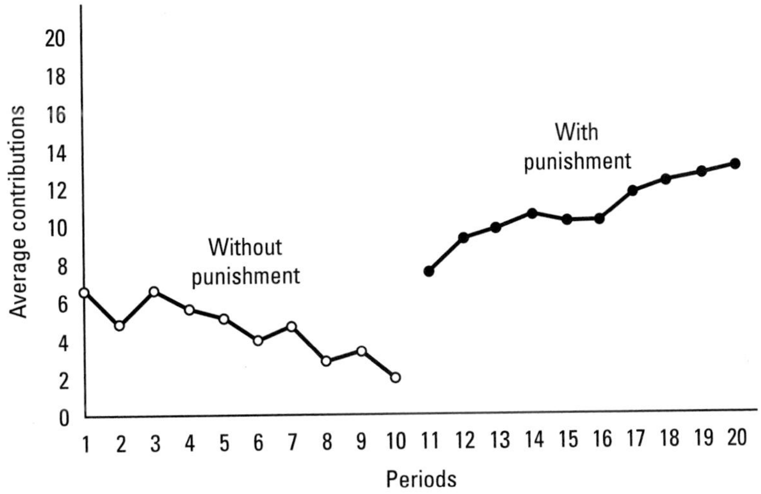

Source: Ernst Fehr and Simon Gachter, "Cooperation and Punishment in Public Goods Experiments," *American Economic Review* 90, no. 4, 2000, pp. 980–994.

gained experience. By the 10th round, players were contributing only about 10 percent of their tokens (2 tokens), on average. Other studies confirm that contributions dwindle as players become more familiar with the voluntary contribution game. Though there is usually a small core of determined contributors, game theory predicts the behavior of experienced subjects reasonably well.

What about rounds 11 through 20? The experimenters changed the game by adding a second stage in which any player could punish any other player. To inflict a punishment, a player had to give up some tokens. For example, reducing another player's payoff by 30 percent cost four tokens. Before reading further, think about what you would do in this two-stage voluntary contribution game. Would you contribute more? Would you punish someone who didn't contribute to the common pool?

With a *credible* threat of punishment, you'd expect people to contribute more. However, in this game, self-interest should guarantee that no one will punish anyone else. Inflicting a punishment is costly. And while it may change the punished player's *future* behavior, it doesn't benefit the punisher because the group assignments change each round. Since the threat of punishment *isn't* credible here, game theory tells us that the addition of punishments shouldn't change the results. (Recall our discussion of strategic credibility in Section 12.4.) Players should contribute nothing and then leave each other alone.

How do people actually play the two-stage voluntary contribution game? Look again at Figure 13.6. As soon as punishments became available (round 11), the contribution rate leaped to nearly 40 percent (8 tokens). As players gained experience with the new stage, *the contribution rate continued to increase.* By the 20th round, the average contribution rate was about 65 percent (13 tokens). So for the two-stage voluntary contribution game, our predictions based on standard game theory are quite far off, even for experienced players.

Does this result mean that game theory is wrong? That's one possibility. Another possibility is that our assumptions about players' preferences are incorrect. In solving the voluntary contribution game with and without punishments, we've assumed that players care only about their own monetary rewards. In fact, they may also care about other things, like fairness. To make sensible predictions, we must take all their motives into account.

The Importance of Social Motives

Since all games involve more than one person, they are necessarily social. In social situations, monetary gain usually isn't the only motive. Some people are altruistic; some value fairness. Others are attracted to efficient outcomes that avoid waste. Some worry about status, and try to create a favorable impression. If treated badly by others, some people react angrily.

An important objective of behavioral economics is to understand these social motives and the ways in which they influence strategic choices. In the following sections we'll highlight some important insights, based on experimental studies of three simple two-player games: the dictator game, the ultimatum game, and the trust game.

In the **dictator game**, one player (the dictator) divides a fixed prize between himself and another player (the recipient) who is a passive participant.

The Dictator Game

In the **dictator game**, one player (the dictator) divides a fixed prize—say $10—between himself and another player (the recipient) who is a passive participant. The dictator and the recipient usually don't know each other, and they have no direct contact during or after the game. Strictly speaking, this isn't really a game at all, since only one player makes a choice. Before reading further, think about what you would do if you played this game in the role of dictator.

If people care only about their own monetary payoffs, every dictator should keep the entire prize for himself. That is not the way people actually behave, however. In one experiment involving $10 prizes and 24 pairs of subjects, only 21 percent of the dictators kept everything for themselves. The same fraction of subjects—21 percent—gave away half the prize ($5). Of the rest, 17 percent ceded $1 to the recipient, 13 percent ceded $2, and 29 percent ceded $3. No one gave away more than half the prize.[35] The specific results have varied a bit from experiment to experiment, depending on the nature of the subject pool, the size of the prize, and other conditions. But most studies have found evidence of significant generosity, even as subjects gained experience. Indeed, a sizable fraction of subjects almost always divides the prize equally.

Results of the dictator game clearly illustrate the potential importance of social motives. Possible explanations include altruism, fairness, and egalitarianism. Concerns about status may also play a role—subjects may want to be *perceived* as generous or fair. Indeed, dictators are considerably less generous when their anonymity is assured.

The Ultimatum Game The **ultimatum game** (also known as **ultimatum bargaining**) starts out just as the dictator game: one player (the proposer) offers to give a second player (the recipient) some share of a fixed prize. The recipient then decides whether to accept or reject the proposal. If he accepts, the pie is divided as specified. If he rejects, both players receive nothing. In other words, this game involves a take-it-or-leave-it offer. Before reading further, think about what you would offer as the proposer (given a prize of, say, $10) and what you would accept as the recipient.

In the **ultimatum game** (also known as **ultimatum bargaining**), one player (the proposer) offers to give the second player (the recipient) some share of a fixed prize. The recipient then decides whether to accept or reject the proposal.

You might expect people to give more under a threat of rejection. But as long as the proposer offers the recipient *something*, a recipient who cares only about his monetary payoff will be better off accepting the offer than rejecting it, so a threat to reject isn't credible. In that case, game theory tells us that the proposer will offer only a tiny fraction of the prize, which the recipient will accept.

How do people actually play this game? When the proposer makes an offer below 20 percent, the recipient rejects it about half of the time. Higher offers are also rejected, but with lower frequency. The threat of rejection results in larger offers than in the dictator game, and recipients enjoy significantly higher payoffs on average, even though some offers are rejected. In an ultimatum game experiment that was otherwise identical to the dictator game experiment discussed in the previous section (the same prize, subject pool, and sample size), 71 percent of proposers divided the $10 prize equally; none proposed keeping it all for themselves. Of the rest, 4 percent offered $1, 4 percent offered $2, 17 percent offered $4, and 4 percent offered $6.[36] As with the dictator game, specific results have varied a bit from experiment to experiment. Even so, virtually every study confirms that many subjects reject very low offers, and the threat of rejection produces larger offers.

Choices in the ultimatum game suggest that in social situations, emotions such as anger and indignation influence economic decisions. People can and often do reject offers that offend their sense of fair play, even if doing so runs contrary to their monetary interests. As a result, many people are careful to avoid giving offense to others.

---

[35]Robert Forsythe, Joel L. Horowitz, N. E. Savin, and Martin Sefton, "Fairness in Simple Bargaining Experiments," *Games and Economic Behavior* 6, 1994, pp. 347–369. The experiment involved undergraduates and MBA students at the University of Iowa.

[36]Robert Forsythe, Joel L. Horowitz, N. E. Savin, and Martin Sefton, "Fairness in Simple Bargaining Experiments," *Games and Economic Behavior* 6, 1994, pp. 347–369. The experiment involved undergraduates and MBA students at the University of Iowa.

Application 13.8

Admitting New States to the Union

The U.S. political system treats each of the 50 states as an equal partner in the federal system of governance. Today we take this equal partnership for granted. But at one time it was a hotly debated issue.

In 1787, delegates from the 13 original states met in Philadelphia to discuss the terms and conditions under which new states would be admitted to the union. A number of them worried that as the western territories were settled, new states might eventually acquire the ability to outvote the original 13. They argued for a two-tier system, with special privileges for the founding states. On the other side of the debate, many of those advocating equal partnership appealed to moral principles. Others offered practical arguments, as George Mason did when he reasoned as follows:

> "[The new states] will have the same pride and other passions which we have, and will either not unite with or will speedily revolt from the Union, if they are not in all respects placed on an equal footing with their brethren."[37]

Mason's argument—that the western territories would reject an unfair take-it-or-leave-it offer—helped to sway the convention in favor of equal partnership.

In the **trust game**, one player (the trustor) decides how much money to invest. A second party (the trustee) divides up the principal and earnings.

The Trust Game In the **trust game**, one player (the trustor) starts out with a fixed amount of money, $\$X$, which he can keep or invest. The investment yields $\$R$ for every dollar invested (where $R > 1$), but the principal and earnings are controlled by a second player (the trustee). The game ends just as the dictator game: the trustee divides the principal and earnings between herself and the trustor. Before reading further, think about what you would invest as the trustor (assuming that $X = 10$ and $R = 3$) and what you would return as the trustee.

You might think that players are more likely to return the money if someone entrusts them with it. But if the trustee cares only about her monetary payoff, she'll keep all the principal and earnings for herself. Anticipating this response, a selfish trustor invests nothing. Since $R > 1$, this result is inefficient. In other words, if players have no motives other than monetary gain, game theory tells us that trustees will be untrustworthy and trustors will forgo potentially profitable investments.

How do people actually play this game? In one experiment involving \$10 prizes and 32 pairs of subjects, only two trustors invested nothing; five of them invested everything. Overall, trustors invested about half their initial funds. Trustees varied widely in their choices. Twenty percent returned nothing and another 27 percent returned only \$1. But others paid back large amounts. Among the 30 trustees who invested something, 11 received more than their investments, 16 received less, and 3 received the same amount. Overall, trustors received about \$0.95 in return for every dollar invested.[38] These results are fairly typical of experimental trust games. Trustors show trust by investing sizable

---

[37]Michael Farrand (ed.). *Records of the Federal Convention*, Vols. I–III. New Haven, Conn.: Yale University Press, 1966, pp. 578–579.

[38]Joyce Berg, John Dickhaut, and Kevin McCabe, "Trust, Reciprocity, and Social History," *Games and Economic Behavior* 10, 1995, pp. 122–142.

amounts. Some trustees prove trustworthy, while others don't. On average, trustors usually come close to breaking even on their investments.

Why is the trust game important? In the real world, people can sometimes enter into binding contracts, which eliminate the need for trust. Here, a contract might specify that the trustor is to provide investment funds of $10, and the trustee is to return $15, keeping $15 for herself. Both parties would come out ahead. But binding contracts don't work well in all situations. A great deal of business is conducted on the basis of handshakes and verbal agreements. The trust game helps us to understand one reason why this approach works. Many (but not all) people do feel obliged to justify the trust shown in them by others. As a result, many are willing to extend trust to others.

13.6 NEUROECONOMICS: A NEW FRONTIER

Like the previous sections of this chapter, the field of behavioral economics is highly compartmentalized. It catalogs noteworthy observations concerning decision making and offers specialized theories to explain many of them. Unlike standard economic theory, it does not proceed from overarching principles, nor does it provide a single unified theory of decision making. Some behavioral economists believe that it may be possible to develop a new unified theory of economic decision making by studying the human neural system, including brain processes. Such speculation has led to a new field of microeconomic research called **neuroeconomics**. Progress to date has been limited, but the field is still in its infancy, and the pace of discovery is accelerating.

Neuroeconomics studies the human neural system, including brain processes, with the object of discovering new principles of economic decision making.

How can the study of human neural processes help with economic modeling? Take the issue of self-control, discussed in Section 13.3. Neuroeconomic research has identified a plausible neurological source of dynamic inconsistency. In one experimental study, subjects made choices involving immediate and delayed rewards while undergoing brain scans.[39] The results suggest that when someone chooses between, say, $10 in two weeks and $12 in six weeks, the brain evaluates both alternatives using the same neural circuitry. However, when someone chooses between $10 immediately and $12 in four weeks (that is, the same alternatives two weeks later), the brain appears to use different circuitry. All alternatives—whether delayed or immediate—activate a portion of the brain that is well-suited to evaluating and comparing abstract rewards (the lateral prefrontal cortex and related structures). But immediate rewards produce more pronounced responses in a part of the brain that is thought to play an important role in many of our emotional responses (the limbic system).

Figure 13.7(a) provides a composite image of multiple brain scans. It highlights areas in which activity is elevated during decision making. Figure 13.7(b) shows how the level of activity in four areas of the brain changes over time once the subject has been asked to choose between two alternatives. Three of these areas are considered limbic structures. The red lines show the level of activity when one of the alternatives provides an immediate reward ("d = today," where d indicates when the earliest reward is available), while the green and blue lines show the level of activity when both alternatives provide delayed

[39] Samuel M. McClure, David I. Laibson, George Loewenstein, and Jonathan D. Cohen, "Separate Neural Systems Value Immediate and Delayed Monetary Rewards," *Science* 306, October 15, 2004, pp. 504–507.

Figure 13.7

Brain Activity during Choices Involving Time. Figure (a), a composite image of multiple brain scans, shows four areas of the brain that are disproportionately activated by immediate rewards. Figure (b) tracks the level of activation in each of these structures in response to various choices. Here, "d" refers to the time delay before the earliest of two rewards. Immediate rewards (d = Today) produce higher activation in all four areas.

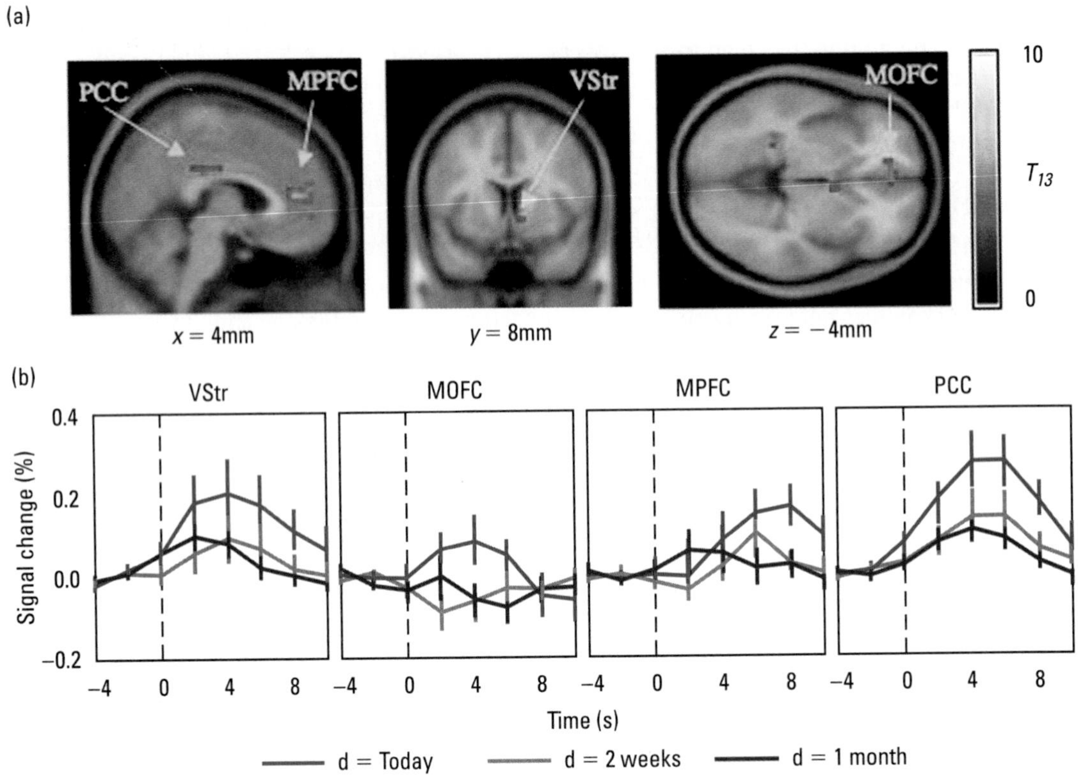

Source: Samuel M. McClure, David I. Laibson, George Loewenstein, and Jonathan D. Cohen, "Separate Neural Systems Value Immediate and Delayed Monetary Rewards," *Science* 306, October 15, 2004, 504–507.

rewards ("d = 2 weeks" and "d = 1 month"). Activity in each of these brain structures is considerably higher when one of the alternatives provides an immediate reward than when rewards are delayed (compare the red lines to the green and blue lines). However, as long as the earliest reward is not immediate, the amount of delay doesn't seem to matter (compare the green lines to the blue lines).

Earlier in this chapter, we emphasized that it is often difficult to determine whether a particular behavioral pattern reflects preferences or mistakes. As Application 13.9 illustrates, another potential benefit of neuroeconomics is that it may help us resolve this issue in particular instances.

Application 13.9

Addiction

The consumption of addictive substances is an important social issue that affects members of all socioeconomic strata in virtually every nation. According to estimates for the United States, nearly half a million deaths each year are attributable to cigarettes, more than 100,000 to alcohol, and roughly 20,000 to various narcotics. Alcohol abuse contributes to 25 to 30 percent of violent crimes.

One school of thought, known as the *theory of rational addiction*, holds that the consumption of addictive substances is simply an expression of consumer preferences.[40] According to this view, addictive substances are distinguished only by the particular pattern of benefits and costs they deliver over time; otherwise, they're just like other goods. While it's true that addictive substances are potentially dangerous, so are hang-gliding, rock climbing, and eating too much fast food. And while it's true that the use of addictive substances sometimes harms other people, the same can be said of automobiles, electricity, and matches. What is the justification for treating addictive substances differently?

There is a growing consensus among neuroscientists that addictive substances interfere with the normal operation of a neural system that generates forecasts of near-term pleasure. Normally, this system learns through feedback—that is, it forecasts pleasure based on past experience. Addictive substances "short circuit" this system, causing it to malfunction. With repeated use of a substance, the cues associated with past consumption cause the system to forecast grossly exaggerated pleasure responses, creating a powerful (and disproportionate) impulse to use.[41]

This new consensus within neuroscience has potentially important implications for the economic analysis of addictive substances. Normally, economists infer consumers' preferences from their choices, and evaluate policies based on these inferred preferences. But in the case of addictive substances, some choices may be attributable to malfunctions of the brain's forecasting circuitry. As a result, they may not reveal consumers' preferences reliably. Indeed, many addicts say they want to quit, and many of them try to quit, but report that they are unable to control their use.

CHAPTER SUMMARY

1. **Objectives and methods of behavioral economics**

   a. There are two main motivations for research in behavioral economics. First, people sometimes make choices that are inconsistent or at least very difficult to reconcile with standard economic theory. Second, in some situations, standard economic theory leads to seemingly unreasonable conclusions about consumer welfare.

   b. The main objective of behavioral economists is to modify, supplement, and enrich standard economic theory by adding insights from psychology. Usually they modify the theory either by making different assumptions about preferences or by assuming that certain actions are mistakes.

   c. For the most part, behavioral economists employ the same tools as other economists, though they tend to rely more on experiments. Experiments offer several potential advantages and disadvantages over other methods.

[40] See Gary Becker and Kevin Murphy, "A Theory of Rational Addiction," *Journal of Political Economy* 96, no. 4, 1988, pp. 675–700.

[41] For a review of the evidence, as well as an elaboration of the policy implications, see B. Douglas Bernheim and Antonio Rangel, "Addiction and Cue-Triggered Decision Processes," *American Economic Review* 94, no. 5, 2004, pp. 1558–1590.

2. **Departures from perfect rationality**

   a. Some experiments call into question the assumption that people have coherent preferences. In some situations, subjects consistently violate the Ranking Principle: in others, their judgments appear to depend on patently irrelevant information.

   b. In some situations, people exhibit a strong attachment to the status quo. For example, they tend to value something more highly when they own it than when they don't. Moreover, when confronted with a menu of alternatives, they sometimes avoid making a choice and end up with the default option. Default effects are apparent in decisions about retirement saving.

   c. People tend to group related items into categories and to draw artificial boundaries around those categories. In making a choice, they tend to consider other items in the same category, and may ignore items in different categories.

   d. Sometimes, people's choices seem to depend on the way the alternatives are presented. Different presentations may convey precisely the same objective information while calling attention to different facts.

   e. When confronted with complex problems, people often rely on simple rules of thumb that have performed reasonably well in the past. Rules of thumb appear to play an important role in decisions concerning saving and portfolio allocation.

3. **Choices involving time**

   a. Some people change their rankings of the alternatives available at some future time as that time approaches. This phenomenon reflects a bias toward immediate gratification, which creates problems involving self-control. That, in turn, leads people to restrict future choices.

   b. People who suffer from present bias may have difficulty exercising the self-control required to save money. If they're aware of their tendencies, they may look for ways to save automatically and lock up funds for retirement—for example, through pension plans.

   c. Though microeconomic theory tells us to ignore sunk costs, people sometimes have difficulty following that principle. For example, they may behave as if the value they attach to an object depends on the price they paid for it.

   d. In some situations, people appear to have trouble accurately forecasting how they'll feel about different outcomes in the future. Instead of making reasonable forecasts, they tend to evaluate future consequences based on their tastes and needs at the moment of decision making.

4. **Choices involving risk**

   a. People tend to make several types of errors in assessing probabilities. Some think that once an event has occurred several times in a row, it is more likely to repeat; others think it is less likely to repeat. Overconfidence causes people to overestimate their abilities and underestimate the uncertainty involved in decisions. This tendency may contribute to the high frequency of business failure.

   b. In some situations, people seem to place disproportionate weight on low-probability events, and are noticeably risk averse, even toward gambles involving very low stakes. These and other puzzles have led to the development of prospect theory.

   c. Prospect theory assumes, first, that people evaluate an outcome based on the change in total resources (rather than on the level of total resources); second, that a person's valuation of an outcome is more sensitive, per dollar, to small losses than to small gains; third, that the impact of enlarging a change on a valuation declines with the size of the change; and fourth, that the weight associated with each potential outcome is greater than its probability for small probabilities and smaller than its probability for large probabilities.

5. **Choices involving strategy**

   a. Predictions of behavior that are based on game theory tend to become more accurate once players have gained some experience with a game, particularly if the rules are relatively simple. However, even experienced players of simple games sometimes appear to behave contrary to their own interests. Many of these failures may be attributable to assumptions about players' payoffs (in particular, that they care only about their own monetary rewards) rather than to problems with game theory itself.

   b. An important objective of behavioral economists is to understand the ways in which social motives influence strategic choices. Results for the dictator game illustrate the potential importance of social motives such as altruism, fairness, egalitarianism, and status. Results for the ultimatum game suggest that emotions such as anger and indignation can also influence economic decisions. Results for the trust game help us to understand one reason why it's possible to conduct a great deal of business based on only handshakes and oral agreements.

6. **Neuroeconomics: a new frontier**

   a. Some economists believe that they will eventually learn to build better models of economic behavior, and perhaps develop a new unified theory of decision making, by studying relevant aspects of the human neural system, including brain processes. For example, researchers have identified a plausible neurological source of dynamic inconsistency.

   b. Neuroeconomics may help us determine whether particular behavioral patterns, such as the consumption of addictive substances, reflect preferences or mistakes.

Exercise 13.1: What are the characteristics of a good economic experiment? What characteristics make an experiment convincing?

Exercise 13.2: Some people use behavioral economics constructively to identify patterns they should watch out for in their own behavior. Based on the material in this chapter, what patterns do you think you should watch out for? Why? How would you detect them?

Exercise 13.3: Some countries (including the United States) require explicit consent for an organ donation; others presume that an individual consents unless he or she explicitly opts out. In countries that require explicit consent, fewer than 30 percent of adults are eligible for organ donation. In most opt-out countries, more than 98 percent are eligible. Interpret this observation in light of the default effect. Why do you think the effect is so strong with regard to organ donation? Can you reconcile this pattern with standard economic theory?

Exercise 13.4: Describe three situations (not including the examples given in the text) in which people use rules of thumb to make complex decisions. What rules do they tend to use? Do those rules strike you as reasonable? Why or why not?

Exercise 13.5: Application 13.4 (on health clubs) shows how a business can make a profit by taking advantage of customers' dynamic inconsistency. Why do health club members allow health clubs to take advantage of them? What else might they do? Can you think of other examples of profitable business strategies (either actual or potential) designed to take advantage of the behavioral patterns discussed in this chapter? For example, do businesses sometimes try to exploit the endowment effect? The anchoring effect? How? Think about advertising and marketing strategies, among other things.

Exercise 13.6: Describe three situations (not including the examples given in the text) in which people may make precommitments. Do they do so because they don't trust themselves to follow through on their plans or intentions, or for some other reason?

Exercise 13.7: Try to think of a situation in which a sunk cost influenced a decision you made. Do you think the decision was a mistake? If you had the opportunity to make a similar decision today, would you choose differently? Why or why not?

Exercise 13.8: Think about a voluntary contribution game with 9 players, in which each player receives 20 tokens. Suppose $M = 0.2$. Let's use R to stand for a player's remaining tokens and C to stand for the number of tokens in the common pool. The dollar payoff is $D = R + 0.2C$, but players are altruistic and rank outcomes according to the value $D + AD^O$, where A is a positive number and D^O stands for the total dollar payoff to every other player. The value of A differs from one player to another. Suppose $A > 0.5$. Will the players have a dominant strategy? What is it? What if $A < 0.5$?

Exercise 13.9: Think about a dictator game in which one player divides \$10 between himself and someone else. Let's use S to stand for the amount he keeps for himself and F for the absolute value of the difference between the amount he keeps, and the amount he gives the other player. For instance, if he keeps \$8, then $F = 6$ (because he gives \$2 to the other player); if he keeps \$4, then $F = 2$ (because he gives \$6 to the other player). Suppose the dictator ranks the outcomes according to the value $S - AF$, where A is a positive number. That is, he cares about both his own dollar payoff and the fairness of the outcome (where greater equality implies greater fairness). What will he do if $A < 0.5$? What will he do if $A > 0.5$?

Exercise 13.10: Think about an ultimatum game in which the proposer divides \$10 and the recipient decides whether to accept or reject the proposal. If the recipient rejects the proposal, neither player receives anything. Let's use F to stand for the absolute value of the difference between the two players' payoffs, as in the last question. Suppose the proposer is selfish and cares only about his own dollar payoff. The receiver, however, cares about fairness—she ranks the outcomes according to the value $R - 0.5F$, where R is her dollar payoff. Which proposals will she accept? Which ones will she reject? Knowing that information, what will the proposer offer?

Exercise 13.11: Think about a trust game in which the trustor starts out with \$10, and an investment yields \$3 for each dollar invested. Let's use F to stand for the absolute value of the difference between the two players' payoffs, as in the last two questions. Suppose the trustor is selfish and cares only about his own dollar payoff. The trustee, however, cares about fairness—she ranks the outcomes according to the value $R - 2F$, where R is her dollar payoff. What will the trustee do if the trustor invests \$2, \$4, \$6, \$8, or \$10? What is the trustor's payoff in each case? What is the trustor's best choice? How would your answer change if the investment yielded \$1.50 for each dollar invested?

MARKETS

part III

Part III In the next eight chapters, we turn our attention to markets. Our objective is to understand how the economic decisions of consumers and firms determine market outcomes, including the prices of goods and the quantities bought and sold. Part IIIA studies perfectly competitive markets, in which consumers and firms treat market prices as fixed. We'll see that perfectly competitive markets can achieve desirable economic outcomes. Part IIIB studies imperfectly competitive markets which fall short of the competitive ideal.

part

IIIA

Competitive Markets

In Chapter 2, we provided a brief introduction to the analysis of competitive markets. The next three chapters examine the nature of competitive equilibrium in greater depth. In Chapter 14 we'll investigate the differences between market equilibrium in the short run and the long run. We'll also analyze the welfare properties of competitive equilibrium outcomes. We'll see that perfectly competitive markets allocate resources efficiently in the sense that it is impossible to make any individual better off without making others worse off. Chapter 15 uses the tools that we develop to study the effects of various government policies. In Chapter 16 we'll broaden the scope of our analysis beyond a single market, and examine competitive equilibrium in many markets simultaneously. We'll see how developments in one market affect others, and how those effects ripple between markets and produce feedback into the original market. We'll also extend our conclusion regarding the efficiency of competitive markets to this more general setting.

chapters

14 EQUILIBRIUM AND EFFICIENCY

LEARNING OBJECTIVES

After reading this chapter, students should be able to:

- Identify the factors that make a market perfectly competitive.
- Determine short- and long-run market demand and supply.
- Analyze changes in market equilibrium due to changes in market conditions in the short and long run.
- Demonstrate how perfectly competitive markets can be considered "efficient" for society.
- Measure aggregate surplus, consumer surplus, and producer surplus using market supply and demand curves.

The fall of the Berlin Wall (above). Soon after (below).

On the night of November 9, 1989, the Berlin Wall came down. Its fall marked the culmination of a revolution in Central Europe, one that gave both political and economic freedom to millions who had lived for years under Soviet-controlled communist regimes. Soon after, the Soviet Union would itself break apart, unable to sustain high military spending and a collapsing economy.

The collapse of communism marked a turning point for the economies of the former Soviet-bloc nations. In the years that followed, many would transition from state-controlled to free-market economies. State-owned firms would be privatized, and new businesses would be allowed to form without hindrance. The economies of those nations that aggressively embraced free markets and privatization soon began to grow rapidly. In Poland, for example, the share of gross domestic product produced by private firms increased from 19 percent in 1988 to 65 percent in 1997. Gross domestic product per capita rose over 150 percent in the ten years from 1990 to 2000.

Economists put a lot of faith in markets. In this chapter, we'll see why. As we noted in Section 1.1, there are many ways for a society to determine what goods are produced, how they are produced, and who consumes them. In the former Soviet-bloc countries, those decisions were made largely by government edict. In a market economy, most of those decisions are made instead by individuals who face market prices. When markets are perfectly competitive, this process, which Adam Smith called the "invisible hand" of the market, produces an outcome that maximizes society's net benefit from the production and consumption of goods. That is not to say that markets always perform flawlessly. In Part IIIB (Chapters 17–21), we'll study circumstances in which markets fail to achieve this ideal, in some cases justifying government intervention.

This chapter covers five topics concerning competitive markets:

1. *What makes a market competitive?* We'll start by discussing the factors that make a market competitive, so that individuals and firms act as price takers, and supply and demand analysis is appropriate.
2. *Market demand and market supply*. In Parts IIA and IIB (Chapters 4–9) we discussed *individual* demand and supply. To find the market demand and market supply, we need to add up those individual demands and supplies. We'll see how to do so, both when the number of firms is fixed, and when firms can freely enter and exit a market.
3. *Short-run and long-run competitive equilibrium*. Once we know the market demand and supply, we can determine the market equilibrium, as discussed in Chapter 2. Here we'll study a topic not covered in Chapter 2, the short-run and long-run adjustments in markets that are characterized by free entry and exit in the long run.
4. *Efficiency of perfectly competitive markets*. A market is only one of many possible ways to allocate a society's scarce resources. Yet with all those possibilities, economists tend to put their faith in markets. We'll show that in a perfectly competitive market, an equilibrium is efficient in the sense that it maximizes "aggregate surplus," society's net benefit from the production and consumption of a good or service.
5. *Measuring surplus using market demand and supply curves*. We'll study how to use market demand and supply curves to measure aggregate surplus, as well as the surpluses enjoyed by consumers and firms. These techniques will prove very useful when we study applications of competitive equilibrium theory in Chapter 15.

14.1 WHAT MAKES A MARKET COMPETITIVE?

When we apply supply and demand analysis to study a market, we assume that buyers and sellers act as price takers. When is this reasonable?

Let's consider buyers first. Usually, a consumer's demand for a good, or a firm's demand for an input, is just a tiny fraction of the overall amount bought and sold. The consumer's or firm's change in the amount purchased has a negligible effect on the balance between total supply and demand, so price remains virtually unchanged. Put slightly differently, because their needs are small relative to the market, each consumer or firm can greatly increase the amount they buy with only a negligible increase in the price they offer to pay sellers. As a result, it is usually reasonable to assume that buyers are price takers. (We discuss some exceptions, however, in Section 17.6.)

What about sellers? Conditions for sellers in markets for their outputs are more varied. Sometimes they act as price takers, and at other times not. We'll study both cases in the remaining chapters of this book.

Economists call the idealized setting in which both buyers and sellers have absolutely no effect on price a *perfectly* competitive market. Three factors cause a market to be perfectly competitive. The first factor is the *absence of transactions costs*. Transactions costs are absent when sellers can easily communicate their prices, buyers can easily locate suppliers and learn their prices, and buyers and sellers can arrange transactions without significant obstacles. This means that when different sellers produce the same product buyers will have no difficulty identifying and purchasing from the seller who offers it at the best terms.

The second factor is **product homogeneity**. Wheat is wheat. For the most part, buyers of wheat don't care who grew it. If any one farmer tries to charge more than the others, buyers will simply get their wheat elsewhere. This means there's only one market for wheat, with a price that applies for wheat grown by every farmer. In contrast, consider a situation in which a small town has two local car dealers, one selling General Motors cars, and the other selling Fords. Consumers are likely to view Ford and General Motors cars as **differentiated products**, products that are not the same. Because consumers will differ in their desire to buy from one dealer versus another, the prices of their cars need not be the same for both to make sales.

Products are **homogeneous** when they are identical in the eyes of purchasers. They are **differentiated** when some purchasers view the products as different.

The third factor is the presence of a *large number of sellers, each of whom accounts for a small fraction of the market supply*. With many small sellers, a single firm can substantially increase or decrease the amount it sells (say doubling it, or halving it) with its profit affected in only a trivial way by the negligible changes in price this may cause. As a result, it will act like a price taker, selling a unit if its price is at least the marginal cost of producing it (see Section 9.3). Economies of scale play a key role in determining when this situation can arise (see Section 8.8 for a review of economies of scale). For many small firms to produce efficiently in a market, the efficient scale of production must be small compared to the overall size of the market, the total amount produced and consumed. The efficient scale in wheat production is indeed a tiny fraction of the overall amount of wheat produced. In contrast, consider the market for concrete in a small town. Because concrete production involves economies of scale, a small town may have only a single firm producing concrete. If so, and if the market demand curve is downward sloping, that firm will recognize that the more it wants to sell, the lower its price must be. It will not be a price taker.[1]

When all three of these factors are present, consumers have many options and buy from the firm that offers the lowest price. No firm can charge more than the price charged by other firms—the market price—without losing virtually all of its customers. Moreover, even substantial changes in the amount a firm sells involve only negligible changes in price. As a result, each firm can essentially take the market price as given and focus only on how much it wants to sell at that price, which leads it to sell a unit precisely when the marginal cost of producing it is no greater than the market price.

[1]In Section 19.6, we'll see more explicitly how the number of firms grows as economies of scale shrink, driving the market outcome toward the outcome predicted by supply and demand analysis.

Factors that Make a Market Perfectly Competitive

1. Buyers and sellers face no transactions costs;
2. Products are homogeneous;
3. There are many suppliers, each accounting for a small fraction of the overall supply of the good.

Few markets are *perfectly* competitive. Consumers usually face at least some transactions costs, the products of different firms usually differ at least a little bit, and many markets have quite a few firms but not an extremely large number (say, 20 firms rather than 100). As a result, firms usually think that their decisions have at least a small effect on price. Economists nonetheless devote a fair amount of attention to models of perfectly competitive markets for two reasons. First, many markets are highly competitive and behave almost as if they're perfectly competitive. Our model of perfect competition therefore helps us predict outcomes in these markets. It provides a useful tool for analyzing how changes in input costs, prices of substitutes, taxes, and other market factors affect the price and quantity sold. Second, we'll see in Section 14.4 (and Chapter 16) that perfect competition leads to outcomes that are, in an important sense, very desirable from the perspective of market participants. As a result, it serves as a useful benchmark against which to compare the performance of markets that are not perfectly competitive, the subject of Part IIIB (Chapters 17–21).

14.2 MARKET DEMAND AND MARKET SUPPLY

In Chapters 4–9 we studied how price-taking consumers and firms determine their individual demand and supply. But to analyze the competitive market for a good, we need to determine the good's *market* demand and *market* supply. Let's start with market demand.

Market Demand

The **market demand** for a product is the sum of the demands of all the individual consumers. Graphically, the **market demand curve** is the horizontal sum of the individual demand curves.

At any given price, the **market demand** for a product is the sum of the demands of all the individual consumers. (For simplicity, in this section we'll assume that all demand comes from consumers and all supply comes from firms.) Graphically, the **market demand curve** is the horizontal sum of the individual demand curves. Example 14.1 illustrates how to add up individual demand to get market demand.

Example 14.1

The Market Demand for Ice Cream Cones

Juan and Emily are the only consumers of ice cream cones. Figure 14.1(a) shows their demand curves, labeled D_{Juan} and D_{Emily}, respectively. Juan's demand function is $Q^d_{Juan} = 10 - 4P$ at prices below \$2.50, and zero at prices above \$2.50.[2] Emily's demand function is $Q^d_{Emily} = 6 - 2P$ at prices below \$3, and zero at prices above \$3. Figure 14.1(b) shows the market demand curve for ice cream cones. At prices equal to or greater than \$2.50, only Emily wants to buy ice cream, so the market demand curve is the same as her individual demand curve. For example, at a price of \$2.50, the market demand is one cone, which is the number Emily demands. Juan demands nothing at that price. At prices below \$2.50, Emily and Juan both want to buy ice cream so the market demand equals the sum of their demands at each price. For example, when the price is \$1.50, Emily wants three cones and Juan wants four cones, so the market demand is seven cones. Since Juan and Emily's demand curves both slope downward, so does the market demand curve.

We can find the market demand function using algebra. At prices below \$2.50, the market demand is $Q^d = Q^d_{Juan} + Q^d_{Emily} = (10 - 4P) + (6 - 2P) = 16 - 6P$. For prices between \$2.50 and \$3.00, only Emily buys ice cream, so the market demand function is $Q^d = Q^d_{Emily} = 6 - 2P$. At prices above \$3.00, neither Emily nor Juan wants a cone. So we can write the market demand function as

$$Q^d = \begin{cases} 0 \text{ for } P > 3.00 \\ 6 - 2P \text{ for } 2.50 < P \leq 3.00 \\ 16 - 6P \text{ for } P \leq 2.50 \end{cases}$$

Figure 14.1

Individual and Market Demand Curves for Ice Cream Cones. Figure (a) shows Juan and Emily's weekly demand curves for ice cream cones. Figure (b) shows the market demand curve, equal to the horizontal sum of Juan and Emily's individual demand curves.

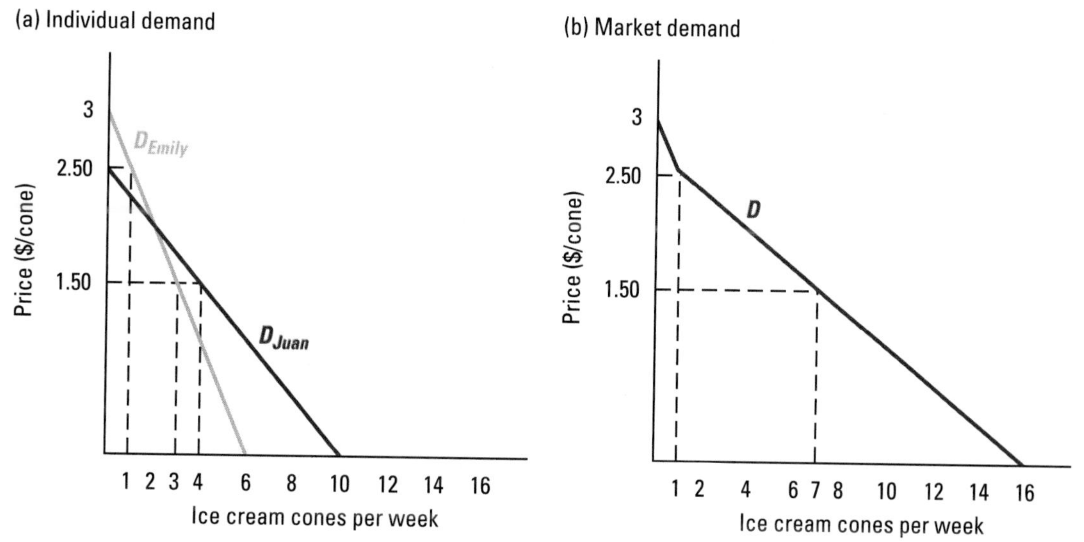

[2]Whenever a demand curve is shown hitting the vertical axis at some price, this should be understood as meaning that demand is zero for all higher prices.

IN-TEXT EXERCISE 14.1 **Juan's demand function for ice cream cones is $Q^d_{Juan} = 20 - 5P$ at prices below \$4, and zero at prices above \$4. Emily's demand function is $Q^d_{Emily} = 6 - 2P$ at prices below \$3, and zero at prices above \$3. What is the market demand function? Graph the individual and market demand curves.**

In Chapter 5 we discussed how a consumer's demand for a product can differ in the short and long run. To find the market demand in the short run, we just add up consumers' short-run demand curves. Similarly, to find the market demand in the long run, we add up consumers' long-run demand curves. Thus, when consumers' demand curves differ in the short and long run, the market demand curve is likely to do so as well.

Market Supply

The **market supply** of a product is the sum of the supply of all the individual sellers. Graphically, the **market supply curve** is the horizontal sum of the individual supply curves.

At any given price, the **market supply** of a product is the sum of all the individual sellers' supplies. Graphically, the **market supply curve** is therefore the horizontal sum of the individual supply curves. Example 14.2 illustrates how to add up individual supplies to get market supply. The procedure is very similar to the way we constructed market demand.

Example 14.2

The Market Supply of Ice Cream Cones

Anitra and Robert are the only sellers of ice cream cones. Figure 14.2(a) shows their supply curves, labeled S_{Anitra} and S_{Robert}, respectively. Anitra's supply function is $Q^s_{Anitra} = 8P - 8$ at prices above \$1, and zero at prices below \$1.[3] Robert's supply function is $Q^s_{Robert} = 3P - 1.50$ at prices above \$0.50, and zero at prices below \$0.50. Figure 14.2(b) shows the market supply curve. At prices below \$0.50, neither of them wants to sell any ice cream. At prices between \$0.50 and \$1, only Robert wants to sell ice cream, so the market supply curve is the same as his individual supply curve. For example, when the price is \$1, the market supply is 1.5 cones per week; all of that supply comes from Robert. At prices above \$1, both Anitra and Robert want to sell ice cream, so the market supply equals the sum of their individual supplies at each price. For example, when the price is \$1.50, Anitra wants to sell four cones and Robert wants to sell three cones. Market supply is therefore seven cones. Since both their supply curves slope upward, so does the market supply curve.

We can find the market supply function using algebra. At prices above \$1, the market supply function is $Q^s = Q^s_{Anitra} + Q^s_{Robert} = (8P - 8) + (3P - 1.50) = 11P - 9.50$. At prices between \$0.50 and \$1, it is $Q^s = Q^s_{Robert} = 3P - 1.50$. At prices below \$0.50, neither Robert nor Anitra wants to supply any ice cream. So we can write the market supply function as

$$Q^s = \begin{cases} 11P - 9.50 \text{ for } P \geq 1.00 \\ 3P - 1.50 \text{ for } 0.50 \leq P < 1.00 \\ 0 \text{ for } P < 0.50 \end{cases}$$

[3] Whenever a supply curve is shown hitting the vertical axis at some price, this should be understood as meaning that supply is zero for all lower prices. In some cases, however, to avoid any possible confusion, we'll explicitly show the portion of a supply curve that reflects zero supply (as we did in Chapter 9 when a firm's supply jumped from zero to a positive quantity when the price reached the lowest level of average cost, AC_{min}).

Figure 14.2

Individual and Market Supply Curves for Ice Cream Cones. Figure (a) shows Anitra and Robert's weekly supply curves for ice cream cones. Figure (b) shows the market supply curve, equal to the horizontal sum of Anitra and Robert's individual supply curves.

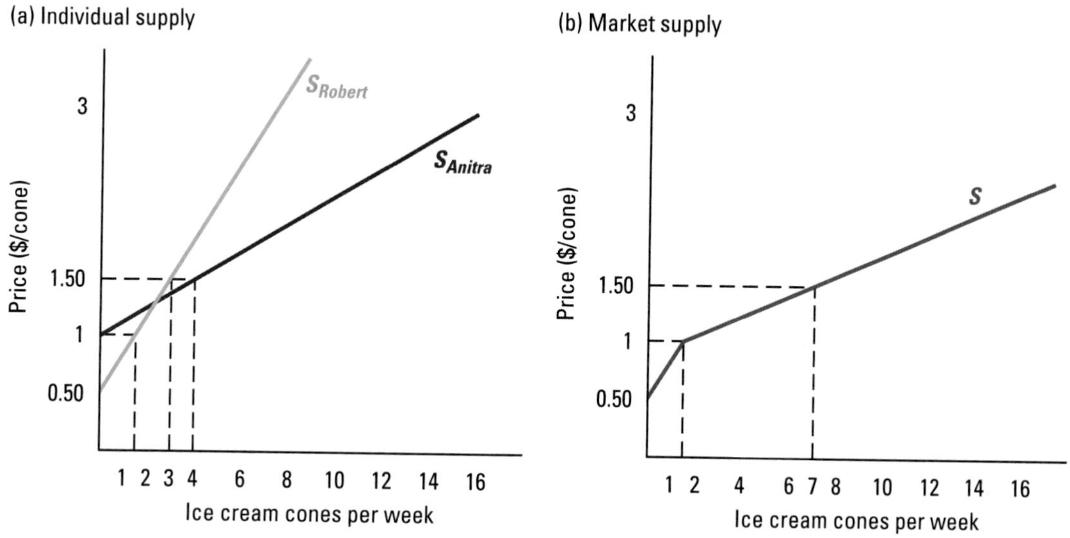

IN-TEXT EXERCISE 14.2 **The supply function of each firm that makes fudge brownies is $Q^s = 100P - 50$ at prices above \$0.50, and zero at prices below \$0.50. Suppose there are 50 brownie manufacturers. What is the market supply function for brownies? Graph the market supply curve. Repeat the exercise supposing instead that there are 100 brownie manufacturers.**

Application 14.1

The U.S. Softwood Lumber Supply in 1998

In Application 9.3 (page 312) we saw how the Softwood Lumber Agreement (SLA) between the United States and Canada affected the export supply curve of lumber producers in Alberta, British Columbia, Ontario, and Quebec. Now let's look at the U.S. market supply of softwood lumber in 1998, one of the five years the agreement was in effect.

The softwood lumber consumed in the United States comes from three sources: domestic (U.S.) producers, Canadian producers in the four provinces subject to the SLA, and other foreign producers (including other Canadian provinces not covered by the SLA). In 1998, U.S. consumption of softwood lumber was 52.9 billion board feet (bbf). U.S. firms produced 65 percent of that total, Canadian firms in the four SLA provinces produced 29 percent, and other imports accounted for the rest.

Figure 14.3 shows the supply curves for these three groups, labeled $S_{U.S.}$ for U.S. producers, S_{Cdn} for the Canadian producers subject to the SLA, and S_{other} for other foreign producers. Each of those curves is the horizontal sum of the individual supply curves of all producers in the group. The light-red dashed line shows what the Canadian supply curve would have looked like at prices above $240 without the Softwood Lumber Agreement.

The supply curve for the Canadian producers who were subject to the SLA reflects the features we studied in Application 9.3. The SLA specified that those producers could freely export in total up to 14.7 bbf a year to the United States; that the next 0.65 bbf would be subject to a tariff of $50 per thousand board feet (collected by the Canadian government); and that any further exports would be subject to a tariff of $100 per thousand board feet. As a result, the SLA shifted the supply curve of those Canadian producers, S_{Cdn}, up by $50 at 14.7 bbf and another $50 at 15.35 bbf.[4] Those jumps imply that there are price ranges over which exports by those producers are insensitive to the price. For example, at all prices between $240 and $290, Canadian producers would export 14.7 bbf to the United States. Only when the price exceeded $290 did it become worthwhile for them to incur the $50 tariff in order to sell more lumber in the United States. Similarly, they would export 15.35 bbf at all prices between $304 and $354.

The U.S. market supply curve of softwood lumber, labeled S in Figure 14.3, is equal to the horizontal sum of the three group supply curves. It is steeper in the price ranges $240–$290 and $304–$354, where Canadian producers from the four affected provinces do not change their exports in response to price changes. The medium-red dashed line shows what the U.S. market supply curve would have looked like at prices above $240 without the Softwood Lumber Agreement.

Figure 14.3

U.S. Market Supply Curve of Softwood Lumber, 1998. The market supply curve S is the sum of the supply curves of three groups: U.S. domestic producers (curve $S_{U.S.}$), Canadian producers subject to the Softwood Lumber Agreement (curve S_{Cdn}), and other foreign producers not subject to the agreement (curve S_{other}). The dashed red lines show what the Canadian and market supply curves would have been at prices above $240 without the Softwood Lumber Agreement.

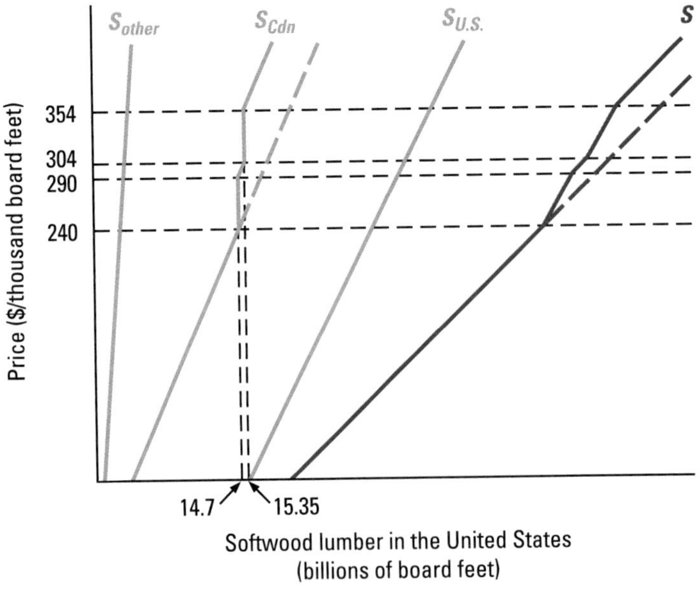

[4]The precise shape of the supply curve S_{Cdn} depends on how the Canadian government distributes the quota limits among the individual suppliers in the four provinces. In constructing it, we've made the simplifying assumption that all of those producers were identical and faced identical fee-free and low-fee limits, so that they had identical individual supply curves like that in Application 9.3. (For example, with 100 producers, each would face the $50 and $100 tariffs once their production reached 1.47 bbf and 1.535 bbf, respectively.)

Short-Run versus Long-Run Market Supply In Section 9.4 we saw that a firm's short-run and long-run supply curves may differ. Since the market supply curve for a product is just the sum of individual sellers' supply curves, the short-run and long-run market supply curves may differ as well.

Short-run and long-run market supply curves may also differ for another reason. Over time, the set of firms that are able to produce in a market may change. In the short run, only those firms that are currently active in the market may be capable of producing. But, in the long run, other firms may be able to begin producing if it is profitable for them to do so. This means that the short-run market supply curve is found by summing the short-run supply curves of the currently active firms, while the long-run market supply curve is found by summing the long-run supply curves of all *potential* suppliers.

Sometimes the number of potential firms is limited; there may be only a small number of firms that have the know-how to produce a product, even in the long run. (End-of-chapter exercise 14.4 asks you to consider such a case.) However, since technological knowledge diffuses over time and patents on production processes, which can prevent others from copying a firm's technology, eventually lapse, we can usually assume that technology is freely available over the long run. When that is so, anyone who wishes to start a firm and enter a market has access to the same technology and opportunities as everyone else—a situation called **free entry**. With free entry, there is in effect an unlimited (that is, infinite) number of firms that can produce a good in the long run.

There is **free entry** in a market when technology is freely available to anyone who wishes to start a firm and entry is unrestricted. In that case, the number of potential firms is unlimited.

How do we add up the supply curves of an unlimited number of potential firms to find the long-run market supply curve with free entry? Figure 14.4 illustrates the procedure.

Figure 14.4

The Long-Run Market Supply Curve for Garden Benches with Free Entry. Figure (a) shows the marginal and average costs and supply function for an individual firm. With 5 or 10 such firms, the market supply curves would be the curves S_5 or S_{10}, respectively, in figure (b). With free entry, the number of potential firms is unlimited, so the market supply curve becomes the horizontal line at a price of \$100 (equal to AC_{min}), labeled S_∞ in figure (b).

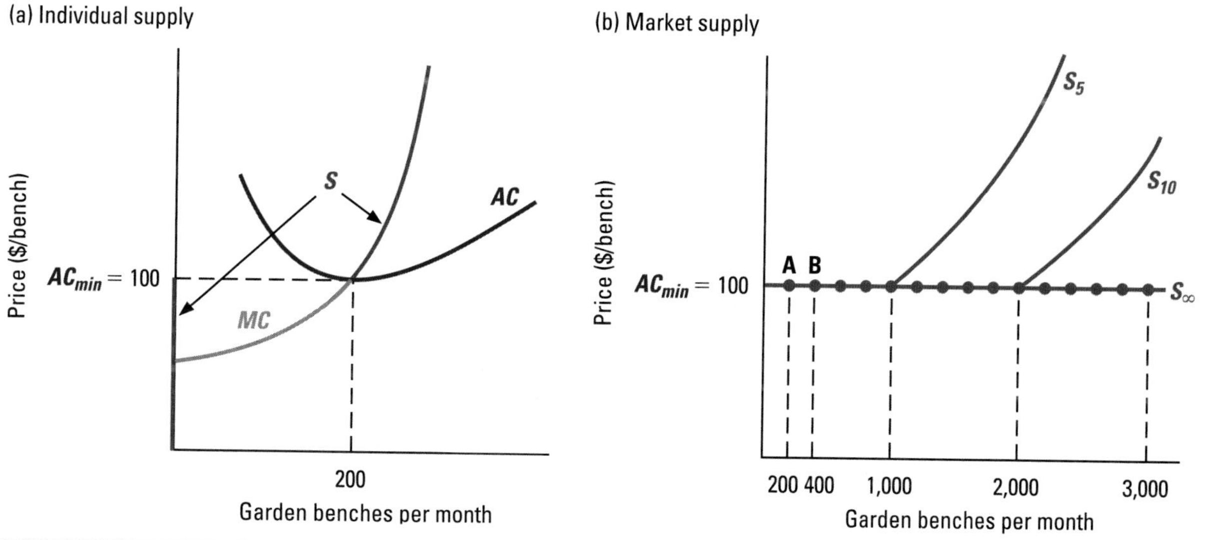

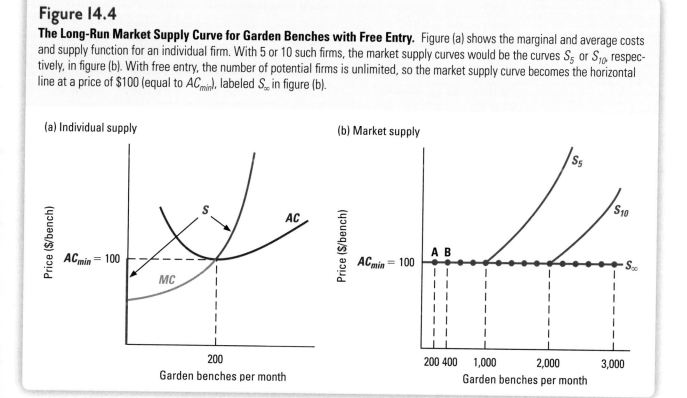

Suppose everyone has access to the same technology for producing garden benches. The (long-run) marginal cost, average cost, and individual firm supply curves are shown in Figure 14.4(a). The level of minimum average cost, AC_{min}, is \$100 per unit. It is achieved at the efficient scale of production, equal to 200 benches per month. (We studied these concepts in Section 8.5.) As the firm's supply curve shows, a firm will produce zero benches if the price is below \$100 and either zero or 200 benches if the price equals \$100. It will produce the amount indicated by the marginal cost curve if the price is above \$100 (that is, the quantity where *MC* equals the price).

Figure 14.4(b) shows the market supply curves if there are 5 firms, 10 firms, and an unlimited number of firms that can produce in the long run. The market supply curve with five firms, labeled S_5, is the horizontal sum of five of the supply curves in Figure 14.4(a). At prices below \$100, supply is zero. At prices above \$100, each of the five firms produces the quantity on its marginal cost curve corresponding to that price. So the market supply curve at prices above \$100 is the horizontal sum of the individual firms' marginal cost curves. What happens when the price equals \$100? Then every firm is willing to supply either 0 or 200 benches. As a result, there are several possibilities for market supply. One firm could produce 200 benches, while the other four firms produce zero. In that case, market supply would be 200 benches, indicated by the dot labeled "A" in Figure 14.4(b). Or two firms could each produce 200 benches, while the other three firms produce zero. Then market supply would be 400, indicated by the dot labeled "B" in Figure 14.4(b). In fact, market supply could be any multiple of 200 benches up to 1,000, which would be the market supply if all five firms produced 200 benches. Those amounts are shown by the set of five dots running up to 1,000 benches.

The same idea applies when there are 10 firms; the market supply curve is then S_{10}. Supply is zero at prices below \$100. At prices above \$100, it coincides with the horizontal sum of the 10 firms' marginal cost curves. At a price of exactly \$100, the market supply curve is shown by the set of 10 dots (spaced in multiples of 200 benches) running up to 2,000.

If we increase the number of firms further, we get more and more dots at a price of \$100. With an unlimited number of potential firms, the long-run market supply curve is the set of dots spaced in multiples of 200 benches that lie along the light red horizontal line at a price equal to \$100, the level of AC_{min}. When the distance between the dots that make up the long-run market supply curve is small compared to total market production, we can safely approximate the long-run market supply curve by the infinitely elastic, horizontal line S_∞.

The fact that with free entry, the long-run market supply curve is a horizontal line at the price AC_{min} makes sense. At any price below AC_{min} no firm can make a profit, so supply is zero. At any price above AC_{min} every firm with access to the technology can make a profit, so that with an unlimited number of potential firms, supply is infinite. When the price exactly equals AC_{min}, a firm with access to the technology can break even (earn zero profit) by producing at its efficient scale, the level at which average cost equals AC_{min}. At that price the market supply can be anything, depending on how many firms choose to produce at the efficient scale and how many choose to produce nothing.

WORKED-OUT PROBLEM 14.1

The Problem Consider the pizza market in Chicago, where the (long-run) daily costs for a pizza company are the same as for Dan's Pizza Company in worked-out problems 9.2 and 9.3 (pages 306 and 308). They include \$845 in avoidable fixed costs and variable costs equal to $VC = 5Q + Q^2/80$, where Q is the number of pizzas produced each day. Marginal cost when producing Q pizzas is $MC = 5 + Q/40$. Suppose that in the long run there is free entry into this market. What is the long-run market supply curve?

The Solution In answering worked-out problem 9.3, we found that the efficient scale of production was 260 pizzas per day. (Recall that we determined that level by finding the output level at which average cost equals marginal cost—look back at worked-out problem 9.3.) At the efficient scale, average cost (AC_{min}) equals \$11.50. Thus, the long-run market supply curve is horizontal at \$11.50. At prices below \$11.50, long-run supply is zero; at prices above \$11.50, it is infinite. When the price exactly equals \$11.50, long-run supply can be any positive quantity that is a multiple of 260.

IN-TEXT EXERCISE 14.3 **Suppose that, in the long run, a pizza firm's variable costs are $VC = Q^2/2$ (where Q is the number of pizzas produced each day), its marginal cost is $MC = Q$, and there is an avoidable fixed cost of \$50 per day. In the long run, there is free entry into the market. What is the long-run market supply curve?**

The time horizon required for long-run adjustments in the number of active firms can differ for different products. It may take a matter of months, for example, to set up a new retail coffee shop. But in the automobile industry, it can take years to open a new plant. The time required for long-run adjustments in a given market may also depend on the types of adjustments required: for example, it may be shorter when existing firms need to shut down than when new ones need to be started.

14.3 SHORT-RUN AND LONG-RUN COMPETITIVE EQUILIBRIUM

Once we've determined market supply and demand, we can find the equilibrium price and quantity (the amount bought and sold), just as we did in Chapter 2. At the equilibrium price, the amounts supplied and demanded are equal. The market clears at that price, with buyers and sellers making all their desired purchases and sales.

To illustrate, consider the market for ice cream cones in Examples 14.1 and 14.2 (pages 498 and 500). Figure 14.5 shows the market demand curve from Figure 14.1(b), labeled D, and the market supply curve from Figure 14.2(b), labeled S. The market clearing price is \$1.50, the price at which the demand and supply curves intersect. At that price, seven cones are bought and sold each week.

Figure 14.5

Market Equilibrium. The market for ice cream cones clears at a price of \$1.50 per cone. At that price demand equals supply, and there is no tendency for the price to either increase or decrease.

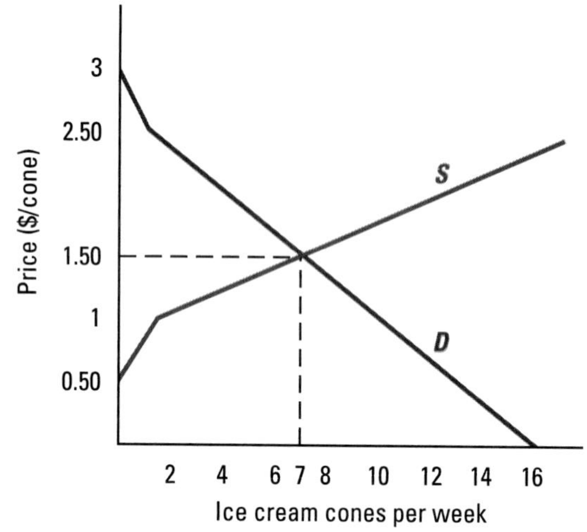

Before you read further, review (or read for the first time) Section 2.3 on the basics of market equilibrium, including how to use algebra to find the market equilibrium and determine changes in the equilibrium in response to shifts in demand or supply. In this section, we'll discuss an issue not covered in Section 2.3, the short-run and long-run adjustment to changes in market conditions in markets with free entry in the long run. We'll begin by considering some of the properties of long-run competitive equilibrium with free entry. (The chapter's appendix examines another issue not covered in Section 2.3, equilibrium in factor markets, the markets for firms' inputs.)

Long-Run Competitive Equilibrium with Free Entry

In Section 14.2 we saw that, with free entry, the supply curve is horizontal at the level of AC_{min}, the minimum average cost level. Figure 14.6 depicts a long-run competitive equilibrium in the garden bench market when there is free entry and all firms have access to the technology shown in Figure 14.4(a) (page 503), so that AC_{min} is \$100 and the efficient scale is 200 garden benches per month. The market demand curve is the medium blue curve, labeled D. The long-run market supply curve is S_{∞}. The long-run equilibrium price is \$100 and 2,000 garden benches are bought and sold per month. Since each active firm must be producing at its efficient scale of 200 garden benches, there are 10 active firms.

More generally, free entry has three important implications for market equilibrium:

Three Properties of Long-Run Competitive Equilibrium with Free Entry

1. The equilibrium price must equal AC_{min}.
2. Firms must earn zero profit.
3. Active firms must produce at their efficient scale of production.

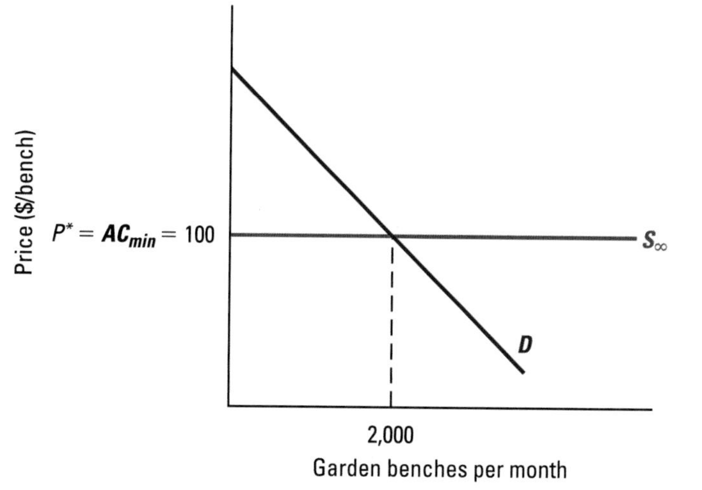

Figure 14.6

Long-Run Market Equilibrium with Free Entry. This figure shows a long-run competitive equilibrium in the garden bench market when there is free entry and all firms have access to the technology in Figure 14.4(a). The equilibrium price equals AC_{min} and 2,000 garden benches are bought and sold each month. Since each firm must produce at its efficient scale (200 garden benches per month), there are 10 active firms.

Figure 14.6 shows why the first implication is true. Because the market supply curve with free entry is horizontal at the price AC_{min}, the equilibrium price must equal AC_{min} regardless of the location or shape of the demand curve.

The second and third points follow from the first. When the price equals AC_{min} a firm can't make a positive profit: there is no output level it might choose at which the price would exceed its average cost. The most it can earn is zero profit, which it does by producing at its efficient scale, the quantity at which average cost equals AC_{min}.

A firm that earns zero economic profit is not doing badly. Remember that economic costs include opportunity costs (see Section 8.2). For example, the firm's economic costs include the opportunity cost of any time the owner spends running the firm. If the firm earns zero economic profit, the owner is being compensated fully for her opportunity cost, which means she can't make more money doing anything else. While the owner would of course prefer to make a positive economic profit, she is earning as much return on her investment of time in the firm as she could earn in other ways. Likewise, if the firm is using capital assets, it is earning exactly the opportunity cost of those assets—that is, the amount it could earn by deploying them in some other way, such as renting them to other firms.

Short-Run and Long-Run Responses to Changes in Demand

To predict the short-run and long-run responses to changes in market conditions, we need to determine how market equilibrium changes in the short run when the number of firms is fixed, as well as in the long run when conditions of free entry hold.

Consider the garden bench market again. Suppose that initially the market is in the long-run equilibrium depicted in Figure 14.6, with 10 active firms, but that the demand curve then shifts outward to the curve labeled $\hat{D}$ in Figure 14.7(a). In the short run, the number of firms is fixed at 10 (its original equilibrium level), so the short-run supply curve is S_{10}. This curve is the sum of the 10 active firms' short-run supply curves [we assume that these firms' fixed costs are sunk in the short run, so these curves coincide with the marginal cost curve in Figure 14.4(a), even at prices below AC_{min}]. So in the short run, the market equilibrium shifts from point A to point B. The price rises above \$100. Because the equilibrium price exceeds the firms' minimum average cost, AC_{min}, they make positive economic profits.

In the long run, however, new firms are free to enter the market. More firms become active in response to the profit opportunity that emerges when the short-run equilibrium price rises above AC_{min}. This entry eventually pushes the price down to a new long-run equilibrium at point C. The price is once again \$100, but the total amount bought and sold is now 4,000 benches. Since each active firm must be producing at its efficient scale, there are now 20 active firms.

Figure 14.7(b) shows the short-run and long-run response to a *reduction* in the demand for garden benches. When demand decreases from D to $\hat{D}$, the market equilibrium adjusts from its initial long-run equilibrium at point A to a new short-run equilibrium at point B. The price falls below \$100, and the active firms incur losses (in the short run, their fixed costs are sunk and they cannot avoid them by exiting). Over time, however, some firms exit and the market adjusts to a new long-run equilibrium at point C. The price is once again \$100 and 1,000 benches are produced and sold each month. Since each active firm

Figure 14.7

Short-Run and Long-Run Responses to a Change in Demand. In the long run, all firms have access to the technology for producing garden benches shown in Figure 14.4(a), and can enter or exit the market. In the short run, however, the number of firms is fixed (and active firms' fixed costs are sunk). Initially, in both figures, the market is at long-run equilibrium at point A, with 10 firms each producing 200 units. When demand changes from D to $\hat{D}$, the short-run equilibrium shifts to point B. In figure (a), where demand increases, the price rises above \$100 and active firms earn a positive profit. In figure (b), where demand decreases, the price falls below \$100 and active firms earn a negative profit. In the long run, however, in both cases the equilibrium shifts to point C in the respective figures and the price returns to \$100. Once again, each active firm is producing 200 units and earning zero economic profit. The new long-run equilibrium involves 20 firms in figure (a) and 5 firms in figure (b).

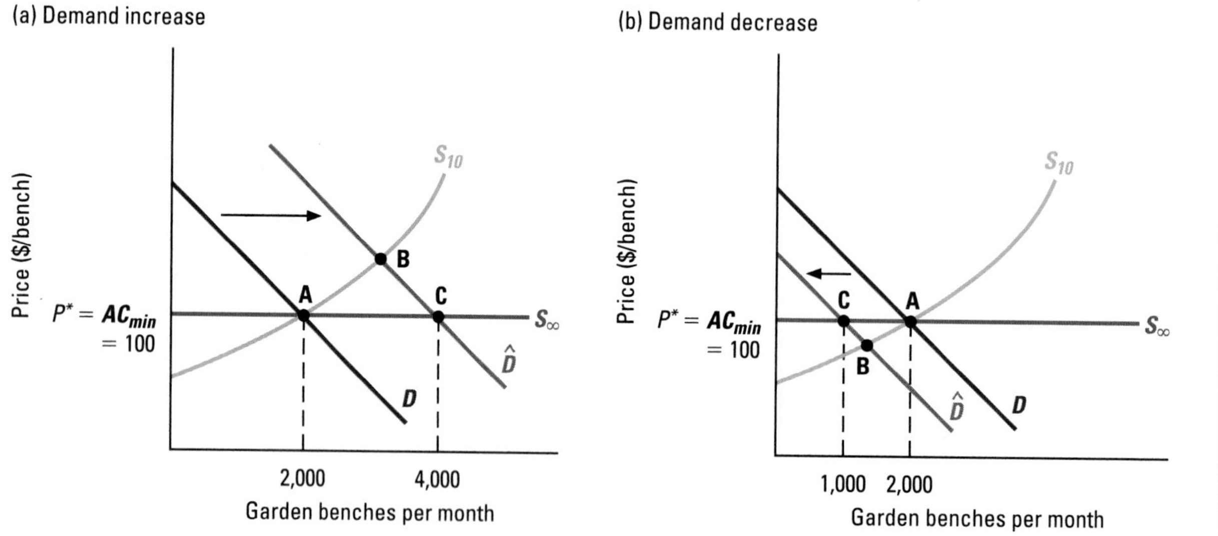

must be producing at its efficient scale of 200 benches a month, only five of the ten original firms remain active; the other five have exited.

We can also solve for short- and long-run changes using algebra instead of graphs. Worked-out problem 14.2 provides an example.

WORKED-OUT PROBLEM 14.2

The Problem Consider again the pizza market in Chicago. Assume the daily demand for pizza is $Q^d = 32{,}900 - 600P$, where P is the price of a pizza. The daily costs for a pizza company are the same as in worked-out problem 14.1. They include \$845 in fixed costs and variable costs equal to $VC = 5Q + Q^2/80$, where Q is the number of pizzas produced in a day. Marginal cost is $MC = 5 + Q/40$. Suppose that in the long run, there is free entry into the market and the fixed cost is avoidable. What are the long-run market equilibrium price and quantity? How many firms are active, and how much do they each produce?

Now suppose that demand doubles to $Q^d = 65{,}800 - 1{,}200P$. If in the short run the number of firms is fixed (so that neither entry nor exit is possible) and fixed costs are sunk, what is the new short-run market equilibrium? What is the new market equilibrium in the long run?

The Solution Recall from worked-out problem 14.1 that the efficient scale of production is 260 pizzas per day, and that AC_{min} equals \$11.50, so that the long-run market supply curve is horizontal at a price of \$11.50.

Step 1: Finding the initial long-run market equilibrium. In a long-run equilibrium, the market price equals AC_{min}, so the price in the initial long-run equilibrium must be \$11.50. The next step is to find out how many pizzas are produced and sold each day in this equilibrium. We can find this quantity from the demand function: when the price is \$11.50, the total amount demanded is $Q^d = 32{,}900 - 600(11.50) = 26{,}000$. Finally, in a long-run equilibrium, each active firm produces 260 pizzas a day, its efficient scale. That means there are 100 active firms in the initial long-run equilibrium.

Step 2: Finding the new short-run market equilibrium. Now suppose that demand doubles. In the short run, the number of active firms is fixed at 100. To find the short-run market supply, we need to first find the supply function for each of these individual firms. In the short-run, their fixed costs are sunk. Each of the firms therefore has the same supply function that we solved for in worked-out problem 9.3 (page 308), in the case with no avoidable fixed cost:

$$S(P) = \begin{Bmatrix} 40P - 200 \text{ if } P \geq 5 \\ 0 \text{ if } P \leq 5 \end{Bmatrix}$$

Since there are 100 such firms, the short-run market supply function is

$$S(P) = \begin{Bmatrix} 4{,}000P - 20{,}000 \text{ if } P \geq 5 \\ 0 \text{ if } P \leq 5 \end{Bmatrix}$$

To find the new short-run market equilibrium, we equate supply and demand and solve for the equilibrium price:

$$65{,}800 - 1{,}200P = 4{,}000P - 20{,}000$$

The solution is $P^* = \$16.50$. The total number of pizzas produced and sold each day in this short-run equilibrium is 46,000 and each active firm sells 460 pizzas. Since the price is above $AC_{min} = \$11.50$, the active firms each make a positive profit.[5]

Step 3: Finding the new long-run market equilibrium. In the long run, the price falls back to $AC_{min} = \$11.50$. Since demand has doubled, the total number of pizzas produced and sold must double to 52,000 a day. And since each active firm is again producing at its efficient scale of 260 pizzas a day, the number of active firms doubles to 200.

IN-TEXT EXERCISE 14.4 **The daily demand for pizzas is $Q^d = 750 - 25P$, where P is the price of a pizza. The daily costs for a pizza company include \$50 in fixed costs, and variable costs equal to $VC = Q^2/2$, where Q is the number of pizzas produced in a day. Marginal cost is $MC = Q$. (These are the costs in in-text exercise 14.3.) Suppose that in the long run there is free entry into the market and the fixed cost is avoidable. What are the long-run market equilibrium price and quantity? How many firms are active, and how much does each produce? If demand doubles to $Q^d = 1{,}500 - 50P$ and, in the short run, the number of firms is fixed (so that neither entry nor exit is possible) and fixed costs are sunk, what is the new short-run market equilibrium? What is the new market equilibrium in the long run?**

Short-Run and Long-Run Responses to Changes in Cost

Let's look now at the short- and long-run response to a change in firms' costs. Suppose that, starting from the long-run equilibrium in Figure 14.6, a garden bench firm's fixed costs decrease while variable costs remain the same. For example, the firm's monthly rent may have decreased, or the opportunity cost of its owner's time may have fallen. Figure 14.8(a) shows that this decrease in fixed cost shifts the average cost curve downward from AC to $\hat{AC}$, decreasing minimum average cost from \$100 to \$70 per table. The firm's minimum efficient scale decreases from 200 to 160.

Figure 14.8(b) shows the resulting short-run and long-run changes in market equilibrium. After the decrease in costs, the short-run market supply curve is S_{10}, the horizontal sum of the firms' marginal cost curves (again, in the short run, the fixed cost is sunk). Since firms' marginal costs have not changed and the number of active firms is fixed, the

[5] Specifically, each of the 100 active firms supplies 460 pizzas (the total amount produced divided by 100). Their revenue is $460 \times 16.50 = \$7{,}590$. Their variable cost is $5(460) + (460)^2/80 = \$4{,}945$, and their fixed cost is \$845. Thus, they each earn \$1,800.

Figure 14.8

Short-Run and Long-Run Responses to a Decrease in Fixed Costs. In the long run, all firms have access to the technology whose cost curves are shown in figure (a), and can enter or exit the market at will. In the short run, however, the number of firms is fixed. Initially, firms' average cost curve is AC, but when fixed costs fall, the average cost curve drops to $\widehat{AC}$ and the efficient scale of production falls from 200 to 160. Initially, the market is in equilibrium at point A in figure (b), with 10 active firms. When fixed costs decrease, the market equilibrium remains at point A in the short run, but shifts to point B in the long run. The price falls to \$70 in the long run.

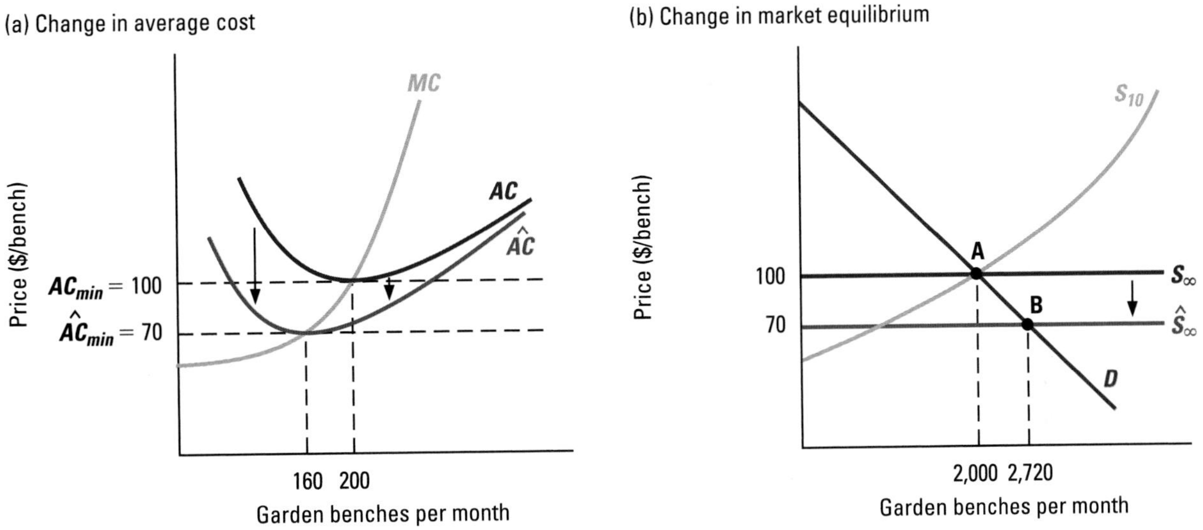

market equilibrium remains at point A over the short run. Active firms make a positive profit because the price is greater than the now-lower minimum average cost level of \$70 per table.

In the long run, however, firms enter the market in response to this profit opportunity. The long-run supply curve is now the horizontal line $\hat{S}_\infty$, and the market equilibrium shifts to point B. The price falls to \$70 per table and 2,720 garden benches are produced and sold each month. Since each firm's efficient scale is now 160 benches a month, all active firms must be producing that amount. Thus, there are 17 active firms in this new long-run equilibrium.

When instead firms' variable costs change, a firm's marginal and average cost curves both shift. This causes the short-run supply curve to shift, in contrast to what happened in Figure 14.8. The basic procedure for identifying short-run and long-run responses is similar, however: find the new short-run equilibrium using the new short-run supply curve of the initially active firms, and then find the new long-run equilibrium using the new long-run market supply curve (which reflects free entry). End-of-chapter exercises 14.8 and 14.9 ask you to identify the short-run and long-run responses to changes in costs using algebra.

Application 14.2

Short- and Long-Run Equilibrium for Ski Resort Condos

Many people enjoy traveling to the mountains to ski in the winter. As a result, large numbers of condominiums have been built near ski resorts. The demand for such units at a particular resort depends on how many people want to ski there. For example, when improvements to the ski trails or heavy snowfall draws additional skiers to an area, demand for condominiums in the area increases. The demand for ski condominiums also depends on the tax treatment of second homes, which has changed over the years.

What effect does an increase in demand, resulting for example from a change in the weather, have on the price of a ski condominium? At many resorts there is a predictable pattern. In the short run, prices rise, sometimes dramatically. But within a few years, new units are built, driving prices back to where they began. Because land around ski resorts is often plentiful and the technology for building condominiums freely available, a condition of free entry holds. Thus, the price of a ski condominium can't exceed the minimum average cost of building one for very long. It can fall lower than that, though, because there is no free exit: once a condominium is built, it's costly to demolish even if its value falls.

Economist William Wheaton has studied the market for condominiums at Loon Mountain, New Hampshire.[6] Figure 14.9 shows two of the factors that affected the demand for ski condominiums in New England between 1980 and 1998. The blue line represents skiers' visits in each year. Note that it fluctuates quite a bit. Its peaks and valleys are closely associated with those of the dark red line, which represents the amount of snowfall each year. But longer-run trends are also evident in skier visits. For example, between 1982 and 1987—two years with about the same snowfall—skier visits increased by about 25 percent. After 1987, visits remained more stable, declining a bit overall. Not shown in Figure 14.9 is one factor that significantly reduced the demand for ski condominiums in the middle of this period: the Tax Reform Act of 1986. That legislation greatly reduced the tax benefits of owning second homes. It was phased in over four years, from 1987 to 1991.

How do we expect prices and condominium construction to change in response to these demand shifts? The theory of short-run and long-run competitive equilibrium suggests that in response to the increase in demand from 1980 to 1987, condominium prices should increase in the short run, creating profit opportunities for builders. In the long run, more condominiums should be built, driving condominium prices back down to their original level. Given the costs of exit (demolishing a condo), however, an event that reduces demand (like the Tax Reform Act of 1986) could push prices below the level prevailing in the initial long-run competitive equilibrium and leave them there for an extended period of time, with little or no new construction occurring.

Figure 14.10 shows the pattern of condominium prices relative to construction costs (the blue line), as well as the number of building permits issued each year for new condominiums (the dark red bars). The blue line shows changes in the ratio of the price per square foot to the construction costs for a typical condominium, including interest costs incurred by the builder. The height of the line shows that price/cost ratio in each year relative to the price/cost ratio in 1980 (so that in 1980 the height of the line is 1). In 1987 the price/cost ratio was 1.32, 32 percent higher than it was in 1980. Clearly, prices increased dramatically relative to costs from 1985 to 1989, most likely because of the increase in demand shown in Figure 14.9, before falling even more dramatically from 1989 to 1994. The price/cost ratio ended the period far below where it had started.

As Figure 14.10 shows, builders responded to these price movements. When prices exploded upward in the mid-1980s, the number of new condominiums soon followed. But the huge increase in supply soon caused prices to fall again. Combined with the reduction in demand following the Tax Reform Act, the increase in supply pushed prices below their original level (relative to costs). By the early 1990s, almost no new units were being built, just as the theory predicts.[7]

[6] W.C. Wheaton, "Resort Real Estate: Does Supply Prevent Appreciation?" *Journal of Real Estate Research* 27, 2005, pp. 1–16.

[7] In contrast to the predictions of the theory, some condomimiums were built in 1991, when prices (relative to costs) were well below their 1980 level. Builders may have sunk some of the costs for these projects before the price fell that low, however. By 1992, essentially no condominiums were being built.

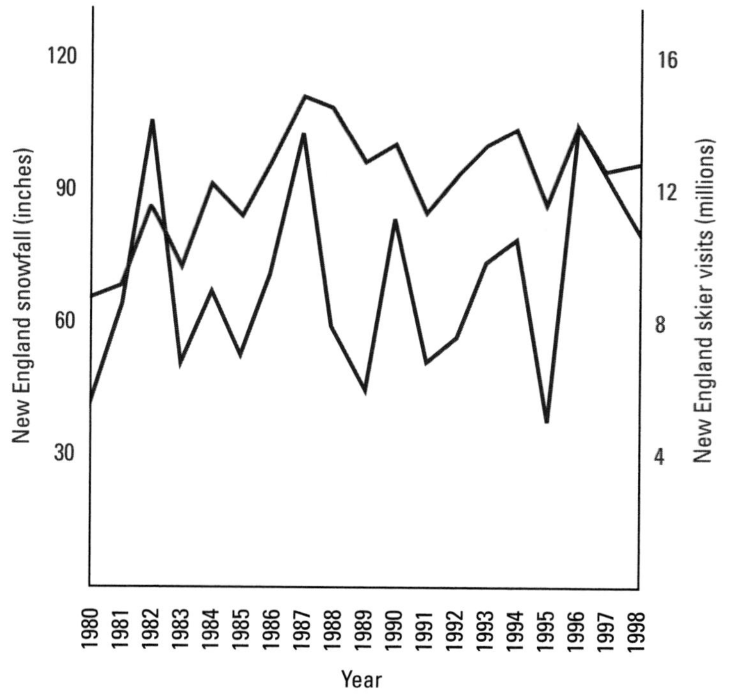

Figure 14.9

New England Snowfall and Skier Visits 1980–1998. The dark red line shows the snowfall in New England each year. The blue line shows skier visits to New England each year.

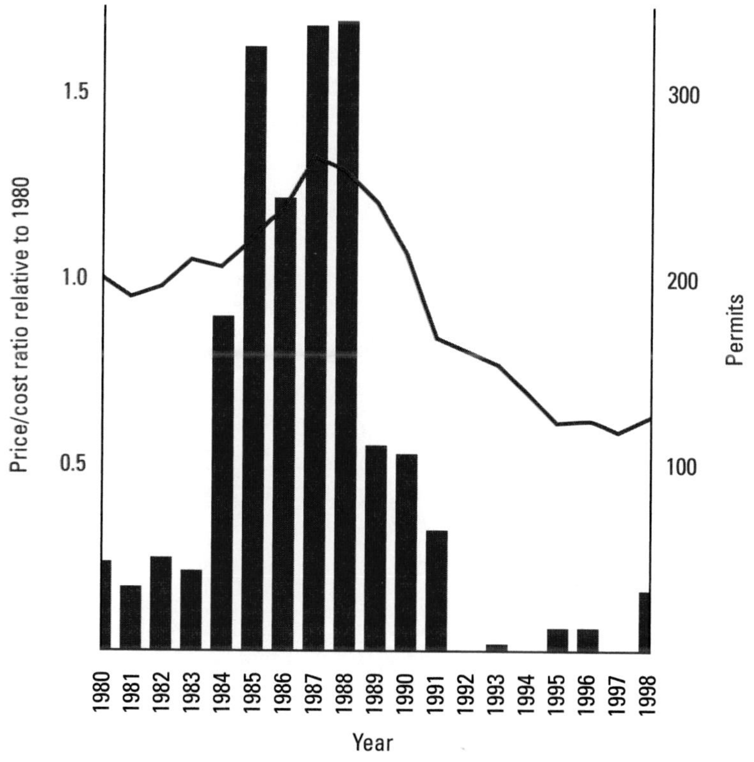

Figure 14.10

Condominium Prices Relative to Costs and New Construction at Loon Mountain, 1980–1998. The blue line shows the ratio of prices to construction costs relative to the base year, 1980. The dark red bars show the number of new building permits issued each year.

Price Changes in the Long Run

In reaching the conclusion that, with free entry, the long-run competitive price is unaffected by changes in demand (always equal to AC_{min}), we've assumed that the prices of firms' inputs do not change. This assumption will be a reasonable one if any increases in the amounts of inputs used are small compared to the sizes of the overall input markets. Then the prices of the inputs will likely not change very much. Our assumption will also be reasonable when the supply in those input markets is very elastic (see Section 2.4 for a discussion of elasticity), since then even large changes in the demand for those inputs will cause only small changes in their prices. In general, though, when the demand for a product increases, the prices of the inputs used to make it may change. This phenomenon is an example of a *general equilibrium effect*—that is, an effect that arises because the market we are studying and the markets for its inputs must *all* be in equilibrium.

We'll study general equilibrium effects in Chapter 16. In the context of input prices, the basic idea is fairly straightforward. Figure 14.11(a) considers again what happens when the demand for garden benches increases. Now, however, we suppose that this drives up the price of the inputs used in producing them. For example, garden bench production might require a special kind of wood that has few other uses. The increase in the price of this wood shifts the long-run market supply curve upward, to the curve $\hat{S}_\infty$. The new long-

Figure 14.11

Price Changes in the Long-Run. Figure (a) shows a case where an increase in the demand for garden benches drives up firms' inputs costs, shifting the long-run supply curve upward and causing the price to increase in the long run. Figure (b) shows a case where instead input prices fall, causing the price of garden benches to fall in the long run.

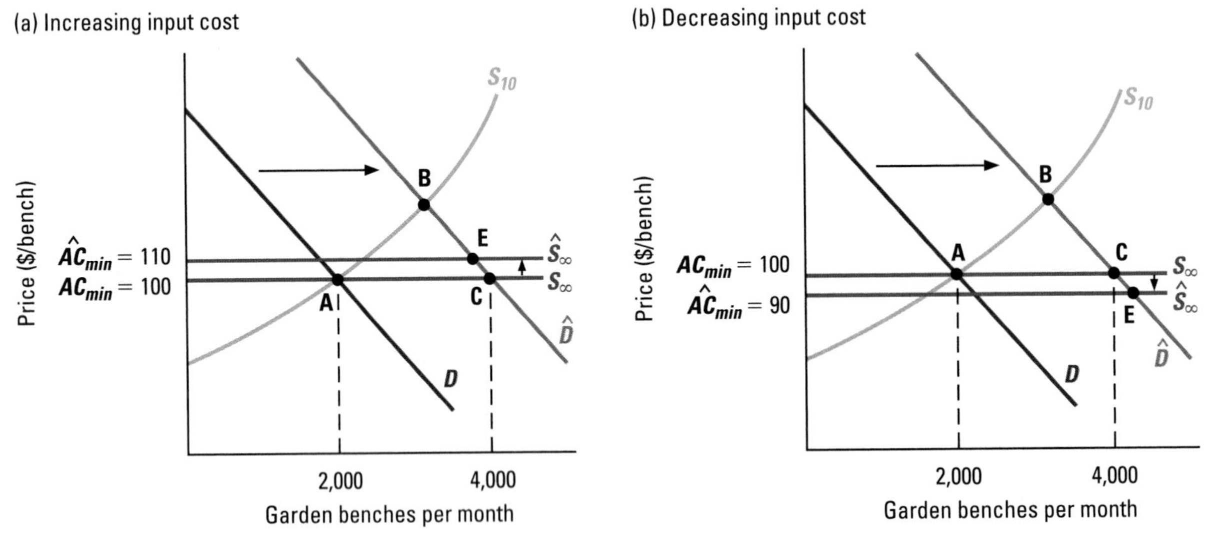

run equilibrium is point E. Thus, once we take account of the induced change in input prices, the increase in demand raises the price of garden benches in the long run.

Sometimes an increase in demand for an input can cause its price to fall. This can't happen if the input market is competitive (since increases in input demand would cause the input price to increase, as we saw in Section 2.3), but we'll see in Section 19.5 that it can happen in an oligopolistic market. In that case, the long-run market supply curve would shift down in response to the increase in demand for garden benches, causing the price of garden benches to fall in the long run, as illustrated in Figure 14.11(b).

14.4 EFFICIENCY OF PERFECTLY COMPETITIVE MARKETS

A market system is only one of many possible ways for a society to determine what goods are produced and consumed, and who will consume and produce them. Instead of privately owned firms producing and selling goods, state-owned firms might produce them, as they did in the former Soviet Union and other Eastern bloc countries. And instead of consumers buying the goods they desire at market prices, the government could allocate goods by edict, a lottery, or on a first-come first-served basis.

Of all the possibilities, why do economists usually prefer markets? Could another economic system achieve a better allocation of resources? In this section we'll provide an answer to this question. We'll see that a perfectly competitive market produces an outcome that is economically efficient, in the sense that it generates the largest possible net benefit from the production and consumption of the good.

Before showing why this statement is true, however, we need to define more carefully what we mean by economic efficiency. For the sake of simplicity, we'll assume that all the buyers in the market are consumers and all the sellers are firms. (The same conclusions would hold even if some or all buyers were firms and some or all sellers were consumers, as in a labor market.)

Aggregate Surplus and Economic Efficiency

If an economic system works well, it creates net benefits: consumers' benefits from the goods they consume exceed the costs of producing them. Economists measure the net benefit created by the production and consumption of a good using the concept of **aggregate surplus** (also called *total surplus* or *social surplus*), which is the total benefit from consumption less the total avoidable cost of production:

Aggregate surplus equals consumers' total willingness to pay for a good less firms' total avoidable cost of production. It captures the net benefit created by the production and consumption of the good.

Aggregate surplus =

$$\text{Total benefit from consumption} - \text{Total avoidable cost of production} \quad \textbf{(1)}$$

Consider, first, the total benefits from consumption, the sum of the benefits enjoyed by all of the consumers of the good. In Section 6.2, we saw that economists measure an individual's benefit from consuming a good by calculating her willingness to pay for the amount she consumes. It follows that:

$$\text{Aggregate surplus} = \text{Total willingness to pay} - \text{Total avoidable cost of production} \quad \textbf{(2)}$$

Figure 14.12

Juan's and Emily's Willingness to Pay for Ice Cream Cones. Juan's and Emily's willingness to pay for four and three ice cream cones a week, respectively, is shown by the shaded areas under their demand curves. Juan's willingness to pay is $8; Emily's is $6.75.

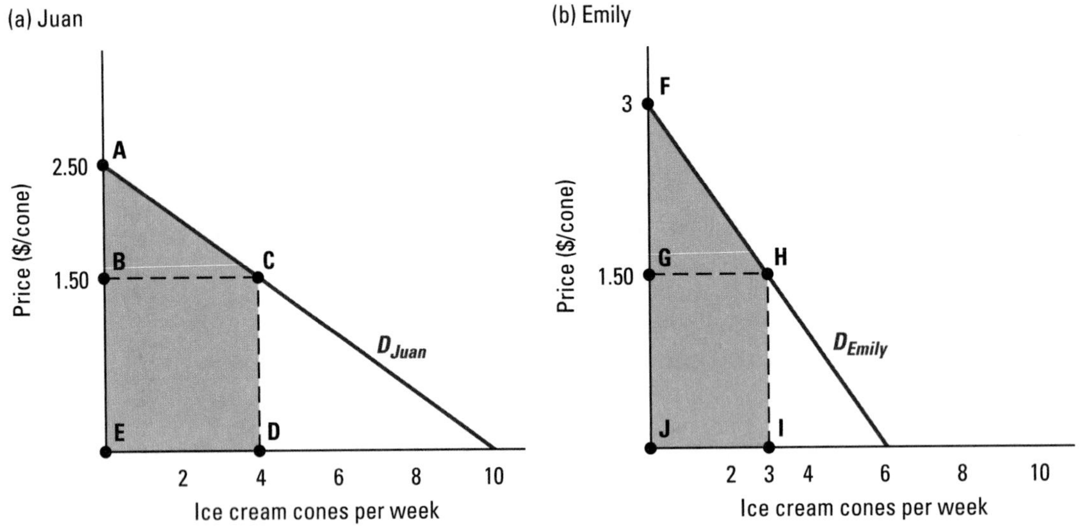

In Section 6.2 we also saw that a consumer's willingness to pay for a particular amount of the good equals the area under the consumer's demand curve up to that quantity.[8] By extension, we can calculate the total willingness to pay of all consumers of a good by adding the areas under those consumers' individual demand curves up to the quantities they each consume. Figure 14.12 shows the total willingness to pay for ice cream cones in Example 14.1 (page 498) when Juan buys four ice cream cones and Emily buys three. Juan's total willingness to pay is $8 (the area of the triangle ABC is 2, and the area of the rectangle BCDE is 6), while Emily's is $6.75 (the area of the triangle FGH is 2.25, and the area of the rectangle GHIJ is 4.50). Their total willingness to pay is therefore $14.75.

Now consider the second part of aggregate surplus in formulas (1) and (2), the total avoidable cost of production. This is the sum of all producers' avoidable costs of producing the good. Avoidable costs include all of a firm's costs other than its sunk costs. Since sunk costs are incurred even if *none* of the good is produced and consumed, by considering only avoidable costs the aggregate surplus truly measures the net benefit from production and consumption of the good.

In Section 9.5 we saw that a firm's avoidable cost of production is equal to the area under its supply curve up to its production level. Figure 14.13 shows the avoidable cost of

[8]In general, the consumer's willingness to pay equals the area under her compensated demand curve (see Section 6.5). However, when the consumer's demand for the good is insensitive to her income, so that there are no income effects, her compensated and uncompensated (ordinary) demand curves coincide, and we can use the area under the consumer's ordinary demand curve. For simplicity, throughout this section we'll assume that there are no income effects, so that we can use ordinary demand curves.

Figure 14.13

Anitra's and Robert's Avoidable Cost of Producing Ice Cream Cones. Anitra's and Robert's avoidable cost of producing four and three ice cream cones a week, respectively, is shown by the shaded areas under their supply curves. Anitra's avoidable cost is $5; Robert's is $3.

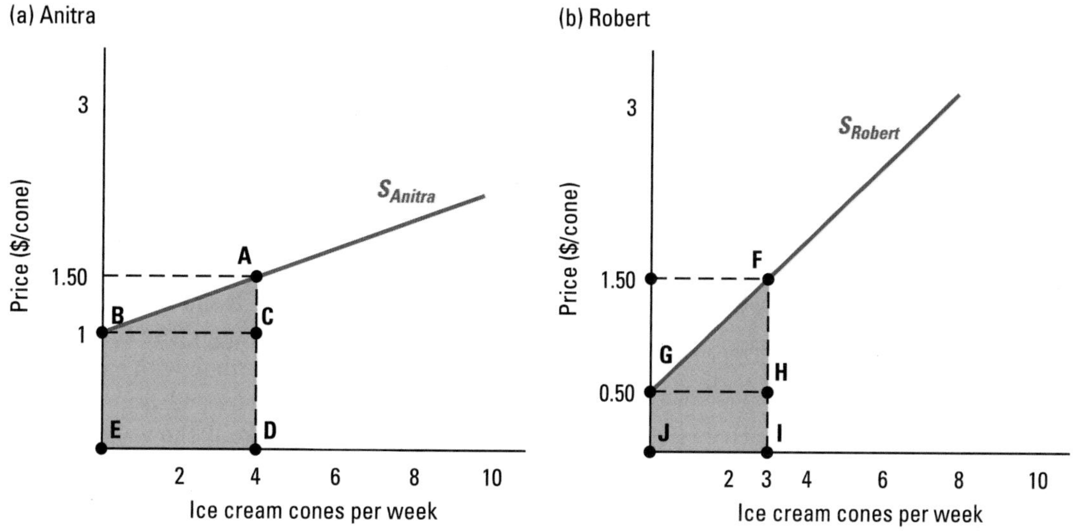

production when Anitra sells four ice cream cones and Robert sells three. Anitra's avoidable cost is $5 (the area of the triangle ABC is 1 and the area of the rectangle BCDE is 4), while Robert's is $3 (the area of the triangle FGH is 1.50 and the area of the rectangle GHIJ is 1.50). The total avoidable cost is therefore $8. Aggregate surplus therefore equals $6.75 (this is consumers' total willingness to pay, $14.75, minus total avoidable costs, $8).

An economic system that maximizes aggregate surplus creates the largest possible net social benefit to be distributed among society's members. Indeed, if an economic outcome maximizes aggregate surplus, it is economically efficient in the following sense: any alternative outcome that makes some members of society better off must make someone else worse off. To see why, think of aggregate surplus as a pie. If an economic system maximizes the size of the pie, any other outcome must make the pie smaller. And if the pie grows smaller, *someone* has to get a smaller slice—that is, someone must be worse off. We'll discuss this notion of economic efficiency, called *Pareto efficiency*, in more detail in Chapter 16.

How Perfectly Competitive Markets Maximize Aggregate Surplus

Economists have long marveled at the workings of competitive markets. Adam Smith, whose insights into the specialization of labor we discussed in Application 7.1, is best known for his observations concerning the efficiency of competitive markets. In his book *The Wealth of Nations* (1776), he commented on the "invisible hand" of the market, through which the self-interested actions of each individual lead to economic efficiency:

> He generally, indeed, neither intends to promote the public interest, nor knows how much he is promoting it. By preferring the support of domestic to that of foreign industry, he intends only his own security; and by directing that industry in such a manner as its produce may be of the greatest value, he intends only his own gain, and he is in this, as in many other cases, led by an invisible hand to promote an end which was no part of his intention. Nor is it always the worse for the society that it was no part of it. By pursuing his own interest he frequently promotes that of the society more effectually than when he really intends to promote it.

Because price equals marginal cost in a perfectly competitive market, a buyer who contemplates consuming one more unit of a good must pay exactly the marginal cost of producing it. Likewise, a seller who contemplates producing another unit of a good, foresees receiving a payment equal to each buyer's marginal willingness to pay for it. Intuitively, this fact means that buyers and sellers face exactly the social costs and benefits of their actions, leading them to make efficient decisions.

"Look, all I'm asking is that we let market forces bring a greater degree of efficiency into our marriage."

In the rest of this section we'll show that perfectly competitive markets do indeed maximize aggregate surplus. Imagine that a competitive market is in equilibrium, with an equilibrium price of P^*. Given that price, consumers and firms each decide how much to consume or produce. We'll show that there is no way to increase aggregate surplus by changing either consumption or production. There are three different ways that we could make such changes:

1. We could change who consumes the good.
2. We could change who produces the good.
3. We could change how much of the good is produced and consumed.

Let's examine the effect of each of these changes on aggregate surplus.[9]

Effects of a Change in Who Consumes the Good Let's think first about changing who consumes the good. Recall that in the market for ice cream cones, the competitive equilibrium involved a price of $1.50. Juan consumed four cones a week and Emily consumed three. Let's see if there is another way to divide up those seven cones that increases aggregate surplus.

Suppose we try to take one cone from Juan and give it to Emily. Could that change increase aggregate surplus? Figure 14.14 demonstrates that the answer is no. Figure 14.14(a) shows Juan's willingness to pay for that ice cream cone (his fourth), represented by the red-shaded area under his demand curve. (We'll use red shading to indicate changes that reduce aggregate surplus and green shading to indicate changes that increase it.) To keep Juan just as happy as he would be at the market equilibrium, we would need to pay him that amount when we take away the fourth ice cream cone. Figure 14.14(b) shows Emily's willingness to pay for one more ice cream cone (her fourth), represented by the green-shaded area under her demand curve. Notice that Emily's green-shaded area is

[9]While we'll continue to assume that income effects are absent, the result holds even with income effects. Indeed, the result follows from the same argument, but using consumers' compensated demand curves (discussed in Section 6.5) instead of their ordinary demand curves.

Figure 14.14

Effects of a Change in Who Consumes an Ice Cream Cone. What happens to aggregate surplus if we change the person who consumes an ice cream cone in a competitive market equilibrium? When we transfer one ice cream cone from Juan to Emily, Juan's willingness to pay for the cone he loses [equal to the red-shaded area in figure (a)] exceeds Emily's willingness to pay for the cone she gains [equal to the green-shaded area in figure (b)]. Aggregate surplus declines as a result of this change.

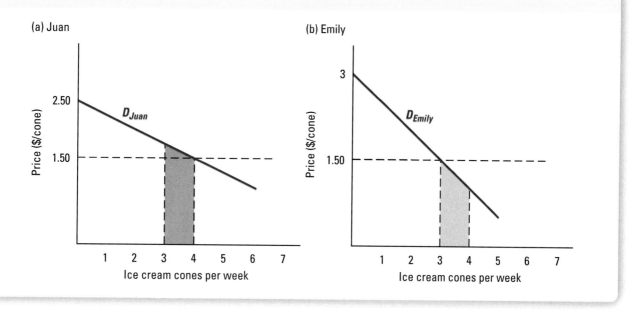

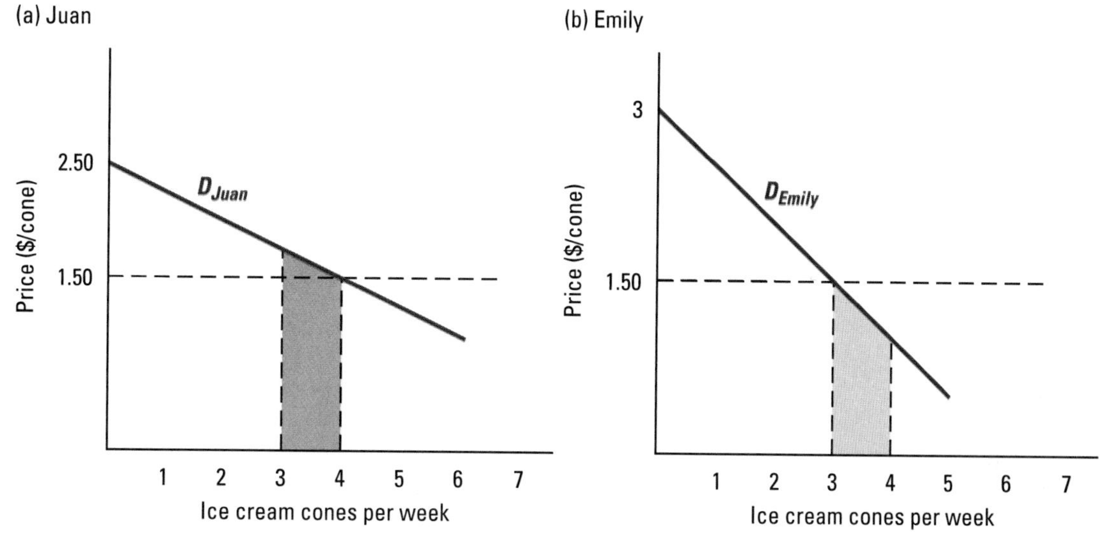

smaller than Juan's red-shaded area. The width of each area equals 1, so the green-shaded area is less than $1.50, while the red-shaded area is greater than $1.50. If we take an ice cream cone from Juan and give it to Emily, the total willingness to pay for the seven cones falls, and aggregate surplus falls with it.

A similar kind of argument applies for *any* number of ice cream cones we might transfer from Juan to Emily, as well as for *any* number we might transfer from Emily to Juan. (Try it.) The reason is that in a competitive equilibrium, the economic value that Juan and Emily attach to any ice cream cones they choose not to buy must be *less* than the market price, $1.50—otherwise they would have bought those cones. Likewise, the value that Juan and Emily attach to any cones they do choose to buy must be greater than the market price: otherwise they would not have bought those cones. Therefore, if we take cones from someone who chose to purchase them at the market price, and give them to someone who chose not to purchase them at the market price, aggregate surplus must fall.

Effects of a Change in Who Produces the Good Changing who produces the cones, like changing who consumes them, can't increase aggregate surplus. Recall that in the competitive equilibrium of the ice cream market, Robert sells three cones; Anitra sells four cones. Can we reassign those sales in a way that would lower the total cost of production and increase aggregate surplus?

Figure 14.15 shows that the answer is no. Suppose we reduce Anitra's sales from four to three cones and increase Robert's from three to four cones. Figure 14.15(a) shows Anitra's cost of producing that ice cream cone, her fourth, as the green-shaded area under her

Figure 14.15

Effects of a Change in Who Produces an Ice Cream Cone. What happens to aggregate surplus if we change the person who produces an ice cream cone in a competitive market equilibrium? When we transfer production of one cone from Anitra to Robert, Anitra's cost of producing that cone [equal to the green-shaded area in figure (a)] is less than Robert's cost of producing it [equal to the red-shaded area in figure (b)]. Aggregate surplus declines as a result of this change.

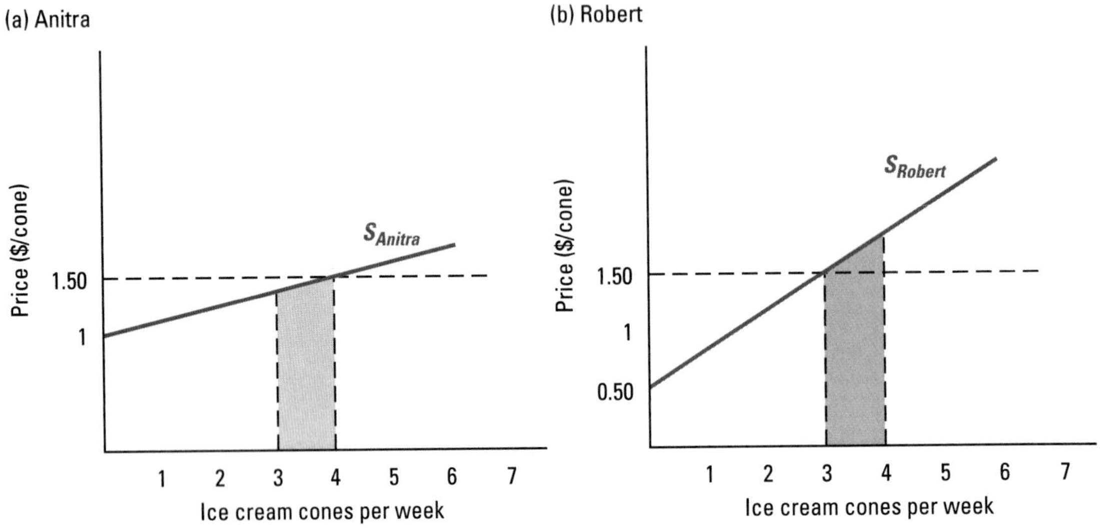

supply curve. Figure 14.15(b) shows Robert's cost of producing an extra cone, his fourth, as the red-shaded area under his supply curve. Since the green-shaded area is smaller than the red-shaded one, the total cost of production increases, so aggregate surplus falls. The same would be true of any change in production that keeps total supply fixed. The cost of producing any ice cream cone that a firm chooses to sell must be less than the equilibrium price of $1.50, and the cost of any cone that a firm chooses not to sell must exceed $1.50. So any shift in production from one firm to another must raise the total cost of production and lower aggregate surplus.

Effects of a Change in the Number of Goods Produced and Consumed

Finally, let's see whether we can increase aggregate surplus by changing the total number of ice cream cones produced and consumed. Suppose, for example, that Robert produces one extra ice cream cone, which Juan consumes. Figure 14.16 shows that this change, too, lowers aggregate surplus. Figure 14.16(a) shows Robert's extra cost of producing that cone, his fourth, as the red-shaded area. Figure 14.16(b) shows Juan's willingness to pay for the extra cone, his fifth, as the green-shaded area. Since the red-shaded area exceeds the green-shaded area, the extra cone costs Robert more to produce than Juan is willing to pay for it. The change therefore lowers aggregate surplus.

The same result holds for any change in the total number of cones. Any cones that are produced and consumed in a competitive market equilibrium must be worth more than the market price of $1.50 to the consumers who buy them. If not, those consumers wouldn't have bought them. They must also cost less than the market price to produce; otherwise

Figure 14.16

Effects of an Increase in the Number of Ice Cream Cones Produced and Consumed. This figure shows the effect on aggregate surplus of an increase in the number of ice cream cones produced and consumed in a competitive market equilibrium. If Robert produces an additional cone that Juan consumes, Robert's cost of producing that cone equals the red-shaded area in figure (a), and Juan's willingness to pay for it equals the smaller green-shaded area in figure (b). Aggregate surplus declines as a result of this change.

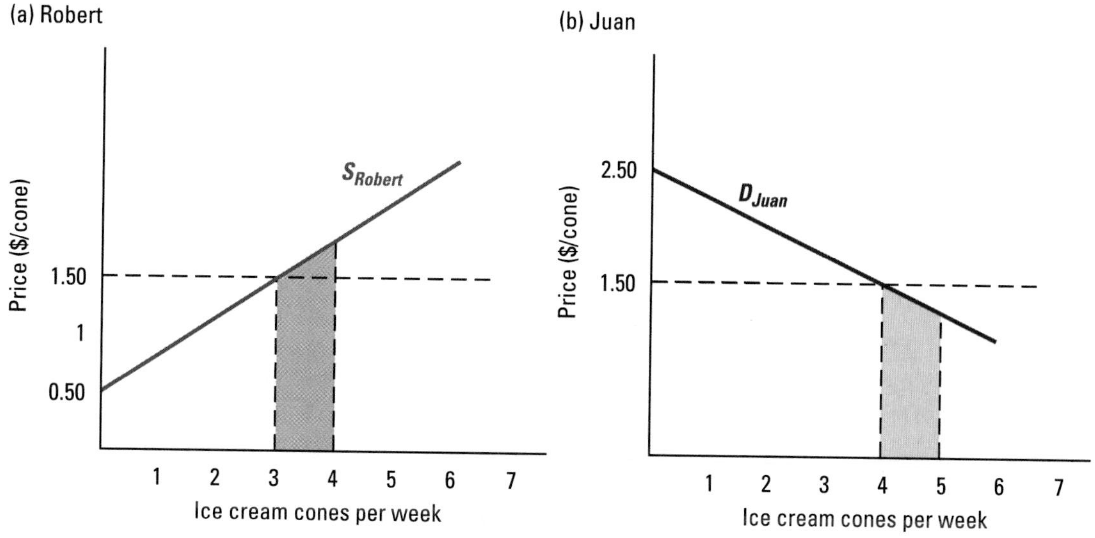

the firms that produced them wouldn't have done so. Those cones must therefore make a positive contribution to aggregate surplus. Similarly, any cones that aren't produced and consumed in a competitive market equilibrium must be worth less than the market price to consumers and must cost more than the market price to produce; otherwise they would have been demanded or produced. Producing and consuming those cones would therefore lower aggregate surplus.

Putting these observations about the effects of the three possible changes in consumption and production together, we can see that a perfectly competitive market equilibrium does indeed maximize aggregate surplus. Any change in who consumes the good, which firms produce it, or the amount that is produced and consumed must lower aggregate surplus and make someone worse off in the process.

This analysis of perfectly competitive market outcomes explains economists' tendency to favor the market over other ways of making production and consumption decisions. At the same time, it does not address questions of *distribution*. If we care about *who* is made better or worse off, we might favor a change that lowers aggregate surplus, as long as it makes the *right* individuals (those considered most deserving) better off.

Need our concerns about equity and efficiency conflict? In principle, no. If the government can costlessly transfer wealth from the rich to the poor, and leave the markets for goods to operate freely, it would get the best of both worlds: aggregate surplus would still be maximized, and we'd achieve an equitable distribution of resources. Intuitively, if we can slice the pie any way we want, making the pie bigger by leaving markets to operate freely means that *everyone* can get a bigger slice.

Unfortunately, in practice, redistribution often ends up interfering with the workings of markets. For example, if the government tries to transfer wealth, it will interfere in the market for savings (in particular, individuals will be discouraged from saving). As a result, balancing equity and efficiency concerns can involve some difficult trade-offs for society. We'll return to this point in Chapter 16.

Application 14.3

The Market for SO_2 Emissions

Acid rain forms when sulfur dioxide (SO_2) and nitrogen oxides (NO_x) react in the atmosphere to form sulfuric and nitric acids. Those acids then fall to the earth when it rains. In the United States, the main source of acid rain is the SO_2 produced by coal-fired electric power plants in the Northeast and Midwest. The SO_2 produced by those plants can cause acid rain to fall hundreds of miles away.

An acid-rain damaged forest

There are two ways to reduce SO_2 emissions. A power plant can switch to using more expensive low-sulfur coal or it can install so-called scrubbers, which reduce the amount of SO_2 that the power plant emits. Traditionally, the U.S. government has regulated SO_2 pollution by limiting the amount of pollution each individual plant can generate.[10] The problem with this type of regulation is that because of differences in location, design, and production rates, power plants differ greatly in the ease and cost with which they can switch to low-sulfur coal or install scrubbers. For example, the cost of switching to low-sulfur coal depends on the cost of transporting it from the nearest low-sulfur coal mine.

In the 1990 Clean Air Act amendments, the government tried a new approach to the problem. The amendments established a program that relied on tradable emissions permits, called *allowances*, to control pollution. Under the program, each generating unit (the typical power plant contains several generating units) receives a certain number of allowances, each of which entitles it to emit one ton of SO_2 per year. The total number of allowances distributed places a cap on the total amount of emissions per year.[11] Once the allowances have been distributed, generators can buy or sell them without restriction.

The idea behind the program is that through trading, the same degree of emissions reduction can be accomplished at a lower cost. In fact, if this market is perfectly competitive (there are, in fact, many buyers and sellers), abatement targets will be reached at the *lowest possible* cost. Why? The value that a power plant places on an emissions allowance is exactly equal to the cost it would incur if it had to buy low-sulfur coal or install scrubbers to reduce its emissions by one ton. We know that every power plant values the allowances it retains or buys in the market equilibrium more than the equilibrium price of an allowance; it values any additional allowances less than the market price. Thus, any transfer of an allowance from a plant

[10] We'll discuss the reasons why government regulation is necessary in Chapter 20.

[11] The program also allows plants to save unused allowances for future use.

that bought or retained it to a plant that did not must increase the total cost of emissions reduction.

Figure 14.17, based on work by economists Richard Schmalensee, Paul Joskow, Denny Ellerman, Juan Pablo Montero, and Elizabeth Bailey, shows the dramatic effects of allowing tradable permits.[12] The black curve represents the predicted amount of SO_2 that different generating units would have emitted in 1996 if the permits had *not* been tradable. The generating units are ordered from left to right along the horizontal axis in terms of their predicted "no trading" emissions, from lowest to highest. The gray vertical bars show the *actual* levels of emissions at each plant in that year after trading of SO_2 allowances. These levels differed dramatically from the no-trading emissions levels. Some generating units bought allowances and used them to produce more SO_2 than their own allowances would have permitted (for those generating units, the gray vertical bar extends above the black curve). Others sold some of their allowances and either bought low-sulfur coal or installed scrubbers to reduce their emissions (for those generating units, the gray vertical bar is below the black curve). Schmalensee et al. estimate that the trading of pollution allowances lowered the cost of reducing SO_2 emissions by 225 to 375 million dollars per year.[13]

Figure 14.17

The Effects of Tradable SO_2 Allowances. The black curve shows the levels of SO_2 that different electric generating units would have emitted in 1996 if allowances could not have been traded. The generating units are ordered from left to right from the lowest to the highest predicted "no-trading" emission rate. The gray-shaded vertical lines show the *actual* emission rates that occurred in 1996 after the trading of SO_2 allowances. Some generating units bought permits to allow them to increase their emissions (for those units, the gray vertical bar extends above the black curve). Others sold permits and emitted less SO_2 (for those units, the gray vertical bar is below the black curve).

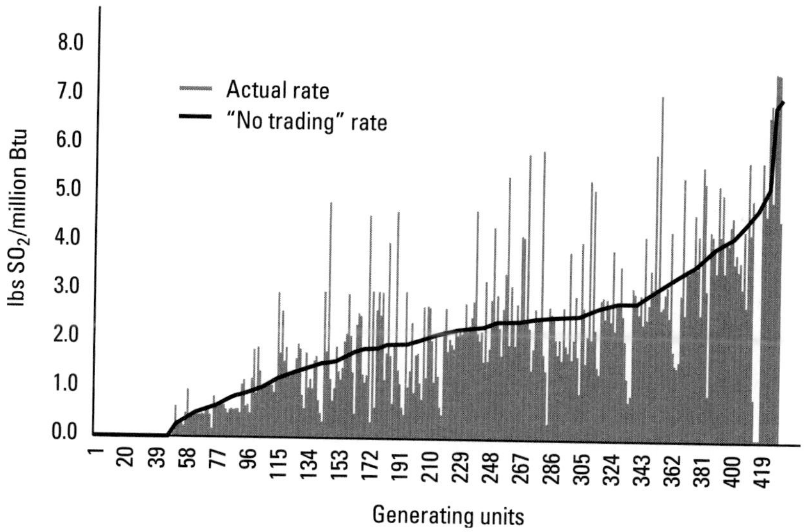

Source: Schmalensee et al. (1998).

[12]Richard Schmalensee et al., "An Interim Evaluation of Sulfur Dioxide Emissions Trading," *Journal of Economic Perspectives* 12, Summer 1998, pp. 53–68.

[13]There is one caveat to the use of such markets: While allowance markets minimize the costs of compliance, the market outcome is insensitive to any differences in the harm done by emissions from different sources. (For example, the damage from one ton of SO_2 emissions may depend on whether the plant is near a city, or whether prevailing winds carry the emissions over sensitive wildlife areas.) The reason these differences don't affect the equilibrium outcome is that the power plants do not care directly about the harm done by their emissions. (In economists' language, there is still an "externality"—see Chapter 20.) For an allowance market to work well, emissions from different sources should create roughly the same level of harm.

14.5 MEASURING SURPLUS USING MARKET DEMAND AND SUPPLY CURVES

We've seen that it's possible to measure aggregate surplus using each consumer's demand curve and each firm's supply curve. That procedure can be cumbersome with large numbers of consumers and firms. Fortunately, there's a more direct and simple procedure. In this section, we explain how to compute aggregate surplus, and how to determine how that surplus is divided between aggregate benefits to consumers and aggregate benefits to producers, using market demand and supply curves. This method will prove very convenient when we discuss the effects of market interventions in Chapter 15.

First let's see how to use the market demand curve to measure total willingness to pay. Figures 14.18(a) and (b) show Emily's and Juan's demand curves for ice cream from Figure 14.1(a). Their willingness to pay for each cone is shown with a shaded vertical bar. For example, in Figure 14.18(a), the heights of the blue vertical bars represent Emily's willingness to pay for each cone, while in Figure 14.18(b), the heights of the red vertical bars represent Juan's willingness to pay for each cone.

Figure 14.18(c) shows the market demand curve [from Figure 14.1(b)] and total willingness to pay for ice cream cones. The willingness to pay for each cone is shown by a vertical bar whose color corresponds to the consumer who demands it. Whenever cones are consumed by the individuals with the highest willingness to pay for them, we can measure the total willingness to pay for the cones they consume by the area under the market demand curve up to that quantity. To illustrate, suppose that three cones are

Figure 14.18

Measuring Total Willingness to Pay Using the Market Demand Curve. Figures (a) and (b) show Emily and Juan's demand curves for ice cream cones. The colored bars represent their approximate willingness to pay for each cone. Figure (c) shows the market demand curve and the corresponding willingness to pay for each cone. The color of each vertical bar indicates whose willingness to pay it represents. At any price, the area under the market demand curve up to the quantity demanded at that price equals consumers' total willingness to pay for the cones they consume.

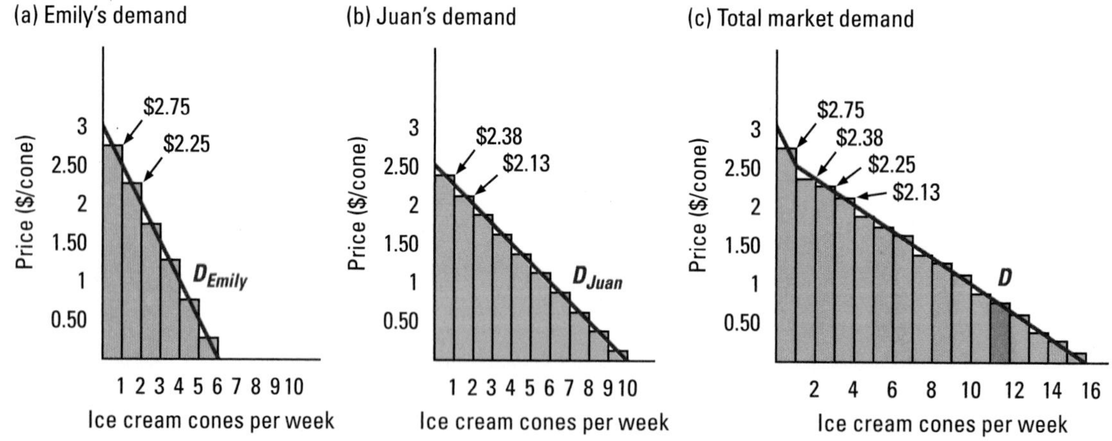

consumed with Emily consuming two and Juan consuming one. In this arrangement, the three cones are consumed by the individuals with the highest willingness to pay for them: Emily has the highest willingness to pay for a cone, \$2.75; Juan has the second highest, \$2.38; and Emily's willingness to pay for her second cone, \$2.25, is the third highest. Their total willingness to pay for these cones is \$7.38, which equals the area under the market demand curve up to three cones.

Cones will always be consumed by the individuals with the highest willingness to pay for them whenever all consumers face the same market price. This follows because the willingness to pay for the cones that are purchased is at least the market price, while the willingness to pay for any cones not purchased is below the market price. For example, if the price of cones in Figure 14.18(c) was \$2.20, three cones would be purchased, two by Emily and one by Juan. The three cones are therefore consumed by the individuals with the highest willingness to pay for them, and the total willingness to pay equals the area under the market demand curve up to three cones.

In similar fashion, whenever the cones that are produced are produced by the firms with the lowest avoidable cost (as occurs whenever all firms in a market face the same price for the goods they sell), we can measure the total avoidable cost of the goods they produce by the area under the market supply curve up to that quantity. We won't draw another set of figures to illustrate but the approach is basically the same as for measuring total willingness to pay.

In sum:

Using Market Demand and Supply Curves to Measure Total Willingness to Pay and Total Avoidable Cost

- Whenever the units of a good are consumed by those individuals with the highest willingness to pay for them, we can measure consumers' total willingness to pay for the units they consume by the area under the market demand curve up to that quantity.
- Whenever the units of a good are produced by the firms with the lowest avoidable cost of producing them, we can measure firms' total avoidable cost for the units they produce by the area under the market supply curve up to that quantity.

Aggregate Surplus

In light of this observation, we can use the market demand and supply curves to measure aggregate surplus whenever consumption is done by the individuals with the highest willingness to pay and production by the firms with the lowest avoidable costs of production.

To illustrate, Figure 14.19(a) shows a situation in which the market demand function for corn is $Q^d = 15 - 2P$ and the market supply function is $Q^s = 5P - 2.50$, both quantities measured in billions of bushels per year, and the market reaches a competitive equilibrium. The demand curve hits the vertical axis at a price of \$7.50 per bushel, while the supply curve hits the vertical axis at a price of \$0.50 per bushel. The equilibrium price is \$2.50 per bushel, and 10 billion bushels of corn are bought and sold.

The figure shows the aggregate surplus in that equilibrium. Since all consumers and firms face the same price, we can measure total willingness to pay and total avoidable

Figure 14.19

Aggregate Surplus, Consumer Surplus, and Producer Surplus in the Market for Corn. Figure (a) shows that aggregate surplus at the market equilibrium for corn, equal to the green-shaded area, is $35 billion per year. Figure (b) shows that this is composed of $25 billion of consumer surplus and $10 billion of producer surplus.

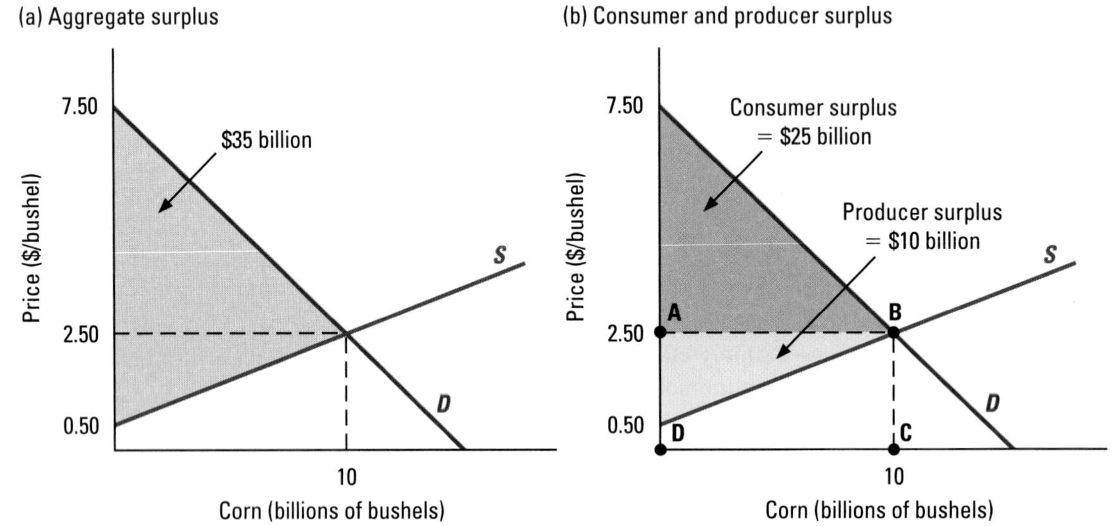

costs—and therefore aggregate surplus—using these curves. Consumers' total willingness to pay for the equilibrium quantity is the area under the demand curve up to 10 billion bushels, while firms' total avoidable cost is the area under the supply curve up to that quantity. Since aggregate surplus is the difference between those two areas, it equals the green-shaded region between the demand and supply curves up to the equilibrium quantity of 10 billion bushels, the point at which the demand and supply curves cross. That region is a triangle, whose area is $35 billion (looking at it sideways, the base of the triangle along the vertical axis has length 7, and the height is 10 billion). So aggregate surplus is $35 billion per year.

A **deadweight loss** is a reduction in aggregate surplus below its maximum possible value.

In Chapter 15 we'll use market demand and supply curves to measure the loss in aggregate surplus associated with various market interventions. Economists call a reduction in aggregate surplus below its maximum possible value a **deadweight loss**. In a competitive market without any interventions, aggregate surplus is maximized, so there is no deadweight loss. Figure 14.20(a) illustrates the deadweight loss that occurs in the corn market if the amount produced differs from 10 billion bushels. Suppose that only 7 billion bushels are produced and consumed, with production being done by the lowest cost farmers and consumption by the individuals with the highest willingness to pay for those bushels. (We'll see examples of how this can happen in Chapter 15.) Because aggregate surplus then equals the area between the demand and supply curves up to only 7 billion bushels (the green-shaded area), the deadweight loss would equal the area of the light red-shaded triangle, $3.15 billion per year. That loss arises because the economy

Figure 14.20

Deadweight Loss and Aggregate Surplus. Figure (a) shows the deadweight losses if either 7 billon or 13 billion bushels of corn are produced and consumed each year (shaded light red and dark red respectively). In each case, the deadweight loss is $3.15 billion per year. Figure (b) shows the relationship between aggregate surplus, deadweight loss, and the amount produced and consumed. Aggregate surplus is largest at 10 billion bushels per year. At that quantity, the deadweight loss is zero.

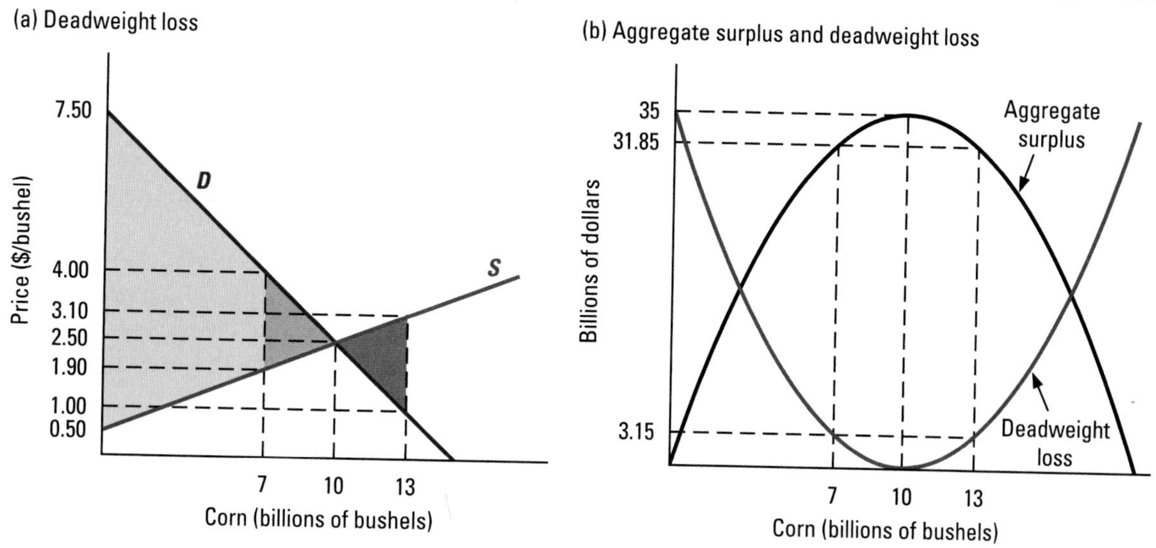

fails to produce 3 billion bushels whose value exceeds their cost. If 13 billion bushels per year were instead produced and consumed, aggregate surplus would equal the sum of the green- and light red-shaded areas *less* the dark red-shaded triangle (we subtract the area of the dark red triangle because above 10 billion bushels the willingness to pay is *less* than the avoidable cost of production). The deadweight loss therefore equals the area of the dark red-shaded triangle, again $3.15 billion per year. This time the loss occurs because the economy produces 3 billion bushels whose cost exceeds their value to consumers.

Figure 14.20(b) shows how aggregate surplus and deadweight loss depend on the amount produced and consumed. Aggregate surplus is largest at 10 billion bushels, the equilibrium quantity (recall Section 14.4). At that quantity, the deadweight loss is zero. At other quantities, the deadweight loss equals the difference between $35 billion, the largest possible aggregate surplus, and the aggregate surplus at the given quantity. For example, the figure shows that when 7 billion bushels are produced and consumed, aggregate surplus is $31.85 billion per year and the deadweight loss is $3.15 billion per year.

Consumer and Producer Surpluses

In Section 6.2 we introduced the notion of consumer surplus. An individual's consumer surplus is equal to her willingness to pay for the goods she consumes less her expenditure on those goods. *Aggregate* consumer surplus is the sum of individual consumers' surpluses, which equals the sum of consumers' total willingness to pay less their total expenditure. Where doing so does not create confusion, we'll call this concept simply the **consumer surplus**.

Consumer surplus equals the sum of consumers' total willingness to pay less their total expenditure.

We can use the market demand curve to measure consumer surplus. Figure 14.19(b) shows the consumer surplus in the competitive equilibrium of the corn market. Total expenditure equals the area of rectangle ABCD (it's \$25 billion, the equilibrium price of \$2.50, times the total amount of corn bought, 10 billion bushels). Since consumer surplus each year is the difference between the total willingness to pay and the total expenditure, each year it equals the area of the blue-shaded triangle, \$25 billion.

In Section 9.5, we introduced the notion of a firm's producer surplus, equal to the firm's total revenue less its avoidable cost. (The firm's profit equals its producer surplus less its sunk costs.) *Aggregate* producer surplus equals the sum of the individual firms' producer surpluses, which equals the sum of firms' revenues less their avoidable costs. Where doing so does not create confusion, we'll refer to this concept simply as **producer surplus**. (Aggregate profit is this amount less firms' sunk costs.)

Producer surplus equals the sum of firms' revenues less their avoidable costs.

We can use the market supply curve to measure producer surplus. Figure 14.19(b) shows the producer surplus in the equilibrium of the corn market. Total revenue, which is the same as the total expenditure by consumers, is the area of the rectangle ABCD. Since producer surplus is the difference between firms' revenue and their avoidable costs, each year it equals the area of the yellow-shaded triangle, \$10 billion.

Comparing Figures 14.19(a) and (b), we can see that the green-shaded area in Figure 14.19(a) equals the sum of the blue- and yellow-shaded areas in Figure 14.19(b), which represent consumer surplus and producer surplus, respectively. So:

$$\text{Aggregate surplus} = \text{Consumer surplus} + \text{Producer surplus} \qquad \textbf{(3)}$$

Formula (3) shows that the aggregate surplus, the total net benefit pie, is composed of the slice consumers get (consumer surplus) plus the slice that firms get (producer surplus).[14] When we study government intervention into markets in Chapter 15, however, we'll also need to take into account the slice of the pie that government gets. Nonetheless, our ability to use market demand and supply curves to measure consumer and producer surplus will prove useful.

IN-TEXT EXERCISE 14.5 **The market demand function for corn is $Q^d = 15 - 2P$ and the market supply function is $Q^s = 5P - 6$, both quantities measured in billions of bushels per year. What are the aggregate surplus, consumer surplus, and producer surplus at the competitive market equilibrium?**

[14]Formula (3) can be derived directly from formula (2) by adding and subtracting total expenditure to rewrite formula (2) as Aggregate surplus = (Total willingness to pay − Total expenditure) + (Total expenditure − Total avoidable cost of production). The first expression in parentheses is consumer surplus; the second is producer surplus (since consumers' total expenditure exactly equals firms' total revenue).

Application 14.4

The Transition from Communism to Capitalism

The transition of many former Soviet-bloc countries from communism to capitalism represented an enormous change in the organization of their economic systems. This was most true of the countries of Eastern Europe, many of which aggressively embraced market-based reforms. For decades in these countries, production decisions were made by government bureaucrats and communist party officials, who were influenced primarily by political concerns. Those officials also set the prices that consumers faced. Goods they considered necessities were priced low; those they considered luxuries (such as cars) were priced extremely high. When not enough of a good was available to satisfy demand at those prices, the available goods were rationed according to the priorities of those officials.

With the transition to capitalism, all of this changed. Goods were traded in markets at market-determined prices. Government-owned firms were sold (or sometimes given) to private investors, managers, and workers. Individuals were allowed to start their own businesses. As Table 14.1 shows, these changes dramatically increased the share of gross domestic product (GDP) produced by private firms in those countries. Indeed, for some of them, that share was approaching the level in the United States by 1997.

Table 14.1

Share of GDP Derived from Private Sources, Six Countries

	1980	1988	1994	1997
Czech Republic	< 1.0%	< 1.0%	65%	75%
Hungary	3.5	7.1	55	75
Poland	15.6	18.8	55	65
Romania	4.5	—	35	60
Slovakia	< 1.0	< 1.0	55	75
United States	79.4	79.6	81.1	82

Source: J.L Saving, "Privatization and the Transition to a Market Economy," Federal Reserve Bank of Dallas *Economic Review*, 1998, pp. 17–25.

Market reforms increased economic efficiency in a number of ways. First, competitive markets pushed firms to become efficient. In state-run firms, production decisions had often reflected political rather than economic motives. Moreover, the state had often heavily subsidized large firms, giving managers little incentive to produce efficiently. In privately owned firms, the desire to maximize profit drives firms to use efficient production technologies (see Chapter 7) and choose least-cost input combinations (see Chapter 8). Second, competitive markets result in an efficient allocation of production across firms. Third, with competitive markets, the amount of each good that is produced and consumed maximizes aggregate surplus, given consumers' willingness to pay and the costs of production. Finally, competitive markets allocate goods to the consumers who value them most.

© The New Yorker Collection 1990 Al Ross from cartoonbank.com. All Rights Reserved.

Figure 14.21 shows the change in aggregate surplus for a good considered a necessity, whose price had been set very low by government officials. For simplicity, it focuses on only the first and third type of gain listed above by assuming that the government had efficiently allocated production and consumption across firms and consumers prior to the transition. (If this assumption is not correct, then the efficiency gains from market reforms are even greater.) Originally, the marginal cost curve was MC_H, the price was $\underline{P}$, and the amount produced and consumed was $\underline{Q}$ (there was no rationing for this good). After the transition to capitalism, the marginal cost of production fell to MC_L and the market reached equilibrium at point B.

The transition increased aggregate surplus by an amount equal to the sum of the green- and red-shaded areas. We can find this change in aggregate surplus in two steps. First, without any change in the marginal cost curve, the transition to a market would shift the amount produced and consumed to point A, with Q_0 units produced and consumed. The red-shaded area represents the increase in aggregate surplus due to that change. The last ($\underline{Q} - Q_0$) units produced under communism were worth less to consumers than they cost to produce; aggregate surplus increases when those units are no longer produced. Second, the reduction in marginal cost shifts the market equilibrium from point A to point B, further increasing aggregate surplus by the green-shaded area.

The gains from a transition to capitalism don't materialize overnight. It can take time for market institutions to develop, for new firms to enter the market, and for consumers and producers to adjust to the new system. Nonetheless, in a relatively short period, many of the Eastern European countries began to grow rapidly. Figure 14.22 shows the growth of GDP per capita in five of those countries from 1990 to 1996. Unfortunately, not all of these countries experienced these benefits. Romania, for example, embraced market reforms only half-heartedly. The situation was even worse in many of the former Soviet Republics (not shown in the figure). The collapse of the Soviet system disrupted their already inefficient economies, causing their per capita GDPs to fall precipitously. Most of these countries adopted less ambitious market reforms than countries such as Poland, Hungary, and the Czech Republic and in many cases their GDPs still haven't recovered to the levels achieved before the fall of communism. One important lesson from this experience is that the transition to a healthy market economy requires many interrelated developments—steps to assure the free formation of businesses, the protection of private property, the ability of shareholders to hold managers accountable, and the general rule of law, among others.

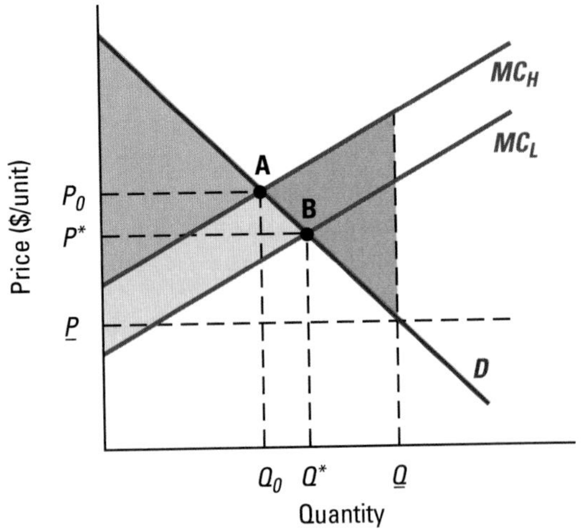

Figure 14.21

Effects of the Transition from Communism to Capitalism. Under communism, the price was set at $\underline{P}$ and the amount consumed was $\underline{Q}$. After the transition to capitalism, the equilibrium price rose to P^* and Q^* units were bought and sold. Aggregate surplus increased by an amount equal to the sum of the red- and green-shaded areas.

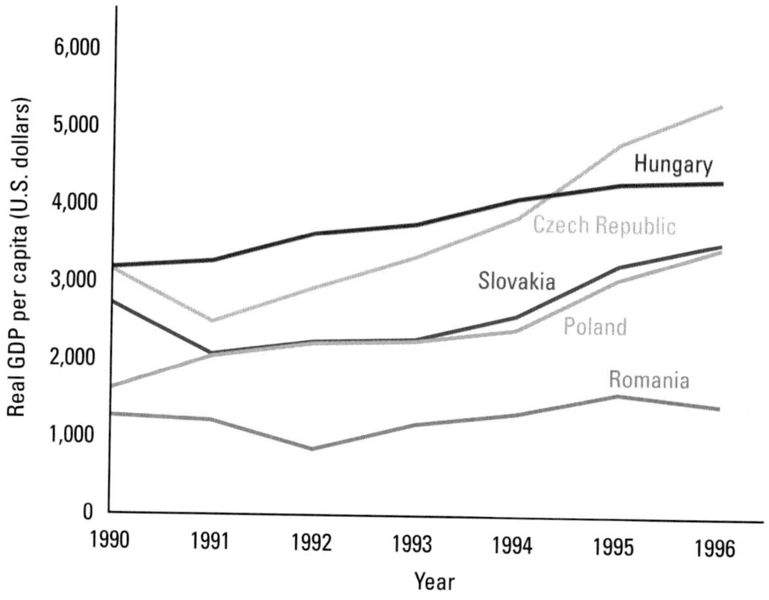

Figure 14.22

The Growth of Real GDP per Capita in Former Soviet-Bloc Countries, 1990–1996. This figure shows the changes in gross domestic product per capita in five former Soviet-bloc countries following the transition to capitalism.

Source: Saving (1998).

CHAPTER SUMMARY

1. **What makes a market competitive?**
   a. A market is perfectly competitive, with firms acting as price takers, when (1) buyers and sellers face no transactions costs, (2) products are homogeneous, and (3) there are many suppliers, each accounting for a small fraction of the overall supply of the good.
   b. For many small firms to produce efficiently in a market, the efficient scale of production must be small compared to the overall size of the market, the total amount produced and consumed.
2. **Market demand and market supply**
   a. The market demand for a product is the sum of the demands of all the individual consumers (or firms, in a factor market). The market demand curve is the horizontal sum of all the individual demand curves.
   b. The market supply for a product is the sum of the supplies of all the individual sellers. The market supply curve is the horizontal sum of all the individual supply curves.
   c. In the short run, the market supply curve includes the supply of all active firms; in the long run it includes the supply of all potential firms.
   d. In the long run, many markets are characterized by free entry, because in the long run technology is freely available to anyone who wishes to start a firm and entry is unrestricted. When this is so, the long-run market supply curve is a horizontal line at the lowest average cost, AC_{min}.
3. **Short-run and long-run competitive equilibrium**
   a. The equilibrium price equates demand and supply.
   b. In a market with free entry: (1) the equilibrium price must equal AC_{min}; (2) firms must earn zero profit; and (3) firms must produce at their efficient scale of production.
   c. The short-run effect of a change in demand or costs is determined using the short-run market supply curve (which includes the supply of all active firms), while in the long run it is determined using the long-run market supply curve (which includes the supply of all potential firms).

d. When there is free entry in the long run, changes in demand have no effect on the price of the good in the long run, assuming input prices are fixed.

e. When a change in the demand for a good affects the price of an input, the good's price can change in the long run even when there is free entry.

4. **Efficiency of perfectly competitive markets**

a. The aggregate surplus from the production and consumption of a good is equal to consumers' total willingness to pay for the goods they consume less firms' total avoidable cost of producing those goods. It captures the net benefit created by the production and consumption of the good.

b. If an economic outcome maximizes aggregate surplus, then any alternative outcome that makes some members of society better off must make someone else worse off.

c. A perfectly competitive equilibrium results in the largest possible level of aggregate surplus.

d. There are three different ways to change the outcome of a perfectly competitive equilibrium: (1) change who consumes the good; (2) change who produces the good; and (3) change the quantity of the good that is produced and consumed. Any of these changes will lower aggregate surplus.

5. **Measuring surplus using market demand and supply curves**

a. Whenever the units of a good are consumed by those individuals with the highest willingness to pay for them, we can measure consumers' total willingness to pay for the units they consume by the area under the market demand curve up to that quantity.

b. Whenever the units of a good are produced by the firms with the lowest avoidable cost of producing them, we can measure firms' total avoidable cost for the units they produce by the area under the market supply curve up to that quantity.

c. Under these conditions, we can use market demand and supply curves to measure aggregate surplus. Aggregate surplus equals the area between these curves up to the quantity produced and consumed. (If the quantity is above the equilibrium quantity, we *subtract* the area between the curves above the equilibrium quantity, where the willingness to pay is less than the avoidable cost of production.)

d. We can use the market demand curve to measure the (aggregate) consumer surplus from a good, which equals the total willingness to pay less total expenditure.

e. We can use the market supply curve to measure the (aggregate) producer surplus, which equals total revenue less firms' total avoidable costs of production. Profit equals the producer surplus less firms' sunk costs.

f. Aggregate surplus equals the sum of consumer surplus and producer surplus.

ADDITIONAL EXERCISES

Exercise 14.1: Juan's demand function for ice cream cones is $Q^d_{Juan} = 10 - 2.5P$ at prices below \$4 and zero at prices above \$4. Emily's demand function is $Q^d_{Emily} = 6 - 1.5P$ at prices below \$4 and zero at prices above \$4. What is the market demand function? Graph the individual and market demand curves.

Exercise 14.2: Anitra's supply function for ice cream is $Q^s_{Anitra} = 6P - 4$ at prices above \$1.50 and zero at prices below \$1.50. Robert's supply function is $Q^d_{Robert} = 4P - 8$ at prices above \$2 and zero at prices below \$2. What is the market supply function? Graph the individual and market supply curves.

Exercise 14.3: The daily cost of producing pizza in New Haven is $C(Q) = 4Q + (Q^2/40)$; the marginal cost is $MC = 4 + (Q/20)$. What is the market supply function if there are 10 firms making pizza? If 20 firms are making pizza? What is the market supply curve under free entry?

Exercise 14.4: Suppose the price of bagels in Allentown is currently \$0.75 per bagel. There are 10 low-cost bakeries that can produce bagels, each of whom has the supply function $Q^s = 200P - 100$. There are 10 high-cost bakeries that can produce bagels, each of whom has the supply function $Q^s = 200P - 200$. (These individual supply functions apply in the short run and the long run.) Which bakeries will be active when the price is \$0.75? If the price rises to \$1.25, what will be the market supply in the short run? In the long run? Graph the short-run and long-run market supply curves.

Exercise 14.5: The daily cost of making pizza in Seattle is $C(Q) = 4Q + (Q^2/40)$, plus an avoidable fixed cost of \$10; marginal cost is $MC = 4 + (Q/20)$. In the long run firms may enter the market freely. What is the long-run market supply curve?

Exercise 14.6: What are the equilibrium price and amount bought and sold when individual demand and supply are as in exercises 14.1 and 14.2?

Exercise 14.7: Suppose the daily demand function for pizza in Berkeley is $Q^d = 1{,}525 - 5P$. The variable cost of making Q pizzas per day is $C(Q) = 3Q + 0.01Q^2$, there is a \$100 fixed cost (which is avoidable in the long run), and the marginal cost is $MC = 3 + 0.02Q$. There is free entry in the long run. What is the long-run market equilibrium in this market? Suppose that demand increases to $Q^d = 2{,}125 - 5P$. If, in the short run, the number of firms is fixed (so that neither entry nor exit is possible) and fixed costs are sunk, what is the new short-run market equilibrium? What is the new long-run market equilibrium if there is free entry in the long run? What if instead demand decreased to $Q^d = 925 - 5P$?

Exercise 14.8: The daily demand for pizzas is $Q^d = 750 - 25P$, where P is the price of a pizza. The daily costs for a pizza company initially include \$50 in fixed costs (which are avoidable in the long run), and variable costs equal to $VC = Q^2/2$, where Q is the number of pizzas produced in a day. Marginal cost is $MC = Q$. Suppose that in the long run there is free entry into the market. If fixed costs fall to \$18 and, in the short run, the number of firms is fixed (so that neither entry nor exit is possible) and fixed costs are sunk, what is the new short-run market equilibrium? What is the new market equilibrium in the long run?

Exercise 14.9: The daily demand for pizzas is $Q^d = 750 - 25P$, where P is the price of a pizza. The daily costs for a pizza company initially include \$50 in fixed costs (which are avoidable in the long run), and variable costs equal to $VC = Q^2/2$, where Q is the number of pizzas produced in a day. Marginal cost is $MC = Q$. Suppose that in the long run there is free entry into the market. If marginal costs rise by \$6 per pizza and, in the short run, the number of firms is fixed (so that neither entry nor exit is possible) and fixed costs are sunk, what is the new short-run market equilibrium? What is the new market equilibrium in the long run?

Exercise 14.10: It is often quicker to exit a market than to enter one. What would change in the answers to exercises 14.8 and 14.9 if active firms could shut down in the short run but inactive firms could enter only in the long run?

Exercise 14.11: After Henry Ford invented the assembly line for manufacturing automobiles, other automobile firms copied his invention. The new technology increased the economies of scale in automobile manufacturing. In the long run, how would it have changed the size of the typical automobile firm?

Exercise 14.12: Suppose the costs of production fall by \$1 per unit at every output level. If the number of firms is fixed in the short run but not in the long run, how would such a change affect the market equilibrium in the short and long run?

Exercise 14.13: At many colleges and business schools, lotteries have long been used to assign seats in highly popular lecture courses. Recently, some schools have switched to systems in which students receive points that they can use to bid for seats in their favorite classes. Why might this new system be more efficient?

Exercise 14.14: For some rock concerts thousands of fans stand in line for hours to purchase tickets. What is the likely effect on aggregate surplus if resale of those tickets in a competitive market is possible? Would aggregate surplus be higher if the concert tickets were priced to begin with at the resale market's equilibrium price?

Exercise 14.15: The market demand function for corn is $Q^d = 21 - 4P$, and the market supply function is $Q^s = 5P - 6$, both quantities measured in billions of bushels per year. What are the aggregate surplus, consumer surplus, and producer surplus at the competitive market equilibrium?

APPENDIX

EQUILIBRIUM IN FACTOR MARKETS

A **factor market** is a market for an input.

A **factor market** is a market for an input, such as labor, physical capital goods (machines), or financial capital. In a factor market, firms are the buyers. Either firms or individual consumers may be the suppliers. For example, many of Dell's personal computers are sold to other firms, which use those computers to produce their own products. In a labor market, however, individuals are the sellers of their labor services. Similarly, when a firm needs to raise financial capital, individuals are often the suppliers of that capital.

In many ways, factor markets work just like the markets for consumption goods that we've been studying. Figure 14.23, for example, shows two examples of equilibrium in a factor market. Figure 14.23(a) shows the demand and supply curves in the labor market for nurses in a large city. The demand for nurses comes from the hospitals and nursing

Figure 14.23

Equilibrium in Factor Markets. Figure (a) shows equilibrium in a labor market for nurses, where the equilibrium weekly wage rate W^* brings the supply and demand for nurses into balance. Figure (b) shows equilibrium in a market for financial capital, where the equilibrium interest rate R^* brings the supply and demand for financial capital into balance.

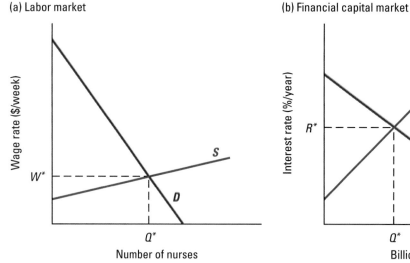

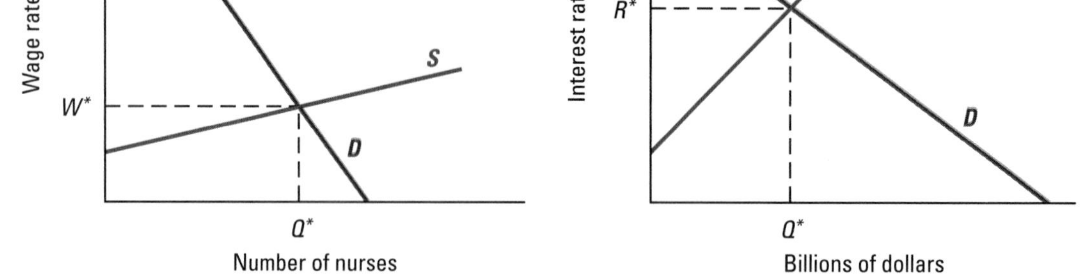

homes that need nurses to take care of their patients and residents. The demand curve is downward sloping: the lower the wage, the more nurses they will want to hire. As the wage decreases, for example, they may decide to provide care with more nurses and fewer doctors, or may decide to offer improved services that require relatively intensive supervision (taking nursing home residents on more walks). They may also decide to increase the number of patients or residents they care for. The supply curve of nurses in Figure 14.23(a), on the other hand, is upward sloping. As the wage increases, more trained nurses may decide to work (rather than stay home), and some may accept a job in this city rather than others. As in other competitive markets, the equilibrium wage brings this supply and demand into balance.

Figure 14.23(b) shows an equilibrium in the market for financial capital (money provided today in return for promised repayments in the future). Here the demanders are entrepreneurs and firms with investment projects. The suppliers are individuals and financial institutions with money to lend. As we discussed in Chapter 10, the price of financial capital is the interest rate. In Figure 14.23(b), the demand curve for financial capital is downward sloping. As the interest rate rises, fewer projects are profitable (have a positive net present value), so the quantity of financial capital demanded falls. In Figure 14.23(b), the supply curve of financial capital is upward sloping. As the interest rate rises, some investors find that lending to others is more lucrative than using the cash for their own projects, and some individuals decide to save for the future by lending money to firms today (or indirectly doing so by putting money in banks, who then lend it to firms). The equilibrium interest rate brings this supply and demand into balance.

Backward-Bending Supply Curves in Factor Markets

The demand and supply curves in Figure 14.23 look just like those we've studied in Chapter 2 and the text of this chapter. However, this need not always be the case in factor markets. One important difference from our previous analysis of competitive markets can arise in factor markets: in some cases, the supply curve can bend backwards in a factor market. That is, the amount supplied can *fall* when the price rises. For example, in Section 6.4, we saw that the supply curve for labor may bend backwards. A similar phenomenon can occur in the markets for financial capital. Firms need money to finance investment. They obtain this money both from other firms and from consumers, who can choose to save some of their money and supply it to the firms, either directly or through banks. We saw in Section 10.2 that saving—and consequently the supply of financial capital from consumers—can either rise or fall when the interest rate rises. Thus, the supply curve for financial capital can also bend backwards. In both of these cases, a similar mechanism is at work: an increase in the price of the input has a positive income effect for consumers, who respond by supplying less.

How does a backward-bending supply curve affect supply and demand analysis? Figure 14.24(a) shows the demand and supply curves in a labor market with a backward-bending supply curve. In this situation, shifts in the demand for labor can have effects that differ from those we discussed in Chapter 2. In Figure 14.24(b), for example, the labor demand curve shifts outward from the dark blue curve labeled D to the light blue curve labeled $\hat{D}$. Following this increase in labor demand, however, firms actually employ *less* labor: the amount of labor hired falls from Q^* to $\hat{Q}^*$. The reason is that the increase in the wage rate, from W^* to $\hat{W}^*$, raises workers' incomes, causing them to supply less labor.

Figure 14.24

Equilibrium in a Labor Market with a Backward-Bending Supply Curve. Because of income effects, the labor supply curve can be backward bending, as in figure (a). As figure (b) shows, this shape can lead to the surprising result that firms may employ less labor after an increase in the demand for labor than before it.

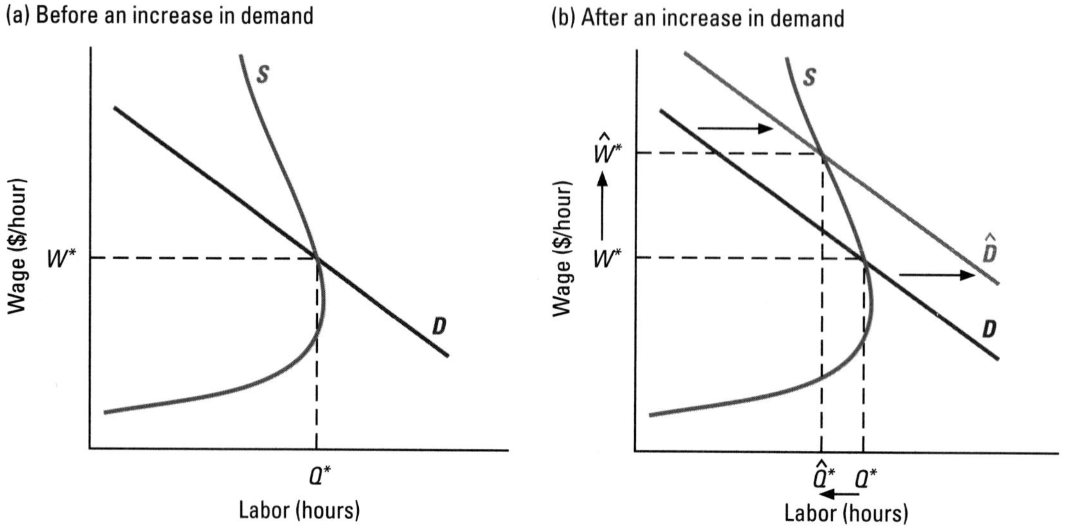

Multiple Equilibria

Another consequence of a backward-bending supply curve is that there may be more than one potential market equilibrium. Figure 14.25 shows an example of this phenomenon in a labor market. Note the triple intersection of the demand and supply curves, one at a high wage (W^{***}) and low employment, one at a medium wage (W^{**}) and medium employment, and one at a low wage (W^*) and high employment. What determines which of these equilibria will arise?

A market equilibrium is **stable** if market pressures near the equilibrium point tend to push the price toward its equilibrium level; it is **unstable** if they tend to push it away.

One factor is the stability of the various equilibria. An equilibrium is **stable** if market pressures near the equilibrium tend to push the market price toward its equilibrium level and **unstable** if they tend to push it away.

The low-wage equilibrium in Figure 14.25 is a stable one. When the wage rate is a little above W^*, supply exceeds demand. Because workers who can't get jobs are willing to work for less, the wage tends to fall back toward W^*. Likewise, when the wage is a little below W^*, demand exceeds supply. Because firms that can't hire enough workers are willing to pay them a little more, the wage tends to rise back toward W^*. The same is true of the high wage equilibrium, which is also stable.

In contrast, the medium-wage equilibrium in Figure 14.25 is not stable. When the wage is a little below W^{**}, supply exceeds demand, causing the wage to fall further below W^{**} as unemployed workers offer to accept lower wages. When the wage is a little above W^{**}, demand exceeds supply, causing the wage to rise further above W^{**} as firms with vacancies try to attract workers. In general, a market equilibrium is stable if demand is greater than supply at prices a little below the equilibrium price, and less than supply at

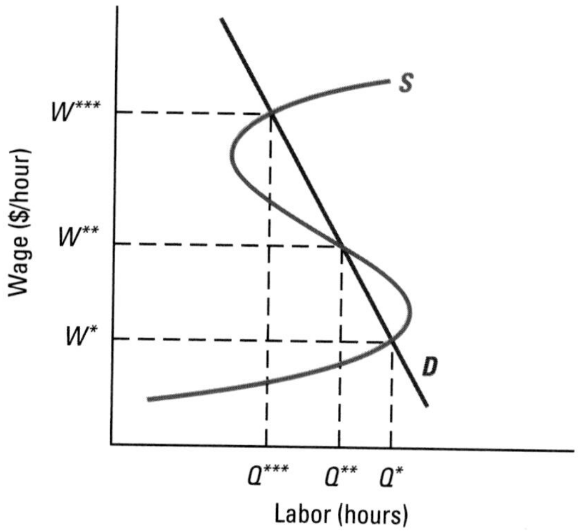

Figure 14.25
Multiple Equilibria in a Labor Market. When the labor supply curve is backward bending, the demand for labor can equal the supply at more than one wage rate.

slightly higher prices. A market is unlikely to settle into an unstable equilibrium, since the market price will tend to move away from the price level in an unstable equilibrium whenever it is close to it.

Another factor that matters is the recent level of prices. For example, in Figure 14.25, if the wage has recently been below W^{**}, the balancing of supply and demand tends to push the wage toward W^{*}. If instead the wage has recently been above W^{**}, that balancing tends to push the wage toward W^{***}.

IN-TEXT EXERCISE 14.6 **Graph the demand and supply in a factor market with three equilibrium prices. Suppose there is a small increase in demand. What will be the effect of this change on each of the three equilibria? Will it differ for stable and unstable equilibria?**

Welfare Analysis in Factor Markets

Section 14.4 discussed welfare properties of competitive markets. How are these properties affected by the presence of a backward-bending supply curve in a factor market? They aren't. A market equilibrium in a perfectly competitive factor market always maximizes aggregate surplus, just as in Section 14.4. In fact, the logic is exactly the same as there: buyers find any units of the factor that they purchase worth more than the equilibrium price and any units that they do not purchase worth less. What about sellers? We can always think of sellers' "costs" in a factor market as the opportunity cost of giving the factor to a buyer. For example, in a labor market this opportunity cost may be the individual's value from leisure or her wage in her best alternative employment. Any units of the factor that are sold must cost less than the equilibrium price, and any units that are not sold must cost more. Thus, as in Section 14.4, any change in who uses the factor, who supplies the factor, or the total amount of the factor bought and sold must lower aggregate surplus. (The analysis in Chapter 16 also implies this same result.)

What about using market demand and supply curves to measure aggregate, consumer, and producer surpluses as in Section 14.5? Does a backward-bending supply curve interfere with doing this? No. To see why, think of a labor market. The supply of labor can bend backwards only if there are income effects in the demand for leisure. But, as we saw in Section 6.5, to properly measure surplus when there are income effects in demand, we need to use compensated demand curves. In the context of factor markets, this translates into using a compensated factor supply curve. Because the compensation removes income effects, compensated factor supply curves always slope upwards, so we can measure surplus using those curves in the same way as in Section 14.5.

MARKET INTERVENTIONS

15

LEARNING OBJECTIVES

After reading this chapter, students should be able to:

- Describe the effects of a tax or subsidy in a competitive market.
- Explain what determines who bears the burden of a tax and the difference between the statutory and economic incidence of the tax.
- Compare the results of price floors, price supports, production quotas, and voluntary price programs.
- Show the effects of a price ceiling.
- Define domestic aggregate surplus and determine the effects of import tariffs and quotas.

President Bush with dairy farmer Dave Kuhle

Senator Kerry with dairy farmer Andrew Dejno

In the 2004 presidential election, the pressing issues were taxes, the deficit, and terrorism. Yet, in Wisconsin, George W. Bush and challenger John Kerry were arguing over cows . . . or perhaps more accurately, over how best to increase the incomes of the farmers who milk them.[1]

In the United States, the dairy industry benefits from an array of government programs. With each election cycle and each new federal farm bill, debate resumes over how large the subsidies will be and how the programs will be structured. In 2004, all dairy farmers wanted large subsidies, but naturally enough, Wisconsin farmers wanted the programs to benefit them in particular.

In Chapter 14 we saw that a perfectly competitive market leads to an efficient outcome, maximizing the level of aggregate surplus generated by the production and consumption of a good. This conclusion suggests

[1]"Where Cow Is Queen, Candidates Milk Dairy Issues," *Milwaukee Sentinel Journal*, October 28, 2004.

that the best government policy would be to let markets function without interference provided they are competitive and don't suffer from any of the other forms of market failure that we'll consider in Part IIIB (Chapters 17–21). Despite the logic of this prescription, however, governments often intervene in competitive markets that have no obvious market failures. Sometimes intervention is necessary, as when government needs to raise tax revenue to finance essential programs. But often intervention results from a political process aimed at benefiting certain constituencies.

Whether government interventions are or are not necessary, and whether they benefit groups in need of protection or groups who make large campaign donations, those interventions usually alter market outcomes. In so doing, they often reduce efficiency and aggregate surplus along with it. In this chapter we'll use the tools we developed in Chapter 14 to examine the effects of market interventions. We'll study three types of intervention:

1. *Taxes (and subsidies)*. Governments tax goods to raise the revenue needed to pay for various public expenditures. We'll see that in a perfectly competitive market, taxation reduces aggregate surplus, creating a deadweight loss. We'll explore the factors that determine the size of the loss, and ask who truly bears the burden of a tax. We'll also examine subsidies, which governments use to encourage certain activities, or to benefit buyers and/or sellers in a market.
2. *Policies designed to raise prices*. Many government interventions are designed to assist those who sell certain goods by raising their prices. Price floors, price supports, production quotas, and voluntary production reduction programs are all meant to raise prices, whether by mandating minimum prices, raising demand, or reducing supply. We'll compare the effects of these different policies. (We'll also briefly discuss their opposites, policies that are designed to benefit buyers by reducing prices, for which similar principles apply.)
3. *Import tariffs and quotas*. Governments also try to assist those who sell certain goods by reducing competition from foreign producers, usually through tariffs or quotas. We'll discuss these policies, paying particular attention to the distinction between overall economic efficiency and the maximization of domestic aggregate surplus.

15.1 TAXES (AND SUBSIDIES)

In many markets, consumers or firms pay taxes to the government when they buy or sell a good. In the United States, the federal government imposes a sales tax on consumers' purchases of gasoline and cigarettes, and an income tax on workers' earnings from the sale of their labor. City, county, and state governments impose sales taxes on goods bought within their limits. In this section we'll study the effects of such taxes on the equilibrium in a perfectly competitive market.

A **specific tax** is a fixed dollar amount that must be paid on each unit bought or sold. An **ad valorem tax** is a tax that is stated as a percentage of the good's price.

Economists distinguish between specific taxes and ad valorem taxes. A **specific tax** is a fixed dollar amount that must be paid on each unit bought or sold. The federal gasoline tax is a specific tax; currently it is 18.4 cents per gallon. An **ad valorem tax** is a tax that is stated as a percentage of the good's price. City sales taxes are ad valorem taxes. San Francisco, for example, assesses a sales tax of 8.5 percent on goods sold within the city.

For the sake of simplicity, we'll focus here mainly on specific taxes. The appendix to the chapter discusses ad valorem taxes.

The Burden of a Tax

Let's consider the effects of a specific tax of T dollars per gallon paid by gas stations on their sales of gasoline. In studying the effects of taxes, it's important to distinguish between the amount a consumer pays for a good and the amount a firm receives. We'll use P_b to stand for the amount a consumer pays and P_s to stand for the amount a firm receives after paying the tax. In the case of gasoline, for example, P_b is the amount posted at the pump. The amount the gas station receives, P_s, equals $P_b - T$.

Figure 15.1 shows one way to determine the tax's effect. The blue and red curves labeled D and S are the market demand and supply curves with no government intervention. Without the tax, consumers pay and firms receive the equilibrium price P_0 and Q_0 gallons are bought and sold. What happens with the tax? We'll first determine the new price paid by consumers, P_b. To do that, we need to determine the demand and supply for each possible level of P_b and then find the price P_b that equates the amounts demanded and supplied.

Figure 15.1 graphs the demand and supply curves with the tax. The vertical axis now measures the price paid by consumers. The demand curve is still given by curve D. What

Figure 15.1

The Effects of a Specific Tax. This figure shows the effects of a specific tax of T per gallon of gas. Without the tax, the market price would be P_0 and Q_0 gallons would be bought and sold. With the vertical axis measuring the price paid by consumers, the tax causes the supply curve to shift upward by the distance T at each quantity. With the tax, consumers pay a total of P_b per gallon, firms receive $P_s = P_b - T$ per gallon, and Q_T gallons are bought and sold. The total tax collected is the gray-shaded area, which equals $T \times Q_T$. The tax causes the price per gallon paid by consumers to increase and the price per gallon received by firms to fall. The sum of the two changes equals T, the amount of the tax.

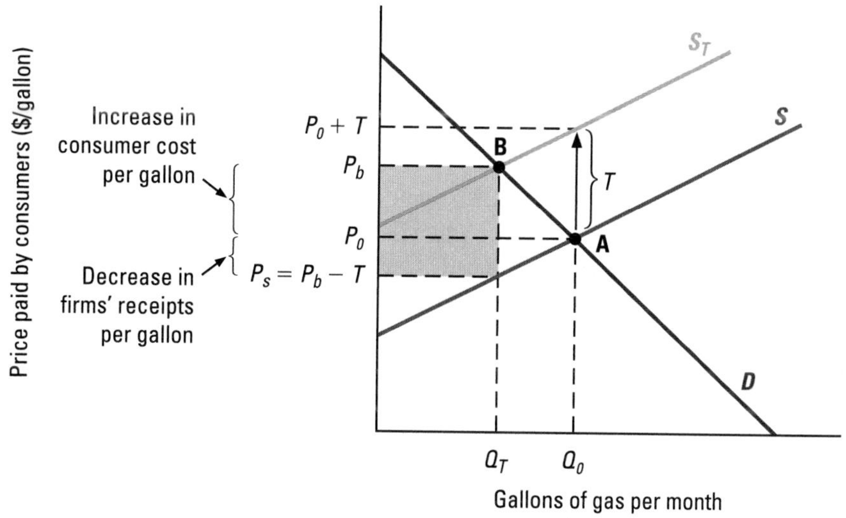

about the supply curve? Intuitively, for any price paid by consumers, firms now receive less than when there is no tax, so they won't be willing to supply as much as before. That is, the supply curve must shift. How do we construct the new supply curve? Consider, for example, the price that elicits a supply of Q_0. Without the tax, a price of P_0 did that. With the tax, the price paid by consumers must be T dollars higher (that is, equal to $P_0 + T$) to give firms the P_0 per gallon that induces them to supply Q_0 gallons. The same idea applies at *every* quantity. Graphically, this means that at each quantity, the supply curve with the tax is located a distance T above the original supply curve: the tax shifts the supply curve up to the light red curve S_T.

The new equilibrium price paid by consumers, P_b, is the price at which the curves D and S_T cross. The tax shifts the market equilibrium from point A to point B, causing the amount bought and sold to fall from Q_0 to Q_T. The amount that firms receive net of the tax is simply $P_s = P_b - T$, also shown in Figure 15.1.

Since P_b is greater than P_0 and P_s is less than P_0, the amount paid by consumers increases, while the amount received by firms (after paying the tax) decreases. However, even though firms pay the tax, the total amount they receive per gallon decreases by less than the amount of the tax, T. Indeed, as Figure 15.1 shows, if we add the extra amount that consumers pay per gallon and the decrease in the amount that firms receive per gallon, the total comes to T dollars, the amount of the tax. Thus, in a competitive market, the burden of the tax is shared by consumers and firms.

The **incidence** of a tax indicates how much of the tax burden is borne by various market participants.

What determines how much of the tax burden is borne by consumers versus firms? Economists call the division of a tax's burden among market participants the tax's **incidence**. The incidence of a tax depends on the shapes of the demand and supply curves. Figure 15.2 shows four extreme cases in which all of the tax is borne by just one side of the market. In Figure 15.2(a), demand is perfectly elastic, so that the tax causes no change in the total price paid by consumers; all of the tax is borne by firms. Firms bear all of the tax in Figure 15.2(b) as well. There, the tax leaves the supply curve unchanged (because it is perfectly inelastic, it remains in the same location when it shifts upward by T dollars). In Figures 15.2(c) and (d), the entire burden of the tax falls instead on consumers, who pay T dollars more per gallon than without the tax. In Figure 15.2(c), consumer demand is perfectly inelastic, while in Figure 15.2(d), firms' supply is perfectly elastic.

As a general matter, the more elastic is demand and the less elastic is supply, the more of the tax is borne by firms. In the appendix to this chapter, we'll show that for small taxes the share of the tax borne by consumers is given by the formula:

$$\text{Consumers' share of tax} = \frac{E^s}{E^s - E^d} \qquad \textbf{(1)}$$

where E^d and E^s are the elasticities of demand and supply, respectively. Consumers bear the larger share of the tax when demand is less elastic than supply, and the smaller share when demand is more elastic than supply (meaning that it is larger in absolute value; recall that E^d is a negative number!). For example, if $E^s = 2$ and $E^d = -1$, then consumers bear two-thirds of the tax's burden, meaning that their price rises by $(2/3)T$ dollars, while firms receive $T/3$ dollars less per gallon. (Check for yourself that the formula gives the right answer for the four cases shown in Figure 15.2.)

The two groups bear the tax equally when demand and supply are equally elastic (so that $E^S = -E^d$). The reason this is so is that consumer and producer prices must change with the tax so that the quantities supplied and demanded change by the same amount—otherwise, the quantities supplied and demanded would no longer be equal after the tax. When the demand and supply elasticities are equal (in absolute value), the quantities

Figure 15.2

Incidence of a Specific Tax: Four Cases. Figures (a) and (b) show two cases in which firms bear the entire burden of the tax. Figures (c) and (d) show two cases in which consumers bear the entire burden of the tax.

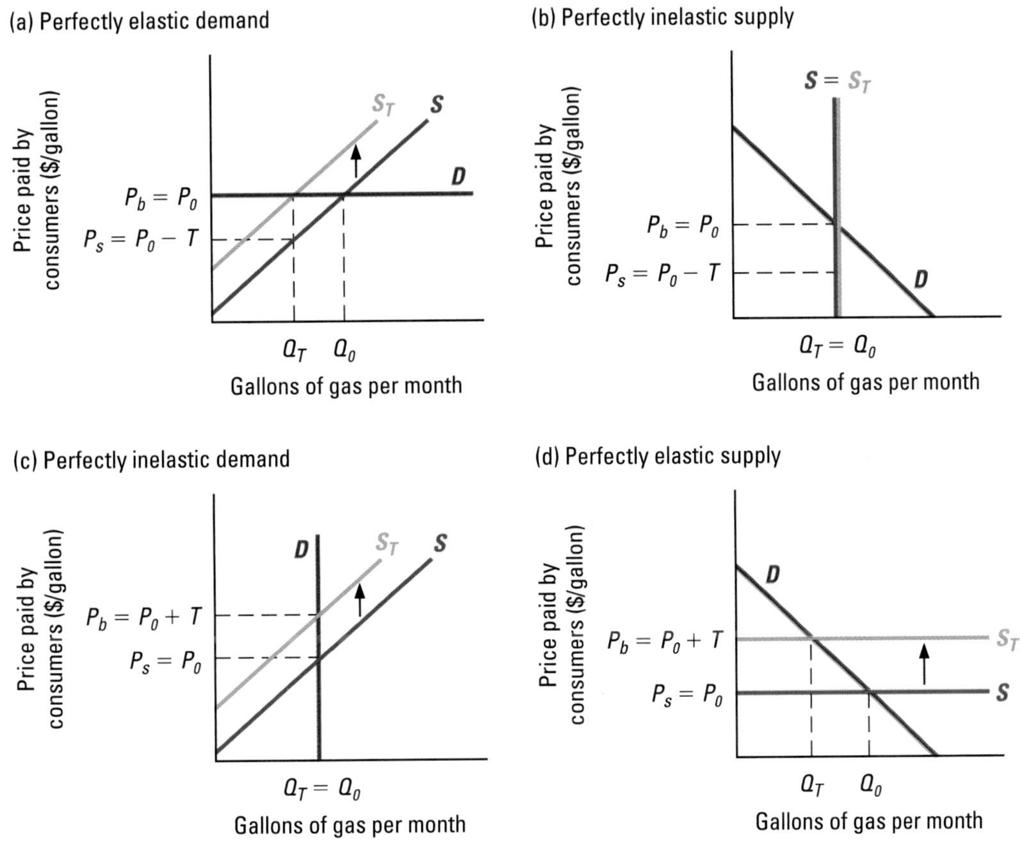

demanded and supplied will change by the same amount if consumer and producer prices change by the same amount. That's why the burden is equally shared. When one group has a bigger elasticity than the other (one farther away from zero), a smaller change in its price is required to produce the same change in quantity, which means it bears a smaller share of the burden.

So far we've focused on a tax paid by firms. What difference would it make if the tax was instead paid by consumers? Surprisingly, perhaps, the answer is *none*. To see why, suppose that instead of the gas station paying the tax, consumers do: for each gallon of gas a consumer buys, she must send T dollars to the government. Let's use demand and supply curves to look at the effect of this tax. We'll continue to let P_b stand for the amount paid by consumers. Now, though, this amount includes both the amount the consumer pays to the firm, P_s, and the tax, T. Let's again graph demand and supply curves as a function of P_b (which now includes the tax) and find the price P_b at which the amounts demanded and supplied are equal. The demand curve is exactly the same as the one shown in Figure 15.1. What about the supply curve? Just as when firms paid the tax, if consumers pay (in total)

P_b per gallon, firms end up receiving $P_s = P_b - T$ per gallon. So the supply curve is once again the curve S_T. Thus, Figure 15.1 also describes the situation in which consumers pay the tax. As a result, the market equilibrium is still point B. Regardless of who hands the tax money over to the government, the incidence of the tax is the same. Another way to put this is that the "statutory incidence" (who by law must pay the tax) has no effect on the "economic incidence" (who really bears the burden of the tax).

Upon reflection, this result is less surprising than it might seem at first. Suppose that instead of having consumers send T dollars to the government for each gallon of gas they buy, the government adopts an "easy pay" program in which gas stations are required to collect and mail in consumers' tax payments. Since the consumer is still the one paying the tax, this change (which involves only the person who puts the envelope in the mail) shouldn't matter. But this new way of collecting taxes is exactly the same as imposing the tax on firms!

The method we have followed in Figure 15.1 is not the only way to determine graphically the effect of the tax. Figure 15.3 shows a second way to do so. There the vertical axis measures the price received by firms, P_s. In that case, the tax leaves the supply curve unchanged, but shifts the demand curve down by a distance of T at each quantity to the curve D_T. Why? Now for any price received by firms, the tax increases the cost to consumers by T dollars per gallon. The price received by firms with the tax (P_s), and the amount bought and sold (Q_T) correspond to the intersection of the curves D_T and S, while the price paid by consumers is T higher than the price received by firms ($P_b = P_s + T$). This outcome is the same as in Figure 15.1.

Figures 15.1 and 15.3 also suggest a third way to find the effect of a specific tax, regardless of who pays it. We can find the amount bought and sold with the tax, Q_T, by

Figure 15.3

The Effects of a Specific Tax: Shifting the Demand Curve. The figure shows another way to find the effect of a specific tax. Now the vertical axis measures the price received by firms, so the tax shifts the demand curve downward by the distance T at each quantity. The outcome identified is the same as in Figure 15.1.

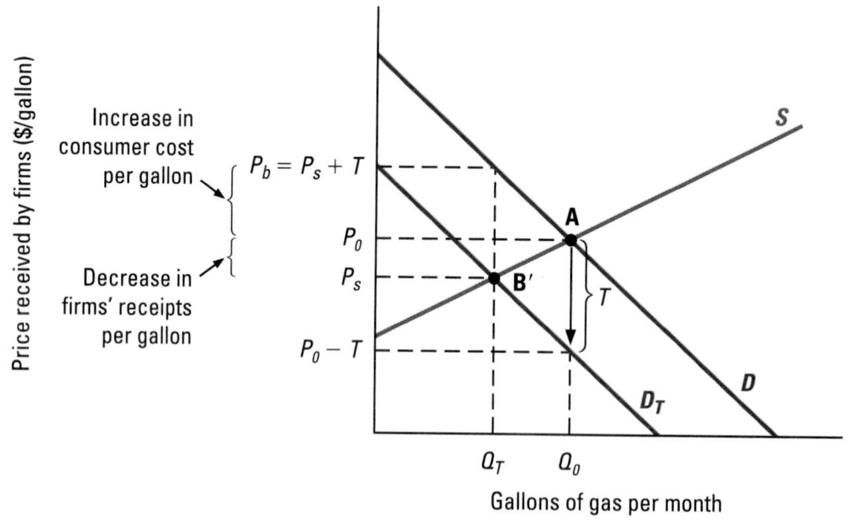

finding the quantity at which the no-tax demand curve, D, is exactly the distance T above the no-tax supply curve, S. Then, once we have done so, we can read the amounts per gallon that consumers pay and firms receive, P_b and P_s, off of the no-tax demand curve D and no-tax supply curve S.

This third approach to finding the effect of a specific tax highlights the fact that the tax creates a "wedge" between the amounts that consumers pay and firms receive. We'll see later in this section that this wedge leads to an inefficiency, because the value of the marginal unit to consumers is T dollars more than firms' marginal cost of producing that unit.

Application 15.1

Statutory versus Economic Incidence: The Evidence

In practice, is the statutory incidence of a tax really irrelevant? Unfortunately, there isn't much evidence on this point. The reason is that policymakers haven't provided the "experiment" that economists need to study this question empirically: a case in which the legal obligation to pay a tax was switched from buyers to sellers, or vice versa, without any other changes that might confound the results.

Given the lack of a real-world example to study, economists have taken the question into the laboratory. In one laboratory experiment, economist John Ruffle created a competitive market environment much like Vernon Smith's experimental markets (see Application 2.1).[2] Ruffle first ran the market experiment several times without any taxes. Then he introduced a tax, sometimes requiring buyers to pay it and sometimes requiring sellers to pay.

Figure 15.4 shows the results of Ruffle's experiments. Each line shows the fluctuations in the median price during a single experimental session, each of which involved a sequence of 20 experimental markets. In all there were 12 sessions, which differed in the numbers of buyers and sellers and in whether buyers or sellers had to pay the tax. In the first eight experimental markets of each session, there was no tax. Given the demand and supply conditions Ruffle created, the predicted market equilibrium price was between 31 and 33 Israeli sheckels.[3] Then, starting with the 9th experimental market in each session and continuing through the 20th, a 10-sheckel tax was imposed on either the buyers or the sellers. In both cases, the predicted market equilibrium price paid by buyers was between 36 and 38 sheckels, and the predicted equilibrium price received by sellers was between 26 and 28 sheckels.

The accompanying figure shows that prices converged fairly rapidly to the predicted ranges. As the theory suggests, the statutory incidence of the tax led to only minor differences in who actually bore its burden.

The prediction that statutory incidence is irrelevant to economic incidence can be extended to market settings that aren't perfectly competitive (see, for example, Exercise 17.21). In some of those settings, however, the theoretical predictions turn out to be less accurate. For example, economists Rudolf Kerschbamer and Georg Kirchsteiger studied the relevance of statutory incidence when sellers face a buyer in one-on-one bargaining, with the power to make take-it-or-leave-it offers (paralleling the ultimatum game discussed in Section 13.5).[4] They found that a seller or buyer who had to pay the tax did worse than the other party. Why might this be the case? In this one-on-one setting, people appear to care about fairness (see Section 13.5). The statutory incidence of a tax may affect their views about what's fair. When a tax is imposed on one party, this may foster a belief that it's fair for that party to bear a larger share of the total burden.

---

[2]Bradley J. Ruffle, "Tax and Subsidy Incidence Equivalence Theories: Experimental Evidence from Competitive Markets," *Journal of Public Economics* 89, August 2005, pp. 1519–1542. Ruffle's experimental procedure did differ somewhat from Smith's, in that it allowed buyers and sellers to engage in direct negotiations. (Smith used an "open outcry" procedure, which resembles commodity trading markets.)

[3]Because the demand and supply curves had a steplike form, all prices in this range were equilibrium prices.

[4]Rudolf Kerschbamer and Georg Kirchsteiger, "Theoretically Robust but Empirically Invalid? An Experimental Investigation into Tax Equivalence," *Economic Theory* 16, 2000, pp. 719–734.

Figure 15.4

An Experimental Study of Tax Incidence. Each line shows the changes in the median price during a single session of the experiment, each consisting of 20 experimental markets. The 12 sessions differed in the number of buyers and sellers who participated, and in who paid the 10-sheckel tax starting in the 9th experimental market. For example, in session "tax13b10," the 10th session, there were 13 buyers and sellers, and the buyers had to pay the tax. The predicted equilibrium price without the tax was 31–33 sheckels. With the tax, the predicted prices paid by the buyers and received by the sellers were in the range of 36–38 and 26–28 sheckels, respectively. As the figure shows, prices converged rapidly to the predicted levels.

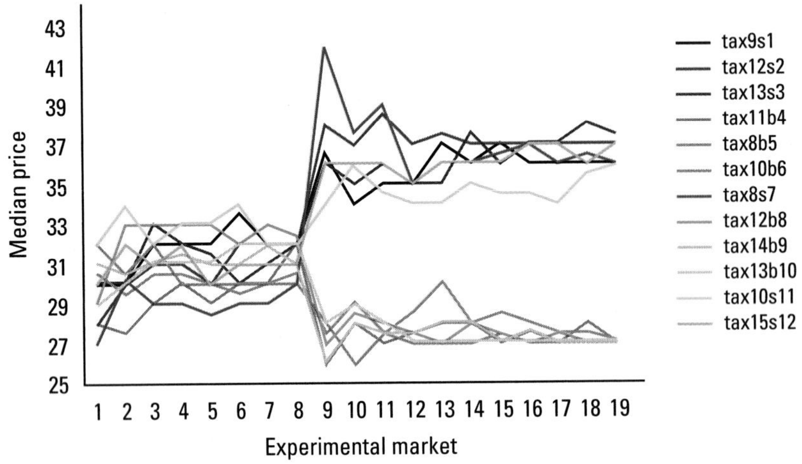

Source: Ruffle (2005).

Application 15.2

The Incidence of the Payroll Tax

If you've ever received a paycheck, you've probably noticed that a significant chunk of your pay was deducted under the heading "FICA." FICA stands for the Federal Insurance Contribution Act, which established a tax to fund the Social Security and Medicare programs.

This tax, also known simply as the *payroll tax*, dates from the start of the Social Security program in the 1930s. Ever since its enactment, both workers and employers have had to make equal contributions. Currently, workers and employers must each pay the federal government 7.65 percent of the worker's total earnings (up to a cap).

When legislators enacted the tax, they decided that it was "fair" for workers and employers to split the tax equally. Economic analysis, however, tells us that the statutory obligation to pay the tax doesn't matter. The statutory incidence may be 50-50, but what is the economic incidence of the tax?

Most of the available evidence suggests that, in the United States, workers bear nearly all the burden of employment-based taxes, such as the payroll tax.[5] This is to be expected, because the elasticity of labor supply is quite low. Among men, for example, there is almost no variety

---

[5]See, for example, Jonathan Gruber, "The Incidence of Mandated Maternity Benefits," *American Economic Review* 84, June 1994, pp. 622–641 and Jonathan Gruber and Alan Krueger, "The Incidence of Mandated Employer-Provided Insurance: Lessons from Workers' Compensation Insurance," in *Tax Policy and the Economy* 5, edited by David Bradford, Cambridge, MA: MIT Press, 1991.

in hours worked in response to changes in the wage, and estimates of the elasticity of women's labor supply are around 0.4. Workers who have full-time jobs simply don't vary their hours of work very much.

For some occupations, however, labor supply is more elastic. For example, those who are employed part time, working in some weeks but not in others, are more responsive than others to increases in the wage. As a result, formula (1) predicts that in occupations staffed largely by this type of worker (for example, cab drivers or temporary help), firms may bear a larger share of the payroll tax than in other types of businesses.

The Welfare Effects of a Tax

Now let's examine the welfare effects of a tax.[6] Figure 15.5 shows the change in aggregate surplus caused by the tax of T dollars per gallon. The no-tax demand curve D and no-tax supply curve S are the same as those in Figures 15.1 and 15.3. The tax reduces the amount bought and sold from Q_0 to Q_T, the quantity at which the distance between the curves D and S is T. We can use the D and S curves to measure aggregate surplus. The area under the no-tax demand curve reflects consumers' willingness to pay, while the area under the no-tax supply curve reflects the avoidable costs of production.[7] As in Section 14.5, aggregate surplus is the area between these curves, up to the equilibrium quantity (the amount bought and sold).

Initially, Q_0 gallons are bought and sold, so aggregate surplus is the sum of the green-shaded area and the red-shaded area. With the tax, only Q_T gallons of gas are bought and sold. So the aggregate surplus with the tax is the green-shaded area. The tax decreases

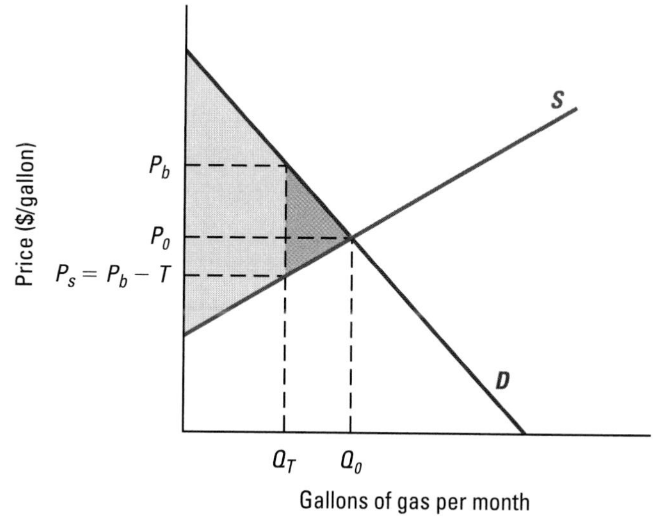

Figure 15.5

The Deadweight Loss of Taxation. This figure shows the deadweight loss from a specific tax of T dollars per gallon of gas. Without the tax, aggregate surplus is the sum of the green-shaded area and the red-shaded area. With the tax, it is the green-shaded area. The deadweight loss (the reduction in aggregate surplus) is therefore the red-shaded area.

[6]Here and throughout the remaining sections of this chapter, we'll assume that there are no income effects, or that they're small so that we can get approximately the right answer using ordinary demand curves. Add-On 15A shows how to measure the welfare effects of a tax when income effects complicate the analysis.

[7]Note that we want to use the no-tax supply curve S for this purpose, *not* the with-tax supply curve S_T. The area under the latter curve includes the costs of the tax, which is not a true social cost of production because the tax is collected by the government. For similar reasons, we want to use the no-tax demand curve, D.

The **deadweight loss of taxation** is the lost aggregate surplus due to a tax.

aggregate surplus by an amount equal to the red-shaded area. That area is the **deadweight loss of taxation**. This deadweight loss arises because the $Q_T - Q_0$ gallons of gas that are not being produced and consumed with the tax cost firms less to produce than consumers are willing to pay.[8]

Figure 15.6 shows how consumers, producers, and the government fare as a result of the tax. Without the tax, consumer surplus equals areas C + D + E; with the tax, it is only C. So the loss to consumers is D + E. Producer surplus equals areas F + G + H without the tax, but only H with the tax, so the loss to producers is F + G. (See Section 14.5 for a discussion of how to use market demand and supply curves to measure consumer and producer surpluses.) The government receives tax revenue equal to areas D + F. Of the amount consumers give up, D + E, the government gets only D. Of the amount producers give up, F + G, the government gets only F. The lost amount, E + G, is the deadweight loss. Taxation is therefore a "leaky bucket"; though it can be used to move resources from the private sector to the government, the government receives less than private parties give up.

Of course, the effect of the tax on welfare depends on what the government does with the revenue. The previous calculation assumes, in effect, that a dollar spent by the government has the same social value as a dollar spent by the typical consumer. (This would

Figure 15.6

The Welfare Effects of a Specific Tax. A specific tax lowers consumer surplus from the sum of areas C + D + E to area C; it lowers producer surplus from the sum of areas F + G + H to area H. (Profit equals producer surplus less sunk costs.) The tax revenue collected is the sum of areas D + F. The amount lost by consumers and firms but not gained by the government equals areas E + G, the deadweight loss of the tax.

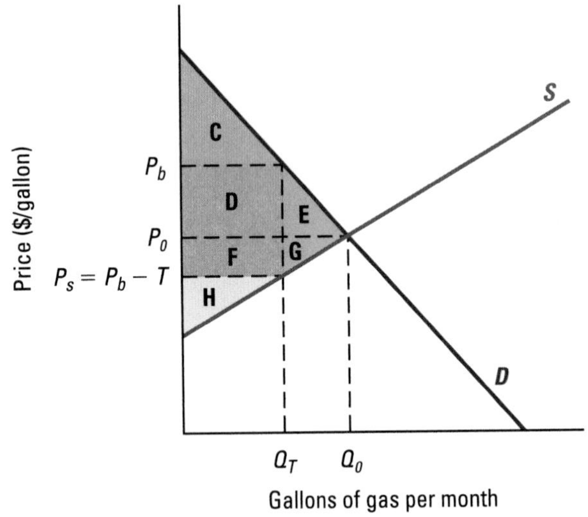

	Without tax	With tax	Gain/Loss with tax
Aggregate surplus	C + D + E + F + G + H	C + D + F + H	E + G
Consumer surplus	C + D + E	C	D + E
Producer surplus	F + G + H	H	F + G
Tax revenue	0	D + F	D + F

[8]For simplicity, we haven't included any administrative costs of collecting the tax, which would increase the deadweight loss.

be the case, for example, if the government simply handed the revenues back to consumers.) If the government wasted the money, then the tax would create an even larger social loss—it would include areas D + F. The loss associated with the tax could be smaller, however—indeed, the tax might even be beneficial—if government spending were more socially valuable on the margin than private spending. This is sometimes possible when there are market failures; see, for example, the discussion of public goods in Chapter 20.

Worked-out problem 15.1 shows how to calculate the welfare effects of a tax.

WORKED-OUT PROBLEM 15.1

The Problem The market demand function for corn is $Q^d = 15 - 2P$ and the market supply function is $Q^s = 5P - 2.5$, both measured in billions of bushels per year. Suppose the government imposes a \$0.70 tax on each bushel of corn. What will be the effects on aggregate surplus, consumer surplus, and producer surplus? What will be the deadweight loss caused by the tax?

The Solution We can find the answer in three steps:

Step 1: Find the market equilibrium without the tax. The equilibrium price without the tax is \$2.50 per bushel and 10 billion bushels of corn are bought and sold each year. (These are the same demand and supply curves that we considered in Section 14.5.) Aggregate surplus is \$35 billion, consumer surplus is \$25 billion, and producer surplus is \$10 billion per year.

At this market equilibrium the elasticity of demand is −0.5 and the elasticity of supply is 1.25. (Check this!) So we should expect that more of the tax will be borne by consumers, and that because demand is inelastic, the tax will cause a relatively small deadweight loss.

Step 2: Find the new market equilibrium with the tax. The tax changes the market supply function to

$$Q^s = 5(P_b - 0.70) - 2.5 = 5P_b - 6$$

where P_b is the price paid by buyers. To find the equilibrium level of P_b, we set demand equal to supply:

$$15 - 2P_b = 5P_b - 6$$

Solving, we find that P_b = \$3 per bushel, which means that sellers receive P_s = \$2.30 per bushel (the price buyers pay, less the tax). So buyers pay \$0.50 more per bushel, and sellers receive \$0.20 less because of the tax. Substituting P_b = \$3 into the demand function tells us that 9 billion bushels are bought and sold each year with the tax. Figure 15.7 shows the new equilibrium.

Step 3: Calculate the new levels of aggregate surplus, consumer surplus, and producer surplus. Figure 15.7 shows the areas that we need to measure. Consumer surplus, equal to the area of the blue triangle, is \$20.25 billion per year. Producer surplus, equal to the area of the yellow triangle, is \$8.1 billion a year. Government revenue, equal to the area of the gray rectangle, is \$6.3 billion a year. Adding these three figures tells us that aggregate surplus is \$34.65 billion a year. Since aggregate surplus without the tax is \$35 billion per year, the deadweight loss from the tax must be \$0.35 billion per year—a relatively small fraction of the original aggregate surplus. Indeed, the tax collects 18 percent of the original aggregate surplus as government revenue, losing only 1 percent of it as deadweight loss. The ratio of deadweight loss to tax revenue is 0.056 (0.35/6.3), so the lost aggregate surplus amounts to 5.6 percent of every tax dollar collected.

We could have calculated aggregate surplus with the tax in two other ways. First, we could have calculated the area of the trapezoid formed by the blue, gray, and yellow areas. Viewed sideways, this trapezoid has a bottom base of 7, a top base of 0.7, and a height of 9, so its area equals ½ × (bottom base + top base) × height, or 34.65. Alternatively, we could have calculated the area of the red deadweight loss triangle, which has a base of 0.7 and a height of 1, so that its area is 0.35. Aggregate surplus with the tax equals the no-tax aggregate surplus (\$35 billion) less this deadweight loss (\$0.35 billion).

IN-TEXT EXERCISE 15.1 **The market demand function for corn is $Q^d = 15 - 2P$ and the market supply function is $Q^s = 5P - 2.5$, both measured in billions of bushels per year. Suppose the government imposes a \$1.40 tax on each bushel of corn. What will be the effects on aggregate surplus, consumer surplus, and producer surplus? What will be the deadweight loss caused by the tax?**

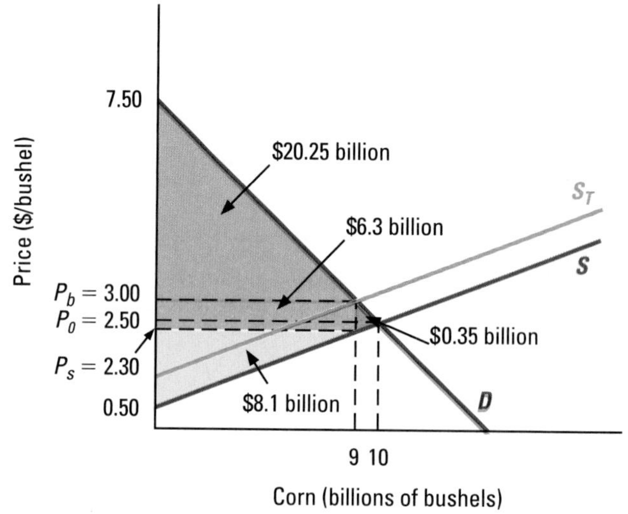

Figure 15.7

The Welfare Effects of a Tax on Corn. The figure shows the welfare effects of a \$0.70 per bushel tax on corn. Consumer surplus falls from \$25 billion per year without the tax (see Figure 14.19 on page 526) to \$20.25 billion with it. Producer surplus falls from \$10 billion per year without the tax to \$8.1 billion with it. The government collects \$6.3 billion per year in tax revenue. Aggregate surplus therefore falls from \$35 billion per year without the tax to \$34.65 billion with it, creating a deadweight loss of \$0.35 billion per year.

Which Goods Should the Government Tax?

The size of the deadweight loss from taxation of a good depends on the shapes of the demand and supply curves. Look at Figure 15.8(a), in which demand is perfectly inelastic, and Figure 15.8(b), in which supply is perfectly inelastic. In both these cases, there is no deadweight loss from taxation, because the tax doesn't change the amount bought and

Figure 15.8

Two Cases of Taxation with No Deadweight Loss. In figure (a), demand is perfectly inelastic; in figure (b), supply is perfectly inelastic. In both cases, a tax causes no change in the amount bought and sold. Aggregate surplus, which equals the green-shaded areas with and without the tax, remains the same.

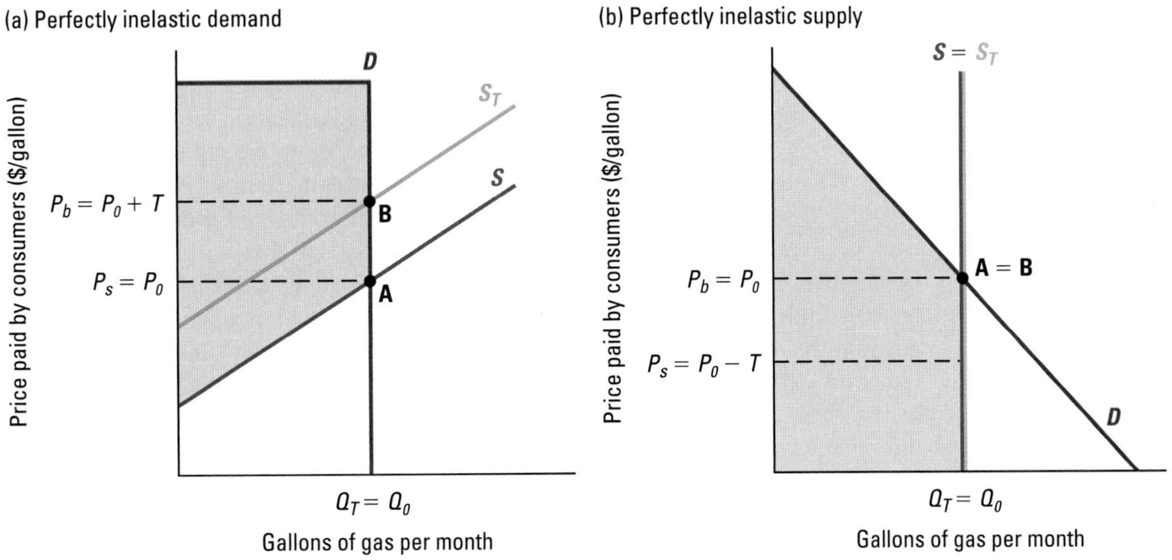

sold. More generally, if either the demand or supply curve is very inelastic, even if not perfectly so, the deadweight loss caused by a tax will be low.

Governments need to raise tax revenue to finance a number of programs, including road and highway improvements, military expenditures, and the administrative functions of government. What goods should the government tax, and in what amounts, to raise this revenue? One important objective should be to tax goods for which the deadweight loss of taxation will be low. Figure 15.8 suggests that this involves choosing goods with inelastic demand or supply. For example, we saw in Chapter 2 that the demand for gasoline is fairly inelastic, which would make gasoline a good product to tax.[9] In Add-On 17B we'll confirm this observation by deriving a general formula for minimizing the deadweight loss of taxation. As an example, suppose that two goods X and Y have the same, constant marginal cost, MC (because marginal cost is constant, the supply curve is infinitely elastic). That formula tells us that the taxes on these two goods, T_X and T_Y, should satisfy

$$\left[\frac{\left(\dfrac{T_X}{MC + T_X}\right)}{\left(\dfrac{T_Y}{MC + T_Y}\right)}\right] = \left(\frac{E_Y^d}{E_X^d}\right)$$

If good X's demand is less elastic than good Y's, the ratio on the right-hand side of this formula is greater than one. So the taxes on the two goods should have $T_X/(MC + T_X) >$

[9]In fact, since both gasoline consumption and driving create externalities, there are also other reasons to tax gasoline (see Chapter 20).

$T_Y/(MC + T_Y)$, which implies that $T_X > T_Y$: the good with the less elastic demand should face a larger tax.

While minimizing deadweight losses is an important objective, it may not be the only one. Distributional considerations can also affect the choice of goods to tax. Many goods with inelastic demand are necessities, such as milk. Taxes on such goods will place a heavy burden on low-income consumers. If there isn't any way to redistribute income without causing deadweight losses, it may make sense to tax instead other goods with more elastic demands.

Finally, for some goods, taxation can actually raise aggregate surplus. In Chapter 20, for example, we'll discuss taxes on pollution. Markets don't necessarily produce efficient outcomes where pollution is concerned. Because polluters don't personally bear all the costs of their actions, they may choose to pollute excessively. (This type of market failure is known as an externality—see Chapter 20.) Taxes can promote efficiency by making activities that generate pollution more costly to polluters. So-called sin taxes on addictive substances such as alcohol or cigarettes may also promote efficiency. One reason is that an addict's substance abuse can harm others (again, an externality). Another possible social benefit is that these taxes discourage youths from developing tastes for addictive substances. In these cases, taxes can not only improve efficiency, but also raise revenue at the same time, eliminating the need to tax other goods whose taxation would cause deadweight losses.

Government Subsidies and Their Effects

A **subsidy** is a payment that reduces the amount that buyers pay for a good or increases the amount that sellers receive.

In some circumstances, governments offer a **subsidy**—a payment that reduces the amount that buyers pay for a good or increases the amount that sellers receive. Subsidies can be either specific (that is, a dollar amount per unit) or ad valorem (that is, a percentage of price). Like taxes, subsidies are sometimes imposed to restore efficiency in response to market failures. Unlike taxes, which usually are observed in perfectly competitive markets without market failures because of the government's need to raise revenue, subsidies in such markets often result from extensive lobbying efforts on behalf of the beneficiaries. For example, the U.S. government subsidizes the production and use of ethanol in gasoline, increasing the incomes of ethanol producers, gasoline refiners, and the farmers who grow the corn that is its primary input. It subsidizes home mortgage loans (and therefore individual purchases of homes) by treating home mortgage interest as tax deductible, increasing the well-being not only of individual home buyers and sellers, but also the firms who build those houses and the real estate agents who arrange the transactions.

Unlike taxes, subsidies usually *increase* sales of the subsidized good. Like taxes, however, they cause deadweight losses. Figure 15.9 shows the effect of a government subsidy of T dollars for each gallon of ethanol produced. Just as with a tax, we can find the equilibrium with the tax by shifting either the supply or demand curve (for example, when we measure the price paid by consumers on the vertical axis, the supply curve shifts *down* by a distance of T, since supply increases with the subsidy) or by looking for the quantity at which the demand curve lies a distance of T below the no-subsidy supply curve (since consumers pay T dollars less than firms receive). The subsidy increases the amount bought and sold from Q_0 to Q_T.

Without the subsidy, aggregate surplus is the green-shaded area. With the subsidy, it is the green-shaded area minus the red-shaded deadweight loss. This deadweight loss arises because the last $Q_T - Q_0$ gallons of ethanol cost more to produce than consumers are willing to pay.

Consumers and firms both benefit from this subsidy. As with a tax, the sum of the reduction in the price paid by consumers and the increase in the price received by firms equals exactly T. How much each group's price falls depends again on the shape of the demand and supply curves. In general, the side of the market whose demand or supply is less elastic has a larger price change. Formula (1) still describes consumers' share of the total price change, but now getting a larger price change is good since with a subsidy it's a reduction in the amount paid for consumers and an increase in the amount received for firms. Since aggregate surplus falls even though both consumers and firms are better off, someone must be worse off. That "someone" is the government, which incurs an expense equal to $T \times Q_T$.

IN-TEXT EXERCISE 15.2 **Graph the changes in consumer surplus, producer surplus, and government revenue caused by a subsidy of T per gallon of ethanol.**

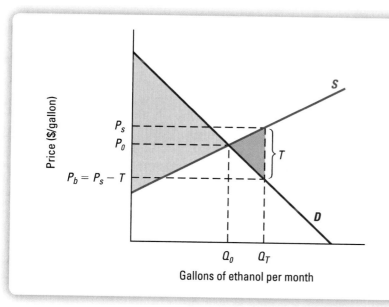

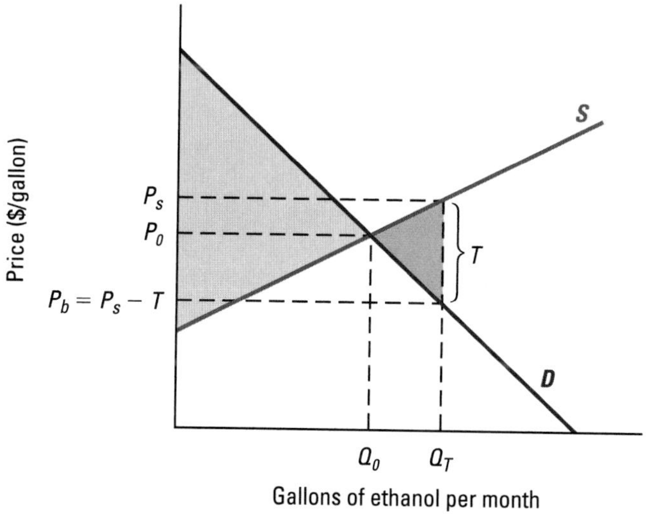

Figure 15.9

The Deadweight Loss from a Per-Unit Subsidy of Ethanol. With a subsidy of T per unit, the amount bought and sold increases from Q_0 to Q_T, producing a deadweight loss equal to the area of the red triangle. As a result of the subsidy, consumers pay less and firms receive more for every gallon of ethanol sold.

Application 15.3

U.S. Dairy Subsidies

Dairy farming is a hard job with long hours. Fortunately for the dairy farmers, their lobbyists work long hours, too. Dairy farmers have been incredibly effective at getting the U.S. Congress to pass legislation that boosts their incomes.[10]

The U.S. dairy program has three parts. One is the Milk Income Loss Contract (MILC) program, which pays farmers a per-unit subsidy equal to 45 percent of the amount by which the price of milk falls below $1.46 per gallon, up to a total of 278,000 gallons per year.[11] In June 2003, for example, the price of milk was only $1.12 per gallon, so farmers received a subsidy of approximately $0.15 per gallon [equal to (0.45)(1.46 – 1.12)], bringing the total amount they received to $1.27 per gallon.

Figure 15.10(a) shows the effect of this subsidy on a large, individual dairy's supply curve. (As we'll see, the dairy's size will affect whether the cap matters for the dairy's supply behavior.) The line connecting points A, B, and C is its supply curve in the absence of any subsidy. With the subsidy, the dairy's supply behavior changes for prices below $1.46 a gallon. If there wasn't a 128,000-gallon cap, the supply curve below $1.46 would be the line segment BD (so the dairy's overall supply curve would be the kinked curve formed by line segments AB and BD). For example, when the price is $0.46, $1 below the $1.46 trigger price for the subsidy, the dairy would receive an extra $0.45 per gallon, for a total receipt of $0.91 per gallon. So its quantity supplied would equal the amount it would want to supply at a price of $0.91 without the subsidy. Finally, the 278,000-gallon cap means that its supply behavior coincides with segment BD below the cap, and then reverts to the no-subsidy supply curve above it. This results in the red supply curve *S* shown in the figure.

For small dairies, which don't supply very much milk, the cap won't be relevant, since it will be above the quantity the dairy would supply at a price of $1.46 [labeled Q_B in Figure 15.10(b)]. (That is, these dairies don't supply 278,000 gallons, even at a price of $1.46.) For large dairies such as the one in Figure 15.10(a), the cap will lie well below the amount they want to supply at a price of $1.46. As a result, at most market prices a large dairy's supply behavior will be exactly the same as if no subsidy program existed. In practice, large dairies that produce beyond the cap make up only 17 percent of all dairy farms, but they produce about 80 percent of the total milk supply. As a result, the cap significantly reduces the degree to which the subsidy increases the milk supply.

Figure 15.11 shows a linear market demand curve and two market supply curves reflecting market conditions in 2003. In that year, the average price was $1.26 per gallon, and 19.8 billion gallons of milk were bought and sold (that is, the market equilibrium was at point E).[12] The market demand function in the figure is

$$Q^d = 31.6 - 9.4P$$

where Q^d is measured in billions of gallons of milk per year. The linear supply curve *S*, which captures the market supply with no subsidy, represents the supply function:[13]

$$Q^s = 6.6 + 10.3P$$

where Q^s is measured in billions of gallons of milk per year. The supply curve *S′* shows the market supply with a subsidy but without a cap. It coincides with the no-subsidy supply curve *S* at prices above $1.46 (that is, above point B), and has a greater supply for prices below $1.46. It reflects the supply function:

$$Q^s_{subsidy} = \begin{Bmatrix} 6.6 + 10.3P_b \text{ if } P_b \geq 1.46 \\ 13.4 + 5.7P_b \text{ if } P_b < 1.46 \end{Bmatrix}$$

Since the cap means that large dairies don't expand their supply unless the price is far below $1.46 [as in Figure 15.10(a)], the actual market supply at prices below $1.46 lies between these two supply curves and intersects the market demand curve at point E.

---

[10]They are not the only farmers who have been successful in this regard; income-boosting programs benefit producers of many other agricultural products.

[11]The cap and price target are actually stated in hundredweight units. A hundredweight, equal to 100 pounds, is equivalent to 11.6 gallons of milk. We use the more familiar gallon units here.

[12]The MILC program payments actually depend on monthly prices and production, but we have stated them in annual terms to simplify the analysis.

[13]The demand and no-subsidy supply functions are linear curves with elasticities of −0.6 and 0.65, respectively, at the observed 2003 price and quantity of milk bought and sold. These elasticities are consistent with published estimates. The supply curve with the subsidy (but no cap) is derived from the no-subsidy supply curve, as in Figure 15.10.

As the figure shows, without the MILC program the equilibrium price in 2003 would have been \$1.27, and 19.7 billion gallons of milk would have been bought and sold. If instead the MILC program had been in place without a cap, the price would have fallen to \$1.21, and 20.2 billion gallons of milk would have been bought and sold. The result would have been a deadweight loss of \$15 million dollars per year, equal to the triangle formed by the light- and dark-red shaded areas. Because of the cap, however, the actual market equilibrium was point E, with a price of \$1.26 per gallon and 19.8 billion gallons bought and sold. This result was very close to the no-subsidy equilibrium, with the price just a penny below the no-subsidy price and only 0.1 billion extra gallons bought and sold. The cap limited the deadweight loss to \$500,000 per year. While the deadweight loss of the MILC program was small, however, the cost to the government certainly was not. Payments covering the years 2002 and 2003 amounted to over \$1.8 billion. So the MILC program amounted to a direct transfer from the government to dairy farmers, with small effects on aggregate surplus but large effects on the well-being of particular members of society.

In addition to minimizing the overall effect of the subsidies on the market equilibrium and aggregate surplus, the cap had different effects on large and small dairies. Small dairies benefited greatly from the program, because all of their production was subsidized. Large dairies received a subsidy on only a small share of their output. States with many small farms, like Wisconsin, received a much larger share of the program's payments than states with many large farms, like California. For example, Wisconsin's dairy farmers produced only about 12 percent of the national milk supply, but received over 20 percent of MILC payments between 2002 and 2004. California's dairy farmers, by contrast, received only about 6 percent of MILC payments, but produced over 20 percent of the national milk supply.

Figure 15.10

Effect of a Subsidy on an Individual Dairy's Milk Supply. This figure shows an individual dairy's supply curve under the MILC program in red. Without the subsidy, the supply curve would be the line ABC. With the subsidy, the supply curve is the same as the no-subsidy supply curve at prices above \$1.46 per gallon. At prices below \$1.46 at which the no-subsidy supply is less than the cap of 278,000 gallons per year, the subsidy increases the dairy's milk supply. Figure (a) shows the situation for a large dairy. The cap is less than its production level unless the price is far below \$1.46. Figure (b) shows the situation for a small dairy that produces less than 278,000 gallons even when the price is \$1.46. For small dairies the cap is irrelevant.

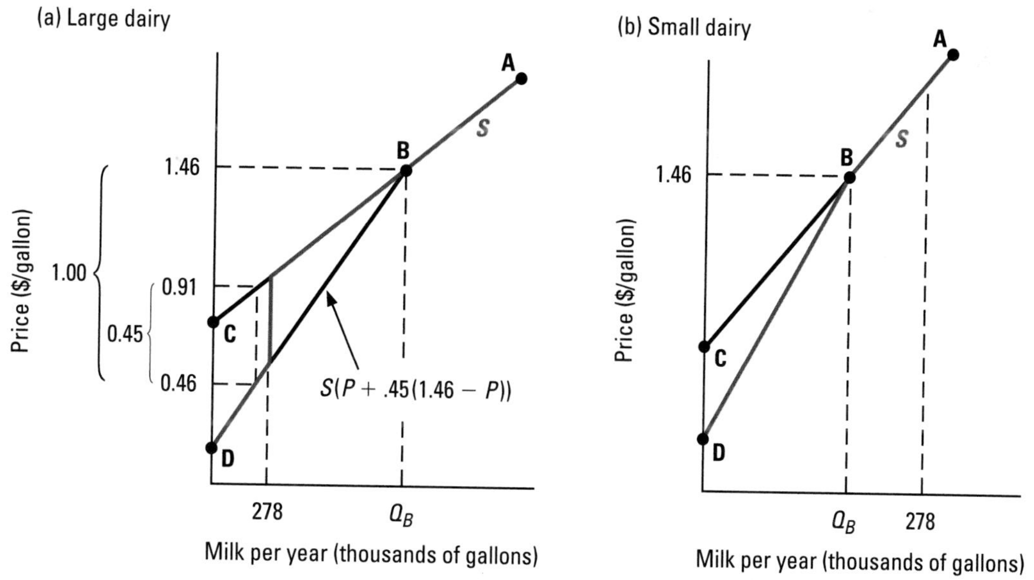

Figure 15.11

The Deadweight Loss from the MILC Program. The triangle formed by the light- and dark-red shaded areas represents the deadweight loss of $15 million a year that would have been caused by the MILC program in 2003 without the 278,000-gallon cap. With the cap, the market supply at prices below $1.46 would lie between the *S* and *S′* curves. The actual market equilibrium was point E, at which 19.8 billion gallons of milk were bought and sold at a price of $1.26 per gallon. The resulting deadweight loss was only $500,000 per year.

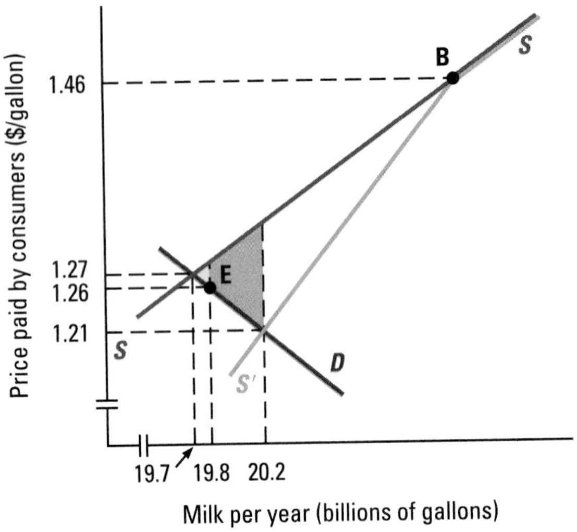

15.2 POLICIES DESIGNED TO RAISE PRICES

Governments often attempt to interfere in markets with the intention of benefiting a particular group. When politicians want to help the sellers in a market, they turn to a variety of policies meant to raise prices. Such policies are particularly prevalent in agricultural markets, where they are intended to raise farmers' incomes. We'll discuss four such policies: price floors, price supports, production quotas, and voluntary production limits.

Price Floors

A **price floor** establishes a minimum price that sellers can charge.

A **price floor** establishes a minimum price that sellers can charge. For example, the United States government establishes minimum prices for milk. Similarly, the United States government, most states, and some cities have minimum wage laws specifying the minimum hourly wage for an employee.

Figure 15.12(a) shows (hypothetical) yearly demand and supply curves for milk. (For simplicity, in this discussion we'll ignore the effects of the MILC subsidy program discussed in Application 15.3.) Absent any intervention, the competitive price would be P_0. Suppose the government sets a price floor above that level, at $\underline{P}$. At that price, the amount supplied exceeds the amount demanded. Since trade requires that both parties agree, the amount of milk bought and sold is Q_1 gallons, determined by the demand curve. (Farmers would like to sell more than Q_1 gallons, but no one is willing to buy them.)

Figure 15.13 shows the welfare implications of this policy (see both the figure and the accompanying table). Aggregate surplus without any intervention, described in the first row of the first column of the table, is the sum of areas A + B + C + D + E. What about with the price floor? Since farmers want to sell Q_2 gallons of milk at a price of $\underline{P}$, the total cost of production depends on *which* farms produce the Q_1 gallons of milk that are bought and sold. If it is the least-cost producers, the total avoidable cost of production is given

Figure 15.12

Three Ways to Raise the Price of Milk. The figure shows three ways to raise the price of milk to $\underline{P}$. In figure (a), the government imposes a price floor of $\underline{P}$, which results in Q_1 gallons being bought and sold. In figure (b), the government increases demand through a price support program in which it buys $Q_2 - Q_1$ gallons a year. Total sales of milk are Q_2 gallons, of which Q_1 gallons are bought by private buyers. In figure (c), the government reduces the supply by convincing farmers to limit their production to Q_1 gallons per year, either by imposing a quota or by instituting a voluntary production reduction program.

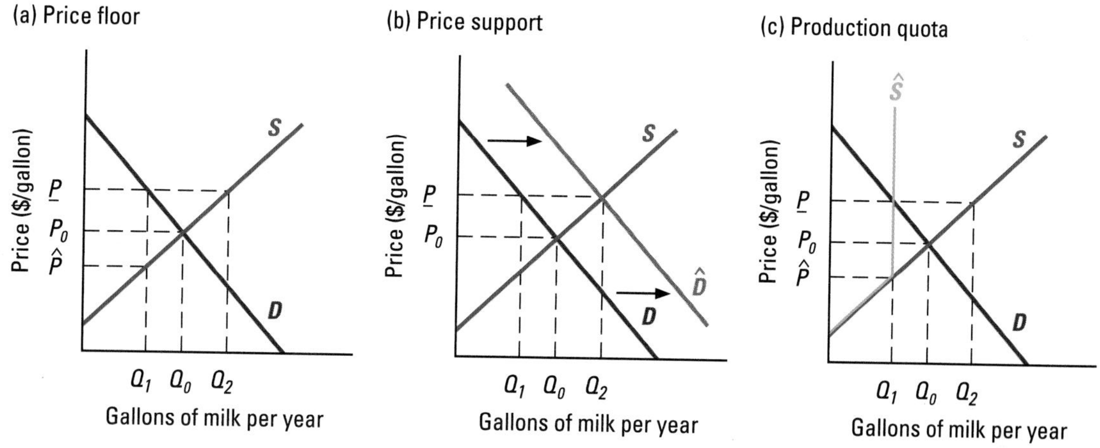

by the area under the supply curve up to Q_1 gallons (see Section 14.5).[14] In that case, the aggregate surplus is areas A + B + D (see the first row of the "Price Floor" column in the table). The deadweight loss from this policy is then areas C + E (shown in the second row of that same column).

Consumers are worse off, because consumer surplus falls from A + B + C without the price floor to only A with it. What about farmers? Certainly, any farmer who is no longer able to sell his goods is worse off, while a farmer who still sells the same amount is better off. What about farmers as a whole? Surprisingly, they may be either better or worse off. With the floor, producer surplus is area B + D; without the floor, it is area D + E. So farmers are better off if area B exceeds area E. In the figure that is so, but it need not be. (Try redrawing the figure with different price floors. You'll see that if the price floor is very high, farmers will make very little money.)

The reason producer surplus need not increase is simple; it relates to our discussion of profit maximization in Chapter 9 (see also Chapter 17). It's just a matter of whether industry profits go up when the price goes up. As we saw in Chapter 9, the highest possible profit occurs where marginal revenue (derived from the market demand curve) equals the marginal cost (which is given by the industry supply curve, *S*). However, the government may set the price floor above or below this profit-maximizing level. If the price floor is too high, it may even yield a *lower* profit than the original market equilibrium. (That said, since these policies are often introduced in response to political pressure from the affected farmers, it's a safe bet that they'll suggest price floors that do in fact raise their profits.)

---

[14]This means that each farm produces those units whose marginal cost is below $\hat{P}$ in Figures 15.12(a) and 15.13.

Figure 15.13

The Welfare Effects of Four Policies Designed to Raise the Price of Milk. All policies represented in this figure raise the price of milk from P_0 to $\underline{P}$, and all create a deadweight loss. The least efficient is the price support program, which causes unused milk to be produced. The other three policies all create the same deadweight loss, but they differ in their benefits to farmers and their cost to the government. The price floor and production quota have the same effects. The voluntary production reduction system gives farmers a larger profit, at the expense of government payments equal to areas C + E + G. Farmers do as well under the voluntary production reduction system as under the price support program, but at a lower cost to the government.

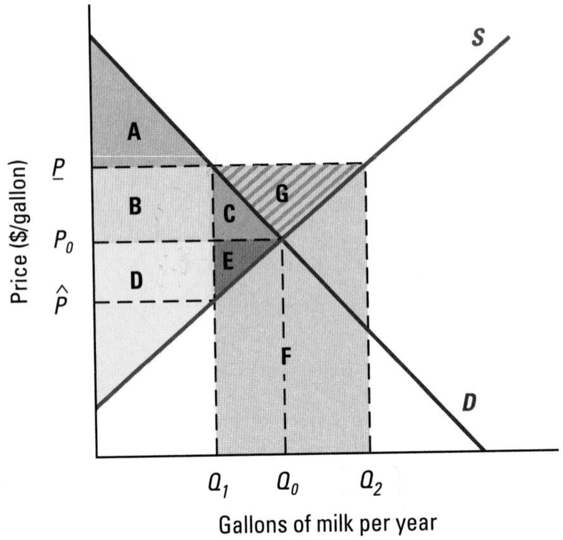

	No intervention	Price floor	Price support	Production quota	Voluntary production reduction
Aggregate surplus	A + B + C + D + E	A + B + D	A + B + D − F	A + B + D	A + B + D
Deadweight loss	0	C + E	C + E + F	C + E	C + E
Consumer surplus	A + B + C	A	A	A	A
Producer surplus	D + E	B + D	B + C + D + E + G	B + D	B + C + D + E + G
Government revenue	0	0	−(C + E + F + G)	0	−(C + E + G)

In some cases, the welfare effects of a price floor can be worse than we have indicated. First, the Q_1 gallons sold with a price floor might not be produced by the least-cost producers. This would raise the costs of production, lowering aggregate surplus. Second, with a binding price floor, producers aren't able to sell as much as they want. Sometimes, they resort to inefficient actions designed to increase their chances of making a sale. For example, under a minimum wage policy that raises the wage above its market equilibrium level, there will be more willing workers than there are jobs. This excess supply of labor can lead to additional inefficiencies, such as workers waiting in line for jobs or filling out excessive numbers of job applications.

Price Supports

Price floors require that the government monitor transactions, since sellers who cannot make sales at the mandated price have an incentive to sell at a lower price. To avoid the need for monitoring, governments often try to increase prices through other means, such as increasing market demand. This policy, known as a **price support** program, is the way the U.S. government has traditionally raised prices for many agricultural crops. For example, the government buys milk powder at an elevated price to support the price of milk. (Unlike liquid milk, milk powder can be stored.) When the government implements price supports, it may end up buying a lot of the good, for which it may have little or no use.

A **price support** program raises the market price by making purchases of the good, thereby increasing demand.

Suppose the government decides to increase the price of milk to $\underline{P}$ using a price support program. As Figure 15.12(b) shows, at that price, the demand is Q_1 gallons per year, while the supply is Q_2 gallons per year. For $\underline{P}$ to be the equilibrium price, the government must therefore buy $Q_2 - Q_1$ gallons of milk each year. By doing so, it shifts the demand curve to $\hat{D}$, as shown in the figure. The amount bought and sold in the new equilibrium is Q_2 gallons. Private parties buy Q_1 gallons, and the government buys the rest.

What are the welfare effects of this policy? That depends on what happens to the gallons that the government buys. If the government has no use for the milk, it will just go to waste. (Officials can't distribute the milk to anyone who would otherwise be willing to buy it at price $\underline{P}$ without undermining the effect of the program.) Figure 15.13 shows the welfare effects of the policy in this case. Aggregate surplus with the price support program is A + B + D − F, so the deadweight loss is C + E + F. The deadweight loss is larger than under the price floor by the amount of area F because, under the price support program, society incurs the cost of producing an extra $Q_2 - Q_1$ gallons of milk that have no use. Consumers are just as well off as with a price floor, but farmers are better off by the amount of areas C + E + G since they get to sell Q_2 instead of Q_1 gallons at price $\underline{P}$. (They are also better off than they would be at the unregulated market equilibrium, by the amount of areas B + C + G.) The government, on the other hand, incurs the expense of buying the extra milk, equal to areas C + E + F + G.

Application 15.4

126 Medallions, 126 Dreams: What Does $292,580.86 Buy You?

Victor Salazar, a 40-year-old Ecuadorian immigrant, was a nervous man in April 2004, just before the City of New York's auction of 126 new taxi medallions.[15] The auction was a rare opportunity to become his own boss, as opposed to just driving for a taxi company. Over the next three years, New York would auction off 900 medallions—the largest

[15]Source: "126 Medallions, 126 Dreams," *The New York Times*, April 24, 2004, p. A11.

increase in the number of medallions since the end of World War II—increasing the total number of cabs from 12,187 to 13,087. Salazar won a medallion in the auction, with a bid that was almost $300,000. The average price of the medallions sold that day was $292,580.86.

The amount Salazar and others were willing to pay tells us that the taxi fares set by New York City's Taxi Commission are a good deal higher than those that would prevail in an unregulated competitive market equilibrium. How much profit would justify spending $292,580.86 on a medallion? At a six percent interest rate, a potential medallion owner could make approximately $17,500 a year by putting that money in the bank. So it's safe to assume that the profit the bidders anticipated was at least that amount.[16]

This knowledge tells us a lot about the degree to which taxi fares in New York exceed the cost of providing taxi service. In 2002, 237 million taxi trips were taken in New York. Total taxi revenue was $1.4 billion, split among 12,187 taxicabs. Thus, the average fare was $5.90 per trip, and each taxi made on average 19,447 trips. If each taxi generated $17,500 a year in profit, it earned a profit of $0.90 per trip. The average cost per trip must therefore be about $5.

Figure 15.14 shows the demand and supply curves for taxi services in New York City. The production of taxi service is simple, requiring little more than a driver and a car. We'll assume, as an approximation, that the supply curve is perfectly elastic. The results of one study of the New York City taxi industry suggest that the elasticity of demand is about −1.2 at the regulated price.[17] Using this elasticity, we can plot a linear demand curve that is consistent with the price of $5.90 per trip and the 237 million trips taken in 2002, along with an elasticity of −1.20. This demand function is $Q^d = 520 - 48P$, where Q^d represents millions of trips demanded per year.[18] As the figure shows, if the price of a taxi trip were instead equal to the $5 marginal cost, 280 million trips would be taken. The deadweight loss, equal to the area of the red triangle, is therefore $19.35 million per year.

Figure 15.14

The Deadweight Loss from Regulated Taxi Fares. Taxi fares set by the New York City Taxi Commission raise price 90 cents above the level that would prevail in a competitive market and lower the number of trips taken by 43 million per year, resulting in an annual deadweight loss of $19.35 million.

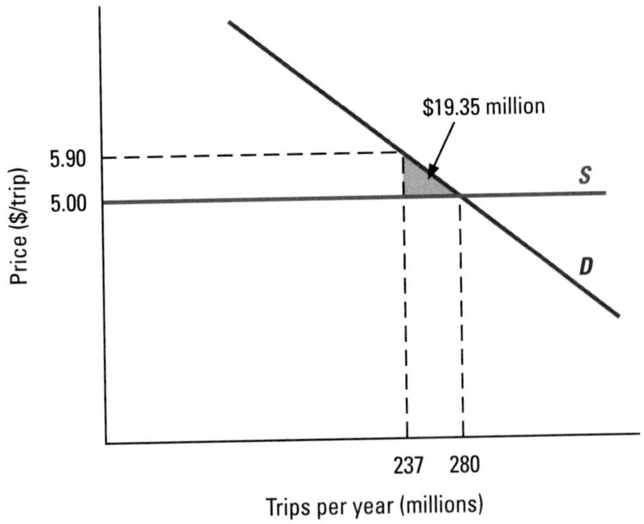

[16]This profit represents the amount bidders could earn above what they would earn if they didn't own a cab and instead worked for a taxi company. That is, it is their profit net of any opportunity cost.

[17]Bruce Schaller, "Elasticities for Taxicab Fares and Service Availability," *Transportation*, 1999, pp. 283–297; Schaller Consulting, *The New York City Taxicab Fact Book*, 2004.

[18]If the demand function has the form $Q^d = A - BP$ and the elasticity of demand is -1.2, then $-1.2 = -B(P/Q) = -B(5.90/237)$, so $B = 48$ (see Section 2.4). Given that, $A = 237 + 48(5.90) = 520$.

Production Quotas

Another way to raise prices without causing the overproduction that occurs under a price support program is to institute **production quotas**. Rather than raising demand, the government limits supply by imposing limits on the quantity that individual firms can produce. For example, the government might pass a law that limits a dairy's production to a certain number of gallons per year. (A quota system was used to raise the price of tobacco for many years, until its elimination in 2004.)

A **production quota** program imposes limits on the quantity that individual firms can produce.

Figure 15.12(c) shows the effect of a production quota that limits farmers to producing a total of Q_l gallons per year. It raises the price to $\underline{P}$ and lowers the amount bought and sold to Q_l. What are the welfare effects of such a quota? The answer depends on how the individual quotas are distributed across individual producers. As long as the individual quotas are assigned to the least-cost producers of the Q_l units, the total avoidable cost of production will equal the area under the market supply curve up to Q_l gallons.[19] As Figure 15.13 shows, in that case aggregate surplus is exactly the same as under a price floor of $\underline{P}$. However, if the quota isn't assigned to the least-cost producers (which could well happen in practice), then the cost of production would be higher, and aggregate surplus lower.

One way to ensure that the Q_l gallons will be produced at the lowest possible cost is to allow producers to trade their quotas, just as in the SO_2 allowance market discussed in Application 14.3 (page 522). The efficiency of a competitive market will guarantee that the quotas will end up in the right hands.

Voluntary Production Reduction Programs

Sometimes the government tries to reduce supply through a **voluntary production reduction** program. In such a program, the government offers inducements to firms to limit their production voluntarily. For example, the government might offer payments to dairy farmers for reducing their production. (For many years the U.S. government paid farmers to leave some of their land unplanted.)

A **voluntary production reduction** program offers firms inducements to reduce their production voluntarily.

To induce a market price of $\underline{P}$, the government must persuade farmers to produce only Q_l gallons. How much money must it offer farmers to reach that goal? Since farmers want to produce Q_2 gallons when the price is $\underline{P}$, they will forgo a profit equal to area C+E+G in Figure 15.13 if they agree to limit their production to Q_l gallons. That is the amount the government must pay them to accept this limit voluntarily.

With this program, the amount bought and sold is Q_l, just as with the quota program. What about the welfare effects? Figure 15.13 shows that aggregate surplus and consumer surplus are the same as under a price floor or quota system (with least-cost production) because the same amount is being produced and consumed in the two cases. But farmers do better than under a price floor or quota system by an amount equal to the government payment. In fact, they do exactly as well as they do under the price support program since the government compensates them to give them the same profit as if they sold their desired output level at price $\underline{P}$. The government, though, does worse than under the quota system since it must make payments to the farmers. Those payments are smaller than under the price support program, however: under the voluntary production reduction program the government must pay farmers only an amount equal to their profit under the price support

[19]Specifically, each farm would be assigned a quota equal to the amount it would supply were the price equal to $\hat{P}$ in Figure 15.12(c). Thus, the total supply would be Q_l, and every gallon supplied would be produced at a marginal cost below $\hat{P}$.

program (area C + E + G); it need not compensate them for the cost of actually producing an additional $Q_2 - Q_1$ gallons (area F).

All these policies create a deadweight loss. The price support program is the worst, because it causes farmers to produce unused milk. The other three programs all create the same deadweight loss (assuming there is least-cost production under the price floor and quota policies). Consumer surplus is the same in all the programs. Farmers do better under price supports or a voluntary production reduction program than under a price floor or quota, but the government does worse since it incurs expenses with those programs. Government expense is lower under a voluntary production reduction program than under a price support program, however.

If all these policies create a deadweight loss, why are they ever enacted? The benefits of raising the price of a good are usually concentrated among a relatively small, easily identified set of people or firms. In contrast, the costs are usually widely dispersed, with only a minute portion borne by each injured party. For example, by one estimate, the U.S. government paid farmers roughly \$3 billion from 1995 to 2005 under its various dairy programs. Yet that amounted to only about \$10 for each American. As a result, those who are negatively affected by such policies may have little economic incentive to oppose their enactment, while those who benefit have an incentive to lobby for them. (Those who are harmed by the policy face a "free rider" problem, which we discuss in Chapter 20.)

Application 15.5

U.S. Dairy Price Supports

In Application 15.3 we studied the effect of the MILC subsidy program. We saw that it tends to increase the supply of milk and to lower the price to some degree. But two other U.S. dairy programs instead ensure that the price of milk will increase rather than decrease. The U.S. Agriculture Department's Milk Marketing Orders set a price floor for milk by region. These price floors are sometimes above and sometimes below the \$1.46 level that triggers MILC program payments. Furthermore, the Dairy Price Support Program (DPSP) allows milk processors to sell processed milk products, such as nonfat dry milk, cheese, and butter, to the government at a set minimum price, so that all the milk produced in response to a relatively high Marketing Order price can be sold. Together, these two programs amount to a price support program. Exercise 15.11 at the end of this chapter asks you to determine their effect using the market demand curve and (MILC-program induced) market supply curve.

WORKED-OUT PROBLEM 15.2

The Problem The market demand function for corn is $Q^d = 15 - 2P$ and the market supply function is $Q^s = 5P - 2.5$, both measured in billions of bushels per year. Suppose the government wants to raise the price to \$3 per bushel. Describe how it could do this with a price ceiling, a price support program, a quota, and a voluntary production reduction program. What would be the welfare consequences of each of these policies?

The Solution As in worked-out problem 15.1 (page 549), the equilibrium absent intervention has a price of \$2.50 per bushel and 10 billion bushels bought and sold each year. At a price of \$3 per bushel, consumers demand 9 billion bushels while farmers want to supply 12.5 billion bushels. The price ceiling policy would simply state that corn can't be sold for less than \$3 per bushel. The price support program would have the government purchase 3.5 billion bushels each year, the difference between the quantities supplied and demanded at a price of \$3. The quota would distribute 9 billion bushels of quotas to farmers (ideally in a manner that minimizes the cost of producing those bushels). In the voluntary production reduction program, the government would pay farmers to reduce their production from 12.5 to 9 billion bushels per year. To calculate the required payment we need to find the area corresponding to C + E + G in Figure 15.13 (using the supply curve for corn). Figure 15.15 shows that the sum of those areas is \$1.23 billion.

The welfare effects from each policy can be found by calculating the areas corresponding to areas A–G in Figure 15.13. Figure 15.15 shows these amounts.

IN-TEXT EXERCISE 15.2 **The market demand function for corn is $Q^d = 15 - 2P$ and the market supply function is $Q^s = 5P - 6$, both measured in billions of bushels per year. Suppose the government wants to raise the price to \$4 per bushel. Describe how it could do this with a price ceiling, a price support program, a quota, and a voluntary production reduction program. What would be the welfare consequences of each of these policies?**

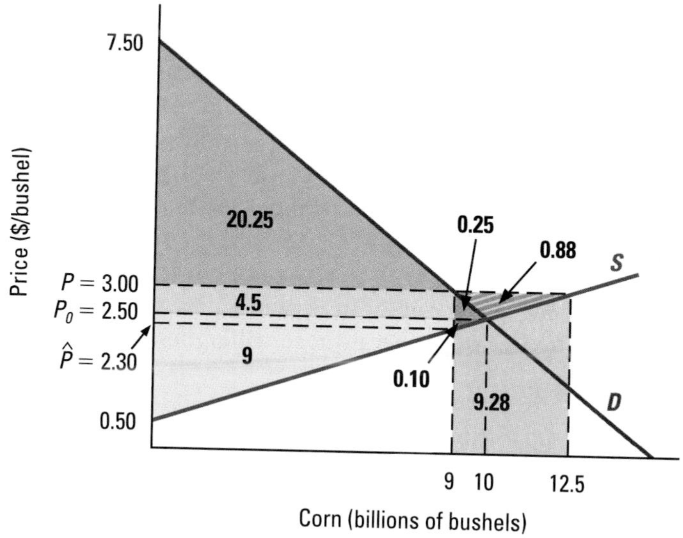

Figure 15.15
Welfare Effects of Raising the Price of Corn. The figure shows the areas corresponding to areas A–G in Figure 15.13 for the demand and supply curves in worked-out problem 15.2.

Policies that Lower Prices

In this section we've focused on policies designed to raise prices. Sometimes governments adopt policies that are designed instead to *lower* prices, in order to improve the

Figure 15.16

A Price Ceiling. If the government imposes a price ceiling on apartment rents equal to $\bar{P}$, the number of available apartments—and hence, the number rented—falls from Q_0 to Q_1. The resulting deadweight loss equals the red-shaded area.

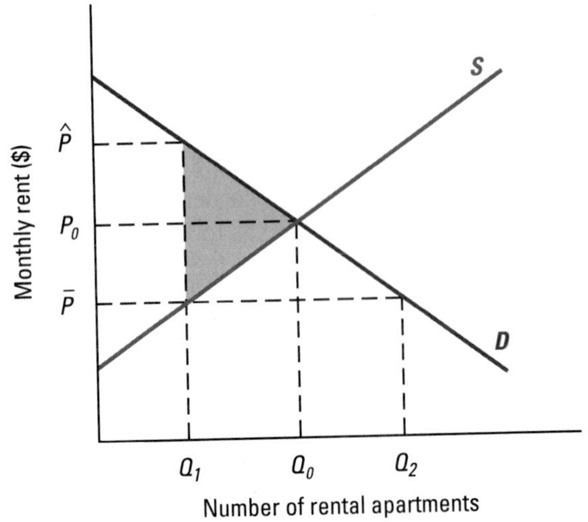

well-being of buyers. For example, some U.S. cities have rent control laws that put a price ceiling on rents. We can analyze the effects of these policies in much the same way that we evaluated the effects of policies that raise prices. As an illustration, Figure 15.16 shows the effects of a price ceiling equal to $\bar{P}$, which is below the unregulated competitive equilibrium monthly rent for an apartment, P_0. (In reality, most cities' rent control policies apply to some, but not all rental apartments; for simplicity, we assume it applies to all apartments here.) Figure 15.16 shows that the policy reduces the number of apartments landlords make available for rent to Q_1. Some former rental apartments may be sold, and fewer new apartments will be built.[20] Since supply is less than demand at the price $\bar{P}$, the amount supplied determines the equilibrium quantity (trade requires both sides to agree). That quantity falls from Q_0 to Q_1. Figure 15.16 also shows the red-shaded deadweight loss, assuming that the Q_1 apartments are rented by the consumers whose willingness to pay for them is greatest.[21] If they are not, then the deadweight loss would be greater.

IN-TEXT EXERCISE 15.3 **Draw a graph to show the effect on the consumer and producer surpluses of the price ceiling in Figure 15.16, assuming that the Q_1 apartments are rented by the consumers whose willingness to pay for them is greatest.**

Because buyers can't buy all that they want at the ceiling price, sometimes they take inefficient actions that increase the deadweight loss. For example, with rent control, renters who want to secure an apartment may wake up at five in the morning to scan the apartment rental ads before others do. There is also another loss that can occur with price ceilings that does not arise with price floors: since sellers face excess demand for their products, each will be able to make sales even if their products are not as good as those of competitors. As a result, sellers have an incentive to inefficiently degrade the quality

[20]Cities adopting rent control often try to limit this reduction by prohibiting currently rented apartments from being sold. Even so, over the long run, the supply of rental apartments is reduced as the policy leads to fewer new apartments being built.

[21]Specifically, the consumers who rent the apartments should be those whose willingness to pay exceeds $\hat{P}$ in the figure.

of their products. For example, a common complaint about rent-controlled apartments is that they receive little maintenance and no renovations.

15.3 IMPORT TARIFFS AND QUOTAS

Many countries discourage the importation of goods through tariffs or quotas. A **tariff** is a tax on imports. For example, the United States imposes a tariff of 29.7 cents on each gallon-equivalent of frozen concentrated orange juice (FCOJ). In June 2003, this tariff was almost 34 percent of the U.S. price of FCOJ. A **quota** directly limits the total amount of a good that can be imported. For example, the U.S. government effectively limits raw sugar imports to 1.227 million metric tons per year.

A **tariff** is a tax on imports. A **quota** directly limits the total quantity of a good that can be imported.

In some cases, governments use a mix of tariffs and quotas. The simplest mixed policy consists of a quota that limits imports, combined with a tariff on those goods allowed into the country. In the United States, cheddar cheese and a number of other dairy products are protected by this type of arrangement. Another example is a policy called a tariff-rate quota under which imports below the quota qualify for a low (or no) tariff; while imports above the quota are subject to a higher tariff. The import fee structure in the U.S.-Canadian Softwood Lumber Agreement (discussed in Applications 9.3 and 14.1, as well as later in this section) is an example of this type of arrangement.

Tariffs

A tariff is a tax on sellers in a market. Unlike the taxes we studied in Section 15.1, however, a tariff is imposed only on *some* sellers—the foreign ones.

Consider the domestic market for sugar. Figure 15.17(a) shows the market supply curve without a tariff or quota. The domestic producers' supply curve is S^d. We'll assume that this country consumes a small share of the world's production of sugar, so that it doesn't affect the world price, P_W. As a result, the import supply curve is horizontal at price P_W. If the domestic price is below P_W, foreign producers won't want to sell anything in this country. If it's above P_W, they'll want to sell all their production here. Without the tariff, the market supply curve is therefore the dark red curve S_0.

Figure 15.17(b) shows the effect of a tariff of T dollars per ton. The vertical axis measures the domestic price (the price paid by consumers and received by domestic firms). The tariff shifts the import supply curve upward by the distance T since foreign firms must now sell their goods for $P_W + T$ to be willing to sell anything in the country. The new market supply curve is therefore the dark red curve S_T. Without the tariff, the domestic equilibrium price equals the world price, $P_0 = P_W$, and domestic consumers buy Q_0 tons of sugar. Of those tons, Q_0^d are supplied by domestic producers; foreign producers supply the remaining $(Q_0 - Q_0^d)$ tons. With the tariff, the domestic equilibrium price rises to $P_T = P_W + T$, and domestic consumers buy only Q_T tons of sugar. However, the amount sold by domestic producers increases to Q_T^d. Imports decline to $(Q_T - Q_T^d)$.

Figure 15.18 shows the welfare effects of this policy. We'll take the perspective of the domestic government, which is concerned only with **domestic aggregate surplus**, the sum of consumer surplus, domestic producer surplus, and government revenue. (A dollar of government revenue counts as a dollar of aggregate surplus.) Without the tariff, consumer surplus equals the area A + B + C + D + E; with the tariff it is only area A. So consumers are worse off under the tariff. Domestic firms, though, are better off: they

Domestic aggregate surplus is the sum of consumer surplus, domestic producer surplus, and government revenue.

Figure 15.17

The Effects of a Tariff. Figure (a) shows the market supply of sugar without a tariff. The domestic producers' supply curve is S^d. Because the country's production is only a small share of world demand, it doesn't affect the world price, P_W. The import supply curve is horizontal at price P_W. The market supply curve is the dark red curve S_0. Figure (b) shows the effect of a tariff. It shifts the import supply curve upward by the distance T, which shifts the market supply to curve S_T. Without the tariff, the price is P_W, and Q_0 tons are bought and sold, of which Q_0^d are supplied by domestic firms. With the tariff, the price rises to $P_W + T$, and Q_T tons are bought and sold, of which Q_T^d are supplied by domestic firms.

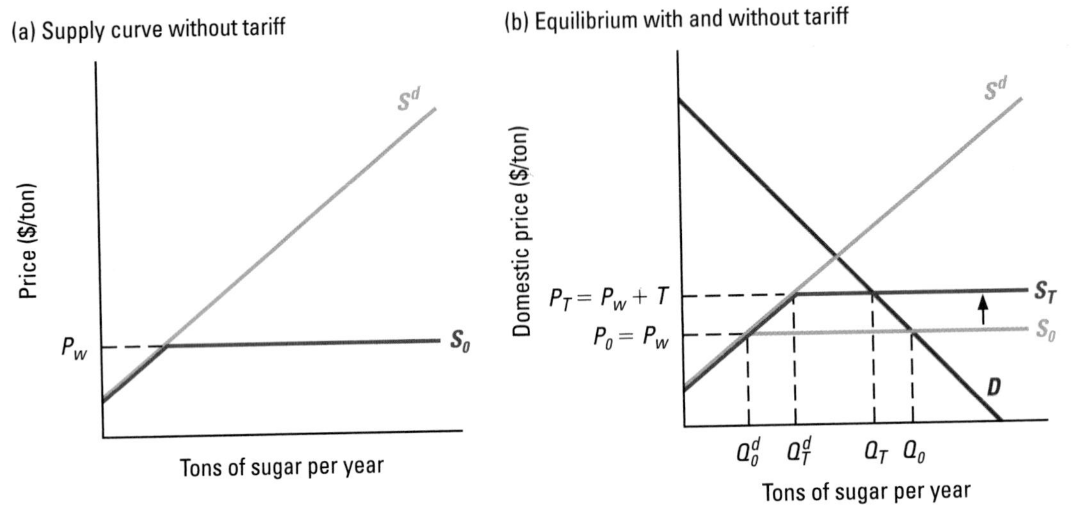

have a producer surplus equal to area B + F with the tariff, compared to area F without it. The government receives revenue equal to the area of rectangle D, which is the quantity of imports $(Q_T - Q_T^d)$ times the tariff T.

While consumers lose areas B + C + D + E under the tariff, only areas B and D are captured by domestic firms and the government. The remaining part of their loss, areas C and E, is the domestic deadweight loss from the tariff. Area E represents the surplus lost because of the reduction in total consumption: it is the difference between consumers' willingness to pay for the $(Q_0 - Q_T)$ tons of sugar they no longer purchase and the cost of that sugar. Since those units are imported, their cost per unit equals the world price P_W. This loss is similar to the deadweight loss from taxation that we encountered in Section 15.1. Area C represents the loss that arises because $(Q_T^d - Q_0^d)$ tons that were previously imported at a cost of P_W per unit are now produced by domestic firms at a higher cost. That is, the tariff causes production to be allocated inefficiently away from foreign producers and toward domestic producers.

Quotas

A quota limits the supply of imports to some maximum $\bar{Q}$. As Figure 15.19 shows, if the government limits imports to a maximum of $(Q_T - Q_T^d)$ tons [the same amounts as in Figure 15.17(b)], the domestic price of sugar will end up being the same $(P_T = P_W + T)$ as if it imposed a tariff of T per ton. That quota produces the market supply curve labeled

Figure 15.18

The Welfare Effects of a Tariff. This figure and the accompanying table summarize the welfare effects of a tariff on sugar. Because of the price increase, consumer surplus decreases by an amount equal to area B + C + D + E. Domestic firms' producer surplus increases by area B, and the government gains tariff revenue equal to area D. Domestic aggregate surplus shrinks by an amount equal to areas C + E.

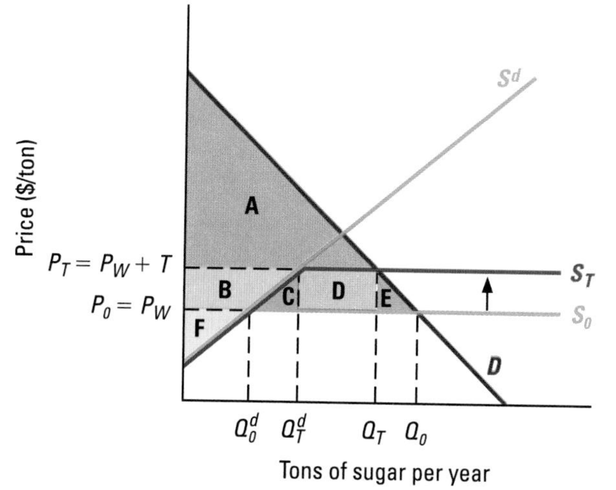

	Without tariff	With tariff
Domestic aggregate surplus	A + B + C + D + E + F	A + B + D + F
Domestic deadweight loss	0	C + E
Consumer surplus	A + B + C + D + E	A
Domestic producer surplus	F	B + F
Government revenue	0	D

S_Q in the figure. (If the price is below P_W, only domestic producers are willing to supply sugar; if the price is above P_W, foreign supply will equal the quota level.)

Consumers and domestic firms are both as well off with the quota as with the tariff. The difference is that with a quota, the government doesn't receive any revenue. Instead, that revenue is earned by whichever foreign firms are lucky enough to be allowed to import their goods. So a quota results in a lower aggregate domestic surplus than a tariff.

If instead, the government were to allocate the right to import those $(Q_T - Q_T^d)$ tons to domestic firms that can buy the good abroad at the world price, then those revenues would increase domestic firms' producer surplus. Aggregate domestic surplus would then be the same with a tariff as with a quota. Another approach with equivalent consequences would be to sell the rights to import those $(Q_T - Q_T^d)$ tons to foreign firms for T dollars per ton.

Beneficial Trade Barriers

When the supply of imports is perfectly elastic, tariffs and quotas must lower aggregate domestic surplus. Sometimes, however, the import supply curve is upward sloping. For example, a large share of Canadian softwood lumber production is exported to the United States. Due to the high cost of shipping lumber overseas, there is not much other foreign demand for that lumber. As a result, changes in U.S. imports from Canada affect the price of Canadian softwood lumber, and the import supply curve of softwood lumber into the United States is upward sloping (see Application 14.1). When the import supply curve

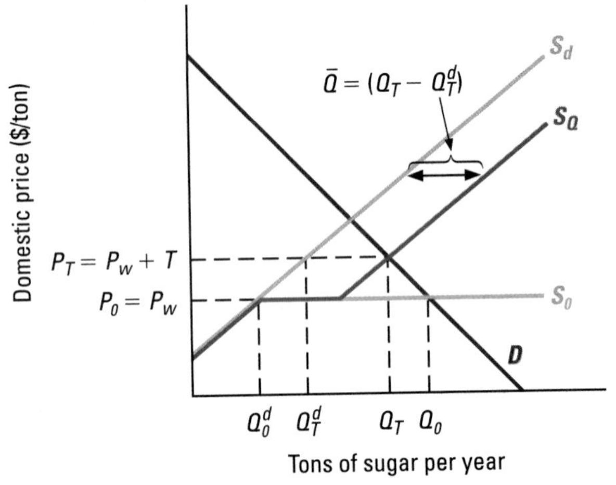

Figure 15.19
The Effects of a Quota. By limiting imports to $(Q_T - Q_T^d)$ tons, a quota produces the same equilibrium price, consumption, and production levels as a tariff of T per ton [compare Figure 15.17(b)]. Consumers and domestic firms are equally well off with a quota as with a tariff. The government, however, earns no tariff revenue with a quota. Instead, that gain goes to the foreign producers who are allowed to import their goods.

is upward sloping, a country can sometimes increase its domestic aggregate surplus by imposing a tariff or quota.

To see why, consider a situation in which there are *no* domestic producers of a good. In that case, a tariff is just a tax on all sellers. Look back now at Figure 15.6 (page 548). The effects of a tariff on welfare will therefore be exactly the same as in that figure. The difference, however, is that this government cares only about domestic aggregate surplus, or the sum of consumer surplus and government revenue (it doesn't count foreign firms' profits). Domestic aggregate surplus equals area C + D + E without the tariff, and area C + D + F with the tariff (consumer surplus is C + D, and the government's tariff revenue is F). If area F is larger than area E, the tariff will increase domestic aggregate surplus.

This idea applies even if there are some domestic producers. The key point is that when the import supply curve is upward sloping, a government can reduce the amount that foreign firms receive for their goods by imposing a tariff.[22] Sometimes the domestic benefit from this effect exceeds the deadweight loss that the tariff creates.

Application 15.6

The Effects of the U.S.-Canadian Softwood Lumber Agreement

In Application 14.1 (page 501), we saw how the U.S.-Canadian Softwood Lumber Agreement (SLA) affected the market supply curve for softwood lumber in the United States in 1998. Let's see now what effect it had on market equilibrium and social welfare.

---

[22] In essence, the domestic government is in the position of a monopsonist relative to the foreign suppliers (see Section 17.6 for a discussion of monopsonists).

Figure 15.20 shows again the market demand curve and various supply curves, both with and without the SLA from Figure 14.3. As before, the dark red curve labeled S is the market supply curve with the SLA, and the dashed dark red line shows how it would differ at prices above \$240 without the SLA. The other supply curves are those of U.S. producers, Canadian producers in the four provinces affected by the SLA, and other foreign producers. The market supply curve is the sum of those three supply curves.

Under the SLA, the market equilibrium in 1998 resulted in a price of \$354 per thousand board feet (point B in Figure 15.20). U.S. consumers bought 52.9 billion board feet of softwood lumber that year. U.S. producers supplied 34.2 billion of that total. Canadian producers from the affected provinces exported 15.35 billion board feet to the United States, coinciding with the quantity at which the fee rises from \$50 to \$100 per thousand board feet. The remaining 3.35 billion came from other foreign sources.

To determine the effects of the SLA, we first need to determine the equilibrium that would have prevailed in its absence. The market demand curve in Figure 15.20 represents the linear function

$$Q^d = 61.9 - 0.0254P$$

This demand function has an elasticity of $-.17$ at the market equilibrium, which matches published elasticity estimates. The supply curves represent linear supply functions chosen to match published elasticity estimates.[23] The U.S. producers' supply function is

$$Q^s_{U.S.} = 15.4 + 0.0531P$$

and the other foreign producers' supply function is

$$Q^s_{other} = 0.8 + 0.0076P$$

Without the SLA, the Canadian producers' supply function is

$$Q^s_{Cdn} = 3.5 + 0.0465P$$

Without the SLA, the market supply function would therefore have been $Q^s = 19.7 + 0.1072P$, the sum of the no-SLA supply functions of the three groups of producers. Setting demand equal to supply,

$$61.9 - 0.0254P = 19.7 + 0.1072P$$

and solving, we find that the no-SLA equilibrium price would have been \$318 per thousand board feet. Substituting that price into the demand function, we see that U.S. consumers would have bought 53.8 billion board feet of softwood lumber without the SLA (point A in Figure 15.20). Substituting the same price into the three groups' supply functions, we see that 32.3 billion of that amount would have been supplied by U.S. producers, 18.3 billion by firms in the four affected Canadian provinces, and 3.2 billion by other foreign producers.

Consumer surplus fell by \$1.9 billion as a result of the SLA. [To calculate this amount, first convert the prices into dollars per board foot. Consumer surplus then equals the area of a trapezoid with a height of \$0.036 = (0.354 − 0.318), one base of 52.9 billion, and another base of 53.8 billion.] Domestic producer surplus increased by \$1.2 billion [equal to the area of a trapezoid with a height of \$0.036, one base of 32.3 billion, and another base of 34.2 billion]. Under the agreement, the Canadian government, not the U.S. government, collected the tariff, so U.S. domestic aggregate surplus fell by \$700 million. So this is a case in which the trade barrier lowered domestic aggregate surplus, even though the import supply curve was upward sloping. (In fact, the Canadian government collected only \$49 million in tariff fees, so domestic aggregate surplus would have fallen even if the U.S. government had received these payments.)

What about Canadian domestic aggregate surplus? Canadian producers from the four affected provinces earned an additional \$606 million (U.S.), not including the SLA fees. Since the \$49 million in fees were just a transfer to the Canadian government, they had no affect on Canada's domestic aggregate surplus. So by raising the price of softwood lumber in the United States, the SLA increased Canada's domestic aggregate surplus by \$606 million. (This analysis ignores any welfare effects arising from induced changes in the market for softwood lumber in Canada.) Other foreign producers' profits increased by \$118 million.

[23]See D. Zhang, "Welfare Impacts of the 1996 United States—Canada Softwood Lumber (Trade) Agreement," *Canadian Journal of Forest Research* 31, November 2001, pp. 1958–1967.

Figure 15.20

The Effects of the U.S.-Canadian Softwood Lumber Agreement in 1998. In 1998, the U.S.-Canadian Softwood Lumber Agreement shifted the market equilibrium from point A to point B. U.S. producer surplus increased by $1.2 billion, but consumer surplus fell by $1.9 billion, reducing domestic aggregate surplus by $700 million. Canadian aggregate surplus, on the other hand, increased by $606 million.

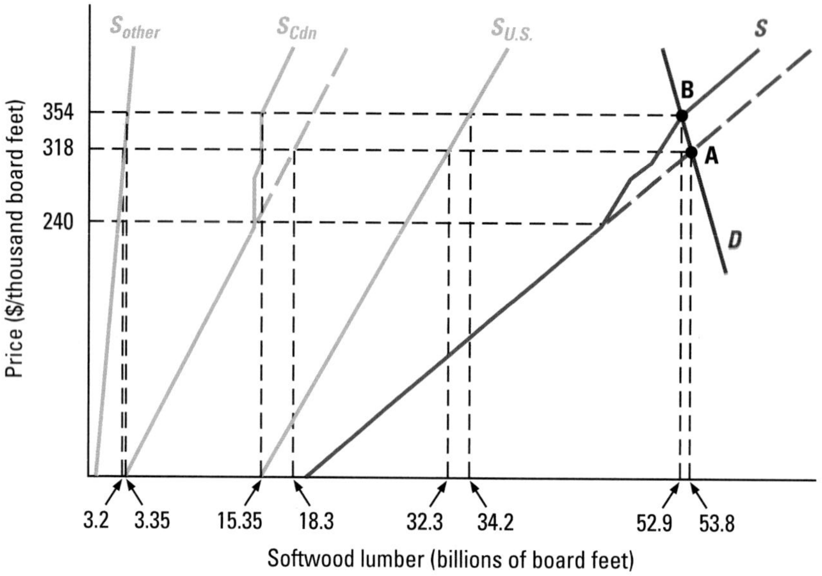

CHAPTER SUMMARY

1. **Taxes (and subsidies)**

   a. A specific tax is a fixed dollar amount that must be paid for each unit bought or sold. An ad valorem tax is a tax that is stated as a percentage of the good's price.

   b. The effects of a tax are independent of who is legally required to pay it, whether buyers or sellers.

   c. A tax lowers the amount of a good bought and sold, raises the total amount that buyers pay per unit, and lowers the amount that sellers receive per unit. It also causes a deadweight loss because some units that buyers value more than the cost of production are not produced.

   d. The economic incidence of a tax depends on the shapes of the demand and supply curves. The more elastic is demand and the less elastic is supply, the smaller the share of the tax borne by consumers. For small taxes, consumers' share of the tax is $E^s/(E^s - E^d)$.

   e. Consumer surplus and producer surplus both fall because of a tax. The amount of this shortfall is greater than the government's revenue from the tax. The difference between the two amounts is the deadweight loss.

   f. To minimize the deadweight loss from taxation, goods that have more inelastic demands and supplies should be taxed more heavily than other goods.

   g. A subsidy is a payment that reduces the amount buyers need to pay or increases the amount sellers receive. Subsidies increase the amount of a good bought and sold. They also create a deadweight loss, because some units that consumers value less than the cost of production are produced and consumed.

2. **Policies designed to raise prices**

a. A price floor establishes a minimum price that sellers can charge. If it is above the equilibrium price without the floor, sellers will want to supply more than buyers are willing to purchase at that price. In principle, a price floor may either raise or lower sellers' total profits.

b. A price support raises the price of a good by increasing the demand for it. Price supports can result in the government buying units for which it has little or no use.

c. A production quota imposes limits on the amount of a good that individual firms can produce.

d. A voluntary production reduction program offers firms an inducement to voluntarily reduce their production.

e. All these ways of raising the price create a deadweight loss. The price support policy creates the largest deadweight loss; the other programs create the same deadweight loss (assuming that quotas are distributed efficiently or can be traded and that production is efficient under the price floor).

f. Sometimes governments instead want to lower the price of a good. A price ceiling is one example of a policy that governments use for this purpose. With a price ceiling that is below the equilibrium price without the floor, sellers will want to supply less than buyers are willing to purchase at that price. The equilibrium quantity falls, creating a deadweight loss.

3. **Import tariffs and quotas**

a. A tariff is a tax on imports. A quota places direct limits on the total amount of a good that can be imported.

b. Domestic aggregate surplus is the sum of consumer surplus, domestic firms' producer surplus, and government revenue.

c. If the import supply curve is horizontal at the world price (that is, if it is infinitely elastic), a tariff will lower domestic aggregate surplus.

d. An appropriately chosen quota can produce the same market equilibrium as a tariff. The only difference is that the government does not receive any revenue with a quota (unless it sells the rights to import the good). Instead, foreign firms lucky enough to import their goods receive the benefit.

e. If the import supply curve is upward sloping, a tariff (or quota) can increase domestic aggregate surplus.

ADDITIONAL EXERCISES

Exercise 15.1: The market demand function for corn is $Q^d = 15 - 2P$ and the market supply function is $Q^s = 5P - 2.5$, both measured in billions of bushels per year. Suppose the government imposes a \$2.10 tax per bushel. What will be the effects on aggregate surplus, consumer surplus, and producer surplus? What will be the deadweight loss created by the tax?

Exercise 15.2: Compare your answers to exercise 15.1 and in-text exercise 15.1 with the answer to worked-out problem 15.1. In each case, compute the ratio of the deadweight loss to tax revenue. What happens as the tax grows larger?

Exercise 15.3: Is a tax on luxury cars a more efficient way to raise revenue (in the sense of creating a small deadweight loss) than a tax on all car purchases? Why or why not?

Exercise 15.4: In a market with free entry and exit, who bears the burden of a tax? Given this fact, how might tax incidence differ in the short and long run?

Exercise 15.5: Consider again worked-out problem 14.2 (page 509). Suppose that starting at the initial long-run equilibrium with a price of \$11.50 and 100 active firms, the government requires firms to pay a tax of \$11.50 per pizza. What is the effect of the tax on the amounts paid by buyers and sellers in the short run? What is the government revenue? What is the deadweight loss? What about in the long run?

Exercise 15.6: Use a graph to show that, when the government increases the tax on a good, the sum of the change in consumer surplus plus the change in producer surplus plus the change in government revenue equals the change in the deadweight loss. Verify that this relationship holds by comparing the answers to worked-out problem 15.1 and in-text exercise 15.1.

Exercise 15.7: The market demand and supply functions for corn are the same as in exercise 15.1. Suppose the government gives corn farmers a \$0.70 subsidy per bushel of corn. What will be the effects on aggregate surplus, consumer surplus, and producer surplus? What will be the deadweight loss created by the subsidy?

Exercise 15.8: Suppose the government passes an operating tax, which requires that each active firm in a market pay an annual fee of F dollars. What effect will this tax have in the short run? In the long run?

Exercise 15.9: The market demand and supply functions for corn are the same as in exercise 15.1. Suppose the government wants to raise the price of corn to \$3. What are the welfare effects of a price floor, price support, production quota, and voluntary production reduction program?

Exercise 15.10: Suppose that the demand function for pizzas is $Q^d = 65{,}800 - 1{,}200P$ and the supply function is $Q^s = 4{,}000P - 20{,}000$. Suppose the pizza parlor lobby is effective at lobbying the government, which institutes a price floor of \$15 on pizzas. Assuming that the least-cost pizza producers are the ones to produce the demanded pizzas, what is the effect on the aggregate, consumer, and producer surpluses? What if instead the government raised the price to \$15 using a price support program?

Exercise 15.11: Suppose that the MILC program (described in Application 15.3) had no cap. Given the demand and supply functions described in Application 15.3, how much would the government need to buy to raise the price of milk to \$1.40 per gallon under a price support program? What would be the effects on aggregate surplus, consumer surplus, producer surplus, and government revenue?

Exercise 15.12: Suppose that the demand function for pizzas is $Q^d = 65{,}800 - 1{,}200P$ and the supply function is $Q^s = 4{,}000P - 20{,}000$. Suppose the College Student Party is elected and places a price ceiling on pizza of \$10 per pizza. How many pizzas will be bought and sold? Assuming that the highest willingness to pay consumers are the ones to consume the supplied pizzas, what will the effect be the effect on the aggregate, consumer, and producer surpluses?

Exercise 15.13: The market demand and supply functions for corn are the same as in exercise 15.1. What would be the welfare effects of a policy that put a cap of \$2 per bushel on the price farmers can charge for corn?

Exercise 15.14: The market demand and domestic supply functions for corn are the same as in exercise 15.1. Suppose the import supply curve is infinitely elastic at a price of \$1.50 per bushel. What would be the welfare effects of a \$0.50 per bushel tariff?

Exercise 15.15: Suppose the import supply curve of a good is infinitely elastic at the world price. Draw a graph to show the welfare effect of a subsidy on imports.

Exercise 15.16: Suppose the supply curve of imports is infinitely elastic at the world price. Using a graph, show how high a tariff the country must set to completely prevent imports from coming into the country.

Exercise 15.17: Is there any benefit to a country (in terms of its domestic aggregate surplus) from subsidizing firms that export to another country when the market in that other country is perfectly competitive?

APPENDIX

TAX INCIDENCE AND AD VALOREM TAXES

In this appendix we discuss two topics. First, we derive formula (1), showing the share of the tax burden borne by consumers with a specific tax. Then, we show how to analyze ad valorem taxes.

Tax Incidence with a Specific Tax

When the government imposes a specific tax of T dollars per unit, the reduction in demand must equal the reduction in supply. For small taxes, the reduction in demand is equal to the elasticity of demand times the percentage change in the price buyers pay, $(\Delta P_b/P_0)$, where P_0 is the initial no-tax equilibrium price and $\Delta P_b = P_b - P_0$ is the increase in the amount buyers pay per unit. So:

$$\text{Change in demand} = E^d\left(\frac{\Delta P_b}{P_0}\right)$$

Likewise, the change in supply is equal to the elasticity of supply times the percentage change in the price firms receive:

$$\text{Change in supply} = E^s\left(\frac{\Delta P_s}{P_0}\right)$$

Since $\Delta P_s = P_s - P_0 = (P_b - T) - P_0 = \Delta P_b - T$, we can rewrite the change in supply as

$$\text{Change in supply} = E^s\left[\left(\frac{\Delta P_b}{P_0}\right) - \left(\frac{T}{P_0}\right)\right]$$

Since the change in demand must equal the change in supply, we know that:

$$E^d\left(\frac{\Delta P_b}{P_0}\right) = E^s\left[\left(\frac{\Delta P_b}{P_0}\right) - \left(\frac{T}{P_0}\right)\right]$$

Solving this formula for ΔP_b we find that:

$$\Delta P_b = \left(\frac{E^s}{E^s - E^d}\right)T$$

That is, the increase in the total amount that buyers pay per unit, ΔP_b, is the fraction $E^s/(E^s - E^d)$ of the per-unit tax T.

Tax Incidence with an Ad Valorem Tax

An ad valorem tax, whether it is paid by consumers or firms, is usually stated as a percentage of the amount received by firms. For example, if a store charges \$100 for a sweater, a 5 percent sales tax requires that the consumer pay \$105 in total.

Figure 15.21 shows the effects of an ad valorem tax on gasoline that requires consumers to pay *t* percent of the amount firms charge. As before, we can find the effect of the tax by identifying the total price paid by consumers, P_b, at which demand equals supply. With the vertical axis measuring the price paid by consumers, the tax shifts the supply curve upward to the curve labeled S_t. For example, without the tax firms supply Q_0 gallons when the price is P_0. With the tax, consumers must pay $P_b = (1 + t)P_0$ for firms to receive P_0 per gallon. So, with the tax, firms supply Q_0 gallons at the price $(1 + t)P_0$.

Note that the higher the price, the larger the shift in the supply curve. To the left of Q_0 (for example, at Q_t), the supply curve shifts upward by less than it does at Q_0. This is because at the lower prices needed to induce firms to supply those smaller quantities, the fixed-percentage tax is a smaller payment. To the right of Q_0, the shift upward is larger, because the fixed-percentage tax is greater at the higher prices needed to induce firms to supply those larger quantities.

With an ad valorem tax, then, the tax collected per gallon depends on the equilibrium price. In Figure 15.21, at the equilibrium point B consumers pay P_b per gallon, including the tax. Firms receive $P_s = P_b/(1 + t)$ per unit. The difference between those two amounts, $P_b - [P_b/(1 + t)] = t[P_b/(1 + t)] = tP_s$, is the tax consumers pay on each gallon of gas they buy. The total tax collected by the government is that amount times the number of gallons consumers buy, Q_t, which equals the gray-shaded area in the figure. As

Figure 15.21

The Effects of an Ad Valorem Tax. Without the ad valorem tax of *t* percent of the amount received by firms, the market price would be P_0 and Q_0 gallons of gas would be bought and sold. The tax causes an upward shift in the supply curve that is larger at higher prices. With the tax, consumers pay P_b per gallon, while firms receive $P_s = P_b/(1 + t)$ per gallon. The gray-shaded area represents the total tax collected. The tax causes consumers to pay more per gallon and firms to receive less per gallon. The total of those two amounts equals the tax per gallon at the new market equilibrium, which equals tP_s.

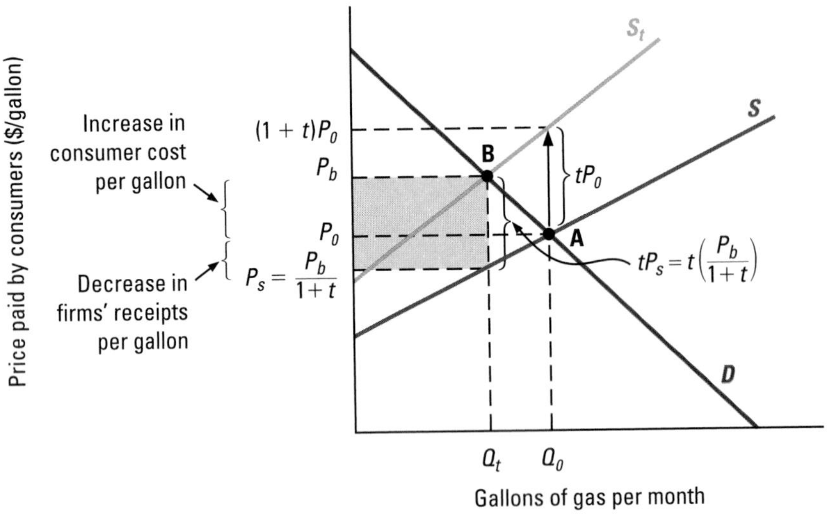

before, consumers pay more in total for each gallon of gas they buy because of the tax (P_b exceeds P_0), and firms receive less for each gallon they sell [$P_s = P_b/(1 + t)$, which is less than P_0]. As the figure shows, the sum of these two amounts equals the tax collected per gallon.

As with a specific tax, the effect of an ad valorem tax is the same no matter who pays it. If firms were to pay a tax of t percent on the amount they charge consumers, the shift in the supply curve would be exactly the same as that shown in Figure 15.21, and the equilibrium point with the tax would also be the same.

16

General Equilibrium, Efficiency, and Equity

Learning Objectives

After reading this chapter, students should be able to:

- Explain how general equilibrium analysis helps economists to understand interdependence among markets.
- Use a simple general equilibrium model to answer positive economic questions.
- Identify criteria for answering normative economic questions.
- Describe how competitive markets achieve efficient exchange and efficient production in general equilibriium.
- Discuss how the goals of equity and efficiency can come into conflict.

Between January 2004 and October 2005, a span of only 19 months, the average price of regular gasoline in the United States nearly doubled, from $1.49 to $2.92 per gallon. The impact on the market for new automobiles was dramatic. American car buyers reconsidered their long-term love affair with gas-guzzling pickup trucks and sport utility vehicles (SUVs), turning instead to smaller, more fuel-efficient models. This development spelled trouble for American car manufacturers like General Motors and Ford, for whom pickup trucks and SUVs had long been a mainstay. Asian rivals like Toyota and Honda, which had placed much greater emphasis on developing more economical vehicles, suddenly found themselves in far better competitive positions. Toyota was unable to keep pace with the booming demand for its ground-breaking hybrid car, the Prius, and even Camrys flew out of showrooms as quickly as dealers could stock them. In July 2006, Toyota overtook Ford as the world's second-largest automobile manufacturer and set its sights on General Motors.

Just as the popularity of pickup trucks and SUVs stimulated the demand for gasoline and contributed to the longer-term rise in gasoline prices, over time the shift to more fuel-efficient cars will reduce the demand for gasoline (or at least moderate the rate of increase) and relieve some of the pressure on gasoline prices. Thus gasoline and automobile markets are highly interdependent.

General equilibrium analysis—the subject of this chapter—provides tools for thinking about the ways in which developments in one market affect others, and how these effects ripple between markets and produce feedback into the original market. It also leads to some important conclusions about the performance of competitive markets and the appropriate economic roles for government. In this chapter we'll cover six topics:

1. *The nature of general equilibrium.* General equilibrium analysis is the study of competitive equilibrium in two or more markets at the same time. As we'll see, it allows us to understand the consequences of interdependence between markets.
2. *Positive analysis of general equilibrium.* Economists are often asked to determine how prices and quantities will respond to changes in the economic environment. Answers based on partial equilibrium analysis are often incomplete. We'll explain how to answer positive questions more accurately through general equilibrium analysis.
3. *Normative criteria for evaluating economic performance.* Good economic institutions avoid waste while treating all members of society fairly. We'll explain how economists think about these two dimensions of economic performance.
4. *General equilibrium and efficient exchange.* Competitive markets allocate consumption goods efficiently among consumers. We'll show why any reallocation of goods in a competitive market hurts at least one consumer.
5. *General equilibrium and efficient production.* Competitive markets also assure efficient production. We'll explain why any other use of the available inputs in a competitive market reduces the output of at least one good, and hurts at least one consumer.
6. *Equity and redistribution.* A competitive equilibrium is only as fair as the initial distribution of resources. We'll investigate the potential for achieving more equitable outcomes through redistribution, and we'll explain how the goals of equity and efficiency can come into conflict.

16.1 THE NATURE OF GENERAL EQUILIBRIUM

In Chapters 14 and 15 we studied the nature of competitive equilibrium in a single market, considered in isolation. That approach is known as **partial equilibrium analysis**. The word *partial* means that the market under consideration is only one part of the economy.

Partial equilibrium analysis concerns competitive equilibrium in a single market, considered in isolation.

Partial equilibrium analysis generates many valuable insights concerning competitive markets. It's especially useful when the supply and demand for a good are largely independent of activities in other markets. In practice, however, markets are often interdependent, as when a change in the price of a good affects the demand for its complements and substitutes.

General equilibrium analysis is the study of competitive equilibrium in many markets at the same time. Unlike partial equilibrium analysis, it allows us to understand the consequences of interdependence among markets. This advantage is important for two reasons. First, factors that affect supply and demand in one market can have significant ripple effects in other markets. In the context of policy making, those ripples can create unintended consequences. Second, the interdependence of markets produces feedback. When a change in price and quantity in one market impacts a second market, the resulting change

General equilibrium analysis is the study of competitive equilibrium in many markets at the same time.

The 19th century French economist Léon Walras (1834–1910) is widely viewed as the father of general equilibrium theory.

in price and quantity in the second market can in turn impact the first. General equilibrium analysis accounts for this feedback between markets; partial equilibrium analysis does not.

Sometimes markets are linked because the price of one good affects the demand for another; sometimes they're linked because the production of one good affects the cost of producing another. For an illustration of a demand-side linkage, consider the case of pie and ice cream. These goods could be either complements (pie is often served a la mode) or substitutes (both are desserts in their own right). Therefore, the location of the demand curve for ice cream depends on the price of pie, and the location of the demand curve for pie depends on the price of ice cream. If we know the price of pie, we can find a partial equilibrium in the ice cream market by looking for the intersection of the supply and demand curves. If we know the price of ice cream, we can find a partial equilibrium in the pie market in exactly the same way. In a general equilibrium, the same pie and ice cream prices clear both markets at the same time.

Figure 16.1 illustrates a general equilibrium in the markets for pie and ice cream. Figure 16.1(a) shows the ice cream market. Assuming that pie costs \$12 per pie, the demand curve for ice cream is D^I. With an ice cream price of \$6 per gallon, the amounts of ice cream supplied and demanded are equal. Figure 16.1(b) shows the pie market. Assuming that ice cream costs \$6 per gallon, the demand curve for pie is D^P. With a pie price of \$12 per pie, the amounts of pie supplied and demanded are equal. Therefore, when the price of

Figure 16.1

General Equilibrium in the Markets for Pie and Ice Cream. Figure (a) shows the ice cream market. When the price of pie is \$12/pie, the demand curve for ice cream intersects the supply curve at a price of \$6/gal. Figure (b) shows the market for pie. When the price of ice cream is \$6/gal., the demand curve for pie intersects the supply curve at a price of \$12/pie. At these prices, both markets are in equilibrium.

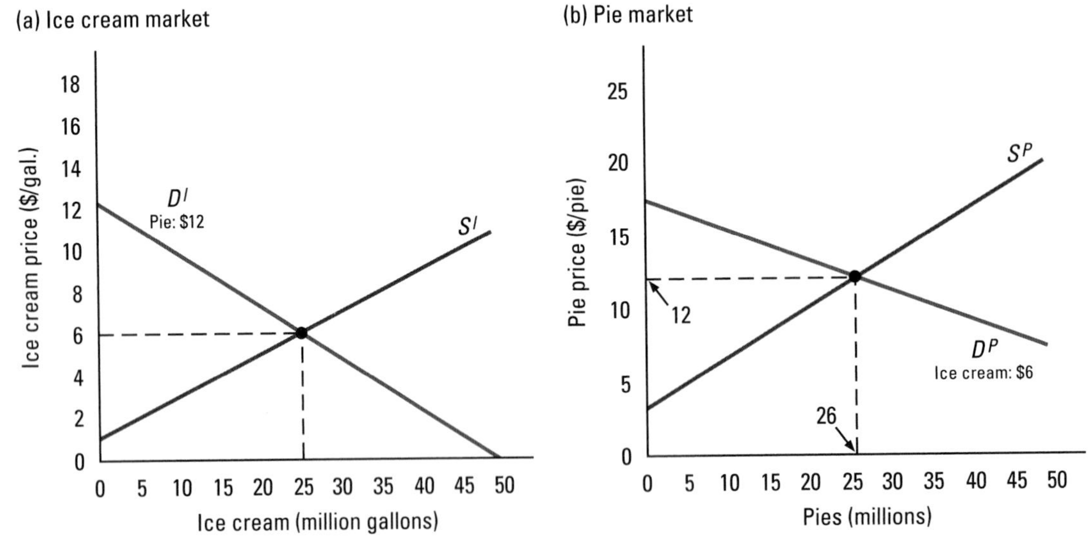

ice cream is \$6 per gallon and the price of pie is \$12 per pie, both markets clear; in other words, we have a general equilibrium. In this equilibrium, there is neither upward nor downward pressure on the price of either good. In contrast, when a general equilibrium does not prevail, the prices of goods will tend to change, rising when demand exceeds supply, and falling when supply exceeds demand.

To be *completely* general, equilibrium analysis would need to encompass every market in the world economy. For most purposes, such an undertaking is obviously impractical. Instead, economists usually focus on markets that are clearly linked, ignoring others. For example, if we're interested in understanding the effect of some development affecting the supply or demand for pie, we might need to consider feedback effects from the ice cream market, but probably not from the market for light bulbs.

The modern treatment of general equilibrium was pioneered by economists Kenneth Arrow (1921–), above, and Gerard Debreu (1921–2004), below, both Nobel Laureates.

16.2 POSITIVE ANALYSIS OF GENERAL EQUILIBRIUM

Economists are often asked to determine how prices and quantities will respond to changes in the economic environment, including the types of policy interventions we studied in Chapter 15. In many cases, answers based on partial equilibrium analysis are incomplete because they ignore the interdependencies between markets. In this section, we explain how to answer positive questions more accurately through general equilibrium analysis.[1]

For the purpose of illustration, we will examine the effects of a sales tax on ice cream. We'll assume here that pie and ice cream are complements. (In-text exercise 16.1 asks you to assume that those goods are substitutes.) We'll also assume that there are no supply linkages between these markets—that is, pie-making costs are independent of ice cream production, and vice versa. (The first exercise at the end of this chapter asks you to consider a case with supply-side linkages.)

The partial equilibrium effects of an ice cream tax are easy to determine: the tax shifts the supply curve upward, causing its intersection with the demand curve and therefore price and quantity, to change (as in Figure 15.1, page 541). In contrast, the general equilibrium effects of an ice cream tax are more difficult to evaluate. First, there is the direct (partial equilibrium) effect on the ice cream market: the price of ice cream rises, and the quantity of ice cream falls. This direct effect produces an indirect effect on the pie market: since the price of ice cream has risen, and since pie and ice cream are complements, the demand curve for pie shifts downward, causing the price of pie to fall. This indirect effect produces a feedback effect on the ice cream market: the falling pie price shifts the demand curve for ice cream upward, causing the price of ice cream to rise further. This feedback effect produces another indirect effect on the pie market, which produces another feedback effect on the ice cream market, which produces another indirect effect on the pie market, and so forth. The effects of the tax ripple back and forth between the two markets in an unending sequence. How can we account for all of those ripples?

In this section, we'll introduce a new tool that helps us determine the prices that prevail in a general equilibrium, accounting for the interdependencies between markets. Then we'll use this tool to evaluate the general equilibrium effects of a sales tax on ice cream.

[1]As we explained in Chapter 1, a positive question concerns what did, will, or would happen; it calls for a factual, descriptive answer.

Figure 16.2

The Market-Clearing Curve for Ice Cream. Figure (a) shows an ice cream supply curve (S^I), three ice cream demand curves (D_1^I, D_2^I, and D_3^I) corresponding to three different pie prices ($6, $12, and $18), and three partial equilibria in the ice cream market (points A_1, A_2, and A_3). Each partial equilibrium shown in figure (a) is associated with a price combination that clears the ice cream market in figure (b): points B_1, B_2, and B_3, respectively. The market-clearing curve for ice cream passes through those points.

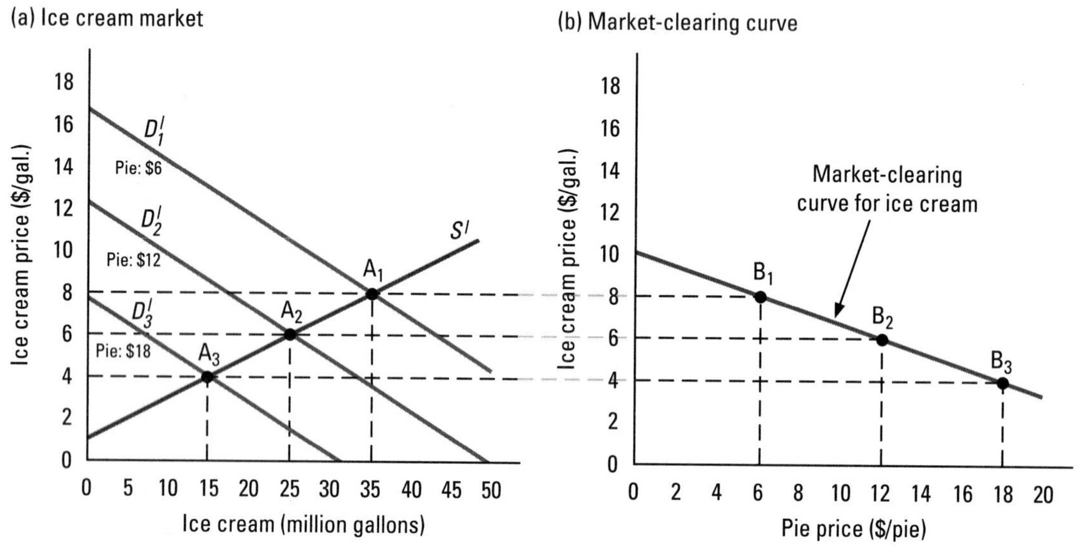

Market-Clearing Curves

The **market-clearing curve** for a good shows the combinations of prices (both for that good and for other related goods) that bring supply and demand for the good into balance.

The first step in our search for a general equilibrium is to identify, for each good, the combinations of prices (both for that good and for other related goods) that bring supply and demand for the good into balance. The **market-clearing curve** for a good shows these price combinations graphically.

Let's start with the ice cream market. Figure 16.2(a) shows a supply curve for ice cream, S^I (in blue), as well as three demand curves (in red). Each demand curve is associated with a different pie price. Since ice cream and pie are complements, the demand curve for ice cream shifts downward as the price of pie rises. When pies cost $6 per pie, the demand curve is D_1^I. The ice cream market clears at point A_1, where consumers purchase 35 million gallons at $8 per gallon. When pies cost $12 per pie, the demand curve is D_2^I and consumers purchase 25 million gallons at $6 per gallon (point A_2). And when pies cost $18 per pie, the demand curve is D_3^I; consumers purchase 15 million gallons at $4 per gallon (point A_3).

Figure 16.2(b) shows the market-clearing curve for ice cream. The horizontal axis shows the price of pie; the vertical axis shows the price of ice cream. Point B_1 corresponds to point A_1 in Figure 16.2(a). It tells us that when the price of pie is $6 per pie, the ice cream market clears at a price of $8 per gallon. Similarly, point B_2 corresponds to point A_2 in Figure 16.2(a). It tells us that when the price of pie is $12 per pie, the ice cream market clears at a price of $6 per gallon. And point B_3 corresponds to point A_3 in Figure 16.2(a). It tells us that when the price of pie is $18 per pie, the ice cream market clears at a price of $4 per gallon. By considering the effects of other pie prices, we can trace out the brown

Figure 16.3

The Market-Clearing Curve for Pie. Figure (a) shows a pie supply curve (S^P), three pie demand curves (D_1^P, D_2^P, and D_3^P) corresponding to three different ice cream prices ($2, $6, and $10), and three partial equilibria in the pie market (points C_1, C_2, *and* C_3). Each partial equilibrium shown in figure (a) is associated with a price combination that clears the pie market in figure (b): points E_1, E_2, and E_3, respectively. The market-clearing curve for pie passes through those points.

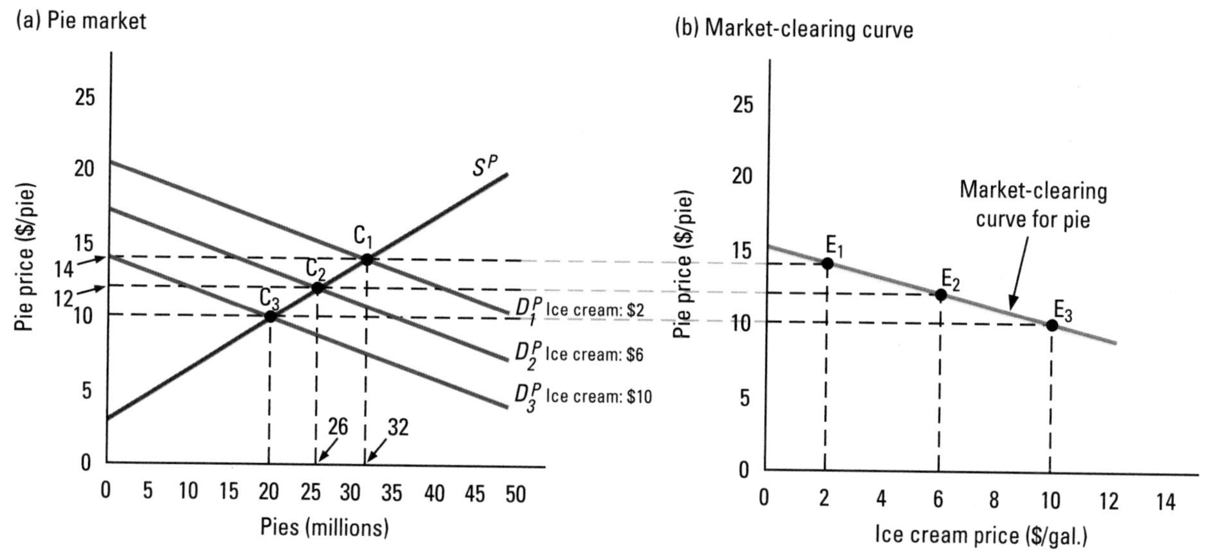

market-clearing curve. At any combination of prices on this curve, the supply of ice cream matches the demand.

Notice that the market-clearing curve for ice cream is downward sloping. Because we've assumed that ice cream and pie are complements, an increase in the price of pie reduces the demand for ice cream, which in turn lowers the partial equilibrium price of ice cream. When the goods in question are substitutes, however, the market-clearing curve is upward sloping (see in-text exercise 16.1, page 586).

Now let's examine the market for pie. Figure 16.3(a) is similar to Figure 16.2(a): it shows a pie supply curve (S^P); three pie demand curves (D_1^P, D_2^P, and D_3^P) corresponding to three different ice cream prices ($2, $6, and $10 per gallon); and three partial equilibria in the pie market (C_1, C_2, and C_3). Each partial equilibrium shown in Figure 16.3(a) is associated with a price combination that clears the pie market in Figure 16.3(b) (points E_1, E_2, and E_3). The green market-clearing curve for pie passes through those price combination points.

A General Equilibrium in Two Markets

At all price combinations on the brown market-clearing curve in Figure 16.2(b), the ice cream market is in equilibrium. At all price combinations on the green market-clearing curve in Figure 16.3(b), the pie market is in equilibrium. If a price combination lies on *both* market-clearing curves, then *both* markets are in equilibrium. In other words, we have a general equilibrium.

Figure 16.4
The General Equilibrium Price Combination. The market-clearing curves for pie and ice cream intersect at a single point, where the pie price is $12 and the ice cream price is $6. These are the general equilibrium prices. According to the market clearing curves, they clear both the pie market and the ice cream market.

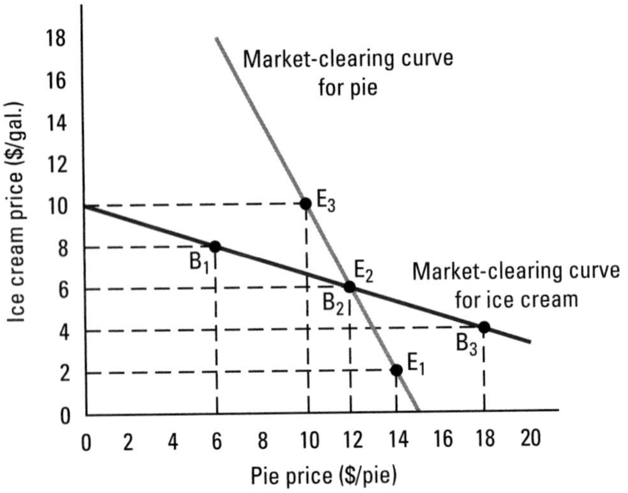

To find a general equilibrium price combination, we can plot both market-clearing curves on the same graph; see Figure 16.4. As in Figure 16.2(b), the horizontal axis shows the price of pie and the vertical axis measures the price of ice cream. The market-clearing curve for pie looks steeper in Figure 16.4 than in Figure 16.3(b) because, compared to Figure 16.3(b), we've reversed the axes. (To confirm that the two curves are the same, check that points E_1, E_2, and E_3 correspond to the same price combinations in both figures.)

Notice that the two market-clearing curves in Figure 16.4 intersect at a single point (labeled B_2 on the ice cream curve and E_2 on the pie curve), where the ice cream price is $6 per gallon and the pie price is $12 per pie. These are the general equilibrium prices. According to the market-clearing curves, the ice cream market and the pie market clear at these prices, exactly as illustrated in Figure 16.1.

The Effects of a Sales Tax

We've said that partial equilibrium analysis, though useful, sometimes overlooks important general equilibrium effects. To illustrate this point, let's examine the effects of a $3 per gallon sales tax on ice cream. First we'll determine the partial equilibrium effects of the tax, starting from the general equilibrium price and quantity described in the previous section. Then we'll find the new general equilibrium.

Let's start with the partial equilibrium effects of the tax. Figure 16.5(a) shows prices and quantities in the ice cream market. The numbers on the vertical axis indicate the price paid by consumers, including the tax, if any. Without a tax, the supply curve S^I (shown in dark blue) intersects the demand curve D_2^I (shown in dark red) at point A_2, producing an initial equilibrium price of $6 per gallon, as in the last section. A $3 per gallon tax on ice cream shifts the ice cream supply curve upward by $3, from S^I to S_T^I, shown in light blue (recall the discussion of sales taxation in Section 15.1). With the price of a pie held fixed at $12, the new partial equilibrium is point F_2, where the demand curve D_2^I crosses the

Figure 16.5

The General Equilibrium Effect of a Tax on Ice Cream, Part 1. In figure (a), a \$3 tax on ice cream shifts the supply curve upward by \$3, from S^I to S^I_T. For the three ice cream demand curves (D^I_1, D^I_2, and D^I_3) corresponding to three different pie prices (\$6, \$12, and \$18), we now have three new partial equilibria (F_1, F_2, and F_3). Each partial equilibrium shown in figure (a) is associated with a price combination that clears the ice cream market, plotted in figure (b) (points G_1, G_2, and G_3, respectively). The market-clearing curve shifts upward by \$1⅔ per gallon, as shown. Point G_4 is the new general equilibrium. The tax increases the price of ice cream by \$2 per gallon (from \$6 to \$8), and reduces the price of pie by \$1 per pie (from \$12 to \$11).

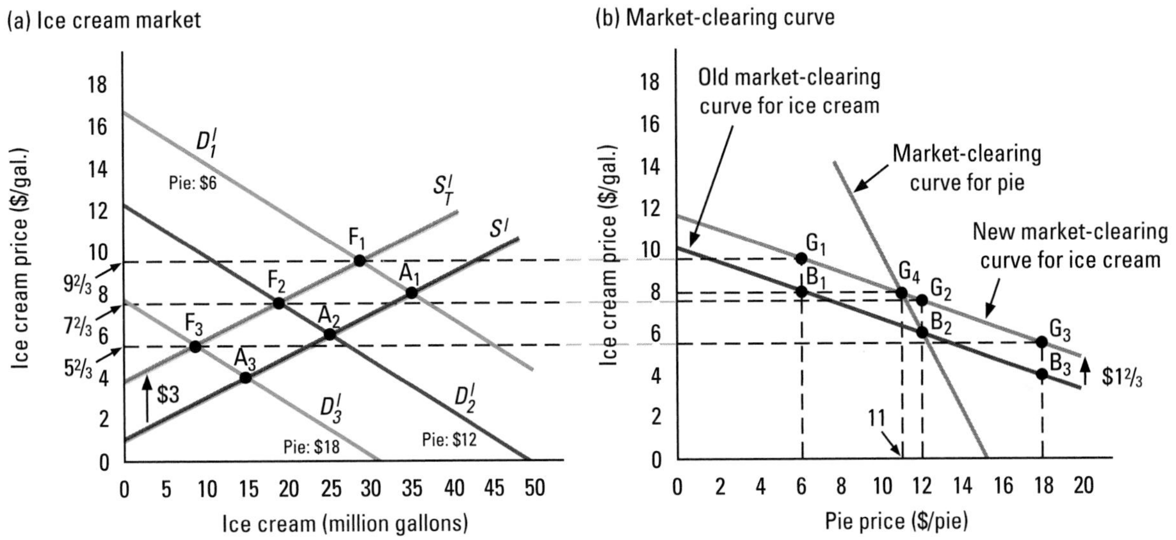

new supply curve S^I_T. The price of ice cream therefore rises by \$1⅔ per gallon (from \$6 to \$7⅔), which is less than the amount of the tax (\$3).

To determine the general equilibrium effects of the ice cream tax, we need to plot a new market clearing curve for ice cream. Notice that Figure 16.5(a) reproduces (in light red) the demand curves D^I_1 (corresponding to a pie price of \$6) and D^I_3 (corresponding to a pie price of \$18) from Figure 16.2(a), as well as the points at which they intersect the supply curve S^I (points A_1 and A_3). When the supply curve shifts from S^I to S^I_T, the partial equilibrium point on D^I_1 moves from A_1 to F_1, and the one on D^I_3 moves from A_3 to F_3. In each case, the tax-inclusive price of ice cream rises by \$1⅔ per gallon.

As shown in Figure 16.5(b), taxing ice cream shifts the market-clearing curve for ice cream upward. The new market clearing curve (shown in tan) lies exactly \$1⅔ above the old one (shown in brown as in Figure 16.2(b)), which means that the magnitude of the shift equals the partial equilibrium effect of the tax. Point G_1 corresponds to point F_1 in Figure 16.5(a); it tells us that when the price of pie is \$6 per pie, the ice cream market clears at a price of \$9⅔ per gallon. Similarly, point G_2 corresponds to point F_2 in Figure 16.5(a), and point G_3 corresponds to point F_3 in Figure 16.5(a).

Figure 16.5(b) also includes the same (green) market-clearing curve for pie that appeared in Figure 16.4. To find the new general equilibrium, we look for an intersection between this curve and the new (tan) market-clearing curve for ice cream. These curves

Figure 16.6

The General Equilibrium Effect of a Tax on Ice Cream, Part 2. Figure (a) shows the ice cream market. When pies cost $11 each, the demand curve for ice cream, D_4^I (shown in light red) intersects the supply curve, S_T^I (shown in light blue), at a price of $8 per gallon. Figure (b) shows the market for pie. When the price of ice cream is $8 per gallon, the demand curve for pie, D_4^P (shown in light red), intersects the supply curve, S^P (shown in blue) at a price of $11 per pie. At these prices, both markets are in equilibrium.

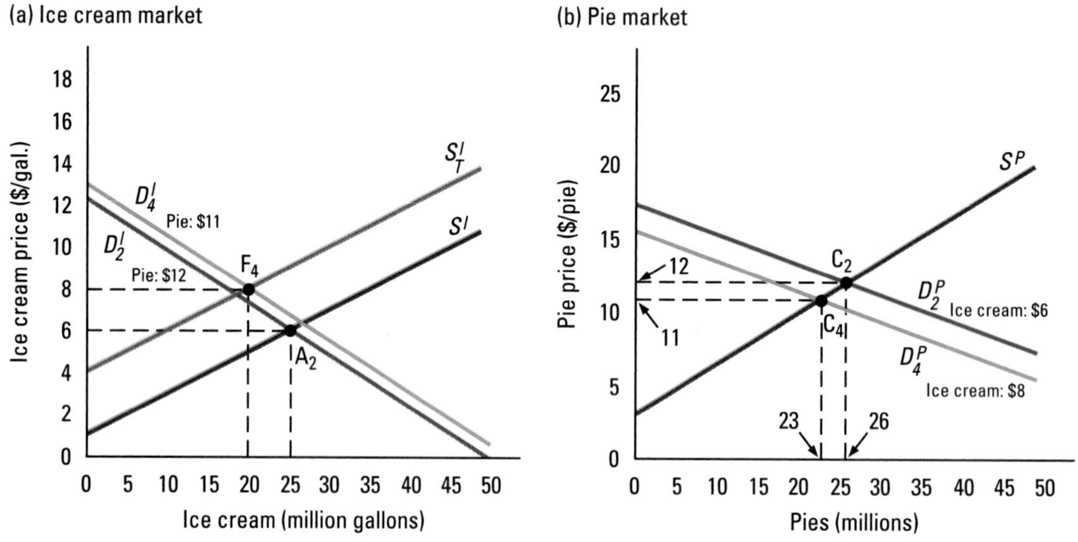

intersect at point G_4, where the pie price is $11 and the ice cream price is $8. These are the new general equilibrium prices: according to the market-clearing curves, they clear both the pie market and the ice cream market.

Figure 16.6 illustrates the new general equilibrium (points F_4 and C_4). We have determined that both markets clear when the price of ice cream is $8 per gallon and the price of pie is $11 per pie. Figure 16.6(a) shows the ice cream market. With pies priced at $11 each, the demand curve for ice cream is D_4^I (shown in light red). With an ice cream price of $8 per gallon, the amounts of ice cream supplied and demanded are equal. Figure 16.6(b) shows the pie market. With ice cream priced at $8 per gallon, the demand curve for pie is D_4^P (shown in light red). With a pie price of $11 per pie, the amounts of pie supplied and demand are equal. Notice that as a result of the tax, the demand curves for both goods shift, moving the general equilibrium from points A_2 and C_2 to points F_4 and C_4.

In this example, we've reached two important conclusions from general equilibrium analysis. First, a sales tax on ice cream reduces the price of a pie by $1 (from $12 to $11). This price reduction occurs because pie and ice cream are complements—a tax on ice cream increases the price of ice cream, which reduces the demand for pie [the shift from D_2^P to D_4^P in Figure 16.6(b)], causing the pie price to fall. Second, partial equilibrium analysis *understates* the effect of the sales tax on the price of ice cream. According to partial equilibrium analysis, the price rises by $\$1^2/_3$, from $6 to $\$7^2/_3$ per gallon. But according to general equilibrium analysis, it rises by $2, from $6 to $8 per gallon.

Why is the general equilibrium effect of the sales tax larger than the partial equilibrium effect in this example? We've concluded that a tax on ice cream causes the pie price to fall. Because ice cream and pie are complements, a lower pie price leads to greater demand for ice cream [the shift from D_2^I to D_4^I in Figure 16.6(a)], which *reinforces* the pressure for the ice cream price to rise. General equilibrium analysis accounts for this feedback from the pie market, but partial equilibrium analysis doesn't.

WORKED-OUT PROBLEM 16.1

The Problem Suppose the following formulas describe the supply and demand for ice cream (where Q_I^d stands for millions of gallons demanded, Q_I^s stands for millions of gallons supplied, P_I stands for the price of ice cream per gallon, and P_P stands for the price per pie):

$$Q_I^d = 85 - 4P_I - 3P_P \quad \textbf{(1)}$$

$$Q_I^s = 5P_I - 5 \quad \textbf{(2)}$$

Also suppose the following formulas describe the supply and demand for pie (where Q_P^d stands for millions of pies demanded and Q_P^s stands for millions of pies supplied):

$$Q_P^d = 110 - 5P_P - 4P_I \quad \textbf{(3)}$$

$$Q_P^s = 3P_P - 10 \quad \textbf{(4)}$$

These formulas correspond to the supply and demand curves in Figures 16.2(a) and 16.3(a) (you should check this).[2] Solve algebraically for the partial and general equilibrium effects of a \$3 sales tax on ice cream.

The Solution When $85 - 4P_I - 3P_P = 5P_I - 5$, the demand for ice cream equals the supply. Solving for P_I, we find that

$$P_I = 10 - \frac{1}{3}P_P \quad \textbf{(5)}$$

This is the formula for the market-clearing curve for ice cream. It corresponds to the brown line in Figure 16.2(b).

Similarly, when $110 - 5P_P - 4P_I = 3P_P - 10$, the demand for pie equals the supply. Solving for P_P, we find that

$$P_P = 15 - \frac{1}{2}P_I \quad \textbf{(6)}$$

This is the formula for the market-clearing curve for pie. It corresponds to the green line in Figure 16.3(b).

Now let's solve for the prices that satisfy both market-clearing formulas at the same time. Substituting formula (5) into (6), we have

$$P_P = 15 - \frac{1}{2}\left(10 - \frac{1}{3}P_P\right)$$

[2]Because quantity cannot be negative, if any of these formulas yields a negative value, the quantity is actually zero.

Solving for P_P yields $P_P = 12$. Substituting this value into formula (5), we find that $P_I = 6$. Plugging these values into either the demand formulas [(1) and (3)] or the supply formulas [(2) and (4)], we learn that in the general equilibrium, consumers purchase 25 million gallons of ice cream and 26 million pies.

The tax changes the supply function for ice cream from formula (2) to:

$$Q_I^s = 5(P_I - 3) - 5 \tag{7}$$

The difference between the supply formulas (7) and (2) reflects the fact that, once the tax is imposed, sellers receive $\$(P_I - 3)$ per gallon, rather than $\$P_I$. (If this isn't clear to you, review Section 15.1, including worked-out problem 15.1 on page 549.) The demand for ice cream equals the supply when $85 - 4P_I - 3P_P = 5(P_I - 3) - 5$. Solving for P_I, we find that

$$P_I = 11^2/_3 - \frac{1}{3}P_P \tag{8}$$

This is the formula for the new market-clearing curve for ice cream. It corresponds to the tan line in Figure 5(b). Comparing formulas (8) and (5), we see that at any pie price, the market-clearing ice cream price is now $\$1^2/_3$ per gallon higher. This is the partial equilibrium effect of the sales tax.

The market-clearing curve for pie, which corresponds to formula (6), is unchanged. We can solve for the prices that satisfy both market-clearing formulas by substituting formula (8) into (6):

$$P_P = 15 - \frac{1}{2}\left(11^2/_3 - \frac{1}{3}P_P\right)$$

Solving for P_P gives us $P_P = 11$. Substituting this value into formula (8), we find that $P_I = 8$. So in general equilibrium, the ice cream price rises by \$2 and the pie price falls by \$1. Plugging these new prices into either the demand formulas [(1) and (3)] or the supply formulas [(7) and (4)], we learn that in the new general equilibrium, consumers purchase 20 million gallons of ice cream and 23 million pies.

IN-TEXT EXERCISE 16.1 **Suppose that the formula for ice cream demand is $Q_I^d = 85 - 4P_I + 6P_P$ and the formula for pie demand is $Q_P^d = 110 - 5P_P + 2P_I$. Here, pie and ice cream are substitutes instead of complements. Continue to assume that formulas (2) and (4) describe the supply of ice cream and pie. (a) Solve for and graph the market-clearing curves for pie and ice cream. Are they downward sloping, as in Figures 16.2(b) and 16.3(b), or upward sloping? Why? (b) Find the general equilibrium prices and levels of consumption. Show the general equilibrium graphically. (c) Solve for the partial and general equilibrium effects of a \$3 sales tax on ice cream. Illustrate these effects graphically. Is the general equilibrium effect on the price of ice cream larger or smaller than the partial equilibrium effect? Why? Does the general equilibrium pie price rise or fall? Why?**

Application 16.1

Do Investment Tax Breaks Benefit the Working Class?

People earn income by supplying labor and/or capital to firms. Most governments raise substantial revenue by taxing that income. Because capital income flows disproportionately to wealthy individuals, many people feel that the tax rate for capital income should be at least as high as the tax rate for labor income. In response, political conservatives often argue that low tax rates for capital income benefit virtually all members of society, including the working class. They reason that a favorable investment climate stimulates business activity, thereby increasing the demand for labor and driving up wage rates. General equilibrium analysis provides the tools we need to assess the validity of this position.

For the sake of simplicity let's suppose that all workers are the same, and that there is only one type of capital. These assumptions allow us to focus our attention on just two markets: one for labor and the other for capital. An individual's labor income is simply the payment he receives when he sells his labor to a firm. Therefore, we can think of a labor income tax as a sales tax on labor. Similarly, because capital income is the payment received when supplying capital to a firm, we can think of a capital income tax as a sales tax on capital. In effect, conservatives argue that a sales tax on capital reduces the price of labor (that is, the wage rate). To evaluate this argument, we can simply apply what we've learned in the previous section.

The price of labor will affect firms' demand for both labor and capital, as will the price of capital. But are labor and capital complements or substitutes? When the price of capital rises, firms substitute labor for capital, which increases the amount of labor demanded. But they also scale back production, which reduces the amount of labor demanded. If the scale effect is large relative to the substitution effect, the demand for labor falls, which means capital and labor are complements. If the opposite is true, the demand for labor rises, which means capital and labor are substitutes.

Let's suppose for the moment that capital and labor are complements. In that case, all we need to do is relabel Figures 16.1 through 16.6. "Ice cream" becomes capital and the "price of ice cream" becomes the cost of capital; "pie" becomes labor and the "price of pie" becomes the wage rate. As Figures 16.5 and 16.6 show, when two goods are complements, a tax on one reduces the general equilibrium price of the other. So a tax on capital will reduce the wage rate. In this case, reducing the tax burden on capital would raise the wage rate, just as political conservatives claim.

Now let's suppose that capital and labor are substitutes. From in-text exercise 16.1, we know that when two goods are substitutes, a tax on one increases the general equilibrium price of the other. So in this case reducing the tax burden on capital would reduce the wage rate, contrary to the politically conservative view. Thus, theory alone cannot resolve whether the conservatives are right or wrong.

A number of economists have attempted to calculate the general equilibrium effects of capital income taxes on wage rates, using estimates of the supply and demand curves for labor and capital. As you might expect, their economic models are more complicated than the one discussed here. For example, a pioneering study by economist Lawrence Summers accounts for the fact that capital accumulates and depreciates gradually over time.[3] It also recognizes that if the government reduces one tax, it must increase another in order to maintain the same total revenue. Still, the basic principles of analysis are essentially the same.

Suppose we replace a tax on capital with a tax on wages that generates the same amount of revenue. What might happen to the wage rate in the long run? According to Summers' calculations, the lower cost of capital would stimulate a great deal of additional investment. Ultimately, the ratio of total capital to total labor would rise by about 78 percent. With capital more plentiful, labor would become more productive, leading to a 15.5 percent increase in the pretax wage rate. Of course, to maintain revenues, the government would need to tax wages at a higher rate. Still, the after-tax wage rate would fall by only 0.25 percent—a tiny fraction of the incremental tax burden that workers would appear to bear if we ignored the general equilibrium effects. If the government balanced its budget by imposing higher taxes on consumption goods instead of wages, some

[3]Lawrence H. Summers, "Capital Taxation and Accumulation in a Life-Cycle Growth Model," *American Economic Review* 71, no. 4, September 1981, pp. 533–544.

of those taxes would fall on purchases made by the owners of capital, and workers would actually *benefit* from a reduction in the capital income tax rate.

Some of Summers' assumptions about the supply and demand for capital and labor are controversial. Other economists have reached different conclusions based on alternative assumptions. General equilibrium analysis is useful here because it allows us to see how different assumptions lead to different outcomes. It shows that the debate over the taxation of capital boils down to scale effects, substitution effects, and supply elasticities, and underscores the importance of measuring those effects accurately.

16.3 NORMATIVE CRITERIA FOR EVALUATING ECONOMIC PERFORMANCE

The most commonly used notion of economic efficiency originated in the writings of the Italian economist Vilfredo Pareto (1848–1923).

Historically, societies have allocated their scarce resources through a wide variety of procedures, including barter, free trade in open markets, restricted trade in regulated markets, central planning, and mixed approaches (such as using markets and central planners to allocate different resources). Every society must set up institutions to govern the allocation of resources. Are there reasons to prefer a free market?

As we noted in Section 14.3, Adam Smith believed that markets are desirable because they lead each individual "by an invisible hand to promote an end which was no part of his intention." Does society in fact benefit from the way in which markets allocate scarce resources? Modern economists have spent a great deal of time and energy investigating this question. The rest of this chapter—and indeed much of the rest of this book— summarizes some key findings concerning the performance of free markets.

Before proceeding, however, it's important to establish criteria for answering normative questions concerning economic performance.[4] Ideally, we would like to achieve an allocation of society's resources that is efficient, in the sense that it avoids waste. But we would also like to achieve an allocation that is equitable, in the sense that it is fair to all members of society. Economists have developed clear criteria for measuring efficiency. However, as we explain, equity and fairness are far more difficult to define and evaluate.

Efficiency

An allocation of resources is **Pareto efficient** if it's impossible to make any consumer better off without hurting someone else.

An economy is wasteful (or inefficient) if we can reallocate resources in a way that will make at least one consumer better off without hurting anyone else.[5] An economy is efficient if there is no waste—that is, if it's *impossible* to make any consumer better off without hurting someone else. This notion of efficiency, known as **Pareto efficiency**, was first proposed by the Italian economist Vilfredo Pareto.

How do we judge whether one allocation makes a consumer better off or worse off than another allocation? With few exceptions, economists use the consumer's own preferences. In other words, we assume that every individual knows what's best for him; we

[4]As we explained in Chapter 1, a normative question concerns what *should* happen; it calls for judgment.

[5]In most situations, this is the equivalent of saying that we can make everyone better off. To see why, suppose there is an allocation that makes one person better off and no one worse off. If we take a sufficiently small amount of some good away from the person who's better off, he'll remain better off. If we then divide what we've taken from him among everyone else, everyone ends up better off.

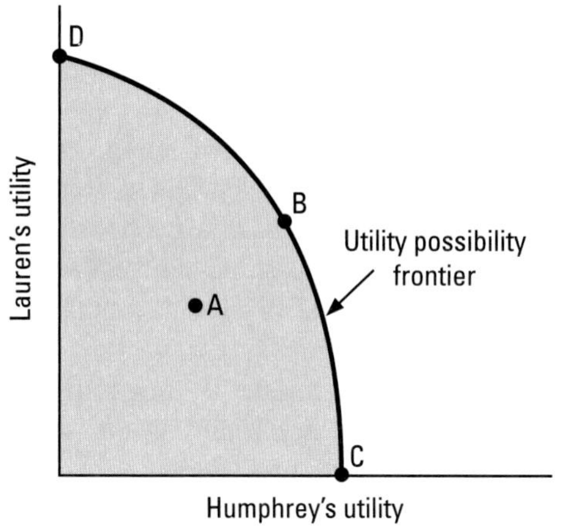

Figure 16.7
Pareto Efficient Outcomes. The green-shaded area shows the utility levels associated with every possible allocation of resources. The northeast boundary of this area, called the utility possibility frontier, contains all the Pareto efficient allocations. Point A is inefficient, while points B, C, and D are all efficient.

don't second-guess any consumer's personal judgment. For example, no matter what we may think of television, we don't take the position that watching television is a waste of time. If someone chooses to watch television, we conclude that doing so must make her better off than her available alternatives.

Figure 16.7 illustrates the concept of Pareto efficiency. Let's assume that the economy consists of two people, Humphrey and Lauren. Suppose we know their preferences, which we can represent with utility functions. Each allocation of society's resources leads to a pair of utility levels, one for Humphrey and one for Lauren. We can plot each of those outcomes as a point in Figure 16.7, like A or B. The green-shaded area shows the utility levels associated with every possible allocation of resources.

The northeast boundary of this area, shown in black, is known as the **utility possibility frontier**.[6] Any allocation associated with a point below this frontier is inefficient. Starting from point A, for example, we can make both Humphrey and Lauren better off by moving to point B. Point A may be inefficient because there's a better way to distribute goods among consumers, or because firms could produce more outputs from the same inputs. Any allocation associated with a point on the utility possibility frontier is Pareto efficient. Starting from point B, for example, we can make Lauren better off only by hurting Humphrey, and we can make Humphrey better off only by hurting Lauren.

The **utility possibility frontier** shows the utility levels associated with all efficient allocations of resources.

As the figure shows, there are many efficient outcomes. Some (like point C) favor Humphrey, while others (like D) favor Lauren. To choose among them, we must rely on normative criteria other than efficiency, like equity.

Equity

Equity is much harder to define and measure than efficiency, because it's a very subjective concept. Different people have different views of what's fair.

[6] As we have drawn it, the utility possibility frontier is concave; that is, it bows outward from the origin. However, since the scale used to measure utility is completely arbitrary (as discussed in Section 4.4), this frontier need not be concave.

Process-oriented notions of equity focus on the procedures used to arrive at an allocation of resources rather than on the allocation itself.

Some notions of equity are **process-oriented**. That is, they focus on the procedures used to arrive at an allocation of resources rather than on the allocation itself. The familiar principle of equal opportunity is an example; it focuses on what people *could* choose rather than on what they *actually* choose.

Some people believe that the free market system is a fair process. They maintain that it fairly rewards people for their effort and ingenuity. Others think that, in practice, markets are unfair. They point out that some people have less opportunity than others to obtain education and marketable skills. They also insist that a person is not less deserving of a comfortable life merely because he or she was born with less talent or intelligence than others.

Outcome-oriented notions of equity focus on whether the process used to allocate resources yields fair results.

Other notions of equity are **outcome-oriented**. That is, they require us to determine whether the process used to allocate resources yields fair results. Most people would agree that some outcomes—like giving everything to a single person—are not fair. Still, there's a lot of room here for subjective judgment and disagreement.

According to the principle of **utilitarianism**, society should place equal weight on the well-being of every individual.

According to the principle of **Rawlsianism**, society should place all weight on the well-being of its worst-off member.

Some outcome-oriented notions of equity focus on the distribution of well-being. In Section 4.4 we mentioned the British moral philosopher Jeremy Bentham, who argued that society should place equal weight on the well-being of every individual. This principle is called **utilitarianism**. John Rawls, a famous contemporary philosopher, has taken a radically different view, arguing that society should place all weight on the well-being of its worst-off member, a principle known as **Rawlsianism**. Utilitarianism and Rawlsianism reflect different subjective judgments concerning equity.

Unfortunately, no one has yet discovered a reliable way to measure an individual's well-being. Indeed, many economists believe that this is an unachievable objective. While the notion of consumer utility is obviously related to well-being, a utility function provides only ordinal information about one individual's preferences, rather than cardinal information (see the discussion on pages 117–118). That is, it assigns higher numbers to preferred alternatives according to some arbitrary scale. Whether one allocation is judged more or less equitable than another shouldn't depend on these arbitrary scales.

This difficulty definitely spells trouble for Rawlsians and utilitarians. Rawlsians assume there's a way to identify society's least happy member. Utilitarians assume it's possible to say whether a change in resource allocation will increase the well-being of one individual more than it decreases the well-being of another. But if we have only ordinal information concerning individual preferences, we can't compare happiness across consumers. For example, we can't say whether Humphrey will be happier with three pounds of food than Lauren will be with two pounds. We can say only that a particular individual likes one consumption bundle better than another.

According to the principle of **egalitarianism**, equal division of society's resources among all members of the population is the most equitable outcome.

Other outcome-oriented notions of equity focus on the distribution of consumption. According to the principle of **egalitarianism**, for example, equal division of society's resources among all members of the population is the most equitable outcome. Unfortunately, egalitarian distributions tend to be extremely inefficient. If you love Coke and hate Pepsi, while your friend loves Pepsi and hates Coke, it makes no sense to give each of you the same amount of Coke and the same amount of Pepsi.[7]

[7]Some people would argue that from a process-oriented perspective, free markets are fair as long as everyone *starts out* with exactly the same resources. Since people have different preferences, they'll make different trades, and the outcome won't be egalitarian. However, everyone will have the same opportunities. Still, the outcomes may seem unfair. If you like Coke and your friend likes Pepsi, starting both of you off with exactly the same resources may seem fair. But what if the prices turn out to be $2 per quart for Pepsi and $20,000 per quart for Coke—does the process still seem fair?

Social Welfare Functions

Economists often use **social welfare functions** to summarize judgments about resource allocations. For each possible allocation, the function assigns a number that indicates the overall level of social welfare. Higher numbers reflect greater social well-being.

A **social welfare function** summarizes judgments about resource allocations. For each possible allocation, the function assigns a number that indicates the overall level of social welfare.

Sometimes, economists break up the calculation of social welfare into two steps. First, they assign utility levels to every consumer using utility functions that represent the consumers' preferences. Second, they apply a function, call it W, that converts those utility levels into social welfare:

$$\text{Social welfare} = W(U_1, U_2, \ldots, U_N) \quad \textbf{(9)}$$

In formula (9), U_i is the level of utility enjoyed by the i-th individual, and N is the number of individuals. Typically, economists assume that higher levels of individual utility imply higher levels of social welfare. The function W is sometimes called a Bergson-Samuelson social welfare function, after economists Abram Bergson and Paul Samuelson, who pioneered this approach.

A Bergson-Samuelson social welfare function can capture concerns for both efficiency and outcome-oriented notions of equity. Let's start with efficiency. Notice that formula (9) is a lot like a utility function. Instead of assigning utility levels to consumption bundles, it assigns welfare levels to "utility bundles." With this analogy in mind, let's return to the problem of allocating resources between Humphrey and Lauren, depicted in Figure 16.7. We've reproduced the feasible outcomes in Figure 16.8, and added social indifference curves to represent the judgments associated with a given social welfare function. Indifference curves that are farther from the origin correspond to higher levels of social welfare. It follows that point A delivers the highest feasible level of social welfare. Since that point lies on the utility possibility frontier, it's Pareto efficient. Thus, the social welfare function reflects a preference for efficiency.

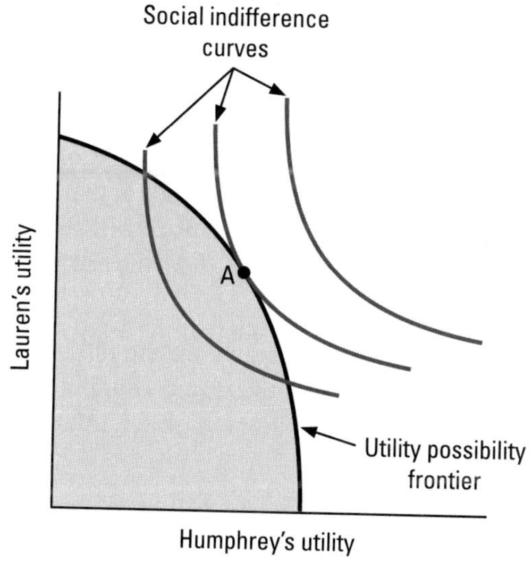

Figure 16.8

Applying Social Welfare Functions. For the social welfare function corresponding to the red social indifference curves, point A is the best possible outcome. Since it lies on the utility possibility frontier, it is Pareto efficient.

It's tempting to interpret a Bergson-Samuelson social welfare function as capturing concerns for outcome-oriented notions of equity that focus on the distribution of well-being.[8] But as we emphasized in the previous section, the utility scale used to measure each individual's well-being is completely arbitrary. How then are we to judge whether one person's "utils" are more or less important than another's?

Instead, economists usually interpret Bergson-Samuelson social welfare functions as capturing concerns for outcome-oriented notions of equity that focus on the distribution of consumption, rather than well-being. We choose the function W in combination with utility scales to summarize judgments about the relative desirability of giving extra goods to different people. For example, a particular Bergson-Samuelson social welfare function, along with particular utility scales, might reflect the judgment that a pound of food received by someone with an income of \$20,000 per year is just as socially valuable as 10 pounds of food received by someone with an income of \$100,000 per year.

How do we arrive at the value judgments captured by a social welfare function? That's a matter for politicians and philosophers. Efforts to develop general economic principles for evaluating and comparing efficient social alternatives have been largely unsuccessful. Indeed, a result known as Arrow's Impossibility Theorem (named after economist Kenneth Arrow, who we mentioned earlier in this chapter) suggests that such efforts are doomed to fail. To learn about Arrow's theorem and the conceptual issues it raises, read Add-On 16A.

16.4 GENERAL EQUILIBRIUM AND EFFICIENT EXCHANGE

In Sections 14.3 and 14.4 we learned that in a single competitive market, partial equilibrium is efficient in the sense that it maximizes the sum of consumer and producer surplus. But what about a general equilibrium with many perfectly competitive markets? When all markets balance at the same time, is the allocation of resources Pareto efficient? In this section, we'll address this question in the context of **exchange economies**—economies in which consumers own and trade goods, but no production takes place. In Section 16.5, we'll expand the analysis to include production.

In an **exchange economy**, people own and trade goods, but no production takes place.

General Equilibrium in Exchange Economies

In an exchange economy, each individual starts out with a bundle of goods called an **endowment**. To meet their needs, consumers buy and sell goods at market prices. A consumer who has too much of one good and too little of another will supply the first and demand the second. If supply matches demand for every good, the economy is in general equilibrium.

An **endowment** is the bundle of goods an individual starts out with before trading.

A Simple Example Suppose Humphrey and Lauren are the only consumers in the economy, and they consume only two goods, food and water. Humphrey starts out with an endowment of eight pounds of food and three gallons of water. Lauren starts out with

[8]To capture utilitarianism, the function W would simply sum up the utility levels of all consumers. That way, an additional unit of utility would be equally valuable regardless of who received it. To capture Rawlsianism, W would simply equal the lowest level of utility enjoyed by any consumer. That way, an additional unit of utility would be valuable only if it was received by society's worst-off member.

Figure 16.9

General Equilibrium in an Exchange Economy. Humphrey starts at point A_H and Lauren starts at point A_L. When food costs \$1 per pound and water costs \$1 per gallon, Humphrey prefers point B_H—he wants to swap 3 pounds of food for 3 gallons of water. Lauren prefers point B_L—she wants to swap 4 pounds of water for 4 gallons of food. Supply doesn't match demand, so this is not an equilibrium. When food costs \$2 per pound and water costs \$1 per gallon, Humphrey prefers point C_H—he wants to swap 2 pounds of food for 4 gallons of water. Lauren prefers point C_L—she wants to swap 4 gallons of water for 2 pounds of food. Supply matches demand, so the economy is in equilibrium.

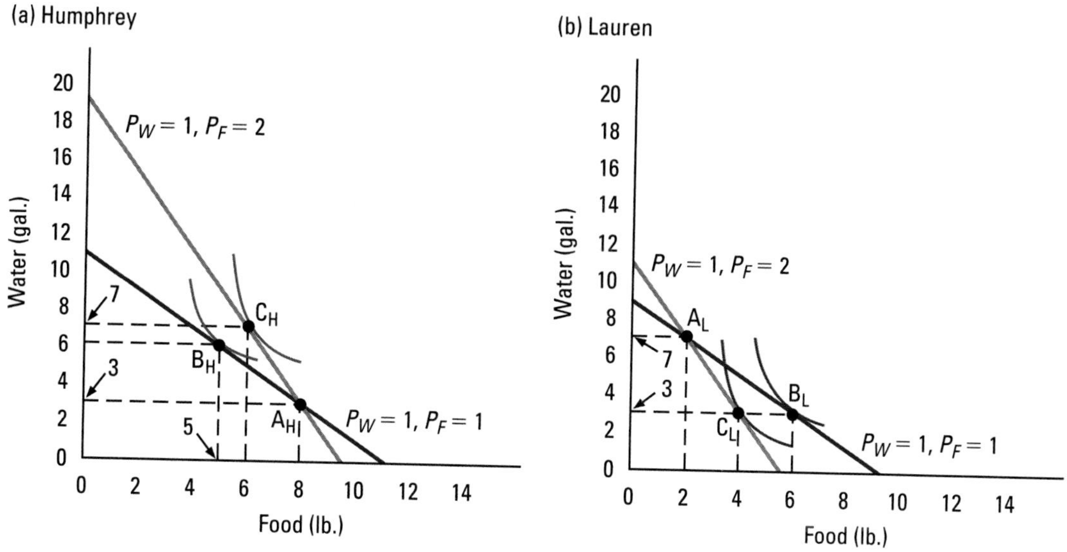

two pounds of food and seven gallons of water. In Figure 16.9(a), Humphrey's endowment corresponds to point A_H; in Figure 16.9(b), Lauren's corresponds to A_L.

For the moment, let's assume that food sells for \$1 per pound and water sells for \$1 per gallon.[9] At those prices, each consumer can trade one pound of food for one gallon of water, or vice versa. The figure shows the resulting budget lines in brown. Judging by the red indifference curves in Figure 16.9(a), Humphrey's favorite point on his budget line is B_H (five pounds of food and six gallons of water). He supplies three pounds of food (eight pounds minus five pounds) and demands three gallons of water (six gallons minus three gallons). Judging by the blue indifference curves in Figure 16.9(b), Lauren's favorite point on her budget line is B_L (six pounds of food and three gallons of water). She demands four pounds of food (six pounds minus two pounds) and supplies four gallons of water (seven gallons minus three gallons). Supply doesn't match demand in either market: Humphrey supplies three pounds of food but Lauren demands four pounds, and Humphrey demands three gallons of water but Lauren supplies four gallons. Consequently, this is not a general equilibrium.

[9] We'll assume too that Humphrey and Lauren are both price takers. With only two consumers in the economy, that is a bit of a stretch—both Humphrey and Lauren should realize that their choices will influence the prices at which markets clear. (If this assumption troubles you, just assume that the economy consists of many identical Humphreys and many identical Laurens, all of whom behave as described in the text.)

Now let's assume that food sells for \$2 per pound and water sells for \$1 per gallon. Consumers can swap one pound of food for two gallons of water or vice versa. The figure shows the resulting budget lines in green. Humphrey chooses point C_H in Figure 16.9(a) (six pounds of food and seven gallons of water), supplying two pounds of food (eight pounds minus six pounds) and demanding four gallons of water (seven gallons minus three gallons). Lauren chooses the point C_L in Figure 16.9(b) (four pounds of food and three gallons of water), demanding two pounds of food (four pounds minus two pounds) and supplying four gallons of water (seven gallons minus three gallons). Because supply and demand match in both markets, this *is* a general equilibrium.

The **Edgeworth box** is a diagram that shows two consumers' opportunities and choices in a single figure.

The Edgeworth Box Economists often illustrate equilibrium in a simple exchange economy using a diagram known as the **Edgeworth box**. First introduced by the British economist Francis Ysidro Edgeworth in the late 19th century, the Edgeworth box is useful because it shows two consumers' opportunities and choices in a single figure.

Figure 16.10 shows the Edgeworth box for the exchange economy discussed in the last section. The box is 10 units wide and 10 units high. Each unit of width represents a pound of food, and each unit of height represents a gallon of water. The width is 10 units because Humphrey and Lauren start out with 10 pounds of food (eight for Humphrey and two for Lauren). Similarly, the height is 10 units because the two start out with 10 gallons of water (three for Humphrey and seven for Lauren).

Each point in the Edgeworth box describes an allocation of resources between Humphrey and Lauren. That is, it specifies the division of food and water between them. For Humphrey, the bottom of the box serves as an axis measuring the amount of food, and the left side serves as an axis measuring the amount of water. For Lauren, the *top* of the box serves as an axis measuring the amount of food, and the *right* side serves as an axis measuring the amount of water. Notice that the numbers on Lauren's axes are read *backward*. On the top, they run from right to left; on the right side, they run from top to bottom.

To illustrate, consider point A. We read Humphrey's consumption from Humphrey's axes: eight pounds of food and three gallons of water. We read Lauren's consumption from Lauren's axes: two pounds of food and seven gallons of water. These are their endowments. In other words, using Humphrey's axes, point A corresponds to point A_H in Figure 16.9(a); using Lauren's axes, point A corresponds to point A_L in Figure 16.9(b).

Next, we'll add budget lines. Suppose food costs \$1 per pound and water costs \$1 per gallon. Starting from his or her endowment, either consumer can swap food for water at the rate of one pound per gallon, or vice versa. To represent these opportunities, we can draw a brown line through the endowment point, A, with a slope of -1. Each consumer can choose any point on this line. Viewed from Humphrey's perspective, this line is identical to the brown one in Figure 16.9(a). Viewed from Lauren's perspective, it's identical to the brown one in Figure 16.9(b). (In effect, we've constructed the Edgeworth box by rotating Figure 16.9(b) 180 degrees, and superimposing it on Figure 16.9(a)).

In 1881, British economist Francis Ysidro Edgeworth (1845–1926) published *Mathematical Psychics: An Essay on the Application of Mathematics to the Moral Sciences.* Though the book was path-breaking, it was also nearly impenetrable. William Jevons, another famous economist of the era, wrote of Edgeworth that "his style, if not obscure, is implicit, so that the reader is left to puzzle out every important sentence like an enigma."

From Figures 16.9(a) and (b), we know that at these prices, Humphrey will trade to point B_H and Lauren will trade to point B_L. We reproduce these points (using Humphrey's axes to plot B_H and Lauren's to plot B_L), as well as the two consumers' indifference curves, in Figure 16.10. (Remember that for Lauren, the picture is upside down, which is why her indifference curve appears to bend the wrong way. If you turn your book upside down, you'll see that it's a normal indifference curve.) We can tell immediately that this economy isn't in equilibrium because points B_H and B_L don't lie on top of each other. At these prices, Humphrey and Lauren together want to consume 11 pounds of food (more than is available), and nine gallons of water (less than is available).

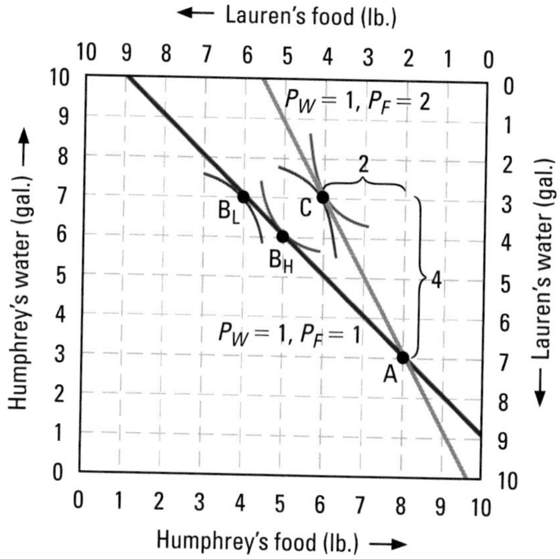

Figure 16.10

Equilibrium in an Edgeworth Box. Humphrey and Lauren start out at point A. When food costs \$1 per pound and water costs \$1 per gallon, Humphrey prefers point B_H and Lauren prefers point B_L. Supply doesn't match demand, so this economy isn't in equilibrium. When food costs \$2 per pound and water costs \$1 per gallon, Humphrey and Lauren both prefer point C. They swap four gallons of water and two pounds of food. Supply matches demand, so this economy is in equilibrium.

Now let's suppose that food costs \$2 per pound and water costs \$1 per gallon. Starting from his or her endowment, either consumer can swap food for water at the rate of one pound for every two gallons, or vice versa. To represent these opportunities, we've drawn a green line through the endowment point, A, with a slope of -2. From Humphrey's perspective, this line is the same as the green budget line in Figure 16.9(a); from Lauren's perspective it's the same as the green budget line in Figure 16.9(b). From Figure 16.9, we know that Humphrey will trade to point C_H and Lauren will trade to point C_L. Those choices correspond to the *same point*, labeled C, in Figure 16.10. As shown, Humphrey supplies and Lauren demands two pounds of food (the horizontal distance between points A and C); likewise, Humphrey demands and Lauren supplies four gallons of water (the vertical distance between points A and C). Since supply matches demand in both markets, this economy is in general equilibrium.

The First Welfare Theorem

We started this section by asking whether in a general equilibrium with many perfectly competitive markets, the allocation of resources is necessarily Pareto efficient. The answer to this question is yes. This important result, known as the **first welfare theorem**, clarifies the sense in which, as Adam Smith put it, the "invisible hand" of the market guides people toward socially desirable choices.

The **first welfare theorem** tells us that, in a general equilibrium with perfect competition, the allocation of resources is Pareto efficient.

To understand why the first welfare theorem holds for exchange economies, look at the Edgeworth box in Figure 16.11. It reproduces the initial allocation (point A) and the equilibrium allocation (point C) from Figure 16.10. Since Humphrey and Lauren face *the same equilibrium prices*, the green line that runs through points A and C serves both as Humphrey's budget line, and as Lauren's budget line. From this critical observation, we can deduce that point C is Pareto efficient:

1. Moving to any allocation to the left of the budget line, like point D, hurts Humphrey. Why? Point D is below Humphrey's budget line (from the perspective of Humphrey's

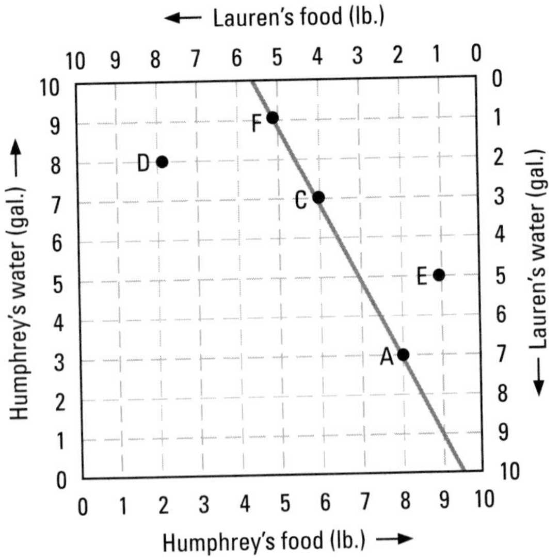

Figure 16.11
The First Welfare Theorem in an Exchange Economy. Suppose that point C is a competitive equilibrium allocation, and that, in equilibrium, the consumers share the green budget line. Humphrey must like point C better than all points to the left of the budget line, like point D. Lauren must like point C better than all points to the right of the budget line, like point E. Both of them must like point C at least as well as all other points on the budget line, like point F. So point C is Pareto efficient.

axes). He could have purchased bundle D, plus a little extra food or water, but he chose bundle C instead. So Humphrey must like bundle C better than bundle D.[10]

2. Moving to any allocation to the right of the budget line, like point E, hurts Lauren. Why? Point E is below Lauren's budget line (from the perspective of Lauren's axes). She could have purchased bundle E, plus a little extra food or water, but she chose bundle C instead. So Lauren must like bundle C more than bundle E.
3. Moving to any other allocation on the budget line, like point F, doesn't help either Humphrey or Lauren. Why not? Either one could have chosen point F, but they both chose point C instead. So they must like point C at least as well as point F.

We conclude that it's impossible to help Humphrey without hurting Lauren, and impossible to help Lauren without hurting Humphrey. That means the general equilibrium is indeed Pareto efficient.

Efficiency in Exchange

What does efficiency entail in an exchange economy? What makes some allocations efficient and others inefficient?

Look at the Edgeworth box in Figure 16.12. Is point G efficient? Two indifference curves pass through point G. The red one (labeled I_0) is Humphrey's and the blue one (labeled I_L) is Lauren's. Because the two indifference curves cross, we can find points that lie above Humphrey's indifference curve and below Lauren's. Any point in the yellow-shaded area will do. Take point H. Since point H lies above the red indifference curve labeled I_0, Humphrey likes it better than point G. Point H also lies below the blue indifference curve labeled I_L, so Lauren also likes it better than point G (remember that the picture is upside down for Lauren). Starting from point G, then, it's possible to make both Humphrey and Lauren better off. That means that point G is inefficient.

[10]This observation reflects the principle of revealed preference, discussed in Section 5.6.

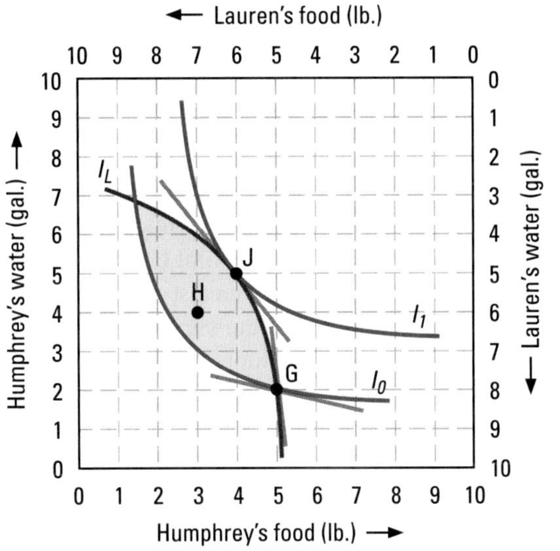

Figure 16.12

A Pareto Efficient Allocation in an Exchange Economy. At point G, Humphrey's indifference curve (in red) crosses Lauren's (in blue). Every point in the yellow-shaded area, such as H, makes both Humphrey and Lauren better off than at point G, so point G is not Pareto efficient. At point J, Humphrey and Lauren's indifference curves touch but do not cross. This is Humphrey's favorite point on Lauren's blue indifference curve. It is also Pareto efficient. At point J, Humphrey and Lauren have the same marginal rate of substitution between food and water. At point G, their marginal rates of substitution differ.

Whenever an allocation is inefficient, there are always potential gains from trade. Starting from the inefficient point G in Figure 16.12, for example, Humphrey and Lauren can reach point H, which they both prefer, by swapping two gallons of Humphrey's food for two gallons of Lauren's water.

Now let's find an efficient allocation. Starting from point G, we'll redistribute resources to make Humphrey as well off as possible without making Lauren worse off. To avoid hurting Lauren, we need to stay on or below the blue indifference curve labeled I_L. Given this restriction, Humphrey's favorite point is J. Notice that one of Humphrey's red indifference curves (labeled I_1) runs through point J, and touches but does not cross the blue indifference curve.

Point J is Pareto efficient. Why? The points that Humphrey likes better than point J lie above the red indifference curve labeled I_1. But all of these points are above the blue indifference curve labeled I_L, which means that Lauren likes point J better. Similarly, the points that Lauren likes better than point J lie below the blue indifference curve labeled I_L. But all of these points are below the red indifference curve labeled I_1, which means that Humphrey likes point J better. So it's impossible to make one of the two consumers better off without hurting the other.

Whenever an allocation is efficient, there are no mutually beneficially trades. Starting from the efficient point J, for example, every conceivable trade makes either Humphrey or Lauren (or both) worse off.

A Condition for Efficiency in Exchange In Section 4.3, we introduced a concept called the marginal rate of substitution (MRS). At point J in Figure 16.12, Humphrey's marginal rate of substitution for food with water (abbreviated MRS_{FW}) is the same as Lauren's. Why? Humphrey and Lauren's indifference curves lie tangent to the *same straight line* at point J (shown in green). The slope of this straight line tells us the rate at which *both* of them are willing to substitute for food with water when the amounts involved are tiny. In contrast, at point G in Figure 16.12, Humphrey and Lauren have different marginal rates of substitution, because their indifference curves lie tangent to different straight lines.

The **exchange efficiency condition** holds if every pair of individuals shares the same marginal rate of substitution for every pair of goods.

If every pair of individuals shares the same marginal rate of substitution for every pair of goods, we say that the allocation satisfies the **exchange efficiency condition**. As long as consumers' indifference curves are smooth (with no kinks) and have declining marginal rates of substitution (see page 110 in Section 4.3), this condition provides a simple test for Pareto efficiency. Allocations that satisfy this condition, like point J, are efficient.[11] Among allocations that assign everyone a positive amount of every good, ones that don't satisfy the exchange efficiency condition, like point G, are inefficient.[12]

We can think of the exchange efficiency condition as a test for the existence of potential gains from trade between consumers.[13] When the consumers' marginal rates of substitution differ, they can both gain by trading goods. Suppose Humphrey's MRS for food with water is $1/2$ and Lauren's is 2. That means Humphrey is willing to trade food for water at the rate of two pounds per gallon, while Lauren is willing to trade water for food at the rate of two gallons per pound. Therefore, if they swap Humphrey's food for Lauren's water at the rate of one gallon per pound, both will be better off. We made a similar point in Example 4.3 (page 111).

In contrast, when marginal rates of substitution are the same, as at point J in Figure 16.12, there are no potential gains to trade. Suppose Humphrey's MRS between food and water is 1, and so is Lauren's. Can Humphrey improve his allocation by trading for an extra gallon of water? He'll be better off only if he gives up slightly less than one pound of food, but Lauren is better off only if she receives slightly more than one pound of food. For similar reasons, Humphrey can't successfully trade for extra food. So there's no way to arrange a mutually beneficial trade.

To illustrate the use of the exchange efficiency condition, let's revisit the first welfare theorem. We've already provided one explanation for the efficiency of a general competitive equilibrium (recall Figure 16.11); here's another. Let's assume that in equilibrium, every consumer purchases a positive amount of every good. If so, then, for each consumer, the marginal rate of substitution between any two goods equals the ratio of their prices (recall equation (4) on page 134). Since every consumer faces the same prices, all their marginal rates of substitution must be the same. So the competitive allocation satisfies the exchange efficiency condition.

For a graphical illustration, look again at Figure 16.10. Notice the similarities between the equilibrium allocation point C in Figure 16.10 and the Pareto efficient point J in Figure 16.12. At point C, each consumer's marginal rate of substitution equals the same price ratio:

$$\text{Humphrey's } MRS_{FW} = \frac{P_F}{P_W} = \text{Lauren's } MRS_{FW}$$

As a result, Humphrey and Lauren's marginal rates of substitution are the same, so the exchange efficiency condition is satisfied.

---

[11] When indifference curves do not have declining marginal rates of substitution, the allocation of consumption goods may not be efficient even if it satisfies the exchange efficiency condition. The principles at work here are similar to those discussed in connection with Figure 5.8 in Section 5.2, page 135.

[12] When at least one individual doesn't consume a positive amount of every good, a corresponding condition involves inequalities between marginal rates of substitution. The principles at work here are similar to those discussed in Section 5.2, in the subsection titled "Boundary Solutions" (page 136). We'll skip this case for the sake of brevity.

[13] To keep things simple, we'll assume here that indifference curves are smooth and that they have declining MRSs. We'll also focus on allocations in which everyone consumes a positive amount of every good.

The Contract Curve We've seen that in Figure 16.12, point J is efficient. But is it the *only* efficient allocation? Plainly not. We found point J by locating Humphrey's favorite point on one of Lauren's indifference curves. To find other efficient allocations, we simply look for Humphrey's favorite points on Lauren's other indifference curves.

Figure 16.13 shows three of Lauren's indifference curves, I_1, I_2, and I_3, in blue. On each of these, we look for a point of tangency with one of Humphrey's indifference curves, shown in red. These three allocations—point K on I_1, point J on I_2, and point L on I_3—are all efficient. If we continued to identify other efficient allocations on Lauren's other indifference curves, we would trace out the black curve in the figure, known as the **contract curve**.[14] The contract curve shows every efficient allocation of consumption goods. At every point on the contract curve, Humphrey and Lauren's indifference curves touch but don't cross, so it is impossible to make both of them better off.

The **contract curve** shows every efficient allocation of consumption goods in an Edgeworth box.

Notice that the contract curve starts at the southwest corner of the Edgeworth box (point M) and ends at the northeast corner (point N). In the southwest corner, Lauren receives all the food and all the water. While that is certainly unfortunate for Humphrey, it is nevertheless Pareto efficient. There isn't any way to help poor Humphrey without taking something away from Lauren, which would make her worse off. The allocation in the northeast corner simply reverses the situation—Humphrey consumes everything, and Lauren goes without.

There is a close relationship between the contract curve shown in Figure 16.13 and the utility possibility frontier shown in Figure 16.7 (page 589). Suppose we have a utility function representing Humphrey's preferences and another representing Lauren's. If so, we can associate each allocation in the Edgeworth box with a pair of utility levels. Every allocation on the contract curve will correspond to a point on the utility possibility frontier, and every point on the utility possibility frontier will correspond to an allocation

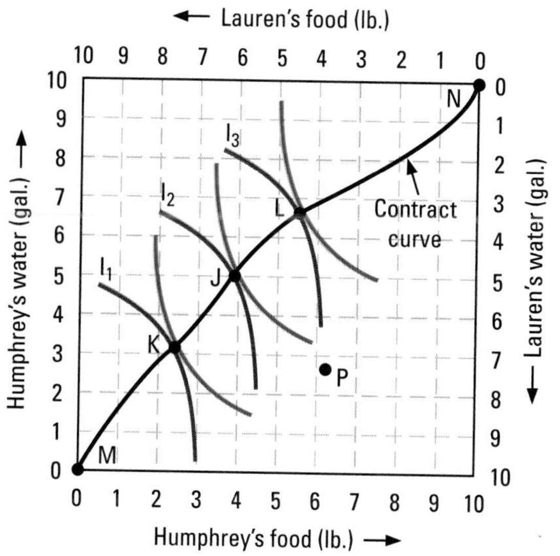

Figure 16.13

The Contract Curve. The contract curve shows every Pareto-efficient allocation of consumption goods. At every point on the contract curve, Humphrey and Lauren's indifference curves touch but don't cross, so it is impossible to make both of them better off.

[14]It is called the contract curve because any efficient contract between Humphrey and Lauren would lead to an allocation on this curve.

on the contract curve. For example, an efficient allocation, like point J in Figure 16.13, will correspond to a point on the utility possibility frontier, like point B in Figure 16.7. An inefficient allocation, like point P in Figure 16.13, will correspond to a point below the utility possibility frontier, like point A in Figure 16.7. Point M in Figure 16.13 corresponds to point D in Figure 16.7: Lauren consumes everything, achieving her highest possible level of utility, while Humphrey consumes nothing, achieving his lowest possible level of utility. Similarly, point N in Figure 16.13 corresponds to point C in Figure 16.7.

If, instead of trading through markets, Humphrey and Lauren were to select an allocation through direct negotiation, they would presumably pick a point on the contract curve. Any other proposal would be met with a counterproposal making both of them better off. The first welfare theorem tells us that a competitive equilibrium also delivers an allocation on the contract curve. To learn more about the relationship between the allocations achieved through competitive markets and through direct negotiation, read Add-on 16B.

WORKED-OUT PROBLEM 16.2

The Problem Humphrey and Lauren must split 10 pounds of food and 10 gallons of water. Suppose we can represent Humphrey's preferences with the utility function $U_H = F_H^2 W_H$ (for which Humphrey's marginal rate of substitution for food with water is $2W_H/F_H$), and Lauren's preferences with the utility function $U_L = \min\{F_L, W_L\}$, where F_H and F_L indicate their food consumption, while W_H and W_L indicate their water consumption. Find and graph the contract curve. Suppose Humphrey and Lauren's initial endowments are $F_H = 2$, $F_L = 8$, $W_H = 5$, and $W_L = 5$. What is the ratio of the price of food to the price of water in competitive equilibrium? To which allocation will Humphrey and Lauren trade?

The Solution In any Pareto efficient allocation, Lauren's food consumption (in pounds) must equal her water consumption (in gallons), that is, $F_L = W_L$. If $F_L > W_L$, we could transfer a small amount of food from Lauren to Humphrey, which would help Humphrey without hurting Lauren. If $F_L < W_L$, we could accomplish the same objective by transferring a small amount of water. Therefore, the contract curve is the diagonal line running between the southwest and northeast corners of the Edgeworth box, as shown in Figure 16.14. Humphrey's indifference curves are shown in red, and Lauren's in blue.

Since a competitive equilibrium is Pareto efficient, Humphrey and Lauren must trade to a point on the contract curve. At every point on that curve, $F_H = W_H$, so Humphrey's $MRS_{FW} = 2$ gallons per pound. We know that, in a competitive equilibrium, Humphrey's $MRS_{FW} = P_F/P_W$, so we conclude that $P_F/P_W = 2$.

To find the allocations to which Humphrey and Lauren trade, we draw a budget line through their endowment point (shown as point A in Figure 16.14). The slope of the budget line is $-P_F/P_W = -2$. Where does this line cross the contract curve? If Humphrey increases his food consumption by one pound (from 2 to 3 pounds), he will have to reduce his water consumption by 2 gallons (from 5 to 3 gallons). This exchange will place him on the contract curve, at point B. As shown in the figure, that is the allocation to which Humphrey and Lauren both wish to trade given their endowments and the equilibrium price ratio.

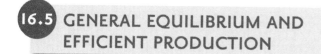

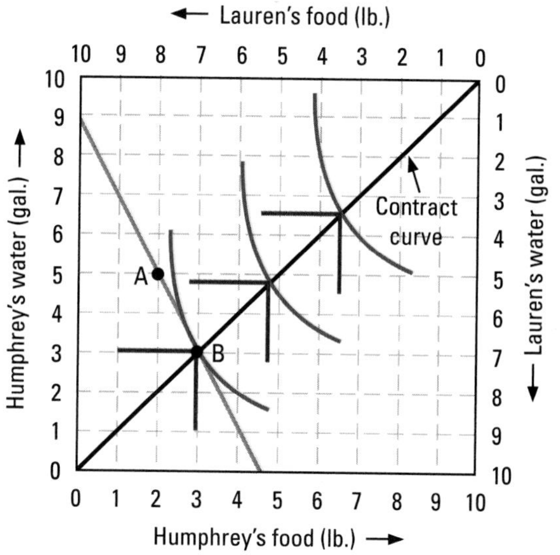

Figure 16.14

Solution to Worked-Out Problem 16.2. Humphrey's indifference curves are shown in red and Lauren's in blue. The contract curve is the diagonal line running between the southwest and northeast corners of the box. The equilibrium ratio of the price of food to the price of water will be 2. Starting from point A, Humphrey and Lauren will trade along the green budget line to point B.

IN-TEXT EXERCISE 16.2 **Repeat worked-out problem 16.2 with the following changes: Humphrey's preferences correspond to the utility function $U_H = F_H W_H$ (which means his $MRS_{FW} = W_H/F_H$) and the consumers' endowments are $F_H = 3$, $F_L = 7$, $W_H = 9$, and $W_L = 1$.**

16.5 GENERAL EQUILIBRIUM AND EFFICIENT PRODUCTION

In Section 16.4, we learned that the competitive equilibrium of an exchange economy is Pareto efficient (the first welfare theorem). We also learned how to tell the difference between efficient and inefficient allocations (the exchange efficiency condition). In this section we'll add production to the mix, and explain why competitive equilibria remain Pareto efficient. First, though, we'll also introduce two new conditions that allow us to distinguish between allocations with efficient versus inefficient production.

Efficiency in Production

What does Pareto efficiency entail in a production economy? It certainly requires efficient exchange. Otherwise, we could help some consumer without hurting anyone else simply by redistributing consumption goods, while holding production fixed. By itself, however, exchange efficiency is not enough; production must also be efficient. As we explain next, there are two requirements for efficient production: input efficiency and output efficiency.

Input efficiency means that holding constant the total amount of each input used in the economy, there is no way to increase any firm's output without decreasing the output of another firm.

Input Efficiency **Input efficiency** means that holding constant the total amount of each input used in the economy, there is no way to increase any firm's output without decreasing the output of another firm. Pareto efficiency requires input efficiency. If an allocation doesn't satisfy input efficiency, then it's possible to produce more of one good and at least as much of every other good using the same inputs. By splitting the extra output among consumers, we could make everyone better off. Thus, the allocation isn't Pareto efficient.

To illustrate this concept, let's examine a simple case involving two firms and two inputs. One firm, MunchieCo, uses labor and capital to produce food. The other, CribCo, uses the same inputs to produce housing. Suppose that between them, the two firms use 50 workers and 25 machines. Which input allocations will achieve input efficiency?

In Section 16.4 we used the Edgeworth box to illustrate allocations of goods between consumers. Here, we can use it to illustrate allocations of inputs between firms. Look at Figure 16.15, which shows an Edgeworth box that is 50 units wide and 25 units high. Each unit of width represents a worker, and each unit of height represents a machine. The width is 50 units because in total, MunchieCo and CribCo use 50 workers. The height is 25 units because in total, the two companies use 25 machines.

Each point in the Edgeworth box describes an allocation of the two inputs between the two firms. For MunchieCo, the bottom of the box serves as the axis that measures the number of workers, and the left side serves as the axis that measures the number of machines. For CribCo, the top of the box serves as the axis that measures the number of workers, and the right side serves as the axis that measures the number of machines.

Now let's consider whether point A, which assigns 25 workers and 8 machines to MunchieCo and 25 workers and 17 machines to CribCo, achieves input efficiency. The figure shows two isoquants crossing at that point, the red one for MunchieCo and the blue one for CribCo. Since the isoquants cross, we can find points that lie above MunchieCo's and below CribCo's, like point B. Because point B lies above the red isoquant, MunchieCo

Figure 16.15

Input Efficiency. This Edgeworth box shows all the possible ways to divide 50 workers and 25 machines between MunchieCo, which produces food, and CribCo, which produces housing. MunchieCo's isoquants are shown in red and CribCo's in blue. Points where the isoquants cross, like point A, are inefficient (point B, for example, allows both firms to increase production). Inputs are allocated efficiently at points C, D, E, F, and G, which lie on the production contract curve.

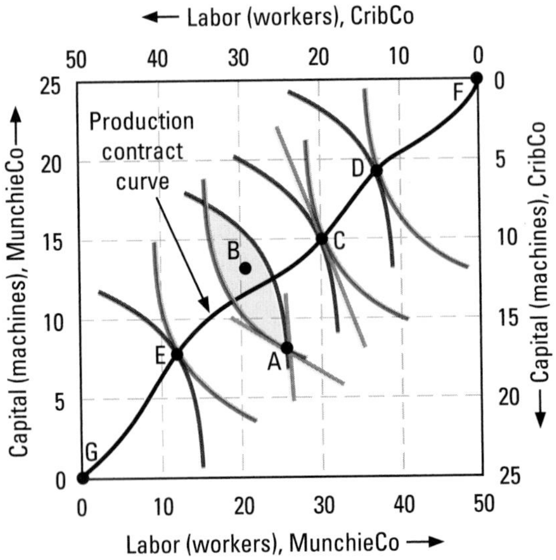

can produce more food at point B than at point A. Likewise, since point B lies below the blue isoquant, CribCo can produce more houses at point B than at point A (remember that for CribCo, the picture is upside down). So starting from point A, it's possible to squeeze more food and more housing out of the same inputs. Therefore, point A is inefficient.

In contrast, at point C, where the two firms' isoquants touch but do not cross, the two inputs are allocated efficiently. Why? Every point other than C is either below the red isoquant that runs through point C (which means that MunchieCo produces less food), above the blue isoquant that runs through point C (which means that CribCo produces fewer houses), or both. There is no way to increase the output of one good without decreasing the output of the other.

Point C isn't the only efficient allocation of inputs. The red and blue isoquants also touch but do not cross at points D and E. These input allocations are also efficient. If we identified all such points, we would trace out the black curve in the figure, known as the **production contract curve**. The production contract curve shows every efficient allocation of inputs between the two firms.

The **production contract curve** shows every efficient allocation of inputs between two firms in an Edgeworth box.

A Condition for Input Efficiency In Section 7.3, we introduced a concept called the marginal rate of technical substitution (MRTS). At the efficient allocations in Figure 16.15, like point C, MunchieCo's marginal rate of technical substitution for labor with capital (abbreviated $MRTS_{LK}$) is the same as CribCo's. Why? At point C, the firms' isoquants lie tangent to the *same straight line* (shown in green). The slope of this line tells us the rate at which *both* firms can substitute labor for capital without changing their output (when the amounts involved are tiny). In other words, it defines their marginal rates of technical substitution. In contrast, at the inefficient allocations in Figure 16.15, like point A, the firms' isoquants lie tangent to different straight lines, so their marginal rates of technical substitution differ.

We say that an allocation satisfies the **input efficiency condition** if every pair of firms shares the same marginal rate of technical substitution between every pair of inputs. As long as the firms' isoquants are smooth (with no kinks) and have declining marginal rates of technical substitution, this condition provides a simple test for input efficiency. Allocations that satisfy this condition, like point C, are efficient.[15] Among allocations that assign every firm a positive amount of every input, ones that don't satisfy the condition, like point A, are inefficient.[16]

The **input efficiency condition** holds if every pair of firms share the same marginal rate of technical substitution between every pair of inputs.

We can think of the input efficiency condition as a test for the existence of potential gains from trade between firms. When the firms' marginal rates of technical substitution differ, they can both gain by trading inputs. For example, suppose that MunchieCo can substitute 5 machines for 10 workers without changing its output, while CribCo can substitute 5 workers for 10 machines. If MunchieCo sends 10 workers to CribCo in exchange for 10 machines, both firms can increase their production. But when the two firms' marginal rates of technical substitution are the same, this potential gain from trade vanishes. As with exchange among consumers, the existence of potential gains from trade implies inefficiency, and vice versa.

---

[15]When isoquants do not have declining MRTSs, the allocation of inputs may not be efficient even if it satisfies the exchange efficiency condition. Here, declining MRTSs play the same role as did declining MRSs in our discussion of exchange efficiency.

[16]When at least one firm doesn't use a positive amount of every input, a corresponding condition involves inequalities between marginal rates of technical substitution. The applicable principles are similar to those discussed in Section 8.4, in the subsection titled "Boundary Solutions" (p. 265). We'll skip this case for brevity.

Figure 16.16

The Production Possibility Frontier. Each of the input allocations in Figure 16.15 corresponds to specific levels of food and housing production, which are plotted in this figure. For example, point A in Figure 16.15 corresponds to A′. The boundary of the green set is the production possibility frontier. Inputs are allocated efficiently at points on the frontier, and inefficiently for points below the frontier. At point C, the marginal rate of transformation between food and clothing is 1.

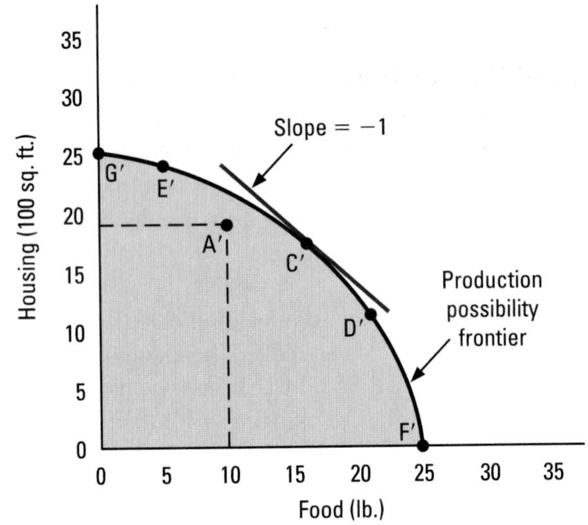

Production Possibilities In Figure 16.15 we focused on inputs. But what about outputs? Look at Figure 16.16. The horizontal axis shows food production and the vertical axis shows housing production. Each input allocation in Figure 16.15 is associated with a level of food production and a level of housing production. We can plot those levels in Figure 16.16. To illustrate, let's assume that with 25 workers and 8 machines, MunchieCo can produce 10 pounds of food, and that, with 25 workers and 17 machines, CribCo can produce 1,800 square feet of housing. In that case, the input allocation labeled A in Figure 16.15 is associated with the outputs labeled A′ in Figure 16.16. Following this procedure, for every possible input, allocation generates the green-shaded area in Figure 16.16. These are the production possibilities for MunchieCo and CribCo, given their technologies and the inputs available to them.

The **production possibility frontier** shows the combinations of outputs that firms can produce when inputs are allocated efficiently among them, given their technologies and the total inputs available.

The northeast boundary of the green-shaded area in Figure 16.16 is known as the **production possibility frontier** (abbreviated PPF). It shows the combinations of outputs firms can produce when inputs are allocated efficiently among them, given their technologies and the total inputs available. The relationship between the PPF and the production contract curve is the same as the relationship between the utility possibility frontier and the contract curve (see Section 16.4). Each input allocation on the production contract curve in Figure 16.15 is associated with a point on the PPF in Figure 16.16, and vice versa. For example, points C, D, E, F, and G in Figure 16.15 are associated, respectively, with points C′, D′, E′, F′, and G′ in Figure 16.16. Points F and F′ represent one extreme: all inputs are allocated to food, and no housing is produced. Points G and G′ represent the opposite extreme: all inputs are allocated to housing, and no food is produced. Inefficient input allocations, like point A in Figure 16.15, are associated with points below the PPF, like A′ in Figure 16.16.

As in Figure 16.16, the PPF always slopes downward. An upward slope would imply that starting at some point on the frontier, it's possible to increase the production of food *and* clothing without changing the total amount of any input. But if that's the case, the allocation of inputs is plainly inefficient. By definition, the PPF includes only those output combinations corresponding to efficient input allocations.

The Marginal Rate of Transformation The downward slope of the PPF reflects the fact that with society's limited inputs, production involves tradeoffs. If we choose to produce more of one good, we must produce less of another. When the units involved are very small, the amount of one good, call it Y, that can be produced by sacrificing an additional unit of a second good, call it X, is known as the **marginal rate of transformation** from X to Y (abbreviated MRT_{XY}).

The **marginal rate of transformation** from good X to good Y is the additional amount of Y that can be produced by sacrificing one unit of X (where the units involved are very small).

At any point on the PPF, the marginal rate of transformation is equal to the slope of a straight line drawn tangent to the frontier at that point, times negative one. For example, at point C′ in Figure 16.16, the slope of the straight line drawn tangent to the PPF is -1, so the marginal rate of transformation from food to housing is 1.

The marginal rate of transformation is related to firms' marginal products. Let's say we want to increase housing production. There are many ways to do so. Here are two possibilities:

1. Shift one worker from MunchieCo to CribCo. MunchieCo's food production falls by its marginal product of labor (abbreviated MP_L^F), and CribCo's housing production rises by its marginal product of labor (abbreviated MP_L^H). The rate at which we can convert food to housing is therefore MP_L^H/MP_L^F.
2. Shift one machine from MunchieCo to CribCo. By the same reasoning, the rate at which we can convert food to housing is MP_K^H/MP_K^F (where MP_K^F is MunchieCo's marginal product of capital and MP_K^H is CribCo's).

At first, the rate at which we can convert food to housing might appear to depend on which input we shift. But in fact, the two rates are identical at any point on the PPF. Remember from Section 7.3 that the marginal rate of technical substitution for labor with capital equals the marginal product of labor divided by the marginal product of capital (page 234). Remember too that on the PPF, inputs are allocated efficiently, so the firms' marginal rates of technical substitution are equal. Putting these facts together, we have:

$$\frac{MP_L^F}{MP_K^F} = \text{MunchieCo's } MRTS_{LK} = \text{CribCo's } MRTS_{LK} = \frac{MP_L^H}{MP_K^H}$$

Rearranging this expression, we discover that $MP_K^H/MP_K^F = MP_L^H/MP_L^F$. In other words, these two ratios are indeed identical. We can therefore use either ratio, reflecting a shift of either input, to define the marginal rate of transformation from food to housing:

$$MRT_{FH} = \frac{MP_K^H}{MP_K^F} = \frac{MP_L^H}{MP_L^F} \tag{10}$$

Note that the PPF in Figure 16.16 bows outward, away from the origin. As we move from left to right, the frontier becomes steeper, which means the marginal rate of transformation from food to housing rises. This change reflects decreasing returns to scale in the production technologies (Section 7.4). As we move from left to right, inputs become more productive in housing (as scale declines) and less productive in food (as scale increases). As a result, the rate at which we gain housing by sacrificing food rises. We can see this relationship in the preceding formula for the MRT_{FH}. If MP_L^H and MP_K^H both rise (due to declining scale) while MP_L^F and MP_K^F both fall (due to increasing scale), the two ratios, MP_K^H/MP_K^F and MP_L^H/MP_L^F, will both rise.

Output efficiency means that, among allocations satisfying exchange efficiency and input efficiency, there is no way to make all consumers better off by shifting production from one good to another.

Output Efficiency **Output efficiency** means that, among allocations satisfying exchange efficiency and input efficiency, there is no way to make all consumers better off by shifting production from one good to another. We've seen that we achieve input efficiency by picking a point on the production contract curve, which is equivalent to picking a point on the PPF. To achieve output efficiency, we need to pick the right point.

Figure 16.17 illustrates the concept of output efficiency for an economy with a single consumer (Humphrey). It shows both the PPF (in black) and Humphrey's indifference curves (in red). Point A satisfies the input efficiency condition because it's on the PPF. However, it doesn't satisfy output efficiency. Why not? Since the indifference curve that runs through point A crosses the PPF, we can make Humphrey better off by moving southeast along the PPF, to a point like B. We reach point B by shifting inputs from housing to food while staying on the production contract curve.

In contrast, point C satisfies both input efficiency and output efficiency. It's on the PPF, and the indifference curve that runs through point C touches but does not cross the PPF. To make Humphrey better off, we would need to move to a point above the indifference curve. But the firms in this economy can't produce any of those points.

A Condition for Output Efficiency At the efficient allocation in Figure 16.17, point C, Humphrey's marginal rate of substitution for food with housing equals the marginal rate of transformation. Why? The indifference curve that runs through point C lies tangent to the same straight line as the PPF. So the slope of that line (shown in dark red) defines both Humphrey's marginal rate of substitution and the marginal rate of transformation at point C.

In contrast, at the inefficient allocations on the PPF, Humphrey's marginal rate of substitution differs from the marginal rate of transformation. At point A, for example, the indifference curve and the PPF lie tangent to different straight lines (as shown in Figure 16.17). The slopes of those lines—which define, respectively, the marginal rate of substitution and the marginal rate of transformation—clearly are not the same.

In an economy with many consumers, when *any* consumer's marginal rate of substitution differs from the marginal rate of transformation, better alternatives are available.

Figure 16.17

Output Efficiency. Point A doesn't achieve output efficiency, because Humphrey's indifference curve crosses the PPF at that point. Since the two curves lie tangent to different straight lines at that point, Humphrey's MRS for food with housing doesn't equal the MRT. Point C achieves output efficiency because the indifference curve touches but does not cross the PPF at that point. At point C, Humphrey's indifference curve and the PPF lie tangent to the same straight line, implying that Humphrey's MRS for food with housing equals the MRT.

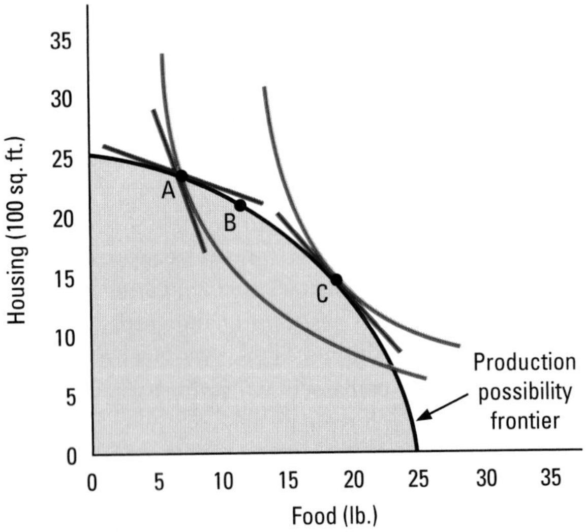

For example, suppose Humphrey is willing to give up 10 square feet of housing to get five pounds of food. Suppose too that it's possible to produce an extra five pounds of food while sacrificing only five square feet of housing. In that case, we can make Humphrey better off without hurting Lauren: reduce both housing production and Humphrey's housing consumption by five square feet, and increase both food production and Humphrey's food consumption by five pounds, while leaving Lauren's consumption unchanged. If we then shift a small amount of housing or food from Humphrey to Lauren, *both* of them will be better off than with the original allocation.

An allocation satisfies the **output efficiency condition** if for every pair of goods, every consumer's marginal rate of substitution equals the marginal rate of transformation. In our example,

$$MRS_{FH} = MRT_{FH}$$

An allocation satisfies the **output efficiency condition** if, for every pair of goods, every consumer's marginal rate of substitution equals the marginal rate of transformation.

When the exchange efficiency condition is satisfied, all consumers share the same marginal rate of substitution; therefore, if the preceding equality holds for one of them, it holds for all of them. As long as (1) the PPF and indifference curves are smooth (with no kinks), (2) indifference curves have declining MRSs, and (3) no production technology yields increasing returns to scale, this condition provides a simple test for output efficiency. Allocations that satisfy this condition, like point C, are efficient.[17] Among allocations that involve positive consumption of every good, ones that don't satisfy the output efficiency condition, like point A, are inefficient.[18]

The output efficiency condition applies both when firms produce different products (like food and housing), and when they produce the same product. For example, suppose that firms A and B both produce food, and that A's product is a perfect substitute for B's. In that case, the output efficiency condition simply tells us to allocate inputs between firms A and B so as to maximize total food production. Here's why. Because consumers are willing to give up exactly one unit of firm A's product to get one unit of firm B's product, the $MRS_{AB} = 1$. Therefore, the output efficiency condition requires that the $MRT_{AB} = 1$. Since we can increase total food output by shifting inputs from firm A to firm B when $MRT_{AB} > 1$, and from firm B to firm A when $MRT_{AB} < 1$, total food production is maximized when the $MRT_{AB} = 1$. The output efficiency condition therefore amounts to the requirement that the allocation of production among food producers maximizes total output. We learned in Section 14.4 that the total output of a good is maximized when all the firms that produce it share the same marginal cost (see Figure 14.15, page 520). That property is equivalent to the output efficiency condition, applied to cases in which different firms produce the same good.[19]

The First Welfare Theorem, Again

We saw in Section 16.4 that the general equilibrium of a competitive exchange economy is Pareto efficient. The same conclusion holds for economies with production.

---

[17]When indifference curves do not have declining MRSs, production may not be efficient even if it satisfies the input and output efficiency conditions. The issues here are the same as those mentioned in the context of exchange efficiency.

[18]When a good is neither produced nor consumed, there is a corresponding condition involving inequalities between the MRS and MRT. We'll skip this case for brevity.

[19]To demonstrate this equivalence, we use the following facts: (1) $MC_A = W/MP_L^A$ and $MC_B = W/MP_L^B$ (see p. 277), and (2) $MRT_{AB} = MP_L^B/MP_L^A$ (see the previous section, formula (10)). Together, these facts imply that $MRT_{AB} = MC_A/MC_B$. In this special case, the output efficiency condition requires $MRT_{AB} = 1$, from which it follows that $MC_A = MC_B$.

Intuitively, why does perfect competition guarantee Pareto efficiency? Let's suppose for the moment that the first welfare theorem is wrong, and that there's a feasible allocation that makes all consumers better off than they are in equilibrium. Then at the equilibrium prices, consumers must not be able to afford the bundles they would consume in that new allocation (otherwise they would purchase those bundles instead of their equilibrium bundles). Consequently, the value of the goods they would purchase from firms must exceed the value of the inputs they would supply to firms, plus any profits they receive in equilibrium as the owners of firms:

$$\begin{matrix}\text{Value of new output bundle} \\ \text{at equilibrium prices}\end{matrix} > \begin{matrix}\text{Value of new input bundle} \\ \text{at equilibrium prices}\end{matrix} + \text{Equilibrium profits}$$

Rearranging this expression, we discover that

$$\begin{matrix}\text{Value of new output bundle} \\ \text{at equilibrium prices}\end{matrix} - \begin{matrix}\text{Value of new input bundle} \\ \text{at equilibrium prices}\end{matrix} > \text{Equilibrium profits}$$

But the difference between the value of outputs and inputs for the new allocation (at equilibrium prices) equals the profits that firms would earn by choosing those output and input levels instead of the equilibrium levels. The preceding expression therefore tells us that, if it's possible to make all consumers better off, and if consumers and firms are facing the same prices, then firms haven't really maximized their profits, which in turn implies that the original allocation isn't a competitive equilibrium after all!

To convince ourselves that a competitive equilibrium is Pareto efficient, we can also check the three efficiency conditions. The exchange efficiency condition holds for the same reasons as in Section 16.4. That leaves us with the input and output efficiency conditions.

We'll start with the input efficiency condition. Let's assume that in equilibrium, every firm uses a positive amount of every input. If so, then for each firm, the marginal rate of technical substitution for one input with another equals the ratio of their prices (as we learned in Section 8.4, p. 264). Since every firm faces the same input prices, all their MRTSs must be the same. So, in our example involving MunchieCo and CribCo:

$$\text{MunchieCo's } MRTS_{LK} = \frac{W}{R} = \text{CribCo's } MRTS_{LK}$$

(where W is the price of labor, and R is the price of capital). Thus, a competitive allocation satisfies the input efficiency condition.

What about the output efficiency condition? Let's assume that in equilibrium, every individual consumes a positive amount of every good. Then for each pair of goods, every consumer's marginal rate of substitution must equal the price ratio (see equation (4) in Section 5.2, p. 134). In our example,

$$MRS_{FH} = \frac{P_F}{P_H}$$

As we learned in Section 9.3, competitive firms will produce up to the point where price equals marginal cost ($P_F = MC_F$ and $P_H = MC_H$), so this last equation implies

$$MRS_{FH} = \frac{MC_F}{MC_H}$$

The marginal cost of each good, in turn, equals the price of any input divided by its marginal product (see Section 8.5, p. 277). In our example, $MC_F = W/MP_L^F$, and

Efficiency as a Justification for Free Markets

Advocates of free markets from Adam Smith to the present argue that the government should not play a significant role in overseeing, directing, or conducting economic activity. Generally, they advocate a "hands off" approach to private commerce. This policy doctrine is known as **laissez-faire**, which is short for *laissez-faire, laissez passer*, a French phrase meaning "let things alone, let them pass."

The doctrine of **laissez-faire** holds that the government should adopt a "hands off" approach to private commerce.

The first welfare theorem provides some support for this position: it tells us that a perfectly competitive economy would produce an efficient outcome. However, this observation does not necessarily imply that laissez-faire is the best policy. Opponents of laissez-faire express two main types of reservations.

First, few if any economists would describe the real economy as perfectly competitive. An imperfectly competitive economy may allocate resources inefficiently. The sources of inefficiency are known as **market failures**. When a market failure occurs, the government may be able to promote economic well-being by intervening in markets. However, even in cases where improvements are possible, governments may introduce new inefficiencies. In some cases, the cure may be worse than the disease. In Part IV of this book, we'll examine the main forms of market failure and their implications in some depth.

A **market failure** is a source of inefficiency in an imperfectly competitive economy.

Second, many people express concerns that free markets can produce inequitable outcomes. Among other things, they point out that laissez-faire leads to extreme wealth and extreme poverty; see, for example, Application 16.3. In the next section, we'll examine potential remedies.

Application 16.3

The Concentration of Wealth

The actual distribution of economic resources favors some people over others. Vast fortunes are the stuff of modern legend. According to *Forbes* magazine, in 2006, 21 Americans owned assets worth more than $10 billion. The list, headed by Microsoft cofounder Bill Gates ($53 billion), included such well-known tycoons such as Warren Buffet of Berkshire Hathaway, Lawrence Ellison of Oracle, Microsoft cofounder Paul Allen, and Michael Dell of Dell Computer. Five Wal-Mart heirs and three heirs of the Mars candy empire also made the list. In 2000, the wealthiest 100 Americans held 2.5 percent of all private wealth in the United States.

Many other Americans enjoy substantial wealth, although not enough to place them on this exclusive list. In 2000, more than 20,000 individuals had a net worth of at least $24 million and more than 200,000 had a net worth of at least $5 million. The wealthiest 1 percent of Americans held 20.8 percent of total private wealth; the wealthiest 0.1 percent held 9 percent; and the wealthiest 0.01 percent held 3.9 percent. In contrast, tens of millions of Americans have little or no wealth.

Popular wisdom holds that the rich grow steadily richer. It is widely believed that the emergence of the personal computer industry in the 1980s, coupled with the explosion of Internet usage during the 1990s—which contributed to the growth of new firms like Microsoft, Apple, and Google—fueled a trend toward inequality. The media have reported a growing gap between the wealthy and the middle class, supported by government statistics on the distribution of income. Yet there has been surprisingly little increase in the concentration of wealth among the very wealthiest Americans. Indeed, by historical standards, the share of wealth held today by the richest Americans is relatively low.

In 1918, John Rockefeller alone accounted for more than half of a percent of total private wealth. To compile the same share in 2000, we would have to combine the fortunes of Bill Gates, Larry Ellison, and Paul Allen, plus a third of Warren Buffet's.

Figure 16.19 shows the fraction of total private wealth held by the richest 1 percent, 0.1 percent, and 0.01 percent of the U.S. population from 1920 to 2000. All three curves exhibit essentially the same pattern. The concentration of wealth peaked in 1930, when the richest 1 percent of Americans held more than 40 percent of private wealth; the richest 0.1 percent held nearly 23 percent; and the richest 0.01 percent held nearly 11 percent. Their shares declined sharply in the 1930s and 1940s due largely to effects of the Great Depression, the New Deal, and World War II. They then remained relatively stable until the 1970s, when they dipped once again. The increase in the concentration of wealth during the 1980s simply restored the levels of concentration that existed before the 1970s. Since then, the concentration of wealth has remained essentially stable, at least through 2000.

Figure 16.19

The Concentration of Wealth in the United States, 1920–2000. This figure shows the fraction of total private wealth held by the richest 1 percent, 0.1 percent, and 0.01 percent of the U.S. population over an 80-year period.

Source: Wojciech Kopczuk and Emmanuel Saez, "Top Wealth Shares in the United States, 1916–2000: Evidence from Estate Tax Returns," *National Tax Journal*, June 2004, pp. 225–487, Table 3.

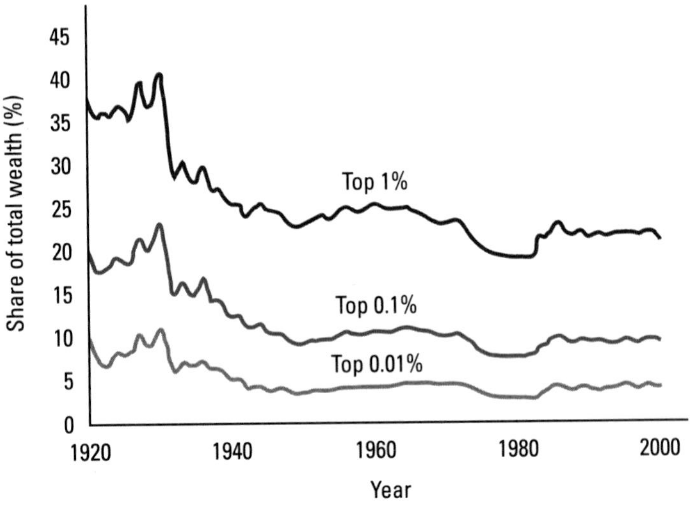

16.6 EQUITY AND REDISTRIBUTION

The first welfare theorem tells us that a competitive equilibrium is Pareto efficient. While this is certainly good news, it may not be enough to convince you that a policy of laissez-faire is desirable. Remember that efficient allocations can be extremely inequitable. Look again at the contract curve in Figure 16.13 (page 599). Every point on that curve is Pareto efficient, including points M and N, which assign everything to a single consumer. Even if the competitive equilibrium allocation lies on the contract curve, there may be other points on that curve that are far more attractive from the perspective of equity. In this section, we examine some of the ways in which a government might achieve a more equitable outcome.

The Second Welfare Theorem

Can competitive markets generate allocations that are not just efficient, but equitable? Another important result, known as the **second welfare theorem**, addresses this question. The second welfare theorem tells us that every Pareto efficient allocation is a competitive equilibrium for some initial allocation of resources.

The **second welfare theorem** tells us that every Pareto efficient allocation is a competitive equilibrium for some initial allocation of resources.

From one perspective, the message of this theorem is discouraging. It tells us that competitive allocations can be extremely inequitable. If the initial distribution of endowments heavily favors certain individuals, the equilibrium will favor them as well.

From another perspective, however, the second welfare theorem carries a positive message. It tells us that in principle, societies can use competitive markets to achieve *both* efficiency *and* equity. If a competitive allocation is inequitable, the problem lies not with the market institutions, but with the initial distribution of resources. If society can redistribute those resources appropriately, then competitive markets will deliver the most equitable Pareto efficient allocation. A society need not sacrifice efficiency—for example, by regulating a market—for the sake of equity. This second interpretation requires many qualifications, and its practical relevance is controversial. We'll explain why later in this section.

To see why the second welfare theorem holds, let's focus on exchange economies. Figure 16.20 reproduces the Edgeworth box presented earlier in this chapter (see Figure 16.13, page 599). Pick any point on the curve—say point J. For which initial allocations of resources is point J a competitive equilibrium? Suppose we give point J to Humphrey and Lauren as their initial endowments. We know that their indifference curves will be tangent to the same straight line (shown in green) at point J. With the right prices for food and water, this straight line will also be their budget line, and both will choose point J. Since neither consumer will supply or demand anything, supply will match demand, creating a competitive equilibrium.

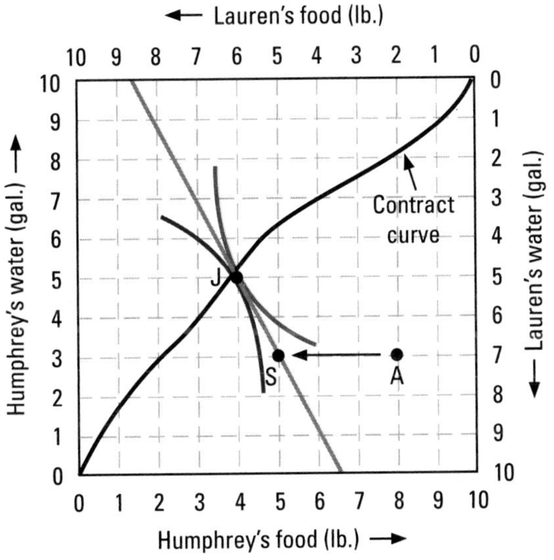

Figure 16.20

The Second Welfare Theorem. Suppose Humphrey and Lauren start out with point J as their endowments. Since point J is efficient, their indifferent curves lie tangent to the same straight line at that point. At the right prices, this line is also their budget line. With this budget line, both consumers choose point J. Since neither consumer supplies or demands anything, supply matches demand, creating a competitive equilibrium. Using any other endowments on the green line, like S, the same prices would lead to the same competitive equilibrium.

Are there other initial allocations of resources for which point J is a competitive equilibrium? Indeed there are. In fact, any point on the straight green line will do. Take point S. At the same prices for food and water as before, the budget line will be unchanged, so both consumers will still pick point J. To reach point J from point S, Humphrey will supply food and demand water, while Lauren will demand food and supply water. Supply will matches demand in both markets, so again we will have a competitive equilibrium.

Now let's suppose the two consumers start out with point A as their endowments. To reach point J, we can replace point A with any endowment on the straight green line, and then allow competitive markets to operate. For example, we can take three pounds of food from Humphrey and give it to Lauren, in which case their endowment will be point S. In the competitive equilibrium that follows, Humphrey and Lauren will trade to point J.

With a **lump-sum transfer**, the amount of resources received or surrendered by each consumer is fixed; it doesn't depend on the consumer's choices.

The redistribution of food that moves Humphrey and Lauren from point A to point S is called a **lump-sum transfer**. All lump-sum transfers have the property that the amount of resources received or surrendered by each consumer is fixed; it doesn't depend on the consumer's choices. Unlike other taxes and transfers, lump-sum transfers don't compromise efficiency because they don't distort choices.

The Conflict between Equity and Efficiency

The second welfare theorem suggests that societies can use competitive markets and lump-sum transfers to achieve both efficiency and equity: we achieve an equitable outcome by transferring resources from consumers with substantial endowments to consumers with modest endowments; we achieve an efficient outcome by allowing competitive markets to operate. This policy prescription assumes, however, that we can observe consumers' endowments, so that we know who to tax and who to subsidize. Is this assumption reasonable?

Since wealth is observable, we could try to achieve an equitable outcome by redistributing resources from the rich to the poor. But wealth isn't an endowment; it depends on a variety of choices involving education, employment, and saving. Therefore, transfers based on wealth aren't lump-sum transfers. While they may be equitable, they distort choices and sacrifice efficiency by reducing consumers' incentives to study, work, and save. The same comments apply to redistribution based on income.

It's difficult to imagine a measure of need that doesn't depend on *any* choice. (Can you come up with one?) As a practical matter, then, we can't use lump-sum transfers to accomplish our distributional objectives. Instead, we need to link such transfers to criteria that reflect choices. Doing so brings equity and efficiency into direct conflict, however. Contrary to the second welfare theorem, we may have to put up with a less efficient outcome to achieve a more equitable one.

Figure 16.21 illustrates the conflict between equity and efficiency in a simple exchange economy consisting of two consumers (Humphrey and Lauren) and two goods (food and water). The endowments (point A in the figure) heavily favor Humphrey, who has all the water and more than half the food. A policy of laissez-faire would lead to a competitive equilibrium at point B. When food sells for \$1 per pound and water sells for \$1 per gallon, the slope of the budget line (shown in black) is -1. At point B, Humphrey's indifference curve (shown in red) lies tangent to the budget line, as does Lauren's (shown in blue). This equilibrium outcome is efficient, but is arguably unfair to Lauren.

What can the government do to promote a more equitable outcome? Here we'll assume that it's impossible to redistribute the endowments. As in the real world, however, the government can tax transactions and transfer revenues to Lauren.

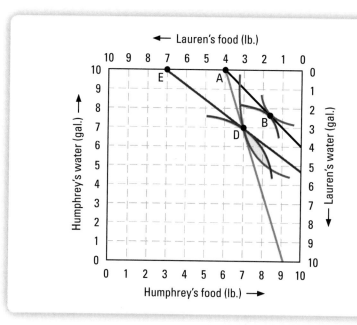

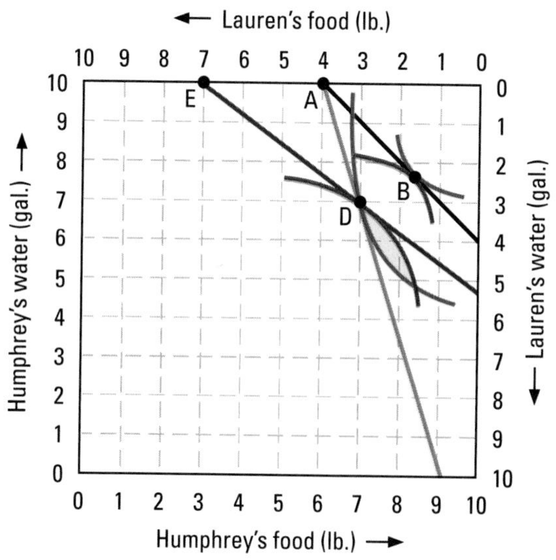

Figure 16.21
Equity versus Efficiency. Humphrey and Lauren start out at point A. Without taxes, food costs \$1/kg and water costs \$1/gallon; point B is the equilibrium. With a 75 percent tax on food (which takes 3 out of every 4 units of food purchased) to fund a distribution to Lauren, food costs \$0.75/kg and water costs \$1/gallon. Humphrey's budget line, in green, passes through points A and D; he chooses D. Lauren's budget line, in brown, passes through points E and D; she too chooses D, so this is an equilibrium. Though the tax-transfer program makes Lauren better off, it is inefficient.

In equilibrium, Humphrey buys food from Lauren. Therefore, the government can try to finance distributions to Lauren by taxing Humphrey's food purchases. Let's see what happens when the government imposes a 75 percent tax on food. For each pound of food Humphrey purchases, the government takes 0.75 pound, leaving him with 0.25 pound. It then gives this food to Lauren.

Figure 16.21 illustrates the new equilibrium. As we've drawn the figure, the equilibrium price of water remains unchanged at \$1 per gallon, while the equilibrium price of food falls to \$0.75. Humphrey and Lauren end up at point D, rather than at point B.

Why do these new prices lead to an equilibrium allocation at point D? Let's start with Humphrey. Since he has to buy four pounds of food in order to keep one pound, in effect he pays \$3 ($4 \times \$0.75$) for each pound of food. The slope of the solid green budget line, -3, equals the after-tax price ratio that Humphrey faces (\$3 per pound of food, divided by \$1 per gallon of water), times negative one. As drawn, D is Humphrey's favorite point on the solid green line. The government collects three pounds of food in tax revenue at that point.

Now consider Lauren. She receives three pounds of food from the government as part of her endowment. The handout shifts her endowment point from point A to E. Since Lauren *sells* food to Humphrey, she doesn't pay the sales tax. As far as she's concerned, the price of food is \$0.75 per pound. The slope of her budget line, shown in brown, is -0.75. Like Humphrey, Lauren chooses point D in the figure, creating an equilibrium. She sells four pounds of food to Humphrey, and buys three gallons of water from him.

Notice that point D is to the southwest of both the blue and red indifference curves that run through point B. Therefore, the tax-transfer policy illustrated in Figure 16.21 makes Lauren better off and Humphrey worse off. Arguably, it produces a more equitable outcome than laissez-faire. However, it's inefficient. At point D, Humphrey and Lauren's indifference curves lie tangent to their budget lines, which have different slopes. As a result, the curves cross. Any point in the yellow-shaded area would make both of them better off. But without lump-sum transfers, there is no way to achieve one of those allocations. Thus, in making the outcome more equitable, the government sacrifices a degree of efficiency.

Application 16.4

Optimal Personal Income Taxation

"Found meat is income."

The personal income tax is the federal government's most important source of funds. In 2006, it raised more than a trillion dollars—nearly 45 percent of total federal revenue, and just under 8 percent of the U.S. gross domestic product (a common measure of total national income).

In addition to providing revenue, the personal income tax also serves the government's distributional objectives. The system is *progressive*, in the sense that the tax rate applied to the last dollar of income rises with the total amount of income received.[21] As a result, affluent people pay more than others, both in absolute terms and as a fraction of their incomes.

Figure 16.22(a) shows the tax rates applicable to married couples (filing jointly) in 2005. The horizontal axis shows taxable income, equal to total income less various deductions and exemptions. The vertical axis shows the tax rate applied to the last dollar received, also known as the *marginal tax rate*. Because of deductions and exemptions, the lowest-income households pay no tax. A 10 percent tax rate applies to the first dollar of taxable income. This rate rises in several steps, reaching a peak of 35 percent for households with incomes exceeding $326,450.

Some would argue that in the interest of equity, the government should increase the top marginal tax rate and reduce rates on lower incomes. That policy would have the effect of redistributing resources from affluent households to the poor and middle class. Others argue that high tax rates discourage people from earning money. In their view, redistribution through the tax system comes at a high cost in terms of economic inefficiency.

At different times, lawmakers have made very different choices concerning the trade-off between equity and efficiency. As Figure 16.22(b) shows, the top marginal tax rate has varied considerably from 1913 (when the Sixteenth Amendment to the U.S. Constitution paved the way for federal income taxation) through 2000. The current top rate of 35 percent is relatively low by historical standards, particularly when compared with the historic peak of 94 percent, reached during World War II.

How should we resolve the trade-off between equity and efficiency, and what does the answer to that question imply for the top marginal tax rate? Many economists have tried to answer these questions by studying simple general equilibrium models that attempt to capture the way income taxation affects the allocation of resources. To evaluate and compare allocations, they apply a social welfare function. Using this approach, economist Emmanuel Saez has developed a general formula for the optimal value of the top tax rate.[22] For the empirically relevant cases, this formula simplifies to the following:

$$T = \frac{1}{1 + 2E_T/(1 - A)}$$

where T is the top marginal tax rate and E_T is the elasticity of taxable income with respect to the tax rate (averaged over the top tax bracket).[23] The remaining term, A, reflects the degree of importance placed on equity. It represents the social value of $1 given as a lump sum to the average person in the top tax bracket, divided by the social value of the same dollar given as a lump sum to the average person in the entire population. Presumably, most people would agree that A is no greater than one. When more importance is attached to equity, A is smaller.

---

[21]Technically, this concept is called *marginal rate progressivity*. In contrast, *average rate progressivity* means that the ratio of total taxes to total income rises as the taxpayer's income increases.

[22]Emmanuel Saez, "Using Elasticities to Derive Optimal Income Tax Rates," *Review of Economic Studies* 68, 2001, pp. 205–229.

[23]Specifically, E_T is the percentage change in taxable income that results from a one percent change in the fraction of income that the taxpayer keeps.

According to Saez's formula, larger values of either E_T or A justify lower tax rates for high income individuals. The effect of E_T on the optimal tax rate reflects concerns for efficiency: when that elasticity is larger, the tax distorts taxpayers' decisions to a greater degree, which makes low tax rates more desirable. The effect of A on the optimal tax rate reflects concerns for equity: when the importance attached to low-income individuals is greater, A is smaller, which makes higher tax rates more desirable.

Many economists have tried to measure E_T empirically, with most estimates falling between 0.25 and 2. While reasonable people may disagree about the appropriate value of A, many would argue that it should be close to zero. Whatever values we use, Saez's formula identifies the optimal value of the top tax rate. To illustrate, let's use $A = 0$, meaning that we attach no social value to extra money received by the wealthiest individuals. In that case, you might think that the best top tax rate would be 100 percent. But such a high rate would cause the wealthy to earn much less income, reducing government revenue, and leaving the poor worse off. In fact, the formula tells us that the top tax rate should be 67 percent if $E_T = 0.25$, 50 percent if $E_T = 0.5$, 33 percent if $E_T = 1$, and 20 percent if $E_T = 2$. Nailing down the value of this elasticity would help policymakers to design the best possible system of personal income taxation.

Figure 16.22

The Federal Personal Income Tax. Part (a) shows the marginal tax rates on different levels of taxable income in 2005. Part (b) shows how the marginal tax rate on the highest incomes has changed over time.

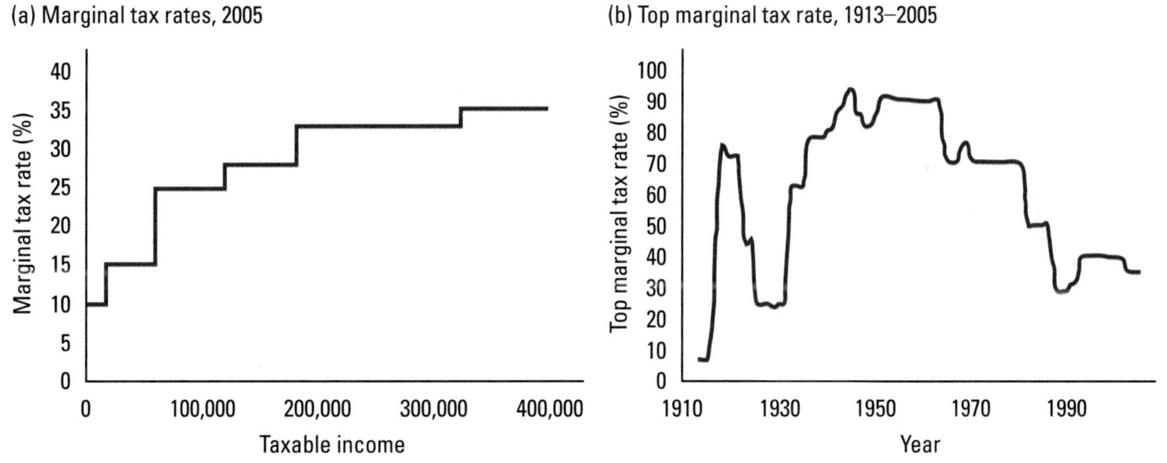

Source: Internal Revenue Service

CHAPTER SUMMARY

1. **The nature of general equilibrium**

   a. Interdependence between markets is important for two reasons. First, factors that affect supply and demand in one market can have significant ripple effects in other markets. Second, interdependence produces feedback.

   b. To be completely general, equilibrium analysis would need to encompass every market in the world economy. For reasons of practicality, economists usually focus on markets that are clearly linked, ignoring others.

2. **Positive analysis of general equilibrium**

   a. In a market with just two goods, general equilibrium corresponds to a point of intersection between two market-clearing curves.

   b. The general equilibrium effects of a tax may differ considerably from the partial equilibrium effects. The effect of a sales tax on the price of a good becomes larger when we account for feedback from the market for a complement, and smaller when we account for feedback from the market for a substitute.

3. **Normative criteria for evaluating economic performance**

   a. Economists evaluate economic performance on the basis of efficiency and equity.

   b. The economy is wasteful (or inefficient) if it's possible to reallocate resources in a way that makes at least one consumer better off without hurting someone else. It is Pareto efficient if there is no waste.

   c. Pareto efficient allocations are associated with utility levels that lie on the utility possibility frontier.

   d. Some notions of equity are process-oriented—for example, the idea that markets are fair because they reward people for effort and ingenuity.

   e. Outcome-oriented notions of equity are based on the distribution of either well-being or consumption and include utilitarianism, Rawlsianism, and egalitarianism. The distribution of well-being may, however, be impossible to measure.

   f. A social welfare function can capture concerns about efficiency, as well as outcome-oriented notions of equity.

4. **General equilibrium and efficient exchange**

   a. To illustrate allocations and competitive equilibrium in an exchange economy, economists often use an Edgeworth box.

   b. The first welfare theorem tells us that competitive general equilibria are Pareto efficient.

   c. To identify efficient allocations of consumption goods in an Edgeworth box, we look for points where two consumers' indifference curves touch but do not cross. At such points, the two curves typically lie tangent to the same straight line, implying that the two consumers have the same marginal rate of substitution. This result is known as the exchange efficiency condition.

   d. Competitive equilibria satisfy the exchange efficiency condition because every consumer chooses a point at which his marginal rate of substitution equals the same price ratio.

   e. When an allocation is inefficient, consumers can mutually benefit from further trade. When an allocation is efficient, no further trade is mutually beneficial.

   f. In an Edgeworth box, each point on the contract curve corresponds to a point on the utility possibility frontier. The contract curve includes both equal and highly unequal allocations.

5. **General equilibrium and efficient production**

   a. To identify efficient allocations of inputs in an Edgeworth box, we look for points where the isoquants for two firms touch but do not cross. Typically, the two curves lie tangent to the same straight line, implying that the two firms have the same marginal rate of technical substitution. This result is known as the *input efficiency condition*.

   b. In an Edgeworth box, each point on the production contract curve corresponds to a point on the production possibility frontier.

   c. To identify efficient levels of production in a one-consumer economy, we look for a point where the PPF and an indifference curve touch but do not cross. Typically, the two curves lie tangent to the same straight line, implying that the firm's marginal rate of transformation equals the consumer's marginal rate of substitution. This result, which also holds with more than one consumer, is known as the *output efficiency condition*.

   d. The first welfare theorem holds in production economies. Competitive equilibria satisfy the input efficiency condition because every firm chooses a point at which its marginal rate of substitution equals the same input price ratio. Competitive equilibria also satisfy the output efficiency condition because firms and consumers face the same prices. Each consumer picks a bundle for which his marginal rate of substitution equals the price ratio for the goods in question. Firms pick production levels at which the marginal rate of transformation equals the same price ratio.

   e. Market failures may prevent free markets from operating efficiently. Also, competitive equilibrium allocations may be extremely unequal across consumers. Either consideration may justify government intervention in markets. However, even in cases where improvements are possible, governments may introduce new inefficiencies.

6. **Equity and redistribution**

a. The second welfare theorem implies that, in principle, societies can use competitive markets to achieve both efficiency and equity. Doing so requires lump-sum transfers to improve the initial allocation of consumption goods.

b. In practice, governments cannot achieve their distributional goals through lump-sum transfers. Instead, taxes and transfers are linked to choices, which creates a trade-off between equity and efficiency.

ADDITIONAL EXERCISES

Exercise 16.1: Suppose that the demand for pie doesn't depend on the price of cake, and that the demand for cake doesn't depend on the price of pie. An increase in the price of pie, however, shifts the supply curve for cake downward, while an increase in the price of cake shifts the supply curve for pie downward (because bakers spend more time making the more profitable product). Assume that demand curves slope downward and supply curves slope upward. Using graphs, show how to construct the market-clearing curves for pie and cake. Do they slope upward or downward? Again using graphs, illustrate the effects of a sales tax on cake. Does the cake price change more in general equilibrium or partial equilibrium?

Exercise 16.2: Should society have economic goals other than equity and efficiency, as those terms are used in the text? If so, what should they be? Explain your reasoning.

Exercise 16.3: Humphrey and Lauren are splitting 10 gallons of soda and six pounds of popcorn. Let's represent Humphrey's preferences with the utility function $U_H = 3S_H + P_H$ and Lauren's preferences with $U_L = 2S_L + 4P_L$, where S_H and S_L indicate their soda consumption, while P_H and P_L indicate their popcorn consumption. Consider the social welfare function $W(U_H, U_L) = U_H + U_L$. According to this social welfare function, which of the following two allocations is better: (1) $S_H = 1$, $S_L = 9$, $P_H = 2$, and $P_L = 4$, or (2) $S_H = 5$, $S_L = 5$, $P_H = 3$, and $P_L = 3$? Which allocation does each consumer prefer? Considering all possible allocations, which is the most socially desirable? (Hint: How is social welfare affected by shifting a gallon of soda between Humphrey and Lauren? What about a pound of popcorn?)

Exercise 16.4: In Section 5.4 we learned about price-consumption curves. Add Humphrey and Lauren's price consumption curves to the Edgeworth Box in Figure 16.10 (page 595). Explain why the competitive equilibrium corresponds to the point at which the price-consumption curves intersect.

Exercise 16.5: In Figure 16.10 (page 595), the competitive equilibrium must lie either to the northwest or southeast of the endowment point A, regardless of the consumers' preferences. Explain why.

Exercise 16.6: Suppose Humphrey starts out with four pounds of food and seven gallons of water, while Lauren starts out with eight pounds of food and five gallons of water. Draw an Edgeworth box that shows all possible allocations of these goods, and plot the endowment points. Now suppose that both Lauren and Humphrey's preferences correspond to the utility function $U(F,W) = \min\{F,W\}$ (where F refers to pounds of food and W refers to gallons of water). This is a case of perfect complements. Add Humphrey and Lauren's indifference curves to the Edgeworth box. Then draw the contract curve. To which points on the contract curve is each consumer willing to trade? Suppose Humphrey starts out with six pounds of food instead of four pounds. How does the picture change? What does the contract curve look like?

Exercise 16.7: For the exchange economy considered in Exercise 16.6, illustrate a competitive equilibrium by adding a budget line to your diagram. Does only one equilibrium exist or are there many? What can you say about general equilibrium prices and the consumption bundles chosen at those prices?

Exercise 16.8: Repeat exercise 16.6, but assume that Humphrey's preferences correspond to the utility function $U(F,W) = 2F + W$, while Lauren's preferences correspond to the utility function $U(F,W) = F + 2W$. This is a case of perfect substitutes.

Exercise 16.9: Repeat exercise 16.7, but assume that Humphrey and Lauren have the preferences described in exercise 16.8.

Exercise 16.10: In an exchange economy with two consumers and two goods, is it possible for one of the markets to clear but not the other? Explain your answer graphically using an Edgeworth box.

Exercise 16.11: Figure 16.17 (page 606) shows why, in an economy with a single consumer, output efficiency requires the marginal rates of substitution and transformation to be identical. How might you modify this figure to make the same point concerning an economy with many consumers?

Exercise 16.12: Suppose an economy produces two goods, food and housing, from two inputs, capital and labor. Explain why in an otherwise competitive economy, a tax on food will violate the output efficiency condition. Illustrate using a graph like Figure 16.17 (page 606).

Exercise 16.13: For each of the following hypothetical policies, indicate which of the three efficiency conditions (exchange, input, and output) are violated, if any. (a) The government bans orange juice. (b) The government assigns a house or apartment to each family and prohibits swapping. (c) The government subsidizes the use of capital for oil exploration.

Exercise 16.14: If the government wanted to reach point J in Figure 16.20 (page 613), it could simply mandate this allocation through centralized control of resources. Why might it be better to set up competitive markets and allow trading? (Hint: What if the government is not completely certain of Humphrey and Lauren's preferences?)

Exercise 16.15: After reading Section 16.6, a student proposes a system of taxes and transfers based on the intelligence quotient (IQ). She argues that intelligence is not chosen, and that it's closely related to economic success. She concludes that redistributing resources from people with high IQs to people with low IQs will promote equity without compromising efficiency. What do you think of this proposal? Why?

Credits

Chapter 2

page 25 (top): © United States Coast Guard
page 25 (bottom): © AP / Wide World Photos
page 33: By permission of the Master and Fellows of St John's College, Cambridge
page 34: © Pascal Le Segretain / Getty Images
page 37: Photo courtesy of Bar Harbor Inn
page 40: © 2007 UDC
page 47 (top): Photo courtesy of Nissan North America
page 47 (bottom): © 2007 BMW of North America, LLC All rights reserved. The BMW trademark, model names and logo are registered trademarks.
page 54: © Brooks Kraft / Corbis
page 56: Courtesy of Honda

Chapter 3

page 70 (left): © Time Inc. / Time Life Pictures / Getty Images
page 70 (right): © AP / Wide World Photos
page 79: © AP / Wide World Photos
page 83: Courtesy of Lemley International

Chapter 4

page 118: © Alamy Images

Chapter 5

page 123: Courtesy of Honda
page 123: © Alvey & Towers Picture Library /Alamy Images
page 154: © McGraw-Hill Companies / Jill Braaten, photographer

Chapter 6

page 176 (left): © The Illustrated London News Picture Library
page 176 (right): Charles Pertwee / The New York Times / Redux
page 195: © Mary Evans Picture Library / The Image Works

Chapter 7

page 212: The Warren J. Samuels Portrait Collection at Duke University
page 213: © Rykoff Collection / Corbis
page 231: Photo courtesy of Cold Hollow Cider Mill, Waterbury Center, Vermont
page 245: Courtesy of Lockheed Martin Aeronautics Company

Chapter 8

page 249: © Profile Books
page 253: © PLITT TODD / CORBIS SYGMA
page 258: Courtesy of the Calpine Corporation
page 290: © AP / Wide World Photos

Chapter 9

page 293: © Blank Archives / Getty Images
page 317: © CBS / Landov

Chapter 10

page 325 (top): Volkswagen of America Inc.
page 325 (bottom): © dpa / Corbis

Chapter 11

page 365: © Icon International

Chapter 12

page 404: Courtesy of World RPS Society
page 415: © AP / Wide World Photos
page 416: R.P. Matthews, Courtesy of Princeton University
page 428: University of Bonn
page 435: © Dan Porges
page 440: © Jane Scherr

Chapter 13

page 447: © The New York Times / Redux
page 467: Giraudon / Art Resource, NY
page 478 (top): Office of Communications, Princeton University
page 478 (bottom): © Stanford University / Stanford News Service
page 480: W.P. Carey, School of Business, Arizona State University
page 488: Courtesy of Samuel McClure, David Laibson, George Loewenstein, Jonathan Cohen

Chapter 14

page 495 (top): © Reuters
page 495 (bottom): Helga Lade GmbH, Germany / Peter Arnold, Inc.
page 522: Courtesy of the Adirondack Council

Chapter 15

page 539 (top): © AP / Wide World Photos
page 539 (bottom): Milwaukee Journal Sentinel

Chapter 16

page 578: The Warren J. Samuels Portrait Collection at Duke University
page 579 (top): Linda A. Cicero / Stanford News Service
page 579 (bottom): © G. Paul Bishop, Jr.